ECONOMICS FOR BUSINESS

Sixth edition

John Sloman
The Economics Network, University of Bristol
Visiting Professor, University of the West of England

Kevin Hinde
Senior Teaching Fellow
University of Durham

Dean Garratt
Principal Lecturer and Course Leader of the Undergraduate
Economics degrees
Nottingham Business School

Additional materials supplied by Andrew Hunt,
University of Plymouth

Harlow, England • London • New York • Boston • San Francisco • Toronto • Sydney
Auckland • Singapore • Hong Kong • Tokyo • Seoul • Taipei • New Delhi
Cape Town • São Paulo • Mexico City • Madrid • Amsterdam • Munich • Paris • Milan

Pearson Education Limited
Edinburgh Gate
Harlow CM20 2JE
United Kingdom
Tel: +44 (0)1279 623623
Web: www.pearson.com/uk

First published by Prentice Hall 1998 (print)
Second edition published 2001 (print)
Third edition published 2004 (print)
Fourth edition published 2007 (print)
Fifth edition published 2010 (print)
Sixth edition published 2013 (print and electronic)

© John Sloman and Mark Sutcliffe 1998, 2001, 2004 (print)
© John Sloman and Kevin Hinde 2007 (print)
© John Sloman, Kevin Hinde and Dean Garratt 2010 (print)
© John Sloman, Dean Garratt and Kevin Hinde 2013 (print and electronic)

Pearson Education is not responsible for the content of third-party internet sites.

The Financial Times. With a worldwide network of highly respected journalists, *The Financial
Times* provides global business news, insightful opinion and expert analysis of business,
finance and politics. With over 500 journalists reporting from 50 countries worldwide,
our in-depth coverage of international news is objectively reported and analysed from
an independent, global perspective. To find out more, visit www.ft.com/pearsonoffer.

ISBN: 978-0-273-79246-8 (print)
      978-0-273-79257-4 (PDF)
      978-0-273-79247-5 (eText)

British Library Cataloguing-in-Publication Data
A catalogue record for the print edition is available from the British Library

Library of Congress Cataloging-in-Publication Data
Sloman, John, 1947-
    Economics for business / John Sloman, The Economics Network, University of Bristol,
Dean Garratt, Nottingham Trent University and Kevin Hinde, Senior Teaching Fellow,
University of Durham. -- Sixth edition
       pages cm
    ISBN 978-0-273-79246-8 -- ISBN 978-0-273-79257-4 (PDF) -- ISBN 978-0-273-79247-5 (eText)
    1. Economics. 2. Business. 3. Commerce. 4. Managerial economics. I. Hinde, Kevin. II. Title.
    HB171.5.S6353 2013
    330--dc23
                                                                    2013008558

10 9 8 7 6 5 4 3 2
17 16 15 14 13

Front cover images and all part and chapter images © John Sloman

Print edition typeset in 8/12pt ITC Stone Serif Std by 35
Print edition printed and bound by L.E.G.O.S.P.A, Italy

NOTE THAT ANY PAGE CROSS REFERENCES REFER TO THE PRINT EDITION

About the authors

John Sloman was Director of the Economics Network (www.economicsnetwork.ac.uk) from 1999 to 2012. The Economics Network is a UK-wide organisation based at the University of Bristol and provides a range of services designed to promote and share good practice in learning and teaching economics. John is now a Visiting Fellow at Bristol and a Senior Associate with the Economics Network.

John is also Visiting Professor at the University of the West of England, Bristol, where, from 1992 to 1999, he was Head of School of Economics. He taught at UWE until 2007.

John has taught a range of courses, including economic principles on social science and business studies degrees, development economics, comparative economic systems, intermediate macroeconomics and managerial economics. He has also taught economics on various professional courses.

He is also co-author with Dean Garratt and Alison Wride, Provost of GSM, London, of *Economics* (Pearson Education, 8th edition 2012); with Dean Garratt of Nottingham Trent University of *Essentials of Economics* (Pearson Education, 6th edition, 2013); with Elizabeth Jones from the University of Warwick of *Economics and the Business*

Environment (3rd edition 2011); and with Peter Smith from the University of Southampton of the *Economics Workbook* designed to accompany *Economics* (Pearson Education, 8th edition, 2009). Translations or editions of the various books are available for a number of different countries with the help of co-authors around the world.

John is very interested in promoting new methods of teaching economics, including group exercises, experiments, role playing, computer-aided learning and use of audience response systems and podcasting in teaching. He has organised and spoken at conferences for both lecturers and students of economics throughout the UK and in many other countries.

As part of his work with the Economics Network he has contributed to its two sites for students and prospective students of economics: Studying Economics (www.studyingeconomics.ac.uk) and Why Study Economics? (www.whystudyeconomics.ac.uk).

From March to June 1997, John was a visiting lecturer at the University of Western Australia. In July and August 2000, he was again a visiting lecturer at the University of Western Australia and also at Murdoch University in Perth.

In 2007, John received a Lifetime Achievement Award as 'outstanding teacher and ambassador of economics' presented jointly by the Higher Education Academy, the Government Economic Service and the Scottish Economic Society.

Kevin Hinde is a Senior Teaching Fellow in economics and strategy at Durham University. Over the years, Kevin has taught or presented on economics and strategy to specialists and non-specialists at undergraduate and postgraduate level in the UK, the Caribbean, Europe, Hong Kong, the Middle East and India. At Durham, Kevin teaches undergraduate economics and intermediate microeconomics, as well as teaching economics to Masters in Management and MBA students on the full time, executive and distance learning programmes. He also supervises undergraduate

and postgraduate dissertations in economics and strategy. Kevin's contribution to teaching and the learning experience have been recognised in prizes and nominations for prizes from peers and students. His main publications are in the areas of microeconomic policy and strategy. He sees these research interests and case studies as essential to developing student learning. Kevin has also published on e-Learning and is an Associate Editor for the international peer-reviewed journal CHEER (Computers in Higher Education Economics Review, now incorporated into the International Review of Economics Education).

Outside work, Kevin enjoys playing golf, hill walking and gardening. His great passions, other than his wife and two sons, are cricket and football, particularly Coventry City FC, his home team.

Dean Garratt is senior lecturer in economics at Nottingham Business School. He joined Nottingham Trent after a spell working as an economic assistant at both HM Treasury and then at the Council of Mortgage Lenders. While at these institutions Dean was briefing on a variety of issues relating to the household sector and to the housing and mortgage markets.

His time as an economic assistant has significantly influenced his approach towards the teaching of economics. This has seen Dean increasingly adopt a problem- or issues-based approach in his teaching of economics. He believes that this approach can help to cultivate amongst students the same interest and fascination that Dean has for economics. Dean believes that a deeper understanding of what it means to think like an economist can be achieved when students can clearly see the relevance and application of economic ideas and principles.

In 2006 Dean received an Outstanding Teaching Award from the Economics Network. The award is given to an academic who demonstrates excellence in course structure, delivery, student response, student performance and peer recognition.

Subsequently, Dean has become an Associate of the Economics Network, helping to promote high quality teaching practices through presentations and workshops. Dean has been involved in projects to develop issued-based learning and teaching resources for economists, including resources for use on first-year quantitative methods and data analysis modules.

Dean teaches economics at a variety of levels both to students on economics programmes and to those taking economics as part of non-economics programmes. In 2008/9 he was the learning and teaching coordinator for the Nottingham Business School. Since 2011 he has been the course leader for the Business School's undergraduate suite of economics courses.

Outside of work, Dean is an avid watcher of most sports. He is a season ticket holder at both Leicester City Football Club and Leicestershire County Cricket Club.

Andrew Hunt is a lecturer in Economics at Plymouth University. He has previously held research and lecturing positions at the universities of Durham and Northumbria. Andrew also holds a Senior Research Fellow position at St Chad's College, Durham University, and is an external examiner for the Economics department at the University of the West of Scotland.

Over the past fifteen years Andrew has taught many aspects of undergraduate and postgraduate economics. His current teaching interests are primarily focussed upon the economics of business strategy, competing approaches to macroeconomics and applied econometrics. Andrew's approach to teaching and learning emphasises the benefits of thinking 'like an economist'. This stresses the need to be able to recognise the essential features of the problem or topic, to be able to apply model-based reasoning and to have the skills to relate this model-based approach to quantitative and qualitative data. Andrew has developed courses for delivery to both specialist economics students and those on business and social science programmes. He also has extensive experience delivering vocational training on the use of economic frameworks and techniques to professional economists and economic development practitioners.

Outside of teaching, Andrew's research has focussed upon the practical application of economics to real world situations. He has undertaken research on behalf of a wide range of public and private sector organisations. Public sector clients include the Department of Business, Innovation and Skills, the North East and North West Development agencies, the Department for Education, the Department for Environment, Food and Rural Affairs and numerous local government organisations. Much of this research has involved the development of bespoke economic modelling tools to address specific research questions. For example, the economic impact of the public sector cuts outlined the 2010 Comprehensive Spending Review upon the North East of England, the wider economic benefits of moving households out of fuel poverty and the commercial property demands generated by economic change. Andrew's current research interests are in the areas of the modelling of regional economies and exploring barriers to small firm formation and growth.

Brief contents

Part A · BUSINESS AND ECONOMICS

Part B · BUSINESS AND MARKETS

Part C · BACKGROUND TO DEMAND

Part D · BACKGROUND TO SUPPLY

Part E · SUPPLY: SHORT-RUN PROFIT MAXIMISATION

Detailed contents

Part G THE FIRM IN THE FACTOR MARKET

Part H THE RELATIONSHIP BETWEEN GOVERNMENT AND BUSINESS

Custom publishing

Custom publishing allows academics to pick and choose content from one or more textbooks for their course and combine it into a definitive course text.

Here are some common examples of custom solutions which have helped over 1000 courses across Europe:

■ different chapters from across our publishing imprints combined into one book;
■ lecturer's own material combined together with textbook chapters or published in a separate booklet;
■ third-party cases and articles that you are keen for your students to read as part of the course;
■ any combination of the above.

The Pearson Education custom text published for your course is professionally produced and bound – just as you would expect from any Pearson Education text. Since many of our titles have online resources accompanying them we can even build a Custom website that matches your course text.

If you are teaching a first year Economics course you may have a large teaching team with different lecturers teaching the micro and macroeconomics sections. Do you find that it can be difficult to agree on one textbook? If you do, you might find combining the macro and micro halves from different Pearson textbooks a useful solution. You may teach a mixed ability class and would like to be able to provide some advanced material from Sloman's larger economics text or perhaps you take more of a business focus where chapters from Sloman's *Economics for Business* might be useful.

Custom publishing has enabled adopters of this text to employ these different solutions.

If, once you have had time to review this title, you feel Custom publishing might benefit you and your course, please do get in contact. However minor, or major the change – we can help you out.

For more details on how to make your chapter selection for your course please go to www.pearsoned.co.uk/sloman and select the custom publishing link.

You can contact us at: **www.pearsoncustom.co.uk** or via your local representative at: **www.pearsoned.co.uk/replocator**.

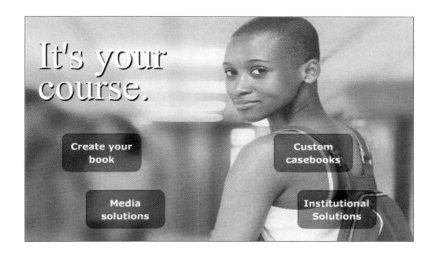

Guided tour

Parts. The book is divided into 11 parts and each part introduction is spread over two pages and contains an introduction to the material covered and an article from the Financial Times about one of the topics.

Chapter introductions begin each chapter by identifying the specific business issues covered in that chapter.

The Sloman News site. This is an excellent resource, and one that you might want to look at on a weekly basis to ensure that your current affairs knowledge is kept up to date. New items are added several times per month. These link to articles in the press and there are questions on each news item and references to the book. There is also a powerful search feature that lets you search for articles by chapter of the book, by topic or by month.

AIDING YOUR UNDERSTANDING

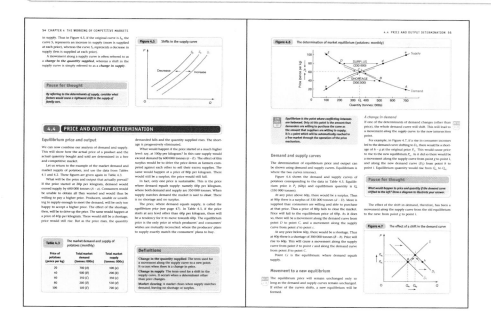

Pause for thought questions help you reflect on what you have just read and to check your understanding.

Definitions for all the key terms are highlighted in the text where they first appear and are defined in definition boxes. This allows you to see the terms used in context and is very useful for revision.

Key ideas are highlighted and explained when they first appear. These ideas make up the key elements of an economist's toolkit. Whenever they recur later in the book an icon appears in the margin. These help you to think like an economist.

Chapter Summaries at the end of each chapter are an ideal revision tool. They allow you to check up on your understanding at frequent intervals.

Glossary terms are clearly defined and easily accessible at the end of the book.

PRACTISING AND TESTING YOUR LEARNING

Review questions can be used for self-testing, in class exercises or debate.

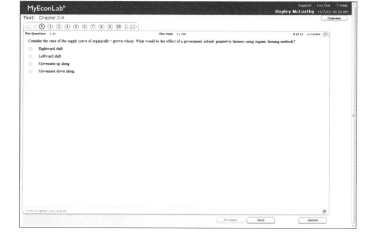

Take the **Chapter Tests in MyEconLab** to generate a personalised Study Plan. You will then be directed to specific resources in MyEconLab to help you focus your studies and improve your grades. For details on how to access MyEconLab visit www.myeconlab.com.

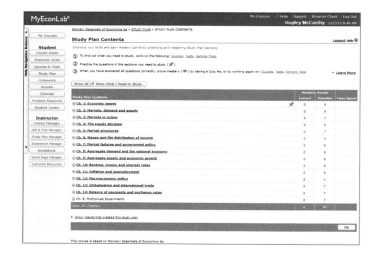

If you have access to MyEconLab you can use your **personalised Study Plan** to assess how well you are doing, and areas you need to concentrate on to improve.

APPLYING ECONOMICS TO THE REAL WORLD

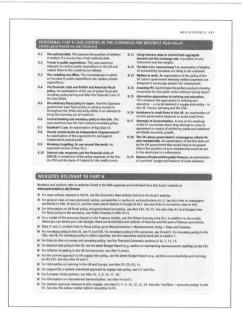

Boxes provide case studies to show how economics can be used to understand particular business problems or aspects of the business environment. The boxes also have questions, which link the material back to the chapter.

Web material at the end of each part lists additional case studies that can be found in MyEconLab along with references to various useful websites.

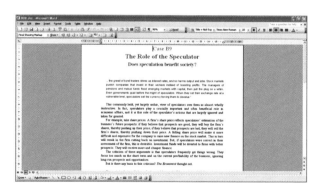

Additional Case Studies relevant to each chapter can be found in MyEconLab.

Guided tour of MyEconLab

MyEconLab is an online assessment and revision tool that puts you in control of your learning through a suite of study and practice tools tied to the online eText.

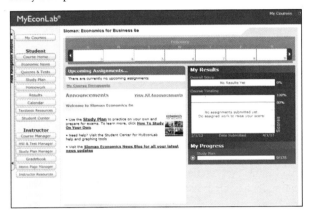

How do I use MyEconLab?

The Course Home page is where you can view announcements from your instructor and see an overview of your personal progress.

View the Calendar to see the dates for online homework, quizzes and tests that your instructor has set for you.

Your lecturer may have chosen **MyEconLab** to provide online homework, quizzes and texts. Check here to access the homework that has been set for you.

Practice tests for each chapter of the textbook enable you to check your understanding and identify the areas in which you need to do further work. Lecturers can customise and assign the practice tests or students can complete the tests on their own.

Keep track of your results in your own gradebook.

Work through the questions in your personalised Study Plan at your own pace. Because the Study Plan is tailored to each student, you will be able to study more efficiently by only reviewing areas where you still need practice. The Study Plan also saves your results, helping you see at a glance exactly which topics you need to review.

Additional instruction is provided in the form of detailed, step-by-step solutions to worked exercises. The figures in many of the exercises in **MyEconLab** are generated algorithmically, containing different values each time they are used. This means that you can practise individual concepts as often as you like.

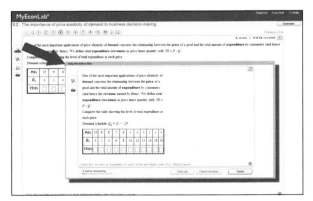

There is also a link to the eText from every question in the Study Plan, so you can easily review and master the content.

View supporting multimedia resources such as links to the eText and Glossary Flashcards.

Lecturer training and support

Our dedicated team of Technology Specialists offer personalised training and support for **MyEconLab, ensuring that** **you can maximise the benefits of MyEconLab**. To make contact with your Technology Specialist please email feedback-cw@pearson.com.

For a visual walkthrough of how to make the most of **MyEconLab**, visit www.myeconlab.com.

To find details of your local sales representatives go to www.pearsoned.co.uk/replocator.

Preface

If you are studying economics on a business degree or diploma, then this book is written for you. Although we cover all the major principles of economics, the focus throughout is on the world of business. For this reason we also cover several topics that do not appear in traditional economics textbooks.

As well as making considerable use of business examples throughout the text, we have included many case studies (in boxes). These illustrate how economics can be used to understand particular business problems or aspects of the business environment. Many of these case studies cover issues that you are likely to read about in the newspapers. Some cover general business issues; others look at specific companies. Nearly all of them cover topical issues including, the rise of online business, the video gaming market, entrepreneurship, competition and growth strategy, the banking crisis of the late 2000s, the sluggish recovery from recession, quantitative easing and increased competition from newly industrialised countries.

The style of writing is direct and straightforward, with short paragraphs to aid rapid comprehension. There are also questions interspersed throughout the text in 'Pause for thought' panels. These encourage you to reflect on what you are learning and to see how the various ideas and theories relate to different issues. Definitions of all key terms are given in definition boxes, with defined terms appearing in bold. Also we have highlighted 43 'Key ideas', which are fundamental to 'thinking like an economist'. We refer back to these every time they recur in the book. This helps you to see how the subject ties together, and also helps you

to develop a toolkit of concepts that can be used in a host of different contexts.

Summaries are given at the end of each chapter, with points numbered according to the section in which they appeared. These summaries should help you in reviewing the material you have covered and in revising for exams. Each chapter finishes with a series of questions. These can be used to check your understanding of the chapter and help you to see how its material can be applied to various business problems. References to various useful websites are listed at the end of each Part of the book.

The book also has a blog, The Sloman Economics News Site, with several postings each week by the authors. The blog discusses topical issues, links to relevant articles, videos and data and asks questions for you to think about.

New to this edition is a 'MyEconLab'. This interactive website is a personalised and innovative online study and testing resource. It also contains additional case studies, answers to 'Pause for Thought' questions and other materials to improve your understanding of concepts and techniques used in economics.

We hope that, in using this book, you will share some of our fascination for economics. It is a subject that is highly relevant to the world in which we live. And it is a world where many of our needs are served by business – whether as employers or as producers of the goods and services we buy. After graduating, you will probably take up employment in business. A thorough grounding in economic principles should prove invaluable in the business decisions you may well have to make.

The aim of this book is to provide a course in economic principles as they apply to the business environment. It is designed to be used by first-year undergraduates on business studies degrees and diplomas where economics is taught from the business perspective. It is also suitable for students studying economics on postgraduate courses in

management, including the MBA, and various professional courses.

Being essentially a book on economics, we cover all the major topics found in standard economics texts – indeed, some of the material in the principles sections is drawn directly from *Economics* (8th edition). But in addition there are several specialist business chapters and sections to build upon and enliven the subject for business studies students. These have been fully updated and revised for this new edition. The following are some examples of these additional topics:

- The business environment
- Business organisations
- Characteristics theory
- Marketing of products
- Business strategy
- Alternative aims of firms
- Growth strategy
- Strategic alliances
- The small-firm sector
- Pricing in practice
- Government and the firm, including policies towards research and development (R&D) and policies towards training
- Government and the market, including environmental policy and transport policy
- Financial markets
- The multinational corporation
- Globalisation and business
- Trading blocs
- Monetary union

The text is split into 32 chapters. Each chapter is kept relatively short to enable the material to be covered in a single lecture or class. Each chapter finishes with review questions, which can be used for seminars or discussion sessions.

The chapters are grouped into 11 Parts:

- Part A Business and economics (Chapters 1–3) establishes the place of business within the economy and the relevance of economics to business decision making.
- Part B Business and markets (Chapters 4 and 5) looks at the operation of markets. It covers supply and demand analysis and examines the importance of the concept of elasticity for business decisions.
- Part C Background to demand (Chapters 6–8) considers the consumer – how consumer behaviour can be predicted and how, via advertising and marketing, consumer demand can be influenced.
- Part D Background to supply (Chapters 9 and 10) focuses on the relationship between the quantity

that businesses produce and their costs, revenue and profits.

- Part E Supply: short-run profit maximisation (Chapters 11 and 12) presents the traditional analysis of market structures and the implications that such structures have for business conduct and performance.
- Part F Supply: alternative strategies (Chapters 13–17) starts by looking at business strategy. It then considers various alternative theories of the firm. It also examines how business size can influence business actions, and why pricing strategies differ from one firm to another and how these strategies are influenced by the market conditions in which firms operate.
- Part G The firm in the factor market (Chapters 18 and 19) focuses on the market for labour and the market for capital. It examines what determines the factor proportions that firms use and how factor prices are determined.
- Part H The relationship between government and business (Chapters 20–22) establishes the theoretical rationale behind government intervention in the economy, and then assesses the relationship between the government and the individual firm and the government and the market.
- Part I Business in the international environment (Chapters 23–25) starts by examining the process of globalisation and the growth of the multinational business. It then turns to international trade and the benefits that accrue from it. It also examines the issue of protection and international moves to advance free trade. Finally it examines the expansion of regional trading agreements.
- Part J The macroeconomic environment (Chapters 26–29) considers the macroeconomic framework in which firms operate. We focus on the principal macroeconomic variables, investigate the role of money in the economy, and briefly outline the theoretical models underpinning the relationships between these variables.
- Part K Macroeconomic policy (Chapters 30–32) examines the mechanics of government intervention at a macro level as well as its impact on business and its potential benefits and drawbacks. Demand-side and supply-side policy and economic policy co-ordination between countries are all considered.

SPECIAL FEATURES

The book contains the following special features:

- A direct and straightforward written style, with short paragraphs to aid rapid comprehension. The aim all the time is to provide maximum clarity.
- Attractive full-colour design. The careful and consistent use of colour and shading makes the text more attractive

to students and easier to use by giving clear signals as to the book's structure.

- Key ideas highlighted and explained where they first appear. There are 43 of these ideas, which are fundamental to the study of economics. Students can see them recurring throughout the book, and an icon appears in the margin to refer back to the page where the idea first appears. Showing how ideas can be used in a variety of contexts helps students to 'think like an economist' and to relate the different parts of the subject together. All 43 Key ideas are defined in a special section at the end of the book.

■ 'Pause for thought' questions integrated throughout the text. These encourage students to reflect on what they have just read and make the learning process a more active one. Answers to these questions appear in the student section of the book's website.

■ Double-page opening spreads for each of the 11 Parts of the book. These contain an introduction to the material covered and an article from the Financial Times on one of the topics.

■ All technical terms are highlighted and clearly defined in definition boxes on the page on which they appear. This feature proved very popular in the first five editions and is especially useful for students when revising.

■ A comprehensive glossary of all technical terms.

■ Additional applied material to that found in the text can be found in the boxes within each chapter. All boxes include questions which relate the material back to the chapter in which the box is located. The extensive use of applied material makes learning much more interesting for students and helps to bring the subject alive. This is particularly important for business students who need to relate economic theory to their other subjects

and to the world of business generally. The boxes are current and include discussion of a range of companies and business topics.

■ Additional case studies appearing in MyEconLab are referred to at the end of each Part.

■ Detailed summaries appear at the end of each chapter with the points numbered by the chapter section in which they are made. These allow students not only to check their comprehension of the chapter's contents, but also to get a clear overview of the material they have been studying.

■ Each chapter concludes with a series of review questions to test students' understanding of the chapter's salient points. These questions can be used for seminars or as set work to be completed in the students' own time.

■ References at the end of each Part to a list of relevant websites, details of which can be found in the Web appendix at the end of the book. You can easily access any of these sites from the book's own website (at www.pearsonblog.campaignserver.co.uk/). When you enter the site, click on 'Hotlinks'. You will find all the sites from the Web appendix listed. Click on the one you want and the 'hotlink' will take you straight to it.

■ A comprehensive index, including reference to all defined terms. This enables students to look up a definition as required and to see it used in context.

SUPPLEMENTS

Blog

Visit the book's blog, The Sloman Economics News Site, at www.pearsonblog.campaignserver.co.uk/ This refers to topical issues in economics and relates them to particular chapters in the book. There are several postings per week, with each one providing an introduction to the topic, and then links to relevant articles, videos, podcasts, data and official documents, and then questions which students and tutors will find relevant for homework or class discussion.

MyEconLab for students

MyEconLab provides a comprehensive set of online re-sources. A student access code card may have been included with this textbook at a reduced cost. If you do not have an access code, you can buy access to MyEconLab and the eText – an online version of the book – at www.myeconlab.com.

Central to MyEconLab is an interactive study plan with questions and answers. You will also find a variety of tools to enable you to assess your own learning. A personalised Study Plan identifies areas to concentrate on to improve

grades, and specific tools are provided to enable you to direct your studies in a more efficient way. Other resources include:

■ Animations of key models with audio explanations

■ 139 case studies with questions for self-study, ordered Part-by-Part and referred to in the text

■ Updated list of over 250 hot links to sites of use for economics

■ Answers to all in-chapter (Pause for Thought) questions

MyEconLab for lecturers and tutors

MyEconLab can be set up by you as a complete virtual learning environment for your course or embedded into Blackboard, WebCT or Moodle. You can customise its look and feel and its availability to students. You can use it to provide support to your students in the following ways:

■ My EconLab's gradebook automatically records each student's time spent and performance on the tests and Study Plan. It also generates reports you can use to monitor your students' progress.

- You can use MyEconLab to build your own test, quizzes and homework assignments from the question base provided to set your own students' assessment.
- Questions are generated algorithmically so they use different values each time they are used.
- You can create your own exercises by using the econ exercise builder.

Additional resources for lecturers and tutors

There are many additional resources for lecturers and tutors that can be downloaded from the lecturer site of MyEconLab. These have been thoroughly revised for the sixth edition. These include:

- PowerPoint® slide shows in full colour for use with a data projector in lectures and classes. These can also be made available to students by loading them on to a local network. There are several types of slideshows:
  - *All figures from the book and most of the tables.* Each figure is built up in a logical sequence, thereby allowing tutors to show them in lectures in an animated form.
  - *Customisable lecture plans.* These are a series of bullet-point lecture plans. There is one for each chapter of the book. Each one can be easily edited, with points added, deleted or moved, so as to suit particular lectures. A consistent use of colour is made to show how the points tie together. They come in various versions:
    - Lecture plans with integrated diagrams. These lecture plans include animated diagrams, charts and tables at the appropriate points.
    - Lecture plans with integrated diagrams and questions. These are like the above but also include multiple-choice questions, allowing lectures to become more interactive. They can be used with or without an audience response system (ARS). ARS versions are available for InterWrite PRS® and TurningPoint® and are ready to use with appropriate 'clickers'.
    - Lecture plans without the diagrams. These allow you to construct your own diagrams on the blackboard or whiteboard or use an OHP.
- Multiple choice questions. This test bank has been thoroughly revised and contains many new questions. It is flexible and easy to use.

- Case studies. These, also available in the student part of MyEconLab, can be reproduced and used for classroom exercises or for student assignments. Answers are also provided (not available on the student site).
- Workshops. There are 22 of these, each one covering one or more chapters. They are in Word® and can be reproduced for use with large groups (up to 200 students) in a lecture theatre or large classroom. Suggestions for use are given in an accompanying file. Answers to all workshops are given in separate Word® files.
- Teaching/learning case studies. There are 20 of these. They examine various approaches to teaching introductory economics and ways to improve student learning of introductory economics.

Answers to:

- all end-of-chapter questions,
- pause for thought questions,
- questions in boxes,
- questions in the case studies in MyEconLab,
- the 22 workshops.

Acknowledgements

As with previous editions, we've had great support from the team at Pearson, including Kate Brewin, Liz Johnson and Rachel Chiles. We'd like to thank all of them for their hard work and encouragement. Thanks too to the many users of the book who have given us feedback. We always value their comments. Please continue to send us your views.

Kevin Hinde and Mark Sutcliffe, co-authors with John on previous editions, have moved on to new ventures. However, many of their wise words and ideas are still embedded in this edition and, for that, we offer a huge thanks. Many thanks also to Andrew Hunt from the University of Plymouth who has contributed many ideas to the first 19 chapters. We really appreciate his input.

Our two families have also been remarkably tolerant and supportive throughout. Thanks especially to Alison and Pat who seem to have perfected a subtle blend of encouragement, humour and patience.

John and Dean

Publisher's acknowledgements

We are grateful to the following for permission to reproduce copyright material:

Figures

Figure 8.2 after *Introduction to Marketing: an administrative approach*, John Wiley & Sons, Inc. (Lipson, H. A. and Darling, J. R. 1971), reproduced with permission; Figure 13.2 reprinted with the permission of Free Press of Simon & Schuster, Inc., from *Competitive Strategy: Techniques for Analyzing Industries and Competitors* by Michael E. Porter. Copyright © 1980, 1988 by the Free Press. All rights reserved; Figures on page 231, page 232 from Cross border mergers and acquisitions, *World Investment Report Annex Tables*, June (UNCTAD 2012), Copyright United Nations; Figure 18.13 from *The Flexible Firm* (Institute of Manpower Studies 1987) Institute for Employment Studies, University of Sussex, Brighton, (IES); Figure on page 342 from *Skills in the UK: The Long-term Challenge*, H. M. Treasury (Leitch Committee Interim Report 2005) December, Chart 3; Figure on page 348 from *Stern Review on the Economics of Climate Change*, Office of Climate Change (OCC) (Stern Review 2006) Executive Summary, Figure 1; Figures 23.1, 23.2 from UNCTAD FDI database, Copyright United Nations; Figure 24.3 from WTO Statistics database, World Trade Organization; Figure 24.4 from *International Trade Statistics 2011* (WTO 2012) Table II.2, World Trade Organization; Figure 26.11 from *Annual Abstract of Statistics Q4 2011* (ONS 2011); Figure on page 466 data showing liabilities of banks and building societies based on series LPMALOA and PRPMTBJF and RPMB3UQ from Statistical Interactive Database (Bank of England), www.bankofengland. co.uk, Bank of England Revisions Policy (http://www. bankofengland.co.uk/mfsd/iadb/notesiadb/Revisions.htm); Figure on page 466 GDP data adapted from Quarterly National Accounts, Q1 2012 (Office for National Statistics); Figure on page 471 based on data from Bank of England Statistical Interactive Database (series LPQB3XE and LPQB3HK), May 2012, www.bankofengland.co.uk, Bank of England Revisions Policy (http://www.bankofengland.co.uk/ mfsd/iadb/notesiadb/Revisions.htm); Figure 28.3 adapted from Statistical Interactive Database (Bank of England). Based on series IUMAMIH and IUMVNEA, www.bankofengland. co.uk, Bank of England Revisions Policy (http://www. bankofengland.co.uk/mfsd/iadb/notesiadb/Revisions.htm); Figure 28.4 based on series LPMAUYN (M4), LPMAVAE (M0), LPMBL22 (reserves) and LPMAVAB (notes and coins) from Statistical Interactive Database (Bank of England), www.bankofengland.co.uk, Bank of England Revisions Policy (http://www.bankofengland.co.uk/mfsd/iadb/notesiadb/ Revisions.htm); Figure on page 515 from *Public Sector Finances Databank*, H. M. Treasury; Figure 30.4 from *Inflation Report* (Bank of England 2012) August, with permission from the Bank of England, www.bankofengland.co.uk.

Tables

Table 1.3 from SME database, Office for National Statistics, 2012; Tables 2.1, 2.2 adapted from *Statistical Annex to European Economy*, Directorate General of Economic and Financial Affairs (ECFIN), European Commission (European Commission 2012), © European Union, 1995–2012; Table 2.3 from Mintel Cider UK Report, February 2012, Mintel Group Ltd; Tables on page 112, page 113 from Private Label Food and Drink – UK – March 2012, http://academic.mintel.com/ display/590059/?highlight=true, Mintel Group Ltd; Table 8.2 based on data in the Advertising Association's, *Advertising Statistics Yearbook 2009*, published by WARC (www.warc. com); Tables 8.3, 8.4 from Nielsen and MPP Consulting. Available from, http://www.rankingthebrands.com, with permission from Nielsen; Table on page 143 from Economies of Scale, *The Single Market Review*, Subseries V, Volume 4 (European Commission/Economists Advisory Group Ltd 1997), Office for Official Publications of the European Communities, Luxembourg, © European Communities, 1995–2010; Tables 16.2, 16.3 from *Business Population Estimates for the UK and Regions* (BIS 2012); Table 16.4 from *Understanding the Small-Business Sector*, Routledge (Storey, D. J. 1994), with permission from Cengage Learning (EMEA) Ltd; Tables 18.1, 18.2 from *Annual Survey of Hours and Earnings*, Office for National Statistics (ONS 2012); Table 22.2 from *Transport Statistics Great Britain 2011* (Department for Transport, National Statistics 2011); Table 23.1 from Yip, George S., *Total Global Strategy II*, 2nd Edition, copyright 2003, pp. 11–12. Reproduced by permission of Pearson Education, Inc., Upper Saddle River, NJ, USA; Table 23.3 from UNCTADstat, Copyright United Nations; Tables 26.1, 26.2 from *United Kingdom National Accounts: The Blue Book – 2011 Edition* (ONS 2011); Table 31.1 adapted from AMECO database, European Commission, DGECFIN, Tables 3.2 and 6.1, © European Union, 1995–2012.

Text

Extract on page 2 from Chinese exporters seek new markets, *The Financial Times*, 12 June 2012 (Jacob, R.), © The Financial Times Limited. All Rights Reserved; Epigraph on page 3 from Everyday economics makes for good fun at parties, *Financial Times*, 2 May 2006 (Kay, J.), © The Financial Times Limited. All Rights Reserved; Box 3.1 from Executive pay: The trickle-up effect, *Financial Times*, 27 July 2011 (Groom, B.), © The Financial Times Limited. All Rights Reserved; Extract on page 44 from A tale of two coffee beans, *Financial Times*, 3 May 2012 (Terazono, E.), © The Financial Times Limited. All Rights Reserved; Epigraph on page 45 reprinted by permission of *Harvard Business Review*. Extract from How to survive in turbulent markets by D. Sull, February 2009. Copyright © 2009 by the Harvard Business School Publishing Corporation; all rights reserved; Box 5.3 from Fundamentals and speculation in commodity markets, *Financial Times*, 16 May 2011 (Davies, G.), © The Financial Times Limited. All Rights Reserved; Extract on page 80 from China Consumers: How to find favour down at the shops, *Financial Times*, 26 October 2011 (Waldmeir, P.), © The Financial Times Limited. All Rights Reserved; Epigraph on page 81 from Preserving and Restoring Trust and Confidence in Markets. Keynote address to the British Institute of International and Comparative Law at the Ninth Annual Trans-Atlantic Antitrust Dialogue. April 30th. Office of Fair Trading (Collins, P. 2009) http://www.oft.gov.uk/shared_oft/speeches/2009/spe0809.pdf; Extract on page 126 from O'Leary looks to skies as he keeps throttle open, *Financial Times*, 3 June 2009 (Done, K.), © The Financial Times Limited. All Rights Reserved; Epigraph on page 127 from *The Global Competitiveness Report 2008–2009*, World Economic Forum, p. 44; Box 10.1 from RWE considers pulling plug on NPower, *Financial Times*, 5th July 2011 (Blair, D., Wiesmann, G. and Sakoui, A.), © The Financial Times Limited. All Rights Reserved; Epigraph on page 159 from HMV expects return to profit in 2013, *Financial Times*, 9 August 2012, © The Financial Times Limited. All Rights Reserved; Extract on page 196 from Back in the grove, *Financial Times*, 31 August 2012 (Aspden, P.), © The Financial Times Limited. All Rights Reserved; Epigraph on page 197 reprinted by permission of *Harvard Business Review*. Extract from The five competitive forces that shape competition by M. E. Porter, January 2008. Copyright © 2008 by the Harvard Business Publishing Corporation; all rights reserved; Quote on page 249 from Our Unique Cocoa Plantation – The Rabot Estate, St Lucia http://www.hotelchocolat.co.uk/cocoa-plantation-ARabot_Uniquecocoa/, Hotel Chocolat Ltd; Extract on page 268 from A German model goes global, *Financial Times*, 21 May 2012 (Bryant, C.), © The Financial Times Limited. All Rights Reserved; Extract on page 308 from Cargo airlines fined for fixing prices, *Financial Times*, 13 April 2009 (Done, K.), © The Financial Times Limited. All Rights Reserved; Epigraph on page 309 from Kroes, N, 30 March 2009, European Commission Competition Commissioner, Competition, The crisis and the road to recovery, Address at Economic Club of Toronto, Copyright European Communities 2009; Extract on page 368 from Big rise in anti-dumping probes, *Financial Times*, 8 May 2009 (Williams, F.), © The Financial Times Limited. All Rights Reserved; Epigraph on page 369 from Why the Critics of Globalization are Mistaken, Hanelsblatt, August, http://www.columbia.edu/~jb38/, Professor Jagdish N. Bhagwati; Extract on page 416 from City confident of recovery amid tide of positive figures, *Financial Times*, 13 June 2009 (Giles, C.), © The Financial Times Limited. All Rights Reserved; Epigraph on page 417 from Mervyn King, Governor of the Bank of England, Finance: A return from risk, speech to the Worshipful Company of International Bankers, at the Mansion House, 17 March 2009, Bank of England Revisions Policy (http://www.bankofengland.co.uk/mfsd/iadb/notesiadb/Revisions.htm); Extract on page 434 from Deflation turns into biggest economic risk, *The Times*, 11 May 2003, © NI Syndication Limited, 2003; Extract on page 508 from Heseltine attempts revamp of regions, *Financial Times*, 29 October 2012 (Groom, B. and Pickard, J.), © The Financial Times Limited. All Rights Reserved; Epigraph on page 509 from Alistair Darling, Chancellor of the Exchequer's Budget speech, 21 April 2009.

Contains public sector information licensed under the Open Government Licence (OGL) v1.0, http://www.nationalarchives.gov.uk/doc/open-government-licence.

In some instances we have been unable to trace the owners of copyright material, and we would appreciate any information that would enable us to do so.

Business and economics

The FT Reports . . .

The Financial Times, 12 June 2012

FT

Chinese exporters seek new markets

By Rahuk Jacob

With hundreds of television sets stacked high, Changhong Electronics' warehouse in Shunde resembles many other storage depots in southern China, but their destinations reveal an important shift in global trade patterns. . . .

Changhong, a Sichuan based company with 80,000 employees, is one of many Chinese companies responding to the eurozone crisis by seeking new markets. Fast growth in developing countries and sluggish western economies are prompting these companies to abandon their obsession with the US and Europe and to try and capitalise on rapidly growing markets in Asia, Africa and Latin America. . . .

Dennis Ng, the owner of Hong Kong-based jewellery maker Polaris, says his Guangzhou factory exports 60 per cent less to Europe than at the end of 2008, while sales to the US have fallen about as much, albeit over seven years.

Polaris has compensated for the decline by boosting sales in developing markets such as Russia where its exports total $35m compared to $10m to the US. The Guangzhou facility, which has so many microscopes for workers poring over precious stones that it looks like a science lab, now concentrates on Russian styles, which means using more gold, red stones and enamel.

Another company, toy manufacturer Maisto which makes 400,000 dinky cars a day in the industrial city of Dongguan, saw sales in Spain and Italy slow dramatically last year. But, Roger Ngan, director of marketing for the family-owned Maisto, says, 'Brazil is popping while Colombia and Peru are all doing very well'. . . .

The trend is redrawing China's trade map, according to China Confidential, the FT's China research service. Trade with Latin America grew by 113 per cent between the end of 2009 to $241.5bn at the end of 2011. . . . China Confidential predicts that if Chinese exporters continue on their current trajectory, Latin America could dislodge the EU as the country's largest trading partner as early as 2017.

The growth in exports to developing markets runs a wide gamut of products. . . . Foreign direct investment by Chinese infrastructure companies in Africa may be responsible for lifting demand in the continent, . . . [Overseas] investment by Chinese infrastructure companies is generating higher exports of capital goods, such as cranes, made by Chinese companies to the developing world. Gavekal Dragonomics, the China economics research firm, argues that a 'second wave' of exports from China has begun, consisting of excavators and turbines. Between 1998 and 2010, Gavekal notes, heavy industry exports to the developing world, grew by 25 per cent annually.

I dread admitting I am an economist. The cab driver quizzes you on what is going to happen to the economy, the dinner companion turns to talk to the person on the other side and the immigration officer says, with heavy sarcasm, that his country needs people like you.

John Kay, Everyday economics makes for good fun at parties
(*Financial Times*, 2 May 2006)

Businesses play a key role in all our lives. Whatever their size, and whatever the goods or services they provide, they depend on us as consumers to buy their products.

But just as businesses rely on us for their income, so equally many of us rely on firms for our income. The wages we earn depend on our employer's success, and that success in turn depends on us as suppliers of labour.

And it is not just as customers and workers that we are affected by business. The success of business in general affects the health of the whole economy and thus the lives of us all.

The extract from the *Financial Times* takes the case of Chinese exporters. To be successful, exporting firms must be capable of responding to changes in the global economy. This requires a thorough understanding of economics. Developing a business strategy that simultaneously responds to the eurozone crisis, high growth rates in parts of Asia and Latin America, the potential for rapid development in parts of Africa, etc. is not an easy task. Fortunately, economics provides frameworks for thinking about these issues, and many more.

In Part A of this book, we consider the relationship between business and economics.

In Chapter 1 we look at the structure of industry and its importance in determining firms' behaviour. We also look at a range of other factors that are likely to affect business decisions and how we can set about analysing the environment in which a firm operates in order to help it devise an appropriate business strategy.

Then, in Chapter 2 we ask what is it that economists do and, in particular, how economists set about analysing the world of business and the things businesses do. In particular, we focus on rational decision making – how to get the best outcome from limited resources.

Finally, in Chapter 3 we look at the different ways in which firms are organised: at their legal structure, at their internal organisation and at their goals.

Key terms

The business environment
PEST analysis
Production
Firms
Industries
Industrial sectors
Standard Industrial
  Classification (SIC)
Industrial concentration
Structure–conduct–
  performance
Scarcity
Factors of production
Macroeconomics
Microeconomics
Opportunity cost
Marginal costs
Marginal benefits
Rational choices
Circular flow of income
Transaction costs
Principal and agent
Business organisation
Price taker
Perfectly competitive
  market
Price mechanism
Demand
Supply

The business environment and business economics

What is business economics?

What is the role of *business economics*? What will you be studying in this book?

An economist's approach to the world of business requires that we examine *firms*: the environment in which they operate, the decisions they make, and the effects of these decisions – on themselves, on their customers, on their employees, on their business rivals and on the public at large.

Firms are essentially concerned with using inputs to make output. Inputs cost money and output earns money. The difference between the revenue earned and the costs incurred constitutes the firm's profit. Firms will normally want to make as much profit as possible, or at the very least to avoid a decline in profits. In order to meet these and other objectives, managers will need to make choices: choices of what types of output to produce, how much to produce and at what price; choices of what techniques of production to use, how many workers to employ and of what type, what suppliers to use for raw materials, equipment, etc. In each case, when weighing up alternatives, managers will want to make the best choices. Business economists study these choices. They study economic decision making by firms.

The study of decision making can be broken down into three stages.

The external influences on the firm (the 'business environment'). Here we are referring to the various factors that affect the firm that are largely outside its direct control. Examples are the competition it faces, the prices it pays for raw materials, the state of the economy (e.g. whether growing or in recession) and the level of interest rates. Businesses will need to obtain a clear understanding of their environment before they can set about making the right decisions.

Internal decisions of the firm. Given a knowledge of these external factors, how do firms then decide on prices, output, inputs, marketing, investment, etc? Here the business economist can play a major role in helping firms achieve their business objectives.

The external effects of business decision making. When the firm has made its decisions and acted on them, how do the results affect the firm's rivals, its customers and the wider public? In other words, what is the impact of a firm's decision making on people outside the firm? Are firms' actions in the public interest, or is there a case for government intervention?

What do business economists do?

Our study of business will involve three types of activity:

■ *Description.* For example, we will be describing the objectives of businesses (e.g. making profit or increasing market share), the types of market in which firms operate (e.g. competitive or non-competitive) and the constraints on decision making (e.g. the costs of production, the level of consumer demand and the state of the economy).

■ *Analysis.* For example, we will analyse how a firm's costs and profits are likely to vary with the amount of output it produces and what would be the consequences of a change in consumer demand or a change in the price charged by rivals. We will also analyse the upswings and downswings in the economy: something that will have a crucial bearing on the profitability of many companies.

■ *Recommendations.* Given the objectives of a firm, the business economist can help to show how those objectives can best be met. For example, if a firm wants to maximise its profits, the business economist can advise on what prices to charge, how much to invest, how much to advertise, etc. Of course, any such recommendations will only be as good as the data on which they are based. In an uncertain environment, recommendations will necessarily be more tentative.

In this chapter, as an introduction to the subject of business economics, we shall consider the place of the firm within its business environment, and assess how these external influences are likely to shape and determine its actions. In order to discuss the relationship between a business's actions and its environment, we first need to define what the business environment is.

1.1 THE BUSINESS ENVIRONMENT

It is normal to identify four dimensions to the business environment: political/legal, economic, social/cultural and technological.

Political/legal factors. Firms will be directly affected by the actions of government and other political events. These might be major events affecting the whole of the business community, such as the collapse of communism, the Iraq War or a change of government. Alternatively, they may be actions affecting just one part of the economy. For example, an anti-smoking campaign by the government will affect the tobacco industry. Similarly, businesses will be affected by the legal framework in which they operate. Examples include industrial relations legislation, product safety standards, regulations governing pricing in the privatised industries and laws preventing collusion between firms to keep prices up.

Economic factors. Economic factors can range from big to small, from local to national to international, from current

to future; from the rising costs of raw materials to the market entry of a new rival, from the forthcoming Budget to the instability of international exchange rates, from the current availability of investment funds to the likely future cash flow from a new product. Business must constantly take such factors into account when devising and acting upon its business strategy.

It is normal to divide the economic environment in which the firm operates into two levels:

■ *The microeconomic environment.* This includes all the economic factors that are *specific* to a particular firm operating in its own particular market. Thus one firm may be operating in a highly competitive market, whereas another may not; one firm may be faced by rapidly changing consumer tastes (e.g. a designer clothing manufacturer), while another may be faced with a virtually constant consumer demand (e.g. a potato merchant); one firm may face rapidly rising costs, whereas another may find that costs are constant or falling.

■ *The macroeconomic environment.* This is the *national* and *international* economic situation in which business as a whole operates. Business in general will fare much better if the economy is growing than if it is in recession. In examining the macroeconomic environment, we will also be looking at the policies that governments adopt in their attempt to steer the economy, since these policies, by affecting things such as taxation, interest rates and exchange rates, will have a major impact on firms.

Social/cultural factors. This aspect of the business environment concerns social attitudes and values. These include attitudes towards working conditions and the length of the working day, equal opportunities for different groups of people (whether by ethnicity, gender, physical attributes, etc.), the nature and purity of products, the use and abuse of animals, and images portrayed in advertising. The social/cultural environment also includes social trends, such as an increase in the average age of the population, or changes in attitudes towards seeking paid employment while bringing up small children. In recent times, various ethical issues, especially concerning the protection of the environment, have had a big impact on the actions of business and the image that many firms seek to present.

Technological factors. Over the past twenty years the pace of technological change has quickened. This has had a huge impact not only on how firms produce products, but also

---

BOX 1.1　THE BIOTECHNOLOGY INDUSTRY

Its business environment

There are few areas of business that cause such controversy as biotechnology. It has generated new medicines, created pest-resistant crops, developed eco-friendly industrial processes and, through genetic mapping, is providing incalculable advances in gene therapy. These developments, however, have raised profound ethical issues. Many areas of biotechnology are uncontentious, but genetic modification and cloning have met with considerable public hostility, colouring many people's views of biotechnology in general.

Biotechnology refers to the application of knowledge about living organisms and their components to make new products and develop new industrial processes. For many it is seen as the next wave in the development of the knowledge-based economy. According to EU estimates, by 2010 the biotechnology sector was worth some €2000 billion.

In global terms, the USA dominates this sector. According to the OECD, the USA has 6213 biotechnology firms, followed by Spain with 1095 and France with 1067. When compared to Europe as a whole, the US biotechnology sector spends over twice as much on research and development ($22 billion) and generates twice as much in revenues. The UK is eighth in the league table with some 496 specialist biotech companies.

The industry is dominated by small and medium-sized businesses. Most biotechnology firms have fewer than 50 employees. However, the larger firms dominate the sector in terms of Research and Development (R&D). In the USA and France, the countries with the largest R&D expenditure, some 88 per cent of this was carried out by firms with over 50 employees. In most countries biotech firms are geographically clustered, forming industry networks around key universities and research institutes. In the UK, such clusters can be found in Cambridge, Oxford and London. The link with universities and research institutes taps into the UK's strong science base.

In addition to such clustering, the biotech industry is well supported by the UK government and other charitable organisations such as the Wellcome Trust. Such support helps to fund what is a highly research-intensive sector. The UK government not only provides finance, but encourages firms to form collaborative agreements, and through such collaboration hopes to encourage better management and use of the results that research generates. It also offers help for biotechnology business start-ups, and guidance on identifying and gaining financial support.

The EU too provides a range of resources to support business within the biotech sector. The EUREKA programme attempts to help create pan-EU partnerships, and the EU Seventh Framework Programme for research (2007–13) provides financing for such collaborative ventures.

Such support by governments is seen as a crucial requirement for the creation of a successful biotechnology sector, as product development within the industry can take up to 12 years.

The majority of funding for the industry comes from 'venture capital' (investment by individuals and firms in new and possibly risky sectors). Even though the UK is Europe's largest venture capital market, such funding is highly volatile. Following significant share price rises in 1999 and 2000, many of the biotech companies listed on the stock market saw their share prices collapse, along with those of various high-tech companies. With a depressed stock market, raising finance becomes much more difficult.

Since 2000 there has been a period of consolidation in the sector. Both public and private biotech companies in Europe have shown an increase in merger and acquisition activity, with 350 mergers between 2000 and 2006. Most of these mergers have been between European firms (49 per cent), although there has also been a significant number of purchases of European companies by US firms (27 per cent). However, the problems in financial markets that began in 2007 led to a collapse in investment in both the EU (−79 per cent) and the US (−62 per cent) biotechnology industry. This had a serious impact on the viability of some businesses in the sector. Some were forced to close and others had to scale back their activities. The sector as a whole weathered the downturn relatively well. Investment recovered quickly. By 2011 the amount of capital raised globally by biotechnology firms was higher than that for any year since 2000. High growth rates in coming years are expected. For example, the biopharmaceuticals sector is projected to grow by 9.9 per cent per annum between 2011 and 2016.

 From the brief outline above, identify the political, economic, social and technological dimensions shaping the biotechnology industry's business environment.

on how their business is organised. The use of robots and other forms of computer-controlled production has changed the nature of work for many workers. It has also created a wide range of new opportunities for businesses, many of which are yet to be realised. The information-technology revolution is also enabling much more rapid communication and making it possible for many workers to do their job from home or while travelling.

The division of the factors affecting a firm into political, economic, social and technological is commonly known as a *PEST analysis* (or PESTEL analysis, where environmental and legal factors need to be examined in more depth). This framework is widely used by organisations to audit their business environment and to help them establish a strategic approach to their business activities. It is nevertheless important to recognise that there is a great overlap and interaction among these sets of factors. Laws and government policies reflect social attitudes; technological factors determine economic ones, such as costs and productivity; technological progress often reflects the desire of researchers to meet social or environmental needs; and so on.

As well as such interaction, we must also be aware of the fact that the business environment is constantly changing.

Some of these changes are gradual, some are revolutionary. To be successful, a business will need to adapt to these changes and, wherever possible, take advantage of them. Ultimately, the better business managers understand the environment in which they operate, the more likely they are to be successful, either in exploiting ever-changing opportunities or in avoiding potential disasters.

> ## Pause for thought
>
> *Under which heading of a PEST analysis would you locate training and education?*

 KEY IDEA 1   *The behaviour and performance of firms is affected by the business environment.* The business environment includes economic, political/legal, social/cultural and technological factors.

Although we shall be touching on political, social and technological factors, it is economic factors which will be our main focus of concern when examining the business environment.

1.2   THE STRUCTURE OF INDUSTRY

One of the most important and influential elements of the business environment is the *structure of industry*. How a firm performs depends on the state of its particular industry and the amount of competition it faces. A knowledge of the structure of an industry is therefore crucial if we are to understand business behaviour and its likely outcomes.

In this section we will consider how the production of different types of goods and services is classified and how firms are located into different industrial groups.

Classifying production

When analysing production it is common to distinguish three broad categories:

- *Primary production*. This refers to the production and extraction of natural resources such as minerals and sources of energy. It also includes output from agriculture.
- *Secondary production*. This refers to the output of the manufacturing and construction sectors of the economy.
- *Tertiary production*. This refers to the production of services, and includes a wide range of sectors such as finance, the leisure industry, retailing and transport.

Figures 1.1 and 1.2 show the share of output (or *gross domestic product (GDP)*) and employment of these three sectors in 1974 and 2011. They illustrate how the tertiary sector has expanded rapidly. In 2011, it contributed some

76.9 per cent to total output and employed 77.0 per cent of all workers. By contrast, the share of output and employment of the secondary sector has declined. In 2008, it accounted for only some 20.0 per cent of output and 19.7 per cent of employment.

This trend is symptomatic of a process known as *deindustrialisation* – a decline in the share of the secondary

> ## Definitions
>
> **PEST analysis** Where the political, economic, social and technological factors shaping a business environment are assessed by a business so as to devise future business strategy.
>
> **Primary production** The production and extraction of natural resources, plus agriculture.
>
> **Secondary production** The production from manufacturing and construction sectors of the economy.
>
> **Tertiary production** The production from the service sector of the economy.
>
> **Gross domestic product (GDP)** The value of output produced within the country over a twelve-month period.
>
> **Deindustrialisation** The decline in the contribution to production of the manufacturing sector of the economy.

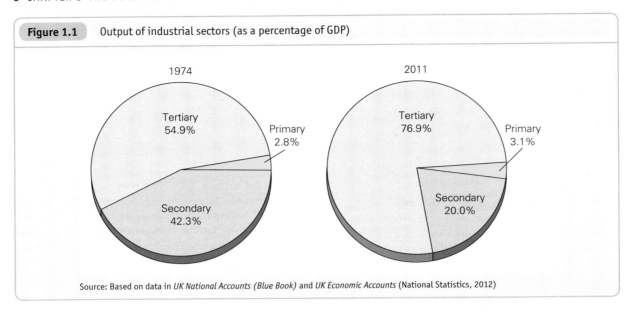

Figure 1.1   Output of industrial sectors (as a percentage of GDP)

Source: Based on data in *UK National Accounts (Blue Book)* and *UK Economic Accounts* (National Statistics, 2012)

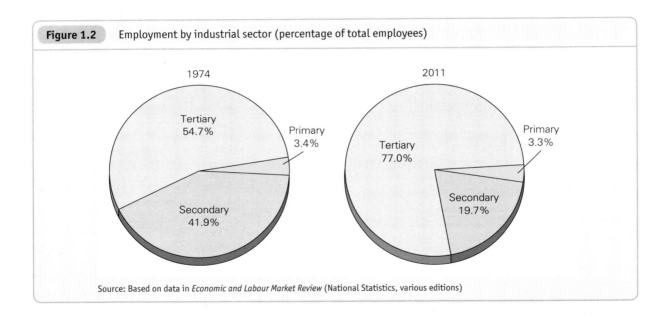

Figure 1.2   Employment by industrial sector (percentage of total employees)

Source: Based on data in *Economic and Labour Market Review* (National Statistics, various editions)

sector in GDP. Many commentators argue that this process of deindustrialisation is inevitable and that the existence of a large and growing tertiary sector in the UK economy reflects its maturity.

The classification of production into primary, secondary and tertiary allows us to consider broad changes in the economy. However, if we require a more comprehensive analysis of the structure of industry and its changes over time, then such a general classification is of little value. What we need to do is to classify firms into particular industries. In the following section we identify the classification process used in the UK and the EU.

Classifying firms into industries

An *industry* refers to a group of firms that produce a particular category of product. Thus we could refer to the electrical goods industry, the holiday industry, the aircraft industry or the insurance industry. Industries can then

Definition

Industry A group of firms producing a particular product or service.

be grouped together into broad *industrial sectors*, such as manufacturing, or mining and quarrying, or construction, or transport.

Classifying firms into industrial groupings and sub-groupings has a number of purposes. It helps us to analyse various trends in the economy and to identify areas of growth and areas of decline. It helps to identify parts of the economy with specific needs, such as training or transport infrastructure. Perhaps most importantly, it helps economists and business people to understand and predict the behaviour of firms that are in direct competition with each other. In such cases, however, it may be necessary to draw the boundaries of an industry quite narrowly.

To illustrate this, take the case of the vehicle industry. The vehicle industry produces cars, lorries, vans and coaches. The common characteristic of these vehicles is that they are self-propelled road transport vehicles. In other words, we could draw the boundaries of an industry in terms of the broad physical or technical characteristics of the products it produces. The problem with this type of categorisation, however, is that these products may not be substitutes in an *economic* sense. If I am thinking of buying a new vehicle to replace my car, I am hardly likely to consider buying a coach or a lorry! Lorries are not in competition with cars. If we are to group together products which are genuine competitors for each other, we will want to divide industries into more narrow categories.

On the other hand, if we draw the boundaries of an industry too narrowly, we may end up ignoring the effects of competition from another closely related industry. For example, if we are to understand the pricing strategies of electricity supply companies in the household market, it might be better to focus on the whole domestic fuel industry.

Thus how narrowly or broadly we draw the boundaries of an industry depends on the purposes of our analysis. You should note that the definition of an industry is based on the *supply* characteristics of firms, not on the qualities that consumers might attribute to products. For example, we could classify cars into several groups according to size, price, engine capacity, design, model (e.g. luxury, saloon, seven-seater and sports), etc. These would be demand-side characteristics of motor cars determined by consumers' tastes. The government, on the other hand, will categorise a company such as Nissan as belonging to the 'motor car' industry because making cars is its principal activity, and it does this even though Nissan produces a variety of models each with numerous features to suit individual consumer needs.

Both demand- and supply-side measures are equally valid ways of analysing the competitive behaviour of firms, and governments will look at both when there is a particular issue of economic importance, such as a merger between car companies. However, the supply-side measure is more simply calculated and is less susceptible to change, thereby making it preferable for general use.

Standard Industrial Classification

The formal system under which firms are grouped into industries is known as the *Standard Industrial Classification (SIC)*. The SIC was first introduced in 1948. Its aim was to promote the collection by various government departments and non-governmental agencies of a uniform and comparable body of data on industry. Since 1948 the SIC has been periodically revised. Revisions to the SIC have been made in order to reflect changes in the UK's industrial structure, such as those resulting from the growth in new products and the new industries associated with them.

The most recent revision in 2007 brings the UK and EU systems of industry classification further into alignment with each other. Such a development is seen as a crucial requirement for the effective monitoring of business in the EU's 'internal market' (the system whereby there are not supposed to be any artificial barriers to trade between EU members).

SIC (2007) is divided into sections (A–U), each representing a production classification (see Table 1.1). The sections are then divided into divisions: for example, the manufacturing sector has 24 divisions (10–33), as shown in Table 1.1. Divisions are divided into groups; groups are divided into classes; and some classes are further divided into subclasses. Table 1.2 gives an example of how a manufacturer of a tufted carpet would be classified according to this system.

In total, SIC (2007) has 21 sections, 88 divisions, 272 groups, 615 classes and 191 subclasses.

Changes in the structure of the UK economy

Given such a classification, how has UK industry changed over time? Figures 1.3 and 1.4 show the changes in output and employment of the various sectors identified by the SIC between 1980 and 2011.

The figures reveal that the services industries (G–S) grew rapidly throughout the period from 1980 to 2008, but with a decline in some sectors by 2011, following the recession of 2009. Construction too (F) grew for most of the period, but again declined in the recent recession and also in that of the early 1990s. Since 1985, there has been only very modest growth in agriculture (A) and a decline since 2005. The value of output of the mining and extraction sector (B) has been quite volatile, reflecting the decline in the coal industry in the mid-1980s, the expansion and then decline

---

Definitions

Industrial sector A grouping of industries producing similar products or services.

Standard Industrial Classification (SIC) The name given to the formal classification of firms into industries used by the government in order to collect data on business and industry trends.

Table 1.1 Standard Industrial Classification (2007)	
Section	**Division (manufacturing)**
A Agriculture, forestry and fishing	
B Mining and quarrying	
C Manufacturing ──────────────────────────→	10 Manufacture of food products
D Electricity, gas, steam and air conditioning supply	11 Manufacture of beverages
E Water supply, sewerage, waste management and	12 Manufacture of tobacco products
remediation activities	13 Manufacture of textiles
F Construction	14 Manufacture of wearing apparel
G Wholesale and retail trade, repair of motor vehicles	15 Manufacture of leather and related goods
and motor cycles	16 Manufacture of wood and of products of wood and cork, except
H Transport and storage	furniture; manufacture of articles of straw and plaiting materials
I Accommodation and food service activities	17 Manufacture of paper and paper products
J Information and communication	18 Printing and reproduction of recorded media
K Financial and insurance activities	19 Manufacture of coke and refined petroleum products
L Real estate activities	20 Manufacture of chemicals and chemical products
M Professional, scientific and technical activities	21 Manufacture of basic pharmaceutical products and
N Administrative and support service activities	pharmaceutical preparations
O Public administration and defence; compulsory social security	22 Manufacture of rubber and plastic products
P Education	23 Manufacture of other non-metallic mineral products
Q Human health and social work activities	24 Manufacture of basic metals
R Arts, entertainment and recreation	25 Manufacture of fabricated metal products, except machinery
S Other service activities	and equipment
T Activities of households as employers; undifferentiated	26 Manufacture of computer, electrical and optical equipment
goods and services producing activities of households	27 Manufacture of electrical equipment
for own use	28 Manufacture of equipment not elsewhere specified
U Extra-territorial organisations and bodies	29 Manufacture of motor vehicles, trailers and semi-trailers
	30 Manufacture of other transport equipment
	31 Manufacture of furniture
	32 Other manufacturing
	33 Repair and installation of machinery and equipment

Source: Based on *Standard Industrial Classification 2007* (National Statistics)

Table 1.2 The classification of the manufacture of a tufted carpet	
Section C	Manufacturing (comprising divisions 10 to 33)
Division 13	Manufacture of textiles
Group 13.9	Manufacture of other textiles
Class 13.93	Manufacture of carpets and rugs
Subclass 13.93/1	Manufacture of woven or tufted carpets and rugs

Source: Based on *Standard Industrial Classification 2007* (National Statistics)

of the oil industry and volatile prices of oil and gas; output has tailed away significantly in recent years. Manufacturing (C) experienced modest growth until the late 1990s. Since then it has experienced a slight decline.

In respect to employment, a similar, although more dramatic, pattern emerges. Only finance and banking (K and L) and retailing and similar customer services (G and I) have seen an increase in employment over the whole 25-year period. In all the other sectors, although some have seen periods of employment growth, employment was lower in

2011 than in 1980, and in mining, quarrying and extraction (B), electricity, gas and water supply (D and E) and manufacturing (C) the fall has been dramatic, with manufacturing seeing a fall throughout the period.

If we examine the subsections and divisions within the SIC, we can get a more detailed picture of how the structure of industry has changed. For example, we find that the process of deindustrialisation has not been experienced by all manufacturing industries. Certain divisions, such as instrument and electrical engineering, are in fact among the fastest growing in the whole UK economy. It is the more traditional manufacturing industries, such as metal manufacturing, which have experienced a substantial decline.

In respect to employment, there are again substantial variations between the parts of each section. Thus whereas the financial services sector has seen a rapid growth in employment, there has been a decline in employment in parts of the retail banking sector (fewer counter staff are required in high street banks, given the growth in cash machines, direct debits, debit cards, etc.). And whereas there has been a decline in traditional manufacturing industries (such as shipbuilding and metal manufacturing), there has been a growth in employment in some of the more 'high-tech' industries.

Figure 1.3   UK GDP by industry (1980 = 100)

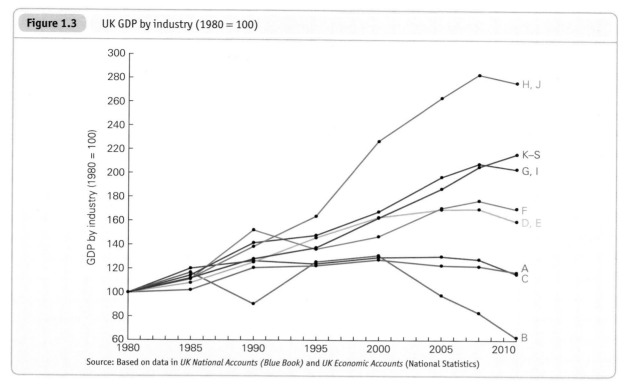

Source: Based on data in *UK National Accounts (Blue Book)* and *UK Economic Accounts* (National Statistics)

Figure 1.4   UK employment by industry (1980 = 100)

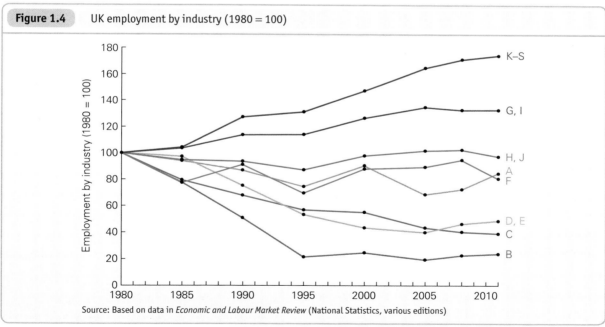

Source: Based on data in *Economic and Labour Market Review* (National Statistics, various editions)

Analysing industrial concentration

The SIC also enables us to address wider issues such as changes in **industrial concentration**.

Definition

Industrial concentration The degree to which an industry is dominated by large business enterprises.

When we examine the size structure of UK industry, we find that some sectors are dominated by large business units (those employing 250 or more people), whereas in others it is small and medium-sized enterprises (SMEs) that dominate.

Table 1.3 shows that in the manufacturing sector (C) 42.9 per cent of all workers were employed by large firms in 2011, and such firms accounted for 66.9 per cent of the sector's turnover. The *number* of large manufacturing firms, however, was a mere 1225, compared with 236 420 SMEs.

Table 1.3 Number of enterprises, employment and turnover by industrial sector: 2011

Sector (SIC2007)	Size of enterprise	Enterprises		Employment % of sector	Turnover % of sector
		Number	% of sector		
All	SMEs[a]	4 536 445	99.9	58.8	48.8
	Large firms[b]	6 320	0.1	41.2	51.2
A	SMEs	149 785	100.0	98.1	97.2
	Large firms	40	0.0	1.9	2.8
B, D, E	SMEs	24 585	99.6	28.0	15.7
	Large firms	110	0.4	72.0	84.3
C	SMEs	236 420	99.5	57.1	33.1
	Large firms	1 225	0.5	42.9	66.9
F	SMEs	875 860	100.0	84.5	72.4
	Large firms	290	0.0	15.5	27.6
G	SMEs	482 830	99.8	44.9	50.0
	Large firms	1 025	0.2	55.1	50.0
I	SMEs	146 810	99.7	57.5	57.8
	Large firms	410	0.3	42.5	42.2
H, J	SMEs	518 885	99.9	49.8	40.4
	Large firms	670	0.1	50.2	59.6
K	SMEs	82 980	99.6	26.4	n/a
	Large firms	320	0.4	73.6	n/a
L, M, N	SMEs	1 031 625	99.8	62.4	62.8
	Large firms	1 590	0.2	37.6	37.2
P	SMEs	230 670	100.0	95.4	95.7
	Large firms	90	0.0	4.6	4.3
Q	SMEs	308 870	99.9	74.2	81.3
	Large firms	315	0.1	25.8	18.7
R, S	SMEs	251 910	100.0	90.8	84.6
	Large firms	50	0.0	9.2	15.4

[a] Enterprises with fewer than 250 employees.
[b] Enterprises with 250 or more employees.
n/a Figures not available.
Source: SME database (Office for National Statistics, 2012). Contains public sector information licensed under the Open Government Licence (OGL) v1.0.
http://www.nationalarchives.gov.uk/doc/open-government-licence.

In some sectors, the bulk of output is produced by small or medium-sized firms. This is especially true in the service sector, but also in agriculture, forestry and fishing, and in construction. In other sectors, production is highly concentrated in just a few firms. This is especially so in industries such as electricity, gas and water supply, and in the mining and quarrying sector. In most of these cases, production involves large-scale capital equipment and thus would not suit small firms.

Pause for thought

Give some examples of things we might learn about the likely behaviour and performance of businesses in an industry by knowing something about the industrial concentration of that industry.

We will be examining industrial structure and the scale of enterprises at several points in the book.

1.3 THE DETERMINANTS OF BUSINESS PERFORMANCE

Structure–conduct–performance

KI 1
p 7

It should be apparent from our analysis thus far that business performance is strongly influenced by the market structure within which the firm operates. This is known as the *structure–conduct–performance paradigm.*

A business operating in a highly competitive market structure will conduct its activities differently from a business in a market with relatively few competitors. For example, the more competitive the market, the more aggressive the business may have to be in order to sell its product and remain competitive. The less competitive the market structure, the greater the chance that collusion between producers might be the preferred strategy, as this reduces the excesses and uncertainties that outright competition might produce.

Such conduct will in turn influence how well businesses perform. Performance can be measured by several different indicators, such as current profitability or profitability over the longer term, market share or growth in market share, and changes in share prices or share prices relative to those of other firms in the industry or to other firms in general, to name some of the most commonly used.

Throughout the book, we shall be seeing how market structure affects business conduct, and how business conduct affects business performance.

It would be wrong, however, to argue that business performance is totally shaped by external factors such as market structure. In fact, the internal aims and organisation of business may be very influential in determining success.

Internal aims and organisation

Economists have traditionally based their analysis of business activity on the assumption that its prime goal is the maximisation of profits. In the past, this was largely true. In the eighteenth and nineteenth centuries, enterprises were managed by the business owner: the true 'entrepreneur'. However, as businesses grew throughout the nineteenth century, and as the range of products became larger and production processes became more complex, so the managerial role became ever more specialist. Owners (the shareholders) and managers became increasingly distinct groups.

This distinction between owners and managers is crucial when we attempt to establish precisely what the objectives

of business might be. Whose objectives are we referring to: those of the owner, or those of the manager who controls the assets of the business enterprise?

KI 7
p 35

The objectives of managers and owners may well be at odds (as we shall see in Chapters 3 and 14). Managers may pursue a range of objectives, and it could well be that these objectives conflict with each other. Thus a manager might like to maximise profits and also to maximise sales. The means to increase sales may be to cut prices, but that may have the effect of reducing profits. Thus managers may have to content themselves with merely achieving a *satisfactory* level of each goal.

> ### Pause for thought
>
> *Other than profit and sales, what other objectives might managers have?*

It is not only the aims of a business that affect its performance. Performance also depends on the following:

- *Internal structure.* The way in which the firm is organised (e.g. into departments or specialised units) will affect its costs, its aggressiveness in the market, its willingness to innovate, etc.
- *Information.* The better informed a business is about its markets, about its costs of production, about alternative techniques and about alternative products it could make, the better will it be able to fulfil its goals.
- *The competence of management.* The performance of a business will depend on the skills, experience, motivation, dedication and sensitivity of its managers.
- *The quality of the workforce.* The more skilled and the better motivated is a company's workforce, the better will be its results.
- *Systems.* The functioning of any organisation will depend on the systems in place: information systems, systems for motivation (rewards, penalties, team spirit, etc.), technical systems (for sequencing production, for quality control, for setting specifications), distributional systems (transport, ordering and supply), financial systems (for accounting and auditing), and so on.

We shall be examining many of these features of internal organisation in subsequent chapters.

SUMMARY

1a Business economics is about the study of economic decisions made by business and the influences upon this. It is also concerned with the effects that this decision making has upon other businesses and the performance of the economy in general.

1b The business environment refers to the environment within which business decision making takes place. It is commonly divided into four dimensions: political, economic, social and technological.

1c The economic dimension of the business environment is divided into two: the microeconomic environment and the macroeconomic environment. The microenvironment analyses factors specific to a particular firm in a particular market. The macroenvironment considers

how national and international economic circumstances affect all business.

2a Production is divided into being primary, secondary or tertiary. Most recently in the UK the tertiary sector has grown and the secondary sector contracted.

2b Firms are classified into industries and industries into sectors. Such classification enables us to chart changes in industrial structure over time and to assess changing patterns of industrial concentration.

3 The performance of a business is determined by a wide range of both internal and external factors, such as business organisation, the aims of owners and managers, and market structure.

REVIEW QUESTIONS

1 Assume you are a Japanese car manufacturer with a plant located in the UK and are seeking to devise a business strategy for the twenty-first century. Conduct a PEST analysis on the UK car industry and evaluate the various strategies that the business might pursue.

2 What is the Standard Industrial Classification (SIC)? In what ways might such a classification system be useful? Can you think of any limitations or problems such a system might have over time?

3 In Chapter 1 we have identified some of the major changes in the UK's industrial structure and concentration in recent times. What were these changes and what might they tell us about changes in the UK economy?

4 Outline the main determinants of business performance. Distinguish whether these are micro or macroeconomic.

Economics and the world of business

Business issues covered in this chapter

- ■ How do economists set about analysing business decision making?
- ■ What are the core economic concepts that are necessary to understand the economic choices that businesses have to make, such as what to produce, what inputs and what technology to use, where to locate their production and how best to compete with other firms?
- ■ What is meant by 'opportunity cost'? How is it relevant when people make economic choices?
- ■ What is the difference between microeconomics and macroeconomics?
- ■ How can you represent simple economic relationships in a graph?
- ■ What are the relative merits of presenting data in a chart or in a table?
- ■ What is meant by a functional relationship?

2.1 WHAT DO ECONOMISTS STUDY?

These are turbulent economic times. As we write (September 2012), the global financial system is undergoing dramatic changes. Following the financial crisis of 2008 a number of banks and other financial institutions failed. Some were nationalised or part-nationalised and several governments offered unprecedented levels of lending and guarantees to the banking sector in a coordinated attempt to ensure that the global wheels of commerce can continue to turn. It will take many years, perhaps decades, for some economies to recover from recent events. Furthermore, considerable reform is needed to reduce the possibility of a similar crisis occurring in the future.

As we look forward, key economic challenges include reforming the financial system and reducing levels of

sovereign debt. The global economy is changing, perhaps more dramatically than in the recent past, but you will be glad to know that most of the principles of economics do not. This book therefore aims to give you a much better understanding of the economic influences on the world of business in a dynamically changing world.

Tackling the problem of scarcity

In the previous chapter we looked at various aspects of the business environment and the influences on firms. We also looked at some of the economic problems that businesses face. But what contribution can economists make to the analysis of these problems and to recommending solutions?

To answer this question we need to go one stage back and ask what it is that economists study in general. What is it that makes a problem an *economic* problem? The answer is that there is one central problem faced by all individuals and all societies. This is the problem of **scarcity**.

> **KEY IDEA 2**
>
> *Scarcity* is the excess of human wants over what can actually be produced. Because of scarcity, various choices have to be made between alternatives.

Of course, we do not all face the problem of scarcity to the same degree. A poor person unable to afford enough to eat or a decent place to live will hardly see it as a 'problem' that a rich person cannot afford a second Ferrari. But economists do not claim that we all face an *equal* problem of scarcity. The point is that people, both rich and poor, want more than they can have and this will cause them to behave in certain ways. Economics studies that behaviour.

Pause for thought

If we would all like more money, why doesn't the government or central bank print a lot more? Could not this solve the problem of scarcity 'at a stroke'?

Two of the key elements in satisfying wants are **consumption** and **production**. As far as consumption is concerned, economics studies how much the population spends; what the pattern of consumption is in the economy; and how much people buy of particular items. The business economist, in particular, studies consumer behaviour; how sensitive consumer demand is to changes in prices, advertising, fashion and other factors; and how the firm can seek to persuade the consumer to buy its products.

As far as production is concerned, economics studies how much the economy produces in total; what influences the rate of growth of production; and why the production of some goods increases and others falls. The business economist tends to focus on the role of the firm in this process: what determines the output of individual businesses and the range of products they produce; what techniques firms use and why; and what determines their investment decisions and how many workers they employ.

The production of goods and services involves the use of inputs, or **factors of production** as they are often called. These are of three broad types:

- Human resources: **labour**. The labour force is limited both in number and in skills.
- Natural resources: **land and raw materials**. The world's land area is limited, as are its raw materials.

- Manufactured resources: **capital**. Capital consists of all those inputs that themselves have had to be produced in the first place. The world has a limited stock of capital: a limited supply of factories, machines, transportation and other equipment. The productivity of capital is limited by the state of technology.

We will be studying the use of these resources by firms for the production of goods and services: production to meet consumer demand – production which will thus help to reduce the problem of scarcity.

Demand and supply

We said that economics is concerned with consumption and production. Another way of looking at this is in terms of *demand* and *supply*. In fact, demand and supply and the relationship between them lie at the very centre of economics. But what do we mean by the terms, and what is their relationship with the problem of scarcity?

Demand is related to wants. If goods and services were free, people would simply demand and consume whatever they wanted. Such wants are virtually boundless: perhaps only limited by people's imagination. *Supply*, on the other hand, is limited. It is related to resources. The amount that firms can supply depends on the resources and technology available.

Given the problem of scarcity, given that human wants exceed what can actually be produced, *potential* demands will exceed *potential* supplies. Society therefore has to find some way of dealing with this problem. Somehow it has to try to match demand and supply. This applies at the level of the economy overall: *aggregate* demand will need to be

KI 2
p 16

Definitions

Scarcity The excess of human wants over what can actually be produced to fulfil these wants.

Consumption The act of using goods and services to satisfy wants. This will normally involve purchasing the goods and services.

Production The transformation of inputs into outputs by firms in order to earn profit (or meet some other objective).

Factors of production (or resources) The inputs into the production of goods and services: labour, land and raw materials, and capital.

Labour All forms of human input, both physical and mental, into current production.

Land (and raw materials) Inputs into production that are provided by nature: e.g. unimproved land and mineral deposits in the ground.

Capital All inputs into production that have themselves been produced: e.g. factories, machines and tools.

balanced against *aggregate* supply. In other words, total spending in the economy must balance total production. It also applies at the level of individual goods and services. The demand and supply of cabbages must balance, as must the demand and supply of DVD recorders, cars, houses and bus journeys.

But if potential demand exceeds potential supply, how are *actual* demand and supply to be made equal? Either demand has to be curtailed or supply has to be increased, or a combination of the two. Economics studies this process. It studies how demand adjusts to available supplies, and how supply adjusts to consumer demands.

The business economist studies the role of firms in this process: how they respond to demand, or, indeed, try to create demand for their products; how they combine their inputs to achieve output in the most efficient way; how they decide the amount to produce and the price to charge their customers; and how they make their investment decisions. Not only this, the business economist also considers the wider environment in which firms operate and how they are affected by it: the effect of changes in the national and international economic climate, such as upswings and downswings in the economy, and changes in interest rates and exchange rates. In short, the business economist studies supply: how firms' output is affected by a range of influences, and how firms can best meet their objectives.

Dividing up the subject

Economics is traditionally divided into two main branches – *macroeconomics* and *microeconomics*, where 'macro' means big, and 'micro' means small.

- *Macroeconomics examines the economy as a whole.* It is thus concerned with **aggregate demand** and **aggregate supply**. By 'aggregate demand' we mean the total amount of spending in the economy, whether by consumers, by overseas customers for our exports, by the government, or by firms when they buy capital equipment or stock up on raw materials. By 'aggregate supply' we mean the total national output of goods and services.
- *Microeconomics examines the individual parts of the economy.* It is concerned with the factors that determine the demand and supply of particular goods and services and resources: cars, butter, clothes and haircuts; electricians, shop assistants, blast furnaces, computers and oil. It explores issues in competition between firms and the rationale for trade.

Business economics, because it studies firms, is largely concerned with microeconomic issues. Nevertheless, given that businesses are affected by what is going on in the economy as a whole, it is still important for the business economist to study the macroeconomic environment and its effects on individual firms.

2.2 BUSINESS ECONOMICS: THE MACROECONOMIC ENVIRONMENT

Because things are scarce, societies are concerned that their resources are being used as *fully as possible*, and that over time the national output should *grow*. Governments are keen to boast to their electorate how much the economy has grown since they have been in charge!

The achievement of growth and the full use of resources is not easy, however, as demonstrated by the periods of high unemployment and stagnation that have occurred from time to time throughout the world (e.g. in the 1930s, the early 1980s, the early 1990s, and the late 2000s). Furthermore, attempts by governments to stimulate growth and employment have often resulted in inflation and a large rise in

imports. Even when societies do achieve growth, it can be short lived. Economies have often experienced cycles, where periods of growth alternate with periods of stagnation, such periods varying from a few months to a few years.

Macroeconomics, then, studies the determination of national output and its growth over time. It also studies the problems of stagnation, unemployment, inflation, the balance of international payments and cyclical instability, and the policies adopted by governments to deal with these problems.

Macroeconomic problems are closely related to the balance between aggregate demand and aggregate supply.

Definitions

Macroeconomics The branch of economics that studies economic aggregates (grand totals): e.g. the overall level of prices, output and employment in the economy.

Aggregate demand The total level of spending in the economy.

Aggregate supply The total amount of output in the economy.

Microeconomics The branch of economics that studies individual units: e.g. households, firms and industries. It studies the interrelationships between these units in determining the pattern of production and distribution of goods and services.

If aggregate demand is *too high* relative to aggregate supply, inflation and balance of payments deficits are likely to result.

■ *Inflation* refers to a general rise in the level of prices throughout the economy. If aggregate demand rises substantially, firms are likely to respond by raising their prices. After all, if demand is high, they can probably still sell as much as before (if not more) even at the higher prices, and thus make more profit. If firms in general put up their prices, inflation results.

■ *Balance of trade deficits* are the excess of imports over exports. If aggregate demand rises, people are likely to buy more imports. In other words, part of the extra expenditure will go on Japanese MP3 players, German cars, Chilean wine, etc. Also if inflation is high, home-produced goods will become uncompetitive with foreign goods. We are likely, therefore, to buy more foreign imports, and foreigners are likely to buy fewer of our exports.

If aggregate demand is *too low* relative to aggregate supply, unemployment and recession may well result.

■ A *recession* is where output in the economy declines: in other words, growth becomes negative. A recession is associated with a low level of consumer spending. If people spend less, shops are likely to find themselves with unsold stocks. As a result they will buy less from the manufacturers, which in turn will cut down on production.

■ *Unemployment* is likely to result from cutbacks in production. If firms are producing less, they will need a smaller labour force.

Government macroeconomic *policy*, therefore, tends to focus on the balance of aggregate demand and aggregate supply. It can be **demand-side policy**, which seeks to influence the level of spending in the economy. This in turn will affect the level of production, prices and employment. Or it can be **supply-side policy**. This is designed to influence the level of production directly: for example, by creating more incentives for businesses to innovate.

Macroeconomic policy and its effects on business

Both demand-side and supply-side policy will affect the business environment. Take demand-side policy. If there is a recession, the government might try to boost the level of spending (aggregate demand) by cutting taxes, increasing government spending or reducing interest rates. If consumers respond by purchasing more, then this will clearly have an effect on businesses. But firms will want to be stocked up ready for an upsurge in consumer demand. Therefore, they will want to estimate the effect on their own particular market of a boost to aggregate demand. Studying the macroeconomic environment and the effects

of government policy, therefore, is vital for firms when forecasting future demand for their product.

It is the same with supply-side policy. The government may introduce tax incentives for firms to invest, or for people to work harder; it may introduce new training schemes; it may build new motorways. These policies will affect firms' costs and hence the profitability of production. So, again, firms will want to predict how government policies are likely to affect them, so that they can plan accordingly.

The circular flow of income

One of the most useful diagrams for illustrating the macro-economic environment and the relationships between producers and consumers is the *circular flow of income* diagram. This is illustrated in Figure 2.1.

The consumers of goods and services are labelled 'households'. Some members of households, of course, are also workers, and in some cases are the owners of other factors of production too, such as land. The producers of goods and services are labelled 'firms'.

Firms and households are in a twin 'demand and supply' relationship.

First, on the right-hand side of the diagram, households demand goods and services, and firms supply goods and services. In the process, exchange takes place. In a money economy (as opposed to a **barter economy**), firms exchange goods and services for money. In other words, money flows from households to firms in the form of consumer expenditure, while goods and services flow the other way – from firms to households.

Definitions

Rate of inflation The percentage increase in the level of prices over a twelve-month period.

Balance of trade Exports of goods and services minus imports of goods and services. If exports exceed imports, there is a 'balance of trade surplus' (a positive figure). If imports exceed exports, there is a 'balance of trade deficit' (a negative figure).

Recession A period where national output falls. The official definition is where output declines for two or more quarters.

Unemployment The number of people who are actively looking for work but are currently without a job. (Note that there is much debate as to who should officially be counted as unemployed.)

Demand-side policy Government policy designed to alter the level of aggregate demand, and thereby the level of output, employment and prices.

Supply-side policy Government policy that attempts to alter the level of aggregate supply directly.

Barter economy An economy where people exchange goods and services directly with one another without any payment of money. Workers would be paid with bundles of goods.

BOX 2.1   LOOKING AT MACROECONOMIC DATA

Assessing different countries' macroeconomic performance

	Unemployment (% of workforce)				Inflation (%)				Economic growth (%)				Balance on current account[1] (% of national income)			
	USA	Japan	Germany	UK	USA	Japan	Germany	UK	USA	Japan	Germany	UK	USA	Japan	Germany	UK
1961–70	4.8	1.3	0.6	1.7	2.4	5.6	2.7	4.0	4.2	10.1	4.4	2.8	0.5	0.6	0.9	0.2
1971–80	6.4	1.8	2.2	3.8	7.0	8.8	5.2	13.4	3.2	4.4	2.9	2.0	0.9	0.5	1.1	−0.7
1981–90	7.1	2.5	6.0	9.6	4.5	1.8	2.6	6.2	3.2	4.6	2.3	2.7	−1.7	2.3	2.6	−1.4
1991–2000	5.6	3.3	7.8	7.9	2.2	0.5	1.8	3.2	3.4	1.2	2.1	2.5	−1.6	2.5	−0.7	−1.5
2001–10	6.1	4.7	8.9	5.6	2.4	−0.3	1.6	2.1	1.6	0.8	0.9	1.7	−4.6	3.4	4.5	−2.2
2011–13[2]	8.0	4.4	5.3	8.7	2.4	−0.2	2.2	3.0	2.2	0.9	2.1	0.8	−4.3	3.1	5.8	−2.2

Sources: Various
Notes: [1] The current account balance is the balance of trade plus other income flows from and to abroad
[2] 2012 and 2013 figures based on forecasts

Rapid economic growth, low unemployment, low inflation and the avoidance of balance of trade deficits are the major macroeconomic policy objectives of most governments round the world. To help them achieve these objectives they employ economic advisers. But when we look at the performance of various economies, the success of government macroeconomic policies seems decidedly 'mixed'.

The table shows data for the USA, Japan, Germany and the UK from 1961 to 2013.

If the government does not have much success in managing the economy, it could be for the following reasons:

■ Economists have incorrectly analysed the problems and hence have given the wrong advice.

■ Economists disagree and hence have given conflicting advice.
■ Economists have based their advice on inaccurate forecasts.
■ Governments have not heeded the advice of economists.
■ There is little else that governments could have done: the problems were insoluble.

1. *Has the UK generally fared better or worse than the other three countries?*
2. *Was there a common pattern in the macroeconomic performance of each of the four countries over this period of just over 50 years?*

Figure 2.1   Circular flow of goods and incomes

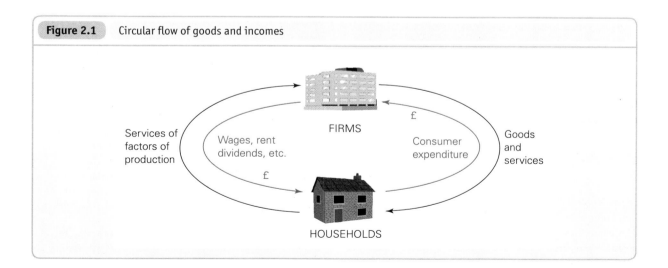

This coming together of buyers and sellers is known as a *market* – whether it be a street market, a shop, an auction, a mail-order system or whatever. Thus we talk about the market for apples, the market for oil, for cars, for houses, for televisions, and so on.

Definition

Market The interaction between buyers and sellers.

Second, firms and households come together in the market for factors of production. This is illustrated on the left-hand side of the diagram. This time the demand and supply roles are reversed. Firms demand the use of factors of production owned by households – labour, land and capital. Households supply them. Thus the services of labour and other factors flow from households to firms, and in exchange firms pay households money – namely, wages, rent, dividends and interest. Just as we referred to particular goods markets, so we can also refer to particular factor markets – the market for bricklayers, for secretaries, for hairdressers, for land, etc.

There is thus a circular flow of incomes. Households earn incomes from firms and firms earn incomes from households. The money circulates. There is also a circular flow of goods and services, but in the opposite direction. Households supply factor services to firms, which then use them to supply goods and services to households.

Macroeconomics is concerned with the total size of the flow. If consumers choose to spend more, firms will earn more from the increased level of sales. They will probably respond by producing more or raising their prices, or some combination of the two. As a result, they will end up paying more out to workers in the form of wages, and to shareholders in the form of profits.

Households will thus have gained additional income. This will then lead to an additional increase in consumer spending, and, therefore, a further boost to production. To summarise: increased spending generates additional income, which, in turn, generates additional spending, and so on as additional incomes flow round and round the circular flow of income.

The effect does not go on indefinitely, however. When households earn additional incomes, not all of it is spent: not all of it recirculates. Some of the additional income will be saved; some will be paid in taxes; and some will be spent on imports (and will not thus stimulate domestic production). The bigger these 'withdrawals', as they are called, the less will production carry on being stimulated.

It is important for firms to estimate the eventual effect of an initial rise in consumer demand (or a rise in government expenditure, for that matter). Will there be a boom in the economy, or will the rise in demand merely fizzle out? A study of macroeconomics helps business people to understand the effects of changes in aggregate demand, and the effects that such changes will have on their own particular business.

We examine the macroeconomic environment and the effects on business of macroeconomic policy in Chapters 26–32.

2.3 BUSINESS ECONOMICS: MICROECONOMIC CHOICES

Microeconomics and choice

Because resources are scarce, choices have to be made. There are three main categories of choice that must be made in any society:

- *What* goods and services are going to be produced and in what quantities, given that there are not enough resources to produce all the things that people desire? How many cars, how much wheat, how much insurance, how many rock concerts, etc. will be produced?
- *How* are things going to be produced, given that there is normally more than one way of producing things? What resources are going to be used and in what quantities? What techniques of production are going to be adopted? Will cars be produced by robots or by assembly-line workers? Will electricity be produced from coal, oil, gas, nuclear fission, renewable resources or a mixture of these?
- *For whom* are things going to be produced? In other words, how is the nation's income going to be distributed? After all, the higher your income, the more you can consume of the nation's output. What will be the wages of farm workers, printers, cleaners and accountants? How much will pensioners receive? How much profit will owners of private companies receive or will state-owned industries make?

All societies have to make these choices, whether they be made by individuals, by groups or by the government. These choices can be seen as *micro*economic choices, since they are concerned not with the *total* amount of national output, but with the *individual* goods and services that make it up: what they are, how they are made, and who gets the incomes to buy them.

Choice and opportunity cost

Choice involves sacrifice. The more food you choose to buy, the less money you will have to spend on other goods. The more food a nation produces, the fewer resources will there be for producing other goods. In other words, the production or consumption of one thing involves the sacrifice of alternatives. This sacrifice of alternatives in the production (or consumption) of a good is known as its **opportunity cost**.

The *opportunity cost* of something is what you give up to get it/do it. In other words, it is cost measured in terms of the best alternative forgone.

Definition

Opportunity cost The cost of any activity measured in terms of the best alternative forgone.

| BOX 2.2 | THE OPPORTUNITY COSTS OF STUDYING ECONOMICS |

What are you sacrificing?

You may not have realised it, but you probably consider opportunity costs many times a day. The reason is that we are constantly making choices: what to buy, what to eat, what to wear, whether to go out, how much to study, and so on. Each time we make a choice to do something, we are in effect rejecting doing some alternative. This alternative forgone is the opportunity cost of our action.

Sometimes the opportunity costs of our actions are the direct monetary costs we incur. Sometimes it is more complicated.

Take the opportunity costs of your choices as a student of economics.

Buying a textbook costing £54.99

This does involve a direct money payment. What you have to consider is the alternatives you could have bought with the £54.99. You then have to weigh up the benefit from the best alternative against the benefit of the textbook.

What might prevent you from making the best decision?

Coming to classes

You may or may not be paying course fees. Even if you are, there is no extra (marginal) monetary cost in coming to classes once the fees have been paid. You will not get a refund by skipping classes!

So are the opportunity costs zero? No: by coming to classes you are *not* working in the library; you are *not* having an extra hour in bed; you are *not* sitting drinking coffee with friends, and so on. If you are making a rational decision to come to classes, then you will consider such possible alternatives.

If there are several other things you could have done, is the opportunity cost the sum of all of them?

Choosing to study at university or college

What are the opportunity costs of being a student in higher education?

At first it might seem that the costs would include the following:

■ Tuition fees.
■ Books, stationery, etc.
■ Accommodation expenses.
■ Transport.
■ Food, entertainment and other living expenses.

But adding these up does not give the opportunity cost. The opportunity cost is the sacrifice entailed by going to university or college rather than doing something else. Let us assume that the alternative is to take a job that has been offered. The correct list of opportunity costs of higher education would include:

■ Tuition fees.
■ Books, stationery, etc.
■ Additional accommodation and transport expenses over what would have been incurred by taking the job.
■ Wages that would have been earned in the job *less* any student grant or loan interest subsidy received.

Note that tuition fees would not be included if they had been paid by someone else: for example, as part of a scholarship or a government grant.

1. *Why is the cost of food not included?*
2. *Make a list of the benefits of higher education.*
3. *Is the opportunity cost to the individual of attending higher education different from the opportunity costs to society as a whole?*

If the workers on a farm can produce either 1000 tonnes of wheat or 2000 tonnes of barley, then the opportunity cost of producing 1 tonne of wheat is the 2 tonnes of barley forgone. The opportunity cost of buying a textbook is the new pair of jeans you also wanted that you have had to go without. The opportunity cost of working overtime is the leisure you have sacrificed.

Rational choices

Economists often refer to **rational choices**. This simply means the weighing-up of the *costs* and *benefits* of any activity, whether it be firms choosing what and how much

to produce, workers choosing whether to take a particular job or to work extra hours, or consumers choosing what to buy.

Pause for thought

Assume that you are looking for a job and are offered two. One is more pleasant to do, but pays less. How would you make a rational choice between the two jobs?

Imagine you are doing your shopping in a supermarket and you want to buy some meat. Do you spend a lot of money and buy best steak, or do you buy cheap mince instead? To make a rational (i.e. sensible) decision, you will need to weigh up the costs and benefits of each alternative. Best steak may give you a lot of enjoyment, but it has a high opportunity cost: because it is expensive, you will need to sacrifice quite a lot of consumption of other goods

Definition

Rational choices Choices that involve weighing up the benefit of any activity against its opportunity cost.

if you decide to buy it. If you buy the mince, however, although you will not enjoy it so much, you will have more money left over to buy other things: it has a lower opportunity cost.

Thus rational decision making, as far as consumers are concerned, involves choosing those items that give you the best value for money: i.e. the *greatest benefit relative to cost*.

The same principles apply to firms when deciding what to produce. For example, should a car firm open up another production line? A rational decision will again involve weighing up the benefits and costs. The benefits are the revenues that the firm will earn from selling the extra cars. The costs will include the extra labour costs, raw material costs, costs of component parts, etc. It will be profitable to open up the new production line only if the revenues earned exceed the costs entailed: in other words, if it earns a profit.

> **KEY IDEA 4**
>
> *Rational decision making involves weighing up the marginal benefit and marginal cost of any activity.* If the marginal benefit exceeds the marginal cost, it is rational to do the activity (or to do more of it). If the marginal cost exceeds the marginal benefit, it is rational not to do it (or to do less of it).

In the more complex situation of deciding which model of car to produce, or how many of each model, the firm must weigh up the relative benefits and costs of each: i.e. it will want to produce the most profitable product mix.

Marginal costs and benefits

In economics we argue that rational choices involve weighing up **marginal costs** and **marginal benefits**. These are the costs and benefits of doing a little bit more or a little bit less of a specific activity. They can be contrasted with the *total* costs and benefits of the activity.

Take a familiar example. What time will you set the alarm clock to go off tomorrow morning? Let us say that you have to leave home at 8.30. Perhaps you will set the alarm for 7.00. That will give you plenty of time to get up and get ready, but it will mean a relatively short night's sleep. Perhaps then you will decide to set it for 7.30 or even 8.00. That will give you a longer night's sleep, but much more of a rush in the morning to get ready.

So how do you make a rational decision about when the alarm should go off? What you have to do is to weigh up the costs and benefits of *additional* sleep. Each extra minute in bed gives you more sleep (the marginal benefit), but gives you more of a rush when you get up (the marginal cost). The decision is therefore based on the costs and benefits of *extra* sleep, not on the *total* costs and benefits of a whole night's sleep.

This same principle applies to rational decisions made by consumers, workers and firms. For example, the car firm we were considering just now will weigh up the marginal costs and benefits of producing cars: in other words, it will compare the costs and revenue of producing *additional* cars. If additional cars add more to the firm's revenue than to its costs, it will be profitable to produce them.

Microeconomic choices and the firm

All economic decisions made by firms involve choices. The business economist studies these choices and their results.

We will look at the choices of how much to produce, what price to charge the customer, how many inputs to use, what types of input to use and in what combination, whether to expand the scale of the firm's operations, whether to invest in new plant, whether to engage in research and development, whether to merge with or take over another company, whether to diversify into other markets, whether to export. The right choices (in terms of best meeting the firm's objectives) will vary according to the type of market in which the firm operates, its predictions about future demand, its degree of power in the market, the actions and reactions of competitors, the degree and type of government intervention, the current tax regime, the availability of finance, and so on. In short, we will be studying the whole range of economic choices made by firms and in a number of different scenarios.

In all these cases, the owners of firms will want the best possible choices to be made: i.e. those choices that best meet the objectives of the firm. Making the best choices, as we have seen, will involve weighing up the marginal benefits against the marginal opportunity costs of each decision.

> ## Definitions
>
> **Marginal costs** The additional cost of doing a little bit more (or *1 unit* more if a unit can be measured) of an activity.
>
> **Marginal benefits** The additional benefits of doing a little bit more (or *1 unit* more if a unit can be measured) of an activity.

SUMMARY

1a The central economic problem is that of scarcity. Given that there is a limited supply of factors of production (labour, land and capital), it is impossible to provide everybody with everything they want. Potential demands exceed potential supplies.

1b The subject of economics is usually divided into two main branches: macroeconomics and microeconomics.

2a Macroeconomics deals with aggregates such as the overall levels of unemployment, output, growth and prices in the economy.

2b The macroeconomic environment will be an important determinant of a business's profitability.

3a Microeconomics deals with the activities of individual units within the economy: firms, industries, consumers, workers, etc. Because resources are scarce, people have to make choices. Society has to choose by some means or other *what* goods and services to produce, *how* to produce them and *for whom* to produce them. Microeconomics studies these choices.

3b Rational choices involve weighing up the marginal benefits of each activity against its marginal opportunity costs. If the marginal benefit exceeds the marginal cost, it is rational to choose to do more of that activity.

3c Businesses are constantly faced with choices: how much to produce, what inputs to use, what price to charge, how much to invest, etc. We will study these choices.

REVIEW QUESTIONS

1 Virtually every good is scarce in the sense we have defined it. There are, however, a few exceptions. Under *certain circumstances*, water and air are not scarce. When and where might this be true for (a) water and (b) air? Why is it important to define water and air very carefully before deciding whether they are scarce or abundant? Under circumstances where they are *not* scarce, would it be possible to charge for them?

2 Which of the following are macroeconomic issues, which are microeconomic ones and which could be either depending on the context?

   (a) Inflation.
   (b) Low wages in certain service industries.
   (c) The rate of exchange between the pound and the euro.
   (d) Why the price of cabbages fluctuates more than that of cars.
   (e) The rate of economic growth this year compared with last year.
   (f) The decline of traditional manufacturing industries.

3 Make a list of three things you did yesterday. What was the opportunity cost of each?

4 A washing machine manufacturer is considering whether to produce an extra batch of 1000 washing machines. How would it set about working out the marginal opportunity cost of so doing?

5 How would a firm use the principle of weighing up marginal costs and marginal benefits when deciding whether (a) to take on an additional worker; (b) to offer overtime to existing workers?

6 We identified three categories of withdrawal from the circular flow of income. What were they? There are also three categories of 'injection' of expenditure into the circular flow of income. What do you think they are?

APPENDIX: SOME TECHNIQUES OF ECONOMIC ANALYSIS

When students first come to economics, many are worried about the amount of mathematics they will encounter. Will it all be equations and graphs, and will there be lots of hard calculations to do and difficult theories to grasp?

As you will see if you glance through the pages of this book, there are many diagrams and tables and a few equations. But this does not mean that there are many mathematical techniques that you will have to master. In fact there are relatively few techniques, but they are ones which we use many times in many different contexts. You will find that, if you are new to the subject, you will very quickly become familiar with these techniques. If you are not new to the subject, perhaps you could reassure your colleagues who are!

Diagrams as pictures

On many occasions, we use diagrams simply to provide a picture of a relationship. Just as a photograph in a newspaper can often provide a much more vivid picture of an event than any description in words, so too a diagram in economics can often picture a relationship with a vividness and clarity that could never be achieved by description alone.

For example, we may observe that as people's incomes rise, they spend a lot more on entertainment and only a little more on food. We can picture this relationship very nicely by the use of a simple graph.

In Figure 2.2, an individual's income is measured along the horizontal axis and the expenditure on food and entertainment is measured up the vertical axis. There are just two lines on this diagram: the one showing how the person's expenditure on entertainment rises as income rises, the other how the expenditure on food rises as income rises. Now we could use a diagram like this to plot actual data.

But we may simply be using it as a sketch – as a picture. In this case we do not necessarily need to put figures on the two axes. We are simply showing the relative *shapes* of the two curves. These shapes tell us that the person's expenditure on entertainment rises more quickly than that on food, and that above a certain level of income the expenditure on entertainment becomes greater than that on food.

If you were to describe in words all the information that this sketch graph depicts, you would need several lines of prose.

Figure 2.1 (the circular flow diagram) was an example of a sketch designed to give a simple, clear picture of a relationship: a picture stripped of all unnecessary detail.

> **Pause for thought**
>
> *What else is the diagram telling us?*

Representing real-life statistics

In many cases we will want to depict real-world data. We may want to show, for example, how the level of business investment has fluctuated over a given period of time, or we may want to depict the market shares of the different firms within a given industry. In the first case we will need to look at time-series data. In the second we will look at cross-section data.

Time-series data

Table 2.1 shows annual percentage changes in investment in the European Union between 1980 and 2013 (the data refer simply to the 15 countries that were members prior to 2004).

Figure 2.2 The effect of a rise in an individual's income on his/her expenditure on food and entertainment

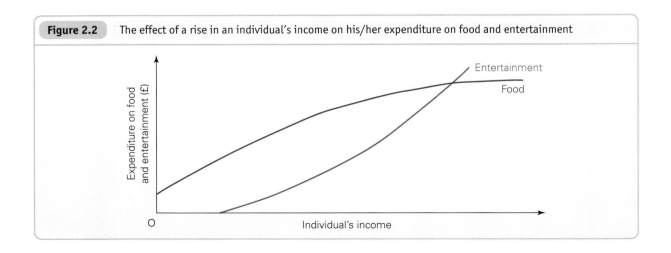

Table 2.1	Investment in the EU(15): percentage changes from previous year at 2000 market prices															
1981	**1982**	**1983**	**1984**	**1985**	**1986**	**1987**	**1988**	**1989**	**1990**	**1991**	**1992**	**1993**	**1994**	**1995**	**1996**	**1997**
−4.4	−1.3	0.2	1.8	3.0	4.1	5.0	8.7	7.0	3.8	−0.2	−0.5	−5.9	3.0	3.2	2.2	3.3
1998	**1999**	**2000**	**2001**	**2002**	**2003**	**2004**	**2005**	**2006**	**2007**	**2008**	**2009**	**2010**	**2011**	**2012**	**2013**	
7.2	5.7	4.7	0.8	−0.7	1.2	2.7	3.3	5.9	4.8	−1.6	−12.2	0.0	1.1	−1.2	2.1	

Source: Adapted from *Statistical Annex of European Economy* (EC, 2012). 2012 and 2013 are forecast

A table like this is a common way of representing *time-series data*. It has the advantage of giving the precise figures, and is thus a useful reference if we want to test any theory and see if it predicts accurately.

Notice that in this particular table the figures are given annually. Depending on the period of time over which we want to see the movement of a variable, it may be more appropriate to use a different interval of time. For example, if we wanted to see how investment had changed over the past 50 years, we might use intervals of five years or more. If, however, we wanted to see how investment had changed over the course of a year, we would probably use monthly figures.

Time-series data can also be shown graphically. In fact the data from a table can be plotted directly on to a graph.

Definition

Time-series data Information depicting how a variable (e.g. the price of eggs) changes over time.

Figure 2.3 plots the data from Table 2.1. Each dot on the graph corresponds to one figure from the table. The dots are then joined up to form a single line.

Thus if you wanted to find the annual percentage change in investment in the EU at any time between 1981 and 2013, you would simply find the appropriate date on the horizontal axis, read vertically upward to the line you have drawn, then read across to find the annual rate of change in investment.

Although a graph like this cannot give you quite such an accurate measurement of each point as a table does, it gives a much more obvious picture of how the figures have moved over time and whether the changes are getting bigger (the curve getting steeper) or smaller (the curve getting flatter). We can also read off what the likely figure would be for some point *between* two observations.

It is also possible to combine *two* sets of time-series data on one graph to show their relative movements over time. Table 2.2 shows annual percentage changes in EU national income (i.e. economic growth rates) for the same time period.

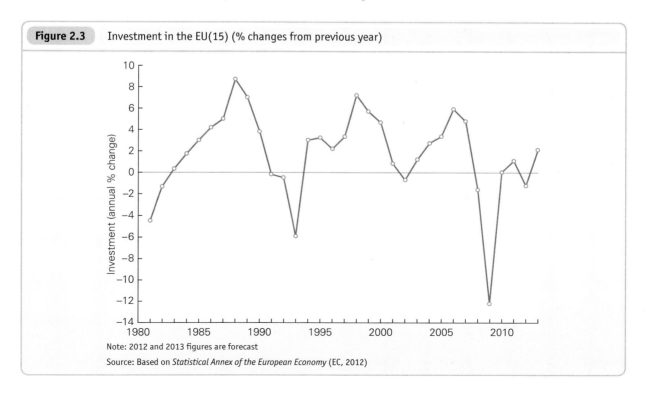

Figure 2.3 Investment in the EU(15) (% changes from previous year)

Note: 2012 and 2013 figures are forecast

Source: Based on *Statistical Annex of the European Economy* (EC, 2012)

| **Figure 2.4** | Economic growth and growth in investment in the EU(15) |

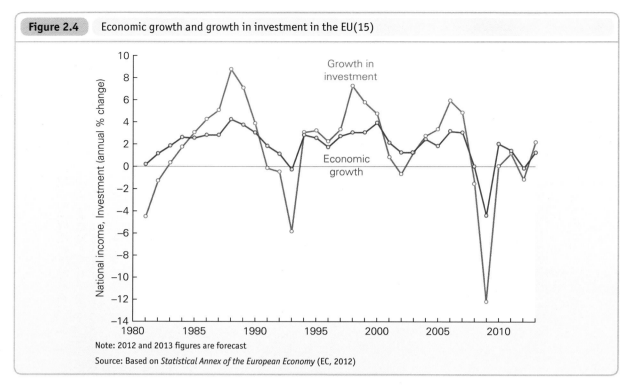

Note: 2012 and 2013 figures are forecast

Source: Based on *Statistical Annex of the European Economy* (EC, 2012)

| **Table 2.2** | National income in the EU(15): percentage changes from previous year (economic growth rates) at 2000 market prices |

1981	1982	1983	1984	1985	1986	1987	1988	1989	1990	1991	1992	1993	1994	1995	1996	1997
0.2	1.1	1.8	2.6	2.5	2.8	2.8	4.2	3.7	3.0	1.8	1.1	−0.3	2.8	2.5	1.7	2.7

1998	1999	2000	2001	2002	2003	2004	2005	2006	2007	2008	2009	2010	2011	2012	2013
3.0	3.0	3.9	2.1	1.2	1.2	2.4	1.8	3.1	3.0	0.0	−4.4	2.0	1.4	−0.2	1.2

Source: Based on *Statistical Annex of the European Economy* (EC, 2012). 2012 and 2013 are forecast

Figure 2.4 plots these data along with those from Table 2.1. This enables us to get a clear picture of how annual percentage changes in investment and in national income moved in relation to each other over the period in question.

Cross-section data

Cross-section data show different observations made at the *same point in time*. For example, they could show the quantities of food and clothing purchased at various levels of household income, or the costs to a firm or industry of producing various quantities of a product.

Table 2.3 gives an example of cross-section data. It shows the percentage shares of the UK's largest cider

Definition

Cross-section data Information showing how a variable (e.g. the consumption of eggs) differs between different groups or different individuals at a given time.

Table 2.3	UK market shares of cider brands	
	2009 (%)	**2011 (%)**
Strongbow	28.5	27.2
Own-label	8.6	7.9
Magners	8.3	7.5
Lambrini	6.5	4.5
Bulmers Original	4.5	3.8
Frosty Jack's	2.9	4.1
Bulmers Pear cider	2.8	2.6
Jacques Fruits De Bois	2.7	2.2
Scrumpy Jack	2.5	2.4
Kopparberg	1.7	2.2
Stella Artois Cidre	n/a	3.2
Others	31.0	32.4
	100.0	100.0

Source: Mintel Cider UK Report, February 2012

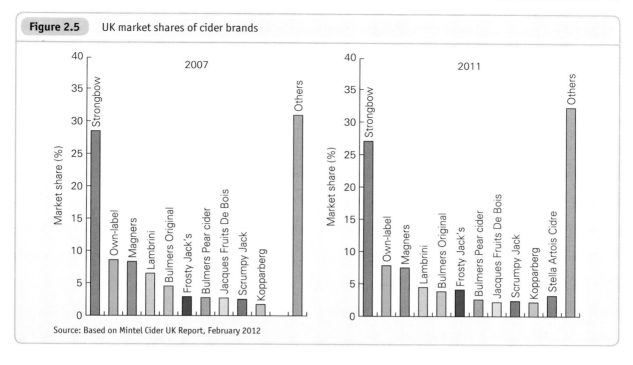

Figure 2.5 UK market shares of cider brands

Source: Based on Mintel Cider UK Report, February 2012

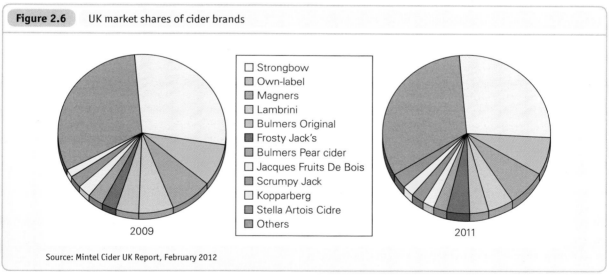

Figure 2.6 UK market shares of cider brands

Source: Mintel Cider UK Report, February 2012

brands in 2009 and 2011. Cross-section data like these are often represented in the form of a chart. Figure 2.5 shows the data as a *bar chart*, and Figure 2.6 as a *pie chart*.

It is possible to represent cross-section data at two or more different points in time, thereby presenting the figures as a time series. In Table 2.3, figures are given for just two years. With a more complete time series we could graph the movement of the market shares of each of the brands over time.

Index numbers

Time-series data are often expressed in terms of *index numbers*. Consider the data in the top row of each part of

Table 2.4. It shows index numbers of manufacturing output in the UK from 1980 to 2011.

One year is selected as the *base year*, and this is given the value of 100. In our example this is 2003. The output for other years is then shown by their percentage variation from 100. For 1981 the index number is 73.9. This means

> **Definitions**
>
> **Index number** The value of a variable expressed as 100 plus or minus its percentage deviation from a base year.
>
> **Base year (for index numbers)** The year whose index number is set at 100.

Table 2.4		UK manufacturing and service industry output at constant 2003 prices: 2003 = 100														
1980	1981	1982	1983	1984	1985	1986	1987	1988	1989	1990	1991	1992	1993	1994	1995
Output of manufacturing															
78.8	73.9	73.8	75.4	78.2	80.4	81.5	85.4	91.6	95.2	95.1	90.4	90.3	91.6	95.9	97.4
Output of services															
49.6	49.8	50.5	52.2	54.1	55.8	58.1	60.5	63.3	64.6	65.5	65.3	65.7	67.7	70.7	73.1
1996	1997	1998	1999	2000	2001	2002	2003	2004	2005	2006	2007	2008	2009	2010	2011
Output of manufacturing															
98.1	99.9	100.5	101.6	103.9	102.5	100.3	100.0	102.1	102.0	103.9	104.9	102.3	92.3	95.8	97.9
Output of services															
75.8	79.0	83.1	86.9	91.1	94.3	96.6	100.0	103.0	107.5	111.0	116.2	116.0	113.5	114.8	116.2

Source: Based on data in *National Accounts*, Blue Book data. Sourced from www.ons.gov.uk

that manufacturing output was 26.1 per cent lower in 1981 than in 2003. The index number for 2004 is 102.2. This means that manufacturing output was 2.2 per cent higher than in 2003.

The use of index numbers allows us to see clearly any upward and downward movements, and to make an easy comparison of one year with another. For example, Table 2.4 shows quite clearly that manufacturing output fell from 2007 to 2009 and had still not reached its 2007 level by 2011.

Index numbers are very useful for comparing two or more time series of data. For example, suppose we wanted to compare the growth of manufacturing output with that of the service industries. To do this we simply express both sets of figures as index numbers with the same base year. This is again illustrated in Table 2.4.

Pause for thought

Does this mean that the value of manufacturing output in 2005 was 2 per cent higher in money terms than in 2003?

The figures show a quite different pattern for the two sectors. The growth of the service industries has been much more steady and more rapid.

Using index numbers to measure percentage changes

To find the annual percentage growth rate in any one year, we simply look at the percentage change in the index from the previous year. To work this out, we use the following formula:

$$\frac{I_t - I_{t-1}}{I_{t-1}} \times 100$$

where I_t is the index in the year in question and I_{t-1} is the index in the previous year.

Thus, using Table 2.4, to find the growth rate in manufacturing output from 1987 to 1988, we first see how much the index has risen, $I_t - I_{t-1}$. The answer is $91.6 - 85.4 = 6.2$.

But this does *not* mean that the growth rate is 6.2 per cent. According to our formula, the growth rate is equal to:

$$\frac{91.6 - 85.4}{85.4} \times 100$$
$$= 6.2/85.4 \times 100$$
$$= 7.3\%$$

The price index

Perhaps the best known of all price indices is the **consumer prices index (CPI)**.[1] It is an index of the prices of goods and services purchased by the average household. Movements in this index, therefore, show how the cost of living has changed. Annual percentage increases in the CPI are the commonest definition of the rate of inflation. Thus if the CPI went up from 100 to 103 over a 12-month period, we would say that the rate of inflation was 3 per cent. If it went up from 150 to 156 over 12 months, the rate of inflation would be $(156 - 150)/150 \times 100 = 4$ per cent.

The use of weighted averages

The CPI is a **weighted average** of the prices of many items. The index of manufacturing output that we looked at above was also a weighted average: an average of the output of many individual products.

To illustrate how a weighted average works, consider the case of a weighted average of the output of just three

Definitions

Consumer prices index (CPI) An index of the prices of goods bought by a typical household.

Weighted average The average of several items where each item is ascribed a weight according to its importance. The weights must add up to 1.

---

[1] Previously another measure, the *retail price index* (RPI), was the major measure of consumer prices. Although the RPI is still used, it has been largely replaced by the CPI, which is a more sophisticated measure.

Table 2.5		Constructing a weighted average index			
		Year 1		Year 2	
Industry	Weight	Index	Index times weight	Index	Index times weight
A	0.7	100	70	90	63
B	0.2	100	20	110	22
C	0.1	100	10	130	13
Total	1.0		100		98

industries, A, B and C. Let us assume that in the base year (year 1) the output of A was £7 million, of B £2 million and of C £1 million, giving a total output of the three industries of £10 million. We now attach weights to the output of each industry to reflect its proportion of total output. Industry A is given a weight of 0.7 because it produces seven-tenths of total output. Industry B is given a weight of 0.2 and industry C of 0.1. We then simply multiply each industry's index by its weight and add up all these figures to give the overall industry index.

The index for each industry in year 1 (the base year) is 100. This means that the weighted average index is also 100. Table 2.5 shows what happens to output in year 2. Industry A's output falls by 10 per cent, giving it an index of 90 in year 2. Industry B's output rises by 10 per cent and industry C's output rises by 30 per cent, giving indices of 110 and 130, respectively. But as you can see from the table, despite the fact that two of the three industries have had a rise in output, the total industry index has *fallen* from 100 to 98. The reason is that industry A is so much larger than the other two that its decline in output outweighs their increase.

The consumer prices index is a little more complicated. This is because it is calculated in two stages. First, products are grouped into categories such as food, clothing and services. A weighted average index is worked out for each group. Thus the index for food would be the weighted average of the indices for bread, potatoes, cooking oil, etc. Second, a weight is attached to each of the groups in order to work out an overall index.

Functional relationships

Business economists frequently examine how one economic variable affects another: how the purchases of cars are affected by their price; how consumer expenditure is affected by taxes, or by incomes; how the cost of producing washing machines is affected by the price of steel; how business investment is affected by changes in interest rates. These relationships are called *functional relationships*. We will need to express these relationships in a precise way. This can be done in the form of a table, as a graph or as an equation.

Simple linear functions
These are relationships which, when plotted on a graph, produce a straight line. Let us take an imaginary example of the relationship between total saving in the economy (S) and the level of national income (Y). This functional relationship can be written as:

$$S = f(Y)$$

This is simply shorthand for saying that saving is a function of (i.e. depends on) the level of national income.

If we want to know just *how much* will be saved at any given level of income, we will need to spell out this functional relationship. Let us do this in each of the three ways.

As a table. Table 2.6 gives a selection of values of Y and the corresponding level of S. It is easy to read off from the table the level of saving at one of the levels of national income listed. It is clearly more difficult to work out the level of saving if national income were £23.4 billion or £47.4 billion.

As a graph. Figure 2.7 plots the data from Table 2.6. Each of the dots corresponds to one of the points in the table. By joining the dots up into a single line we can easily read off the value for saving at some level of income other than those listed in the table. A graph also has the advantage of allowing us to see the relationship at a glance.

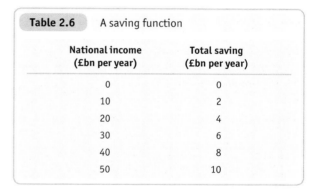

Table 2.6	A saving function	
	National income (£bn per year)	Total saving (£bn per year)
	0	0
	10	2
	20	4
	30	6
	40	8
	50	10

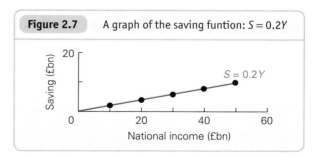

Figure 2.7 A graph of the saving funtion: $S = 0.2Y$

Definition

Functional relationships The mathematical relationships showing how one variable is affected by one or more others.

It is usual to plot the *independent variable* (i.e. the one that does not depend on the other) on the horizontal or *x*-axis, and the *dependent variable* on the vertical or *y*-axis. In our example, saving *depends* on national income. Thus saving is the dependent variable and national income is the independent variable.

As an equation. The data in the table can be expressed in the equation:

$$S = 0.2Y$$

This has the major advantage of being precise. We could work out *exactly* how much would be saved at any given level of national income.

This particular function starts at the origin of the graph (i.e. the bottom left-hand corner). This means that when the value of the independent variable is zero, so too is the value of the dependent variable. Frequently, however, this is not the case in functional relationships. For example, when people have a zero income, they will still have to live, and thus will draw from their past savings: they will have *negative* saving.

When a graph does not pass through the origin, its equation will have the form:

$$y = a + bx$$

where this time *y* stands for the dependent variable (not 'income') and *x* for the independent variable, and *a* and *b*

will have numbers assigned in an actual equation. For example, the equation might be:

$$y = 4 + 2x$$

This would give Table 2.7 and Figure 2.8.

Notice two things about the relationship between the equation and the graph:

■ The point where the line crosses the vertical axis (at a value of 4) is given by the constant (*a*) term. If the *a* term were negative, the line would cross the vertical axis *below* the horizontal axis.

■ The slope of the line is given by the *b* term. The slope is 2/1: for every 1 unit increase in *x* there is a 2 unit increase in *y*.

Non-linear functions

These are functions where the equation involves a squared term (or other power terms). Such functions will give a curved line when plotted on a graph. As an example, consider the following equation:

$$y = 4 + 10x - x^2$$

Table 2.8 and Figure 2.9 are based on it.

As you can see, *y* rises at a decelerating rate and eventually begins to fall. This is because the negative x^2 term is becoming more and more influential as *x* rises, and eventually begins to outweigh the 10*x* term.

Table 2.7	$y = 4 + 2x$
x	**y**
0	4
1	6
2	8
3	10
4	12
5	14
.	.
.	.
.	.

Table 2.8	$y = 4 + 10x - x^2$
x	**y**
0	4
1	13
2	20
3	25
4	28
5	29
6	28
.	.
.	.
.	.

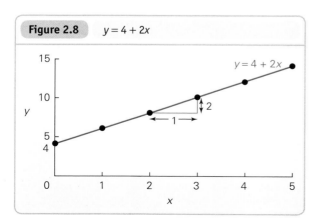

Figure 2.8 $y = 4 + 2x$

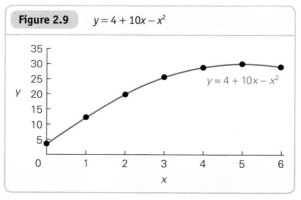

Figure 2.9 $y = 4 + 10x - x^2$

SUMMARY TO APPENDIX

1   Diagrams in economics can be used as pictures: to sketch a relationship so that its essentials can be perceived at a glance.

2   Tables, graphs and charts are also used to portray real-life data. These can be time-series data or cross-section data or both.

3   Presenting time-series data as index numbers gives a clear impression of trends and is a good way of comparing how two or more series (perhaps originally measured in different units) have changed over the same time period. A base year is chosen and the index for that year is set at 100. The percentage change in the value of a variable is given by the percentage change in the index. The formula is:

$$\frac{I_t - I_{t-1}}{I_{t-1}} \times 100$$

4   Several items can be included in one index by using a weighted value for each of the items. The weights must add up to 1 and each weight will reflect the relative importance of that particular item in the index.

5   Functional relationships can be expressed as an equation, a table or a graph. In the linear (straight-line) equation $y = a + bx$, the a term gives the vertical intercept (the point where the graph crosses the vertical axis) and the b term gives the slope. When there is a power term (e.g. $y = a + bx + cx^2$), the graph will be a curve.

REVIEW QUESTIONS TO APPENDIX

1   What are the relative advantages and disadvantages of presenting information in (a) a table; (b) a graph; (c) an equation?

2   If the CPI went up from 125 to 130 over 12 months, what would be the rate of inflation over that period?

3   On a diagram like Figure 2.8, draw the graphs for the following equations.

$$y = -3 + 4x$$
$$y = 15 - 3x$$

4   What shaped graph would you get from the following equations?

$$y = -6 + 3x + 2x^2$$
$$y = 10 - 4x + x^2$$

If you cannot work out the answer, construct a table like Table 2.8 and then plot the figures on a graph.

3 Chapter

Business organisations

Business issues covered in this chapter

- How are businesses organised and structured?
- What are the aims of business?
- Will owners, managers and other employees necessarily have the same aims? How can those working in the firm be persuaded to achieve the objectives of their employers?
- What are the various legal categories of business and how do different legal forms suit different types of business?
- How do businesses differ in their internal organisation? What are the relative merits of alternative forms of organisation?

If you decide to grow strawberries in your garden or allotment, or if you decide to put up a set of shelves in your home, then you have made a production decision. Most production decisions, however, are not made by the individuals who will consume the product. Most production decisions are made by firms: whether by small one-person businesses or by giant multinational corporations, such as General Motors or Sony.

In this chapter we are going to investigate the firm: what is its role in the economy; what are the goals of firms; how do firms differ in respect to their legal status; and in what ways are they organised internally?

3.1 THE NATURE OF FIRMS

Economists have traditionally paid little attention to the ways in which firms operate and to the different roles they might take. Firms were often seen merely as organisations for producing output and employing inputs in response to market forces. Virtually no attention was paid to how firms were organised and how different forms of organisation would influence their behaviour. The firm was seen as a 'black box': inputs were fed in one end, they were used in the most efficient way, and output then emerged from the other end. But do firms have a more significant function to play in respect to resource allocation and production, and does their internal organisation affect their decisions? The answer to these questions is clearly yes.

Complex production

Very few goods or services are produced by one person alone. Most products require a complex production process that will involve many individuals. But how are these individuals to be organised in order to produce such goods and services? Two very different ways are:

- within markets via price signals;
- within firms via a hierarchy of managerial authority.

In the first of these two ways, each stage of production would involve establishing a distinct contract with each separate producer. Assume that you wanted to produce a woollen jumper. You would need to enter a series of separate contracts: to have the jumper designed, to buy the wool, to get the wool spun, to get it dyed, to have the jumper knitted. There are many other stages in the production and distribution process that might also be considered. With each contract a price will have to be determined, and that price will reflect current market conditions. In most cases, such a form of economic organisation would prove to be highly inefficient and totally impractical. Consider the number of contracts that might be necessary if you wished to produce a motor car!

With the second way of organising production, a single *firm* (or just a few firms) replaces the market. The coordination of the conversion of inputs into output takes place *within* the firm: not through the market mechanism, but by management issuing orders as to what to produce and the manner in which this is to take place. Hence the distinguishing feature of the firm is that the price mechanism plays little if any role in allocating resources within it.

The benefits of organising production within firms

The function of the firm is to bring together a series of production and distribution operations, doing away with the need for individuals to enter into narrowly specified contracts. If you want a woollen jumper, you go to a woollen jumper retailer.

According to Ronald Coase,[1] the key advantage of organising production and distribution through firms, as opposed to the market, is that it involves lower **transaction costs**. Transaction costs are the costs of making economic arrangements about production, distribution and sales.

> **KEY IDEA 5**
>
> ***Transaction costs.*** The costs incurred when firms buy inputs or services from other firms as opposed to producing them themselves. They include the costs of searching for the best firm to do business with, the costs of negotiating, drawing up, monitoring and enforcing contracts, and the costs of transporting and handling products between the firms. These costs should be weighed against the benefits of outsourcing through the market.

The transaction costs associated with individual contracts made through the market are likely to be substantial for the following reasons:

- The *uncertainty* in framing contracts. It is unlikely that decision makers will have perfect knowledge of the production process. Given, then, that such contracts are established on imperfect information, they are consequently subject to error.

- The *complexity* of contracts. Many products require many stages of production. The more complex the product, the greater the number of contracts that would have to be made. The specifications within contracts may also become more complex, requiring high levels of understanding and knowledge of the production process, which raises the possibility of error in writing them. As contracts become more complex they raise a firm's costs of production and make it difficult to determine the correct price for a transaction.

- *Monitoring* contracts. Entering into a contract with another person may require that you monitor whether the terms of the contract are fulfilled. This may incur a significant time cost for the individual, especially if a large number of contracts require monitoring.

- *Enforcing* contracts. If one party breaks its contract, the legal expense of enforcing the contract or recouping any losses may be significant. Many individuals might find such costs prohibitive, and as a consequence be unable to pursue broken contracts through the legal system.

What is apparent is that, for most goods, the firm represents a superior way to organise production. The actions of management replace the price signals of the market and overcome many of the associated transaction costs.

Goals of the firm

Economists have traditionally assumed that firms will want to maximise profits. The 'traditional theory of the firm', as it is called, shows how much output firms should produce and at what price, in order to make as much profit as possible. But do firms necessarily want to maximise profits?

It is reasonable to assume that the *owners* of firms will want to maximise profits: this much most of the critics of the traditional theory accept. The question is, however, whether the owners make the decisions about how much to produce and at what price.

The divorce of ownership from control

As businesses steadily grew over the eighteenth and nineteenth centuries, many owner-managers were forced, however reluctantly, to devolve some responsibility for the running of the business to other individuals. These new managers brought with them technical skills and business expertise, a crucial prerequisite for a modern successful

KI 7 p35

> **Definitions**
>
> **The firm** An economic organisation that coordinates the process of production and distribution.
>
> **Transaction costs** Those costs incurred when making economic contracts in the marketplace.

[1] Ronald H. Coase, 'The Nature of the Firm', *Economica*, Vol. 4, No. 16, Nov. 1937, pp. 386–405.

business enterprise. The managerial revolution that was to follow, in which business owners (shareholders) and managers became distinct groups, called into question what the precise goals of the business enterprise might now be. This debate was to be further fuelled by the development of the *joint-stock company*, in which the ownership of the enterprise was progressively dispersed over a large number of shareholders. The growth in the joint-stock company was a direct consequence of business owners looking to raise large amounts of investment capital in order to maintain or expand business activity.

This twin process of managerial expansion and widening share ownership led Berle and Means[2] to argue that the *ownership* of stocks and shares in an enterprise no longer meant *control* over its assets. They subsequently drew a distinction between 'nominal ownership', namely getting a return from investing in a business, and 'effective ownership', which is the ability to control and direct the assets of the business. The more dispersed nominal ownership becomes, the less and less likely it is that there will be effective ownership by shareholders. (This issue will be considered in more detail in Chapter 14.)

The modern company is *legally* separate from its owners (as you will discover in section 3.2). Hence the assets are legally owned by the business itself. Consequently, the group *in charge* of the business is that which controls the use of these assets: i.e. the group which determines the business's objectives and implements the necessary procedures to secure them. In most companies this group is the managers.

Berle and Means argued that, as a consequence of this transition from owner to manager control, conflicts are likely to develop between the goals of managers and those of the owners. But what are the objectives of managers? Will they want to maximise profits, or will they have some other aim?

Managers may be assumed to want to maximise their *own* interests. This may well involve pursuits that conflict with profit maximisation. They may, for example, pursue higher salaries, greater power or prestige, greater sales, better working conditions or greater popularity with their subordinates. Different managers in the same firm may well pursue different aims.

Managers will still have to ensure that *sufficient* profits are made to keep shareholders happy, but that may be very different from *maximising* profits. Alternative theories of the firm to those of profit maximisation, therefore, tend to assume that large firms are profit 'satisficers'. That is, managers strive hard for a minimum target level of profit, but are less interested in profits above this level.

Such theories fall into two categories: first, those theories that assume that firms attempt to maximise some other aim, provided that sufficient profits are achieved; and second, those theories that assume that firms pursue a number of potentially conflicting aims, of which sufficient profit is merely one. (These alternative theories are examined more fully in Chapter 14.)

(These alternative theories are examined more fully in Chapter 14.)

Pause for thought

Make a list of six possible aims that a manager of a high street department store might have. Identify some conflicts that might arise between these aims.

 KEY IDEA 6

The nature of institutions and organisations is likely to influence behaviour. There are various forces influencing people's decisions in complex organisations. Assumptions that an organisation will follow one simple objective (e.g. short-run profit maximisation) are thus too simplistic in many cases.

The principal–agent relationship

Can the owners of a firm ever be sure that their managers will pursue the business strategy most appropriate to achieving the owners' goals (which traditional economic theory tells us is the maximisation of profit)? This is an example of what is known as the *principal–agent problem*. One of the features of a complex modern economy is that people (principals) have to employ others (agents) to carry out their wishes. If you want to go on holiday, it is easier to go to a travel agent to sort out the arrangements than to do it all yourself. Likewise, if you want to buy a house, it is more convenient to go to an estate agent.

The crucial advantage that agents have over their principals is specialist knowledge and information. This is frequently the basis upon which agents are employed. For example, owners employ managers for their specialist knowledge of a market or their understanding of business practice. But this situation of *asymmetric information* – that one party (the agent) knows more than the other (the principal) – means that it will be very difficult for the principal to judge in whose interest the agent is operating. Are the manager's own goals rather than the goals of the owner being pursued? It is the same in other walks of life. The estate agent selling your house may try to convince you that it is necessary to accept a lower price, while the

---

Definitions

Joint-stock company A company where ownership is distributed between a large number of shareholders.

Principal–agent problem One where people (principals), as a result of lack of knowledge, cannot ensure that their best interests are served by their agents.

Asymmetric information A situation in which one party in an economic relationship knows more than another.

---

[2] A. A. Berle and G. C. Means, *The Modern Corporation and Private Property* (Macmillan, 1933).

real reason is to save the agent time, effort and expense. A second-hand car dealer may 'neglect' to tell you about the rust on the underside of the car, or that it had a history of unreliability.

> **KEY IDEA 7**
>
> *The principal–agent problem.* Where people (principals), as a result of a lack of knowledge, cannot ensure that their best interests are served by their agents. Agents may take advantage of this situation to the disadvantage of the principals.

Principals may attempt to reconcile the fact that they have imperfect information, and are thus in an inherently weak position, in the following ways:

- *Monitoring* the performance of the agent. Shareholders could monitor the performance of their senior managers through attending annual general meetings. The managers could be questioned by shareholders and ultimately replaced if their performance is seen as unsatisfactory.
- Establishing a series of *incentives* to ensure that agents act in the principals' best interest. For example, managerial pay could be closely linked to business performance (e.g. profitability).

Within any firm there will exist a complex chain of principal–agent relationships – between workers and managers, between junior managers and senior managers, between senior managers and directors, and between directors and shareholders. All groups will hold some specialist knowledge which might be used to further their own distinct goals. Predictably, the development of effective monitoring and evaluation programmes and the creation of performance-related pay schemes have been two central themes in the development of business practices in recent years – a sign that the principal is looking to fight back.

Staying in business

Aiming for profits, sales, salaries, power, etc. will be useless if the firm does not survive! Trying to *maximise* any of the various objectives may be risky. For example, if a firm tries to maximise its market share by aggressive advertising or price cutting, it might invoke a strong response from its rivals. The resulting war may drive it out of business. Some of the managers may easily move to other jobs and may actually gain from the experience, but the majority are likely to lose. Concern with survival, therefore, may make firms cautious.

Not all firms, however, make survival the top priority. Some are adventurous and are prepared to take risks. Adventurous firms are most likely to be those dominated by a powerful and ambitious individual – an individual prepared to take gambles.

The more dispersed the decision-making power is in the firm, and the more worried managers are about their own survival, the more cautious are their policies likely to be: preferring 'tried and trusted' methods of production, preferring to stick with products that have proved to be popular, and preferring to expand slowly and steadily.

If a firm is too cautious, however, it may not after all survive. It may find that it loses markets to more innovative or aggressive competitors. Ultimately, therefore, if a firm is concerned to survive, it must be careful to balance caution against keeping up with competitors, ensuring that the customer is sufficiently satisfied and that costs are kept sufficiently low by efficient management and the introduction of new technology.

The efficient operation of the firm may be strongly influenced by its internal organisational structure. We will consider this in more detail (see section 3.3), but first we must consider how the *legal* structure of the firm might influence its conduct within the marketplace.

3.2 THE FIRM AS A LEGAL ENTITY

 The legal structure of the firm is likely to have a significant impact on its conduct, and subsequent performance, within the marketplace. In the UK, there are several types of firm, each with a distinct legal status.

The sole proprietor

This is where the business is owned by just one person. Usually such businesses are small, with only a few employees. Retailing, construction and farming are typical areas where sole proprietorships are found. Such businesses are easy to set up and may require only a relatively small initial capital investment. They may well flourish if the owner is highly committed to the business, and can respond to changing market conditions. They suffer two main disadvantages, however:

- *Limited scope for expansion.* Finance is limited to what the owner can raise personally. Also there is a limit to the size of an organisation that one person can effectively control.
- *Unlimited liability.* The owner is personally liable for any losses that the business might make. This could result in the owner's house, car and other assets being seized to pay off any outstanding debts.

The partnership

This is where two or more people own the business. In most partnerships there is a legal limit of 20 partners. Partnerships are common in the same fields as sole proprietorships. They are also common in the professions: solicitors, accountants, surveyors, etc. With more owners, there is more scope for expansion. More finance can be raised and the partners can each specialise in one aspect of the business.

BOX 3.1 **MANAGERS AND PERFORMANCE**

Are high CEO salaries justified?

In 2011, the average pay, including bonuses and long-term incentive plans, for a chief executive of the top 100 UK companies was some £4.8 million. Average earnings in the UK in the same year were just over £26,000. Thus, the average chief executive was paid 184 times more than an average UK worker. What is more, the average annual increase in executive pay in 2011 was 12.0 per cent at a time when many employees' pay was falling in real terms.[1]

The awards given to executive 'fat cats' have met with considerable protest in recent years. So how can such high pay awards to top executives be justified? The two main arguments put forward to justify such generosity are as follows:

- 'The best cost money.' Failure to offer high rewards may encourage the top executives within an industry to move elsewhere.
- 'High rewards motivate.' High rewards are likely to motivate not only top executives, but also those below them. Managers, especially those in the middle of the business hierarchy, will compete for promotion and seek to do well with such high rewards on offer.

However, this view has been challenged, not least by the Business Secretary, Vince Cable.

> Vince Cable, Britain's outspoken business secretary, is fulminating about 'outrageous' executive pay awards. . . . 'There's a serious problem, because executive pay has got way out of line with company performance . . .'.

> Is the link between executive pay and performance as broken as critics say – and if it is, can anything meaningful be done?

> The phenomenon has been building for years. FTSE 100 chief executives' pay was 47 times that of average employees in 1998 but had risen to 120 times by 2010. . . . Bosses' packages have more than doubled

in value over that period, while share prices have barely changed. . . .

> The High Pay Commission says the growth of performance-related pay has itself added to the complexity of remuneration and boosted the amount that can be received. . . . Some academics argue that over-powerful executives have been able to extract excessive awards.

Not everyone agrees with the consensus view, however. Thomas Noe, professor of management studies at Oxford's Said Business School, says it is fundamentally incorrect. . . . In the US, he argues – and probably in the UK, too – most of the increase in executive pay can be accounted for by an increase in company size. . . . for a large company, it can make sense to pay a premium for a chief executive who may deliver a slightly better performance than its rivals. 'You are much more willing to pay for tiny differences in performance, because now they are getting multiplied by a much bigger base.' . . . 'If shareholders were unhappy', he adds, 'they would vote against company pay policies.'

Robert Talbut, chief investment officer at Royal London Asset Management and a member of the High Pay Commission says: 'Shareholders are engaging but the tools available to them are very limited, because all we do is get an advisory vote once the remuneration committee have decided what they want to do.'

The real problem, he says, is that remuneration committees are showing 'insufficient steel' and not doing the job that shareholders want them to do. 'The whole system gives the impression of having been captured by the insiders.'[2]

1. *Explain how excessive executive remuneration might illustrate the principal–agent problem.*
2. *In the UK, many of the highest-paid executives head former public utilities. Why might the giving of very high rewards to such individuals be a source of public concern?*

[1] *Guardian*, 11 June 2012.

[2] Brian Groom, 'Executive pay: The trickle-up effect' *Financial Times*, 27 July 2011. © The Financial Times Limited. All Rights Reserved.

Although since 2001 it has been possible to form limited liability partnerships, many partnerships still have unlimited liability. This problem could be very serious. The mistakes of one partner could jeopardise the personal assets of all the other partners.

Where large amounts of capital are required and/or when the risks of business failure are relatively high, partnerships without limited liability are not an appropriate form of organisation. In such cases it is best to form a company (or 'joint-stock company' to give it its full title).

Companies

A company is legally separate from its owners. This means that it can enter into contracts and own property. Any debts are *its* debts, not the owners'.

Each owner has a share in the company. The size of their shareholdings will vary from one shareholder to another and will depend on the amount they invest. Each shareholder will receive his or her share of the company's distributed profit. The payments to shareholders are called 'dividends'.

The owners have only *limited liability*. This means that, if the company goes bankrupt, the owners will lose the amount of money they have invested in the company, but no more. Their personal assets cannot be seized. This has the advantage of encouraging people to become shareholders, and indeed large companies may have thousands of shareholders – some with very small holdings and others, including institutional shareholders such as pension funds, with very large holdings. Without the protection of limited liability, many of these investors would never put their money into any company that involved even the slightest risk.

Shareholders often take no part in the running of the firm. They may elect a board of directors which decides broad issues of company policy. The board of directors in turn appoints managers who make the day-to-day decisions. There are two types of company: public and private.

Public limited companies. Don't be confused by the title. A public limited company is still a private enterprise: it is not a nationalised industry. It is 'public' because it can offer new shares publicly: by issuing a prospectus, it can invite the public to subscribe to a new share issue. In addition, many public limited companies are quoted on a stock exchange. This means that existing shareholders can sell some or all of their shares on the stock exchange. The prices of these shares will be determined by demand and supply. A public limited company must hold an annual shareholders' meeting. Examples of well-known UK public limited companies are Marks & Spencer, BP, Barclays, BSkyB and Tesco.

Private limited companies. Private limited companies cannot offer their shares publicly. Shares have to be sold privately. This makes it more difficult for private limited companies to raise finance, and consequently they tend to be smaller than public companies. They are, however, easier to set up than public companies. One of the most famous examples of a private limited company was Manchester United football club (which used to be a public limited company until it was bought out by the Glazer family in 2005). It then became a public limited company again in August 2012 when 10 per cent of the shares were floated on the New York Stock Exchange.

Consortia of firms

It is common, especially in large civil engineering projects that involve very high risks, for many firms to work together as a consortium. The Channel Tunnel and Thames Barrier are products of this form of business organisation. Within the consortium one firm may act as the managing contractor, while the other members may provide specialist services. Alternatively, management may be more equally shared.

Cooperatives

These are of two types.

Consumer cooperatives. These, like the old high street Co-ops, are officially owned by the consumers. Consumers in fact play no part in the running of these cooperatives. They are run by professional managers.

Producer cooperatives. These are firms that are owned by their workers, who share in the firm's profit according to some agreed formula. They are sometimes formed by people in the same trade coming together: for example, producers of handicraft goods. At other times they are formed by workers buying out their factory from the owners; this is most likely if it is due to close, with a resultant loss of jobs. Producer cooperatives, although still relatively few in number, have grown in recent years. One of the most famous is the department store chain, John Lewis, with its supermarket division, Waitrose.

Public corporations

These are state-owned enterprises such as the BBC, the Bank of England and nationalised industries.

Public corporations have a legal identity separate from the government. They are run by a board, but the members of the board are appointed by the relevant government minister. The boards have to act within various terms of reference laid down by Act of Parliament. Profits of public corporations that are not reinvested accrue to the Treasury. Since 1980 most public corporations have been 'privatised': that is, they have been sold directly to other firms in the private sector (such as Austin Rover to British Aerospace) or to the general public through a public issue of shares (such as British Gas). However, in response to turmoil in the financial markets, the UK government nationalised two banks in 2008, Northern Rock (see Box 15.3) and Bradford and Bingley. It also partly nationalised two others, the Royal Bank of Scotland and the Lloyds Banking Group (HBOS and Lloyds TSB).

The issue of privatisation is considered in Chapter 22.

3.3 THE INTERNAL ORGANISATION OF THE FIRM

The internal operating structures of firms are frequently governed by their size. Small firms tend to be centrally managed, with decision making operating through a clear managerial hierarchy. In large firms, however, the organisational structure tends to be more complex, although technological change is forcing many organisations to reassess the most suitable organisational structure for their business.

> **Pause for thought**
>
> *Before you read on, consider in what ways technology might influence the organisational structure of a business.*

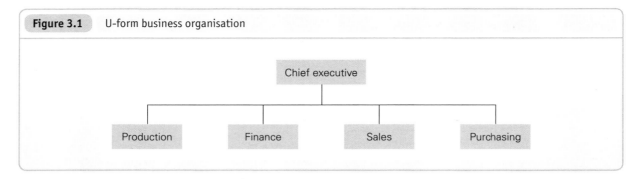

Figure 3.1   U-form business organisation

U-form

In small to medium-sized firms, the managers of the various departments – marketing, finance, production, etc. – are normally directly responsible to a chief executive, whose function is to coordinate their activities: relaying the firm's overall strategy to them and being responsible for inter-departmental communication. We call this type of structure *U (unitary) form* (see Figure 3.1).

When firms expand beyond a certain size, however, a U-form structure is likely to become inefficient. This inefficiency arises from difficulties in communication, coordination and control. It becomes too difficult to manage the whole organisation from the centre. The problem is that the chief executive suffers from ***bounded rationality*** – a limit on the rate at which information can be absorbed and processed. When facing complex decisions they typically make satisfactory rather than optimal decisions, relying on rules-of-thumb and tried and tested methods. As the firm grows, more decisions are required. This leads to less time per decision and ultimately poorer decisions. The chief executive effectively loses control of the firm.

 KEY IDEA 8   *Good decision making requires good information. Where information is poor, or poorly used, decisions and their outcomes may be poor. This may be the result of bounded rationality.*

In attempting to regain control, it is likely that a further managerial layer will be inserted. The chain of command thus becomes lengthened as the chief executive must now coordinate and communicate via this intermediate managerial level. This leads to the following problems:

- Communication costs increase.
- Messages and decisions may be misinterpreted and distorted.
- The firm experiences a decline in organisational efficiency as various departmental managers, freed from central control, seek to maximise their personal departmental goals.

M-form

To overcome these organisational problems, the firm can adopt an ***M (multi-divisional) form*** of managerial structure (see Figure 3.2).

This suits medium to large firms. The firm is divided into a number of 'divisions'. Each division could be responsible for a particular product or group of products, or a particular market (e.g. a specific country). The day-to-day running and even certain long-term decisions of each division would be the responsibility of the divisional manager(s). This leads to the following benefits:

- Reduced length of information flows.
- The chief executive being able to concentrate on overall strategic planning.
- An enhanced level of control, with each division being run as a mini 'firm', competing with other divisions for the limited amount of company resources available.

The flat organisation

The shift towards the M-form organisational structure was primarily motivated by a desire to improve the process of decision making within the business. This involved adding layers of management. Recent technological innovations, especially in respect to computer systems such as e-mail and management information systems, have encouraged many organisations to think again about how to establish an efficient and effective organisational structure. The ***flat organisation*** is one that fully embraces the latest

Definitions

U-form business organisation One in which the central organisation of the firm (the chief executive or a managerial team) is responsible both for the firm's day-to-day administration and for formulating its business strategy.

Bounded rationality Individuals are limited in their ability to absorb and process information. People think in ways conditioned by their experiences (family, education, peer groups, etc.).

M-form business organisation One in which the business is organised into separate departments, such that responsibility for the day-to-day management enterprise is separated from the formulation of the business's strategic plan.

Flat organisation One in which technology enables senior managers to communicate directly with those lower in the organisational structure. Middle managers are bypassed.

Figure 3.2 M-form business organisation

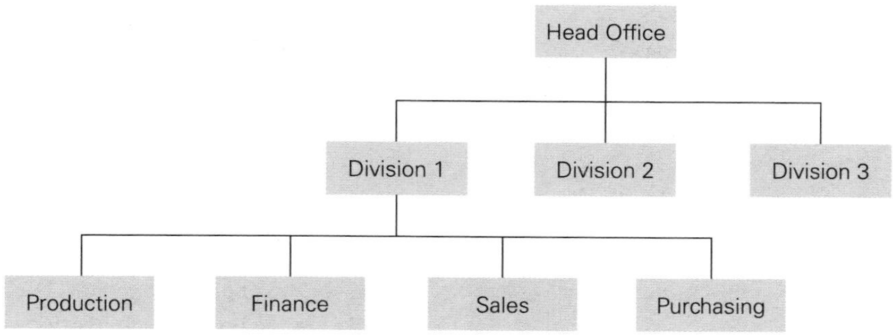

developments in information technology, and by so doing is able to reduce the need for a large group of middle managers. Senior managers, through these new information systems, can communicate easily and directly with those lower in the organisational structure. Middle managers are effectively bypassed.

The speed of information flows reduces the impact of bounded rationality on the decision-making process. Senior managers are able to re-establish and, in certain cases, widen their span of control over the business organisation.

In many respects the flat organisation represents a return to the U-form structure. It is yet to be seen whether we also have a return to the problems associated with this type of organisation.

Multinationals and business organisation

Further types of business organisation which we might identify are closely linked to the expansion and development of the multinational enterprise. Such organisational structures have developed as a response to these businesses attempting to control their business activities on a global scale. Three forms of multinational business organisation are identified below.

H-form. The H-form or **holding company** is in many respects a variation on the M-form structure. A holding company (or parent company) is one which owns a controlling interest in other subsidiary companies. These subsidiaries, in turn, may also have controlling interests in other companies.

H-form organisational structures can be highly complex. While the parent company has ultimate control over its various subsidiaries, it is likely that both tactical and strategic decision making is left to the individual companies within the organisation. Many multinationals are organised along the lines of an international holding company, where overseas subsidiaries pursue their own independent strategy. The Walt Disney Company (Holding Company) represents a

good example of an H-form business organisation. Figure 3.3 shows the firm's organisational structure and the range of assets it owns.

Integrated international enterprise. The **integrated international enterprise** is an organisational structure where a company's international subsidiaries, rather than pursuing independent business strategies, coordinate and integrate their activities in pursuit of shared corporate aims and objectives. The coordination of such activities can be either at a regional level – for example, within the European market – or on a truly global scale. In such an organisation, the distinction between parent company and subsidiary is of less relevance than the identification of a clear corporate philosophy which dominates business goals and policy.

Transnational association. A further form of multinational business organisation is the **transnational association**. Here the business headquarters holds little equity investment in its subsidiaries. These are largely owned and managed by local people. These subsidiaries receive from the headquarters managerial and technical assistance, in exchange for contractual agreements that output produced by the subsidiary is sold to the headquarters. Such output is most

Definitions

Holding company A business organisation in which the present company holds interests in a number of other companies or subsidiaries.

Integrated international enterprise One in which an international company pursues a single business strategy. It coordinates the business activities of its subsidiaries across different countries.

Transnational association A form of business organisation in which the subsidiaries of a company in different countries are contractually bound to the parent company to provide output to or receive inputs from other subsidiaries.

Figure 3.3 Organisational structure of The Walt Disney Company (Holding Company)

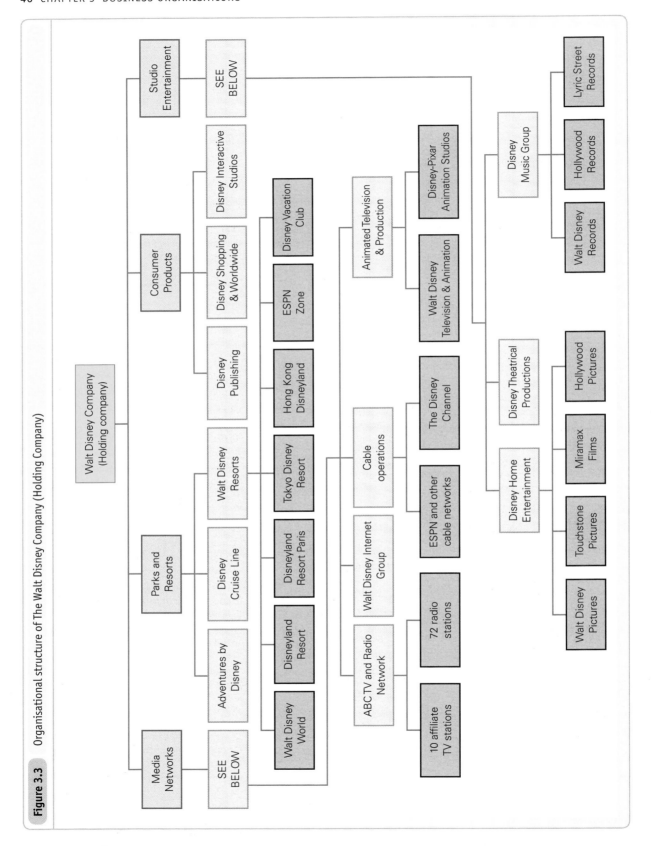

BOX 3.2 **THE CHANGING NATURE OF BUSINESS**

Knowledge rules

In the knowledge-driven economy, innovation has become central to achievement in the business world. With this growth in importance, organisations large and small have begun to re-evaluate their products, their services, even their corporate culture in the attempt to maintain their competitiveness in the global markets of today. The more forward-thinking companies have recognised that only through such root and branch reform can they hope to survive in the face of increasing competition.

European Commission, Directorate-General for Enterprise, *Innovation Management and the Knowledge-Driven Economy* (ECSC-EC-EAEC Brussels-Luxembourg, 2004)

Knowledge is fundamental to economic success in many industries, and for most firms, key knowledge resides in skilled members of the workforce. The result is a market in knowledge, with those having the knowledge being able to command high salaries and often being 'head hunted'. The 'knowledge economy' is affecting people from all walks of life, and fundamentally changing the nature, organisation and practice of business.

The traditional business corporation was based around five fundamental principles:

- Individual workers needed the business and the income it provided more than the business needed them. After all, employers could always find alternative workers. As such, the corporation was the dominant partner in the employment relationship.
- Employees who worked for the corporation tended to be full time, and depended upon the work as their sole source of income.
- The corporation was integrated, with a single management structure overseeing all the various stages of production. This was seen as the most efficient way to organise productive activity.
- Suppliers, and especially manufacturers, had considerable power over the customer by controlling information about their product or service.
- Technology relevant to an industry was developed within the industry.

In more recent times, with the advent of the knowledge economy, the principles above have all but been turned on their head.

- The key factor of production in a knowledge economy is knowledge itself, and the workers that hold such knowledge. Without such workers, the corporation is unlikely to succeed. As such, the balance of power between the business and the worker in today's economy is far more equal.
- Even though the vast majority of employees still work full time, the diversity in employment contracts, such

as part-time and short-term contracts and consultancy, means that full-time work is not the only option. (We examine this in section 18.7.) The result is an increasing number of workers offering their services to business in non-conventional ways.
- As the domestic economy increasingly spills into the global economy, the complexity of the marketplace facing business means that few businesses have the expertise to provide an integrated product. With communication costs that are largely insignificant, businesses are likely to be more efficient and flexible if they outsource and de-integrate. Not only are businesses outsourcing various stages of production, but many are employing specialist companies to provide key areas of management, such as HRM (human resource management): hiring, firing, training, benefits, etc.
- Whereas in the past businesses controlled information, today access to information via sources such as the Internet means that power is shifting towards the consumer.
- Today, unlike in previous decades, technological developments are less specific to industries. Knowledge developments diffuse and cut across industry boundaries. What this means for business, in a knowledge-driven economy, is that they must look beyond their own industry if they are to develop and grow. We frequently see partnerships and joint ventures between businesses that cut across industry types and technology.

What is clear from the above is that the dynamics of the knowledge economy require a quite fundamental change in the nature of business. Organisationally it needs to be more flexible, helping it to respond to the ever-changing market conditions it faces. Successful companies draw upon their *core* competencies to achieve market advantage, and thus ultimately specialise in what they do best. Businesses must learn to work with others, either through outsourcing specialist tasks, or through more formal strategic partnerships.

Within this new business model the key assets are the specialist people in the organisation – its knowledge workers. How will businesses attract, retain and motivate the best? Will financial rewards be sufficient, or will workers seek more from their work and the organisation they work for?

With such issues facing the corporation we can expect to see a radical reinterpretation of what business looks like and how it is practised over the coming years.

 How is the development of the knowledge economy likely to affect the distribution of wage income? Will it become more equal or less equal?

likely to take the form of product components rather than finished products. The headquarters then acts as an assembler, marketer or distributor of such output, or some combination of all three. The main advantage of organising international business in this way is that it reduces costs. This form of organisation is known as *global sourcing* and involves the international business using distinct production sites to produce large numbers of single components. With the transnational association, the headquarters still retains the decisive role in integrating business activity.

We shall investigate the organisational structures and issues surrounding multinational corporations more fully (see Chapter 23).

Definition

Global sourcing Where a company uses production sites in different parts of the world to provide particular components for a final product.

SUMMARY

1a The firm's role in the economy is to eliminate the need for making individual contracts through the market, and to provide a more efficient way to organise production.

1b Using the market to establish a contract is not costless. Transaction costs will mean that the market is normally less efficient than the firm as an allocator of resources.

1c The divorce of ownership from control implies that the objectives of owners and managers may diverge, and similarly the objectives of one manager from another. Hence the goals of firms may be diverse. What is more, as ownership becomes more dispersed, so the degree of control by owners diminishes yet further.

1d Managers might pursue maximisation goals other than profit, or look to achieve a wide range of targets in which profit acts as a constraint on other business aims.

1e The problem of managers not pursuing the same goals as the owners is an example of the *principal–agent problem*. Agents (in this case the managers) may not always carry out the wishes of their principals (in this case the owners). Because of asymmetric information, managers are able to pursue their own aims, just so long as they produce results that will satisfy the owners. The solution for owners is for there to be better means of monitoring the performance of managers, and incentives for the managers to behave in the owners' interests.

2a The legal status of the firm will influence both its actions and performance within the marketplace.

2b There are several types of legal organisation of firms: the sole proprietorship, the partnership, the private limited company, the public limited company, consortia of firms, cooperatives and public corporations. In the first two cases, the owners have unlimited liability: the owners are personally liable for any losses the business might make. With companies, however, shareholders' liability is limited to the amount they have invested. This reduced risk encourages people to invest in companies.

3a The relative success of a business organisation will be strongly influenced by its organisational structure. As a firm grows, its organisational structure will need to evolve in order to account for the business's growing complexity. This is particularly so if the business looks to expand overseas.

3b As firms grow, so they tend to move from a U-form to an M-form structure. In recent years, however, with the advance of information technology, many firms have adopted a flat organisation – a return to U-form.

3c Multinational companies often adopt relatively complex forms of organisation. These vary from a holding company (H-form) structure, to the integrated international enterprise, to transnational associations.

REVIEW QUESTIONS

1 What is meant by the term 'transaction costs'? Explain why the firm represents a more efficient way of organising economic life than relying on individual contracts.

2 Explain why the business objectives of owners and managers are likely to diverge. How might owners attempt to ensure that managers act in their interests and not in the managers' own interests?

3 Compare and contrast the relative strengths and weaknesses of the partnership and the public limited company.

4 Conduct an investigation into a recent large building project, such as the 2012 London Olympics. Identify what firms were involved and the roles and responsibilities they had. Outline the advantages and disadvantages that such business consortia might have.

5 If a business is thinking of reorganisation, why and in what ways might new technology be an important factor in such considerations?

6 What problems are multinational corporations, as opposed to domestic firms, likely to have in respect to organising their business activity? What alternative organisational models might multinationals adopt? To what extent do they overcome the problems you have identified?

ADDITIONAL PART A CASE STUDIES IN THE *ECONOMICS FOR BUSINESS* MyEconLab (www.pearsoned.co.uk/sloman)

A.1 **The UK defence industry.** A PEST analysis of the changes in the defence industry in recent years.

A.2 **Scarcity and abundance.** If scarcity is the central economic problem, is anything truly abundant?

A.3 **Global economics.** This examines how macroeconomics and microeconomics apply at the global level and identifies some key issues.

A.4 **Buddhist economics.** A different perspective on economic problems and economic activity.

A.5 **Downsizing and business reorganisation.** Many companies in recent years have 'downsized' their operations and focused on their core competencies. This looks particularly at the case of IBM.

A.6 **Positive and normative statements.** A crucial distinction when considering matters of economic policy.

WEBSITES RELEVANT TO PART A

Numbers and sections refer to websites listed in the Web appendix and hotlinked from this book's website at **www.pearsoned.co.uk/sloman**

■ For a tutorial on finding the best economics websites, see site C8 (*The Internet Economist*).

■ For news articles relevant to Part A, see the *Economics News Articles* link from the book's website.

■ For general economics news sources, see websites in section A of the Web appendix at the end of the book, and particularly A1–9, 24, 38, 39. See also A38, 39 and 43 for links to newspapers worldwide; and A42 for links to economics news articles from newspapers worldwide.

■ For business news items, again see websites in section A of the Web appendix at the end of the book, and particularly A1–3, 20–26, 35, 36.

■ For sources of economic and business data, see sites in section B and particularly B1–4, 33, 34.

■ For general sites for students of economics for business, see sites in section C and particularly C1–7.

■ For sites giving links to relevant economics and business websites, organised by topic, see sites I4, 7, 8, 11, 12, 17, 18.

■ For details on companies, see sites B2 and A3.

Business and markets

The FT Reports . . .

The Financial Times, 3 May 2012

FT

A tale of two coffee beans

By Emiko Terazono

For coffee traders, this year has been a tale of two beans.

Since the start of the year, prices for arabica, the high-quality bean beloved of the espresso cognoscenti, have plummeted more than 20 per cent, while robusta, used mainly for instant coffee, has risen nearly 10 per cent.

Both markets weakened at the end of last year on expectations of good harvests: in Brazil for arabica, and in Vietnam for robusta. But this year Vietnamese farmers have held back their crop, refusing to sell [at low prices]. Added to that, strong demand for lower-quality beans has pushed up robusta prices. . . .

The slump in arabica is a far cry from last year, when prices hit a 34-year high in March amid a shortage caused by bad weather in Colombia, one of the leading producers of high-quality beans. Having hit $3.089 per pound over a year ago, prices are down more than 40 per cent to $1.82 per pound.

Brazil is the world's largest coffee producer and the outlook for a large crop has prompted hedge funds and other speculators to bet on lower prices – or short positions. Hedge funds replaced their bullish bets, or long positions, on arabica for bearish bets after mid-January, when Brazilian producers started to forward sell their crop to lock in prices. . . .

The robusta market in London, on the other hand, has been supported by rising demand in developing countries – particularly in robusta producers such as Mexico, where they now drink a large share of their harvest. Indonesians, in particular, have been big importers of Vietnamese coffee after domestic production fell by a third in 2011. In Europe, traders and analysts have noted the rise in robusta in coffee blends offered by coffee makers as the economic slump has depressed the value of ordinary consumers' shopping baskets. . . .

After hefty profits in the first quarter placing simultaneously bullish bets for robusta coffee and bearish bets for arabica beans, hedge funds are now a little more hesitant as the outlook for the two coffee markets starts to change.

The key is whether robusta prices will fall back, tracking the downward trend of the arabica bean.

Uncertainty is also the defining characteristic of business competition today. Competing in volatile markets can feel a lot like entering the ring against George Foreman in his prime – or, even worse, like stumbling into a barroom brawl. The punches come from all directions, include a steady barrage of body blows and periodic haymakers, and are thrown by a rotating cast of characters who swing bottles and bar stools as well as fists.

Donald Sull, 'How to survive in turbulent markets', *Harvard Business Review*, February 2009, p. 80

Markets dominate economic life, from buying and selling raw materials, to supplying the final product to the customer. It would be difficult to imagine a world without markets. In fact we talk about economies today as 'market economies', with economic decisions made primarily by business, consumers and employees interacting with each other in a market environment.

The determination of a market price is a complex business and often subject to great fluctuation (as the *Financial Times* article illustrates). This is particularly so when you consider commodities, such as coffee, which are highly dependent upon the weather and subject to considerable speculative buying and selling.

In Part B of this book we shall explore how the market system operates. In Chapter 4 we will consider those factors that influence both demand and supply, and how via their interaction we are able to derive a market price. We see how markets transmit information from consumers to producers and from producers to consumers. We see how prices act as an incentive – for example, if consumers want more mobile phones, how this increased demand leads to an increase in their price and hence to an incentive for firms to increase their production.

Changes in price affect the quantity demanded and supplied. But how much? How much will the demand for DVDs go up if the price of DVDs comes down? How much will the supply of new houses go up if the price of houses rises? In Chapter 5 we develop the concept of *elasticity* of demand and supply to examine this responsiveness. We also consider some of the issues the market raises for business, such as the effects on a business's revenue of a change in the price of the product, the impact of time on demand and supply and how businesses deal with the risk and uncertainty markets generate. We also look at speculation – people attempting to gain by anticipating price changes.

Key terms

Price mechanism
Demand and demand curves
Income and substitution effects
Supply and supply curves
Equilibrium price and quantity
Shifts in demand and supply curves
Price elasticity of demand
Income elasticity of demand
Cross-price elasticity of demand
Price elasticity of supply
Speculation
Risk and uncertainty
Spot and futures markets

4

The working of competitive markets

Business issues covered in this chapter

- How do markets operate?
- How are market prices determined and when are they likely to rise or fall?
- Under what circumstances do firms have to accept a price given by the market rather than being able to set the price themselves?
- What are the influences on consumer demand?
- What factors determine the amount of supply coming on to the market?
- How do markets respond to changes in demand or supply?

4.1 BUSINESS IN A COMPETITIVE MARKET

If a firm wants to increase its profits, should it raise its prices, or should it lower them? Should it increase its output, or should it reduce it? Should it modify its product, or should it keep the product unchanged? The answer to these and many other questions is that it depends on the market in which the firm operates. If the market is buoyant, it may well be a good idea for the firm to increase its output in anticipation of greater sales. It may also be a good idea to raise the price of its product in the belief that consumers will be willing to pay more. If, however, the market is declining, the firm may well decide to reduce output, or cut prices, or diversify across into an alternative product.

The firm is thus greatly affected by its market environment, an environment that is often outside the firm's control and subject to frequent changes. For many firms, prices are determined not by them, but by the market. Even where they do have some influence over prices, the

influence is only slight. They may be able to put prices up a small amount, but if they raise them too much, they will find that they lose sales to their rivals.

The market dominates a firm's activities. The more competitive the market, the greater this domination becomes. In the extreme case, the firm may have no power at all to change its price: it is what we call a **price taker**. It has to accept the market price as given. If the firm attempts to raise the price above the market price, it will simply be unable to sell its product: it will lose all its sales to its competitors. Take the case of farmers selling wheat. They have to accept the price as dictated by the market. If individually they try to sell above the market price, no one will buy.

In competitive markets, consumers too are price takers. When we go into shops we have no control over prices. We have to accept the price as given. For example, when you get to the supermarket checkout, you cannot start haggling with the checkout operator over the price of a can of beans or a tub of margarine.

So how does a competitive market work? For simplicity we will examine the case of a *perfectly competitive market*. This is where both producers and consumers are too numerous to have any control over prices whatsoever: a situation where everyone is a price taker.

Clearly, in other markets, firms will have some discretion over the prices they charge. For example, a manufacturing company such as Ford will have some discretion over the prices it charges for its Fiestas or Mondeos. In such cases the firm has some 'market power'. (We will examine different degrees of market power in Chapters 11 and 12.)

The price mechanism

In a *free market* individuals are free to make their own economic decisions. Consumers are free to decide what to buy with their incomes: free to make demand decisions. Firms are free to choose what to sell and what production methods to use: free to make supply decisions. The resulting demand and supply decisions of consumers and firms are transmitted to each other through their effect on *prices*: through the *price mechanism*.

The price mechanism works as follows. Prices respond to *shortages* and *surpluses*. Shortages cause prices to rise. Surpluses cause prices to fall.

If consumers decide they want more of a good (or if producers decide to cut back supply), demand will exceed supply. The resulting *shortage* will cause *the price of the good to rise*. This will act as an incentive to producers to supply more, since production will now be more profitable. At the same time, it will discourage consumers from buying so much. *The price will continue rising until the shortage has thereby been eliminated.*

If, on the other hand, consumers decide they want less of a good (or if producers decide to produce more), supply will exceed demand. The resulting *surplus* will cause *the price of the good to fall*. This will act as a disincentive to producers, who will supply less, since production will now be less profitable. It will encourage consumers to buy more.

The price will continue falling until the surplus has thereby been eliminated.

This price, where demand equals supply, is called the *equilibrium price*. By *equilibrium* we mean a point of balance or a point of rest: in other words, a point towards which there is a tendency to move.

The same analysis can be applied to labour markets (and those for other factors of production), except that here the demand and supply roles are reversed. Firms are the demanders of labour. Households are the suppliers. If the demand for a particular type of labour exceeded its supply, the resulting shortage would drive up the wage rate (i.e. the price of labour), thus reducing firms' demand for that type of labour and encouraging more workers to take up that type of job. Wages would continue rising until demand equalled supply: until the shortage was eliminated.

Likewise if there were a surplus of a particular type of labour, the wage would fall until demand equalled supply. As with price, the wage rate where the demand for labour equals the supply is known as the *equilibrium* wage rate.

The response of demand and supply to changes in price illustrates a very important feature of how economies work.

 KEY IDEA 9 *People respond to incentives.* It is important, therefore, that incentives are appropriate and have the desired effect.

The effect of changes in demand and supply

How will the price mechanism respond to changes in consumer demand or producer supply? After all, the pattern of consumer demand changes over time. For example, people may decide they want more downloadable music and fewer CDs. Likewise the pattern of supply also changes. For example, changes in technology may allow the mass production of microchips at lower cost, while the production of hand-built furniture becomes relatively expensive.

In all cases of changes in demand and supply, the resulting changes in *price* act as both *signals* and *incentives*.

Definitions

Price taker A person or firm with no power to be able to influence the market price.

Perfectly competitive market (preliminary definition) A market in which all producers and consumers of the product are price takers. There are other features of a perfectly competitive market; these are examined in Chapter 11.

Free market One in which there is an absence of government intervention. Individual producers and consumers are free to make their own economic decisions.

The price mechanism The system in a market economy whereby changes in price in response to changes in demand and supply have the effect of making demand equal to supply.

Equilibrium price The price where the quantity demanded equals the quantity supplied: the price where there is no shortage or surplus.

Equilibrium A position of balance. A position from which there is no inherent tendency to move away from current prices and quantities.

A change in demand

A rise in demand is signalled by a rise in price. This then acts as an incentive for firms to produce more of the good: the quantity supplied rises. Firms divert resources from goods with lower prices relative to costs (and hence lower profits) to those goods that are more profitable.

A fall in demand is signalled by a fall in price. This then acts as an incentive for firms to produce less: such goods are now less profitable to produce.

A change in supply

A rise in supply is signalled by a fall in price. This then acts as an incentive for consumers to buy more: the quantity demanded rises. A fall in supply is signalled by a rise in price. This then acts as an incentive for consumers to buy less: the quantity demanded falls.

> **KEY IDEA 10**
> *Changes in demand or supply cause markets to adjust.* Whenever such changes occur, the resulting 'disequilibrium' will bring an automatic change in prices, thereby restoring equilibrium (i.e. a balance of demand and supply).

The interdependence of markets

The interdependence of goods and factor markets

A rise in demand for a good will raise its price and profitability. Firms will respond by supplying more. But to do this they will require more inputs. Thus the demand for the inputs will rise, which, in turn, will raise the price of the inputs. The suppliers of inputs will respond to this incentive by supplying more. This can be summarised as follows:

Goods market

- Demand for the good rises.
- This creates a shortage.
- This causes the price of the good to rise.
- This eliminates the shortage by choking off some of the demand and encouraging firms to produce more.

Factor market

- The increased supply of the good causes an increase in the demand for factors of production (i.e. inputs) used in making it.
- This causes a shortage of those inputs.
- This causes their prices to rise.
- This eliminates their shortage by choking off some of the demand and encouraging the suppliers of inputs to supply more.

Goods markets thus affect factor markets. Figure 4.1 summarises this sequence of events. (It is common in economics to summarise an argument like this by using symbols.)

Interdependence exists in the other direction too: factor markets affect goods markets. For example, the discovery of raw materials will lower their price. This will lower the costs of production of firms using these raw materials and increase the supply of the finished goods. The resulting surplus will lower the price of the good, which, in turn, will encourage consumers to buy more.

The interdependence of different goods markets

A rise in the price of one good will encourage consumers to buy alternatives. This will drive up the price of alternatives. This in turn will encourage producers to supply more of the alternatives.

Let us now turn to examine each side of the market – demand and supply – in more detail.

Figure 4.1   The price mechanism: the effect of a rise in demand

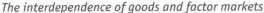

Goods market

$$D_g \uparrow \longrightarrow \text{shortage} \ (D_g > S_g) \longrightarrow P_g \uparrow \nearrow{S_g \uparrow} \searrow_{D_g \downarrow} \ \text{until } D_g = S_g$$

Factor market

$$S_g \uparrow \longrightarrow D_i \uparrow \longrightarrow \text{shortage} \ (D_i > S_i) \longrightarrow P_i \uparrow \nearrow{S_i \uparrow} \searrow_{D_i \downarrow} \ \text{until } D_i = S_i$$

(where D = demand, S = supply, P = price, g = the good, i = inputs, $\longrightarrow$ means 'leads to')

4.2 DEMAND

The relationship between demand and price

The headlines announce, 'Major crop failures in Brazil and East Africa: coffee prices soar.' Shortly afterwards you find that coffee prices have doubled in the shops. What do you do? Presumably you will cut back on the amount of coffee you drink. Perhaps you will reduce it from, say, six cups per day to two. Perhaps you will give up drinking coffee altogether.

This is simply an illustration of the general relationship between price and consumption: *when the price of a good rises, the quantity demanded will fall*. This relationship is known as the *law of demand*. There are two reasons for this law:

■ People will feel poorer. They will not be able to afford to buy so much of the good with their money. The purchasing power of their income (their *real income*) has fallen. This is called the *income effect* of a price rise.
■ The good will now be dearer relative to other goods. People will thus switch to alternative or 'substitute' goods. This is called the *substitution effect* of a price rise.

Similarly, when the price of a good falls, the quantity demanded will rise. People can afford to buy more (the income effect), and they will switch away from consuming alternative goods (the substitution effect).

Therefore, returning to our example of the increase in the price of coffee, we will not be able to afford to buy as much

as before, and we will probably drink more tea, cocoa, fruit juices or even water instead.

A word of warning: be careful about the meaning of the words *quantity demanded*. They refer to the amount consumers are willing and able to purchase at a given price over a given time period (for example, a week, or a month, or a year). They do *not* refer to what people would simply *like* to consume. You might like to own a luxury yacht, but your demand for luxury yachts will almost certainly be zero.

The demand curve

Consider the hypothetical data in Table 4.1. The table shows how many kilos of potatoes per month would be purchased at various prices.

Columns (2) and (3) show the *demand schedules* for two individuals, Tracey and Darren. Column (4), by contrast, shows the total *market demand schedule*. This is the total demand by all consumers. To obtain the market demand schedule for potatoes, we simply add up the quantities demanded at each price by *all* consumers: i.e. Tracey, Darren and everyone else who demands potatoes. Notice that we are talking about demand *over a period of time* (not at a *point* in time). Thus we would talk about daily demand or weekly demand or annual demand or whatever.

	Price (pence per kg) (1)	Tracey's demand (kg) (2)	Darren's demand (kg) (3)	Total market demand (tonnes: 000s) (4)
Table 4.1	**The demand for potatoes (monthly)**			
A	20	28	16	700
B	40	15	11	500
C	60	5	9	350
D	80	1	7	200
E	100	0	6	100

Definitions

The law of demand The quantity of a good demanded per period of time will fall as the price rises and rise as the price falls, other things being equal (*ceteris paribus*).

Income effect The effect of a change in price on quantity demanded arising from the consumer becoming better or worse off as a result of the price change.

Substitution effect The effect of a change in price on quantity demanded arising from the consumer switching to or from alternative (substitute) products.

Quantity demanded The amount of a good that a consumer is willing and able to buy at a given price over a given period of time.

Demand schedule for an individual A table showing the different quantities of a good that a person is willing and able to buy at various prices over a given period of time.

Market demand schedule A table showing the different total quantities of a good that consumers are willing and able to buy at various prices over a given period of time.

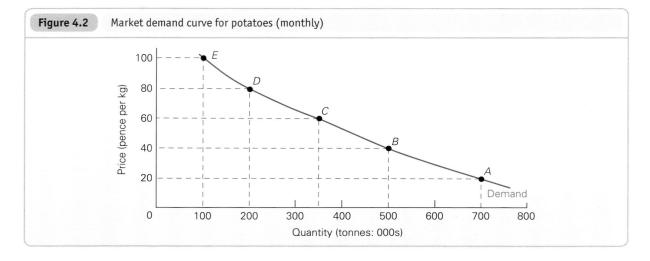

Figure 4.2   Market demand curve for potatoes (monthly)

The demand schedule can be represented graphically as a **demand curve**. Figure 4.2 shows the market demand curve for potatoes corresponding to the schedule in Table 4.1. The price of potatoes is plotted on the vertical axis. The quantity demanded is plotted on the horizontal axis.

Point *E* shows that at a price of 100p per kilo, 100 000 tonnes of potatoes are demanded each month. When the price falls to 80p we move down the curve to point *D*. This shows that the quantity demanded has now risen to 200 000 tonnes per month. Similarly, if the price falls to 60p, we move down the curve again to point *C*: 350 000 tonnes are now demanded. The five points on the graph (*A–E*) correspond to the figures in columns (1) and (4) of Table 4.1. The graph also enables us to read off the likely quantities demanded at prices other than those in the table.

A demand curve could also be drawn for an individual consumer. Like market demand curves, individuals' demand curves generally slope downward from left to right (they have negative slope): the lower the price of a product, the more is a person likely to buy.

Two points should be noted at this stage:

■ In textbooks, demand curves (and other curves too) are only occasionally used to plot specific data. More frequently they are used to illustrate general theoretical arguments. In such cases the axes will simply be price and quantity, with the units unspecified.

■ The term 'curve' is used even when the graph is a straight line! In fact, when using demand curves to illustrate arguments we frequently draw them as straight lines – it's easier.

Other determinants of demand

Price is not the only factor that determines how much of a good people will buy. Demand is also affected by the following.

Tastes. The more desirable people find the good, the more they will demand. Tastes are affected by factor such as advertising, fashion, observations of other consumers, considerations of health and experiences from consuming the good on previous occasions.

The number and price of substitute goods (i.e. competitive goods). The higher the price of **substitute goods**, the higher will be the demand for this good as people switch from the substitutes. For example, the demand for coffee will depend on the price of tea. If tea goes up in price, the demand for coffee will rise.

The number and price of complementary goods. **Complementary goods** are those that are consumed together: cars and petrol, shoes and polish, bread and butter. The higher the price of complementary goods, the fewer of them will be bought and hence the less the demand for this good. For example, the demand for compact discs will depend on the price of CD players. If the price of CD players goes up, so that fewer are bought, the demand for CDs will fall.

Income. As people's incomes rise, their demand for most goods will rise. Such goods are called **normal goods**. There are exceptions to this general rule, however. As people get richer, they spend less on **inferior goods**, such as cheap margarine, and switch to better-quality goods.

Distribution of income. If, for example, national income were redistributed from the poor to the rich, the demand

Definition

Demand curve A graph showing the relationship between the price of a good and the quantity of the good demanded over a given time period. Price is measured on the vertical axis; quantity demanded is measured on the horizontal axis. A demand curve can be for an individual consumer or a group of consumers, or more usually for the whole market.

for luxury goods would rise. At the same time, as the poor got poorer, they might have to turn to buying inferior goods, whose demand would thus rise too.

Expectations of future price changes. If people think that prices are going to rise in the future, they are likely to buy more now before the price does go up.

> ### Pause for thought
>
> 1. By referring to each of these six determinants of demand, consider what factors would cause a rise in the demand for butter.
> 2. Do all these six determinants of demand affect both an individual's demand and the market demand for a product?

Movements along and shifts in the demand curve

A demand curve is constructed on the assumption that 'other things remain equal' (*ceteris paribus*). In other words, it is assumed that none of the determinants of demand, other than price, changes. The effect of a change in price is then simply illustrated by a movement along the demand curve: for example, from point *B* to point *D* in Figure 4.2 when price rises from 40p to 80p per kilo.

What happens, then, when one of these other determinants does change? The answer is that we have to construct a whole new demand curve: the curve shifts. If a change in one of the other determinants causes demand to rise – say, income rises – the whole curve will shift to the right. This shows that at each price more will be demanded than before. Thus in Figure 4.3 at a price of P, a quantity of Q_0 was originally

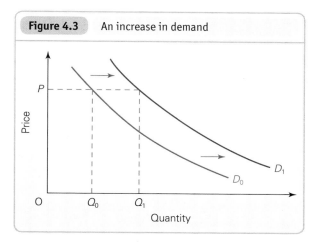

Figure 4.3 An increase in demand

demanded. But now, after the increase in demand, Q_1 is demanded. (Note that D_1 is not necessarily parallel to D_0.)

If a change in a determinant other than price causes demand to fall, the whole curve will shift to the left.

To distinguish between shifts in and movements along demand curves, it is usual to distinguish between a change in *demand* and a change in the *quantity demanded*. A shift in demand is referred to as a **change in demand**, whereas a movement along the demand curve as a result of a change in price is referred to as a **change in the quantity demanded**.

> ### Pause for thought
>
> By referring to the determinants of demand, consider what factors would cause a rightward shift in the demand for family cars.

> ### Definitions
>
> **Substitute goods** A pair of goods which are considered by consumers to be alternatives to each other. As the price of one goes up, the demand for the other rises.
>
> **Complementary goods** A pair of goods consumed together. As the price of one goes up, the demand for both goods will fall.
>
> **Normal goods** Goods whose demand rises as people's incomes rise.
>
> **Inferior goods** Goods whose demand falls as people's incomes rise.
>
> **Change in demand** The term used for a shift in the demand curve. It occurs when a determinant of demand *other* than price changes.
>
> **Change in the quantity demanded** The term used for a movement along the demand curve to a new point. It occurs when there is a change in price.

4.3 SUPPLY

Supply and price

Imagine you are a farmer deciding what to do with your land. Part of your land is in a fertile valley. Part is on a hillside where the soil is poor. Perhaps, then, you will consider growing vegetables in the valley and keeping sheep on the hillside.

Your decision will depend to a large extent on the price that various vegetables will fetch in the market, and likewise the price you can expect to get from sheep and wool. As far as the valley is concerned, you will plant the vegetables that give the best return. If, for example, the price of potatoes is high, you will probably use a lot of the valley for growing potatoes. If the price gets higher, you may well use the whole of the valley, perhaps being prepared to run the risk of potato disease. If the price is very high indeed, you may even consider growing potatoes on the hillside, even though the yield per acre is much lower there. In other words, the higher the price of a particular crop, the more you are likely to grow in preference to other crops.

This illustrates the general relationship between supply and price: *when the price of a good rises, the quantity supplied will also rise*. There are three reasons for this:

■ As firms supply more, they are likely to find that, beyond a certain level of output, costs rise more and more rapidly. Only if price rises will it be worth producing more and incurring these higher costs.

In the case of the farm we have just considered, once potatoes have to be grown on the hillside, the costs of producing them will increase. Also if the land has to be used more intensively, say by the use of more and more fertilisers, again the cost of producing extra potatoes is likely to rise quite rapidly. It is the same for manufacturers. Beyond a certain level of output, costs are likely to rise rapidly as workers have to be paid overtime and as machines approach their full capacity. If higher output involves higher costs of production, producers will need to get a higher price if they are to be persuaded to produce extra output.

■ The higher the price of the good, the more profitable it becomes to produce. Firms will thus be encouraged to produce more of it by switching from producing less profitable goods.

■ Given time, if the price of a good remains high, new producers will be encouraged to set up in production. Total market supply thus rises.

The first two determinants affect supply in the short run. The third affects supply in the long run. (We distinguish between short-run and long-run supply later, in section 5.4.)

The supply curve

The amount that producers would like to supply at various prices can be shown in a *supply schedule*. Table 4.2 shows a monthly supply schedule for potatoes, both for an individual farmer (farmer X) and for all farmers together (the whole market).

The supply schedule can be represented graphically as a *supply curve*. A supply curve may be an individual firm's supply curve or a market supply curve (i.e. that of the whole industry).

Figure 4.4 shows the *market* supply curve of potatoes. As with demand curves, price is plotted on the vertical axis and quantity on the horizontal axis. Each of the points a–e

Definitions

Supply schedule A table showing the different quantities of a good that producers are willing and able to supply at various prices over a given time period. A supply schedule can be for an individual producer or group of producers, or for all producers (the market supply schedule).

Supply curve A graph showing the relationship between the price of a good and the quantity of the good supplied over a given period of time.

Table 4.2 The supply of potatoes (monthly)

	Price of potatoes (pence per kg)	Farmer X's supply (tonnes)	Total market supply (tonnes: 000s)
a	20	50	100
b	40	70	200
c	60	100	350
d	80	120	530
e	100	130	700

Figure 4.4 Market supply curve of potatoes (monthly)

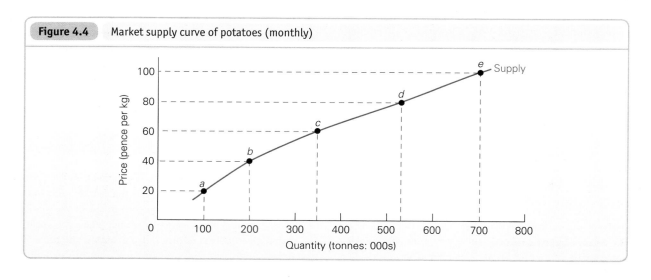

corresponds to a figure in Table 4.2. Thus for example, a price rise from 60p per kilogram to 80p per kilogram will cause a movement along the supply curve from point *c* to point *d*: total market supply will rise from 350 000 tonnes per month to 530 000 tonnes per month.

Not all supply curves will be upward sloping (positively sloped). Sometimes they will be vertical, or horizontal, or even downward sloping. This will depend largely on the time period over which firms' response to price changes is considered. This question is examined in Chapter 5 (pages 69–70).

(pages 69–70).

Pause for thought

1. *How much would be supplied at a price of 70p per kilo?*
2. *Draw a supply curve for farmer X. Are the axes drawn to the same scale as in Figure 4.4?*

Other determinants of supply

Like demand, supply is not determined simply by price. The other determinants of supply are as follows.

The costs of production. The higher the costs of production, the less profit will be made at any price. As costs rise, firms will cut back on production, probably switching to alternative products whose costs have not risen so much.

The main reasons for a change in costs are as follows:

- Change in input prices: costs of production will rise if wages, raw material prices, rents, interest rates or any other input prices rise.
- Change in technology: technological advances can fundamentally alter the costs of production. Consider, for example, how the microchip revolution has changed production methods and information handling in virtually every industry in the world.
- Organisational changes: various cost savings can be made in many firms by reorganising production.
- Government policy: costs will be lowered by government subsidies and raised by various taxes.

The profitability of alternative products (substitutes in supply). If some alternative product (a **substitute in supply**) becomes more profitable to supply than before, producers are likely to switch from the first good to this alternative. Supply of the first good falls. Other goods are likely to become more profitable if their prices rise or their costs of production fall. For example, if the price of carrots goes up, or the cost of producing carrots comes down, farmers may decide to produce more carrots. The supply of potatoes is therefore likely to fall.

The profitability of goods in joint supply. Sometimes when one good is produced, another good is also produced at the same time. These are said to be **goods in joint supply**. An example is the refining of crude oil to produce petrol. Other grade fuels will be produced as well, such as diesel and paraffin. If more petrol is produced, due to a rise in demand, then the supply of these other fuels will rise too.

Nature, 'random shocks' and other unpredictable events. In this category we would include the weather and diseases affecting farm output, wars affecting the supply of imported raw materials, the breakdown of machinery, industrial disputes, earthquakes, floods and fire, etc.

The aims of producers. A profit-maximising firm will supply a different quantity from a firm that has a different aim, such as maximising sales.

Pause for thought

By reference to each of the above determinants of supply, identify what would cause (a) the supply of potatoes to fall and (b) the supply of leather to rise.

Expectations of future price changes. If price is expected to rise, producers may temporarily reduce the amount they sell. Instead they are likely to build up their stocks and only release them on to the market when the price does rise. At the same time they may plan to produce more, by installing new machines, or taking on more labour, so that they can be ready to supply more when the price has risen.

The number of suppliers. If new firms enter the market, supply is likely to rise.

Movements along and shifts in the supply curve

The principle here is the same as with demand curves. The effect of a change in price is illustrated by a movement along the supply curve: for example, from point *d* to point *e* in Figure 4.4 when price rises from 80p to 100p. Quantity supplied rises from 530 000 to 700 000 tonnes.

If any other determinant of supply changes, the whole supply curve will shift. A rightward shift illustrates an increase in supply. A leftward shift illustrates a decrease

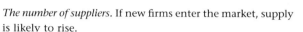

Definitions

Substitutes in supply These are two goods where an increased production of one means diverting resources away from producing the other.

Goods in joint supply These are two goods where the production of more of one leads to the production of more of the other.

in supply. Thus in Figure 4.5, if the original curve is S_0, the curve S_1 represents an increase in supply (more is supplied at each price), whereas the curve S_2 represents a decrease in supply (less is supplied at each price).

A movement along a supply curve is often referred to as a *change in the quantity supplied*, whereas a shift in the supply curve is simply referred to as a *change in supply*.

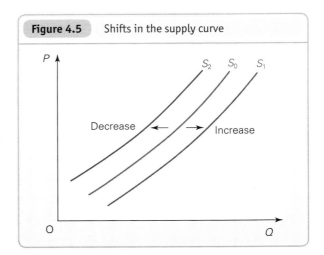

Figure 4.5   Shifts in the supply curve

Pause for thought

By referring to the determinants of supply, consider what factors would cause a rightward shift in the supply of family cars.

4.4   PRICE AND OUTPUT DETERMINATION

Equilibrium price and output

We can now combine our analysis of demand and supply. This will show how the actual price of a product and the actual quantity bought and sold are determined in a free and competitive market.

Let us return to the example of the market demand and market supply of potatoes, and use the data from Tables 4.1 and 4.2. These figures are given again in Table 4.3.

What will be the price and output that actually prevail? If the price started at 20p per kilogram, demand would exceed supply by 600 000 tonnes ($A - a$). Consumers would be unable to obtain all they wanted and would thus be willing to pay a higher price. Producers, unable or unwilling to supply enough to meet the demand, will be only too happy to accept a higher price. The effect of the shortage, then, will be to drive up the price. The same would happen at a price of 40p per kilogram. There would still be a shortage; price would still rise. But as the price rises, the quantity

demanded falls and the quantity supplied rises. The shortage is progressively eliminated.

What would happen if the price started at a much higher level: say, at 100p per kilogram? In this case supply would exceed demand by 600 000 tonnes ($e - E$). The effect of this surplus would be to drive the price down as farmers competed against each other to sell their excess supplies. The same would happen at a price of 80p per kilogram. There would still be a surplus; the price would still fall.

In fact, only one price is sustainable. This is the price where demand equals supply: namely 60p per kilogram, where both demand and supply are 350 000 tonnes. When supply matches demand the market is said to *clear*. There is no shortage and no surplus.

The price, where demand equals supply, is called the *equilibrium price* (see page 47). In Table 4.3, if the price starts at any level other than 60p per kilogram, there will be a tendency for it to move towards 60p. The equilibrium price is the only price at which producers' and consumers' wishes are mutually reconciled: where the producers' plans to supply exactly match the consumers' plans to buy.

Table 4.3	The market demand and supply of potatoes (monthly)	
Price of potatoes (pence per kg)	**Total market demand (tonnes: 000s)**	**Total market supply (tonnes: 000s)**
20	700 (A)	100 (a)
40	500 (B)	200 (b)
60	350 (C)	350 (c)
80	200 (D)	530 (d)
100	100 (E)	700 (e)

Definitions

Change in the quantity supplied The term used for a movement along the supply curve to a new point. It occurs when there is a change in price.

Change in supply The term used for a shift in the supply curve. It occurs when a determinant other than price changes.

Market clearing A market clears when supply matches demand, leaving no shortage or surplus.

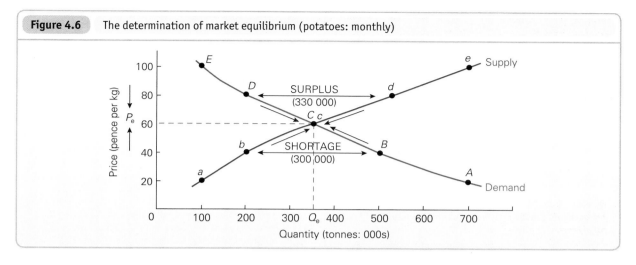

Figure 4.6 The determination of market equilibrium (potatoes: monthly)

KEY IDEA 11

Equilibrium is the point where conflicting interests are balanced. Only at this point is the amount that demanders are willing to purchase the same as the amount that suppliers are willing to supply. It is a point which will be automatically reached in a free market through the operation of the price mechanism.

Demand and supply curves

The determination of equilibrium price and output can be shown using demand and supply curves. Equilibrium is where the two curves intersect.

Figure 4.6 shows the demand and supply curves of potatoes corresponding to the data in Table 4.3. Equilibrium price is P_e (60p) and equilibrium quantity is Q_e (350 000 tonnes).

At any price above 60p, there would be a surplus. Thus at 80p there is a surplus of 330 000 tonnes ($d - D$). More is supplied than consumers are willing and able to purchase at that price. Thus a price of 80p fails to clear the market. Price will fall to the equilibrium price of 60p. As it does so, there will be a movement along the demand curve from point D to point C, and a movement along the supply curve from point d to point c.

At any price below 60p, there would be a shortage. Thus at 40p there is a shortage of 300 000 tonnes ($B - b$). Price will rise to 60p. This will cause a movement along the supply curve from point b to point c and along the demand curve from point B to point C.

Point Cc is the equilibrium: where demand equals supply.

Movement to a new equilibrium

KI 11 p 55

The equilibrium price will remain unchanged only so long as the demand and supply curves remain unchanged. If either of the curves shifts, a new equilibrium will be formed.

A change in demand

If one of the determinants of demand changes (other than price), the whole demand curve will shift. This will lead to a movement *along* the *supply* curve to the new intersection point.

KI 10 p 48

For example, in Figure 4.7, if a rise in consumer incomes led to the demand curve shifting to D_2, there would be a shortage of $h - g$ at the original price P_{e_1}. This would cause price to rise to the new equilibrium P_{e_2}. As it did so there would be a movement along the supply curve from point g to point i, and along the new demand curve (D_2) from point h to point i. Equilibrium quantity would rise from Q_{e_1} to Q_{e_2}.

Pause for thought

What would happen to price and quantity if the demand curve shifted to the left? Draw a diagram to illustrate your answer.

The effect of the shift in demand, therefore, has been a movement *along* the supply curve from the old equilibrium to the new: from point g to point i.

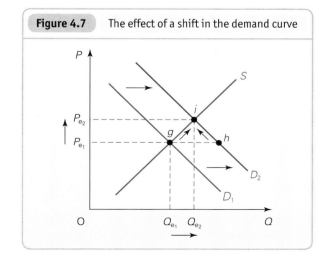

Figure 4.7 The effect of a shift in the demand curve

BOX 4.1   UK HOUSE PRICES

The ups and downs of the housing market

If you are thinking of buying a house sometime in the future, then you may well follow the fortunes of the housing market with some trepidation. In the late 1980s there was a housing price explosion in the UK: between 1984 and 1989 house prices doubled. After several years of falling or gently rising house prices in the early and mid-1990s, there was another boom from 1996 to 2007, with house prices tripling in value over that period. For those on low incomes, owning a home of their own was becoming increasingly difficult.

However, from 2008 to 2009 the return of falling house prices induced many people to postpone buying in the hope of paying lower prices if they waited. Further price falls in 2011 and 2012 led many to continuing deferring purchases as long as prices kept falling.

House prices since the early 1980s

The diagram shows what happened to house prices in the period 1983 to 2012. Initially, there was rapid house price inflation up to 1989, reaching a peak in 1988.

In their rush to buy a house before prices rose any further, many people in this period borrowed as much as they were able. Building societies and banks at that time had plenty of money to lend and were only too willing to do so. Many people, therefore, took out very large mortgages. In 1983 the average new mortgage was 2.08 times average annual earnings. By 1989 this figure had risen to 3.44.

After 1989 there followed a period of *falling* prices. From 1990 to 1995, house prices fell by 12.2 per cent. As a result of this, many people found themselves in a position of *negative equity*. This is the situation where the size of

their mortgage is greater than the value of their house. In other words, if they sold their house, they would end up still owing money! For this reason many people found that they could not move house.

Then, in 1996, house prices began to recover and for the next three years rose moderately – by around 5 per cent per annum. But then they started rising rapidly again, and by 2003, house price inflation had returned to rates similar to those in the 1980s. Was this good news or bad news? For those trapped in negative equity, it was good news. It was good news also for old people who wished to move into a retirement home and who had a house to sell. It was bad news, however, for the first-time buyer! In the mid-1990s the gross house price to earnings ratio for first-time buyers was just over 2 but by 2007 the price of a house was over 5 times higher than a first-time buyer's earnings. It became increasingly difficult for younger people to get on to the housing ladder.

Since 2008 prices have fallen overall. While this appears to be good news for first-time buyers, many remain reluctant to buy for fear of future prices falls and hence a return to the negative equity problems of the early 1990s. As we shall see in many parts of this book, what is good news for one person is often bad news for another.

The determinants of house prices

House prices are determined by demand and supply. If demand rises (i.e. shifts to the right) or if supply falls (i.e. shifts to the left), the equilibrium price of houses will rise. Similarly, if demand falls or supply rises, the equilibrium price will fall.

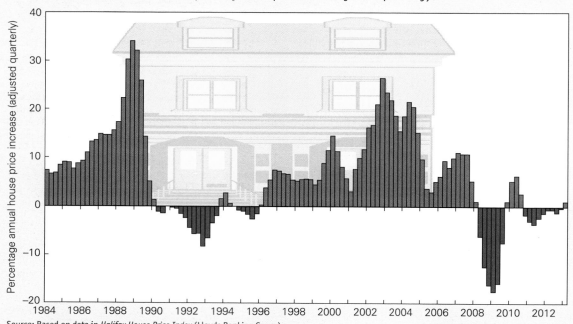

UK house price inflation (annual %, adjusted quarterly)

Source: Based on data in *Halifax House Price Index* (Lloyds Banking Group)

So why did UK house prices rise so rapidly in the 1980s, only to fall in the early 1990s and then rise rapidly again in the late 1990s through to 2007? The answer lies primarily in changes in the *demand* for housing. Let us examine the various factors that affected the demand for houses.

Incomes (actual and anticipated). The second half of the 1980s and from 1996 to 2007 were periods of rapidly rising incomes. The economy was experiencing economic 'boom' during these times. Many people wanted to spend their extra incomes on housing: either buying a house for the first time, or moving to a better one. What is more, many people thought that their incomes would continue to grow, and were thus prepared to stretch themselves financially in the short term by buying an expensive house, confident that their mortgage payments would become more and more affordable over time.

The early 1990s and from 2008 to 2012, by contrast, were periods of low or negative growth, with rising unemployment and falling incomes. People had much less confidence about their ability to afford large mortgages.

The desire for home ownership. The desire for home ownership has increased over the years. In recent times this has been fuelled by a host of television programmes focused on buying and selling property.

The cost of mortgages. During the second half of the 1980s, mortgage interest rates were generally falling. This meant that people could afford larger mortgages, and thus afford to buy more expensive houses. In 1989, however, this trend was reversed. Mortgage interest rates were now rising. Many people found it difficult to maintain existing payments, let alone to take on a larger mortgage. From 1996 to 2003 mortgage rates were generally reduced again, once more fuelling the demand for houses. From 2003 to 2007 interest rates rose again, but this was not enough to deter the demand for housing. From 2008 to 2012 interest rates remained low, although this did not cause an increase in housing demand due to the continued economic uncertainty created by the financial crisis and banks being cautious over their lending.

The availability of mortgages. In the late 1980s, mortgages were readily available. Banks and building societies were prepared to accept smaller deposits on houses, and to grant mortgages of $3\frac{1}{2}$ times a person's annual income, compared with $2\frac{1}{2}$ times in the early 1980s. In the early 1990s, however, banks and building societies were more cautious about granting mortgages. They were aware that, with falling house prices, rising unemployment and the growing problem of negative equity, there was a growing danger that borrowers would default on payments.

With the recovery of the economy in the mid-1990s, however, and with a growing number of mortgage lenders, mortgages became more readily available and for greater amounts relative to people's income. This pushed up prices. In 2001 the average house price was 3.4 times greater than a person's earnings, but this rose steadily to reach 5.74 times a person's earnings in 2007. From late 2007 to 2012, however, problems in acquiring loans from the banking sector, falling house prices and rising unemployment all signalled a repeat of the early 1990s.

Speculation. A belief that house prices will continue to move in a particular direction can exacerbate house price movements. In other words, speculation tends to increase house price volatility. In the 1980s and from the mid-1990s to 2007, people generally believed that house prices would continue rising. This encouraged people to buy as soon as possible, and to take out the biggest mortgage possible, before prices went up any further. There was also an effect on supply. Those with houses to sell held back until the last possible moment in the hope of getting a higher price. The net effect was for a rightward shift in the demand curve for houses and a leftward shift in the supply curve. The effect of this speculation, therefore, was to help bring about the very effect that people were predicting (see section 5.4).

In the early 1990s, and again from 2008, the opposite occurred. People thinking of buying houses held back, hoping to buy at a lower price. People with houses to sell tried to sell as quickly as possible before prices fell any further. Again the effect of this speculation was to aggravate the change in prices – this time a fall in prices.

A global dimension to falling house prices

The fall in UK house prices in 2008 had global origins. The dramatic growth in mortgage lending in the UK was also a feature of many other industrialised countries at this time, most notably the USA, where there had been similar dramatic rises in house prices.

Banks and other mortgage lenders bundled up these large mortgage debts into 'financial instruments' and sold them on to other global financial institutions so that they could meet their everyday liquidity requirements of paying bills and meeting customers' demands for cash. This worked well while there was economic prosperity and people could pay their mortgages. However, it became apparent in 2007 that many of the mortgages sold, notably in the USA, were to people who could not meet their repayments.

As the number of mortgage defaults increased, the value of the mortgage-laden financial instruments sold on to other financial institutions fell. As banks found it increasingly difficult to meet their liquidity requirements, they reduced the number of mortgages to potential home owners. By the beginning of 2013, UK prices had fallen by nearly 20 per cent since the peak in 2007. The uncertainty over how far house prices might fall was discouraging consumers from moving home and, as the financial crisis turned into economic recession, house building fell dramatically and construction firms were laying off workers.

1. *Draw supply and demand diagrams to illustrate what was happening to house prices (a) in the second half of the 1980s and from the late 1990s to 2007; (b) in the early 1990s and 2008–12.*
2. *Are there any factors on the supply side that contribute to changes in house prices? If so, what are they?*
3. *Find out what has happened to house prices over the past three years. Attempt an explanation of what has happened.*

BOX 4.2	STOCK MARKET PRICES

Demand and supply in action

Firms that are quoted on the stock market (see page 37 and section 19.5) can raise money by issuing shares. These are sold on the 'primary stock market'. People who own the shares receive a 'dividend' on them, normally paid six-monthly. This varies with the profitability of the company.

People or institutions that buy these shares, however, may not wish to hold on to them for ever. This is where the 'secondary stock market' comes in. It is where existing shares are bought and sold. There are stock markets, primary and secondary, in all the major countries of the world.

There are more than 2500 companies whose shares are listed on the London Stock Exchange and shares are traded each Monday to Friday (excluding bank holidays). The prices of shares depend on demand and supply. For example, if the demand for Tesco shares at any one time exceeds the supply on offer, the price will rise until demand and supply are equal. Share prices fluctuate throughout the trading day and sometimes price changes can be substantial.

To give an overall impression of share price movements, stock exchanges publish share price indices. The best known one in the UK is the FTSE 100, which stands for the 'Financial Times Stock Exchange' index of the 100 largest

companies' shares. The index represents an average price of these 100 shares. The chart shows movements in the FTSE 100 from 1995 to 2012. The index was first calculated on 3 January 1984 with a base level of 1000 points. It reached a peak of 6930 points on 30 December 1999 and fell to 3287 on 12 March 2003; it then rose again, reaching a high of 6730 on 12 October 2007. In the midst of the financial crisis the index fell to a low of 3781 on 21 November 2008, but by early 2010 it partially recovered, passing 6000 for a brief period, before levelling out and fluctuating around an average of 5500 to mid-2012, only to rise above 6000 again at the start of 2013.

But what causes share prices to change? Why were they so high in 1999, but only just over half that value just three years later, and why has this trend repeated itself in the late 2000s? The answer lies in the determinants of the demand and supply of shares.

Demand

There are five main factors that affect the demand for shares.

The dividend yield. This is the dividend on a share as a percentage of its price. The higher the dividend yields on

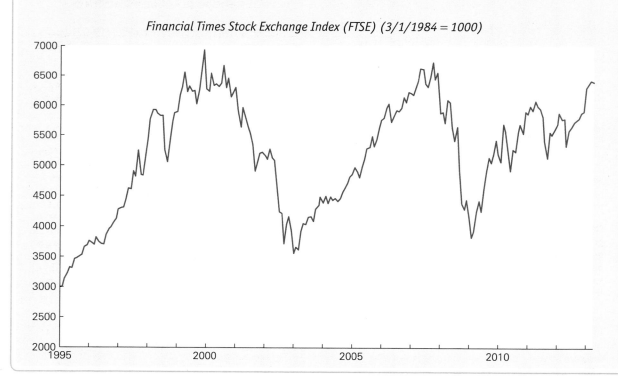

Financial Times Stock Exchange Index (FTSE) (3/1/1984 = 1000)

shares the more attractive they are as a form of saving. One of the main explanations of rising stock market prices from 2003 to 2007 was high profits and resulting high dividends. Similarly, the slowdown in the world economy after 2007 led to falling profits and falling dividends.

The price of and/or return on substitutes. The main substitutes for shares in specific companies are other shares. Thus if, in comparison with other shares, Tesco shares are expected to pay high dividends relative to the share price, people will buy Tesco shares. As far as shares in general are concerned, the main substitutes are other forms of saving. Thus if the interest rate on savings accounts in banks and building societies fell, people with such accounts would be tempted to take their money out and buy shares instead. Another major substitute is property. If house prices rise rapidly, as they did from the late 1990s to 2007, this will reduce the demand for shares as many people switch to buying property in anticipation of even higher prices. If house prices level off, this makes shares relatively more attractive as an investment and can boost the demand for them.

From late 2007, when house prices and share prices fell dramatically, investors looked towards other, safer, investments such as gold, government debt (Treasury bills and gilts) or even holding cash.

Incomes. If the economy is growing rapidly and people's incomes are thus rising rapidly, they are likely to buy more shares. Thus in the mid to late 1990s, when UK incomes were rising at an average annual rate of over 3 per cent, share prices rose rapidly (see chart). As growth rates fell in the early 2000s, so share prices fell. Similarly, when economic growth improved from 2003 to 2007 shares prices increased, but they fell back with the global financial crisis in 2007/8 and the onset of recession and declining real incomes from 2008.

Wealth. 'Wealth' is people's accumulated savings and property. Wealth rose in the 1990s and 2000s, and many people used their increased wealth to buy shares.

Expectations. From 2003 to 2007 people expected share prices to go on rising. They were optimistic about continued growth in the economy. But as people bought shares, this pushed their prices up even more, thereby fuelling further speculation that they would go on rising and encouraging further share buying. In recent years, by contrast, confidence has been shaken. A global banking crisis and fears of impending recession started a dramatic fall in share prices. Uncertainty over how and when the global economy will recover has caused share prices to be volatile in the past few years.

Supply

The factors affecting supply in the secondary market are largely the same as those affecting demand, but in the opposite direction.

If the return on alternative forms of saving falls, people with shares are likely to hold on to them, as they represent a better form of saving. The supply of shares to the market will fall. If incomes or wealth rise, people again are likely to want to hold on to their shares.

As far as expectations are concerned, if people believe that share prices will rise, they will hold on to the shares they have. Supply to the market will fall, thereby pushing up prices. If, however, they believe that prices will fall (as they did in 2008), they will sell their shares now before prices do fall. Supply will increase, driving down the price.

Share prices and business

Companies are crucially affected by their share price. If a company's share price falls, this is taken as a sign that 'the market' is losing confidence in the company. This will make it more difficult to raise finance, not only by issuing additional shares in the primary market, but also from banks.

It will also make the company more vulnerable to a takeover bid. This is where one company seeks to buy out another by offering to buy all its shares. A takeover will succeed if the owners of more than half of the company's shares vote to accept the offered price. Shareholders are more likely to agree to the takeover if the company's share price has not been performing very well.

Can you buck the market?

Many individuals like to play the market, thinking that they can make easy profits. However, beware! The 'efficient markets hypothesis' predicts that historical share price information, such as that shown in the chart or in the pages of today's financial press, provides no help whatsoever in determining future share prices. Why? Because the current share price *already* reflects what people anticipate will happen. Future share price movements will occur only as *new* (unanticipated) information arrives – and it's pure chance if you can predict the unanticipated! In this purist view, the market for shares is said to be a perfectly efficient market (see section 19.5 for further analysis).

 If the rate of economic growth in the economy is 3 per cent in a particular year, why are share prices likely to rise by more than 3 per cent that year?

A change in supply

KI 10
p 48

Likewise, if one of the determinants of supply changes (other than price), the whole supply curve will shift. This will lead to a movement *along* the *demand* curve to the new intersection point.

For example, in Figure 4.8, if costs of production rose, the supply curve would shift to the left: to S_2. There would be a shortage of $g - j$ at the old price of P_{e_1}. Price would rise from P_{e_1} to P_{e_3}. Quantity would fall from Q_{e_1} to Q_{e_3}. In other words, there would be a movement along the demand curve from point g to point k, and along the new supply curve (S_2) from point j to point k.

To summarise: a shift in one curve leads to a movement along the other curve to the new intersection point.

KI 11
p 55

Sometimes a number of determinants might change. This may lead to a shift in *both* curves. When this happens, equilibrium simply moves from the point where the old curves intersected to the point where the new ones intersect.

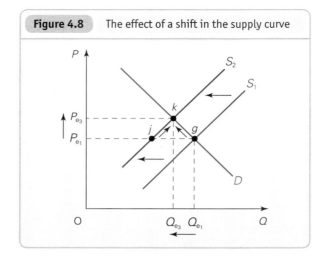

Figure 4.8 The effect of a shift in the supply curve

SUMMARY

1a A firm is greatly affected by its market environment. The more competitive the market, the less discretion the firm has in determining its price. In the extreme case of a perfect market, the price is entirely outside the firm's control. The price is determined by demand and supply in the market, and the firm has to accept this price: the firm is a price taker.

1b In a perfect market, price changes act as the mechanism whereby demand and supply are balanced. If there is a shortage, price will rise until the shortage is eliminated. If there is a surplus, price will fall until that is eliminated.

2a When the price of a good rises, the quantity demanded per period of time will fall. This is known as the 'law of demand'. It applies both to individuals' demand and to the whole market demand.

2b The law of demand is explained by the income and substitution effects of a price change.

2c The relationship between price and quantity demanded per period of time can be shown in a table (or 'schedule') or as a graph. On the graph, price is plotted on the vertical axis and quantity demanded per period of time on the horizontal axis. The resulting demand curve is downward sloping (negatively sloped).

2d Other determinants of demand include tastes, the number and price of substitute goods, the number and price of complementary goods, income, the distribution of income and expectations of future price changes.

2e If price changes, the effect is shown by a movement along the demand curve. We call this effect 'a change in the quantity demanded'.

2f If any other determinant of demand changes, the whole curve will shift. We call this effect 'a change in demand'. A rightward shift represents an increase in demand; a leftward shift represents a decrease in demand.

3a When the price of a good rises, the quantity supplied per period of time will usually also rise. This applies both to individual producers' supply and to the whole market supply.

3b There are two reasons in the short run why a higher price encourages producers to supply more: (a) they are now willing to incur higher costs per unit associated with producing more; (b) they will switch to producing this product and away from now less profitable ones. In the long run there is a third reason: new producers will be attracted into the market.

3c The relationship between price and quantity supplied per period of time can be shown in a table (or schedule) or as a graph. As with a demand curve, price is plotted on the vertical axis and quantity per period of time on the horizontal axis. The resulting supply curve is upward sloping (positively sloped).

3d Other determinants of supply include the costs of production, the profitability of alternative products, the profitability of goods in joint supply, random shocks and expectations of future price changes.

3e If price changes, the effect is shown by a movement along the supply curve. We call this effect 'a change in the quantity supplied'.

3f If any determinant *other* than price changes, the effect is shown by a shift in the whole supply curve. We call this effect 'a change in supply'. A rightward shift represents an increase in supply; a leftward shift represents a decrease in supply.

4a If the demand for a good exceeds the supply, there will be a shortage. This will lead to a rise in the price of the good.

4b If the supply of a good exceeds the demand, there will be a surplus. This will lead to a fall in the price.

4c Price will settle at the equilibrium. The equilibrium price is the one that clears the market: the price where demand equals supply. This is shown in a demand and supply diagram by the point where the two curves intersect.

4d If the demand or supply curve shifts, this will lead either to a shortage or to a surplus. Price will therefore either rise or fall until a new equilibrium is reached at the position where the supply and demand curves *now* intersect.

REVIEW QUESTIONS

1 Using a diagram like Figure 4.1, summarise the effect of (a) a reduction in the demand for a good; (b) a reduction in the costs of production of a good.

2 Referring to Table 4.1, assume that there are 200 consumers in the market. Of these, 100 have schedules like Tracey's and 100 have schedules like Darren's. What would be the total market demand schedule for potatoes now?

3 Again referring to Table 4.1, draw Tracey's and Darren's demand curves for potatoes on one diagram. (Note that you will use the same vertical scale as in Figure 4.2, but you will need a quite different horizontal scale.) At what price is their demand the same? What explanations could there be for the quite different shapes of their two demand curves? (This question is explored in Chapter 5.)

4 The price of pork rises and yet it is observed that the sales of pork increase. Does this mean that the demand curve for pork is upward sloping? Explain.

5 This question is concerned with the supply of oil for central heating. In each case consider whether there is a movement along the supply curve (and in which direction) or a shift in it (and whether left or right): (a) new oil fields start up in production; (b) the demand for central heating rises; (c) the price of gas falls; (d) oil companies anticipate an upsurge in the demand for central-heating oil; (e) the demand for petrol rises; (f) new technology decreases the costs of oil refining; (g) all oil products become more expensive.

6 For what reasons might the price of foreign holidays rise? In each case, identify whether these are reasons affecting demand or supply (or both).

7 The price of cod is much higher today than it was 20 years ago. Using demand and supply diagrams, explain why this should be so.

8 The number of owners of compact disc players has grown rapidly and hence the demand for compact discs has also grown rapidly. Yet the price of CDs has fallen. Why? Use a supply and demand diagram to illustrate your answer.

9 What will happen to the equilibrium price and quantity of butter in each of the following cases? You should state whether demand or supply or both have shifted and in which direction: (a) a rise in the price of margarine; (b) a rise in the demand for yoghurt; (c) a rise in the price of bread; (d) a rise in the demand for bread; (e) an expected increase in the price of butter in the near future; (f) a tax on butter production; (g) the invention of a new, but expensive, process of removing all cholesterol from butter, plus the passing of a law which states that butter producers must use this process. In each case, assume *ceteris paribus*.

10 If both demand and supply change, and if we know in which direction they have shifted but not by how much, why is it that we will be able to predict the direction in which *either* price or quantity will change, but not both? (Clue: consider the four possible combinations and sketch them if necessary: *D* left, *S* left; *D* right, *S* right; *D* left, *S* right; *D* right, *S* left.)

5
Chapter

Business in a market environment

Business issues covered in this chapter

■ How responsive is consumer demand to changes in the market price? How responsive is it to changes in consumer incomes and to the prices of competitor products?
■ How is a firm's sales revenue affected by a change in price?
■ How responsive is business output to changes in price?
■ How does the responsiveness (or 'elasticity') of demand and supply to changes in price affect the working of markets?
■ Why are markets likely to be more responsive in the long run than in the short run to changes in demand or supply?
■ What is meant by 'risk' and 'uncertainty' and what is their significance to business?
■ How do firms deal with uncertainty about future market movements?

In Chapter 4 we examined how prices are determined in perfectly competitive markets: by the interaction of market demand and market supply. In such markets, although the *market* demand curve is downward sloping, the demand curve faced by the individual firm will be horizontal. This is illustrated in Figure 5.1.

The market price is P_m. The individual firm can sell as much as it likes at this market price: it is too small to have any influence on the market – it is a price taker. It will not force the price down by producing more because, in terms of the total market, this extra would be an infinitesimally small amount. If a farmer doubled the output of wheat sent to the market, it would be too small an increase to affect the world price of wheat!

In practice, however, many firms are not price takers; they have some discretion in choosing their price. Such firms will face a downward-sloping demand curve. If they raise their price, they will sell less; if they lower their price, they will sell more. But firms will want to know more than this. They will want to know just *how much* the quantity demanded will fall. In other words, they will want to know how *responsive* demand is to a rise in price. This responsiveness is measured using a concept called 'elasticity'.

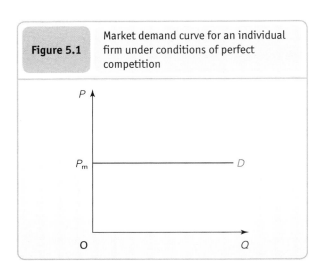

Figure 5.1	Market demand curve for an individual firm under conditions of perfect competition

KEY IDEA 12

Elasticity. The responsiveness of one variable (e.g. demand) to a change in another (e.g. price). This concept is fundamental to understanding how markets work. The more elastic variables are, the more responsive is the market to changing circumstances.

5.1 PRICE ELASTICITY OF DEMAND

The responsiveness of quantity demanded to a change in price

The demand for an individual firm

For any firm considering changing its price, it is vital to know the likely effect on the quantity demanded. Take the case of two firms facing very different demand curves. These are shown in Figure 5.2.

Firm A can raise its price quite substantially – from £6 to £10 – and yet its level of sales only falls by a relatively small amount – from 100 units to 90 units. This firm will probably be quite keen to raise its price. After all, it could make significantly more profit on each unit sold (assuming no rise in costs per unit), and yet sell only slightly fewer units.

Firm B, however, will think twice about raising its price. Even a relatively modest increase in price – from £6 to £7 – will lead to a substantial fall in sales from 100 units to 40 units. What is the point of making a bit more profit on those units it manages to sell, if in the process it ends up selling a lot fewer units? In such circumstances the firm may contemplate lowering its price.

The responsiveness of market demand

KI 10 p 48

Economists too will want to know how responsive demand is to a change in price: except in this case it is the responsiveness of *market* demand that is being considered. This information is necessary to enable them to predict the effects of a shift in supply on the market price of a product.

Figure 5.3 shows the effect of a shift in supply with two quite different demand curves (*D* and *D'*). Assume that

initially the supply curve is S_1, and that it intersects with both demand curves at point *a*, at a price of P_1 and a quantity of Q_1. Now supply shifts to S_2. What will happen to price and quantity? Economists will want to know! The answer is that it depends on the shape of the demand curve. In the case of demand curve *D*, there is a relatively large rise in price (to P_2) and a relatively small fall in quantity (to Q_2): equilibrium is at point *b*. In the case of demand curve *D'*, however, there is only a relatively small rise in price (to P_3), but a relatively large fall in quantity (to Q_3): equilibrium is at point *c*.

Given the importance of knowing the responsiveness of demand to a change in price, we will need some way of measuring this responsiveness. *Elasticity* is the measure we use.

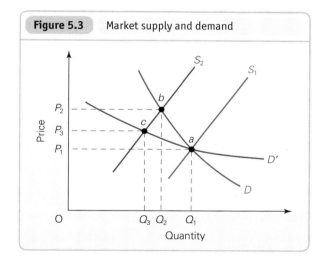

Figure 5.3 Market supply and demand

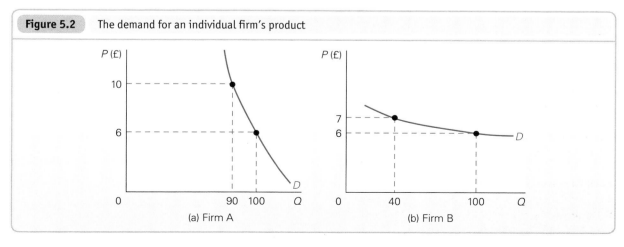

Figure 5.2 The demand for an individual firm's product

(a) Firm A

(b) Firm B

Defining price elasticity of demand

What we will want to compare is the size of the change in quantity demanded of a given product with the size of the change in price. **Price elasticity of demand** does just this. It is defined as follows:

$$Pe_D = \frac{\text{proportionate (or percentage) change in quantity demanded}}{\text{proportionate (or percentage) change in price}}$$

If, for example, a 20 per cent rise in the price of a product causes a 10 per cent fall in the quantity demanded, the price elasticity of demand will be:

$$-10\%/20\% = -0.5$$

Three things should be noted at this stage about the figure that is calculated for elasticity.

The use of proportionate or percentage measures

Elasticity is measured in proportionate or percentage terms for the following reasons:

- It allows comparison of changes in two qualitatively different things, which are thus measured in two different types of unit: i.e. it allows comparison of quantity changes (quantity demanded) with monetary changes (price).
- It is the only sensible way of deciding *how big* a change in price or quantity is. Take a simple example. An item goes up in price by £1. Is this a big increase or a small increase? We can answer this only if we know what the original price was. If a can of beans goes up in price by £1, that is a huge price increase. If, however, the price of a house goes up by £1, that is a tiny price increase. In other words, it is the percentage or proportionate increase in price that we look at in deciding how big a price rise it is.

The sign (positive or negative)

If price increases (a positive figure), the quantity demanded will fall (a negative figure). If price falls (a negative figure), the quantity demanded will rise (a positive figure). Thus price elasticity of demand will be negative: a positive figure is being divided by a negative figure (or vice versa).

The value (greater or less than 1)

If we now ignore the sign and just concentrate on the value of the figure, this tells us whether demand is *elastic* or *inelastic*.

Elastic ($\varepsilon > 1$). This is where a change in price causes a proportionately larger change in the quantity demanded. In this case the price elasticity of demand will be greater than 1, since we are dividing a larger figure by a smaller figure.

Inelastic ($\varepsilon < 1$). This is where a change in price causes a proportionately smaller change in the quantity demanded. In this case the price elasticity of demand will be less than 1, since we are dividing a smaller figure by a larger figure.

Unit elastic ($\varepsilon = 1$). **Unit elasticity** is where the quantity demanded changes proportionately the same as price. This will give an elasticity equal to 1, since we are dividing a figure by itself.

The determinants of price elasticity of demand

The price elasticity of demand varies enormously from one product to another. But why do some products have a highly elastic demand, whereas others have a highly *in*elastic demand? What determines price elasticity of demand?

The number and closeness of substitute goods

This is the most important determinant. The more substitutes there are for a good, and the closer they are, the more will people switch to these alternatives when the price of the good rises: the greater, therefore, will be the price elasticity of demand.

For example, the price elasticity of demand for a particular brand of a product will probably be fairly high, especially if there are many other, similar brands. If its price goes up, people can simply switch to another brand: there is a large substitution effect. By contrast, the demand for a product in general will normally be pretty inelastic. If the price of food in general goes up, demand for food will fall only slightly. People will buy a little less, since they cannot now afford so much: this is the *income* effect of the price rise. But there is no alternative to food that can satisfy our hunger: there is therefore virtually no *substitution* effect.

Definitions

Price elasticity of demand A measure of the responsiveness of quantity demanded to a change in price.

Elastic If demand is (price) elastic, then any change in price will cause the quantity demanded to change proportionately more. (Ignoring the negative sign) it will have a value greater than 1.

Inelastic If demand is (price) inelastic, then any change will cause the quantity demanded to change by a proportionately smaller amount. (Ignoring the negative sign) it will have a value less than 1.

Unit elasticity When the price elasticity of demand is unity, this is where quantity demanded changes by the same proportion as the price. Price elasticity is equal to 1.

The proportion of income spent on the good

The higher the proportion of our income we spend on a good, the more we will be forced to cut consumption when its price rises: the bigger will be the income effect and the more elastic will be the demand.

Thus salt has a very low price elasticity of demand. This is because we spend such a tiny fraction of our income on salt that we would find little difficulty in paying a relatively large percentage increase in its price: the income effect of a price rise would be very small. By contrast, there will be a much bigger income effect when a major item of expenditure rises in price. For example, if mortgage interest rates rise (the 'price' of loans for house purchases), people may have to cut down substantially on their demand for housing – being forced to buy somewhere much smaller and cheaper, or to live in rented accommodation.

> ### Pause for thought
>
> *Think of two products and estimate which is likely to have the higher price elasticity of demand. Explain your answer.*

The time period

When price rises, people may take a time to adjust their consumption patterns and find alternatives. The longer the time period after a price change, then, the more elastic is the demand likely to be.

5.2 THE IMPORTANCE OF PRICE ELASTICITY OF DEMAND TO BUSINESS DECISION MAKING

A firm's sales revenue

One of the most important applications of price elasticity of demand concerns its relationship with a firm's sales revenue. The **total sales revenue (TR)** of a firm is simply price times quantity:

$$TR = P \times Q$$

For example, 3000 units (Q) sold at £2 per unit (P) will earn the firm £6000 (TR).

Let us assume that a firm wants to increase its total revenue. What should it do? Should it raise its price or lower it? The answer depends on the price elasticity of demand.

Elastic demand and sales revenue

As price rises, so quantity demanded falls, and vice versa. When demand is elastic, quantity changes proportionately more than price. Thus the change in quantity has a bigger effect on total revenue than does the change in price. This can be summarised as follows:

P rises; *Q* falls proportionately more; therefore *TR* falls.
P falls; *Q* rises proportionately more; therefore *TR* rises.

In other words, total revenue changes in the same direction as *quantity*.

This is illustrated in Figure 5.4. The areas of the rectangles in the diagram represent total revenue. But why? The area of a rectangle is its height multiplied by its length. In this case, this is price multiplied by quantity purchased, which, as we have seen, gives total revenue.

Demand is elastic between points *a* and *b*. A rise in price from £4 to £5 causes a proportionately larger fall in quantity demanded: from 20 to 10. Total revenue *falls* from £80 (the striped area) to £50 (the shaded area).

When demand is elastic, then, a rise in price will cause a fall in total revenue. If a firm wants to increase its revenue, it should *lower* its price.

> ### Pause for thought
>
> *If a firm faces an elastic demand curve, why will it not necessarily be in the firm's interests to produce more? (Clue: you will need to distinguish between revenue and profit. We will explore this relationship in Chapter 6.)*

> **Figure 5.4**   Elastic demand between two points
>
>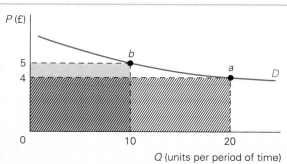

> ### Definition
>
> **Total (sales) revenue (TR)** The amount a firm earns from its sales of a product at a particular price. TR = P × Q. Note that we are referring to *gross* revenue: that is, revenue before the deduction of taxes or any other costs.

KI 12
p 63

Inelastic demand and sales revenue

When demand is inelastic, it is the other way around. Price changes proportionately more than quantity. Thus the change in price has a bigger effect on total revenue than does the change in quantity. To summarise the effects:

P rises; Q falls proportionately less; TR rises.
P falls; Q rises proportionately less; TR falls.

In other words, total revenue changes in the same direction as price.

This is illustrated in Figure 5.5. Demand is inelastic between points a and c. A rise in price from £4 to £8 causes a proportionately smaller fall in quantity demanded: from 20 to 15. Total revenue *rises* from £80 (the striped area) to £120 (the shaded area).

If a firm wants to increase its revenue in this case, therefore, it should *raise* its price.

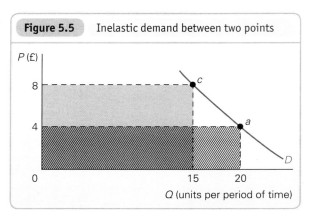

Figure 5.5 Inelastic demand between two points

Special cases

Figure 5.6 shows three special cases: (a) a totally inelastic demand ($P\varepsilon_D = 0$), (b) an infinitely elastic demand ($P\varepsilon_D = 1$) and (c) a unit elastic demand ($P\varepsilon_D = -1$).

BOX 5.1   THE MEASUREMENT OF ELASTICITY

An optional technical box

We have defined price elasticity as the percentage or proportionate change in quantity demanded divided by the percentage or proportionate change in price. But how, in practice, do we measure these changes for a specific demand curve?

A common mistake that students make is to think that you can talk about the elasticity of a whole *curve*. The mistake here is that in most cases the elasticity will vary along the length of the curve.

Take the case of the demand curve illustrated in diagram (a). Between points a and b, total revenue rises ($P_2Q_2 > P_1Q_1$): demand is thus elastic between these two points. Between points b and c, however, total revenue falls ($P_3Q_3 < P_2Q_2$). Demand here is inelastic.

Normally, then, we can refer to the elasticity only of a *portion* of the demand curve, not of the *whole* curve.

There is, however, an exception to this rule. This is when the elasticity just so happens to be the same all the way along a curve, as in the three special cases illustrated in Figure 5.6.

Although we cannot normally talk about the elasticity of a whole curve, we can nevertheless talk about the elasticity between any two points on it. Remember the formula we used was:

$$\frac{\% \text{ or proportionate } \Delta Q}{\% \text{ or proportionate } \Delta P}$$

(where Δ means 'change in').

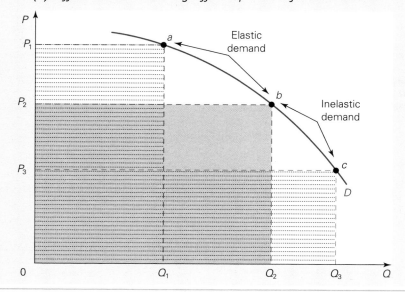

(a) Different elasticities along different portions of a demand curve

Figure 5.6 (a) Totally inelastic demand ($P\varepsilon_D = 0$); (b) Infinitely elastic demand ($P\varepsilon_D = \infty$); (c) Unit elastic demand ($P\varepsilon_D = -1$)

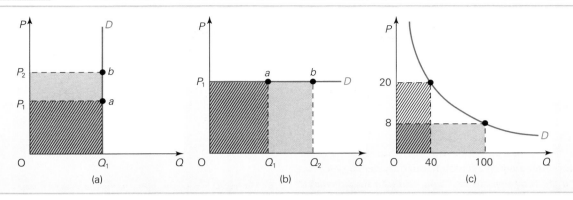

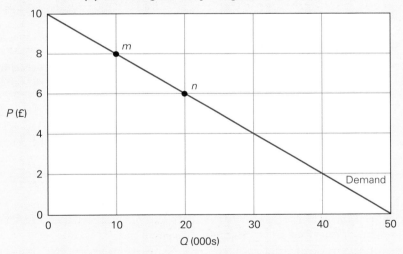

(b) Measuring elasticity using the arc method

The way we measure a *proportionate* change in quantity is to divide that change by the level of Q: i.e. $\Delta Q/Q$. Similarly, we measure a proportionate change in price by dividing that change by the level of P: i.e. $\Delta P/Q$. Price elasticity of demand can thus now be rewritten as:

$$\frac{\Delta Q}{Q} \div \frac{\Delta P}{P}$$

But just what value do we give to P and Q? Consider the demand curve in diagram (b). What is the elasticity of demand between points *m* and *n*? Price has fallen by £2 (from £8 to £6), but what is the proportionate change? Is it −2/8 or −2/6? The convention is to express the change as a proportion of the average of the two prices, £8 and £6: in other words to take the mid-point price, £7. Thus the proportionate change is −2/7.

Similarly the proportionate change in quantity between points *m* and *n* is 10/15, since 15 is mid-way between 10 and 20.

Thus using the *average (or 'mid-point') formula*, elasticity between *m* and *n* is given by:

$$\frac{\Delta Q}{\text{average } Q} \div \frac{\Delta P}{\text{average } P} = \frac{10}{15} \div \frac{-2}{7} = -2.33$$

Since 2.33 is greater than 1, demand is elastic between *m* and *n*.

 Referring again to diagram (b), what is the price elasticity of demand between a price of (a) £6 and £4; (b) £4 and £2? What do you conclude about the elasticity of a straight-line demand curve as you move down it?

Totally inelastic demand

This is shown by a vertical straight line. No matter what happens to price, quantity demanded remains the same. It is obvious that the more the price is raised, the bigger will be the revenue. Thus in Figure 5.6(a), P_2 will earn a bigger revenue than P_1.

Infinitely elastic demand

This is shown by a horizontal straight line. At any price above P_1 demand is zero. But at P_1 (or any price below) demand is 'infinitely' large.

This seemingly unlikely demand curve is in fact relatively common. Many firms that are very small (like the small-scale grain farmer) are price takers. They have to accept the price as given by supply and demand in the *whole market*. If individual farmers were to try to sell above this price, they would sell nothing at all. At this price, however, they can sell to the market all they produce. (Demand is not *literally* infinite, but as far as the farmer is concerned it is.) In this case, the more the individual farmer produces, the more revenue will be earned. In Figure 5.6(b), more revenue is earned at Q_2 than at Q_1.

Unit elastic demand

This is where price and quantity change in exactly the same proportion. Any rise in price will be exactly offset by a fall in quantity, leaving total revenue unchanged. In Figure 5.6(c), the striped area is exactly equal to the shaded area: in both cases total revenue is £800.

You might have thought that a demand curve with unit elasticity would be a straight line at 45° to the axes. Instead it is a curve called a *rectangular hyperbola*. The reason for its shape is that the proportionate *rise* in quantity must equal the proportionate *fall* in price (and vice versa). As we move down the demand curve, in order for the *proportionate* (or percentage) change in both price and quantity to remain constant, there must be a bigger and bigger *absolute* rise in quantity and a smaller and smaller absolute fall in price. For example, a rise in quantity from 200 to 400 is the same proportionate change as a rise from 100 to 200, but its absolute size is double. A fall in price from £5 to £2.50 is the same percentage as a fall from £10 to £5, but its absolute size is only half.

> ### Pause for thought
>
> *Two customers go to the fish counter at a supermarket to buy some cod. Neither looks at the price. Customer A orders 1 kilo of cod. Customer B orders £3 worth of cod. What is the price elasticity of demand of each of the two customers?*

5.3 OTHER ELASTICITIES

Firms are interested to know the responsiveness of demand not just to a change in price: they will also want to know the responsiveness of demand to changes in other determinants, such as consumers' incomes and the prices of goods that are substitute or complementary to theirs. They will want to know the **income elasticity of demand** – the responsiveness of demand to a change in consumers' incomes (Y); and the **cross-price elasticity of demand** – the responsiveness of demand for their good to a change in the price of another (whether a substitute or a complement).

Income elasticity of demand ($Y\varepsilon_D$)

We define the income elasticity of demand for a good as follows:

$$Y\varepsilon_D = \frac{\text{proportionate (or percentage) change in quantity demanded}}{\text{proportionate (or percentage) change in income}}$$

For example, if a 2 per cent rise in consumer incomes causes an 8 per cent rise in a product's demand, then its income elasticity of demand will be:

8%/2% = 4

The major determinant of income elasticity of demand is the degree of 'necessity' of the good.

In a developed country, the demand for luxury goods expands rapidly as people's incomes rise, whereas the demand for more basic goods, such as bread, rises only a little. Thus items such as cars and foreign holidays have a high income elasticity of demand, whereas items such as potatoes and bus journeys have a low income elasticity of demand.

The demand for some goods actually decreases as income rises. These are inferior goods such as cheap margarine. As people earn more, so they switch to butter or better-quality

> ### Definitions
>
> **Income elasticity of demand** The responsiveness of demand to a change in consumer incomes: the proportionate change in demand divided by the proportionate change in income.
>
> **Cross-price elasticity of demand** The responsiveness of demand for one good to a change in the price of another: the proportionate change in demand for one good divided by the proportionate change in price of the other.

margarine. Unlike normal goods, which have a positive income elasticity of demand, inferior goods have a negative income elasticity of demand (a rise in income leads to a *fall* in demand).

Income elasticity of demand and the firm

Income elasticity of demand is an important concept to firms considering the future size of the market for their product. If the product has a high income elasticity of demand, sales are likely to expand rapidly as national income rises, but may also fall significantly if the economy moves into recession.

Firms may also find that some parts of their market have a higher income elasticity of demand than others, and may thus choose to target their marketing campaigns on this group. For example, middle-income groups may have a higher income elasticity of demand for certain high-tech products than lower-income groups (who are unlikely to be able to afford such products even if their incomes rise somewhat) or higher-income groups (who can probably afford them anyway, and thus would not buy much more if their incomes rose).

> ### Pause for thought
>
> *Assume that you decide to spend a quarter of your income on clothes. What is (a) your income elasticity of demand; (b) your price elasticity of demand?*

Cross-price elasticity of demand ($C\varepsilon_{D_{ab}}$)

This is often known by its less cumbersome title of 'cross elasticity of demand'. It is a measure of the responsiveness of demand for one product to a change in the price of another (either a substitute or a complement). It enables us to predict how much the demand curve for the first product will shift when the price of the second product changes. For example, knowledge of the cross elasticity of demand for Coca-Cola with respect to the price of Pepsi would allow Coca-Cola to predict the effect on its own sales if the price of Pepsi were to change.

We define cross-price elasticity as follows:

$$C\varepsilon_D = \frac{\text{proportionate (or percentage)}}{\text{proportionate (or percentage) change}}$$
$$\frac{\text{change in demand for good a}}{\text{in price of good b}}$$

If good b is a *substitute* for good a, a's demand will *rise* as b's price rises. For example, the demand for bicycles will rise as the price of public transport rises. In this case, cross elasticity will be a positive figure. If b is *complementary* to a, however, a's demand will *fall* as b's price rises and thus as the quantity of b demanded falls. For example, the demand for petrol falls as the price of cars rises. In this case, cross elasticity will be a negative figure.

Cross-price elasticity of demand and the firm

The major determinant of cross elasticity of demand is the closeness of the substitute or complement. The closer it is, the bigger will be the effect on the first good of a change in the price of the substitute or complement, and hence the greater will be the cross elasticity – either positive or negative.

Firms will wish to know the cross elasticity of demand for their product when considering the effect on the demand for their product of a change in the price of a rival's product (a substitute). If firm b cuts its price, will this make significant inroads into the sales of firm a? If so, firm a may feel forced to cut its prices too; if not, then firm a may keep its price unchanged. The cross-price elasticities of demand between a firm's product and those of each of its rivals are thus vital pieces of information for a firm when making its production, pricing and marketing plans.

Similarly, a firm will wish to know the cross-price elasticity of demand for its product with any complementary good. Car producers will wish to know the effect of petrol price increases on the sales of their cars.

Price elasticity of supply ($P\varepsilon_S$)

Just as we can measure the responsiveness of demand to a change in one of the determinants of demand, so too we can measure the responsiveness of supply to a change in one of the determinants of supply. The *price elasticity of supply* refers to the responsiveness of supply to a change in price. We define it as follows:

$$P\varepsilon_S = \frac{\text{proportionate (or percentage)}}{\text{change in quantity supplied}}$$
$$\frac{\text{change in quantity supplied}}{\text{proportionate (or percentage) change in price}}$$

Thus if a 15 per cent rise in the price of a product causes a 30 per cent rise in the quantity supplied, the price elasticity of supply will be:

30%/15% = 2

In Figure 5.7, curve S_2 is more elastic between any two prices than curve S_1. Thus, when price rises from P_1 to P_2 there is a larger increase in quantity supplied with S_2 (namely, Q_1 to Q_3) than there is with S_1 (namely, Q_1 to Q_2).

Determinants of price elasticity of supply

The amount that costs rise as output rises. The less the additional costs of producing additional output, the more firms

> ### Definition
>
> **Price elasticity of supply** The responsiveness of quantity supplied to a change in price: the proportionate change in quantity supplied divided by the proportionate change in price.

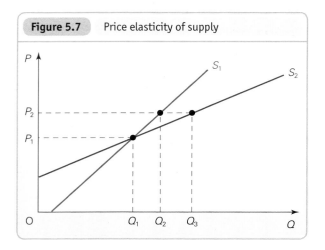

Figure 5.7 Price elasticity of supply

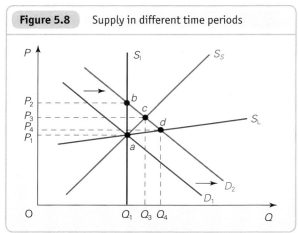

Figure 5.8 Supply in different time periods

will be encouraged to produce for a given price rise: the more elastic will supply be.

Supply is thus likely to be elastic if firms have plenty of spare capacity, if they can readily get extra supplies of raw materials, if they can easily switch away from producing alternative products and if they can avoid having to introduce overtime working (at higher rates of pay). If all these conditions hold, costs will be little affected by a rise in output, and supply will be relatively elastic. The less these conditions apply, the less elastic will supply be.

Time period (see Figure 5.8)

- Immediate time period. Firms are unlikely to be able to increase supply by much immediately. Supply is virtually fixed, or can vary only according to available stocks. Hence, supply is highly inelastic. In the diagram S_I is drawn with $P\varepsilon_S = 0$. If demand increases to D_2, supply will

not be able to respond. Price will rise to P_2. Quantity will remain at Q_1. Equilibrium will move to point b.
- Short run. If a slightly longer time period is allowed to elapse, some inputs can be increased (e.g. raw materials), while others will remain fixed (e.g. heavy machinery). Supply can increase somewhat. This is illustrated by S_S. Equilibrium will move to point c with price falling again, to P_3, and quantity rising to Q_3.
- Long run. In the long run, there will be sufficient time for all inputs to be increased and for new firms to enter the industry. Supply, therefore, is likely to be highly elastic. This is illustrated by curve S_L. Long-run equilibrium will be at point d with price falling back even further, to P_4, and quantity rising all the way to Q_4. In some circumstances the supply curve may even slope downward. (See the section on economies of scale in Chapter 9, pages 136–7.)

5.4 THE TIME DIMENSION OF MARKET ADJUSTMENT

The full adjustment of price, demand and supply to a situation of disequilibrium will not be instantaneous. It is necessary, therefore, to analyse the time path which supply takes in responding to changes in demand, and which demand takes in responding to changes in supply.

Short-run and long-run adjustment

As we have already seen, elasticity varies with the time period under consideration. The reason is that producers and consumers take time to respond to a change in price. The longer the time period, the bigger the response, and thus the greater the elasticity of supply and demand.

This is illustrated in Figures 5.9 and 5.10. In both cases, as equilibrium moves from points a to b to c, there is a large short-run price change (P_1 to P_2) and a small

short-run quantity change (Q_1 to Q_2), but a small long-run price change (P_1 to P_3) and a large long-run quantity change (Q_1 to Q_3).

Price expectations and speculation

In a world of shifting demand and supply curves, prices do not stay the same. Sometimes they go up; sometimes they come down. If prices are likely to change in the foreseeable future, this will affect the behaviour of buyers and sellers *now*. If, for example, it is now December and you are thinking of buying a new winter coat, you might decide to wait until the January sales, and in the meantime make do with your old coat. If, on the other hand, when January comes you see a new summer jacket in the sales, you might well buy it now and not wait until the summer, for fear

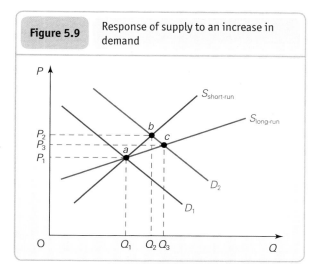

Figure 5.9 Response of supply to an increase in demand

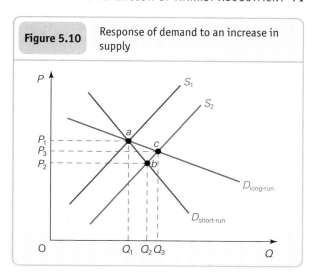

Figure 5.10 Response of demand to an increase in supply

that the price will have gone up by then. Thus a belief that prices will go up will cause people to buy now; a belief that prices will come down will cause them to wait.

The reverse applies to sellers. If you are thinking of selling your house and prices are falling, you will want to sell it as quickly as possible. If, on the other hand, prices are rising sharply, you will wait as long as possible so as to get the highest price. Thus a belief that prices will come down will cause people to sell now; a belief that prices will go up will cause them to wait.

KEY IDEA 13

People's actions are influenced by their expectations. People respond not just to what is happening now (such as a change in price), but to what they anticipate will happen in the future.

This behaviour of looking into the future and making buying and selling decisions based on your predictions is called *speculation*. Speculation is often partly based on current trends in price behaviour. If prices are currently rising, people may try to decide whether they are about to peak and go back down again, or whether they are likely to go on rising. Having made their prediction, they will then act on it. This speculation will thus affect demand and supply, which in turn will affect price. Speculation is commonplace in many markets: the stock exchange (see Box 4.2), the foreign exchange market and the housing market (see Box 4.1) are three examples. Large firms often employ specialist buyers who choose the right time to buy inputs, depending on what they anticipate will happen to their price.

Speculation tends to be *self-fulfilling*. In other words, the actions of speculators tend to bring about the very effect on prices that speculators had anticipated. For example, if speculators believe that the price of BP shares is about to rise, they will buy more BP shares, shifting demand to the right. But by doing this they will ensure that the price *will* rise. The prophecy has become self-fulfilling.

Speculation can either help to reduce price fluctuations or aggravate them: it can be stabilising or destabilising.

Stabilising speculation

Speculation will tend to have a ***stabilising*** effect on price fluctuations when suppliers and/or demanders believe that a change in price is only *temporary*.

Assume, for example, that there has recently been a rise in price, caused, say, by an increase in demand. In Figure 5.11(a) demand has shifted from D_1 to D_2. Equilibrium has moved from point a to point b, and price has risen from P_1 to P_2. How do people react to this rise in price?

Given that they believe this rise in price to be only temporary, suppliers bring their goods to market now, before price falls again. Supply shifts from S_1 to S_2. Demanders, however, hold back until price does fall. Demand shifts from D_2 to D_3. The equilibrium moves to point c, with price falling back towards P_1.

A good example of stabilising speculation is that which occurs in agricultural commodity markets. Take the case of wheat. When it is harvested in the autumn there will be a plentiful supply. If all this wheat were to be put on the market, the price would fall to a very low level. Later in the year, when most of the wheat would have been sold, the price would then rise to a very high level. This is all easily predictable.

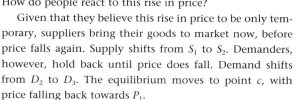

Definitions

Speculation This is where people make buying or selling decisions based on their anticipations of future prices.

Self-fulfilling speculation The actions of speculators tend to cause the very effect that they had anticipated.

Stabilising speculation This is where the actions of speculators tend to reduce price fluctuations.

BOX 5.2 ADJUSTING TO OIL PRICE SHOCKS

Short-run and long-run demand and supply responses

Between December 1973 and June 1974, the Organization of Petroleum Exporting Countries (OPEC) put up the price of oil from $3 to $12 per barrel. It was further raised to over $30 in 1979. In the 1980s the price fluctuated, but the trend was downward. Except for a sharp rise at the time of the Gulf War in 1990, the trend continued through most of the 1990s, at times falling as low as $11.

In the early 2000s, oil prices were generally higher, first fluctuating between $19 and $33 per barrel and then, from 2004 to 2006, steadily rising. The price then increased dramatically from January 2007, when it was just over $50 per barrel, to mid-2008 when it reached $147 per barrel. By late 2008 the price had fallen back sharply to under $50 per barrel as fears of a world recession cut the demand for oil. As the global economy began to recover, the oil price rose steadily, reaching $128 per barrel by early 2011. Since then prices have remained relatively stable and stood at around $100 in July 2012.

The price movements can be explained using simple demand and supply analysis.

The initial rise in price

In the 1970s OPEC raised the price from P_1 to P_2 (see diagram (a)). To prevent surplus at that price, OPEC members restricted their output by agreed amounts. This had the effect of shifting the supply curve to S_2, with Q_2 being produced. This reduction in output needed to be only relatively small because the short-run demand for oil was highly price inelastic: for most uses there are no substitutes in the short run.

Long-run effects on demand

The long-run demand for oil was more elastic (see diagram (b)). With high oil prices persisting, people tried to find ways of cutting back on consumption. People bought smaller cars. They converted to gas or solid-fuel central heating. Firms switched to other fuels. Less use was made of oil-fired power

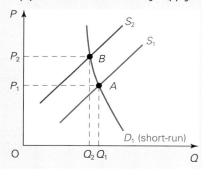

(a) An initial restriction of supply

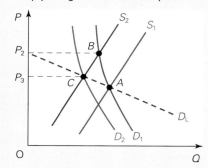

(b) Long-run demand response

Figure 5.11 Speculation (initial rise in price)

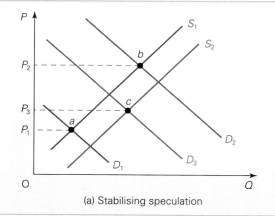

(a) Stabilising speculation

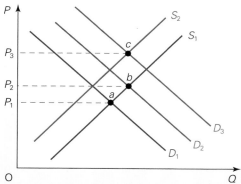

(b) Destabilising speculation

stations for electricity generation. Energy-saving schemes became widespread both in firms and in the home.

This had the effect of shifting the short-run demand curve from D_1 to D_2. Price fell back from P_2 to P_3. This gave a long-run demand curve of D_L: the curve that joins points A and C.

The fall in demand was made bigger by a world recession in the early 1980s.

Long-run effects on supply

With oil production so much more profitable, there was an incentive for non-OPEC oil producers to produce oil. Prospecting went on all over the world and large oil fields were discovered and opened up in the North Sea, Alaska, Mexico, China and elsewhere. In addition, OPEC members were tempted to break their 'quotas' (their allotted output) and sell more oil.

The net effect was an increase in world oil supplies. In terms of the diagrams, the supply curve of oil started to shift to the right from the mid-1980s onwards, causing oil prices to fall through most of the period up to 1998.

Back to square one?

By the late 1990s, with the oil price as low as $10 per barrel, OPEC once more cut back supply. The story had come full circle. This cut-back is once more illustrated in diagram (a).

The trouble this time was that worldwide economic growth was picking up. Demand was shifting to the right. The result was a rise in oil prices to around $33, which then fell back again in 2001 as the world slipped into recession and the demand curve shifted to the left.

There were then some very large price increases, first as a result of OPEC in late 2001 attempting once more to restrict supply (a leftward shift in supply), and then, before the Iraq

war of 2003, because of worries about possible adverse effects on oil supplies (a rightward shift in demand as countries stocked up on oil). The worries about long-run security of supply continued after the invasion of Iraq and the continuing political uncertainty in the region.

The rises in the price of oil from 2004 through to mid-2008 were fuelled partly by rapidly expanding demand (a rightward shift in short-run demand), especially in countries such as China and India, and by speculation on the future price of oil. On the supply side, producers could not respond rapidly to meet this demand and there has been further disruption to supply in some oil-producing countries, including Nigeria and Algeria (a leftward shift in short-run supply). However, the dramatic rise in oil prices fuelled inflation across the world. Consumers and industry faced much higher costs and looked at methods to conserve fuel.

In late 2008, the global financial crisis was followed by recession. The price of oil began to fall back as the demand curve for oil shifted leftwards. It fell from a peak of $147 per barrel in July 2008 to a mere $34 per barrel by the end of the year. But then, as the world economy slowly recovered, and the demand for oil rose, so oil prices rose again. By early 2011, oil was trading at around $128 per barrel.

With both demand and supply being price *inelastic* in the short run, large fluctuations in price are only to be expected. And these are amplified by speculation.

The problem is made worse by an income elastic demand for oil. Demand can rise rapidly in times when the global economy is booming, only to fall back substantially in times of recession.

 Give some examples of things that could make the demand for oil more elastic. What specific policies could the government introduce to make demand more elastic?

So what do farmers do? The answer is that they speculate. When the wheat is harvested they know its price will tend to fall, and so instead of bringing it all to market they put a lot of it into store *anticipating that the price will later rise*. But this holding back of supplies prevents prices from falling. In other words, it stabilises prices.

Later in the year, when the price begins to rise, they will gradually release grain on to the market from the stores. The more the price rises, the more will they release on to the market *anticipating that the price will fall again by the time of the next harvest*. But this releasing of supplies will again stabilise prices by preventing them rising so much.

Destabilising speculation

Speculation will tend to have a ***destabilising*** effect on price fluctuations when suppliers and/or buyers believe that a change in price heralds similar changes to come.

Assume again that there has recently been a rise in price, caused by an increase in demand. In Figure 5.11(b), demand

has shifted from D_1 to D_2 and price has risen from P_1 to P_2. This time, however, believing that the rise in price heralds further rises to come, suppliers wait until the price rises further. Supply shifts from S_1 to S_2. Demanders buy now before any further rise in price. Demand shifts from D_2 to D_3. As a result the price continues to rise: to P_3.

Box 4.1 examined the housing market. In this market, speculation is frequently destabilising. Assume that people see house prices beginning to move upward. This might be the result of increased demand brought about by a cut in mortgage interest rates or by growth in the economy. People may well believe that the rise in house prices signals a boom in the housing market: that prices will go on rising. Potential buyers will thus try to buy as soon as possible

Definition

Destabilising speculation This is where the actions of speculators tend to make price movements larger.

before prices rise any further. This increased demand (as in Figure 5.11(b)) will thus lead to even bigger price rises. This is precisely what happened in the UK housing market in 1999–2007.

Pause for thought

Draw two diagrams like Figures 5.11(a) and (b), only this time assume an initial fall in demand and hence price. The first diagram should show the effects of stabilising speculation and the second the effect of destabilising speculation.

Conclusion

In some circumstances, then, the action of speculators can help keep price fluctuations to a minimum (stabilising speculation). This is most likely when markets are relatively stable in the first place, with only moderate underlying shifts in demand and supply.

Pause for thought

What are the advantages and disadvantages of speculation from the point of view of (a) the consumer; (b) firms?

In other circumstances, however, speculation can make price fluctuations much worse. This is most likely in times of uncertainty, when there are significant changes in the determinants of demand and supply. Given this uncertainty, people may see price changes as signifying some trend. They then 'jump on the bandwagon' and do what the rest are doing, further fuelling the rise or fall in price.

5.5 DEALING WITH UNCERTAINTY

Risk and uncertainty

When price changes are likely to occur, buyers and sellers will try to anticipate them. Unfortunately, on many occasions no one can be certain just what these price changes will be. Take the case of stocks and shares. If you anticipate that the price of, say, BP shares is likely to go up substantially in the near future, you may well decide to buy some now and then sell them later after the price has risen. But you cannot be certain that they will go up in price: they may fall instead. If you buy the shares, therefore, you will be taking a gamble.

Now gambles can be of two types. The first is where you know the odds. Let us take the simplest case of a gamble on the toss of a coin. Heads you win; tails you lose. You know that the odds of winning are precisely 50 per cent. If you bet on the toss of a coin, you are said to be operating under conditions of **risk**. *Risk is when the probability of an outcome is known.* Risk itself is a measure of the *variability* of an outcome. For example, if you bet £1 on the toss of a coin, such that heads you win £1 and tails you lose £1, then the variability is −£1 to +£1.

The second form of gamble is the more usual. This is where the odds are not known or are known only roughly. Gambling on the Stock Exchange is like this. You may have a good idea that a share will go up in price, but is it a 90 per cent chance, an 80 per cent chance or what? You are not certain. Gambling under these sorts of conditions is known as operating under **uncertainty**. *This is when the probability of an outcome is not known.*

You may well disapprove of gambling and want to dismiss people who engage in it as foolish or morally wrong. But 'gambling' is not just confined to horses, cards, roulette and the like. Risk and uncertainty pervade the whole of economic life and decisions are constantly having to be made whose outcome cannot be known for certain. Even the most morally upright person will still have to decide which career to go into, whether and when to buy a house, or even something as trivial as whether or not to take an umbrella when going out. Each of these decisions and thousands of others are made under conditions of uncertainty (or occasionally risk).

People's actions are influenced by their attitudes towards risk. Many decisions are taken under conditions of risk or uncertainty. Generally, the lower the probability of (or the more uncertain) the desired outcome of an action, the less likely will people be to undertake the action.

We shall be examining how risk and uncertainty affect economic decisions at several points throughout the book. For example, in the next chapter we will see how it affects people's attitudes and actions as consumers, and how taking out insurance can help to reduce their uncertainty. At this point, however, let us focus on firms' attitudes when supplying goods.

Definitions

Risk This is when an outcome may or may not occur, but where its probability of occurring is known.

Uncertainty This is when an outcome may or may not occur and where its probability of occurring is not known.

Stock holding as a way of reducing the problem of uncertainty. A simple way that suppliers can reduce risks is by holding stocks. Take the case of the wheat farmers we saw in the previous section. At the time when they are planting the wheat in the spring, they are uncertain as to what the price of wheat will be when they bring it to market. If they keep no stores of wheat, they will just have to accept whatever the market price happens to be at harvest time. If, however, they have storage facilities, they can put the wheat into store if the price is low and then wait until it goes up. Alternatively, if the price of wheat is high at harvest time, they can sell it straight away. In other words, they can wait until the price is right.

> ### Pause for thought
>
> *The demand for pears is more price elastic than the demand for bread and yet the price of pears fluctuates more than that of bread. Why should this be so? If pears could be stored as long and as cheaply as flour, would this affect the relative price fluctuations? If so, how?*

Purchasing information. One way of reducing uncertainty is to buy information. A firm could commission various forms of market research or purchase the information from specialist organisations. It is similar for consumers. You might take advice on shares from a stockbroker, or buy a copy of a consumer magazine, such as *Which?*. The buying and selling of information in this way helps substantially to reduce uncertainty.

Better information can also, under certain circumstances, help to make any speculation more stabilising. With poor information, people are much more likely to be guided by rumour or fear, which could well make speculation destabilising as people 'jump on the bandwagon'. If people generally are better informed, however, this is likely to make prices go more directly to a long-run stable equilibrium.

Dealing in futures markets

Another way of reducing or even eliminating uncertainty is by dealing in *futures* or *forward markets*. Let us examine the activities first of sellers and then of buyers.

Sellers

Suppose you are a farmer and want to store grain to sell some time in the future, expecting to get a better price then than now. The trouble is that there is a chance that the price will go down. Given this uncertainty, you may be unwilling to take a gamble.

An answer to your problem is provided by the *commodity futures market*. This is a market where prices are agreed between sellers and buyers *today* for delivery at some specified date in the *future*.

For example, if it is 20 October today, you could be quoted a price *today* for delivery in six months' time (i.e.

on 20 April). This is known as the six-month *future price*. Assume that the six-month future price for wheat is £60 per tonne. If you agree to this price and make a six-month forward contract, you are agreeing to sell a specified amount of wheat at £60 on 20 April. No matter what happens to the *spot price* (i.e. the current market price) in the meantime, your selling price has been agreed. The spot price could have fallen to £30 (or risen to £100) by April, but your selling price when 20 April arrives is fixed at £60. There is thus *no risk to you whatsoever of the price going down*. You will, of course, lose out if the spot price is *more* than £60 in April.

Buyers

Now suppose that you are a flour miller. In order to plan your expenditures, you would like to know the price you will have to pay for wheat, not just today, but also at various future dates. In other words, if you want to take delivery of wheat at some time in the future, you would like a price quoted *now*. You would like the risks removed of prices going *up*.

Let us assume that today (20 October) you want to *buy* the same amount of wheat on 20 April that a farmer wishes to sell on that same date. If you agree to the £60 future price, a future contract can be made with the farmer. You are then guaranteed that purchase price, no matter what happens to the spot price in the meantime. There is thus *no risk to you whatsoever of the price going up*. You will, of course, lose out if the spot price is *less* than £60 in April.

The determination of the future price

Prices in the futures market are determined in the same way as in other markets: by demand and supply. For example, the six-month wheat price or the three-month coffee price will be that which equates the demand for those futures with the supply. If the five-month sugar price is currently £200 per tonne and people expect by then, because of an anticipated good beet harvest, that the spot price for sugar will be £150 per tonne, there will be few who will want to buy the futures at £200 (and many who will want to sell). This excess of supply of futures over demand will push the price down.

Speculators

Many people operate in the futures market who never actually handle the commodities themselves. They are

> ### Definitions
>
> **Futures or forward market** A market in which contracts are made to buy or sell at some future date at a price agreed today.
>
> **Future price** A price agreed today at which an item (e.g. commodities) will be exchanged at some set date in the future.
>
> **Spot price** The current market price.

BOX 5.3   DON'T SHOOT THE SPECULATOR

Well not yet, anyway!

In February 2008 the United Nations Food and Agricultural Organisation stated that the price of cereals had risen 83 per cent over the previous 12 months, with dire consequences for developing nations in particular. In July 2008 the price of oil rose to the unprecedented high of $147 per barrel, with devastating consequences for the millions of users of oil and oil-based products. Between early September and late October 2008 the FTSE 100 fell by 35 per cent, from a high of 5646 to a low of 3665 (see Box 4.2), a fall that had not been seen since October 1987, offering misery to millions of ordinary investors and those with pensions.

Much of the blame for these dramatic changes is placed on speculators who are seen as exacerbating the problem. They are seen as greedy and acting immorally, and affecting the lives of millions of ordinary people through their actions. Thankfully, no one in power has yet adopted Vladimir Lenin's declaration to a meeting at the Petrograd Soviet in 1918 that 'Speculators who are caught and fully exposed as such shall be shot . . . on the spot.' However, religious leaders, politicians and regulators have been calling for, and getting, stricter controls over their operations.

This commonly held view of the speculator, however, is not held by everyone. Consider the following taken from *The Financial Times* in regard to the rapid rise in commodity prices in early 2011.

> . . . where are commodity prices headed next?
>
> There are many problems in understanding, let alone forecasting, the behaviour of commodity prices. In the long term, which means decades, the real price of commodities is determined by the supply side costs of extraction, . . . over shorter term horizons, these factors are incapable of explaining commodity price fluctuations, because they change so slowly. Prices, on the other hand, can change dramatically over short periods. Since demand and supply curves are both very steep (especially for oil), a very small shift in either curve can have very large effects on oil prices, making them very hard to predict.
>
> There are two possible explanations for the surge in commodity prices since last August. The first and 'fundamental' explanation is that the growth in global industrial production has been maintained at levels well above long term trends. . . .
>
> The second, and 'speculative' explanation is that the Fed's decision to expand liquidity has leaked into all risk assets, including commodities, via financial market demand for these assets. . . . Paul Krugman and others have argued that the 'speculative' explanation can be eliminated on a priori grounds, because financial operators never take delivery of physical commodities. Ultimately they do not increase the real demand for commodities, and therefore they can have no effect on the price. Financial demand can of course alter the prices for futures and options on commodities, but since the prices of these derivative contracts must eventually home in on the price for the physical, this will eventually be a zero sum game. On this argument, financial speculation is irrelevant.
>
> . . . but it seems to me that for short periods . . . rising futures prices could lead to the expectation of higher prices for physical commodities, in which case physical players might decide to 'hoard' stocks, and reduce the rate of extraction so that they can benefit from the subsequent rise in prices. By changing inventory levels and extraction rates, this type of real activity could tighten the physical market and, at least for a time, raise prices. . . .
>
> So which of these explanations best fits the evidence? . . . The calculations suggest that while a large part of the rise in oil and other commodity prices may have been caused by fundamentals, nevertheless commodity prices may have overshot their 'equilibrium' levels at times in recent months. . . .[1]

Are speculators largely adjusting their decisions in line with changing circumstances? In other words, are they being efficient? Or are they being inefficient and causing increased price volatility?

 How might it be beneficial for the economy if speculators were less efficient?

[1] Gavyn Davies, 'Fundamentals and speculation in commodity markets' *The Financial Times* 16 May 2011. © The Financial Times Limited. All Rights Reserved.

---

neither producers nor users of the commodities. They merely speculate. Such speculators may be individuals, but they are more likely to be financial institutions.

Let us take a simple example. Suppose that the six-month (April) coffee price is £1000 per tonne and that you, as a speculator, believe that the spot price of coffee is likely to rise above that level between now (October) and six months' time. You thus decide to buy 20 tonnes of April coffee futures now.

But you have no intention of taking delivery. After four months, let us say, true to your prediction, the spot price (February) has risen and as a result the April price (and other future prices) have risen too. You thus decide to *sell* 20 tonnes of April (two-month) coffee futures, whose price, let us say, is £1200. You are now 'covered'.

When April comes, what happens? You have agreed to buy 20 tonnes of coffee at £1000 per tonne and to sell 20 tonnes of coffee at £1200 per tonne. All you do is hand the futures contract to buy to the person to whom you agreed to sell. They sort out delivery between them and you make £200 per tonne profit.

If, however, your prediction had been wrong and the price had *fallen*, you would have made a loss. You would have been forced to sell coffee contracts at a lower price than you had bought them.

Speculators in the futures market thus incur risks, unlike the sellers and buyers of the commodities, for whom the futures market eliminates risk. Financial institutions offering futures contracts will charge for the service: for taking on the risks.

SUMMARY

1a Price elasticity of demand measures the responsiveness of demand to a change in price. It is defined as the proportionate (or percentage) change in quantity demanded divided by the proportionate (or percentage) change in price.

1b If quantity demanded changes proportionately more than price, the figure for elasticity will be greater than 1 (ignoring the sign): it is elastic. If the quantity demanded changes proportionately less than price, the figure for elasticity will be less than 1: it is inelastic. If they change by the same proportion, the elasticity has a value of 1: it is unit elastic.

1c Given that demand curves are downward sloping, price elasticity of demand will have a negative value.

1d Demand will be more elastic the greater the number and closeness of substitute goods, the higher the proportion of income spent on the good and the longer the time period that elapses after the change in price.

1e Demand curves normally have different elasticities along their length. We can thus normally refer only to the specific value for elasticity between two points on the curve or at a single point.

2a It is important for firms to know the price elasticity of demand for their product whenever they are considering a price change. The reason is that the effect of the price change on the firm's sales revenue will depend on the product's price elasticity.

2b When the demand for a firm's product is price elastic, a rise in price will lead to a reduction in consumer expenditure on the good and hence to a reduction in the total revenue of the firm.

2c When demand is price inelastic, however, a rise in price will lead to an increase in total revenue for the firm.

3a Income elasticity of demand measures the responsiveness of demand to a change in income. For normal goods it has a positive value. Demand will be more income elastic the more luxurious the good and the less rapidly demand is satisfied as consumption increases.

3b Cross-price elasticity of demand measures the responsiveness of demand for one good to a change in the price of another. For substitute goods the value will be positive; for complements it will be negative. The cross-price elasticity will be greater the closer the two goods are as substitutes or complements.

3c Price elasticity of supply measures the responsiveness of supply to a change in price. It has a positive value. Supply will be more elastic the less costs per unit rise as output rises and the longer the time period.

4a A complete understanding of markets must take into account the time dimension.

4b Given that producers and consumers take a time to respond fully to price changes, we can identify different equilibria after the elapse of different lengths of time. Generally, short-run supply and demand tend to be less price elastic than long-run supply and demand. As a result any shifts in demand or supply curves tend to have a relatively bigger effect on price in the short run and a relatively bigger effect on quantity in the long run.

4c People often anticipate price changes and this will affect the amount they demand or supply. This speculation will tend to stabilise price fluctuations if people believe that the price changes are only temporary. However, speculation will tend to destabilise these fluctuations (i.e. make them more severe) if people believe that prices are likely to continue to move in the same direction as at present (at least for some time).

5a A lot of economic decision making is made under conditions of risk or uncertainty.

5b Risk is when the probability of an outcome occurring is known. Uncertainty is when the probability is not known.

5c One way of reducing risks is to hold stocks. If the price of a firm's product falls unexpectedly, it can build up stocks rather than releasing its product on to the market. If the price later rises, it can then release stocks on to the market. Similarly with inputs: if their price falls unexpectedly, firms can build up their stocks, only to draw on them later if input prices rise.

5d A way of eliminating risk and uncertainty is to deal in the futures markets. When firms are planning to buy or sell at some point in the future, there is the danger that price could rise or fall unexpectedly in the meantime. By agreeing to buy or sell at some particular point in the future at a price agreed today (a 'future' price), this danger can be eliminated. The bank or other institution offering the price (the 'speculator') is taking on the risk, and will charge for this service.

REVIEW QUESTIONS

1 Why does price elasticity of demand have a negative value, whereas price elasticity of supply has a positive value?

2 Rank the following in ascending order of elasticity: jeans, black Levi jeans, black jeans, black Levi 501 jeans, trousers, outer garments, clothes.

3 How might a firm set about making the demand for its brand less elastic?

4 Will a general item of expenditure like food or clothing have a price elastic or inelastic demand?

5 Assuming that a firm faces an inelastic demand and wants to increase its total revenue, how much should it raise its price? Is there any limit?

6 Can you think of any examples of goods which have a totally inelastic demand (a) at all prices; (b) over a particular price range?

7 Which of these two pairs are likely to have the highest cross-price elasticity of demand: two brands of coffee, or coffee and tea?

8 Why are both the price elasticity of demand and the price elasticity of supply likely to be greater in the long run?

9 Redraw Figure 5.11, only this time assume that it was an initial shift in supply that caused the price to change in the first place.

10 Give some examples of decisions you have taken recently that were made under conditions of uncertainty. With hindsight, do you think you made the right decisions? Explain.

11 What methods can a firm use to reduce risk and uncertainty?

12 If speculators believed that the price of cocoa in six months was going to be below the six-month future price quoted today, how would they act?

ADDITIONAL PART B CASE STUDIES IN THE *ECONOMICS FOR BUSINESS* MyEconLab (www.pearsoned.co.uk/sloman)

B.1 **The interdependence of markets.** A case study of the operation of markets, examining the effects on a local economy of the discovery of a large coal deposit.

B.2 **Adam Smith (1723–1790).** Smith, the founder of modern economics, argued that markets act like an 'invisible hand' guiding production and consumption.

B.3 **Shall we put up our price?** Some examples of firms charging high prices in markets where demand is relatively inelastic.

B.4 **Any more fares?** Pricing on the buses: an illustration of the relationship between price and total revenue.

B.5 **Elasticities of demand for various foodstuffs.** An examination of the evidence about price and income elasticities of demand for food in the UK.

B.6 **Adjusting to oil price shocks.** A case study showing how demand and supply analysis can be used to examine the price changes in the oil market since 1973.

B.7 **Income elasticity of demand and the balance of payments.** This examines how a low income elasticity of demand for the exports of many developing countries can help to explain their chronic balance of payments problems.

B.8 **The cobweb.** An outline of the theory that explains price fluctuations in terms of time lags in supply.

B.9 **The role of the speculator.** This assesses whether the activities of speculators are beneficial or harmful to the rest of society.

B.10 **Rationing.** A case study in the use of rationing as an alternative to the price mechanism. In particular, it looks at the use of rationing in the UK during the Second World War.

B.11 **Rent control.** This shows how setting (low) maximum rents is likely to lead to a shortage of rented accommodation.

B.12 **Agriculture and minimum prices.** This shows how setting (high) minimum prices is likely to lead to surpluses.

B.13 **The fallacy of composition.** An illustration from agricultural markets of the fallacy of composition: 'what applies in one case will not necessarily apply when repeated in all cases'.

B.14 **Coffee prices.** An examination of the coffee market and the implications of fluctuations in the coffee harvest for growers and coffee drinkers.

B.15 **Response to changes in petrol and ethanol prices in Brazil.** This case examines how drivers with 'flex-fuel' cars responded to changes in the relative prices of two fuels: petrol and ethanol (made from sugar cane).

WEBSITES RELEVANT TO PART B

Numbers and sections refer to websites listed in the Web appendix and hotlinked from this book's website at
www.pearsoned.co.uk/sloman

■ For news articles relevant to Part B, see the *Economics News Articles* link from the book's website.

■ For general news on markets, see websites in section A, and particularly A2, 3, 4, 5, 8, 9, 18, 20–26, 35, 36. See also site A42 for links to economics news articles from newspapers worldwide.

■ For links to sites on markets, see the relevant sections of I4, 7, 11, 17.

■ For data on the housing market (Box 4.1), see sites B7, 8, 11.

■ For student resources relevant to Part B, see sites C1–7, 9, 10, 19; D3.

■ For sites favouring the free market, see C17 and E34.

Background to demand

The FT Reports . . .

The Financial Times, 26 October 2011

FT

Chinese Consumers: How to find favour down at the shops

By Patti Waldmeir

Chinese consumers tend to know exactly what they want to buy – and it is not always what multinational companies want to sell them. . . .

The Chinese love foreign brands – but especially those that have learnt to act local.

Best Buy, the US retailer, is a perfect example: it is looking for a way to re-enter the Chinese market after failing ignominiously with its own-brand stores, which were closed this year. Retail analysts across the board agreed that Best Buy's mistake was, in a way, its all-American arrogance.

Torsten Stocker, head of the China consumer goods practice at Monitor Group, the strategy consulting firm, says: 'Best Buy tried to replicate the US model, providing a premium shopping experience that consumers were ultimately not willing to pay for.' . . .

KFC has been more successful in China than McDonald's, partly because it has localised its menu and management, retail analysts say: the average KFC in China serves rice gruel with pork and thousand-year-old egg for breakfast – not a staple item on US menus. . . .

Indeed, Chinese consumers are now so important to some multinational companies that their tastes and preferences are shaping how consumer products are designed and marketed, not just in China but around the world.

Carmakers have long given cars more leg room in the back seat, to accommodate the chauffeur-driven Chinese entrepreneur, only to find – as GM did with its newly designed Buick LaCrosse sedan – that others, too, like a more spacious back seat as much as Chinese passengers. The LaCrosse sold in Detroit has a back seat influenced by Shanghai.

Now China's passion for high-tech multi-tasking has begun to influence even something as mundane as the lavatory. The $6,400 'smart' toilet from Kohler, the plumbing fixtures company, has several features inspired primarily by China's entertainment-obsessed consumers.

The heated footrest, designed for chilly Chinese water closets, has proved one of its most popular features globally, says David Kohler, president of the family company founded by his great-grandfather in 1873. The toilets' sleek iTouch-style remote – which controls an internal music system and the temperature of the seat – has also proved popular outside China, he says.

Kohler also has a remote-controlled bidet seat which allows users to Skype, play video games, go online and read ebooks while abluting. . . .

As the country urbanises – and its middle class grows wealthier – Chinese tastes are likely to influence more of the things the rest of the world buys. Rolls-Royce Motor Cars says China's love for back seat drinks cabinets and champagne refrigerators has spurred the company to offer these perks also in other markets.

Consumers, that is, the 'demand side', are just as important as the supply side: after all, it is they who ultimately pay for the goods and services provided, while the shape and size of their current and future demand choices is critical to the investment decisions that businesses make.

Philip Collins (2009) Chairman of the Office of Fair Trading, Preserving and Restoring Trust and Confidence in Markets. Keynote address to the British Institute of International and Comparative Law at the Ninth Annual Trans-Atlantic Antitrust Dialogue. April 30th. Available at http://www.oft.gov.uk/shared_oft/speeches/2009/spe0809.pdf

If a business is to be successful, it must be able to predict the strength of demand for its products and be able to respond to any changes in consumer tastes, particularly when the economic environment is uncertain. It will also want to know how its customers are likely to react to changes in its price or its competitors' prices, or to changes in income. In other words, it will want to know the price, cross-price and income elasticities of demand for its product. The better the firm's knowledge of its market, the better will it be able to plan its output to meet demand, and the more able will it be to choose its optimum price, product design, marketing campaigns, etc.

In Chapter 6 we will go behind the demand curve to gain a better understanding of consumer behaviour. We will consider how economists analyse consumer satisfaction and how it varies with the amount consumed. We will then relate this to the shape of the demand curve.

Then, in Chapter 7, we will investigate how data on consumer behaviour can be collected and the problems that businesses face in analysing such information and using it to forecast changes in demand.

Chapter 8 explores how firms can expand and develop their markets by the use of various types of non-price competition. It looks at ways in which firms can differentiate their products from those of their rivals. The chapter also considers how a business sets about deriving a marketing strategy, and assesses the role and implications of product advertising. As the *Financial Times* article shows, businesses have to find new ways to get consumers to part with their money in difficult economic environments.

Key terms

Marginal utility
Diminishing marginal utility
Consumer surplus
Rational consumer
Adverse selection
Moral hazard
Product characteristics
Indifference curves
Efficiency frontier
Market surveys
Market experiments
Demand function
Forecasting
Non-price competition
Product differentiation
Product marketing
Advertising

6 chapter

Demand and the consumer

Business issues covered in this chapter

- What determines the amount of a product that consumers wish to buy at each price? How does consumer satisfaction or 'utility' affect purchasing decisions?
- Why are purchasing decisions sometimes risky for consumers?
- How do attitudes towards risk vary between consumers?
- How can insurance help to reduce or remove the level of risk?
- Why may insurance companies have to beware of high-risk consumers being more likely to take out insurance ('adverse selection') and people behaving less carefully when they have insurance ('moral hazard')?
- How do product characteristics influence consumer choice?
- How will changing a product's characteristics and/or its price influence consumers' choices between products?

Given our limited incomes, we have to make choices about what to buy. You may have to choose between that new economics textbook you feel you ought to buy and going to a rock concert, between a new pair of jeans and a meal out, between saving up for a car and having more money to spend on everyday items, and so on. Business managers are interested in finding out what influences your decisions to consume, and how they might price or package their product to increase their sales.

In this section it is assumed that as consumers we behave 'rationally': that we consider the relative costs and benefits of our purchases in order to gain the maximum satisfaction possible from our limited incomes. Sometimes we may act 'irrationally'. We may purchase goods impetuously with little thought to their price or quality. In general, however, it is a reasonably accurate assumption that people behave rationally.

This does not mean that you get a calculator out every time you go shopping! When you go round the supermarket, you are hardly likely to look at every item on the shelf and weigh up the satisfaction you think you would get from it against the price on the label. Nevertheless, you have probably learned over time the sort of things you like and the prices they cost. You can probably make out a 'rational' shopping list quite quickly.

With major items of expenditure such as a house, a car, a carpet or a foreign holiday, we are likely to take much more care. Take the case of a foreign holiday: you will probably spend quite a long time browsing through brochures comparing the relative merits of various holidays against their relative costs, looking for a holiday that gives good value for money. This is rational behaviour.

6.1 MARGINAL UTILITY THEORY

Total and marginal utility

People buy goods and services because they get satisfaction from them. Economists call this satisfaction 'utility'.

An important distinction must be made between *total utility* and *marginal utility*.

Total utility (*TU*) is the total satisfaction that a person gains from all those units of a commodity consumed within a given time period. Thus if Tracey drank 10 cups of tea a day, her daily total utility from tea would be the satisfaction derived from those 10 cups.

Marginal utility (*MU*) is the additional satisfaction gained from consuming one *extra* unit within a given period of time. Thus we might refer to the marginal utility that Tracey gains from her third cup of tea of the day or her eleventh cup.

Diminishing marginal utility

Up to a point, the more of a commodity you consume, the greater will be your total utility. However, as you become more satisfied, each extra unit you consume will probably give you less additional utility than previous units. In other words, your marginal utility falls as you consume more. This is known as the **principle of diminishing marginal utility**. For example, the second cup of tea in the morning gives you less additional satisfaction than the first cup. The third cup gives less satisfaction still.

 KEY IDEA 15

The principle of diminishing marginal utility. The more of a product a person consumes over a given period of time, the less will be the additional utility gained from one more unit.

Pause for thought

Are there any goods or services where consumers do not experience diminishing marginal utility?

At some level of consumption, your total utility will be at a maximum. No extra satisfaction can be gained by the consumption of further units within that period of time. Thus marginal utility will be zero. Your desire for tea may be fully satisfied at twelve cups per day. A thirteenth cup will yield no extra utility. It may even give you displeasure (i.e. negative marginal utility).

The optimum level of consumption: the simplest case – one commodity

Just how much of a good should people consume if they are to make the best use of their limited income? To answer this question we must tackle the problem of how to measure utility. The problem is that utility is subjective. There is no way of knowing what another person's experiences are really like. Just how satisfying does Brian find his first cup of tea in the morning? How does his utility compare with Tracey's? We do not have utility meters that can answer these questions!

One solution to the problem is to measure utility with money. In this case, total utility becomes the value that people place on their consumption, and marginal utility becomes the amount of money that a person would be prepared to pay to obtain one more unit: in other words, what that extra unit is worth to that person. If Darren is prepared to pay 30p to obtain an extra packet of crisps, then that packet yields him 30p worth of utility: $MU = 30p$.

So how many packets should he consume if he is to act rationally? To answer this we need to introduce the concept of **consumer surplus**.

Marginal consumer surplus

Marginal consumer surplus (*MCS*) is the difference between what you are willing to pay for one more unit of a good and what you are actually charged. If Darren was willing to pay 30p for another packet of crisps which in fact cost him only 25p, he would be getting a marginal consumer surplus of 5p.

$$MCS = MU - P$$

Definitions

Total utility The total satisfaction a consumer gets from the consumption of all the units of a good consumed within a given time period.

Marginal utility The extra satisfaction gained from consuming one extra unit of a good within a given time period.

Principle of diminishing marginal utility As more units of a good are consumed, additional units will provide less additional satisfaction than previous units.

Consumer surplus The excess of what a person would have been prepared to pay for a good (i.e. the utility) over what that person actually pays.

Marginal consumer surplus The excess of utility from the consumption of one more unit of a good (*MU*) over the price paid: $MCS = MU - P$.

Total consumer surplus

Total consumer surplus (*TCS*) is the sum of all the marginal consumer surpluses you have obtained from all the units of a good you have consumed. It is the difference between the total utility from all the units and your expenditure on them. If Darren consumes 4 packets of crisps, and if he would have been prepared to spend £1.40 on them and only had to spend £1.00, then his total consumer surplus is 40p.

$$TCS = TU - TE$$

where *TE* is the total expenditure on a good: i.e. $P \times Q$.

(Note that total expenditure (*TE*) is a similar concept to total revenue (*TR*). They are both defined as $P \times Q$. But in the case of total expenditure, *Q* is the quantity *purchased* by the consumer(s) in question, whereas in the case of total revenue, *Q* is the quantity *sold* by the firm(s) in question.)

Rational consumer behaviour

KI 4
p 22
Let us define **rational consumer behaviour** as the attempt to maximise (total) consumer surplus.

The process of maximising consumer surplus can be shown graphically. Let us take the case of Tina's annual purchases of petrol. Tina has her own car, but as an alternative she can use public transport or walk. To keep the analysis simple, let us assume that Tina's parents bought her the car and pay the licence duty, and that Tina does not have the option of selling the car. She does, however, have to buy the petrol. The current price is 130p per litre. Figure 6.1 shows her consumer surplus.

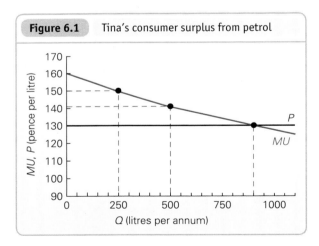

Figure 6.1 Tina's consumer surplus from petrol

Definitions

Total consumer surplus The excess of a person's total utility from the consumption of a good (*TU*) over the amount that person spends on it (*TE*): *TCS = TU – TE*.

Rational consumer behaviour The attempt to maximise total consumer surplus.

If she were to use just a few litres per year, she would use them for very important journeys for which no convenient alternative exists. For such trips she may be prepared to pay up to 160p per litre. For the first few litres, then, she is getting a marginal utility of around 160p per litre, and hence a marginal consumer surplus of around 30p (i.e. 160p – 130p).

By the time her annual purchase is around 250 litres, she would only be prepared to pay around 150p for additional litres. The additional journeys, although still important, would be less vital. Perhaps these are journeys where she could have taken public transport, albeit at some inconvenience. Her marginal consumer surplus at 250 litres is 20p (i.e. 150p – 130p).

Gradually additional litres give less and less additional utility as fewer and fewer important journeys are undertaken. The 500th litre yields 141p worth of extra utility. Marginal consumer surplus is now 11p (i.e. 141p – 130p).

KI 15
p 83

By the time she gets to the 900th litre, Tina's marginal utility has fallen to 130p. There is no additional consumer surplus to be gained. Her total consumer surplus is at a maximum. She thus buys 900 litres, where $P = MU$.

Her total consumer surplus is the sum of all the marginal consumer surpluses: the sum of all the 900 vertical lines between the price and the *MU* curve. This is represented by the total *area* between the dashed *P* line and the *MU* curve.

This analysis can be expressed in general terms. In Figure 6.2, if the price of a commodity is P_1, the consumer will consume Q_1. The person's total expenditure (*TE*) is P_1Q_1, shown by area 1. Total utility (*TU*) is the area under the marginal utility curve: i.e. areas 1 + 2. Total consumer surplus (*TU – TE*) is shown by area 2.

We can now state the general rule for maximising total consumer surplus. If $MU > P$ people should buy more. As they do so, however, *MU* will fall (diminishing marginal utility). People should stop buying more when *MU* has fallen to equal *P*. At that point, total consumer surplus is maximised.

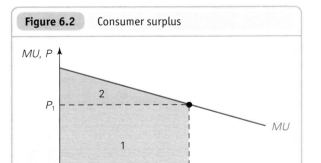

Figure 6.2 Consumer surplus

Marginal utility and the demand curve for a good

An individual's demand curve

Individual people's demand curves for any good will be the same as their marginal utility curve for that good, measured in terms of money.

This is demonstrated in Figure 6.3, which shows the marginal utility curve for a particular person and a particular good. If the price of the good were P_1, the person would consume Q_1: where $MU = P_1$. Thus point a would be one point on that person's demand curve. If the price fell to P_2, consumption would rise to Q_2, since this is where $MU = P_2$. Thus point b is a second point on the demand curve. Likewise if price fell to P_3, Q_3 would be consumed. Point c is a third point on the demand curve.

Thus as long as individuals seek to maximise consumer surplus and hence consume where $P = MU$, their demand curve will be along the same line as their marginal utility curve.

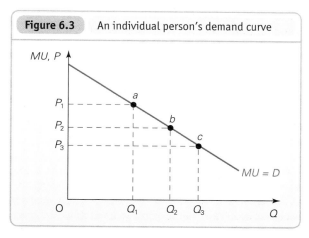

Figure 6.3 An individual person's demand curve

The market demand curve

The market demand curve will simply be the (horizontal) sum of all individuals' demand curves and hence MU curves.

BOX 6.1   **THE MARGINAL UTILITY REVOLUTION: JEVONS, MENGER, WALRAS**

Solving the diamonds–water paradox

What determines the market value of a good? We already know the answer: demand and supply. So if we find out what determines the position of the demand and supply curves, we will at the same time be finding out what determines a good's market value.

This might seem obvious. Yet for years economists puzzled over just what determines a good's value.

Some economists like Karl Marx and David Ricardo concentrated on the supply side. For them, value depended on the amount of resources used in producing a good. This could be further reduced to the amount of *labour* time embodied in the good. Thus, according to the *labour theory of value*, the more labour that was directly involved in producing the good, or indirectly in producing the capital equipment used to make the good, the more valuable would the good be.

Other economists looked at the demand side. But here they came across a paradox. Adam Smith in the 1760s gave the example of water and diamonds. 'How is it', he asked, 'that water which is so essential to human life, and thus has such a high "value-in-use", has such a low market value (or "value-in-exchange")? And how is it that diamonds which are relatively so trivial have such a high market value?' The answer to this paradox had to wait over a hundred years until the marginal utility revolution of the 1870s. William Stanley Jevons (1835–82) in England, Carl Menger (1840–1921) in Austria, and Leon Walras (1834–1910) in Switzerland all independently claimed that the source of the market value of a good was its *marginal* utility, not its *total* utility.

This was the solution to the diamonds–water paradox. Water, being so essential, has a high total utility: a high 'value in use'. But for most of us, given that we consume so much already, it has a very low marginal utility. Do you leave the cold tap running when you clean your teeth? If you do, it shows just how trivial water is to you *at the margin*. Diamonds, on the other hand, although they have a much

lower total utility, have a much higher marginal utility. There are so few diamonds in the world, and thus people have so few of them, that they are very valuable at the margin. If, however, a new technique were to be discovered of producing diamonds cheaply from coal, their market value would fall rapidly. As people had more of them, so their marginal utility would rapidly diminish.

Marginal utility still only gives the demand side of the story. The reason why the marginal utility of water is so low is that *supply* is so plentiful. Water is very expensive in Saudi Arabia! In other words, the full explanation of value must take into account both demand *and* supply.

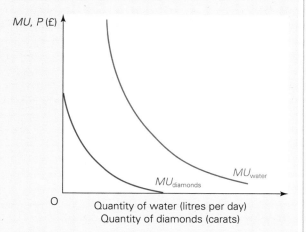

The diagram illustrates a person's MU curves of water and diamonds. Assume that diamonds are more expensive than water. Show how the MU of diamonds will be greater than the MU of water. Show also how the TU of diamonds will be less than the TU of water. (Remember: TU is the area under the MU curve.)

The shape of the demand curve. The price elasticity of demand will reflect the rate at which *MU* diminishes. If there are close substitutes for a good, it is likely to have an elastic demand, and its *MU* will diminish slowly as consumption increases. The reason is that increased consumption of this product will be accompanied by *decreased* consumption of the alternative product(s). Since total consumption of this product *plus* the alternatives has increased only slightly (if at all), the marginal utility will fall only slowly.

For example, the demand for a given brand of petrol is likely to have a fairly high price elasticity, since other brands are substitutes. If there is a cut in the price of Texaco petrol (assuming the prices of other brands stay constant), consumption of Texaco will increase a lot. The *MU* of Texaco petrol will fall slowly, since people consume less of other brands. Petrol consumption *in total* may be only slightly greater and hence the *MU* of petrol only slightly lower.

Shifts in the demand curve. How do *shifts* in demand relate to marginal utility? For example, how would the marginal utility of (and hence demand for) margarine be affected by a rise in the price of butter? The higher price of butter would cause less butter to be consumed. This would increase the marginal utility of margarine, since if people are using less butter, their desire for margarine is higher. The *MU* curve (and hence the demand curve) for margarine thus shifts to the right.

Weaknesses of the one-commodity version of marginal utility theory

A change in the consumption of one good will affect the marginal utility of substitute and complementary goods. It will also affect the amount of income left over to be spent on other goods. Thus a more satisfactory explanation of demand would involve an analysis of choices between goods, rather than looking at one good in isolation. (We examine such choices in section 6.3.)

Nevertheless, the assumptions of diminishing marginal utility and of the consumer making rational choices by considering whether it is 'worth' paying the price being charged are quite realistic assumptions about consumer behaviour. It is important for businesses to realise that the demand for their product tends to reflect consumers' perceptions of the *marginal* utility they expect to gain, rather than the *total* utility.

6.2 DEMAND UNDER CONDITIONS OF RISK AND UNCERTAINTY

The problem of imperfect information

So far we have assumed that when people buy goods and services, they know exactly what price they will pay and how much utility they will gain. In many cases this is a reasonable assumption. When you buy a bar of chocolate, you clearly do know how much you are paying for it and have a very good idea how much you will like it. But what about a DVD player, or a car, or a washing machine, or any other **consumer durable**? In each of these cases you are buying something that will last you a long time, and the further into the future you look, the less certain you will be of its costs and benefits to you.

Take the case of a washing machine costing you £400. If you pay cash, your immediate outlay involves no uncertainty: it is £400. But washing machines can break down. In two years' time you could find yourself with a repair bill of £100. This cannot be predicted and yet it is a price you will have to pay, just like the original £400. In other words, when you buy the washing machine, you are uncertain as to the full 'price' it will entail over its lifetime.

Not only are the costs of the washing machine uncertain, so too are the benefits. You might have been attracted to buy it in the first place by the manufacturer's glossy brochure, or by the look of it, or by adverts on TV, in magazines, etc. When you have used it for a while, however, you will probably discover things you had not anticipated. The spin dryer does not get your clothes as dry as you had hoped; it is noisy; it leaks; the door sticks; and so on.

Buying consumer durables thus involves uncertainty. So too does the purchase of assets, whether a physical asset such as a house or financial assets such as shares. In the case of assets, the uncertainty is over their future *price*, which you cannot know for certain.

Attitudes towards risk and uncertainty

So how will uncertainty affect people's behaviour? The answer is that it depends on their attitudes towards taking a gamble. To examine these attitudes let us assume that a person does at least know the *odds* of the gamble. In other words, the person is operating under conditions of *risk* rather than *uncertainty*.

To illustrate different attitudes towards risk, consider the case of gambling that a particular number will come up on the throw of a dice. There is a one in six chance of this happening. Would you gamble? It depends on what odds you were offered and on your attitude to risk.

Odds can be of three types. They can be *favourable* odds. This is where on average you will gain. If, for example, you

Definition

Consumer durable A consumer good that lasts a period of time, during which the consumer can continue gaining utility from it.

were offered odds of 10 to 1 on the throw of a dice, then for a £1 bet you would get nothing if you lost, but you would get £10 if your number came up. Since your number should come up on average one time in every six, on average you will gain. The longer you go on playing, the more money you are likely to win. If the odds were 6 to 1, they would be *fair* odds. On average you would break even. If, however, they were less than 6 to 1, they would be described as *unfavourable*. On average you would lose.

There are three possible categories of attitude towards risk.

- *Risk neutral*. This is where a person will take a gamble if the odds are favourable; not take a gamble if the odds are unfavourable; and be indifferent about taking a gamble if the odds are fair.
- *Risk loving*. This is where a person is prepared to take a gamble even if the odds are unfavourable. The more risk loving a person is, the worse the odds he or she will be prepared to accept.
- *Risk averse*. This is where a person may not be prepared to take a gamble even if the odds are favourable. The more risk averse the person is, the better would have to be the odds before he or she could be enticed to take a gamble. Few people are *totally risk averse* and thus totally unwilling to take a gamble. If I offered people a bet on the toss of a coin such that tails they pay me 10p and heads I pay them £100, few would refuse (unless on moral grounds).

Diminishing marginal utility of income and attitudes towards risk taking

Avid gamblers may be risk lovers. People who spend hours in the betting shop or at the race track may enjoy the risks, knowing that there is always the chance that they might win. On average, however, such people will lose. After all, the bookmakers have to take their cut and thus the odds are generally unfavourable.

Most people, however, for most of the time are risk averters. We prefer to avoid insecurity. But why? Is there a simple reason for this? Economists use marginal utility analysis to explain why.

Pause for thought

Which gamble would you be more likely to accept, a 60:40 chance of gaining or losing £10 000, or a 40:60 chance of gaining or losing £1? Explain why.

They argue that the gain in utility to people from an extra £100 is less than the loss of utility from forgoing £100. Imagine your own position. You have probably adjusted your standard of living to your income (or are trying to!). If you unexpectedly gained £100, that would be very nice:

you could buy some new clothes or have a weekend away. But if you lost £100, it could be very hard indeed. You might have very serious difficulties in making ends meet. Thus if you were offered the gamble of a 50:50 chance of winning or losing £100, you would probably decline the gamble.

This risk-averting behaviour accords with the principle of *diminishing marginal utility*. Up to now in this chapter we have been focusing on the utility from the consumption of individual goods: Tracey and her cups of tea; Darren and his packets of crisps. In the case of each individual good, the more we consume, the less satisfaction we gain from each additional unit: the marginal utility falls. But the same principle applies if we look at our *total* consumption. The higher our level of total consumption, the less additional satisfaction will be gained from each additional £1 spent. What we are saying here is that there is a **diminishing marginal utility of income**. The more you earn, the lower will be the utility from each *extra* £1. If people on low incomes earn an extra £100, they will feel a lot better off: the marginal utility they will get from that income will be very high. If rich people earn an extra £100, however, their gain in utility will be less.

Why, then, does a diminishing marginal utility of income make us risk averters? The answer is illustrated in Figure 6.4, which shows the *total* utility you get from your income.

The slope of this curve gives the *marginal* utility of your income. As the marginal utility of income diminishes, so the curve gets flatter. A rise in income from £5000 to £10 000 will cause a movement along the curve from point *a* to point *b*. Total utility rises from U_1 to U_2. A similar rise in income from £10 000 to £15 000, however, will lead to a move from point *b* to point *c*, and hence a *smaller* rise in total utility from U_2 to U_3.

Now assume that your income is £10 000 and you are offered a chance of gambling £5000 of it. You are offered the fair odds of a 50:50 chance of gaining an extra £5000 (i.e. doubling it) or losing it. Effectively, then, you have an equal chance of your income rising to £15 000 or falling to £5000.

At an income of £10 000, your total utility is U_2. If your gamble pays off and as a result your income rises to £15 000, your total utility will rise to U_3. If it does not pay off, you will be left with only £5000 and a utility of U_1. Given that you have a 50:50 chance of winning, your *average* expected utility will be midway between U_1 and U_3 i.e. $= \dfrac{U_1 + U_3}{2} = U_4$. But this is the utility that would be gained from an income of £8000. Given that you would

Definition

Diminishing marginal utility of income Where each additional pound earned yields less additional utility.

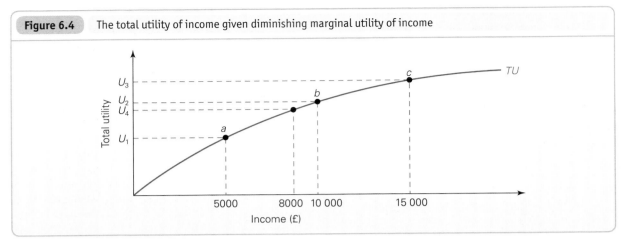

Figure 6.4   The total utility of income given diminishing marginal utility of income

prefer U_2 to U_4 you will choose not to take the gamble. Thus risk aversion is part of rational utility-maximising behaviour.

On most occasions we will not know the odds of taking a gamble. In other words, we will be operating under conditions of *uncertainty*. This could make us very cautious indeed. The more pessimistic we are, the more cautious we will be.

Insurance: a way of removing risks

Insurance is the opposite of gambling. It takes the risk away. If, for example, you risk losing your job if you are injured, you can remove the risk of loss of income by taking out an appropriate insurance policy.

Given that people are risk averters, they will be prepared to pay the premiums even though they give them 'unfair odds'. The total premiums paid to insurance companies will be *more* than the amount the insurance companies pay out: that is, after all, how the companies make a profit.

But does this mean that the insurance companies are less risk averse than their customers? Why is it that the insurance companies are prepared to shoulder the risks that their customers were not? The answer is that the insurance company is able to ***spread its risks***.

The spreading of risks

If there is a one in a hundred chance of your house burning down each year, although it is only a small chance it would be so disastrous that you are simply not prepared to take the risk. You thus take out house insurance and are prepared to pay a premium of *more than* 1 per cent (one in a hundred).

The insurance company, however, is not just insuring you. It is insuring many others at the same time. If your house burns down, there will be approximately 99 others that do not. The premiums the insurance company has collected will be more than enough to cover its payments. The more houses it insures, the smaller will be the variation in the proportion that actually burn down each year.

This is an application of the **law of large numbers**. What is unpredictable for an individual becomes highly predictable in the mass. The more people the insurance company insures, the more predictable is the total outcome.

What is more, the insurance company will be in a position to estimate just what the risks are. It can thus work out what premiums it must charge in order to make a profit. With individuals, however, the precise risk is rarely known. Do you know your chances of living to 70? Almost certainly you do not. But a life assurance company will know precisely the chances of an average person of your age, sex and occupation living to 70! It will have the statistical data to show this. In other words, an insurance company will be able to convert your *uncertainty* into their *risk*.

The spreading of risks does not just require that there should be a large number of policies. It also requires that the risks should be **independent**. If any insurance company insured 1000 houses *all in the same neighbourhood*, and then there were a major fire in the area, the claims would be enormous. The risks of fire were not independent. The company would, in fact, have been taking a gamble on a single event. If, however, it provides fire insurance for houses scattered all over the country, the risks *are* independent.

Definitions

Spreading risks (for an insurance company) The more policies an insurance company issues and the more independent the risks of claims from these policies are, the more predictable will be the number of claims.

Law of large numbers The larger the number of events of a particular type, the more predictable will be their average outcome.

Independent risks Where two risky events are unconnected. The occurrence of one will not affect the likelihood of the occurrence of the other.

KI 14
p 74

Another way in which insurance companies can spread their risks is by *diversification*. The more types of insurance a company offers (car, house, life, health, etc.), the greater is likely to be the independence of the risks.

Problems for unwary insurance companies

There are two main issues that companies who offer insurance need to confront – *adverse selection* and *moral hazard*.

Adverse selection

This is where the people most likely to take out insurance are those who have the highest risk. It arises because consumers of insurance have more information about their situation than the insurance companies. Unless the companies screen applicants, individuals with higher risk will select to take out insurance policies and this will have adverse effects on the average person.

For example, suppose that a company offers medical insurance. It surveys the population and works out that the average person requires £200 of treatment per year. The company thus sets the premium at £250 (the extra £50 to cover its costs and provide a profit). But it is probable that the people most likely to take out the insurance are those most likely to fall sick: those who have been ill before, those whose families have a history of illness, those in jobs that are hazardous to health, etc. These people on average may require £500 of treatment per year. The insurance company would soon make a loss.

But cannot the company then simply raise premiums to £550 or £600? It can, but the problem is that it will thereby be depriving the person of *average* health of reasonably priced insurance.

> ## Pause for thought
>
> *What details does an insurance company require to know before it will insure a person to drive a car?*

The answer is for the company to discriminate more carefully between people. You may have to fill out a questionnaire so that the company can assess your own particular risk and set an appropriate premium. There may need to be legal penalties for people caught lying!

 KEY IDEA 16

Adverse selection. Where information is imperfect, high-risk groups will be attracted to profitable market opportunities to the disadvantage of the average buyer (or seller). In the context of insurance, it refers to those who are most likely to take out insurance posing the greatest risks to the insurer.

Moral hazard

This occurs because the insurance company does not have perfect information about the behaviour of policy holders once they have taken out insurance. Thus, having insurance can make an individual less careful and increases their risk to the company.

For example, if your bicycle is insured against theft, you may be less concerned to go through the hassle of chaining it up each time you leave it.

Again, if insurance companies work out risks by looking at the *total* number of bicycle thefts, these figures will understate the risks to the company because they will include thefts from *uninsured* people who are likely to be more careful.

> ## Pause for thought
>
> *How will the following reduce the moral hazard problem?*
>
> *(a) A no-claims bonus.*
> *(b) Your having to pay the first so many pounds of any claim.*
> *(c) Offering lower premiums to those less likely to claim (e.g. lower house contents premiums for those with burglar alarms).*

 KEY IDEA 17

Moral hazard. Following a deal, there is an increased likelihood that one party will engage in problematic (immoral and hazardous) behaviour to the detriment of another. In the context of insurance, it refers to people taking more risks when they have insurance.

The problem of moral hazard occurs in many other walks of life. A good example is that of debt. If someone else is willing to pay your debts (e.g. your parents) it is likely to make you less careful in your spending! This argument has been used by some rich countries for not cancelling the debts of poor countries. See Box 6.2 for another example.

> ## Definitions
>
> **Diversification** Where a firm expands into new types of business.
>
> **Adverse selection** Where information is imperfect, high-risk groups will be attracted to profitable market opportunities to the disadvantage of the average buyer (or seller).
>
> **Moral hazard** Following a deal, there is an increased likelihood that one party will engage in problematic (immoral and hazardous) behaviour to the detriment of another.

BOX 6.2 ROGUE TRADERS

Buyer beware!

Markets are usually an efficient way of letting buyers and sellers exchange goods and services. However, this does not stop consumers making complaints about the quality of the goods or services they receive.

It is impossible to get a true measure of customer dissatisfaction because aggrieved consumers do not always complain and data are collected by a number of separate agencies. Particular sectors though seem to be more vulnerable to 'rogue traders' than others.

Ombudsman Services is an organisation that provides independent dispute resolution for the communications, energy, property and copyright industries. They deal with more than a quarter of a million queries and resolve around 25 000 formal complaints each year.

In 2011/12 Ombudsman Services accepted 15 571 complaints in the area of communications (landlines, mobiles, internet providers etc.), up from 13 165 in 2010/11. These complaints cover a broad range of areas. The largest number of queries related to the standard of customer service, followed by disputes over charges and the quality of service (see the table).

Around one-third of these complaints were resolved informally, with mutually acceptable settlements being reached. However, two-thirds of the complaints required a formal investigation; of these, 68 per cent necessitated a financial settlement to acknowledge shortfalls in customer service and a further 20 per cent required a non-financial solution (such as a apology or change in service provision).

Queries responded to by Ombudsman Services in the communications sector 2011/12

	Percentage of queries
Consumer service	38
Disputed charges	19
Service	17
Contract issues	15
Billing	7
Equipment	3
Other	1

Additional data from Ombudsman Services show that a large number of complaints were received in relation to the property sector (with the majority relating to the quality of surveys and valuations) and energy sector (mainly in relation to billing).

 Which other sectors would you expect to have a large number of customer complaints? Why?

Consumer complaints are also of concern to cross-border sales as the growth of buying over the Internet has blossomed in recent times. Data gathered by econsumer.gov covering 21 countries show that the largest proportion of complaints relating to e-commerce transactions concern clothing, catalogue sales, computing, lotteries, Internet auction sites, Internet access services, credit cards, banking, telephones and travel. Interestingly, only 706 of the 17 729 complaints were reported by UK consumers, while 1832 complaints were against UK online retailers!

The chart shows the types of consumer complaints about e-commerce. The percentages are based on the 25 513 e-consumer law violations during 2011, not the total number of complaints; one complaint may have multiple law violations.

Adverse selection and moral hazard

But why does a market, which you would think would respond to consumer wishes, give rise to consumer complaints? Why is it that rogue traders can continue in business? The answer can be found in the concepts of adverse selection and moral hazard. In both cases, the problem is essentially one of 'information asymmetries' and is an example of the 'principal–agent problem'. The buyer (the 'principal') has poorer information about the product than the agent (the 'seller').

Information asymmetries. Complaints by consumers are likely to be few if the product is fairly simple and information about the exchange process is publicly available. For example, if I buy apples from a market trader but subsequently return them because some are damaged, they are likely to exchange the apples, or offer a full refund, because failure to do so would lead to the trader's sales falling as information gets out that they sell poor-quality fruit. Here information asymmetries are minimal.

However, where the product is more complex, perhaps with consumers making large outlays, and information is more private, the situation can be very different. The greater the information 'gap' between sellers and consumers, the greater the scope for deception and fraud and the more likely are rogue traders to thrive. In these situations the number of consumer complaints increases.

Consider the sale of a conservatory, a large extension to a house usually comprising a number of various building products, including double-glazed windows and doors. A product such as this involves an expensive outlay for consumers, but they may have very limited information about the price of materials and labour, as well as the method of building a conservatory.

Assume that there is a standard-sized conservatory and that a high-quality seller would be prepared to supply this product at a price of £10 000. Such a price would reflect the quality of their work and would keep them in the business of selling high-quality products. On the other hand, assume that a poor-quality supplier, a 'rogue trader', could provide this conservatory at £5000.

Given information asymmetry, let us assume that consumers are not aware of who is a high-quality or low-quality seller. Assume, however, that they believe that 90 per cent of traders sell the high-quality product and 10 per cent are 'rogue traders'. This means that the 'risk-neutral' consumer will be willing to pay £9500, i.e. (£10 000 × 0.9) + (£5000 × 0.1), for a standard-sized conservatory.

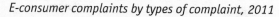

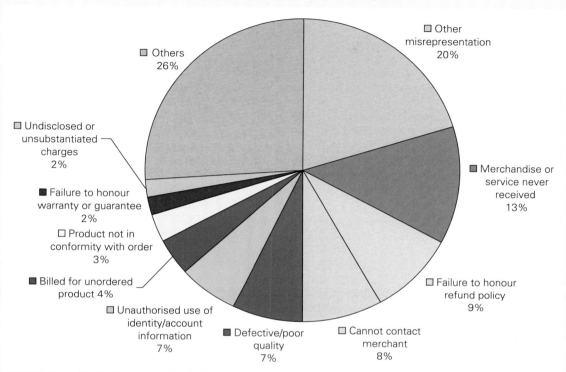

E-consumer complaints by types of complaint, 2011

Source: www.econsumer.gov

Adverse selection. This price of £9500, however, is not enough to cover the costs of high-quality sellers, and so they will not want to offer their services to build high-quality conservatories. On the other hand, 'rogue traders' will find this price very profitable and it will attract a higher than normal number of such sellers into the market. Of course, if consumers know that the only sellers in the market are likely to be 'rogue traders', they will not buy conservatories and the market will collapse.

The problem just described is an example of adverse selection. In this case a group of sellers ('rogue traders') have been attracted to the market by prices considerably greater than their costs even before any transactions have taken place.

Moral hazard. Of course, the market in conservatories is thriving. Consumers do try to find out about sellers before they buy and most consumers get a good product. However, 'rogue traders' also make sales.

Once a contract has been signed, the problem of moral hazard occurs. In our example, the rogue trader might initially agree to supply and install the conservatory to meet particular high standards of quality for a particular price. However, unless the buyer has full information about the construction of conservatories or can keep a constant watch over the work, defective materials or poor-quality workmanship may be supplied. But the buyer will not know this until a later date when problems start to appear with the conservatory!

Moral hazard results because the seller has acted inappropriately (immorally) and to the detriment of the buyer. The 'hazard' arises because of imperfect information on the part of the consumer. Rogue traders are tempted to supply an inferior product, believing that they can get away with it.

Usually, the process of law would work in favour of the buyer because a contract had been established, but in many cases involving 'rogue traders' the business has been declared bankrupt or the costs to buyers of pursuing a legal case are too great.

Consider the customer complaints in the communications sector (telephones, Internet, etc.) received by Ombudsman Services (see table). Use the concepts of adverse selection and moral hazard to explain why this sector may be predisposed to a high number of complaints.

Solutions

So how can sellers signal to buyers that they offer high-quality products? And how can consumers trust this information? A number of methods exist.

Establishing a reputation. A single firm can establish a reputation for selling high-quality goods, usually over a number of years, or perhaps they have created a valued brand name through advertising. Alternatively, firms can offer guarantees and warranties on their products, although a ten-year guarantee on the building work associated with a conservatory is of no use if the firm has gone bankrupt!

Trade associations and other third parties. Firms can also band together collectively and establish a trade association. Examples include the Federation of Master Builders and the Association of British Travel Agents (ABTA). Firms that belong to a trade association have benefits that can extend beyond that of acting alone. For example, if one firm provides a poor-quality product, then consumers may get compensation via the association. ABTA, for example, guarantees to make sure customers will complete their holiday, or obtain a refund, if they have purchased it from a member that has gone bankrupt.

Trade associations are a means by which firms can demonstrate that they regulate themselves rather than have governments impose rules on them.

Sometimes third parties can help firms to signal high quality. The online auction site eBay, for example, has provided a feedback system for buyers and sellers so they can register their happiness or otherwise with sales. Likewise, the Office of Fair Trading, under the auspices of the Enterprise Act (2002), has created an Approved Codes of Practice scheme

whereby trade associations and their members will guarantee that customers will receive high-quality service. Successful associations can display an OFT Approved Codes logo.

Government intervention. On the whole, government does not like to intervene in particular industries, preferring a sector to regulate itself. However, in the case of the financial services industry, the government has directly intervened because the impact of the industry on consumers in recent times has been widespread and financially devastating. Following a number of financial scandals, including the mis-selling of pensions and mortgages, the government replaced ineffective self-regulation in 2000 with the Financial Services Authority, an independent industry regulator with statutory powers, whose board is appointed by and accountable to the Treasury. In this instance the level of product complexity and information asymmetry between buyer and seller was viewed to be too great for the industry to control itself.

 What are the disadvantages of trade associations?

6.3 THE CHARACTERISTICS APPROACH TO ANALYSING CONSUMER DEMAND

This section is optional. You may skip straight to the next chapter if you prefer.

To get a better understanding of consumer demand, we need to analyse how consumers choose *between* products (as we concluded in section 6.1). In other words, we must look at products, not in isolation, but in relation to other products. Any firm wanting to understand the basis on which consumers demand its products will want to know why they might choose *its* product rather than those of its rivals. A car manufacturer will want to know why consumers might choose one of its models rather than those of its competitors.

 Such choices depend not only on price but on the characteristics of the products. If you were buying a car, in addition to its price you would consider features such as style, performance, comfort, reliability, durability, fuel economy, safety and various added features (such as air conditioning, stereo system, air bags, electric windows, etc.). Car manufacturers will thus design their cars to make them as attractive as possible to consumers, relative to the cost of manufacture. In fact, most firms will constantly try to find ways of improving their products to make them more appealing to consumers.

 What we are saying here is that consumers derive utility from the various characteristics that a product possesses. To understand choices, then, we need to look at the attributes of different products and how these influence consumer choices between them. ***Characteristics theory*** (sometimes

called 'attributes theory') was developed by the economist Kelvin Lancaster[1] in the mid-1960s to analyse such choices and to relate them to the demand for a product.

Characteristics theory is based on four key assumptions:

■ All products possess various characteristics.
■ Different brands possess them in different proportions.
■ The characteristics are measurable: they are 'objective'.
■ The characteristics, along with price and consumers' incomes, determine consumer choice.

Identifying and plotting products' characteristics

Let us take a simple case of a product where consumers base their choice between brands on price and just two characteristics. For example, assume that consumers choose

> ### Definition
>
> **Characteristics (or attributes) theory** The theory that demonstrates how consumer choice between different varieties of a product depends on the characteristics of these varieties, along with prices of the different varieties, the consumer's budget and the consumer's tastes.

---

[1] K. Lancaster, 'A new approach to consumer theory', *Journal of Political Economy*, 74 (April 1966), pp. 132–57.

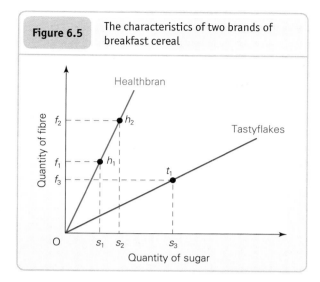

Figure 6.5 The characteristics of two brands of breakfast cereal

between different brands of breakfast cereal on the basis of taste and health-giving properties. To keep the analysis simple, let us assume that taste is related to the amount of sugar in the cereal and that health-giving properties are related to the amount of fibre.

Plotting the characteristics of different brands

The combinations of these two characteristics, sugar and fibre, can be measured on a diagram. In Figure 6.5, the quantity of sugar is measured on the horizontal axis and the quantity of fibre on the vertical axis. One brand, Healthbran, contains a lot of fibre, but only a little sugar. Another, Tastyflakes, contains a lot of sugar, but only a little fibre.

The ratio of the two attributes, fibre and sugar, in each of the two brands is given by the slope of the two rays out from the origin. Thus by consuming a certain amount of Healthbran, given by point h_1 on the Healthbran ray, the consumer is getting f_1 of fibre and s_1 of sugar. The consumption of more Healthbran is shown by a movement up the ray, say to h_2. At this point the consumer gets f_2 of fibre and s_2 of sugar. Notice that the ratio of fibre to sugar is the same in both cases. The ratio is given by f_1/s_1 (= f_2/s_2), which is simply the slope of the Healthbran ray.

The consumer of Tastyflakes can get relatively more sugar, but less fibre. Thus consumption at point t_1 gives s_3 of sugar, but only f_3 of fibre. The ratio of fibre to sugar for Tastyflakes is given by the slope of its ray, which is f_3/s_3.

Any number of rays can be put on the diagram, each one representing a particular brand. In each case, the ratio of fibre to sugar is given by the slope of the ray.

Changes in a product's characteristics. If a firm decides to change the mix of characteristics of a product, the slope of the ray will change. Thus if Healthbran were made sweeter, its ray would become shallower.

The budget constraint

The amount that a consumer buys of a brand will depend in part on the consumer's budget and on the price of the product. Assume that, given the current price of Healthbran, Jane's budget for breakfast cereals allows her to buy at h_1 per month: in other words, the amount of Healthbran that gives f_1 of fibre and s_1 of sugar. (This assumes that she only buys Healthbran and not some other brand too.)

A change in the budget. If she allocates more of her income to buying breakfast cereal, and sticks with Healthbran, she would move up the ray: say, to h_2. In other words, by buying more Healthbran, she would be buying more fibre and more sugar. Similarly, a reduction in expenditure on a product would be represented by a movement down its ray.

A change in price. If a product rises in price and the budget allocated to it remains the same, less will be purchased. There will be a movement down its ray.

The efficiency frontier

In practice, many consumers will buy a mixture of brands. Some days you may prefer one type of breakfast cereal, some days you may prefer another type. People get fed up with consuming too much of one brand or variety: they experience diminishing marginal utility from that particular mix of characteristics. You may allocate a certain amount of money for a summer holiday each year, but you may well want to go to a different place each year, since each place has a different mix of characteristics.

Assume that, given her current budget for breakfast cereals, the prices of Healthbran and Tastyflakes allow Jane to buy at either point *a* or point *b* in Figure 6.6. By switching completely from Healthbran to Tastyflakes, her consumption of fibre would go down from f_1 to f_2, and her consumption of sugar would go up from s_1 to s_2. She could, however, spend part of her budget on Healthbran and part on Tastyflakes. In fact, she could consume anywhere along the straight line joining points *a* and *b*. This line is known

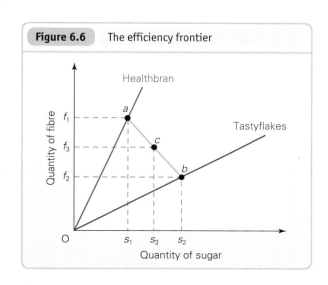

Figure 6.6 The efficiency frontier

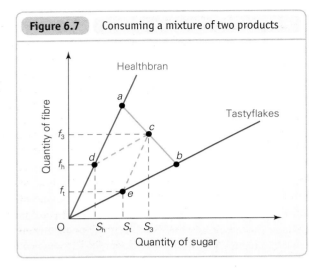

Figure 6.7 Consuming a mixture of two products

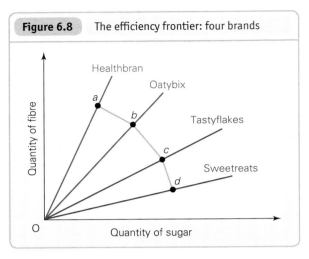

Figure 6.8 The efficiency frontier: four brands

as the *efficiency frontier*. For example, by buying some of each brand, she could consume at point *c*, giving her f_3 of fibre and s_3 of sugar.

If she did consume at point *c*, how much of the two characteristics would she get from each of the two brands? This is shown in Figure 6.7 by drawing two lines from point *c*, each one parallel to one of the two rays. Consumption of the two brands takes place at points *d* and *e* respectively, giving her f_h units of fibre and s_h units of sugar from Healthbran, and f_t units of fibre and s_t units of sugar from Tastyflakes. The total amount of fibre and sugar from the two brands will be f_3 (= f_h + f_t) and s_3 (= s_h + s_t).[2]

It is easily possible to show an efficiency frontier between several brands, each with their own particular blend of characteristics. This is illustrated in Figure 6.8, which shows the case of four breakfast cereals, each with different combinations of fibre and sugar.

Any of the four points through which the efficiency frontier passes can change if the price of that brand changes. So if Oatybix went up in price, point *b* would move down the Oatybix ray, thereby altering the shape of the efficiency frontier.

If any of the brands changed their mix of characteristics, then the respective ray would pivot. If the consumer's budget changed, then the whole efficiency frontier would move parallel up or down all the rays.

The optimum level of consumption

Indifference curves

We have seen that by switching between brands, consumers can obtain different mixtures of characteristics. But what, for any given consumer, is the optimum mixture? This can

be shown by examining a consumer's preferences, and the way we do this is to construct **indifference curves**. This is illustrated in Figure 6.9, which shows five indifference curves, labelled I_1 to I_5.

An indifference curve shows all the different combinations of the two characteristics that yield an equal amount of satisfaction or utility. Thus any combination of characteristics along curve I_1 represents the same given level of utility. The consumer is, therefore, 'indifferent' between all points along curve I_1. Although the actual level

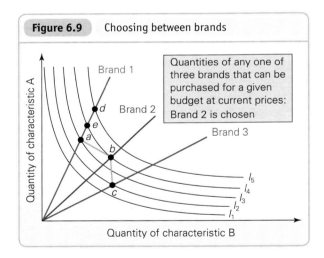

Figure 6.9 Choosing between brands

Definitions

Efficiency frontier A line showing the maximum attainable combinations of two characteristics for a given budget. These characteristics can be obtained by consuming one or a mixture of two brands or varieties of a product.

Indifference curve A line showing all those combinations of two characteristics of a good between which a consumer is indifferent: i.e. those combinations that give a particular level of utility.

---

[2] This follows because of the shape of the parallelogram O*dce*. Being a parallelogram makes the distance f_3–f_h equal to f_t–O. Thus adding f_h and f_t gives f_3, which must correspond to point *c*. Similarly the distance s_3–s_t must equal s_h–O. Thus adding s_h and s_t gives s_3, which also must correspond to point *c*.

of utility is not measured in the diagram, the further out the curve, the higher the level of utility. Thus all points on curve I_5 are preferred to all points along curve I_4, and all points along curve I_4 are preferred to all points along curve I_3, and so on. In fact, indifference curves are rather like contours on a map. Each contour represents all points on the ground that are a particular height above sea level. You can have as many contours as you like on the map, depending at what interval you draw them: 100 metre, 25 metre, 10 metre, or whatever. Similarly you could have as many indifference curves as you like on an **indifference map**. In Figure 6.9, we have drawn just five such curves, as that is all that is necessary to illustrate consumer choice, in this example.

The shape of indifference curves. Indifference curves are drawn as downward sloping. The reason is that if consumers get less of one characteristic, they would need more of the other to compensate, if their total level of utility was to stay the same. Take the case of washing powder. For any given expenditure, you would only be prepared to give up a certain amount of one characteristic, say whiteness, if you got more of another characteristic, such as softness.

Notice that the indifference curves are not drawn as straight lines. They are bowed in towards the origin. The reason is that people generally are willing to give up less and less of one characteristic for each additional unit of another. For example, if you were buying a new PC, you might be prepared to give up some RAM to get extra hard disk space, but for each extra GB of disk space you would probably be prepared to give up less and less RAM. We call this a **diminishing marginal rate of substitution** between the two characteristics. The reason is that you get diminishing marginal utility from any characteristic the more of it you consume, and are thus prepared to give up less and less of another characteristic (whose marginal utility rises as you have less of it).

KI 15
p 83

KI 4
p 22

Indifference curves for different consumers. Different consumers will have different indifference maps. The indifference map in Figure 6.9 is drawn for a particular consumer, say James. If another consumer, Henry, gets relatively more satisfaction from characteristic B than does James, Henry's indifference curves would be steeper. In other words, he would be prepared to give up more units of A to get a certain amount of B than would James.

The optimum combination of characteristics

We are now in a position to see how a 'rational' consumer would choose between brands. Figure 6.9 shows the rays for three brands of a product, with, at given prices, the efficiency frontier passing through points *a*, *b* and *c*. The consumer would choose to consume Brand 2, since point *b* is on a higher indifference curve than point *a* (Brand 1), which in turn is on a higher indifference curve than point *c* (Brand 3).

Sometimes the consumer will choose to purchase a mixture of brands. This is shown in Figure 6.10, which takes the simple case of just two brands in the market. By consuming at point *a* (i.e. a combination of point *b* on the Brand 1 ray and point *c* on the Brand 2 ray), the consumer is on a higher indifference curve than by consuming only Brand 1 (point *d*) or Brand 2 (point *e*).

Response to changes

We can now show how consumers would respond to changes in price, income, product characteristics and tastes.

Changes in price

Referring back to Figure 6.9, if the price of a brand changes, there is a shift in the efficiency frontier, so that it crosses the ray for that brand at a different point. For example, if the price of Brand 1 fell, there would be a movement of the efficiency frontier up the Brand 1 ray from point *a*. If the price fell far enough that the efficiency frontier now passed through point *d*, the consumer would switch from consuming just Brand 2 to just Brand 1. If the price fell less

Pause for thought

Can you think of any instances where the indifference curve will not be bowed in towards the origin?

Definitions

Indifference map A diagram showing a whole set of indifference curves. The further away a particular curve is from the origin, the higher the level of utility it represents.

Diminishing marginal rate of substitution of characteristics The more a consumer gets of characteristic A and the less of characteristic B, the less and less of B the consumer will be willing to give up to get an extra unit of A.

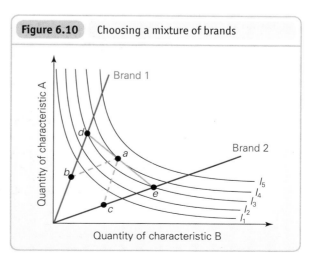

Figure 6.10 Choosing a mixture of brands

than this, so that the efficiency frontier passed through point *e*, then the consumer would buy a mixture of both brands. The optimum consumption point would lie on an indifference curve a little above I_4.

We can relate this analysis to the concept of cross-price elasticity of demand (see page 69). If two products are very close substitutes, they will have a high cross-price elasticity of demand. But what makes them close substitutes? The answer is that they are likely to have similar characteristics; their rays will have a similar slope. Even a slight rise in the price of one of them (i.e. a small movement along its ray) can lead the consumer to switch to the other. This will occur when the rays are close together: when they have a similar slope.

Changes in income

If there is a change in consumer incomes, so that people allocate a bigger budget to the product in question, then there will be a parallel movement outwards of the efficiency frontier. Whether this will involve consumers switching between brands depends on the shape of the indifference map.

Changes in the characteristics of a product (real or perceived)

If consumers believe that a brand now yields relatively more of characteristic B than A, the ray will become less steep. How far out will the efficiency point be on this new ray? This depends on the total perceived amount of the two characteristics that is obtained from the given budget spent on this brand.

To illustrate this, consider Figure 6.11. The firm producing Brand 1 changes its specifications, so that for a given budget a lot more characteristic B can be obtained and a little more characteristic A. The result is that the brand's ray shifts inwards and the efficiency frontier which originally connected points *a* and *b* now connects points *c* and *b*. In this case the consumer represented by the indifference curves shown switches consumption from Brand 2 at point *b* to Brand 1 at point *c*.

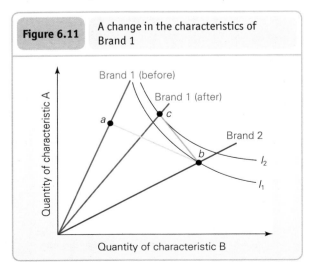

Figure 6.11   A change in the characteristics of Brand 1

If there is a proportionate increase in both characteristics (i.e. the brand has generally improved), the slope of the ray will not change. Instead, there will be a movement of the efficiency frontier outward along the ray. Graphically the effect is the same as a fall in the price of the product: more of both characteristics can be obtained for a given budget.

Changes in tastes

If consumers' tastes change, their whole indifference map will change. If characteristic B now gives more utility relative to A than before, the curves will become steeper, and the consumer is likely to choose a product which yields relatively more of characteristic B (i.e. one with a relatively shallow ray).

Clearly firms will attempt to predict such changes in tastes and will try, through product design, advertising and marketing, to shift the ray for their brand in the desired direction (downwards in the above case). They will also try to persuade consumers that the product is generally better (i.e. has more of all characteristics) and thereby move outward the point where the efficiency frontier crosses the brand's ray.

Business and the characteristics approach

Characteristics analysis can help us understand the nature of consumer choice. When we go shopping and compare one product with another, it is the differences in the features of the various brands, along with price, that determine which products we end up buying. If firms, therefore, want to compete effectively with their rivals, it is not enough to compete solely in terms of price; it is important to focus on the specifications of their product and how these compare with those of their rivals' products.

Characteristics analysis can help firms study the implications of changing their product's specifications (and of their rivals changing theirs). It also allows firms to analyse the effects of changes in their price, or their rivals' prices; the effects of changes in the budgets of various types of consumer; the effects of changes in consumer tastes; and the effects of repositioning themselves in the market.

Take the producer of Brand 1 in Figure 6.12. Clearly the firm would like to persuade consumers like the one illustrated to switch away from Brand 2 to Brand 1. It could do this by lowering its price. But a small reduction in price will have no effect on this consumer. Only when the price has fallen far enough for the efficiency frontier to rise nearly to point *d* will the consumer start switching; and only when the price has fallen further still, so that the efficiency frontier passes through a point a little above point *d*, will the consumer switch completely.

An alternative would be for the firm to reposition its product. It could introduce more of characteristic B into its product, thereby swinging the Brand 1 ray clockwise towards the Brand 2 ray. Clearly, it would have to be careful about its price too. The closer its brand became in quality to Brand 2, the more elastic would demand become, since

KI 8
p 38

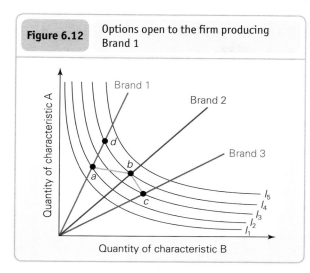

Figure 6.12 Options open to the firm producing Brand 1

Brand 1 would now be a closer substitute for Brand 2. In the extreme case of its ray becoming the same as that for Brand 2, its price would have to be low enough for the consumer to buy at or above point *b*. Depending on consumer tastes (and hence the shape of the indifference curves), it may choose to reposition its brand between the Brand 2 and Brand 3 rays. Again, a careful mix of product characteristics and price may enable it to capture a larger share of the market.

Another alternative would be for the firm to attempt to influence consumer tastes. In Figure 6.12, if it could persuade consumers to attach more value to characteristic A, the indifference curves would become shallower (i.e. less characteristic A would now be needed to give consumers a given level of utility). If the curves swung downwards enough, point *a* could be now on a higher indifference curve than point *b*. The consumer concerned would switch from Brand 2 to Brand 1. Clearly, the more consumers are influenced in this way, the more will sales of Brand 1 rise.

If a firm is thinking of launching a new product, again it will need to see how the characteristics of its product compare with those of the existing firms in the market. It will need to see where its ray would be compared with those of other firms, and whether the price it is thinking of charging would enable it to take sales off its rivals.

Limitations of characteristics analysis

Characteristics analysis, as we have seen, can help firms to understand their position in the market and the effects of changing their strategy. Nevertheless it cannot provide firms with a complete analysis of demand. There are four key limitations of the approach:

- It is sometimes difficult to identify and measure characteristics in a clear and unambiguous way. Take the look or design of a product, whether it be furniture, clothing, a painting or a car. What makes it visually appealing depends on the personal tastes of the consumer, and such tastes are virtually impossible to quantify.
- Most products have several characteristics. The analysis we have been examining, however, is limited to just two characteristics: one on each axis. By using mathematical analysis it is possible to extend the number of characteristics, but the more characteristics that are included in the analysis, the more complex it becomes.
- Indifference curves, while being a good means of understanding consumer choice in theory, have practical limitations. To draw an indifference map for just one consumer would be very difficult, given that consumers would often find it hard having to imagine a series of combinations of characteristics between which they were indifferent. To draw indifference curves for millions of consumers would be virtually impossible. At best, therefore, they can provide a rough guide to consumer choice.
- Consumer tastes change. In what ways consumer tastes will change, and how these changes will influence the shape of the indifference curves, are very difficult to predict.

Despite these problems, there are many useful insights that firms can gain from the analysis. Firms, through their market research, could gain considerable information about consumer attitudes towards their products' characteristics and thus the general shape, if not precise position, of indifference curves.

What is more, many markets divide into different *market segments* with consumers in each segment having similar tastes (and hence similar sets of indifference curves). For example, different models of car fall into different groups (such as medium-sized saloons, high-performance small cars, people carriers and small 'tall' cars), as do different types of restaurant and different types of holiday. Thus a tour operator will first identify the particular segment of the market it is aiming for (e.g. a young person's package holiday with the characteristics of guaranteed sunshine and plenty of nightlife) and then position itself in that particular market relative to its rival tour operators.

What is clear is that firms need good information about the demand for their products and to develop a careful marketing strategy. In Chapter 7 we look at how firms attempt to get information about demand, and in Chapter 8 we examine how firms set about developing, marketing and advertising their products.

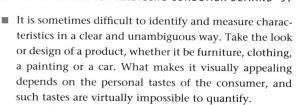

Definition

Market segment A part of a market for a product where the demand is for a particular variety of that product.

SUMMARY

1a Economists call consumer satisfaction 'utility'. Marginal utility diminishes as consumption increases. This means that total utility will rise less and less rapidly as people consume more. At a certain point, total utility will reach a maximum, at which point marginal utility will be zero. Beyond this point, total utility will fall; marginal utility will be negative.

1b Consumers will attempt to maximise their total utility. They will do this by consuming more of a good as long as its marginal utility to them (measured in terms of the price they are prepared to pay for it) exceeds its price. They will stop buying additional amounts once MU has fallen to equal the price. At this point, the consumer's surplus will be maximised.

1c An individual's demand curve lies along the same line as the individual's marginal utility curve. The market demand curve is the sum of all individuals' marginal utility curves.

2a When people buy consumer durables they may be uncertain of their benefits and any additional repair and maintenance costs. When they buy financial assets they may be uncertain of what will happen to their price in the future. Buying under these conditions of imperfect knowledge is therefore a form of gambling. When we take such gambles, if we know the odds, we are said to be operating under conditions of *risk*. If we do not know the odds, we are said to be operating under conditions of *uncertainty*.

2b People can be divided into risk lovers, risk averters and those who are risk neutral. Because of the diminishing marginal utility of income it is rational for people to be risk averters (unless gambling is itself pleasurable).

2c Insurance is a way of eliminating risks for policy-holders. Being risk averters, people are prepared to pay premiums in order to obtain insurance. Insurance companies, on the other hand, are prepared to take on these risks because they can spread them over a large number of policies. According to the law of large numbers, what is unpredictable for a single policy-holder becomes highly predictable for a large number of them provided that their risks are independent of each other.

2d When information is imperfect and the product is complex, buyers and sellers can experience the problems of adverse selection and moral hazard. For example, insurance companies that offer health insurance without taking into account the health of their potential policy-holders will attract those individuals who are most likely to benefit from a health policy, i.e. those prone to illness and injury. This is the problem of adverse selection. Further, once individuals have taken out an insurance policy, they may engage in more risky behaviour. This is the problem of moral hazard.

3a Consumers buy products for their characteristics. Characteristics can be plotted on a diagram and a ray drawn out from the origin for each product. The slope of the ray gives the amount of the characteristic measured on the vertical axis relative to the amount measured on the horizontal axis.

3b The amount purchased will depend on the consumer's budget. An efficiency frontier can be drawn showing the maximum quantity of various alternative brands (or combinations of them) that can be purchased for that budget.

3c An indifference map can be drawn on the same diagram. The map shows a series of indifference curves, each one measuring all the alternative combinations of two characteristics that give the consumer a given level of utility. The consumer is thus indifferent between all combinations along an indifference curve. Indifference curves further out to the right represent higher levels of utility and thus preferred combinations. Indifference curves are bowed in to the origin. This reflects a diminishing marginal rate of substitution between characteristics.

3d The optimum combination of characteristics is where the efficiency frontier is tangential to (i.e. just touches) the highest indifference curve. The 'rational' consumer will thus purchase at this point.

3e A change in a product's price, or a change in the consumer's budget, is represented by a movement along the product's ray. A change in the mix of characteristics of a product is represented by a swing in the ray (i.e. a change in its slope). A change in consumer tastes is represented by a shift in the indifference curves. They will become steeper if tastes shift towards the characteristic measured on the horizontal axis.

3f Although (a) some characteristics are difficult or impossible to measure, (b) only two characteristics can be measured on a simple two-dimensional diagram and (c) the position of indifference curves is difficult to identify in practice, characteristics theory gives useful insights into the process of consumer choice. It can help firms analyse the implications of changing their or their rivals' product specifications, changes in consumer tastes and changes in their or their rivals' prices.

REVIEW QUESTIONS

1 Do you ever purchase things irrationally? If so, what are they and why is your behaviour irrational?

2 If you buy something in the shop on the corner when you know that the same item could have been bought more cheaply two miles up the road in the supermarket, is your behaviour irrational? Explain.

3 How would marginal utility and market demand be affected by a rise in the price of a complementary good?

4 Why do we get less consumer surplus from goods where our demand is relatively price elastic?

5 Explain why the price of a good is no reflection of the *total* value that consumers put on it.

6 Give some examples of risk taking or gambling where the odds are (a) unfavourable; (b) fair; (c) favourable.

7 If people are generally risk averse, why do so many people around the world take part in national lotteries?

8 Why are insurance companies unwilling to provide insurance against losses arising from war or 'civil insurrection'? Name some other events where it would be impossible to obtain insurance.

9 Make a list of characteristics of shoes. Which of these could be easily measured and which are more 'subjective'?

10 If two houses had identical characteristics, except that one was near a noisy airport and the other was in a quiet location, and if the market price of the first house was £300 000 and the second was £400 000, how would that help us to put a value on the characteristic of peace and quiet?

11 Assume that Rachel is attending university and likes to eat a meal at lunchtime. Assume that she has three options of where to eat: the university refectory, a nearby pub or a nearby restaurant. Apart from price, she takes into account the quality of the food and the pleasantness of the surroundings when choosing where to eat.

Sketch her indifference map for the two characteristics, food quality and pleasantness of surroundings. Now, making your own assumptions about which locations provide which characteristics, the prices they charge and Rachel's weekly budget for lunches, sketch the rays for the three locations and draw a weekly efficiency frontier. Mark Rachel's optimum consumption point.

Now illustrate the following (you might need to draw separate diagrams):

(a) A rise in the price of meals at the local pub, but no change in the price of meals at the other two locations.

(b) A shift in Rachel's tastes in favour of food quality relative to pleasantness of surroundings.

(c) The refectory is refurbished and is now a much more attractive place to eat.

12 Why would consumption at a point inside the efficiency frontier not be 'rational'?

WEB APPENDIX IN THE CASE STUDIES SECTION OF MyEconLab

Indifference analysis. This examines the choices consumers make between products and shows how these choices are affected by the prices of the products. It is the traditional analysis on which Characteristics Theory (examined in section 6.3) is based.

Demand and the firm

Business issues covered in this chapter

- How can businesses set about estimating the strength of demand for their products?
- How do businesses set about gathering information on consumer attitudes and behaviour?
- How do businesses calculate the importance of various factors (such as tastes, consumer incomes and rivals' prices) in determining the level of demand?
- What methods can they use to forecast the demand for their products?
- How useful are past trends in predicting future ones?

Given our analysis in Chapter 6, how might a business set about discovering the wants of consumers and hence the intensity of demand? The more effectively a business can identify such wants, the more likely it is to increase its sales and be successful. The clearer idea it can gain of the rate at which the typical consumer's utility will decline as consumption increases, the better estimate it can make of the product's price elasticity.

Also the more it can assess the relative utility to the consumer of its product compared with those of its rivals, the more effectively will it be able to compete by differentiating its product from theirs. In this chapter we shall consider the alternative strategies open to business for collecting data on consumer behaviour, and how it can help business managers to estimate and forecast patterns of demand.

7.1 ESTIMATING DEMAND FUNCTIONS

KI 8
p 38

If a business is to make sound strategic decisions, it must have a good understanding of its market. It must be able to predict things such as the impact of an advertising campaign, or the consequences of changing a brand's price or specifications. It must also be able to predict the likely growth (or decline) in consumer demand, both in the near future and over the longer term.

The problem is that information on consumer behaviour can be costly and time consuming to acquire, and there is no guarantee as to its accuracy. As a result, business managers are frequently making strategic decisions with imperfect knowledge, never fully knowing whether the decision they have made is the 'best' one: i.e. the one which yields the most profit or sales, or best meets some other more specific strategic objective (such as driving a competitor from a segment of a market).

But despite the fact that the information which a firm acquires is bound to be imperfect, it is still usually better than relying on hunches or 'instinct'. The firm having obtained information on consumer behaviour, there are two main uses to which it can be put:

- *Estimating demand functions.* Here the information is used to show the relationship between the quantity demanded and the various determinants of demand, such as price, consumers' incomes, advertising, the price of substitute and complementary goods, etc. Once this relationship (known as a *demand function*) has been established, it can be used to predict what would happen to demand if one of its determinants changed.
- *Forecasting future demand.* Here the information is used to project future sales potential. This can then be used as the basis for output and investment plans.

In this section we concentrate on the first of these two uses. We examine methods for gathering data on consumer behaviour and then see how these data can be used to estimate a demand function. (Forecasting is considered in section 7.2.)

Methods of collecting data on consumer behaviour

There are three general approaches to gathering information about consumers. These are: **observations of market behaviour**, **market surveys** and **market experiments**.

Market observations

The firm can gather data on how demand for its product has changed over time. Virtually all firms will have detailed information of their sales broken down by week, and/or month, and/or year. They will probably also have information on how sales have varied from one part of the market to another.

In addition, the firm will need to obtain data on how the various determinants of demand (such as price, advertising and the price of competitors' products) have themselves changed over time. Firms are likely to have much of this information already: for example, the amount spent on advertising and the prices of competitors' products. Other information might be relatively easy to obtain by paying an agency to do the research.

Having obtained this information, the firm can then use it to estimate how changes in the various determinants have affected demand in the past, and hence what effect they will be likely to have in the future (we examine this estimation process later in this section).

Even the most sophisticated analysis based on market observations, however, will suffer from one major drawback. Relationships that held in the past will not necessarily hold in the future. Consumers are human, and humans change their minds. Their perceptions of products change (something that the advertising industry relies on!) and their tastes change. It is for this reason that many firms turn to market surveys or market experiments to gain more information about the future.

Market surveys

It is not uncommon to be stopped in a city centre, or to have a knock at the door, and be asked whether you would kindly answer the questions of some market researcher. If the research interviewer misses you, then a postal questionnaire may well seek out the same type of information. A vast quantity of information can be collected in this way. It is a relatively quick and cheap method of data collection. Questions concerning all aspects of consumer behaviour might be asked, such as those relating to present and future patterns of expenditure, or how a buyer might respond to changing product specifications or price, both of the firm in question and of its rivals.

A key feature of the market survey is that it can be targeted at distinct consumer groups, thereby reflecting the specific information requirements of a business. For example, businesses selling luxury goods will be interested only in consumers falling within higher income brackets. Other samples might be drawn from a particular age group or gender, or from those with a particular lifestyle, such as eating habits.

The major drawback with this technique concerns the accuracy of the information acquired. Accurate information requires various conditions to be met.

A random sample. If the sample is not randomly selected, it may fail to represent a cross-section of the population being surveyed. As a result, it may be subject to various forms of research bias. For example, the sample might not contain the correct gender and racial balance. The information might then over-emphasise the views of a particular group (e.g. white men).

Clarity of the questions. It is important for the questions to be phrased in an unambiguous way, so as not to mislead the respondent.

Definitions

Observations of market behaviour Information gathered about consumers from the day-to-day activities of the business within the market.

Market surveys Information gathered about consumers, usually via a questionnaire, that attempts to enhance the business's understanding of consumer behaviour.

Market experiments Information gathered about consumers under artificial or simulated conditions. A method used widely in assessing the effects of advertising on consumers.

Avoidance of leading questions. It is very easy for the respondent to be led into giving the answer the firm wants to hear. For example, when asking whether the person would buy a new product that the firm is thinking of launching, the questionnaire might make the product sound really desirable. The respondents might, as a result, say that they would buy the product, but later, when they see the product in the shops, they might realise that they do not want it.

Willingness of respondents. People might refuse to answer particular questions, possibly due to their personal nature. This may then lead to partial or distorted information.

Truthful response. It is very tempting for respondents who are 'keen to please' to give the answer that they think the questioner wants, or for other somewhat reluctant respondents to give 'mischievous' answers. In other words, people may lie!

Stability of demand. By the time the product is launched, or the changes to an existing product are made, time will have elapsed. The information may then be out of date. Consumer demand may have changed, as tastes and fashions have shifted, or as a result of the actions of competitors. The essence of the problem of market surveys is that they ask consumers what they are likely to do. People can and do change their mind.

As well as surveying consumers, businesses might survey other businesses, or panels of experts within a particular market. Both could yield potentially valuable information to the business.

Market experiments

Rather than asking consumers questions and getting them to *imagine* how they *would* behave, the market experiment involves observing consumer *behaviour* under simulated conditions. It can be used to observe consumer reactions to a new product or to changes in an existing product.

A simple experiment might involve consumers being asked to conduct a blind taste test for a new brand of toothpaste. The experimenter will ensure that the same amount of paste is applied to the brush, and that the subjects swill their mouths prior to tasting a further brand. Once the experiment is over, the 'consumers' are quizzed about their perceptions of the product.

More sophisticated experiments could be conducted. For example, a *laboratory shop* might be set up to simulate a real shopping experience. People could be given a certain amount of money to spend in the 'shop' and their reactions to changes in prices, packaging, display, etc. could be monitored.

The major drawback with such 'laboratories' is that consumers might behave differently because they are being observed. For example, they might spend more time comparing prices than they otherwise would, simply because they think that this is what a *good*, rational consumer should do. With real shopping, however, it might simply be habit,

or something 'irrational' such as the colour of the packaging, that determines which product they select.

Another type of market experiment involves confining a marketing campaign to a particular town or region. The campaign could involve advertising, or giving out free samples, or discounting the price, or introducing an improved version of the product, but each confined to that particular locality. Sales in that area are then compared with sales in other areas in order to assess the effectiveness of the various campaigns.

> ### Pause for thought
>
> *Before you read on, try to identify some other drawbacks in using market experiments to gather data on consumer behaviour.*

Using the data to estimate demand functions

Once the business has undertaken its market analysis, what will it do with the information? How can it use its new knowledge to aid its decision making?

One way the information might be used is for the business to attempt to estimate the relationship between the quantity demanded and the various factors that influence demand. This would then enable the firm to predict how the demand for the product would be likely to change if one or more of the determinants of demand changed.

We can represent the relationship between the demand for a product and the determinants of demand in the form of an equation. This is called a ***demand function***. It can be expressed in general terms or with specific values attached to the determinants.

General form of a demand function

In its general form the demand function is effectively a list of the various determinants of demand.

$$Q_d = f(P_g;\ T;\ P_{s_1},\ P_{s_2} \ldots P_{s_n};\ P_{c_1},\ P_{c_2} \ldots P_{c_m};\ Y;\ P^e_{g_{t+1}};\ U)$$

This is merely saying in symbols that the quantity demanded (Q_d) is a 'function of' (f) – i.e. depends on – the price of the good itself (P_g), tastes (T), the price of a number of substitute goods ($P_{s_1},\ P_{s_2} \ldots P_{s_n}$), the price of a number of complementary goods ($P_{c_1},\ P_{c_2} \ldots P_{c_m}$), total consumer incomes (Y), the expected price of the good (P^e_g) at some future time ($t + 1$) and other factors (U) such as the distribution of income, the demographic profile of the population, etc. The equation is thus just a form of shorthand.

> ### Definition
>
> **Demand function** An equation showing the relationship between the demand for a product and its principal determinants.

Note that this function could be extended by dividing determinants into sub-categories. For example, income could be broken down by household type, age, gender or any other characteristic. Similarly, instead of having one term labelled 'tastes', we could identify various characteristics of the product or its marketing that determine tastes.

In this general form, there are no numerical values attached to each of the determinants. As such, the function has no predictive value for the firm.

Estimating demand equations

To make predictions, the firm must use its survey or experimental data to assign *values* to each of the determinants. These values show just how much demand will change if any one of the determinants changes (while the rest are held constant). For example, suppose that an electricity distributor believes that there are three main determinants of demand (Q_d) for the electricity it supplies: its price (P), total consumer incomes (Y) and the price of gas (P_g). It will wish to assign values to the terms *a*, *b*, *c* and *d* (known as *coefficients*) in the following equation:

$$Q_d = a + bP + cY + dP_g$$

But how are the values of the coefficients to be estimated? This is done using a statistical technique called **regression analysis**. To conduct regression analysis, a number of observations must be used. For example, the electricity company could use its market observations (or the results from various surveys or experiments).

To show how these observations are used, let us consider the very simplest case: that of the effects of changes in just one determinant – for example, price. In this case the demand equation would simply be of the form $Q_d = a + bP$ (where the value of *b* would be a negative number).

The observations might be like those illustrated in Figure 7.1. The points show the amounts of electricity per time period actually consumed at different prices. We could, by eye, construct a demand curve through these points. Regression analysis is a technique that allows us to

obtain the line of best fit. (We do not explain regression analysis in this book, but most business statistics texts cover the topic.)

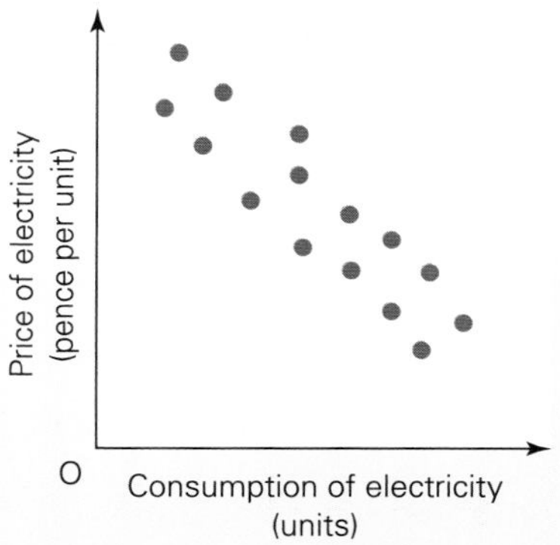

Of course, in reality, there are many determinants of the demand for electricity. That is one reason why the observed points in Figure 7.1 do not all fall exactly along the line. Demand varies at each different price according to what is happening to the other determinants. The other major reason is if the observed points are based on different samples, where each sample is not identical in composition and tastes.

Regression analysis can also be used to determine more complex relationships: to derive the equation that best fits the data on changes in a number of variables. Unlike a curve on a diagram, which simply shows the relationship between two variables, an equation can show the relationship between several variables. Regression analysis can be used to find the 'best fit' equation from data on changes in a number of variables.

For example, regression analysis could be applied to data showing the quantity of electricity consumed at various levels of price, consumer incomes and the price of gas. An equation similar to the following might be estimated:

$$Q_d = 2000 - 500P + 0.4Y + 200P_g$$

where Q_d is measured in millions of gigawatts per annum, P in pence per kilowatt hour, Y in £ millions and P_g in pence per kilowatt hour.

Thus if the price of electricity were 5p per kilowatt hour, consumer incomes were £20 billion and the price of gas were 2p per kilowatt hour, then the demand for electricity would be 7900 million gigawatts per annum. This is calculated as follows:

$$
\begin{aligned}
Q_d &= 2000 - (500 \times 5) + (0.4 \times 20\,000) + (200 \times 2) \\
&= 2000 - 2500 + 8000 + 400 \\
&= 7900
\end{aligned}
$$

The branch of economics that applies statistical techniques to economic data is known as **econometrics**. The problem with using such techniques, however, is that they cannot produce equations and graphs that allow totally reliable predictions to be made. The data on which the equations are based are often incomplete or unreliable, and the underlying relationships on which they are based (often ones of human behaviour) may well change over time. Thus econometrics cannot provide a business manager with 'the answer', but when properly applied it is more reliable than relying on 'hunches' and instinct.

Figure 7.1   Consumption of electricity at different prices

Definitions

Regression analysis A statistical technique which shows how one variable is related to one or more other variables.

Econometrics The branch of economics which applies statistical techniques to economic data.

BOX 7.1 **THE DEMAND FOR LAMB**

A real-world demand function

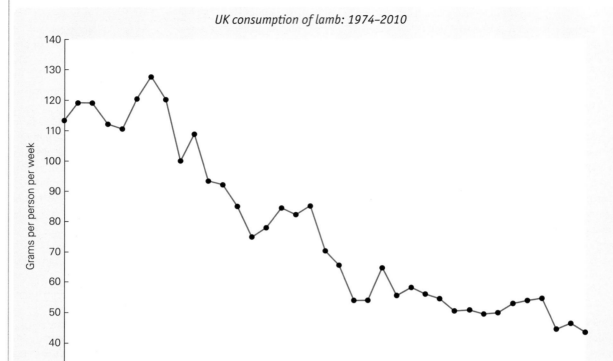

UK consumption of lamb: 1974–2010

Source: Based on family food datasets (defra)

The diagram shows what happened to the consumption of lamb in the UK over the period 1974–2010. How can we explain this dramatic fall in consumption? One way of exploring this issue is to make use of a regression model, which should help us to see which variables are relevant and how they are likely to affect demand.

The following is an initial model fitted (using *Gretl,* a free, open source, statistical software package) to annual data for the years 1974–2010.

$$Q_L = 144.0 - 0.137P_L - 0.034P_B + 0.214P_P - 0.00513Y \quad (1)$$

where:

Q_L is the quantity of lamb sold in grams per person per week;
P_L is the 'real' price of lamb (in pence per kg, 2000 prices);
P_B is the 'real' price of beef (in pence per kg, 2000 prices);

P_P is the 'real' price of pork (in pence per kg, 2000 prices);
Y is households' real disposable income per head (£ per year, 2000 prices).

This model makes it possible to predict what would happen to the demand for lamb if any one of the four explanatory variables changed, assuming that the other variables remained constant.

Using equation (1), calculate what would happen – ceteris paribus – to the demand for lamb if:
(a) the real price of lamb went up by 10p per kg;
(b) the real price of beef went up by 10p per kg;
(c) the real price of pork fell by 10p per kg;
(d) real disposable income per head rose by £100 per annum.
Are the results as you would expect?

7.2 FORECASTING DEMAND

Demand functions are useful in that they show what will happen to demand *if* one of the determinants changes. But businesses will want to know more than the answer to an 'If . . . then' question. They will want to know what will

actually happen to the determinants and, more importantly, what will happen to demand itself as the determinants change. In other words, they will want *forecasts* of future demand. After all, if demand is going to increase, they

KI 1
p 7

There is a serious problem with estimated demand functions like these: they assume that *other* determinants of demand (i.e. those not included in the model) have not changed. In the case of this demand-for-lamb function, one of the other determinants *did* change. This was tastes – during the 37-year period there was a shift in demand away from lamb and other meats, partly for health reasons, and partly because of an expansion in the availability of and demand for vegetarian and low-meat alternatives.

On the assumption that this shift in taste took place steadily over time, a new demand equation was estimated for the same years:

$$Q_L = 121.4 - 0.151P_L - 0.0213P_B + 0.180P_P \\ - 0.000391Y - 1.728TIME \qquad (2)$$

where $TIME = 1$ in 1974, 2 in 1975, 3 in 1976, etc.

1. *How does the introduction of the variable* TIME *affect the relationship between the demand for lamb and (a) its real price; (b) real disposable income per head?*
2. *Does lamb appear to be a normal good or an inferior good?*
3. *What does the negative coefficient of* P_B *indicate?*

Model (2) is a better model than model (1) in two major respects. The first point is that it has a better 'goodness of fit'. This can be shown by the 'R-squared'. $R^2 = 1$ represents a perfect fit, whereas $R^2 = 0$ shows that the model has no explanatory power whatsoever. In model (2), $R^2 = 0.913$ compared with 0.908 for model (1). This means that model (2) can explain 91.3 per cent of the variation in the consumption of lamb during the period 1974 to 2010, whereas model (1) can explained 90.8 per cent.

While model (2) is clearly an improvement on model (1), it is by no means perfect. The second model still has problems. For example, the coefficient of Y remains positive. The estimated coefficient is much smaller and very close to zero, suggesting that household income has little effect on demand. Is this realistic?

Another problem is that P_B should have a positive coefficient, since beef is surely a substitute for lamb. More importantly, the model takes no account of the fact that consumers' purchases of lamb this year are likely to be strongly influenced by what they were consuming last year. Finally, while the model includes the real prices of two substitutes for lamb, it does not include the real prices of any complements. By omitting these variables from model (1) and (2) we mis-specified the

models and introduced a bias into the estimated coefficients. By including *all* variables that we believe are relevant we hope to remove this bias.

To take the above points into account, the following third model was estimated, using data for 1975 to 2010.

$$Q_L = -37.520 - 0.128P_L + 0.0757P_B + 0.122P_P \\ + 0.00415Y - 1.529TIME + 0.679LQ_L - 0.0519P_C \qquad (3)$$

where LQ_L is the lagged consumption of lamb (i.e. consumption in the previous year) and P_C is the real price of a complement (potatoes). $R^2 = 0.958$.

1. *To what extent is model (3) an improvement on model (2)? (Hint: is lamb now a normal or inferior good?)*
2. *Use the three equations and also the data given in the table below to estimate the demand for lamb in 2000 and 2010. Which model works the best in each case? Why? Explain why the models are all subject to error in their predictions.*
3. *Use model (3) and the data given in the table to explain why the demand for lamb fell so dramatically between 1980 and 2010.*
4. *The formula for the elasticity of demand (price elasticity, income elasticity or cross elasticity) can be written as* $dQ/dX \div Q/X$, *where* dQ/dX *represents the coefficient for a given variable,* X. *For example, in equation (3),* 0.0757 *gives the value of the term* dQ_L/dP_B *when working out the cross-price elasticity of demand for lamb with respect to changes in the price of beef. Using equation (3) and the table below, work out the following for 2010:*
   (a) *the price elasticity of demand for lamb;*
   (b) *the income elasticity of demand for lamb;*
   (c) *the cross-price elasticity of demand for lamb with respect to (i) beef, (ii) pork, (iii) potatoes.*

	Q_L	LQ_L	P_L	P_B	P_P	Y	$TIME$	P_C
1980	128	121	421.7	546.0	414.6	10 498	7	26.7
2000	54	56	467.0	480.5	381.1	17 797	27	44.9
2010	44	46	506.2	470.1	381.1	19 776	37	53.5

Sources: Nominal food prices were calculated by dividing expenditure by consumption. These nominal prices in pence per kg were then adjusted to 'real' prices by dividing by the RPI (retail price index) for total food (2000 = 100) and multiplying by 100. http://www.defra.gov.uk/statistics/foodfarm/food/familyfood/datasets/ (expenditure and consumption) http://www.ons.gov.uk/ (income and RPI food)

may well want to invest *now* so that they have the extra capacity to meet the extra demand. But it will be a costly mistake to invest in extra capacity if demand is not going to increase.

We now, therefore, turn to examine some of the forecasting techniques used by business.

Simple time-series analysis

Simple time-series analysis involves directly projecting from past sales data into the future. Thus if it is observed that sales of a firm's product have been growing steadily by 3 per cent per annum for the last few years, the firm can use this to predict that sales will continue to grow at approximately the same rate in the future. Similarly, if it is observed that there are clear seasonal fluctuations in demand, as in the case of the demand for holidays or ice cream or winter coats, then again it can be assumed that fluctuations of a similar magnitude will continue into the future. In other words, using simple time-series analysis assumes that demand in the future will continue to behave in the same way as in the past.

Using simple time-series analysis in this way can be described as 'black box' forecasting. No *explanation* is offered as to *why* demand is behaving in this way: any underlying model of demand is 'hidden in a black box'. In a highly stable market environment, where the various factors affecting demand change very little or, if they do, change very steadily or regularly, such time-series analysis can supply reasonably accurate forecasts. The problem is that, without closer examination of the market, the firm cannot know whether changes in demand of the same magnitude as in the past will continue into the future. Just because demand has followed a clear pattern in the past, it does not follow that it will continue to exhibit the same pattern in the future. After all, the determinants of demand may well change. Successful forecasting, therefore, will usually involve a more sophisticated analysis of trends.

The decomposition of time paths

One way in which the analysis of past data can be made more sophisticated is to identify different elements in the time path of sales. Figure 7.2 illustrates one such time path: the (imaginary) sales of woollen jumpers by firm X. It is shown by the continuous red line, labelled 'Actual sales'.

Four different sets of factors normally determine the shape of a time path like this.

Trends. These are increases or decreases in demand over a number of years. In our example, there is a long-term decrease in demand for this firm's woollen jumpers up to year 7 and then a slight recovery in demand thereafter.

Trends may reflect longer-term factors such as changes in population structure, or technological innovation or longer-term changes in fashion. Thus if wool were to become more expensive over time compared with other fibres, or if there were a gradual shift in tastes away from woollen jumpers and towards acrylic or cotton jumpers, or towards sweatshirts, this could explain the long-term decline in demand up to year 7. A gradual shift in tastes back towards natural fibres, and to wool in particular, or a gradual reduction in the price of wool, could then explain the subsequent recovery in demand.

Alternatively, trends may reflect changes over time in the structure of an industry. For example, an industry might become more and more competitive with new firms joining. This would tend to reduce sales for existing firms (unless the market were expanding very rapidly).

Cyclical fluctuations. In practice, the level of actual sales will not follow the trend line precisely. One reason for this is the cyclical upswings and downswings in business activity in the economy as a whole. In some years, incomes are rising rapidly and thus demand is buoyant. In other years, the economy will be in recession, with incomes falling. In these years, demand may well also fall. In our example, in boom years people may spend much more on clothes (including woollen jumpers), whereas in a recession, people may make do with their old clothes. The cyclical variations line thus rises above the trend line in boom years and falls below the trend line during a recession.

Seasonal fluctuations. The demand for many products also depends on the time of year. In the case of woollen jumpers, the peak demand is likely to be as winter approaches or just before Christmas. Thus the seasonal variations line is above the cyclical variations line in winter and below it in summer.

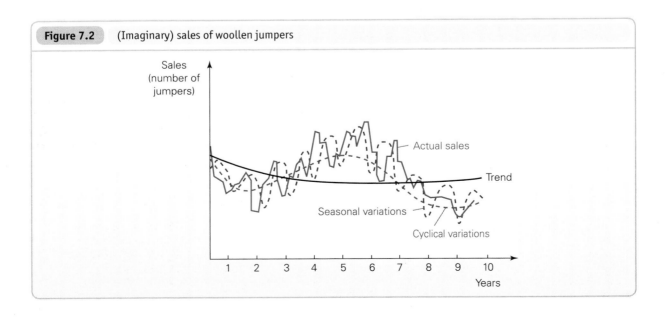

Figure 7.2 (Imaginary) sales of woollen jumpers

Short-term shifts in demand or supply. Finally, the actual sales line will also reflect various short-term shifts in demand or supply, causing it to diverge from the smooth seasonal variations line.

There are many reasons why the demand curve might shift. A competitor might increase its price, or there may be a sudden change in fashion, caused, say, by a pop group deciding to wear woollen jumpers for their new video: what was once seen as unfashionable by many people now suddenly becomes fashionable! Alternatively, there may be an unusually cold or hot, or wet or dry spell of weather.

Likewise there are various reasons for sudden shifts in supply conditions. For example, there may be a sheep disease which ruins the wool of infected sheep. As a result, the price of wool goes up, and sales of woollen jumpers falls.

These sudden shifts in demand or supply conditions are often referred to as 'random shocks' because they are usually unpredictable and temporarily move sales away from the trend. (Note that *long-term* shifts in demand and supply will be shown by a change in the trend line itself.)

Even with sophisticated time-series analysis, which breaks time paths into their constituent elements, there is still one major weakness: time-series analysis is merely a projection of the *past*. Most businesses will want to anticipate *changes* to sales trends – to forecast any deviations from the current time path. One method for doing this is *barometric forecasting*.

Barometric forecasting

Assume that you are a manager of a furniture business and are wondering whether to invest in new capital equipment. You would only want to do this if the demand for your product was likely to rise. You will probably, therefore, look for some indication of this. A good barometer of future demand for furniture would be the number of new houses being built. People will tend to buy new furniture some months after the building of their new house has commenced.

It is common for businesses to use **leading indicators** such as 'housing starts' (the number of houses built measured at the time when building starts rather than when it is completed) when attempting to predict the future. In fact some leading indicators, such as increased activity in the construction industry, rises in Stock Exchange prices, a depreciation of the rate of exchange and a rise in industrial confidence, are good indicators of a general upturn in the economy.

Barometric forecasting is a technique whereby forecasts of demand in industry A are based on an analysis of time-series data for industry (or sector, or indicator) B, where changes in B normally precede changes in the demand for A. If B rises by *x* per cent, it can be assumed (other things being equal) that the demand for A will change by *y* per cent.

Barometric forecasting is widely used to predict *cyclical* changes: the effects of the upswings and downswings in the economy. It is thus useful not only for individual firms, but also for governments, which need to plan their policies to counteract the effects of the business cycle: the unemployment associated with recessions, or the inflation associated with booms in the economy.

Barometric forecasting suffers from two major weaknesses. The first is that it only allows forecasting a few months ahead – as far ahead as is the time lag between the change in the leading indicator and the variable being forecasted. The second is that it can only give a general indication of changes in demand. It is simply another form of time-series analysis. Just because a relationship existed in the past between a leading indicator and the variable being forecasted, it cannot be assumed that exactly the same relationship will exist in the future.

Normally, then, firms use barometric forecasting merely to give them a rough guide as to likely changes in demand for their product: i.e. whether it is likely to expand or contract, and by 'a lot' or by 'a little'. Nevertheless information on leading indicators is readily available in government or trade statistics.

To get a more precise forecast, firms must turn to their demand function, and estimate the effects of predicted changes in the determinants of the demand for their product.

Using demand functions in forecasts

We have seen (section 7.1) how demand functions can be used to show the effects of changes in the determinants of demand. For example, in the following model:

$$Q_d = a + bP + cP_s + dY + eA$$

where the demand for the product (Q_d) is determined by its price (P), the price of a substitute product (P_s), consumer incomes (Y) and advertising (A), the parameters (b, c, d and e) show the effects on Q_d of changes in the determinants.

In order to forecast the demand for its product (the **dependent variable**), the firm will need to obtain values for P, P_s, Y and A (the **independent variables**). The firm itself

---

Definitions

Leading indicators Indicators that help predict future trends in the economy.

Barometric forecasting A technique used to predict future economic trends based upon analysing patterns of time-series data.

Dependent variable That variable whose outcome is determined by other variables within an equation.

Independent variables Those variables that determine the dependent variable, but are themselves determined independently of the equation they are in.

chooses what price to charge and how much to advertise, and thus will decide the values of P and A. Forecasts of consumer incomes are readily available from the government's Office for National Statistics (ONS) or from private forecasting agencies. As far as P_s is concerned, here the firm will have to make an informed guess. Most firms will have a pretty good idea of the likely policies of their competitors.

Obviously, the accuracy of the forecasts will depend on the accuracy of the model as a description of the past relationship between demand and its determinants. Fortunately, this can be tested using various econometric techniques, and the reliability of the model can be determined. What is more, once the forecast is made, it can be compared with the actual outcome and the new data can be used to refine the model and improve its predictive power for next time.

The major strength of these econometric models is that they attempt to show how the many determinants affect demand. They also allow firms to feed in different assumptions to see how they will affect the outcome. Thus one forecast might be based on the assumption that the major competitor raises its price by x per cent, another that it raises its price by y per cent, and another that it leaves its price unchanged. The firm can then see how sensitive its sales will be to these possible changes. This is called *sensitivity analysis* and its use allows the firm to assess just how critical its assumptions are: would a rise in its rival's price by x per cent rather than y per cent make all the difference between a profit and a loss, or would it make little difference?

Econometric models can be highly complex, involving several equations and many variables. For example, there might be a separate variable for each of the prices and specifications of all the various products in competition with this one.

Definitions

Sensitivity analysis Assesses how sensitive an outcome is to different variables within an equation.

Problems with econometric forecasting

But despite the apparent sophistication of some of the econometric models used by firms or by forecasting agencies, the forecasts are often wrong.

One reason for this is that the variables specified in the model cannot explain all the variation in the demand for the product. In order to take some account of these missing independent variables, it is normal to include an *error term* (r). But this error term will probably cover a number of unspecified determinants which are unlikely to move together over time. It does not therefore represent a stable or predictable 'determinant'. The larger the error term, the less confident we can be about using the equation to predict future demand.

Another reason for the inaccuracy of forecasts is that certain key determinants are difficult, if not impossible, to measure with any accuracy. This is a particular problem with subjective variables like taste and fashion. How can taste be modelled?

Perhaps the biggest weakness of using demand functions for forecasting is that the forecasts are themselves based on forecasts of what will happen to the various determinants. Take the cases of just two determinants: the specifications of competitors' products and consumer tastes. Just what changes will competitors make to their products? Just how will tastes change in the future? Consider the problems a clothing manufacturer might have in forecasting demand for a range of clothing! Income, advertising and the prices of the clothing will all be significant factors determining demand, but so too will be the range offered by other manufacturers and also people's perception of what is and what is not fashionable. But predicting changes in competitors' products and changes in fashion is notoriously difficult.

This is not to say that firms should give up in their attempt to forecast demand. Rather it suggests that they might need to conduct more sophisticated market research, and even then to accept that forecasts can only give an approximate indication of likely changes to demand.

SUMMARY

1a Businesses seek information on consumer behaviour so as to predict market trends and improve strategic decision making.

1b One source of data is the firm's own information on how its sales have varied in the past with changes in the various determinants of demand, such as consumer incomes and the prices of competitors' products.

1c Another source of data is market surveys. These can generate a large quantity of cheap information. Care should be taken, however, to ensure that the sample of consumers investigated reflects the target consumer group.

1d Market experiments involve investigating consumer behaviour within a controlled environment. This method is particularly useful when considering new products where information is scarce.

1e Armed with data drawn from one or more of these sources, the business manager can attempt to estimate consumer demand using various statistical techniques, such as regression analysis.

1f The estimation of the effects on demand of a change in a particular variable, such as price, depends upon the assumption that all other factors that influence demand remain constant. However, factors that influence the demand for a product are constantly changing, hence there will always be the possibility of error when estimating the impact of change.

2a It is not enough to know what will happen to demand if a determinant changes. Businesses will want to forecast what will actually happen to demand. To do this they can use a variety of methods: time-series analysis, barometric forecasting and econometric modelling.

2b Time-series analysis bases future trends on past events. Time-series data can be decomposed into different elements: trends, seasonal fluctuations, cyclical fluctuations and random shocks.

2c Barometric forecasting involves making predictions based upon changes in key leading indicators.

2d If a firm has estimated its demand function (using econometric techniques), it can then feed into this model forecasts of changes in the various determinants of demand and use the model to predict the effect on demand. The two main problems with this approach are: the reliability of the demand function (although this can be tested using econometric techniques), and the reliability of forecasts of changes in the various determinants of demand.

REVIEW QUESTIONS

1 What are the relative strengths and weaknesses of using (a) market observations, (b) market surveys and (c) market experiments as means of gathering evidence on consumer demand?

2 You are working for a record company which is thinking of signing up some new bands. What market observations, market surveys and market experiments could you conduct to help you decide which bands to sign?

3 You are about to launch a new range of cosmetics, but you are still to decide upon the content and structure of your advertising campaign. Consider how market surveys and market experiments might be used to help you assess consumer perceptions of the product. What limitations might each of the research methods have in helping you gather data?

4 The following is an estimate of an historical UK market demand curve for instant coffee. It has been derived (using a computer regression package) from actual data for the years 1973–85.

$$Q_c = 0.042 + 0.068P_c + 0.136P_T + 0.0067Y$$

where:

Q_c is the quantity of instant coffee purchased in ounces per person per week;

P_c and P_T are respectively the 'real' prices of instant coffee and tea, calculated by dividing their market prices in pence per lb by the retail price index for all food (RPI) (1980 = 100);

Y is an index of real personal disposable income (1980 = 100): i.e. household income after tax.

The following table gives the prices of coffee and tea and real disposable income for three years (1973, 1985 and 1990).

Year	Market price of coffee (MP_c) (pence per lb)	RPI of all food (1980 = 100)	Real price of coffee ($P_c = MP_c/RPI \times 100$)	Market price of tea (MP_T) (pence per lb)	Real price of tea ($P_T = MP_T/RPI \times 100$)	Index of real disposable income (Y) (1980 = 100)
1973	111.33	35.20		35.53		89.30
1985	511.65	131.40		184.39		106.10
1990	585.19	165.89		212.77		128.62

(a) Fill in the columns for the real price of coffee (P_c) and the real price of tea (P_T).

(b) Use the above equation to estimate the demand for instant coffee in 1973.

(c) Calculate the percentage growth in the market over the 13-year sample period (1973–85).

(d) The equation was used to forecast the demand for instant coffee in 1990. Purchases were estimated at 0.7543 ounces per person per week.
  (i) Verify this from the equation.

  (ii) The actual level of purchases is recorded as 0.48 ounces per week. Suggest reasons why the equation seriously over-estimates the level of demand for 1990.

5 Outline the alternative methods a business might use to forecast demand. How reliable do you think such methods are?

6 Imagine that you are an airline attempting to forecast demand for seats over the next two or three years. What, do you think, could be used as leading indicators?

Products, marketing and advertising

Business issues covered in this chapter

■ In what ways can firms differentiate their products from those of their rivals?
■ What strategies can firms adopt for gaining market share, developing their products and marketing them?
■ What elements are likely to be contained in a marketing strategy?
■ How extensive is advertising in the UK and how does it vary from product to product?
■ What are the effects of advertising and what makes a successful advertising campaign?

For most firms, selling their product is not simply a question of estimating demand and then choosing an appropriate price and level of production. In other words, they do not simply take their market as given. Instead they will seek to *influence* demand. They will do this by developing their product and differentiating it from those of their rivals, and then marketing it by advertising and other forms of product promotion.

What firms are engaging in here is *non-price competition*. In such situations the job of the manager can be quite complex. It is likely to involve making a series of strategic decisions, not just concerning price, but also concerning each product's design and quality, its marketing and advertising, and the provision of various forms of after-sales service.

Central to non-price competition is *product differentiation*. Most firms' products differ in various ways from those of their rivals. Take the case of washing machines. Although all washing machines wash clothes, and as such are close substitutes for each other, there are many differences between brands. They differ not only in price, but also in their capacity, their styling, their range of programmes, their economy in the use of electricity, hot water and detergent, their reliability, their noise, their after-sales service, etc. Firms will attempt to design their product so that they can stress its advantages (real or imaginary) over the competitor brands. Just think of the specific features of particular models of car, hi-fi equipment or brands of cosmetic, and then consider the ways in which these features are stressed by advertisements. In fact, think of virtually any advertisement and consider how it stresses the features of that particular brand.

Definitions

Non-price competition Competition in terms of product promotion (advertising, packaging, etc.) or product development.

Product differentiation Where a firm's product is in some way distinct from its rivals' products.

8.1 PRODUCT DIFFERENTIATION

Features of a product

A product has many dimensions, and a strategy to differentiate a product may focus on one or more of these dimensions.

- *Technical standards.* These relate to the product's level of technical sophistication: how advanced it is in relation to the current state of technology. This would be a very important product dimension if, for example, you were purchasing a PC.
- *Quality standards.* These relate to aspects such as the quality of the materials used in the product's construction and the care taken in assembly. These will affect the product's durability and reliability. The purchase of consumer durables, such as televisions, hi-fi and toys, will be strongly influenced by quality standards.
- *Design characteristics.* These relate to the product's direct appeal to the consumer in terms of appearance or operating features. Examples of design characteristics are colour, style and even packaging. The demand for fashion products such as clothing will be strongly influenced by design characteristics.
- *Service characteristics.* This aspect is not directly concerned with the product itself, but with the support and back-up given to the customer after the product has been sold. Servicing, product maintenance and guarantees would be included under this heading. When purchasing a new car, the quality of after-sales service might strongly influence the choice you make.

Any given product will possess a 'bundle' of the above attributes. Within any product category, each brand is likely to have a different mix of technical and quality standards and design and service characteristics. Consumers will select the bundle of attributes or characteristics they most prefer (see section 6.3). The fact that these different dimensions exist means that producers can focus the marketing of their product on factors other than price – they can engage in non-price competition.

Vertical and horizontal product differentiation

When firms are seeking to differentiate their product from those of their rivals (product differentiation), one important distinction they must consider is that between *vertical* and *horizontal* differentiation.

Vertical product differentiation. This is where products differ in quality, with some being perceived as superior and others as inferior. In general, the better the quality, the more expensive will the product be. Take the case of a DVD recorder. The cheaper (inferior) models will just have basic functions. More expensive models will have more and better functions, such as picture zooming, editing facilities, Dolby 5.1 'surround sound' and thumbnail outlines of recorded films.

Vertical product differentiation will usually be in terms of the quantity and quality of functions and/or the durability of the product (often a reflection of the quality of the materials used and the care spent in making the product). Thus a garment will normally be regarded as superior if it is better made and uses high-quality cloth. In general, the vertical quality differences between products will tend to reflect differences in production costs.

Horizontal product differentiation. This refers to differences between products that are not generally regarded as superior or inferior, but merely reflections of the different tastes of different consumers. One person may prefer black shoes and another brown. One may prefer milk chocolate, another plain. Within any product range there may be varieties which differ in respect to style, design, flavour, colour, etc. Such attributes are neither better, nor worse, simply different.

Horizontal differences within a range do not significantly alter the costs of production, and it is common for the different varieties to have the same price. A pot of red paint is likely to be the same price as a pot of blue (of the same brand). The point is that the products, although horizontally different, are of comparable quality.

> ### Pause for thought
>
> *Identify two other products that are vertically differentiated, two that are horizontally differentiated and two that are both.*

In practice, most product ranges will have a mixture of horizontal and vertical differentiation. For example, some of the differences between different makes and models of motor car will be vertical (e.g. luxury or basic internal fittings, acceleration and fuel consumption); some will be horizontal (e.g. hatchback or saloon, colour and style).

> ### Definitions
>
> **Vertical product differentiation** Where a firm's product differs from its rivals' products with respect to quality.
>
> **Horizontal product differentiation** Where a firm's product differs from its rivals' products, although the products are seen to be of a similar quality.

Market segmentation

Different features of a product will appeal to different consumers. This applies both to vertically differentiated features and to horizontally differentiated ones. Where features are quite distinct, and where particular features or groups of features can be seen to appeal to a particular category of consumers, it might be useful for producers to divide the market into segments. Taking the example of

cars again, the market could be divided into luxury cars, large, medium and small family cars, sports cars, multi-terrain vehicles, six-seater people carriers, etc. Each type of car occupies a distinct market segment, and within each segment the individual models are likely to be both horizontally and vertically differentiated from competitor models.

When consumer tastes change over time, or where existing models do not cater for every taste, a firm may be

---

| BOX 8.1 | THE BATTLE OF THE BRANDS |

The rise, fall and rise of own-label brands

From fairly humble beginnings, supermarket own-label brands really took off in the late 1980s and early 1990s. By 1995 they accounted for over half of supermarket sales in the UK.

However, by the mid-2000s own-label brands' share of supermarket sales had fallen to around one third. By the late 2000s, however, own-label supermarket brands had become popular once again. The market shares of own-label products varies from close to 100 per cent in categories where it is difficult to 'add value' such as fresh fruit to below 10 per cent for products such as energy drinks and chocolate.

So, how do own-label brands compete? Why have their fortunes fluctuated over time?

They don't have significant differences in costs of production . . .

Branded manufacturers were always thought to be able to take advantage of large economies of scale in sourcing and production. However, new technologies and close working relationships between retailers and suppliers have allowed supermarkets to provide own-label products in smaller batches but at lower costs, thus offsetting any advantage that brand manufacturers may have. Technology has also helped to improve the quality of products, making it possible for own-label producers to imitate the ideas of brand manufacturers and engage in their own innovations.

. . . but they do offer different product characteristics

Branded and own-label products are perceived by consumers as offering different product characteristics (table (a)). According to Mintel, branded goods are typically associated with positive associations, such as being trustworthy and authentic, when compared to own-label goods. Own label products, however, are much more likely to be seen as offering value for money and being family friendly, when compared to the branded alternatives.

The major supermarket chains such as Tesco, Asda, Sainsbury's and Morrisons have all developed their own premium brands, either to compete in particular segments, for example in healthy eating ranges, such as 'Be Good to Yourself' or 'Taste the Difference', or more generally, for example Tesco's 'Finest' range. Mintel states that these ranges are seen as having strong value-for-money

(a) Perceived characteristics of branded and own-label products, 2011

| | Percentage of respondents | |
Characteristic	Branded product	Own-label product
Trustworthy	52	32
Traditional	51	22
Authentic	41	25
Family friendly	28	45
Healthy	19	17
Value for money	16	82
Bland	2	28

Source: Mintel 2011

credentials, suggesting that products within them are viewed as competitive by consumers. However, some of the 'value' own-label brands are not seen as offering superior value for money than the branded alternative. This suggests that, by 2011, although many customers see these products as low cost, the lower quality may not always justify the price! This weakens the ability of the supermarket to use these products as a competitive tool.

They take advantage of changing economic prosperity

The decline in market share of own-brands from the early 1990s to 2007 was partly due a period of prolonged economic growth. The rise in disposable income during this period led to increased conspicuous consumption, and many branded goods are associated with affluence and increased quality of lifestyle.

The recessions of the early 1990s and from 2008, by contrast, saw a growth in market share of own-label brands as consumers sought to economise. Supermarkets were able to tap into the price sensitivity of consumers with a range of good value-for-money own-label products; branded products failed to follow suit.

Nevertheless, customers still value brands. Brand manufacturers rely on consumers developing a loyal attachment to a product over a number of years. This is

able to identify a new segment of the market – a *market niche*. Having identified the appropriate market niche for its product, the marketing division within the firm will then set about targeting the relevant consumer group(s) and developing an appropriate strategy for promoting the product. (In the next section we will explore more closely those factors which are likely to influence a business's marketing strategy.)

Definition

Market niche A part of a market (or new market) that has not been filled by an existing brand or business.

---

strengthened by substantial investments in advertising and marketing. Branding is concerned with conveying an image and a style of living, as well as showing the product's function, its convenience and its value. All this takes time to develop, and successful brands, such as Kelloggs and Hovis, have been popular for over 100 years.

Brands dominate many market segments . . .

While the trend in recent times has been back towards own-label brands, it is important to recognise that there is still substantial variability in own-label penetration across products. As Table (b) illustrates, in some product segments, the penetration of supermarkets' own-brands is considerable (e.g. fruit, vegetables and nuts). In others, however, branded products dominate (e.g. cereal bars and confectionary).

Where products are viewed as fairly homogeneous, at least in the eyes of the consumer, or requiring limited technological input, product differentiation by brand is difficult to achieve. There are no real cost advantages and supermarket own-label brands can compete keenly on price.

On the other hand, where products are more differentiated, consumers may identify their particular product by branding. Examples include products targeted at a particular group (defined by gender, age or socioeconomic status), products

that reflect a certain style of living (e.g. healthy eating), products that embody high quality or innovative characteristics, or have a long history. In these markets, own-label brands compete actively by differentiating their products. They do not have to compete strictly on price because sophisticated products command a greater premium.

The disadvantage for supermarkets is that their advertising expenditures are largely concerned with branding the store *as a whole*, rather than particular own-label lines. Their promotional expenditures are thus somewhat diluted. Brand manufacturers, on the other hand, are specialists in targeting their advertising and promotional expenditures towards particular markets. They achieve economies from marketing the brand, with the result that their sales per pound of promotional expenditure are higher. Economies of scale in marketing provide a powerful competitive advantage for brand manufacturers.

. . . but brand manufacturers still have to be responsive to competitive pressures from low-cost own-label rivals

The leading supermarkets use own-label brands to promote their store name but they recognise how important brands are to customers. Likewise, the success of own-labels, particularly value lines, in times of recession, stimulates manufacturers of branded goods to compete fiercely. For example, Unilever recently announced, along with Procter and Gamble and L'Oréal, that they would extend their product ranges to include more 'value lines'. They have also restructured their businesses to reduce cost. Thus, own-label brands keep prices keen and quality high and that means consumers have more choice.

(b) Market penetration of own-label brands in selected UK markets, 2011

Market segment	Market share (%)
Fresh fruit and vegetables	96
Nuts	74
Dried fruits	67
Cakes and cake bars	50
Biscuits	22
Crisps and snacks	21
Yoghurt	19
Sugar confectionary	14
Cereal bars	8
Chocolate confectionary	8

Source: *Mintel* reports (2011)

1. *How has the improvement in the quality of own-brands affected the price elasticity of demand for branded products? What implications does this have for the pricing strategy of brand manufacturers?*
2. *Why don't brand manufacturers readily engage in the production of supermarket own-label products?*
3. *How might brand manufacturers respond to the development of a new product line?*

8.2 MARKETING THE PRODUCT

What is marketing?

There is no single accepted definition of marketing. It is generally agreed, however, that marketing covers the following activities: establishing the strength of consumer demand in existing parts of the market, and potential demand in new niches; developing an attractive and distinct image for the product; informing potential consumers of various features of the product; fostering a desire by consumers for the product; and, in the light of all these, persuading consumers to buy the product.

Clearly, marketing must be seen within the overall goals of the firm. There would be little point in spending vast sums of money in promoting a product if it led to only a modest increase in sales and sales revenue.

Figure 8.1 Growth vector components

		Product	
		Current	*New*
Market	*Current*	**A** Market penetration	**B** Product development
	New	**C** Market development	**D** Diversification

Source: I. Ansoff, *Corporate Strategy* (McGraw-Hill, 1965); 'Strategies for diversification', *Harvard Business Review* (September–October 1957)

Product/market strategy

Once the nature and strength of consumer demand (both current and potential) have been identified, the business will set about meeting and influencing this demand. In most cases it will be hoping to achieve a growth in sales. To do this, one of the first things the firm must decide is its *product/market strategy*. This will involve addressing two major questions:

KI 23 p 181

- Should it focus on promoting its existing product, or should it develop new products?
- Should it focus on gaining a bigger share of its existing market, or should it seek to break into new markets?

In 1957 Igor Ansoff illustrated these choices in what he called a ***growth vector matrix***. This is illustrated in Figure 8.1.

The four boxes show the possible combinations of answers to the above questions: Box A – *market penetration* (current product, current market); Box B – *product development* (new product, current market); Box C – *market development* (current product, new market); Box D – *diversification* (new product, new market).

- *Market penetration.* In the market penetration strategy, the business will seek not only to retain existing customers, but to expand its customer base with current products in current markets. Of the four strategies, this is generally the least risky: the business will be able to play to its product strengths and draw on its knowledge of the market. The business's marketing strategy will tend to focus upon aggressive product promotion and distribution. Such a strategy, however, is likely to lead to fierce competition from current business rivals, especially if the overall market is not expanding and if the firm can therefore gain an increase in sales only by taking market share from its rivals.
- *Product development.* Product development strategies will involve introducing new models and designs in current markets. This may involve either vertical differentiation (e.g. the introduction of an upgraded model) or horizontal differentiation (e.g. the introduction of a new style).
- *Market development.* With a market development strategy the business will seek increased sales of current products by expanding into new markets. These may be in a different geographical location (e.g. overseas), or new market segments. Alternatively, the strategy may involve finding new uses and applications for the product.
- *Diversification.* A diversification strategy will involve the business expanding into new markets with new products. Of all the strategies, this is the most risky given the unknown factors that the business is likely to face.

Once the product/market strategy has been decided upon, the business will then attempt to devise a suitable *marketing strategy*. This will involve looking at the marketing mix.

Definition

Growth vector matrix A means by which a business might assess its product/market strategy.

Pause for thought

What unknown factors is the business likely to face following a diversification strategy?

The marketing mix

In order to differentiate the firm's product from those of its rivals, there are four variables that can be adjusted. These are as follows:

- product;
- price;
- place (distribution);
- promotion.

The particular combination of these variables, known as 'the four Ps', represents the business's **marketing mix**, and it is around a manipulation of them that the business will devise its marketing strategy.

Figure 8.2 illustrates the various considerations that might be taken into account when looking at product, price, place and promotion.

Definition

Marketing mix The mix of product, price, place (distribution) and promotion that will determine a business's marketing strategy.

- *Product considerations.* These involve issues such as quality and reliability, as well as branding, packaging and after-sales service.
- *Pricing considerations.* These involve not only the product's basic price in relation to those of competitors' products, but also opportunities for practising price discrimination (the practice of charging different prices in different parts of the market: see Chapter 17), offering discounts to particular customers, and adjusting the terms of payment for the product.
- *Place considerations.* These focus on the product's distribution network, and involve issues such as where the business's retail outlets should be located, what warehouse facilities the business might require, and how the product should be transported to the market.
- *Promotion considerations.* These focus primarily upon the amount and type of advertising the business should use. In addition, promotion issues might also include selling techniques, special offers, trial discounts and various other public relations 'gimmicks'.

Every product is likely to have a distinct marketing *mix* of these four variables. Thus we cannot talk about an ideal value for one (e.g. the best price), without considering the

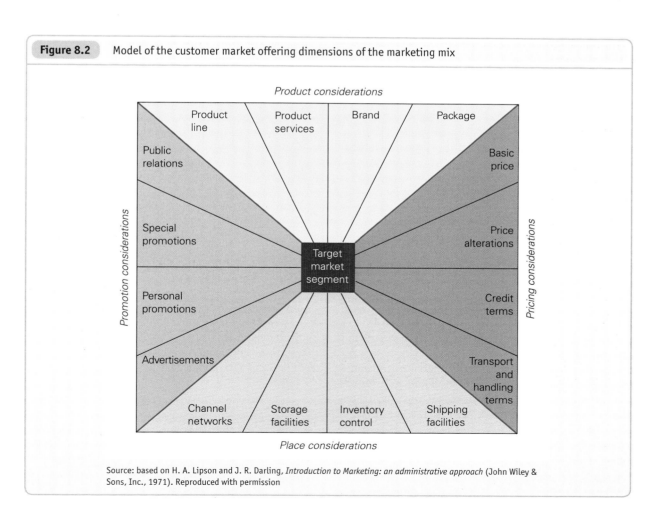

Figure 8.2 Model of the customer market offering dimensions of the marketing mix

Source: based on H. A. Lipson and J. R. Darling, *Introduction to Marketing: an administrative approach* (John Wiley & Sons, Inc., 1971). Reproduced with permission

other three. What is more, the most appropriate mix will vary from product to product and from market to market. If you wanted to sell a Rolls-Royce, you would be unlikely to sell any more by offering free promotional gifts or expanding the number of retail outlets. You might sell more Rolls-Royces, however, if you were to improve their specifications or offer more favourable methods of payment.

What the firm must seek to do is to estimate how sensitive demand is to the various aspects of marketing. The greater the sensitivity (elasticity) in each case, the more the firms should focus on that particular aspect. It must be careful, however, that changing one aspect of marketing does not conflict with another. For example, there would be little point in improving the product's quality if, at the same time, the product was promoted by the use of marketing gimmicks that led consumers to believe they were buying an inferior, 'mass consumption' product.

Another consideration that must be taken into account is the stage in the product's life cycle (see section 17.6). The most appropriate marketing mix for a new and hence unfamiliar product, and one which may be facing little in the way of competition, may well be totally inappropriate for a product that is long established and may be struggling against competitors to maintain its market share.

8.3 ADVERTISING

One of the most important aspects of marketing is advertising. The major aim of advertising is to sell more products, and business spends a vast quantity of money on advertising to achieve this goal. By advertising, the business will not only be informing the consumer of the product's existence and availability, but also deliberately attempting to persuade and entice the consumer to purchase the good. In doing so, it will tend to stress the specific and unique qualities of this firm's product over those of its rivals. This will be discussed in more detail below.

Advertising facts and figures

Advertising and the state of the economy

Advertising expenditure, like other business expenditure, is subject to the cyclical movement of the national economy. Indeed, advertising is particularly sensitive to the ups and downs in the economy. In times of rising demand and growing profitability of business, expenditure on advertising tends to rise substantially. Conversely, when economic growth slows, and product demand falls, advertising budgets will be cut. Thus between 1984 and 1989, when GDP in real terms (i.e. after accounting for inflation) increased by 22 per cent, advertising expenditure increased by 48 per cent in real terms. Similarly, in the long period of economic growth from 1992 to 2000, advertising expenditure in real terms grew faster, accounting for a higher and higher proportion of household expenditure (see Table 8.1).

Conversely, in times of recession or very low economic growth, advertising budgets will be cut. Thus there was a 15 per cent fall in advertising expenditure in real terms between 1989 (the peak of the 1980s boom) and 1991 (a year of recession), and a fall of nearly 20 per cent from 2007–9 as the economy experienced another downturn.

Advertising media

When considering advertising expenditure by the main categories of media, there has been a long historical trend over which total press advertising has fallen from a high of 84.7 per cent in 1938 (although it reached a peak of nearly 90 per cent in 1953) to 27.4 per cent in 2010. By contrast, advertising on television (which only started in the UK in the mid-1950s) now accounts for some 26 per cent of total advertising expenditure and direct mail for about 11 per cent. Other types of advertising – posters, radio and cinema – account for less than 10 per cent between them. The most dramatic growth in advertising expenditure, however, is on the Internet, which increased from virtually nothing in 1998 to 26.1 per cent in 2012. Figure 8.3 compares the proportions in 2010 with 2005.

Product sectors

The distribution of advertising expenditure by product sectors shows that some 21 per cent of advertising expenditure is for consumables: i.e. food, drink, cosmetics, etc. A further 16.7 per cent is for consumer durables such as household appliances and equipment, and 14.2 per cent for retailers, such as supermarkets. Both these sectors tend to be dominated by just a few firms producing each type of product. This type of market is known as an 'oligopoly', which is Greek for 'few sellers'. Oligopolists often compete heavily in terms of product differentiation and advertising. (Oligopoly is examined in Chapter 12.)

Details of the allocation of advertising expenditure between the different product sectors are given in Table 8.2.

If we take the 20 companies with the highest advertising expenditure, most are within the consumables, consumer durables and retail sectors. The same applies to the 20 most valuable brands (see Table 8.3).

Pause for thought

Try to use the ideas of the growth vector matrix and marketing mix to explain the reasons for the high advertising expenditures of a few of the companies in Table 8.3.

Table 8.1 UK total advertising expenditure

	At current prices (£bn)	At constant (2008) prices (£bn)	As percentage of GDP	As percentage of household expenditure
1988	6.95	11.90	1.46	2.42
1990	8.17	12.40	1.43	2.38
1992	8.05	10.90	1.29	2.10
1994	9.21	11.92	1.33	2.16
1996	10.95	13.48	1.40	2.27
1998	13.10	15.60	1.49	2.40
2000	15.37	17.92	1.57	2.49
2002	15.24	17.32	1.42	2.24
2004	16.81	18.61	1.40	2.25
2006	16.33	17.32	1.22	1.99
2007	17.08	17.70	1.21	1.98
2008	16.59	16.59	1.15	1.89
2009	14.50	14.20	1.03	1.69
2010	15.68	14.86	1.07	1.73
2011	16.10	14.61	1.06	1.73
2012*	16.80	14.87	1.09	1.78

Note: * = forecast

Source: Based on data in *Advertising Statistics Yearbook 2009* (NTC Publications, 2009), *The Advertising Expenditure Report 2011* (Advertising Association), OFCOM site (2012). Advertising Association/WARC, reproduced with permission

Figure 8.3 Distribution of UK advertising expenditure by sector

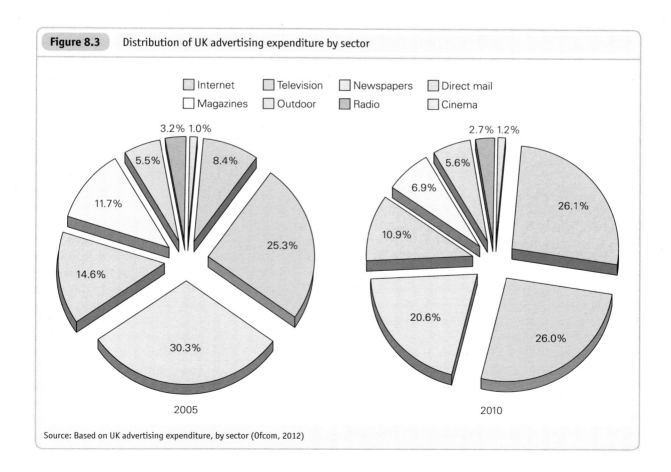

Source: Based on UK advertising expenditure, by sector (Ofcom, 2012)

Table 8.2	UK advertising expenditure by product sector (percentage of total advertising expenditure)					
	1986	**1990**	**1995**	**2000**	**2005**	**2008**
Retail	13.8	12.4	17.9	13.5	14.5	14.2
Industrial	8.7	7.4	7.7	16.7	12.9	12.3
Financial	10.2	10.5	9.7	11.7	13.9	12.9
Government	3.3	3.2	2.5	2.4	5.4	6.4
Services	8.5	10.8	10.7	11.1	16.2	16.7
Durables	20.5	19.6	20.2	21.4	17.2	16.7
Consumables	35.0	36.1	31.2	23.5	19.9	20.8
Total	100.0	100.0	100.0	100.0	100.0	100.0

Source: Based on data in *Advertising Statistics Yearbook 2009* (NTC Publications, 2009). Advertising Association/WARC, reproduced with permission

The advertising/sales ratio

If we wished to consider the intensity of advertising within a given product sector, we could construct an ***advertising/sales ratio***. This relates the total expenditure on advertising for a particular product to the total value of product sales. A selection of products and their advertising/sales ratios in the USA can be seen in Table 8.4.

Transportation services have the highest advertising/sales ratio at 22.2 per cent. This tells us that 22.2 per cent of all earnings by firms supplying transportation services (rail, air, taxis, etc.) go on advertising their product. At the other extreme, companies producing and/or selling industrial organic chemicals spend only 0.1 per cent of their sales revenue on advertising their products.

The wide variation in advertising intensity can be put down to two factors: market structure and product characteristics. As mentioned above, oligopolistic markets are likely to see high advertising outlays. But what types of product will be the most heavily advertised? There are three main categories here.

Definition

Advertising/sales ratio A ratio that reflects the intensity of advertising within a market.

Table 8.3	The top advertisers and advertising brands in the UK (2011)

(a) The top 20 advertisers in the UK

Advertiser	Total spending on advertising (£m)	Advertiser	Total spending on advertising (£m)
1. Procter & Gamble	203.92	11. Morrisons	73.61
2. British Sky Broadcasting	145.14	12. L'Oréal	70.21
3. Unilever	125.53	13. Marks & Spencer	68.72
4. Tesco	114.65	14. Sainsbury's	68.21
5. Asda	113.36	15. Nestlé	67.41
6. COI (Central Office of Information)	105.41	16. Argos	67.32
7. DFS	94.37	17. GlaxoSmithKline	61.41
8. Reckitt Benckiser	80.98	18. B&Q	57.33
9. BT	79.43	19. O2	49.00
10. Kellogg's	76.99	20. McDonald's	48.82

(b) The top 20 brands in the UK

Brand	Market value ($m)	Brand	Market value ($m)
1. Vodafone	19 832	11. Kit Kat	2 180
2. Virgin	8 005	12. Aquafresh	2 013
3. O2	7 830	13. Lipton	1 787
4. BP	7 320	14. Fairy	1 628
5. Orange	6 518	15. Rolls-Royce	1 521
6. Tesco	4 370	16. Bentley	1 448
7. Sainsbury's	3 255	17. Skittles	1 393
8. HSBC	3 134	18. Innocent drinks	1 372
9. Reebok	2 820	19. Marks & Spencer	1 348
10. Barclays	2 769	20. Ariel	1 296

Source: Nielsen and MPP Consulting. Available from www.rankingthebrands.com, reproduced with permission

Table 8.4 US Advertising/sales ratio: 2010

Product category	Advertising/sales ratio (%)	Product category	Advertising/sales ratio (%)
Transportation services	22.2	Investment advice	2.5
Perfumes, Cosmetics, etc	20.1	Motor vehicles and Car bodies	2.3
Motion picture, Videotape production	19.4	Hotels and Motels	2.2
Food and kindred products	11.5	Household appliances	1.7
Educational services	9.8	Accident and health insurance	1.1
Soap, Detergent, Toilet preparations	9.2	Farm machinery and equipment	1.0
Fats and Oils	8.9	Management consulting services	1.0
Amusement parks	8.0	Computer and office equipment	0.7
Beverages	6.1	Personal credit institutions	0.7
Household furniture	6.0	Hospitals	0.6
Department stores	5.0	Ball and roller bearings	0.4
Sugar and Confectionery products	3.3	Computer storage devices	0.3
Paints, Varnishes, Lacquers	3.0	Aircraft	0.2
Dairy products	2.5	Industrial organic chemicals	0.1

Source: Nielsen and MPP Consulting. Available from http://www.rankingthebrands.com, reproduced with permission

The first category is goods that represent a large outlay for consumers (e.g. furniture, electrical goods and other consumer durables). Consumers will not want to make a wrong decision: it would be an expensive mistake. They will thus tend to be cautious in their purchasing decision and will be likely to search for information before selecting a particular product. Advertisers will seek to provide information (but, of course, only information relating to their particular product).

The second category is new products which producers are attempting to establish on the market. The third category is goods, such as educational services, which experience constant changes in their customer base.

Products with the lowest advertising/sales ratio will, by contrast, tend to be those goods whose specifications change very little, or where competition is minimal, or where they are selling to just a few large companies who will be familiar with the equipment or other inputs they are buying. For example, industrial organic chemicals have a ratio of just 0.1 per cent.

The intended effects of advertising

We have argued that the main aim of advertising is to sell more of the product. But when we are told that brand X will make us more beautiful, enrich our lives, wash our clothes whiter, give us get-up-and-go, give us a new taste sensation or make us the envy of our friends, just what are the advertisers up to? Are they merely trying to persuade consumers to buy more?

In fact, there is a bit more to it than this. Advertisers are trying to do two things:

- Shift the product's demand curve to the right.
- Make it less price elastic.

This is illustrated in Figure 8.4. D_1 shows the original demand curve with price at P_1 and sales at Q_1. D_2 shows the curve after an advertising campaign. The rightward shift allows an increased quantity (Q_2) to be sold at the original price. If, at the same time, the demand is made less elastic, the firm can also raise its price and still experience an increase in sales. Thus in the diagram, price can be raised to P_2 and sales will be Q_3 – still substantially above Q_1. The total gain in revenue is shown by the shaded area.

How can advertising bring about this new demand curve?

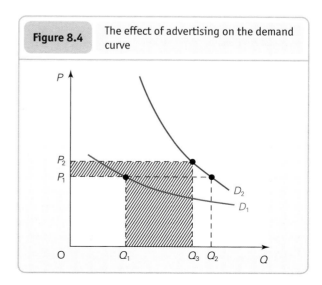

Figure 8.4 The effect of advertising on the demand curve

BOX 8.2	ADVERTISING AND THE LONG RUN

Promoting quality

It is relatively straightforward to measure the short-term impact of an advertising campaign; a simple before and after assessment of sales will normally give a good indication of the advertising's effectiveness. But what about the medium- and longer-term effects of an advertising campaign? How will sales and profits be affected over, say, a five-year period?

The typical impact of advertising on a product's sales is shown in Figure (a). Assume that there is an advertising campaign for the product between time T_1 and T_2. There is a direct effect on sales while the advertising lasts and shortly afterwards. Sales rise from S_1 to S_2. After a while (beyond time T_3), the direct effect of the advertising begins to wear off, and wears off completely by time T_4. This is illustrated by the dashed line. But the higher level of sales declines much more slowly, given that many of the new customers continue to buy the product out of habit. Sales will eventually level off (at point T_5). It is likely, however, that sales will not return to the original level of S_1; there will be some new customers who will stick with the product over the long term. This long-term effect is shown by the increase in sales from S_1 to S_3.

But just what is this long-term effect? One way to explore the impact of advertising over the long run is to evaluate how advertising and profitability in general are linked.

In Figure (b) the argument is made that advertising shapes the key element of profitability, namely relative customer value. Customer value is determined by the product's perceived quality (and hence utility) relative to price. The more that advertising can enhance the perceived

quality of a product, the more it will increase the product's profitability.

How this benefits the business over the longer term is best seen through examples.

Purina Petcare is the world's leading pet care company. It produces a range of pet-food brands, including Felix, Winalot, Go Cat, Bonio and Bakers. Bakers is a success story of a long-term advertising campaign that began in 1994, when the dog-food market was dominated by tinned meat and Bakers was one of a small number of dry dog-food brands. Working with a small advertising agency, Purina developed an advertising campaign around the idea that 'dogs would choose Bakers'. This campaign was awarded a gold medal by the Institute of Practitioners in Advertising, the UK trade body and professional institute, which noted:

> 10 years on, this powerful campaign is still running. Bakers achieved both its short-term objective of becoming the market leader and long-term objective of increasing the size of the market. The length of the campaign is testament to the strong sales response, having so far delivered an estimated £58.3 million for the brand.[1]

---

[1] www.ipaeffectivenessawards.co.uk/pdfs/Embargoed_2005_winners_release.pdf

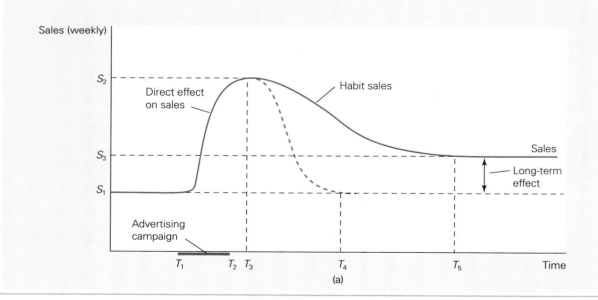

(a)

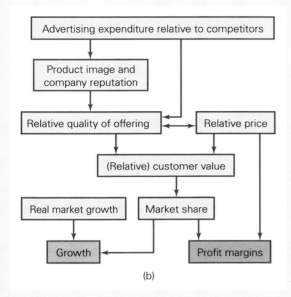

(b)

PG Tips, launched in 1930, is another brand that leads its respective market. The UK tea market has been dominated by PG Tips since 1958, when it became market leader, a position it still holds today, with some 27 per cent of the 'traditional' tea market in 2011. The 'chimp' adverts, then the Aardman T-Birds and more recently Johnny Vegas and Monkey, have established a clear brand image, enabling PG Tips to hold its ground in a highly competitive market and charge a price premium. (Blind tests have revealed that consumers cannot distinguish between any of the leading tea brands!) Market analysis shows that PG Tips has a price elasticity of demand of −0.4 compared with its nearest rival, Tetley, which has an elasticity of −1.4. It was estimated that between 1980 and 2000 advertising the PG Tips brand cost £100 million but generated in the region of £2 billion in extra sales.

Another example of a successful long-term campaign is Audi, which was one of the winners of the 2011 Institute of Practitioners in Advertising (IPA) Effectiveness Awards. Praising the advertising campaign's focus on design, performance and innovation, the IPA acknowledged that 'Audi went from being the understated alternative to Mercedes and BMW, to the fastest growing prestige car brand of the last eight years. In 1999, against ambitious growth targets, the communications strategy was overhauled to position Audi as the leader in the prestige sector. "Vorsprung durch Technik" – the relentless desire to challenge and evolve – became the focus of the campaign which generated an incremental 50 000 car sales and payback of £7.50 for every

£1 spent.'[2] In 2000, Audi had a 1.5 per cent share of the UK market. By 2010, this had grown to 5.3 per cent.

An alternative way to illustrate the impact of advertising on longer-term profitability is to assess how companies approach advertising in a recession. What happens when advertising expenditure is cut, and how does profitability return once the recession is over and advertising expenditure once again begins to rise?

Recessions place many firms under significant pressures due to declining consumer demand. A study[3] published in 2011 examined the impact of marketing, in recessionary periods, upon long-term profitability. It reviewed 18 previous academic articles and reports. Firm-wide pressures to cut costs often result in large declines in advertising expenditure. However, the study finds that these cutbacks may be short-sighted. The long-term prospects of some firms can be improved during economic downturns. Firms that are able to engage in marketing activities during recessions are associated with superior shareholder value, customer loyalty and long-term profitability. Those which rein in expenditures put future profits, and perhaps ultimately their survival, at risk.

During the recent downturn many media-savvy companies have attempted to maintain advertising activity despite their declining budgets. Increasing use has been made of Internet-based advertising. Websites such as YouTube and Facebook have been used as platforms to support 'viral' or word-of-mouth campaigns. For example, the Cadbury's Dairy Milk chocolate brand was rejuvenated in 2008, following the re-launch of its long-standing 'glass and a half' adverts. The successful 'drumming gorilla' advert substantially increased sales. Although the campaign made use of traditional media, it was launched online. The advert has been viewed millions of times, on various websites, at no cost to the company.

The message is that advertising should seek to continually promote a product's quality. This is the key to long-term sales and profits. What is also apparent is that successful brands have advertising campaigns which have been consistent over time. A brand image of quality is not created overnight, and once it is established, it requires continued investment if it is to endure and yield profits over the longer term.

1. How are long-run profits and advertising linked?
2. Why does quality 'win out' in the end?

2 www.ipaeffectivenessawards.co.uk/IPA-Brand-Films
3 L. O'Malley, V. Story and V. O'Sullivan, 'Marketing in a recession: retrench or invest', *Journal of Strategic Marketing*, 19(3) (2011).

Shifting the demand curve to the right. This will occur if the advertising brings the product to more people's attention and if it increases people's desire for the product.

Making the demand curve less elastic. This will occur if the advertising creates greater brand loyalty (i.e. lowering the product's cross-elasticity of demand). People must be led to believe (rightly or wrongly) that competitors' brands are inferior. This will allow the firm to raise its price above that of its rivals with no significant fall in sales. There will be only a small substitution effect of this price rise because consumers have been led to believe that there are no close substitutes.

The more successful an advertising campaign is, the more it will shift the demand curve to the right and the more it will reduce the price elasticity of demand.

Assessing the effects of advertising

The supporters of advertising claim that not only is it an important freedom for firms, but also it provides specific benefits for the consumer. By contrast, critics of advertising suggest that it can impose serious costs on the consumer and on society in general. In this section we will assess the basis of this difference.

> ### Pause for thought
>
> *Before considering the points listed below, see if you can identify the main arguments both for and against the use of advertising.*

The arguments put forward in favour of advertising include the following:

- Advertising provides information to consumers on what products are available.
- Advertising may be necessary in order to introduce new products. Without it, firms would find it difficult to break into markets in which there were established brands. In other words, it is a means of breaking down barriers to the entry of new firms and products.
- It can aid product development by helping the firm emphasise the special features of its product.
- It may encourage price competition, if prices feature significantly in the advertisement.
- By increasing sales, it may allow the firm to gain economies of scale (see section 9.4), which in turn will help to keep prices down.

On the other side, the following arguments are put forward against advertising:

- Advertising is designed to persuade people to buy the product. Consumers do not have perfect information and may thus be misled into purchasing goods whose qualities may be inferior to those goods which are not advertised.
- Scarcity is defined as the excess of human wants over the means of fulfilling them. Advertising is used to *create* wants. It could thus be argued to increase scarcity.
- It increases materialism.
- Advertising costs money: it uses resources. These resources could be put to alternative uses in producing more goods.
- If there are no reductions in costs to be gained from producing on a larger scale, the costs of advertising will tend to raise the price paid by the consumer. Even if the firm has potential economies of scale, it may be prevented from expanding its sales by retaliatory advertising from its rivals.
- Advertising can create a barrier to the entry of new firms by promoting brand loyalty to *existing* firms' products. New firms may not be able to afford the large amount of advertising necessary to create a new brand image, whereas existing firms can spread the cost of their advertising over their already large number of sales. In other words, there are economies of scale in advertising which act as a barrier to entry (see page 167).

    This barrier is strengthened if existing firms sell many brands each (for example, in the washing powder industry many brands are produced by just two firms). This makes it even harder for new firms to introduce a new brand successfully, since the consumer already has so many to choose from.

    The fewer the competitors, the less elastic will be the demand for each individual firm, and the higher will be the profit-maximising price (see Chapter 12).

- People are constantly subjected to advertisements, whether on television, in magazines, on bill-boards, etc., and often find them annoying, tasteless or unsightly. Thus advertising imposes costs on society in general. These costs are external to the firm: that is, they do not cost the firm money, and hence are normally ignored by the firm.

The effects of advertising on competition, costs and prices are largely an empirical issue (an issue of *fact*), and clearly these effects will differ from one product to another. However, many of the arguments presented here involve judgements as to whether the effects are socially desirable or undesirable. Such judgements involve questions of taste and morality: things that are questions of opinion and cannot be resolved by a simple appeal to the facts.

SUMMARY

1a When firms seek to differentiate their product from those of their competitors, they can adjust one or more of four dimensions of the product: its technical standards, its quality, its design characteristics, and the level of customer service.

1b Products can be vertically and horizontally differentiated from one another. Vertical differentiation is where products are superior or inferior to others. Horizontal differentiation is where products differ, but are of a similar quality.

2a Marketing involves developing a product image and then persuading consumers to purchase it.

2b A business must choose an appropriate product/market strategy. Four such strategies can be identified: market penetration (focusing on current product and market); product development (new product in current market); market development (current product in new markets); diversification (new products in new markets).

2c The marketing strategy of a product involves the manipulation of four key variables: product, price, place and promotion. Every product has a distinct marketing mix. The marketing mix is likely to change over the product's life cycle.

3a Advertising expenditure is cyclical, expanding and contracting with the upswings and downswings of the economy.

3b Most advertising expenditure goes on consumables and durable goods.

3c The advertising intensity within a given product sector can be estimated by considering the advertising/sales ratio. The advertising/sales ratio is likely to be higher the more oligopolistic the market, the more expensive the product, the newer the product, and the more that the customer base for a product is subject to change.

3d The aims of advertising are to increase demand and make the product less price elastic.

3e Supporters of advertising claim that it: provides consumers with information; brings new products to consumers' attention; aids product development; encourages price competition; and generates economies of scale through increasing sales.

3f Critics of advertising claim that it: distorts consumption decisions; creates wants; pushes up prices; creates barriers to entry; and produces unwanted side-effects, such as being unsightly.

REVIEW QUESTIONS

1 How might we account for the growth in non-price competition within the modern developed economy?

2 Distinguish between vertical and horizontal product differentiation. Give examples of goods that fall into each category.

3 Consider how the selection of the product/market strategy (market penetration, market development, product development and diversification) will influence the business's marketing mix. Identify which elements in the marketing mix would be most significant in developing a successful marketing strategy.

4 Why might the advertising/sales ratio be a poor guide to the degree of exposure of the consumer to advertisements for a particular category of product?

5 Imagine that 'Sunshine' sunflower margarine, a well-known brand, is advertised with the slogan, 'It helps you live longer' (the implication being that butter and margarines high in saturates shorten your life). What do you think would happen to the demand curve for a supermarket's own brand of sunflower margarine? Consider both the direction of shift and the effect on elasticity. Will the elasticity differ markedly at different prices? How will this affect the pricing policy and sales of the super-market's own brand? Could the supermarket respond other than by adjusting the price of its margarine?

6 On balance, does advertising benefit (a) the consumer; (b) society in general?

ADDITIONAL PART C CASE STUDIES IN THE *ECONOMICS FOR BUSINESS* MyEconLab (www.pearsoned.co.uk/sloman)

C.1 **Bentham and the philosophy of utilitarianism.** This looks at the historical and philosophical underpinning of the ideas of utility maximisation.

C.2 **Choices within the household.** Is what is best for the individual best for the family?

C.3 **Taking account of time.** The importance of the time dimension in consumption decisions.

C.4 **The demand for butter.** An examination of a real-world demand function.

C.5 **What we pay to watch sport.** Consideration of the demand function for season tickets to watch spectator sports such as football.

WEBSITES RELEVANT TO PART C

Numbers and sections refer to websites listed in the Web appendix and hotlinked from this book's website at
www.pearsoned.co.uk/sloman

■ For news articles relevant to Part C, see the *Economics News Articles* link from the book's website.

■ For general news on demand, consumers and marketing, see websites in section A, and particularly A2, 3, 4, 8, 9, 11, 12, 23, 25, 36. See also site A41 for links to economics news articles and to search particular topics (e.g. advertising).

■ For data, information and sites on products and marketing, see sites B2, 10, 11, 13, 17.

■ For student resources relevant to Part C, see sites C1–7, 19.

■ For data on advertising, see site E37.

■ For links to sites on various aspects of advertising and marketing, see section *Industry and Commerce > Consumer Protection > Advertising* in sites I7 and 11.

Background to supply

The FT Reports . . .

The Financial Times, 3 June 2009

FT

O'Leary looks to skies as he keeps throttle open

By Kevin Done

So far the recession has been good for Ryanair and its iconoclastic leader Michael O'Leary. In the space of 15 years as chief executive, he has taken a small lossmaking airline from the fringes of Europe and has built it into the world's second most valuable carrier by market capitalisation, after Singapore Airlines.

In the past 12 months it has overtaken both Air France KLM and Germany's Lufthansa – British Airways was left in the slipstream long ago – to become the biggest European short-haul carrier, measured by passenger numbers. And in the depth of the recession, it is stretching its lead.

As most carriers in Europe cut capacity, Ryanair is still adding more aircraft, confident that with the lowest costs in the industry it can continue to drive down fares, gaining market share to fill its rising number of seats . . .

Ryanair's low-cost airline business model is again demonstrating it can develop robustly during recession. Even with a 59 per cent rise in fuel costs last year and an 8 per cent drop in average fares, the group stayed in profit at an underlying level.

To the discomfiture of rivals Mr O'Leary is keeping the throttle open. Ryanair has led the low-cost airline revolution in Europe. It did not invent the model, which originated in the US with Southwest Airlines, but it has implemented it with unmatched zeal and discipline.

The immediate outlook is promising. Mr O'Leary forecast yesterday that under-lying net profits would at least double to between €200 m and €300 m this year. The flipside of having made bad hedging decisions in the previous two years is that Ryanair was free to lock in relatively low fuel prices for much of the current financial year, when the oil price plunged in recent months.

Mr O'Leary is also still driving down non-fuel costs as he squeezes airport and handling costs around Europe, and he has locked in reduced prices for acquiring new aircraft thanks to the strength of the euro against the dollar.

With one of the strongest balance sheets in the industry, Ryanair has also secured financing for new aircraft to September 2010.

While many airline chief executives claim they are fighting for survival in the worst trading conditions they have ever faced, Mr O'Leary was confidently sticking yesterday to prerecession forecasts that Ryanair would double its profits and passenger numbers between 2007 and 2012 . . .

Prosperity is determined by the productivity of an economy, which is measured by the value of goods and services produced per unit of the nation's human, capital, and natural resources. Productivity depends both on the value of a nation's products and services, measured by the prices they can command in open markets, and the efficiency with which these products can be produced. Productivity supports high wages, a strong currency, and attractive returns to capital – and with them a high standard of living. Competitiveness, then, is measured by productivity.

The Global Competitiveness Report 2008–2009, p. 44

In Part D we turn to supply. In other words, we will focus on the amount that firms produce. In Parts E and F we shall see how the supply decision is affected by the environment in which a firm operates, and in particular by the amount of competition it faces. In this part of the book, however, we take a more general look at supply and its relationship to profit.

Profit is made by firms earning more from the sale of goods than the goods cost to produce. A firm's total profit ($T\Pi$) is thus the difference between its total sales revenue (TR) and its total costs of production (TC):

$$T\Pi = TR - TC$$

(Note that we use the Greek Π (pi) for 'profit'.)

Businesses can increase their profitability either by increasing their revenue (by selling more of their product or adjusting their price) or by reducing their costs of production. As the *Financial Times* article opposite illustrates in the case of Ryanair, the low-cost, low-price business model has been successful in increasing profit and market share.

In order, then, to discover how a firm can maximise its profit, or even get a sufficient level of profit, we must first consider what determines costs and revenue. Chapter 9 examines production, productivity and costs. Chapter 10 considers revenue, and then puts costs and revenue together to examine profit. We will discover the output at which profits are maximised and how much profit is made at that output.

Key terms

Opportunity cost
Explicit and implicit costs
Short and long run
Law of diminishing
  (marginal) returns
Returns to scale
  (increasing, constant
  and decreasing)
Economies of scale
  (internal)
External economies
  of scale
Diseconomies of scale
Specialisation and division
  of labour
Fixed and variable factors
Fixed and variable costs
Total average and
  marginal costs and
  revenue
Price takers and price
  makers/choosers
Profit maximisation
Normal profit
Supernormal profit

Costs of production

Business issues covered in this chapter

- What do profits consist of?
- How are costs of production measured?
- What is the relationship between inputs and outputs in both the short and long run?
- How do costs vary with output in both the short and long run?
- What are meant by 'economies of scale' and what are the reasons for such economies?
- How can a business combine its inputs in the most efficient way?

9.1 THE MEANING OF COSTS

Opportunity cost

When measuring costs, economists always use the concept of *opportunity cost*. Opportunity cost is the cost of any activity measured in terms of the sacrifice made in doing it: in other words, the cost measured in terms of the opportunities forgone (see Chapter 2). If a car manufacturer can produce 10 small saloon cars with the same amount of inputs as it takes to produce 6 large saloon cars, then the opportunity cost of producing 1 small car is 0.6 of a large car. If a taxi and car hire firm uses its cars as taxis, then the opportunity cost includes not only the cost of employing taxi drivers and buying fuel, but also the sacrifice of rental income from hiring its vehicles out.

Measuring a firm's opportunity costs

Just how do we measure a firm's opportunity cost? First we must discover what factors of production it has used. Then we must measure the sacrifice involved in using

them. To do this it is necessary to put factors into two categories.

Factors not owned by the firm: explicit costs

The opportunity cost of those factors not already owned by the firm is simply the price that the firm has to pay for them. Thus if the firm uses £100 worth of electricity, the opportunity cost is £100. The firm has sacrificed £100 which could have been spent on something else.

These costs are called *explicit costs* because they involve direct payment of money by firms.

Definitions

Opportunity cost Cost measured in terms of the next best alternative forgone.

Explicit costs The payments to outside suppliers of inputs.

Factors already owned by the firm: implicit costs

When the firm already owns factors (e.g. machinery), it does not as a rule have to pay out money to use them. Their opportunity costs are thus *implicit costs*. They are equal to what the factors *could* earn for the firm in some alternative use, either within the firm or hired out to some other firm.

Here are some examples of implicit costs:

- A firm owns some buildings. The opportunity cost of using them is the rent it could have received by letting them out to another firm.
- A firm draws £100 000 from the bank out of its savings in order to invest in new plant and equipment. The opportunity cost of this investment is not just the £100 000 (an explicit cost), but also the interest it thereby forgoes (an implicit cost).
- The owner of the firm could have earned £15 000 per annum by working for someone else. This £15 000 is the opportunity cost of the owner's time.

If there is no alternative use for a factor of production, as in the case of a machine designed to produce a specific product, and if it has no scrap value, the opportunity cost of using it is *zero*. In such a case, if the output from the machine is worth more than the cost of all the *other* inputs involved, the firm might as well use the machine rather than let it stand idle.

What the firm paid for the machine – its *historic cost* – is irrelevant. Not using the machine will not bring that money back. It has been spent. These are sometimes referred to as *sunk costs*.

> #### Pause for thought
>
> *Assume that a farmer decides to grow wheat on land that could be used for growing barley. Barley sells for £100 per tonne. Wheat sells for £150 per tonne. Seed, fertiliser, labour and other costs of growing crops are £80 per tonne for both wheat and barley. What are the farmer's costs and profit per tonne of growing wheat?*

KEY IDEA 18 — *The 'bygones' principle* states that sunk (fixed) costs should be ignored when deciding whether to produce or sell more or less of a product. Only variable costs should be taken into account.

Likewise, the *replacement cost* is irrelevant. That should be taken into account only when the firm is considering replacing the machine.

> #### Definitions
>
> **Implicit costs** Costs which do not involve a direct payment of money to a third party, but which nevertheless involve a sacrifice of some alternative.
>
> **Historic costs** The original amount the firm paid for factors it now owns.
>
> **Sunk costs** Costs that cannot be recouped (e.g. by transferring assets to other uses).
>
> **Replacement costs** What the firm would have to pay to replace factors it currently owns.

BOX 9.1 | **THE FALLACY OF USING HISTORIC COSTS**

Or there's no point crying over spilt milk

'What's done is done.'

'Write it off to experience.'

'You might as well make the best of a bad job.'

These familiar sayings are all everyday examples of a simple fact of life: once something has happened, you cannot change the past. You have to take things as they are *now*.

If you fall over and break your leg, there is little point in saying, 'If only I hadn't done that I could have gone on that skiing holiday; I could have taken part in that race; I could have done so many other things (sigh).' Wishing things were different won't change history. You have to manage as well as you can *with* your broken leg.

It is the same for a firm. Once it has purchased some inputs, it is no good then wishing it hadn't. It has to accept that it has now got them, and make the best decisions about what to do with them.

Take a simple example. The local convenience store in early December decides to buy 100 Christmas trees for £10 each.

At the time of purchase this represents an opportunity cost of £10 each, since the £10 could have been spent on something else. The shopkeeper estimates that there is enough local demand to sell all 100 trees at £20 each, thereby making a reasonable profit (even after allowing for handling costs).

But the estimate turns out to be wrong. On 23 December there are still 50 trees unsold. What should be done? At this stage the £10 that was paid for the trees is irrelevant. It is a historic cost. It cannot be recouped: the trees cannot be sold back to the wholesaler!

In fact the opportunity cost is now zero. It might even be negative if the shopkeeper has to pay to dispose of any unsold trees. It might, therefore, be worth selling the trees at £10, £5 or even £1. Last thing on Christmas Eve it might even be worth giving away any unsold trees.

 Why is the correct price to charge (for the unsold trees) the one at which the price elasticity of demand equals –1? (Assume no disposal costs.)

 KI 3 p 20

9.2 PRODUCTION IN THE SHORT RUN

The cost of producing any level of output will depend on the amount of inputs used and the price that the firm must pay for them. Let us first focus on the quantity of inputs used.

 KEY IDEA 19 *Output depends on the amount of resources and how they are used.* Different amounts and combinations of inputs will lead to different amounts of output. If output is to be produced efficiently, then inputs should be combined in the optimum proportions.

Short-run and long-run changes in production

If a firm wants to increase production, it will take time to acquire a greater quantity of certain inputs. For example, a manufacturer can use more electricity by turning on switches, but it might take a long time to obtain and install more machines, and longer still to build a second or third factory.

If, then, the firm wants to increase output in a hurry, it will only be able to increase the quantity of certain inputs. It can use more raw materials, more fuel, more tools and possibly more labour (by hiring extra workers or offering overtime to its existing workforce). But it will have to make do with its existing buildings and most of its machinery.

The distinction we are making here is between *fixed factors* and *variable factors*. A *fixed* factor is an input that cannot be increased within a given time period (e.g. buildings). A *variable* factor is one that can.

The distinction between fixed and variable factors allows us to distinguish between the *short run* and the *long run*.

The short run is a time period during which at least one factor of production is fixed. In the short run, then, output can be increased only by using more variable factors. For example, if a shipping line wanted to carry more passengers in response to a rise in demand, it could accommodate more passengers on existing sailings if there was space. It could increase the number of sailings with its existing fleet, by hiring more crew and using more fuel. But in the short run it could not buy more ships: there would not be time for them to be built.

The long run is a time period long enough for all inputs to be varied. Given long enough, the shipping company can have a new ship built, making all factors of production variable.

The actual length of the short run will differ from firm to firm. It is not a fixed period of time. Thus if it takes a farmer a year to obtain new land, buildings and equipment, the short run is any time period up to a year and the long run is any time period longer than a year. But if it takes a shipping company three years to obtain an extra ship, the short run is any period up to three years and the long run is any period longer than three years.

For this and the next section we will concentrate on *short-run* production and costs. We will look at the long run in sections 9.4 and 9.5.

Pause for thought

How will the length of the short run for the shipping company depend on the state of the shipbuilding industry?

Production in the short run: the law of diminishing returns

Production in the short run is subject to *diminishing returns*. You may well have heard of 'the law of diminishing returns': it is one of the most famous of all 'laws' of economics. To illustrate how this law underlies short-run production, let us take the simplest possible case where there are just two factors: one fixed and one variable.

Take the case of a farm. Assume the fixed factor is land and the variable factor is labour. Since the land is fixed in supply, output per period of time can be increased only by increasing the number of workers employed. But imagine what would happen as more and more workers crowded on to a fixed area of land. The land cannot go on yielding more and more output indefinitely. After a point the additions to output from each extra worker will begin to diminish.

We can now state the *law of diminishing (marginal) returns*.

 KEY IDEA 20 *The law of diminishing marginal returns.* When increasing amounts of a variable factor are used with a given amount of a fixed factor, there will come a point when each extra unit of the variable factor will produce less additional output than the previous unit.

Definitions

Fixed factor An input that cannot be increased in supply within a given time period.

Variable factor An input that *can* be increased in supply within a given time period.

Short run The period of time over which at least one factor is fixed.

Long run The period of time long enough for *all* factors to be varied.

Law of diminishing (marginal) returns When one or more factors are held fixed, there will come a point beyond which the extra output from additional units of the variable factor will diminish.

A good example of the law of diminishing returns is given in Case D.3 in MyEconLab. The case looks at diminishing returns to the application of nitrogen fertiliser on farmland.

The short-run production function: total product

Let us now see how the law of diminishing returns affects total output or **total physical product** (TPP).

The relationship between inputs and output is shown in a **production function**. In the simple case of the farm with only two factors – namely, a fixed supply of land ($\bar{L}n$) and a variable supply of farm workers (Lb) – the production function would be:

$$TPP = f(\bar{L}n, Lb)$$

Definitions

Total physical product The total output of a product per period of time that is obtained from a given amount of inputs.

Production function The mathematical relationship between the output of a good and the inputs used to produce it. It shows how output will be affected by changes in the quantity of one or more of the inputs.

	Table 9.1	Wheat production per year from a particular farm (tonnes)		
	Number of workers (*Lb*)	*TPP*	*APP* (= *TPP/Lb*)	*MPP* (= *ΔTPP/ΔLb*)
a	0	0	–	
	1	3	3	3
	2	10	5	7
b	3	24	8	14
c	4	36	9	12
	5	40	8	4
	6	42	7	2
d	7	42	6	0
	8	40	5	-2

This states that total physical product (i.e. the output of the farm) over a given period of time is a function of (i.e. depends on) the quantity of land and labour employed.

The production function can also be expressed in the form of a table or a graph. Table 9.1 and Figure 9.1 show a hypothetical production function for a farm producing wheat. The first two columns of Table 9.1 and the top diagram in Figure 9.1 show how wheat output per year varies as extra workers are employed on a fixed amount of land.

Figure 9.1   Wheat production per year (tonnes) from a particular farm

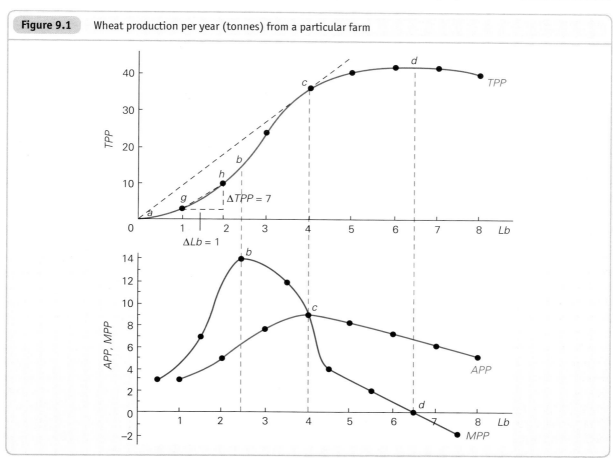

With nobody working on the land, output will be zero (point *a*). As the first farm workers are taken on, wheat output initially rises more and more rapidly. The assumption behind this is that with only one or two workers efficiency is low, since the workers are spread thinly across multiple tasks. With more workers, however, they can work as a team – each, perhaps, doing some specialist job – and thus they can use the land more efficiently. In the top diagram of Figure 9.1, output rises more and more rapidly up to the employment of the third worker (point *b*).

After point *b*, however, diminishing marginal returns set in: output rises less and less rapidly, and the *TPP* curve correspondingly becomes less steeply sloped.

When point *d* is reached, wheat output is at a maximum: the land is yielding as much as it can. Any more workers employed after that are likely to get in each other's way. Thus beyond point *d*, output is likely to fall again: eight workers produce less than seven workers.

The short-run production function: average and marginal product

In addition to total physical product, two other important concepts are illustrated by a production function: namely, **average physical product (APP)** and **marginal physical product (MPP)**.

Average physical product

This is output (*TPP*) per unit of the variable factor (*Qv*). In the case of the farm, it is the output of wheat per worker.

$$APP = TPP/Qv$$

Thus in Table 9.1, the average physical product of labour when four workers are employed is 36/4 = 9 tonnes per year.

Marginal physical product

This is the *extra* output (Δ*TPP*) produced by employing *one more* unit of the variable factor, (where the symbol Δ denotes 'a change in').

Thus in Table 9.1 the marginal physical product of the fourth worker is 12 tonnes. The reason is that, by employing the fourth worker, wheat output has risen from 24 tonnes to 36 tonnes: a rise of 12 tonnes.

In symbols, marginal physical product is given by:

$$MPP = \Delta TPP/\Delta Qv$$

Thus in our example:

$$MPP = 12/1 = 12$$

The reason why we divide the increase in output (Δ*TPP*) by the increase in the quantity of the variable factor (Δ*Qv*) is that some variable factors can be increased only in multiple units. For example, if we wanted to know the *MPP* of fertiliser and we found out how much extra wheat was produced by using an extra 20 kg bag, we would have to divide this output by 20 (Δ*Qv*) to find the *MPP* of *one* more kilogram.

Note that in Table 9.1 the figures for *MPP* are entered in the spaces between the other figures. The reason is that *MPP* can be seen as the *difference* in output *between* one level of input and another. Thus in the table the difference in output between five and six workers is 2 tonnes.

The figures for *APP* and *MPP* are plotted in the lower diagram of Figure 9.1. We can draw a number of conclusions from these two diagrams.

- The *MPP* between two points is equal to the slope of the *TPP* curve between those two points. For example, when the number of workers increases from 1 to 2 (Δ*Lb* = 1), *TPP* rises from 3 to 10 tonnes (Δ*TPP* = 7). *MPP* is thus 7: the slope of the line between points *g* and *h*.
- *MPP* rises at first: the slope of the *TPP* curve gets steeper.
- *MPP* reaches a maximum at point *b*. At that point the slope of the *TPP* curve is at its steepest.
- After point *b*, diminishing returns set in. *MPP* falls. *TPP* becomes less steep.
- *APP* rises at first. It continues rising as long as the addition to output from the last worker (*MPP*) is greater than the average output (*APP*): the *MPP* pulls the *APP* up. This continues beyond point *b*. Even though *MPP* is now falling, the *APP* goes on rising as long as the *MPP* is still above the *APP*. Thus *APP* goes on rising to point *c*.
- Beyond point *c*, *MPP* is below *APP*. New workers add less to output than the average. This pulls the average down: *APP* falls.
- As long as *MPP* is greater than zero, *TPP* will go on rising: new workers add to total output.
- At point *d*, *TPP* is at a maximum (its slope is zero). An additional worker will add nothing to output: *MPP* is zero.
- Beyond point *d*, *TPP* falls. *MPP* is negative.

Pause for thought

What is the significance of the slope of the line ac in the top part of Figure 9.1?

Definitions

Average physical product (*APP*) Total output (*TPP*) per unit of the variable factor (*Qv*) in question: *APP = TPP/Qv*.

Marginal physical product (*MPP*) The extra output gained by the employment of one more unit of the variable factor: *MPP = ΔTPP/ΔQv*.

9.3 COSTS IN THE SHORT RUN

Having looked at the background to costs in the short run, we now turn to examine short-run costs themselves. We will be examining how costs change as a firm changes the amount it produces. Obviously, if it is to decide how much to produce, it will need to know just what the level of costs will be at each level of output.

Costs and inputs

A firm's costs of production will depend on the factors of production it uses. The more factors it uses, the greater will its costs be. More precisely, this relationship depends on two elements.

KI 19
p 130 *The productivity of the factors.* The greater their physical productivity, the smaller will be the quantity of them that is needed to produce a given level of output, and hence the lower will be the cost of that output. In other words, there is a direct link between *TPP*, *APP* and *MPP* and the costs of production.

The price of the factors. The higher their price, the higher will be the costs of production. In the short run, some factors are fixed in supply. Their total costs, therefore, are fixed, in the sense that they do not vary with output. For example, rent on land is a *fixed cost*. It is the same whether the firm produces a lot, a little or nothing.

The cost of variable factors, however, does vary with output. The cost of raw materials is a *variable cost*. The more that is produced, the more raw materials are used and therefore the higher is their total cost.

Total cost

The *total cost (TC)* of production is the sum of the *total variable costs* (TVC) and the *total fixed costs* (TFC) of production.

$$TC = TVC + TFC$$

Consider Table 9.2 and Figure 9.2. They show the total costs for an imaginary firm for producing different levels

Table 9.2	Total costs for firm X		
Output (Q)	**TFC (£)**	**TVC (£)**	**TC (£)**
0	12	0	12
1	12	10	22
2	12	16	28
3	12	21	33
4	12	28	40
5	12	40	52
6	12	60	72
7	12	91	103

Definitions

Fixed costs Total costs that do not vary with the amount of output produced.

Variable costs Total costs that do vary with the amount of output produced.

Total cost (TC) The sum of total fixed costs (TFC) and total variable costs (TVC): TC = TFC + TVC.

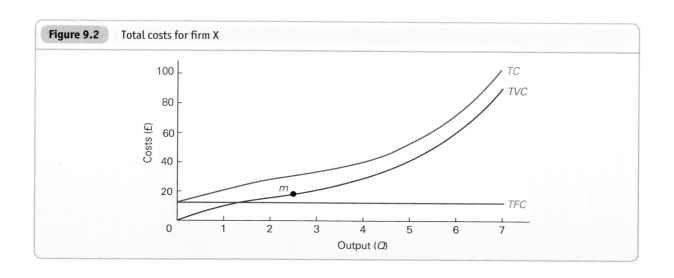

Figure 9.2 Total costs for firm X

of output (Q). Let us examine each of the three cost curves in turn.

Total fixed cost (TFC)

In our example, total fixed cost is assumed to be £12. Since this does not vary with output, it is shown by a horizontal straight line.

Total variable cost (TVC)

With a zero output, no variable factors will be used. Thus $TVC = 0$. The TVC curve, therefore, starts from the origin.

The shape of the TVC curve follows from the law of diminishing returns. Initially, *before* diminishing returns set in, TVC rises less and less rapidly as more variable factors are added. For example, in the case of a factory with a fixed supply of machinery, initially as more workers are taken on the workers can do increasingly specialist tasks and make a fuller use of the capital equipment. This corresponds to the portion of the TPP curve that rises more rapidly (up to point b in the top diagram of Figure 9.1).

As output is increased beyond point m in Figure 9.2, diminishing returns set in. Given that extra workers (the extra variable factors) are producing less and less extra output, the extra units of output they do produce will be costing more and more in terms of wage costs. Thus TVC rises more and more rapidly. The TVC curve gets steeper. This corresponds to the portion of the TPP curve that rises less rapidly (between points b and d in Figure 9.1).

Total cost (TC)

Since $TC = TVC + TFC$, the TC curve is simply the TVC curve shifted vertically upwards by £12.

Average and marginal cost

Average cost (AC) is cost per unit of production.

$$AC = TC/Q$$

Thus if it costs a firm £2000 to produce 100 units of a product, the average cost would be £20 for each unit (£2000/100).

Like total cost, average cost can be divided into the two components, fixed and variable. In other words, average cost equals *average fixed cost* ($AFC = TFC/Q$) plus *average variable cost* ($AVC = TVC/Q$).

$$AC = AFC + AVC$$

Marginal cost (MC) is the *extra* cost of producing *one more unit*: that is, the rise in total cost per one unit rise in output.

$$MC = \frac{\Delta TC}{\Delta Q}$$

where Δ means 'a change in'.

For example, assume that a firm is currently producing 1 000 000 boxes of matches a month. It now increases output by 1000 boxes (another batch): $\Delta Q = 1000$. As a result its total costs rise by £30: $\Delta TC = £30$. What is the cost of producing *one* more box of matches? It is:

$$MC = \frac{\Delta TC}{\Delta Q} = \frac{£30}{1000} = 3p$$

(Note that all marginal costs are variable, since, by definition, there can be no extra fixed costs as output rises.)

Given the TFC, TVC and TC for each output, it is possible to derive the AFC, AVC, AC and MC for each output using the above definitions. For example, using the data of Table 9.2, Table 9.3 can be constructed.

What will be the shapes of the MC, AFC, AVC and AC curves? These follow from the nature of the MPP and APP curves (which we looked at in section 9.2).

Definitions

Average (total) cost (AC) Total cost (fixed plus variable) per unit of output: $AC = TC/Q = AFC + AVC$.

Average fixed cost (AFC) Total fixed cost per unit of output: $AFC = TFC/Q$.

Average variable cost (AVC) Total variable cost per unit of output: $AVC = TVC/Q$.

Marginal cost (MC) The cost of producing one more unit of output: $MC = \Delta TC/\Delta Q$.

Table 9.3	Costs						
Output (Q) (units)	TFC (£)	AFC (TFC/Q) (£)	TVC (£)	AVC (TVC/Q) (£)	TC (TFC + TVC) (£)	AC (TC/Q) (£)	MC (ΔTC/ΔQ) (£)
0	12	–	0	–	12	–	
							10
1	12	12	10	10	22	22	
							6
2	12	6	16	8	28	14	
							5
3	12	4	21	7	33	11	
							7
4	12	3	28	7	40	10	
							12
5	12	2.4	40	8	52	10.4	
							20
6	12	2	60	10	72	12	
							31
7	12	1.7	91	13	103	14.7	

KI 20
p 130

Marginal cost (MC)

KI 20
p 130
The shape of the *MC* curve follows directly from the law of diminishing returns. Initially, in Figure 9.3, as more of the variable factor is used, extra units of output cost less than previous units. *MC* falls. This corresponds to the portion of the *TVC* curve in Figure 9.2 to the left of point *m*.

Beyond a certain level of output, diminishing returns set in. This is shown as point *x* in Figure 9.3 and corresponds to point *m* in Figure 9.2. Thereafter *MC* rises. Additional units of output cost more and more to produce, since they require ever-increasing amounts of the variable factor.

Average fixed cost (AFC)

This falls continuously as output rises, since *total* fixed costs are being spread over a greater and greater output.

Average variable cost (AVC)

The shape of the *AVC* curve depends on the shape of the *APP* curve. As the average product of workers rises, the average labour cost per unit of output (the *AVC*) falls: up to point *y* in Figure 9.3. Thereafter, as *APP* falls, *AVC* must rise.

Average (total) cost (AC)

This is simply the vertical sum of the *AFC* and *AVC* curves. Note that, as *AFC* gets less, the gap between *AVC* and *AC* narrows.

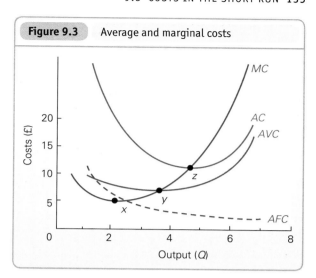

Figure 9.3 Average and marginal costs

The relationship between average cost and marginal cost

This is simply another illustration of the relationship that applies between *all* averages and marginals.

BOX 9.2   SHORT-RUN COST CURVES IN PRACTICE

When fixed factors are divisible

Are short-run cost curves always the shape depicted in this chapter? The answer is no. Sometimes, rather than being U-shaped, the *AVC* and *MC* curves are flat bottomed, like the curves in the diagram. Indeed, they may be constant (and equal to each other) over a *substantial* range of output.

The reason for this is that sometimes fixed factors may not have to be in full use all the time. Take the case of a firm with 100 identical machines, each one requiring one person to operate it. Although the firm cannot use *more* than the 100 machines, it could use fewer: in other words, some of the machines could be left idle. Assume, for example, that instead of using 100 machines, the firm uses only 90. It would need only 90 operatives and 90 per cent of the raw

materials. Similarly, if it used only 20 machines, its total variable costs (labour and raw materials) would be only 20 per cent of those incurred at full capacity. What we are saying here is that *average* variable cost remains constant – and over a very large range of output: using anything from 1 machine to 100 machines.

The reason for the constant *AVC* (and *MC*) is that by varying the amount of fixed capital used, the *proportions* used of capital, labour and raw materials can be kept the same and hence the average and marginal productivity of labour and raw materials will remain constant.

Only when all machines are in use (at Q_1) will *AVC* start to rise if output is further expanded. Machines may then have to work beyond their optimal speed, using more raw materials per unit of output (diminishing returns to raw materials), or workers may have to work longer shifts with higher (overtime) pay.

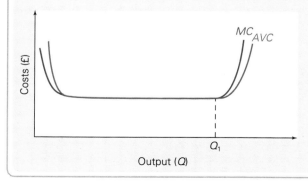

1. *Assume that a firm has 5 identical machines, each operating independently. Assume that with all 5 machines operating normally, 100 units of output are produced each day. Below what level of output will AVC and MC rise?*
2. *Manufacturing firms like the one we have been describing will have other fixed costs (such as rent and managerial overheads). Does the existence of these affect the argument that the AVC curve will be flat bottomed?*

As long as the cost of additional units of output is less than the average, their production must pull the average cost down. That is, if *MC* is less than *AC*, *AC* must be falling. Likewise, if additional units cost more than the average, their production must drive the average up. That is, if *MC* is greater than *AC*, *AC* must be rising. Therefore, the *MC* crosses the *AC* at its minimum point (point *z* in Figure 9.3).

Pause for thought

Before you read on, can you explain why the marginal cost curve will always cut the average cost curve at its lowest point?

Since all marginal costs are variable, the same relationship holds between *MC* and *AVC*.

9.4 PRODUCTION IN THE LONG RUN

In the long run *all* factors of production are variable. There is time for the firm to build a new factory (maybe in a different part of the country), to install new machines, to use different techniques of production, and in general to combine its inputs in whatever proportion and in whatever quantities it chooses.

When planning for the long run, then, a firm will have to make a number of decisions: about the scale of its operations, the location of its operations and the techniques of production it will use. These decisions will affect the costs of production. It is important, therefore, to get them right.

The scale of production

If a firm were to double all of its inputs – something it could do in the long run – would it double its output? Or would output more than double or less than double? We can distinguish three possible situations.

- *Constant returns to scale*. This is where a given percentage increase in inputs will lead to the same percentage increase in output.
- *Increasing returns to scale*. This is where a given percentage increase in inputs will lead to a larger percentage increase in output.
- *Decreasing returns to scale*. This is where a given percentage increase in inputs will lead to a smaller percentage increase in output.

Notice the terminology here. The words 'to scale' mean that *all* inputs increase by the same proportion. Decreasing returns to *scale* are therefore quite different from *diminishing* marginal returns (where only the *variable* factor increases). The differences between marginal returns to a variable factor and returns to scale are illustrated in Table 9.4.

In the short run, input 1 is assumed to be fixed in supply (at 3 units). Output can be increased only by using more of the variable factor (input 2). In the long run, however, both input 1 and input 2 are variable.

In the short-run situation, diminishing returns can be seen from the fact that output increases at a decreasing rate (25 to 45 to 60 to 70 to 75) as input 2 is increased. In the

Table 9.4	Short-run and long-run increases in output					
	Short run			**Long run**		
	Input 1	Input 2	Output	Input 1	Input 2	Output
	3	1	25	1	1	15
	3	2	45	2	2	35
	3	3	60	3	3	60
	3	4	70	4	4	90
	3	5	75	5	5	125

long-run situation, the table illustrates increasing returns to scale. Output increases at an *increasing* rate (15 to 35 to 60 to 90 to 125) as both inputs are increased.

Economies of scale

The concept of increasing returns to scale is closely linked to that of *economies of scale*. A firm experiences economies of scale if costs per unit of output fall as the scale of production increases. Clearly, if a firm is getting increasing returns to scale from its factors of production, then as it produces more, it will be using smaller and smaller amounts of factors per unit of output. Other things being equal, this means that it will be producing at a lower unit cost.

There are a number of reasons why firms are likely to experience economies of scale. Some are due to increasing returns to scale; some are not.

Specialisation and division of labour. In large-scale plants, workers can do more simple, repetitive jobs. With this *specialisation and division of labour*, less training is

Definitions

Economies of scale When increasing the scale of production leads to a lower cost per unit of output.

Specialisation and division of labour Where production is broken down into a number of simpler, more specialised tasks, thus allowing workers to acquire a high degree of efficiency.

needed; workers can become highly efficient in their particular job, especially with long production runs; there is less time lost in workers switching from one operation to another; supervision is easier. Workers and managers who have specific skills in specific areas can be employed.

Indivisibilities. Some inputs are of a minimum size. They are indivisible. The most obvious example is machinery. Take the case of a combine harvester. A small-scale farmer could not make full use of one. They only become economical to use, therefore, on farms above a certain size. The problem of **indivisibilities** is made worse when different machines, each of which is part of the production process, are of a different size. For example, assume there are two types of machine, one producing a maximum of 6 units a day, the other packaging a maximum of 4 units a day. If all machines are to be fully utilised, a minimum of 12 units per day will have to be produced, involving two production machines and three packaging machines.

The 'container principle'. Any capital equipment that contains things (blast furnaces, oil tankers, pipes, vats, etc.) will tend to cost less per unit of output, the larger its size. The reason has to do with the relationship between a container's volume and its surface area. A container's cost will depend largely on the materials used to build it and hence roughly on its *surface area*. Its output will depend largely on its *volume*. Large containers have a bigger volume relative to surface area than do small containers. For example, a container with a bottom, top and four sides, with each side measuring 1 metre, has a volume of 1 cubic metre and a surface area of 6 square metres (6 surfaces of 1 square metre each). If each side were now to be doubled in length to 2 metres, the volume would be 8 cubic metres and the surface area 24 square metres (6 surfaces of 4 square metres each). Thus an eightfold increase in capacity has been gained at only a fourfold increase in the container's surface area, and hence an approximate fourfold increase in cost.

Greater efficiency of large machines. Large machines may be more efficient, in the sense that more output can be gained for a given amount of inputs. For example, only one worker may be required to operate a machine whether it be large or small. Also, a large machine may make more efficient use of raw materials.

By-products. With production on a large scale, there may be sufficient waste products to enable them to make some by-product. For example, a wood mill may produce sufficient saw dust to make products such as charcoal briquettes or paper.

Multistage production. A large factory may be able to take a product through several stages in its manufacture. This saves time and cost moving the semi-finished product from one firm or factory to another. For example, a large cardboard-manufacturing firm may be able to convert trees or waste paper into cardboard and then into cardboard boxes in a continuous sequence.

All the above are examples of *plant economies of scale*. They are due to an individual factory or workplace or machine being large. There are other economies of scale that are associated with the firm being large – perhaps with many factories.

Organisational. With a large firm, individual plants can specialise in particular functions. There can also be centralised administration of the firms. Often, after a merger between two firms, savings can be made by **rationalising** their activities in this way.

Spreading overheads. Some expenditures are economic only when the *firm* is large, such as research and development: only a large firm can afford to set up a research laboratory. This is another example of indivisibilities, only this time at the level of the firm rather than the plant. The greater the firm's output, the more these **overhead costs** are spread.

Financial economies. Large firms may be able to obtain finance at lower interest rates than small firms, as they are perceived as having lower default risks. Additionally they may be able to obtain certain inputs cheaper by purchasing in bulk.

Economies of scope. Often a firm is large because it produces a range of products. This can result in each individual product being produced more cheaply than if it was produced in a single-product firm. The reason for these *economies of scope* is that various overhead costs and financial and organisational economies can be shared between the products. For example, a firm that produces a whole range of CD players, DVD players and recorders, games consoles, TVs and so on can benefit from shared marketing and distribution costs and the bulk purchase of electronic components.

Definitions

Indivisibilities The impossibility of dividing a factor of production into smaller units.

Plant economies of scale Economies of scale that arise because of the large size of the factory.

Rationalisation The reorganising of production (often after a merger) so as to cut out waste and duplication and generally to reduce costs.

Overheads Costs arising from the general running of an organisation, and only indirectly related to the level of output.

Economies of scope When increasing the range of products produced by a firm reduces the cost of producing each one.

Diseconomies of scale

When firms get beyond a certain size, costs per unit of output may start to increase. There are several reasons for such **diseconomies of scale**:

- Management problems of coordination may increase as the firm becomes larger and more complex, and as lines of communication get longer. There may be a lack of personal involvement and oversight by management.
- Workers may feel 'alienated' if their jobs are boring and repetitive, and if they feel an insignificant, and under-valued, small part of a large organisation. Poor motivation may lead to shoddy work.
- Industrial relations may deteriorate as a result of these factors and also as a result of the more complex inter-relationships between different categories of worker.
- Production-line processes and the complex interdepend-encies of mass production can lead to great disruption if there are hold-ups in any one part of the firm.

Whether firms experience economies or diseconomies of scale will depend on the conditions applying in each individual firm.

Location

In the long run, a firm can move to a different location. The location will affect the cost of production, since locations differ in terms of the availability and cost of raw materials, suitable land and power supply, the qualifications, skills and experience of the labour force, wage rates, transport and communications networks, the cost of local services, and banking and financial facilities. In short, locations differ in terms of the availability, suitability and cost of the factors of production.

Transport costs will be an important influence on a firm's location. Ideally, a firm will wish to be as near as possible to both its raw materials and the market for its finished product. When market and raw materials are in different locations, the firm will minimise its transport costs by locating somewhere between the two. In general, if the raw materials are more expensive to transport than the finished product, the firm should locate as near as pos-sible to the raw materials. This will normally apply to firms whose raw materials are heavier or more bulky than the finished product. Thus heavy industry, which uses large quantities of coal and various ores, tends to be concen-trated near the coal fields or near the ports. If, on the other hand, the finished product is more expensive to transport (e.g. bread or beer), the firm will probably be located as near as possible to its market.

When raw materials or markets are in many different locations, transport costs will be minimised at the 'centre of gravity'. This location will be nearer to those raw materials and markets whose transport costs are greater per mile.

The size of the whole industry

As an *industry* grows in size, this can lead to **external economies of scale** for its member firms. This is where a firm, whatever its own individual size, benefits from the *whole industry* being large. For example, the firm may benefit from having access to specialist raw material or component suppliers, labour with specific skills, firms that specialise in marketing the finished product, and banks and other financial institutions with experience of the industry's requirements. What we are referring to here is the **industry's infrastructure**: the facilities, support services, skills and experience that can be shared by its members.

The member firms of a particular industry might experi-ence **external diseconomies of scale**. For example, as an industry grows larger, this may create a growing shortage of specific raw materials or skilled labour. This will push up their prices, and hence the firms' costs.

The optimum combination of factors

In the long run, all factors can be varied. The firm can thus choose what techniques of production to use: what design of factory to build, what types of machine to buy, how to organise the factory, and whether to use highly automated processes or more labour-intensive techniques. It must be very careful in making these decisions. Once it has built its factory and installed the machinery, these then become fixed factors of production, maybe for many years: the subsequent 'short-run' time period may in practice last a very long time!

For any given scale, how should the firm decide what technique to use? How should it decide the optimum 'mix' of factors of production?

Definitions

Diseconomies of scale Where costs per unit of output increase as the scale of production increases.

External economies of scale Where a firm's costs per unit of output decrease as the size of the whole *industry* grows.

Industry's infrastructure The network of supply agents, communications, skills, training facilities, distribution channels, specialised financial services, etc. that support a particular industry.

External diseconomies of scale Where a firm's costs per unit of output increase as the size of the whole industry increases.

The profit-maximising firm will obviously want to use the least costly combination of factors to produce any given output. It will therefore substitute factors, one for another, if by so doing it can reduce the cost of a given output. What, then, is the optimum combination of factors?

The simple two-factor case

Take first the simplest case where a firm uses just two factors: labour (L) and capital (K). The least-cost combination of the two will be where:

$$\frac{MPP_L}{P_L} = \frac{MPP_K}{P_K}$$

In other words, it is where the extra product (MPP) from the last pound spent on each factor is equal. But why should this be so? The easiest way to answer this is to consider what would happen if they were not equal.

If they were not equal, it would be possible to reduce cost per unit of output, by using a different combination of labour and capital. For example, if:

$$\frac{MPP_L}{P_L} > \frac{MPP_K}{P_K}$$

more labour should be used relative to capital, since the firm is getting a greater physical return for its money from extra workers than from extra capital. As more labour is used per unit of capital, however, diminishing returns to labour set in. Thus MPP_L will fall. Likewise, as less capital is used per unit of labour, the MPP_K will rise. This will continue until:

$$\frac{MPP_L}{P_L} = \frac{MPP_K}{P_K}$$

At this point, the firm will stop substituting labour for capital.

Since no further gain can be made by substituting one factor for another, this combination of factors or 'choice of techniques' can be said to be the most efficient. It is the least-cost way of combining factors for any given output. Efficiency in this sense of using the optimum factor proportions is known as **technical or productive efficiency**.

The multifactor case

Where a firm uses many different factors, the least-cost combination of factors will be where:

$$\frac{MPP_a}{P_a} = \frac{MPP_b}{P_b} = \frac{MPP_c}{P_c} \cdots = \frac{MPP_n}{P_n}$$

where a . . . n are different factors of production.

The reasons are the same as in the two-factor case. If any inequality exists between the MPP/P ratios, a firm will be able to reduce its costs by using more of those factors with a high MPP/P ratio and less of those with a low MPP/P ratio until the ratios all become equal. A major problem for a firm in choosing the least-cost technique is in predicting future factor price changes.

If the price of a factor were to change, the MPP/P ratios would cease to be equal. The firm, to minimise costs, would then like to alter its factor combinations until the MPP/P ratios once more become equal. The trouble is that, once it has committed itself to a particular technique, it may be several years before it can switch to an alternative one. Thus if a firm invests in labour-intensive methods of production and is then faced with an unexpected wage rise, it may regret not having chosen a more capital-intensive technique.

Postscript: decision making in different time periods

We have distinguished between the short run and the long run. Let us introduce two more time periods to complete the picture. The complete list then reads as follows.

Very short run (immediate run). All factors are fixed. Output is fixed. The supply curve is vertical. On a day-to-day basis, a firm may not be able to vary output at all. For example, a flower seller, once the day's flowers have been purchased from the wholesaler, cannot alter the amount of flowers available for sale on that day. In the very short run, all that may remain for a producer to do is to sell an already-produced good.

Short run. At least one factor is fixed in supply. More can be produced, but the firm will come up against the law of diminishing returns as it tries to do so.

Long run. All factors are variable. The firm may experience constant, increasing or decreasing returns to scale. But although all factors can be increased or decreased, they are of a fixed *quality*.

Very long run. All factors are variable, *and* their quality and hence productivity can change. Labour productivity can increase as a result of education, training, experience and social factors. The productivity of capital can increase as a result of new inventions (new discoveries) and innovation (putting inventions into practice).

Improvements in factor quality will increase the output they produce: *TPP*, *APP* and *MPP* will rise. These curves will shift vertically upward.

Just how long the 'very long run' is will vary from firm to firm. It will depend on how long it takes to develop new techniques, new skills or new work practices.

It is important to realise that decisions *for* all four time periods can be made *at* the same time. Firms do not

---

Definition

Technical or productive efficiency The least-cost combination of factors for a given output.

BOX 9.3   UK COMPETITIVENESS: MOVING TO THE NEXT STAGE

The importance of location

In May 2003 Professor Michael Porter and Christian Ketels of Harvard Business School published a review of the UK's competitiveness on behalf of the UK government. The authors declared that since 1980 the UK had done remarkably well in halting its economic decline on world markets, and had in fact matched and even bettered its main rivals in many industrial sectors. However, they were quick to sound a note of caution.

> The UK currently faces a transition to a new phase of economic development. The old approach to economic development is reaching the limits of its effectiveness, and government, companies, and other institutions need to rethink their policy priorities. This rethinking is not a sign of the past strategy's failure; it is a necessary part of graduating to the new stage.[1]

Porter's view is that economic development is achieved through a series of stages. The factor-driven stage identifies factors of production as the basis of competitive advantage: you have an advantage in those industries where you have a plentiful supply of the relevant factors of production. The investment-driven stage of development focuses upon efficiency and productivity as the key to competitive success. The third stage, into which Porter believes the UK is shifting, is innovation-driven. Here competitive advantage is achieved through the production of innovative products and services.

The importance of industrial clusters

One of the key characteristics of a successful innovation-led development strategy is the existence of industrial clusters.

> Clusters are geographically proximate groups of interconnected companies, suppliers, service providers, and associated institutions in a particular field, linked by commonalties and complementarities.[2]

Porter suggests that clusters are vital for competitiveness in three crucial respects:

- Clusters improve productivity. The close proximity of suppliers and other service providers enhances flexibility.
- Clusters aid innovation. Interaction among businesses within a cluster stimulates new ideas and aids their dissemination.
- Clusters contribute to new business formation. Clusters are self-reinforcing, in so far as specialist factors such as

dedicated venture capital, and labour skills, help reduce costs and lower the risks of new business start-up.

Given that national economies tend to specialise in certain industrial clusters, we can identify where clusters occur and their importance, by considering their share of national output and export earnings. Export earnings in particular are a good indicator of how globally competitive a cluster might be.

The UK's industrial clusters were seen by Porter as being relatively weak, and in fact many traditional clusters, such as steel and car manufacturing, had thinned to the point where they now lacked critical mass and failed to benefit from the clustering effect. Where the UK had strengths were in the areas of services, such as financial services and media, defence, products for personal use, health care and telecommunications.

Porter and Katels concluded that, to improve its competitiveness, the UK must not only support what clusters it has but 'mount a sustained programme of cluster development to create a more conducive environment for productivity growth and innovation through the collective action of companies and other institutions'.[3]

The UK government responded to this report and currently supports cluster development in a number of ways, including through the creation of Enterprise Zones. These zones include the Humber Estuary Renewable Energy Cluster and The Modern Manufacturing and Technology Growth area in Sheffield. Eligible companies within these zones receive benefits such as reductions in business rates and simplified planning regulations. Cluster development has become an integral part of the remit of other policy areas, including science and innovation, export and foreign investment promotion and small and medium-sized enterprise policies.

Recent evidence

The performance of UK clusters has not changed greatly since the earlier report by Porter and Katels, but more information is coming to light. The European Cluster Observatory, an EU project, has identified locations where employment is highly concentrated in particular industrial clusters across Europe.[4]

The table shows the UK position. Information from the Observatory also shows that the UK leads the rest of Europe in cluster developments in areas such as Education and

---

[1] M. E. Porter and C. H. M. Ketels, UK Competitiveness: moving to the next stage (DTI and ESRC, May 2003), p. 5.
[2] Ibid., p. 27.

[3] Ibid., p. 46.
[4] See www.clusterobservatory.eu

---

make short-run decisions *in* the short run and long-run decisions *in* the long run. They can make both short-run and long-run decisions today. For example, assume that a firm experiences an increase in consumer demand and anticipates that it will continue into the foreseeable future. It thus wants to increase output. Consequently, it makes the following four decisions *today*:

- *(Very short run)* It accepts that for a few days it will not be able to increase output. It informs its customers that they will have to wait. It may temporarily raise prices to choke off some of the demand.
- *(Short run)* It negotiates with labour to introduce overtime working as soon as possible, to tide it over the next few weeks. It orders extra raw materials from its suppliers. It launches a recruitment drive for new

The Top UK industry clusters ranked by employment, 2009

Region	Cluster category	Employees	Size (%)	Specialisation (quotient)	Focus (%)
Inner London	Financial services	233 734	4.25	3.04	9.82
Inner London	Business services	219 044	3.64	2.59	9.21
Outer London	Business services	122 757	2.04	2.07	7.33
Outer London	Transportation and logistics	100 707	2.02	2.04	6.02
Berks, Bucks and Oxon	Business services	95 295	1.58	2.44	8.66
Inner London	Education and knowledge creation	89 444	3.31	2.35	3.76
Surrey, E and W Sussex	Business services	81 724	1.36	2.02	7.18
Inner London	Media and publishing	76 111	3.92	2.80	3.20
Hants and Isle of Wight	Business services	62 199	1.03	2.10	7.47
Beds and Herts	Business services	60 947	1.01	2.31	8.20
E Scotland	Financial services	59 747	1.09	2.05	6.62
Berks, Bucks and Oxon	Education and knowledge creation	58 363	2.16	3.32	5.30
E Anglia	Education and knowledge creation	36 276	1.34	2.36	3.78
W Midlands	Automotive	35 419	1.62	2.30	2.97
E Scotland	Education and knowledge creation	34 416	1.27	2.39	3.81
W Yorks	Education and knowledge creation	31 638	1.17	2.01	3.21
Berks, Bucks and Oxon	IT	30 184	1.96	3.01	2.74
NE Scotland	Oil and gas	11 792	3.98	25.22	4.45

Source: Based on EU Cluster Observatory, www.clusterobservatory.eu

Notes:
The European Cluster Observatory uses three measures to define a cluster, all based on employment. The three measures are size, specialisation and focus. If, for each measure, a location meets a specific criterion it is awarded a star. Only industries that achieved three stars are included in the above table.

The criteria for awarding a star are as follows:
Size: This gives employment in the cluster as a percentage of European employment in that industry. If a cluster is in the top 10 per cent of similar clusters in Europe in terms of employees, it receives a star (Europe is defined as the EU-27, Iceland, Israel, Norway, Switzerland and Turkey)
Specialisation: If a specialisation quotient of 2 or more achieved, it is awarded a star. The specialisation quotient is given by

$$\frac{\text{UK employment in a region in a cluster category/total UK employment}}{\text{European employment in a cluster category/total European employment}}$$

Focus: This shows the extent to which the regional economy is focused upon the industries comprising the cluster category. This measure shows employment in the cluster as a percentage of total employment in the region. The top 10 per cent of clusters which account for the largest proportion of their region's total employment receive a star.

Knowledge Creation, Business Services, Finance and Transportation and Logistical Services, with most of these clusters occurring in London and the South East.

The UK has been very successful relative to the rest of Europe in developing clusters in the provision of Education and Knowledge Creation, notably in Oxford, Cambridge and East Scotland. Outside of these sectors the UK advantage relative to the rest of Europe is very limited, although there are pockets of success. For example, the UK has achieved some success in IT (around Oxford and the south coast of England),

oil and gas (around Aberdeen in Scotland) and the automotive industry (in the West Midlands). These locations have achieved the size, specialisation and focus that have enabled them to develop positive spillovers and linkages which create local prosperity. Much more, though, has to be done.

 What policies or initiatives might a 'programme of cluster development' involve? Distinguish between policies that government and business might initiate.

labour so as to avoid paying overtime longer than is necessary.
- *(Long run)* It starts proceedings to build a new factory. The first step may be to discuss requirements with a firm of consultants.
- *(Very long run)* It institutes a programme of research and development and/or training in an attempt to increase productivity.

Pause for thought

1. *What will the long-run market supply curve for a product look like? How will the shape of the long-run curve depend on returns to scale?*
2. *Why would it be difficult to construct a very-long run supply curve?*

Although we distinguish these four time periods, it is the middle two we are primarily concerned with. The reason for this is that there is very little that the firm can do in the very short run. And in the very long run, although the firm will obviously want to increase the productivity of its inputs, it will not be in a position to make precise calculations of how to do it. It will not know precisely what inventions will be made, or just what will be the results of its own research and development.

9.5 COSTS IN THE LONG RUN

When it comes to making long-run production decisions, the firm has much more flexibility. It does not have to operate with plant and equipment of a fixed size. It can expand the whole scale of its operations. All its inputs are variable, and thus the law of diminishing returns does not apply. The firm may experience economies of scale or diseconomies of scale, or its average costs may stay constant as it expands the scale of its operations.

Since there are no fixed factors in the long run, there are no long-run fixed costs. For example, the firm may rent

---

BOX 9.4 MINIMUM EFFICIENT SCALE

The extent of economies of scale in practice

Two of the most important studies of economies of scale have been those made by C. F. Pratten[1] in the late 1980s and by a group advising the European Commission[2] in 1997. Both studies found strong evidence that many firms, especially in manufacturing, experienced substantial economies of scale.

In a few cases long-run average costs fell continuously as output increased. For most firms, however, they fell up to a certain level of output and then remained constant.

The extent of economies of scale can be measured by looking at a firm's *minimum efficient scale* (*MES*). The *MES* is the size beyond which no significant additional economies of scale can be achieved: in other words, the point where the *LRAC* curve flattens off. In Pratten's studies he defined this level as the minimum scale above which any possible doubling in scale would reduce average costs by less than 5 per cent (i.e. virtually the bottom of the *LRAC* curve). In the diagram *MES* is shown at point *a*.

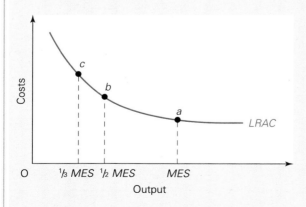

Table (a)

Product	MES as % of production		% additional cost at $^1/_2$ MES
	UK	**EU**	
Individual plants			
Cellulose fibres	125	16	3
Rolled aluminium semi-manufactures	114	15	15
Refrigerators	85	11	4
Steel	72	10	6
Electric motors	60	6	15
TV sets	40	9	9
Cigarettes	24	6	1.4
Ball-bearings	20	2	6
Beer	12	3	7
Nylon	4	1	12
Bricks	1	0.2	25
Tufted carpets	0.3	0.04	10
Shoes	0.3	0.03	1
Firms			
Cars	200	20	9
Lorries	104	21	7.5
Mainframe computers	>100	n.a.	5
Aircraft	100	n.a.	5
Tractors	98	19	6

Sources: Based on Pratten, F. and Emerson, M. (1988) *The Economics of 1992*, Oxford University Press, data from Tables on pp. 126–40, Section 6.1 'Size phenomena: economies of scale'

The *MES* can be expressed in terms either of an individual factory or of the whole firm. Where it refers to the minimum efficient scale of an individual factory, the *MES* is known as *the minimum efficient plant size* (*MEPS*).

[1] C. F. Pratten, 'A survey of the economies of scale', in *Research on the 'Costs of Non-Europe'*, vol. 2 (Office for Official Publications of the European Communities, 1988).

[2] European Commission/Economists Advisory Group Ltd, 'Economies of scale', The Single Market Review, Subseries V, Volume 4 (Office for Official Publications of the European Communities, 1997).

more land in order to expand its operations. Its rent bill therefore goes up as it expands its output. All costs, then, in the long run are variable costs.

Long-run average costs

Although it is possible to draw long-run total, marginal and average cost curves, we will concentrate on *long-run average cost (LRAC) curves*. These curves can take various shapes, but a typical one is shown in Figure 9.4.

It is often assumed that, as a firm expands, it will initially experience economies of scale and thus face a downward-sloping *LRAC* curve. After a point (Q_1 in Figure 9.4), however, all such economies will have been achieved and thus the curve will flatten out. Then, possibly after a period of constant *LRAC* (between Q_1 and Q_2), the firm will get so large

that it will start experiencing diseconomies of scale and thus a rising *LRAC*. At this stage, production and financial economies begin to be offset by the managerial problems of running a giant organisation. The effect of this is to give an L-shaped or saucer-shaped curve.

> ### Definition
>
> **Long-run average cost (*LRAC*) curve** A curve that shows how average cost varies with output on the assumption that *all* factors are variable. (It is assumed that the least-cost method of production will be chosen for each output.)

Table (b)

Plants	MES as % of total EU production
Aerospace	12.19
Tractors and agricultural machinery	6.57
Electric lighting	3.76
Steel tubes	2.42
Shipbuilding	1.63
Rubber	1.06
Radio and TV	0.69
Footwear	0.08
Carpets	0.03

Source: see footnote 2

The *MES* can then be expressed as a percentage of the total size of the market or of total domestic production. Table (a), based on the Pratten study, shows *MES* for plants and firms in various industries. The first column shows *MES* as a percentage of total UK production. The second column shows *MES* as a percentage of total EU production. Table (b), based on the 1997 study, shows *MES* for various plants as a percentage of total EU production.

Expressing *MES* as a percentage of total output gives an indication of how competitive the industry could be. In some industries (such as footwear and carpets), economies of scale were exhausted (i.e. *MES* was reached) with plants or firms that were still small relative to total UK production and even smaller relative to total EU production. In such industries there would be room for many firms and thus scope for considerable competition.

In other industries, however, even if a single plant or firm were large enough to produce the whole output of the industry in the UK, it would still not be large enough to experience the full potential economies of scale: the *MES* is greater than 100 per cent. Examples from Table (a) include factories producing cellulose fibres, and car manufacturers.

In such industries there is no possibility of competition. In fact, as long as the *MES* exceeds 50 per cent there will not be room for more than one firm large enough to gain full economies of scale. In this case the industry is said to be *a natural monopoly*. As we shall see in the next few chapters, when competition is lacking, consumers may suffer by firms charging prices considerably above costs.

A second way of measuring the extent of economies of scale is to see how much costs would increase if production were reduced to a certain fraction of *MES*. The normal fractions used are $^1/_2$ or $^1/_3$ *MES*. This is illustrated in the diagram. Point *b* corresponds to $^1/_2$ *MES*; point *c* to $^1/_3$ *MES*. The greater the percentage by which *LRAC* at point *b* or *c* is higher than at point *a*, the greater will be the economies of scale to be gained by producing at *MES* rather than at $^1/_2$ *MES* or $^1/_3$ *MES*. For example, in the table there are greater economies of scale to be gained from moving from $^1/_2$ *MES* to *MES* in the production of electric motors than in cigarettes.

The main purpose of the studies was to determine whether the single EU market is big enough to allow both economies of scale and competition. The tables suggest that in all cases, other things being equal, the EU market is large enough for firms to gain the full economies of scale *and* for there to be enough firms for the market to be competitive.

The second study also found that 47 of the 53 manufacturing sectors analysed had scope for further exploitation of economies of scale.

In the 2007–13 Research Framework, the European Commission agreed to fund a number of research projects. These will conduct further investigations of *MES* across different industries and consider the impact of the expansion of the EU.

1. *Why might a firm operating with one plant achieve* MEPS *and yet not be large enough to achieve* MES*? (Clue: are all economies of scale achieved at plant level?)*
2. *Why might a firm producing bricks have an* MES *which is only 0.2 per cent of total EU production and yet face little effective competition from other EU countries?*

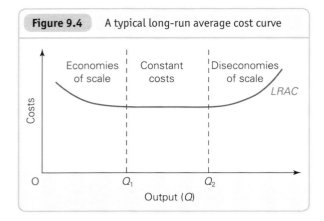

Figure 9.4   A typical long-run average cost curve

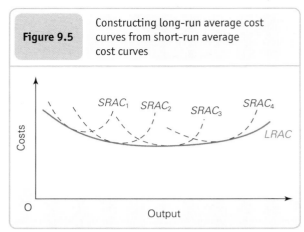

Figure 9.5   Constructing long-run average cost curves from short-run average cost curves

Firms do experience economies of scale. Some experience continuously falling *LRAC* curves. Others experience economies of scale up to a certain output and thereafter constant returns to scale. However, evidence is inconclusive on the question of diseconomies of scale. There is little evidence to suggest the existence of technical diseconomies, but the possibility of diseconomies due to managerial and industrial relations problems cannot be ruled out.

Assumptions behind the long-run average cost curve

We make three key assumptions when constructing long-run average cost curves.

Factor prices are given. At each level of output, a firm will be faced with a given set of factor prices. If factor prices *change*, therefore, both short- and long-run cost curves will shift. For example, an increase in wages would shift the curves vertically upwards.

However, factor prices might be different at *different* levels of output. For example, one of the economies of scale that many firms enjoy is the ability to obtain bulk discount on raw materials and other supplies. In such cases the curve does *not* shift. The different factor prices are merely experienced at different points along the curve, and are reflected in the shape of the curve. Factor prices are still given for any particular level of output.

The state of technology and factor quality are given. These are assumed to change only in the very long run. If a firm gains economies of scale, it is because it is being able to exploit *existing* technologies and make better use of the existing availability of factors of production. As technology improves the curves will shift downwards.

Firms choose the least-cost combination of factors for each output. The assumption here is that firms operate efficiently: that they choose the cheapest possible way of producing any level of output. In other words, at every point along the *LRAC* curve the firm will adhere to the cost-minimising formula:

$$\frac{MPP_a}{P_a} = \frac{MPP_b}{P_b} = \frac{MPP_c}{P_c} \cdots = \frac{MPP_n}{P_n}$$

where a . . . n are the various factors that the firm uses.

If the firm did not choose the optimum factor combination, it would be producing at a point above the *LRAC* curve.

The relationship between long-run and short-run average cost curves

Take the case of a firm which has just one factory and faces a short-run average cost curve illustrated by $SRAC_1$ in Figure 9.5.

In the long run, it can build more factories or expand its existing facilities. If it thereby experiences economies of scale (due, say, to savings on administration), each successive factory will allow it to produce with a new lower *SRAC* curve. Thus with two factories it will face curve $SRAC_2$; with three factories curve $SRAC_3$, and so on. Each *SRAC* curve corresponds to a particular amount of the factor that is fixed in the short run: in this case, the factory. (There are many more *SRAC* curves that could be drawn between the ones shown, since factories of different sizes could be built or existing ones could be expanded.)

From this succession of short-run average cost curves we can construct a long-run average cost curve. This is shown in Figure 9.5 and is known as the ***envelope curve***, since it envelops the short-run curves.

> **Pause for thought**
>
> *Will the envelope curve be tangential to the bottom of each of the short-run average cost curves? Explain why it should or should not be.*

> **Definition**
>
> **Envelope curve** A long-run average cost curve drawn as the tangency points of a series of short-run average cost curves.

BOX 9.5 FASHION CYCLES

Costs and prices in the clothing industry

For many products, style is a key component of their success. A good example is clothing. If manufacturers can successfully predict or even drive a new fashion, then sales growth can be substantial.

With any new fashion, growth is likely to be slow at first. Then as the fashion 'catches on' and people want to be seen wearing this fashionable item, sales grow until a peak is eventually reached. In the case of clothing, if it is 'this year's fashion' then the peak will be reached within a couple of months. Then, as the market becomes saturated and people await the next season's fashions, so sales will fall.

This rise and fall is known as the 'fashion cycle' and is illustrated in the following diagram, which shows five stages: introduction of a style; growth in popularity; peak in popularity; decline in popularity; obsolescence.

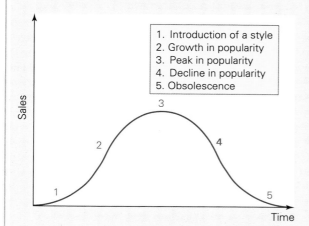

The variation of costs and prices over the fashion cycle

Costs and prices tend to vary with the stages of the fashion cycle. At the introductory stage, average costs are likely to be high. Within that stage, the fixed costs of design, setting up production lines, etc. are being spread over a relatively small output; average fixed costs are high. Also, there is a risk to producers that the fashion will not catch on and thus they are likely to factor in this risk when estimating costs. Finally, demand from those wishing to be ahead in fashion and wearing the very latest thing is likely to be relatively price inelastic; they will be willing to pay a high price to obtain such items. The result of all these factors is that price is likely to be high in the introductory stage.

Assuming the fashion catches on, average costs will begin to fall and the fashion is likely to be taken up by cheaper High Street chains. Prices will correspondingly fall.

Beyond the peak, costs are unlikely to fall much further, but intense competition between retailers is likely to continue driving prices down. The garments may end up on sales rails. (Note that with fashions that do not catch on, the price may fall rapidly quite early on as producers seek to cut their losses.)

Then, with the new season's fashions, the cycle begins again.

The greater the importance of fashion for a particular type of garment, the greater is likely to be the seasonable price variability. The taller the 'bell' in the diagram, i.e. the greater the rise and fall in sales, the greater is likely to be the difference in price between the different stages.

Technology and the fashion cycle

We have seen that costs are an important element in the fashion cycle and in prices and sales through the different phases of the cycle. Fixed costs are highly dependent on technology. Advances in the textile industry have included more easily adaptable machines which are relatively easily programmed and design software which allows designers to change fashion parameters on the screen rather than with physical materials. These advances have meant that the fixed costs of introducing new fashions have come down. With lower fixed costs, average costs will tend to decline less steeply as output rises.

1. If consumers are aware that fashion clothing will fall in price as the season progresses, why do they buy when prices are set high at the start of the season? What does this tell us about the shape of the demand curve for a given fashion product (a) at the start, and (b) at the end of the season?

2. How might we account for the changing magnitudes of the fashion price cycles of clothing? What role do fixed costs play in the explanation?

3. Despite new technology in the car industry, changing the design and shape of cars has risen as a share of the total production costs. How is this likely to have affected the fashion cycle in the car industry?

SUMMARY

1a When measuring costs of production, we should be careful to use the concept of opportunity cost.

1b In the case of factors not owned by the firm, the opportunity cost is simply the explicit cost of purchasing or hiring them. It is the price paid for them.

1c In the case of factors already owned by the firm, it is the implicit cost of what the factor could have earned for the firm in its next best alternative use.

2a A production function shows the relationship between the amount of inputs used and the amount of output produced from them (per period of time).

2b In the short run it is assumed that one or more factors (inputs) are fixed in supply. The actual length of the short run will vary from industry to industry.

2c Production in the short run is subject to diminishing returns. As greater quantities of the variable factor(s) are used, so each additional unit of the variable factor will add less to output than previous units: total physical product will rise less and less rapidly.

2d As long as marginal physical product is above average physical product, average physical product will rise. Once MPP has fallen below APP, however, APP will fall.

3a With some factors fixed in supply in the short run, their total costs will be fixed with respect to output. In the case of variable factors, their total cost will increase as more output is produced and hence as more of them are used.

3b Total cost can be divided into total fixed and total variable cost. Total variable cost will tend to increase less rapidly at first as more is produced, but then, when diminishing returns set in, it will increase more and more rapidly.

3c Marginal cost is the cost of producing one more unit of output. It will probably fall at first (corresponding to the part of the TVC curve where the slope is getting shallower), but will start to rise as soon as diminishing returns set in.

3d Average cost, like total cost, can be divided into fixed and variable costs. Average fixed cost will decline as more output is produced. The reason is that the total fixed cost is being spread over a greater and greater number of units of output. Average variable cost will tend to decline at first, but once the marginal cost has risen above it, it must then rise.

4a In the long run, a firm is able to vary the quantity it uses of all factors of production. There are no fixed factors.

4b If it increases all factors by the same proportion, it may experience constant, increasing or decreasing returns to scale.

4c Economies of scale occur when costs per unit of output fall as the scale of production increases. This can be due to a number of factors, some of which are directly caused by increasing (physical) returns to scale. These include the benefits of specialisation and division of labour, the use of larger and more efficient machines, and the ability to have a more integrated system of production. Other economies of scale arise from the financial and administrative benefits of large-scale organisations having a range of products (economies of scope).

4d Long-run costs are also influenced by a firm's location. The firm will have to balance the need to be as near as possible both to the supply of its raw materials and to its market. The optimum balance will depend on the relative costs of transporting the inputs and the finished product.

4e To minimise costs per unit of output, a firm should choose that combination of factors which gives an equal marginal product for each factor relative to its price: i.e. $MPP_a/P_a = MPP_b/P_b = MPP_c/P_c$, etc. (where a, b and c are different factors). If the MPP/P ratio for any factor is greater than that for another, more of the first should be used relative to the second.

4f Four distinct time periods can be distinguished. In addition to the short- and long-run periods, we can also distinguish the very-short- and very-long-run periods. The very short run is when all factors are fixed. The very long run is where not only the quantity of factors but also their quality is variable (as a result of changing technology, etc.).

5a In the long run, all factors are variable. There are thus no long-run fixed costs.

5b When constructing long-run cost curves, it is assumed that factor prices are given, that the state of technology is given and that firms will choose the least-cost combination of factors for each given output.

5c The LRAC curve can be downward sloping, upward sloping or horizontal, depending in turn on whether there are economies of scale, diseconomies of scale or neither. Typically, LRAC curves are drawn as saucer-shaped or L-shaped. As output expands, initially there are economies of scale. When these are exhausted, the curve will become flat. When the firm becomes very large, it may begin to experience diseconomies of scale. If this happens, the LRAC curve will begin to slope upward again.

5d An envelope curve can be drawn which shows the relationship between short-run and long-run average cost curves. The LRAC curve envelops the short-run AC curves: it is tangential to them.

REVIEW QUESTIONS

1 Are all explicit costs variable costs? Are all variable costs explicit costs?

2 Up to roughly how long is the short run in the following cases?

(a) A mobile disco firm.
(b) Electricity power generation.
(c) A small grocery retailing business.
(d) 'Superstore Hypermarkets plc'.

In each case, specify your assumptions.

3 Given that there is a fixed supply of land in the world, what implications can you draw from Figure 9.1 about the effects of an increase in world population for food output per head?

4 The following are some costs incurred by a shoe manufacturer. Decide whether each one is a fixed cost or a variable cost or has some element of both.

(a) The cost of leather.
(b) The fee paid to an advertising agency.
(c) Wear and tear on machinery.
(d) Business rates on the factory.
(e) Electricity for heating and lighting.
(f) Electricity for running the machines.
(g) Basic minimum wages agreed with the union.
(h) Overtime pay.
(i) Depreciation of machines as a result purely of their age (irrespective of their condition).

5 Assume that you are required to draw a TVC curve corresponding to Figure 9.1. What will happen to this TVC curve beyond point d?

6 Why is the minimum point of the AVC curve at a lower level of output than the minimum point of the AC curve?

7 Which economies of scale are due to increasing returns to scale and which are due to other factors?

8 What economies of scale is a large department store likely to experience?

9 Why are many firms likely to experience economies of scale up to a certain size and then diseconomies of scale after some point beyond that?

10 Why are bread and beer more expensive to transport per mile than the raw materials used in their manufacture?

11 Name some industries where external economies of scale are gained. What are the specific external economies in each case?

12 How is the opening up of trade and investment between eastern and western Europe likely to affect the location of industries within Europe that have (a) substantial economies of scale; (b) little or no economies of scale?

13 If factor X costs twice as much as factor Y ($P_X/P_Y = 2$), what can be said about the relationship between the MPPs of the two factors if the optimum combination of factors is used?

14 Could the long run and the very long run ever be the same length of time?

15 Examine Figure 9.4. What would (a) the firm's long-run total cost curve and (b) its long-run marginal cost curve look like?

16 Under what circumstances is a firm likely to experience a flat-bottomed $LRAC$ curve?

10 Chapter

Revenue and profit

Business issues covered in this chapter

- How does a business's sales revenue vary with output?
- How does the relationship between output and sales revenue depend on the type of market in which a business is operating?
- How do we measure profits?
- At what output will a firm maximise its profits? How much profit will it make at this output?
- At what point should a business call it a day and shut down?

In this chapter we will identify the output and price at which a firm will maximise its profits, and how much profit will be made at that level. Remember that we defined a firm's total profit ($T\Pi$) as its total revenue minus its total costs of production.

$$T\Pi = TR - TC$$

In the previous chapter we have looked at costs in some detail. We must now turn to the revenue side of the equation. As with costs, we distinguish between three revenue concepts: total revenue (TR), average revenue (AR) and marginal revenue (MR).

10.1 REVENUE

Total, average and marginal revenue

Total revenue (TR)

Total revenue is the firm's total earnings per period of time from the sale of a particular amount of output (Q).

For example, if a firm sells 1000 units (Q) per month at a price of £5 each (P), then its monthly total revenue will be £5000: in other words, £5 × 1000 ($P \times Q$). Thus:

$$TR = P \times Q$$

Definition

Total revenue A firm's total earnings from a specified level of sales within a specified period: $TR = P \times Q$.

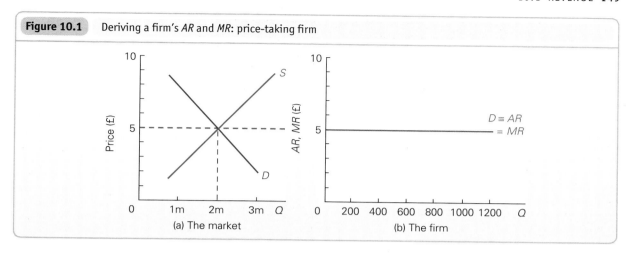

Figure 10.1 Deriving a firm's *AR* and *MR*: price-taking firm

(a) The market

(b) The firm

Average revenue (AR)

Average revenue is the average amount the firm earns per unit sold. Thus:

$$AR = TR/Q$$

So if the firm earns £5000 (*TR*) from selling 1000 units (*Q*), it will earn £5 per unit. But this is simply the price! Thus:

$$AR = P$$

The only exception to this is when the firm is selling its products at different prices to different consumers. In this case *AR* is simply the (weighted) average price.

Marginal revenue (MR)

Marginal revenue is the extra total revenue gained by selling one more unit, per time period. So if a firm sells an extra 20 units this month compared with what it expected to sell, and in the process earns an extra £100, then it is getting an extra £5 for each extra unit sold: *MR* = £5. Thus:

$$MR = \Delta TR/\Delta Q$$

We now need to see how each of these three revenue concepts (*TR*, *AR* and *MR*) varies with output. We can show this relationship graphically in the same way as we did with costs.

The relationship will depend on the market conditions under which a firm operates. A firm which is too small to be able to affect market price will have differently shaped revenue curves from a firm which is able to choose the price it charges. Let us examine each of these two situations in turn.

Revenue curves when price is not affected by the firm's output

Average revenue

If a firm is very small relative to the whole market, it is likely to be a *price taker*. That is, it has to accept the price

given by the intersection of demand and supply in the whole market. If the firm chose to charge a higher price it would lose all its sales to competitors. Charging a lower price would not be rational as the firm can sell as much as it is capable of producing at the prevailing price. This is illustrated in Figure 10.1.

Diagram (a) shows market demand and supply. Equilibrium price is £5. Diagram (b) looks at the demand for an individual firm which is tiny relative to the whole market. (Look at the difference in the scale of the horizontal axes in the two diagrams.)

Being so small, any change in the firm's output will be too insignificant to affect the market price. The firm thus faces a horizontal demand 'curve' at this price. It can sell 200 units, 600 units, 1200 units, or any other amount it is capable of producing, without affecting this £5 price.

Average revenue is thus constant at £5. The firm's average revenue curve must therefore lie along exactly the same line as its demand curve.

Marginal revenue

In the case of a horizontal demand curve, the marginal revenue curve will be the same as the average revenue curve, since selling one more unit at a constant price (*AR*) merely adds that amount to total revenue. If an extra unit is sold at a constant price of £5, an extra £5 is earned.

Definitions

Average revenue Total revenue per unit of output. When all output is sold at the same price, average revenue will be the same as price: $AR = TR/Q = P$.

Marginal revenue The extra revenue gained by selling one or more unit per time period: $MR = \Delta TR/\Delta Q$.

Price taker A firm that is too small to be able to influence the market price.

Table 10.1 Deriving total revenue

Quantity (units)	Price = AR = MR (£)	TR (£)
0	5	0
200	5	1000
400	5	2000
600	5	3000
800	5	4000
1000	5	5000
1200	5	6000
.	.	.

Table 10.2 Revenues for a firm facing a downward-sloping demand curve

Q (units)	P = AR (£)	TR (£)	MR (£)
1	8	8	
			6
2	7	14	
			4
3	6	18	
			2
4	5	20	
			0
5	4	20	
			−2
6	3	18	
			−4
7	2	14	
.	.	.	.

Figure 10.2 Total revenue curve for a price-taking firm

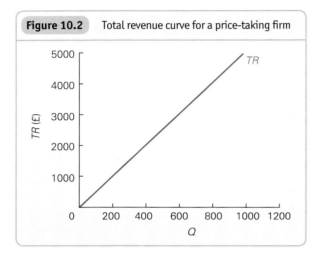

Total revenue

Table 10.1 shows the effect on total revenue of different levels of sales with a constant price of £5 per unit.

As price is constant, total revenue will rise at a constant rate as more is sold. The *TR* 'curve' will therefore be a straight line through the origin, as in Figure 10.2.

Pause for thought

What would happen to the **TR** *curve if the market price rose to £10? Try drawing it.*

Revenue curves when price varies with output

The three curves (*TR*, *AR* and *MR*) will look quite different when price does vary with the firm's output.

If a firm has a relatively large share of the market, it will face a downward-sloping demand curve. This means that if it is to sell more, it must lower the price. But it could also choose to raise its price. If it does so, however, it will have to accept a fall in sales. When a firm faces a

downward-sloping demand curve it is referred to as a *price maker* (or *price chooser*).

Average revenue

Remember that average revenue equals price. If, therefore, the price has to be reduced to sell more output, average revenue will fall as output increases.

Table 10.2 gives an example of a firm facing a downward-sloping demand curve. The demand curve (which shows how much is sold at each price) is given by the first two columns.

Note that, as in the case of a price-taking firm, the demand curve and the *AR* curve lie along exactly the same line. The reason for this is simple: *AR* = *P*, and thus the curve relating price to quantity (the demand curve) must be the same as that relating average revenue to quantity (the *AR* curve).

Pause for thought

Consider the items you have recently purchased. Classify them into products purchased from markets where sellers were price takers and those where the sellers were price makers.

Marginal revenue

When a firm faces a downward-sloping demand curve, marginal revenue will be less than average revenue, and may even be negative. But why?

If a firm is to sell more per time period, it must lower its price (assuming it does not advertise). This will mean

Definition

Price maker (Price chooser) A firm that has the ability to influence the price charged for its good or service.

lowering the price not just for the extra units it hopes to sell, but also for those units it would have sold had it not lowered the price.

Thus the marginal revenue is the price at which it sells the last unit, *minus* the loss in revenue it has incurred by reducing the price on those units it could otherwise have sold at the higher price. This can be illustrated with Table 10.2.

Assume that price is currently £7. Two units are thus sold. The firm now wishes to sell an extra unit. It lowers the price to £6. It thus gains £6 from the sale of the third unit, but loses £2 by having to reduce the price by £1 on the two units it could otherwise have sold at £7. Its net gain is therefore £6 − £2 = £4. This is the marginal revenue: it is the extra revenue gained by the firm from selling one more unit. Try using this method to check out the remaining figures for *MR* in Table 10.2. (Note that in the table the figures for *MR* are entered in the spaces between the figures for the other three columns.)

There is a simple relationship between marginal revenue and *price elasticity of demand*. Remember from Chapter 5 (see pages 65–6) that if demand is price elastic, a *decrease* in price will lead to a proportionately larger increase in the quantity demanded and hence an *increase* in revenue. Marginal revenue will thus be positive. If, however, demand is inelastic, a decrease in price will lead to a proportionately smaller increase in sales. In this case the price reduction will more than offset the increase in sales and as a result revenue will fall. Marginal revenue will be negative.

If, then, marginal revenue is a positive figure (i.e. if sales per time period are 4 units or fewer in Figure 10.3), the demand curve will be elastic at that point, since a rise in quantity sold (as a result of a reduction in price) would lead to a rise in total revenue. If, on the other hand, marginal

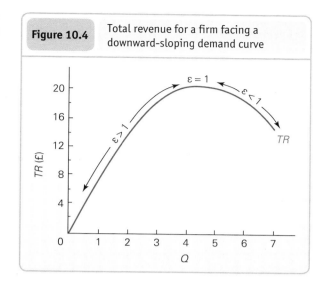

Figure 10.4 Total revenue for a firm facing a downward-sloping demand curve

revenue is negative (i.e. at a level of sales of 5 or more units in Figure 10.3), the demand curve will be inelastic at that point, since a rise in quantity sold would lead to a *fall* in total revenue.

Thus the demand (*AR*) curve of Figure 10.3 is elastic to the left of point *r* and inelastic to the right.

Total revenue

Total revenue equals price times quantity. This is illustrated in Table 10.2. The *TR* column from Table 10.2 is plotted in Figure 10.4.

Unlike in the case of a price-taking firm, the *TR* curve is not a straight line. It is a curve that rises at first and then falls. But why? As long as marginal revenue is positive (and hence demand is price elastic), a rise in output will raise total revenue. However, once marginal revenue becomes negative (and hence demand is inelastic), total revenue will fall. The peak of the *TR* curve will be where *MR* = 0. At this point, the price elasticity of demand will be equal to −1.

Shifts in revenue curves

We saw (Chapter 4) that a change in *price* will cause a movement along a demand curve. It is similar with revenue curves, except that here the causal connection is in the other direction. Here we ask what happens to revenue when there is a change in the firm's *output*. Again the effect is shown by a movement along the curves.

A change in any *other* determinant of demand, such as tastes, income or the price of other goods, will shift the demand curve. By affecting the price at which each level of output can be sold, it will cause a shift in all three revenue curves. An increase in revenue is shown by a vertical shift upwards; a decrease by a shift downwards.

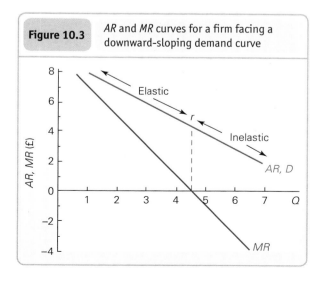

Figure 10.3 *AR* and *MR* curves for a firm facing a downward-sloping demand curve

10.2 PROFIT MAXIMISATION

We are now in a position to put costs and revenue together to find the output at which profit is maximised, and also to find out how much that profit will be.

There are two ways of doing this. The first and simpler method is to use total cost and total revenue curves. The second method is to use marginal and average cost and marginal and average revenue curves. Although this method is a little more complicated, it makes things easier when we come to compare profit maximising under different market conditions (see Chapters 11 and 12).

We will look at each method in turn. In both cases we will concentrate on the short run: namely, that period in which one or more factors are fixed in supply. In both cases we take the case of a firm facing a downward-sloping demand curve: i.e. a price maker.

Short-run profit maximisation: using total curves

Table 10.3 shows the total revenue figures from Table 10.2. It also shows figures for total cost. These figures have been chosen so as to produce a *TC* curve of a typical shape.

Total profit (*TΠ*) is found by subtracting *TC* from *TR*. This can be seen in Table 10.3. Where (*TΠ*) is negative, the firm is making a loss. Total profit is maximised at an output of 3 units: namely, where there is the greatest gap between total revenue and total costs. At this output, total profit is £4 (£18 − £14).

The *TR*, *TC* and (*TΠ*) curves are plotted in Figure 10.5. The size of the maximum profit is shown by the arrows.

Short-run profit maximisation: using average and marginal curves

Finding the maximum profit that a firm can make is a two-stage process. The first stage is to find the profit-maximising

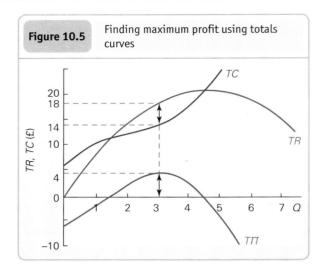

Figure 10.5 Finding maximum profit using totals curves

output. To do this we use the *MC* and *MR* curves. The second stage is to find out just how much profit is at this output. To do this we use the *AR* and *AC* curves.

Stage 1: Using marginal curves to arrive at the profit-maximising output

There is a very simple **profit-maximising rule**: if profits are to be maximised, *MR must equal MC*. From Table 10.4 it can be seen that *MR = MC* at an output of 3 (Table 10.4 is based on the figures in Table 10.3). This is shown as point *e* in Figure 10.6.

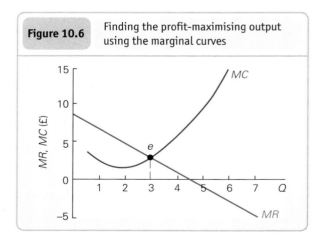

Figure 10.6 Finding the profit-maximising output using the marginal curves

Table 10.3			
Q (units)	**TR (£)**	**TC (£)**	**TΠ (£)**
0	0	6	−6
1	8	10	−2
2	14	12	2
3	18	14	4
4	20	18	2
5	20	25	−5
6	18	36	−18
7	14	56	−42
.	.	.	.

Definition

Profit-maximising rule Profit is maximised where marginal revenue equals marginal cost.

Table 10.4

Q (units)	P = AR (£)	TR (£)	MR (£)	TC (£)	AC (£)	MC (£)	TΠ (£)	AΠ (£)
0	9	0		6	–		–6	–
			8			4		
1	8	8		10	10		–2	–2
			6			2		
2	7	14		12	6		2	1
			4			2		
3	6	18		14	$4^2/_3$		4	$-1^1/_3$
			2			4		
4	5	20		18	$4^1/_2$		2	$^1/_2$
			0			7		
5	4	20		25	5		–5	–1
			–2			11		
6	3	18		36	6		–18	–3
			–4			20		
7	2	14		56	8		–42	–6
.	.	.	.	.	.	.	.	.

KI 4
p 22

Pause for thought

Why are the figures for MR and MC entered in the spaces between the lines in Table 10.4?

But why are profits maximised when $MR = MC$? The simplest way of answering this is to see what the position would be if MR did not equal MC.

Referring to Figure 10.6, at a level of output below 3, MR exceeds MC. This means that by producing more units there will be a bigger addition to revenue (MR) than to cost (MC). Total profit will *increase*. As long as MR *exceeds* MC, *profit can be increased by increasing production.*

At a level of output above 3, MC exceeds MR. All levels of output above 3 thus add more to cost than to revenue and hence *reduce* profit. As long as MC *exceeds* MR, *profit can be increased by cutting back on production.*

Profits are thus maximised where $MC = MR$: at an output of 3. This can be confirmed by examining the $T\Pi$ column in Table 10.4.

Students worry sometimes about the argument that profits are maximised when $MR = MC$. Surely, they say, if the last unit is making no profit, how can profit be at a *maximum*? The answer is very simple. If you cannot *add* anything more to a total, the total must be at the maximum. Take the simple analogy of going up a hill. When you cannot go any higher, you must be at the top.

Stage 2: Using average curves to measure the size of the profit

Once the profit-maximising output has been discovered, we now use the average curves to measure the *amount* of profit at the maximum. Both marginal and average curves corresponding to the data in Table 10.4 are plotted in Figure 10.7.

First, average profit ($A\Pi$) is found. This is simply $AR - AC$. At the profit-maximising output of 3, this gives a figure for

$A\Pi$ of £6 − £$4^2/_2$ = £$1^1/_3$. Then total profit is obtained by multiplying average profit by output:

$$T\Pi = A\Pi \times Q$$

This is shown as the shaded area. It equals £$1^1/_3 \times 3$ = £4. This can again be confirmed by reference to the $T\Pi$ column in Table 10.4.

Pause for thought

What will be the effect on a firm's profit-maximising output of a rise in fixed costs?

Some qualifications

Long-run profit maximisation

Assuming that the AR and MR curves are the same in the long run as in the short run, long-run profits will be maximised at the output where MR equals the *long-run MC*. The reasoning is the same as with the short-run case.

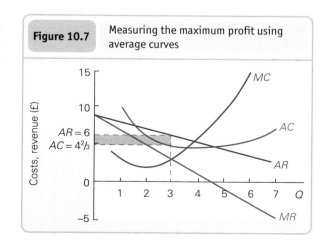

Figure 10.7 Measuring the maximum profit using average curves

The meaning of 'profit'

One element of cost is the opportunity cost to the owners of the firm incurred by being in business. This is the minimum return that the owners must make on their capital in order to prevent them from eventually deciding to close down and perhaps move into some alternative business. It is a *cost* since, just as with wages, rent, etc., it has to be covered if the firm is to continue poducing. This opportunity cost to the owners is sometimes known as **normal profit**, and *is included in the cost curves.*

What determines this normal rate of profit? It has two components. First, someone setting up in business invests capital in it. There is thus an opportunity cost of capital. This is the interest that could have been earned by lending it in some riskless form (e.g. by putting it in a savings account in a bank). Nobody would set up a business unless they expected to earn at least this rate of profit. Running a business is far from riskless, however, and hence a second element is a return to compensate for risk. Thus:

$$\text{normal profit (\%)} = \text{rate of interest on a riskless loan} + \text{a risk premium}$$

The risk premium varies according to the line of business. In those with fairly predictable patterns, such as food retailing, it is relatively low. Where outcomes are very uncertain, such as mineral exploration or the manufacture of fashion garments, it is relatively high.

Thus if owners of a business earn normal profit, they will (just) be content to remain in that industry. If they earn more than normal profit, they will also (obviously) prefer to stay in this business. If they earn less than normal profit, then after a time they will consider leaving and using their capital for some other purpose.

Given that normal profits are included in costs, any profit that is shown diagrammatically (e.g. the shaded area in Figure 10.7) must therefore be over and above normal profit. It is known by several alternative names: **supernormal profit**, **pure profit**, **economic profit**, **abnormal profit** or sometimes simply **profit**. They all mean the same thing: the excess of profit over normal profit.

Loss minimising

It may be that there is no output at which the firm can make a profit. Such a situation is illustrated in Figure 10.8: the *AC* curve is above the *AR* curve at all levels of output.

Definitions

Normal profit The opportunity cost of being in business. It consists of the interest that could be earned on a riskless asset, plus a return for risk-taking in this particular industry. It is counted as a cost of production.

Supernormal profit (also known as **pure profit**, **economic profit**, **abnormal profit** or simply **profit**) The excess of total profit above normal profit.

BOX 10.1 | OPPORTUNITY COST OF CAPITAL IN PRACTICE

Opportunity costs of capital and company structures

Opportunity costs of capital play an important role in determining the structure of large corporations. The RWE Group is one of Europe's largest electricity and gas companies. Its core operations are in Germany, the Netherlands and the UK. In the UK it operates through its NPower subsidiary, which it purchased in 2002.

By 2011 Jürgen Grossmann, RWE's chief executive, was considering if NPower should remain part of the RWE portfolio. According to the *Financial Times*:

> RWE has been reviewing its strategic options, advised by Goldman Sachs, as it grapples with net debt of €27.5bn (£24.7bn).
>
> To reduce this burden, Mr Grossmann has pledged asset disposals of up to €8bn a year between 2011 and 2013. Selling NPower, which generates about 9 per cent of the UK's electricity, will go a long way towards hitting this target. . . .
>
> Analysts point out that NPower has significantly underperformed its counterparts in RWE. Last year, NPower's return on capital employed was 5.3 per cent, making Britain the worst performing geographical area in the RWE group.
>
> Last year, RWE's annual report showed that NPower's return fell below the group's cost of capital of 9 per cent

before tax, ... [However] NPower remains a cash-generating business, achieving an operating profit of €277m last year.[1]

When making his decision Mr Grossmann will not look at past performance alone. He will also assess NPower's prospects for the future. On the demand side, there is a consumer perception that gas and electricity companies are charging 'unfair' prices. This is making producers reluctant to raise prices, fearing the effects of negative publicity. On the supply side, distribution costs are rising and from 2013 more powerful emissions regulations will exert additional upward pressure on costs.

Finally, the decision must also take into account the prospects for the rest of the RWE Group. Are the prospects of the other constituent parts better or worse than NPower's?

1. *Explain why, even though NPower generated €277 million in profit in 2010, it may make sense for RWE to sell the company.*
2. *Under what circumstances would another company consider buying NPower?*

---

[1] David Blair, Gerrit Wiesmann and Ausha Sakoui, RWE considers pulling plug on NPower (*The Financial Times*, 5 July 2011). © The Financial Times Limited. All Rights Reserved.

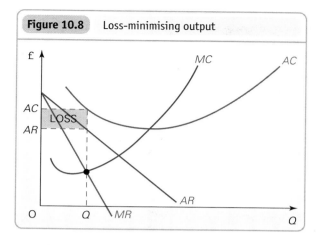

Figure 10.8 Loss-minimising output

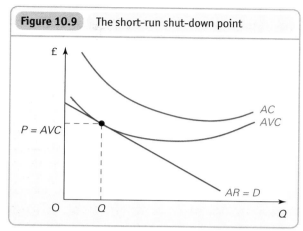

Figure 10.9 The short-run shut-down point

In this case, the output where $MR = MC$ will be the loss-minimising output. The amount of loss at the point where $MR = MC$ is shown by the shaded area in Figure 10.8.

Whether or not to produce at all

The short run. Fixed costs have to be paid even if the firm is producing nothing at all. Rent has to be paid, business rates have to be paid, etc. Providing, therefore, that the firm is more than covering its *variable* costs, it can go some way to paying off these fixed costs and therefore will continue to produce.

It will shut down if it cannot cover its variable costs: that is, if the *AVC* curve is above, or the *AR* curve is below, that illustrated in Figure 10.9. This situation is known as the **short-run shut-down point**.

The long run. All costs are variable in the long run. If, therefore, the firm cannot cover its long-run average costs (which include normal profit), it will close down. The **long-run shut-down point** will be where the *AR* curve is tangential to the *LRAC* curve.

> #### Pause for thought
>
> *Why might it make sense for a firm which cannot sell its output at a profit to continue in production for the time being?*

> #### Definitions
>
> **Short-run shut-down point** This is where the *AR* curve is tangential to the *AVC* curve. The firm can only just cover its variable costs. Any fall in revenue below this level will cause a profit-maximising firm to shut down immediately.
>
> **Long-run shut-down point** This is where the *AR* curve is tangential to the *LRAC* curve. The firm can just make normal profits. Any fall in revenue below this level will cause a profit-maximising firm to shut down once all costs have become variable.

BOX 10.2 SELLING ICE CREAM WHEN I WAS A STUDENT

John's experience of competition

When I was a student, my parents lived in Exeter in Devon, and at that time, the city's bypass became completely jammed on a summer Saturday as holidaymakers made their way to the coast. Traffic queues were several miles long.

For a summer job, I drove a small ice-cream van. Early on, I had the idea of selling ice cream from a tray to the people queuing in their cars. I made more money on a Saturday than the rest of the week put together. I thought I was on to a good thing.

But news of this lucrative market soon spread, and each week new ice-cream sellers appeared – each one reducing my earnings! By the middle of August there were over 30 ice-cream sellers from five different ice-cream companies. Most tried to get to the beginning of the queue, to get ahead of their rivals.

Imagine the scene. A family driving to the coast rounds a bend and is suddenly met by a traffic jam and several

ice-cream sellers all jostling to sell them an ice cream. It was quite surreal. Not surprisingly, many of the potential customers refused to buy, feeling somewhat intimidated by the spectacle. It was not long before most of us realised that it was best to disperse and find a section of the road where there were no other sellers.

But with so many ice-cream sellers, no one made much money. My supernormal earnings had been reduced to a normal level. I made about the same on Saturday selling to people stuck in queues as I would have done if I had driven my van around the streets.

 Imagine that you live in a popular and sunny seaside town and that the local council awarded you the only licence to sell ice cream in the town. Would you be earning normal or supernormal profit? Explain your answer.

SUMMARY

1a Just as we could identify total, average and marginal costs, so too we can identify total, average and marginal revenue.

1b Total revenue (*TR*) is the total amount a firm earns from its sales in a given time period. It is simply price times quantity: $TR = P \times Q$.

1c Average revenue (*AR*) is total revenue per unit: $AR = TR/Q$. In other words, $AR = P$.

1d Marginal revenue is the extra revenue earned from the sale of one more unit per time period.

1e The *AR* curve will be the same as the demand curve for the firm's product. In the case of a price taker, the demand curve and hence the *AR* curve will be a horizontal straight line and will also be the same as the *MR* curve. The *TR* curve is an upward-sloping straight line from the origin.

1f A firm that faces a downward-sloping demand curve must obviously also face the same downward-sloping *AR* curve. The *MR* curve will also slope downwards, but will be below the *AR* curve and steeper than it. The *TR* curve will be an arch shape starting from the origin.

1g When demand is price elastic, marginal revenue will be positive and the *TR* curve will be upward sloping. When demand is price inelastic, marginal revenue will be negative and the *TR* curve will be downward sloping.

1h A change in output is represented by a movement along the revenue curves. A change in any other determinant of revenue will shift the curves up or down.

2a Total profit equals total revenue minus total cost. By definition, then, a firm's profits will be maximised at the point where there is the greatest gap between total revenue and total cost.

2b Another way of finding the maximum-profit point is to find the output where marginal revenue equals marginal cost. Having found this output, the level of maximum profit can be found by finding the average profit ($AR - AC$) and then multiplying it by the level of output.

2c Normal profit is the minimum profit that must be made to persuade a firm to stay in business in the long run. It is counted as part of the firm's cost. Supernormal profit is any profit over and above normal profit.

2d For a firm that cannot make a profit at any level of output, the point where $MR = MC$ represents the loss-minimising output.

2e In the short run, a firm will close down if it cannot cover its variable costs. In the long run, it will close down if it cannot make normal profits.

REVIEW QUESTIONS

1 Draw a downward-sloping demand curve. Now put in scales of your own choosing for both axes. Read off various points on the demand curve and use them to construct a table showing price and quantity. Use this table to work out the figures for a marginal revenue column. Now use these figures to draw an *MR* curve.

2 Copy Figures 10.3 and 10.4 (which are based on Table 10.2). Now assume that incomes have risen and that, as a result, two more units per time period can be sold at each price. Draw a new table and plot the resulting new *AR*, *MR* and *TR* curves on your diagrams. Are the new curves parallel to the old ones? Explain.

3 What can we say about the slope of the *TR* and *TC* curves at the maximum-profit point? What does this tell us about marginal revenue and marginal cost?

4 Using the following information, construct a table like Table 10.3.

Q	0	1	2	3	4	5	6	7
P	12	11	10	9	8	7	6	5
TC	2	6	9	12	16	21	28	38

Use your table to draw diagrams like Figures 10.5 and 10.7. Use these two diagrams to show the profit-maximising output and the level of maximum profit. Confirm your findings by reference to the table you have constructed.

5 The following table shows the average cost and average revenue (price) for a firm at each level of output.

(a) Construct a table to show *TC*, *MC*, *TR* and *MR* at each level of output (put the figures for *MC* and *MR* midway between the output figures).

(b) Using *MC* and *MR* figures, find the profit-maximising output.

(c) Using *TC* and *TR* figures, check your answer to (b).

(d) Plot the *AC*, *MC*, *AR* and *MR* figures on a graph.

(e) Mark the profit-maximising output and the *AR* and *AC* at this output.

(f) Shade in an area to represent the level of profits at this output.

Output	1	2	3	4	5	6	7	8	9	10
AC (£)	7.00	5.00	4.00	3.30	3.00	3.10	3.50	4.20	5.00	6.00
AR (£)	10.00	9.50	9.00	8.50	8.00	7.50	7.00	6.50	6.00	5.50

6 Normal profits are regarded as a cost (and are included in the cost curves). Explain why.

7 What determines the size of normal profit? Will it vary with the general state of the economy?

8 A firm will continue producing in the short run even if it is making a loss, providing it can cover its variable costs. Explain why. Just how long will it be willing to continue making such a loss?

9 Would there ever be a point in a firm attempting to continue in production if it could not cover its *long-run average (total)* costs?

10 The price of pocket calculators and digital watches fell significantly in the years after they were first introduced and at the same time demand for them increased substantially. Use cost and revenue diagrams to illustrate these events. Explain the reasoning behind the diagram(s) you have drawn.

11 In February 2000, Unilever, the giant consumer products company, announced that it was to cut 25 000 jobs, close 100 plants and rely more on the Internet to purchase its supplies. It would use part of the money saved to increase promotion of its leading brands, such as Dove skincare products, Lipton tea, Omo detergents and Calvin Klein cosmetics. The hope was to boost sales and increase profits. If it meets these targets, what is likely to have happened to its total costs, total revenue, average costs and average revenue? Give reasons for your answer.

ADDITIONAL PART D CASE STUDIES IN THE *ECONOMICS FOR BUSINESS* MyEconLab (www.pearsoned.co.uk/sloman)

D.1 **Malthus and the dismal science of economics.** A gloomy warning, made over 200 years ago by Robert Malthus, that diminishing returns to labour would lead to famine for much of the world's population.

D.2 **Division of labour in a pin factory.** This is the famous example of division of labour given by Adam Smith in his *Wealth of Nations* (1776).

D.3 **Diminishing returns to nitrogen fertiliser.** This case study provides a good illustration of diminishing returns in practice by showing the effects on grass yields of the application of increasing amounts of nitrogen fertiliser.

D.4 **Diminishing returns in the bread shop.** An illustration of the law of diminishing returns.

D.5 **The relationship between averages and marginals.** An examination of the rules showing how an average curve relates to a marginal curve.

D.6 **Deriving cost curves from total physical product information.** This shows how total, average and marginal costs can be derived from a total product information and the price of inputs.

WEBSITES RELEVANT TO PART D

Numbers and sections refer to websites listed in the Web appendix and hotlinked from this book's website at **www.pearsoned.co.uk/sloman**

- For news articles relevant to Part D, see the Economics News Articles link from the book's website.

- For student resources relevant to Part D, see sites C1–7, 9, 10, 14, 19, 20.

- For a case study examining costs, see site D2.

- For sites that look at companies, their scale of operation and market share, see B2; E4, 10; G7, 8.

- For links to sites on various aspects of production and costs, see section Microeconomics > Production in site I7 and 11.

Supply: short-run profit maximisation

The FT Reports . . .

The Financial Times, 14 August 2012

FT

The British boozer is pulling pints again

By Luke Johnson

Pubs are a quintessential British institution and the classic small enterprise. They remain the social heart of most communities, with millions of regulars going to their local every week. . . . Their evolution reflects the various cycles of capitalism and parallel changes in legislation, social tastes and economics. . . .

Brewing started as a cottage industry and gradually achieved scale within a region. The sector was fragmented and, like most other forms of commercial activity, has continued to amalgamate relentlessly.

As certain brewers grew, so they started to vertically integrate by buying pubs. They worked with housebuilders to construct new taverns in the booming cities of the industrial revolution in the 18th and 19th centuries. Economies of scale enabled the big companies to dominate territories. Samuel Whitbread opened the first purpose-built, mass-production brewery in east London in 1750. Others followed, and brewing in retail alehouses declined steadily.

Free houses became rare and more publicans served as tenants of the breweries. They were free agents who paid rent to the brewery and bought their beer. Eventually, the industry became subject to regulation, while consolidation continued relentlessly. Guinness went public in 1886, while Bass & Co floated two years later. They used the capital raised to increase their control further over beer sales.

Margaret Thatcher's beer orders broke up the vertically integrated brewers. Small pubs became increasingly unviable and started to close; supermarkets increasingly sold cheap alcohol for consumption at home; tough drink-drive laws made life harder still for publicans.

There have been further shifts in the past decade. Thanks to endless mergers, large-scale brewing is dominated worldwide by four international corporations: Anheuser-Busch InBev, SABMiller, Heineken and Carlsberg – together they make more than half the world's beer. . . . [However, large brewery-owned pub chains] proved to be the wrong model in tough times. Now the huge pub companies are shrinking materially to reduce debt and so the ownership of Britain's pubs has become more dispersed.

Alongside this there has been a revival of craft brewers and independent proprietors of public houses. . . . Many establishments have converted themselves into pub restaurants and their dependence on beer sales has fallen as consumers have turned to wine, coffee, cocktails and other drinks. Across the licensed trade there are thousands of small businesses who are leading a reinvention of an ancient facility, making it relevant and attractive to today's customers. They are investing their own equity to bring novel ideas to the business of providing refreshment – and in many cases succeeding. . . .

HMV, the struggling high street retailer, said it expected to return to profit next year despite posting heavy losses for 2012 as its core market of DVDs and audio continued to decline. . . . Despite improving technology sales, HMV's core markets of DVDs and music continued to wilt, with the group's management predicting a decline of 10–13 per cent and 20 per cent, respectively, over the coming year. . . . Kate Calvert, an analyst at Seymour Pierce, said: '[HMV's] markets are under structural pressures, with the move online and the supermarkets' aggressive pricing. The move into technology has helped them but does not differentiate them. It's not going to drive new footfall.'

'HMV expects return to profit', *The Financial Times*, 9 August 2012. © The Financial Times Limited. All Rights Reserved

As we saw in Chapter 10, a firm's profits are maximised where its marginal cost equals its marginal revenue. But we will want to know more than this.

- What determines the *amount* of profit that a firm will make? Will profits be large, or just enough for the firm to survive, or so low that it will be forced out of business?
- Will the firm produce a high level of output or a low level?
- Will it be producing efficiently?
- Will the price charged to the consumer be high or low?
- And, more generally, will the consumer benefit from the decisions that a firm makes?

The answers to all these questions depend on the amount of *competition* that a firm faces. A firm in a highly competitive environment will behave quite differently from a firm facing little or no competition.

In Part E we will look at *different types of market structure*: from highly competitive markets at one end of the spectrum ('perfect competition'), to ones with no competition at all at the other ('monopoly'). We will also look at the intermediate cases of 'imperfect competition': monopolistic competition (where there are quite a lot of firms competing against each other) and oligopoly (where there are just a few).

As the article from the *Financial Times* opposite and the quote above show, there is intense competition even within industries where only a few firms dominate the market. Indeed, the presence of alternative *types* of product can even affect firms that have a monopoly of a particular product. However, it is also the case that firms may collude to restrict competition and the development of new technology, as we will see in this Part and Chapter 21. Consumers may then end up with less choice and paying higher prices.

Key terms

Market structures
Perfect competition
Monopoly
Natural monopoly
Competition for corporate control
Barriers to entry
Contestable markets
Sunk costs
Monopolistic competition
Product differentiation
Oligopoly
Interdependence
Collusive and non-collusive oligopoly
Open and tacit collusion
Price leadership
Benchmark pricing
Game theory
Dominant and non-dominant strategy games
Prisoners' dilemma
Nash equilibrium
Credible threat
First-mover advantage
Decision tree
Countervailing power

Profit maximisation under perfect competition and monopoly

Business issues covered in this chapter

- What determines the degree of market power of a firm?
- Why does operating under conditions of perfect competition make being in business a constant battle for survival?
- How do firms get to become monopolies and remain so?
- At what price and output will a monopolist maximise profits and how much profit will it make?
- How well or badly do monopolies serve the consumer compared with competitive firms?
- Why will the size of entry barriers to an industry (the degree of 'contestability' of a market) affect the amount of profit a monopolist can make?

11.1 ALTERNATIVE MARKET STRUCTURES

It is traditional to divide industries into categories according to the degree of competition that exists between the firms within the industry. There are four such categories.

At the most competitive extreme is a market structure referred to as *perfect competition*. This is a situation where there are a large number of firms competing. Each firm is so small relative to the whole industry that it has no power to influence market price. It is a price taker. At the least competitive extreme is *monopoly*, where there is just one firm in the industry, and hence no competition from *within* the industry. In the middle comes *monopolistic competition*, which involves quite a lot of firms competing and where there is freedom for new firms to enter the industry, and *oligopoly*, where there are only a few firms and where entry of new firms is difficult.

To distinguish more precisely between these four categories, the following must be considered:

Definitions

Perfect competition A market structure in which there are many firms; where there is freedom of entry to the industry; where all firms produce an identical product; and where all firms are price takers.

Monopoly A market structure where there is only one firm in the industry.

Monopolistic competition A market structure where, like perfect competition, there are many firms and freedom of entry into the industry, but where each firm produces a differentiated product and thus has some control over its price.

Oligopoly A market structure where there are few enough firms to enable barriers to be erected against the entry of new firms.

- How freely can firms enter the industry: is entry free or restricted? If it is restricted, just how great are the barriers to the entry of new firms?
- The nature of the product. Do all firms produce an identical product, or do firms produce their own particular brand or model or variety?
- The degree of control the firm has over price. Is the firm a price taker or can it choose its price, and if it can, how will changing its price affect its profits? What we are talking about here is the nature of the demand curve it faces. How elastic is it? If it puts up its price, will it lose (a) all its sales (a horizontal demand curve), or (b) a large proportion of its sales (a relatively elastic demand curve), or (c) just a small proportion of its sales (a relatively inelastic demand curve)?

> **KEY IDEA 21**
>
> ***Market power benefits the powerful at the expense of others.*** When firms have market power over prices, they can use this to raise prices and profits above the perfectly competitive level. Other things being equal, the firm will gain at the expense of the consumer. Similarly, if consumers or workers have market power, they can use this to their own benefit.

Table 11.1 shows the differences between the four categories.

The market structure under which a firm operates will determine its behaviour. Firms under perfect competition behave quite differently from firms that are monopolists, which behave differently again from firms under oligopoly or monopolistic competition.

This behaviour, or conduct, will in turn affect the firm's performance: its prices, profits, efficiency, etc. In many cases it will also affect other firms' performance: *their* prices, profits, efficiency, etc. The collective conduct of all the firms in the industry will affect the whole industry's performance.

Some economists thus see a causal chain running from market structure, through conduct, to the performance of that industry.

Structure → Conduct → Performance

This does not mean, however, that all firms operating in a particular market structure will behave in exactly the same way. For example, some firms under oligopoly may be highly competitive, whereas others may collude with each other to keep prices high. This conduct may then, in turn, influence the development of the market structure. For example, the interaction between firms may influence the development of new products or new production methods, and may encourage or discourage the entrance of new firms into the industry.

> **Pause for thought**
>
> *Give one more example in each of the four market categories in Table 11.1.*

It is for this reason that government policy towards firms – known as 'competition policy' – prefers to focus on the *conduct* of individual firms, rather than simply on the market structure within which they operate. Regulators focus on aspects of conduct such as price fixing and other forms of collusion. Indeed, competition policy in most countries accepts that market structures evolve naturally (e.g. because of economies of scale or changing consumer preferences) and do not necessarily give rise to competition problems.

Nevertheless, market structure still influences firms' behaviour and the performance of the industry, even though it does not, in the case of oligopoly and monopoly, rigidly determine it. We look at these influences in this chapter and the next. First, we look at the two extreme market structures: perfect competition and monopoly.

Table 11.1 Features of the four market structures

Type of market	Number of firms	Freedom of entry	Nature of product	Examples	Implication for demand curve for firm
Perfect competition	Very many	Unrestricted	Homogeneous (undifferentiated)	Cabbages, carrots (these approximate to perfect competition)	Horizontal. The firm is a price taker
Monopolistic competition	Many/several	Unrestricted	Differentiated	Builders, restaurants	Downward sloping, but relatively elastic. The firm has some control over price
Oligopoly	Few	Restricted	1. Undifferentiated or 2. Differentiated	1. Cement 2. Cars, electrical appliances	Downward sloping, relatively inelastic but depends on reactions of rivals to a price change
Monopoly	One	Restricted or completely blocked	Unique	Local water company, many prescription drugs	Downward sloping, more inelastic than oligopoly. Firm has considerable control over price

BOX 11.1 CONCENTRATION RATIOS

Measuring the degree of competition

We can get some indication of how competitive a market is by observing the number of firms: the more firms, the more competitive the market would seem to be. However, this does not tell us anything about how *concentrated* the market might be. There may be *many* firms (suggesting a situation of perfect competition or monopolistic competition), but the largest two firms might produce 95 per cent of total output. This would make these two firms more like oligopolists.

Thus even though a large number of producers may make the market *seem* highly competitive, this could be deceiving. Another approach, therefore, to measuring the degree of competition is to focus on the level of concentration of firms.

The simplest measure of industrial concentration involves adding together the market share of the largest so many firms: e.g. the largest three, five or fifteen. This would give what is known as the '3-firm', '5-firm' or '15-firm concentration ratio'. The resulting figures can be used to assess whether or not the largest firms in an industry dominate the market. There are different ways of estimating market share: by revenue, by output, by profit, etc.

The table shows the 5-firm concentration ratios of selected industries in the UK by output. As you can see, there is an enormous variation in the degree of concentration from one industry to another.

One of the main reasons for this is differences in the percentage of total industry output at which economies of scale are exhausted (see Box 9.4). If this occurs at a low level of output, there will be room for several firms in the industry which are all benefiting from the maximum economies of scale.

The degree of concentration will also depend on the barriers to entry of other firms into the industry (see pages 167–8) and on various factors such as transport costs and historical accident. It will also depend on how varied the products are within any one industrial category. For example, in categories as large as furniture and construction there is room for many firms, each producing a specialised range of products.

So is the degree of concentration a good guide to the degree of competitiveness of the industry? The answer is that it is *some* guide, but on its own it can be misleading. In particular, it ignores the degree of competition from abroad, and from other industries within the country.

1. *What are the advantages and disadvantages of using a 5-firm concentration ratio rather than a 10-firm, 3-firm or even a 1-firm ratio?*
2. *Why are some industries like bread baking and brewing relatively concentrated, in that a few firms produce a large proportion of total output (see case studies E8 and E9 in MyEconLab), and yet there are also many small producers?*

Concentration ratios for business by industry (2004)

Industry	5-firm ratio	15-firm ratio	Industry	5-firm ratio	15-firm ratio
Sugar	99	99	Alcoholic beverages	50	78
Tobacco products	99	99	Soap and toiletries	40	64
Oils and fats	88	95	Accountancy services	36	47
Confectionary	81	91	Motor vehicles	34	54
Gas distribution	82	87	Glass and glass products	26	49
Soft drinks, mineral water	75	93	Fishing	16	19
Postal/courier services	65	75	Advertising	10	20
Telecommunications	61	75	Wholesale distribution	6	11
Inorganic chemicals	57	80	Furniture	5	13

Source: based on data in Table 8.31 of *United Kingdom Input–Output Analyses* 2006 (National Statistics)

Then we turn to look at the two intermediate cases of monopolistic competition and oligopoly (Chapter 12).

These two intermediate cases are sometimes referred to collectively as ***imperfect competition***. The vast majority of firms in the real world operate under imperfect competition. It is still worth studying the two extreme cases, however,

because they provide a framework within which to understand the real world. They provide important benchmarks for comparison. For example, regulators would find it difficult to identify anti-competitive behaviour if they could not show how outcomes would differ in a more competitive environment.

Some industries tend more to the competitive extreme, and thus their performance corresponds to some extent to perfect competition. Other industries tend more to the other extreme: for example, when there is one dominant firm and a few much smaller firms. In such cases, their performance corresponds more to monopoly.

Definition

Imperfect competition The collective name for monopolistic competition and oligopoly.

The theory of perfect competition illustrates an extreme form of capitalism. In it firms are entirely subject to market forces. They have no power whatsoever to affect the price of the product. The price they face is that determined by the interaction of demand and supply in the whole *market*.

Assumptions

The model of perfect competition is built on four assumptions:

1. Firms are *price takers*. There are so many firms in the industry that each one produces an insignificantly small proportion of total industry supply, and therefore has *no power whatsoever* to affect the price of the product. Hence it faces a horizontal (perfectly elastic) demand 'curve' at the market price: the price determined by the interaction of demand and supply in the whole market.

2. There is complete *freedom of entry* into the industry for new firms. Existing firms are unable to stop new firms setting up in business. Setting up a business takes time, however. Freedom of entry therefore applies in the long run.

3. All firms produce an *identical product*. The product is 'homogeneous' i.e. all products in the market are identical and are perfect substitutes for each other. There is therefore no branding or advertising.

4. Producers and consumers have *perfect knowledge* of the market. That is, producers are fully aware of prices, costs, technology and market opportunities. Consumers are fully aware of price, quality and availability of the product.

These assumptions are very strict. Few, if any, industries in the real world meet these conditions. Certain agricultural markets perhaps are closest to perfect competition. The market for fresh vegetables is an example.

Pause for thought

It is sometimes claimed that the market for various stocks and shares is perfectly competitive, or nearly so. Take the case of the market for shares in a large company, such as BP. Go through each of the four assumptions above and see if they apply in this case. (Don't be misled by the first assumption. The 'firm' in this case is not BP itself, but rather the owners of the shares.)

The short-run equilibrium of the firm

In the **short run**, we assume that the number of firms in the industry cannot be increased; there is simply no time for new firms to enter the market.

Figure 11.1 shows a short-run equilibrium for both industry and a firm under perfect competition. Both parts of the diagram have the same scale for the vertical axis. The horizontal axes have totally different scales, however. For example, if the horizontal axis for the firm were measured in, say, thousands of units, the horizontal axis for the whole industry might be measured in millions or tens of millions of units, depending on the number of firms in the industry.

Let us examine the determination of price, output and profit in turn.

Definition

The short run under perfect competition The period during which there is too little time for new firms to enter the industry.

Figure 11.1 Short-run equilibrium of industry and firm under perfect competition

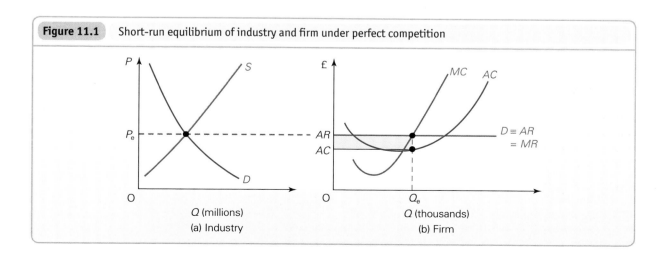

(a) Industry

(b) Firm

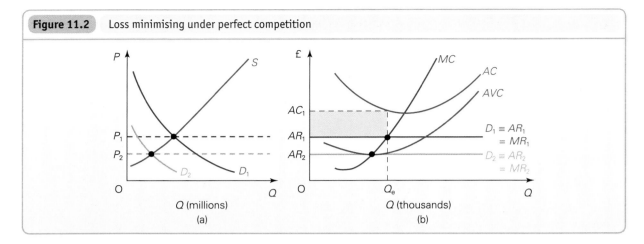

Figure 11.2   Loss minimising under perfect competition

Q (millions)
(a)

Q (thousands)
(b)

Price

The price is determined in the industry by the intersection of market demand and supply. The firm faces a horizontal demand (or average revenue) 'curve' at this price. It can sell all it can produce at the market price (P_e). It would sell nothing at a price above P_e, however, since competitors would be selling identical products at a lower price.

Output

The firm will maximise profit where marginal cost equals marginal revenue ($MR = MC$), at an output of Q_e. Note that, since the price is not affected by the firm's output, marginal revenue will equal price (see page 149 and Figure 10.1). Thus the firm's MR 'curve' and AR 'curve' (= demand 'curve') are the same horizontal straight line.

Profit

If the average cost (AC) curve (which includes normal profit) dips below the average revenue (AR) 'curve', the firm will earn supernormal profit. Supernormal profit per unit at Q_e is the vertical difference between AR and AC at Q_e. Total supernormal profit is the shaded rectangle in Figure 11.1 (i.e. profit per unit times quantity sold).

What happens if the firm cannot make a profit at *any* level of output? This situation would occur if the AC curve were above the AR curve at all points. This is illustrated in Figure 11.2 where the market price is P_1. In this case, the point where $MC = MR$ represents the *loss-minimising* point (where loss is defined as anything less than normal profit). This amount of the loss is represented by the shaded rectangle.

As we saw in Chapter 10, whether the firm is prepared to continue making a loss in the short run or whether it will close down immediately depends on whether it can cover its *variable* costs. Provided price is above average variable cost (AVC), the firm will continue producing in the short run: it can pay its variable costs and go some way to paying its fixed costs. It will shut down in the short run only if the market price falls below P_2 in Figure 11.2: i.e. when variable costs of production cannot be covered.

The long-run equilibrium of the firm

In the **long run**, if typical firms are making supernormal profits, new firms will be attracted into the industry. Likewise, if existing firms can make supernormal profits by increasing the scale of their operations, they will do so, since all factors of production are variable in the long run.

The effect of the entry of new firms and/or the expansion of existing firms is to increase industry supply, meaning that at every price level the quantity produced would be higher. This is illustrated in Figure 11.3.

> **Pause for thought**
>
> *Before you read on, can you explain why perfect competition and substantial economies of scale are likely to be incompatible?*

The industry supply curve shifts to the right. This in turn leads to a fall in price. Supply will go on increasing, and price falling, until firms are making only normal profits. This will be when price has fallen to the point where the demand 'curve' for the firm just touches the bottom of its long-run average cost curve. Q_L is thus the long-run equilibrium output of the firm, with P_L the long-run equilibrium price.

Since the $LRAC$ curve is tangential to all possible short-run AC curves (see section 9.5), the full long-run equilibrium will be as shown in Figure 11.4 where:

$$LRAC = AC = MC = MR = AR$$

> **Definitions**
>
> **The long run under perfect competition** The period of time which is long enough for new firms to enter the industry.

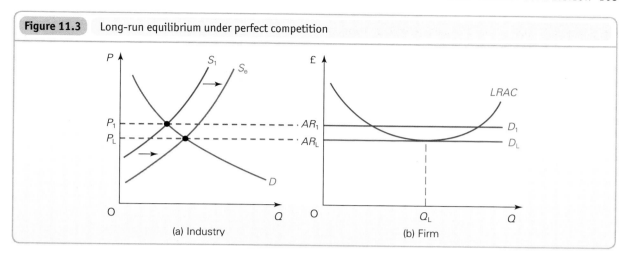

Figure 11.3 Long-run equilibrium under perfect competition

(a) Industry

(b) Firm

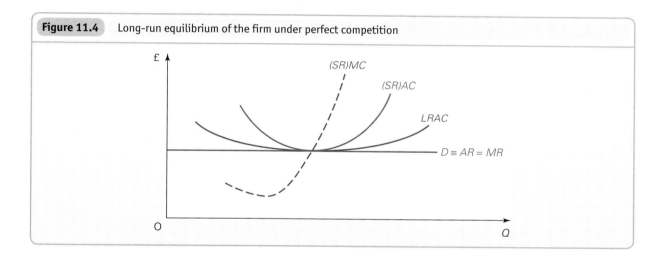

Figure 11.4 Long-run equilibrium of the firm under perfect competition

The incompatibility of perfect competition and substantial economies of scale

Why is perfect competition so rare in the real world – if it even exists at all? One important reason for this has to do with economies of scale.

In many industries, firms may have to be quite large if they are to experience the full potential economies of scale. But perfect competition requires there to be *many* firms. Firms must therefore be small under perfect competition: too small in most cases for them to achieve economies of scale.

Once a firm expands sufficiently to achieve economies of scale, it will usually gain market power. It will be able to undercut the prices of smaller firms, which will thus be driven out of business. Perfect competition is destroyed. Perfect competition could only exist in any industry, therefore, if there were no (or virtually no) economies of scale.

Does the firm benefit from operating under perfect competition?

Under perfect competition the firm faces a constant battle for survival. If it becomes less efficient than other firms, it will make less than normal profits and be driven out of business. If it becomes more efficient, it will earn super-normal profits. But these supernormal profits will not last for long. Soon other firms, in order to survive themselves, will be forced to copy the more efficient methods of the new firm. They are able to do this because the perfect knowledge assumption implies that new methods can be copied by all producers.

KEY IDEA 22

Economic efficiency is achieved when each good is produced at the minimum cost and where consumers get maximum benefit from their income.

BOX 11.2 **E-COMMERCE**

A modern form of perfect competition?

The relentless drive towards big business in recent decades has seen many markets become more concentrated and increasingly dominated by large producers. However, forces are at work that are undermining this dominance and bringing more competition to markets. One of these forces is *e-commerce*.

In this case study, we will consider just how far e-commerce is returning 'power to the people'.

Moving markets back towards perfect competition?

To see the extent to which e-commerce is making markets more competitive, let's look at the assumptions of perfect competition.

Large number of firms. The growth of e-commerce has led to many new firms starting up in business. It's not just large firms like Amazon.com that are providing increased competition for established firms, but the thousands of small online companies that are being established every year. Many of these firms are selling directly to us as consumers. This is known as 'B2C' (business-to-consumers) e-commerce. But many more are selling to other firms ('B2B'). More and more companies, from the biggest to the smallest, are transferring their purchasing to the Web and are keen to get value for money.

The reach of the Web is global. This means that firms, whether conventional or web-based, have to keep an eye on the prices and products of competitors in the rest of the world, not just in the local neighbourhood. Firms' demand curves are thus becoming more price elastic. This is especially so for goods that are cheap to transport, or for services such as insurance and banking where no transport is required.

Perfect knowledge. There are various ways in which e-commerce is adding to the consumer's knowledge. There is greater price transparency, with consumers able to compare prices on-line. Online shopping agents, such as Kelkoo, Shopzilla and Google Shopping, can quickly locate a list of alternative suppliers. There is greater information on product availability and quality and this information is available at very little cost to the consumer. Virtual shopping malls, full of e-retailers, place the high street retailer under intense competitive pressure.

The pressure is even greater in the market for intermediate products. Many firms are constantly searching for cheaper sources of supply, and the Internet provides a cheap and easy means of conducting such searches.

Freedom of entry. Internet companies often have lower start-up costs than their conventional rivals. Their premises are generally much smaller, with no 'shop-front' costs and lower levels of stockholding; in fact many of these businesses are initially operated from their owners' homes. Marketing costs can also be relatively low, especially given the ease with which companies can be located with search engines. Internet companies are often smaller and more specialist, relying on Internet 'outsourcing' (buying parts, equipment and other supplies through the Internet), rather than making everything themselves. They are also more likely to use delivery firms rather than having their own transport fleet. All this makes it relatively cheap for new firms to set up and begin trading over the Internet.

One consequence of e-commerce is that the distinction between firms and consumers is becoming increasingly blurred. With the rise of eBay, more and more people are finding going into business incredibly easy. Some people are finding a market for all the junk they've collected over the

---

It is the same with the development of new products. If a firm is able to produce a new product that is popular with consumers, it will be able to gain a temporary advantage over its rivals. But again, any supernormal profits will last only as long as it takes other firms to respond. Soon the increase in supply of the new product will drive the price down and eliminate these supernormal profits. Similarly, the firm must be quick to copy new products developed by its rivals. If it does not, it will soon make a loss and be driven out of the market.

Thus being in perfect competition is a constant battle for survival. It might benefit the consumer, due to the lower prices and higher quantities. However, most firms in such an environment would love to be able to gain some market power: power to be able to restrict competition and to retain supernormal profits into the long run.

The extreme case of market power is that of monopoly: a firm that faces no competition – at least not from *within* its industry. Monopoly is the subject of the next section.

11.3 MONOPOLY

What is a monopoly?

This may seem a strange question because the answer seems obvious. A monopoly exists when there is only one firm in the industry.

But whether an industry can be classed as a monopoly is not always clear. It depends how narrowly the industry is defined. For example, a textile company may have a monopoly on certain types of fabric, but it does not have a monopoly on fabrics in general. The consumer can buy

years, while others are selling products they produce at home and yet others specialise in selling on products using the marketing power of eBay. As a consequence there are over 100 million active eBay users worldwide, and hundreds of thousands of people make a full-time living from buying and selling on eBay. In 2011 the total value of goods sold on eBay was $68.6 billion having grown over 600 per cent from a figure of $9.3 billion ten years earlier.

Not only do these factors make markets more price competitive, they also bring other benefits. Costs are driven down, as firms economise on stockholding, rely more on outsourcing and develop more efficient relationships with suppliers. 'Procurement hubs', online exchanges and trading communities are now well established in many industries. The competition also encourages innovation, which improves quality and the range of products.

What are the limits to e-commerce?

In 20 years, will we be doing all our shopping on the Internet? Will the only shopping malls be virtual ones? Although e-commerce is revolutionising some markets, it is unlikely that things will go anything like that far.

The benefits of 'shop shopping' are that you get to see the good, touch it and use it. You can buy the good there and then, and take instant possession of it: you don't have to wait. Shopping is also an enjoyable experience. Many people like wandering round the shops, meeting friends, seeing what takes their fancy, trying on clothes, browsing through DVDs, and so on. 'Retail therapy' for many is a leisure activity. Many consumers are willing to pay a 'premium' for these advantages.

Online shopping is limited by current technology and infrastructure. The quality of Internet access has improved significantly as broadband has become widely available.

However, you still have to wait for goods to be delivered; and what if deliveries are late or fail completely? (See Box 6.2.) The busiest time for Internet shopping is in the run-up to Christmas. In 2011 Yodel, the UK's second largest household delivery company (after the Royal Mail), failed to deliver around 15 000 parcels per day as Christmas approached.[1] Their delivery infrastructure simply could not cope with the increase in demand. Additionally, online shopping requires access to a credit or debit card, which might not be available to everyone, particularly younger consumers and those on low incomes.

Also costs might not always be as low as expected. How efficient is it to have many small deliveries of goods? How significant are the lost cost savings from economies of scale that larger producers or retailers are likely to generate?

Nevertheless, e-commerce has made many markets, both retail and B2B, more competitive. This is especially so for services and for goods whose quality is easy to identify online. Many firms are being forced to face up to having their prices determined by the market.

1. *Why may the Internet work better for replacement buys than for new purchases?*
2. *Give three examples of products that are particularly suitable for selling over the Internet and three that are not. Explain your answer.*
3. *In 2008 eBay sellers called for a boycott of the site, following changes in the fees being charged and the removal of their ability to leave feedback on buyers. Explain how eBay can both increase competition across the economy and simultaneously acquire very substantial monopoly power.*

[1] Surge in online orders hits deliveries Financial Times, 23/12/11.

---

fabrics other than those supplied by the company. A rail company may have a monopoly over rail services between two cities, but it does not have a monopoly over public transport between these two cities. People can travel by coach or air. They could also use private transport.

To some extent, the boundaries of an industry are arbitrary. What is more important for a firm is the amount of monopoly *power* it has, and that depends on the closeness of substitutes produced by rival industries. The Post Office, before 2006, had a monopoly over the delivery of letters, but it faces competition in communications from telephone, faxes and e-mail.

Barriers to entry

For a firm to maintain its monopoly position, there must be barriers to the entry of new firms. Barriers also exist under oligopoly, but in the case of monopoly they must be high enough to block the entry of new firms. Barriers can take various forms.

Economies of scale. If the monopolist's average costs go on falling significantly up to the output that satisfies the whole market, the industry may not be able to support more than one producer. This case is known as **natural monopoly**. This is more likely if the market is small. For example, two bus companies might find it unprofitable to serve the same routes, each running with perhaps only half-full buses, whereas one company with a monopoly of the routes could make a profit. Electricity transmission via a national grid is another example of a natural monopoly.

Even if a market could support more than one firm, a new entrant is unlikely to be able to start up on a very large scale. Thus the monopolist which is already experiencing

Definition

Natural monopoly A situation where long-run average costs would be lower if an industry were under monopoly than if it were shared between two or more competitors.

economies of scale can charge a price below the cost of the new entrant and drive it out of business. If, however, the new entrant is a firm already established in another industry, it may be able to survive this competition.

Economies of scope. A firm that produces a range of products is also likely to experience a lower average cost of production due to economies of scope. For example, a large pharmaceutical company producing a range of drugs and toiletries can use shared research, marketing, storage and transport facilities across its range of products. These lower costs make it difficult for a new single-product entrant to the market, since the large firm will be able to undercut its price and drive it out of the market.

Product differentiation and brand loyalty. If a firm produces a clearly differentiated product, where the consumer associates the product with the brand, it will be very difficult for a new firm to break into that market. Rank Xerox invented, and patented, the plain paper photocopier. After this legal monopoly (see below) ran out, people still associated photocopiers with Rank Xerox. It is still not unusual to hear someone say that they are going to 'Xerox the article' or, for that matter, 'Hoover their carpet'. Other examples of strong brand image include Guinness, Kelloggs Cornflakes, Coca-Cola, Nescafé and Sellotape.

Lower costs for an established firm. An established monopoly is likely to have developed specialised production and marketing skills. It is more likely to be aware of the most efficient techniques and the most reliable and/or cheapest suppliers. It is likely to have access to cheaper finance. It is thus operating on a lower average total cost curve. New firms would therefore find it hard to compete on price and would be likely to lose any price war.

Pause for thought

Illustrate the situation described above using AC curves for both a new entrant and an established firm.

Ownership of, or control over, key inputs or outlets. If a firm governs the supply of vital inputs (say, by owning the sole supplier of some component part), it can deny access to these inputs to potential rivals. On a world scale, the de Beers company has a monopoly in fine diamonds because all diamond producers market their diamonds through de Beers.

Similarly, if a firm controls the outlets through which the product must be sold, it can prevent potential rivals from gaining access to consumers. For example, Birds Eye Walls used to supply freezers free to shops on the condition that they stocked only Wall's ice cream in them.

Legal protection. The firm's monopoly position may be protected by patents on essential processes, by copyright, by

various forms of licensing (allowing, say, only one firm to operate in a particular area) and by tariffs (i.e. customs duties) and other trade restrictions to keep out foreign competitors. Examples of monopolies, or near monopolies, protected by patents include most new medicines developed by pharmaceutical companies (e.g. anti-AIDS drugs), Microsoft's Windows operating systems and agro-chemical companies, such as Monsanto, with various genetically modified plant varieties and pesticides.

Mergers and takeovers. The monopolist can put in a takeover bid for any new entrant. The sheer threat of takeovers may discourage new entrants.

Aggressive tactics. An established monopolist can probably sustain losses for longer than a new entrant. Thus it could start a price war, mount massive advertising campaigns, offer attractive after-sales service, introduce new brands to compete with new entrants, and so on.

Equilibrium price and output

Since there is, by definition, only one firm in the industry, the firm's demand curve is also the industry demand curve.

Compared with other market structures, demand under monopoly will be relatively inelastic at each price. The monopolist can raise its price and consumers have no alternative firm to turn to within the industry. They either pay the higher price, or go without the good altogether.

Unlike the firm under perfect competition, the monopoly firm is thus a 'price maker'. It can choose what price to charge. Nevertheless, it is still constrained by its demand curve. A rise in price will reduce the quantity demanded.

As with firms in other market structures, a monopolist will maximise profit where $MR = MC$. In Figure 11.5 profit is maximised by producing a quantity of Q_m. The supernormal profit obtained is shown by the shaded area.

These profits will tend to be larger, the less elastic is the demand curve (and hence the steeper is the MR curve), and

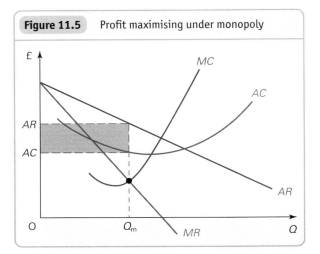

Figure 11.5 Profit maximising under monopoly

thus the bigger is the gap between *MR* and price (*AR*). The actual elasticity will depend on whether reasonably close substitutes are available in *other* industries. The demand for a rail service will be much less elastic (and the potential for profit greater) if there is no bus service between the same destinations.

KI 21
p 161

Since there are barriers to the entry of new firms, a monopolist's supernormal profits will not be competed away in the long run. The only difference, therefore, between short-run and long-run equilibrium is that in the long run the firm will produce where *MR = long-run MC*.

Comparing monopoly with perfect competition

Because it faces a different type of market environment, the monopolist will produce a quite different output and at a quite different price from a perfectly competitive industry. Let us compare the two.

KI 21
p 161

The monopolist will produce a lower output at a higher price in the short run. Figure 11.6 compares the profit-maximising position for an industry under monopoly with that under perfect competition. Note that we are comparing the monopoly with the whole *industry* under perfect competition. That way we can assume, for the sake of comparison, that they both face the same demand curve. We also assume for the moment that they both face the same cost curves.

The monopolist will produce Q_1 at a price of P_1. This is where *MC = MR*.

If the same industry were under perfect competition, however, it would produce at Q_2 and P_2 – a higher output and a lower price. But why? The reason for this is that for each of the firms in the industry – and it is at this level that the decisions are made – marginal revenue is the same as

price. Remember that the *firm* under perfect competition faces a perfectly elastic demand (*AR*) curve, which also equals *MR* (see Figure 11.1). Thus producing where *MC = MR* also means producing where *MC = P*. When *all* firms under perfect competition do this, price and quantity in the *industry* will be given by P_2 and Q_2 in Figure 11.6.

The monopolist may also produce a lower output at a higher price in the long run. Under perfect competition, freedom of entry eliminates supernormal profit and forces firms to produce at the bottom of their *LRAC* curve. The effect, therefore, is to keep long-run prices down. Under monopoly, however, barriers to entry allow profits to remain supernormal in the long run. The monopolist is not forced to operate at the bottom of the *AC* curve. Thus, other things being equal, long-run prices will tend to be higher, and hence output lower, under monopoly. (In section 20.2 we examine this in more detail by considering the impact of monopoly on consumer and producer surplus. You might wish to take a preliminary look at pages 314–5 now.)

> ### Pause for thought
>
> *If the shares in a monopoly (such as a water company) were very widely distributed among the population, would the shareholders necessarily want the firm to use its monopoly power to make larger profits?*

Costs under monopoly. The sheer survival of a firm in the long run under perfect competition requires that it uses the most efficient known technique, and develops new techniques wherever possible. The monopolist, however, sheltered by barriers to entry, can still make large profits even if it is not using the most efficient technique. It has less incentive, therefore, to be efficient.

On the other hand, the monopoly may be able to achieve substantial economies of scale due to larger plant, centralised administration and the avoidance of unnecessary duplication (e.g. a monopoly water company would eliminate the need for several sets of rival water mains under each street). If this results in an *MC* curve substantially below that of the same industry under perfect competition, the monopoly may even produce a *higher* output at a *lower* price.

Another reason why a monopolist may operate with lower costs is that it can use part of its supernormal profits for research and development and investment. It may not have the same *incentive* to become efficient as the perfectly competitive firm which is fighting for survival, but it may have a much greater *ability* to become efficient than has the small firm with limited funds.

Although a monopoly faces no competition in the goods market, it may face an alternative form of competition in

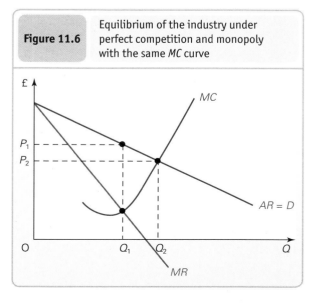

Figure 11.6 Equilibrium of the industry under perfect competition and monopoly with the same *MC* curve

BOX 11.3   WINDOWS CLEANING

The Microsoft Monopoly under challenge?

In March 2004 the European Commission fined Microsoft €497 million for an Abuse of a Dominant Position in the operating system market. It found that Microsoft had harmed competition in the media player market by bundling *Windows Media Player* with its operating system. Further, Microsoft had refused to supply information about its secret software code to suppliers of alternative network software at reasonable rates. Such code was needed to allow non-Windows network software to be interoperable with ('talk' to) Windows network software. Without it, firms who had purchased *Windows Network* servers would be solely tied in to Microsoft server software. This, in turn, would discourage the development of application software products by Microsoft's rivals.

In April 2006, Microsoft launched an appeal against the judgment claiming that the EU's ruling violated international law by forcing the company to share information with rivals. However, the Court of First Instance found in the Commission's favour. Microsoft complied with the first ruling and unbundled *Windows Media Player* from its operating systems, much to the annoyance of computer suppliers who argued that their customers could easily upload alternative media players from the Web.

However, until October 2007 Microsoft continued to charge high royalty rates and fees for interoperability information that would allow competitors to access secret source code on the *Windows Network System*. As a result, in February 2008 the Commission penalised Microsoft a further €899 million for non-compliance with its 2004 decision and Microsoft became the first company in fifty years of EU competition policy to be fined for non-compliance with a Commission decision.[1] Microsoft took the Commission to court in an attempt to overturn the fine, losing its case in 2012.

This is not the end of Microsoft's dealings with the European Commission. In 2009 the Commission announced an investigation into the bundling of *Internet Explorer* with *Windows*. The bundling was thought to be restricting competition in the market for web browsers.[2] Microsoft took the Commission seriously and agreed to remove *Explorer* from the European versions of *Windows 7*. To promote competition they offered users an option of downloading one browser from a list of twelve. However, only three years later Microsoft may once again be engaging in anti-competitive behaviour. The Commission is examining the possibility that *Windows 8* will discourage, or even prevent, users from using other browsers. In July 2012 the Commission publicly

threatened Microsoft with severe penalties if it breaks the 2009 bundling agreement with its *Windows 8* product.

Is Microsoft playing a 'game' with the competition authorities – maximising profits by pushing as hard as possible against the legal framework?

Earlier anti-monopoly rulings in other countries

Microsoft is no stranger to anti-monopoly lawsuits. In 2005 Microsoft was fined 33bn Won ($32 million; £18.4 million) by South Korea's Fair Trade Commission for breaches of anti-monopoly legislation that covered very similar issues to those in the EU investigation.

In August 2008, Microsoft was investigated by Taiwan's Fair Trade Commission because of its monopoly position in the operating system market.

Perhaps the most famous investigation began on 18 May 1998, when the US government accused Microsoft of abusing its market power and seeking to crush its rivals. The US Justice Department alleged that Microsoft had committed the following anti-competitive actions:

- In May 1995 Microsoft attempted to collude with Netscape Communications to divide the Internet browser market. Netscape Communications refused.
- Microsoft had forced personal computer manufacturers to install *Internet Explorer* in order to obtain a *Windows 95* operating licence.
- Microsoft insisted that PC manufacturers conformed to a Microsoft front screen for *Windows*. This included specified icons, one of which was Microsoft's *Internet Explorer*.
- It had set up reciprocal advertising arrangements with America's largest Internet service providers, such as America Online. Here Microsoft would promote America Online via *Windows*. In return, America Online would not promote Netscape's browsers.

One solution, posed by Federal Judge Thomas Penfield Jackson in 2000, was that Microsoft be split in two to prevent it operating as a monopoly. One company would produce and market the *Windows* operating system; the other would produce and market the applications software, such as *Microsoft Office* and the web browser, *Internet Explorer*.

This was overturned on appeal in June 2001 and Microsoft agreed to provide technical information about *Windows* to other companies so that potential rivals could write software that would compete with Microsoft's own software. Also Microsoft would not be allowed to retaliate against computer manufacturers that installed rival products or removed icons for Microsoft applications.

Microsoft and the public interest

These lawsuits raise an important issue: is Microsoft acting for or against the public interest?

---

[1] See Antitrust: Commission imposes €899 million penalty on Microsoft for non-compliance with March 2004 Decision, IP/08/318, 27 February 2008.

[2] See Antitrust: Commission confirms sending of a Statement of Objections to Microsoft on the tying of Internet Explorer to Windows Reference, MEMO/09/15, 17 Janurary 2009.

---

financial markets. A monopoly, with potentially low costs, which is currently run inefficiently, is likely to be subject to a takeover bid from another company. This **competition for corporate control** may thus force the monopoly to be efficient in order to prevent being taken over.

Definition

Competition for corporate control The competition for the control of companies through takeovers.

The classic case against monopoly suppliers is that they charge higher prices and offer lower quantities to consumers than would be the case under perfect competition. In addition, the supernormal profit that monopolies earn may be detrimental to society if it is used to continue to support the monopoly position, say by lobbying or bribing government officials. Further, if no competition prevails then monopoly suppliers may become more inefficient.

However, the competition authorities have never penalised Microsoft simply for possessing monopoly power. It has been fined when it has *abused* its market power. That is, it is not the monopoly market structure that matters per se to competition authorities; rather, it is the behaviour of the firm when it has monopoly power. Through its actions, Microsoft had raised barriers to entry by restricting the opportunities for potential rival firms to offer alternative products to customers. Choice was thereby restricted.

In its defence, Microsoft has argued that it has continually sought to reinvest its profits in new product development and offered a number of innovative solutions over the past 30 years for individuals and businesses alike. (Can you think of all the versions of *Windows* and the 'free updates' there have been?)

Further, in an environment where technology is changing rapidly, Microsoft's control over standards gives the user a measure of stability, knowing that any new products and applications will be compatible with existing ones. In other words, new software can be incorporated into existing systems. In this respect Microsoft can be viewed as operating in society's interest. Microsoft would argue that it has a right to protect its in-house software code from competitors and receive a fair price for it. Indeed, it is a natural response for a firm to protect its intellectual property rights. Failure to do so could lead to the firm's demise.

Network effects

Microsoft is a vertically integrated firm (see pages 227–9), with a dominant position in the operating system market (i.e. *Windows*) and in certain application software (*Office* and *Windows Media Player*) markets. It has built this position by creating networks of users. These networks bring both benefits and costs to society.

Network effects arise when consumers of a product benefit from it being used by *other* consumers. In the case of Microsoft's products, firms benefit from lower training costs because individuals who have learnt to use Microsoft products elsewhere can be readily absorbed into the firm. Individuals benefit too because they do not have to learn to use new software when they move to another organisation and the learning costs are fairly low as a new version of the software is introduced.

The negative aspect of developing strong networks is that users can get 'locked in' to using the software and they become reluctant to switch to alternative systems. Protecting the network is vital to Microsoft's competitive edge.

Challenges to Microsoft monopoly

Microsoft is facing increasing competitive pressure. The recent challenges from competition authorities (referred to above) have opened up the browser market, for example. Microsoft's *Internet Explorer* is no longer the dominant browser; since the mid-2000s its market share has fallen significantly as other browsers have become widely used. In July 2003, it had an 82.7 per cent share of the global browser market; by July 2012, this had fallen to 16.3 per cent – third behind Google's Chrome (42.9%) and Firefox (33.7%).[3]

There is also a growing challenge from new Internet firms, such as Google and Facebook. Both Google and Facebook have created enormous networks of users who are then targeted with tailored adverts paid for by firms who want to reach these vast audiences.

This is a very different business model from that of Microsoft and, as part of the desire to create large networks of users, free products are being released that will compete with that of Microsoft. For example, Google's *Google Docs* and Apache's *Open Office* compete with Microsoft's *Office*. These are becoming increasingly well known and have growing market shares.

Microsoft still dominates the operating system market. In July 2012, the various versions of *Windows* had a 69 per cent market share. Apple's *Mac* has been the only serious contender for standalone computers – its market share was 8 per cent. However, with the rise of tablet computers and smart phones, Linux's open-source operating system, *Android*, had gained a market share of nearly 7 per cent – a share likely to increase substantially in the future.[4]

You might want to follow subsequent events as the news unfolds (see section A of the Hotlinks section of this text's website for links to newspaper sites).

1. In what respects might Microsoft's behaviour be deemed to have been: (a) against the public interest; (b) in the public interest?
2. Being locked in to a product or technology is only a problem if such a product can be clearly shown to be inferior to an alternative. What difficulties might there be in establishing such a case?

[3] For figures on browser usage, see http://www.w3schools.com/browsers/browsers_stats.asp
[4] *Wikimedia Traffic Analysis Report – Operating Systems* (July 2012).

Innovation and new products. The promise of supernormal profits, protected perhaps by patents, may encourage the development of new (monopoly) industries producing new products. It is this chance of making monopoly profits that encourages many people to take the risks of going into business.

11.4 POTENTIAL COMPETITION OR POTENTIAL MONOPOLY? THE THEORY OF CONTESTABLE MARKETS

Potential competition

In recent years, economists have developed the theory of contestable markets. This theory argues that what is crucial in determining price and output is not whether an industry is *actually* a monopoly or competitive, but whether there is the real *threat* of competition.

If a monopoly is protected by high barriers to entry – say that it owns all the raw materials – then it will be able to make supernormal profits with no fear of competition.

If, however, another firm *could* take over from it with little difficulty, it will behave much more like a competitive firm. The threat of competition has a similar effect to actual competition.

As an example, consider a catering company that is given permission by a factory to run its canteen. The catering company has a monopoly over the supply of food to

---

Bidding for the UK National Lottery

Since its launch in November 1994, the UK National Lottery has struck at the heart of the British psyche because it offers the opportunity to win a fortune and support worthwhile ventures. By the middle of 2012 the lottery had created over 2900 millionaires. It had also generated over £28 billion for 'Good Causes' and contributed £2.2 billion to the 2012 London Olympic and Paralympic Games.

Around 70 per cent of UK adults play the lottery, spending on average about £3 per week. Around £41 billion had been paid out in prize money by March 2012. On average, for every pound spent on the lottery, 50p is paid in prizes, 28p goes to the National Lottery Distribution Fund, which is distributed to arts, sports and charities that bid for it, 12p goes to the government in the form of Lottery Tax, 5p goes to the retailer and 5p goes to Camelot, the operator, and its Canadian parent company, Ontario Teachers' Pension Plan.

Sales of lottery tickets grew dramatically in the early years of operation but waned around the turn of the century. In the past decade there has been a recovery following the launch of a second lottery in 2002. Sales have grown by 12 per cent in the five years to 2012 and continue to grow. Sales in the quarter-year to 30 June 2012 were £1.67 billion – a 9.5 per cent increase on the previous year.

The institutional framework

There are a number of institutions involved in providing the lottery. The Department of Culture, Media and Sport oversees the lottery as directed by the National Lottery Act and dictates its strategic direction. It appoints the National Lottery Commission (NLC), which ensures that bids for the lottery licence and the running of the lottery games maximise the returns for 'Good Causes'. There are also a number of distribution bodies that provide lottery funds to thousands of local projects.

The main point of contact for lottery buyers is Camelot, which runs the lotto and scratchcard games via retail outlets, mobile phones, digital television and the Internet. Camelot won the first, second and third licences for the right to run the UK National Lottery from 1994, 2002 and 2009 respectively. Camelot's extended third-term licence will expire in 2023.

The rationale for a monopoly supplier

Camelot is a monopoly supplier of the UK National Lottery, although it need not be so. The legislation currently allows for two licences, one to operate the infrastructure and another to run the games. It is possible for other companies to run games on the computer network owned by Camelot, much in the same way that Network Rail owns the railway tracks, tunnels, etc. and allows competition between firms on particular routes on the network. Indeed, this option was briefly undertaken by Camelot in 1998, when Vernons Pools sold its 'Easy Play' game using the National Lottery retailer network. Its sales, though, were poor and it was scrapped in May 1999.

However, the government has a strong preference for a single owner of the infrastructure and a single supplier of National Lottery games. The rationale for having a single owner of the infrastructure is fairly standard; this is a natural monopoly and it would be pointless having two lottery computer networks, just as it would be having two separately owned rail lines from Edinburgh to London. With one firm controlling the infrastructure, economies of scale can be reaped.

One of the arguments for having a single supplier of games is known, rather bizarrely, as 'peculiar economies of scale'.[1] This is a situation in which a company that offered a portfolio of innovative lottery games would be more likely to induce additional players to participate in games because they can raise the size of the prize to be won. In other words, good game design can lead to more and bigger jackpots and thus more people buying lottery tickets. This reduces the average costs of supplying tickets and raises the money for 'Good Causes'.

Arguably, more than one firm may be able to supply an innovative portfolio of games if the market is large enough. However, the government is concerned about the risks involved in regulating relationships between network owners and network users (a problem that has occurred in regulating

---

[1] See, for example, P. Daffern, 'Assessment of the effects of competition on the National Lottery', Technical Paper No. 6, Department of Culture, Media and Sport, 2006.

the workers in that factory. If, however, it starts charging high prices or providing a poor service, the factory could offer the running of the canteen to an alternative catering company. This threat may force the original catering company to charge 'reasonable' prices and offer a good service.

Perfectly contestable markets

A market is *perfectly contestable* when the costs of entry and exit by potential rivals are zero, and when such entry can be made very rapidly. In such cases, the moment the possibility of earning supernormal profits occurs, new firms will enter, thus driving profits down to a normal level. The sheer threat of this happening, so the theory goes, will ensure that the firm already in the market will (a) keep its prices down, so that it just makes normal profits, and (b) produce as efficiently as possible, taking advantage of any economies of scale and any new technology. If the existing firm did not do this, entry would take place and potential competition would become actual competition.

> ### Definition
>
> **Perfectly contestable market** A market where there is free and costless entry and exit.

---

the railways – see Box 22.3). For example, there might be a lengthy legal dispute if a supplier of games is accused of unacceptable performance but it, in turn, accuses the network owner of poor service. This would then have a detrimental effect on the money raised for 'Good Causes'. Thus the government has always preferred a single firm framework for running the National Lottery.

Bidding for the National Lottery monopoly

Unlike auctions to run national rail franchises or a local bus route, bidding for the lottery does not involve any payment on the part of the successful bidder. The bid is purely a detailed business plan outlining all aspects of running the lottery, but its main emphasis is on providing likely revenue scenarios from games that would maximise money for 'Good Causes' and safeguard players. It was the uncertainty over future revenue flows that led the government in 1994 to require a paper-based bidding scheme for the first lottery licence. This view did not change when subsequent licences came up for renewal.

The NLC is responsible for evaluating the bids and awarding the licence. There were seven bidders for the first licence but for the second licence there were only two tabled 'bids', one from Camelot and other from Sir Richard Branson's The People's Lottery (and initially the NLC rejected both before settling on the incumbent).

For the third licence, the NLC tried to encourage as many bids as possible to come forward. Only one other bidder, Sugal and Dumani UK Ltd, submitted a bid. Camelot won because the NLC believed that, at a similar level of sales, they would be slightly more generous to Good Causes and that 'there was a higher probability that they would achieve higher sales over the length of the licence'.[2]

Clearly, incumbent firms like Camelot have considerable advantages over potential rivals when contracts have to be renewed and thus the number of new bidders is likely to be low. Two problems, in particular, stand out for rivals.

The 'Winner's Curse'. If a potential entrant outbids the incumbent in an auction to run (say) a local bus service, then it could be that winner has paid too much. After all, the incumbent has more knowledge about running the bus service and the likely revenues that may prevail. This situation is known as the 'Winner's Curse' and a similar scenario may occur in respect of the lottery. Potential bidders may be put off from bidding because they don't have the same knowledge about the UK lottery market.

Arguably, the lottery market might be considered a mature market and more is now known about lottery sales and the gaming market in general. However, there are strong incentives for risk-averse regulators to continue with accepting bids from incumbent firms because they are known to provide a certain level of sales and service.

The handover problem. If Camelot were to lose the lottery licence, there would be some large risks in transferring to the new bidder. Arguably, Camelot could sell its infrastructure to the new lottery provider, but there is a valuation dilemma. In terms of opportunity cost, Camelot would value the infrastructure at scrap value (if it has no alternative use for it), whereas a winner with no alternative source for such infrastructure would value Camelot's assets at close to their replacement value. This could lead to some difficult negotiations.

Because of this difficulty, the NLC did require bidders for the third lottery licence to provide new infrastructure, but recognised that this would take time to have in place (imagine trying to replace 30 000 retail terminals as well as to make online, television and mobile games work well). Given this difficulty, it is not surprising that there was only one rival bidder to Camelot.

Camelot managed to achieve a first-mover advantage (see page 192) by winning the initial lottery licence in 1994. It is now to continue providing the UK National Lottery until 2023 and so will have been sole monopoly provider for 29 years. Removing Camelot after that date could prove to be difficult.

---

[2] NLC press release, 'Preferred bidder announced for the third National Lottery licence', 7/8/2007. Available at www.natlotcomm.gov.uk/CLIENT/ news_item.ASP?NewsId=49

1. *If Camelot is maximising revenue, what is the price elasticity of demand for lottery tickets?*
2. *To what extent is the National Lottery market a contestable market?*

Contestable markets and natural monopolies

So why in such cases are the markets not *actually* perfectly competitive? Why do they remain monopolies?

The most likely reason has to do with economies of scale and the size of the market. To operate on a minimum efficient scale, the firm may have to be so large relative to the market that there is only room for one such firm in the industry. If a new firm does come into the market, then one or other of the two firms will not survive the competition. The market is simply not big enough for both of them.

If, however, there are no entry or exit costs, new firms will be perfectly willing to enter even though there is only room for one firm, provided they believe that they are more efficient than the existing firm. The existing firm, knowing this, will be forced to produce as efficiently as possible and with only normal profit.

The importance of costless exit

Setting up in a new business usually involves large expenditures on plant and machinery. Once this money has been spent, it becomes fixed costs. If these fixed costs are no higher than those of the existing firm, then the new firm could win the battle. But, of course, there is always the risk that it might lose.

But does losing the battle really matter? Can the firm not simply move to another market?

It does matter if there are substantial costs of exit. This will be the case if the capital equipment cannot be transferred to other uses. In this case these fixed costs are known as **sunk costs**. The losing firm is left with capital equipment it cannot use. The firm may therefore be put off entering in the first place. The market is not perfectly contestable, and the established firm can make supernormal profit.

If, however, the capital equipment can be transferred, the exit costs will be zero (or at least very low), and new firms will be more willing to take the risks of entry. For example, a rival coach company may open up a service on a route previously operated by only one company, and where there is still only room for one operator. If the new firm loses the resulting battle, it can still use the coaches it has purchased. It simply uses them for a different route or sells them for a fair price on the second-hand market. The cost of the coaches is not a sunk cost.

Costless exit, therefore, encourages firms to enter an industry, knowing that, if unsuccessful, they can always transfer their capital elsewhere.

The lower the exit costs, the more contestable the market. This implies that firms already established in other similar markets may provide more effective competition against monopolists, since they can simply transfer capital from one market to another. For example, studies of airlines in the USA show that entry to a particular route may be much easier for an established airline, which can simply transfer planes from one route to another.

Assessment of the theory

Simple monopoly theory merely focuses on the existing structure of the industry and makes no allowance for potential competition. The theory of contestable markets, however, goes much further and examines the *size* of entry barriers and exit costs. The bigger these are, the less contestable the market and therefore the greater the monopoly power of the existing firm. Various attempts have been made to measure monopoly power in this way.

One criticism of the theory, however, is that it does not take sufficient account of the possible reactions of the established firm. There may be no cost barriers to entry or exit (i.e. a perfectly contestable market), but the established firm may let it be known that any firm that dares to enter will face all-out war! This may act as a deterrent to entry. In the meantime, the established firm may charge high prices and make supernormal profits.

If a monopoly operates in a perfectly contestable market, it might bring the 'best of both worlds' for the consumer. Not only will it be able to achieve low costs through economies of scale, but also the potential competition will keep profits and hence prices down.

Definition

Sunk costs Costs that cannot be recouped (e.g. by transferring assets to other uses).

Pause for thought

Think of two examples of highly contestable monopolies (or oligopolies). How well is the consumer's interest served?

SUMMARY

1a There are four alternative market structures under which firms operate. In ascending order of firms' market power, they are: perfect competition, monopolistic competition, oligopoly and monopoly.

1b The market structure under which a firm operates will affect its conduct and its performance.

2a The assumptions of perfect competition are: a very large number of firms, complete freedom of entry, a homogeneous product and perfect knowledge of the good and its market by both producers and consumers.

2b In the short run, there is not time for new firms to enter the market, and thus supernormal profits can persist. In the long run, however, any supernormal profits will be competed away by the entry of new firms.

2c The short-run equilibrium for the firm will be where the price, as determined by demand and supply in the market, is equal to marginal cost. At this output the firm will be maximising profit.

2d The long-run equilibrium will be where the market price is just equal to firms' long-run average cost.

2e There are no substantial economies of scale to be gained in a perfectly competitive industry. If there were, the industry would cease to be perfectly competitive as the large, low-cost firms drove the small, high-cost ones out of business.

3a A monopoly is where there is only one firm in an industry. In practice, it is difficult to determine where a monopoly exists because it depends on how narrowly an industry is defined.

3b Barriers to the entry of new firms will normally be necessary to protect a monopoly from competition.

Such barriers include economies of scale (making the firm a natural monopoly or at least giving it a cost advantage over new (small) competitors), control over supplies of inputs or over outlets, patents or copyright, and tactics to eliminate competition (such as takeovers or aggressive advertising).

3c Profits for the monopolist (as for other firms) will be maximised where $MC = MR$.

3d If demand and cost curves are the same in a monopoly and a perfectly competitive industry, the monopoly will produce a lower output and at a higher price than the perfectly competitive industry.

3e On the other hand, any economies of scale will in part be passed on to consumers in lower prices, and the monopolist's high profits may be used for research and development and investment, which in turn may lead to better products at possibly lower prices.

4a Potential competition may be as important as actual competition in determining a firm's price and output strategy.

4b The threat of this competition is greater, the lower are the entry and exit costs to and from the industry. If the entry and exit costs are zero, the market is said to be *perfectly* contestable. Under such circumstances, an existing monopolist will be forced to keep its profits down to the normal level if it is to resist entry of new firms. Exit costs will be lower, the lower are the sunk costs of the firm.

4c The theory of contestable markets provides a more realistic analysis of firms' behaviour than theories based simply on the *existing* number of firms in the industry.

REVIEW QUESTIONS

1 Why do economists treat normal profit as a cost of production? What determines (a) the level and (b) the rate of normal profit for a particular firm?

2 Why is perfect competition so rare?

3 Why does the market for fresh vegetables approximate to perfect competition, whereas that for frozen or tinned ones does not?

4 Illustrate on a diagram similar to Figure 11.3 what would happen in the long run if price were initially below P_L.

5 As an illustration of the difficulty in identifying monopolies, try to decide which of the following are monopolies: a train-operating company; your local evening newspaper; British Gas; the village post office; the Royal Mail; Interflora; the London Underground; ice creams in the cinema; Guinness; food on trains; TippEx; the board game 'Monopoly'.

6 Try this brain teaser. A monopoly would be expected to face an inelastic demand. After all, there are no direct substitutes. And yet, if it produces where $MR = MC$, MR must be positive, demand must therefore be elastic. Therefore the monopolist must face an elastic demand! Can you solve this conundrum?

7 For what reasons would you expect a monopoly to charge (a) a higher price and (b) a lower price than if the industry were operating under perfect competition?

8 In which of the following industries are exit costs likely to be low: (a) steel production; (b) market gardening; (c) nuclear power generation; (d) specialist financial advisory services; (e) production of fashion dolls; (f) production of a new drug; (g) contract catering; (h) mobile discos; (i) car ferry operators? Are these exit costs dependent on how narrowly the industry is defined?

9 Think of three examples of monopolies (local or national) and consider how contestable their markets are.

Profit maximisation under imperfect competition

Business issues covered in this chapter

- How will firms behave under monopolistic competition (i.e. where there are many firms competing, but where they produce differentiated products)?
- Why will firms under monopolistic competition make only normal profits in the long run?
- How are firms likely to behave when there are just a few of them competing ('oligopolies')?
- What determines whether oligopolies will engage in all-out competition or instead collude with each other?
- What strategic games are oligopolists likely to play in their attempt to out-do their rivals?
- Why might such games lead to an outcome where all the players are worse off than if they had colluded?
- Does oligopoly serve the consumer's interests?

Very few markets in practice can be classified as perfectly competitive or as a pure monopoly. The vast majority of firms do compete with other firms, often quite aggressively, and yet they are not price takers: they do have some degree of market power. Most markets, therefore, lie between the two extremes of monopoly and perfect competition, in the realm of 'imperfect competition'. There are two types of imperfect competition: namely, monopolistic competition and oligopoly (see section 11.1).

12.1 MONOPOLISTIC COMPETITION

Monopolistic competition is nearer to the competitive end of the spectrum. It can best be understood as a situation where there are a lot of firms competing, but where each firm does nevertheless have some degree of market power (hence the term 'monopolistic' competition): each firm has some discretion as to what price to charge for its products.

Assumptions of monopolistic competition

- There is *quite a large number of firms*. As a result, each firm has only a small share of the market and, therefore,

its actions are unlikely to affect its rivals to any great extent. What this means is that each firm in making its decisions does not have to worry about how its rivals will react. It assumes that what its rivals choose to do will not be influenced by what it does.

This is known as the assumption of *independence*. (As we shall see later, this is not the case under oligopoly. There we assume that firms believe that their decisions do affect their rivals, and that their rivals' decisions will affect them. Under oligopoly we assume that firms are interdependent.)

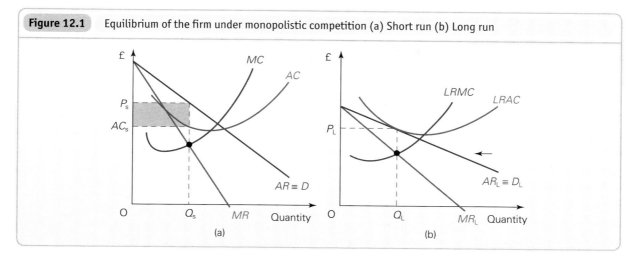

Figure 12.1 Equilibrium of the firm under monopolistic competition (a) Short run (b) Long run

(a)

(b)

■ There is freedom of entry of new firms into the industry. If any firm wants to set up in business in this market, it is free to do so.

In these two respects, therefore, monopolistic competition is like perfect competition.

■ Unlike perfect competition, however, each firm produces a product or provides a service that is in some way different from its rivals. As a result, it can raise its price without losing all its customers. Thus its demand curve is downward sloping, albeit relatively elastic given the large number of competitors to whom customers can turn. This is known as the assumption of *product differentiation*.

Petrol stations, restaurants, hairdressers and builders are all examples of monopolistic competition.

When considering monopolistic competition it is important to take account of the distance consumers are willing to travel to buy a product. In other words, the geographical size of the market matters. For example, McDonald's is a major global and national fast-food restaurant. However, in any one location it experiences intense competition in the 'informal eating-out' market from Indian, Chinese, Italian and other restaurants (see Box 12.1). So in any one local area, there is competition between firms each offering differentiated products.

Definitions

Independence (of firms in a market) When the decisions of one firm in a market will not have any significant effect on the demand curves of its rivals.

Product differentiation When one firm's product is sufficiently different from its rivals' to allow it to raise the price of the product without customers all switching to the rivals' products. A situation where a firm faces a downward-sloping demand curve.

Equilibrium of the firm

Short run

As with other market structures, profits are maximised at the output where $MC = MR$. The diagram will be the same as for the monopolist, except that the AR and MR curves will be more elastic. This is illustrated in Figure 12.1(a). As with perfect competition, it is possible for the monopolistically competitive firm to make supernormal profit in the short run. This is shown as the shaded area.

Just how much profit the firm will make in the short run depends on the strength of demand: the position and elasticity of the demand curve. The further to the right the demand curve is relative to the average cost curve, and the less elastic the demand curve is, the greater will be the firm's short-run profit. Thus a firm facing little competition and whose product is considerably differentiated from its rivals may be able to earn considerable short-run profits.

Pause for thought

Which of these two items is a petrol station more likely to sell at a discount: (a) engine oil; (b) sweets? Why?

Long run

If typical firms are earning supernormal profit, new firms will enter the industry in the long run. As new firms enter, they will take some of the customers away from established firms. The demand for the established firms' products will therefore fall. Their demand (AR) curve will shift to the left, and will continue doing so as long as supernormal profits remain and thus new firms continue entering.

Long-run equilibrium will be reached when only normal profits remain: when there is no further incentive for new firms to enter. This is illustrated in Figure 12.1(b). The firm's demand curve settles at D_L, where it is tangential to (i.e. just touches) the firm's LRAC curve. Output will be Q_L: where

$AR_L = LRAC$. (At any other output, $LRAC$ is greater than AR and thus less than normal profit would be made.)

Limitations of the model

There are various problems in applying the model of monopolistic competition to the real world:

- Information may be imperfect. Firms will not enter an industry if they are unaware of the supernormal profits currently being made, or if they underestimate the demand for the particular product they are considering selling.
- Firms are likely to differ from each other, not only in the product they produce or the service they offer, but also in their size and in their cost structure. What is more, entry may not be completely unrestricted. For example, two petrol stations could not set up in exactly the same place – on a busy crossroads, say – because of local authority planning controls. Thus although the typical or 'representative' firm may only earn normal profit in the long run, other firms may be able to earn long-run supernormal profit. They may have some cost advantage or produce a product that is impossible to duplicate perfectly.

- Existing firms may make supernormal profits, but if a new firm entered, this might reduce everyone's profits below the normal level. Thus a new firm will not enter and supernormal profits will persist into the long run. An example would be a small town with two chemist shops. They may both make more than enough profit to persuade them to stay in business. But if a third set up (say midway between the other two), there would not be enough total sales to allow them all to earn even normal profit. This is a problem of indivisibilities. Given the overheads of a chemist shop, it is not possible to set up one small enough to take away just enough customers to leave the other two with normal profits.
- One of the biggest problems with the simple model outlined above is that it concentrates on price and output

---

BOX 12.1　EATING OUT IN BRITAIN

A monopolistically competitive sector

The 'eating-out' sector (i.e. takeaways, cafés and restaurants) is a highly competitive market in the UK, with sales, in 2010, of some £72.1 billion, according to the Office for National Statistics.[1] The sector has grown less strongly in recent years than in the late 1990s. The value of its sales grew at an average rate of just 3.2 per cent per annum over the decade from 2000 – barely enough to cover the effects of inflation.

The sector exhibits many of the characteristics of a monopolistically competitive market.

- *Large number of local buyers*. According to a Mintel survey in 2008, around 93 per cent of UK adults had eaten out within the previous three months.
- *Large number of firms*. In 2011 there were nearly 121 000 hotel, restaurant, takeaway and pub enterprises in the UK. These firms employed 1 362 000 individuals. Although the sector has some large national and global chains, these are usually competing in local markets.
- *Competitive prices*. Margins are very tight because firms have to price very competitively to catch local custom. Only around 60 per cent of these businesses survive longer than three years.
- *Differentiated products*. To attract customers, suppliers must each differentiate their product in various ways, such as food type, ambience, comfort, service, quality, advertising and opening hours. Firms have to cater for the dynamic nature of consumer preferences and respond to the behaviour of competitors. They must constantly adapt or go under.

Lunchtime food

A significant growth area in the eating-out sector has been the sandwich and lunchtime food sector. Lunch is seen by many as a refuelling exercise rather than leisure activity.

This means that consumers value convenience, fast service and value for money.

In recent years the sector has been ferociously competitive with the advent of meal deals and price promotions. Mintel[2] reports that the sector grew rapidly through the mid-2000s, but reached maturity by around 2009. Competition in the mature market has forced some high-profile closures (e.g. O'Brian's) and allowed others to expand (e.g. Subway).

Only around 40 per cent of consumers eat lunch at home every day. These tend to be those not working and the retired. Hence there is a large lunchtime food market for the remaining 60 per cent of people, about half of whom state that they always buy food (rather than bring food from home).

In 2011 the most popular lunchtime foods were sandwiches and wraps, fruit, soup and salads. Most of these lunches are not consumed at the place of purchase. Only 3 per cent of those consuming weekday lunches found the time to sit down in a restaurant, café or bar. Niche take-out markets are becoming increasingly popular, for example sushi and burritos, especially in areas with high populations, such as London. For more price-conscious consumers the recent downturn has triggered a growth in 'classic' sandwiches, since they often represent better value for money.

However, the consumer is still looking for the retailer to 'add value'. The 75 pence jam sandwich offered by Marks and Spencer's was a failure and quickly withdrawn from the market! Consumers who focus on value added are often willing to pay a premium to have sandwiches made in front of them, perceiving this as providing them with greater choice and a fresher final product.

---

[1] Input-Output Supply and Use Tables, ONS (2012).

[2] Sandwiches and Lunchtime Foods, Mintel (2011).

decisions. In practice, the profit-maximising firm under monopolistic competition will also need to decide the exact variety of product to produce, and how much to spend on advertising it. This will lead the firm to take part in non-price competition (which we examined in Chapter 8).

Comparing monopolistic competition with perfect competition and monopoly

Comparison with perfect competition

It is often argued that monopolistic competition leads to a less efficient allocation of resources than perfect competition.

Figure 12.2 compares the long-run equilibrium positions for two firms. One firm is under perfect competition and thus faces a horizontal demand curve. It will produce an output of Q_1 at a price of P_1. The other is under monopolistic competition and thus faces a downward-sloping demand curve. It will produce the lower output of Q_2 at the higher

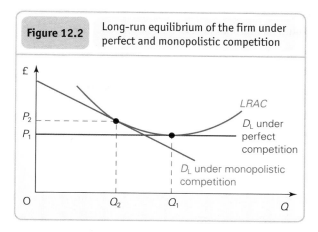

Figure 12.2 Long-run equilibrium of the firm under perfect and monopolistic competition

price of P_2. A crucial assumption here is that a firm would have the *same* long-run average cost (*LRAC*) curve in both cases. Given this assumption, we can make the following two predictions about monopolistic competition:

In addition to having to fight for customers, lunchtime food sellers are facing problems on the supply side. The sector has been hit by rising food costs. Smaller sellers are finding it hard to compete due, in part, to the sheer number of outlets of the largest players, including supermarkets and grocery stores, which dominate the 'channels to market'.

The Indian restaurant

The traditional Indian curry house – the institution that made curry the UK's favourite dish – accounted for 24 per cent of meals eaten out by UK adults in 2007. In recent times, however, Indian restaurants have suffered from changing British preferences and supply-side pressures. They are also facing direct competition from ready-to-eat curries sold in local supermarkets and the sale of curry in local pubs. For example, JD Wetherspoon's offers a one night a week 'curry club' menu at a price comfortably undercutting most curry houses.

Competition to attract the discerning local customer has been keen *within* the Indian restaurant trade. In the 1990s 'Curry Wars' developed around the country, with local Indian restaurants undercutting each other's prices. Profits tumbled. Eventually, strong cultural ties among the local Asian communities helped to avert such cut-throat competition. It was realised that, as prices in Indian restaurants were considerably less than in Italian and French ones, fixing minimum curry prices would raise incomes. In effect 'curry cartels' were being proposed.

Such activity – however well intentioned – is illegal in the UK. It is also unlikely to last for long as other segments of the market develop to undercut curry-house prices or attract consumers with a new culinary offering.

The Indian restaurant has had to relaunch its appeal. One reported method of attracting customers to Birmingham's

'Balti Belt' in the early 2000s was for rival Indian restaurants to have the most visible Las Vegas-style neon sign. This, however, has not been a common response and the lower end of the market is still stagnating. Many restaurants claimed to have received awards, often with an unclear provenance. These proclaimed the outstanding quality of the food or the chef's capabilities. However, consumers quickly cottoned on to this practice and such awards are slowly disappearing from many towns and cities.

In some parts of the UK Indian restaurants have recognised that only promoting themselves in a way that threatens rivals may not be the best option. Traders in some localities have chosen to act collectively, attempting to alter consumer tastes in their favour, aiming to increase the total market size. For example, Bradford's curry houses achieve significant publicity through an annual public vote for the best Asian restaurant. There are also equivalent national activities based around organisations such as the Federation of Specialist Restaurants.

Innovation is starting to develop in the premium end of the market where returns are greatest. Mintel reports, for example, that some of the high-end Indian restaurants in London have achieved Michelin stars. There is growth in this market segment but there is some debate about the sustainability of these high-end ventures, given the nature of international competition for high-quality chefs.

It will be interesting to see how the market develops over the next 10 years.

1. *What has happened to the price elasticity of demand for Indian restaurant curries over time? What can be said about cross-price elasticity of demand for pub meals?*
2. *Collusion between restaurants would suggest that they are operating under oligopoly, not monopolistic competition. Do you agree?*

■ Less will be sold and at a higher price.
■ Firms will not be producing at the least-cost point.

By producing more, firms would move to a lower point on their *LRAC* curve. Thus firms under monopolistic competition are said to have **excess capacity**. In Figure 12.2 this excess capacity is shown as $Q_1 - Q_2$. In other words, monopolistic competition is typified by quite a large number of firms (e.g. petrol stations), all operating at less than optimum output, and thus being forced to charge a price above that which they could charge if they had a bigger turnover.

> ### Pause for thought
>
> *Which would you rather have: five restaurants to choose from, each with very different menus and each having spare tables so that you could always guarantee getting one; or just two restaurants to choose from, charging a bit less but with less choice and making it necessary to book well in advance?*

So how does this affect the consumer? Although the firm under monopolistic competition may charge a higher price than under perfect competition, the difference may be very small. Although the firm's demand curve is downward sloping, it is still likely to be highly elastic due to the large number of substitutes. Furthermore, the consumer may benefit from monopolistic competition by having a greater variety of products to choose from. Each firm may satisfy some particular requirement of particular consumers.

Comparison with monopoly

The arguments are very similar here to those when comparing perfect competition and monopoly.

On the one hand, freedom of entry for new firms and hence the lack of long-run supernormal profits under monopolistic competition are likely to help keep prices down for the consumer and encourage cost saving. On the other hand, monopolies are likely to achieve greater economies of scale and have more funds for investment and research and development.

12.2 OLIGOPOLY

Oligopoly occurs when just a few firms between them share a large proportion of the industry. Some of the best-known companies are oligopolists, including Ford, Coca-Cola, BP and Nintendo.

There are, however, significant differences in the structure of industries under oligopoly, and similarly significant differences in the behaviour of firms. The firms may produce a virtually identical product (e.g. metals, chemicals, sugar, petrol). Most oligopolists, however, produce differentiated products (e.g. cars, soap powder, soft drinks, electrical appliances). Much of the competition between such oligopolists is in terms of the marketing of their particular brand. Marketing practices may differ considerably from one industry to another.

The two key features of oligopoly

Despite the differences between oligopolies, there are two crucial features that distinguish oligopoly from other market structures.

Barriers to entry

Unlike firms under monopolistic competition, there are various barriers to the entry of new firms. These are similar to those under monopoly (see pages 167–8). The size of the barriers, however, will vary from industry to industry. In some cases entry is relatively easy, whereas in others it is virtually impossible, perhaps due to patent protection or prohibitive research and development costs.

Interdependence of the firms

Because there are only a few firms under oligopoly, each firm will take account of the behaviour of the others when making its own decisions. This means that they are mutually dependent: they are **interdependent**. Each firm is affected by its rivals' actions. If a firm changes the price or specification of its product, for example, or the amount of its advertising, the sales of its rivals will be affected. The rivals may then respond by changing their price, specification or advertising. No firm can therefore afford to ignore the actions and reactions of other firms in the industry.

KI 1
p 7

> ### Definitions
>
> **Excess capacity (under monopolistic competition)** In the long run, firms under monopolistic competition will produce at an output below that which minimises average cost per unit.
>
> **Interdependence (under oligopoly)** Each firm will be affected by its rivals' decisions. Likewise its decisions will affect its rivals. Firms recognise the importance of this interdependence and it affects their decisions. It is one of the two key features of oligopoly.

People often think and behave strategically. How you think others will respond to your actions is likely to influence your own behaviour. Firms, for example, when considering a price or product change will often take into account the likely reactions of their rivals.

It is impossible, therefore, to predict the effect on a firm's sales of, say, a change in its price without first making some assumption about the reactions of other firms. Different assumptions will yield different predictions. For this reason there is no single, generally accepted theory of oligopoly. Firms may react differently and unpredictably.

Competition and collusion

Oligopolists are pulled in two different directions:

- The interdependence of firms may make them wish to *collude* with each other. If they can club together and act as if they were a monopoly, they could jointly maximise industry profits.
- On the other hand, they will be tempted to *compete* with their rivals to gain a bigger share of industry profits for themselves.

These two policies are incompatible. The more fiercely firms compete to gain a bigger share of industry profits, the smaller these industry profits will become! For example, price competition drives down the average industry price, while competition through advertising raises industry costs. Either way, industry profits fall.

Sometimes firms will collude. Sometimes they will not. The following sections examine first *collusive oligopoly* (both explicit and tacit), and then *non-collusive oligopoly*.

Collusive oligopoly

KI 21 p 161 When firms under oligopoly engage in collusion, they may agree on prices, market share, advertising expenditure, etc. Such collusion reduces the uncertainty they face. It reduces the fear of engaging in competitive price cutting or retaliatory advertising, both of which could reduce total industry profits.

Cartels

A formal collusive agreement is called a *cartel*. The cartel will maximise profits if it acts like a monopoly: if the members behave as if they were a single firm. This is illustrated in Figure 12.3.

KI 4 p 22 The total market demand curve is shown with the corresponding market *MR* curve. The cartel's *MC* curve is

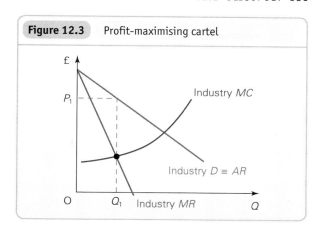

Figure 12.3 Profit-maximising cartel

the *horizontal* sum of the *MC* curves of its members (since we are adding the *output* of each of the cartel members at each level of marginal cost). Profits are maximised at Q_1 where $MC = MR$. The cartel must therefore set a price of P_1 (at which Q_1 will be demanded).

Having agreed on the cartel price, the members may then compete against each other using *non-price competition*, to gain as big a share of resulting sales (Q_1) as they can.

Alternatively, the cartel members may somehow agree to divide the market between them. Each member would be given a **quota**. The sum of all the quotas must add up to Q_1. If the quotas exceeded Q_1, either there would be output unsold if price remained fixed at P_1, or the price would fall to clear the market.

But if quotas are to be set by the cartel, how will it decide the level of each individual member's quota? The most likely method is for the cartel to divide the market between the members according to their current market share. That is the solution most likely to be accepted as 'fair'.

In many countries cartels are illegal, being seen by the government as a means of driving up prices and profits and thereby as being against the public interest. (Government policy towards cartels is examined in Chapter 21.)

Definitions

Collusive oligopoly When oligopolists agree, formally or informally, to limit competition between themselves. They may set output quotas, fix prices, limit product promotion or development, or agree not to 'poach' each other's markets.

Non-collusive oligopoly When oligopolists have no agreement between themselves – formal, informal or tacit.

Cartel A formal collusive agreement.

Quota (set by a cartel) The output that a given member of a cartel is allowed to produce (production quota) or sell (sales quota).

Where open collusion is illegal, firms may simply break the law, or get round it. Alternatively, firms may stay within the law, but still *tacitly* collude by watching each other's prices and keeping theirs similar. Firms may tacitly 'agree' to avoid price wars or aggressive advertising campaigns.

Pause for thought

If this 'fair' solution were adopted, what effect would it have on the industry MC curve in Figure 12.3?

Tacit collusion

One form of **tacit collusion** is where firms keep to the price that is set by an established leader. The leader may be the largest firm: the firm which dominates the industry. This is known as **dominant firm price leadership**. Alternatively, the price leader may simply be the one that has proved to be the most reliable one to follow: the one that is the best barometer of market conditions. This is known as **barometric firm price leadership**. Let us examine each of these two types of price leadership in turn.

Dominant firm price leadership. How does the leader set the price? This depends on the assumptions it makes about its rivals' reactions to its price changes. If it assumes that rivals will simply follow it by making exactly the same percentage price changes up or down, then a simple model can be constructed. This is illustrated in Figure 12.4. The leader assumes that it will maintain a constant market share (say 50 per cent).

The leader will maximise profits where its marginal revenue is equal to its marginal cost. It knows its current position on its demand curve (say, point *a*). It then estimates how responsive its demand will be to industry-wide price changes and thus constructs its demand and *MR* curves on that basis. It then chooses to produce Q_L at a price of P_L: at point *l* on its demand curve (where $MC = MR$). Other firms then follow that price. Total market demand will be Q_T, with followers supplying that portion of the market not supplied by the leader: namely, $Q_T - Q_L$.

There is one problem with this model. That is the assumption that the followers will want to maintain a constant

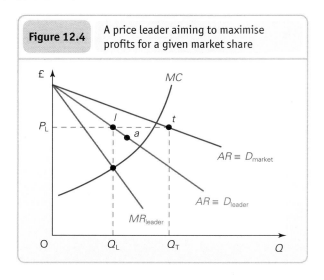

Figure 12.4 A price leader aiming to maximise profits for a given market share

market share. It is possible that, if the leader raises its price, the followers may want to supply more, given that the new price (= *MR* for a price-taking follower) may well be above their marginal cost. On the other hand, the followers may decide merely to maintain their market share for fear of invoking retaliation from the leader, in the form of price cuts or an aggressive advertising campaign.

Barometric firm price leadership. A similar exercise can be conducted by a barometric firm. Although the firm is not dominating the industry, its price will be followed by the others. It merely tries to estimate its demand and *MR* curves – assuming, again, a constant market share – and then produces where $MR = MC$ and sets price accordingly.

In practice, which firm is taken as the barometer may frequently change. Whether we are talking about oil companies, car producers or banks, any firm may take the initiative in raising prices. If the other firms are merely waiting for someone to take the lead – say, because costs have risen – they will all quickly follow suit. For example, if one of the bigger building societies or banks raises its mortgage rates by 1 per cent, this is likely to stimulate the others to follow suit.

Other forms of tacit collusion. An alternative to having an established leader is for there to be an established set of simple 'rules of thumb' that everyone follows.

One such example is **average cost pricing**. Here producers, instead of equating *MC* and *MR*, simply add a certain percentage for profit on top of average costs. Thus, if average costs rise by 10 per cent, prices will automatically be raised by 10 per cent. This is a particularly useful rule of thumb in times of inflation, when all firms will be experiencing similar cost increases.

Another rule of thumb is to have certain **price benchmarks**. Thus clothes may sell for £9.95, £24.95 or £39.95 (but not, say, £12.31 or £36.42). If costs rise, then firms simply raise their price to the next benchmark, knowing that other firms will do the same. (Average cost pricing and other pricing strategies are considered in more detail in Chapter 17.)

Definitions

Tacit collusion A situation where firms have an unspoken agreement to engage in a joint strategy. For example, oligopolists take care not to engage in price cutting, excessive advertising or other forms of competition. There may be unwritten 'rules' of collusive behaviour such as price leadership.

Dominant firm price leadership When firms (the followers) choose the same price as that set by a dominant firm in the industry (the leader).

Barometric firm price leadership Where the price leader is the one whose prices are believed to reflect market conditions in the most satisfactory way.

Rules of thumb can also be applied to advertising (e.g. you do not criticise other firms' products, only praise your own); or to the design of the product (e.g. lighting manufacturers tacitly agreeing not to bring out an everlasting light bulb).

> ### Pause for thought
>
> *If a firm has a typical-shaped average cost curve and sets prices 10 per cent above average cost, what will its supply curve look like?*

Factors favouring collusion

Collusion between firms, whether formal or tacit, is more likely when firms can clearly identify with each other or some leader and when they trust each other not to break agreements. It will be easier for firms to collude if the following conditions apply:

- There are only very few firms, all well known to each other.
- They are open with each other about costs and production methods.
- They have similar production methods and average costs, and are thus likely to want to change prices at the same time and by the same percentage.
- They produce similar products and can thus more easily reach agreements on price.
- There is a dominant firm.
- There are significant barriers to entry and thus there is little fear of disruption by new firms.
- The market is stable. If industry demand or production costs fluctuate wildly, it will be difficult to make agreements, partly due to difficulties in predicting and partly because agreements may frequently have to be amended. There is a particular problem in a declining market where firms may be tempted to undercut each other's price in order to maintain their sales.
- There are no government measures to curb collusion.

Non-collusive oligopoly: the breakdown of collusion

In some oligopolies, there may be only a few (if any) factors favouring collusion. In such cases, the likelihood of price competition is greater.

Even if there is collusion, there will always be the temptation for individual oligopolists to 'cheat', by cutting prices or by selling more than their allotted quota. The danger, of course, is that this would invite retaliation from the other members of the cartel, with a resulting price war. Price would then fall and the cartel could well break up in disarray.

When considering whether to break a collusive agreement, even if only a tacit one, a firm will ask: (1) 'How much can we get away with without inviting retaliation?' and (2) 'If a price war does result, will we be the winners? Will we succeed in driving some or all of our rivals out of business and yet survive ourselves, and thereby gain greater market power?'

The position of rival firms, therefore, is rather like that of generals of opposing armies or the players in a game. It is a question of choosing the appropriate *strategy*: the strategy that will best succeed in outwitting your opponents. The strategy that a firm adopts will, of course, be concerned not just with price, but also with advertising and product development.

Non-collusive oligopoly: assumptions about rivals' behaviour

Even though oligopolists might not collude, they will still need to take account of rivals' likely behaviour when deciding their own strategy. In doing so they will probably look at rivals' past behaviour and make assumptions based on it. There are three well-known models, each based on a different set of assumptions.

Assumption that rivals produce a given quantity: the Cournot model

One assumption is that rivals will produce a particular *quantity*. This is most likely when the market is stable and the rivals have been producing a relatively constant quantity for some time. The task, then, for the individual oligopolist is to decide its own price and quantity given the presumed output of its competitors.

The earliest model based on this assumption was developed by the French economist Augustin Cournot in 1838. The **Cournot model** (which is developed in Web Appendix 4.2) takes the simple case of just two firms (a **duopoly**) producing an identical product: for example, two electricity generating companies supplying the whole country.

Definitions

Average cost pricing Where a firm sets its price by adding a certain percentage for (average) profit on top of average cost.

Price benchmark This is a price which is typically used. Firms, when raising prices, will usually raise them from one benchmark to another.

Cournot model A model of duopoly where each firm makes its price and output decisions on the assumption that its rival will produce a particular quantity.

Duopoly An oligopoly where there are just two firms in the market.

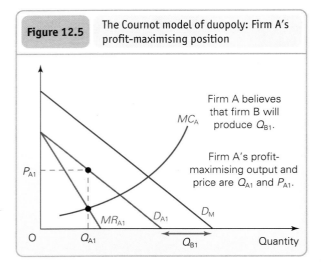

Figure 12.5 The Cournot model of duopoly: Firm A's profit-maximising position

This is illustrated in Figure 12.5, which shows the profit-maximising price and output for firm A. The total market demand curve is shown as D_M. Assume that firm A believes that its rival, firm B, will produce Q_{B1} units. Thus firm A perceives its own demand curve (D_{A1}) to be Q_{B1} units less than total market demand. In other words, the horizontal gap between D_M and D_{A1} is Q_{B1} units. Given its perceived demand curve of D_{A1}, its marginal revenue curve will be MR_{A1} and the profit-maximising output will be Q_{A1}, where $MR_{A1} = MC_A$. The profit-maximising price will be P_{A1}.

If firm A believed that firm B would produce *more* than Q_{B1}, its perceived demand and *MR* curves would be further to the left and the profit-maximising quantity and price would both be lower.

Profits in the Cournot model. Industry profits will be *less* than under a monopoly or a cartel. The reason is that price will be lower than the monopoly price. This can be seen from Figure 12.5. If this were a monopoly, then to find the profit-maximising output, we would need to construct an *MR* curve corresponding to the market demand curve (D_M). This would intersect with the *MC* curve at a higher output than Q_{A1} and a *higher* price (given by D_M). Nevertheless, profits in the Cournot model will be higher than under perfect competition, since price is still above marginal cost.

Assumption that rivals set a particular price: the Bertrand model

An alternative assumption is that rival firms set a particular price and stick to it. This scenario is more realistic when firms do not want to upset customers by frequent price changes or want to produce catalogues which specify prices. The task, then, for a given oligopolist is to choose its own price and quantity in the light of the prices set by rivals.

The most famous model based on this assumption was developed by another French economist, Joseph Bertrand, in 1883. Bertrand again took the simple case of a duopoly,

but its conclusions apply equally to oligopolies with three or more firms.

The outcome is one of price cutting until all supernormal profits are competed away. The reason is simple. If firm A assumes that its rival, firm B, will hold price constant, then firm A should undercut this price by a small amount and as a result gain a large share of the market. At this point, firm B will be forced to respond by cutting its price. What we end up with is a price war until price is forced down to the level of average cost, with only normal profits remaining.

Nash equilibrium. The equilibrium outcome in either the Cournot or Bertrand models is not in the *joint* interests of the firms. In each case, total profits are less than under a monopoly or cartel. But, in the absence of collusion, the outcome is the result of each firm doing the best it can, given its assumptions about what its rivals are doing. The resulting equilibrium is known as a **Nash equilibrium**, after John Nash, a US mathematician (and subject of the film *A Beautiful Mind*) who introduced the concept in 1951.

In practice, when competition is intense, as in the Bertrand model, the firms may seek to collude long before profits have been reduced to a normal level. Alternatively, firms may put in a **takeover bid** for their rival(s).

The kinked demand-curve assumption

In 1939 a theory of non-collusive oligopoly was developed simultaneously on both sides of the Atlantic: in the USA by Paul Sweezy and in Britain by R. L. Hall and C. J. Hitch. This **kinked demand theory** has since become perhaps the most famous of all theories of oligopoly. The model seeks to explain how it is that, even when there is no collusion at all between oligopolists, prices can nevertheless remain stable.

The theory is based on two asymmetrical assumptions:

- If an oligopolist cuts its price, its rivals will feel forced to follow suit and cut theirs, to prevent losing customers to the first firm.
- If an oligopolist raises its price, its rivals will *not* follow suit since, by keeping their prices the same, they will thereby gain customers from the first firm.

Definitions

Nash equilibrium The position resulting from everyone making their optimal decision based on their assumptions about their rivals' decisions.

Takeover bid Where one firm attempts to purchase another by offering to buy the shares of that company from its shareholders.

Kinked demand theory The theory that oligopolists face a demand curve that is kinked at the current price: demand being significantly more elastic above the current price than below. The effect of this is to create a situation of price stability.

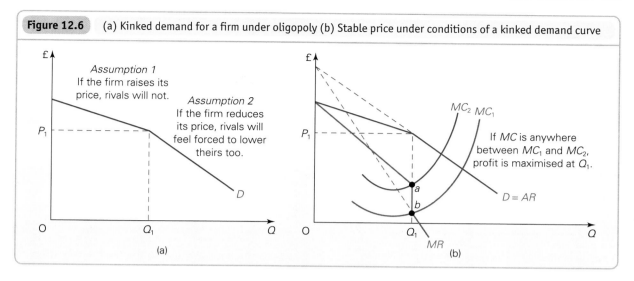

Figure 12.6 (a) Kinked demand for a firm under oligopoly (b) Stable price under conditions of a kinked demand curve

On these assumptions, each oligopolist will face a demand curve that is *kinked* at the current price and output (see Figure 12.6(a)). A rise in price will lead to a large fall in sales as customers switch to the now relatively lower-priced rivals. The firm will thus be reluctant to raise its price. Demand is relatively elastic above the kink. On the other hand, a fall in price will bring only a modest increase in sales, since rivals lower their prices too and therefore customers do not switch. The firm will thus also be reluctant to lower its price. Demand is relatively inelastic below the kink. Thus oligopolists will be reluctant to change prices at all.

This price stability can be shown formally by drawing in the firm's marginal revenue curve, as in Figure 12.6(b).

To see how this is done, imagine dividing the diagram into two parts either side of Q_1. At quantities less than Q_1 (the left-hand part of the diagram), the MR curve will correspond to the shallow part of the AR curve. At quantities greater than Q_1 (the right-hand part), the MR curve will correspond to the steep part of the AR curve. To see how this part of the MR curve is constructed, imagine extending the steep part of the AR curve back to the vertical axis. This and the corresponding MR curve are shown by the dotted lines in Figure 12.6(b).

As you can see, there will be a gap between points a and b. In other words, there is a vertical section of the MR curve between these two points.

Profits are maximised where $MC = MR$. Thus, if the MC curve lies anywhere between MC_1 and MC_2 (i.e. between points a and b), the profit-maximising price and output will be P_1 and Q_1. Thus prices will remain stable *even with a considerable change in costs*.

Oligopoly and the consumer

If oligopolists act collusively and jointly maximise industry profits, they will in effect be acting together as a monopoly. In such cases, prices may be very high. This is clearly not in the best interests of consumers.

Furthermore, in two respects, oligopoly may be more disadvantageous than monopoly:

- Depending on the size of the individual oligopolists, there may be less scope for economies of scale to lower costs and mitigate the effects of market power.
- Oligopolists are likely to engage in much more extensive advertising than a monopolist. This is likely to raise costs and prices.

These problems will be less severe, however, if oligopolists do not collude, if there is some degree of price competition and if barriers to entry are weak.

Moreover, the power of oligopolists in certain markets may to some extent be offset if they sell their product to other powerful firms. Thus oligopolistic producers of baked beans or soap powder sell a large proportion of their output to giant supermarket chains, which can use their market power to keep down the price at which they purchase these products. This phenomenon is known as ***countervailing power***.

In some respects, oligopoly may be more beneficial to the consumer than other market structures:

Pause for thought

Assume that two brewers announce that they are about to merge. What information would you need to help you decide whether the merger would be in the consumer's interests?

Definition

Countervailing power When the power of a monopolistic/oligopolistic seller is offset by powerful buyers who can prevent the price from being pushed up.

BOX 12.2 REINING IN BIG BUSINESS

Market power in oligopolistic industries

In recent years the car industry, the large supermarket chains and BT in charging broadband suppliers for using its fibre optic cables have all been charged with 'ripping off' the consumer. Such has been the level of concern, that all three industries were referred to the UK Competition Commission (see section 20.1). In this box we consider developments in each sector in turn.

Car industry

The Competition Commission report, published in April 2000, found that car buyers in Britain were paying on average some 10 to 12 per cent more than those in France, Germany and Italy for the same models.[1] The price discrepancies between Britain and mainland Europe were maintained by car manufacturers blocking cheaper European cars coming into the UK. This was achieved by threatening mainland European car dealers with losing their dealership if they sold to British buyers, and delaying the delivery date of right-hand-drive models to European dealers in the hope that British buyers would change their minds and go back to a British dealership.

As the problem involved more than one EU country, the European Commission (EC) also examined the issue. It concluded that the motor vehicle manufacturers had agreements with distributors that were too restrictive. In 2002, the EC changed the 'Block Exemption' regulations governing the sector to allow distributors to set up in different countries and to sell multiple brands of car within their showrooms. Furthermore, distributors which are offered an exclusive 'sales territory' distribution agreement by car manufacturers are now allowed to resell cars to other distributors which are not part of the manufacturer's network. This has helped to develop other sales outlets such as car supermarkets and Internet retailers. In addition, the regulation has opened up the repair and spare parts sector to more firms.

Changes in the regulations, and the addition of ten new EU member states in 2004 and another two in 2007, have made the car market more competitive by increasing the sources of supply. Slowly, prices of new car prices have been converging across the EU towards the lower-price markets.[2]

With the recession of 2008/9, the demand for new cars plummeted. Competition became intense and new cars were heavily discounted. Some dealers went out of business and

there were mergers of car manufacturers, such as Fiat and Chrysler. Many car factories went on to short-time working. In the first half of 2012, new car registrations were down in all major Continental European countries, with the exception of Germany where registrations remained stable.

But what about the UK? In the first half of 2012 the UK market for new cars was growing. New registrations were up around 3 per cent on the previous year. However, sales were still 15 per cent below levels achieved in 2007. This said, some car producers have done well during the downturn, especially UK-based manufacturers such as Jaguar Land Rover, Nissan and Toyota, which have all expanded production through 2011/12, creating thousands of jobs. It will be interesting to see whether all of these events will make the car market more, or less, competitive when the world economy expands again.

Supermarkets

Consumers, suppliers and regulators have commented upon the use (or abuse) of market power in the supermarket sector during recent times. Three major areas of concern have arisen.

Barriers to entry. The most important barrier to entry is the difficulty in getting planning permission to open a new supermarket, thus restricting consumer choice. Furthermore, supermarkets own covenants on land ('land banks') suitable for siting new stores and by not releasing them to competitors they thereby restrict competition.

Another barrier is the large economies of scale and the huge buying power of the established supermarkets, which make it virtually impossible for a new player or for the smaller convenience stores to match their low costs. Indeed, the big supermarkets have used their scale to enter the convenience sector with considerable effect. Thus brands like 'Tesco Metro' and 'Sainsbury's Local' have been successful in driving out many small stores from the market.

Relationships with suppliers. One of the most contentious issues concerns the major supermarket chains' huge buying power. They have been able to drive costs down by forcing suppliers to offer discounts. Many suppliers, such as growers, have found their profit margins cut to the bone. However, in many cases these cost savings to the supermarkets have not been passed on to shoppers.

Price competition. National advertising campaigns tell us that supermarkets are concerned about keeping prices lower than their competitors on a number of items. However, this can often mask certain pricing concerns. For some goods the supermarkets have, on occasion, adopted a system of 'shadow pricing', a form of tacit collusion whereby they all observe each other's prices and ensure that they remain at

---

[1] Competition Commission (2000), 'New cars: a report on the supply of new motor cars within the UK' (Cm 4660). Available at www.competition-commission.org.uk/rep_pub/reports/2000/439cars.htm

[2] http://ec.europa.eu/competition/sectors/motor_vehicles/prices/report.htmlx

similar levels – often similarly high levels rather than similarly low levels! This has limited the extent of true price competition, and the resulting high prices have seen profits grow as costs have been driven ever downwards. Somewhat perversely, this activity may be presented to consumers as competitive behaviour – 'we will not charge you more than our competitors'!

Moreover, the supermarkets have been observed charging high prices where there is little or no competition, notably in rural locations, and charging lower prices on some items, often below cost, where competition is more intense.

But intense price competition tends to be only over basic items, such as the own-brand 'value' products. To get to the basic items, you normally have to pass the more luxurious ones, which are much more highly priced. Supermarkets rely on shoppers making impulse buys of the more expensive lines: lines that have much higher profit margins.

In response to these claims, the Competition Commission reported in 2008 that it found little evidence of tacit collusion.[3] Further, the nature of below-cost selling on grocery items by the supermarkets did not mislead consumers in relation to the overall cost of shopping at a particular store. Indeed, temporary promotions on some products, including fuel, may represent effective competition between supermarkets and lower the average price of a basket of goods for customers.

However, the Commission did have some concerns in relation to the existence of a number of stores owned by the same supermarket chain in a particular location (e.g. Tesco Metro and Tesco Superstore) and the covenants on land owned by supermarkets that restrict entry by competitors. To this end it proposed a 'competition test' in planning decisions and action to prevent land agreements, both of which would lessen the market power of supermarkets in local areas. The Commission also found that the supermarkets had substantial buying power and that the drive to lower supply prices may have had an inhibiting effect on innovation.

The Commission proposed the creation of a new strengthened and extended Groceries Supply Code of Practice that would be enforced by an independent ombudsman and incorporated the bigger firms. Following failed attempts to create a voluntary code of practice between the supermarkets and government, consultation on the creation of an ombudsman occurred in 2010. Parliamentary time has been set aside with the hope of creating this statutory body by 2013. We await the outcome of this with interest.

Broadband

In 2011 Ofcom, the independent regulator and competition authority for the UK communications industries, decided that BT should cut the price of its wholesale broadband product. The wholesale broadband market allows competitors such as TalkTalk and SkyBroadband to use the BT network in certain parts of the UK. The ruling was expected to lead to cheaper Internet access, mainly for customers in rural areas, where there is little competition.

Granting competitors access to the BT network was allowed following a European Commission decision in 2008. At the time, BT was wary of this decision, pointing out that it would only invest in expanding the broadband network if it could achieve satisfactory returns. This would partly depend on the price it charged rivals for accessing its fibre optic networks.

BT was unhappy with the 2011 Ofcom ruling and asked the Competition Commission to review the decision. In June 2012 the Competition Commission ruled that Ofcom had reached the correct judgment.[4]

The ruling centred around the appropriateness of BT including 'deficit repair charges' in its wholesale broadband costs. The 'deficit repair charge' was to assist the filling of a £3 billion deficit in the BT pension scheme. By levying this charge on companies such as TalkTalk and SkyBroadband, BT was forcing them to assist in funding its pension liabilities. The regulator's decision came down to its judgment on the cause of BT's pension deficit. Was it due to poor management on the part of BT? Or, was it a legitimate business cost? If the deficit was a result of poor management then shareholders ought to bear the costs, not competitors.[5]

The Commission concluded that BT had managed its pension scheme poorly. Hence 'deficit repair charges' should not be part of wholesale broadband access fees. By including them, providers such as TalkTalk and SkyBroadband were not being charged in relation to the true cost of the fibre optic networks. The charges were anti-competitive. BT is currently 'considering its position'.

1. *Identify the main barriers to entry in each of the three sectors.*
2. *Update each of the cases and consider the economic implications for consumers.*

---

[3] Competition Commission (2008), 'Market investigation into the supply of groceries in the UK'. Available at www.competition-commission.org.uk/inquiries/ref2006/grocery/index.htm

[4] Competition Commission (2012) 'British Telecommunications plc v Ofcom telecommunications price control appeal: Wholesale broadband access charge control' (1187/3/3/11, June). Available at www.competition-commission.org.uk/

[5] BT rebuffed on pensions cost (*Financial Times* 24 June 2012).

- Oligopolists, like monopolists, can use part of their super-normal profit for research and development. Unlike monopolists, however, oligopolists will have a considerable *incentive* to do so. If the product design is improved, this may allow the firm to capture a larger share of the market, and it may be some time before rivals can respond with a similarly improved product. If, in addition, costs are reduced by technological improvement, the resulting higher profits will improve the firm's capacity to withstand a price war.

- Non-price competition through product differentiation may result in greater choice for the consumer. Take the case of stereo equipment. Non-price competition has led to a huge range of different products of many different specifications, each meeting the specific requirements of different consumers.

It is difficult to draw any general conclusions, since oligopolies differ so much in their performance.

Oligopoly and contestable markets

The theory of contestable markets has been applied to oligopoly as well as to monopoly, and similar conclusions are drawn.

The lower the entry and exit costs for new firms, the more difficult it will be for oligopolists to collude and make supernormal profits. If oligopolists do form a cartel (whether legal or illegal), this will be difficult to maintain if it very soon faces competition from new entrants. What a cartel has to do in such a situation is to erect entry barriers, thereby making the 'contest' more difficult. For example, the cartel could form a common research laboratory, denied to outsiders. It might attempt to control the distribution of the finished product by buying up wholesale or retail outlets. Or it might simply let it be known to potential entrants that they will face all-out price, advertising and product competition from all the members if they should dare to set up in competition.

The industry is thus likely to behave competitively if entry and exit costs are low, with all the benefits and costs to the consumer of such competition – even if the new firms do not actually enter. However, if entry and/or exit costs are high, the degree of competition will simply depend on the relations between existing members of the industry.

> ### Pause for thought
>
> *Which of the following markets do you think are contestable: (a) credit cards; (b) brewing; (c) petrol retailing; (d) insurance services; (e) compact discs?*

12.3 GAME THEORY

As we have seen, the behaviour of a firm under non-collusive oligopoly depends, in part, on how it thinks its rivals will react to its decisions. When considering whether to cut prices in order to gain a larger market share, a firm will ask itself two key questions: first, how much it can get away with, without inciting retaliation; second, if its rivals do retaliate and a price-war ensues, whether it will be able to 'see off' some or all of its rivals, while surviving itself.

Economists use *game theory* to examine the best strategy a firm can adopt for each assumption about its rivals' behaviour.

Single-move games

The simplest type of 'game' is a single-move or single-period game, sometimes known as a normal-form game.

> ### Definition
>
> **Game theory (or the theory of games)** The study of alternative strategies that oligopolists may choose to adopt, depending on their assumptions about their rivals' behaviour.

This involves just one 'move' by each firm in the game. For example, two or more firms are bidding for a contract which will be awarded to the lowest bidder. When the bids are all made, the contract will be awarded to the lowest bidder; the 'game' is over.

Simple dominant strategy games

Many single-period games have predictable outcomes, no matter what assumptions each firm makes about its rivals' behaviour. Such games are known as dominant strategy games. The simplest case is where there are just two firms with identical costs, products and demand. They are both considering which of two alternative prices to charge. Table 12.1 shows typical profits they could each make.

Let us assume that at present both firms (X and Y) are charging a price of £2 and that they are each making a profit of £10 million, giving a total industry profit of £20 million. This is shown in the top left-hand cell (A).

Now assume they are both (independently) considering reducing their price to £1.80. In making this decision, they will need to take into account what their rival might do, and how this will affect them. Let us consider X's position. In our simple example there are just two things that its rival, firm Y, might do. Either Y could cut its price to £1.80, or it could leave its price at £2. What should X do?

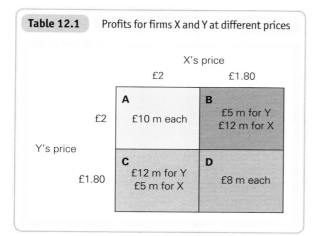

Table 12.1 Profits for firms X and Y at different prices

		X's price	
		£2	£1.80
Y's price	£2	**A** £10 m each	**B** £5 m for Y £12 m for X
	£1.80	**C** £12 m for Y £5 m for X	**D** £8 m each

One alternative is to go for the *cautious* approach and think of the worst thing that its rival could do. If X kept its price at £2, the worst thing for X would be if its rival Y cut its price. This is shown by cell C: X's profit falls to £5 million. If, however, X cut its price to £1.80, the worst outcome would again be for Y to cut its price, but this time X's profit only falls to £8 million. In this case, then, if X is cautious, it will *cut its price to £1.80*. Note that Y will argue along similar lines, and if it is cautious, it too will cut its price to £1.80. This policy of adopting the safer approach is known as *maximin*. Following a maximin approach, the firm will opt for the alternative that will *maxi*mise its *min*imum possible profit.

An alternative is to go for the *optimistic* approach and assume that your rivals react in the way most favourable to you. Here the firm will go for the strategy that yields the highest possible profit. In X's case this will be again to cut price, only this time on the optimistic assumption that firm Y will leave its price unchanged. If firm X is correct in its assumption, it will move to cell B and achieve the maximum possible profit of £12 million. This approach of going for the maximum possible profit is known as *maximax*. Note that again the same argument applies to Y. Its maximax strategy will be to cut price and hopefully end up in cell C.

Given that in this 'game' *both* approaches, maximin and maximax, lead to the *same* strategy (namely, cutting price), this is known as a *dominant strategy game*. The result is that the firms will end up in cell D, earning a lower profit (£8 million each) than if they had charged the higher price (£10 million each in cell A).

As we saw, the equilibrium outcome of a game where there is no collusion between the players is known as a *Nash equilibrium*. The Nash equilibrium in this game is cell D.

KEY IDEA 24

> **Nash equilibrium.** The position resulting from everyone making their optimal decision based on their assumptions about their rivals' decisions. Without collusion, there is no incentive for any firm to move from this position.

In our example, collusion rather than a price war would have benefited both firms. Yet, even if they did collude, both would be tempted to cheat, or renege, on the agreement and cut prices. This is known as the *prisoners' dilemma* (see Box 12.3).

More complex games with no dominant strategy

More complex 'games' can be devised with more than two firms, many alternative prices, differentiated products and various forms of non-price competition (e.g. advertising). In such cases, the cautious (maximin) strategy may suggest a different policy (e.g. do nothing) from the high-risk (maximax) strategy (e.g. cut prices substantially).

In many situations, firms will have a number of different options open to them and a number of possible reactions by rivals. In such cases, the choices facing firms may be many. They may opt for a compromise strategy between maximax and maximin. This could be a strategy that is more risky than the maximin one, but with the chance of a higher profit; but not as risky as the maximax one, but where the maximum profit possible is not so high.

Multiple-move games

In many situations, firms will *react* to what their rivals do; their rivals, in turn, will react to what they do. In other words, the game moves back and forth from one 'player' to the other like a game of chess or cards. Firms will still have to think strategically (as you do in chess), considering the likely responses of their rivals to their own actions. These multiple-move games are known as *repeated games* or *extensive-form games*.

One of the simplest repeated games is the *tit-for-tat*. This is where a firm will cut prices, or make some other aggressive move, *only* if the rival does so first. To illustrate this in a multiple-move situation let us look again at the example

---

Definitions

Maximin The strategy of choosing the policy whose worst possible outcome is the least bad.

Maximax The strategy of choosing the policy which has the best possible outcome.

Dominant strategy game Where different assumptions about rivals' behaviour lead to the adoption of the same strategy.

Prisoners' dilemma Where two or more firms (or people), by attempting independently to choose the best strategy, based upon what other(s) are likely to do, end up in a worse position than if they had cooperated from the start.

Tit-for-tat Where a firm will cut prices, or make some other aggressive move, *only* if the rival does so first. If the rival knows this, it will be less likely to make an initial aggressive move.

we considered in Table 12.1, but this time we will extend it beyond one time period.

Assume that firm X is adopting the tit-for-tat strategy. If firm Y cuts its price from £2.00 to £1.80, then firm X will respond in round 2 by also cutting its price. The two firms will end up in cell D – worse off than if neither had cut their price. If, however, firm Y had left its price at £2.00 then firm X would respond by leaving its price unchanged too. Both firms would remain in cell A with a higher profit than cell D.

As long as firm Y knows that firm X will respond in this way, it has an incentive not to cut its price. Thus it is in X's interests to make sure that Y clearly 'understands' how X will react to any price cut. To do this X can make a threat.

The importance of threats and promises

In many situations, an oligopolist will make a threat or promise that it will act in a certain way. As long as the threat or promise is *credible* (i.e. its competitors believe it), the firm can gain and it will influence its rivals' behaviour.

Take the simple situation where a large oil company, such as Esso, states that it will match the price charged by

---

> ### Definition
>
> **Credible threat (or promise)** One that is believable to rivals because it is in the threatener's interests to carry it out.

BOX 12.3   THE PRISONERS' DILEMMA

Game theory is relevant not just to economics. A famous non-economic example is the prisoners' dilemma.

Nigel and Amanda have been arrested for a joint crime of serious fraud. They are both guilty. Each is interviewed separately and given the following alternatives:

- First, if they say nothing, the court has enough evidence to sentence both to a year's imprisonment.
- Second, if either Nigel or Amanda alone confesses, he or she is likely to get only a three-month sentence but the partner could get up to ten years.
- Third, if both confess, they are likely to get three years each.

What should Nigel and Amanda do?

Let us consider Nigel's dilemma. Should he confess in order to get the short sentence (the maximax strategy)? This is better than the year he would get for not confessing. There is, however, an even better reason for confessing. Suppose Nigel doesn't confess but, unknown to him, Amanda does confess. Then Nigel ends up with the long sentence. Better than this is to confess and to get no more than three years: this is the safest (maximin) strategy.

Amanda is in the same dilemma. The result is simple. When both prisoners act selfishly by confessing, they both end up in position D with relatively long prison terms. Only when they collude will they end up in position A with relatively short prison terms, the best combined solution.

Of course the police know this and will do their best to prevent any collusion. They will keep Nigel and Amanda in separate cells and try to persuade each of them that the other is bound to confess.

Thus the choice of strategy depends on:

- Nigel's and Amanda's risk attitudes: i.e. are they 'risk lovers' or 'risk averse'?
- Nigel's and Amanda's estimates of how likely the other is to own up.

1. *Why is this a dominant strategy game?*
2. *How would Nigel's choice of strategy be affected if he had instead been involved in a joint crime with Adam, Ashok, Diana and Rikki, and they had all been caught?*

Let us now look at two real-world examples of the prisoners' dilemma.

Standing at concerts

When people go to some public event, such as a concert or a match, they often stand in order to get a better view. But once people start standing, everyone is likely to do so: after all, if they stayed sitting, they would not see at all. In this Nash equilibrium, most people are worse off, since, except for tall people, their view is likely to be worse and they lose the comfort of sitting down.

Too much advertising

Why do firms spend so much on advertising? If they are aggressive, they do so to get ahead of their rivals (the maximax approach). If they are cautious, they do so in case their rivals increase their advertising (the maximin approach). Although in both cases it may be in the individual firm's best interests to increase advertising, the resulting Nash equilibrium is likely to be one of excessive advertising: the total spent on advertising (by all firms) is not recouped in additional sales.

Give one or two other examples (economic or non-economic) of the prisoners' dilemma.

		Amanda's alternatives	
		Not confess	Confess
Nigel's alternatives	Not confess	**A** Each gets 1 year	**B** Nigel gets 10 years Amanda gets 3 months
	Confess	**C** Nigel gets 3 months Amanda gets 10 years	**D** Each gets 3 years

Figure 12.7 A decision tree

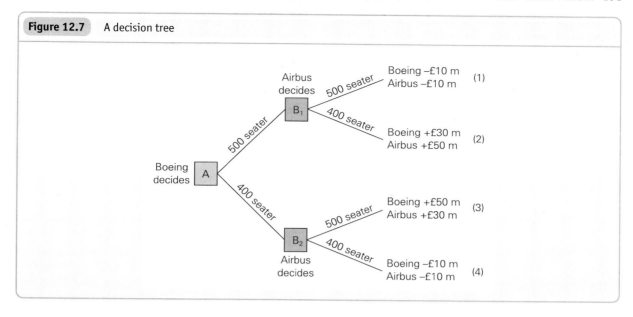

any competitor within a given radius. Assume that competitors believe this 'price promise' but also that Esso will not try to *undercut* their price. In the simple situation where there is only one other filling station in the area, what price should it charge? Clearly it should charge the price which would maximise its profits, assuming that Esso will charge the *same* price. In the absence of other filling stations in the area, this is likely to be a relatively high price.

Now assume that there are several filling stations in the area. What should the company do now? Its best choice is probably to charge the same price as Esso and hope that no other company charges a lower price and forces Esso to cut its price. Assuming that Esso's threat is credible, other companies are likely to reason in a similar way. Hence Esso's credible threat has the effect of keeping fuel prices high.

Pause for thought

Assume that there are two major oil companies operating filling stations in an area. The first promises to match the other's prices. The other promises to sell at 1p per litre cheaper than the first. Describe the likely sequence of events in this 'game' and the likely eventual outcome. Could the promise of the second company be seen as credible?

The importance of timing

Most decisions by oligopolists are made by one firm at a time rather than simultaneously by all firms. Sometimes a firm will take the initiative. At other times it will respond to decisions taken by other firms.

Take the case of a new generation of large passenger aircraft which can fly further without refuelling. Assume that there is a market for a 500-seater version of this type of aircraft and a 400-seater version, but that the individual

markets for each aircraft are not big enough for the two manufacturers, Boeing and Airbus, to share them profitably. Let us also assume that the 400-seater market would give an annual profit of £50 million to a single manufacturer and the 500-seater would give an annual profit of £30 million, but that if both manufacturers produced the same version, they would each make an annual loss of £10 million.

Assume that Boeing announces that it is building the 400-seater plane. What should Airbus do? The choice is illustrated in Figure 12.7. This diagram is called a ***decision tree*** and shows the sequence of events. The small square at the left of the diagram is Boeing's decision point (point A). If it had decided to build the 500-seater plane, we would move up the top branch. Airbus would now have to make a decision (point B_1). If it too built the 500-seater plane, we would move to outcome 1: a loss of £10 million for both manufacturers. Clearly, with Boeing building a 500-seater plane, Airbus would choose the 400-seater plane: we would move to outcome 2, with Boeing making a profit of £30 million and Airbus a profit £50 million. Airbus would be very pleased!

Boeing's best strategy at point A, however, would be to build the 400-seater plane. We would then move to Airbus's decision point B_2. In this case, it is in Airbus's interests to build the 500-seater plane. Its profit would be only £30 million (outcome 3), but this is better than a £10 million loss if it too built the 400-seater plane (outcome 4). With Boeing deciding first, the Nash equilibrium will thus be outcome 3.

Definition

Decision tree (or game tree) A diagram showing the sequence of possible decisions by competitor firms and the outcome of each combination of decisions.

There is clearly a ***first-mover advantage*** here. Once Boeing has decided to build the more profitable version of the plane, Airbus is forced to build the less profitable one. Naturally, Airbus would like to build the more profitable one and be the first mover. Which company succeeds in going first depends on how advanced they are in their research and development and in their production capacity.

More complex decision trees. The aircraft example is the simplest version of a decision tree, with just two companies and each one making only one key decision. In many business situations, much more complex trees could be constructed. The 'game' would be more like one of chess, with many moves and several options on each move. If there were more than two companies, the decision tree would be more complex still.

> ### Pause for thought
>
> *Give an example of decisions that two firms could make in sequence, each one affecting the other's next decision.*

The usefulness of game theory

The advantage of the game-theory approach is that the firm does not need to know which response its rivals will make. It does, however, need to be able to measure the effect of each possible response. This will be virtually impossible to do when there are many firms competing and many different responses that could be made. The approach is only useful, therefore, in relatively simple cases, and even here the estimates of profit from each outcome may amount to no more than a rough guess.

It is thus difficult for an economist to predict with any accuracy what price, output and level of advertising the firm will choose. This problem is compounded by the difficulty of predicting the type of strategy – safe, high risk, compromise – that the firm will adopt.

In some cases, firms may compete hard for a time (in price or non-price terms) and then realise that maybe no one is winning. Firms may then jointly raise prices and reduce advertising. Later, after a period of tacit collusion, competition may break out again. This may be sparked off by the entry of a new firm, by the development of a new product design, by a change in market demand, or simply by one or more firms no longer being able to resist the temptation to 'cheat'. In short, the behaviour of particular oligopolists may change quite radically over time.

> ### Definition
>
> **First-mover advantage** When a firm gains from being the first one to take action.

SUMMARY

1a Monopolistic competition occurs where there is free entry to the industry and quite a large number of firms operating independently of each other, but where each firm has some market power as a result of producing differentiated products or services.

1b In the short run, firms can make supernormal profits. In the long run, however, freedom of entry will drive profits down to the normal level. The long-run equilibrium of the firm is where the (downward-sloping) demand curve is tangential to the long-run average cost curve.

1c The long-run equilibrium is one of excess capacity. Given that the demand curve is downward sloping, its tangency point with the *LRAC* curve will not be at the bottom of the *LRAC* curve. Increased production would thus be possible at *lower* average cost.

1d In practice, supernormal profits may persist into the long run: firms have imperfect information; entry may not be completely unrestricted; there may be a problem of indivisibilities; firms may use non-price competition to maintain an advantage over their rivals.

1e Monopolistically competitive firms, because of excess capacity, may have higher costs, and thus higher prices, than perfectly competitive firms, but consumers may gain from a greater diversity of products.

1f Monopolistically competitive firms may have less economies of scale than monopolies and conduct less research and development, but the competition may keep prices lower than under monopoly. Whether there will be more or less choice for the consumer is debatable.

2a An oligopoly is where there are just a few firms in the industry with barriers to the entry of new firms. Firms recognise their mutual dependence.

2b Oligopolists will want to maximise their joint profits. This will tend to make them collude to keep prices high. On the other hand, they will want the biggest share of industry profits for themselves. This will tend to make them compete.

2c They are more likely to collude: if there are few of them; if they are open with each other; if they have similar products and cost structures; if there is a dominant firm; if there are significant entry barriers; if the market is stable; and if there is no government legislation to prevent collusion.

2d Collusion can be open or tacit.

2e A formal collusive agreement is called a 'cartel'. A cartel aims to act as a monopoly. It can set the price and leave the members to compete for market share, or it can assign quotas. There is always a temptation for cartel members to 'cheat' by undercutting the cartel price if they think they can get away with it and not trigger a price war.

2f Tacit collusion can take the form of price leadership. This is where firms follow the price set by either a dominant firm in the industry or one seen as a reliable 'barometer' of market conditions. Alternatively, tacit collusion can simply involve following various rules of thumb such as average cost pricing and benchmark pricing.

2g Even when firms do not collude they will still have to take into account their rivals' behaviour. In the Cournot model, firms assume that their rivals' output is given and then choose the profit-maximising price and output in the light of this assumption. The resulting price and profit are lower than under monopoly, but still higher than under perfect competition. In the Bertrand model, firms assume that their rivals' price is given. This will result in prices being competed down until only normal profits remain.

2h In the kinked-demand curve model, firms are likely to keep their prices stable unless there is a large shift in costs or demand.

2i Non-collusive oligopolists will have to work out a price strategy. This will depend on their attitudes towards risk and on the assumptions they make about the behaviour of their rivals.

2j Whether consumers benefit from oligopoly depends on: the particular oligopoly and how competitive it is; whether there is any countervailing power; whether the firms engage in extensive advertising and of what type; whether product differentiation results in a wide range of choice for the consumer; how much of the profits are ploughed back into research and development; and how contestable the market is. Since these conditions vary substantially from oligopoly to oligopoly, it is impossible to state just how well or how badly oligopoly in general serves the consumer's interest.

3a Game theory is a way of modelling behaviour in strategic situations where the outcome for an individual or firm depends on the choices made by others. Thus game theory examines various strategies that firms can adopt when the outcome of each is not certain.

3b The simplest type of 'game' is a single-move or single-period game, sometimes known as a normal-form game. Many single-period games have predictable outcomes, no matter what assumptions each firm makes about its rivals' behaviour. Such games are known as dominant strategy games.

3c Non-collusive oligopolists will have to work out a price strategy. They can adopt a low-risk 'maximin' strategy of choosing the policy that has the least-bad worst outcome, or a high-risk 'maximax' strategy of choosing the policy with the best possible outcome, or some compromise. Either way, a 'Nash' equilibrium is likely to be reached which is not in the best interests of the firms collectively. It will entail a lower level of profit than if they had colluded.

3d In multiple-move games, play is passed from one 'player' to the other sequentially. Firms will respond not only to what firms do, but also to what they say they will do. To this end, a firm's threats or promises must be credible if they are to influence rivals' decisions.

3e A firm may gain a strategic advantage over its rivals by being the first one to take action (e.g. launch a new product). A decision tree can be constructed to show the possible sequence of moves in a multiple-move game.

REVIEW QUESTIONS

1 Think of ten different products or services and estimate roughly how many firms there are in the market. You will need to decide whether 'the market' is a local one, a national one or an international one. In what ways do the firms compete in each of the cases you have identified?

2 Imagine there are two types of potential customer for jam sold by a small food shop. One is the person who has just run out and wants some now. The other is the person who looks in the cupboard, sees that the pot of jam is less than half full and thinks, 'I will soon need some more.' How will the price elasticity of demand differ between these two customers?

3 Why may a food shop charge higher prices than supermarkets for 'essential items' and yet very similar prices for delicatessen items?

4 How will the position and shape of a firm's short-run demand curve depend on the prices that rivals charge?

5 Assuming that a firm under monopolistic competition can make supernormal profits in the short run, will there be any difference in the long-run and short-run elasticity of demand? Explain.

6 Firms under monopolistic competition generally have spare capacity. Does this imply that if, say, half of the petrol stations were closed down, the consumer would benefit? Explain.

7 Will competition between oligopolists always reduce total industry profits?

8 In which of the following industries is collusion likely to occur: bricks, beer, margarine, cement, crisps, washing powder, blank audio or video cassettes, carpets?

9 Draw a diagram like Figure 12.4. Illustrate what would happen if there were a rise in market demand.

10 Devise a box diagram like that in Table 12.1, only this time assume that there are three firms, each considering the two strategies of keeping price the same or reducing it by a set amount. Is the game still a 'dominant strategy game'?

11 What are the limitations of game theory in predicting oligopoly behaviour?

12 Which of the following are examples of effective countervailing power?

   (a) A power station buying coal from a large local coal mine.
   (b) A large factory hiring a photocopier from Rank Xerox.
   (c) Marks and Spencer buying clothes from a garment manufacturer.
   (d) A small village store (but the only one for miles around) buying food from a wholesaler.

   Is it the size of the purchasing firm that is important in determining its power to keep down the prices charged by its suppliers?

ADDITIONAL PART E CASE STUDIES IN THE *ECONOMICS FOR BUSINESS* MyEconLab (www.pearsoned.co.uk/sloman)

E.1 **Is perfect best?** An examination of the meaning of the word 'perfect' in perfect competition.

E.2 **B2B electronic marketplaces.** This case study examines the growth of firms trading with each other over the Internet (business to business or 'B2B') and considers the effects on competition.

E.3 **Measuring monopoly power.** An examination of how the degree of monopoly power possessed by a firm can be measured.

E.4 **X-inefficiency.** A type of inefficiency suffered by many large firms, resulting in a wasteful use of resources.

E.5 **Competition in the pipeline.** An examination of attempts to introduce competition into the gas industry in the UK.

E.6 **Airline deregulation in the USA and Europe.** Whether the deregulation of various routes has led to more competition and lower prices.

E.7 **The motor vehicle repair and servicing industry.** A case study of monopolistic competition.

E.8 **Bakeries: oligopoly or monopolistic competition.** A case study on the bread industry, showing that small-scale local bakeries can exist alongside giant national bakeries.

E.9 **Oligopoly in the brewing industry.** A case study showing how the UK brewing industry is becoming more concentrated.

E.10 **OPEC.** A case study examining OPEC's influence over oil prices from the early 1970s to the current day.

E.11 **Cut throat competition.** An examination of the barriers to entry to the UK razor market.

WEBSITES RELEVANT TO PART E

Numbers and sections refer to websites listed in the Web appendix and hotlinked from this book's website at **www.pearsoned.co.uk/sloman**

- For news articles relevant to Part E, see the Economics News Articles link from the book's website.

- For general news on companies and markets, see websites in section A, and particularly A1, 2, 3, 4, 5, 8, 9, 18, 23, 24, 25, 26, 35, 36. See also A38, 39 and 43 for links to newspapers worldwide; and A42 for links to economics news articles from newspapers worldwide.

- For sites that look at competition and market power, see B2; E4, 10, 18; G7, 8. See also links in I7, 11, 14 and 17. In particular see the following links in sites I7: Microeconomics > Competition and Monopoly.

- For a site on game theory, see A40 including its home page. See also D4; C20; I17 and 4 (in the EconDirectory section).

Supply: alternative strategies

The FT Reports . . .

The Financial Times, 31 August 2012

FT

Back in the groove

By Peter Aspden

The digital era: a miraculous time for information, accessibility, storage and portability; a bad time for the album. The entity that started life 60 years ago as the Long Playing Record is in crisis. Figures released by the British Phonographic Industry in July revealed that despite much-trumpeted growth in the digital market, UK album sales fell by 12.7 per cent year-on-year in the second quarter of 2012. Total first-half 2012 album sales were 43.6m, a 13.8 per cent fall on the 50.5m albums sold in the first half of 2011. There is a similar pattern worldwide.

Those gloomy figures came just a couple of months after it was announced that digital format sales had overtaken physical product sales for the first time, accounting for 55.5 per cent of UK trade revenues in the first quarter of 2012. . . . Nevertheless, it is a fact that we are buying less and less music. And the album – the industry's mainstay for that golden period of rock music which started in the 1960s and fizzled out some time at the turn of the millennium – is fast becoming a musical irrelevance.

Nonsense, say those in denial over the decline, countering with a single word: Adele. The British singer's second album *21* has performed astonishingly since its release at the beginning of 2011. It has slowly been gaining ground on the highest-selling UK albums of all time, moving past Michael Jackson's *Thriller* in May to clinch fifth place. . . .

It took time for the album to find its existential confidence in the world of popular music, however. Initially, albums were regarded as vehicles on which to load best-selling singles, . . .

The introduction of the compact disc in the 1980s only served to boost the album's supremacy. Sold by the promise of indestructibility, superior sound quality (no crackles!) and compactness, record-buyers flocked, in many cases, to buy their record collections all over again. . . .

The speed of the information super-highway turned out to be a game-changer. . . . Artists themselves responded by working in shorter formats: video singles trailed on YouTube, EPs. . . . The relentless march of iTunes towards the domination of music distribution made the need for albums almost obsolete: the pick-and-mix culture was here to stay. . . .

The competitive forces reveal the drivers of industry competition. A company strategist who understands that competition extends well beyond existing rivals will detect wider competitive threats and be better equipped to address them. At the same time, thinking comprehensively about an industry's structure can uncover opportunities: differences in customers, suppliers, substitutes, potential entrants, and rivals that can become the basis for distinct strategies yielding superior performance. In a world of more open competition and relentless change, it is more important than ever to think structurally about competition.

Michael E. Porter, 'The five competitive forces that shape competition', *Harvard Business Review*, January 2008, p. 93

Many small companies, especially those facing fierce competition, may be forced to pursue profit as their overriding goal, merely to survive. With large companies, however, where mere survival is not the overriding concern, the pursuit of short-run profit is likely to be only one of many business objectives.

The modern business enterprise is often a complex organisation, with many different departments and divisions. What is more, the ownership and control of the firm are often in totally different hands: i.e. shareholders and managers. With many competing interests there are often several objectives being pursued simultaneously.

In Part F we will consider what these alternative objectives might be and the strategies that businesses might adopt in their pursuit. Having the correct strategy is crucial for business survival. For example, a strategy that worked well selling music in the late twentieth century may be tantamount to commercial suicide in today's environment (see the *Financial Times* article on the left).

We start, in Chapter 13, by introducing you to the world of business strategy. We show how crucial the degree of competition is in shaping not only business success but the strategic approaches open to business.

In Chapter 14 we will outline various alternative theories of the firm – alternative, that is, to the traditional theory of short-run profit maximisation. Then, in Chapter 15, we will focus on one particular strategy: that of growth. Should a firm seek to grow by simply expanding the scale of its operations, or should it merge with other firms or enter into alliances with them? Chapter 16 looks at the small-firm sector, and compares the objectives and behaviour of small firms with those of their bigger rivals.

Finally, in Chapter 17, we will look at alternative pricing strategies and how they vary with market structure and the different aims that firms might pursue.

Key terms
Porter's five forces
Strategic management
Value chain
Core competence
Profit satisficing
Managerial utility
Behavioural theories of the firm
Organisational slack
Internal expansion
External expansion
Transaction costs
Takeover constraint
Horizontal and vertical integration
Vertical restraints
Diversification
Merger
Enterprise
Strategic alliance
Networks
Logistics
SME
Cost-based pricing
Price discrimination
Transfer pricing
Peak-load pricing
Inter-temporal pricing
Product life cycle

An introduction to business strategy

Business issues covered in this chapter

- What are the objectives of strategic management?
- What are the key competitive forces affecting a business?
- What choices of strategy towards competitors are open to a business?
- What internal strategic choices are open to a business and how can it make best use of its core competencies when deciding on its internal organisation?
- How does a business's strategy relate to its vision and mission? What is the role of various stakeholders in shaping strategy?
- Should a business 'go global'?

Ben & Jerry's is founded on and dedicated to a sustainable corporate concept of linked prosperity. Our mission consists of 3 interrelated parts:

- Social Mission: To operate the Company in a way that actively recognizes the central role that business plays in society by initiating innovative ways to improve the quality of life locally, nationally and internationally.
- Product Mission: To make, distribute and sell the finest quality all natural ice cream and euphoric concoctions with a continued commitment to incorporating wholesome, natural ingredients and promoting business practices that respect the Earth and the Environment.
- Economic Mission: To operate the Company on a sustainable financial basis of profitable growth, increasing value for our stakeholders and expanding opportunities for development and career growth for our employees.

Underlying the mission of Ben & Jerry's is the determination to seek new and creative ways of addressing all three parts, while holding a deep respect for individuals inside and outside the company and for the communities of which they are a part.

Source: © Ben & Jerry's Homemade Holdings Inc.

Being a successful business means what? According to its mission statement, for Ben & Jerry's it means producing a high-quality product, returning a profit, presiding over business growth and enhancing shareholder value. The company also claims that a successful business rests upon a 'deep respect for individuals' and that it wants to initiate ways of improving the quality of life. What strategy or strategies will Ben & Jerry's need to adopt in order to achieve these goals?

Ben & Jerry's was formed in 1978 by Ben Cohen and Jerry Greenfield. In 2000, it was taken over by Unilever, the Anglo-Dutch multinational, but it still maintains its identity and its mission. Since its early years as a two-person operation, Ben & Jerry's has expanded to have operations in 26 countries. However, as the mission statement suggests, the founders of Ben & Jerry's were in search of more than profits from their business activities. With a clear philosophy of social responsibility, the business strategy has been one in which the search for profit has been regulated by a wider set of social and environmental goals.

13.1 WHAT IS STRATEGY?

Defining strategy

Business strategy describes the way in which an organisation addresses its fundamental challenges over the medium to long term. Usually, the term 'strategy' is applied to the decision-making processes of the senior management team, but it can be applied at all levels of the organisation.

The term can also be applied to a number of everyday situations. Thus, an individual may have a strategy to keep fit that involves a healthy diet and going to the gym. A student may have a career strategy that involves passing examinations.

Businesses use strategy in an attempt to be more competitive than their rivals. Sometimes these strategies are successful: businesses outperform their competitors. Similarly, individuals' strategy may be successful: people keep their weight under control; students pass exams.

Sometimes, however, strategies fail. Businesses underperform; individuals put on weight; students fail their exams. If this is the case, then a re-evaluation of existing goals and strategies has to take place with new strategies being developed to meet long-term objectives. For a business that has failed to perform, this is an opportunity to regain its competitive position.

Clearly the type of business 'strategy' that is appropriate depends upon the context in which the strategy is being developed. In an attempt to capture the diversity of the term, Henry Mintzberg (1987)[1] suggests that we need to look at the 'five Ps' of business strategy. A strategy can be:

- a **p**lan
- a **p**loy
- a **p**attern of behaviour
- a **p**osition with respect to others
- a **p**erspective

A plan. This represents the most common use of the term strategy. It involves, as Mintzberg states, a 'consciously intended course of action to deal with a situation'. Plans most commonly operate over a given period of time, in which the business outlines where it would like to be at a given point in the future. This might be in terms of its market share or its level of profitability, or some other combination of criteria upon which business progress or success might be evaluated. As such, plans tend to focus on long-term issues facing the business rather than operational details.

A ploy. In contrast to the long-term nature of the plan, strategy as a ploy is generally short term in its application. It often focuses on a specific manoeuvre by business in order to outwit or counteract the behaviour of rivals. Aggressive pricing policy and the use of special offers by supermarkets is a frequently adopted ploy to gain, or more commonly protect, market share. Such a strategy may have limited objectives and be liable to frequent changes.

A pattern of behaviour. Rather than a consciously planned framework of action, business strategy may in fact emerge naturally from a consistent response to events: e.g. introducing a new product variety each year. Such consistent action involves a pattern of behaviour, which takes on a strategic form. Such strategies tend to evolve as circumstances change. There is no clear long-term objective; unlike plan and ploy, here strategy just happens.

A position with respect to others. Here strategy is determined by the position of the business in its market. For example, a firm may attempt to gain or defend market share. Thus a car company such as BMW may set out to defend its position as a manufacturer of high-quality motorcars by focusing on design and performance in its product development and advertising campaigns. Conversely, Asda Wal-Mart might focus on defending and developing its claim to have some of the lowest prices in grocery retailing.

A perspective. In this respect strategy is based upon establishing a common way of perceiving the world, primarily within the organisation itself. It may be that this perspective of the world is based on the views of a forceful leader or a strong senior management team, though it can also involve a consensus between stakeholders in the organisation. Businesses with strong ethical and environmental objectives, such as Ben & Jerry's, would see a shared perspective as an important part of their business strategy. Employees are encouraged to take on board the company's philosophy. This, it is hoped, will not only contribute to the business's

---

[1] Henry Mintzberg, 'The strategy concept I: five ps for strategy', *California Management Review*, vol. 30, no. 1, autumn 1987, pp. 11–24.

BOX 13.1 BUSINESS STRATEGY THE SAMSUNG WAY

Staying ahead of the game

Samsung is a major South Korean conglomerate involved in a number of industries, including the machinery and heavy engineering, chemical, financial services and consumer electronic sectors. In its various divisions it has over 300 000 employees globally and is a major international investor and exporter.

This box outlines some of the strategic initiatives that have been taken in recent times by one of its most successful divisions, Samsung Electronics, which is the world's largest producer of televisions, colour monitors, TFT-LCDs and mobile phones and the second largest producer of memory chips (after Intel), and employs over 200 000 people.

Samsung's success over the past few years is quite an achievement, given the massive financial problems it faced following the Asian financial crisis in the late 1990s. Since that time it has managed not only to shake off its debts and post significant improvements in profits, but also to reposition itself in the upmarket segment of the consumer electronics industry.

The key features of Samsung's strategy

How has Samsung achieved this? What have been the keys to its success? First, it has a strong management team led by Mr Kwon Oh-Hyun, vice-chairman and CEO of Samsung Electronics. Together they have a clear vision of the future of the sector.

Second, there has been a dramatic streamlining of the business and the decision-making structure following poor financial performance in the mid-1990s and an association with low-end brands in televisions and air-conditioning units. The management team took aggressive measures to improve the division's finances by cutting jobs, closing unprofitable factories, reducing inventory levels and selling corporate assets. They then 'delayered' the company, ensuring that managers had to go through fewer layers of bureaucracy, thereby speeding up the approval of new products, budgets and marketing plans.

Third, Samsung Electronics has been investing heavily in research and development (R&D) to increase its product portfolio and reduce the lead time from product conception to product launch. In 2011 it employed 53 320 people in its R&D units. These employees were spread over 42 research facilities around the world. It has engaged in a number of strategic alliances with major players such as Sony, IBM and Hewlett-Packard to share R&D costs, and for every year from 2006 to 2011 Samsung ranked second in obtaining patent approvals in the USA, behind International Business Machines (IBM). By 2011 Samsung Electronics had registered approximately 100 000 patents.

Samsung has a vision of achieving $400 billion in revenue and becoming one of the world's top five brands by 2020. To achieve this end, Mr Kwon Oh-Hyun and his team recognised that most of its flagship products will be obsolete in ten years' time. This is why innovation is central to Samsung's 2020 vision. The company intends to build on its existing capabilities in three areas: new technology, innovate products and creative solutions.

Fourth, Samsung is concerned about volumes from which it can achieve economies of scale. To this end it invests heavily in modern factories that can cope with large production runs. To help achieve these economies, Samsung also supplies components to its competitors as well as making them for its own product range. For example, it sells flash memory chips for Apple's iPod, Nokia phones and digital cameras. Further, production systems are flexible enough to allow customisation for individual buyers, ensuring that selling prices are above the industry average.

Alongside longer production runs, Samsung is concerned with ensuring that production costs are minimised by making its own business units compete with external rivals. For example, Samsung buys colour filters from Sumitomo Chemical Company of Japan and from its own factories.

Finally, Samsung has been developing its global brand name in consumer electronics and marketing, particularly sports marketing. For example, it currently sponsors Chelsea football club and was one of the eleven official partners of the London 2012 Olympics.

Thus, whilst Samsung makes most of its profits from semiconductors, investment in less profitable consumer products with a clear brand identity helps to raise the profile of all products. As a result of these changes, Samsung Electronics rose from 42nd in BusinessWeek/Interbrand's list of the top 100 global brands in 2001 to 17th in 2011.

The dramatic growth of Samsung Electronics has been largely achieved since the turn of the twenty-first century. In 2010 the company altered its top management team to include a slightly younger team. It also restructured some of its divisions, producing a better fit with changes in the market and product offerings. This was intended to support Samsung in maintaining its growth into the foreseeable future.

However, Samsung was hit by a major setback in August 2012. The US courts decided the company should pay Apple $1.03 billion in damages for infringing several of its software and design patents. This triggered an immediate 7.5 per cent drop in Samsung's share price, wiping $12 billion from its market value. Samsung will appeal against this decision, but it will take some time for this dispute to be finally settled. One thing is for sure, Samsung's reputation will have been tarnished, whatever the final legal outcome.

1. *What dangers do you see with Samsung's recent business strategy?*
2. *Given Mintzberg's five Ps, which would you say fit(s) Samsung's approach to strategy most closely and why?*

success through motivation and commitment, but also encourage employees to feel good about what they do.

Mintzberg notes in his analysis of the term 'strategy' that businesses might adopt any number of approaches to strategic behaviour. Pursuing strategy as a plan, for example, does not preclude using strategy as a ploy or as a position in respect to others. Businesses may interpret strategy in a number of ways simultaneously. What these different understandings of strategy do is to enable us to analyse different aspects of business behaviour and organisation.

Strategic management

For most of the time, most managers have as their primary function the managing of the routine day-to-day activities of the business, such as dealing with personnel issues, checking budgets and looking for ways to enhance efficiency. In other words, they are involved in the detailed operational activities of the business.

Some managers, however, especially those high up in the business organisation, such as the managing director, will be busy in a different way, thinking about big, potentially complex issues, which affect the whole company. For example, they might be analysing the behaviour of competitors, or evaluating the company's share price or considering ways to expand the business. In other words, these managers are involved in the strategic long-term activities of the business.

Both types of management are equally important in the management process, as each contributes in its own way to the business's overall success. However, what is clear is that strategic and operational management are quite distinct managerial functions.

Strategic management comprises three main components.

■ *Strategic analysis* is concerned with examining those factors which underpin an organisation's mission (or purpose) and its long-term vision. These factors are key in determining a business's performance and include internal factors, such as the development of business skills and knowledge, and external factors, such as the competitive environment, resource availability and changes in technology.
■ *Strategic choice*, by contrast, is primarily concerned with the formulation and evaluation of alternative courses of action that might be adopted in order to achieve the business's strategic objectives. What strategic choices

are available? How suitable are such strategies, given their risks and constraints such as time, cost and the business's values?
■ *Strategic implementation* is concerned with how strategic choices might be put into effect. In other words, it considers how a strategy might be translated into action. Who is responsible for its implementation? How will it be managed? How is its success or otherwise to be monitored?

In the following sections of this chapter we are going to consider these three dimensions of strategic management and the issues they raise for the conduct of business. Before we do so, it is worth considering what strategic management means for different business types. How might businesses differ in respect to their analysis, choice and implementation of strategy?

Big business/small business. The strategic requirements of a small local computer assembler and Microsoft are clearly going to be massively different. A small business, operating in a niche market, providing a limited range of products or services, would certainly not require the complex strategic assessment of a large business operating in many markets and providing a whole range of products. Not only would the strategy for a small business be generally simpler, it would probably be easier to formulate, given that the managers of small businesses are often the owners and generally the principal creators of the businesses strategy.

Manufacturing business/service provider business. Although in many respects the strategic commitments of both a manufacturer and a service-sector business might be similar, in some crucial respects the focus of strategy will differ. Manufacturers will tend to focus a large part of their strategy effort on product issues (technology, design, inputs, etc.), whereas service providers will tend to focus on strategic issues related to the customer, especially in the area of retailing.

Domestic business/multinational business. The crucial difference in strategic thinking between a domestic business and a multinational business concerns the geographic spread of the multinational corporation. The multinational will need to focus its strategy not only in global terms but possibly within the context of each international market within which it operates. Depending upon the diversity of these markets, this may require a quite distinct strategic approach within each. Similarly, a business serving a national market will have more complex strategic issues to consider than one serving a local market.

Private-sector business/public-sector business. Quite clearly the strategic considerations of the National Health Service will in many respects be quite different from, say, Ford, but how different will they be from those of BUPA, the private-sector medical care provider? Increasingly, public-sector organisations, like their private-sector counterparts, are having to adopt a more business-orientated approach to service provision. Stakeholders may be different and profit may not be the principal motivation of business activity, but efficiency, targets and accountability are increasingly becoming public-sector as well as private-sector organisational goals.

For-profit organisations/not-for-profit organisations. Not-for-profit businesses such as charities are essentially based upon a mission underpinned by principles of value. In shaping their strategic goals, such values will be paramount in determining the direction and focus of strategic behaviour.

13.2 STRATEGIC ANALYSIS

In order for an organisation to make strategic decisions, it must first analyse what the organisation is about (its mission) and how it envisages where it wants to be (its vision). In other words, the mission and vision will affect the strategic choices made. Take the case of Ben & Jerry's. Its proclaimed ethical stance limits potential strategic avenues.

Strategic choices also depend on an analysis of (a) the external business environment and (b) the organisation's internal capabilities.

- How much competition does the firm face and what forms does it take?
- What other external factors, such as laws and regulations, technological changes and changes in consumer tastes, are likely to affect the firm's decisions?
- Similarly, what internal factors drive an organisation's performance?

In the case of Ben & Jerry's, the nature of its supply chain is likely to affect not only the quality of the product but the ability of the company to develop and grow.

Vision and mission

At the beginning of this chapter, we referred to the mission statement of Ben & Jerry's, in which the company clearly expresses a purpose for its business: a purpose that goes far beyond simply making a profit. Such wider social, environmental and ethical considerations are increasingly shaping business thinking, as expectations regarding corporate responsibility grow.

It is now widely expected that a business must look beyond 'the bottom line' (i.e. profitability) and take account of the interests of a wide group of stakeholders, such as employees, customers, creditors and the local community, and not just the owners of the business. It would be a risky business strategy indeed that pursued profit without taking into account the social, environmental and ethical implications that this might entail (see section 20.5). As such, the formulation of strategy must take into account the purpose of the organisation and the values and objectives that such a purpose involves. Organisational purpose is most often found in a business's mission statement, which is in turn shaped by a number of distinct influences (see Figure 13.1).

Corporate governance. Corporate governance refers to the way in which a business is run and the structure of decision making. It also includes the monitoring and supervising, and in some cases regulation, of executive decisions. The way a business is run depends on the purposes of the business and in *whose interests* it is run.

Stakeholders. Stakeholders differ in power and influence, but ultimately they might all shape the purpose of the organisation in certain respects. Given the wide number of stakeholders, many conflicts of interest can arise.

Business ethics. A business's ethical position might, as in the case of Ben & Jerry's, be driven by the values of its founders. Alternatively, ethics might be determined and shaped by wider cultural values and standards regarding what is and what is not acceptable behaviour. As previously remarked, business today would find it very difficult to pursue a strategy that failed to exhibit a degree of social responsibility.

Various high-profile cases, such as those concerning Nike, Reebok and Royal Dutch Shell, in which ethical standards were sacrificed in the pursuit of profit, have had a significant impact on their reputation and standing in

Figure 13.1 Factors influencing organisational purpose

both the business community and society in general. All three companies are trying to clean up their image and present a more socially responsible approach to business. They recognise that ethically sound behaviour is good for business and the bottom line.

Cultural context. How does the cultural context of the organisation influence its objectives? Not only will national culture be significant here, but also the subculture of managers. Wider questions are also raised given the growth in multinational business activity, and the cross-cultural nature of such organisations. Recognising differing cultural contexts might be crucial in shaping business success within such increasingly global markets.

The business environment

We considered the various dimensions of the business environment and how they shape and influenced business activity (Chapter 1). We divided the business environment into four distinct sets of factors: political, economic, social and technological. Such factors comprise what we call a PEST analysis. In this section we will take our analysis of the business environment forward and consider more closely those factors that are likely to influence the competitive advantage of the organisation.

> ### Pause for thought
>
> *Give some examples of cultural differences between countries or regions which might influence business strategy.*

The Five Forces Model of competition

Developed by Professor Michael Porter of Harvard Business School in 1980, the Five Forces Model sets out to identify those factors which are likely to affect an organisation's competitiveness (see Figure 13.2). This then helps a firm choose an appropriate strategy to enhance its competitive opportunities and to protect itself from competitive threats. The five forces that Porter identifies are:

- the bargaining power of suppliers;
- the bargaining power of buyers;
- the threat of potential new entrants;
- the threat of substitutes;
- the extent of competitive rivalry.

The bargaining power of suppliers. Most business organisations depend upon suppliers to some extent, whether to provide raw materials or simply stationery. Indeed, many businesses have extensive supply or 'value chain' networks (as we shall discuss later in this section). Such suppliers can have a significant and powerful effect on a business when:

- there are relatively few suppliers in the market, reducing the ability of the firm to switch from one supply source to another;
- there are no alternatives to the supplies they offer;
- the prices of suppliers form a large part of the firm's total costs;
- a supplier's customers are small and fragmented, and as such have little power over the supplying business.

Car dealers often find that car manufacturers can exert considerable pressure over them in terms of pricing, display and after-sales service.

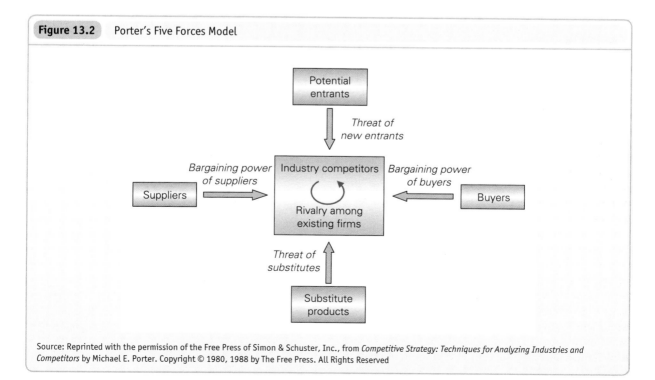

| Figure 13.2 | Porter's Five Forces Model |

The bargaining power of buyers. The bargaining power of companies that purchase a firm's products will be greater when:

- these purchasing companies are large and there are relatively few of them;
- there are many other firms competing for their custom, and hence a firm that produces an undifferentiated product is likely to be more prone to 'buyer power' than one that produces a unique or differentiated product;
- the costs for the purchasing companies of switching to other suppliers are low;
- purchasing companies are able to backward integrate and effectively displace the supplying firm.

The UK grocery-retailing sector is dominated by a small number of large supermarket chains such as Tesco, Sainsbury and Asda Wal-Mart. These exert massive levels of buyer power over farmers and food processors. Not only do such supermarkets dominate the market, but they can normally find many alternative supply sources, both domestic and international, at relatively low switching costs. Also, all the supermarkets sell own-brand labels, either produced themselves or through agreement with existing manufacturers, and these are often sold at prices considerably below those of equivalent branded products (see Box 8.1 on page 112).

The threat of potential new entrants. The ability of new entrants to enter the marketplace depends largely upon the existence and effectiveness of various barriers to entry. These barriers to entry were described fully in section 11.3 (pages 167–8), but are listed here as a reminder:

- economies of scale and scope;
- product differentiation;
- capital requirements;
- lower costs of established firm;
- ownership of/control over key factors of production;
- ownership of/control over wholesale or retail outlets;
- legal protection;
- aggressive tactics and retaliation.

Barriers to entry tend to be very industry, product and market specific. Nevertheless, two useful generalisations can be made. First, companies with products that have a strong brand identity will often attempt to use this form of product differentiation to restrict competition; second, manufacturers will tend to rely on economies of scale and low costs as a basis for restricting competitive pressure.

The threat of substitutes. The availability of substitutes can be a major threat to a business and its profitability. Issues that businesses need to consider in relation to the availability of substitute products are:

- the ability of and cost to customers of switching to the substitute;
- the threat of competitors bringing out a more advanced or up-to-date product;

- the impact that substitute products are likely to have on pricing policy.

The market for standalone CD players and blank CDs is a good example of one that has been greatly affected by the arrival of a substitute in the form of MP3 players and digital music files. As MP3 players have fallen in price and digital music files have become more widely available, the CD market has shrunk. Early switching costs, such as the cost of obtaining high-quality music files, have largely been overcome through sellers such as iTunes and Amazon MP3. Clearly CDs are not facing imminent obsolescence. However, firms operating in the CD market will need to reconsider their strategies as the market continues to change.

The extent of competitive rivalry. The previous two chapters focused on market structure and were primarily concerned with how businesses respond to differing levels of competition. Clearly the degree of competition a firm faces is a crucial element in shaping its strategic analysis. Competitive rivalry will be enhanced when there is the potential for new firms to enter the market, when there is a real threat from substitute products and when buyers and suppliers have some element of influence over the firm's performance. In addition to this, competitive rivalry is likely to be enhanced in the following circumstances:

- Competitors are of equal size.
- Markets are growing slowly. This makes it difficult to acquire additional sales without taking market share from rivals.
- There are high fixed costs, which require the firm to gain a large market share in order to break even.
- Productive capacity in an industry increases in large increments, often resulting in over-production in the short term. This adds to competitive pressure by putting downward pressure on prices.
- Product differentiation is difficult to achieve; hence product switching by consumers is a real threat.
- There are high exit costs. When a business invests in non-transferable fixed assets, such as highly specialist capital equipment, it may be reluctant to leave a market. It may thus compete fiercely to maintain its market position. On the other hand, as we have seen in the section on contestable markets (page 174), high exit costs may deter firms from entering a market in the first place and thus make the market less contestable.
- There exists the possibility for merger and acquisition. This competition for corporate control may have considerable influence on the firm's strategy.

Pause for thought

Given that the stronger the competitive forces, the lower the profit potential for firms, describe what five force characteristics an attractive and unattractive industry might have.

BOX 13.2 | **HYBRID STRATEGY**

Stuck in the middle?

Michael Porter,[1] in his analysis of alternative business strategies, suggested that it could be disastrous for a business to be 'stuck in the middle', having no clear strategic direction. Attempting both to differentiate its product and to offer lower prices would be a serious strategic error. According to Porter, consumers would be confused, as the business would have no clear market identity to which they could relate. His advice was to pick one strategy and stick with it exclusively.

But is a single generic strategy always the best choice? Is a mixed strategy always inappropriate? Consumers often demand a range of product characteristics that cover not only issues such as quality and reliability, but also price and convenience. As such, businesses are often forced to adopt a strategic position that attempts to capture both difference and low prices simultaneously.

Hybrid theories that focus on a combination of strategy are greatly influenced by the market within which business is

operating. Grocery retailing in the UK offers a clear example of hybrid strategy. The various supermarket chains not only look to differentiate themselves from their rivals in terms of the look and feel of their stores, customer service, and loyalty schemes such as Sainsbury's Nectar card and Tesco's Clubcard, but also compete fiercely over price.

Then there is the range of their products. At the 'bottom' end of the range, with their own-branded 'basic' products, the supermarkets compete primarily in terms of price (e.g. the Tesco 'Value' and Morrisons 'M Savers' ranges). But with more upmarket products, they compete in terms of the variety of lines stocked and their quality (e.g. Asda's 'Extra Special' and Sainsbury's 'Taste the Difference' ranges).

1. *Choose three supermarket chains and identify the strategy or strategies they adopt.*
2. *Do you feel the classification of business strategy options into cost leadership, differentiation and focus is adequate to describe the strategic approaches that businesses might adopt?*

---

[1] M. E. Porter, *Competitive Advantage: Creating and Sustaining Superior Performance* (Free Press, 1985).

Limitations of the Five Forces Model

One of the great values of the Five Forces Model is that it creates a structured framework for a business to analyse the strategic issues that it faces. However, it does have a number of weaknesses.

First, the Five Forces Model presents a largely static view of the business environment, whereas in reality it is likely to be constantly changing.

Second, the model starts from the premise that the business environment is a competitive threat to the business organisation, which, if the business is to be successful, needs to be manipulated in particular ways. Often, however, success might be achievable not via competition but rather through cooperation and collaboration. For example, a business might set up close links with one of its major buyers; or businesses in an industry might establish links either to build barriers or to share costs via some form of collaborative research and development. In such instances, the business environment of the Five Forces Model might be viewed as a collaborative opportunity rather than a competitive threat. (The section on strategic alliances in Chapter 15 (section 15.6) will offer a fuller evaluation of collaborative business agreements.)

Finally, critics of the model argue that it fails to take sufficient account of the microenvironment of the organisation and its human resources. For example, factors such as country culture and management skills might have a decisive impact on a firm's choice of strategy and its successful implementation.

Value chain analysis and sustainable competitive advantage

As with the Five Forces Model, value chain analysis was developed by Michael Porter, and as such the two concepts are closely related. A *value chain* shows how value is added to a product as it moves through each stage of production: from the raw material stage to its purchase by the final consumer. Value chain analysis is concerned with evaluating how each of the various operations within and around an organisation, such as handling inputs, manufacturing the product and marketing it, contributes to the competitive position of the business. Ultimately it is these value-creating activities which shape a firm's strategic capabilities. A firm's value chain can be split into two separate sets of activities: primary and support (see Figure 13.3).

Primary activities

Primary activities are those directly concerned with the production, distribution and sales of the firm's product. Such primary activities can be grouped into five categories:

Definition

Value chain The stages or activities that help to create product value.

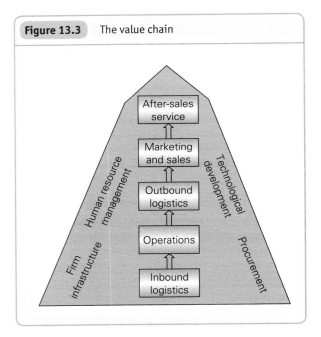

Figure 13.3 The value chain

■ *Inbound **logistics***. Here we are concerned with the handling of inputs, storage and distribution of such inputs throughout the business.
■ *Operations*. These activities involve the conversion of inputs into the final product or service. Operations might include manufacturing, packaging and assembly.
■ *Outbound logistics*. These are concerned with transferring the final product to the consumer. Such activities would include warehousing and transport.
■ *Marketing and sales*. This section of the value chain is concerned with bringing the product to the consumer's attention and would involve product advertising and promotion.
■ *Service*. This can include activities such as installation and repair, as well as customer requirements such as training.

A business might attempt to add value to its activities by improving its performance in one or more of the above

---

Definition

Logistics The process of managing the supply of inputs to a firm and the outputs from a firm to its customers.

---

categories. For example, it might attempt to lower production costs or be more efficient in outbound logistics.

Support activities
Such primary activities are underpinned by support activities. These are activities that do not add value directly to any particular stage within the value chain. They do, however, provide support to such a chain and ensure that its various stages are undertaken effectively. Support activities include:

■ *Procurement*. This involves the acquisition of inputs by the firm.
■ *Technological development*. This includes activities within the business that support new product and process developments, such as the use of research departments.
■ *Human resource management*. Activities in this category include things such as recruitment, training, and the negotiation and determination of wage rates.
■ *Firm infrastructure*. This category includes activities such as financial planning and control systems, quality control and information management.

As well as creating value directly themselves, most firms buy in certain value chain activities, such as employing another firm to do its advertising, or using an external delivery firm to distribute its products. The outsourcing of these activities might prove to be far more beneficial to a business than providing the activities itself. You can employ the best advertisers or the most efficient and reliable distributors.

Thus the value system extends beyond the individual organisation and encompasses the value chains of all those individual businesses that the organisation might deal with. The implication is that the value chain and the value system may be highly complex, and the competitive position of a business may extend well beyond the immediate value chain of the organisation. This will have significant implications for the formulation and choice of business strategy.

Having now discussed the background to strategic analysis, we can shift our focus to consider strategic choice and implementation. What strategies are potentially open to businesses and how do they choose the right ones and set about implementing them?

13.3 STRATEGIC CHOICE

Theories of strategic choice fall into two main categories: market based and resources based.

Market-based theories argue that strategic choices are ultimately determined by the competitive environment that the business faces. As such, understanding this competitive

environment and identifying appropriate ways to deal with it will determine whether you are successful or not.

Resource-based theory also looks at the firm's competitive position, but focuses on its internal situation. It considers how strategic decision making is affected by the ownership, control and use of an organisation's resources. It is seen that such resources ultimately deliver profits and it is through a manipulation of such resources that a business can maintain and enhance its competitive position.

Clearly market- and resource-based explanations of strategic choice overlap and interact, and in practice, most businesses will attempt to evaluate *both* their resource base and the threats posed by competitors. However, the two types of explanation do address the issue of strategic choice from quite distinct starting points and this, as we shall see, affects the strategic solutions they offer.

Environment or market-based strategy

As with many other areas in this field, our analysis of market-based theory starts with the observations of Michael Porter. As an extension of his Five Forces Model of competition, Porter argued that there are three fundamental (or 'generic') strategies that a business might adopt:

- cost leadership;
- differentiation;
- focus.

In order to identify which of these was the most appropriate strategy, a business would need to establish two things: (a) the basis of its competitive advantage – whether it lies in lower costs or differentiation; (b) the nature of the target market – is it broad or a distinct market niche?

Cost leadership

As the title implies, a business that is a low-cost leader is able to manufacture and deliver its product more cheaply than its rivals, thereby gaining competitive advantage. The strategic emphasis here is on driving out inefficiency at every stage of the value chain. 'No-frills' budget airlines, such as easyJet and Ryanair, are classic examples of companies that pursue a cost-leadership strategy.

A strategy based upon cost leadership may require a fundamentally different use of resources or organisational structure if the firm is to stay ahead of its rivals. Wal-Mart's hub and spoke distribution system would be an example in point. Here the company distributes its products to shops from regional depots in order to minimise transport costs.

In addition, firms which base their operations on low costs in order to achieve low prices (although that may not necessarily be the aim of low costs) are unlikely to have a high level of brand loyalty. In other words, if customer choice is going to be driven largely by price, demand is likely to be relatively price elastic. Other virtues of the product that might tie in buyers, such as quality or after-sales service, are largely absent from such firms' strategic goals.

Differentiation

A differentiation strategy aims to emphasise and promote the uniqueness of the firm's product. As such, high rather than low prices are often attached to such products. Product characteristics such as quality, design and reliability are the basis of the firm's competitive advantage. Hence a strategy that adds to such differences and creates value for the customer needs to be identified.

Such a strategy might result in higher costs, especially in the short term, as the firm pursues constant product development through innovation, design and research. However, with the ability to charge premium prices, revenues may increase more than costs: in other words, the firm may achieve higher profits. Games console manufacturers, such as Nintendo with its Wii, Sony with its PlayStation3 and Microsoft with its Xbox 360, are a good example (see Box 14.1). Even though they are in fierce competition with each other, both manufacturers focus their strategy on trying to differentiate their products from their rival's. This differentiation is in terms of features and performance, not price. Processor speed, online capabilities, software support and product image are all characteristics used in the competitive battle.

Differentiation strategies are not, however, risk free. Pricing differentiated products can be problematic. At what point does the price premium for the product deter potential buyers, such that the differentiated nature of the product is insufficient to outweigh such price considerations? The fact that tastes and fashion change could also have a significant impact upon the sales of a differentiated product.

Laura Ashley clothing was a case in point. In an attempt to differentiate itself from other high street clothing rivals, Laura Ashley promoted a strategy producing rather exclusive good-quality clothing for women, which was very feminine and rooted in a country lifestyle. During the early 1980s Laura Ashley's profits grew as its differentiated product attracted a large following. But the fickle nature of fashion had turned by the early 1990s and Laura Ashley's fashion products were seen as dated and stuffy.

But while its differentiated product and brand image had become somewhat of a liability *in the clothing market*, the company has successfully diversified into the home decorations and furniture market. Here the existing brand image was used to create an affluent customer base.

Focus strategy

Rather than considering a whole market as a potential for sales, a focus strategy involves identifying market niches and designing and promoting products for such niches. Such a strategy may or may not be applicable to other niches. As such, a business might pursue any number of different strategies simultaneously for different market niches. In such cases, a business that does not hold a competitive advantage in a market in general may be able to identify distinct market segments in which it might exploit some advantage it might have over its rivals, whether in terms of costs, or product difference. Ben & Jerry's ice cream would be a case in point. The mass low-cost ice-cream market is served by a number of large multinational food manufacturers and processors, but the existence of niche high-quality ice-cream markets offers opportunities for companies like Ben & Jerry's and Häagen-Dazs. By focusing on such consumers they are able to sell and market their product at premium prices.

Niche markets, however profitable, are by their nature small and as such are limited in their growth potential. Hence firms that focus upon niche market opportunities are likely to have limited growth prospects. There is also the possibility that niches shift or over time disappear. This would require businesses to be flexible in setting out their strategic position.

Sometimes a focus strategy may be combined with a cost-leadership strategy to develop a niche market into a mass market. Amazon.com, the online bookseller, was until relatively recently a business that had a clear cost focus strategy. With low overheads it was able to sell books at knockdown prices to online customers (its niche market segment) and over time, thanks to lower costs, lower prices and the spread of the Internet, this has become a mass market.

Resource-based strategy

Resource-based strategy, as already mentioned, focuses on exploiting a firm's internal organisation and production processes in order to develop its competitive advantage. It is the firm's *distinctiveness* that sets it apart from its competitors. If a business does not have a distinctive feature then it needs to set about creating one.

Core competencies

Core competencies are those skills, knowledge and technologies that underpin the organisation's competitive advantage. These competencies are likely to differ from one business to another, reflecting the uniqueness of each individual organisation, and ultimately determining its potential for success. Given these differences, how does a firm select an appropriate strategy?

When a firm has unique competencies, its strategy should seek to sustain and exploit these, whether in the design of the product or in its methods of production. In many cases, however, firms do not have any competencies that give them a distinctive competitive advantage, even though they may still be profitable. In such instances, strategy often focuses upon either developing such resources or more effectively using the resources the firm already has.

What defines a core competence?

A core competence must satisfy the following four capabilities to serve as a source of competitive advantage for the business. It must be:

- *valuable*: a competence that helps the firm deal with threats or contributes to business opportunities;
- *rare*: a competence or resource that is not possessed by competitors;
- *costly to imitate*: a competence or resource that other firms find difficult to develop and copy;
- *non-substitutable*: a competence or resource for which there is no alternative.

> **Pause for thought**
>
> *Referring back to Box 13.1, what core competencies does Samsung have? Remember, you must justify a core competence in terms of all four listed criteria.*

 KEY IDEA 25

Core competencies. The key skills of a business that underpin its competitive advantage. A core competence is valuable, rare, costly to imitate and non-substitutable. Firms will normally gain from exploiting their core competencies.

Clearly then, whether we adopt a market-based view of strategic choice or a resource-based view will have significant implications for how a firm can develop and exploit competitive advantage.

Before we consider issues of how to implement strategy, there is one dimension of the business environment that we need to consider and that is the impact of globalisation on the world economy in general and business activity in particular. Few businesses have been left untouched by the phenomenon. So how has globalisation affected strategic analysis and strategic choice?

> **Definition**
>
> **Core competence** The key skills of a business that underpin its competitive advantage.

13.4 BUSINESS STRATEGY IN A GLOBAL ECONOMY

In many respects a firm's global strategy is simply an extension of its strategy within its own domestic market. However, opening up to global markets can present many new business opportunities: access to new markets, new customers, new supply sources, new ideas and skills. In addition to such opportunities, the global marketplace can also present competitive threats, as new market entrants from abroad arrive with lower costs, innovative products and marketing, or some other core competency which the domestic firm finds difficult to match. In this section we explore the strategic implications for business in facing up to the global economic system.

Why go global?

The following are reasons why a business may wish to expand beyond its domestic market.

Market size

International markets can potentially offer a business massive new opportunities for growth and expansion. Such markets would be particularly attractive to a business where domestic growth opportunities are limited as a result of either the maturity of the market or shifting consumer taste. Businesses that conduct extensive research and development (R&D) would also be attracted to larger markets as potential returns can be used to offset the firm's R&D investment costs and risk.

Increased profitability

Expanding beyond the domestic economy offers a number of opportunities for increasing profits.

Location economies. The internationalisation of a firm's value chain would enable it to place each value-creating activity in the most appropriate or effective geographic location. So if production costs are lower in one country, it could locate production there. If another country has the specialist skills to offer superior product design and research facilities, then these functions could be located there. Nike, the US training shoe and sportswear manufacturer, undertakes most of its manufacturing at production sites in south-east Asia. However, product innovation and research, along with marketing and promotion, are largely undertaken in the USA. As businesses relocate many dimensions of their value chain, the structure and organisation of the business takes on a web-like appearance, with its various operations being spread throughout the world.

> ### Pause for thought
>
> *Identify some of the potential strengths and weaknesses of businesses having their value chains located in a variety of different countries.*

Scope for significant cost reductions. It is widely observed that over the life cycle of a product a firm's average costs fall. This is partly the result of economies of scale as the firm gets bigger and plants can specialise in particular functions. Clearly, these cost reductions can be greater by expanding globally.

Cost reductions over time are also the result of what is known as 'learning by doing'. This is where skills and productivity improve with experience. Such learning effects apply not only to workers in production, sales, distribution, etc., but also to managers, who learn to develop more efficient forms of organisation. When a firm expands globally, there may be more scope for learning by doing. For example, if a firm employs low-cost labour in developing countries, initially the lower cost per worker will to some extent be offset by lower productivity. As learning by doing takes place, and productivity increases, so initial small cost advantages may become much more substantial.

Using core competencies. A firm may be able to exploit its core competencies in competing effectively in global markets. The firm might look to expanding first in those countries where it has a clear competitive advantage over already established companies. Wal-Mart's logistic expertise is one example of a business that might exploit such an advantage in particular overseas markets.

Learning from experience in diverse markets. Successful businesses will learn from their global operations, copying or amending production techniques, organisation, marketing, etc. from one country to another as appropriate. In other words, they can draw lessons from experiences in one country for use in another.

Spreading risk (diversification)

Clearly one of the main reasons a business might have for going global is to spread risk, avoiding being overly reliant on any specific market or geographic region. As such, falling profitability in one region of the global economy might be effectively offset by improved or more favourable economic conditions elsewhere. A large number of German and Japanese businesses have diversified globally in order to reduce their reliance on domestic markets, which in recent years have been growing very slowly and, in the case of Japan, has been suffering from a significant squeeze on prices. For example, Toyota and Honda, the two largest Japanese car manufacturers, both showed record profits for 2002 despite the depressed state of the Japanese economy. They were able to do this by focusing on production in foreign markets – in particular the USA, where three-quarters of the cars sold by Honda and Toyota are also manufactured.

Keeping up with rivals

Increasingly it seems that the globalisation of business is like a game of competitive leapfrog, with businesses having to look overseas in order to maintain their competitive position in respect to their rivals. A fiercely competitive global environment, in which small cost differences or design improvements can mean the difference between business success and failure, ensures that strategic thinking within a global context is high on the business agenda.

It would seem that at this point we need to raise a few notes of caution regarding the adoption of a global strategy. It is clearly not without its potential pitfalls. Within any global strategy there exists a high degree of both economic and political risk. Investing in developing economies or emerging markets, such as China, is likely to be much riskier than investing in developed market economies. However, it is often within emerging markets that the greatest returns are achieved. It is essentially this trade-off between potential returns and risk that a firm needs to consider in its strategic decisions.

A global business will need a strategy for effectively embracing foreign cultures and traditions into its working practices, and for devising an efficient system for global logistics. Some businesses may be more suited to deal with such global issues than others.

The global strategy trade-off

A firm's drive to reduce costs and enhance profitability by embracing a global strategy is tempered by one critical consideration – the need to meet the demands of customers in foreign markets. To minimise costs, a firm may seek to standardise its product and its operations throughout the world. However, to meet foreign buyers' needs and respond to local market conditions, a firm may be required to differentiate both its product and its operations, such as marketing. In such cases, customisation will *add* to costs and generate a degree of duplication within the business. If a business is required to respond to local market conditions in many different markets, it might be faced with significantly higher costs. But if it fails to take into account the uniqueness of the market in which it wishes to sell, it may lose market share.

The trade-off between cost reduction and local responsiveness can be a key strategic consideration for a firm when selling or producing overseas. As a general rule we tend to find that cost pressures are greatest in those markets where price is the principal competitive weapon. Where product differentiation is high, and attributes such as quality or some other non-price factor predominates within the competitive process, local responsiveness will tend to shape business thinking. In other words, cost considerations will tend to be secondary.

KI 3
p 20

13.5 STRATEGY: EVALUATION AND IMPLEMENTATION

Evaluation

In deciding what strategy to pursue, global or otherwise, the business will need to evaluate the alternatives open to it. How feasible are they? Are they acceptable strategic goals given the business's mission and vision and other stakeholder demands? How will the strategy contribute to the business's competitive position?

If the choice of strategy is deliberate or prescriptive, i.e. planned in advance, then evaluation tools such as investment appraisal and cost–benefit analysis (CBA) might be used to help identify the best strategy (see section 19.3). Most strategies, however, tend to be emergent: in other words, they evolve over time as conditions change and as the success or otherwise of the firm's decisions becomes apparent. The result is that techniques such as investment appraisal have limited value, given the incomplete information available at the time an appraisal is conducted.

KI 8
p 38

Implementation

When a business considers implementing a strategy this often involves an assessment of three areas:

- resourcing;
- business culture and structure;
- managing change.

Resourcing

All businesses need to evaluate the resource implications of their strategic choices. What resources will be required? Where might such resources be drawn from within the organisation? What new resources will need to be brought into the organisation? From where will the finance for such resources come? Predictably, the more adventurous the strategy, the greater the impact on resources it is likely to have.

Business culture and structure

Similarly, the more radical the strategic shift, the greater the impact this is likely to have on a business's culture and structure. Is the organisation of the business flexible enough to adapt to the new strategic demands placed upon it? This might be particularly relevant if the strategic shift in the business is towards a greater focus on the global marketplace.

Managing change

Managing change can be both difficult and time consuming. With change often comes uncertainty for employees, especially if the changes are not understood or managers are not trusted. The more the uncertainty, the more difficult managing change becomes. In addition to barriers to change from employees, there may be organisational barriers. Entrenched power structures and control systems may be quite unsuitable for the new strategy. There may need to be fundamental organisational restructuring before the new strategy can be implemented.

In this chapter we have introduced you to the basic principles underpinning the determination, choice and evaluation of business strategy. This is a massive subject area, and we can but hope to cover a small fraction of the material

KI 1
p 7

here. However, from what we have covered you can see how the market environment in which a business operates has a significant impact on its strategic behaviour – and it is such behaviour that ultimately determines its success.

As we have seen, one key factor in determining a business's choice of strategy is its vision and mission – in other words, its aims. In traditional microeconomic theory the firm is assumed to aim for maximum profit. In the next chapter we turn to 'alternative theories of the firm'. These examine the effects of pursuing aims other than simple profit maximisation, especially on prices and output.

SUMMARY

1a Business strategy describes the way in which an organisation addresses its fundamental challenges over the medium to long term.

1b Strategy can be understood in many ways. It can be a plan, a ploy, a pattern of behaviour, a position in respect to others, a perspective, or any combination of them.

1c Strategic management differs from operational management (the day-to-day running of the business) as it focuses on issues which affect the whole business, usually over the long term.

1d Strategic management is composed of three components: strategic analysis (factors affecting business performance), strategic choice (the formulation and evaluation of alternative sources of action), and strategic implementation (how strategic choices are put into effect).

1e Different strategic issues will face different types of business, depending on whether they are large or small, manufacturing or service providers, domestic or multinational, private sector or public sector, and whether they are for-profit or not-for-profit organisations.

2a The Five Forces Model of competition identifies those factors that are most likely to influence the competitive environment of a business. The five forces are: the bargaining power of suppliers, the bargaining power of buyers, the threat of potential new entrants, the threat of substitutes, and the extent of competitive rivalry.

2b The weakness of the Five Forces Model is that not only is it a static view of the business environment, but also it does not see the business environment as a collaborative opportunity but merely as a competitive threat. Critics also argue that it underplays the impact of country culture and management skills on strategic choice and implementation.

2c A business value chain shapes its strategic capabilities. The value chain can be split into primary and support activities. Primary activities are those that directly create value, such as operations and marketing and sales. Support activities are those that underpin value creation in other areas, such as procurement and human resource management.

2d A business's vision and mission are shaped by a number of considerations: in whose interest the business is run, the influence of different stakeholder groups, the prevailing ethical expectations of society or the business owners, and the cultural context of the environment in which the organisation operates.

3a Strategic choices are determined either by the competitive nature of the environment within which the organisation operates, or by the internal resources controlled by the business. Strategic choice often involves a consideration of both internal and external factors.

3b Environment- or market-based strategies are of three types: cost-leadership strategy, where competitiveness is achieved by lower costs; differentiation strategy, where the business promotes the uniqueness of its product; focus strategy, where competitiveness is achieved by identifying market niches and tailoring products for different groups of consumers.

3c The resource-based view of strategy involves identifying core competencies as the key to a business's competitive advantage. A core competence will be valuable, rare, costly to imitate and non-substitutable.

4a A firm might go global in order to increase market size, increase profitability, spread risk and keep up with rivals.

4b When a firm does go global it must weigh up the potential benefits against ensuring it meets the local markets' needs. There is a trade-off between cost reduction and local responsiveness.

5a The impact of a chosen strategy is difficult to evaluate, as the strategy often evolves over time as conditions change.

5b When implementing a strategy, a business must consider the following: the resource implications of the strategic choice, how the strategic choice might fit (or not fit) into existing business culture and structure, and the difficulties in managing the change resulting from the new strategic direction of the business.

REVIEW QUESTIONS

1 What do you understand by the term 'business strategy'?

2 Explain why different types of business will see strategic management in different ways. Give examples.

3 Outline the Five Forces Model of competition. Identify both the strengths and weaknesses of analysing industry in this manner.

4 Distinguish between a business's primary and support activities in its value chain. Why might a business be inclined to outsource its support activities? Can you see any weaknesses in doing this?

5 Explain what is meant by a business's vision and mission. What implications might different missions have for its strategic decision making?

6 Distinguish between a market-based and a resource-based view of strategic choice.

7 What do you understand by the term 'core competence' when applied to a business?

8 How might going global affect a business's strategic decision making?

9 'Going global, thinking local.' Explain this phrase, and identify the potential conflicts for a business in behaving in this way.

10 Why is the choice of business strategy and its potential for success difficult to evaluate?

11 When implementing a business strategy, what issues does it raise for a firm?

Alternative theories of the firm

14.1 PROBLEMS WITH TRADITIONAL THEORY

The traditional profit-maximising theories of the firm have been criticised for being unrealistic. The criticisms are mainly of two sorts: (a) that firms wish to maximise profits, but for some reason or other are unable to do so; or (b) that firms have aims other than profit maximisation. Let us examine each in turn.

Difficulties in maximising profit

One criticism of traditional theory sometimes put forward is that firms do not use *MR* and *MC* concepts. This may be true, but firms could still arrive at maximum profit by trial and error adjustments of price, or by finding the output where *TR* and *TC* are furthest apart. Provided they end up maximising profits, they will be equating *MC* and *MR*, even if they do not know it!

In mature industries, where all firms have access to similar technology, an evolutionary process may ensure that the firms who survive are the ones closest to profit maximisation. Firms that are not maximising profits will be forced out of the market by their more profitable rivals. In this case, traditional models will still be useful in predicting price and output.

Lack of information

The main difficulty in trying to maximise profits is a lack of information.

Firms may well use accountants' cost concepts not based on opportunity cost (see section 9.1). If it is thereby impossible to measure true profit, a firm will not be able to maximise profit except by chance.

More importantly, firms are unlikely to know precisely (or even approximately) their demand curves and hence their *MR* curves. Even though (presumably) they will know how much they are selling at the moment, this only gives them one point on their demand curve and no point at all on their *MR* curve. In order to make even an informed guess about marginal revenue, they must have some idea of how responsive demand will be to a change in price. But how are they to estimate this price elasticity? Market research may help. But even this is frequently very unreliable.

The biggest problem in estimating the firm's demand curve is in estimating the actions and reactions of *other* firms and their effects. Collusion between oligopolists or price leadership would help, but there will still be a considerable area of uncertainty, especially if the firm faces competition from abroad or from other industries.

 Game theory may help a firm decide its price and output strategy: it may choose to sacrifice the chance of getting the absolute maximum profit (the high-risk, maximax option), and instead go for the safe strategy of getting probably at least reasonable profits (maximin). But even this assumes that it knows the consequences for its profits of each of the possible reactions of its rivals. In reality, it will not even have this information to any degree of certainty, because it simply will not be able to predict just how consumers will respond to each of its rivals' alternative reactions.

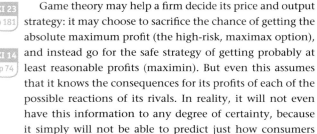

Pause for thought

What cost concepts are there other than those based on opportunity cost? Would the use of these concepts be likely to lead to an output greater or less than the profit-maximising one?

Time period

Finally, there is the problem in deciding the *time period* over which the firm should be seeking to maximise profits. Firms operate in a changing environment. Demand curves shift; supply curves shift. Some of these shifts occur as a result of factors outside the firm's control, such as changes in competitors' prices and products, or changes in technology. Some, however, change as a direct result of a firm's policies, such as an advertising campaign, the development of a new improved product, or the installation of new equipment. The firm is not, therefore, faced with static cost and revenue curves from which it can read off its profit-maximising price and output. Instead it is faced with a changing (and often highly unpredictable) set of curves. If it chooses a price and an output that maximise profits this year, it may as a result jeopardise profits in the future.

Take a simple example. The firm may be considering whether to invest in new expensive equipment. If it does, its costs will rise in the short run and thus short-run profits will fall. On the other hand, if the quality of the product thereby increases, demand is likely to increase over the longer run. Also variable costs are likely to decrease if the new equipment is more efficient. In other words, long-run

profit is likely to increase, but probably by a highly uncertain amount.

Given these extreme problems in deciding profit-maximising price and output, firms may adopt simple rules of thumb for pricing. (These are examined in Chapter 17.)

Alternative aims

An even more fundamental attack on the traditional theory of the firm is that firms do not even *aim* to maximise profits (even if they could).

The traditional theory of the firm assumes that it is the *owners* of the firm that make price and output decisions. It is reasonable to assume that owners *will* want to maximise profits: this much most of the critics of the traditional theory accept. The question is, however, whether the owners do in fact make the decisions.

In Chapter 3 we saw that in public limited companies there is generally a separation of ownership and control. The shareholders are the owners and presumably will want the firm to maximise profits so as to increase their dividends and the value of their shares. Shareholders elect directors. Directors in turn employ professional managers, who are often given considerable discretion in making decisions. But what are the objectives of managers? Will *they* want to maximise profits, or will they have some other aim?

Managers may be assumed to want to *maximise their own utility*. This may well involve pursuits that conflict with profit maximisation. They may, for example, pursue higher salaries, greater power or prestige, better working conditions, greater sales, etc. Different managers in the same firm may well pursue different aims.

Managers will still have to ensure that *sufficient* profits are made to keep shareholders happy, but that may be very different from *maximising* profits.

Alternative theories of the firm to those of profit maximisation, therefore, tend to assume that large firms are **profit satisficers**. That is, managers strive hard for a minimum target level of profit, but are less interested in profits above this level.

Such theories fall into two categories: first, those theories that assume that firms attempt to maximise some other aim, provided that sufficient profits are achieved (these are examined in section 14.2); and second, those theories that assume that firms pursue a number of potentially conflicting aims, of which sufficient profit is merely one (these theories are examined in section 14.3).

Definition

Profit satisficing Where decision-makers in a firm aim for a target level of profit rather than the absolute maximum level.

14.2 ALTERNATIVE MAXIMISING THEORIES

Long-run profit maximisation

The traditional theory of the firm is based on the assumption of *short-run* profit maximisation. Many actions of firms may be seen to conflict with this aim and yet could be consistent with the aim of **long-run profit maximisation**. For example, policies to increase the size of the firm or the firm's share of the market may involve heavy advertising or low prices to the detriment of short-run profits. But if this results in the firm becoming larger, with a larger share of the market, the resulting economic power may enable the firm to make larger profits in the long run.

At first sight, a theory of long-run profit maximisation would seem to be a realistic alternative to the traditional short-run profit-maximisation theory. In practice, however, the theory is not a very useful predictor of firms' behaviour and is very difficult to test.

A claim by managers that they were attempting to maximise long-run profits could be an excuse for virtually any policy. When challenged as to why the firm had, say, undertaken expensive research, or high-cost investment, or engaged in a damaging price war, the managers could reply, 'Ah, yes, but in the long run it will pay off.' This is very difficult to refute (until it is too late!).

Even if long-run profit maximisation *is* the prime aim, the means of achieving it are extremely complex. The firm will need a plan of action for prices, output, investment, etc., stretching from now into the future. But today's prices and marketing decisions affect tomorrow's demand. Therefore, future demand curves cannot be taken as given. Similarly, today's investment decisions will affect tomorrow's costs. Therefore, future cost curves cannot be taken as given. These shifts in demand and cost curves will be very difficult to estimate with any precision. Quite apart from this, the actions of competitors, suppliers, unions and so on are difficult to predict. Thus the picture of firms making precise calculations of long-run profit-maximising prices and outputs is a false one.

It may be useful, however, simply to observe that firms, when making current price, output and investment decisions, try to judge the approximate effect on new entrants, consumer demand, future costs, etc., and try to avoid decisions that would appear to conflict with long-run profits. Often this will simply involve avoiding making decisions (e.g. cutting price) that may stimulate an unfavourable reaction from rivals (e.g. rivals cutting their price).

Managerial utility maximisation

One of the most influential of the alternative theories of the firm, **managerial utility maximisation**, was developed by O.E. Williamson[1] in the 1960s. Williamson argued that, provided satisfactory levels of profit are achieved, managers often have the discretion to choose what policies to pursue. In other words, they are free to pursue their own interests. And what are the managers' interests? To maximise their own utility, argued Williamson.

Williamson identified a number of factors that affect a manager's utility. The four main ones were salary, job security, dominance (including status, power and prestige) and professional excellence.

Of these only salary is *directly* measurable. The rest have to be measured indirectly. One way of doing this is to examine managers' expenditure on various items, and in particular on *staff*, on *perks* (such as a company car and a plush office) and on *discretionary investment*. The greater the level of expenditure by managers on these items, the greater is likely to be their status, power, prestige, professional excellence and job security, and hence utility.

Having identified the factors that influence a manager's utility, Williamson developed several models in which managers seek to maximise their utility. He used these models to predict managerial behaviour under various conditions and argued that they performed better than traditional profit-maximising theory.

One important conclusion was that average costs are likely to be higher when managers have the discretion to pursue their own utility. For example, perks and unnecessarily high staffing levels add to costs. On the other hand, the resulting 'slack' allows managers to rein in these costs in times of low demand (see page 220). This enables them to maintain their profit levels. To support these claims he conducted a number of case studies. These did indeed show that staff and perks were cut during recessions and expanded during booms, and that new managers were frequently able to reduce staff levels without influencing the productivity of firms.

KI 6
p43

---

[1] *The Economics of Discretionary Behaviour* (Prentice Hall, 1964), p. 3.

Definitions

Long-run profit maximisation An alternative theory which assumes that managers aim to shift cost and revenue curves so as to maximise profits over some longer time period.

Managerial utility maximisation An alternative theory which assumes that managers are motivated by self-interest. They will adopt whatever policies are perceived to maximise their own utility.

BOX 14.1 | IN SEARCH OF LONG-RUN PROFITS

The video games war

Traditional economic theory argues that firms will seek to maximise their short-run profits, and therefore adopt a range of strategies to achieve this goal. There are, however, plenty of examples from the world of business to suggest that firms often take a longer-term perspective. One example is the long-running video games war between Sony, Nintendo and Microsoft.

The static games console market

Market share in the static console games market fluctuates between the three main consoles (see chart). In 2012, Sony sold 11.3 million units of its PlayStation 3 (43.4 per cent of the market); Microsoft was next, selling 9.8 million units of its Xbox 360 (37.7 per cent), followed by Nintendo, which sold 4.9 million Wiis (18.9 per cent).[1]

---

[1] '2013 Year on Year Sales and Market Share Update to January 12th', http://www.vgchartz.com/article/250686/2013-year-on-year-sales-and-market-share-update-to-january-12th/

New console developments, which occur every few years, have a dramatic impact on the shape of the industry. For example, Nintendo was the industry leader with its GameCube until the mid-1990s when Sony launched its PlayStation 1. Sony managed to increase its sales from 2000 when it launched PlayStation 2 but it suffered a set back in 2005 when, because of technical difficulties, it failed to deliver PlayStation 3 on schedule.

Microsoft launched Xbox 360 in November 2005 at prices between £209 and £279.99, depending on whether a basic or premium model was purchased, and it quickly became the market leader. However, when Nintendo launched the Wii in 2006 at a price of £179, targeting a much wider audience than the traditional male gamer aged 16 to 24, it was catapulted into first place in the market. In response, Microsoft slashed prices below that of Nintendo, but took a while to impact on market shares, with Nintendo remaining in first place through to 2010 (see chart).

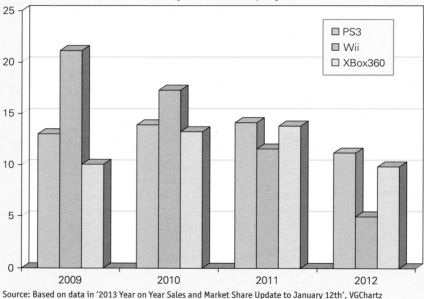

Number of consoles sold per year

Source: Based on data in '2013 Year on Year Sales and Market Share Update to January 12th', VGChartz

Sales revenue maximisation (short run)

Perhaps the most famous of all alternative theories of the firm is that developed by William Baumol in the late 1950s. This is the theory of *sales revenue maximisation*. Unlike the theories of long-run profit maximisation and

Definition

Sales revenue maximisation An alternative theory of the firm which assumes that managers aim to maximise the firm's short-run total revenue.

managerial utility maximisation, it is easy to identify the price and output that meet this aim – at least in the short run.

So why should managers want to maximise their firm's sales revenue? The answer is that the success of managers, and especially sales managers, may be judged according to the level of the firm's sales. Sales figures are an obvious barometer of the firm's health. Managers' salaries, power and prestige may depend directly on sales revenue. The firm's sales representatives may be paid commission on their sales. Thus sales revenue maximisation may be a more dominant aim in the firm than profit maximisation, particularly if it has a dominant sales department.

The market for mobile gaming hardware

The other strand of the gaming market is the handheld or mobile gaming sector, but Microsoft is notably absent from this segment thus far. Mobile gaming is dominated today by Nintendo, primarily because of its main product, the DS and, more recently, the 3DS, which between them had global sales of 17.4 million units in 2012 (73 percent of the handheld market). Sony successfully entered the market in 2004 with its own mobile gaming handset, the PSP, and later the PS Vita, the combined sales of which were 6.7 million units in 2012 (27 percent of the handheld market). Both companies have seen annual sales fall, however, as their markets become saturated, even with the launch of the new '8th generation' devices (the 3DS and PS Vita). In 2009, sales of DS and PSP were 29.7 million and 14.0 million respectively.

They are also facing new competitive pressure from firms such as Apple, which manufactures the iPhone and iPod Touch. These two devices have gaming capability because users can upload games software from the online 'App Store'. Some 100 days after Apple launched its online App Store in late 2008, there were 200 million downloads from the store. By June 2012 this figure had risen to a staggering 30 billion downloads. Seventeen of the most frequently downloaded paid-for Apps for iPhones were games, the comparable figure for iPads was 6.[2]

It is difficult to say what impact Apple or other potential entrants will have on the mobile gaming market – the primary function of the iPhone and the iPod Touch is not gaming – but clearly technologies such as phones, cameras, media players, office organisers and games machines can be converged on to one handheld device because that is what many consumers like.

The secret of success

The gaming market is a rich source of income and has grown rapidly in recent times. Mintel[3] reports that the number of Internet users in the UK over 16 years old who consider themselves regular gamers in 2011 was 30 per cent. The video game market in the UK is projected to be worth £1.3 billion in 2012, rising to over £1.5 billion by 2014. Higher income

[2] 'Apple Reveals New "All-Time Top Apps" Following 25 Billion Downloads', www.macstories.net, 3 March 2012.
[3] Video Games – UK, Mintel, November 2011.
[4] Ibid.

groups are the largest users of computer games and women are no longer peripheral users of games.

Static and mobile console sales are only successful if they play games and have other features that are attractive to consumers. Strong vertical relationships with gaming software companies are essential. Only technologically sophisticated games that appeal to particular audiences are chosen by console manufacturers. Console manufacturers reportedly earn a royalty of approximately $10 per sale from the licence they grant to the software developer, and so getting the right games is essential. This helps lower the substantial set-up costs in console development but, more importantly, good games generate greater software sales and create a network of loyal users.

Most games are now available to download, and sales through this medium have risen rapidly. Rockstar Games (producer of games such as Grand Theft Auto and Max Payne) reported that revenue from digitally distributed content rose 49 per cent in the year to June 2011.[4] By 2012, 40 per cent of online games revenue worldwide came from digital distribution and this is expected to rise to between 60 and 70 per cent by 2017. The convenience of downloading for gamers is likely to drive sales.

Another important feature of these best-selling static and mobile gaming machines is online gaming capability and global connectivity. Console owners can play a favourite game online against a stranger in another part of the world. Moreover, connection to the Internet has facilitated a move towards the use of consoles as 'digital entertainment centres', in which users can download content, including TV channels, films and music. These developments will continue as long as broadband Internet connectivity improves and remains fairly cheap to use.

All three companies – Nintendo, Sony and Microsoft – know how to be successful in the gaming industry: technological excellence and innovation, appropriate pricing strategies and visionary marketing. There are high costs, but high rewards if the business is a long-term venture.

1. What can you say about the price and income elasticity of demand for new technologies such as the Nintendo 3DS?
2. How does the maximisation of long-run profits conflict with the maximisation of short-run profits?
3. What factors might favour collusion in the video games market? What factors might make collusion unlikely?

Sales revenue will be maximised at the top of the *TR* curve at output Q_1 in Figure 14.1. Profits, by contrast, would be maximised at Q_2. Thus, for given total revenue and total cost curves, sales revenue maximisation will tend to lead to a higher output and a lower price than profit maximisation.

The firm will still have to make sufficient profits, however, to keep the shareholders happy. Thus firms can be seen to be operating with a profit constraint. They are *profit satisficers*.

The effect of this profit constraint is illustrated in Figure 14.2. The diagram shows a total profit curve. (This is found by simply taking the difference between *TR* and *TC* at each output.) Assume that the minimum acceptable profit is *Π* (whatever the output). Any output greater than

Q_3 will give a profit less than *Π*. Thus the sales revenue maximiser who is also a profit satisficer will produce Q_3 not Q_1. Note, however, that this output is still greater than the profit-maximising output Q_2.

If the firm could maximise sales revenue and still make more than the minimum acceptable profit, it would probably spend this surplus profit on advertising to increase revenue further. This would have the effect of shifting the *TR* curve upward and also the *TC* curve (since advertising costs money).

Sales revenue maximisation will tend to involve more advertising than profit maximisation. Ideally the profit-maximising firm will advertise up to the point where

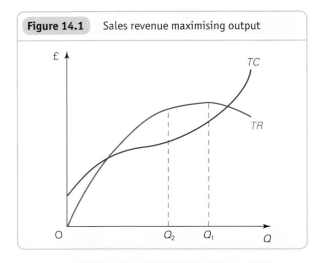

Figure 14.1 Sales revenue maximising output

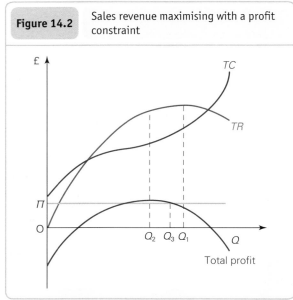

Figure 14.2 Sales revenue maximising with a profit constraint

the marginal revenue of advertising equals the marginal cost of advertising (assuming diminishing returns to advertising). The firm aiming to maximise sales revenue will go beyond this, since further advertising, although costing more than it earns the firm, will still add to total revenue. The firm will continue advertising until surplus profits above the minimum have been used up.

Growth maximisation

Rather than aiming to maximise *short-run* revenue, managers may take a longer-term perspective and aim for *growth maximisation* in the size of the firm. They may gain utility

Definition

Growth maximisation An alternative theory which assumes that managers seek to maximise the growth in sales revenue (or the capital value of the firm) over time.

directly from being part of a rapidly growing 'dynamic' organisation; promotion prospects are greater in an expanding organisation, since new posts tend to be created; large firms may pay higher salaries; managers may obtain greater power in a large firm.

Growth is probably best measured in terms of a growth in sales revenue, since sales revenue (or 'turnover') is the simplest way of measuring the size of a business. An alternative would be to measure the capital value of a firm, but this will depend on the ups and downs of the stock market and is thus a rather unreliable method.

If a firm is to maximise growth, it needs to be clear about the time period over which it is setting itself this objective. For example, maximum growth over the next two or three years might be obtained by running factories to absolute maximum capacity, cramming in as many machines and workers as possible, and backing this up with massive advertising campaigns and price cuts. Such policies, however, may not be sustainable in the longer run. The firm may simply not be able to finance them. A longer-term perspective (say, 5–10 years) may therefore require the firm to 'pace' itself, and perhaps to direct resources away from current production and sales into the development of new products that have a potentially high and growing long-term demand.

Equilibrium for a growth-maximising firm

What will a growth-maximising firm's price and output be? Unfortunately, there is no simple formula for predicting this.

In the short run, the firm may choose the profit-maximising price and output – so as to provide the greatest funds for investment. On the other hand, it may be prepared to sacrifice some short-term profits in order to mount an advertising campaign. It all depends on the strategy it considers most suitable to achieve growth.

In the long run, prediction is more difficult still. The policies that a firm adopts will depend crucially on the assessments of market opportunities made by managers. But this involves judgement, not fine calculation. Different managers will judge a situation differently.

One prediction can be made. Growth-maximising firms are likely to diversify into different products, especially as they approach the limits to expansion in existing markets. (Alternative growth strategies are considered in Chapter 15.)

Alternative maximising theories and the consumer

It is difficult to draw firm conclusions about how the behaviour of firms in these alternative maximising theories will affect the consumer's interest.

In the case of sales revenue maximisation, a higher output will be produced than under profit maximisation, but the consumer will not necessarily benefit from lower

KI 21
p 161

prices, since more will be spent on advertising – costs that will be passed on to the consumer.

In the case of growth and long-run profit maximisation, there are many possible policies that a firm could pursue. To the extent that a concern for the long run encourages firms to look to improved products, new products and new techniques, the consumer may benefit from such a concern. To the extent, however, that growth encourages a greater level of industrial concentration through merger, the consumer may lose from the resulting greater level of monopoly power.

As with the traditional theory of the firm, the degree of competition that a firm faces is a crucial factor in determining just how responsive it will be to the wishes of the consumer.

> **Pause for thought**
>
> *How will competition between growth-maximising firms benefit the consumer?*

14.3 MULTIPLE AIMS

Satisficing and the setting of targets

Firms may have more than one aim. For example, they may try to achieve increased sales revenue *and* increased profit. The problem with this is that, if two aims conflict, it will not be possible to maximise both of them. For example, sales revenue will probably be maximised at a different price and output from that at which profits are maximised. Where firms have two or more aims, a compromise may be for targets to be set for individual aims which are low enough to achieve simultaneously, and yet which are sufficient to satisfy the interested parties. This is known as 'satisficing' (as opposed to maximising) behaviour.

Such target setting is also likely when the maximum value of a particular aim is unknown. If, for example, the maximum achievable profit is unknown, the firm may well set a target for profit which it feels is both satisfactory and achievable.

Behavioural theories of the firm: the setting of targets

A major advance in alternative theories of the firm has been the development of **behavioural theories**.[2] Rather than setting up a model to show how various objectives could in theory be achieved, behavioural theories of the firm are based on observations of how firms *actually* behave.

KI 6
p 34

Large firms are often complex institutions with several departments (sales, production, design, purchasing, personnel, finance, etc.). Each department is likely to have its own specific set of aims and objectives, which may possibly come into conflict with those of other departments. These aims in turn will be constrained by the interests of shareholders, workers, customers and creditors (collectively known as **stakeholders**), who will need to be kept sufficiently happy.

Behavioural theories do not lay down rules of how to *achieve* these aims, but rather examine what these aims are, the motivations underlying them, the conflicts that can arise between aims, and how these conflicts are resolved.

In many firms, targets are set for production, sales, profit, stockholding, etc. If, in practice, target levels are not achieved, a 'search' procedure will be started to find what went wrong and how to rectify it. If the problem cannot be rectified, managers will probably adjust the target downwards. If, on the other hand, targets are easily achieved, managers may adjust them upwards. Thus the targets to which managers aspire depend to a large extent on the success in achieving *previous* targets. Targets are also influenced by expectations of demand and costs, by the achievements of competitors and by expectations of competitors' future behaviour. For example, if it is expected that the economy is likely to move into recession, sales and profit targets may be adjusted downwards.

If targets conflict, the conflict will be settled by a bargaining process between managers. The outcome of the bargaining, however, will depend on the power and ability of the individual managers concerned. Thus a similar set of conflicting targets may be resolved differently in different firms.

> **Definitions**
>
> **Behavioural theories of the firm** Theories that attempt to predict the actions of firms by studying the behaviour of various groups of people within the firm and their interactions under conditions of potentially conflicting interests.
>
> **Stakeholders (in a company)** People who are affected by a company's activities and/or performance (customers, employees, owners, creditors, people living in the neighbourhood, etc.). They may or may not be in a position to take decisions, or influence decision taking, in the firm.

---

[2] See in particular: R. M. Cyert and J. G. March, *A Behavioural Theory of the Firm* (Prentice Hall, 1963).

Behavioural theories of the firm: organisational slack

Since changing targets often involves search procedures and bargaining processes and is therefore time consuming, and since many managers prefer to avoid conflict, targets tend to be changed fairly infrequently. Business conditions, however, often change rapidly. To avoid the need to change targets, therefore, managers will tend to be fairly conservative in their aspirations. This leads to the phenomenon known as **organisational slack**.

When the firm does better than planned, it will allow slack to develop. This slack can then be taken up if the firm does worse than planned. For example, if the firm produces more than it planned, it will build up stocks of finished goods and draw on them if production subsequently falls. It would not, in the meantime, increase its sales target or reduce its production target. If it did, and production then fell below target, the production department might not be able to supply the sales department with its full requirement.

Thus keeping targets fairly low and allowing slack to develop allows all targets to be met with minimum conflict.

Organisational slack, however, adds to a firm's costs. If firms are operating in a competitive environment, they may be forced to cut slack in order to survive. In the 1970s, many Japanese firms succeeded in cutting slack by using **just-in-time** methods of production. These involve keeping stocks to a minimum and ensuring that inputs are delivered as required. Clearly, this requires that production is tightly

> ### Definitions
>
> **Organisational slack** When managers allow spare capacity to exist, thereby enabling them to respond more easily to changed circumstances.
>
> **Just-in-time methods** Where a firm purchases supplies and produces both components and finished products as they are required. This minimises stockholding and its associated costs.

BOX 14.2 STAKEHOLDER POWER

Who governs the firm?

The concept of the 'stakeholder economy' became fashionable in the late 1990s. Rather than the economy being governed by big business, and rather than businesses being governed in the interests of shareholders (many of whom are big institutions, such as insurance companies and pension funds), the economy should serve the interests of everyone. But what does this mean for the governance of firms?

The stakeholders of a firm include customers, employees (from senior managers to the lowest-paid workers), shareholders, suppliers, lenders and the local and national communities.

The supporters of a stakeholding economy argue that *all* these interest groups ought to have a say in the decisions of the firm. Trade unions or workers' councils ought to be included in decisions affecting the workforce, or indeed all company decisions. They could be represented on decision-making bodies and perhaps have seats on the board of directors. Alternatively, the workforce might be given the power to elect managers.

Banks or other institutions lending to firms ought to be included in investment decisions. In Germany, where banks finance a large proportion of investment, banks are represented on the boards of most large companies.

Local communities ought to have a say in any projects (such as new buildings or the discharge of effluent) that affect the local environment. Customers ought to have more say in the quality of products being produced, for example by being given legal protection against the production of shoddy or unsafe goods. Where interest groups cannot be directly represented in decision making, then companies ought to be regulated by the government in order to protect the interests of the various groups. For example, if farmers and other

suppliers to supermarkets are paid very low prices, then the purchasing behaviour of the supermarkets could be regulated by some government agency.

But is this vision of a stakeholder economy likely to become reality? Trends in the international economy suggest that the opposite might be occurring. The growth of multinational corporations, with their ability to move finance and production to wherever it is most profitable, has weakened the power of employees, local interest groups and even national governments.

Employees in one part of the multinational may have little in the way of common interests with employees in another. In fact, they may vie with each other, for example over which plant should be expanded or closed down. What is more, many firms are employing a larger and larger proportion of casual, part-time, temporary or agency workers. With these new 'flexible labour markets' such employees have far less say in the company than permanent members of staff: they are 'outsiders' to decision making within the firm (see section 18.7).

Also, the widespread introduction of share incentive schemes for managers (whereby managers are rewarded with shares) has increasingly made profits their driving goal. Finally, the policies of opening up markets and deregulation, policies that were adopted by many governments round the world up to the mid-1990s, have again weakened the power of many stakeholders.

 Are customers' interests best served by profit-maximising firms, answerable primarily to shareholders, or by firms where various stakeholder groups are represented in decision taking?

controlled and that suppliers are reliable. Many firms today have successfully cut their warehouse costs by using such methods. (These methods are examined in section 18.7.)

Multiple goals: some predictions of behaviour

Conservatism

Some firms may be wary of unnecessary change. Change is risky. They may prefer to stick with tried and tested practices. 'If it works, stick with it.' This could apply to pricing policies, marketing techniques, product design and range, internal organisation of the firm, etc.

If something does not work, however, managers will probably change it, but again they may be conservative and only try a cautious change: perhaps imitating successful competitors.

This safe, satisficing approach makes prediction of any given firm's behaviour relatively easy. You simply examine its past behaviour. Making generalisations about all such cautious firms, however, is more difficult. Different firms are likely to have established different rules of behaviour depending on their own particular experiences of their market.

Comparison with other firms

Managers may judge their success by comparing their firm's performance with that of rival firms. For example, growing market share may be seen as a more important indicator of 'success' than simple growth in sales. Similarly, they may compare their profits, their product design, their technology or their industrial relations with those of rivals. To many managers it is *relative* performance that matters, rather than absolute performance.

What predictions can be made if this is how managers behave? The answer is that it depends on the nature of competition in the industry. The more profitable, innova-tive and efficient are the competitors, the more profitable, innovative and efficient will managers try to make their particular firm.

The further ahead of their rivals that firms try to stay, the more likely it is that there will be a 'snowballing' effect: each firm trying to outdo the other.

> ### Pause for thought
>
> *Will this type of behaviour tend to lead to profit maximisation?*

Satisficing and the consumer's interest

Firms with multiple goals will be satisficers. The greater the number of goals of the different managers, the greater is the chance of conflict and the more likely it is that organisational slack will develop. Satisficing firms are therefore likely to be less responsive to changes in consumer demand and changes in costs than profit-maximising firms. They may thus be less efficient.

On the other hand, such firms may be less eager to exploit their economic power by charging high prices, or to use aggressive advertising, or to pay low wages.

The extent to which satisficing firms do act in the public interest will, as in the case of other types of firm, depend to a large extent on the amount and type of competition they face, and their attitudes towards this competition. Firms that compare their performance with that of their rivals are more likely to be responsive to consumer wishes than firms that prefer to stick to well-established practices. On the other hand, they may be more concerned to 'manipulate' consumer tastes than the more traditional firm.

SUMMARY

1a There are two major types of criticism of the traditional profit-maximising theory: (a) firms may not have the information to maximise profits; (b) they may not even want to maximise profits.

1b Lack of information on demand and costs and on the actions and reactions of rivals, and a lack of use of opportunity cost concepts, may mean that firms adopt simple 'rules of thumb' for pricing.

1c In large companies there is likely to be a divorce between ownership and control. The shareholders (the owners) may want maximum profits, but it is the managers who make the decisions, and managers are likely to aim to maximise their own utility rather than that of the shareholders. This leads to profit 'satisficing'. This is where managers aim to achieve sufficient profits to keep shareholders happy, but this is a secondary aim to one or more alternative aims.

1d Some alternative theories assume that there is a single alternative aim that firms seek to maximise. Others assume that managers have a series of (possibly conflicting) aims.

2a Rather than seeking to maximise short-run profits, a firm may take a longer-term perspective. It is very difficult, however, to predict the behaviour of a long-run profit-maximising firm, since (a) different managers are likely to make different judgements about how to achieve maximum profits, and (b) demand and cost curves may shift unpredictably both in response to the firm's own policies and as a result of external factors.

2b Managers may seek to maximise their own utility, which, in turn, will depend on factors such as salary, job security, power within the organisation and the achievement of professional excellence. Given, however, that managerial utility depends on a range of variables,

▶

2c Managers may gain utility from maximising sales revenue. However, they will still have to ensure that a satisfactory level of profit is achieved. The output of a firm which seeks to maximise sales revenue will be higher than that for a profit-maximising firm. Its level of advertising will also tend to be higher. Whether price will be higher or lower depends on the relative effects on demand and the cost of the additional advertising.

2d Many managers aim for maximum growth of their organisation, believing that this will help their salaries, power, prestige, etc.

2e As with long-run profit-maximising theories, it is difficult to predict the price and output strategies of a growth-maximising firm. Much depends on the judgements of particular managers about growth opportunities.

3a In large firms, decisions are taken by, or influenced by, a number of different people, including various managers, shareholders, workers, customers, suppliers and creditors. If these different people have different aims, then a conflict between them is likely to arise. A firm cannot maximise more than one of these conflicting

(it is difficult to use the theory to make general predictions of firms' behaviour.)

aims. The alternative is to seek to achieve a satisfactory target level of a number of aims.

3b Behavioural theories of the firm examine how managers and other interest groups actually behave, rather than merely identifying various equilibrium positions for output, price, investment, etc.

3c If targets were easily achieved last year, they are likely to be made more ambitious next year. If they were not achieved, a search procedure will be conducted to identify how to rectify the problem. This may mean adjusting targets downwards, in which case there will be some form of bargaining process between managers.

3d Life is made easier for managers if conflict can be avoided. This will be possible if slack is allowed to develop in various parts of the firm. If targets are not being met, the slack can then be taken up without requiring adjustments in other targets.

3e Satisficing firms may be less innovative, less aggressive and less willing to initiate change. If they do change, it is more likely to be in response to changes made by their competitors. Managers may judge their performance by comparing it with that of rivals.

3f Satisficing firms may be less aggressive in exploiting a position of market power. On the other hand, they may suffer from greater inefficiency.

REVIEW QUESTIONS

1 In the traditional theory of the firm, decision makers are often assumed to have perfect knowledge and to be able to act, therefore, with complete certainty. It is now widely accepted that in practice firms will be certain about very few things. Of the following: (a) production costs; (b) demand; (c) elasticity; (d) supply; (e) consumer tastes; (f) technology; (g) government policy, which might they be certain of? Which might they be uncertain of?

2 Make a list of six aims that a manager of a high street department store might have. Identify some conflicts that might arise between these aims.

3 When are increased profits in a manager's personal interest?

4 Draw a diagram with *MC* and *MR* curves. Mark the output (a) at which profits are maximised; (b) at which sales revenue is maximised.

5 Since advertising increases a firm's costs, will prices necessarily be lower with sales revenue maximisation than with profit maximisation?

6 We have seen that a firm aiming to maximise sales revenue will tend to produce more than a profit-maximising firm. This conclusion certainly applies under monopoly and oligopoly. Will it also apply under (a) perfect competition and (b) monopolistic competition, where in both cases there is freedom of entry?

7 A frequent complaint of junior and some senior managers is that they are frequently faced with new targets from above, and that this makes their life difficult. If their complaint is true, does this conflict with the hypothesis that managers will try to build in slack?

8 What evidence about firms' behaviour could be used to refute the argument that firms will tend to build in organisational slack and as a result be inherently conservative?

15 Chapter

Growth strategy

Business issues covered in this chapter

- Why do many businesses want to grow larger?
- What is the relationship between business growth and profitability?
- What constraints on its growth is a business likely to face?
- What alternative growth strategies can a business pursue?
- Why will some firms pursue a growth strategy of internal expansion whereas others will pursue a strategy of merging with or taking over other firms?
- As far as internal expansion is concerned, why will some firms expand through a process of vertical integration whereas others will prefer to diversify?
- Under what circumstances might a business want to form a strategic alliance with other firms?

Whether businesses wish to grow or not, many are forced to. The dynamic competitive process of the market drives producers on to expand in order to remain in the marketplace. If a business fails to grow, this may benefit its more aggressive rivals. They may secure a greater share of the market, leaving the first firm with reduced profits. Thus business growth is often vital if a firm is to survive.

The goal of business growth is closely linked to the key objectives of managers. Managerial status, prestige, promotion and salary might be more directly related to such a goal rather than to that of profit maximisation (as mentioned in Chapter 14). Business growth might also be essential if the business is successfully to manage change and deal with many of the inherent uncertainties of the business environment.

In this chapter we shall consider the various growth strategies open to firms and assess their respective advantages and disadvantages. First, however, we shall need to look at the relationship between a firm's growth and its profitability, and also at those factors which are likely to constrain the growth of the business.

15.1 GROWTH AND PROFITABILITY

In using traditional theories of the firm, economists often assume that there is a limit to the expansion of the firm: that there is a level of output beyond which profits will start to fall. The justification for this view can be found on both the supply side and the demand side.

On the supply side, it is assumed that if a firm grows beyond a certain size, it will experience rising long-run average costs. In other words, the long-run average cost curve is assumed to be U-shaped, possibly with a horizontal section at the bottom (see pages 143–4). This argument is often based on the assumption that it is *managerial* diseconomies of scale which start driving costs up once a firm has expanded beyond a certain point: there are no more plant economies to be achieved (the firm has passed its *minimum efficient scale (MES)* – see Box 9.4); instead, the firm is faced with a more complex form of organisation, with longer lines of management, more difficult labour relations and a greater possibility of lack of effort going unnoticed.

On the demand side it is assumed that the firm faces a downward-sloping demand curve (and hence marginal revenue curve) for its product. Although this demand curve can be shifted by advertising and other forms of product promotion, finite demand naturally places a constraint on the expansion of the firm.

These two assumptions can be challenged, however. On the supply side, with a multidivisional form of organisation and systems in place for monitoring performance, it is quite possible to avoid diseconomies of scale.

As far as demand is concerned, although the demand (or at least its rate of growth) for any one product may be limited, the firm could diversify into new markets.

It is thus incorrect to say that there is a limit to the size of a business. An individual business may be able to go on expanding its capacity or diversifying its interests indefinitely. There does, however, exist an upper limit on the firm's *rate* of growth – the *speed* at which it can expand its capacity or diversify. The reason behind this constraint is that growth is determined by the profitability of the business. The growth rate/profitability relationship can operate in two ways:

■ *Growth depends upon profitability*. The more profitable the firm, the more likely it is to be able to raise finance for investment.

■ *Growth affects profitability*. In the short run, growth above a certain rate may *reduce* profitability. Some of the finance for the investment necessary to achieve growth may have to come from the firm's sales revenue. A firm wishing to expand its operations in an existing market will require greater advertising and marketing; and a firm seeking to diversify may have to spend considerable sums on market research and employing managers with specialist knowledge and skills. In both cases, investment is likely to be needed in new plant and machinery. In other words, the firm may have to sacrifice some of its short-run profits for the long-run gains that greater growth might yield.

But what about long-run profits? Will growth increase or decrease these? The answer depends on the nature of the growth. If growth leads to expansion into new markets in which demand is growing, or to increased market power, or to increased economies of scale, then growth may well increase long-run profits – not only total profits, but the rate of profit on capital, or the ratio of profits to revenue. If, however, growth leads to diseconomies of scale, or to investment in risky projects, then growth may well be at the expense of long-run profitability.

To summarise: greater profitability may lead to higher growth, but higher growth, at least in the short run, may be at the expense of profits.

15.2 CONSTRAINTS ON GROWTH

However much a firm may want to grow, it might simply not be possible. There are several factors that can restrict the ability of a business to expand.

Pause for thought

Before you read on, what constraints on its growth do you feel a business might experience?

Financial conditions. Financial conditions determine the ability of a firm to fund its growth. Growth can be financed in three distinct ways: from internal funds, from borrowing or from the issue of new shares.

The largest source of finance for investment in the UK is *internal funds* (i.e. ploughed-back profit). The principal limitation in achieving growth via this means is that such funds are linked to business profitability, and this in turn is subject to the cyclical nature of economic activity – to the booms and slumps that the economy experiences. Profitability tends to fall in a recession along with the level of sales. In such times it is often difficult for a firm to afford new investment.

The *borrowing* of finance to fund expansion may be constrained by a wide range of factors, from the availability of finance in the banking sector to the credit-worthiness of the business.

Definitions

Minimum efficient scale (MES) The size of the individual factory or of the whole firm, beyond which no significant additional economies of scale can be gained. For an individual factory the MES is known as the *minimum efficient plant size* (MEPS).

Internal funds Funds used for business expansion that come from ploughed-back profit.

The *issuing of new shares* to fund growth depends not only on confidence within the stock market in general, but on the stock market's assessment of the potential performance of the individual firm in particular. It should be noted that finance from this source is not open to all firms. For most small and medium-sized enterprises (i.e. those not listed on the Stock Exchange), raising finance through issuing new shares must be done privately, and normally this source of finance is very limited and hence difficult to access.

(We will examine the financing of investment in more detail in sections 19.4 and 19.5.)

Shareholder confidence. Whichever way growth is financed – internal funds, borrowing or new share issues – the likely outcome in the short run is a reduction in the firm's share dividend. If the firm *retains* too much *profit*, there will be less to pay out in dividends. Similarly, if the firm *borrows* too much, the interest payments that it incurs are likely to make it difficult to maintain the level of dividends to shareholders. Finally, if it attempts to raise capital by a *new issue of shares*, the distributed profits will have to be divided between a larger number of shares.

Whichever way it finances investment, therefore, the more it invests, the more the dividends on shares in the short run will probably fall. Unless shareholders are confident that *long*-run profits and hence dividends will rise again, thus causing the share price to remain high in the long run, they may well sell their shares. This will cause share prices to fall. If they fall too far, the firm runs the risk of being taken over and certain managers risk losing their jobs.

This risk of takeover gives rise to a concept referred to as the **takeover constraint**. The takeover constraint requires that the growth-maximising firm needs to distribute sufficient profits to avoid being taken over. Hence the rate of business growth is influenced not only by market opportunities but also by shareholder demands and expectations and the fear of takeover.

The converse of this situation is also true. If a business fails to grow fast enough, it may be that a potential buyer sees the firm as a valuable acquisition, whose resources might be put to more profitable use over the longer term. Hence businesses must avoid being overcautious and paying high share dividends, but, as a result, failing to invest and failing to exploit their true potential.

The likelihood of takeover depends in large part on the stock market's assessment of the firm's potential: how is the firm's investment strategy perceived to affect its future performance and profitability? The views of the stock market are reflected in the **valuation ratio** of the firm. This is the ratio of the stock market value of the firm's shares (the number of issued shares times the current share price) to the book value of the firm's assets. This is sometimes referred to as the **price to book ratio**. A low ratio means that the real assets of the business are effectively undervalued: that they can be purchased at a low market price. The business is thus likely to be more attractive to potential bidders. Conversely, firms with a high valuation ratio are seen as overvalued and are unlikely to be the target of takeover bids.

In the long run, a rapidly growing firm may find its profits increasing, especially if it can achieve economies of scale and a bigger share of the market. These profits can then be used to finance further growth. The firm will still not have unlimited finance, however, and therefore will still be faced by the takeover constraint if it attempts to grow too rapidly.

Demand conditions. Our analysis of business growth has shown that finance for growth is largely dependent upon the business's profitability. The more profit it makes, the more it can draw on internal funds; the more likely financial institutions will be to lend; and the more readily will new share issues be purchased by the market. The profitability of a business is in turn dependent upon market demand and demand growth. If the firm is operating in an expanding market, profits are likely to grow and finance will be relatively easy to obtain.

If, on the other hand, the firm's existing market is not expanding, it will find that profits and sales are unlikely to rise unless it diversifies into related or non-related markets. One means of overcoming this demand constraint is to expand overseas, either by attempting to increase export sales or by locating new production facilities in foreign markets.

Managerial conditions. The growth of a firm is usually a planned process, and as such must be managed. But the management team might lack entrepreneurial vision, or various organisational skills.

Equally, as with other resources within the business, the management team might grow, or alternatively its composition might change in order to reflect the new needs of the growing business. However, new managers take time to be incorporated into, and become part of, an effective management team. They must undergo a period of training and become integrated into their new firm and its culture. It takes time to integrate into a team of managers already accustomed to working together. The rate of growth of business is thus constrained by this process of managerial expansion.

In the sections below we will explore the alternative growth strategies open to businesses and the various advantages and limitations that such strategies present.

Definitions

Takeover constraint The effect that the fear of being taken over has on a firm's willingness to undertake projects that reduce distributed profits.

Valuation ratio or **price to book ratio** The ratio of stock market value to book value. The stock market value is an assessment of the firm's past and anticipated future performance. The book value is a calculation of the current value of the firm's assets.

15.3 ALTERNATIVE GROWTH STRATEGIES

In pursuit of growth, a firm will seek to increase its markets: whether at home or internationally. In either case the firm will need to increase its capacity. This may be achieved by internal or external expansion.

Internal expansion. This is where a business looks to expand its productive capacity by adding to existing plant or by building new plant. There are three main ways of doing this:

- The firm can expand or ***differentiate its product*** within existing markets, by, for example, updating or restyling its product, or improving its technical characteristics.
- Alternatively, the business might seek to expand via ***vertical integration***. This involves the firm expanding within the same product market, but at a different stage of production. For example, a car manufacturer might wish to produce its own components. This is known as 'backward' vertical integration (sometimes called 'upstream' integration). Alternatively, it might decide to distribute and sell its own car models. This is described as 'forward' (or 'downstream') vertical integration.
- As a third option, the business might seek to expand outside of its current product range, and move into new markets. This is known as a process of ***diversification***.

External expansion. This is where the firm engages with another in order to expand its activities. It may do this in one of two ways:

- It can join with another firm to form a single legal identity either by merger or by acquisition (takeover).
- Alternatively, it may form a ***strategic alliance*** with one or more firms. Here firms retain their separate identities.

The term 'strategic alliance' is used to cover a wide range of alternative collaborative arrangements. A strategic alliance might involve a joint venture between one or more firms to complete a particular project or to produce a particular product. It might also involve firms making an informal or a contractual agreement to supply or distribute goods. A key characteristic of a strategic alliance is that the parties involved retain their own legal identity outside of the alliance.

As with internal expansion, external expansion, whether by merger or alliance, can be vertical or horizontal, or involve diversification. In the case of mergers, we use the terms 'horizontal merger', 'vertical merger' and 'conglomerate merger'.

Figure 15.1 outlines the main routes to a firm's growth and the various stages at which it can take place. These will be considered in the following sections.

A further dimension of business growth that we should note at this point is that all of the above-mentioned growth paths can be achieved by the business looking beyond its national markets. In other words, the business might decide to become multinational and invest in expansion overseas. This raises a further set of advantages, issues and problems that a business might face. (These will be discussed in Chapter 23 when we consider multinational business.)

We have already considered business expansion through product differentiation (see Chapter 8). In this chapter, therefore, we will focus on the other possibilities facing the firm: internal expansion via vertical integration or diversification, and external expansion via merger or takeover (whether horizontal, vertical or conglomerate). We will also investigate the increasing tendency for business to enter into strategic alliances with other businesses as an alternative to all of the above.

Definitions

Internal expansion Where a business increases its productive capacity by adding to existing plant or by building new plant.

Product differentiation In the context of growth strategies, this is where a business upgrades existing products or services so as to make them different from those of rival firms.

Vertical integration A business growth strategy that involves expanding within an existing market, but at a different stage of production. Vertical integration can be 'forward', such as moving into distribution or retail, or 'backward', such as expanding into extracting raw materials or producing components.

Diversification A business growth strategy in which a business expands into new markets outside of its current interests.

External expansion Where business growth is achieved by merger, takeover, joint venture or an agreement with one or more other firms.

Strategic alliance Where two firms work together, formally or informally, to achieve a mutually desirable goal.

Figure 15.1 Alternative growth strategy

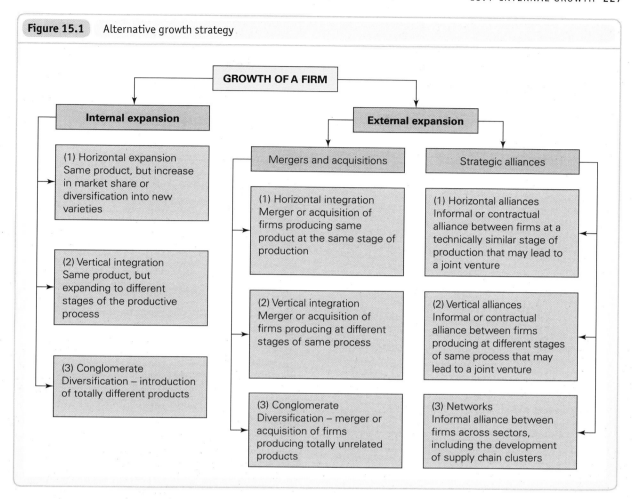

15.4 INTERNAL GROWTH

Firms can extend their product range in a number of ways and for a number of reasons. One method is that of horizontal expansion. This involves the firm producing multiple products within a similar and related activity for which there may be economies of scope (see page 137). Likewise there may be gains for the firm in providing different varieties of the product as discussed in Chapter 8. Given our extensive discussions on this method of internal growth therefore, we concentrate in the next two sections on vertical integration and conglomerate diversification.

Growth through vertical integration

We can identify a number of specific reasons why a business might wish to expand via vertical integration. (These reasons also apply to external expansion by merger or acquisition.)

Greater efficiency. When vertical integration results in a fall in a business's long-run average costs, it is effectively experiencing various economies of scale. We can identify four

categories under which vertical integration might lead to cost savings.

■ *Production economies*. These occur when a business, through integration, lowers its costs by performing *complementary* stages of production within a single business unit. The classic example of this is the steel manufacturer combining the furnacing and milling stages of production, saving the costs that would have been required to reheat the iron had such operations been undertaken by independent businesses. Clearly, for most firms, performing more than one stage on a single site is likely to reduce transport costs, as semi-finished products no longer have to be moved from one plant to another.

■ *Coordination economies*. Such economies arise from the internal structure of the business and its ability to transfer intermediate products between its various divisions. The business is able to avoid purchasing and selling expenses, including those related to the marketing and

KI 22
p 165

advertising of the product(s). If a firm can accurately forecast its intermediate product demand it may be able to reduce costs by holding lower stocks of intermediate products.

■ *Managerial economies.* Even though each production stage or division might have its own management or administrative team, economies can be gained from having a single source of supervision.

■ *Financial economies.* A vertically integrated business may gain various financial economies. Given the link between vertical integration and business size, such companies may be more able to negotiate favourable deals from key suppliers and secure lower borrowing rates of interest from the financial markets.

(For a more detailed analysis of economies of scale, you should refer back to Chapter 9.)

Reduced uncertainty. A business that is not vertically integrated may find itself subject to various uncertainties in the marketplace. Examples include: uncertainty over future price movements, supply reliability or access to markets.

Backward vertical integration will enable the business to control its supply chain. Without such integration the firm may feel very vulnerable, especially if there are only a few suppliers within the market. In such cases the suppliers would be able to exert considerable control over price. Alternatively, suppliers may be unreliable.

Forward vertical integration creates greater certainty in so far as it gives the business guaranteed access to distribution and retailing on its own terms. As with supply, forward markets might be dominated by large monopsonists (monopoly buyers) which are able not only to dictate price, but also to threaten market foreclosure (being shut out from a market). Forward vertical integration can remove the possibility of such events occurring.

Innovation. Having a more integrated supply chain may lead to more innovation and higher rates of technical change. Enclosing multiple stages of production within the same business should improve communication between component producers and consumers. Dialogue between component designers, manufacturers and users leads to increased possibilities for the development of productivity-improving innovations.

Monopoly power. Forward or backward vertical integration may allow the business to acquire a greater monopoly/monopsony position in the market. Depending upon the type of vertical integration, the business might be able to set prices both for final products and for factor inputs.

Barriers to entry. Vertical integration may give the firm greater power in the market by enabling it to erect entry barriers to potential competitors. For example, a firm that undertakes backward vertical integration and acquires a key input resource can effectively close the market to potential new entrants, either by simply refusing to supply a competitor, or by charging a very high price for the factor such that new firms face an absolute cost disadvantage.

A further barrier to entry might arise from an increase in the minimum efficient size of the business. As the firm becomes more integrated, it is likely to experience greater economies of scale (i.e. long-run average costs that go on falling below their previous minimum level). New entrants are then forced to come into the market at the level of integration that existing firms are operating under. Failure to do so will mean that new entrants will be operating at an instant cost disadvantage, and hence will be less competitive.

Problems with vertical integration

The major problem with vertical integration as a form of expansion is that the security it gives the business may reduce its ability to respond to changing market demands. A business that integrates, either backward or forward, ties itself to particular supply sources or particular retail outlets. If, by contrast, it were free to choose between suppliers, inputs might be obtained at a lower price than the firm could achieve by supplying itself. Equally, the ability to shift between retail outlets would allow the firm to locate in the best market positions. This may not be possible if it is tied to its own retail network.

As with all business strategy, one course of action may well preclude the pursuit of an alternative. The decision of the business to expand its operations via vertical integration means that resources will be diverted to this goal. The potential advantages from other growth strategies, such as the spreading of risk through diversification, are lost. This is not a problem of vertical integration as such, but it represents the opportunity costs of selecting this strategy to the *exclusion* of others.

Tapered vertical integration

How can a firm gain the benefits of vertical integration but avoid the costs? One alternative means of expansion is **tapered vertical integration**. This is where a business begins producing some of an input itself, while still buying some from another firm (often through subcontracting). This growth strategy is different from a situation where you are relying totally on subcontractors to provide supply (which we will explore in section 15.7). For example, Coca-Cola and Pepsi are large vertically integrated enterprises. They have, as part of their operations, wholly-owned bottling subsidiaries. However, in certain markets they subcontract to independent bottlers both to produce and to market their product.

> ### Definition
>
> **Tapered vertical integration** Where a firm is partially integrated with an earlier stage of production: where it produces *some* of an input itself and buys some from another firm.

The advantages of both making and buying an input are:

- The firm, by making an input or providing a service in-house, will have information concerning the costs and profitability of such an operation. Such information helps in the negotiation of contracts with independent producers. In addition, the firm will be able to use the threat of producing more itself to ensure that independent suppliers do not exploit their supply position, which they might be able to do if they held a monopolistic position within the supply chain. The firm is not totally at the mercy of an independent third party over which it has no control.
- The firm does not require the same level of capital outlay that would be required if it were to rely solely on an input or service produced by itself. As such it is able to externalise some of the costs and risks of its business operations.

The major drawback with this growth strategy is that shared production might fail to generate economies of scale, and is hence less efficient than might otherwise be the case. In other words, if Coca-Cola bottled all its own cola, then it might achieve significantly greater economies of scale than by sharing bottling with other firms. None might be large enough to achieve the efficiency gains that a single production site might generate.

Other significant costs with subcontracting are largely borne by the firm doing the subcontracted work, not by the contractor. Many small and medium-sized enterprises (SMEs), which might see doing subcontracted work for a large firm as a means of expanding their business and hence of growing themselves, find that the relationship between them and the large firm is often a highly unequal one. SMEs find that they not only bear some of the large firm's risk, but are easily expendable. Such vulnerability intensifies, the greater the proportion of the SME's production that is done for a particular customer. When a high level of reliance occurs, the SME finds that its business is, in essence, vertically integrated with its customer, but without the benefits that such a position should confer.

Growth through diversification

Diversification is the process whereby a firm shifts from being a single-product to a multiproduct producer. Such products need not cover similar activities. We can in fact identify four directions in which diversification might be undertaken:

- using the existing technological base and market area;
- using the existing technological base and new market area;

- using a new technological base and existing market area;
- using a new technological base and new market area.

Categorising the strategies in this way would suggest that the direction of diversification is largely dependent upon both the nature of technology and the market opportunities open to the firm. But the ability to capitalise on these features depends on the experience, skills and market knowledge of the managers of the business. In general, diversification is likely to occur in areas where the business can use and adapt existing technology and knowledge to its advantage.

A good example of a highly diversified company is Virgin. The brand began as the name of a small record shop in London. It now embraces an airline, trains, banking and finance, gift 'experiences', holidays, hotels, soft drinks, mobile phones, a digital television service, Internet service provision, radio, online books, an online wine store, cosmetics, health clubs, balloon rides and even, with its Virgin Galactic brand, space travel!

Why diversification?

There are three principal factors which might encourage a business to diversify.

- *Stability*. So long as a business produces a single product in a single market, it is vulnerable to changes in that market's conditions. If a farmer produces nothing but potatoes, and the potato harvest fails, the farmer is ruined. If however, the farmer produces a whole range of vegetable products, or even diversifies into livestock, then he or she is less subject to the forces of nature and the unpredictability of the market. Diversification therefore enables the business to *spread risk*.
- *Maintaining profitability*. Businesses might also be encouraged to diversify if they wish to protect existing profit levels. It may be that the market in which a business is currently located is saturated and that current profitability is perceived to be at a maximum. Alternatively, the business might be in a market where demand is stagnant or declining. In such cases the business is likely to see a greater return on its investment by diversifying into new product ranges located in dynamic expanding markets.
- *Growth*. If the current market is saturated, stagnant or in decline, diversification might be the only avenue open to the business if it wishes to maintain a high growth performance. In other words, it is not only the level of profits that may be limited in the current market, but also the growth of sales.

15.5 EXTERNAL GROWTH THROUGH MERGER

A *merger* is a situation in which, as a result of mutual agreement, two firms decide to bring together their business operations. A merger is distinct from a **takeover** in so far as a takeover involves one firm bidding for another's shares (often against the will of the directors of the target firm). One firm thereby acquires another.

The distinction between merger and takeover is an important one. For example, an important difference is that, in order to acquire a firm, a business will require finance, whereas a merger might simply involve two firms swapping their existing shares for shares in the newly created merged company. A further difference might concern managerial relations between the two businesses. A merger implies that managers, through negotiation, have reached an agreement acceptable to both sides, whereas a takeover involves one group of managers, working in opposition to another group, looking to fend off the aggressor. The acquired firm usually finds its management team dismissed following such action!

In order to avoid confusion at this stage, we will use the term 'merger' to refer to *both* mergers ('mutual agreements') and takeovers ('acquisitions'), although where necessary we will draw a distinction between the two. Before proceeding we need to give some consideration to the types of merger and acquisition. We distinguished three types in Figure 15.1.

Definitions

Merger The outcome of a mutual agreement made by two firms to combine their business activities.

Takeover Where one business acquires another. A takeover may not necessarily involve mutual agreement between the two parties. In such cases, the takeover might be viewed as 'hostile'.

BOX 15.1 GLOBAL MERGER ACTIVITY

An international perspective

What have been the trends, patterns and driving factors in mergers and acquisitions (M&A) around the world in recent years? An overview of cross-border M&A is given in Chart (a).

The 1990s saw a rapid growth in M&A as the world economy boomed. Then with a slowing down in economic growth after 2000, M&A activity declined, both in value and in the number of deals, but from 2004 to 2007 they rose back dramatically with the rapid growth in the world economy. But then in 2008, there was a global banking crisis followed by the credit crunch and recession. M&A activity fell substantially. From 2009 M&A activity started to rise again as firms restructured following the crisis (see Chart (a)). Many large firms attempted to acquire weakened competitors or purchase undervalued complementary businesses.

The 1990s

The early years of the 1990s saw relatively low M&A activity as the world was in recession, but as world economic growth picked up, so worldwide M&A activity increased. Economic growth was particularly rapid in the USA, which became the major target for acquisitions.

There was also an acceleration in the process of 'globalisation'. With the dismantling of trade barriers around the world and increasing financial deregulation, so international competition increased. Companies felt the need to become bigger in order to compete more effectively.

In Europe, M&A activity was boosted by the development of the single European market, which came into being in January 1993. Companies took advantage of the abolition of trade barriers in the EU, which made it easier for them to operate on an EU-wide basis. As 1999 approached, and with

it the arrival of the euro, so European merger activity reached fever pitch, stimulated also by the strong economic growth experienced throughout the EU.

By 2000, the number of annual worldwide M&As was some three times the level of 1990. Around this time there were some very large mergers indeed. These included a $67 billion marriage of pharmaceutical companies Zeneca of the UK and Astra of Sweden in 1998, a $183 billion takeover of telecoms giant Mannesmann of Germany by Vodafone of the UK in 1999 and a $40.3 billion takeover of Orange of the UK by France Telecom in 2000.

Other sectors in which merger activity was rife included financial services and the privatised utilities sector. In the UK, in particular, most of the privatised water and electricity companies were taken over, with buyers attracted by the sector's monopoly profits. French and US buyers were prominent.

The 2000s

Then, with a worldwide economic slowdown after 2000, there was a fall in both the number and value of mergers throughout most of the world. However, both increased again from 2003 onwards.

In 2008 and 2009, as recession took hold, the number and value of cross-border M&As fell quite dramatically. Recession is a difficult time for deal making and the number of withdrawn mergers – that is, where two firms agree in principle to merge but later pull out of a deal – increased. M&As in 2009 totalled $2059 billion, which was down 29 per cent from 2008 and down 51 per cent from the record high in 2007. Chart (a) shows an even bigger percentage fall in

- A *horizontal merger* is where two firms at the same stage of production within an industry merge. An example of this would be the merger in 2008 of Lloyds-TSB and HBOS, two major British banks.
- A *vertical merger* is where businesses at different stages of production within the same industry merge. As such we might identify backward and forward vertical mergers for any given firm involved in the merger. One example of this is where TomTom, the Dutch producer of portable navigation devices (e.g. satnavs in cars), bought TeleAtlas, the Dutch provider of navigable maps, in 2008.
- A *conglomerate merger* is where firms in totally unrelated industries merge. Many of the big multinational corporations operate in a number of sectors and regularly buy other firms. For example, in 2004 the US conglomerate group General Electric purchased Vivendi, the conglomerate multimedia firm which owned the US media and entertainment firms NBC and Universal.

Why merge?

Why do firms want to merge with or take over others? Is it purely that they want to grow: are mergers simply evidence of the hypothesis that firms are growth maximisers? Or are there other motives that influence the predatory drive?

Merger for growth. Mergers provide a much quicker means to growth than does internal expansion. Not only does the firm acquire new capacity, but also it acquires additional consumer demand. Building up this level of consumer

Definitions

Horizontal merger Where two firms in the same industry at the same stage of the production process merge.

Vertical merger Where two firms in the same industry at different stages of the production process merge.

Conglomerate merger Where two firms in different industries merge.

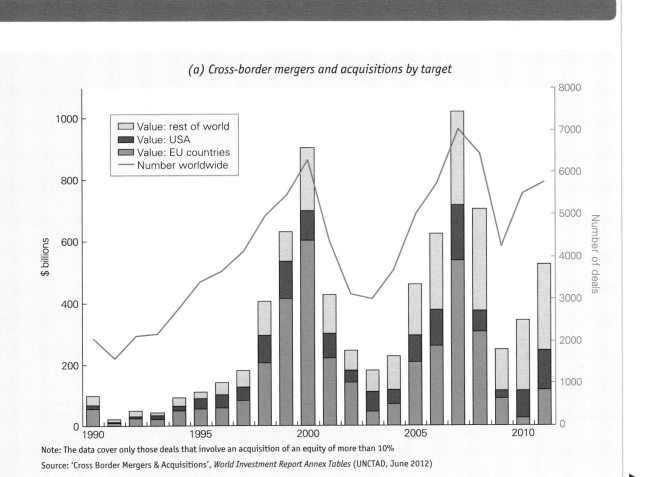

(a) Cross-border mergers and acquisitions by target

Note: The data cover only those deals that involve an acquisition of an equity of more than 10%

Source: 'Cross Border Mergers & Acquisitions', *World Investment Report Annex Tables* (UNCTAD, June 2012)

cross-border M&A. With the faltering recovery of 2010, however, there was a small increase in global M&A.

What is more, the worldwide pattern of cross-border M&A activity had changed between the mid-1990s and the post financial crisis period of 2008–11. Chart (b) illustrates three interesting trends.

First, North America saw a small proportionate growth in its global share of cross-border M&As from 21.0 per cent in the mid-1990s to 22.9 per cent from 2008–11, although its share measured by value fell from 33.3 per cent to 24.3 per cent.

Second, Asian countries saw a dramatic growth in their share of the number of cross-border M&As from 8.6 per cent to 15.6 per cent over the period 1994–7 to 2008–11 and an even more dramatic growth in their share of the value, from 5.1 per cent to 17.6 per cent. Two nations in the region, China and India, have been particularly attractive because their economies are growing rapidly; they have low costs, notably cheap skilled labour and low tax rates; and they are

becoming more receptive to all forms of foreign direct investment, including M&As.

Third, the EU-15 (i.e. those fifteen countries which were EU members before the accession of ten new countries in 2004 and another two in 2007) saw a reduction in their share of the number of cross-border M&As, as well as a fall in their share of the value, from 42.0 per cent to 28.8 per cent. In 2007, the biggest completed cross-border M&A was the €70 billion ($98.3 billion) purchase of the Dutch Bank ABN-AMRO by RFS Holdings, a consortium of the Royal Bank of Scotland, Santander and Fortis, just before the banking crisis – an acquisition that put huge strain on the finances of the acquiring companies and was a major contributing factor to RBS having to be bailed out by the UK government in October 2008.

There were also some high-value cross-border M&As in the EU-15 nations during this latter period, and some of these were M&As between firms in the EU-15 nations. In 2001, for example, the biggest completed cross-border M&A was the

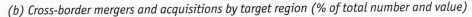

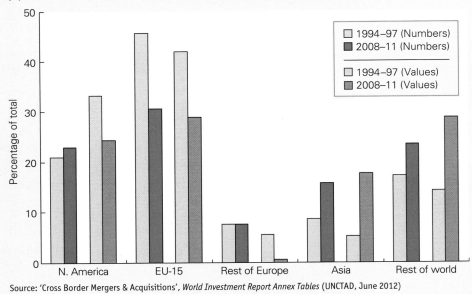

(b) Cross-border mergers and acquisitions by target region (% of total number and value)

Source: 'Cross Border Mergers & Acquisitions', *World Investment Report Annex Tables* (UNCTAD, June 2012)

demand by internal expansion might have taken a considerable length of time.

The telecommunications, media and technology sector has seen many mergers in recent times where companies in different market segments have come together. The acquisition of Time Warner by America Online (AOL), the Internet group, brought together a firm strong in media distribution with a media content provider. The two businesses were clearly complementary and allowed AOL to grow and expand its range of media-based interests.

Merger for economies of scale. Once the merger has taken place, the constituent parts can be reorganised through a

process of 'rationalisation'. The result can be a reduction in costs. For example, only one head office will now be needed. On the marketing side, the two parts of the newly merged company may now share distribution and retail channels, benefiting from each other's knowledge and operation in distinct market segments or geographical locations.

The merger of SBC Communications Inc. and AT&T Corp. in 2005 has made the new company, AT&T Inc., the largest telecommunications company in the USA and one of the largest in the world. According to the *Financial Times* in February 2006, the merger was expected ultimately to result in total cost savings of $18 billion, largely

$25.1 billion purchase of GDF Suez Energy, a natural gas transmission company, by International Power PLC. Other big cross-border purchases of EU-15 firms included Weather Investments Srl (Italy) by VimpelCom Ltd (Netherlands) for $22.4 billion and Nycomed International Management GmbH (Switzerland) by Takeda Pharmaceutical Co Ltd of Japan for $13.7 billion.[1]

Some consequences of cross-border M&A activity

When viewed in terms of long-run trends, cross-border M&As are becoming more common as globalisation gathers pace. In the UK, cross-border deals are more frequent than internal deals. The Office for National Statistics reported that in the first half of 2012 there were 151 acquisitions by UK companies abroad or by foreign companies into the UK. By contrast, there were 133 acquisitions of UK companies by other UK companies.[2]

M&As are a rapid entry strategy for firms that want to gain an immediate entry hold on an overseas market. However, they can raise concerns about national sovereignty, i.e. the extent to which governments have control over their industrial base when foreign firms are present in the domestic economy. For example, the takeover of the nuclear electricity generator, British Energy, by the French firm EDF in 2008 raises issues about the direction of long-term nuclear energy strategy in the UK.

Horizontal cross-border mergers. A horizontal merger or acquisition of a domestic firm by an overseas firm may not alter the number of firms competing in the sector if the foreign firm is new to the market and merely replaces an existing firm. However, its presence may generate greater competition and innovation in the industry if the new owners bring with them fresh techniques and ways of doing business.

On the other hand, if the foreign firm is already present in the domestic economy and it then takes over a rival, the number of firms in the industry is reduced. Again, this may be beneficial for consumers if the costs of the merged firms fall and they subsequently compete vigorously with other firms in the domestic market on price and product range. However, as

Chapters 11 and 12 show, it is also possible that fewer firms in the industry means less competition and higher prices.

Vertical cross-border mergers. Vertical and conglomerate cross-border M&As are less common than their horizontal counterparts but they too come with potential costs as well as benefits. For example, a backward vertical M&A can help a firm compete globally by reducing its supply costs, but it can impose harsh terms on suppliers in the domestic economy where it operates in order to achieve this. Forward vertical M&A into, say, the retail sector can help a foreign firm secure a domestic market and offer customers a better service, but they may now move away from supplying rival retailers on comparable terms so that customer choice is reduced.

Conglomerate cross-border mergers. Conglomerate M&As can have the same positive and detrimental impacts as those associated with horizontal and vertical M&A. However, the large size and diverse product range of the conglomerate bring with it additional costs and benefits.

For example, acquired subsidiaries of conglomerates can gain access to considerable managerial expertise and other resources, including technology and cheaper finance. This can mean greater benefits for customers if competition prevails. But if acquired subsidiaries can access cheaper finance than domestic firms, this may deter new investment by home-based firms, thereby reducing competition.

In addition, access to cheaper finance may allow conglomerate subsidiaries the opportunity to engage in predatory pricing behaviour, i.e. offering prices below cost in order to drive rival businesses out of the market. Once rivals have left the sector, the predator firm can raise prices once again (see pages 262 and 334).

Most cross-border M&As are good for society. That they exist is a sign of healthy global capital markets, where funds can be borrowed or shares purchased in order that new firms can replace older, possibly under-performing firms. Whilst there are often job losses through M&As, new owners often provide stability and generate new employment growth. That said, to maximise the benefits of cross-border M&As, governments have to be wary of the potential downsides.

[1] *World Investment Report*, Annex Tables (UNCTAD, September 2012).
[2] *Mergers and Acquisitions involving UK Companies*, Q2 2012 (ONS, September 2012).

1. *Are the motives for merger likely to be different in a recession from in a period of rapid economic growth?*
2. *Use newspaper and other resources to identify the costs and benefits of a recent cross-border merger or acquisition.*

as a result of rationalisation in the combined business. It also resulted in dramatic growth in parts of the business as customers saw the benefits of being on a larger telecommunications network.

Many mergers are motivated by potential cost savings and increased revenue. However, a survey of executives in 2002 by the management consultants, McKinsey, noted that 70 per cent of mergers failed to achieve the predicted revenue gains, while cost savings were overestimated by at least 25 per cent in a quarter of mergers. The reasons for this absence of cost savings may be either that potential economies of scale are not exploited due to a lack of rationalisation, or diseconomies result from the disruptions

of reorganisation. New managers installed by the parent company are often seen as unsympathetic, and morale may go down. Nevertheless, although many mergers are not always as successful as planned, there is evidence that many mergers do lead to increased plant productivity.

Pause for thought

Which of the three types of merger (horizontal, vertical and conglomerate) are most likely to lead to (a) reductions in average costs; (b) increased market power?

KI 21
p 161

Merger for monopoly power. Here the motive is to reduce competition and thereby gain greater market power and larger profits. With less competition, the firm will face a less elastic demand and be able to charge a higher percentage above marginal cost. What is more, the new more powerful company will be in a stronger position to regulate entry into the market by erecting effective entry barriers, thereby enhancing its monopoly position yet further.

Merger for increased market valuation. A merger can benefit shareholders of *both* firms if it leads to an increase in the stock market valuation of the merged firm. If both sets of shareholders believe that they will make a capital gain on their shares, then they are more likely to give the go-ahead for the merger.

In practice, however, there is little evidence to show that mergers lead to a capital gain. One possible reason for this is the lack of reduction in costs referred to above. In the early stages of a merger boom, such as 2005–6, when some good deals may be had, the share price of acquiring firms may rise. But as the merger boom develops, more marginal firms are acquired. Take the merger boom of the late 1990s. In some 80 per cent of cases, there was a significant fall in the share value of the acquiring firm.

KI 14
p 74

Merger to reduce uncertainty. Firms face uncertainty at two levels. The first is in their own markets. The behaviour of rivals may be highly unpredictable. Mergers, by reducing the number of rivals, can correspondingly reduce uncertainty. At the same time, they can reduce the *costs* of competition (e.g. reducing the need to advertise).

The second source of uncertainty is the economic environment. In a period of rapid change, such as often accompanies a boom, firms may seek to protect themselves by merging with others.

Merger due to opportunity. A widely held theory concerning merger activity is that it occurs simply as a consequence of opportunities that may arise: opportunities that are often unforeseen. Therefore business mergers are largely unplanned and, as such, virtually impossible to predict. Dynamic business organisations will be constantly on the lookout for new business opportunities as they arise.

Other motives. Other motives for mergers include:

■ Getting bigger so as to become less likely to be taken over oneself.
■ Merging with another firm so as to defend it from an unwanted predator (the 'White Knight' strategy).
■ Asset stripping. This is where a firm takes over another and then breaks it up, selling off the profitable bits and probably closing down the remainder.
■ Empire building. This is where owners or managers favour takeovers because of the power or prestige of owning or controlling several (preferably well-known) companies.
■ Geographical expansion. The motive here is to broaden the geographical base of the company by merging with a firm in a different part of the country or the world.

Mergers will generally have the effect of increasing the market power of those firms involved. This could lead to less choice and higher prices for the consumer. For this reason, mergers have become the target for government competition policy. (Such policy is the subject of Chapter 21.)

15.6 EXTERNAL GROWTH THROUGH STRATEGIC ALLIANCE

We noted (section 15.3) that a major form of growth for firms was that of strategic alliances – a broad term that covers a number of collaborative arrangements across one or more sectors. These alliances may involve some joint ownership and sharing of resources; they may be contractual arrangements or agreements based on trust between parties to supply and distribute goods. Strategic alliances may be horizontal or vertical, or involve networks of firms across industries (see Figure 15.1).

Horizontal strategic alliances. These are formal or informal arrangements between firms to cooperate on a particular activity at the same stage of production. This may involve the establishment of a ***joint venture***. Examples of this include the decision by Samsung and Sony to cooperate and build LCD screens in Korea or the Sony–NEC joint venture to produce hard disk drives.

Figure 15.2 shows the current status of the major strategic alliances in the airline industry. In addition to the global alliances illustrated in Figure 15.2, there are many bilateral arrangements between the airlines on specific routes. Indeed, many airlines see these as more significant than belonging to one of the three global airline alliances. For example, Emirates, whilst refusing to join one of the three global alliances, formed a 10-year strategic alliance with Qantas in September 2012 to align ticket prices and flight schedules between Europe and Australia. This

> ### Definitions
>
> **Horizontal strategic alliances** A formal or informal arrangement between firms jointly to provide a particular activity at a similar stage of the same technical process.
>
> **Joint venture** Where two or more firms set up and jointly own a new independent firm.

Figure 15.2 Airline strategic alliances

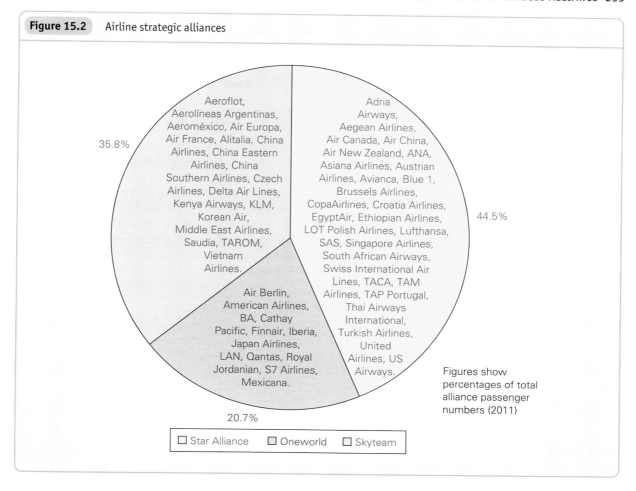

35.8%

Aeroflot, Aerolíneas Argentinas, Aeroméxico, Air Europa, Air France, Alitalia, China Airlines, China Eastern Airlines, China Southern Airlines, Czech Airlines, Delta Air Lines, Kenya Airways, KLM, Korean Air, Middle East Airlines, Saudia, TAROM, Vietnam Airlines.

44.5%

Adria Airways, Aegean Airlines, Air Canada, Air China, Air New Zealand, ANA, Asiana Airlines, Austrian Airlines, Avianca, Blue 1, Brussels Airlines, CopaAirlines, Croatia Airlines, EgyptAir, Ethiopian Airlines, LOT Polish Airlines, Lufthansa, SAS, Singapore Airlines, South African Airways, Swiss International Air Lines, TACA, TAM Airlines, TAP Portugal, Thai Airways International, Turkish Airlines, United Airlines, US Airways.

Air Berlin, American Airlines, BA, Cathay Pacific, Finnair, Iberia, Japan Airlines, LAN, Qantas, Royal Jordanian, S7 Airlines, Mexicana.

20.7%

Figures show percentages of total alliance passenger numbers (2011)

☐ Star Alliance ☐ Oneworld ☐ Skyteam

replaced a similar arrangement between Qantas and BA. Nevertheless, Qantas remained in the One World Alliance and continued to cross-sell seats with BA.

Contractual agreements between firms at the same stage of production include the establishment of a *franchise* (though there are also vertical franchise agreements). A franchise usually involves another party agreeing to take on the product format of the franchisor in return for a fee. A well-known example of a horizontal franchise business in the UK is the design, printing and copying company, Prontaprint. Another form of contractual agreement is that of *licensing*. Some lagers and beers sold in the UK, for example, are brewed under licence.

Some informal horizontal agreements might focus upon very specific stages in the supply chain. An example here is the decision by three of the world's largest steel manufacturers, NKK, Kawasaki and ThyssenKrupp, to share information on the technology for producing car panels.

Vertical strategic alliances. These are formal or informal arrangements between firms operating at different stages of an activity to provide jointly a particular product or service. Examples of vertical joint ventures include the company FilmFlex, a movie-on-demand service, provided for cable TV viewers in the UK. This service is provided

jointly by Walt Disney Television International and Sony Pictures Television. In the UK it operates services with Virgin Media, Channel 4 and HMV. The venture brings film and TV makers into a specialist retail sector. Customers can order and watch a particular film or TV programme from their own home when it is convenient for them.

Where a number of companies join together to provide a good or service, the term *consortium* is used. In recent years, many consortia have been created. A consortium is usually created for very specific projects, such as a large

---

Definitions

Franchise A formal agreement whereby a company uses another company to produce or sell some or all of its product.

Licensing Where the owner of a patented product allows another firm to produce it for a fee.

Vertical strategic alliance A formal or informal arrangement between firms operating at different stages of an activity jointly to provide a product or service.

Consortium Where two or more firms work together on a specific project and create a separate company to run the project.

civil engineering work. As such they have a very focused objective and once the project is completed the consortium is usually dissolved. TransManche Link, the Anglo-French company that built the Channel Tunnel, is an example of a defunct consortium. Camelot, the company that runs the UK National Lottery, was previously owned in equal shares by Cadbury Schweppes, De La Rue, Fujitsu Services, Royal Mail Enterprises and Thales Electronics, each of which had particular expertise to bring to the consortium.

It is also possible for firms at different stages of production to form contractual agreements. For example, there are licensing deals between suppliers of mobile phones and software companies such as Adobe. Similarly, Edios and Square, which create and manufacture games for the PlayStation 3, have been given licences by Sony. There are also licensing agreements between manufacturers of cosmetics and retailers as well as car manufacturers and car dealers. These are sometimes known in competition policy language as **vertical restraints** because the dealer is restrained by the manufacturer as to how and where it can sell the product.

One of the best-known forms of vertical contractual alliance is that of **outsourcing** or **subcontracting**. When a business outsources, it employs an independent business to manufacture or supply some service rather than conduct the activity itself. Car manufacturers are major subcontractors. Given the multitude and complexity of components that are required to manufacture a car, the use of subcontractors to supply specialist items, such as brakes and lights, seems a logical way to organise the business. Nissan in the UK, for example, has set up a supplier park so that it can get its inputs at the right price and quality and available 'just-in-time', thereby keeping inventory costs to a minimum. Box 15.2 explores some of the issues associated with outsourcing the Apple iPhone.

Networks. These consist of multi-firm alliances across sectors between organisations, some of which may be formal and others informal. Sony is a good example of a company that has expanded abroad over the years through the formation of joint ventures, licensing and informal arrangements with other firms across a number of sectors. Firms in the motor vehicle, electronics, pharmaceutical and other high-tech sectors have similar arrangements.

Some networks of firms are very large and reflect expansion through internal growth as well as via mergers, acquisitions and strategic alliances. Being part of a network may give firms access to technology and resources at lower costs. It may also give greater access to global markets. However, network development is also important at the local level. Many firms have developed supply-chain clusters to support their operations and they rely increasingly on other organisations from outside the sector, such as banks, insurance companies and government. Thus, the establishment of networks allows firms to develop competitive advantage through their core business activities

and other less formal means, including conversations with influential individuals and groups.

Why form strategic alliances?

There are many reasons why firms may decide to set up a strategic alliance. Often these reasons are specific to a particular time or set of circumstances.

New markets. As a business expands, possibly internationally, it may well be advantageous to join with an existing player in the market. Such a business would have local knowledge and an established network of suppliers and distributors. Similar arguments apply if a business is seeking to diversify. Rather than developing the skills, knowledge and networks necessary to succeed, the process might be curtailed by establishing an alliance with a firm already operating in the market.

Risk sharing. Many business ventures might just be too risky for a solitary firm. Creating some form of strategic alliance spreads risk and creates opportunity. The Channel Tunnel and the consortium of firms that built it is one such example. The construction of the Channel Tunnel was a massive undertaking and far too risky for any single firm to embark upon. With the creation of a consortium, risk was spread, and the various consortium members were able to specialise in their areas of expertise.

Capital pooling. Projects that might have prohibitively high start-up costs, or running costs, may become feasible if firms cooperate and pool their capital. In addition, an alliance of firms, with their combined assets and credibility, may find it easier to generate finance, whether from investors in the stock market or from the banking sector.

The past 20 years have seen a flourishing of strategic alliances. They have become a key growth strategy for business both domestically and internationally. They are seen as a way of expanding business operations quickly without the difficulties associated with the more aggressive approach of acquisition or the more lengthy process of merger.

> ### Pause for thought
>
> *What are the difficulties associated with acquisitions and mergers?*

> ### Definitions
>
> **Vertical restraints** Where a dealer is restrained by a manufacturer as to how and where it can sell a product.
>
> **Outsourcing or subcontracting** Where a firm employs another firm to produce part of its output or some of its input(s).
>
> **Network** The establishment of formal and informal multi-firm alliances across sectors.

BOX 15.2   HOW MANY FIRMS DOES IT TAKE TO MAKE AN iPHONE?

Quite a lot actually

Outsourcing is a growing and strategically important activity for modern businesses. Making decisions about what products to make in-house and what to outsource has important implications for a firm's profitability and growth.

Take the case of the iPhone. The original iPhone was introduced in 2007, and the sixth generation iPhone 5 was launched in Autumn 2012. iPhones are not manufactured by Apple. Rather, production is managed by Apple, using hundreds of parts manufactured and assembled by a range of different companies across three continents, especially in Taiwan and China.

Apple's main contribution is the design of the product. A design team designs the look and feel of the phone and its various features. Apple's engineers design the internal workings of the phone – the hardware and the necessary software – to meet the specifications of the design team. Not surprisingly, there is a lot of negotiation between these two teams before an initial specification is agreed.

Then the supply chain team comes in. The engineering team will itemise the range of components and other materials that are needed and the assembly requirements. The supply chain team will then have to estimate the costs of sourcing the components and their assembly from a range of potential suppliers.

'Apple's consistently reliable and profitable operations has made their supply chain team . . . one of the most envied in the industry – they develop and source from hundreds of suppliers from around the world; manage assembly contractors; set challenging production schedules and deliver better than most in their industry.'[1]

Companies within the supply chain do not stay constant between models. The suppliers chosen by Apple are those that offer the best deal, where 'best' includes not just cost, but quality, reliability and capacity.

Take the iPhone 4S, introduced in Autumn 2011. It has display panels manufactured by LG Display, Samsung and CMI; A5 processors and NAND flash chips by Samsung; DRAM by Elpida Memory, Hynix and Samsung; camera modules by Sharp and LG Innotek; camera lenses by Largan Precision and Genius Electrical Optical; CMOS sensors by Sony; touch screens by Corning, TPK Holdings and Wintek; touchscreen controllers by Texas Instruments; transmit modules by Skyworks, TriQuint and Avago; CPU architecture by ARM Holdings; power management by Fairchild Semiconductor; aluminium frames by Catcher. Several other manufacturers supply other parts. Manufacture (i.e. assembly) is in mainland China by two Taiwanese companies, Foxconn (a subsidiary of Hon Hai Precision Industry) and Pegatron.

With the launch of iPhone 5, although many of the suppliers remained the same, some had bigger roles to play than previously and some had smaller ones. For example, Sony supplies the battery in the iPhone 5, rather than Amperex which supplied the iPhone 4S one.   SanDisk was one of the biggest gainers, supplying flash memory for the first time. Samsung has a smaller role, following protracted court battles between Samsung and Apple over software patents.

Power and value added

With such as large share of the market, Apple has considerable market power when negotiating with suppliers. The components Apple purchases for the 16 GB iPhone 5 cost around $200 and assembly adds a further $8. When this is subtracted from the price of around $650, this leaves Apple with around $442 of value added to cover R&D, administration, marketing, distribution and pre-tax profit. Estimates for the pre-tax profit vary from $250 to $400 per iPhone. Apple makes around $30 billion in pre-tax profit from iPhones, making them one of the, if not the, most profitable products in the world.

Apple's market power works two ways.

First, with suppliers eager to supply parts to such a large purchaser, Apple can use this competition to drive down component and assembly prices. Most of the parts are pretty generic and Apple thus has a choice of suppliers.

Second, with a buoyant demand for iPhones (and other Apple products), Apple can take advantage of this and charge a premium price. It has a monopoly on its specific designs and thus demand for the finished product is relatively inelastic.

The story of iPhones applies also to iPods, iPads and Macs. Each uses parts sourced from around the world and each features unique design properties that give the product a loyal following.

1. *What factors determine the size of Apple's value added?*
2. *Is value added the same as normal or supernormal profit?*

---

[1] Ram Ganeshan, 'The iPhone 4 Supply Chain', *Operations Buzz* (28/11/2010).

15.7 EXPLAINING EXTERNAL FIRM GROWTH: A TRANSACTION COSTS APPROACH

By way of concluding this chapter it is worth considering a theoretical approach to understanding how external growth may occur. We examined the transaction cost approach (see Chapter 3) when explaining why firms exist. This approach, developed by the economist Oliver Williamson, can also be useful in illustrating the

---

BOX 15.3   THE DAY THE WORLD STOPPED

Northern Rock: a cautionary tale of business growth

In 1997 Northern Rock converted from a building society – a residential mortgage lender owned by its savers and borrowers – into a bank quoted on the stock market. During the next ten years it reduced the number of branches from 128 to 76 but expanded its online banking capabilities and mortgage business dramatically.

In January 2007 the bank announced pre-tax profits of £627 million for 2006, 27 per cent above 2005 levels. Its share of the UK mortgage market had grown from 11 per cent in 2006 to 13.4 per cent in December 2006 and to 18.9 per cent in June 2007. Northern Rock had grown from being a small local lender in the north-east of England to being the fifth largest supplier of mortgages in the UK.

However, all was not well. On 13 September 2007 Northern Rock was granted emergency financial support from the Bank of England in its role as lender of the last resort. The share price plummeted (see figure).

The following day saw the beginning of a 'run on the bank', something that had not occurred since 1866 when Overend, Gurney & Co. went to the wall. Not only were there queues outside the branch offices of Northern Rock, but the online banking website crashed as depositors withdrew their savings.

Over the next few months the government issued some £25 billion in loans so that the bank could continue operating. In spite of several attempts to find a private-sector 'white knight' to take it over, the government decided to take it into full public ownership on 22 February 2008 and shares were finally suspended.

What went wrong?

Commercial retail banks have two major objectives. They should make profit for their shareholders by engaging in activities that include lending but have sufficient liquidity (e.g. cash) in order to meet the requirements of their customers (see Chapter 28).

Northern Rock relied largely on making profit through mortgage lending, which was in marked contrast to the strategy of other commercial banks which had a more diversified range of services. Northern Rock had an exceptional IT system that not only lowered the costs of mortgage services but showed mortgage brokers and independent financial advisers, the principal source of their mortgage business, that the company had cheap mortgages for sale.

While house prices were rising (see Box 4.1) the demand for mortgages kept rising, but this also meant that individuals needed bigger mortgages. If an individual wanted a 100 per cent (or even 125 per cent) mortgage at competitive rates,

Northern Rock would provide it if they were viewed as being able to pay it back.

A bank makes profit on the interest that it earns from mortgage customers. However, in providing high-value mortgages, banks have to find money from deposits to pay house sellers or borrow from elsewhere. Northern Rock largely adopted the latter strategy, because attracting new deposits is a more costly exercise. The bank bundled its mortgages together and packaged them as financial instruments (bonds), which it then sold to investors on money markets around the world at a favourable interest rate, at least initially. These loans were largely accepted as secure investments in money markets because investors believed that Northern Rock customers were unlikely to default on their mortgages.

This practice of 'securitisation' is legitimate and allowed under international banking regulations, but Northern Rock engaged in extremely high levels of money market lending. According to the BBC, 61 per cent of its lending was from the money market. This was far in excess of its rivals such as HBOS (33 per cent), RBS (23 per cent), Barclays (20 per cent) and Lloyds (16 per cent).[1] In using the money markets to borrow money at low interest rates, it gained a competitive edge over its rivals. The more money it borrowed, the more mortgages it could afford to provide and the more profit it would make. Mortgage lending backed by securitised assets was the 'goose that laid the golden egg', and so Northern Rock continued to focus its business efforts in this direction. Even though there had been some disquiet among financial commentators about this strategy, the risks were viewed at the time as acceptable by the UK financial regulators – the Financial Services Authority and the Bank of England.

In 2007, as monetary policy in the UK tightened faster than expected, Northern Rock issued a tranche of mortgages at interest rates that were lower than those it had to pay in the market to finance them. The bank issued a profits warning in June and its share price fell.

Then the market for obtaining finance from securitised assets crumbled as it became clear that similar mortgage-backed assets in the USA had high levels of repayment arrears and property prices were falling rapidly. Anyone who now held a mortgage-backed asset (bond) would be highly unsure whether they could recoup its value in the presence of mortgage defaults. Thus, credit, once freely available, dried

---

[1] See BBC The downturn in facts and figures. Available at http://news.bbc.co.uk/1/hi/business/7250498.stm

growth of firms, particularly by strategic alliance or vertical integration.

Consider two firms, one a motor vehicle manufacturer, the other a supplier of car exhausts. These two parties will have invested heavily in a highly specific set of assets which have little or no alternative use outside of making cars or exhausts, respectively. In other words, they both have sunk costs. Both the car and the exhaust manufacturer will also be involved in frequent transactions with each other. The car manufacturer sells a lot of cars and so will need a lot of exhausts on a regular basis. In addition, if the economic environment is uncertain and there is information asymmetry in the exchange then the potential for moral hazard exists (see pages 89–91).

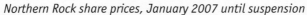

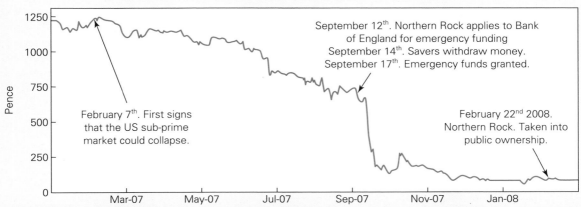

Northern Rock share prices, January 2007 until suspension

February 7th. First signs that the US sub-prime market could collapse.

September 12th. Northern Rock applies to Bank of England for emergency funding
September 14th. Savers withdraw money.
September 17th. Emergency funds granted.

February 22nd 2008. Northern Rock. Taken into public ownership.

Source: Based on data available from http://timesonline.hemscott.com/timesonline/timesonline.jsp?page=company-chart&companyId=3497&from=1/1/2007&to=22/2/2008&returnPeriod=2

up and the term 'credit crunch' has become part of the lexicon of everyday life. Northern Rock now had mortgages that were not covered by money market loans. The goose had been mortally wounded.

The chief executive of Northern Rock had a vivid recollection of the day in 2007 when he realised the business strategy had failed.

'The world stopped on August 9. It's been astonishing, gobsmacking. Look across the full range of financial products, across the full geography of the world, the entire system has frozen.'[2]

The world is different now

The world of Northern Rock is very different four and a half years after nationalisation. Questions were asked in the press and Parliament about the risks involved in the Northern Rock business strategy and about the role of the Financial Services Authority, the Bank of England and the Treasury as regulators. Questions are also being raised about the Basel II arrangements which provide guidance, rules and standards in respect of risk management and supervision at an international level (see Chapter 28, pages 467–8).

In 2010 the bank was split into two parts. The first, Northern Rock Asset Management, holds the bank's historic mortgage portfolio and toxic loans. The second, Northern Rock PLC,

holds the retail and wholesale deposit business. These two banks are informally referred to by staff as 'bad bank' and 'good bank'. The 'good bank' was sold to Virgin Money in November 2011, for around £1 billion, substantially below the amount pumped into the bank by the government to secure its solvency. The bank continues to make strides towards being profitable and retains a network of 74 branches. It made a loss of £110.9 million in 2011 compared to a loss of £188.3 million in 2010. However, the size of the bank is much reduced. In 2007 Northern Rock employed around 6500 staff; the current figure is below 2000.

'Bad bank' remains under government ownership. This business has no customer branches and is closed to new business. It only services what remains of the residential mortgage book.

In an attempt to reduce the risk of a similar situation in the future, the government intends to amend legislation and establish two new regulators. A new macro-level regulator, the Financial Policy Committee, will be a subsidiary of the Bank of England. It also plans to create a micro-level (or firm-level) regulator, the Financial Conduct Authority. It is hoped that the necessary legislation will be in place by 2017, ten years after the run on Northern Rock.

1. *What are the strengths and weaknesses of diversification as a business growth strategy?*
2. *Follow the story of the successors to Northern Rock using materials from the media and consider how they have developed since Northern Rock was split.*

---

[2] 'Why Northern Rock was doomed to fail', *Daily Telegraph*, 17 September 2007.

KI 17
p 89

Consider the following. The car manufacturer is looking for a supplier of exhausts. It puts out an invitation to tender for the contract. A number of potential suppliers put in bids and one supplier is chosen because it offers the best price and can deliver the best quality, and does so 'just-in-time' to keep inventory costs low. Once the contract has been signed, the two parties to the exchange become 'locked in' to the contract. It is at this stage that one or both of the parties could act opportunistically and exploit the situation because they have different sets of information about the markets in which they operate.

For example, the motor vehicle manufacturer could say to the supplier of exhausts that car sales are poorer than expected because of a fall in demand. As a result it might ask the exhaust manufacturer to lower the price at which it sells exhausts. Alternatively, the exhaust manufacturer may claim that it needs a higher price for its exhausts because the cost of steel has risen. The possibility of this renegotiation of the contract arises because each party to the exchange has a different set of information. But what should either party do if they were faced with this problem?

Both firms have invested in highly specific equipment that may have been specially tailored to meet this contract. It would take some time for the parties to find another partner. Williamson suggested that one party might take over or merge with the other – a vertically integrated merger would occur.

However, it is also possible that the parties engage in some other action short of a merger, largely because they want to carry out business transactions in a more civilised manner. Contracts can be useful devices for managing the exchange process but they can also be very difficult instruments to apply because they do not allow flexibility.

Williamson suggested, therefore, that many firms would form some intermediate arrangement – a strategic alliance – that might rely partly on contract and also on trust. Parties will have to signal to the other that they want a long-term business relationship as a means of building that trust.

A number of companies, particularly Japanese firms, have these sorts of arrangements. For example, there may be an opportunity for senior executives from each firm to sit on the boards of the other, or there may be meetings between business partners to discuss key issues. Indeed, in our example above, buyers from the car manufacturer might go out on visits with their exhaust manufacturer counterparts so that they can explain to raw materials suppliers the consequences of higher prices further up the supply chain.

Further, firms that signal that they are trustworthy business partners and that they have successfully developed resources over the long term are also more likely to engage in joint ventures.

Thus, where there are large and uncertain costs associated with market transactions, it can be beneficial to have some form of merger or an alliance. The conditions in which these might occur are often specific to the parties involved and depend on the nature of the industry as well as the prevailing and anticipated economic conditions.

In this chapter we have considered the growth of firms and the forms it may take. Although we identified various constraints on growth (section 15.2), a word of caution is still required. There can be real dangers associated with a strategy of rapid external business growth in turbulent or largely unknown environments, as the case of Northern Rock in Box 15.3 demonstrates.

SUMMARY

1a Business growth and business profitability are likely to be inversely related in the short run. A growing firm will bear certain additional costs, such as higher advertising and marketing bills.

1b In the long run, the relationship could be positive. A growing firm may take advantage of new market opportunities and may achieve greater economies of scale and increased market power. On the other hand, a rapidly growing firm may embark on various risky projects or projects with a low rate of return.

2a Constraints on business growth include (i) financial conditions, (ii) shareholder confidence, (iii) the level and growth of market demand and (iv) managerial conditions.

2b (i) Financial conditions determine the business's ability to raise finance. (ii) Shareholder confidence is likely to be jeopardised if a firm ploughs back too much profit into investment and distributes too little to shareholders. (iii) A firm is unlikely to be able to grow unless it faces a growing demand: either in its existing market, or by

diversifying into new markets. (iv) The knowledge, skills and dynamism of the management team will be an important determinant of the firm's growth.

3a A business can expand either internally or externally.

3b Internal expansion involves one or more of the following: expanding the market through product promotion and differentiation; vertical integration; diversification.

3c External expansion entails the firm expanding by merger/acquisition or by strategic alliance.

4a Vertical integration can reduce a firm's costs through various economies of scale. It can also help to reduce uncertainty, as the vertically integrated business can hopefully secure supply routes and/or retail outlets. This strategy can also enhance the business's market power by enabling it to erect various barriers to entry.

4b A vertically integrated business will trade off the security of such a strategy with the reduced ability to respond to change and to exploit the advantages that the market might present.

4c Through a process of tapered vertical integration, many firms make part of a given input themselves and subcontract the production of the remainder to one or more other firms. By making a certain amount of an input itself, the firm is less reliant on suppliers, but does not require as much capital equipment as if it produced all the input itself.

4d The nature and direction of diversification depend upon the skills and abilities of managers, and the type of technology employed.

4e Diversification offers the business a growth strategy that not only frees it from the limitations of a particular market, but also enables it to spread its risks, and seek profit in potentially fast-growing markets.

5a There are three types of merger: horizontal, vertical and conglomerate. The type of merger adopted will be determined by the aims of business: that is, whether to increase market power, improve business security or spread risks.

5b There is a wide range of motives for merger. Some have more statistical backing than others.

6a One means of achieving growth is through the formation of strategic alliances with other firms. They are a means whereby business operations can be expanded relatively quickly and at relatively low cost.

6b Types of strategic alliance include: horizontal and vertical strategic alliances and networks. They may take a number of forms: joint ventures, consortia, franchising, licensing, subcontracting and informal agreements based on trust between the parties.

6c Advantages of strategic alliances include easier access to new markets, risk sharing and capital pooling.

7 An important explanation of business growth relates to the transaction costs in markets where there are large sunk costs, frequent transactions and information differences on both sides of the exchange. This is particularly relevant in explaining the development of strategic alliances and vertical integration.

REVIEW QUESTIONS

1 Explain the relationship between a business's rate of growth and its profitability.

2 'Business managers must constantly tread a fine line between investing in business growth and paying shareholders an "adequate" dividend on their holdings.' Explain why this is such a crucial consideration.

3 Distinguish between internal and external growth strategy. Identify a range of factors which might determine whether an internal or external strategy is pursued.

4 What is meant by the term 'vertical integration'? Why might a business wish to pursue such a growth strategy?

5 A firm can grow by merging with or taking over another firm. Such mergers or takeovers can be of three types: horizontal, vertical or conglomerate. Which of the following is an example of which type of merger (takeover)?

(a) A soft drinks manufacturer merges with a pharmaceutical company.

(b) A car manufacturer merges with a car distribution company.

(c) A large supermarket chain takes over a number of independent grocers.

6 To what extent will consumers gain or lose from the three different types of merger identified above?

7 Assume that an independent film company, which has up to now specialised in producing documentaries for a particular television broadcasting company, wishes to expand. Identify some possible horizontal, vertical and other closely related fields. What types of strategic alliance might it seek to form and with what types of company? What possible drawbacks might there be for it in such alliances?

The small-firm sector

Business issues covered in this chapter

- How are small and medium-sized businesses defined?
- How large is the small-firm sector in the UK?
- What competitive advantages do small businesses have?
- What problems are they likely to face?
- What determines how rapidly small businesses are likely to grow?
- What policies towards small businesses do governments pursue?

KI 6
p 34

How often do you hear of small business making it big? Not very often, and yet many of the world's major corporations began life as small businesses. From acorns have grown oak trees! But small and large businesses are usually organised and run quite differently and face very different problems.

In this chapter we consider the place of small firms in the economy: their strengths and weaknesses, their ability to grow and the factors that limit expansion. We also consider the small-business policies of governments, both in the UK and in the European Union.

16.1 DEFINING THE SMALL-FIRM SECTOR

Unfortunately, there is no single agreed definition of a 'small' firm. In fact, a firm considered to be small in one sector of business, such as manufacturing, may be considerably different in size from one in, say, the road haulage business. Nevertheless, the most widely used definition is that adopted by the EU for its statistical data. Three categories of SME (small and medium enterprise) are distinguished. These are shown in Table 16.1.

This subdivision of small firms into three categories allows us to distinguish features of enterprises that vary with the degree of smallness (e.g. practices of hiring and firing, pricing and investment strategies, competition and collusion, innovation). It also enables us to show changes over time in the size and composition of the small-firm sector. However,

Table 16.1 EU SME definitions

Criterion	Micro	Small	Medium
Maximum number of employees	9	49	249
Maximum annual turnover	€2 million	€10 million	€50 million
Maximum annual balance sheet total	€2 million	€10 million	€43 million
Maximum % owned by one, or jointly by several, enterprise(s) not satisfying the same criteria	25%	25%	25%

Note: To qualify as an SME, both the employee and the independence criteria must be satisfied and either the turnover or the balance sheet total criteria

Table 16.2 Number of UK businesses, employment and turnover by number of employees (2011)

Size (number of employees)	Businesses (number)	Employment (000s)	Turnover[a] (£m ex VAT)	Businesses (%)	Employment (%)	Turnover (%)
0–9 (micro)	4 384 570	7 477	615 226	95.0	24.4	18.8
10–49 (small)	185 520	3 713	471 950	4.0	12.2	14.4
50–249 (medium)	34 445	3 409	443 119	0.7	11.2	13.5
250+ (large)	8 590	15 927	1 747 273	0.2	52.2	53.3
All	4 613 125	30 526	3 277 607	100.0	100.0	100.0

[a] Excluding finance sector (Sector K) as data are not available on a comparable basis.

Source: *Business Population Estimates for the UK and Regions* (BIS, 2012). Contains public sector information licensed under the Open Government Licence (OGL) v1.0. http://www.nationalarchives.gov.uk/doc/open-government-licence.

we might still question the adequacy of such a definition, given the diversity that can be found in business activity, organisational structure and patterns of ownership within the small-firm sector.

The small-firm sector in the UK

In the UK, firms are divided into four categories by number of employees: micro (0–9 employees), small (0–49 employees) (includes micro), medium (50–249 employees), large (250 or more employees). The Department for Business, Innovation and Skills publishes annual business population estimates, which are available from their website (www.bis.gov.uk). Table 16.2 is taken from the 2011 dataset.

The most significant feature of the data is that micro businesses (between 0 and 9 employees) accounted for 95.0 per cent of all businesses and provided 24.4 per cent of all employment. The table also shows that there were 4 570 090 micro and small businesses out of a total of 4 613 125 businesses: i.e. 99.1 per cent. Micro and small businesses also accounted for 36.7 per cent of employment and 33.2 per cent of turnover. From such information we can see that the small-firm sector clearly represents a very important part of the UK's industrial structure.

There are significant variations between sectors in the percentage of SMEs, whether by number of firms, employment or turnover. This is illustrated in Table 16.3.

Table 16.3 SME share of UK private-sector businesses, employment and turnover by industrial sector (2012)

Industrial sector SIC 2007	Businesses		Employment		Turnover	
	Total number	SME (% share)	Total employment (000s)	SME (% share)	Total turnover (£m)	SME (% share)
All industries	4 794 105	99.9	23 893	59.1	3 131 549	48.8
A Agriculture, forestry and fishing	152 085	100.0	437	95.4	35 481	90.0
B, D, E Mining, electricity, gas, water	25 655	99.6	340	n.a.	203 916	n.a.
C Manufacturing	230 970	99.5	2 553	56.8	508 676	32.9
F Construction	907 480	100.0	1 985	85.1	227 669	72.9
G Wholesale, retail and repairs	514 805	99.8	4 810	45.3	1 109 921	49.3
H Transportation and storage	269 945	99.9	1 363	44.8	149 726	43.3
I Hotels and restaurants	166 555	99.7	1 841	58.7	77 696	56.8
J Information and Communication	289 075	99.9	1 186	57.6	188 896	41.2
K Financial and insurance activities	76 380	99.6	1 107	25.3	n.a.	n.a.
L Real estate activities	91 810	99.8	422	74.4	44 474	77.7
M Professional, scientific and technical activities	665 625	99.9	2 127	76.9	221 135	66.8
N Administrative and support service activities	378 735	99.8	2 470	48.1	169 250	59.7
P Education	243 220	99.9	488	84.4	19 346	n.a.
Q Health and social work	303 540	99.9	1 522	73.3	61 943	80.0
R Arts, entertainment and recreation	209 430	99.9	618	65.4	84 550	25.5
S Other service activities	268 805	100.0	624	n.a.	30 869	n.a.

Note: n.a. = not available.

Source: *Business Population Estimates for the UK and Regions* (BIS, 2012). Contains public sector information licensed under the Open Government Licence (OGL) v1.0. http://www.nationalarchives.gov.uk/doc/open-government-licence.

BOX 16.1 CAPTURING GLOBAL ENTREPRENEURIAL SPIRIT

Stimulating the growth of SMEs

There has been considerable interest in the notion of entrepreneurship in recent times and governments around the world have increasingly made it a focus of their economic strategy. For example, in 2012, the UK government launched the *Business in You* campaign. This aims to raise awareness of the opportunities for entrepreneurship and the support that is available to promote new firm formation and SME growth. Policies in this area include providing information, guidance and support to entrepreneurs, improving access to external finance, awarding grants and promoting an entrepreneurial 'culture'.

But what exactly is an entrepreneur? Entrepreneurs are sources of new ideas and new ways of doing things. That is, they are at the forefront of invention and innovation, providing new products and developing markets.

The GEM

The Global Entrepreneurship Monitor (GEM) provides a framework for analysing entrepreneurship. It suggests that entrepreneurship is a complex phenomenon that can exist at various stages of the development of a business. So, someone who is just starting a venture and trying to make it in a highly competitive environment is entrepreneurial. And so too, but in a different way, are established business owners if they are innovative, competitive and growth-minded. Focusing on different stages of the 'entrepreneurial cycle' allows many of the dynamic elements of SMEs to be identified and analysed.

GEM measures the stage of the life cycle of entrepreneurship by dividing entrepreneurs into nascent, new and established business owners. Nascent owners are those who have established a business within the last three months. New owners are those who have been in business between 3 and 42 months. Together, nascent and new business owners make up 'early stage entrepreneurs', while 'established owners' – those in business for more than 42 months – will have come through the traumas of the initial birth and the early development stages of the firm.

The Global Report[1] measures entrepreneurial activity in a country by the percentage of those aged 18 to 64 who are business owners, whether early stage or established. In 2011, the prevalence of all entrepreneurial activity was highest in Thailand, where 50.6 per cent of those surveyed indicated entrepreneurial tendencies, and lowest in Russia where only 7.5 per cent of those surveyed showed an enterprising disposition (see diagram (a)). The average for all the countries surveyed was 14.2 per cent.

Among the 13 European countries cited in the GEM survey of 2011, the UK appears about midway, with 14.5 per cent noted as early stage or established entrepreneurs. The UK was ahead of France (8.2 per cent), Germany (11.4 per cent) and Norway (13.6 per cent) but behind Spain (14.7 per cent),

---

[1] D. Kelly, S. Singer and M. Herrington, *Global Entrepreneurship Monitor, 2011 Executive Report* (GERA, 2012).

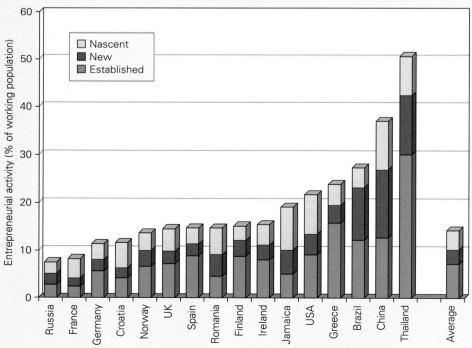

(a) Entrepreneurial activity

Note: Average is of 54 countries

Source: Based on data in *Global Entrepreneurship Monitor 2011, Executive Report* (Global Enterprise Research Association, 2012)

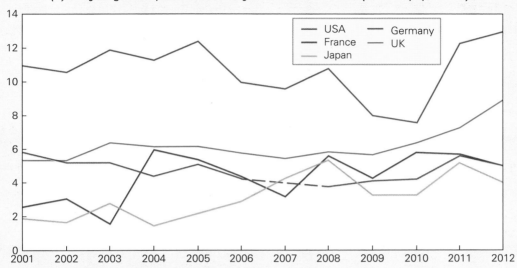

(b) Early stage entrepreneurial activity in selected countries (% adult population)

Note: Survey data was not available for Germany in 2007

Source: Data accessed 2013 from *Key Indicators database, Global Entrepreneurship Monitor* (Global Entrepreneurship Research Association)

Ireland (15.4 per cent) and Greece (23.9 per cent). It was also behind the USA (21.7 per cent) and China (37.0 per cent) in all measures of entrepreneurship.

Unfortunately, consistent time-series data are not available. Not all countries report every year and the concept of 'established entrepreneurs' was only introduced in 2005. However, there are data relevant for comparison purposes on nascent and new business owners (early stage entrepreneurial activity) for industrialised countries over the period 2001 to 2011. Diagram (b) illustrates that the UK is above France, Germany and Japan but below the USA in being involved in new venture creation.

Information from the 2011 version of the GEM report indicates that the proportion of entrepreneurs in the UK who established a business because of new opportunities, rather than out of economic necessity, was higher than in France or Germany, but lower than in the USA, (some 6.0 per cent compared to 4.2, 4.2 and 9.1 per cent, respectively).[2]

Challenges for UK entrepreneurs

Thus, the UK seems to be performing fairly well compared to similar nations. However, challenges remain.

First, longer-term survival has to be improved – a particularly difficult task given that the onset of the recession in 2008 led to dramatic increases in the company insolvency rate.[3] In the years prior to this, there had been some improvement in the three-year survival rates. The Office for National

Statistics reported in November 2008 that the three-year survival rate of UK VAT-registered businesses that started in 2004 (i.e. which were still active in 2007) was 65.3 per cent.[4] However, the five-year survival rate was still low, with only 44.4 per cent of businesses born in 2005 still active in 2010. The survival rate varied substantially by sector, ranging from a high of 58.3 per cent for businesses related to health and education to a low of 33.6 per cent in the hotel and catering industry.

Improving survival rates is important because fear of failure is commonly cited as part of the explanation for differences in enterprise and business formation rates between the UK and USA: 36.1 per cent of people seeking entrepreneurial opportunities in the UK, compared with 31.2 per cent in the USA, said that fear of failure would prevent them from starting a business.[5]

Second, the UK needs to address the issue of female entrepreneurship. The UK GEM report for 2011 shows that rates of establishing a business in the UK for women was 4.1 per cent but in the USA it was 6.8 per cent. The Small Business Survey for 2010 reports that 14 per cent of SMEs were led by women, and this figure had remained constant since 2006. The corresponding figure for the USA was around 30 per cent. Further, if the UK matched the USA's levels of female entrepreneurship there would be 700 000 more businesses in the UK and the enterprise gap between the USA and the UK would be virtually eliminated.[6]

[2] J. Levie and M. Hart, *Global Entrepreneurship Monitor, 2011* (GERA, 2012).
[3] 'Statistics release: insolvencies in the fourth quarter 2008', INS/COM/31 (Insolvency service, 6 February 2009). Available at www.insolvency.gov.uk/otherinformation/statistics/200902/index.htm

[4] 'Business demography 2010' (Office for National Statistics, December 2011).
[5] D. Kelly, S. Singer and M. Herrington, *Global Entrepreneurship Monitor, 2011 Executive Report* (GERA, 2012).
[6] 'Enterprise: unlocking Britain's talent' (BERR, March 2008), p. 16. Available at www.berr.gov.uk/files/file44992.pdf

The UK does seem to have a large number of high-growth SMEs (see Box 16.2 for an example). The 2010 Small Business Survey reported that 74 per cent of SMEs planned to grow over the period to 2012/3. The OECD defines high-growth firms as those with annual growth rates of at least 20 per cent (of either turnover or employment) over a three-year period, and having more than ten employees at the beginning of the observation period. A subset of these high-growth firms – those which were less than five years old – are referred to as 'gazelles'.

High-growth firms contribute dramatically to an economy's employment, innovation and growth and their presence in large numbers demonstrates a higher order of entrepreneurial dynamism within an economy. A survey of 100 fast-growing firms in the UK revealed that 93 could be classified as small and medium-sized enterprises, with most belonging to the latter category. Almost half were in the broad services sector, producing services ranging from road gritting to recruitment. The second largest group was companies in the retail sector, many of whom were selling a large portion of their output via the internet.[7]

However, it seems difficult to turn fast-growing small firms in the UK from 'gazelles' into 'gorillas' – firms less than 10 (perhaps 15) years old with a presence in at least three countries and employing over 500 people. In the USA, companies such as Google, Facebook, eBay and Amazon stand out as recent examples of firms that have developed from gazelles into gorillas. In the UK, however, these beasts are much more elusive.

1. *Under what economic conditions is 'necessity' entrepreneurship likely to increase?*
2. *Is business failure necessarily a 'bad thing' for a country?*

---

[7] 'Sunday Times Fast Track 100 Research Report 2011' (Fast Track, December 2011).

Service providers (categories G to S in Table 16.3) contribute the overwhelming number of micro and small firms within the economy, accounting for 3 254 445 businesses, or 71.6 per cent of all small firms.

Changes over time

How has the small-firm sector changed over time? The problems associated with definition and data collection make time-series analysis of the small-firm sector very difficult and prone to various inconsistencies. However, it is possible to identify certain trends. The percentage of small firms fell from the early part of the twentieth century, but from the mid-1960s began to rise again.

Pause for thought

What inconsistencies might there be in time-series data on the small-firm sector?

What is the explanation for this rise in small businesses in recent years? A wide range of factors have been advanced to explain this phenomenon, and include the following:

- *The growth in the service sector of the economy.* Many services are, by their nature, small in scale and/or specialist. For example, many small businesses have developed in the area of computer support and back-up.
- *The growth in niche markets.* Rising consumer affluence creates a growing demand for specialist products and services. Key examples might be in textiles and in other fashion/craft-based markets. Such goods and services are likely to be supplied by small firms, in which economies of scale and hence price considerations are of less relevance.
- *New working practices which require greater labour force flexibility.* Forms of employment such as **subcontracting** have become more pronounced, as businesses attempt to achieve certain cost and flexibility advantages over their rivals. This often forces individuals either to set up their own companies to provide such services, or to become self-employed.
- *Rises in the level of unemployment.* The higher the level of unemployment, the more people turn to self-employment as an alternative to trying to find work with an employer. The rise in unemployment in the 1980s, early 1990s and from 2008 all saw rises in self-employment. According to the Office for National Statistics, in the second quarter of 2012, 4.18 million individuals were self-employed. This was an all-time high, representing 14.3 per cent of total employment.
- *The role of government.* Government attitudes and policy initiatives shifted in favour of small business creation during the 1980s. The development of an **enterprise culture**, in which individuals were to be given the opportunity, and various financial incentives, to start their own businesses, has been one of the principal aims of all governments in recent times. (In section 16.3 we shall consider government policy initiatives in more detail.)

The growth in small businesses in the UK has been pronounced since the early 1970s. But has a similar trend been apparent in other developed economies?

Definitions

Subcontracting The business practice where various forms of labour (frequently specialist) are hired for a given period of time. Such workers are not directly employed by the hiring business, but either employed by a third party or self-employed.

Enterprise culture One in which individuals are encouraged to become wealth creators through their own initiative and effort.

International comparisons

Poor-quality data have made international comparisons very difficult in the past. There have been no agreed definitions on what constitutes a small firm or what is meant by entrepreneurship. However, this challenge is starting to be met because of their importance in job creation (look at Tables 16.2 and 16.3 again), in productivity, in innovation and, ultimately, economic growth. For example, a consortium of academics in universities across the world has compiled a Global Entrepreneurial Monitor (GEM). This is reported on in Box 16.1.

16.2 THE SURVIVAL, GROWTH AND FAILURE OF SMALL BUSINESSES

Evidence suggests that a small business stands a significantly higher chance of failure than a large business, and yet many small businesses survive and some grow. What characteristics distinguish a successful small business from one that is likely to fail? The following section looks at this issue.

Competitive advantage and the small-firm sector

The following have been found to be the key competitive advantages that small firms might hold.

> **Pause for thought**
>
> *Before you read on, try to identify what competitive advantages a small business might have over larger rivals.*

- *Flexibility.* Small firms are more able to respond to changes in market conditions and to meet customer requirements effectively. For example, they may be able to develop or adapt products for specific needs. Small firms may also be able to make decisions quickly, avoiding the bureaucratic and formal decision-making processes that typify many larger companies.
- *Quality of service.* Small firms are more able to deal with customers in a personal manner and offer a more effective after-sales service.
- *Production efficiency and low overhead costs.* Small firms can avoid some of the diseconomies of scale that beset large companies. A small firm can benefit from: management that avoids waste; good labour relations; the employment of a skilled and motivated workforce; lower accommodation costs.
- *Product development.* As we have seen, many small businesses operate in niche markets, offering specialist goods or services. The distinctiveness of such products gives the small firm a crucial advantage over its larger rivals. A successful small business strategy, therefore, would be to produce products that are clearly differentiated from those of large firms in the market, thereby avoiding head-on competition – competition which the small firm would probably not be able to survive.
- *Innovation.* Small businesses, especially those located in high-technology markets, are frequently product or process innovators. Such businesses, usually through entrepreneurial vision, manage successfully to match such innovations to changing market needs. Many small businesses are, in this respect, path breakers or market leaders.

Small businesses do, however, suffer from a number of significant limitations.

Problems facing small businesses

The following points have been found to hinder the success of small firms. They are often collectively referred to as the 'liabilities of smallness'.

- *Selling and marketing.* Small firms face many problems in selling and marketing their products, especially overseas. Small firms are perceived by their customers to be less stable and reliable than their larger rivals. This lack of credibility is likely to hinder their ability to trade. This is a particular problem for 'new' small firms which have not had long enough to establish a sound reputation.
- *Funding R&D.* Given the specialist nature of many small firms, their long-run survival may depend upon developing new products and processes in order to keep pace with changing market needs. Such developments may require significant R&D investment. However, the ability of small firms to attract finance is limited, as many of them have virtually no collateral and they are frequently perceived by banks as a highly risky investment.
- *Management skills.* A crucial element in ensuring that small businesses not only survive but grow is the quality of management. If key management skills, such as being able to market a product effectively, are limited, then this will limit the success of the business.
- *Economies of scale.* Small firms will have fewer opportunities and scope to gain economies of scale, and hence their costs are likely to be somewhat higher than those of their larger rivals. This will obviously limit their ability to compete on price.

The question often arises whether it is possible to distinguish between those small businesses which are likely to grow and prosper and those that are likely to fail. In the section below we will consider not only how businesses grow, but whether there is a key to success.

Table 16.4	Management role and style in the five stages of small business growth		
Stage	**Top management role**	**Management style**	**Organisation structure**
1 Inception	Direct supervision	Entrepreneurial, individualistic	Unstructured
2 Survival	Supervised supervision	Entrepreneurial, administrative	Simple
3 Growth	Delegation/coordination	Entrepreneurial, coordinate	Functional, centralised
4 Expansion	Decentralisation	Professional, administrative	Functional, decentralised
5 Maturity	Decentralisation	Watchdog	Decentralised, functional/product

Source: D. J. Storey, *Understanding the Small-Business Sector* (Routledge, 1994). Reproduced with permission of Cengage Learning (EMEA) Ltd.

How do small businesses grow?

It is commonly assumed that all businesses wish to grow. But is it true? Do small businesses want to become big businesses? It may well be that the owners of a small firm have no aspirations to expand the operations of their enterprise. They might earn sufficient profits and experience a level of job satisfaction that would in no way be enhanced with a bigger business operation. In fact the negative aspects of big business – formalised management structure, less customer contact and a fear of failure – might reduce the owner's level of satisfaction.

If growth is a small business objective, what are the chances of success? Evidence from the UK and the USA suggests that for every 100 firms established, after a five-year period only 44 and 51, respectively, will survive; but they are more likely to survive if they have grown.

The process of growth

Small businesses are frequently perceived to grow in five stages. These are shown in Table 16.4.

In the initial stage, *inception*, the entrepreneur plays the key role in managing the enterprise with little if any formalised management structure. In the next two stages we see the firm establish itself (the *survival* stage) and then *begin to grow*. The entrepreneur devolves management responsibility to non-owner managers. Such non-owner managers are able to add certain skills to the business which might enhance its chances of growth and success. The fourth and fifth phases, *expansion* and *maturity*, see the firm become more bureaucratic and rationalised; power within the organisation becomes more dispersed.

This picture of the growth of small businesses is *descriptive* rather than explanatory. To *explain* why a small firm grows we need to examine a number of factors. It is useful to group them under three headings – the entrepreneur, the firm and strategy.

The entrepreneur

Factors in this section relate predominantly to the attributes and experience of the individual entrepreneur. They include the following.

- *Entrepreneurial motivation and a desire to succeed.* Motivation, drive and determination are clearly important attributes for a successful entrepreneur. On their own, however, they are unlikely to be sufficient. If motivation is not complemented with things such as good business knowledge and decision making, then a business is likely to fail irrespective of its owner's motives.
- *Educational attainment.* Although educational attainment does not necessarily generate business success (indeed, it is often claimed that running a business is not an 'intellectual' activity), the level of education of an entrepreneur is positively related to the rate of growth of the firm.
- *Prior management experience and business knowledge.* Previous experience by the owner in the same or a related industry is likely to offer a small firm a far greater chance of survival and growth. 'Learning by doing' will enable the new business owner to avoid past mistakes or to take advantage of missed previous opportunities.

The firm

The following are the key characteristics of a small business that determine its rate of growth.

- *The age of the business.* New businesses grow faster than mature businesses.
- *The sector of the economy in which the business is operating.* A firm is more likely to experience growth if it is operating in a growing market. Examples include the financial services sector during the 1980s, and specialist high-technology sectors today.
- *Legal forms.* Limited companies have been found to grow faster than sole proprietorships or partnerships. Evidence suggests that limited companies tend to have greater market credibility with both banks and customers.
- *Location.* Small firms tend to be highly dependent for their performance on a localised market. Being in the right place is thus a key determinant of a small business's growth.

BOX 16.2   HOTEL CHOCOLAT

A small, fast-growing, ethical business

Hotel Chocolat is a UK-based luxury chocolate manufacturer founded in 1993 by Angus Thirwell and Peter Harris. They had previous experience of the confectionery sector, beginning in 1988 by selling peppermints to the corporate market before moving into the chocolate business as Choc Express.

Their initial sales were primarily from mail-order catalogue-based customers. They then developed an online store to complement their catalogue sales but, in 2003, Choc Express was rebranded as Hotel Chocolat, and they embraced a new means of selling when their first retail store was launched. By September 2012 they had 66 retail outlets in the UK and four overseas; had built up a loyal following of over 100 000 members across Europe through their Tasting Club; and had established successful UK and US online stores. The company is currently developing a franchising system to allow it to expand further its retail operations outside of the UK.

The company's growth has been based on premium chocolates with authentic, wholesome ingredients, i.e. without artificial flavourings or hydrogenated fats. The product range covers chocolate slabs, boxed chocolates, gift boxes and chocolate fancies, such as chocolate-covered 'Ameretto and Almond Sultanas' and 'Dark with Chilli and Cocoa Nibs'. They cover occasions such as Easter, Valentine's Day, dinner party and 'thank you' gifts and can offer products for the corporate sector, vegetarians, vegans and diabetics. They also produce a hot chocolate drink.

Fair trading

In 2004 the Hotel Chocolat engaged in backward vertical integration and purchased a 140-acre cocoa plantation on the Caribbean island of St Lucia. As part of the first phase of developing the St Lucia plantation, the company has refurbished the estate, begun to plant new seedlings and is working towards gaining full organic accreditation. It has also started phase 2 of the project, the establishment of a chocolate factory in St Lucia, and it has developed a hotel on the plantation.

The company realised early on in St Lucia that developing a sustainable industry for the long term, offering a high-quality and consistent supply of cocoa, required that it support local cocoa growers. For over 20 years prior to the purchase of the plantation, cocoa in St Lucia had been in decline. Local growers had no guarantee that harvested crops would be bought and, when crops were sold, payment could take up to six months to arrive. Under these circumstances cocoa production was loss making.

The company has developed a programme of 'engaged ethics' to develop sustainable production and fair standards. Hotel Chocolat now guarantees that farmers who embrace the programme will be able to sell all the cocoa they produce at 30 to 40 per cent above the market price and will be paid within one week. The company buys all of the cocoa 'wet' (unfermented), to ensure consistent quality, allowing farmers to concentrate on growing and replanting. All of this is supported by advice and technical expertise. By early 2009, 42 farmers had benefited from the programme.

As it develops the chocolate factory, Hotel Chocolat plans to bring other St Lucians into the supply chain, including chocolate workers, drivers, tour guides, engineers, and support staff, all of whom will be trained and developed.

In October 2010 a hurricane passed through the estate. Co-founder Angus Thirlwell takes-up the story:

> There were two main things I saw which gave me real confidence about the strength of our Engaged Ethics culture in Saint Lucia: Firstly, the day after the devastating hurricane, we opened our fermentation station as usual. It was essential that farmers who were not badly hit and who could make it with wet cocoa deliveries, could keep on doing business with us and earning much needed funds to help with rebuilding and replanting. It would have been all too easy to have kept it closed, but our team made exceptional efforts to keep the promises we made – we will buy all your cocoa, you can rely on us – fantastic to see! Secondly, the day after the hurricane we despatched our carpenters and stone-masons into the community to help put new roofs on, clear roads and distribute food. We had our own building programme to finish off but more important to help people in desperate straits first.[1]

This programme of engaged ethics has also been a mainstay of the company's approach in Ghana, the world's second largest cocoa producer. In 2002 the company began sourcing cocoa in the Osuben Basin Region. Here it provided direct funding and management skills to help launch and sustain projects that would help cocoa growers: for example, by subsidising health insurance, supporting local schools and sinking bore-holes for clean drinking water.

Tapping into a growing market

The chocolate market in the UK has been growing rapidly in recent times. According to Mintel, in 2011 this market was worth £3967 million and is forecast to grow to £5245 by 2016.[2] Hotel Chocolat's approach to excellence in chocolate products and its strong sense of corporate and social responsibility have clearly helped it to tap into this growing market and appeal to the ethical consumer.

Much of the company's rapid growth has come in recent times. Hotel Chocolat's retail operations grew from 32 domestic outlets in 2009 to 66 in 2012: a remarkable growth rate, given the depressed state of consumer spending during this period.

Its success is largely due to its retail growth, where it competes directly with Thorntons on the high street. *Retail Week* awarded it 'Emerging Retailer of the Year' in 2007 and it was nominated as one of the UK's 'Coolbrands' in 2007/8. In 2008 most of its stores were located in the south of England but the company planned its retail growth upon the low price of property in key UK locations, notably Guildford, Harrogate and Oxford. It has also taken advantage of depressed rental costs during the downturn, having more recently opened stores in prime locations in cities such as Edinburgh, Newcastle and Plymouth.

1. *What conditions existed to enable Hotel Chocolat's small business to do so well in such a short period of time?*
2. *What dangers do you see in the growth strategy adopted by Hotel Chocolat?*

---

[1] *Our Unique Cocoa Plantation – The Rabot Estate, St Lucia* (http://www.hotelchocolat.co.uk, September 2012).
[2] *Chocolate Confectionery – UK* (Mintel, April 2012).

Strategy

Various strategies adopted by the small firm will affect its rate of growth. Strategies that are likely to lead to fast growth include the following:

- *Workforce and management training.* Training is a form of investment. It adds to the firm's stock of human capital, and thereby increases the quantity, and possibly also the quality, of output per head. This, in turn, is likely to increase the long-term growth of the firm.
- *The use of external finance.* Taking on additional partners, or, more significantly, taking on shareholders, will increase the finance available to firms and therefore allow a more rapid expansion.
- *Product innovation.* Firms that introduce new products have been found on the whole to grow faster than those that do not.
- *Export markets.* Even though small firms tend to export relatively little, export markets can frequently offer additional opportunities for growth. This is especially important when the firm faces stiff competition in the domestic market.

- *The use of professional managers.* The devolving of power to non-owning managers is identified as a major characteristic of fast-growth small firms. Such managers, as previously mentioned, widen the skills and knowledge base of the organisation, and shift the reliance of the business away from the entrepreneur, whose skills might be limited to specific areas.

What the above factors suggest is that, if a small business is to be successful and subsequently grow, it must consider its business strategy – the organisation of the business, and the utilisation of individuals' abilities and experience. It is a combination of these factors which is likely to generate success, and only those businesses that coordinate such characteristics are likely to grow. Conversely, those businesses that fail to embrace these key characteristics are likely to fall by the wayside.

A potentially crucial factor in aiding success is the contribution and role of public policy. In the next section we shall consider the attitude of the UK government to small business and the policy initiatives it has introduced. We will also assess how such initiatives differ from, complement or duplicate those provided by the EU.

16.3 GOVERNMENT ASSISTANCE AND THE SMALL FIRM

When the UK Conservative-Liberal coalition government was elected in 2001, it stated that its principal economic objective was to develop a strategy that would enable the country to achieve its full economic potential. A key element of the strategy was the encouragement and promotion of entrepreneurial talent; and one way of achieving this was by supporting small and medium-sized enterprises.

SME policy in the UK

UK governments in recent years have recognised the strategic importance of small firms to the economy and have introduced various forms of advisory services and tax concessions. In particular, they have tried to encourage the establishment of new small firms. In the UK, the level of small business start-ups is about three businesses per 100 adults. In the USA, it is over seven businesses per 100 adults.

> ### Pause for thought
>
> *Why might the government wish to distinguish SME start-up policies from SME growth and performance policies?*

Under the previous Labour administration, in June 2009, a new Department for Business, Innovation and

Skills (BIS) was created. This became the lead authority for small business policy. The Treasury, however, provides the financial opportunities and establishes the macroeconomic policy framework for industry, including small firms. The government and the EU also offer grants and other forms of assistance through regional, urban, social and industrial policy that small firms may be able to tap into (see sections 21.2, 21.3, 31.3 and 31.4). In this section we concentrate on the strategic framework and specific policies aimed at SMEs.

Strategic framework

In October 2010 the UK government launched a new vision for growth and enterprise, entitled 'Local growth: realising every place's potential'. This set out how it intended to support enterprise, innovation, global trade and inward investment. It developed a framework centred around the idea of 'Local Enterprise Partnerships'. These are joint bodies bringing together the private and public sector to promote the economic interests of each part of the country.

The government has been critical of past policies that focused on a narrow range of sectors: e.g. the financial sector. Local Enterprise Partnerships aim to create a more balanced economy. The intention is to support businesses across a wider range of sectors, with support varying across locations, depending on each area's needs.

Forms of government support to small business in the UK

Enterprise Finance Guarantee (EFG). The government has guaranteed to cover 75 per cent of loans made by banks to viable SMEs through the EFG. The scheme is open to businesses with an annual turnover of up to £44 million which are not able easily to access the finance they need for new loans. The scheme enables businesses to secure loans of between £1000 and £1 million for up to ten years. There is a similar scheme that provides shorter-term finance for companies which are exporting.

Equity finance. Since 2006, the government has established a multi-million-pound equity finance scheme, currently administered through Capital for Enterprise, to enable funding of up to £2 million for businesses that require investment. These businesses often fall within the 'equity gap' – more than private individuals ('business angels') can supply and less than venture capital firms would consider.

Corporate venturing. In an attempt to draw in private venture capital funds, a programme to encourage 'corporate venturing' was introduced and some of this has been aimed at deprived local communities. Corporate venturing involves investment by larger companies in new or expanding small businesses. Investors are able to claim corporation tax relief at 20 per cent on all investments in the smaller firm.

Grants. There is a large range of grants on offer via Business Link. Some are regionally specific or sourced from the EU. In the 'Solutions for Business' portfolio, for example, there are grants to help individuals and SMEs research and develop new products and processes and develop the skills of their workforce. For example, the 'Smart' scheme provides grants of between £10 000 and £500 000 to support the research and development of new technologies and the testing of their commercial viability.

Tax concessions. Every year the Chancellor of the Exchequer sets out the tax rates and exemptions for the economy. In most instances there are some tax concessions to encourage enterprise and SME development. For example, in the year from April 2012 small firms with a turnover of up to £300 000 pay a 20 per cent rate of corporation tax compared with 24 per cent for larger companies.

Regulations. The coalition government has introduced the 'red tape challenge'. Businesses are invited to indicate the regulations which they think could be simplified or removed. Small firms are also subject to fewer planning and other bureaucratic controls than large companies.

Mentoring. There are several business mentoring schemes available to eligible SMEs. For example, the 'Designing Demand' programme provides up to 10 days of design and innovation mentoring, to eligible entrepreneurs, over a 6- to 18-month period. There is also the 'Growth Accelerator' programme which provides mentoring to assist SMEs in developing and acting upon growth plans.

Small-firm policy in the EU

The need for an EU policy for SMEs was first recognised in the Colonna report on industrial policy back in 1970. However, it was not until 1985 that the European Council gave top priority to SME policy.

Limited assistance was available for SMEs within the EU between 1970 and 1985. A division within DG-3[1] (the part of the European Commission dealing with industrial policy) was set up to work with the Business Co-operation Centre, which helped SMEs to establish cooperative ventures with other firms, and also provided limited subsidies for certain trade activities.

Further assistance might have been gained from other divisions. DG-1 (External Relations) gave SMEs priority budget allocations that promoted international business. DG-16 (Regional Development) provided a wide range of grants for business creation projects in depressed regions. DG-5 (Employment, Social Affairs and Education) encouraged local employment initiatives, with small business being seen as a prime source of job creation.

Such initiatives as these were not coordinated, but instead were pursued as largely separate strategies. However, in 1983, the 'European Year of the SME and Craft Industry', the European Parliament focused its attention on the needs of SMEs and the crucial requirement of a coordinated and independent policy. As a result, an SME taskforce was established in June 1986. This taskforce had two functions:

■ To coordinate the various policies towards SMEs within the different EU divisions.
■ To develop a general programme to aid SMEs which did not substitute or interfere with national actions within the EU, but rather operated in a complementary way.

The EU's *SME Action Programme* was set out in 1986. Its thirteen points fell into two categories. The first seven points considered regulatory and administrative issues; the final six points considered ways to help the creation and development of SMEs. The thirteen points of the Action Programme are outlined in Table 16.5.

A more significant move towards a fully integrated SME policy occurred in 1993 when, as part of the EU's enterprise policy, SME initiatives were given an independent budget of ECU112.2 billion (where 1 ECU = €1) for the period 1993 to 1996. In conjunction with this, it was stated that the impact of community policies on SMEs was to be more tightly monitored, coordinated and scrutinised.

---

[1] DG stands for 'Directorate General'. There are 36 DGs in the European Commission, each headed by a director-general, who reports to one of 20 Commissioners. DGs are no longer known by number but by name: e.g. Economic and Financial Affairs, Social Affairs, Consumer Protection, Enterprise.

Table 16.5	EU SME Action Programme
Regulatory and administrative matters	**Initiatives to encourage the establishment and development of SMEs**
1 Promoting the spirit of enterprise	7 Improving the social environment of SMEs
2 Improving the administrative environment	8 Training
3 Monitoring the completion of the internal market	9 Information
4 Adapting company law	10 Exports
5 Adapting competition law	11 Encouraging new firms and innovation
6 Improving the tax environment	12 Cooperation between firms and regions
	13 Provision of capital

By June 2008 the Union had reached the point of adopting the Small Business Act, the EUs first comprehensive SME policy framework aiming to level the playing field for SMEs across the EU. This act focused upon issues such as access to finance, the time taken to set up a company and how the public sector interacts with SMEs.

In 2011 the original act was revisited, with the Commission taking stock of progress and proposing new actions to be implemented. These new actions included strengthening loan guarantee schemes, improving access to venture capital markets and streamlining legislation.

The major sources of financial support for SMEs are the Structural Funds and the European Investment Bank (EIB).

The Structural Funds provide finance to help correct regional imbalance within the EU. Structural Funds are managed by EU member states and they determine the amount of money allocated to SMEs. Some €16 billion from the EU's Structural Funds were allocated to SME-targeted projects for the period 2002–6. In the 2007–13 period, €350 billion has been allocated to the Structural Fund, of which some €55 billion is intended to be used to support SMEs.

The EIB provides loans to SMEs via commercial banks. Between 2008 and 2011 it lent over £33 billion to more than 180 000 SMEs and midcap companies. The loans were for between 2 and 12 years and capped at a maximum of €12.5 million per loan. The EIB also indirectly finances SMEs through loans to selected venture capital operators, which then invest in the SMEs.

A wide range of policy initiatives has also been adopted in order to encourage SMEs to participate in the EU's technology programme. In the Cohesion Policy Programmes (2007–15), SMEs have been allocated €27 billion to support entrepreneurship, access to finance, technology transfer and access to information technology. A number of schemes have been developed in this regard, including the provision of financial instruments through the European Investment Fund to support businesses at every phase of their life cycle; a network of business and innovation service centres which offer advice and other services; and initiatives to support and foster innovation, including eco-innovation.

The EU's commitment to SMEs has clearly grown in recent years. The EU provides not only 'hard' support, such as providing direct financial support to individual investments, but also 'soft' support such as fostering the development of business networks and clusters.

The EU has recognised the valuable role that SMEs play within the economy, not only as employers and contributors to output, but in respect of their ability to innovate and initiate technological change – vital components in a successful and thriving regional economy. However, it also recognises that there is more to be done.

SUMMARY

1a The small-firm sector is difficult to define. Different criteria might be used. However, the level of employment tends to be the most widely used.

1b The difficulties in defining what a small firm is mean that measuring the size of the small-firm sector is also difficult and subject to a degree of error. However, it appears that in the UK the small-firm sector has been growing since the mid-1960s. This is the result of a variety of influences including: industrial structure, working practices, the level of unemployment, the role of government and consumer affluence.

1c The growth in the small-firm sector in the UK is not mirrored elsewhere in the major European nations other than in Italy.

2a Small firms survive because they provide or hold distinct advantages over their larger rivals. Such advantages include: greater flexibility, greater quality of service, production efficiency, low overhead costs and product innovation.

2b Small businesses are prone to high rates of failure, however. This is due to problems of credibility, finance and limited management skills.

2c Of those small businesses that manage to survive, a small fraction will grow. The growth of business tends to proceed through a series of stages, in which the organisation and management of the firm evolves, becoming less and less dependent upon the owner-manager.

2d Those small businesses that do grow are likely to have distinct characteristics relating to individual abilities, business organisation and business strategy. Combinations of variables from these three categories will tend to favour growth of the SME.

3a Government policy aimed at the small firm within the UK is particularly concerned with business start-ups, although we can also identify initiatives that look to stimulate growth and improve performance.

3b Small business policy within the EU seeks to complement national programmes. It provides a wide range of grants, projects and information for SMEs. A large emphasis is placed upon the development and transmission of technological innovations within the SME sector.

REVIEW QUESTIONS

1 Why is it so difficult to define the small-firm sector? What problems does this create?

2 'Small businesses are crucial to the vitality of the economy.' Explain.

3 Compare and contrast the competitive advantages held by both small and big business.

4 It is often argued that the success of a small business depends upon a number of conditions. Such conditions can be placed under the general headings of: the entrepreneur, the firm and the strategy. How are conditions under each of these headings likely to contribute to small business success?

5 Compare and contrast UK and EU approaches to SME policy.

17 Chapter

Pricing strategy

Business issues covered in this chapter

- How are prices determined in practice?
- What determines the power that a firm has to determine its prices?
- Why do some firms base prices on average costs of production?
- Why do firms sometimes charge different prices to different customers for the same product (e.g. seats on a plane)? What forms can such 'price discrimination' take?
- What types of pricing strategy is a firm likely to pursue if it is producing multiple products?
- How does pricing vary with the stage in the life of a product? Will newly launched products be priced differently from products that have been on the market a long time?

How are prices determined in practice? Is there such a thing as an 'equilibrium price' for a product, which will be charged to all customers and by all firms in the industry? In most cases the answer is no.

Take the case of the price of a rail ticket. On asking, 'What's the train fare to London?', you are likely to receive any of the following replies: Do you want an 'Advance' ticket? Do you want a single or return? How old are you? Do you have a railcard (family & friends, young person's, student, senior)? Do you want an off-peak or Anytime return? Will you be travelling out before 10 a.m.? Will you be leaving London between 4 p.m. and 6 p.m.? Do you want to reserve a seat? Do you want to take advantage of our special low-priced winter Saturday fare?

How you respond to the above questions will determine the price you pay, a price that can vary several hundred per cent from the lowest to the highest. And it is not just train fares that vary in this way: air fares and holidays are other examples. Selling the same product to different groups of consumers at different prices is known as *price discrimination*. (We shall examine price discrimination in detail later in this chapter.) But prices for a product do not just vary according to the customer. They vary according to a number of other factors as well.

- *The life cycle of the product*. When a firm launches a product, it may charge a very different price from when the product has become established in the market, or, later, when it is beginning to be replaced by more up-to-date products.

Definition

Price discrimination Where a firm sells the same product at different prices.

- *The aims of the firm.* Is the firm aiming to maximise profits, or is it seeking to maximise sales or growth, or does it have a series of aims? Which aim or aims that it pursues will determine the price it charges?
- *The competition that the firm faces.* Firms operating under monopoly or collusive oligopoly are likely to charge very different prices from firms operating in highly competitive markets.
- *Information on costs and demand.* Firms in the real world may have very scant information about the elasticity of demand for their product and for the products of their competitors, and how demand is likely to change. It is the same with information on costs: firms may have only a rough idea of how costs are likely to change over time. The picture of a firm choosing its price by a careful calculation of marginal cost and marginal revenue may be far from reality.

In this chapter we will explore the pricing strategies of business. We will identify different pricing models, show how a firm's pricing policy is likely to change over a product's life cycle, and how and under what circumstances businesses might practise price discrimination. We will also consider a number of other pricing issues, such as those linked to a multiproduct business and the use of a practice known as 'transfer pricing'.

17.1 PRICING AND MARKET STRUCTURE

The firm's power over prices

In a free and competitive market we know that the quantity bought and sold, and the actual price of the product, are determined by the forces of supply and demand. If demand is in excess of supply, the consequent market shortage will cause the price level to rise. Equally, if supply is in excess of demand, the resulting market surplus will cause the market price to fall. At some point we have an equilibrium or market-clearing price, to which the market will naturally move. In such an environment, the firm cannot have a 'pricing strategy': the price is set for it by the market. It is a price taker.

But, even if a firm were able to identify the market demand and supply schedules, which is not at all certain given the problem of acquiring accurate market information, the market equilibrium price is likely to be short lived as market conditions change and demand and supply shift. This would be particularly the case for those goods or services that are fashionable and subject to changing consumer preferences, or where production technology is undergoing a period of innovation, influencing both the cost structure of the product and the potential output decisions open to the business. The best business could hope for, given the uncertainty of demand and supply, is to be flexible enough to continue making a profit when market conditions shift.

When a firm has a degree of market power, however, it will have some discretion over the price it can charge for its product. The smaller the number of competitors, and the more distinct its product is from those of its rivals, the more inelastic will the firm's demand become and the greater will be its control over price.

We saw (Chapter 12) that, in oligopolistic markets, firms are dependent on each other: what one firm does, in

terms of pricing, product design, product promotion, etc., will affect its rivals. The degree of interdependence, and the extent to which firms acknowledge it, will affect the degree to which they either compete or collude. This, in turn, will affect their pricing strategy. The result is that prices may be very difficult to predict in advance and bear little resemblance to those that would have been determined through the operation of free-market forces.

At one time there may be an all-out price war, with firms madly trying to undercut each other in order to grab market share, or even drive their rivals out of business. At other times, prices may be very high, with the oligopolists colluding with each other to achieve maximum industry profits. In such cases the price may be even higher than if the industry were an unregulated monopoly because there might still be considerable *non*-price competition, which would add to costs and hence to the profit-maximising price.

Pause for thought

Would prices generally be lower or higher if a business was aiming to maximise long-run growth rather than short-run profits?

It is clear from this that, under oligopoly, pricing is likely to be highly strategic. One of the key strategic issues is the effect of prices on potential new entrants, and here it is not only the oligopolist, but also the monopolist that must think strategically. If the firm sets its prices too high, will new firms take the risk of entering the market? If so, should the firm keep its price down and thereby deliberately limit the size of its profits so as not to attract new entrants?

BOX 17.1 EASY PRICING

Getting the most revenue from the demand curve

Low-cost airlines, such as easyJet and Ryanair adopted an approach to pricing in the late 1990s that was novel at the time, but is now being increasingly used by other airlines and in other industries. The approach is a form of price discrimination.

The principal is simple: with a fixed number of seats per flight, as the seats are sold, so the prices go up. Thus the first few seats are sold at a really low prices. Indeed, when particular flights first come on sale, many people go online very quickly to try to get the lowest priced seats. This rush to purchase seats at reasonable prices helps to drive sales and gets people to commit to a purchase when otherwise they may have waited and perhaps changed their minds.

The idea is also to take advantage of the different prices people are willing to pay. Business passengers, for example, may be willing to pay very high prices (or at least their employers may) but might want to book a flight at the last minute. The pricing model means that with a plane that is nearly fully booked at that stage, the price will be high and the airline will be able to charge a price closer to the business passenger's willingness to pay.

In fact, in the perfect case of such a pricing model, each passenger is paying the maximum they would be willing to pay – a case of first-degree price discrimination. This means that all the consumer surplus (see pages 83–4) that would have gone to the consumer, instead goes as revenue to the airline. This is illustrated in the diagram. Assume that the plane has 156 seats (the typical easyJet Airbus A319-100 configuration) and that the demand for seats is given by the demand curve (D). If each passenger pays what he or she would be willing to pay, the total revenue from a full

plane is given by the total grey and pink shaded areas. If, by contrast, a single price were charged to fill the plane, this would have to be P1, giving total revenue of just the pink area, with passengers gaining consumer surplus of the grey area.

The easyGroup

Stelios Haji-Ioannou, the original owner of easyJet, founded the easyGroup holding company of 'easy' subsidiaries in 1998. In addition to easyJet, these include or have included easyCinema, easyMobile and easyCruise amongst others. In several of these easyGroup companies prices rise as sales increase, just as with easyJet. Take the case of easyCinema. Prices started very low and then rose as the cinema filled up for any given screening. EasyCinema customers had no tickets: they booked online and printed out a bar-coded entry pass..

Unfortunately, for Mr Haji-Ioannou, the easyCinema venture failed. Faced with an effective cartel of film distributors, which chose not to sell to the cut-price easyCinema, it could only show old or less popular films. It was forced to close in 2006.

Other similar ventures, such as easyCruise and easyMobile have also closed or been sold. Nevertheless, the number of ventures in easyGroup now number over 20, including easyCar, easyVan, easyOffice (serviced office rental), easyJobs (employment agency), easyGym and easyBus (airport transfers).

But the most successful of the easyGroup businesses remains easyJet, the UK's largest. It has seen turnover grow in every year since 2000. Its load factor has steadily increased, with an average seat occupancy in 2012 of 88.7 per cent.

Unlike Ryanair, it has targeted the business market and flies to main airports rather than small ones in remote locations. The pricing model particularly suits easyJet's market, with holiday makers being able to take advantage of low-priced seats booked a long time in advance and business travellers having the flexibility of buying tickets at the last minute, but at much higher prices.

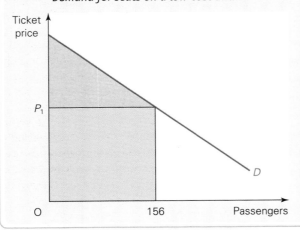

Demand for seats on a low-cost airline

1. *Distinguish between first- and third-degree price discrimination.*
2. *Is easyJet's pricing model one of pure first-degree price discrimination? Explain whether or not the total revenue for a full plane will be the full amount shown by the grey and pink areas in the diagram.*
3. *What other policies of easyJet have made it so successful?*

Limit pricing

This policy of *limit pricing* is illustrated in Figure 17.1. Two *AC* curves are drawn: one for the existing firm and one for a new entrant. The existing firm, being experienced and with a capital base and established supply channels, is shown having a lower *AC* curve. Any new entrant, if it is to compete successfully with the existing firm, must charge the same price or a lower one. Thus provided the existing firm does not raise price above P_L, the other firm, unable to make supernormal profit, will not be attracted into the industry.

P_L may well be below the existing firm's short-run profit-maximising price, but it may prefer to limit its price to P_L to protect its long-run profits from damage by competition.

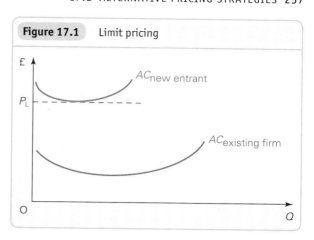

Figure 17.1 Limit pricing

17.2 ALTERNATIVE PRICING STRATEGIES

What is the typical procedure by which firms set prices? Do they construct marginal cost and marginal revenue curves (or equations) and find the output where they are equal? Do they then use an average revenue curve (or equation) to work out the price at that output?

To do this requires a detailed knowledge of costs and revenues that few firms possess. To work out *marginal* revenue, the firm requires information not just on current price and sales. It must know what will happen to demand if price *changes*. In other words, it must know the price elasticity of demand for its product. Similarly, to work out *marginal* cost, the firm must know how costs will *change* as output changes. In reality this is highly unlikely. The business environment is in a constant state of change and uncertainty. The costs of production and the potential revenues from sales will be difficult to predict, shaped as they are by many complex and interrelated variables (changes in tastes, advertising, technological innovation, etc.). Under oligopoly in particular, it is virtually impossible to identify a demand curve for the firm's product. Demand for one firm's product will depend on what its rivals do: and that can never be predicted with any certainty. As a consequence, managers' 'knowledge' of future demand and costs will take the form of estimates (or even 'guesstimates'). Trying to equate marginal costs and marginal revenue, therefore, is likely to be a highly unreliable means of achieving maximum profits (if, indeed, that were the aim).

If, then, the marginalist principle of traditional theory is not followed by most businesses, what alternative pricing strategy can be adopted? In practice, firms look for rules of pricing that are relatively simple to apply.

Cost-based pricing

One alternative to marginalist pricing is average-cost or *mark-up pricing*. In this case, producers derive a price by simply adding a certain percentage (mark-up) for profit on top of average costs (average fixed costs plus average variable costs).

$$P = AFC + AVC + \text{profit mark-up}$$

The size of the profit mark-up will depend on the firm's aims: whether it is aiming for high or even maximum profits, or merely a target based on previous profit.

Choosing the level of output

Although calculating price in this manner does away with the firm's need to know its marginal cost and revenue curves, it still requires the firm to estimate how much output it intends to produce. The reason is that average cost varies with output. If the firm estimates that it will be working to full capacity, its average cost is likely to be quite different from that if it only works at 80 or 60 per cent of capacity.

Businesses tend to base their mark-up on *short-run* average costs. This is because estimates of short-run costs are more reliable than those of long-run costs. Long-run costs are based on *all* factors being variable, including capital. But by the time new capital investment has taken place, factors such as technological change and changes in factor prices will have shifted the long-run average cost curve, thereby making initial estimations inaccurate.

Definitions

Limit pricing Where a business keeps prices low, restricting its profits, so as to deter new rivals entering the market.

Mark-up pricing A pricing strategy adopted by business in which a profit mark-up is added to average costs.

Figure 17.2	A firm's short-run average cost curve

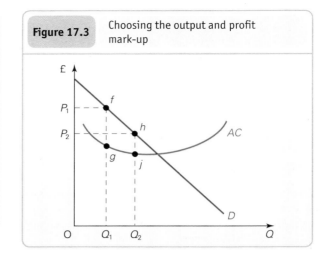

Figure 17.3   Choosing the output and profit mark-up

Figure 17.2 shows a firm's typical short-run average cost curves. The AVC curve is assumed to be saucer shaped. It falls at first as a result of a more efficient deployment of resources; then is probably flat, or virtually so, over a range of output; then rises as a result of diminishing marginal returns and possibly the need to pay overtime. The flat range of the average variable cost curve reflects the ***reserve capacity*** held by the business. This is spare capacity that the business can draw upon, if needed, to respond to changes in the market. For example, demand for the product may be subject to seasonal variation. The point is that many businesses can accommodate such changes with very little change in their average variable costs.

Most firms that use average-cost pricing will base their price on this horizontal section of the AVC curve (between points a and b in Figure 17.2). This section represents the firm's *normal* range of output. This normal range of output is that within which the plant has been designed to operate, and the business expects to be producing.

Average fixed costs will carry on falling as more is produced: overheads are spread over a greater output. This is illustrated in Figure 17.2. The result is that average (total) cost (AC) will continue falling over the range of output where AVC is constant, with minimum AC being reached at point c – beyond the flat section of the AVC curve. In practice, many firms do not regard average fixed costs in this way. Instead, they focus on average variable costs and then just add an element for overheads (AFC).

Choosing the mark-up

The level of profit mark-up on top of average cost will be influenced by a range of possible considerations, such

as fairness and the response of rivals. However, the most significant consideration is likely to be the implications of price for the level of market demand.

If a firm could estimate its demand curve, it could then set its output and profit mark-up at levels to avoid a shortage or surplus. Thus in Figure 17.3 it could choose a lower output (Q_1) with a higher mark-up (fg), or a higher output (Q_2) with a lower mark-up (hj). If a firm could not estimate its demand curve, then it could adjust its mark-up and output over time by a process of trial and error, according to its success in meeting profit and sales aims.

One problem here is that prices have to be set in advance of the firm knowing just how much it will sell and therefore how much it will need to produce. In practice, firms will usually base their assumptions about next year's sales on this year's figures, add a certain percentage to allow for growth in demand and then finally adjust this up or down if they decide to change the mark-up.

Variations in the mark-up

In most firms, the mark-up is not rigid. In expanding markets, or markets where firms have monopoly/oligopoly power, the size of the mark-up is likely to be greater. In contracting markets, or under conditions of rising costs and constant demand, a firm may well be forced to accept lower profits and thus reduce the mark-up.

Multiproduct firms often have different mark-ups for their different products depending on their various market conditions. Such firms will often distribute their overhead costs unequally among their products. The potentially most profitable products, often those with the least elastic demands, will probably be required to make the greatest contribution to overheads.

The firm is likely to take account of the actions and possible reactions of its competitors. It may well be unwilling to change prices when costs or demand change, for fear of the reactions of competitors (see the kinked demand curve

Definition

Reserve capacity A range of output over which business costs will tend to remain relatively constant.

theory on pages 184–5). If prices are kept constant and yet costs change, either due to a movement along the *AC* curve in response to a change in demand, or due to a shift in the *AC* curve, the firm must necessarily change the size of the mark-up.

> ### Pause for thought
>
> *If the firm adjusts the size of its mark-up according to changes in demand and the actions of competitors, could its actions approximate to setting price and output where MC = MR?*

17.3 PRICE DISCRIMINATION

Up to now we have assumed that a firm will sell its output at a single price. Sometimes, however, firms may practise price discrimination, of which there are three broad types: first, second and third degree.

First-degree price discrimination

First-degree price discrimination is where the firm charges each consumer the maximum price he or she is prepared to pay for each unit. This is a common occurrence in modern business. For example, stall-holders in a bazaar will attempt to do this when bartering with their customers. So will car dealers who sell new cars to customers. The car they offer for sale to each customer may be the same, but they can sell it at a different price because they recognise that some individuals are willing to pay slightly more than others.

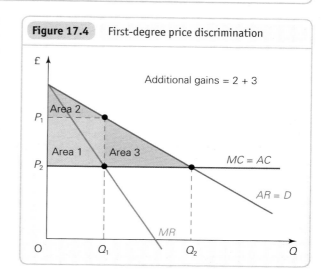

Figure 17.4 First-degree price discrimination

> ### Pause for thought
>
> *Is the pricing system adopted by the 'easy' group of companies a form of first-degree price discrimination (see Box 17.1 on page 256)?*

Indeed, first-degree price discrimination is likely in any sector where there is some scope for bargaining over price. Accountants, lawyers, architects and other firms offering professional services are often able to charge different prices to different people: through discussion and negotiation they can obtain a more intimate knowledge of their customers' willingness to pay.

Figure 17.4 demonstrates how first-degree price discrimination works. To simplify the explanation, we assume that marginal cost (*MC*) is constant and that there are no fixed costs, so that average cost $AC = MC$. If the profit-maximising firm charged one price, it would be P_1 and output would correspondingly be Q_1. Area 1 would therefore represent supernormal profit for the firm which did not discriminate between customers on price. However, if the firm knew the demand curve, it could sell every unit at the maximum price that each consumer was prepared to pay and so make additional gains. For any consumer who is willing to pay above the price of P_1, the firm could also extract area 2 in additional revenue. Likewise, if the

firm were prepared to offer consumers prices lower than P_1 then it could also increase its revenue by area 3. These consumers would gain by this pricing strategy, for they would not have bought this product otherwise.

In practice, pure first-degree price discrimination, where the firm knows every customer's willingness to pay, is normally unrealistic because it would require both parties to the exchange having considerable amounts of information.

Second-degree price discrimination

Second-degree price discrimination is where the firm charges customers different prices according to how much they purchase. It may charge a high price for the first so many units, a lower price for the next so many units, a lower price again for the next, and so on. This method of price

> ### Definitions
>
> **First-degree price discrimination** Where a firm charges each consumer for each unit the maximum price which that consumer is willing to pay for that unit.
>
> **Second-degree price discrimination** Where a firm charges a consumer so much for the first so many units purchased, a different price for the next so many units purchased, and so on.

discrimination is a common marketing strategy for firms. For example, a product may be offered as a 'buy two, get one free' deal or 'buy six and get a 5 per cent discount'. With such incentives, more customers may be induced to buy the product than if a single price was being charged, because the average price of a product is lower if more is bought.

Similarly, electricity companies in some countries charge a high price for the first so many kilowatts. This is the amount of electricity that would typically be used for lighting and running appliances: in other words, the uses for which there is no substitute fuel. Additional kilowatts are charged at a much lower rate. This is electricity that is typically used for heating and cooking, where there are alternative fuels.

Second-degree price discrimination is particularly useful where firms face a downward-sloping average cost curve. Figure 17.5 illustrates the situation. If a firm charges a single price, it will be P^* and output will be Q^* (where $MC = MR$). However, by offering a range of prices to induce customers to buy more – in Figure 17.5 these are P^*, P_1, P_2 and P_3 – the firm can get the benefit of achieving economies of scale and extracting more revenue from customers.

Notice that this pricing strategy also helps customers because, as with first-degree price discrimination, the pricing strategy reflects their willingness to pay for the product. However, those customers paying above P^* will lose as they would be paying more than if a single price had been charged.

Third-degree price discrimination

Third-degree price discrimination is where consumers are grouped into two or more independent markets and a separate price is charged in each market. Examples include different-priced seats on buses for adults, children and pensioners, and different prices charged for the same product in different countries. Third-degree price discrimination is common practice in trade between firms.

To see how it operates, assume that a firm sells an identical product in two separate markets X and Y with demand and MR curves as shown in Figure 17.6. Diagram (c) shows the MC and MR curves for the firm as a whole. This MR curve is found by adding the amounts sold in the two markets at each level of MR (in other words, the horizontal addition of the two MR curves). Thus, for example, with output of 1000 units in market X and 2000 in market Y, making 3000 in total, revenue would increase by £5 if one extra unit were sold, whether in market X or Y.

Total profit is maximised where $MC = MR$: i.e. at an output of 3000 units in total. This output must then be divided between the two markets so that MC is equal to MR in each market: i.e. $MC = MR = £5$ in each market. MR must be the same in both markets, otherwise revenue could be

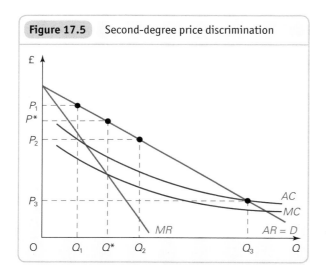

Figure 17.5 Second-degree price discrimination

Definition

Third-degree price discrimination Where a firm divides consumers into different groups and charges a different price to consumers in different groups, but the same price to all the consumers within a group.

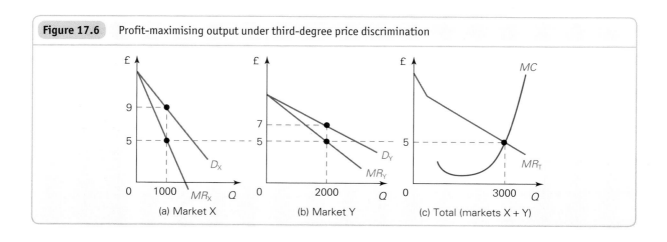

Figure 17.6 Profit-maximising output under third-degree price discrimination

(a) Market X (b) Market Y (c) Total (markets X + Y)

BOX 17.2 HOW DO EUROPEAN COMPANIES SET PRICES?

In 2005 the European Central Bank published a summary of surveys of the pricing behaviour of 11 000 firms by the national central banks of nine countries in the eurozone (Austria, Belgium, France, Germany, Italy, Luxembourg, the Netherlands, Portugal and Spain).[1] This work mirrored much of the work carried out in other countries, including a study of pricing by UK firms in the mid-1990s.[2]

A number of questions were asked. Among these were: how do firms set prices? The findings, illustrated in table (a), show that firms engage largely in imperfect competition. For the eurozone as a whole, over half of firms engage in mark-up pricing, and for German firms this proportion is as high as 73 per cent. Where the country surveys asked firms to distinguish between constant and variable mark-up, the latter type dominates. Moreover, the survey revealed that the lower the level of competition, the more frequently mark-up pricing is used.

More recently published evidence for the UK economy supports the finding that firms operate under conditions of imperfect competition.[3] Sixty-eight per cent of UK firms said that competitor price levels were important when determining their own prices. Fifty-eight per cent of firms said variable mark-ups, and 44 per cent said fixed mark-ups, were important considerations when setting prices.

(a) How do firms set prices? (%)

	Belgium	Germany	Spain	France	Italy	Netherlands	Portugal	Eurozone
Mark-up	46	73	52	40	42	56	65	54
Competitors' price	36	17	27	38	32	22	13	27
Other (mainly customer and regulator set)	18	10	21	22	26	21	23	18

Figures do not necessarily add up to 100 per cent because of rounding.

Another question asked in the European surveys was whether firms charged a uniform price to each customer, or based their pricing on the quantity that each firm bought, or whether they priced on a case-by-case basis. The survey found that, on average, 80 per cent of eurozone firms use price discrimination tactics, setting prices on case-by-case or quantity sold basis. Figures range from 92 per cent of German firms to 65 per cent of Spanish firms.

There seems to be no clear relationship between the size of firm and price discrimination, though Luxembourg reported a positive relationship. If anything, smaller firms seem to differentiate their prices in France, Italy and Portugal. There was also no overall pattern as to the relationship between the frequency of price discrimination and the degree of competition in the domestic market. However, firms in the retail and wholesale trade were more likely to use uniform pricing.

Surveys conducted in Belgium, Spain and Luxembourg included questions directed at firms operating in foreign as well as domestic markets. Table (b) reveals the pricing behaviour of these firms. The survey suggests that some of the differences in pricing between markets seem to be accounted for by exchange rate movements, transport costs, market rules and the tax system. However, two of the most important determinants of overseas pricing by these firms are the prices charged by competitors and the cyclical nature of demand in these locations. In other words, pricing in foreign markets is determined more by the market power of the firms than by costs of transacting abroad.

The survey also sought to establish those factors which could cause prices to change – either up or down. The summary results are presented in table (c). Changes in costs are the main factor underlying price increases, whereas changes in market conditions, such as competitors' prices and demand, are more important explanations of price reductions. Furthermore, prices seem to be more flexible downwards in response to demand shocks, while the opposite holds true in the case of cost shocks. Generally, prices did not seem to be sensitive to the economic outlook prevailing at the time the surveys were conducted.

(c) Factors leading to a rise or fall in price in the eurozone (mean scores: 4 = very important; 1 = completely unimportant)

	Rise	Fall
Labour costs	3.0	2.1
Costs of raw materials	3.1	2.6
Financial costs, including interest rates	2.2	1.9
Demand	2.2	2.6
Competitors' price	2.4	2.8

(b) Pricing behaviour in foreign markets (%)

	Belgium	Spain	Luxembourg
Price in euros is same for all countries	33	47	56
Price in euros is same for eurozone countries	9	6	5
Price in euros is different for all countries	58	47	39

1. Which of the following is more likely to be consistent with the aim of maximising profits: pricing on the basis of
   (a) cost per unit plus a variable percentage mark-up;
   (b) cost per unit plus a fixed percentage mark-up?
2. Explain the differences between the importance attached to the different factors leading to price increases and those leading to price reductions.
3. What type of price discrimination is occurring, according to table (b), where firms have the possibility of charging different prices in different locations?
4. Why might we require a more detailed analysis of firm size and the different industrial sectors within the survey in order to evaluate the price-setting data presented above?

[1] *The Pricing Behaviour of Firms in the Euro Area: New Survey Evidence* (Eurosystem Inflation Persistence Network, Working Paper series, no. 535, European Central Bank, October 2005).

[2] S. Hall, M. Walsh and T. Yates, 'How do UK companies set prices?', *Bank of England Quarterly Bulletin*, May 1996.

[3] J. Greenslade and M. Parker, 'New Insights into Price-Setting Behaviour in the UK: Introduction and Survey Results', *The Economic Journal*, February 2012.

increased by switching some units of output to the market with the higher *MR*.

The profit-maximising price in each market will be given by the relevant demand curve. Thus, in market X, 1000 units will be sold at £9 each, and in market Y, 2000 units will be sold at £7 each. Note that the higher price is charged in the market with the less elastic demand curve.

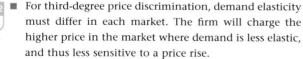

Pause for thought

How would profit-maximising output and price be determined under third-degree price discrimination if there were three separate markets? Draw a diagram to illustrate your answer.

Price discrimination by the non-profit-maximising firm

If a firm does not set a profit-maximising price, either because it has some alternative aim, or because it uses cost-based methods of pricing, which, owing to a lack of information, do not lead to the profit-maximising price, then we cannot predict precisely what the discriminatory prices will be. All we can say is that price discrimination will allow the firm to achieve higher profits, which most firms will prefer to lower profits.

Conditions necessary for price discrimination to operate

As we have seen, a firm is able to increase its profits if it can engage in price discrimination. But under what circumstances will it be able to charge discriminatory prices? There are three conditions that must be met:

- The firm must have market power: in other words, it must face a downward-sloping demand curve and hence can set its price. Thus price discrimination would be impossible under perfect competition, where firms are price takers.
- There must be no opportunity (or, in the case of first-degree price discrimination, willingness) to resell the product for a higher price. For example, children must not be able to resell a half-priced child's cinema ticket for use by an adult.
- For third-degree price discrimination, demand elasticity must differ in each market. The firm will charge the higher price in the market where demand is less elastic, and thus less sensitive to a price rise.

Price discrimination and the consumer

No clear-cut decision can be made over the desirability of price discrimination from the point of view of the consumer. Some people will benefit from it; others will lose. This leaves the net effect on the consumer indeterminate. This can be illustrated by considering the effects of price discrimination on the following aspects of the market.

Distribution

Those paying the higher price will probably feel that price discrimination is unfair to them. On the other hand, those charged the lower price may thereby be able to obtain a good or service that they could otherwise not afford: e.g. concessionary bus fares for old-age pensioners. Price discrimination is likely to increase output and make the good or service available to more people.

Competition

It is possible that a firm may use price discrimination to drive competitors out of business. This is known as ***predatory pricing***. Under this practice, a company charges a price below average cost in one market by cross-subsidising that part of the business with profits from another part of the business. It does this until its rival stops competing in that market.

Predatory pricing, however, is illegal under UK and European competition law. Even though consumers gain from lower prices in the short run, the long-run strategy of predatory firms is to raise their prices once their competitor has been driven from the market.

On the other hand, a firm that engages in price discrimination might use its profits from its high-priced market to break into another market and withstand a possible price war. This would increase competition and hence consumer welfare. Alternatively, it might use the higher profits to invest in new and improved products that enhance consumer choice.

Other pricing strategies

There are numerous other pricing strategies used by firms and we briefly mention these here. Each involves an element of price discrimination. They include the following.

Peak-load pricing. This is where people are charged more at times of peak demand and less at off-peak times (see Case Study F.6 in MyEconLab). For example, bus and train fares are often highest during the 'rush hours' in which consumers want to get to work. Similarly, the price of telephone calls is highest during the working day. During 'off-peak' times, prices are lower.

Part of the reason for this practice is the lower price elasticity of demand at peak times. For example, many commuters have little option but to pay higher rail fares at peak times. This is genuine price discrimination. But part of the reason has to do with higher marginal costs incurred at peak times, as capacity limits are reached.

Definition

Predatory pricing Where a firm sets its average price below average cost in order to drive competitors out of business.

Inter-temporal pricing. This occurs where different groups have different price elasticities of demand for a product at different points in time. When a product is launched, some consumers have an inelastic demand for it. They want it and are willing to pay a higher price for it. For example, some consumers want to have the most up-to-date technology and are willing to pay more for a new mobile phone that is released with innovative features. Similarly, when computers are available with a new, faster processing chip, the price tends to be higher. Later the price of such products is reduced, thereby selling to people less anxious to switch to the latest version.

However, it is not just high-tech items that attract such pricing strategies. A book written by a celebrity author is usually released in the higher-priced, and more profitable, hardback form to capture the desire of more avid fans before being released in the lower-price paperback version sometime later.

As with peak-load pricing, inter-temporal pricing is only partly to do with price elasticity of demand and hence only partly genuine (third-degree) price discrimination. Part of

the reason has to do with the reduction in costs over the longer term as firms experience economies of scale or a reduction in the price of key inputs (such as chips).

Two-part tariff. This is a pricing system that requires customers to pay an access and a usage price for a product. This practice is used in a variety of settings but particularly in the telecommunications and energy sectors. For example, most customers who use gas have to pay a fixed standing charge per period of time and then pay so much per therm of gas used.

The aim of these schemes is to increase the firm's revenue, by giving it a lump-sum payment per customer (particularly relevant where the firm has high fixed costs) on top of the price per unit. The problem is setting the appropriate two-part tariff. This is particularly difficult when there is a lot of competition between firms and when customers are quite prepared to switch supplier. It is for this reason that there are a number of mobile phone two-part tariff plans for customers with an average to high usage, as well as a 'Pay-As-You-Go' option aimed at lighter users.

17.4 MULTIPLE PRODUCT PRICING

Thus far in our analysis of pricing strategy, we have been concerned only with a single product produced by a single firm. However, many businesses produce a range of products. Such products might be totally distinct and sold in different markets, or the firm might offer a range of models in the same market that differ in design and performance. For example, a vacuum cleaner manufacturer might also produce other household appliances such as irons, as well as offering a range of vacuums with different suction abilities and design features.

Each of these products and product ranges will require its own distinct price, and probably a longer-term pricing strategy. However, multiproduct pricing raises a wider set of issues due to the interrelated nature of demand and production.

Interrelated demand

Many of the large supermarkets or DIY stores are in fierce competition for business. It is quite normal to see them offering 'bargain buys', whose prices are cut dramatically in order to attract customers to the store. Often their price is even below average cost. Such cases are known as *loss leaders*. The hope is that customers will purchase not just the loss leader, but additional amounts of other products with full profit mark-ups, thereby bringing a net gain in profits.

This strategy is known as *full-range pricing* and involves the business assessing the prices of all its products together,

and deciding from this how it might improve its profit performance. One of the most important considerations is the price elasticity of demand for the loss leader. The more elastic it is, the more customers will tend to be attracted into the store by the bargain. The business will also consider additional factors such as advertising the loss leaders and their positioning in the store, so as to attract customers to see other items at full price that they had not intended to buy.

KI 12
p 63

Definitions

Peak-load pricing The practice of charging higher prices at times when demand is highest because the constraints on capacity lead to higher marginal cost.

Inter-temporal pricing This occurs where different groups have different price elasticities of demand for a product at different points in time.

Two-part tariff A pricing system that requires customers to pay both an access and a usage price for a product.

Loss leader A product whose price is cut by the business in order to attract custom.

Full-range pricing A pricing strategy in which a business, seeking to improve its profit performance, assesses the pricing of its goods as a whole rather than individually.

Other demand interrelations that might influence the pricing policy of a business are where a business produces either complementary or substitute products. If a business produces complementary products, then increased sales of one product, such as Apple's iPod, will raise the revenue gained from the other, such as the use of the iTunes store. Alternatively, if the products produced by a business are substitutes, such as those of a breakfast cereal manufacturer like Kellogg's, then the increased sales of one product within its range may well detract from the revenue gained from the others. Businesses like Apple and Kellogg's should therefore determine the prices of all their substitute and complementary products jointly so as to assess the total revenue implications. Here it is vital for the firm to have estimates of the cross-price elasticities of demand for their products (see section 5.3).

Interrelated production

The production of **by-products** is the most common form of interrelated production. A by-product is a good or service that is produced as a consequence of producing another good or service. For example, whey is a by-product of cheese. By-products have their own distinct market demand. However, the by-product is only produced following demand for the main production good: it may well not be profitable to produce as a separate product.

To consider whether the by-product is profitable to sell, it is important to allocate the correct costs to its production.

The raw materials and much of the other inputs to produce it can be considered to have a zero cost, since they have already been paid in producing the main product. But packaging, marketing and distributing the by-product clearly involve costs that have to be allocated directly to it, and the price it sells for must more than cover these costs.

It is not as simple as this, however, since the pricing of the by-product, and the subsequent revenue gained from its sale, might significantly influence the pricing of the main production good. Given that the two products share joint costs, a business must carefully consider how to allocate costs between them and what pricing policy it is going to pursue.

If it is aiming to maximise profits, it should add the marginal costs from both products to get an *MC* curve for the 'combined' product. Similarly, it should add the marginal revenues from both products at each output to get an *MR* curve for the combined product. It should then choose the combined output where the combined *MC* equals the combined *MR*. It should read off the price at this output for each of the two products from their separate demand curves.

In practice, many firms simply decide on the viability of selling by-products *after* a decision has been made on producing the main product. If the specific costs associated with the by-product can be more than covered, then the firm will go ahead and sell it.

17.5 TRANSFER PRICING

The growth of modern business, both national and international, has meant that its organisation has become ever more complex. In an attempt to reduce the diseconomies that stem from coordinating such large business enterprises, the setting of price and output levels is frequently decentralised to individual divisions or profit centres. Such divisions or profit centres are assumed to operate in a semi-independent way, aiming to maximise their individual performance and, in so doing, benefit the business as a whole.

However, the decentralisation of pricing and output decision making can become problematic. This is particularly the case when the various divisions within the firm represent distinct stages in the production process. In these instances, certain divisions may well produce intermediate products that they will sell to other divisions within the business. There then arises the difficulty of how such intermediate products should be priced. This is known as the problem of **transfer** pricing.

One implication of this is that a division which is seeking to maximise its own profits when selling to another division will attempt to exploit its 'monopoly' position

and increase the transfer price. As it does so, the purchasing division, unless it, in turn, can pass on the higher cost, will see its profits fall. Indeed, if it could, the purchasing division would seek to drive down the purchase price as low as possible.

This conflict between divisions may not necessarily be in the interests of the business as a whole. The solution to this problem is for divisions to base their pricing of intermediate products on marginal costs. The marginal cost of the final product produced by the business will then be a 'true' marginal cost. If the business is seeking to maximise overall profits, it can then compare this final marginal cost

Definitions

By-product A good or service that is produced as a consequence of producing another good or service.

Transfer pricing The pricing system used within a business organisation to transfer intermediate products between the business's various divisions.

with marginal revenue in order to decide on the level of total output. The lesson is that, for maximum company profits, individual divisions should seek to be efficient and produce with the lowest possible marginal costs, but not seek to maximise their own division's profits.

Transfer pricing within multinational companies is an area of concern for tax authorities. The price used to transfer goods between plants located in different countries is not determined by a market. The price could be set to avoid tax, ensuring that profits appear in countries where taxes on profits are lowest. OECD countries have agreed that tax liabilities on profits should be calculated using prices that would have arisen if the transfers had taken place between independent firms, rather than within one firm. In practice this is difficult to achieve and extremely hard to police. We examine this issue further in section 23.6 (see pages 384–5).

17.6 PRICING AND THE PRODUCT LIFE CYCLE

New products are launched and then become established. Later they may be replaced by more up-to-date products. Many products go through such a 'life cycle'. Four stages can be identified in a typical life cycle (see Figure 17.7):

1. Being launched.
2. A rapid growth in sales.
3. Maturity: a levelling off in sales.
4. Decline: sales begin to fall as the market becomes saturated, or as the product becomes out of date.

Analogue televisions, audio cassettes and traditional mobile phones have all reached stage 4. Writable CDs, DIY products and automatic washing machines have reached stage 3. Large LED TVs, speed-dating events, fairtrade herbal teas, induction hobs, music downloads and smart phones are probably still in stage 2. Electric cars, HD multimedia entertainment devices and biodiesel are probably still in stage 1 (at least they were when we wrote this – but things move quickly!).

At each stage, the firm is likely to be faced with quite different market conditions: not only in terms of consumer demand, but also in terms of competition from rivals. What does this mean for pricing strategy?

The launch stage

In this stage the firm will probably have a monopoly (unless there is a simultaneous launch by rivals).

Given the lack of substitutes, the firm may be able to charge very high prices and make large profits. This will be especially true if it is a radically new product – like the ballpoint pen, the home computer and the mobile phone were. Such products are likely to have a rapidly expanding and price-inelastic demand.

Pause for thought

If entry barriers are high, should a firm always charge a high price during this phase?

The danger of a high-price policy is that the resulting high profits may tempt competitors to break into the

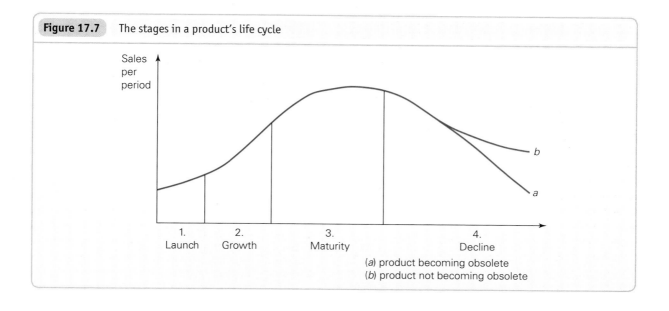

Figure 17.7 The stages in a product's life cycle

(a) product becoming obsolete
(b) product not becoming obsolete

industry, even if barriers are quite high. As an alternative, then, the firm may go for maximum 'market penetration': keeping the price low to get as many sales and as much brand loyalty as possible, before rivals can become established.

Which policy the firm adopts will depend on its assessment of its current price elasticity of demand and the likelihood of an early entry by rivals.

The growth stage

Unless entry barriers are very high, the rapid growth in sales will attract new firms. The industry becomes oligopolistic.

Despite the growth in the number of firms, sales are expanding so rapidly that all firms can increase their sales. Some price competition may emerge, but it is unlikely to be intense at this stage. New entrants may choose to compete in terms of minor product differences, while following the price lead set by the original firm.

The maturity stage

Now that the market has grown large, there are many firms competing. New firms – or, more likely, firms diversifying into this market – will be entering to get 'a piece of the action'. At the same time, the growth in sales is slowing down.

Competition is now likely to be more intense and collusion may well begin to break down. Pricing policy may become more aggressive as businesses attempt to hold on to their market share. Price wars may break out, only to be followed later by a 'truce' and a degree of price collusion.

It is in this stage particularly that firms may invest considerably in product innovation in order to 'breathe new life' into old products, especially if there is competition from new types of product. Thus the upgrading of hi-fi cassette recorders, with additional features such as Dolby S, was one way in which it was hoped to beat off competition from digital cassette recorders.

The decline stage

Eventually, as the market becomes saturated, or as new superior alternative products are launched, sales will start to fall. For example, once most households had a fridge, the demand for fridges fell back as people simply bought them to replace worn-out ones, or to obtain a more up-to-date one. Initially in this stage, competition is likely to be intense. All sorts of price offers, extended guarantees, better after-sales service, added features, etc., will be introduced as firms seek to maintain their sales. Some firms may be driven out of the market, unable to survive the competition.

After a time, however, the level of sales may stop falling. Provided the product has not become obsolete, people still need replacements. This is illustrated in Figure 17.7 by line *b*. The market may thus return to a stable oligopoly with a high degree of tacit price collusion.

Alternatively, the product becomes obsolete (line *a*) and sales dry up. Firms will leave the market. It is pointless trying to compete.

SUMMARY

1a Prices are determined by a wide range of factors, principal among which are demand and supply, market structure and the aims of managers.

1b Firms with market power will not always attempt to maximise short-run profits, even if maximum profit is the aim. They may well limit prices so as to forestall the entry of new firms.

2a Traditional economic theory assumes that businesses will set prices corresponding to the output where the marginal costs of production are equal to marginal revenue. They will do so in pursuit of maximum profits.

2b The difficulties that a business faces in deriving its marginal cost and revenue curves suggest that this is unlikely to be a widely practised pricing strategy.

2c Cost-based pricing involves the business adding a profit mark-up to its average costs of production. The profit mark-up set by the business is likely to alter depending upon market conditions, such as the level of consumer demand and the degree of market competition.

3a Many businesses practise price discrimination, in an attempt to maximise profits from the sale of a product. There are different types of price discrimination that a business might practise.

3b For a business to practise price discrimination it must be able to set prices, separate markets so as to prevent resale from the cheap to the expensive market, and identify distinct demand elasticities in each market.

3c Whether price discrimination is in the consumer's interest or not is uncertain. Some individuals will gain and some will lose.

4 Businesses that produce many products need to consider the demand and production interrelations between them when setting prices.

5a The organisation of a business as a series of divisions, each pursuing an independent strategy, has implications for pricing policy, especially when products are sold within a business enterprise.

5b The optimum transfer price between divisions from the point of view of the whole organisation is likely to be equal to marginal cost.

6a Products will be priced differently depending upon where they are in the product's life cycle.

6b New products can be priced cheaply so as to gain market share, or priced expensively to recoup cost. Later on in the product's life cycle, prices will have to reflect the degree of competition, which may become intense as the market stabilises or even declines.

REVIEW QUESTIONS

1 Explain why a business will find it difficult to set prices following the $MC = MR$ rule of traditional economic theory.

2 'Basing prices on average cost is no less problematical than using marginal cost and marginal revenue.' Assess this statement.

3 Outline the main factors that might influence the size of the profit mark-up set by a business.

4 If a cinema could sell all its seats to adults in the evenings at the end of the week, but only a few on Mondays and Tuesdays, what price discrimination policy would you recommend to the cinema in order for it to maximise its weekly revenue?

5 What is the role of a loss leader and what lessons might a business learn when pricing a range of products? Are there any supermarket products that would *not* be suitable to sell as loss leaders?

6 How will a business's pricing strategy differ at each stage of its product's life cycle? First assume that the business has a monopoly position at the launch stage; then assume that it faces a high degree of competition right from the outset.

ADDITIONAL PART F CASE STUDIES IN THE *ECONOMICS FOR BUSINESS* MyEconLab (www.pearsoned.co.uk/sloman)

F.1 **What do you maximise?** An examination of 'rational' behaviour from an individual's point of view – including individual managers.

F.2 **When is a theory not a theory?** A light-hearted examination of the difficulties of formulating theories from evidence.

F.3 **Business divorce.** A case study of the demergers of ICI and Hanson.

F.4 **Enron.** A cautionary tale of business growth.

F.5 **Hypergrowth companies.** Why do some companies grow quickly and are they likely to be a long-term success?

F.6 **Peak load pricing.** An example of price discrimination: charging more when it costs more to produce.

F.7 **Price discrimination in the cinema.** An illustration of why it might be in a cinema's interests to offer concessionary prices at off-peak times, but not at peak times.

F.8 **How do UK companies set prices?** The findings of a Bank of England survey.

WEBSITES RELEVANT TO PART F

Numbers and sections refer to websites listed in the Web appendix and hotlinked from this book's website at **www.pearsoned.co.uk/sloman**

■ For news articles relevant to Part F, see the *Economics News Articles* link from the book's website.

■ For general news relevant to alternative strategies, see websites in section A, and particularly A2, 3, 8, 9, 23, 24, 25, 26, 35, 36. See also A38, 39 and 43 for links to newspapers worldwide; and A42 for links to economics news articles on particular search topics from newspapers worldwide.

■ For student resources relevant to Part F, see sites C1–7, 9, 10, 19.

■ For information on mergers, see sites E4, 10, 18, 20.

■ For data on SME, see the SME database in B3 or E10.

■ For information on pricing, see site E10 and the sites of the regulators of the privatised industries: E16, 19, 21, 22, 25.

■ Sites I7 and 11 in the Business section contain links to *Business > Management > Organisational Management*.

The firm in the factor market

The FT Reports . . .

The Financial Times, 21 May 2012

FT

A German model goes global

By Chris Bryant

Mercedes-Benz began building cars near Tuscaloosa, Alabama more than 15 years ago. Over time, US sales and the technological complexity of its vehicles accelerated but the company faced a bigger challenge: the supply of skilled labour did not keep pace and the German company feared driving headlong into a wall. 'Producing a Mercedes car is a hugely technical task in terms of the materials and process involved such as automation technology, laser welding and gluing,' says Marcus Schaefer, chief executive of Mercedes-Benz US International. 'That ultimately requires high-quality trained people who can manage the technology in the plant. But there was a gap between what we could get from the labour market and what we needed in the plant.'

Mercedes-Benz decided to take matters into its own hands and set up an apprenticeship scheme based on the German dual system, which emphasises a combination of theoretical training in the classroom and hands-on technical experience on the factory floor. In January, 40 Alabama high-school graduates began a seven-semester programme at the plant.

In Germany, apprentice schemes such as this are the norm. About 60 per cent of the country's school leavers begin an apprenticeship, which lasts up to three and a half years. . . .

Meanwhile, as students in western countries emerge from university with huge debts and dim job prospects, the ability of the German system to match young people's skills to those required by the labour market is seen as attractive. . . .

To do this requires adapting the German model to the local market. . . . German companies also seek to involve local partners, especially local colleges, both to help train the apprentices and to develop the curriculum. . . .

Many companies also find that creating an apprenticeship scheme can be cheaper than scouring the labour market for talent. Trainees tend to be more loyal and the programmes are also good for their corporate image. . . .

'It's never been about finding cheaper labour,' [says Schaefer]. 'The focus has always been on high-tech processes, efficiency and quality output. That requires skilled people and so I think more and more companies will create their own apprenticeship programmes.'

Since 1970 women have filled two new jobs for every one taken by a man. Back-of-the-envelope calculations suggest that the employment of extra women has not only added more to GDP than new jobs for men but has also chipped in more than either capital investment or increased productivity.

'Women and the world economy: A guide to womenomics', *The Economist*, 15 April 2006

So far we have considered the role of the firm as a supplier of goods and services. In other words, we have looked at the operation of firms in the goods market. But to produce goods and services involves using factors of production: labour, capital and raw materials. In Part G, therefore, we turn to examine the behaviour of firms in factor markets and, in particular, the market for labour and the market for capital.

In factor markets, the supply and demand roles are reversed. The firm is *demanding* factors of production in order to *produce* goods and services. This demand for factors is thus a *derived* demand: one that is derived from consumers' demand for the firm's products. Households, on the other hand, in order to earn the money to buy goods and services, are *supplying* labour. Chapter 18 focuses upon labour and the determination of wage rates. It also shows how the existence of power, whether of employers or trade unions, affects the wage rate and the level of employment in a given labour market. In addition to the issue of wage determination, we will consider the problem of low pay and discrimination, and the implications for the labour market of growing levels of flexibility in employment practices (see the *Financial Times* article). We also look at the effects of the minimum wage.

In Chapter 19 we will consider the employment of capital by firms and look at the relationship between the business and investment. We will consider how businesses appraise the profitability of investment. We will also examine the various sources of finance for investment. The chapter finishes by examining the stock market. We ask whether it is an efficient means of allocating capital.

Key terms

Derived demand
Wage taker
Wage setter
Marginal revenue product
Monopsony
Bilateral monopoly
Trade union
Collective bargaining
Efficiency wages
Minimum wage rates
Discrimination
The flexible firm
Core and peripheral
  workers
Insiders and outsiders
Capital
Capital services
Investment
Discounting
Net present value
Financial intermediaries
Maturity transformation
Risk transformation
Retail and wholesale
  banking
Efficient capital markets
Weak, semi-strong and
  strong efficiency
Random walk

18 Chapter

Labour markets, wages and industrial relations

Business issues covered in this chapter

■ How has the UK labour market changed over the years?

■ How are wage rates determined in a perfect labour market?

■ What are the determinants of the demand and supply of labour and their respective elasticities?

■ What forms of market power exist in the labour market and what determines the power of employers and labour?

■ What effects do powerful employers and trade unions have on wages and employment?

■ What are the causes of low pay?

■ How has the minimum wage affected business and employment?

■ What is meant by a 'flexible' labour market and how has increased flexibility affected working practices, employment and wages?

In this chapter we will consider how labour markets operate. In particular, we will focus on the determination of wage rates in different types of market: ones where employers are wage takers, ones where they can choose the wage rate, and ones where wage rates are determined by a process of collective bargaining.

We start by examining some of the key trends in the structure of the labour market.

18.1 THE UK LABOUR MARKET

The labour market has undergone great change in recent years. Advances in technology, changes in the pattern of output, a need to be competitive in international markets and various social changes have all contributed to changes in work practices and in the structure and composition of the workforce.

Major changes in the UK include the following:

■ A shift from agricultural and manufacturing to service-sector employment. Figure 18.1 reveals that employment in agriculture has been falling over a long historical period (until very recently). The fall in

manufacturing employment, however, has been more recent, starting in the 1960s and gathering pace through the 1970s, 1980s and 1990s. By contrast, employment in the service industries has grown steadily since 1946. In fact, since 1980 it has expanded by some 8.5 million jobs.

■ A rise in part-time employment. In 1971, 17 per cent of those in employment worked part time; by June 2012 this had risen to 27 per cent. In the EU as a whole, the figure is around 20 per cent. The growth in part-time work reflects the growth in the service sector, where many jobs are part time.

Figure 18.1   Employment in different sectors of the UK economy

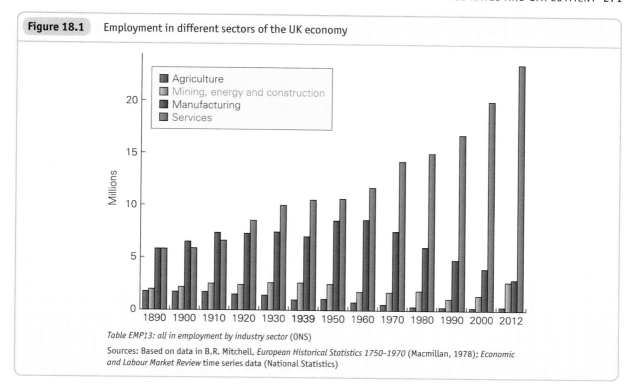

Table EMP13: all in employment by industry sector (ONS)

Sources: Based on data in B.R. Mitchell, *European Historical Statistics 1750–1970* (Macmillan, 1978); *Economic and Labour Market Review* time series data (National Statistics)

■ A rise in female participation rates. Women now constitute approximately half of the paid labour force. The rise in participation rates is strongly associated with the growth in the service sector and the creation of part-time positions. Some 43 per cent of female workers, about 5.9 million, are in part-time work. In the EU as a whole, 33 per cent of female workers work part time.

■ A rise in the proportion of workers employed on fixed-term contracts, or on a temporary or casual basis. Many firms nowadays prefer to employ only their core workers/managers on a permanent ('continuing') basis. They feel that it gives them more flexibility to respond to changing market conditions to have the remainder of their workers employed on a short-term basis and, perhaps, to make use of agency staff or to contract out work.

■ *Downsizing*. It has become very fashionable in recent years for companies to try to 'trim' the numbers of their employees in order to reduce costs. There is now, however, a growing consensus that the process may have gone too far. The cost of reducing its workforce may be that a company loses revenue: if it cuts back on people employed to market its products, develop new products or ensure that quality is maintained, then it is likely to lose market share. It might reduce unit costs, but total profits could nevertheless fall, not rise.

18.2 MARKET-DETERMINED WAGE RATES AND EMPLOYMENT

Perfect labour markets

When looking at the market for labour, it is useful to make a similar distinction to that made in the theory of the firm: the distinction between perfect and imperfect markets. Although in practice few labour markets are totally perfect, many do at least approximate to it.

The key assumption of a perfect labour market is that everyone is a *wage taker*. In other words, neither employers nor employees have any economic power to affect wage rates. This situation is not uncommon. Small employers are likely to have to pay the 'going wage rate' to their employees, especially where the employee is of a clear category, such as an electrician, a bar worker, a secretary or a porter. As far as employees are concerned, being a wage taker means not being a member of a union and therefore not being able to use collective bargaining to push up the wage rate.

> ### Definitions
>
> **Downsizing** Where a business reorganises and reduces its size, especially in respect to levels of employment, in order to cut costs.
>
> **Wage taker** The wage rate is determined by market forces.

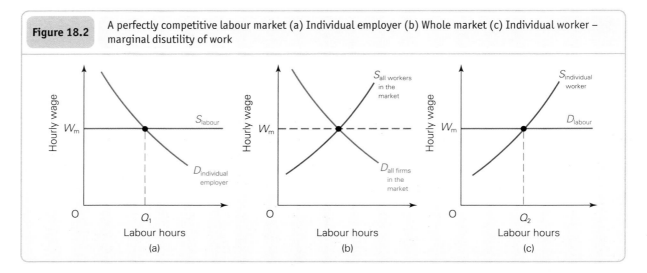

Figure 18.2 A perfectly competitive labour market (a) Individual employer (b) Whole market (c) Individual worker – marginal disutility of work

The other assumptions of a perfect labour market are as follows:

- *Freedom of entry.* There are no restrictions on the movement of labour. For example, workers are free to move to alternative jobs or to areas of the country where wage rates are higher. There are no barriers erected by, say, unions, professional associations or the government. Of course, it takes time for workers to change jobs and maybe to retrain. This assumption therefore applies only in the long run.
- *Perfect knowledge.* Workers are fully aware of what jobs are available at what wage rates and with what conditions of employment. Likewise employers know what labour is available and how productive that labour is.
- *Homogeneous labour.* It is usually assumed that, in perfect markets, workers of a given category are identical in terms of productivity. For example, it would be assumed that all bricklayers are equally skilled and motivated.

Pause for thought

Which of these assumptions do you think would be correct in each of the following cases? (a) Supermarket checkout operators. (b) Agricultural workers. (c) Crane operators. (d) Business studies teachers. (e) Call centre workers.

KI 11
p 55
Wage rates and employment under perfect competition are determined by the interaction of the market demand and supply of labour. This is illustrated in Figure 18.2(b).

Generally it would be expected that the supply and demand curves slope the same way as in goods markets. The higher the wage paid for a certain type of job, the

more workers will want to do that job. This gives an upward-sloping supply curve of labour. On the other hand, the higher the wage that employers have to pay, the less labour they will want to employ. Either they will simply produce less output, or they will substitute other factors of production, like machinery, for labour. Thus the demand curve for labour slopes downwards.

Figure 18.2(a) shows how an individual employer has to accept this wage. The supply of labour to that employer is infinitely elastic. In other words, at the market wage W_m, there is no limit to the number of workers available to that employer (but no workers at all will be available below it: they will all be working elsewhere). At the market wage W_m, the employer will employ Q_1 hours of labour.

Figure 18.2(c) shows how an individual worker also has to accept this wage. In this case it is the demand curve for that worker that is infinitely elastic. In other words, there is as much work as the worker cares to do at this wage (but none at all above it).

We now turn to look at the supply and demand for labour in more detail.

The supply of labour

We can look at the supply of labour at three levels: the supply of hours by an individual worker (Figure 18.2(c)), the supply of workers to an individual employer (Figure 18.2(a)) and the total market supply of a given category of labour (Figure 18.2(b)). Let us examine each in turn.

The supply of hours by an individual worker

Work involves two major costs (or 'disutilities') to the worker:

- When people work they sacrifice leisure.
- The work itself may be unpleasant.

KI 9
p 47

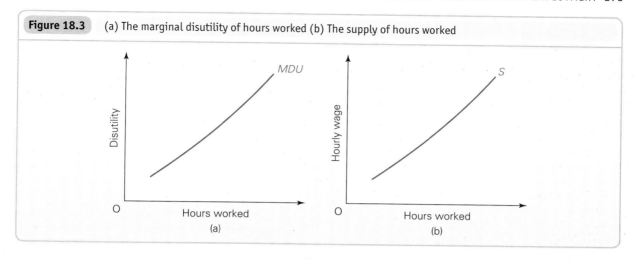

Figure 18.3 (a) The marginal disutility of hours worked (b) The supply of hours worked

KI 15
p 83
Each extra hour worked will involve additional disutility. This *marginal disutility of work* (*MDU*) will tend to *increase* as people work more hours. There are two reasons for this. First, the less the leisure they have left, the greater the disutility they experience in sacrificing a further hour of leisure. Second, the unpleasantness they experience in doing the job will tend to increase due to boredom or tiredness.

This increasing marginal disutility (see Figure 18.3(a)) will tend to give an upward-sloping supply curve of hours by an individual worker (see Figure 18.3(b)). The reason is that, in order to persuade people to work more hours, a higher hourly wage must be paid to compensate for the higher marginal disutility incurred. This helps explain why overtime rates are higher than standard rates.

Under certain circumstances, however, the supply of hours curve might bend backwards (see Figure 18.4). The reason is that, when wage rates go up, there will be two opposing forces operating on the individual's labour supply.

On the one hand, with higher wage rates people will tend to work more hours, since leisure would now involve a greater sacrifice of income and hence consumption. They substitute income for leisure. This is called the *substitution effect* of the increase in wage rates.

On the other hand, people may feel that with higher wage rates they can afford to work less and have more leisure. This is called the *income effect*.

The relative magnitude of these two effects determines the slope of the individual's supply curve. It is normally assumed that the substitution effect outweighs the income effect, especially at lower wage rates. A rise in wage rates acts as an incentive: it encourages a person to work more hours. It is possible, however, that the income effect will outweigh the substitution effect. Particularly at very high wage rates people say, 'There's not so much point now in doing overtime. I can afford to spend more time at home.'

If the wage rate becomes high enough for the income effect to dominate, the supply curve will begin to slope backward. This occurs above a wage rate of W_1 in Figure 18.4.

These considerations are particularly important for a government considering tax cuts. The Conservative governments of the 1980s and 1990s and the Coalition government from 2010 have argued that cuts in income taxes are like giving people a pay rise, and thus provide an incentive for people to work harder. This analysis is only correct, however, if the substitution effect dominates. If the income effect dominates, people will work less after the tax cut.

Figure 18.4 Backward-bending supply curve of labour

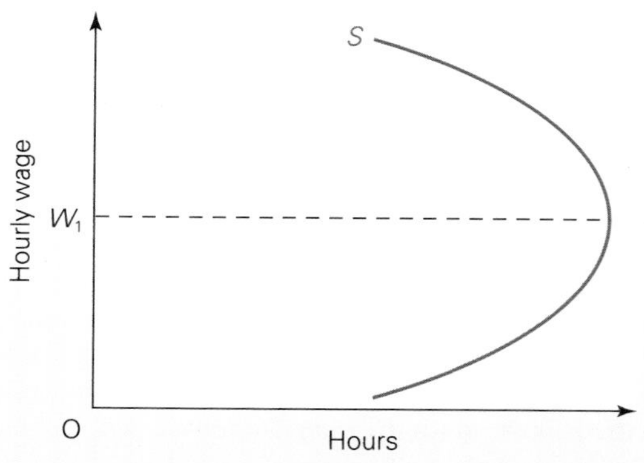

Definitions

Marginal disutility of work The extra sacrifice/hardship to a worker of working an extra unit of time in any given time period (e.g. an extra hour per day).

Substitution effect of a rise in wages Workers will tend to substitute income for leisure as leisure now has a higher opportunity cost. This effect leads to *more* hours being worked as wages rise.

Income effect of a rise in wages Workers get a higher income for a given number of hours worked and may thus feel they need to work fewer hours as wages rise.

BOX 18.1 'TELECOMMUTERS'

The electronic cottage

The increasing sophistication of information technology, with direct computer linking, broadband access to the Internet, fax machines and mobile phones, has meant that many people can work at home. The number of these 'telecommuters' has grown steadily since the information technology revolution of the early 1980s.

It has been found that where 'telecommuting networks' have been established, gains in productivity levels have been significant, when compared with comparable office workers. Most studies indicate rises in productivity of over 35 per cent. With fewer interruptions and less chatting with fellow workers, less working time is lost. Add to this the stress-free environment, free from the strain of commuting, and the individual worker's performance is enhanced.

With further savings in time, in the renting and maintenance of offices (often in high-cost inner-city locations) and in heating and lighting costs, the economic arguments in favour of telecommuting seem very persuasive.

These technological developments have been the equivalent of an increase in labour mobility. Work can be taken to the workers rather than the workers coming to the work. The effect is to reduce the premium that needs to be paid to workers in commercial centres, such as the City of London.

Then there are the broader gains to society. Telecommuting opens up the labour market to a wider group of workers who might find it relatively difficult to leave the home – groups such as single parents and the disabled. Also, concerns that managers lose control over their employees, and that the

quality of work falls, appear unfounded. In fact the reverse seems to have occurred: the quality of work in many cases has improved.

But do such employees feel isolated? For many people, work is an important part of their social environment, providing them with an opportunity to meet others and to work as a team. For those who are unable to leave the home, however, telecommuting may be the *only* means of earning a living: the choice of travelling to work may simply not be open to them. The existence of video call software, such as Skype, has reduced some of these problems. However, for many, this technology is a poor substitute for being in the same room.

There is no reason, of course, why telecommuters cannot work in different countries. Increasingly companies in developed countries are employing low-wage workers in the developing world to do data processing, telesales and various types of 'back-office' work.

However, telecommuters can be exploited. In 2008, for example, the Low Pay Commission has found that many homeworkers are paid well below the minimum wage. The main reason is that employers pay by the amount of work done and underestimate the amount of time it takes to complete work.

1. ↑*What effects are such developments likely to have on (a) trade union membership; (b) trade union power?*
2. *How is a growth in telecommuting likely to affect relative house prices between capital cities and the regions?*

The supply of labour to an individual employer

Under perfect competition, the supply of labour to a particular firm will be perfectly elastic, as in Figure 18.2(a). The firm is a 'wage taker' and thus has no power to influence wages.

The market supply of a given type of labour

This will typically be upward sloping. The higher the wage rate offered in a particular type of job, the more people will want to do that job.

The *position* of the market supply curve of labour will depend on the number of people willing and able to do the job at each given wage rate. This depends on three things:

- the number of qualified people;
- the non-wage benefits or costs of the job, such as the pleasantness or otherwise of the working environment, job satisfaction or dissatisfaction, status, power, the

degree of job security, holidays, perks and other fringe benefits;
- the wages and non-wage benefits in alternative jobs.

Pause for thought

Which way will the supply curve shift if the wage rates in alternative jobs rise?

A change in the wage rate will cause a movement along the supply curve. A change in any of these other three determinants will shift the whole curve.

The elasticity of the market supply of labour

How *responsive* will the supply of labour be to a change in the wage rate? If the market wage rate goes up, will a lot more labour become available or only a little? This responsiveness (elasticity) depends on (a) the difficulties and costs of changing jobs and (b) the time period.

Another way of looking at the elasticity of supply of labour is in terms of the **mobility of labour**: the willingness and ability of labour to move to another job, whether in a different location (geographical mobility) or in a different industry (occupational mobility). The mobility of labour (and hence the elasticity of supply of labour) will be higher when there are alternative jobs in the same location, when alternative jobs require similar skills and when people have good information about these jobs.

It is also much higher in the long run, when people have the time to acquire new skills and when the education system has had time to adapt to the changing demands of industry.

The demand for labour: the marginal productivity theory

The traditional 'neoclassical' theory of the firm assumes that firms aim to maximise profits. The same assumption is made in the neoclassical theory of labour demand. This theory is generally known as the **marginal productivity theory**.

The profit-maximising approach

How many workers will a profit-maximising firm want to employ? The firm will answer this question by weighing up the costs of employing extra labour against the benefits. It will use exactly the same principles as in deciding how much output to produce.

In the goods market, the firm will maximise profits where the marginal cost of an extra unit of *goods* produced equals the marginal revenue from selling it: $MC = MR$.

In the labour market, the firm will maximise profits where the marginal cost of employing an extra *worker* equals the marginal revenue that the worker's output earns for the firm: MC of labour = MR of labour. The reasoning is simple. If an extra worker adds more to a firm's revenue than to its costs, the firm's profits will increase. It will be worth employing that worker. But as more workers are employed, diminishing returns to labour will set in (see page 130). Each extra worker will produce less than the previous one, and thus earn less revenue for the firm. Eventually the marginal revenue from extra workers will fall to the level of their marginal cost. At that point the firm will stop employing extra workers. There are no additional profits to be gained. Profits are at a maximum.

Measuring the marginal cost and revenue of labour

Marginal cost of labour (MC_L). This is the extra cost of employing one more worker. Under perfect competition the firm is too small to affect the market wage. It faces a horizontal supply curve (see Figure 18.2(a)). In other words, it can employ as many workers as it chooses at the market wage rate. Thus the additional cost of employing one more person will simply be the wage rate: $MC_L = W$.

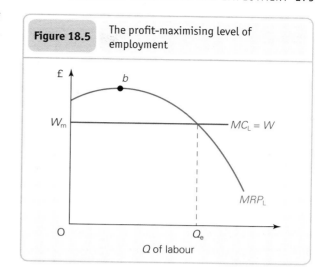

Figure 18.5 The profit-maximising level of employment

Marginal revenue of labour (MRP_L). The marginal revenue that the firm gains from employing one more worker is called the **marginal revenue product of labour** (MRP_L). The MRP_L is found by multiplying two elements – the *marginal physical product* of labour (MPP_L) and the marginal revenue gained by selling one more unit of output (MR).

$$MRP_L = MPP_L \times MR$$

The MPP_L is the extra output produced by the last worker. Thus if the last worker produces 100 tonnes of output per week (MPP_L), and if the firm earns an extra £2 for each additional tonne sold (MR), then the worker's MRP is £200. This extra worker is adding £200 to the firm's revenue.

The profit-maximising level of employment for a firm

The MRP_L curve is illustrated in Figure 18.5. As more workers are employed, there will come a point when diminishing returns set in (point *b*). Thereafter the MRP_L curve slopes downwards. The figure also shows the MC_L 'curve' at the current market wage W_m.

Definitions

Mobility of labour The ease with which labour can either shift between jobs (occupational mobility) or move to other parts of the country in search of work (geographical mobility).

Marginal productivity theory The theory that the demand for a factor depends on its marginal revenue product.

Marginal revenue product of labour The extra revenue a firm earns from employing one more unit of labour.

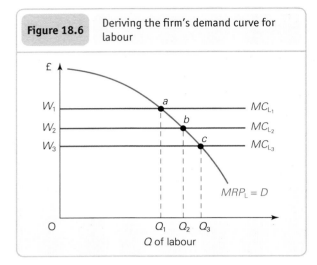

Figure 18.6 Deriving the firm's demand curve for labour

KI 4
p 22

Profits are maximised at an employment level of Q_e, where MC_L (i.e. W) = MRP_L. Why? At levels of employment below Q_e, MRP_L exceeds MC_L. The firm will increase profits by employing more labour. At levels of employment above Q_e, MC_L exceeds MRP_L. In this case the firm will increase profits by reducing employment.

Derivation of the firm's demand curve for labour

No matter what the wage rate, the quantity of labour demanded will be found from the intersection of W and MRP_L (see Figure 18.6). At a wage rate of W_1, Q_1 labour is demanded (point a); at W_2, Q_2 is demanded (point b); at W_3, Q_3 is demanded (point c).

Thus the MRP_L curve shows the quantity of labour employed at each wage rate. But this is just what the demand curve for labour shows. Thus the MRP_L curve is the demand curve for labour.

There are three determinants of the demand for labour:

- *The wage rate.* This determines the position *on* the demand curve. (Strictly speaking, we would refer here to the wage determining the 'quantity demanded' rather than the 'demand'.)
- *The productivity of labour (MPP_L).* This determines the position *of* the demand curve.
- *The demand for the good.* The higher the market demand for the good, the higher will be its market price, and hence the higher will be the MR, and thus the MRP_L. This too determines the position of the demand curve. It shows how the demand for labour (and other factors) is a **derived demand**: i.e. one derived from the demand for the good. For example, the higher the demand for houses, and hence the higher their price, the higher will be the demand for bricklayers.

KI 12
p 63

Pause for thought

If the productivity of a group of workers rises by 10 per cent, will the wage rate they are paid also rise by 10 per cent? Explain why or why not.

A change in the wage rate is represented by a movement *along* the demand curve for labour. A change in the productivity of labour or in the demand for the good *shifts* the curve.

The elasticity of demand for labour

The elasticity of demand for labour (with respect to changes in the wage rate) will be greater:

The greater the price elasticity of demand for the good. A rise in the wage rate, being a cost of production, will drive up the price of the good. If the market demand for the good is elastic, this rise in price will lead to a lot less being sold and hence a lot fewer people being employed.

The easier it is to substitute labour for other factors and vice versa. If labour can be readily replaced by other inputs (e.g. machinery), then a rise in the wage rate will lead to a large reduction in labour as workers are replaced by these other inputs.

The greater the wage cost as a proportion of total costs. If wages are a large proportion of total costs and the wage rate rises, total costs will rise significantly; therefore production will fall significantly, and so too will the demand for labour.

The longer the time period. Given sufficient time, firms can respond to a rise in wage rates by reorganising their production processes. For example, they could introduce robotic production lines.

Wages and profits under perfect competition

The wage rate (W) is determined by the interaction of demand and supply in the labour market. This will be equal to the value of the output that the last person produces (MRP_L).

Profits to the individual firm will arise from the fact that the MRP_L curve slopes downward (diminishing returns).

Definition

Derived demand The demand for a factor of production depends on the demand for the good which uses it.

Thus the last worker adds less to the revenue of firms than previous workers already employed.

If *all* workers in the firm receive a wage equal to the *MRP* of the *last* worker, everyone but the last worker will receive a wage less than their *MRP*. This excess of MRP_L over *W* of previous workers provides a surplus to the firm over its wages bill (see Figure 18.7). Part of this will be required for paying non-wage costs; part will be the profits for the firm.

Perfect competition between firms will ensure that profits are kept down to *normal* profits. If the surplus over wages is such that *supernormal* profits are made, new firms will enter the industry. The price of the good (and hence MRP_L) will fall, and the wage will be bid up, until only normal profits remain.

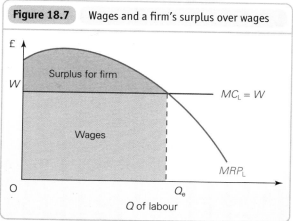

Figure 18.7 Wages and a firm's surplus over wages

18.3 FIRMS WITH POWER IN THE LABOUR MARKET

In the real world, many firms have the power to influence wage rates: they are not wage takers. This is one of the major types of labour market 'imperfection'.

When a firm is the only employer of a particular type of labour, this situation is called a **monopsony**. The Post Office used to be a monopsony employer of postal workers. Another example is when a factory is the only employer of certain types of labour in that district. It therefore has local monopsony power. When there are just a few employers, this is called **oligopsony**.

Monopsonists (and oligopsonists too) are 'wage setters', not 'wage takers'. Thus a large employer in a small town may have considerable power to resist wage increases or even to force wage rates down.

Such firms face an upward-sloping supply curve of labour. This is illustrated in Figure 18.8. If the firm wants to take on more labour, it will have to pay a higher wage rate to attract workers away from other industries. But conversely, by employing less labour it can get away with paying a lower wage rate.

The supply curve shows the wage that must be paid to attract a given quantity of labour. The wage it pays is the *average cost* to the firm of employing labour (AC_L): i.e. the cost per worker. The supply curve is also therefore the AC_L curve.

The *marginal* cost of employing one more worker (MC_L) will be above the wage (AC_L): see Figure 18.8. The reason is that the wage rate has to be raised to attract extra workers. The MC_L will thus be the new higher wage paid to the new employee *plus* the small rise in the total wages bill for existing employees: after all, they will be paid the higher wage too.

The profit-maximising employment of labour would be at Q_1, where $MC_L = MRP_L$. The wage (found from the AC_L curve) would thus be W_1.

If this had been a perfectly competitive labour market, employment would have been at the higher level Q_2, with the wage rate at the higher level W_2, where $W = MRP_L$. What in effect the monopsonist is doing, therefore, is forcing the wage rate down by restricting the number of workers employed.

KI 4
p 22

KI 21
p 161

Definitions

Monopsony A market with a single buyer or employer.

Oligopsony A market with just a few buyers or employers.

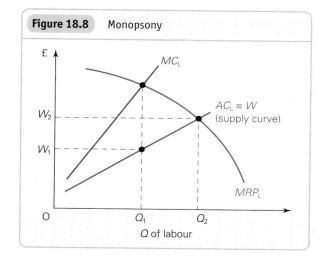

Figure 18.8 Monopsony

18.4 THE ROLE OF TRADE UNIONS

How can unions influence the determination of wages, and what might be the consequences of their actions?

The extent to which unions will succeed in pushing up wage rates depends on their power and militancy. It also depends on the power of firms to resist and on their ability to pay higher wages. In particular, the scope for unions to gain a better deal for their members depends on the sort of market in which the employers are producing.

Unions facing competitive employers

If the employers are producing under perfect or monopolistic competition, unions can raise wages only at the expense of employment. Firms are only earning normal profit. Thus if unions force up wages, the marginal firms will go bankrupt and leave the industry. Fewer workers will be employed. The fall in output will lead to higher prices. This will enable the remaining firms to pay a higher wage rate.

KI 21
p 161

Pause for thought

Which of the following unions find themselves in a weak bargaining position for the reasons given?

(a) The maritime workers union (Nautilus).
(b) The shopworkers' union (USDAW).
(c) The National Union of Mineworkers (NUM).
(d) The farmworkers' union (part of the Unite Union).

Figure 18.9 illustrates these effects. If unions force the wage rate up from W_1 to W_2, employment will fall from Q_1 to Q_2. There will be a surplus of people ($Q_3 - Q_2$) wishing to work in this industry, for whom no jobs are available.

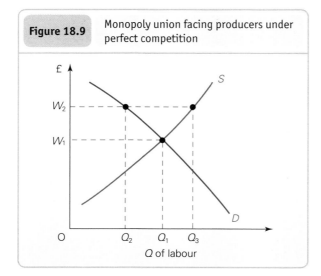

Figure 18.9 Monopoly union facing producers under perfect competition

The union is in a doubly weak position. Not only will jobs be lost as a result of forcing up the wage rate, but also there is a danger that these unemployed people could undercut the union wage, unless the union can prevent firms employing non-unionised labour.

In a competitive market, then, the union is faced with the choice between wages and jobs. Its actions will depend on its objectives.

Wages can be increased without a reduction in the level of employment only if, as part of the bargain, the productivity of labour is increased. This is called a **productivity deal**. The *MRP* curve, and hence the demand curve in Figure 18.9, shifts to the right.

Bilateral monopoly

What happens when a union monopoly faces a monopsony employer? What will the wage rate be? What will the level of employment be? Unfortunately, economic theory cannot give a precise answer to these questions. There is no 'equilibrium' level as such. Ultimately, the wage rate and level of employment will depend on the relative bargaining strengths and skills of unions and management.

Strange as it may seem, unions may be in a stronger position to make substantial gains for their members when they are facing a powerful employer. There is often considerable scope for them to increase wage rates *without* this leading to a reduction in employment, or even for them to increase both the wage rate *and* employment. Figure 18.10 shows how this can be so.

Assume first that there is no union. The monopsonist will maximise profits by employing Q_1 workers at a wage rate of W_1 (Q_1 is where $MRP_L = MC_L$).

What happens when a union is introduced into this situation? Wages will now be set by negotiation between unions and management. Once the wage rate has been agreed, the employer can no longer drive the wage rate down by employing fewer workers. If it tried to pay less than the agreed wage, it could well be faced by a strike, and thus have a zero supply of labour!

Similarly, if the employer decided to take on *more* workers, it would not have to *increase* the wage rate as long as the negotiated wage was above the free-market wage: as long as the wage rate was above that given by the supply curve S_1.

Definition

Productivity deal Where, in return for a wage increase, a union agrees to changes in working practices that will increase output per worker.

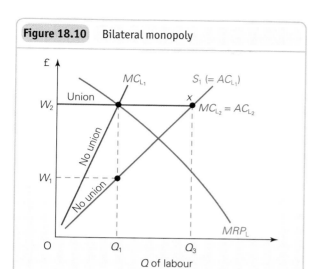

Figure 18.10 Bilateral monopoly

The effect of this is to give a new supply curve that is horizontal up to the point where it meets the original supply curve. For example, let us assume that the union succeeds in negotiating a wage rate of W_2 in Figure 18.10. The supply curve will be horizontal at this level to the left of point x. To the right of this point it will follow the original supply curve S_1, since to acquire more than Q_3 workers the employer would have to raise the wage rate above W_2.

If the supply curve is horizontal to the left of point x at a level of W_2, so too will be the MC_L curve. The reason is simply that the extra cost to the employer of taking on an extra worker (up to Q_3) is merely the negotiated wage rate: no rise has to be given to existing employees. If MC_L is equal to the wage, the profit-maximising employment ($MC_L = MRP_L$) will now be where $W = MRP_L$. At a negotiated wage rate of W_2, the firm will therefore choose to employ Q_1 workers.

What this means is that the union can push the wage right up from W_1 to W_2 and the firm will still *want* to employ Q_1. In other words, a wage rise can be obtained *without* a reduction in employment.

The union could go further still. By threatening industrial action, it may be able to push the wage rate above W_2 and still insist that Q_1 workers are employed (i.e. no redundancies). The firm may be prepared to see profits drop right down to normal level rather than face a strike and risk losses. The absolute upper limit to the wage rate will be that at which the firm is forced to close down.

The actual wage rate under bilateral monopoly is usually determined through a process of negotiation or 'collective bargaining'. The outcome of this bargaining will depend on a wide range of factors, which vary substantially from one industry or firm to another.

Collective bargaining

Sometimes when unions and management negotiate, *both* sides can gain from the resulting agreement. For example,

the introduction of new technology may allow higher wages, improved working conditions and higher profits. Usually, however, one side's gain is the other's loss. Higher wages mean lower profits. Either way, both sides will want to gain the maximum for themselves.

The outcome of the negotiations will depend on the relative bargaining strengths of both sides. In bargaining there are various threats or promises that either side can make. For these to be effective, of course, the other side must believe that they will be carried out.

Union *threats* might include strike action, *picketing*, *working to rule* or refusing to cooperate with management, for example in the introduction of new technology. Alternatively, in return for higher wages or better working conditions, unions might *offer* no strike agreements (or an informal promise not to take industrial action), increased productivity, reductions in the workforce or long-term deals over pay.

In turn, employers might threaten employees with plant closure, *lock-outs*, redundancies or the employment of non-union labour. Or they might offer, in return for lower wage increases, various 'perks' such as productivity bonuses, profit-sharing schemes, better working conditions, more overtime, better holidays or security of employment.

Strikes, lock-outs and other forms of industrial action impose costs on both unions and firms. Unions lose pay. Firms lose revenue. It is usually in both sides' interests, therefore, to settle by negotiation. Nevertheless, to gain the maximum advantage, each side must persuade the other that it will carry out its threats if pushed.

The approach described so far has essentially been one of confrontation. The alternative is for both sides to concentrate on increasing the total net income of the firm by cooperating on ways to increase efficiency or the quality of the product. This approach is more likely when unions and management have built up an atmosphere of trust over time.

The role of government

The government can influence the outcome of collective bargaining in a number of ways. One is to try to set an example. It may take a tough line in resisting wage demands

---

Definitions

Picketing Where people on strike gather at the entrance to the firm and attempt to dissuade workers or delivery vehicles from entering.

Working to rule Workers do no more than they are supposed to, as set out in their job descriptions.

Lock-outs Union members are temporarily laid off until they are prepared to agree to the firm's conditions.

by public-sector workers, hoping thereby to persuade employers in the private sector to do likewise.

Alternatively, it could set up arbitration or conciliation machinery. For example, in the UK, the Advisory Conciliation and Arbitration Service (ACAS) conciliates in around one thousand disputes each year, roughly half of these involving pay-related issues. It also provides, on request by both sides, an arbitration service, where its findings will be binding.

Another approach is to use legislation. The government could pass laws that restrict the behaviour of employers or unions. It could pass laws that set a minimum wage rate (see pages 282–4), or prevent discrimination against workers on various grounds. Similarly, it could pass laws that curtail the power of unions. The Conservative governments between 1979 and 1997 put considerable emphasis on reducing the power of trade unions and making labour markets more 'flexible'. Several Acts of Parliament were passed during these years and included the following measures:

- Employees were given the right to join any union, or not to join a union at all. This effectively ended ***closed-shop*** agreements.
- Secret postal ballots of the union membership were made mandatory for the operation of a political fund, the election of senior union officials, and strikes and other official industrial action.
- Political strikes, sympathy action and action against other non-unionised companies were made illegal.
- Lawful action would be confined to that against workers' own direct employers, even to their own particular place of work. All ***secondary action*** was made unlawful.
- It was made unlawful for employers to penalise workers for choosing to join or refusing to join a trade union. It was also made unlawful for employers to deny employment on the grounds that an applicant does not belong to a union.

The effect of these measures was considerably to weaken the power of trade unions in the UK.

18.5 THE EFFICIENCY WAGE HYPOTHESIS

We have seen that a union may be able to force an employer to pay a wage above the market-clearing rate. But it may well be in an employer's interests to do so, even in non-unionised sectors.

One explanation for this phenomenon is the ***efficiency wage hypothesis***. This states that the productivity of workers rises as the wage rate rises. As a result, employers are frequently prepared to offer wage rates above the market-clearing level, attempting to balance increased wage costs against gains in productivity. But why may higher wage rates lead to higher productivity? There are three main explanations.

Less 'shirking'. In many jobs it is difficult to monitor the effort that individuals put into their work. Workers may thus get away with shirking or careless behaviour. The business could attempt to reduce shirking by imposing a series of sanctions, the most serious of which would be dismissal. The greater the wage rate currently received, the greater will be the cost to the individual of dismissal, and the less likely it is that workers will shirk. The business will benefit not only from the additional output, but also from a reduction in the costs of having to monitor workers' performance. As a consequence the ***efficiency wage rate*** for the business will lie above the market-determined wage rate.

Reduced labour turnover. If workers receive on-the-job training or retraining, then to lose a worker once the training has been completed is a significant cost to the business. Labour turnover, and hence its associated costs, can be reduced by paying a wage above the market-clearing rate. By paying such a wage, the business is seeking a degree of loyalty from its employees.

Morale. A simple reason for offering wage rates above the market-clearing level is to motivate the workforce – to create the feeling that the firm is a 'good' employer that cares about its employees. As a consequence, workers might be more industrious, show more initiative and be more willing to accept the introduction of new technology (with the reorganisation that it involves).

The paying of efficiency wages above the market-clearing wage will depend upon the type of work involved. Workers who occupy skilled positions, especially where the business has invested time in their training (thus making them costly to replace) are likely to receive efficiency wages considerably above the market wage. By contrast, workers in unskilled positions, where shirking can be easily monitored, little training takes place and workers can be easily replaced, are unlikely to command an 'efficiency wage premium'. In such situations, rather than keeping wage rates high, the business will probably try to pay as little as possible.

Definitions

Closed shop Where a firm agrees to employ only members of a recognised union.

Secondary action Industrial action taken against a firm not directly involved in the dispute.

Efficiency wage hypothesis A hypothesis that states that a worker's productivity is linked to the wage he or she receives.

Efficiency wage rate The profit-maximising wage rate for the firm after taking into account the effects of wage rates on worker motivation, turnover and recruitment.

18.6 LOW PAY AND DISCRIMINATION

Low pay

Identifying workers as being low paid clearly involves making certain value judgements about what constitutes 'low'.

One way is to consider pay relative to living standards. The problem here, though, is that pay is only one of the determinants of living standards. Pay of a certain level may give a reasonable living standard for a single person, especially if he or she has property, such as a house and furniture. The same pay may result in dire poverty for a large household with several dependants on that one income, and considerable outgoings.

It is more usual, therefore, to define low pay relative to average rates of pay. Low pay will be anything below a certain percentage of the average wage rate. The larger the percentage selected, the bigger the low-paid sector will become.

The Council of Europe defines low pay as anything below 60 per cent of a country's mean net (i.e. post-tax) earnings. It refers to this as the 'decency threshold'. Previously the decency threshold was defined as anything below 68 per cent of a country's mean gross wage rate, which gave a higher figure. If a minimum hourly wage were to be based on even the new lower decency threshold, then in the UK it would be set at around £8.60 in 2012, and would raise wages for about 35 per cent of workers. Other studies have identified the low-pay threshold at two-thirds of *median* hourly earnings of *male* workers.[1] A minimum hourly wage set at this level would be around £8.90 for full-time workers in 2012.

In practice, as we shall see below, the UK defines low pay as being below the minimum wage, which in October 2012 was set at £6.19 per hour for those aged 21 and over, £4.98 per hour for those aged 18–20 and £3.68 for 16- and 17-year-olds. In 2011/12 the minimum wage was 54.9 per cent of the median hourly wage for all workers and 48.4 per cent of that for full-time workers. In 1999, the year that the minimum wage was introduced, it was 45.6 per cent of the median for all workers, but when evidence suggested that the minimum wage seemed to be having little effect on unemployment, it was raised faster than wages, to reach over 52 per cent of the median wage by 2008.

Another approach to the analysis of low pay is to see how the wage rates of the lowest-paid workers have changed over time compared to the average worker. Evidence from various editions of the *Annual Survey of Hours and Earnings* (National Statistics) indicates that inequality in pay in the UK has widened. The lowest 10 per cent of wage earners saw hourly wage rates fall from 70 per cent of the median wage in 1979 to 57 per cent in 2011. By contrast, hourly wage rates of the top 10 per cent rose from 167 to 225 per cent of the median over the same period.

Low pay tends to be concentrated in certain sectors and occupations. Sales and customer service workers are a classic example. Weekly wages of workers in these occupations are only 64 per cent of the UK average. Low pay also occurs disproportionately between women and men. In 2011, the median hourly wage for women was £9.90; the figure for men was 25.4 per cent higher at £12.41, although for full-time workers it was 11.67 per cent higher, reflecting the lower pay for part-time workers and the higher proportion of women working part time.

The growth in low pay

A number of factors have contributed to the progressive rise in the size of the low-paid sector and the widening disparity between high and low income earners over the past 30 years.

Recessions of the 1980s and 1990s. Very high rates of unemployment in the early 1980s and early 1990s shifted the balance of power from workers to employers – a trend that was not reversed with the falling unemployment in the late 1990s and early 2000s. Employers have been able to force many wage rates downwards, especially of unskilled and semi-skilled workers.

Technological change. Changes in technology have led industry to shift its demand for labour away from unskilled to skilled workers. As might be expected, wage rates for skilled workers have generally risen (except for those with older, now irrelevant skills), while relative employment rates of the unskilled have worsened.

Competition in the goods market from developing countries. The rapid growth in imports of manufactured goods from China, Brazil, India and other developing countries has led to a decline in competing domestic industries. Many skilled workers in these industries have lost their jobs, adding to the total supply of workers seeking low-skilled or unskilled work. This has pushed down wage rates across the low-paid sector.

Competition in labour markets from developing countries. Recent years have seen considerable outsourcing of jobs to India and other developing countries. These include not just call-centre work, but also 'back-office', IT and other technical jobs. This has competed down wages in similar jobs in the UK.

KI 32
p 311

---

[1] The mean hourly wage is the arithmetical average: i.e. the total level of gross wage payments divided by the total number of hours worked by the population (over a specified time period). The median hourly wage is found by ranking the working population from lowest to highest paid, and then finding the hourly pay of the middle person in the ranking.

Figure 18.11   Minimum hourly wage rates (2011)

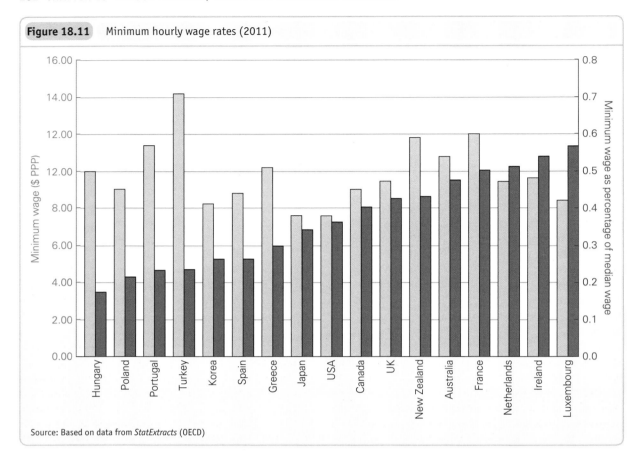

Source: Based on data from *StatExtracts* (OECD)

Growth in part-time employment. Changes in the structure of the UK economy – in particular, the growth of the service sector and the growing proportion of women seeking work – have led to an increase in part-time work. Many part-time workers do not receive the same rights, privileges and hourly pay as their full-time equivalents.

Changes in labour laws. The abolition of wages councils in 1993, which had set legally enforceable minimum hourly rates in various low-paid industries, and the introduction of various new laws to reduce the power of labour (see page 280) had taken away what little protection there was for low-paid workers.

The introduction of the UK national minimum wage in 1999 has gone some way to arresting the growth in low pay. But just what are the costs and benefits of minimum wages? We examine this issue in the next section.

Minimum wages

Minimum wages are used widely in developed countries. Figure 18.11 shows the minimum wage rates in a number of countries in 2011. The red bars show real minimum wages. They are converted to US dollars at 'purchasing-power parity (PPP)' exchange rates, which adjust the market exchange rate to reflect purchasing power: i.e. the exchange

rates at which one dollar would be worth the same in purchasing power in each country. This allows more meaningful comparisons between countries. The blue bars show minimum hourly wage rates as a percentage of each country's median hourly wage rate.

Critics of a national minimum wage argue that it can cause unemployment and with it a *rise* in poverty. Supporters argue that it not only helps to reduce poverty among the low paid, but also has little or no adverse effects on employment. Some go further. They argue that it actually *increases* employment.

In order to assess the background to this debate, we need to revisit our earlier analysis of the demand and supply of labour.

Minimum wages in a competitive labour market

In a competitive labour market, workers will be hired up to the point where the marginal revenue product of labour (MRP_L), i.e. the demand for labour, is equal to the marginal cost of labour (MC_L), which gives the supply curve. Referring back to Figure 18.9 on page 278, the free-market equilibrium wage is W_1 and the level of employment is Q_1. A national minimum wage, set at W_2, will reduce the level of employment to Q_2 and increase the supply of labour to Q_3, thereby creating unemployment of the amount $Q_3 - Q_2$.

The level of unemployment created as a result of the national minimum wage will be determined not only by the level of the minimum wage, but also by the elasticity of labour demand and supply. The more elastic the demand and supply of labour, the bigger the unemployment effect will be. Evidence suggests that the demand for low-skilled workers is likely to be relatively wage sensitive. The most likely reason for this is that many of the goods or services produced by low-paid workers are very price sensitive, the firms frequently operating in very competitive markets. It would seem at first sight, therefore, that any increase in wage rates is likely to force up prices and thereby reduce output and employment.

It is important to be careful in using this argument, however. What is relevant is not so much the price elasticity of demand for *individual* firms' products, but rather for the products of the low-paid sector as a whole. If one firm alone raised its prices, it might well lose a considerable number of sales. But with minimum wage legislation applying to *all* firms, if all the firms in an industry or sector put up their prices, demand for any one firm would fall much less. Here the problem of consumers switching away from a firm's products, and hence of that firm being forced to reduce its workforce, would mainly occur (a) if there were cheaper competitor products from abroad, where the new minimum wage legislation would not apply, or (b) if other firms produced the products with more capital-intensive techniques, involving fewer workers to whom the minimum wage legislation applied.

Minimum wages and monopsony employers

In an imperfect labour market where the employer has some influence over rates of pay, the impact of the

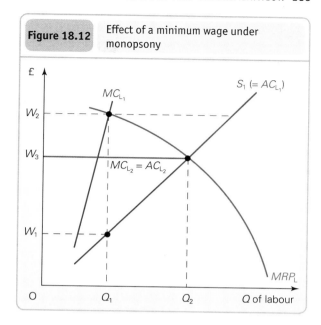

Figure 18.12 Effect of a minimum wage under monopsony

national minimum wage on levels of employment is even less clear cut.

The situation is illustrated in Figure 18.12 (which is similar to Figure 18.10 on page 279). A monopsonistic employer will employ Q_1 workers: where MC_{L_1} is equal to MRP_L. At this point the firm is maximising its return from the labour it employs. Remember that the MC_L curve lies above the supply of labour curve (AC_L), since the additional cost of employing one more unit of labour involves paying all existing employees the new wage. The wage rate paid by the monopsonist will be W_1.

BOX 18.2   THE UK NATIONAL MINIMUM WAGE

The answer to low pay?

Despite the adoption of national minimum wage rates in most of the developed world, the Conservative government in the UK (1979–97), following its philosophy of free-market economics, resisted introducing such a policy. But the number of low-paid workers was increasing. There were many people working as cleaners, kitchen hands, garment workers, security guards and shop assistants who were receiving pittance rates of pay, sometimes less than £2 per hour.

The incoming Labour government in 1997 was committed to introducing a minimum wage, which it did in April 1999 at a rate of £3.60 per hour. There was a lower 'development rate' of £3.00 for those between 18 and 21. The government had sought advice from the Low Pay Commission, which argued that a £3.60 rate would 'offer real benefits to the low paid, while avoiding unnecessary risks to business and jobs'. The minimum wage has been raised in October each year (standing at £6.19 in 2012/13), with equivalent rises in the development rate for those aged 18 to 20 (£4.98 in 2012/13). In October 2004 a new development rate for

16- and 17-year-olds was introduced at a rate of £3.00. This stood at £3.68 in 2012/13.

Some 1.2 million workers benefit from the minimum wage and there have been virtually no adverse effects on unemployment. The main beneficiaries have been women, the majority of whom work part time and many of whom are lone parents, and people from ethnic minorities. Even the Conservative Party, previously staunch opponents of a minimum wage, has dropped its opposition.

1. *If an increase in wage rates for the low paid led to their being more motivated, how would this affect the marginal revenue product and the demand for such workers? What implications does your answer have for the effect on employment in such cases?*

2. *If minimum wages encourage employers to substitute machines for workers, will this necessarily lead to higher long-term unemployment in (a) that industry and (b) the economy in general?*

If the minimum wage is set above W_1 (but below W_2), the level of employment within the firm is likely to grow! Why should this be so? The reason is that the minimum wage cannot be bid down by the monopsonist cutting back on its workforce. Assume, for example, that the minimum wage was set at a rate of W_3. The minimum wage rate is thus both the new AC_{L_2} and also the new MC_{L_2}: the additional cost of employing one more worker (up to Q_2) is simply the minimum wage rate. The $MC_{L_2} = AC_{L_2}$ line is thus a horizontal straight line up to the original supply curve ($S_1 = AC_1$). The level of employment that maximises the monopsonist's profits will be found from the intersection of this new $MC_L = AC_L$ line with the MRP_L curve: namely, an employment level of Q_2. In fact, with a wage rate anywhere between W_1 and W_2 this intersection will be to the right of Q_1: i.e. the imposition of a minimum wage rate will *increase* the level of employment.

Clearly, if the minimum wage rate were very high, then, other things being equal, the level of employment would fall. This would occur in Figure 18.12 if the minimum wage rate were above W_3. But even this argument is not clear cut, given that (a) a higher wage rate may increase labour productivity by improving worker motivation and (b) other firms, with which the firm might compete in the product market, will also be faced with paying the higher minimum wage rate. The resulting rise in prices is likely to shift the MRP_L curve to the right.

On the other hand, to the extent that the imposition of a minimum wage rate reduces a firm's profits, this may lead it to cut down on investment, which may threaten long-term employment prospects.

Evidence on the effect of minimum wages

Which of the views concerning the effects of a national minimum wage are we to believe? Evidence from the USA and other countries suggests that modest increases in the minimum wage have had a neutral effect upon employment. It has been found that there exists a 'range of indeterminacy' over which wage rates can fluctuate with little impact upon levels of employment. Even above this 'range', research findings have suggested that, whereas some employers might reduce the quantity of labour they employ, others might respond to their higher wage bill, and hence higher costs, by improving productive efficiency.

Since the introduction of the minimum wage in the UK in 1999 (see Box 18.2), there is little evidence to suggest that employers have responded by employing fewer workers. In fact, until 2008, unemployment rates fell. This, however, can be explained by a buoyant economy and increasing labour market flexibility (see section 18.7).

With the recession of 2009/10, however, many employers were claiming that it would be difficult to pay the minimum wage without reducing their workforce, given falling demand for their products and, in some cases, falling prices. Also, firms may make significant cuts in employment if the minimum wage were to rise substantially. The issue here is

how *high* can the minimum wage be set before unemployment begins to rise?

Gender and the labour market

Women earn less than men. How much less depends on how earnings are measured, but on the most widely used definition, mean earnings per hour (see Table 18.1), women in the UK earned some 15 per cent less per hour than men in 2011. The gender wage gap has narrowed over the years, however. In 1970, women earned 37 per cent less than men.

> **Pause for thought**
>
> *If we were to look at weekly rather than hourly pay and included the effects of overtime, what do you think would happen to the pay differentials in Table 18.1?*

In the EU, the gender pay gap in 2010 was 16.4 per cent, although the size of the gap varied substantially between member states. In Germany it was 23.1 per cent, whereas in Italy it was only 5.5 per cent.

The inequality between male and female earnings can in part be explained by the fact that men and women are occupationally segregated. Seeing that women predominate in poorly paid occupations, the difference in earnings is somewhat to be expected. But if you consider Table 18.2, you can see that quite substantial earning differentials persist *within* particular occupations, partly because a smaller proportion of women are in senior positions.

So why has this inequality persisted? There are a number of possible reasons:

- The marginal productivity of labour in typically female occupations may be lower than in typically male occupations. This may in small part be due to simple questions of physical strength. More often, however, it is due to the fact that women tend to work in more labour-intensive occupations. If there is less capital equipment per female worker than there is per male worker, then the marginal product of a woman is likely to be less than that of a man. Evidence from the EU as a whole suggests that occupational segregation is a significant factor in explaining pay differences.

Table 18.1	Women's pay as a percentage of men's (average hourly pay, excluding overtime, for full-time UK employees, aged 18 and over)				
1970	**1980**	**1990**	**2000**	**2011**
63.1	73.5	76.6	79.8	85.2

Source: *Annual Survey of Hours and Earnings* (Office for National Statistics, 2012). Contains public sector information licensed under the Open Government Licence (OGL) v1.0. http://www.nationalarchives.gov.uk/doc/open-government-licence.

Table 18.2	Average gross hourly pay, excluding overtime, for selected occupations, full-time UK employees on adult rates, 2011		

Occupation	Men	Women	Women's pay as a % of men's
	(£ per hour)		
Car park attendants	8.08	10.82	133.9
Security guards and related occupations	9.09	11.24	123.7
Electrical/electronic engineers	12.84	13.88	108.1
Midwives	17.91	18.51	103.4
Bar staff	6.67	6.57	98.5
Social workers	17.15	16.66	97.1
Chiropodists	17.60	16.80	95.5
Communication operators	14.05	13.18	93.8
Chefs, cooks	8.61	8.05	93.5
Police officers (sergeant and below)	18.39	16.97	92.3
Secondary school teachers	23.47	21.59	92.0
Hairdressers, barbers	8.34	7.65	91.7
Librarians	16.38	14.42	88.1
Assemblers and routine operatives	10.18	8.34	82.1
Management consultants, economists	26.52	21.51	81.1
Medical practitioners	38.25	30.30	79.2
Directors/CEOs of major organisations	66.02	52.19	79.1
Laboratory technicians	13.58	10.63	78.3
Sales representatives	15.97	12.44	77.9
Electrical engineers	21.87	16.74	76.5
Solicitors, lawyers, judges and coroners	34.25	26.06	76.1
Office managers	23.38	16.60	71.0
All occupations	**16.44**	**14.00**	**85.2**
Average gross weekly pay (incl. overtime)	659.30	521.80	79.1
Average weekly hours worked (incl. overtime)	40.2	37.3	
Average weekly overtime	1.5	0.5	

Source: *Annual Survey of Hours and Earnings* (Office for National Statistics, 2012). Contains public sector information licensed under the Open Government Licence (OGL) v1.0. http://www.nationalarchives.gov.uk/doc/open-government-licence

■ Many women take career breaks to have children. For this reason, employers are sometimes more willing to invest money in training men (thereby increasing their marginal productivity), and more willing to promote men.

■ Women tend to be less geographically mobile than men. If social norms are such that the man's job is seen as somehow more 'important' than the woman's, then a couple will often move if that is necessary for the man to get promotion. The woman, however, will have to settle for whatever job she can get in the same locality as her partner. Additionally this may reduce a woman's bargaining power when negotiating for wage increases in her current job, if her employer knows that her outside options are more limited than a man's would be.

■ A smaller proportion of women workers are members of unions than men. Even when they are members of unions, they are often in jobs where unions are weak (e.g. clothing industry workers, shop assistants and secretaries).

■ Part-time workers (mainly women) have less bargaining power, less influence and less chance of obtaining promotion.

■ Custom and practice. Despite equal pay legislation, many jobs done wholly or mainly by women continue to be low paid, irrespective of questions of productivity.

■ Prejudice. In many jobs women are discriminated against when it comes to promotion, especially to senior positions. A report published in 2011 for the UK government[2] confirmed that women remain seriously under-represented in boardrooms. This phenomenon is known as the 'glass ceiling'. It is very difficult to legislate against, however, when the employer can simply claim that the 'better' person was given the job.

---

[2] http://www.bis.gov.uk/assets/biscore/business-law/docs/w/11-745-women-on-boards.pdf

Which of the above reasons could be counted as economically 'irrational' (i.e. paying different wage rates to women and men for other than purely economic reasons)? Certainly the last two would qualify. Paying different wage rates on these grounds would *not* be in the profit interests of the employer.

Some of the others, however, are more difficult to classify. The causes of inequality in wage rates may be traced back beyond the workplace: perhaps to the educational system, or to a culture which discourages women from being so aggressive in seeking promotion or to more generous maternity than paternity leave. Even if it is a manifestation of profit-maximising behaviour by employers that women in some circumstances are paid less than their male counterparts, the reason *why* it is more profitable for employers to pay men more than women may indeed reflect discrimination elsewhere or at some other point in time.

> ### Pause for thought
>
> *If employers were forced to give genuinely equal pay for equal work, how would this affect the employment of women and men? What would determine the magnitude of these effects?*

18.7 THE FLEXIBLE FIRM AND THE MARKET FOR LABOUR

The past 25 years have seen sweeping changes in the ways that firms organise their workforce. Three world recessions combined with rapid changes in technology have led many firms to question the wisdom of appointing workers on a permanent basis to specific jobs. Instead, they want to have the greatest flexibility possible to respond to new situations. If demand falls, they want to be able to 'shed' labour without facing large redundancy costs. If demand rises, they want rapid access to additional labour supplies. If technology changes, say with the introduction of new computerised processes, they want to have the flexibility to move workers around, or to take on new workers in some areas and lose workers in others.

What many firms seek, therefore, is flexibility in employing and allocating labour. What countries are experiencing is an increasingly flexible labour market, as workers and employment agencies respond to the new 'flexible firm'.

There are three main types of flexibility in the use of labour:

- *Functional flexibility*. This is where an employer is able to transfer labour between different tasks within the production process. It contrasts with traditional forms of organisation where people were employed to do a specific job, and then stuck to it. A functionally flexible labour force will tend to be multi-skilled and relatively highly trained.

- *Numerical flexibility*. This is where the firm is able to adjust the size and composition of its workforce according to changing market conditions. To achieve this, the firm is likely to employ a large proportion of its labour on a part-time or casual basis, or even subcontract out specialist requirements, rather than employing such labour skills itself.

- *Financial flexibility*. This is where the firm has flexibility in its wage costs. In large part it is a result of functional and numerical flexibility. Financial flexibility can be achieved by rewarding individual effort and productivity rather than paying a given rate for a particular job. Such rates of pay are increasingly negotiated at the local level rather than being nationally set. The result is not only a widening of pay differentials between skilled and unskilled workers, but also growing differentials in pay between workers within the same industry but in different parts of the country.

Figure 18.13 shows how these three forms of flexibility are reflected in the organisation of a *flexible firm*, an organisation quite different from that of the traditional firm.

>
> **KEY IDEA 26**
>
> *Flexible firm.* A firm that has the flexibility to respond to changing market conditions by changing the composition of its workforce and its working practices.

Definitions

Functional flexibility Where employers can switch workers from job to job as requirements change.

Numerical flexibility Where employers can change the size of their workforce as their labour requirements change.

Financial flexibility Where employers can vary their wage costs by changing the composition of their workforce or the terms on which workers are employed.

Flexible firm A firm that has the flexibility to respond to changing market conditions.

Figure 18.13 The flexible firm

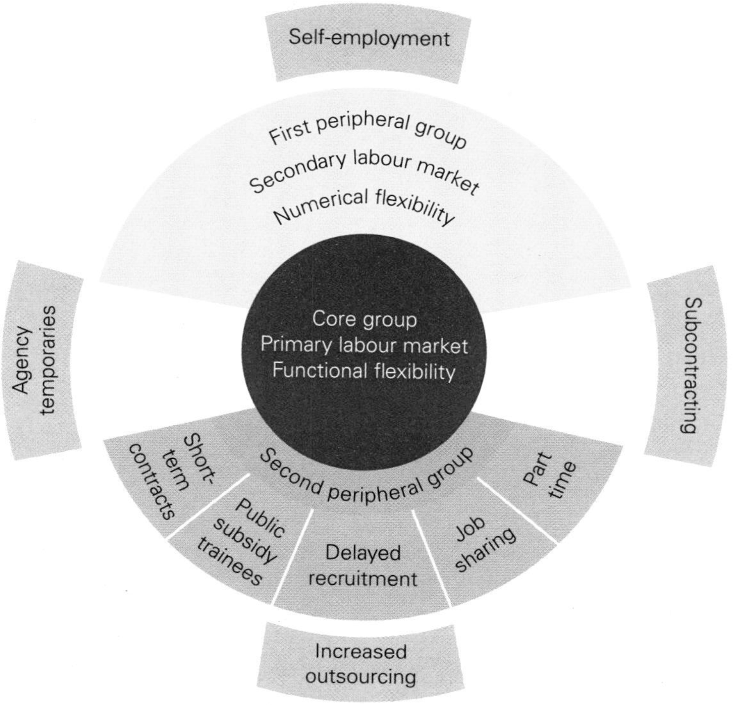

Source: From the Institute of Manpower Studies, *The Flexible Firm* (MS, 1984). Reproduced with permission

The most significant difference is that the labour force is segmented. The core group, drawn from the **primary labour market**, will be composed of *functionally* flexible workers, who have relatively secure employment and are generally on full-time permanent contracts. Such workers will be relatively well paid and receive wages reflecting their scarce skills.

The periphery, drawn from the **secondary labour market**, is more fragmented than the core, and can be subdivided into a first and a second peripheral group. The first peripheral group is composed of workers with a lower level of skill than those in the core, skills that tend to be general rather than firm specific. Thus workers in the first peripheral group can usually be drawn from the external labour market. Such workers may be employed on full-time contracts, but they will generally face less secure employment than those workers in the core.

The business gains a greater level of numerical flexibility by drawing labour from the second peripheral group. Here workers are employed on a variety of short-term, part-time contracts, often through a recruitment agency. Some of these workers may be working from home, or online from another country, such as India, where wage rates are much lower. Workers in the second peripheral group have little job security.

As well as supplementing the level of labour in the first peripheral group, the second periphery can also provide high-level specialist skills that supplement the core. In this instance the business can subcontract or hire self-employed labour, minimising its commitment to such workers. The business thereby gains both functional and numerical flexibility simultaneously.

Pause for thought

How is the advent of flexible firms likely to alter the gender balance of employment and unemployment?

Definitions

Primary labour market The market for permanent full-time core workers.

Secondary labour market The market for peripheral workers, usually employed on a temporary or part-time basis, or a less secure 'permanent' basis.

The Japanese model

The application of new flexible working patterns is becoming more prevalent in businesses in the UK and elsewhere in Europe and North America. In Japan, flexibility has been part of the business way of life for many years and was crucial in shaping the country's economic success in the 1970s and 1980s. In fact we now talk of a Japanese model of business organisation, which many of its competitors seek to emulate.

The model is based around four principles:

■ *Total quality management (TQM).* This involves all employees working towards continuously improving all aspects of quality, both of the finished product and of methods of production.

■ *Elimination of waste.* According to the 'just-in-time' (JIT) principle, businesses should take delivery of just sufficient quantities of raw materials and parts, at the right time and place. Stocks are kept to a minimum and hence the whole system of production runs with little, if any, slack. For example, supermarkets today have smaller storerooms relative to the total shopping area than they did in the past, and take more frequent deliveries.

■ *A belief in the superiority of team work in the core group.* Collective effort is a vital element in Japanese working practices. Team work is seen not only to enhance individual performance, but also to involve the individual in the running of the business, and thus to create a sense of commitment.

■ *Functional and numerical flexibility.* Both are seen as vital components in maintaining high levels of productivity.

The principles of this model are now widely accepted as being important in creating and maintaining a competitive business in a competitive marketplace.

Within the EU, the UK has been one of the most successful in cutting unemployment and creating jobs. Much of this has been attributed to increased labour market flexibility. As a result, other EU countries, such as Italy and Germany, are seeking to emulate many of the measures the UK has adopted.

BOX 18.3   THE INTERNET AND LABOUR MOBILITY

Online flexibility

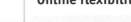

A firm may wish to be flexible, but is the *labour market* sufficiently flexible to meet the firm's needs?

It is all well and good a firm looking to expand employment in a prosperous period, but how will it find the individuals it needs, whether they be self-employed, subcontracted or added to the core labour group? This question becomes far more critical, the more highly skilled (and hence scarce) are the workers that the firm requires. Generally, it is the core/skilled workers that flexible firms find most difficulty in recruiting.

A solution to enhancing labour market flexibility, it seems, may lie in the development of online recruitment technologies.

Keynote, a market research company, reports that in 2012, 44 per cent of survey respondents had used the Internet for job search.[1] Firms not only have their own online vacancy boards but are also using social networking sites to target different audiences. Four per cent of respondents had used social media sites to search for jobs. This figure is expected to increase in coming years. Many candidates use online sites such as Monster.co.uk and Fish4jobs.com to register for job alerts by e-mail or mobile phone and to register their CV. On the downside, Keynote reports that use of e-recruitment is leading to increased numbers of unsuitable candidates applying for vacancies. Filtering out these candidates wastes time and money.

The Internet improves the efficiency with which information is relayed to the employers and suppliers of labour and increases their search horizons. Almost one in three firms

had searched for recruits online according to evidence cited by the CIPD,[2] and nearly a further 30 per cent of firms stated that they would do so in the future. As well as reaching a wider and more targeted audience, recruitment costs are lowered and the recruitment cycle is shortened and made more efficient by the use of Internet technologies. A large number of companies have been established which provide software that can manage e-recruitment processes: e.g. jobtrain.co.uk and rectuitactive.com. These companies offer services such as managing the application process, online psychometric testing, online advertising etc.

There are big benefits for job seekers too. It may lead to increased spatial search for employment. For example, workers based in London no longer have to travel to Manchester and scout around; they can peruse jobs online.

It can also widen the range of industries that firms and individuals might target. So, shipyard workers might look to use their welding skills in the offshore industry. It can also enhance the likelihood of matching the skills of the unemployed with job vacancies and so lower the average length of time it takes to fill a vacancy.

The days of pounding the streets, looking in employment agency windows, or circling a vacancy in the newspaper with a pen are not over, but the opportunity afforded by online recruitment is dramatically enhancing labour market flexibility.

Explain how a flexible firm's flexibility would be enhanced by online recruitment.

---

[1] 'E-Recruitment Market Assessment 2012' (Keynote, 2012). Available at www.keynote.co.uk/market-intelligence/view/product/10553/e-recruitment

[2] 'E-recruitment' (CIPD, 2009). Available at www.cipd.co.uk/subjects/recruitmen/onlnrcruit/onlrec.htm

SUMMARY

1   Major changes in the UK labour market over recent years include: the movement towards service-sector employment; the rise in part-time working; the growth in female employment levels; a rise in the proportion of temporary, short-term contracts and casual employment; and downsizing.

2a Wages in a competitive labour market are determined by the interaction of demand and supply. The individual's supply of labour will be determined by the substitution and income effects from a given increase in the wage rate. At low wage levels, it is likely that individuals will substitute work for leisure. At high wage levels, it is possible that individuals will work less and consume more leisure time, giving a backward-bending supply curve of labour by the individual.

2b The elasticity of labour supply will largely depend upon the geographical and occupational mobility of labour. The more readily labour can transfer between jobs and regions, the more elastic the supply.

2c The demand for labour is traditionally assumed to be based upon labour's productivity. Marginal productivity theory assumes that the employer will demand labour up to the point where the cost of employing one additional worker (MC_L) is equal to the revenue earned from the output of that worker (MRP_L). The firm's demand curve for labour is its MRP_L curve.

2d The elasticity of demand for labour is determined by: the price elasticity of demand for the good that labour produces; the substitutability of labour for other factors; the proportion of wages to total costs; and time.

3   In an imperfect labour market, where a business has monopoly power in employing labour, it is known as a monopsonist. Such a firm will employ workers to the point where the $MRP_L = MC_L$. Since the wage is below the MC_L, the monopsonist, other things being equal, will employ fewer workers at a lower wage than would be employed in a perfectly competitive labour market.

4a If a union has monopoly power, its power to raise wages will be limited if the employer operates under perfect or monopolistic competition in the goods market. A rise in wage rates will force the employer to cut back on employment, unless there is a corresponding rise in productivity.

4b In a situation of bilateral monopoly (where a monopoly union faces a monopsony employer), the union may have considerable scope to raise wages above the monopsony level, without the employer wishing to reduce the level of employment. There is no unique equilibrium wage. The wage will depend on the outcome of a process of collective bargaining between union and management.

5   The efficiency wage hypothesis states that business might hold wages above the market-clearing wage rate so as to: reduce shirking; reduce labour turnover; improve the quality of labour recruited; and stimulate worker morale. The level of efficiency wage will be determined largely by the type of job the worker does, and the level and scarcity of skill they possess.

6a Low pay is difficult to define. There is no accepted definition. The widening disparity in wages between high and low income earners is due to: unemployment resulting from recession; unemployment resulting from a shift in technology; the growth in part-time employment; and changes in labour market legislation.

6b A statutory minimum wage is one way of tackling the problem of low pay. It is argued, however, that in a perfect labour market, where employers are forced to accept the wage as determined by the marketplace, any attempt to impose a minimum wage above this level will create unemployment. In an imperfect labour market, where an employer has some monopsonistic power, the impact of a minimum wage is uncertain. The impact will depend largely upon how much workers are currently paid below their MRP and whether a higher wage encourages them to work more productively.

6c Differences between male and female earnings between occupations can in part be explained by differences in the types of work that men and women do; they are occupationally segregated. Differences within occupations are less easily accounted for. It would seem that some measure of discrimination is being practised.

7a Changes in technology have had a massive impact upon the process of production and the experience of work. Labour markets and business organisations have become more flexible as a consequence. There are three major forms of flexibility: functional, numerical and financial. The flexible firm will incorporate these different forms of flexibility into its business operations. It will organise production around a core workforce, to which it will supplement workers and skills drawn from a periphery. Peripheral workers will tend to hold general skills rather than firm-specific skills, and be employed on part-time and temporary contracts.

7b The application of the flexible firm model is closely mirrored in the practices of Japanese business. Commitments to improve quality, reduce waste, build teamwork and introduce flexible labour markets are seen as key components in the success of Japanese business organisation.

REVIEW QUESTIONS

1 If a firm faces a shortage of workers with very specific skills, it may decide to undertake the necessary training itself. If, on the other hand, it faces a shortage of unskilled workers, it may well offer a small wage increase in order to obtain the extra labour. In the first case it is responding to an increase in demand for labour by attempting to shift the supply curve. In the second case it is merely allowing a movement along the supply curve. Use a demand and supply diagram to illustrate each case. Given that elasticity of supply is different in each case, do you think that these are the best policies for the firm to follow?

2 The wage rate a firm has to pay and the output it can produce varies with the number of workers as follows (all figures are hourly):

Number of workers	1	2	3	4	5	6	7	8
Wage rate (AC_L) (£)	3	4	5	6	7	8	9	10
Total output (TPP_L)	10	22	32	40	46	50	52	52

Assume that output sells at £2 per unit.

(a) Copy the table and add additional rows for TC_L, MC_L, TRP_L and MRP_L. Put the figures for MC_L and MRP_L in the spaces between the columns.

(b) How many workers will the firm employ in order to maximise profits?

(c) What will be its hourly wage bill at this level of employment?

(d) How much hourly revenue will it earn at this level of employment?

(e) Assuming that the firm faces other (fixed) costs of £30 per hour, how much hourly profit will it make?

(f) Assume that the workers now form a union and that the firm agrees to pay the negotiated wage rate to all employees. What is the maximum to which the hourly wage rate could rise without causing the firm to try to reduce employment below that in (b) above? (See Figure 18.10.)

(g) What would be the firm's hourly profit now?

3 If, unlike a perfectly competitive employer, a monopsonist has to pay a higher wage to attract more workers, why, other things being equal, will a monopsonist pay a lower wage than a perfectly competitive employer?

4 The following are figures for a monopsonist employer:

Number of workers (1)	Wage rate (£) (2)	Total cost of labour (£) (3)	Marginal cost of labour (£) (4)	Marginal revenue product (£) (5)
1	100	100		
			110	230
2	105	210		
			120	240
3	110	230		
				240
4	115			
				230
5	120			
				210
6	125			
				190
7	130			
				170
8	135			
				150
9	140			
				130
10	145			

Fill in the missing figures for columns (3) and (4). How many workers should the firm employ if it wishes to maximise profits?

5 To what extent could a trade union succeed in gaining a pay increase from an employer with no loss in employment?

6 Do any of the following contradict marginal productivity theory: wage scales related to length of service (incremental scales), nationally negotiated wage rates, discrimination, firms taking the lead from other firms in determining this year's pay increase?

7 What is the efficiency wage hypothesis? Explain what employers might gain from paying wages above the market-clearing level.

8 'Minimum wages will cause unemployment.' Is this so?

9 How might we explain why men earn more than women?

10 Identify the potential costs and benefits of the flexible firm to (a) employers and (b) employees.

Investment and the employment of capital

Business issues covered in this chapter

- What determines the amount of capital a firm will employ?
- How can a firm judge whether a proposed investment should go ahead? What techniques are there for investment appraisal?
- How can investment be financed? What types of financial institution are involved in financing investment?
- What are the relative merits of alternative sources of finance?
- What are the functions of the stock market?
- Is the stock market efficient as a means of allocating capital?

19.1 THE PRICING OF CAPITAL AND CAPITAL SERVICES

Capital includes all manufactured products that are used to produce goods and services. Thus capital includes such diverse items as a blast furnace, a bus, a cinema projector, a computer, a factory building and a screwdriver.

The capital goods described above are physical assets and are known as *physical* capital. The word 'capital' is also used to refer to various *paper* assets, such as shares and bonds. These are the means by which firms raise finance to purchase physical capital, and are known as *financial* capital. Being merely paper assets, however, they do not count as factors of production. Nevertheless, financial markets have an important role in determining the level of investment in physical capital, and we shall be examining these markets in the final two sections of this chapter.

The price of capital versus the price of capital services

A feature of most manufactured factors of production is that they last a period of time. A machine may last 10 years; a

factory may last 20 years or more. This leads to an important distinction: the income for the owner from *selling* capital and the income from *using* it or *hiring* it out.

- The income from selling capital is its *price*. It is a once-and-for-all payment. Thus a factory might sell for £1 million, a machine for £20 000 or a screwdriver for £1.
- The income gained from using capital is its *return*, and the income gained from hiring it out is its *rental*. This income therefore represents the value or price of the *services* of capital, expressed per period of time. Thus a firm might have to pay a rental of £1000 per year for a photocopier.

Obviously the price of capital will be linked to the value of its services: to its return. A highly productive machine will sell for a higher price than one producing a lower output and hence yielding a lower return.

The discussion of the rewards to capital leads to a very important distinction: that between stocks and flows.

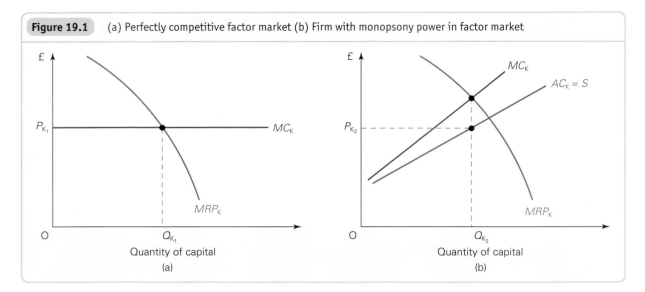

Figure 19.1 (a) Perfectly competitive factor market (b) Firm with monopsony power in factor market

A *stock* is a quantity of something held. You may have £1000 in a savings account. A factory may contain 100 machines. These are both stocks: they are quantities held at a given point in time. A *flow* is an increase or decrease in quantity over a specified time period. You may save £10 per month. The factory may invest in another 20 machines next year.

> **KEY IDEA 27**
>
> *Stocks and flows.* A stock is a quantity of something at a given point in time. A flow is an increase or decrease in something over a specified period of time. This is an important distinction and a common cause of confusion.

Wages, rental and interest are all rewards to *flows*. Wages are the amount paid not to purchase a person (as a slave!), but for the services of that person's labour for a period of time. Rental is the amount paid per period of time to use the services of machinery or equipment, not to buy it outright. Likewise interest is the reward paid to people per year for the use of their money.

> **Pause for thought**
>
> *Which of the following are stocks and which are flows?*
>
> (a) Unemployment.
> (b) Redundancies.
> (c) Profits.
> (d) A firm's stock market valuation.
> (e) The value of property after a period of inflation.

An important example of stocks and flows arises with capital and investment. If a firm has 100 machines, that is a stock of capital. It may choose to build up its stock by investing. Investment is a flow concept. The firm may choose to invest in 10 new machines each year. This may

not add 10 to the stock of machines, however, as some may be wearing out (a negative flow).

The profit-maximising employment of capital

On the demand side, the same rules apply for capital as for labour, if a firm wishes to maximise profits. Namely, it should demand additional capital (K) up to the point where the **marginal cost of capital** equals its **marginal revenue product**: $MC_K = MRP_K$. This same rule applies whether the firm is buying the capital outright, or merely hiring it.

Figure 19.1 illustrates the two cases of perfect competition and monopsony. In both diagrams the MRP curve slopes downwards. This is just another illustration of the law of diminishing returns, but this time applied to capital. If a firm increases the amount of capital while *holding other factors constant*, diminishing returns to capital will occur. Diminishing returns will equally apply whether the firm is buying the extra capital or hiring it.

In diagram (a) the firm is a price taker. The capital price is given at P_{K_1}. Profits are maximised at Q_{K_1} where $MRP_K = P_K$ (since $P_K = MC_K$).

In diagram (b) the firm has monopsony power. The price it pays for capital will vary, therefore, with the amount

> **Definitions**
>
> **Stock** The quantity of something held.
>
> **Flow** An increase or decrease in quantity over a specified period.
>
> **Marginal cost of capital** The cost of one additional unit of capital.
>
> **Marginal revenue product** The additional revenue earned from employing one additional unit of capital.

it uses. The firm will again buy or hire capital to the point where $MRP_K = MC_K$. In this case, it will mean using Q_{K_2} at a price of P_{K_2}.

What is the difference when applying these principles between buying capital and hiring it? Although the $MRP_K = MC_K$ rule remains the same, there are differences. As far as buying capital is concerned, MC_K is the extra

outlay for the firm in *purchasing* one more unit of capital – say, a machine – and MRP_K is all the revenue produced by that machine over its *whole life* (but measured in terms of what this is worth when purchased: see section 19.3). In the case of hiring the machine, MC_K is the extra outlay for the firm in rental *per period of time*, while MRP_K is the extra revenue earned from it *per period of time*.

19.2 THE DEMAND FOR AND SUPPLY OF CAPITAL SERVICES

In this section we will consider the *hiring* of capital equipment for a given period of time.

Demand for capital services

The analysis is virtually identical to that of the demand for labour. As with labour we can distinguish between an individual firm's demand for capital services (K) and the whole market demand for capital services.

Individual firm's demand

Take the case of a small painting and decorating firm that requires some scaffolding in order to complete a job. It could use ladders, but the job would take longer to complete. It goes along to a company that hires out scaffolding and is quoted a daily rate.

If it hires the scaffolding for one day, it can perhaps shorten the job by two or three days. If it hires it for a second day, it can perhaps save another one or two days. Hiring it for additional days may save extra still. But diminishing returns are occurring: the longer the scaffolding is up, the less intensively it will be used, and the less additional time it will save. Perhaps for some of the time it will be used when ladders could have been used equally easily.

The time saved allows the firm to take on extra work. Thus each extra day the scaffolding is hired gives the firm extra revenue. This is the scaffolding's marginal revenue product of

capital (MRP_K). Diminishing returns to the scaffolding mean that the MRP_K curve has the normal downward-sloping shape (see Figure 19.1).

Market demand

The market demand for capital services depends on the demand by individual firms (determined by the productivity of the capital and the price of the product it produces). The higher the MRP_K for individual firms, the greater will be the market demand.

Supply of capital services

It is necessary to distinguish (a) the supply *to* a single firm, (b) the supply *by* a single firm and (c) the market supply.

Supply to a single firm

This is illustrated in Figure 19.2(a). The small firm renting capital equipment is probably a price taker. If so, it faces a horizontal supply curve at the going rental rate (R_e). This is the firm's AC_K and MC_K curve. If, however, it has monopsony power, it will face an upward-sloping supply curve as in Figure 19.1(b).

Supply by a single firm

This is illustrated in Figure 19.2(c). Here the firm supplying the capital equipment is likely to be a price taker, facing a horizontal demand curve. It has to accept the going rental

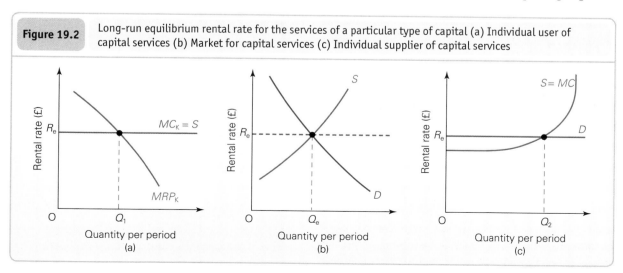

| **Figure 19.2** | Long-run equilibrium rental rate for the services of a particular type of capital (a) Individual user of capital services (b) Market for capital services (c) Individual supplier of capital services |

rate (R_e) established in the market. If it tries to charge more, then customers are likely to turn to rival suppliers.

It will maximise profit by supplying an amount Q_2, where the market rental rate is equal to the marginal cost of supplying the equipment. This is the profit-maximising rule for perfect competition that we established on page 164.

There is a problem, however, in working out the marginal cost of renting out capital equipment: the piece of equipment probably cost a lot to buy in the first place, but lasts a long time. How are these large costs to be apportioned to each new rental? The answer is that it depends on the time period under consideration.

The short run. In the short run the hire company is not buying any new equipment: it is simply hiring out its existing equipment. In the case of our scaffolding firm, the marginal costs of doing this will include the following:

■ *Depreciation.* Scaffolding has second-hand value. Each time the scaffolding is hired out it deteriorates, and thus its second-hand value falls. This loss in value is called 'depreciation'.

■ *Maintenance and handling.* When equipment is hired out, it can get damaged and thus incur repair costs. The equipment might need servicing. Also, hiring out equipment involves labour time (e.g. in the office) and possibly transport costs.

Pause for thought

Assume now that the firm has monopoly power in hiring out equipment, and thus faces a downward-sloping demand curve. Draw in two such demand curves on a diagram like Figure 19.2(c), one crossing the MC curve in the horizontal section, and one in the vertical section. How much will the firm supply in each case and at what price? (You will need to draw in MR curves too.) Is the MC curve still the supply curve?

These marginal costs are likely to rise relatively slowly. In other words, for each extra day a piece of equipment is hired out, the company will incur the same or only slightly higher additional costs. This gives a relatively flat supply curve of

capital services in Figure 19.2(c) up to the hire company's maximum capacity. Once the scaffolding firm is hiring out all its scaffolding, the supply curve becomes vertical.

The long run. In the long run, the hire company will consider purchasing additional equipment. It can therefore supply as much as it likes in the long run. The supply curve will be relatively elastic, or if it is a price taker itself (i.e. if the scaffolding firm simply buys scaffolding at the market price), the supply curve will be horizontal (i.e. perfectly elastic). This long-run supply curve will be vertically higher than the short-run curve, since the long-run *MC* includes the cost of purchasing each additional piece of equipment.

Market supply

This is illustrated in Figure 19.2(b). The market supply curve of capital services is the sum of the quantities supplied by all the individual firms.

In the short run, the market supply will be relatively inelastic, given that it takes time to manufacture new equipment and that stocks of equipment currently held by manufacturers are likely to be relatively small. Moreover, hire companies may be unwilling to purchase (expensive) new equipment immediately there is a rise in demand: after all, the upsurge in demand may turn out to be short lived.

In the long run, the supply curve will be more elastic because extra capital equipment can be produced.

Determination of the price of capital services

As Figure 19.2(b) shows, in a perfect market the market rental rate for capital services will be determined by the interaction of market demand and supply.

KI 11
p 55

If there is monopsony power on the part of the users of hired capital, this will have the effect of depressing the rental rate below the MRP_K (see Figure 19.1(b)). If, on the other hand, there is monopoly power on the part of hire companies, the analysis is similar to that of monopoly in the goods market (see Figure 11.5 on page 168). The firm, by reducing the supply of capital for hire, can drive up the rental rate. It will maximise profit where the marginal revenue from hiring out the equipment is equal to the marginal cost of so doing: at a rental rate (price) *above* the marginal cost.

19.3 INVESTMENT APPRAISAL

The alternative to hiring capital is to buy it outright. This section examines the demand and supply of capital for purchase.

The demand for capital: investment

How many computers will an engineering firm want to buy? Should a steelworks install another blast furnace? Should a removal firm buy another furniture lorry? Should it buy

another warehouse? These are all *investment* decisions. Investment is the purchasing of additional capital.

Definition

Investment The purchase by the firm of equipment or materials that will add to its stock of capital.

The demand for capital, or 'investment demand', by a profit-maximising firm is based on exactly the same principles as the demand for labour or the demand for capital services. The firm must weigh up the marginal revenue product of that investment (i.e. the money it will earn for the firm) against its marginal cost.

However, capital is durable. It goes on producing goods, and hence yielding revenue for the firm, for a considerable period of time. Calculating these benefits, therefore, involves taking account of their *timing*.

There are two ways of approaching this question of timing: the **present value approach** and the **rate of return approach**. In both cases the firm is comparing the marginal benefits with the marginal costs of the investment.

Present value approach

To work out the benefit of an investment (its *MRP*), the firm must estimate all the future earnings it will bring and then convert them to a *present value*. Let us take a simple example.

Assume that a firm is considering buying a machine. It will produce profits of £1000 per year for four years and then wear out and sell for £1000 as scrap. What is the benefit of this machine to the firm? At first sight the answer would seem to be £5000. This, after all, is the total income earned from the machine. Unfortunately, it is not as simple as this. The reason is that money earned in the future is less beneficial to the firm than having the same amount of money today: after all, if the firm has the money today, it can earn interest on it by putting it in the bank or reinvesting it in some other project. (Note that this has nothing to do with inflation. In the case we are considering, we are assuming constant prices.)

To illustrate this, assume that you have £100 today and can earn 10 per cent interest by putting it in a bank. In one year's time that £100 will have grown to £110, in two years' time to £121, in three years' time to £133.10, and so on. This process is known as **compounding**.

It follows that, if someone offered to give you £121 in two years' time, it would be no better than giving you £100 today, since, with interest, £100 would grow to £121 in two years. What we say, then, is that with a 10 per cent interest rate, £121 in two years' time has a *present value* of £100.

The procedure of reducing future values back to a present value is known as **discounting**.

> **KEY IDEA 28**
> **The principle of discounting.** People generally prefer to have benefits today than in the future. Thus future benefits have to be reduced (discounted) to give them a present value.

When we do discounting, the rate which we use is called the **rate of discount**: in this case 10 per cent. The formula for discounting is given by:

$$PV = \sum \frac{X_t}{(1+r)^t}$$

where PV is the present value
      X_t is the earnings from the investment in year t
      r is the rate of discount (expressed as a decimal: i.e. 10 per cent = 0.1)
      Σ is the sum of each of the years' discounted earnings.

So what is the present value of the investment in the machine that produced £1000 for four years and then is sold as scrap for £1000 at the end of the four years? According to the formula it is:

$$\frac{£1000}{1.1} + \frac{£1000}{(1.1)^2} + \frac{£1000}{(1.1)^3} + \frac{£2000}{(1.1)^4}$$
$$= £909 + £826 + £751 + £1366$$
$$= £3852$$

Thus the present value of the investment (i.e. its *MRP*) is £3852, *not* £5000 as it might seem at first sight. In other words, if the firm had £3852 today and deposited it in a bank at a 10 per cent interest rate, the firm would earn exactly the same as it would by investing in the machine.

> ## Pause for thought
>
> *What is the present value of a machine that lasts three years, earns £100 in year 1, £200 in year 2, and £200 in year 3, and then has a scrap value of £100? Assume that the rate of discount is 5 per cent. If the machine costs £500, is the investment worthwhile? Would it be worthwhile if the rate of discount were 10 per cent?*

So is the investment worthwhile? It is now simply a question of comparing the £3852 benefit with the cost of buying the machine. If the machine costs less than £3852, it will be worth buying. If it costs more, the firm would be better off keeping its money in the bank and earning the 10 per cent rate of interest.

BOX 19.1 INVESTING IN ROADS

The assessment of costs and benefits

In the UK, the Department of Transport uses the following procedure to evaluate new road schemes, a procedure very similar to that used in many countries.

Estimating demand

The first thing to be done is to estimate likely future traffic flows. These are based on the government's National Road Traffic Forecast. This makes two predictions: a 'low-growth case', based on the assumption of low economic growth and high fuel prices, and a 'high-growth case', based on the assumption of high economic growth and low fuel prices. The actual growth in traffic, therefore, is likely to lie between the two.

Identifying possible schemes

Various road construction and improvement schemes are constantly under examination by the government, especially in parts of the network where traffic growth is predicted to be high and where congestion is likely to occur. In each case forecasts are then made of the likely use of the new roads and the diversion of traffic away from existing parts of the network. Again, two forecasts are made in each case: a 'low-growth' and a 'high-growth' one.

The use of cost–benefit analysis

The costs and benefits of each scheme are assigned monetary values and are compared with those of merely maintaining the existing network. The government uses a computer program known as COBA to assist it in the calculations.

Estimating the benefits of a scheme (relative to the existing network)

Three types of benefit are included in the analysis:

■ *Time saved*. This is broken down into two categories: working time and non-working time (including travelling to and from work). The evaluation of working time is based on average national wage rates, while that of non-working time is based on surveys and the examination of traveller behaviour (the aim being to assess the value placed by the traveller on time saved). This results in non-working time per minute being given a value of approximately a quarter of that given to working time.
■ *Reductions in vehicle operating costs*. These include: fuel, oil, tyres, maintenance and depreciation from usage. There will be savings if the scheme reduces the distance of journeys or allows a more economical speed to be maintained.
■ *Reductions in accidents*. There are two types of benefit here: (a) the reduction in the human costs of casualties (divided into three categories – fatal, serious non-fatal, and slight); and (b) the reduction in monetary costs, such as lost output, vehicle repair or replacement, medical costs and police, fire service and ambulance costs.

The reductions in monetary costs are relatively easy to estimate. The human benefits from the reduction in casualties are more difficult. The current method of evaluating them is based on the amount people are prepared to pay to reduce the risks of accidents. This clearly has the drawback that people are often unaware of the risks of accidents or of the extent of the resulting pain and suffering.

The following figures are used to value each accident prevented (in 2010 prices and up-rated each year for inflation, changes in fuel costs, etc.): fatal, £1 653 687; serious non-fatal, £185 831; slight, £14 320. The human cost element for each type of accident was valued at £1 084 230, £150 661 and £11 025 respectively.[1]

Estimating the costs of the scheme (relative to the existing network)

There are two main categories of cost: construction costs and additional road maintenance costs. If the new scheme results in a saving in road maintenance compared with merely retaining the existing network, then the maintenance costs will be negative.

The analysis

The costs and benefits of the scheme are assessed for the period of construction and for a standard life (in the UK this is 30 years). The costs and benefits are discounted back to a present value. The rate of discount recommended by the UK Treasury is 3.5 per cent. If the discounted benefits exceed the discounted costs, there is a positive net present value, and the scheme is regarded as justified on economic grounds. If there is more than one scheme, then their net present values will be compared so as to identify the preferable scheme.

It is only at this final stage that environmental considerations are taken into account. In other words, they are not included in the calculation of costs and benefits, but may have some influence in determining the choice between schemes. Clearly, if a socially efficient allocation of road space is to be determined, such externalities need to be included in the cost and benefit calculations.

 Are there any other drawbacks of using a willingness to pay principle to evaluate human costs?

---

[1] *The Accidents Sub-Objective, TAG Unit 3.4.1*, Table 1 (Department for Transport, August 2012).

The difference between the present value of the benefits (PV_b) of the investment and its cost (C) is known as the **net present value (NPV)**.

$$NPV = PV_b - C$$

If the *NPV* is positive, the investment is worthwhile.

Rate of return approach

$$PV = \sum \frac{X_t}{(1+r)^t}$$

The alternative approach when estimating whether an investment is worthwhile is to calculate the investment's *rate of return*. This rate of return is known as the firm's **marginal efficiency of capital (MEC)** or **internal rate of return (IRR)**.

We use the same formula as for calculating present value and then calculate what value of r would make the PV equal to the cost of investment: in other words, the rate of discount that would make the investment just break even. Say this worked out at 20 per cent. What we would be saying is that the investment will just cover its costs if the current rate of interest (rate of discount) is 20 per cent. In other words, this investment is equivalent to receiving 20 per cent interest: it has a 20 per cent rate of return (*IRR*).

So should the investment go ahead? Yes, if the actual rate of interest (i) is less than 20 per cent. The firm is better off investing its money in this project than keeping its money in the bank: i.e. if $IRR > i$, the investment should go ahead.

This is just one more application of the general rule that if $MRP_K > MC_K$ then more capital should be used: only in this case MRP_K is expressed as a rate of return (*IRR*), and the MC_K is expressed as a rate of interest (i).

The risks of investment

One of the problems with investment is that the future is uncertain. The return on an investment will depend on the value of the goods it produces, which will depend on the goods market. For example, the return on investment in the car industry will depend on the demand and price of cars. But future markets cannot be predicted with accuracy: they depend on consumer tastes, the actions of rivals and the whole state of the economy. Investment is thus risky.

Risk may also be incurred in terms of the output from an investment. Take the case of prospecting for oil. An oil company may be lucky and have a major strike, but it may simply drill dry well after dry well. If it does get a major strike and

hence earn a large return on its investment, these profits will not be competed away by competitors prospecting in other fields, because they too still run the risk of drilling dry holes.

How is this risk accounted for when calculating the benefits of an investment? The answer is to use a higher rate of discount. The higher the risk, the bigger the premium that must be added to the rate.

The supply of capital

It is important to distinguish between the supply of *physical* capital and the supply of *finance* to be used by firms for the purchase of capital.

Supply of physical capital. The principles here are just the same as those in the goods market. It does not matter whether a firm is supplying lorries (capital) or cars (a consumer good): it will still produce up to the point where $MC = MR$ if it wishes to maximise profits.

Supply of finance. When firms borrow to invest, this creates a demand for finance (or 'loanable funds'). The supply of loanable funds comes from the deposits that individuals and firms make in financial institutions. These deposits are savings, the level of which depends on the rate of interest that depositors receive. The higher the rate of interest, the more people will be encouraged to save. This is illustrated by an upward-sloping supply curve of loanable funds, as shown in Figure 19.3.

Saving also depends on the level of people's incomes, their expectations of future price changes, and their general level of 'thriftiness' (their willingness to forgo present consumption in order to be able to have more in the future). A change in any of these other determinants will shift the supply curve.

Determination of the rate of interest

The rate of interest is determined by the interaction of supply and demand in the market for loanable funds. This is illustrated in Figure 19.3.

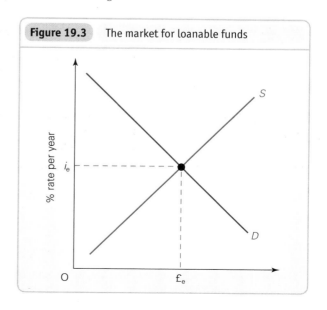

Figure 19.3 The market for loanable funds

Definitions

Net present value of an investment (NPV) The discounted benefits of an investment minus the cost of the investment.

Marginal efficiency of capital (MEC) or **internal rate of return (IRR)** The rate of return of an investment: the discount rate that makes the net present value of an investment equal to zero.

As we have seen, supply represents accumulated savings. The demand curve includes the demand by households for credit and the demand by firms for funds to finance their investment. This demand curve slopes downward for two reasons. First, households will borrow more at lower rates of interest. It effectively makes goods cheaper for them to buy. Second, it reflects the falling rate of return on investment as investment increases. This is simply due to diminishing returns to investment. As rates of interest fall, it will now become profitable for firms to invest in projects that have a lower rate of return: the quantity of loanable funds demanded thus rises.

Equilibrium will be achieved where demand equals supply at an interest rate of i_e and a quantity of loanable funds £$_e$.

How will this market adjust to a change in demand or supply? Assume that there is a rise in demand for capital equipment, due, say, to an improvement in technology which increases the productivity of capital. There is thus an increase in demand for loanable funds. The demand curve shifts to the right in Figure 19.3. The equilibrium rate of interest will rise and this will encourage more savings. The end result is that more money will be spent on capital equipment.

Calculating the costs of capital

When calculating the net present value or internal rate of return of an investment, it is clearly important for the firm to estimate the cost of the investment. The cost does not just include the cost of the equipment that the firm buys: it also includes the costs of raising the finance to pay for the investment.

A firm can finance investment from three major sources:

- retaining profits;
- borrowing from the banking sector – either domestic or overseas;
- issuing new shares (equities) or debentures (fixed-interest loan stock).

It is quite common for a firm to raise finance for a particular project from a mixture of all three sources. The problem is that each source of finance will have a different cost. What is needed, then, for each project is a weighted average of the interest rate (or equivalent) charged or implied by each component of finance.

For investment financed by retained profits, the opportunity cost depends on what would have been done with the profits as the next best alternative. It might be the interest forgone by not putting the money into a bank or other financial institution, or by not purchasing assets. If the next best alternative was to distribute the profits to shareholders, then the opportunity cost would be the cost associated with the increased risks of the firm's share price falling, and the consequent risks of a takeover by another company. (Share prices would fall if shareholders, disillusioned with the reduced dividends, sold their shares.)

For a bank loan, or for debentures, the cost is simply the rate of interest paid on the loan. The only estimation problem here is that of forecasting future rates of interest on loans where the rate of interest is variable.

For equity finance, the cost is the rate of return that must be paid to shareholders to persuade them not to sell their shares. This will depend on the rate of return on shares elsewhere. The greater the return on shares generally, the higher must be the dividends paid by any given firm in order to persuade its shareholders not to switch into other companies' shares.

Leverage and the cost of capital

The cost of capital will increase as the risks for those supplying finance to the company increase: they will need a higher rate of return to warrant incurring the higher risks. One of the most important determinants of the risk to suppliers of finance is the company's leverage. *Leverage* is a measure of the extent to which the company relies on debt finance (i.e. loans) as opposed to equity finance.

There are two common measures of leverage. The first is the *gearing ratio*. This is the ratio of debt finance (debentures and borrowing from banks) to total finance. The other is the *debt/equity ratio*. This is the ratio of debt finance to equity finance.

The higher the company's leverage, the higher will be the risks to creditors and hence the higher will be the interest charged (see Figure 19.4). But why should this be so? The reason is that interest on loans (bank loans and debentures) has to be paid, irrespective of the company's profits. If there is a downturn in the company's profits, then, if it has 'low gearing' (i.e. a low debt/equity ratio), it can simply cut its dividends and as a result will find it relatively easy to make its interest payments. If, however, it is 'highly geared', it may find it impossible to pay all the interest due, even by cutting dividends, in which case it will be forced into receivership.

Given that a highly geared company poses greater risks to creditors, they will demand a higher interest rate to compensate. Similarly with shareholders: given that dividends are likely to fluctuate more with a highly geared company, shareholders will require a higher average dividend over the years. In other words, investors in a highly geared company – whether banks, debenture holders or shareholders – will demand a higher *risk premium*. As gearing increases, so the risk premium, and hence the average cost of capital, will rise at an accelerating rate (see Figure 19.4).

KI 13
p 71

KI 14
p 74

Definitions

Leverage The extent to which a company relies upon debt finance as opposed to equity finance.

Gearing ratio The ratio of debt finance to total finance.

Debt/equity ratio The ratio of debt finance to equity finance.

Risk premium As a business's gearing rises, investors require a higher average dividend from their investment.

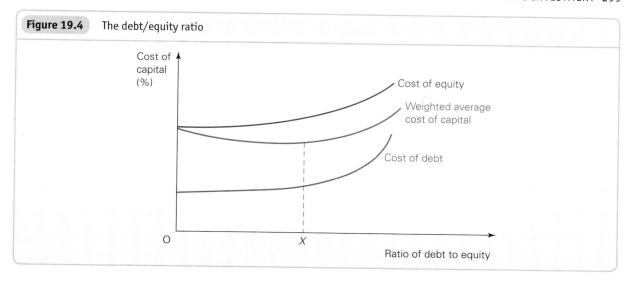

Figure 19.4 The debt/equity ratio

19.4 FINANCING INVESTMENT

It is often claimed that the UK has 'fair weather' bankers: that is, bankers who are prepared to lend when things are going well, but less inclined to lend when times are hard. This criticism has intensified in recent years, with banks accused of holding back recovery in the economy by being reluctant to lend to many businesses, especially SMEs. They are also accused of taking a short-term perspective in their lending practices and of being over-eager to charge high rates of interest on loans, thereby discouraging investment.

But the problem for business does not end there. Dealers on the stock market are also accused of focusing their speculative behaviour on short-run returns (see Box 5.3), thereby generating volatility in share prices and creating business caution, as firms seek ways of maintaining shareholder confidence in their stock (usually through paying high dividends).

In this section we will consider the sources from which business might draw finance, and the roles played by the various UK financial institutions. We will assess the extent to which 'short-termism' is an endemic problem in the capital market.

Sources of business finance

The firm can finance growth by borrowing, by retaining profits or by a new issue of shares (see section 19.3).

Internal funds

As we noted (see Chapter 15), the largest source of finance for investment in the UK is firms' own internal funds (i.e. ploughed-back profit). Given that business profitability depends in large part on the general state of the economy, internal funds as a source of business finance are likely to show considerable cyclical variation. When profits are squeezed in a recession, this source of investment will decline – but so also will the *demand* for investment: after all, what is the point in investing if your market is declining?

External funds

Other sources of finance, which include borrowing and the issue of shares and debentures, are known as 'external funds'. These are then categorised as short-term, medium-term or long-term sources of finance.

Short-term finance. This is usually in the form of a short-term bank loan or overdraft facility, and is used by firms as a form of working capital to aid them in their day-to-day business operations. Another way of borrowing for a short period of time is for a firm to issue *commercial bills of exchange* (see page 465).

Medium-term finance. Again, this is provided largely by banks, is usually in the form of a loan with set repayment targets. It is common for such loans to be made at a fixed rate of interest, with repayments being designed to fit in with the business's expected cash flow. Bank lending tends to be the most volatile source of business finance, and has been particularly sensitive to the state of the economy. While part of the reason is the lower demand for loans during a recession, part of the reason is the caution of banks in granting loans if prospects for the economy are poor.

Long-term finance. Especially in the UK, this tends to be acquired through the stock and bond markets. The proportion of business financing from this source clearly depends on the state of the stock market. In the late 1990s, with a buoyant stock market, the proportion of funds obtained through share issue increased. Then with a decline in stock market prices from 2000 to 2003, this proportion fell, only to rise again as the stock market surged ahead after 2004. From late 2007 through to early 2009, however, with growing worries about difficulties of raising finance following the 'credit crunch' (see Chapter 28) and fears of an impending recession, the stock market plummeted once more. By 2012 the stock market remained below pre-credit-crunch levels (see the diagram in Box 4.2 on page 58) as many investors preferred to keep their assets in less risky form. This, in turn, led to greater uncertainty for long-term finance of business growth through, for example, mergers and acquisitions (see Box 15.1).

Despite the traditional reliance on the stock market for external long-term sources of finance, there has been a growing involvement of banks in recent years. Banks have become more willing to provide finance for business start-ups and for diversification. Nevertheless, there is a concern that banks are still overly cautious. There is a popular perception that, in the years following the credit crunch, banks have become more cautious still. This results in a problem of short-termism, with bankers often demanding a quick return on their money or charging high interest rates, and being less concerned to finance long-term investment.

Other sources of long-term finance include various forms of grants from government, local authorities and the EU. These are often for specific purposes, such as R&D or training; some are available only to SMEs.

Another source is 'venture capital'. This is where an established business or a 'business angel' invests in a new business or small business seeking to expand. They provide capital in exchange for a share of the business.

Another source of finance is that from outside the country. Part of this is direct investment by externally based companies in the domestic economy. Part is finance from foreign financial institutions. In either case, a major determinant of the amount of finance from this source is the current state of the economy and predictions of its future state relative to other countries. One of the major considerations here is anticipated changes in the exchange rate (see Chapter 27). If the exchange rate is expected to rise, this will increase the value of any given profit in terms of foreign currency. As would be expected, this source of finance is particularly volatile.

Comparison of the UK with other European countries

In other European countries, notably Germany and France, the attitude towards business funding is quite different from that in the UK. In these countries, banks provide a significant amount of *long-term*, fixed interest rate finance. While this tends to increase companies' gearing ratios and thus increases the risk of bankruptcy, it does provide a much more stable source of finance and creates an environment where banks are much more committed to the long-run health of companies. For this reason the net effect may be to *reduce* the risks associated with financing investment.

The role of the financial sector

Before we look at the financial institutions operating within the UK, and assess their differing financial roles, it should be noted that they all have the common function of providing a link between those who wish to lend and those who wish to borrow. In other words, they act as the mechanism whereby the supply of funds is matched to the demand for funds.

As *financial intermediaries*, these institutions provide four important services.

Expert advice

Financial intermediaries can advise their customers on financial matters: on the best way of investing their funds and on alternative ways of obtaining finance. This should help to encourage the flow of savings and the efficient use of them. As far as businesses are concerned, banks often play a central role in advising on investment and on possible mergers and acquisitions. They also support small firms, for example, in assisting with the development of business plans. There is considerable competition between banks in terms of the advisory services that they offer to businesses.

Expertise in channelling funds

Financial intermediaries have the specialist knowledge to be able to channel funds to those areas that yield the highest return. This too encourages the flow of saving as it gives savers the confidence that their savings will earn a good rate of interest. Financial intermediaries help to ensure that projects that are potentially profitable, at least in the short run, are able to obtain finance. They thereby help to increase allocative efficiency.

Maturity transformation

Many people and firms want to borrow money for long periods of time, and yet many depositors want to be able to withdraw their deposits on demand or at short notice. If people had to rely on borrowing directly from other people, there would be a problem: the lenders would not be prepared to lend for a long enough period. If you had £100 000 of savings, would you be prepared to lend it to a friend to buy a house if the friend was going to take 25 years to pay it back? Even if there was no risk whatsoever of your friend defaulting, most people would be totally unwilling to tie up their savings for so long.

Definition

Financial intermediaries The general name for financial institutions (banks, building societies, etc.) which act as a means of channelling funds from depositors to borrowers.

BOX 19.2   FINANCING INNOVATION

A flourishing domestic economy is, in no small part, the result of firms successfully innovating and responding to the changing conditions and technologies within the marketplace. Through such adaptation and innovation the economy prospers, stimulating growth, income and employment. Conversely, an economy that fails to innovate and respond to change is likely to be set upon the rocky road to stagnation and decline.

Given the stark contrast in these alternative realities, not only is the development of new ideas and their diffusion throughout the economy crucial to its vitality, but it is essential that the financial system supports such innovation, and does so in the most efficient way. It must ensure not only that finance is available, but that it goes to those projects with the greatest potential.

Unfortunately, the projects with the greatest potential may involve considerable risk and uncertainty. Because of this, the private sector may be unwilling to fund their development. It may also be unwilling to finance various forms of research, where the outcomes are uncertain: something that is inevitable in much basic research.

As a result of this reluctance by the private sector, innovation funding has traditionally operated at three levels:

■ Level one: government financing of 'upstream' or basic research, where outcomes are likely to yield few if any financial returns.
■ Level two: self-financed business R&D (i.e. financed out of ploughed-back profit), where the profitability of such R&D activity is difficult to assess, especially by those outside of the business, and thus where banks and other financial institutions would be reluctant to provide finance.
■ Level three: external financing using accepted financial assessment criteria for risk and uncertainty.

In this traditional model, the state's role in financing innovation and investment does not end at the level of basic research. It will also compensate for market failures at later stages of the innovation-financing process. For example, it may adopt measures to improve the self-financing capacity of firms (e.g. tax relief), or measures to facilitate easier access to external finance (e.g. interest rate subsidies), or measures to extend and protect the ownership of intellectual property rights (e.g. tightening up and/or extending patent or copyright legislation).

The offshore wind generation sector is an excellent example of a sector currently moving from level one to level two. When compared to onshore facilities, offshore wind farms offer considerable potential. There is more energy to capture and planning regulations are less restrictive. However, this potential needs to be offset against the high costs of offshore production. At present these costs remain prohibitively high. However, the technology is improving rapidly and costs are expected to decline substantially.

If the potential for the offshore wind sector is to be realised, a significant amount of investment will be required. Estimates suggest that around £100 billion will be needed in the UK between 2012 and 2020. Much of this investment will need to make a commercial return. However, for such an amount of investment to occur, continued public subsidy will be necessary. This subsidy will help to overcome the private sector's unwillingness to bear the risk and uncertainty of investing in the emerging technology. Once the technology becomes recognised as commercially viable, the sector will have entered level two, or even level three, and the government subsidy can be removed.

There is much to suggest, however, that this traditional model is changing, and, along with it, the perceived role of the state in the process of conducting, funding and supporting the innovation process. The most significant of these changes can be found in the liberalisation of global finance.

Three of the major effects of financial liberalisation on innovation financing are as follows:

■ Channels of finance have diversified, widening the range of potential investment sources.
■ Financial innovations have increased the ability of potential innovators to locate and negotiate favourable financial deals.
■ Government regulations over capital market activities have diminished.

The implications of these changes have been to increase the efficiency and flexibility of the financial system. This has resulted in a reduction in international differences in the costs of capital for any businesses having access to global financing. Projects with high earning potential, but high risk, have been able to raise finance from a wider range of sources, national and international.

Although such financial globalisation has not removed the need for state support, it appears that financial changes are certainly diminishing its significance as a supporter of innovation finance.

1. *What market failures could account for a less than optimal amount of innovation in the absence of government support?*
2. *If financial markets were perfectly competitive and could price risk accurately, would there be any case at all for government support of innovation?*

This is where a bank or building society comes in. It borrows money from a vast number of small savers, who are able to withdraw their money on demand or at short notice. It then lends the money to house purchasers for a long period of time by granting mortgages (typically these are paid back over 20 to 30 years).

This process whereby financial intermediaries lend for longer periods of time than they borrow is known as *maturity transformation*. They are able to do this because with a large number of depositors it is highly unlikely that

Definition

Maturity transformation The transformation of deposits into loans of a longer maturity.

they would all want to withdraw their deposits at the same time. On any one day, although some people will be withdrawing money, others will be making new deposits.

There is still the problem, however, that long-term loans by banks, especially to industry, often carry greater risks. With banking tradition, especially in the UK, being to err on the side of caution, this can limit the extent to which maturity transformation takes place, and can result in a less than optimum amount of investment finance, when viewed from a long-term perspective.

Risk transformation

You may be unwilling to lend money directly to another person in case they do not pay up. You are unwilling to take the risk. Financial intermediaries, however, by lending to large numbers of people, are willing to risk the odd case of default. They can absorb the loss because of the interest they earn on all the other loans. This spreading of risk is known as **risk transformation**. What is more, financial intermediaries may have the expertise to be able to assess just how risky a loan is. Again, however, banks in the UK have been accused of being too cautious, and too unwilling to lend to industry for long-term investment, given the risks associated with such loans.

Pause for thought

Which of the above are examples of economies of scale?

In addition to channelling funds from depositors to borrowers, certain financial institutions have another important function. This is to provide a means of transmitting payments. Thus by the use of debit cards, credit cards, cheques, standing orders, etc., money can be transferred from one person or institution to another without having to rely on cash.

The banking system

Banking can be divided into two main types: *retail banking* and *wholesale banking*. Most banks today conduct both types of business and are thus known as 'universal banks'.

Retail banking. This is the business conducted by the familiar high street banks, such as Barclays, Lloyds TSB, HSBC, Royal Bank of Scotland, NatWest (part of the RBS group) and Santander. They operate bank accounts for individuals

and businesses, attracting deposits and granting loans at published rates of interest. Some of these accounts are accessed through the banks' branches and some via telephone or Internet banking.

Wholesale banking. This involves receiving large deposits from and making large loans to companies or other banks and financial institutions; these are known as **wholesale deposits and loans**.

As far as companies are concerned, these may be for short periods of time to account for the non-matching of a firm's payments and receipts from its business. They may be for longer periods of time, for various investment purposes. As these wholesale deposits and loans are very large sums of money, banks compete against each other for them and negotiate individual terms with the firm to suit the firm's particular requirements. The rates of interest negotiated will reflect the current market rates of interest and the terms of the particular loan/deposit. Very large loans to firms are often divided ('syndicated') among several banks.

In the past, there were many independent wholesale banks, known as *investment banks*. These included famous names such as Morgan Stanley, Rothschild, S. G. Hambros and Goldman Sachs. In recent years, however, most of the independent investment banks merged with universal banks, so that today most wholesale banking is conducted in a division of the major universal banks.

Banks also lend and borrow wholesale funds to and from each other. Banks that are short of funds borrow large sums from others with surplus funds, thus ensuring that the banking sector as a whole does not have funds surplus to its requirements. The rate at which they lend to each other is known as the IBOR (inter-bank offer rate). The IBOR has a major influence on the other rates that banks charge. In the eurozone, the IBOR is known as Euribor. In the UK, it is known as LIBOR (where 'L' stands for 'London'). As inter-bank loans can be anything from overnight to 12 months, the IBOR will vary from one length of loan to another.

Since the deregulation of the mid-1980s, banks have diversified their business, and each one now provides a range of financial services, often through one or more of its subsidiaries. These services include insurance, share dealing, pensions, mortgages and estate agency.

One of the major causes of the banking crisis of 2008 was the growth in dealing in highly complex financial products by the investment arms of universal banks. Many of

Definitions

Risk transformation The process whereby banks can spread the risks of lending by having a large number of borrowers.

Retail banking Branch, telephone, postal and Internet banking for individuals and businesses at published rates of interest and charges. Retail banking involves the operation of extensive branch networks.

Wholesale banking Where banks deal in large-scale deposits and loans, mainly with companies and other banks and financial institutions. Interest rates and charges may be negotiable.

Wholesale deposits and loans Large-scale deposits and loans made by and to firms at negotiated interest rates.

these products bundled up sound assets with highly risky ones, such as mortgage loans to borrowers in the USA who had little change of repaying, especially with the fall in US house prices. These 'toxic' assets caused serious problems for many banks and forced governments around the world to intervene to rescue ailing banks (we look at this in more detail in Chapter 28). In the aftermath of the crisis, governments have sought ways of 'ring-fencing' the risky investment (or 'casino') divisions of banks from their more traditional retail arms.

19.5 THE STOCK MARKET

In this section, we will look at the role of the stock market and consider the advantages and limitations of raising finance through it. We will also consider whether the stock market is efficient.

The role of the Stock Exchange

The London Stock Exchange operates as both a primary and secondary market in capital.

As a ***primary market*** it is where public limited companies (see page 37) can raise finance by issuing new shares, whether to new shareholders or to existing ones. To raise finance on the Stock Exchange a business must be 'listed'. The Listing Agreement involves directors agreeing to abide by a strict set of rules governing behaviour and levels of reporting to shareholders. Companies must have at least three years' trading experience and make at least 25 per cent of their shares available to the public. At the end of 2012, there were 1009 UK and 318 international companies on the Main Market List. During 2012, companies on this list raised £11.5 billion of equity capital on the London Stock Exchange, £5.8 billion of which was raised by international companies.

As well as those on the Main Market List, there are some 1110 companies on what is known as the Alternative Investment Market (AIM). Companies listed here tend to be young but with growth potential, and do not have to meet the strict criteria or pay such high costs as companies on the Main Market List. In 2012, companies on the AIM list raised £3.1 billion of new capital, a figure slightly down on 2011, when £3.7 billion was raised, and considerably down on 2007 when £16.2 billion was raised. The reason for this fall had been the persistence of economic uncertainty created by the recession that began in 2008.

As a *secondary market*, the Stock Exchange operates as a market where investors can sell existing shares to one another. In 2012, on an average day's trading, around £4 billion worth of trades in listed equities took place.

The advantages and disadvantages of using the stock market to raise capital

As a market for raising capital the stock market has a number of advantages:

- It brings together those who wish to invest and those who seek investment. It thus represents a way that savings can be mobilised to create output, and does so in a relatively low-cost way.
- Firms that are listed on the stock exchange are subject to strict regulations. This is likely to stimulate investor confidence, making it easier for business to raise finance.
- The process of merger and acquisition is facilitated by having a share system. It enables business more effectively to pursue this as a growth strategy.

The main weaknesses of the stock market for raising capital are:

- The cost to a business of getting listed can be immense, not only in a financial sense, but also in being open to public scrutiny. Directors' and senior managers' decisions will often be driven by how the market is likely to react, rather than by what they perceive to be in the business's best interests. They always have to think about the reactions of those large shareholders in the City that control a large proportion of their shares.
- It is often claimed that the stock market suffers from ***short-termism***. Investors on the Stock Exchange are more concerned with a company's short-term performance and its share value. In responding to this, the business might neglect its long-term performance and potential.

Is the stock market efficient?

One of the arguments made in favour of the stock market is that it acts as an arena within which share values can be accurately or efficiently priced. If new information comes on to the market concerning a business and its performance,

---

Definitions

Primary market in capital Where shares are sold by the issuer of the shares (i.e. the firm) and where, therefore, finance is channelled directly from the purchasers (i.e. the shareholders) to the firm.

Secondary market in capital Where shareholders sell shares to others. This is thus a market in 'second-hand' shares.

Short-termism Where firms and investors take decisions based on the likely short-term performance of a company, rather than on its long-term prospects. Firms may thus sacrifice long-term profits and growth for the sake of quick return.

this will be quickly and rationally transferred into the business's share value. This is known as the *efficient market hypothesis*. So, for example, if an investment analyst found that, in terms of its actual and expected dividends, a particular share was underpriced and thus represented a 'bargain', the analyst would advise investors to buy. As people then bought the shares, their price would rise, pushing their value up to their full worth. So by attempting to gain from inefficiently priced securities, investors will encourage the market to become more efficient.

 KEY IDEA 29 *Efficient capital markets.* Capital markets are efficient when the prices of shares accurately reflect information about companies' current and expected future performance.

So how efficient is the stock market in pricing securities? Is information rationally and quickly conveyed into the share's price? Or are investors able to prosper from the stock market's inefficiencies?

We can identify three levels of efficiency.

Weak form of efficiency. Share prices often move in cycles which do not reflect the underlying performance of the firm. If information is imperfect, those with a better understanding of such cycles gain from buying shares at the trough and selling them at the peak of the cycles. They are taking advantage of the market's inefficiency.

The technical analysis used by investment analysts to track share cycles is a complex science, but more and more analysts are using the techniques. As they do so and knowledge becomes more perfect, so the market will become more efficient and the cycles will tend to disappear. But why?

As more people buy a company's shares as the price falls towards its trough, so this extra demand will prevent the price falling so far. Similarly, as people sell as the price rises towards its peak, so this extra supply will prevent the price rising so far. This is an example of stabilising speculation (see pages 72–3). As more and more people react in this way, so the cycle all but disappears. When this happens, *weak efficiency* has been achieved.

The semi-strong form of efficiency. **Semi-strong efficiency** is when share prices adjust fully to publicly available information. In practice, not all investors will interpret such information correctly: their knowledge is imperfect. But as investors become more and more sophisticated, and as more and more advice is available to shareholders (through stockbrokers, newspapers, published accounts, etc.), and as many shares are purchased by professional fund managers, so the interpretation of public information becomes more and more perfect and the market becomes more and more efficient in the semi-strong sense.

If the market were efficient in the semi-strong sense, then no gain could be made from studying a company's performance and prospects, as any such information would *already* be included in the current share price. In selecting shares, you would do just as well by pinning the financial pages of a newspaper on the wall, throwing darts at them, and buying the shares the darts hit!

The strong form of efficiency. If the stock market showed the **strong form of efficiency**, then share prices would fully reflect *all* available information – whether public or not. For this to be so, all 'inside' information would have to be reflected in the share price the moment the information is available.

If the market is *not* efficient at this level, then people who have access to privileged information will be able to make large returns from their investments by acting on such information. For example, directors of a company would know if the company was soon to announce better than expected profits. In the meantime, they could gain by buying shares in the company, knowing that the share price would rise when the information about the profits became public. Gains made from such 'insider dealing' are illegal, but proving whether individuals are engaging in it is very difficult. Nevertheless, there are people in prison for insider dealing: so it does happen!

Given the penalties for insider dealing and the amount of private information that firms possess, it is unlikely that all such information will be reflected in share prices. Thus the strong form of stock market efficiency is unlikely to hold.

If stock markets were fully efficient, the expected returns from every share would be the same. The return is referred to as the *yield*: this is measured as the dividends paid on the share as a percentage of the share's market price. For KI 29 p 304

Definitions

Efficient (capital) market hypothesis The hypothesis that new information about a company's current or future performance will be quickly and accurately reflected in its share price.

Weak efficiency (of share markets) Where share dealing prevents cyclical movements in shares.

Semi-strong efficiency (of share markets) Where share prices adjust quickly, fully and accurately to publicly available information.

Strong efficiency (of share markets) Where share prices adjust quickly, fully and accurately to all available information, both public and that available only to insiders.

Yield on a share The dividend received per share expressed as a percentage of the current market price of the share.

example, if you hold shares whose market price is £1 per share and you receive an annual dividend of 3p per share, then the yield on the shares is 3 per cent. But why should the expected returns on shares be the same? If any share was expected to yield a higher-than-average return, people would buy it; its price would rise and its yield would correspondingly fall.

It is only unanticipated information, therefore, that would cause share prices to deviate from that which reflected expected average yields. Such information must, by its nature, be random, and as such would cause share prices to deviate randomly from their expected price, or follow what we call a *random walk*. Evidence suggests that share prices do tend to follow random patterns.

Pause for thought

Would the stock market be more efficient if insider dealing were made legal?

Definition

Random walk Where fluctuations in the value of a share away from its 'correct' value are random: i.e. have no systematic pattern. When charted over time, these share price movements would appear like a 'random walk': like the path of someone staggering along drunk!

SUMMARY

1a We need to distinguish between factor prices and factor services. A factor's price is income from its sale, whereas a factor's service is the income from its use.

1b The profit-maximising employment of capital will be at the point where the marginal cost of capital equals the marginal revenue product.

2a The demand for capital services will be equal to MRP_K. As a result of diminishing returns, this will decline as more capital is used.

2b The supply of capital services to a firm will be horizontal or upward sloping, depending on whether the firm is perfectly competitive or has monopsony power.

2c The supply curve of capital services *by* a firm in the short run will be relatively elastic up to capacity supply. In the long run, the supply curve will be very elastic, but at a higher rental rate than in the short run, given that the cost of purchasing the equipment must be taken into account in the rental rate.

2d The market supply of capital services is likely to be highly inelastic in the short run, given that capital equipment tends to have very specific uses and cannot normally be transferred from one use to another. In the long run it will be more elastic.

2e The price of capital services will be determined by the interaction of demand and supply.

3a The demand for capital for purchase will depend on the return it earns for the firm. To calculate the return, all future earnings from the investment have to be reduced to present value by discounting at a market rate of interest. If the present value exceeds the cost of the investment, the investment is worthwhile. Alternatively, a rate of return from the investment (IRR) can be calculated and then this can be compared with the return that the firm could have earned by investing elsewhere.

3b The supply of finance for investment depends on the supply of loanable funds, which in turn depends, in large part, on the rate of interest.

3c The rate of interest will be determined by the demand and supply of loanable funds.

3d The costs of capital supplied to the firm will rise the more it is in debt, and hence the more risky the investment becomes.

4a Business finance can come from internal and external sources. Sources external to the firm include borrowing, the issue of shares, venture capital and government grants.

4b The role of the financial sector is to act as a financial intermediary between those who wish to borrow and those who wish to lend.

4c UK financial institutions specialise in different types of deposit taking and lending. It is useful to distinguish between retail and wholesale banking.

5a The stock market operates as both a primary and secondary market in capital. As a primary market it channels finance to companies as people purchase new shares. It is also a market for existing shares.

5b It helps to stimulate growth and investment by bringing together companies and people who want to invest in them. By regulating firms and by keeping transaction costs of investment low, it helps to ensure that investment is efficient.

5c It does impose costs on firms, however. It is expensive for firms to be listed and the public exposure may make them too keen to 'please' the market. It can also foster short-termism.

5d The stock market is relatively efficient. It achieves weak efficiency by reducing cyclical movements in share prices. It achieves semi-strong efficiency by allowing share prices to respond quickly and fully to publicly available information. Whether it achieves strong efficiency by adjusting quickly and fully to *all* information (both public or insider), however, is more doubtful.

REVIEW QUESTIONS

1 Draw the MRP_K, AC_K and MC_K curves for a firm which has monopsony power when hiring capital equipment. Mark the amount of capital equipment it will choose to hire and show what hire charge it will pay.

2 Using a diagram like Figure 19.2, demonstrate what will happen under perfect competition (in the short run) when there is an increase in the productivity of a particular type of capital. Consider the effects on the demand, price (rental rate) and quantity supplied of the services of this type of capital. In what way will the long-run effect differ from the short-run one that you have illustrated?

3 Suppose an investment costs £12 000 and yields £5000 per year for three years. At the end of the three years, the equipment has no value. Work out whether the investment will be profitable if the rate of discount is: (a) 5% (b) 10% (c) 20%.

4 If a project's costs occur throughout the life of the project, how will this affect the appraisal of whether the project is profitable?

5 What factors would cause a rise in the market rate of interest?

6 What is meant by the two terms 'gearing ratio' and 'debt/equity ratio'? What is their significance?

7 Explain the various roles that financial intermediaries play within the finance sector.

8 In what circumstances is the stock market likely to be 'efficient' in the various senses of the term?

ADDITIONAL PART G CASE STUDIES IN THE *ECONOMICS FOR BUSINESS* MyEconLab (www.pearsoned.co.uk/sloman)

G.1 **Stocks and flows.** This examines one of the most important distinctions in economics and one which we shall come across on several occasions.

G.2 **Poverty in the past.** Extreme poverty in Victorian England.

G.3 **The rise and decline of the labour movement.** A brief history of trade unions in the UK.

G.4 **How useful is marginal productivity theory?** How accurately does the theory describe employment decisions by firms?

G.5 **Profit sharing.** An examination of the case for and against profit sharing as a means of rewarding workers.

G.6 **How can we define poverty?** This examines different definitions of poverty and, in particular, distinguishes between absolute and relative measures of poverty.

G.7 **How to reverse the UK's increased inequality.** Recommendations of the Rowntree Foundation.

G.8 **Calculating net present value.** A numerical example using discounting techniques to show how net present value is calculated.

G.9 **Catastrophic risk.** This examines the difficulties in assigning a monetary value to the remote chance of a catastrophe happening (such as an explosion at a nuclear power station).

WEBSITES RELEVANT TO PART G

Numbers and sections refer to websites listed in the Web appendix and hotlinked from this book's website at **www.pearsoned.co.uk/sloman**

■ For news articles relevant to Part G, see the *Economics News Articles* link from the book's website.

■ For general news on labour and capital markets, see websites in section A, and particularly A1–5, 7, 8, 21–26, 35, 36. See also A42 for links to economics news articles from newspapers worldwide.

■ For data on labour markets, see links in B1 or 2, especially to *Labour Market Trends* on the National Statistics site. Also see B9 and links in B19. Also see the labour topic in B33 and the *resources > statistics* links in H3.

■ For information on international labour standards and employment rights, see site H3.

■ Sites I7 and 11 contain links to *Labour economics, Labour force and markets* and *Labour unions* in the *Microeconomics* section and to *Distribution of income and wealth* in the *Macroeconomics* section. Site I4 has links in the *Directory* section to *Labor* and *Labor Economics*. Site I17 in the *Labor Economics* section has links to various topics, such as *Labor Unions, Minimum Wage, Poverty* and *Work*.

■ Links to the TUC and Confederation of British Industry sites can be found at E32 and 33.

■ For information on poverty and inequality, see sites B18; E9, 13.

■ For information on taxes, benefits and the redistribution of income, see E9, 30, 36; G5, 13. See also *The Virtual Economy* at D1.

■ For information on stock markets, see sites F18 and A3.

■ Sites I7 and 11 contain links to *Financial Economics*.

■ For student resources relevant to Part G, see sites C1–7, 9, 10, 19; D3.

The relationship between government and business

The FT Reports . . .

The Financial Times, 13 April 2009

FT

Cargo airlines fined for fixing prices

By Kevin Done

Three cargo airlines have agreed to pay fines totalling $214 m for their roles in a global conspiracy to fix prices for air freight.

The penalties are the latest imposed following one of the biggest cartel probes led by the US justice department. It has led to the prosecution of 15 airlines and has resulted in total fines of more than $1.6 bn against the aviation industry.

In addition, three senior air cargo industry executives agreed to serve jail terms.

Cargolux, which is based in Luxembourg; Nippon Cargo Airlines of Japan; and Korea's Asiana Airlines have each agreed to plead guilty and pay criminal fines for conspiring to fix prices.

The fixing of cargo rates for international air shipments began as early as September 2001 and continued until February 2006.

Cargolux will pay a fine of $119 m; Nippon Cargo, $45 m; and Asiana, $50 m. The DoJ said Asiana had admitted to engaging in a conspiracy to fix passenger fares from as early as January 2000.

The plea agreements are still subject to final court approval. All three carriers have agreed to co-operate in the continuing investigation.

Scott Hammond, acting assistant attorney-general, who is in charge of the Department of Justice's antitrust division, said the investigation would continue 'into this criminal conduct until all co-conspirators are brought to justice'.

Other carriers to have admitted criminal guilt and paid fines in the US include British Airways; Korean Airlines; Qantas; Japan Airlines; Martinair (a subsidiary of Air France-KLM); Cathay Pacific; SAS Scandinavian Airlines; Air France and KLM; LAN Cargo; Aerolinhas Brasileiras and El Al Israel Airlines.

Three executives from BA, Qantas and SAS have previously pleaded guilty and have been given jail terms.

According to the DoJ, the airlines participated in 'meetings, conversations and communications' to agree some components of the cargo rates to be charged on certain routes to and from the US. They conspired to monitor and enforce adherence to the prices.

Competition officials from around the world including from the US, the European Union and Australia are investigating the global price-fixing conspiracy in the air freight industry in what has become one of the world's biggest cartel probes.

The EU is expected to bring further charges against airlines; several other airline executives are under investigation in the US and in the UK . . .

> *While I have been a lifelong capitalist, I could never accept that laissez faire is a good solution for a society. It was John Ralston Saul who said that 'unregulated competition is just a naïve metaphor for anarchy' – we don't need that. What we need are regulated markets. And the challenge is to maximise our prosperity by finding the most efficient ways to regulate them.*

Neelie Kroes, European Commission Competition Commissioner, 'Competition, the crisis and the road to recovery', Address at the Economic Club of Toronto, 30 March 2009

Despite the fact that most countries today can be classified as 'market economies', governments nevertheless intervene substantially in the activities of business in order to protect the interests of consumers, workers or the environment.

Firms might collude to fix prices (see the *Financial Times* article), use misleading advertising, create pollution, produce unsafe products, or use unacceptable employment practices. In such cases, government is expected to intervene to correct for the failings of the market system: for example, by outlawing collusion, by establishing advertising standards, by taxing or otherwise penalising polluting firms, by imposing safety standards on firms' behaviour and products, or by protecting employment rights.

In Part H, we explore the relationship between business and government. In Chapter 20 we will consider how markets might fail to achieve ideal outcomes, and what government can do to correct such problems. We will also consider how far firms should go in adopting a more socially responsible position.

In Chapter 21 we will focus upon the relationship between the government and the individual firm, and consider three policy areas: monopolies and oligopolies, research and technology, and training.

In Chapter 22, we will broaden our analysis and look at government policy aimed at the level of the market, and its impact upon all firms. Here we will consider environmental policy, transport policy and the issue of privatisation and regulation.

Perhaps, like Neelie Kroes (see the quote above), you believe that markets need government intervention in order to make them more efficient. There is, however, a problem. Unless government intervention is carefully designed, it can have unintended consequences. The 'cure' might even be worse than the 'disease'.

Key terms

Social efficiency
Equity
Market failure
Externalities
Private and social costs and benefits
Deadweight welfare loss
Public goods
Free-rider problem
Merit goods
Government intervention
Coase theorem
Laissez-faire
Social responsibility
Competition policy
Restrictive practices
Technology policy
Training policy
Environmental policy
Green taxes
Tradable permits
Cost–benefit analysis
Road pricing
Transport policy
Privatisation
Regulation
Price-cap regulation
Deregulation
Franchising

Reasons for government intervention in the market

Business issues covered in this chapter

- ■ To what extent does business meet the interests of consumers and society in general?
- ■ In what sense are perfect markets 'socially efficient' and why do most markets fail to achieve social efficiency?
- ■ In what ways do governments intervene in markets and attempt to influence business behaviour?
- ■ Can taxation be used to correct the shortcomings of markets, or is it better to use the law?
- ■ What are the drawbacks of government intervention?
- ■ What is meant by 'corporate social responsibility' and what determines firms' attitudes towards society and the environment?
- ■ What is the relationship between business ethics and business performance?

20.1 MARKETS AND THE ROLE OF GOVERNMENT

Government intervention and social objectives

In order to decide the optimum amount of government intervention, it is first necessary to identify the various social goals that intervention is designed to meet. Two of the major objectives of government intervention identified by economists are *social efficiency* and *equity*.

Social efficiency. If the marginal benefits to society – or 'marginal social benefits' (*MSB*) – of producing any given

good or service exceed the marginal costs to society or 'marginal social costs' (*MSC*), it is said to be socially efficient to produce more. For example, if people's gains from having additional motorways exceed *all* the additional costs to society (both financial and non-financial) then it is socially efficient to construct more motorways.

If, however, the marginal social costs of producing any good or service exceed the marginal social benefits, then it is socially efficient to produce less.

It follows that if the marginal social benefits of any activity are equal to the marginal social costs, then the current level is the optimum. To summarise: for social efficiency in the production of any good or service:

$MSB > MSC \rightarrow$ produce more

$MSC > MSB \rightarrow$ produce less

$MSB = MSC \rightarrow$ keep production at its current level

Definitions

Social efficiency Production and consumption at the point where $MSB = MSC$.

Equity The fair distribution of a society's resources.

Similar rules apply to consumption. For example, if the marginal social benefits of consuming more of any good or service exceed the marginal social costs, then society would benefit from more of the good being consumed.

Social efficiency is an example of 'allocative efficiency': in other words, the best allocation of resources between alternative uses.

> **KEY IDEA 30**
>
> *Allocative efficiency in any activity is achieved where any reallocation would lead to a decline in net benefit.* It is achieved where marginal benefit equals marginal cost. Private efficiency is achieved where marginal private benefit equals marginal private cost ($MB = MC$). Social efficiency is achieved where marginal social benefit equals marginal social cost ($MSB = MSC$).

In the real world, the market rarely leads to social efficiency: the marginal social benefits of most goods and services do not equal the marginal social costs. In this chapter we examine why the free market fails to lead to social efficiency and what the government can do to rectify the situation. We also examine why the government itself may fail to achieve social efficiency.

> **KEY IDEA 31**
>
> *Markets generally fail to achieve social efficiency.* There are various types of market failure. Market failures provide one of the major justifications for government intervention in the economy.

Equity. Most people would argue that the free market fails to lead to a *fair* distribution of resources, if it results in some people living in great affluence while others live in dire poverty. Clearly what constitutes 'fairness' is a highly contentious issue: those on the political right generally have a quite different view from those on the political left. Nevertheless, most people would argue that the government does have some duty to redistribute incomes from the rich to the poor through the tax and benefit system, and perhaps to provide various forms of legal protection for the poor (such as a minimum wage rate).

> **KEY IDEA 32**
>
> *Equity* is where income is distributed in a way that is considered to be fair or just. Note that an equitable distribution is not the same as a totally equal distribution and that different people have different views on what is equitable.

Although our prime concern in this chapter is the question of social efficiency, we will be touching on questions of distribution too.

20.2 TYPES OF MARKET FAILURE

Externalities

The market will not lead to social efficiency if the actions of producers or consumers affect people *other than themselves*. These effects on other people are known as *externalities*: they are the side-effects, or 'third-party' effects, of production or consumption. Externalities can be either desirable or undesirable. Whenever other people are affected beneficially, there are said to be *external benefits*. Whenever other people are affected adversely, there are said to be *external costs*.

> **KEY IDEA 33**
>
> *Externalities are spillover costs or benefits.* Where these exist, even an otherwise perfect market will fail to achieve social efficiency.

Thus the full cost to society (the *social cost*) of the production of any good or service is the private cost faced by firms plus any externalities of production (positive or negative). Likewise the full benefit to society (the *social benefit*) from the consumption of any good is the private benefit enjoyed by consumers plus any externalities of consumption (positive or negative).

There are four major types of externality.

External costs of production (MSC > MC)

When a chemical firm dumps waste in a river or pollutes the air, the community bears costs additional to those borne by the firm. The marginal *social* cost (*MSC*) of chemical production exceeds the marginal private cost (*MC*). Diagrammatically, the *MSC* curve is above the *MC* curve. This is shown in Figure 20.1(a), which assumes that the firm in other respects is operating in a perfect market, and is therefore a price taker (i.e. faces a horizontal demand curve).

> ### Definitions
>
> **Externalities** Costs or benefits of production or consumption experienced by society but not by the producers or consumers themselves. Sometimes referred to as 'spillover' or 'third-party' costs or benefits.
>
> **External benefits** Benefits from production (or consumption) experienced by people *other* than the producer (or consumer).
>
> **External costs** Costs of production (or consumption) borne by people *other* than the producer (or consumer).
>
> **Social cost** Private cost plus externalities in production.
>
> **Social benefit** Private benefit plus externalities in consumption.

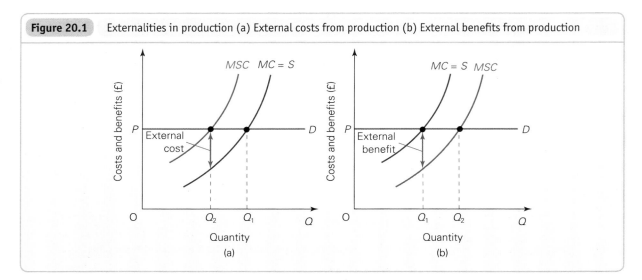

Figure 20.1 Externalities in production (a) External costs from production (b) External benefits from production

The firm maximises profits at Q_1: the output where marginal cost equals price (see section 11.2). The price is what people buying the good are prepared to pay for one more unit (if it wasn't, they wouldn't buy it) and therefore reflects their marginal benefit. We assume no externalities from consumption, and therefore the marginal benefit to consumers is the same as the marginal *social* benefit (MSB).

The socially optimum output would be Q_2, where P (i.e. MSB) = MSC. The firm, however, produces Q_1, which is more than the optimum. Thus external costs lead to over-production from society's point of view.

The problem of external costs arises in a free-market economy because no one has legal ownership of the air or rivers and no one, therefore, can prevent or charge for their use as a dump for waste. Such a 'market' is missing. Control must, therefore, be left to the government or local authorities.

Other examples include extensive farming that destroys hedgerows and wildlife, and global warming caused by CO_2 emissions from power stations.

External benefits of production (MSC < MC)

If a forestry company plants new woodlands, there is a benefit not only to the company itself, but also to the world through a reduction of CO_2 in the atmosphere (forests are a carbon sink). The marginal *social* cost of providing timber, therefore, is less than the marginal *private* cost to the company.

In Figure 20.1(b), the MSC curve is *below* the MC curve. The level of output provided by a forestry company is Q_1, where $P = MC$, a *lower* level than the social optimum, Q_2, where $P = MSC$.

Another example of external benefits in production is that of research and development. If other firms have access to the results of the research, then clearly the benefits extend beyond the firm which finances it. Since the firm only receives the private benefits, it will conduct a less

than optimal amount of research. In turn, this may reduce the pace of innovation and so negatively affect economic growth over the longer term.

External costs of consumption (MSB < MB)

When people use their cars, other people suffer from their exhaust, the added congestion, the noise, etc. These 'negative externalities' make the marginal social benefit of using cars less than the marginal private benefit (i.e. marginal utility to the car user).

Figure 20.2(a) shows the marginal utility and price to a motorist (i.e. the consumer) of using a car. The optimal distance travelled for this motorist will be Q_1 miles: i.e. where $MU = P$ (where price is the cost of petrol, oil, wear and tear, etc. per mile). The *social* optimum, however, would be less than this, namely Q_2, where $MSB = P$.

Other examples of negative externalities of consumption include noisy radios in public places, the smoke from cigarettes, and litter.

External benefits of consumption (MSB > MB)

When people travel by train rather than by car, other people benefit by there being less congestion and exhaust fumes and fewer accidents on the roads. Thus the marginal social benefit of rail travel is *greater* than the marginal private benefit (i.e. the marginal utility to the rail passenger). There are external benefits from rail travel. In Figure 20.2(b), the MSB curve is *above* the private MB curve. The actual level of consumption (Q_1) is thus below the socially optimal level of consumption (Q_2).

Other examples include the beneficial effects for other people of deodorants, vaccinations and attractive clothing.

To summarise: whenever there are external benefits, there will be too little produced or consumed. Whenever there are external costs, there will be too much produced or consumed. The market will not equate MSB and MSC.

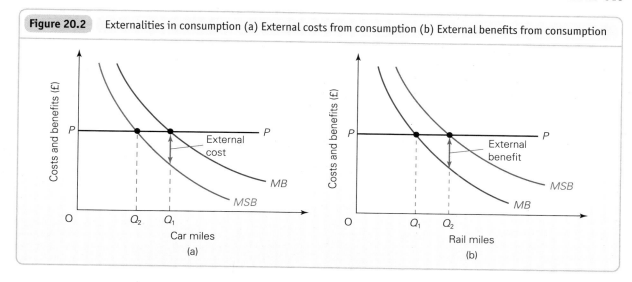

Figure 20.2 Externalities in consumption (a) External costs from consumption (b) External benefits from consumption

The above arguments have been developed in the context of perfect competition with prices given to the producer or consumer by the market. Externalities also occur in all other types of market.

Pause for thought

Give other examples of each of the four types of externality.

Public goods

There is a category of goods where the positive externalities are so great that the free market, whether perfect or imperfect, may not produce at all. They are called *public goods*. Examples include lighthouses, pavements, flood control dams, public drainage, public services such as the police and even government itself.

Pause for thought

Which of the following have the property of non-rivalry: (a) a can of drink; (b) public transport; (c) a commercial radio broadcast; (d) the sight of flowers in a public park?

Public goods have two important characteristics: *non-rivalry* and *non-excludability*:

- If I consume a bar of chocolate, it cannot then be consumed by someone else. If, however, I enjoy the benefits of street lighting, it does not prevent you or anyone else doing the same. There is thus what we call *non-rivalry* in the consumption of such goods. These goods tend to have large external benefits relative to private benefits. This makes them socially desirable, but privately unprofitable. No one person on their own would pay

to have a pavement built along his or her street. The private benefit would be too small relative to the cost. And yet the social benefit to all the other people using the pavement may far outweigh the cost.

- If I spend money erecting a flood control dam to protect my house, my neighbours will also be protected by the dam. I cannot prevent them enjoying the benefits of my expenditure. This feature of *non-excludability* means that they would get the benefits free, and would therefore have no incentive to pay themselves. This is known as the *free-rider problem*.

 KEY IDEA 34

The free-rider problem. People are often unwilling to pay for things if they can make use of things other people have bought. This problem can lead to people not purchasing things which would be to the benefit of them and other members of society to have.

When goods have these two features, the free market will simply not provide them. Thus these public goods can only be provided by the government or by the government subsidising private firms. (Note that not all goods and

Definitions

Public good A good or service which has the features of non-rivalry and non-excludability and as a result would not be provided by the free market.

Non-rivalry Where the consumption of a good or service by one person will not prevent others from enjoying it.

Non-excludability Where it is not possible to provide a good or service to one person without it thereby being available for others to enjoy.

Free-rider problem When it is not possible to exclude other people from consuming a good that someone has bought.

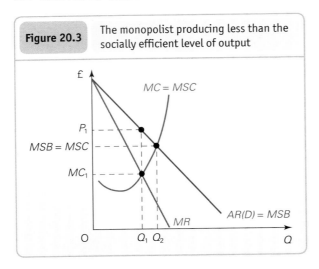

Figure 20.3 The monopolist producing less than the socially efficient level of output

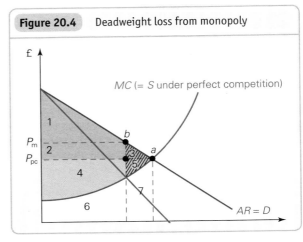

Figure 20.4 Deadweight loss from monopoly

services produced by the public sector come into the category of public goods and services: thus education and health are publicly provided, but they *can* be, and indeed are, privately provided.)

Market power

Whenever markets are imperfect, whether as pure monopoly or monopsony or whether as some form of imperfect competition, the market will fail to equate *MSB* and *MSC*, even if there are no externalities.

Take the case of monopoly. A monopoly will produce less than the socially efficient output. This is illustrated in Figure 20.3. A monopoly faces a downward-sloping demand curve, and therefore marginal revenue is below average revenue (= P = *MSB*). Profits are maximised at an output of Q_1, where marginal revenue equals marginal cost (see Figure 11.6 on page 169). If there are no externalities, the socially efficient output will be at the higher level of Q_2, where *MSB* = *MSC*.

Deadweight loss under monopoly

One way of analysing the welfare loss that occurs under monopoly is to use the concepts of *consumer* and *producer surplus*. The two concepts are illustrated in Figure 20.4. The diagram shows an industry which is initially under perfect competition and then becomes a monopoly (but faces the same revenue and cost curves).

Consumer surplus. **Consumer surplus** from a good is the difference between the total utility (satisfaction) received by consumers and their total expenditure on the good (see pages 83–4). Under *perfect competition* the industry will produce an output of Q_{pc} at a price of P_{pc}, where $MC(= S) = P(= AR)$: i.e. at point *a*. Consumers' total utility is given by the area under the demand (*MU*) curve (the sum of all the areas 1–7). Consumers' total expenditure is $P_{pc} \times Q_{pc}$ (areas 4 + 5 + 6 + 7). Consumers' surplus is thus the area between the price and the demand curve (areas 1 + 2 + 3).

Producer surplus. **Producer surplus** is similar to profit. It is the difference between total revenue and total variable cost. (It will be more than profit if there are any fixed costs.) Total revenue is $P_{pc} \times Q_{pc}$ (areas 4 + 5 + 6 + 7). Total cost is the area under the *MC* curve (areas 6 + 7). The reason for this is that each point on the marginal cost curve shows what the last unit costs to produce. The area under the *MC* curve thus gives all the marginal costs starting from an output of zero to the current output: i.e. it gives total costs. Producer surplus is thus the area between the price and the *MC* curve (areas 4 + 5).

Total (private) surplus. Total consumer plus producer surplus is therefore the area between the demand and *MC* curves. This is shown by the total shaded area (areas 1 + 2 + 3 + 4 + 5).

The effect of monopoly on total surplus

What happens when the industry is under *monopoly*? The firm will produce where $MC = MR$, at an output of Q_m and a price of P_m (at point *b* on the demand curve). Total revenue is $P_m \times Q_m$ (areas 2 + 4 + 6). Total cost is the area under the *MC* curve (area 6). Thus the producer surplus is areas 2 + 4. This is clearly a *larger* surplus than under perfect competition (since area 2 is larger than area 5): monopoly profits are larger than profits under perfect competition.

Consumer surplus, however, will be much smaller. With consumption at Q_m, total utility is given by areas 1 + 2 + 4 + 6,

---

Definitions

Consumer surplus The excess of what a person would have been prepared to pay for a good (i.e. the utility measured in money terms) over what that person actually pays. Total consumer surplus equals total utility minus total expenditure.

Producer surplus The excess of a firm's total revenue over its total (variable) cost.

whereas consumer expenditure is given by areas 2 + 4 + 6. Consumer surplus, then, is simply area 1. (Note that area 2 has been transformed from consumer surplus to producer surplus.)

Total surplus under monopoly is therefore areas 1 + 2 + 4: a smaller surplus than under perfect competition. 'Monopolisation' of the industry has resulted in a loss of total surplus of areas 3 + 5. The producer's gain has been more than offset by the consumers' loss. This loss of surplus is known as *deadweight welfare loss* of monopoly.

Ignorance and uncertainty

Perfect competition assumes that consumers, firms and factor suppliers have perfect knowledge of costs and benefits.

Definition

Deadweight welfare loss The loss of consumer plus producer surplus in imperfect markets (when compared with perfect competition).

BOX 20.1 CAN THE MARKET PROVIDE ADEQUATE PROTECTION FOR THE ENVIRONMENT?

In recent years people have become acutely aware of the damage being done to the environment by pollution. But if the tipping of chemicals and sewage into the rivers and seas and the spewing of toxic gases into the atmosphere cause so much damage, why does it continue? If we all suffer from these activities, both consumers and producers alike, then why will a pure market system not deal with the problem? After all, a market should respond to people's interests.

The reason is that the costs of pollution are largely *external* costs. They are borne by society at large and only very slightly (if at all) by the polluter. If, for example, 10 000 people suffer from the smoke from a factory (including the factory owner), then that owner will bear only approximately 1/10 000 of the suffering. That personal cost may be quite insignificant when the owner is deciding whether the factory is profitable. And if the owner lives far away, the personal cost of the pollution will be zero.

Thus the *social* costs of polluting activities exceed the *private* costs. If people behave selfishly and only take into account the effect their actions have on themselves, there will be an *overproduction* of polluting activities.

Thus it is argued that governments must intervene to prevent or regulate pollution, or alternatively to tax the polluting activities or subsidise measures to reduce the pollution (see section 22.1).

But if people are purely selfish, why do they buy 'green' products? Why do they buy, for example, 'ozone-friendly' aerosols? After all, the amount of damage done to the ozone layer from their own personal use of 'non-friendly' aerosols would be absolutely minute. The answer is that many people have a social conscience. They *do* sometimes take into account the effect their actions have on other people. They are not totally selfish. They like to do their own little bit, however small, towards protecting the environment.

Nevertheless, to rely on people's consciences may be a very unsatisfactory method of controlling pollution. In a market environment where people are all the time being encouraged to consume more and more goods and where materialism is the religion of the age, there would have to be a massive shift towards 'green thinking' if the market were to be a sufficient answer to the problem of pollution.

Certain types of environmental problem may get high priority in the media, such as global warming or toxic waste. However, the sheer range of polluting activities makes reliance on people's awareness of the problems and their social consciences far too arbitrary.

The table gives the costs and benefits of an imaginary firm operating under perfect competition whose activities create a certain amount of pollution. (It is assumed that the costs of this pollution to society can be accurately measured.)

(a) What is the profit-maximising level of output for this firm?

(b) What is the socially efficient level of output?

(c) Why might the marginal pollution costs increase in the way illustrated in this example?

Output (units)	Price per unit (MSB) (£)	Marginal (private) costs to the firm (MC) (£)	Marginal external (pollution) costs (MEC) (£)	Marginal social costs (MSC = MC + MEC) (£)
1	100	30	20	50
2	100	30	22	52
3	100	35	25	60
4	100	45	30	75
5	100	60	40	100
6	100	78	55	133
7	100	100	77	177
8	100	130	110	240

In the real world there is often a great deal of ignorance and uncertainty. Thus people are unable to equate marginal benefit with marginal cost.

Consumers purchase many goods only once or a few times in a lifetime. Cars, washing machines, televisions and other consumer durables fall into this category. Consumers may not be aware of the quality of such goods until they have purchased them, by which time it is too late. Advertising may contribute to people's ignorance by misleading them as to the benefits of a good.

Firms are often ignorant of market opportunities, prices, costs, the productivity of workers (especially white-collar workers), the activity of rivals, etc.

Many economic decisions are based on expected future conditions. Since the future can never be known for certain, many decisions may turn out to be wrong.

Asymmetric information

 One form of imperfect information is when the different sides in an economic relationship have different amounts of information. This is known as 'asymmetric information' (see page 34) and is at the heart of the *principal–agent problem*.

Take the case of a firm (the principal) using the services of a bank (the agent) to finance its investments. The bank is likely to have a much better knowledge of its range of products and of the current state of financial markets and may mis-sell products to the firm in order to earn a larger profit for the bank. For example, it could provide loans at fixed rates of interest, knowing that rates were likely to fall. The firm would end up being locked into paying a higher rate of interest than if it had taken out a variable rate loan and the bank would consequently make more profit. This practice came to light in 2012, with banks accused of mis-selling such products to some 28 000 SMEs.

Immobility of factors and time-lags in response

Even under conditions of perfect competition, factors may be very slow to respond to changes in demand or supply. Labour, for example, may be highly immobile both occupationally and geographically. This can lead to large price

changes and hence to large supernormal profits and high wages for those in the sectors of rising demand or falling costs. The long run may be a very long time coming!

In the meantime, there will be further changes in the conditions of demand and supply. Thus the economy is in a constant state of disequilibrium and the long run never comes. As firms and consumers respond to market signals and move towards equilibrium, so the equilibrium position moves and the social optimum is never achieved.

 The problem of time lags. Many economic actions can take a long time to take effect. This can cause problems of instability and an inability of the economy to achieve social efficiency.

Whenever monopoly/monopsony power exists, the problem is made worse as firms or unions put up barriers to the entry of new firms or factors of production.

Protecting people's interests

The government may feel that people need protecting from poor economic decisions that they make on their *own* behalf. It may feel that in a free market people will consume too many harmful things. Thus if the government wants to discourage smoking and drinking, it can put taxes on tobacco and alcohol. In more extreme cases it could make various activities illegal: activities such as prostitution, certain types of gambling, and the sale and consumption of drugs.

On the other hand, the government may feel that people consume too little of things that are good for them: things such as education, health care and sports facilities. Such goods are known as **merit goods**. The government could either provide them free or subsidise their production.

Definition

Merit goods Goods which the government feels that people will underconsume and which therefore ought to be subsidised or provided free.

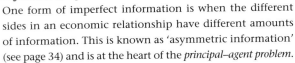
20.3 GOVERNMENT INTERVENTION IN THE MARKET

Faced with all the problems of the free market, what is a government to do?

There are several policy instruments that the government can use. At one extreme, it can totally replace the market by providing goods and services itself. At the other extreme, it can merely seek to persuade producers, consumers or workers to act differently. Between the two extremes the government has a number of instruments it can use to change the way markets operate. These include taxes,

subsidies, laws and regulatory bodies. In this section we examine these different forms of government intervention.

 Government intervention may be able to rectify various failings of the market. Government intervention in the market can be used to achieve various economic objectives which may not be best achieved by the market. Governments, however, are not perfect, and their actions may bring adverse as well as beneficial consequences.

Taxes and subsidies

KI 31
p 311
When there are imperfections in the market, social efficiency will not be achieved. Marginal social benefit (*MSB*) will not equal marginal social cost (*MSC*). A different level of output would be more desirable.

Taxes and subsidies can be used to correct these imperfections. Essentially the approach is to tax those goods or activities where the market produces too much, and subsidise those where the market produces too little.

KI 33
p 311
Taxes and subsidies to correct externalities. The rule here is simple: the government should impose a tax equal to the marginal external cost (or grant a subsidy equal to the marginal external benefit).

Assume, for example, that a chemical works emits smoke from a chimney and thus pollutes the atmosphere. This creates external costs for the people who breathe in the smoke. The marginal social cost of producing the chemicals thus exceeds the marginal private cost to the firm: $MSC > MC$.

This is illustrated in Figure 20.5. The marginal pollution cost (the externality) is shown by the vertical distance between the MC and MSC curves. For simplicity, it is assumed that the firm is a price taker. It produces Q_1 where $P = MC$ (its profit-maximising output), but in doing so takes no account of the external pollution costs it imposes on society.

If the government now imposes a tax on production equal to the marginal pollution cost, it will effectively 'internalise' the externality. The firm will have to pay an amount equal to the external cost it creates. It will therefore now maximise profits at Q_2, which is the socially optimum output where $MSB = MSC$.

Taxes and subsidies to correct for monopoly. If the problem of monopoly that the government wishes to tackle is that of *excessive profits*, it can impose a lump-sum tax on the monopolist: that is, a tax of a fixed absolute amount irrespective of how much the monopolist produces, or the price it charges. Since a lump-sum tax is an additional *fixed* cost to the firm, and hence will not affect the firm's marginal cost, it will not reduce the amount that the monopolist

produces (which *would* be the case with a per-unit tax). Two examples of such taxes are the 'windfall taxes' imposed by the UK Labour government. The first, in 1997, was on the profits of various privatised utilities. The second, in 2005, was on the 'excess' profits of oil companies operating in the North Sea. These had been the result of large increases in world oil prices.

If the government is concerned that the monopolist produces *less* than the socially efficient output, it could give the monopolist a per-unit *subsidy* (which would encourage the monopolist to produce more). But would this not *increase* the monopolist's profit? The answer to this is to impose a harsh lump-sum tax in addition to the subsidy. The tax would not undo the subsidy's benefit of encouraging the monopolist to produce more, but it could be used to reduce the monopolist's profits below the original (i.e. pre-subsidy) level.

Advantages of taxes and subsidies

Many economists favour the tax/subsidy solution to market imperfections (especially the problem of externalities) because it still allows the market to operate. It forces firms to take on board the full social costs and benefits of their actions. It is also adjustable according to the magnitude of the problem.

KI 9
p 47
What is more, by taxing firms for polluting, say, they are encouraged to find cleaner ways of producing. The tax thus acts as an incentive over the longer run to reduce pollution: the more a firm can reduce its pollution, the more taxes it can save.

Likewise, when *good* practices are subsidised, firms are given the incentive to adopt more good practices.

Disadvantages of taxes and subsidies

Infeasible to use different tax and subsidy rates. Each firm produces different levels and types of externality and operates under different degrees of imperfect competition. It would be expensive and administratively very difficult, if not impossible, to charge every offending firm its own particular tax rate (or grant every relevant firm its own particular rate of subsidy).

> **Pause for thought**
>
> *Why is it easier to use taxes and subsidies to tackle the problem of car exhaust pollution than to tackle the problem of peak-time traffic congestion in cities?*

Lack of knowledge. Even if a government did decide to charge a tax equal to each offending firm's marginal external costs, it would still have the problem of measuring that cost and apportioning blame. The damage to lakes and forests from acid rain has been a major concern since the beginning of the 1980s. But just how serious is that damage? What is its current monetary cost? How long lasting is the damage?

Figure 20.5	Using taxes to correct a distortion: the first-best world

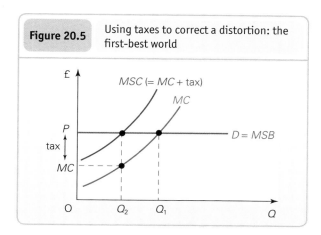

Just what and who are to blame? These are questions that cannot be answered precisely. It is thus impossible to fix the 'correct' pollution tax on, say, a particular coal-fired power station.

Despite these problems, it is nevertheless possible to charge firms by the amount of a particular emission. For example, firms could be charged for chimney smoke by so many parts per million of a given pollutant. Although it is difficult to 'fine-tune' such a system so that the charge reflects the precise number of people affected by the pollutant and by how much, it does go some way to internalising the externality.

Changes in property rights

One cause of market failure is the limited nature of property rights. If someone dumps a load of rubble in your garden, you can insist that it is removed. If, however, someone dumps a load of rubble in his or her *own* garden, which is next door to yours, what can you do? You can still see it from your window. It is still an eyesore. But you have no property rights over the next-door garden.

Property rights define who owns property, to what uses it can be put, the rights other people have over it and how it may be transferred. By *extending* these rights, individuals may be able to prevent other people imposing costs on them, or charge them for doing so.

> ### Pause for thought
>
> *If the sufferers had no property rights, show how it would still be in their interests to 'bribe' the firm to produce the socially efficient level of output.*

The socially efficient level of charge would be one that was equal to the marginal external cost (and would have the same effect as the government charging a tax on the firm of that amount (see Figure 20.5). The **Coase theorem**[1] states that in an otherwise perfectly competitive market, the socially efficient charge *will* be levied. But why?

Let us take the case of river pollution by a chemical works that imposes a cost on people fishing in the river. If property rights to the river were now given to the fishing community, they could impose a charge on the chemical works per unit of output. If they charged *less* than the marginal external cost, they would suffer more from the last unit (in terms of lost fish) than they were being compensated. If they charged *more*, and thereby caused the firm to cut back its output below the socially efficient level, they would be sacrificing receiving charges that would be greater than the marginal suffering. It will be in the sufferers'

best interests, therefore, to charge an amount *equal* to the marginal externality.

In most instances, however, this type of solution is totally impractical. It is impractical when *many* people are *slightly* inconvenienced, especially if there are many culprits imposing the costs. For example, if I were disturbed by noisy lorries outside my home, it would not be practical to negotiate with every haulage company involved. What if I wanted to ban the lorries from the street, but my next-door neighbour wanted to charge them 10p per journey? Who gets their way?

The extension of private property rights becomes a more practical solution where the culprits are few in number, are easily identifiable and impose clearly defined costs. Thus a noise abatement act could be passed which allowed me to prevent my neighbours playing noisy radios, having noisy parties or otherwise disturbing the peace in my home. The onus would be on me to report them. Or I could agree not to report them if they paid me adequate compensation.

But even in cases where only a few people are involved, there may still be the problem of litigation. I may have to incur the time and expense of taking people to court. Justice may not be free, and there is thus a conflict with equity. The rich can afford 'better' justice. They can employ top lawyers. Thus even if I have a right to sue a large company for dumping toxic waste near me, I may not have the legal muscle to win.

Finally, there is the broader question of *equity*. The extension of private property rights may favour the rich (who tend to have more property) at the expense of the poor. Ramblers may get great pleasure from strolling across a great country estate, along public rights of way. This may annoy the owner. If the owner's property rights were now extended to exclude the ramblers, is this a social gain?

Of course, equity considerations can also be dealt with by altering property rights, but in a different way. *Public* property like parks, open spaces, libraries and historic buildings could be extended. Also the property of the rich could be redistributed to the poor. Here it is less a question of the rights that ownership confers, and more a question of altering the ownership itself.

> ### Pause for thought
>
> *Would it be a good idea to extend countries' territorial waters in order to bring key open seas fishing grounds within countries' territory? Could it help to solve the problem of overfishing?*

> ### Definition
>
> **Coase theorem** When sufferers from externalities do deals with perpetrators (by levying charges or offering bribes), the externality will be 'internalised' and the socially efficient level of output will be achieved.

---

[1] Named after Ronald Coase, who developed the theory. See his article, 'The problem of social cost', *Journal of Law and Economics* (1960).

BOX 20.2 **DEADWEIGHT LOSS FROM TAXES ON GOODS AND SERVICES**

The excess burden of taxes

Taxation can be used to correct market failures, but taxes can have adverse effects themselves. One such effect is the deadweight loss that results when taxes are imposed on goods and services.

The diagram shows the demand and supply of a particular good. Equilibrium is initially at a price of P_1 and a level of sales of Q_1 (i.e. where $D = S$). Now an excise tax is imposed on the good. The supply curve shifts upwards by the amount of the tax, to S + tax. Equilibrium price rises to P_2 and equilibrium quantity falls to Q_2. Producers receive an after-tax price of $P_2 - tax$.

Consumer surplus falls from areas $1 + 2 + 3$, to area 1 (the upper grey area). Producer surplus falls from areas $4 + 5 + 6$ to area 6 (the lower grey area). Does this mean, therefore,

that total surplus falls by areas $2 + 3 + 4 + 5$? The answer is no, because there is a gain to the government from the tax revenue (and hence a gain to the population from the resulting government expenditure). The revenue from the tax is known as the *government surplus*. It is given by areas $2 + 4$ (the blue area).

But, even after including government surplus, there is still a fall in total surplus of areas $3 + 5$ (the pink area). This is the deadweight loss of the tax. It is sometimes known as the *excess burden* of the tax.

Does this loss of total surplus from taxation imply that taxes on goods are always a 'bad thing'? The answer is no. This conclusion would only follow in a 'first-best' world where there were no market failures: where competition was perfect, where there were no externalities and where income distribution was optimum. In such a world, the loss of surplus from imposing a tax on a good would represent a reduction in welfare.

In the real world of imperfect markets and inequality, taxes can do more good than harm. As we have shown in this section, they can help to correct for externalities. They can also be used as a means of redistributing incomes. Nevertheless, the excess burden of taxes is something that ideally ought to be considered when weighing up the desirability of imposing taxes on goods and services, or of increasing their rate.

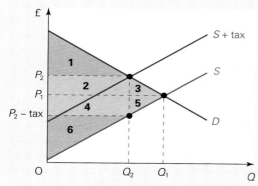

Deadweight loss from an indirect tax

1. How would the burden of taxation change if (a) demand was more inelastic and (b) supply was more inelastic?
2. How far can an economist contribute to this highly political debate over the desirability of an excise tax?

Laws prohibiting or regulating undesirable structures or behaviour

Laws are frequently used to correct market imperfections. Laws can be of three main types: those that prohibit or regulate behaviour that imposes external costs, those that prevent firms providing false or misleading information, and those that prevent or regulate monopolies and oligopolies (see Chapter 21).

Advantages of legal restrictions

■ They are usually simple and clear to understand and are often relatively easy to administer. For example, various polluting activities could be banned or restricted.

■ When the danger is very great, it might be much safer to ban various practices altogether (e.g. the use of various toxic chemicals) rather than to rely on taxes or on individuals attempting to assert their property rights through the civil courts.

■ When a decision needs to be taken quickly, it might be possible to invoke emergency action. For example, in a city like Athens it has been found to be simpler to ban or restrict the use of private cars during a chemical smog emergency than to tax their use.

■ Because consumers suffer from imperfect information, consumer protection laws can make it illegal for firms to sell shoddy or unsafe goods, or to make false or misleading claims about their products.

Definitions

Government surplus (from a tax on a good) The total tax revenue earned by the government from sales of a good.

Excess burden (of a tax on a good) The amount by which the loss in consumer plus producer surplus exceeds the government surplus.

Disadvantages of legal restrictions

The main problem is that legal restrictions tend to be a rather blunt weapon. If, for example, a firm were required to reduce the effluent of a toxic chemical to 20 tonnes per week, there would be no incentive for the firm to reduce it further. With a tax on the effluent, however, the more the firm reduced the effluent, the less tax it would pay. Thus with a system of taxes there is a *continuing* incentive to cut pollution, to improve safety, or whatever.

Regulatory bodies

Rather than using the blunt weapon of general legislation to ban or restrict various activities, a more 'subtle' approach can be adopted. This involves the use of various regulatory bodies. Having identified possible cases where action might be required (e.g. potential cases of pollution, misleading information or the abuse of monopoly power), the regulatory body would probably conduct an investigation and then prepare a report containing its findings and recommendations. It might also have the power to enforce its decisions.

In the UK there are regulatory bodies for each of the major privatised utilities (see section 22.3). More generally, the current legislative framework for UK competition policy is provided by the *1998 Competition Act* and the *2002 Enterprise Act*. These Acts charged the Office of Fair Trading (OFT) with investigating and reporting on suspected cases of anti-competitive practices. It could order firms to cease or modify their practices. Alternatively it could refer them to the Competition Commission (CC), which could conduct an investigation and make a ruling.

In March 2011 the UK government set up a consultation process on its proposed changes to competition regulation in the UK. While retaining the principles and broad procedures of the 1998 and 2002 Acts, it proposed that the Office of Fair Trading and the Competition Commission be merged. The merged body would provide a single regulator for the UK, the Competition and Markets Authority (CMA). The intention was to reduce duplication of processes and costs and to increase business confidence in regulation. The government said that it hoped these proposals would make it easier to tackle anti-competitive mergers and to reform anti-trust rules. (UK and EU competition policy is discussed further in Section 21.1).

The advantage of regulatory bodies like the OFT or the CMA is that a case-by-case approach can be adopted and, as a result, the most appropriate solution adopted. However, investigations may be expensive and time consuming; only a few cases may be examined; and offending firms may make various promises of good behaviour which may not in fact be carried out owing to a lack of follow-up by the regulatory body.

Pause for thought

What other forms of intervention are likely to be necessary to back up the work of regulatory bodies?

Price controls

Price controls can be used either to raise prices above, or to reduce them below, the free-market level.

Prices could be raised above the market equilibrium to support the incomes of certain suppliers. For example, until recently, under the Common Agricultural Policy of the European Union, high prices for food were set so as to raise farmers' incomes above the free-market level.

Prices could be lowered in order to protect consumers' interests. For example, the government, or another body, may prevent a monopoly or oligopoly from charging excessive prices. This is one of the major roles of the regulatory bodies for the privatised utilities. Typically, an industry has not been allowed to raise its prices by more than a certain amount below the rate of inflation. However, above-inflation increases are permitted where it can be argued to be in the wider social interest to do so. For example, in recent years water companies have been permitted to raise some charges by more than inflation to fund investment in infrastructure.

Provision of information

When ignorance is a reason for market failure, the direct provision of information by the government or one of its agencies may help to correct that failure. An example is the information on jobs provided by job centres to those looking for work. They thus help the labour market to work better and increase the elasticity of supply of labour. Another example is the provision of consumer information: for example, on the effects of smoking, or of eating certain foodstuffs. Another is the provision of government statistics on prices, costs, employment, sales trends, etc. This enables firms to plan with greater certainty.

The direct provision of goods and services

In the case of public goods and services, such as streets, pavements, seaside illumination and national defence, the market may completely fail to provide. In this case the government must take over the role of provision. Central government, local government or some other public agency could provide these goods and services directly. Alternatively, they could pay private firms to do so. The public would pay through central and local taxation.

The government could also provide goods and services directly which are *not* public goods. Examples include health and education. There are four reasons why such things are provided free or at well below cost.

Social justice. Society may feel that these things should not be provided according to ability to pay. Rather they should be provided as of right: an equal right based on need. KI 32 p311

Large positive externalities. People other than the consumer may benefit substantially. If a person decides to get KI 33 p311 treatment for an infectious disease, other people benefit by not being infected. A free health service thus helps to combat the spread of disease.

Dependants. If education were not free, and if the quality of education depended on the amount spent, and if parents could choose how much or little to buy, then the quality of children's education would depend not just on their parents' income, but also on how much they cared. A government

may choose to provide such things free in order to protect children from 'bad' parents. A similar argument is used for providing free prescriptions and dental treatment for all children.

Ignorance. Consumers may not realise how much they will benefit. If they have to pay, they may choose (unwisely) to go without. Providing health care free may persuade people to consult their doctors before a complaint becomes serious.

20.4 THE CASE FOR LESS GOVERNMENT INTERVENTION

Government intervention in the market can itself lead to problems. The case for less government intervention is not that the market is the *perfect* means of achieving given social goals, but rather that the problems created by intervention are greater than the problems overcome by that intervention.

Drawbacks of government intervention

Shortages and surpluses. If the government intervenes by fixing prices at levels other than the equilibrium, this will create either shortages or surpluses.

If the price is fixed *below* the equilibrium, there will be a shortage. For example, if the rent of council houses is fixed below the equilibrium in order to provide cheap housing for poor people, demand will exceed supply. In the case of such shortages the government will have to adopt a system of waiting lists, or rationing, or giving certain people preferential treatment. Alternatively it will have to allow allocation to be on a first-come, first-served basis or allow queues to develop. Underground markets are likely to occur.

If the price is fixed *above* the equilibrium price, there will be a surplus. For example, if the price of food is fixed above the equilibrium in order to support farmers' incomes, supply will exceed demand. Either government will have to purchase such surpluses and then perhaps store them, throw them away or sell them cheaply in another market, or it will have to ration suppliers by allowing them to produce only a certain quota, or allow them to sell to whom they can.

Poor information. The government may not know the full costs and benefits of its policies. It may genuinely wish to pursue the interests of consumers or any other group and yet may be unaware of people's wishes or misinterpret their behaviour.

Bureaucracy and inefficiency. Government intervention involves administrative costs. The more wide reaching and detailed the intervention, the greater the number of people and material resources that will be involved. These resources may be used wastefully.

Lack of market incentives. If government intervention removes market forces or cushions their effect (by the use of subsidies, welfare provisions, guaranteed prices or wages, etc.), it may remove certain useful incentives. Subsidies may allow inefficient firms to survive. Welfare payments may discourage effort. The market may be imperfect, but it does tend to encourage efficiency by allowing the efficient to receive greater rewards.

Shifts in government policy. The economic efficiency of industry may suffer if government intervention changes too frequently. It makes it difficult for firms to plan if they cannot predict tax rates, subsidies, price and wage controls, etc.

Lack of freedom for the individual. Government intervention involves a loss of freedom for individuals to make economic choices. The argument is not just that the pursuit of individual gain is seen to lead to the social good, but that it is desirable in itself that individuals should be as free as possible to pursue their own interests with the minimum of government interference: that minimum being largely confined to the maintenance of laws consistent with the protection of life, liberty and property.

Advantages of the free market

Although markets in the real world are not perfect, even imperfect markets can be argued to have positive advantages over government provision or even government regulation. These might include the following.

Automatic adjustments. Government intervention requires administration. A free-market economy, on the other hand, leads to the automatic, albeit imperfect, adjustment to demand and supply changes.

Dynamic advantages of capitalism. The chances of making high monopoly/oligopoly profits will encourage entrepreneurs to invest in new products and new techniques. Prices may be high initially, but consumers will gain from the extra choice of products. Furthermore, if profits are high, new firms will sooner or later break into the market and competition will ensue.

> **Pause for thought**
>
> *Are there any features of the free market that would discourage innovation?*

A high degree of competition even under monopoly/oligopoly. Even though an industry at first sight may seem to be highly monopolistic, competitive forces may still work as a result of the following:

- A fear that excessively high profits might encourage firms to attempt to break into the industry (assuming that the market is contestable).

- Competition from closely related industries (e.g. coach services for rail services, or electricity for gas).
- The threat of foreign competition.
- Countervailing powers (see page 185). Large powerful producers often sell to large powerful buyers. For example, the power of detergent manufacturers to drive up the price of washing powder is countered by the power of supermarket chains to drive down the price at which they purchase it. Thus power is to some extent neutralised.
- The competition for corporate control (see page 170).

20.5 FIRMS AND SOCIAL RESPONSIBILITY

It is often assumed that firms are simply concerned to maximise profits: that they are not concerned with broader issues of **corporate social responsibility (CSR)**. What this assumption means is that firms are only concerned with the interests of shareholders (or managers) and are not concerned for the well-being of the community at large.

It is then argued, however, that competitive forces could result in society *benefiting* from the self-interested behaviour of firms: i.e. that profit maximisation will lead to social efficiency under conditions of perfect competition and the absence of externalities.

KI 31
p 311 But, as we have seen, in the real world markets are not perfect and there are often considerable externalities. In such cases, a lack of social responsibility on the part of firms can have profoundly adverse effects on society. Indeed, many forms of market failure can be attributed directly to business practices that could not be classified as 'socially responsible': advertising campaigns that seek to misinform, or in some way deceive the consumer; monopoly producers exploiting their monopoly position through charging excessively high prices; the conscious decision to ignore water and air pollution limits, knowing that the chances of being caught are slim.

So should businesses be simply concerned with profit, or should they take broader social issues into account? If they do behave in an anti-social way, is the only answer to rely on government intervention, or are there any social pressures that can be brought to bear to persuade businesses to modify their behaviour?

Two views of corporate social responsibility

The classical view. According to this view, business managers are responsible only to their shareholders, and as such should be concerned solely with profit maximisation. If managers in their business decisions take into account a wider set of social responsibilities, not only will they tend

to undermine the market mechanism, but they will be making social policy decisions in fields where they may have little skill or expertise. If being socially responsible ultimately reduces profits, then the shareholder loses and managers have failed to discharge their duty. By diluting their purpose in pursuit of *social* goals, businesses extend their influence over society as a whole, which cannot be good given the lack of public accountability to which business leaders are subject.

The socioeconomic view. This view argues that the role of modern business has changed, and that society expects business to adhere to certain moral and social responsibilities. Modern businesses are seen as more than economic institutions, as they are actively involved in society's social, political and legal environments. As such, all businesses are responsible not only to their shareholders but to all **stakeholders**. Stakeholders are all those affected by the business's operations: not only shareholders, but workers, customers, suppliers, creditors and people living in the neighbourhood. Given the far-reaching environmental effects of many businesses, stakeholding might extend to the whole of society.

In this view of corporate social responsibility, it is not just a moral argument that managers should take into account broader social and environmental issues, but also a financial one. It is argued that a business will maximise profits over the *long term* only if its various social responsibilities are taken into account. If a business is seen as ignoring the

> **Definitions**
>
> **Corporate social responsibility** Where a firm takes into account the interests and concerns of a community rather than just its shareholders.
>
> **Stakeholder** An individual affected by the operations of a business.

interests of the wider community and failing to protect society's welfare, then this will be 'bad for business': the firm's reputation and image will suffer.

In many top corporations, **environmental scanning** is now an integral part of the planning process. This involves the business surveying changing political, economic, social, technological, environmental and legal trends in the external environment in order to remain in tune with consumer concerns (see section 1.1). For example, the general public's growing concern over 'green' issues has significantly influenced many businesses' product development programmes and R&D strategies (see Box 20.3). The more successful a business is in being able to associate the image of 'environmentally friendly' to a particular product or brand, the more likely it is to enhance its sales or establish a measure of brand loyalty, and thereby to strengthen its competitive position.

Several companies in recent years have made great play of their social responsibility. For instance, in 2007, Marks and Spencer launched its 'Plan A'. The original plan centred on meeting 100 social and environmental targets across 5 areas: climate change, waste, natural resources, ethical trading and health and well-being. In 2010, M&S announced that it was adding a further 80 commitments and extending some of its original commitments.[2]

What we increasingly observe today is business feeling that it is not enough to be seen merely *complying* with laws on the environment, product standards or workplace conditions: i.e. just to be doing the legal minimum. Hence, there is a growing philosophy of 'compliance plus' which motivates businesses to compete against each other in terms of their social image.

The virtue matrix: generating corporate social responsibility

In an article in the *Harvard Business Review*,[3] Roger L. Martin developed a framework for analysing corporate social responsibility and the factors that influence it. The framework is the 'virtue matrix' and an adaptation of it is illustrated in Figure 20.6.

The matrix is divided into four cells, each of which shows types of action taken by a firm that have social effects.

Definition

Environmental scanning Where a business surveys political, economic, social, technological, environmental and legal trends in the external environment to aid its decision-making process.

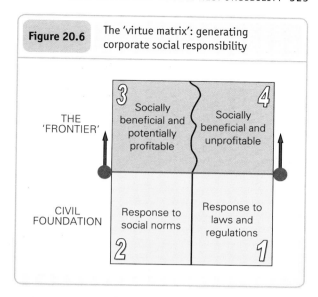

Figure 20.6 The 'virtue matrix': generating corporate social responsibility

The civil foundation

The bottom two cells are in what is termed *the civil foundation*. They refer to socially responsible actions that society expects firms to take and firms will normally do so.

Cell 1 refers to actions in response to laws and regulations. For example, firms may control the emissions of toxic waste because they are obliged to do so by law. Similarly, they may provide a clean and safe environment for their workers because of health and safety legislation.

Cell 2 refers to the types of behaviour expected of firms by society and where firms would come in for criticism, or even condemnation, if they did not abide by these social norms. For example, employers may operate flexible working hours or set up nursery facilities to help workers with small children; manufacturers may landscape the surroundings to their factories or build factories of a pleasant design so as to make them more attractive to local residents and visitors. They are not obliged to take such actions by law, but feel that it is expected of them.

A key point about actions in the civil foundation is that they are likely to be consistent with the aim of profit maximisation or maximising shareholder value. In other words, shareholders' and society's interests are likely to coincide. This is obvious in the case of abiding by the law. Except in cases where breaking the law can go undetected, firms must abide by the law if they are to avoid prosecution with all the risks to profits that this entails. But abiding by social norms (cell 2) is also likely to contribute towards profit. The extra costs associated with such actions will probably be recouped from extra sales associated with achieving a good public image or extra productivity from a contented workforce.

The frontier

The top two cells represent *the frontier*. These refer to activities that are not directly in the interests of shareholders, but have a moral or social motivation.

[2] http://plana.marksandspencer.com/about
[3] Roger L. Martin 'The virtue matrix: calculating the return on corporate responsibility', *Harvard Business Review*, March 2002.

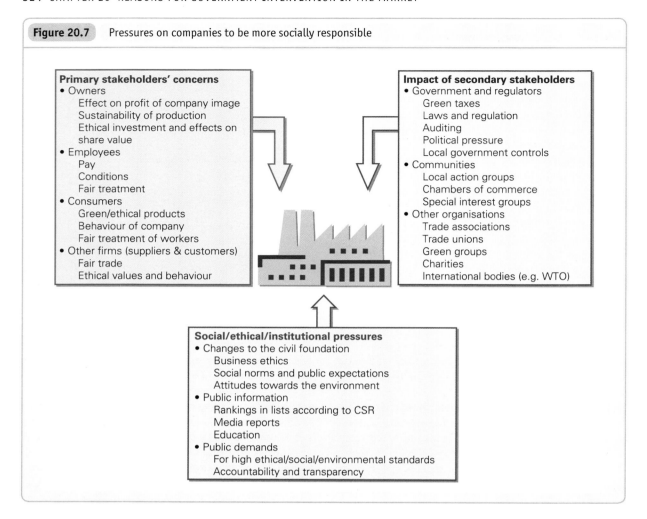

Figure 20.7 Pressures on companies to be more socially responsible

Cell 3 represents those actions that are not immediately profitable, but could possibly become so in the future because of positive reactions from consumers, employees, competitors or government. To quote from Martin, 'When Prudential allowed people with AIDS to tap the death benefits in their life assurance policies to pay for medical expenses, the move generated so much goodwill that competing insurers soon offered [such] settlements as well. Very quickly, corporate behavior that had seemed radical became business as usual throughout the insurance industry.'[4] Generally activities in cell 3 are risky and the willingness of firms to engage in them depends on their attitudes towards risk.

Cell 4 represents the most radical departure from shareholders' interests. Here managers take action that benefits society but at the *expense* of profit. Managers are not always ruthless profit maximisers (see Chapter 14). They can be motivated by a range of objectives. One of these is 'to do the right thing' by employees, customers or society generally. For example, improving working conditions for employees

is seen not just as a way of improving productivity, but as a moral duty towards the workforce. Likewise managers may control toxic emissions beyond the legal minimum requirement because of their genuine concern for the environment.

The development of corporate social responsibility over time

Pressures from various stakeholders are likely to increase corporate social responsibility over time. These pressures are summarised in Figure 20.7. They come from three sources: from the primary stakeholders, such as shareholders, employees, customers and suppliers; from secondary stakeholders, such as the government and other local, national and international organisations; and from changes to the whole civil foundation, with its norms and values and what is regarded as 'acceptable' corporate behaviour.

These pressures have tended to grow over time. This has resulted in the boundary between the civil foundation and the frontier moving upwards as activities that start in the frontier and then are copied by competitor firms become the norm. The norms of corporate behaviour in Victorian Britain would seem totally unacceptable in Britain today.

[4] Ibid., page 8.

The long hours, child labour, appalling working conditions, lack of redress for grievances, the filthy conditions of the workplace, the smoke and other pollution pouring from factories are not only illegal nowadays, but totally alien to the norms of society.

Although the boundary tends to move upwards, this is not necessarily the case. Martin gives the example of Russia in the immediate post-communist period, where a collapse of the old order and the development of 'cowboy' capitalism led to a decline in standards and the non-enforcement of many regulations governing things such as working conditions and child labour. Many developing countries have a very much lower boundary, which is constantly in danger of being pushed lower by ruthless forces of globalisation and non-representative governments conniving in the process.

Another factor leading to the development of corporate social responsibility is the movement of activities from cell 4 to cell 3. Activities that start as socially desirable but unprofitable tend to become profitable as consumers come to expect firms to behave in socially responsible ways and punish firms that do not by boycotting their products. Thus companies such as Nestlé, McDonald's and Nike have been very concerned to 'clean up' their corporate image because of adverse publicity. Of course, part of the reaction of companies to social pressure may be simply to improve their public relations, but part may be a genuine improvement in their behaviour.

Globalisation and corporate social responsibility

As the world economy becomes ever more intertwined, many companies in rich countries, with a relatively deep civil foundation, are outsourcing much of their production to developing countries, which have a relatively shallow and less secure civil foundation. This can have the effect of either levelling up or levelling down. Nike and Gap, which produce much of their footwear and clothing in south-east Asia, have been accused of operating sweatshops in these countries, with low wages and poor working conditions – a case of levelling down to the civil foundation of these developing countries. Nike and Gap reply that, compared with other factories in these countries, pay and conditions are better – a case of levelling up.

Economic performance and social responsibility

If corporate social responsibility has grown as a business objective, has this in any way impinged upon business performance? Studies, empirical and otherwise, suggest that rather than detracting from business performance and harming shareholder value, in fact the opposite appears to be the case. Corporate social responsibility appears to offer a positive contribution to business performance, especially over the longer term.

The following factors have been identified as some of the positive economic benefits that firms have gained from adopting a more socially responsible position.

Improved economic performance

A large number of studies have attempted to identify and evaluate the economic returns from social responsibility. Factors that have been considered include business growth rates, stock prices and sales and revenue. A survey by van Beurden and Gössling[5] evaluated the findings of 34 studies that considered the link between business ethics and enhanced profits. They concluded that 23 studies showed a positive link, 9 suggested neutral effects or were inconclusive, and the remaining 2 suggested that there was a negative relationship.

Although this evidence would on balance favour an argument that corporate social responsibility is good business practice, the whole area of linking ethics and responsibility to profit is a contentious one. When considering ethics and social responsibility, what are we including within this definition? Is the business merely complying with a business code, developed either within the business or by a third party? Such codes essentially state 'what is not acceptable business behaviour', such as taking bribes or pursuing anti-competitive behaviour. They can be seen as lying in the civil foundation. Or does the understanding of an 'ethical business' go further and entail positive social actions, ranging from giving money to good causes to contributing to particular programmes in which the business has competency? For example, a pharmaceutical company might develop a drug that benefits the populations of the world's poorest countries, with no possibility of profit. Such actions lie in the frontier.

So at what level do we identify an ethical business, and to what degree might this level of responsibility influence profitability?

The concept of profitability is also contentious, most crucially in respect to the time frame over which the assessment takes place. Linking long-run profitability with an ethical or socially responsible programme is fraught with difficulties. How are all the other factors that influence business performance over the longer term accounted for? How do you attribute a given percentage or contribution to profit to the adoption of a more socially responsible business position? Can it ever be this precise, or are we merely left with intimating that a link exists, and is this good enough?

Enhancing the brand

Related to profitability is the issue of how far corporate social responsibility enhances brand image and the firm's reputation. This would not only strengthen consumer

5 P. van Beurden and T. Gössling, 'The worth of values – a literature review on the relation between corporate social and financial performance', *Journal of Business Ethics*, vol. 82, no. 2, October 2008, pp. 407–24.

loyalty but also aid the firm in raising finance and attracting trading partners.

Surveys have identified that the ethical dimension of the firm is becoming increasingly important in consumer buying decisions. For example, the Cooperative Bank Ethical Consumerism Report shows that the total value of *ethical consumerism*, where consumer decisions, including those concerning financial investments, are motivated by concerns over human rights, social justice, the environment or animal welfare, was some £46.8 billion in 2011. This was 191 per cent higher than in 2000, when ethical consumerism was recorded at £16.1 billion.

The survey also shows that the proportion of people who purchased a product at least once a year for ethical reasons rose from 29 per cent in 2000 to 46 per cent in 2011.[6] The report also shows that, in 2011, 55 per cent of people surveyed avoided buying a product or service from a company because of its reputation; the comparable figure in 2000 was 44 per cent. Moreover, 24 per cent of people had actively campaigned on a social or environmental issue in 2011 compared with 15 per cent in 2000.

Thus, environmental responsibility and active participation in the community are the social factors most likely to influence consumers' purchasing behaviour.

Firms may be further encouraged to develop the social image of their brand with the increasing number of awards given to recognise and promote corporate social responsibility. 'Most admired companies' lists, such as those presented by *Management Today* in the UK and *Fortune* in America, are based on criteria such as reputation for ethics and honesty, use of corporate assets, and community and environmental responsibility. The public relations and marketing potential that can be gained from such awards help firms to strengthen further their socially responsible image.

Attracting and retaining employees

It increasingly appears to be the case that companies with clear ethical and social positions find it easier not only to recruit, but to hold on to their employees. In a number of surveys of graduate employment intentions, students have claimed that they would be prepared to take a lower salary in order to work for a business with high ethical standards and a commitment to socially responsible business practices.

An international survey in 2005 in 15 European, Middle Eastern and African countries[7] showed that 28 per cent of job seekers considered the ethical conduct and values of an employer to be an important factor in deciding whether to apply for work there. (Top of the list was security and stability (47 per cent), followed by pay (42 per cent).)

Access to capital

Investment in ethically screened investment funds has grown rapidly in recent years. This has been driven not only by the demands of shareholders for ethical funds, but also by a realisation from investors generally that socially responsible business has the potential to be hugely profitable.

The 2011 Cooperative Bank Ethical Consumerism Report shows that the value of funds invested by households in ethical financial products had risen from £6.5 billion in 2000 to £21.1 billion in 2011, an increase of 225 per cent.

The likelihood of returns being lower in ethically screened funds has been questioned by a number of papers.[8] Indeed, evidence shows that investing in ethical funds in the UK, USA, Germany and Canada does not lead to returns that are significantly different from those obtained from conventional funds.[9] It is difficult to ascertain precisely why this is. However, it could be that environmental performance is a good indicator of general management quality, which is the main determinant of stock price.

Social responsibility appears not only to bring a range of benefits to business and society, but also to be generally profitable. It is likely to enhance business performance, strengthen brand image, reduce employee turnover and increase access to stock market funds. Box 20.3 gives an example of a company that built its reputation on being socially and environmentally responsible – The Body Shop. (See also Box 16.2 on page 249.)

However, perhaps what is even more important is the cost of *not* being socially responsible. In 2010, the massive oil spill from the Deepwater Horizon rig in the Gulf of Mexico, which killed 11 workers, was blamed on poor safety standards and taking excessive risks with the environment. From the blowout on 20 April to the final capping in August, some 4.9 million barrels of oil leaked into the Gulf, causing immense environmental damage and destroying the livelihoods of people in the fishing and tourist industries. It cost the owner, BP,

---

Definition

Ethical consumerism Where consumers' decisions about what to buy are influenced by ethical concerns such as the producer's human rights record and care for the environment.

[6] Cooperative Bank, *The Ethical Consumerism Report* (2011). Available at www.goodwithmoney.co.uk

[7] *What Makes a Great Employer?* (MORI survey for Manpower, October 2005).
[8] See, for example, MISTRA, The Foundation for Strategic Environmental Research, *Screening of Screening Companies* (2001) and P. Rivoli, 'Making a difference or making a statement? Finance research and socially responsible investment', *Business Ethics Quarterly* 13(3), 2003, pp. 271–87.
[9] See R. Bauer, J. Derwall and R. Otten, 'The ethical mutual fund performance debate: new evidence from Canada', *Journal of Business Ethics*, 70, 2007, pp. 111–124; and R. Bauer, K. Koedijk and R. Otten, 'International evidence on ethical mutual fund performance and investment style', *Journal of Banking and Finance* 29, 2005, pp. 1751–67.

BOX 20.3   THE BODY SHOP

Is it 'worth it'?

The Body Shop shot to fame in the 1980s. It stood for environmental awareness and an ethical approach to business. But its success had as much to do with what it sold as what it stood for. It sold natural cosmetics, Raspberry Ripple Bathing Bubbles and Camomile Shampoo, products that were immensely popular with consumers.

Its profits increased from a little over €1.7 million in 1985 to nearly €64 million in 2007. Sales, meanwhile, grew even more dramatically, from €8.4 million to €756 million in 2008. By the end of 2008, The Body Shop had 2550 stores worldwide, opening 124 stores in the year.

What makes this success so remarkable is that The Body Shop did virtually no advertising. Its promotion has largely stemmed from the activities and environmental campaigning of its founder, Anita Roddick, and the company's uncompromising claims that it sold only 'green' products and conducted its business operations with high ethical standards. It actively supported green causes, such as saving whales and protecting rainforests, and it refused to allow its products to be tested on animals. Perhaps most surprising in the world of big business was its high-profile initiative 'trade not aid', whereby it claimed to pay 'fair' prices for its ingredients, especially those supplied from people in developing countries, who were open to exploitation by large companies.

The growth strategy of The Body Shop, since its founding in 1976, has focused upon developing a distinctive and highly innovative product range, and at the same time identifying such products with major social issues of the day such as the environment and animal rights.

Its initial expansion was based on a process of franchising.

> . . . franchising. We didn't know what it was, but all these women came to us and said, 'if you can do this and you can't even read a balance sheet, then we can do it'. I had a cabal of female friends all around Brighton, Hove and Chichester, and they started opening little units, all called the Body Shop. I just supplied them with gallons of products – we only had 19 different products, but we made it look like more as we sold them in five different sizes![1]

In 1984 the company went public. In the 1990s, however, sales growth was less rapid and in 1998 Anita Roddick stepped down as chief executive, but for a while she and her husband remained as co-chairmen. In 2003 she was awarded a knighthood and became Dame Anita Roddick. Sales began to grow rapidly from 2004 to 2006 from €553 million to €709 million.

---
[1] Anita Roddick interview, Startups.co.uk

Acquisition of the Body Shop by L'Oréal

A dramatic strategic event occurred in 2006 when The Body Shop was sold to the French cosmetics giant L'Oréal, which was 26 per cent owned by Nestlé. The event resulted in the magazine, *Ethical Consumer*, downgrading The Body Shop's ethical rating from 11 out of 20 to a mere 2.5 and calling for a boycott of the company.

There were a number of reasons for this. L'Oréal's animal-testing policies conflict with that of The Body Shop and L'Oréal has been accused of being involved in price fixing with other French perfume houses. L'Oréal's part-owner, Nestlé, has also been subject to various criticisms for ethical misconduct, including promoting formula milk to mothers with babies in poor countries rather than breast milk and using slave labour in cocoa farms in West Africa.

Anita Roddick, however, believed that, by taking over The Body Shop, L'Oréal would develop a more ethical approach to business. L'Oréal has publicly recognised that it would have to develop its ethical policies.

Sadly, Anita Roddick died in 2007 and so has not been able to witness changes. L'Oréal though has begun to address its ethical approach. It adopted a new Code of Business Ethics in 2007 and it is gaining some external accreditation for its approach to sustainability and ethics. Notably, L'Oréal was ranked as one of the world's 100 most ethical companies by Ethisphere in 2007. It has also allowed The Body Shop to continue with its ethical policies.

L'Oréal has, however, looked to inject greater finance into the company aimed at improving the marketing of products. In autumn 2006 a transactional website was launched and there have been greater press marketing campaigns. Profits continued to rise in 2006 and 2007, but fell back quite dramatically from €64 million in 2007 to €36 million in 2008 as recession hit the high street. Despite the continued fragility of economic growth, profits recovered in 2011 to €68.1 million (equivalent to 8.9 per cent of its sales turnover).

So, it is probably too early to answer the question of 'Why did L'Oréal acquire the Body Shop?' with the answer from its own advertising slogan, 'Because they're worth it' – but time will tell.

1. *What assumptions has The Body Shop made about the 'rational consumer'?*
2. *How has The Body Shop's economic performance been affected by its attitudes towards ethical issues? (You could do an Internet search to find further evidence about its performance and the effects of its sale to L'Oréal.)*

---

some $3.5 billion in containment and clear-up operations, although the final cost to the company could be many times that amount. Its reputation plummeted in the USA, with motorists boycotting fuel stations. Its share price plummeted from £628 in April 2010 to £296 just three months later.

Despite the concern about cases like this and evidence that firms are increasingly competing with others over their social image, there are still many firms and consumers who care relatively little about the social or natural environment. There is thus a strong case for government intervention to correct market failures.

SUMMARY

1   Government intervention in the market sets out to attain two goals: social efficiency and equity. Social efficiency is achieved at the point where the marginal benefits to society for either production or consumption are equal to the marginal costs of either production or consumption. Issues of equity are difficult to judge due to the subjective assessment of what is, and what is not, a fair distribution of resources.

2a Externalities are spillover costs or benefits. Whenever there are external costs, the market will (other things being equal) lead to a level of production and consumption above the socially efficient level. Whenever there are external benefits, the market will (other things being equal) lead to a level of production and consumption below the socially efficient level.

2b Public goods will be underprovided by the market. The problem is that they have large external benefits relative to private benefits, and without government intervention it would not be possible to prevent people having a 'free ride' and thereby escaping contributing to their cost of production.

2c Monopoly power will (other things being equal) lead to a level of output below the socially efficient level. It will lead to a deadweight welfare loss: a loss of consumer plus producer surplus.

2d Ignorance and uncertainty may prevent people from consuming or producing at the levels they would otherwise choose. Information may sometimes be provided (at a price) by the market, but it may be imperfect; in some cases it may not be available at all.

2e Markets may respond sluggishly to changes in demand and supply. The time lags in adjustment can lead to a permanent state of disequilibrium and to problems of instability.

2f In a free market there may be inadequate provision for dependants and an inadequate output of merit goods.

3a Taxes and subsidies are one means of correcting market distortions. Externalities can be corrected by imposing tax rates equal to the size of the marginal external cost, and granting rates of subsidy equal to marginal external benefits.

3b Taxes and subsidies can also be used to affect monopoly price, output and profit. Subsidies can be used to persuade a monopolist to increase output to the competitive level. Lump-sum taxes can be used to reduce monopoly profits without affecting price or output.

3c Taxes and subsidies have the advantages of 'internalising' externalities and of providing incentives to reduce external costs. On the other hand, they may be impractical to use when different rates are required for each case, or when it is impossible to know the full effects of the activities that the taxes or subsidies are being used to correct.

3d An extension of property rights may allow individuals to prevent others from imposing costs on them. This is not practical, however, when many people are affected to a small degree, or where several people are affected but differ in their attitudes towards what they want doing about the 'problem'.

3e Laws can be used to regulate activities that impose external costs, to regulate monopolies and oligopolies, and to provide consumer protection. Legal controls are often simpler and easier to operate than taxes, and are safer when the danger is potentially great. However, they tend to be rather a blunt weapon.

3f Regulatory bodies can be set up to monitor and control activities that are against the public interest (e.g. anti-competitive behaviour of oligopolists). They can conduct investigations of specific cases, but these may be expensive and time consuming, and may not be acted on by the authorities.

3g The government may provide information in cases where the private sector fails to provide an adequate level. It may also provide goods and services directly. These could be either public goods or other goods where the government feels that provision by the market is inadequate. The government could also influence production in publicly owned industries.

4a Government intervention in the market may lead to shortages or surpluses; it may be based on poor information; it may be costly in terms of administration; it may stifle incentives; it may be disruptive if government policies change too frequently; it may not represent the majority of voters' interests if the government is elected by a minority, or if voters did not fully understand the issues at election time, or if the policies were not in the government's manifesto; it may remove certain liberties.

4b By contrast, a free market leads to automatic adjustments to changes in economic conditions; the prospect of monopoly/oligopoly profits may stimulate risk taking and hence research and development and innovation, and this advantage may outweigh any problems of resource misallocation; there may still be a high degree of actual or potential competition under monopoly and oligopoly.

5a There are two views of corporate social responsibility (CSR). The first states that it should be of no concern to business, which would do best for society by serving the interests of its shareholders. Social policy should be left to politicians. The alternative view is that business needs to consider the impact of its actions upon society, and to take changing social and political considerations into account when making decisions. This, anyway, is generally good business.

5b The virtue matrix is a means of illustrating the drivers of CSR. Firms will take socially responsible actions if they are required to by law or if social norms dictate. These pressures on firms represent the 'civil foundation'. Some firms will take corporate social responsibility further and thus move into the 'frontier'. Here they may do things that are socially beneficial and may only possibly lead to higher profits, or may even clearly reduce profits. As firms become more socially responsible over time and as social pressures on business increase, so the civil foundation is likely to grow.

5c Evidence suggests that economic performance is likely to be enhanced as the corporate responsibility of firms grows.

REVIEW QUESTIONS

1 Assume that a firm discharges waste into a river. As a result, the marginal social costs (*MSC*) are greater than the firm's marginal (private) costs (*MC*). The following table shows how *MC*, *MSC*, *AR* and *MR* vary with output.

Output	1	2	3	4	5	6	7	8
MC(£)	23	21	23	25	27	30	35	42
MSC(£)	35	34	38	42	46	52	60	72
TR(£)	60	102	138	168	195	219	238	252
AR(£)	60	51	46	42	39	36.5	34	31.5
MR(£)	60	42	36	30	27	24	19	14

(a) How much will the firm produce if it seeks to maximise profits?

(b) What is the socially efficient level of output (assuming no externalities on the demand side)?

(c) How much is the marginal external cost at this level of output?

(d) What size tax would be necessary for the firm to reduce its output to the socially efficient level?

(e) Why is the tax less than the marginal externality?

(f) Why might it be equitable to impose a lump-sum tax on this firm?

(g) Why will a lump-sum tax not affect the firm's output (assuming that in the long run the firm can still make at least normal profit)?

2 Distinguish between publicly provided goods, public goods and merit goods.

3 Name some goods or services provided by the government or local authorities that are not public goods.

4 Some roads could be regarded as a public good, but some could be provided by the market. Which types of road could be provided by the market? Why? Would it be a good idea?

5 Assume that you wanted the information given in (a)–(h) below. In which cases could you (i) buy perfect information; (ii) buy imperfect information; (iii) be able to obtain information without paying for it; (iv) not be able to obtain information?

(a) Which washing machine is the most reliable?

(b) Which of two jobs that are vacant is the most satisfying?

(c) Which builder will repair my roof most cheaply?

(d) Which builder will make the best job of repairing my roof?

(e) Which builder is best value for money?

(f) How big a mortgage would it be wise for me to take out?

(g) What course of higher education should I follow?

(h) What brand of washing powder washes whiter?

In which cases are there non-monetary costs to you of finding out the information? How can you know whether the information you acquire is accurate or not?

6 Make a list of pieces of information a firm might want to know and consider whether it could buy the information and how reliable that information might be.

7 Why might it be better to ban certain activities that cause environmental damage rather than to tax them?

8 Consider the advantages and disadvantages of extending property rights so that everyone would have the right to prevent people imposing any costs on them whatsoever (or charging them to do so).

9 How suitable are legal restrictions in the following cases?

(a) Ensuring adequate vehicle safety (e.g. that tyres have sufficient tread or that the vehicle is roadworthy).

(b) Reducing traffic congestion.

(c) Preventing the use of monopoly power.

(d) Ensuring that mergers are in the public interest.

(e) Ensuring that firms charge a price equal to marginal cost.

10 Evaluate the following statement: 'Despite the weaknesses of a free market, the replacing of the market by the government generally makes the problem worse.'

11 In what ways might business be socially responsible?

12 What economic costs and benefits might a business experience if it decided to adopt a more socially responsible position? How might such costs and benefits change over the longer term?

21 Chapter

Government and the firm

Business issues covered in this chapter

- ■ How do governments attempt to prevent both the abuse of monopoly power and collusion by oligopolists through competition policy?
- ■ How effective is competition policy?
- ■ Why does a free market fail to achieve the optimal amount of research and development?
- ■ What can the government do to encourage technological development and innovation?
- ■ Why is training so important for a country's economic performance?
- ■ Why do governments pursue a training policy and not just leave it to employers?
- ■ How do training policies differ between countries?

KI 36
p 316

In this chapter we shall consider the relationship between government and the individual firm. This relationship is not simply one of regulation and control, but can involve the active intervention of government in attempting to improve the economic performance of business. We shall consider government attitudes and policy towards enhancing research and technology development, and training, as well as the more punitive area of business regulation through the use of monopolies and mergers legislation.

21.1 COMPETITION POLICY

Competition, monopoly and the public interest

KI 21
p 161

Most markets in the real world are imperfect, with firms having varying degrees of market power. But will this power be against the public interest? This question has been addressed by successive governments in framing legislation to deal with monopolies and oligopolies.

It might be thought that market power is always 'a bad thing', certainly as far as the consumer is concerned. After all, it enables firms to make supernormal profit, thereby 'exploiting' the consumer. The greater the firm's power, the higher prices will be relative to the costs of production. Also, a lack of competition removes the incentive to become more efficient.

But market power is not necessarily a bad thing. Firms may not fully exploit their position of power – perhaps for fear that very high profits would eventually lead to other firms overcoming entry barriers, or perhaps because they are not aggressive profit maximisers. Even if they do make large supernormal profits, they may still charge a lower price than more competitive sectors of the industry because of their economies of scale. Finally, they may use their profits for research and development and for capital investment. The consumer might then benefit from improved products at lower prices.

Competition policy could seek to ban various structures. For example, it could ban mergers leading to market share of more than a certain amount. Most countries, however, prefer to focus on whether the *practices* of particular monopolists or oligopolists are anti-competitive. Some of these practices may be made illegal, such as price fixing by oligopolists; others may be assessed on a case-by-case approach to determine whether or not they should be permitted. Such an approach does not presume that the mere possession of power is against the public interest, but rather that certain uses of that power may be.

There are three possible targets of competition policy:

- *monopoly policy* – the abuse of the existing power of monopolies and oligopolies;
- *merger policy* – the growth of power through mergers and acquisitions;
- *restrictive practices policy* – oligopolistic collusion.

Competition policy in the European Union

EU competition legislation is contained in Articles 101 and 102 of the Treaty of Lisbon (formerly Articles 81 and 82 of the Treaty of Amsterdam) and in additional regulations covering mergers, which came into force in 1990 and were amended in 2004.

Article 101 is concerned with restrictive practices and Article 102 with the abuse of market power. The Articles are largely confined to firms trading between EU members and thus do not cover monopolies or oligopolies operating solely within a member country. The policy is implemented by the European Commission. If any firm appears to be breaking the provisions of either of the Articles, the Commission can refer it to the European Court of Justice.

EU restrictive practices policy

Article 101 covers *agreements* between firms, *joint decisions*, and concerted *practices* which prevent, restrict or distort competition. In other words it covers all types of oligopolistic collusion that are against the interests of consumers.

Article 101 is not designed to prevent oligopolistic *structures* (i.e. the simple existence of cooperation between firms), but rather collusive *behaviour*. No matter what form collusion takes, if the European Commission finds that firms are committing anti-competitive *practices*, they will be banned from doing so and possibly fined (up to 10 per cent of annual turnover), although firms do have the right of appeal to the European Court of Justice.

Practices considered anti-competitive include firms colluding to do any of the following:

- fix prices (i.e. above competitive levels);
- limit production, markets, technical development or investment;
- share out markets or sources of supply;
- charge discriminatory prices or operate discriminatory trading conditions, such as to benefit the colluding parties and disadvantage others;
- make other firms who sign contracts with any of the colluding firms accept unfavourable obligations which, by their nature, have no connection with the subject of such contracts.

In recent years, the Commission has adopted a tough stance and has fined many firms.

It has also streamlined its procedures for dealing with cartel cases. During 2008, it introduced new settlement procedures. In doing so it acknowledged that existing procedures were unwieldy, resulting in extremely long investigations and limiting the number that could be undertaken. Under the new procedures, parties involved are shown the evidence against them. They then have the opportunity to acknowledge their 'guilt'. In return any fines imposed are reduced by 10 per cent. The intention was to simplify administrative processes and to reduce the number of cases going to the courts. Box 21.1 considers some of the settlements made since the new procedures were implemented.

EU monopoly policy

Article 102 relates to the abuse of market power and has also been extended to cover mergers. As with Article 101, it is the *behaviour* of firms that is the target of the legislation. The following are cited as examples of abuse of market power:

- charging unfairly high prices to consumers, or paying unfairly low prices to suppliers;
- limiting production, markets or technical developments to the detriment of consumers;
- using price discrimination or other discriminatory practices to the detriment of certain parties;
- making other firms that sign contracts with it accept unfavourable obligations which, by their nature, have no connection with the subject of such contracts.

As you can see, these abuses are very similar to those in Article 101.

Under Article 102, such practices can be banned and firms can be fined where they are found to have abused a dominant position (see Box 11.3 for an example in relation to Microsoft). A firm does not need to have some specified minimum market share before Article 102 can be invoked. Instead, if firms are able to conduct anti-competitive practices, it is simply assumed that they must be in a position of market power. This approach is sensible, given the difficulties of identifying the boundaries of a market, either in terms of geography or in terms of type of product.

EU merger policy

The 1990 merger control measures tightened up the legislation in Article 102. They cover mergers where combined worldwide annual sales exceed €5 billion; where EU sales of at least two of the companies exceed €250 million; and where at least one of the companies conducts no more than two-thirds of its EU-wide business in a single member state. (Less than 4 per cent of mergers involving European companies meet these conditions.)

Relevant mergers must be notified to the Commission, which must then conduct preliminary investigations (Phase 1). A decision must then be made, normally within 25 working days, whether to conduct a formal investigation (Phase 2) or to let the merger proceed. A formal investigation must normally be completed within a further 90 working days (or 110 days in complex cases).

The process of EU merger control is thus very rapid and administratively inexpensive. The regulations are also potentially quite tough. Mergers are disallowed if they result in 'a concentration which would significantly impede effective competition, in particular by the creation or strengthening of a dominant position'. But the regulations are also flexible, since they recognise that mergers *may* be in the interests of consumers if they result in cost reductions. In such cases they are permitted.

The merger investigation process is now overseen by a Chief Competition Economist and a panel to scrutinise the investigating team's conclusions. One concern of this panel is that the Commission, in being willing to show flexibility, must not be too easily persuaded by firms, and impose conditions on them which are too lax and rely too much on the firms' cooperation. From 1990 to June 2012, close to 5000 mergers were notified, with around 5 per cent proceeding to Phase 2, but only 22 were prohibited. In many cases (too many, claim critics), the Commission accepted the undertakings of firms.

There is considerable disagreement in the EU between those who want to encourage competition *within* the EU and those who want to see European companies being world leaders. For them, the ability to compete in *world* markets normally requires that companies are large, which may well imply having monopoly power within the EU.

> **Pause for thought**
>
> *To what extent is Article 102 consistent with both these points of view?*

UK competition policy

There have been substantial changes to UK competition policy since the first legislation was introduced in 1948 (see Table 21.1). The current approach is based on the 1998 Competition Act and the 2002 Enterprise Act.

The Competition Act brought UK policy in line with EU policy, detailed above. The Act has two key sets (or 'chapters') of prohibitions. Chapter I prohibits various restrictive practices, and mirrors Article 101. Chapter II prohibits various abuses of monopoly power, and mirrors Article 102.

Table 21.1	UK competition legislation	
Year	**Act**	**Provisions**
1948	Monopolies and Restrictive Practices Act	Set up Monopolies and Restrictive Practices Commission (MRC) to investigate suspected cases of abuse by a firm or group of firms of a dominant market position.
1956, 1968, 1976	Restrictive Trade Practices Acts	Set up Restrictive Practices Court (RPC). All restrictive practices had to be registered. These would then have to be justified to the RPC. MRC renamed Monopolies Commission.
1964, 1976	Resale Prices Acts	Resale price maintenance banned unless firm could demonstrate to the RPC that it was in the public interest.
1965	Monopolies and Mergers Act	Role of Monopolies Commission now extended to examine mergers that would lead to a dominant market position.
1973	Fair Trading Act	Office of Fair Trading established. Its Director-General (DGFT) is responsible for referrals to the RPC or the renamed Monopolies and Mergers Commission (MMC).
1980	Competition Act	Various types of anti-competitive practice were specified. OFT would investigate alleged cases of such practices and possibly refer to MMC.
1989	Companies Act	Simplified and speeded up mergers investigation procedures.
1998	Competition Act	Brought UK legislation in line with EU legislation. Chapter I prohibition applies to restrictive practices. Chapter II prohibition applies to the abuse of a dominant position. MMC replaced by Competition Commission (CC).
2002	Enterprise Act	Made OFT and CC independent of government. Made various cartel agreements a criminal offence. Mergers investigated by OFT and referred, if necessary, to CC for ruling. In 2011 a consultation process begins over proposed merger of OFT and CC to create the Competition and Markets Authority (CMA).

The Enterprise Act strengthened the Competition Act and introduced new measures for the control of mergers.

Under the two Acts, the body charged with ensuring that the prohibitions are carried out is the Office of Fair Trading (OFT). The OFT can investigate any firms suspected of engaging in one or more of the prohibited practices. Its officers have the power to enter and search premises and can require the production and explanation of documents. Where the OFT decides that an infringement of one of the prohibitions has occurred, it can direct the offending firms to modify their behaviour or cease their practices altogether. Companies in breach of a prohibition are liable to fines of up to 10 per cent of their annual UK turnover. Third parties adversely affected by such breaches can seek compensation through the courts.

The Competition Act also set up a Competition Commission (CC) to which the OFT can refer cases for further investigation. The CC is charged with determining whether the structure of an industry or the practices of firms within it are detrimental to competition.

The Enterprise Act made the OFT and CC independent of government. It also set up a Markets and Policy Initiatives Division (MPI) of the OFT. This carries out investigations into particular markets suspected of not working in the best interests of consumers. The MPI's investigations could lead to the OFT enforcing its findings if anti-competitive practices were taking place (see below). Alternatively, the MPI could refer the case to the CC or make proposals to the government for changes in the law.

If a case is referred to the Competition Commission, it will carry out an investigation to establish whether competition is adversely affected. If it finds that it is, it will decide on the appropriate remedies, such as prohibiting various practices.

Firms affected by an OFT or CC ruling have the right of appeal to the Competition Appeal Tribunal (CAT), which can uphold or quash the original decision. The CAT is entirely independent of the CC and OFT.

UK restrictive practices policy

Under the 2002 Enterprise Act it is a *criminal* offence to engage in cartel agreements (i.e. horizontal, rather than vertical, collusive agreements between firms), irrespective of whether there are appreciable effects on competition. Convicted offenders may receive a prison sentence of up to five years and/or an unlimited fine. Prosecutions may be brought by the Serious Fraud Office or the OFT. The Act strengthened the OFT's power to enter premises, seize documents and require people to answer questions or provide information. In 2008, three British citizens were jailed under the Enterprise Act for organising a cartel: the first such prosecutions in the UK.

But what practices constitute 'cartel agreements'? These involve one or more of the following: price fixing, limiting supply, sharing out markets, limiting supply or bid-rigging. In more detail these include:

- Horizontal price-fixing agreements. These are agreements between competitors to set one or more of the following: fixed prices, minimum prices, the amount or percentage by which prices may be increased, or a range outside which prices may not move. The object is to restrict price competition and thus to keep prices higher than they would otherwise be.
- Agreements to share out markets. These may be by geographical area, type or size of customer, or nature of outlet. By limiting or even eliminating competition within each part of the market, such agreements can be an effective means of keeping prices high (or quality low).
- Agreements to limit production. This may involve output quotas or a looser agreement not to increase output wherever this would drive down prices.
- Agreements to limit or coordinate investment. By restraining capacity, this will help firms to keep output down and prices up.
- *Collusive tendering*. This is where two or more firms put in a tender for a contract at secretly agreed (high) prices. A well-known case throughout most of the 1980s and 1990s was that of firms supplying ready-mixed concrete agreeing on prices they would tender to local authorities (see Case Study H.5 in MyEconLab).
- Agreements between purchasers. These could be to reduce prices paid to suppliers. For example, large supermarkets could collude to keep prices low to farmers. An alternative form of agreement would be to deal with certain suppliers only.
- Agreements to boycott suppliers or distributors that deal with competitors to the colluding firms.

Pause for thought

Are all such agreements necessarily against the interests of consumers?

In the case of other types of agreement, the OFT has the discretion to decide, on a case-by-case basis, whether or not competition is appreciably restricted, and whether, therefore, they should be terminated or the firms should be exempted. Such cases include the following:

- Vertical price-fixing agreements. These are price agreements between purchasing firms and their suppliers. An example of this is *resale price maintenance*. This is

---

Definitions

Collusive tendering Where two or more firms secretly agree on the prices they will tender for a contract. These prices will be above those which would be put in under a genuinely competitive tendering process.

Resale price maintenance Where the manufacturer of a product (legally) insists that the product should be sold at a specified retail price.

where a manufacturer or distributor sets the price for retailers to charge. It may well distribute a price list to retailers (e.g. a car manufacturer may distribute a price list to car showrooms). Resale price maintenance is a way of preventing competition between retailers driving down retail prices and ultimately the price they pay to the manufacturer. Both manufacturers and retailers, therefore, are likely to gain from resale price maintenance.

■ Agreements to exchange information that could have the effect of reducing competition. For example, if producers exchange information on their price intentions, it is a way of allowing price leadership, a form of tacit collusion, to continue.

UK monopoly policy

Under the Chapter II prohibition of the 1998 Competition Act, it is illegal for a dominant firm to exercise its market power in such a way as to reduce competition. Any suspected case is investigated by the OFT, which uses a two-stage process in deciding whether an abuse has taken place.

The first stage is to establish whether a firm has a position of dominance. The firm does not literally have to be a monopoly. Rather 'dominance' normally involves the firm having at least a 40 per cent share of the market (national or local, whichever is appropriate), although this figure will vary from industry to industry. Also dominance depends on the barriers to entry to new competitors. The higher the barriers to the entry of new firms, the less contestable will be the market (see section 11.4), and the more dominant a firm is likely to be for any given current market share.

If the firm *is* deemed to be dominant, the second stage involves the OFT then deciding whether the firm's practices constitute an abuse of its position. As with restrictive practices, Chapter II follows EU legislation. It specifies the same four types of market abuse as does Article 102 (see above). Within these four categories, the OFT identifies the following practices as being overtly anti-competitive:

KI 23
p 181

■ *Charging excessively high prices*. These are prices above those the firm would charge if it faced effective competition. One sign of excessively high prices is abnormally high rates of profit.

■ *Price discrimination*. This is regarded as an abuse only to the extent that the higher prices are excessive or the lower prices are used to exclude competitors.

■ *Predatory pricing*. This is where prices are set at loss-making levels, so as to drive competitors out of business (see page 262). The test is to look at the dominant firm's price in relation to its average costs. If its price is below average variable cost, predation would be assumed. If its price is above average variable cost, but below average total cost, then the Director General would need to establish whether the reason was to eliminate a competitor.

In November 2008 the OFT decided that Cardiff Bus engaged in predatory conduct intended to eliminate a competitor, 2 Travel, during the period April 2004 to February 2005. Before 2 Travel's entry into the market, Cardiff Bus had a substantial market share, carrying 80 000 passengers per day. However, 'Cardiff Bus responded to the introduction of a new no-frills bus service by another bus company, 2 Travel, by introducing its own no-frills bus services which ran on the same routes, at similar times as 2 Travel's services and made a loss for Cardiff Bus. Shortly after 2 Travel's exit from the market Cardiff Bus withdrew its own no-frills services.'[1]

■ *Vertical restraints*. This is where a supplying firm imposes conditions on a purchasing firm (or vice versa). For example, a manufacturer may impose rules on retailers about displaying the product or the provision of after-sales service, or it may refuse to supply certain outlets (e.g. perfume manufacturers refusing to supply discount chains, such as Superdrug). Another example is *tie-in sales*. This is where a firm controlling the supply of a first product insists that its customers buy a second product from it rather than from its rivals.

The simple *existence* of any of these practices may not constitute an abuse. The OFT has to decide whether their *effect* is to restrict competition.

If the case is not straightforward, the OFT can refer it to the Competition Commission (CC). The CC will then carry out a detailed investigation to establish whether competition is restricted or distorted. If it is, the CC will rule what actions must be taken to remedy the situation.

UK merger policy

Merger policy is covered by the 2002 Enterprise Act. It seeks to prevent mergers that are likely to result in a substantial lessening of competition.

A merger or takeover will be investigated by the OFT if the target company has a turnover of £70 million or more, or if the merger results in the new company having a market share of 25 per cent or more. The OFT conducts a preliminary investigation to see whether competition is likely to be threatened. If it is, and if there are unlikely to be any substantial compensating benefits to consumers, the OFT refers the case to the Competition Commission.

> ## Definitions
>
> **Vertical restraints** Conditions imposed by one firm on another which is either its supplier or its customer.
>
> **Tie-in-sales** Where a firm is only prepared to sell a first product on the condition that its customers buy a second product from it.

---

[1] *'Cardiff Bus engaged in predatory conduct against competitor, OFT decides'* (OFT press release, 133/08. 18 November 2008). In this instance, the OFT decided not to fine Cardiff Bus because its turnover did not exceed £50 million at the time of the infringement of Chapter II of the Competition Act 1998.

BOX 21.1 **FROM MICROCHIPS TO SOAP POWDER, THE UMPIRE STRIKES BACK**

New EU procedures for dealing with cartels

EU competition policy applies to companies operating in two or more EU countries. The policy is implemented by the European Commission, which has the power to levy substantial fines on companies found to be in breach of the legislation. However, in 2008, in order to simplify administrative processes and to reduce the number of cases going to the courts, new settlement procedures were introduced. If, on seeing the evidence against them, firms cooperate, then fines can be reduced by 10 per cent. Meanwhile, firms who have participated in a cartel but who reveal its existence can be granted immunity from fines.

Between the introduction of the new procedures in 2008 and June 2012, six cartel cases were settled. The following table summarises these six cases.

Date	Industry/sector	Number of firms involved	Commission fine, €m
May 2010	Memory chips	10	331.3
July 2010	Animal feed phosphates	13	175.6
April 2011	Detergents	3	315.2
October 2011	Cathode ray tubes	4	128.0
December 2011	Refrigeration compresses	10	161.2
June 2012	Water management products	3	13.6

Squeaky clean competition

The first case settled under the new arrangements involved 10 companies which were found to have restricted competition of microchips to manufacturers of PCs. The collective fine imposed was €331.3 million – the largest of the six settlements.

However, one of the better-known cases involves detergent manufacturers. In April 2011, the Commission announced fines totalling €315.2 million against Procter & Gamble and Unilever. They had been accused of operating a cartel with a third company, Henkel, in an EC investigation called 'Purity'. The three were the largest soap powder producers in Europe. Henkel was granted immunity from the fines, after revealing the existence of the cartel to the Commission in 2008. The company said that the cartel arrangements were detected by internal audit procedures and that it immediately informed the authorities.

The Commission announced that the three companies had operated a cartel for three years and across eight EU countries. The aim had been to stabilise their market positions and to coordinate prices. They found that the soap powder cartel started when the companies implemented a genuine and legal initiative through their trade association to improve the environmental performance of detergent products. But, in the course of this initiative, the companies strayed into illegal territory, agreeing measures to protect their market share, to maintain prices and, ultimately, to fix prices. Henkel, Procter & Gamble and Unilever did this on their own initiative and at their own risk.[1]

Joaquín Almunia, Vice-President of the Commission in charge of competition policy, said: 'By acknowledging their participation in the cartel, the companies enabled the Commission to swiftly conclude its investigation, and for this they got a reduction of the fine. But companies should be under no illusion that the Commission will pursue its relentless fight against cartels, which extract higher prices from consumers than if companies compete fairly and on the merits.'

 Why might global cartels be harder to identify and eradicate than cartels solely located within the domestic economy? What problems does this raise for competition policy?

[1] Europa Press Release IP 11/473 13 April 2011 (http://europa.eu/rapid/pressReleasesAction.do?reference=IP/11/473)

If reference is made to the CC, it conducts a detailed investigation to establish whether the merger is likely to lead to a significant reduction in competition. If so, it can prohibit the merger. Alternatively, it can require the merged firm to behave in certain ways in order to protect consumers' interests. In such cases, the OFT then monitors the firm to ensure that it is abiding by the CC's conditions. CC investigations must normally be completed within 24 weeks.

The 2002 Act tightened up merger legislation. In the past, the vast majority of mergers were not referred to the CC (or its predecessor, the Monopolies and Mergers Commission). Yet studies had shown that mergers were generally *not* in the public interest. Mergers had contributed to a growing degree of market concentration in the UK. The 2002 Act sought to rectify this problem.

Between 2005 and 2008 a number of mergers were referred to the CC; these included the merger of Heinz and HP Foods, the purchase of 115 Morrisons stores by Somerfield, and Sky's purchase of a 17.9 per cent stake in ITV.

However, in the autumn of 2008, following the announcement that a merger was proposed between Lloyds TSB and the troubled bank HBOS, the government said that it would overrule any objections raised by the competition authorities. This highlights the fact that governments may sometimes prefer to take a pragmatic view of competition policy, particularly in times of economic crisis.

In March 2011 the UK government set up a consultation process on its proposed changes to competition regulation in the UK. While retaining the principles and broad procedures of the 1998 and 2002 Acts, it proposed that the Office of Fair Trading and the Competition Commission should be merged. The merged body would provide a single regulator for the UK, the Competition and Markets Authority (CMA). The intention was to reduce duplication of processes and costs and to increase business confidence in regulation. The government said that it hoped these proposals would make it easier to tackle anti-competitive mergers and to reform anti-trust rules.

Assessment of EU and UK competition policy

With UK competition legislation having been brought in line with EU legislation, it is possible to consider the two together.

It is generally agreed by commentators that the policy is correct to concentrate on anti-competitive *practices* and their *effects* rather than simply on the existence of agreements or on the size of a firm's market share. After all, economic power is only a problem when it is abused. When, by contrast, it enables firms to achieve economies of scale, or more finance for investment, the result can be to the benefit of consumers. In other words, the assumption that structure determines conduct and performance (see pages 13 and 161) is not necessarily true, and certainly it is not necessarily true that market power is always bad or competitive industries are always good.

Secondly, most commentators favour the system of certain practices being *prohibited*, with fines applicable to the first offence. This acts as an important deterrent to anti-competitive behaviour.

Similar conclusions have been reached in the USA, where the application of competition law has undergone changes in recent years. In the past, the focus was on the structure of an industry. Under the Sherman Act of 1890, oligopolistic collusion in the 'restraint of trade' was made illegal, as was any attempt to establish a monopoly. Although, under the Clayton Act of 1914, various potentially anti-competitive practices (such as price discrimination) were only illegal when they substantially lessened competition, the application of these two 'anti-trust' laws was largely directed to breaking up large firms. Today, the approach is to focus on efficiency, rather than on market share; and on the effects on consumers of any collusion or cooperation between firms, rather than on the simple collusion itself.

A problem with any policy to deal with collusion is the difficulty in rooting it out. When firms do all their deals 'behind closed doors' and are careful not to keep records or give clues, then collusion can be very hard to spot. The cases that have come to light, such as that of collusive tendering between firms supplying ready-mixed concrete, may be just the tip of an iceberg.

21.2 POLICIES TOWARDS RESEARCH AND DEVELOPMENT (R&D)

The impact of technology, not only on the practice of business but on the economy in general, is vividly illustrated by the development and use of the Internet. In 1997, worldwide some 40 million people and 25 000 firms used the Internet. By 2012, there were 2.3 billion users (33 per cent of the world's population).

The commercial possibilities of the Internet range from the selling of information and services to global forms of catalogue shopping. The Internet is just one example of how technology and technological change are shaping the whole structure and organisation of business (see Chapter 3 on the flat organisation), the experience of work for the worker, and the productivity of business and hence the competitive performance of national economies.

If a business fails to embrace new technology, its productivity and profitability will almost certainly lag behind those businesses that do.

It is the same for countries. Unless they embrace new technology, the productivity gap between them and those that do is likely to widen. Once such a gap has been opened, it will prove very difficult to close. Those countries ahead in the technological race will tend to get further ahead as the dynamic forces of technology enhance their competitiveness, improve their profits and provide yet greater potential for technological advance. In other words, the rate of technological advance can have dramatic effects on a country's living standards. This helps to explain why understanding the nature and drivers of technological advance is an important part of the literature on long-term economic growth. So how can countries compete more effectively in the technological race? *Technology policy* refers to a series of government initiatives to affect the process of technological change and its rate of adoption. The nature of the policy will depend on which stage of the introduction of new technology it is designed to affect. Three stages can be identified:

■ *Invention*. In this initial stage, research leads to new ideas and new products. Sometimes the ideas arise from general research; sometimes the research is directed towards a particular goal, such as the development of a new type of car engine or computer chip.

■ *Innovation*. In this stage, the new ideas are put into practice. A firm will introduce the new technology, and will hopefully gain a commercial advantage from so doing.

Definition

Technology policy Involves government initiatives to affect the process and rate of technological change.

■ *Diffusion*. In the final stage, the new products and processes are copied, and possibly adapted, by competitor firms. The effects of the new technology thus spread throughout the economy, affecting general productivity levels and competitiveness.

Technology policy can be focused on any or all of these stages of technological change.

Technological change and market failure

Why is a technology policy needed in the first place? The main reason is that the market system might fail to provide those factors vital to initiate technological change, and there are a number of reasons for this, including the following.

R&D free riders. If an individual business can benefit from the results of *other* businesses conducting R&D, with all its associated costs and risks, then it is less likely to conduct R&D itself. It will simply 'free ride' on such activity. As a consequence, it would be in the interest of the firm conducting R&D to keep its findings secret or under some kind of property right, such as a patent, so as to gain as much competitive advantage as possible from its investment.

Although it is desirable to encourage firms to conduct R&D, and for this purpose it may be necessary to have a strict patent system in force, it is also desirable that there is the maximum *social* benefit from such R&D. This would occur only if such findings were widely disseminated. It is thus important that technology policy finds the optimum balance between the two objectives of (a) encouraging individual firms to conduct research and (b) disseminating the results.

Monopolistic and oligopolistic market structures. The more a market is dominated by a few large producers, the less incentive they will have to conduct R&D and innovate as a means of reducing costs or developing innovative new products or experiences for consumers. The problem is most acute under monopoly. Nevertheless, despite a lower incentive to innovate, the higher profits of firms with monopoly power will at least put them in a position of being more able to afford to conduct research.

Duplication. Not only is it likely that there is too little R&D being conducted, there is also the danger that resources may be wasted in duplicating research. The more firms there are conducting R&D, the greater the likelihood of some form of duplication. Given the scarcity of R&D resources, any duplication would be a highly inefficient way to organise production.

Risk and uncertainty. Because the payoffs from R&D activity are so uncertain, there will tend to be a natural caution on the part of both the business conducting R&D and (if different) the financier. Only R&D activity which has a clear market potential, or is of low risk, is likely to be considered. It has been found that financial markets in particular will tend to adopt a risk-averting strategy and fail to provide an adequate pool of long-term funds. (This is another manifestation of the 'short-termism' we considered in section 19.4.)

Forms of intervention

Attempts to correct the above market failures and develop a technology policy might include the use of the following.

The patent system. The strengthening of legal rights over the development of new products will encourage businesses to conduct R&D, as they will be able to reap greater rewards from successful R&D investment.

> ### Pause for thought
>
> *Before you read on, can you identify the main forms of intervention the government might use in order to encourage and support R&D?*

Public provision. In an attempt to overcome the free-rider problem and the inefficiency of R&D duplication, government might provide R&D itself, either through its own research institutions or via funding to universities and other research organisations. This is of particular importance in the case of basic research, where the potential outcomes are far less certain than those of applied research.

R&D subsidies. If the government provided subsidies to businesses conducting R&D activity, it not only would reduce the cost and hence the risk for business, but could ensure that the outcome from the R&D activity is more rapidly diffused throughout the economy than might otherwise be expected. This would help improve general levels of technological innovation.

Cooperative R&D. Given that the benefits of technological developments are of widespread use, the government could encourage cooperative R&D. The government could take various roles here, from being actively involved in the R&D process to acting as a facilitator, bringing private-sector businesses together. The key advantages of this policy are that it will not only reduce the potential for duplication, but also encourage the pooling of scarce R&D resources.

Diffusion policies. Such policies tend to be of two types: the provision of information concerning new technology, and the use of subsidies to encourage businesses to adopt new technology.

Other policies. A wide range of other policies, primarily adopted for other purposes, might also influence R&D. These might include: education and training policy; competition policy; national defence policies and initiatives; and policies on standards and compatibility.

Technology policy in the UK and EU

The UK's poor technological performance since 1945 can be attributed to many factors, from a lack of entrepreneurial vision on the part of business to the excessive short-termism of the UK's financial institutions. There also appears to have been a failure on the part of government to initiate suitable strategies to overcome such problems.

In the UK, the attitude towards technology policy has tended to be market-driven, with the role of government relatively limited. More interventionist strategies have typically been kept to a minimum, focusing largely on military and defence technologies. Recent UK governments have looked to provide financial support for R&D by enabling companies to reduce their profits liable to corporation tax by a proportion of their R&D expenditure (see section 31.2).

BOX 21.2　**THE R&D SCOREBOARD**

For many years, it has been suggested that the UK's poor international competitive record has been in no small part due to its failure to invest in research and development. The UK's R&D intensity – that is, the ratio of R&D spending to sales – has been considerably lower than that of its main economic rivals.

Each year the European Union publishes the *EU Industrial R&D Investment Scoreboard*. This gives details of the R&D expenditures by the top R&D spending companies both in the EU and worldwide. It also investigates emerging trends and patterns in R&D spending. The Scoreboard is composed of the 1000 leading R&D-spending EU companies and the 1000 leading non-EU global R&D spenders. From this sample, the report also focuses on the world's largest 1400 R&D-spending companies. In 2010, 79 of these 1400 companies were based in the UK with 400 across the whole of the EU.

Here we look at some of the patterns that emerge from the 2011 Scoreboard. The Scoreboard focuses on financial year 2010.

Geographical concentration

During 2010, R&D spending by the world's top 1400 companies rose by 4 per cent to €456 billion. This followed a 1.9 per cent decline during the global economic recession of 2009. However, there were significant geographic differences in growth rates. The R&D decline of 2009 centred on the EU (−2.6 per cent) and the US (−5.1 per cent). While there was a R&D rebound of 2.6 per cent by EU companies and 5.1 per cent by US companies, this was dwarfed by increases in R&D expenditure of 29.5 per cent by Chinese companies, 20.5 per cent by South Korean companies and 17.8 per cent by those based in Taiwan.

Of the top 1400 R&D-spending companies, 1082 are registered in just seven countries – the USA (487), Japan (267), Germany (101), the UK (79), France (58), Taiwan (50) and Switzerland (40). They contribute 83 per cent of the R&D spending of the top 1400.

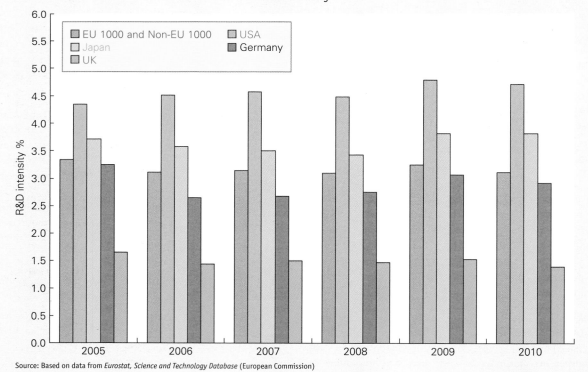

R&D intensity

Source: Based on data from *Eurostat, Science and Technology Database* (European Commission)

Despite a sizeable number of UK-based companies regularly making a list of the world's largest R&D-spending companies, the UK's R&D performance compares less favourably when measured relative to GDP. In part, this reflects the limited R&D expenditure by government. But, it also reflects the low R&D intensity across the private sector. In other words, total R&D expenditure by British firms is low *relative* to the income generated by sales (see Box 21.2).

Since 1995, UK gross expenditure on research and development as a percentage of GDP has been lower than that of its main economic rivals (see Figure 21.1). For instance, the UK's share of R&D expenditure in GDP has typically been only 72 per cent of that in Germany and only 57 per cent of that in Japan.

As Figure 21.1 shows, the aggregate level of R&D spending across the 27 member states of the EU is relatively low,

Research and development by sector

Sector	Expenditure, €m	Intensity, % of net sales	Investment per employee, €
Pharmaceuticals	77 820	14.8	53 898
Automobiles and parts	68 572	4.1	13 845
Semi-conductors	28 190	13.1	38 929
Telecommunications equipment	27 436	11.8	31 651
Software	21 632	14.0	31 090
Electronic equipment	20 824	4.2	18 560
Chemicals	20 184	3.1	14 324
Aerospace and defence	16 153	4.0	9 711
Leisure goods	14 480	6.2	16 307
Computer hardware	14 001	3.2	12 360
General industrials	13 666	2.4	6 751
Computer services	10 495	5.4	10 368
Electrical components and equipment	10 055	4.3	6 977
Biotechnology	9 485	20.9	88 476
Health care, equipment and services	9 364	6.1	11 750
Fixed line communications	9 077	1.7	4 825

Source: Based on data from *2011 EU Industrial R&D Investment Scorecard*, (European Commission)

R&D intensity

Across the highest-spending 1000 EU and 1000 non-EU companies, R&D intensity stood at 3.1 per cent in 2010. In other words, the value of R&D expenditure was equivalent to 3.1 per cent of their sales. As the chart shows, this is little changed since 2005. In contrast, R&D intensity in the UK is considerably lower, averaging 1.5 per cent across the period. This compares especially unfavourably with the USA and Japan, where the R&D intensity averaged 4.6 and 3.6 per cent, respectively, over the period.

R&D by sector

R&D investment is heavily concentrated in three sectors: *pharmaceuticals, technology hardware and equipment* and *automobiles and parts*. The table above ranks R&D expenditure by industrial sector for the world's 1400 largest R&D spenders. The pharmaceuticals and the automobile and parts sectors account between them for one-third of R&D expenditure. In 2010 the largest two R&D spenders, Roche (Switzerland) and Pfizer (USA), were both pharmaceutical companies, each spending just over €7 billion.

The table also shows how the intensity of R&D, as measured relative to sales, varies across industrial sectors.

Unsurprisingly, we find that the biotechnology (21 per cent) and pharmaceutical sectors (15 per cent) are especially R&D intensive. Another way of measuring the relative investment in R&D is to estimate R&D expenditure per employee. Under this measure we once again see how highly R&D focused the pharmaceutical and biotechnology sectors are.

The largest two R&D-spending companies based in the UK were, in 2010, both pharmaceutical companies. GlaxoSmithKline and AstraZeneca spent €4.4 billion and €3.2 billion, respectively, with a combined R&D intensity of 13 per cent of net sales. This level of capital intensity is considerably higher than the aggregate across all British companies. These two companies alone contributed 34 per cent of R&D spending by UK companies in 2010. The next biggest spender, BT, invested €962 million in R&D.

1. *What are the economic costs and benefits of R&D spending to the national economy? Distinguish between the short and long run.*
2. *R&D is only one indicator, albeit an important one, of innovation potential. What other factors are likely to affect innovation?*
3. *What is the economic case for and against government intervention in the field of R&D?*

Figure 21.1   Gross expenditure on R&D as a percentage of GDP

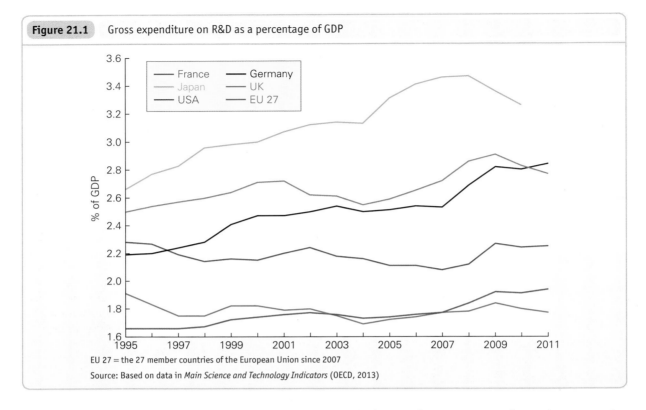

EU 27 = the 27 member countries of the European Union since 2007

Source: Based on data in *Main Science and Technology Indicators* (OECD, 2013)

averaging only 1.75 per cent of GDP since 1995. Member countries, however, have been encouraged to invest 3 per cent of their GDP in R&D (2 per cent private investment, 1 per cent public finding). The principal EU fund for allocating funds for R&D is the *EU framework for Research and Technological Development*. The budget for the Seventh Framework Programme from 2007 to 2013 was €50.5 billion, while that for the Eighth Framework Programme from 2014 to 2020 has been raised to €80 billion.

The framework programmes are designed, amongst other things, to foster collaboration in research, including between academia and industry, to fund frontier science, help develop knowledge and science clusters, provide scholarships for young researchers and to fund R&D by small businesses. In doing so, the intention is to improve the EU's competitive stance and to promote new growth and jobs. The hope is that this interventionist approach will raise the productive potential of the wider EU economy not only in the short term, but also in the longer term.

21.3 POLICIES TOWARDS TRAINING

It is generally recognised by economists and politicians alike that improvements in training and education can yield significant supply-side gains. Indeed, the UK's failure to invest as much in training as many of its major competitors is seen as a key explanation for the country's poor economic performance since the early 1970s. OECD figures[2] show that in the UK the percentage of the population aged 25 to 64 with at least upper secondary education, such as A-levels or vocational equivalents, is 74 per cent. By contrast in Germany it is 85 per cent.

Training and economic performance

Training and economic performance are linked in three main ways.

Labour productivity. In various studies comparing the productivity of UK and German industry, education and training was seen as the principal reason for the productivity gap between the two countries (see Box 21.3).

Innovation and change. A key factor in shaping a firm's willingness to introduce new products or processes will be the adaptability and skills of its workforce. If the firm has to spend a lot of money on retraining, or on attracting skilled workers away from other firms, the costs may prove prohibitive.

---
[2] Education at a Glance 2011 (OECD).

Costs of production. A shortage of skilled workers will quickly create labour bottlenecks and cause production costs to increase. This will stifle economic growth.

Training policy

If training is left to the employer, the benefits will become an externality if the workers leave to work elsewhere. Society has benefited from the training, but the firm has not. The free market, therefore, will provide a less than optimal amount of training. The more mobile the labour force, and the more 'transferable' the skills acquired from training, the more likely it is that workers will leave, and the less willing will firms be to invest in training.

In the UK, there is a high level of labour turnover. What is more, wage differentials between skilled and unskilled workers are narrower than in many other countries, and so there is less incentive for workers to train.

How can increased training be achieved? There are three broad approaches:

- Workers could be encouraged to stay with their employer so that employers would be more willing to invest in training. Externalities would be reduced.
- The government could provide subsidies for training. Alternatively, the government or some other agency could provide education and training directly.
- Firms could cooperate to prevent 'poaching' and set up industry-wide training programmes, perhaps in partnership with the government and unions.

Training policy in various countries

As far as the first approach is concerned, most countries have seen a movement towards *greater* labour mobility. The rise in the 'flexible firm' has involved the employment of fewer permanent workers and more part-time and temporary workers. Some countries, such as Japan and Germany, however, have a generally lower rate of labour turnover than most. In Japan, in particular, it is common for workers to stay with one employer throughout their career. There the relationship between employer and employee extends well beyond a simple short-term economic arrangement. Workers give loyalty and commitment to their employer, which in return virtually guarantees long-term employment and provides various fringe benefits (such as housing, child care, holiday schemes and health care). It is not surprising that Japanese firms invest highly in training.

In the USA, labour turnover is very high and yet there is little in the way of industry-wide training. Instead, by having a high percentage of young people in further and higher education, the US government hopes that sufficient numbers and quality of workers are available for industry. As of 2009, approximately 70 per cent of the US population were entering higher education, slightly higher than in the UK where the figure was 61 per cent. The percentage of the population taking vocational training courses is very low.

Total public-sector expenditure on all types of training programmes averaged just 0.05 per cent of GDP between 2005 and 2010.

In Germany, 40 per cent of the population in 2009 entered higher education, considerably lower than in the USA (and the UK). However, public-sector expenditure on training accounts for 0.3 per cent of GDP, six times larger than the share in the USA. Three-quarters of this training is categorised as institutional training, whereby young people who do not enter higher education embark on some form of apprenticeship, attending college for part of the week and receiving work-based training for the rest.

In the German model, the state, unions and employers' associations work closely in determining training provision, and they have developed a set of vocational qualifications based around the apprenticeship system. Given that virtually all firms are involved in training, the 'free-rider' problem of firms poaching labour without themselves paying for training is virtually eliminated. The result is that the German workforce is highly skilled. Many of the skills, however, are highly specific. This is a problem when the demand for particular skills declines.

The UK approach

There has been considerable concern in the UK about the quantity and appropriateness of training. For instance, in 2004 the Labour government set up a committee under Lord Leitch to consider the most effective forms of training for increasing economic prosperity and productivity, and improving social justice. The assessment was rather gloomy; the Leitch Committee stated in its interim report that the UK had to 'raise its game' (see Box 21.3). So to what extent has the UK approach to training evolved?

The approach adopted by the Conservative government elected in 1979 was initially influenced by its free-market approach. Training was to be left largely to employers. However, with growing worries over the UK's *productivity gap* (see Box 31.2 for empirical evidence), the government set up Training and Enterprise Councils (TECs) in 1988. The TECs identified regional skills needs, organised training and financed work-based training schemes.

> ### Pause for thought
>
> *What advantages and drawbacks are there in leaving training provision to employers? Clue: think about how training provision might be influenced by the business cycle (the cycle of booms and recessions in the economy).*

In 2001, the Labour government (1997–2010) replaced the TECs by the Learning and Skills Council (LSC). This had a budget of over £10 billion and was responsible for planning and funding training in sixth forms and

BOX 21.3 **THE UK NEEDS TO 'RAISE ITS GAME'**

The Leitch Review of future skill needs

In his pre-Budget speech in November 2005, the Chancellor of the Exchequer announced the publication of an interim review of the UK's future skill needs by Lord Leitch, Chairman of the National Employment Panel. The report noted that the UK had to 'raise its game' if it was to be successful in the increasingly competitive global economy. The following extracts are taken from the executive summary of the *Leitch Review*.[1]

Skills in the UK in 2005

The UK starts from a strong economic position. It is the fourth largest economy in the world and has the highest employment rate in the G7 group of industrialised nations. Despite this strong performance, the UK today faces important economic challenges. In particular, despite some recent improvements, the UK continues to have relatively poor productivity performance which still trails some of the UK's main comparator nations. Output per hour worked is almost 30 per cent higher in France and more than 10 per cent higher in Germany and the USA than it is in the UK.

Evidence shows that a significant contributory factor to the UK's relatively poor productivity performance is its low overall level of skills. For example, one fifth of the

gap with France and Germany is a result of the UK's comparatively poor skills. Low levels of skills in the UK constrain growth and innovation in firms . . .

Today, the UK's human capital is poor in relation to key comparator nations:

■ the proportion of adults in the UK without a basic school-leaving qualification is double that of Canada and Germany;

■ over 5 million people of working age in the UK have no qualification at all; and

■ one in six adults do not have the literacy skills expected of an 11-year-old. Almost half do not have these levels of functional numeracy; only half of adults who lack these functional skills are in work.

Although the position in higher-level skills is better, with over one quarter of adults in the UK holding a degree-level qualification, other countries such as USA, Japan and Canada are still in a superior position (see the chart).

Skill deficiencies are reflected in employers' experiences. In survey evidence from across the UK, employers report significant skills shortages within their own workforce and in the pool of labour from which they recruit. Recent evidence shows persistent recruitment difficulties across the skills spectrum, in low skilled service jobs as well as in skilled craft jobs. This affects the ability of firms to grow and become more productive and profitable. Almost one third of firms who report skills gaps in their workforce say that these gaps prevent them from modernising their

[1] HM Treasury (2005) *Skills in the UK: The Long-term Challenge* (Leitch Committee interim report, December 2005) (HMSO, December 2005). © Crown Copyright 2005. Crown copyright material is reproduced with permission of the Controller of Her Majesty's Stationery Office (HMSO).

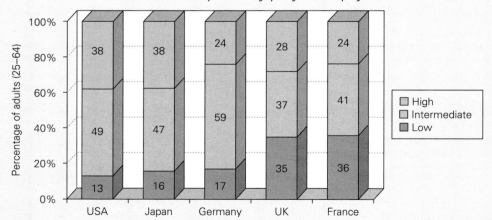

International comparisons of qualifications profiles

Source: H. M. Treasury, *Skills in the UK: The Long-term Challenge* (Leitch Committee interim report, December 2005), Chart 3 (based on data in *Education at a glance*, OECD, 2005). Contains public sector information licensed under the Open Government Licence (OGL) v1.0. http://www.nationalarchives.gov.uk/doc/open-government-licence.

business to move into higher value added – and more productive – economic activity.

Skill levels have an important impact on employment and social welfare. For example, only half of those people with no qualifications are in work compared to 90 per cent of adults qualified to at least degree level. Low skills levels are particularly pronounced in certain groups. For example, over 40 per cent of people with a disability have no qualifications at all. The unequal distribution of skills has adverse effects on income equality and constrains social mobility, which has deteriorated in the UK over the past two decades. Evidence suggests that skills gaps exacerbate social deprivation including poverty, poor health and crime . . .

Over the last decade, the UK has made real improvements to its skills profile. The proportion of the working age population with a degree has increased from one fifth to over one quarter. The proportion of adults who hold no qualifications has fallen by one third, from one fifth of the working age population to 14 per cent.

These changes are primarily due to younger, better-qualified people flowing into the workforce, while older and less well-qualified people retire. One in ten 25–34-year-olds has no qualifications compared to one in four 55–64-year-olds. Over the last decade, there has been a significant decrease in the proportion of people who lack a qualification at the equivalent level to five good GCSEs, falling by almost one half from 43 per cent to 23 per cent.

The Government has set ambitious targets to further improve the skills profile of the UK. These include addressing the stock of adults who lack basic literacy and numeracy skills; reducing the stock of adults without the equivalent of a good school-leaving qualification; and increasing the numbers of young people with a degree. Meeting these targets will bring significant improvements to the stock of skills in the UK. However, the Review believes that, on current trends, achieving these targets will be extremely challenging.

Looking forward to 2020

- [F]urther improvements [in] the skills of young people alone will not [raise] the UK's overall skills profile significantly enough by 2020 because:
- 70 per cent of the working age population in 2020 have already completed their compulsory school education; and
- half of the working age population in 2020 is already over 25 years old. This is beyond the age when people are likely to participate in the traditional education route from school through to university.

By 2020, there will be about 3.5 million more people in the working age population and the population will have aged significantly. Adults aged 50–65 years will account for 60 per cent of the growth in the working age population. The contribution of older people to the labour market will become increasingly important. By 2020, 30 per cent of the working age population will be over 50, compared with 25 per cent today. These demographic changes make it essential to improve the skills of older groups in the workforce.

The Review has undertaken new analysis to assess the UK's current trajectory in developing its skills profile and the likely stock of skills in 2020 if all current targets are met. The most marked changes over the next 15 years will occur at each end of the skills spectrum:

- by 2020, the proportion of working age adults without any qualifications will fall to 4 per cent;
- the proportion without qualifications at the equivalent level to five good GCSEs will halve from 31 per cent today to 16 per cent in 2020; and
- the proportion holding a degree or better would increase from 27 per cent to 38 per cent of the working age population.

The Review's analysis suggests that the economic benefits from meeting these current ambitions would be substantial. Productivity could be 3 per cent higher compared to what it would otherwise be and the employment rate could increase by 0.75 per cent. This is a net benefit to the economy of an average £3 billion each year – equivalent to 0.3 per cent of gross domestic product (GDP). One fifth of this benefit is due to increased employment; the rest is due to adults who are already in work improving their skills further and becoming more productive.

However, even if the Government's current ambitious targets were met, significant problems would remain with the UK's skills base in 2020. At least 4 million adults will still not have literacy skills expected of an 11-year-old, at least 12 million will be without numeracy skills at this level (equivalent to three in ten adults) and 6.5 million adults will not have qualifications at the equivalent level to five good GCSEs. In comparative terms, the UK will continue to be an 'average performer' – positioned at best, in the middle of the OECD ranking. It will continue to have smaller proportions of intermediate and higher-level skills than key comparator countries such as France and the USA.

1. *What other factors help to raise long-term productivity in the UK?*
2. *To what extent is the UK on target to achieve the ambitions set out in the Leitch Committee reports? Explore the UK government websites and other sources to help you come to a view.*

further education colleges, work-based training for young people aged 16 to 24 ('Apprenticeships' and 'Advanced Apprenticeships'), adult and community learning, the provision of information, advice and guidance for adults, and developing links between education and business.

In addition, a support service called 'Connexions' offered training and employment advice and support for young people between the ages of 13 and 19. In 2012, this was replaced by the National Careers Service. This is a single point of access for both young people and adults. Dedicated national Careers Direct advisers for young people are available online or by phone. Although careers advice is still provided by some local authorities, many of the Connexions centres have closed.

In March 2008, it was announced that the LSC was to be abolished. Funding responsibilities for 16- to 19-year-olds were transferred to local education authorities. A newly created Skills Funding Agency took responsibility for the funding and regulation of further education and training for adults in England.

Qualifications. The past 20 years have seen various new vocational qualifications introduced. The National Vocational Qualification (NVQ) was launched in 1991 specifically to support workplace learning for young people. A young person works for an employer and receives on-the-job training. They also attend college on an occasional basis. The NVQ is awarded when they have achieved sufficient competence. In addition, the government launched General National Vocational Qualifications (GNVQs). These further-education qualifications were aimed to bridge the gap between education and work, by ensuring that education was more work relevant.

The GNVQ system was modelled on that in France, where a clear vocational educational route is seen as the key to reducing skills shortages. At the age of 14, French students can choose to pursue academic or vocational education routes. The vocational route provides high-level, broad-based skills (unlike in Germany, where skills tend to be more job specific).

However, GNVQs were competing alongside other well-established vocational qualifications such as City and Guilds and BTEC certificates and diplomas. Such competition led to the withdrawal of the GNVQ by October 2007. The NVQ survives largely because it complements other vocational qualifications, for example on apprenticeship schemes.

In 2008, 14–19 diplomas were launched. By 2011, these were offered in 14 vocational areas or 'lines of learning', such as engineering, IT, hair and beauty studies, retail business, construction and hospitality. They are studied in schools or colleges. All Diplomas are available at three levels: Foundation (level 1), Higher (level 2: equivalent to GCSE grades A* to C) and Advanced (level 3: equivalent to 3¹/₂ A-levels).

Another approach adopted by the Labour government was to encourage 'lifelong learning'. Measures included setting up the following:

- A University for Industry, which through its 'Learndirect' brand offers online courses in a range of business, technical and IT subjects.
- Some 700 UK Online centres. These offer access to the Internet, and helpers are on hand to provide basic IT, literacy and numeracy support. Today there are nearly 4000 such centres.
- Two-year foundation degrees, offered by universities or higher education colleges. These are designed in conjunction with employers to meet various skill shortages. They are taken at the university or an associated college, normally on a part-time basis, and often include work-based study with local employers.

The final report of the Leitch Review released in December 2006 argued that all young people should continue in learning until they are 18. This has now been widely accepted across the political spectrum. The Coalition government formed in 2010 announced that it would be increasing the age to which all young people must continue in either education or training. The 'participation age' was increased to 17 in 2013 and 18 in 2015. Local authorities have a statutory duty to provide sufficient education and training provision for those young people aged 16 to 18.

Apprenticeships are not only forming an increasingly important plank of training for young people in the UK, but for older age groups too. Figure 21.2 shows the steady

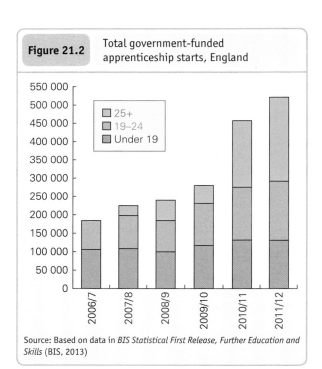

Figure 21.2 Total government-funded apprenticeship starts, England

Source: Based on data in *BIS Statistical First Release, Further Education and Skills* (BIS, 2013)

expansion of government-funded apprenticeships in England between 2006/7 and 2009/10 followed by a more significant expansion in 2010/11 and 2011/12. While each age group has seen an increase in the number of apprenticeships, the growth in the number of learners aged 25 and over starting apprenticeships has been particularly rapid.

The expansion of apprenticeships follows a series of government initiatives. At the time of writing, the public funds 100 per cent of the training costs for young people aged 16 to 18, up to 50 per cent for those aged 19 to 24, and up to 40 per cent for those aged 25 and over.

In 2011, the government announced a £25 million Higher Apprenticeship fund to help further an expansion of 'higher apprenticeships', which were first introduced in 2009. These are designed to meet employers' need for higher-level skills. They have been identified as one way for professionals, such as those in engineering and accountancy, to become fully qualified.

In November 2011, as part of its 'Youth Contract', the government announced a one-year scheme to run from February 2012 to March 2013 to provide up to 40 000 apprenticeship grants for small and medium-sized enterprises (firms with fewer than 250 employees). The scheme offered SMEs an incentive payment of £1500 and employers could make up to three grant requests. The aim was to encourage more SMEs to take on apprentices aged 16 to 24 and, in doing so, reduce the number in this age bracket not in education, employment or training – so-called 'NEETs'.

It appears that UK governments have begun to take on the challenge offered in the Leitch Review. We await with interest the extent to which the UK will have 'raised its game' by 2020.

SUMMARY

1a Competition policy in most countries recognises that monopolies, mergers and restrictive practices can bring both costs and benefits to the consumer. Generally, though, restrictive practices tend to be more damaging to consumers' interests than simple monopoly power or mergers.

1b European Union legislation applies to firms trading between EU countries. Article 101 applies to restrictive practices. Article 102 applies to dominant firms. There are also separate merger control provisions.

1c UK legislation is largely covered by the 1998 Competition Act and 2002 Enterprise Act. The Chapter I prohibition of the 1998 Act applies to restrictive practices and is similar to Article 101. The Chapter II prohibition applies to dominant firms and is similar to Article 102. The 2002 Act made certain cartel agreements a criminal offence and required mergers over a certain size to be investigated by the Office of Fair Trading with possible reference to the Competition Commission. Both the OFT and CC were made independent of government. In 2011, the government announced proposals to merge the OFT and CC to create the Competition and Markets Authority.

1d The focus of both EU and UK legislation is on anti-competitive practices rather than on the simple existence of agreements between firms or market dominance. Practices that are found after investigation to be detrimental to competition are prohibited and heavy fines can be imposed, even for a first offence. Since 2008 the EU has operated a streamlined settlement procedure for firms suspected of operating in cartels. Cooperation results in fines being reduced and firms acting as 'whistle-blowers' can receive immunity from fines.

2a The importance of technology in determining national economic success is growing. There is now a need for government to formulate a technology policy to ensure that the national economy has every chance to remain competitive.

2b Technological change, when left to the market, is unlikely to proceed rapidly enough or to a socially desirable level. Reasons for this include R&D free riders, monopolistic market structures, duplication of R&D activities, and risk and uncertainty.

2c Government technology policy might involve intervention at different levels of the technology process (invention, innovation and diffusion). Such intervention might involve extending ownership rights over new products, providing R&D directly or using subsidies to encourage third parties. Government might also act in an advisory/coordinating capacity.

2d Technology policy in the UK has tended to emphasise the market as the principal provider of technological change. Where possible, government's role has been kept to a minimum. Within the EU, policy has been more interventionist and a wide range of initiatives have been launched to encourage greater levels of R&D.

3a A well-trained workforce contributes to economic performance by enhancing productivity, encouraging and enabling change and, in respect to supplying scarce skills to the workplace, helps to reduce wage costs.

3b Training policy in the UK has largely been the responsibility of industry. The result has been a less than optimum amount of training. In other countries, such as Germany, the state plays a far greater role in training provision. Since 1979 training and education policy in the UK has become increasingly vocational. The number of apprenticeships has grown particularly strongly in recent years.

REVIEW QUESTIONS

1 Try to formulate a definition of the public interest.

2 What are the advantages and disadvantages of the current system of controlling restrictive practices?

3 What problems are likely to arise in identifying which firms' practices are anti-competitive? Should regulators take firms' assurances into account when deciding whether to grant an exemption?

4 If anti-monopoly legislation is effective enough, is there ever any need to prevent mergers from going ahead?

5 If two or more firms were charging similar prices, what types of evidence would you look for to prove that this was collusion rather than mere coincidence?

6 Should governments or regulators always attempt to eliminate the supernormal profits of monopolists/oligopolists?

7 We can distinguish three clear stages in the development and application of technology: invention, innovation and diffusion. How might forms of technology policy intervention change at each stage of this process?

8 Governments and educationalists generally regard it as desirable that trainees acquire transferable skills. Why may many employers disagree?

9 There are externalities (benefits) when employers provide training. What externalities are there from the undergoing of training by the individual? Do they imply that individuals will choose to receive more or less than the socially optimal amount of training?

Government and the market

In the previous chapter we considered examples of the relationship between the government and the individual firm. In this chapter we turn to examine government policy at the level of the whole market. Although such policies are generally directed at a whole industry or sector, they nevertheless still affect individual businesses, and indeed the effects may well vary from one firm to another.

22.1 ENVIRONMENTAL POLICY

Growing concerns over global warming, industrial and domestic waste, traffic fumes and other forms of pollution have made the protection of the environment a major political and economic issue. The subject of environmental degradation lies clearly within the realm of economics, since it is a direct consequence of production and consumption decisions. So how can economic analysis help us to understand the nature of the problem and design effective policies for sustainable development? What will be the impact of such policies on business?

The environment and production

We considered (see section 20.2) how pollution could be classified as a 'negative externality' of production or consumption. In the case of production, this means that the marginal social costs (MSC) are greater than the marginal

private costs (MC) to the polluter. The failure of the market system to equate MSC and marginal social benefit (MSB) is due to the lack of property rights of those suffering the pollution. The fact that no charge is levied on the producer for use of the air or rivers means that the environment is effectively a free good, and as such is overused.

In order to ensure that the environment is taken sufficiently into account by both firms and consumers, the government must intervene. It must devise an appropriate **environmental policy**. Such a policy will involve measures

Definition

Environmental policy Initiatives by government to ensure a specified minimum level of environmental quality.

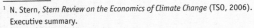

BOX 22.1 A STERN REBUKE ABOUT CLIMATE CHANGE INACTION

It's cheaper to act now

The analysis of global warming is not just for climate scientists. Economists have a major part to play in examining its causes and consequences and the possible solutions. And these solutions are likely to have a major impact on business.

Perhaps the most influential study of climate change in recent times has been the Stern Review. This was an independent review, commissioned by the UK Chancellor of the Exchequer, and headed by Sir Nicholas Stern, head of the Government Economic Service and former chief economist of the World Bank. Here was an economist using the methods of economics to analyse perhaps the most serious problem facing the world.

> Climate change presents a unique challenge for economics: it is the greatest and widest-ranging market failure ever seen. The economic analysis must therefore be global, deal with long time horizons, have the economics of risk and uncertainty at centre stage, and examine the possibility of major, non-marginal change. To meet these requirements, the Review draws on ideas and techniques from most of the important areas of economics, including many recent advances.[1]

First the bad news . . .

According to the Stern Report, if no action is taken, global temperatures will rise by some 2–3°C within the next fifty years. As a result the world economy will shrink by up to 20 per cent – and that would be just the average. The economies of the countries most seriously affected by floods, drought and crop failure could shrink by considerably more. These tend to be the poorest countries, least able to bear the costs of these changes.

Rising sea levels could displace some 200 million people; droughts could create tens or even hundreds of millions of 'climate refugees'. 'Ecosystems will be particularly vulnerable to climate change, with around 15–40 per cent of species potentially facing extinction after only 2°C of warming.'[2]

Then the good news . . .

If action is taken now, these consequences could be averted – and at relatively low cost. According to the Stern Report, a sacrifice of just 1 per cent of global GDP (global income) could, if correctly targeted, be enough to stabilise greenhouse gases to an equivalent of 500–550 ppm of CO_2 – a level generally considered to be sustainable. To achieve this, action would need to be taken to cut emissions from their various sources (see the chart). This would involve a mixture of four things:

---
[1] N. Stern, *Stern Review on the Economics of Climate Change* (TSO, 2006). Executive summary.
[2] Ibid.

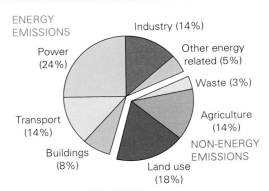

Greenhouse gas emissions in 2000, by source

Total emissions in 2000: 42 GtCO₂e.

Energy emissions are mostly CO_2 (some non-CO_2 in industry and other energy related).

Non-energy emissions are CO_2 (land use) and non-CO_2 (agriculture and waste).

Source: Stern Review on the Economics of Climate Change. Office of Climate Change (OCC) (Stem Review, 2006), Executive Summary, Figure 1 based on data drawn from World Resources Institute *Climate Analysis Indicators Tool* (CAIT) on-line database version 3.0

- reducing consumer demand for emissions-intensive goods and services;
- increased efficiency, which can save both money and emissions;
- action on non-energy emissions, such as avoiding deforestation;
- switching to lower-carbon technologies for power, heat and transport.

What policies did Sir Nicholas recommend to achieve these four objectives? Essentially the answer is to alter incentives. This could involve taxing polluting activities; subsidising green alternatives, including the development of green technology; establishing a price for carbon through trading carbon (see section on tradable permits on pages 352–3) and regulating its production; and encouraging behavioural change through education, better labelling of products, imposing minimum standards for building and encouraging public debate.

We consider some of these alternatives in this chapter.

1. *Would it be in the interests of a business to reduce its carbon emissions if this involved an increase in costs.*
2. *How is the concept of 'opportunity cost' relevant in analysing the impact of business decisions on the environment?*

---

to ensure that at least a specified minimum level of environmental quality is achieved. Ideally, however, the policy would ensure that all externalities are fully 'internalised'. This means that firms and consumers are forced to pay the *full* costs of production or consumption: i.e. their marginal private costs *plus* any external costs.

Problems with policy intervention

Valuing the environment

The principal difficulty facing government in constructing its environmental policy is that of *valuing* the environment and hence of estimating the costs of its pollution. If policy

KI 8
p 38

is based upon the principle that the polluter pays, then an accurate assessment of pollution costs is vital if the policy is to establish a socially efficient level of production.

Three common methods used for valuing environmental damage are: the financial costs to *other* users; revealed preferences; and 'contingent valuation' (or stated preference).

The financial costs to other users. In this method, environmental costs are calculated by considering the financial costs imposed on other businesses or individuals by polluting activities. For example, if firm A feeds chemical waste into a local stream, then firm B, which is downstream and requires a clean water supply, may have to introduce a water purification process. The expense of this to firm B can be seen as an external cost of firm A.

The main problem with this method is that not all external costs entail a direct financial cost for the sufferers. Many external costs may therefore be overlooked.

Revealed preferences. If the direct financial costs of pollution are difficult to identify, let alone calculate, then an alternative approach to valuing the environment might be to consider how individuals or businesses change their *behaviour* in response to environmental changes. Such changes in behaviour frequently carry a financial cost, which makes calculation easier. For example, the building of a new superstore on a greenfield site overlooked by your house might cause you to move. Moving house entails a financial cost, including the loss in value of your property resulting from the opening of the store. Clearly, in such a case, by choosing to move you would be regarding the cost of moving to be less than the cost to you of the deterioration in your environment.

Contingency valuation. In this method, people likely to be affected are asked to evaluate the effect on them of any proposed change to their environment. In the case of the superstore, local residents might be asked how much they would be willing to pay in order for the development not to take place, or alternatively, how much they would need to be compensated if it were to take place.

The principal concern with this method is how reliable the answers are to the questionnaires. There are two major problems:

- *Ignorance.* People will not know just how much they will suffer *until* the project goes ahead.
- *Dishonesty.* People will tend to exaggerate the compensation they would need. After all, if compensation is actually going to be paid, people will want to get as much as possible. But even if it is not, the more people exaggerate the costs to them, the more likely it is that they can get the project stopped.

These problems can be lessened if people who have already experienced a similar project elsewhere are questioned. They are more knowledgeable and have less to gain from being dishonest.

Research on contingency valuation has focused heavily on the questioning process and how monetary values of costs and benefits might be accurately established. Of all the methods, contingency valuation has grown most in popularity over recent years, despite its limitations.

Other problems

As well as the problems of value, other aspects of environmental damage make policy making particularly difficult. These include the following:

- *Spatial issues.* The place where pollution is produced and the places where it is deposited may be geographically very far apart. Pollution crosses borders (e.g. acid rain) or can be global (e.g. greenhouse gases). In both cases, national policies might be of little value, especially if you are a receiver of others' pollution! In such circumstances, international agreements would be needed, and these can be very difficult to reach.
- *Temporal issues.* Environmental problems such as acid rain and the depletion of the ozone layer have been occurring over many decades. Thus the full effect of pollution on the environment may be identifiable only in the long term. As a consequence, policy initiatives are required to be forward looking and proactive, if the cumulative effects of pollution are to be avoided. Most policy tends to be reactive, however, dealing only with problems as they arise. In such cases, damage to the environment may have already been done.
- *Irreversibility issues.* Much environmental damage might be irreversible: once a species is extinct, for example, it cannot normally be reintroduced.

Environmental policy options

Environmental policy can take many forms. However, it is useful to put the different types of policy into three broad categories: market based, non-market based, and mixed. The most important market-based solution is to use taxes and subsidies. Non-market-based solutions usually involve imposing regulations and controls. The most important mixed system is that of tradable permits. Let us examine each of these three categories in turn.

Market-based environmental policy: taxation

Market-based solutions attempt to internalise the costs of the externality, and ensure that the polluter pays. The most common market-based approach to environmental policy is to impose indirect taxes on specific types of polluting activity, such as the use of carbon-based fuels. To achieve a socially efficient output, the rate of tax should be equal to the marginal external cost (see Figure 20.5 on page 317).

Taxes have the advantage of relating the size of the penalty to the amount of pollution. This means that there is continuous pressure to cut down on production or consumption of polluting products or activities in order to save tax.

Table 22.1 Types of environmental taxes and charges

Motor fuels
Leaded/unleaded
Diesel (quality differential)
Carbon/energy taxation
Sulphur tax
Other energy products
Carbon/energy tax
Sulphur tax or charge
NO_2 charge
Methane charge
Agricultural inputs
Fertilisers
Pesticides
Manure
Vehicle-related taxation
Sales tax depends on car size
Road tax depends on car size

Other goods
Batteries
Plastic carrier bags
Glass containers
Drink cans
Tyres
CFCs/halons
Disposable razors/cameras
Lubricant oil charge
Oil pollutant charge
Solvents
Waste disposal
Municipal waste charges
Waste-disposal charges
Hazardous waste charges
Landfill tax or charges
Duties on waste water

Air transport
Noise charges
Aviation fuels
Water
Water charges
Sewage charges
Water effluent charges
Manure charges
Direct tax provisions
Tax relief on green investment
Taxation on free company cars
Employer-paid commuting expenses taxable
Employer-paid parking expenses taxable
Commuter use of public transport tax deductible

One approach is to modify *existing* taxes. In most developed countries there are now higher taxes on high-emission cars.

Increasingly, however, countries are introducing *new* 'green' taxes in order to discourage pollution as goods are produced, consumed or disposed of. Table 22.1 shows the wide range of green taxes and charges used around the world and Figure 22.1 shows green tax revenues as a percentage of GDP in various countries. As you can see, they are higher than average in the Netherlands and the Scandinavian nations, reflecting the strength of their environmental

concerns. They are lowest in the USA. By far the largest green tax revenues come from fuel taxes. Fuel taxes are relatively high in the UK and so, therefore, are green tax revenues.

There are various problems with using taxes in the fight against pollution.

Identifying the socially efficient tax rate. It will be difficult to identify the marginal pollution cost of each firm, given that each one is likely to produce different amounts of pollutants for any given level of output. Even if two firms produce identical amounts of pollutants, the environmental damage

Figure 22.1 Green tax revenues as a percentage of GDP

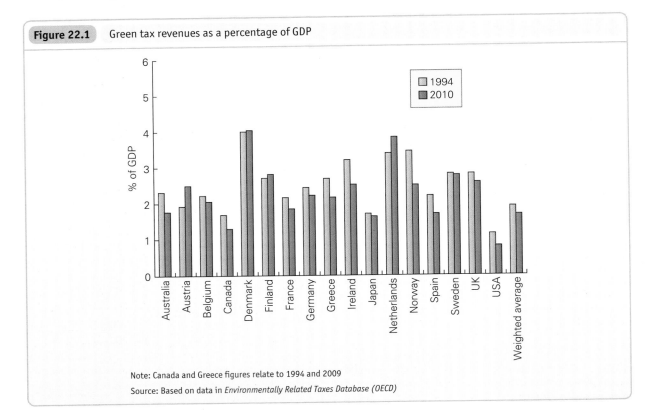

Note: Canada and Greece figures relate to 1994 and 2009

Source: Based on data in *Environmentally Related Taxes Database (OECD)*

might be quite different, because the ability of the environment to cope with it will differ between the two locations. Also, the number of people suffering will differ (a factor that is very important when considering the *human* impact of pollution). What is more, the harmful effects are likely to build up over time, and predicting these effects is fraught with difficulty.

 Problems of demand inelasticity. The less elastic the demand for the product, the less effective will a tax be in cutting production and hence in cutting pollution. Thus taxes on petrol would have to be very high indeed to make significant reductions in the consumption of petrol and hence significant reductions in the exhaust gases that contribute towards global warming and acid rain.

Redistributive effects. The poor spend a higher proportion of their income on domestic fuel than the rich. A 'carbon tax' on such fuel will, therefore, have the effect of redistributing incomes away from the poor. The poor also spend a larger proportion of their income on food than do the rich. Taxes on agriculture, designed to reduce intensive use of fertilisers and pesticides, will again tend to hit the poor proportionately more than the rich.

However, not all green taxes hit the poor more than the rich. The rich spend a higher proportion of their income on motoring than the poor. Thus petrol and other motoring taxes could help to reduce inequality.

Problems with international trade. If a country imposes pollution taxes on its industries, its products will become less competitive in world trade. To compensate for this, the industries may need to be given tax rebates for exports. Also taxes would need to be imposed on imports of competitors' products from countries where there is no equivalent green tax.

Evidence on the adverse effect of environmental taxes on a country's exports is inconclusive, however. Over the long term, in countries with high environmental taxes (or other tough environmental measures), firms will be stimulated to invest in low-pollution processes and products. This will later give such countries a competitive advantage if *other* countries then impose tougher environmental standards.

Effects on employment. Reduced output in the industries affected by green taxes will lead to a reduction in employment. If, however, the effect was to encourage investment in new cleaner technology, employment might not fall. Furthermore, employment opportunities could be generated elsewhere if the extra revenues from the green taxes were spent on alternative products, such as buses and trains rather than cars.

Non-market-based environmental policy: command-and-control systems (laws and regulations)

The traditional way of tackling pollution has been to set maximum permitted levels of emission or resource use, or minimum acceptable levels of environmental quality, and then to fine firms contravening these limits. Measures of this type are known as ***command-and-control (CAC) systems***. Clearly, there have to be inspectors to monitor the amount of pollution, and the fines have to be large enough to deter firms from exceeding the limit.

Virtually all countries have environmental regulations of one sort or another. For example, the EU has over 200 items of legislation covering areas such as air and water pollution, noise, the marketing and use of dangerous chemicals, waste management, the environmental impacts of new projects (such as power stations, roads and quarries), recycling, depletion of the ozone layer and global warming.

Typically there are three approaches to devising CAC systems.[1]

- ***Technology-based standards.*** The focus could be on the amount of pollution generated, irrespective of its environmental impact. As technology for reducing pollutants improves, so tougher standards could be imposed, based on the 'best available technology' (as long as the cost was not excessive). Thus car manufacturers could be required to ensure that new car engines meet lower CO_2 emission levels as the technology enabled them to do so.
- ***Ambient-based standards.*** Here the focus is on the environmental impact. For example, standards could be set for air or water purity. Depending on the location and the number of polluters in that area, a given standard would be achieved with different levels of discharge. If the object is a cleaner environment, then this approach is more efficient than technology-based standards.
- ***Social-impact standards.*** Here the focus is on the effect on people. Thus tougher standards would be imposed in densely populated areas. Whether this approach is more efficient than that of ambient-based standards depends on the approach to sustainability. If the objective is to achieve social efficiency, then human-impact standards

Definitions

Command-and-control (CAC) systems The use of laws or regulations backed up by inspections and penalties (such as fines) for non-compliance.

Technology-based standards Pollution control that requires firms' emissions to reflect the levels that could be achieved from using the best available pollution control technology.

Ambient-based standards Pollution control that requires firms to meet minimum standards for the environment (e.g. air or water quality).

Social-impact standards Pollution control that focuses on the effects on people (e.g. on health or happiness).

[1] See R. K. Turner, D. Pearce and I. Bateman, *Environmental Economics* (Harvester Wheatsheaf, 1994), p. 198.

are preferable. If the objective is to protect the environment for its own sake (a 'deeper green' approach), then ambient standards would be preferable.

Assessing CAC systems. Given the uncertainty over the environmental impacts of pollutants, especially over the longer term, it is often better to play safe and set tough emissions or ambient standards. These could always be relaxed at a later stage if the effects turn out not to be so damaging, but it might be too late to reverse damage if the effects turn out to be more serious. Taxes may be a more sophisticated means of reaching a socially efficient output, but CAC methods are usually more straightforward to devise, easier to understand by firms and easier to implement.

Where command-and-control systems are weak is that they fail to offer business any incentive to do better than the legally specified level. By contrast, with a pollution tax, the lower the pollution level, the less tax there will be to pay. There is thus a continuing incentive for businesses progressively to cut pollution levels and introduce cleaner technology.

Tradable permits

A policy measure that has grown in popularity in recent years is that of **tradable permits**. This is a combination of command-and-control and market-based systems. A maximum permitted level of emission is set for a given pollutant for a given factory, and the firm is given a permit to emit up to this amount. If it emits less than this amount, it is given a credit for the difference, which it can then use in another of its factories. Alternatively it can sell the credits. The firms buying them are then allowed to emit that amount *over* their permitted level. Thus the overall level of emissions is set by CAC methods, whereas their distribution is determined by the market.

Take the example of firms A and B, which are currently producing 12 units of a pollutant each. Now assume that a standard is set permitting them to produce only 10 units each. If firm A managed to reduce the pollutant to 8 units, it would be given a credit for 2 units. It could then sell this to firm B, enabling B to continue emitting 12 units. The effect would still be a total reduction of 4 units between the two firms. However, the trade in pollution allows pollution reduction to be concentrated where it can be achieved at

lowest cost. In our example, if it cost firm B more to reduce its pollution than firm A, then the permits could be sold from A to B at a price that was profitable to both (i.e. at a price above the cost of emission reduction to A, but below the cost of emission reduction to B).

> ### Pause for thought
>
> *To what extent will the introduction of tradable permits lead to a lower level of total pollution (as opposed to its redistribution)?*

The principle of tradable permits can be used as the basis of international agreements on pollution reduction. Each country could be required to achieve a certain percentage reduction in a pollutant (e.g. CO_2 or SO_2), but any country exceeding its reduction could sell its right to these emissions to other (presumably richer) countries.

A similar principle can be adopted for using natural resources. Thus fish quotas could be assigned to fishing boats or fleets or countries. Any parts of these quotas not used could then be sold.

How are the permitted pollution levels (or fish quotas) to be decided? The way that seems to be the most acceptable is to base them on firms' *current* levels, with any subsequent reduction in total permitted pollution being achieved by requiring firms to reduce their emissions by the *same* percentage. This approach is known as **grandfathering**. The main problem with this approach is that it could be seen as unfair by those firms that are already using cleaner technology. Why should they be required to make the same reductions as firms using dirty technology?

The EU carbon trading system. In the EU, a carbon Emissions Trading Scheme (ETS) started in January 2005 as part of the EU's approach to meeting its targets under the Kyoto Treaty. This is known as a 'cap and trade' scheme. It operates across the 27 EU member states and also Iceland, Norway and Liechtenstein.

The first phase of the scheme ran from January 2005 until December 2007. Around 12 000 industrial plants were allocated CO_2 emissions allowances, or credits, by their respective governments. These installations were collectively responsible for around 40 per cent of the EU's CO_2 emissions each year. Companies that exceeded their limits could purchase credits to cover the difference, while those that reduced their emissions were able to sell their surplus credits for a profit. Companies were able to trade directly with each other or via brokers operating throughout Europe.

At the end of December 2007 all existing allowances became invalid and the second Trading Period began, to last until the end of 2012. Although this was run under the same general principles as Trading Period 1, it also allowed companies to offset emissions in the EU against emission reductions they achieved in countries outside the EU.

> ### Definitions
>
> **Tradable permits** Each firm is given a permit to produce a given level of pollution. If less than the permitted amount is produced, the firm is given a credit. This can then be sold to another firm, allowing it to exceed its original limit.
>
> **Grandfathering** Where each firm's emission permit is based on its *current* levels of emission (e.g. permitted levels for all firms could be 80 per cent of their current levels).

In January 2008 the European Commission published proposals for ETS Phase III, to run from 2013 to 2020. The long lead-in time ensured that all involved would be aware of proposed changes to the system and thus could adapt strategies and processes in anticipation. These changes included a move to a centralised allocation of allowances rather than an allocation by national governments, and from a free allocation of allowances to one where, by the end of the period, all allowances would be auctioned. Furthermore, the period should see the inclusion of other greenhouse gases in addition to CO_2.

KI 22
p 165

Assessing the system of tradable permits. The main advantage of tradable permits is that they combine the simplicity of CAC methods with the benefits of achieving pollution reduction in the most efficient way. There is also the advantage that firms have a financial incentive to cut pollution. This might then make it easier for governments to impose tougher standards (i.e. impose lower permitted levels of emission).

> ### Pause for thought
>
> *What determines the size of the administrative costs of a system of tradable permits? For what reasons might green taxes be cheaper to administer than a system of tradable permits?*

There are, however, various general problems with tradable permits. One is how to distribute the permissions in a way that all firms and indeed countries regard as fair. The system could be seen by participants as inequitable if some countries set tough targets while others set more generous limits and if pollution is concentrated in certain geographical areas or certain industries. As we have seen, the EU system is addressing this in Phase III through the removal of national allocation plans. From 2013 there will be a single, EU-wide cap. This is to be at a level which will result in a 21 per cent reduction in total emissions between 2005 and 2020 in the sectors covered by the scheme.

The system will lead to significant cuts in pollution only if the permitted levels are low. Once the system is in place, the government might then feel that the pressure to *reduce* the permitted levels is off. This was a major criticism of the first trading period of the EU's ETS from 2005 to 2007. Emissions allowances were relatively generous. As a result many firms found it easy to produce surplus credits, which pushed their price to a low level, reaching a minuscule €0.02 per tonne by the end of 2007. This, in turn, made it cheap for 'dirty' firms to buy credits and thus reduced the pressure on them to cut pollution. In answer to this, the allowances were tightened in the second trading period (2008–12). Until the global downturn of 2009 depressed activity and hence pollution levels, the tightening of allowances saw emission prices rise. By mid-2008, carbon was trading at around €28 per tonne.

Environmental policy in the UK and EU

UK policy

In the UK, current policy is embodied in the 1990 Environmental Protection Act, the 1995 Environment Act (which set up the Environment Agency), the 2003 Waste and Emissions Trading Act and the 2005 Neighbourhoods and Environment Act. The Acts are an attempt to establish an integrated pollution control strategy. This has been the approach in other European countries, notably the Netherlands.

Following a number of energy White Papers and Reviews, the UK government introduced the Climate Change and Sustainable Energy Act and Climate Change Programme in 2006. This obliged government to report to Parliament on greenhouse gas emissions and measures taken to reduce these emissions.

In 2008 the Climate Change Act established legally binding targets on the UK to achieve reductions in greenhouse gases of at least 80 per cent by 2050 on 1990 levels, and a 26 per cent reduction in carbon dioxide emissions by 2020. This will be achieved through carbon budgets which will set caps on emissions affecting all businesses, including shipping and aviation. There is also scope within the Act for the government to introduce local emission trading schemes if required and powers to provide financial incentives to reduce household waste in England. The UK is the first country to establish a long-range carbon reduction target in law.

EU policy

A major plank of EU environmental policy is its carbon trading scheme. The broader framework for environmental policy has typically been detailed in EU Environment Action Programmes. There have been a series of such programmes since 1973. The Sixth Programme was designed to run from 2002 to 2012. The programme identifies four main areas to which environmental policy should be directed: climate change; nature and biodiversity; environment and health and quality of life; and sustainable use and management of natural resources and waste.

The Sixth Programme advocates the use of various policy instruments, such as legislation, inspection, taxation and information. The choice of instrument should be one that tackles the problem at source and is both efficient and effective. The programme identified 156 areas where action was needed and these were delivered by 2007. However, while the policy framework was in place, the 2007 Environmental Policy Review revealed that implementation was often slow and incomplete, often because of resistance from member states.

At the time of writing, the details of a seventh environmental action programme remain under discussion, illustrating the difficulties that policy-makers often face in balancing the interests of different stakeholders with different priorities.

22.2 TRANSPORT POLICY

Traffic congestion is a challenge for all nations, particularly in the large cities and at certain peak times. This problem has become more acute as our lives have become increasingly dominated by the motor car. Sitting in a traffic jam is both time wasting and frustrating. It adds considerably to the costs and stress of modern living.

And it is not only the motorist that suffers. Congested streets make life less pleasant for the pedestrian, and increased traffic leads to increased accidents. What is more, the inexorable growth of traffic has led to significant problems of pollution. Traffic is noisy and car fumes are unpleasant and lead to substantial environmental damage.

Between 1950 and 2010 road traffic in Great Britain rose by 529 per cent, whereas the length of public roads rose by only 33 per cent (albeit some roads were widened). Most passenger and freight transport is by road. In 2010, 91 per cent of passenger kilometres and 68 per cent of domestic freight tonnage kilometres in Great Britain were by road, whereas rail accounted for a mere 8 per cent of passenger traffic and 9 per cent of freight tonnage. Of road passenger kilometres, 92 per cent was by car in 2010, and, as Table 22.2 shows, this proportion has been growing. In 2010, motoring costs amounted to some 14 per cent of average weekly household expenditure.

But should the government do anything about the problem? Is traffic congestion a price worth paying for the benefits we gain from using cars? Or are there things that can be done to ease the problem without greatly inconveniencing the traveller?

The existing system of allocating road space

The allocation of road space depends on both demand and supply. Demand is by individuals who base their decisions on largely private considerations. Supply, by contrast, is usually by the central government or local authorities. Let us examine each in turn.

Demand for road space (by car users)

The demand for road space can be seen largely as a *derived* demand. What people want is not the car journey for its own sake, but to get to their destination. The greater the benefit they gain at their destination, the greater the benefit they gain from using their car to get there.

The demand for road space, like the demand for other goods and services, has a number of determinants. If congestion is to be reduced, it is important to know how responsive demand is to a change in any of these: it is important to consider the various elasticities of demand.

Price. This is the *marginal cost* to the motorist of a journey. It includes petrol, oil, maintenance, depreciation and any toll charges.

The price elasticity of demand for motoring tends to be relatively low. There can thus be a substantial rise in the price of petrol and there will be only a modest fall in traffic.

Recent estimates of the short-run price elasticity of demand for road fuel in industrialised countries typically range from −0.15 to −0.28. Long-run elasticities are somewhat higher, but are still generally inelastic.[2] The low price elasticity of demand suggests that any schemes to tackle traffic congestion that merely involve raising the costs of motoring will have only limited success.

Income. The demand for road space also depends on people's income. As incomes rise, so car ownership and hence car usage increase substantially. Demand is elastic with respect to income. Figure 22.2 shows the increase in car ownership in various countries.

Price of substitutes. If bus and train fares came down, people might switch from travelling by car. The cross-price elasticity is likely to be relatively low, however, given that most people regard these alternatives as a poor substitute for

---

[2] *See Environmentally Related Taxes in OECD Countries: Issues and Strategies* (OECD, 2001), pp. 99–103.

Table 22.2	Passenger transport in Great Britain: percentage of passenger kilometres by mode of transport					
Year	**Cars**	**Motor cycles**	**Buses and coaches**	**Bicycles**	**Rail**	**Air**
1960	49	4	28	4	14	0.3
1970	74	2	15	1	9	0.5
1980	79	1	11	1	7	0.5
1990	85	1	7	1	6	0.8
2000	85	1	6	1	6	1.0
2010	84	1	6	1	8	1.0

Source: *Transport Statistics Great Britain 2011* (Department for Transport, National Statistics 2011). Contains public sector information licensed under the Open Government Licence (OGL) v1.0. http://www.nationalarchives.gov.uk/doc/open-government-licence

Figure 22.2 Increase in car ownership in various European countries

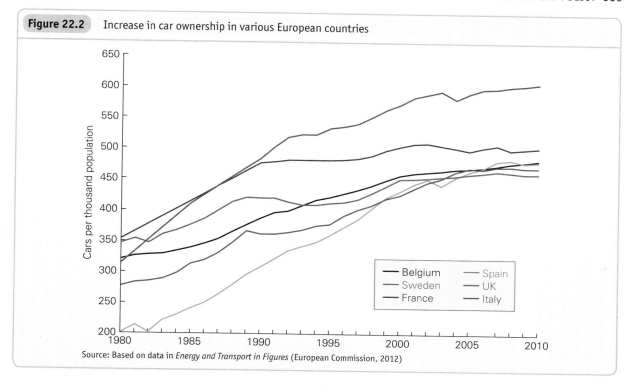

Source: Based on data in *Energy and Transport in Figures* (European Commission, 2012)

travelling in their own car. Cars are seen as more comfortable and convenient.

Price of complements. Demand for road space will depend on the price of cars. The higher the price of cars, the fewer people will own cars and thus the fewer will be the cars on the road.

Pause for thought

Go through each of the determinants we have identified so far and show how the respective elasticity of demand makes the problem of traffic congestion difficult to tackle.

Demand will also depend on the price of complementary services, such as parking. A rise in car parking charges will reduce the demand for car journeys. But here again the cross-elasticity is likely to be relatively low. In most cases, the motorist will either pay the higher charge or park elsewhere, such as in side streets.

Tastes/utility. Another factor explaining the preference of many people for travelling by car is the pleasure they gain from it compared with alternative modes of transport. Car ownership is regarded by many people as highly desirable, and once accustomed to travelling in their own car, most people are highly reluctant to give it up.

One important feature of the demand for road space is that it fluctuates. There will be periods of peak demand, such as during the rush hour or at holiday weekends. At

such times, roads can get totally jammed. At other times, however, the same roads may be virtually empty.

Supply of road space

The supply of road space can be examined in two contexts: the short run and the long run.

The short run. In the short run, the supply of road space is constant. When there is no congestion, supply is more than enough to satisfy demand. There is spare road capacity. At times of congestion, however, there is pressure on this fixed supply. Maximum supply for any given road is reached at the point where there is the maximum flow of vehicles per minute along the road.

The long run. In the long run, the authorities can build new roads or improve existing ones. This will require an assessment of the costs and benefits of such schemes.

Identifying a socially efficient level of road usage (short run)

The existing system of *government* provision of roads and *private* ownership of cars is unlikely to lead to an optimum allocation of road space. So how do we set about identifying just what the social optimum is?

In the short run, the supply of road space is fixed. The question of the short-run optimum allocation of road space, therefore, is one of the optimum usage of existing road space. It is a question of *consumption* rather than supply. For this reason we must focus on the road user, rather than on road provision.

A socially efficient level of consumption occurs where the marginal social benefit of consumption equals its marginal social cost ($MSB = MSC$). So what are the marginal social benefits and costs of using a car?

Marginal social benefit of road usage

Marginal social benefit equals marginal private benefit plus externalities.

Marginal private benefit is the direct benefit to the car user and is reflected in the demand for car journeys, the determinants of which we examined above. External benefits are few. The one major exception occurs when drivers give lifts to other people.

Marginal social cost of road usage

Marginal social cost equals marginal private cost plus externalities.

Marginal private costs to the motorist were identified when we looked at demand. They include the costs of petrol, wear and tear, and tolls. They also include the time costs of travel.

There may also be substantial external costs. These include the following.

Congestion costs: time. When a person uses a car on a congested road, it will add to the congestion. This will therefore slow down the traffic even more and increase the journey time of *other* car users.

Congestion costs: monetary. Congestion increases fuel consumption, and the stopping and starting increases the costs of wear and tear. So when a motorist adds to congestion, there will be additional monetary costs imposed on other motorists.

Environmental costs. When motorists use a road, they reduce the quality of the environment for others. Cars emit fumes and create noise. This is bad enough for pedestrians and other car users, but can be particularly distressing for people living along the road. Driving can cause accidents, a problem that increases as drivers become more impatient as a result of delays.

The socially efficient level of road usage

The optimum level of road use is where the marginal social benefit is equal to the marginal social cost. In Figure 22.3 costs and benefits are shown on the vertical axis and are measured in money terms. Thus any non-monetary costs or benefits (such as time costs) must be given a monetary value. The horizontal axis measures road usage in terms of cars per minute passing a specified point on the road.

For simplicity it is assumed that there are no external benefits from car use and that therefore marginal private and marginal social benefits are the same. The MSB curve is shown as downward sloping. The reason for this is that different road users put a different value on this particular journey. If the marginal (private) cost of making the journey were high, only those for whom the journey had a high

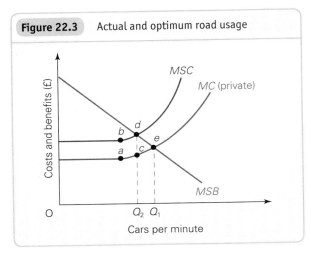

Figure 22.3   Actual and optimum road usage

marginal benefit would travel along the road. If the marginal cost of making the journey fell, more people would make the journey: people would choose to make the journey at the point at which the marginal cost of using their car had fallen to the level of their marginal benefit. Thus, the greater the number of cars, the lower the marginal benefit.

The marginal (private) cost curve (MC) is likely to be constant up to the level of traffic flow at which congestion begins to occur. This is shown as point *a* in Figure 22.3. Beyond this point, marginal cost is likely to rise as time costs increase and as fuel consumption rises.

The marginal *social* cost curve (MSC) is drawn above the marginal private cost curve. The vertical difference between the two represents the external costs. Up to point *b*, external costs are simply the environmental costs. Beyond point *b*, there are also external congestion costs, since additional road users slow down the journey of *other* road users. These external costs get progressively greater as the level of traffic increases.

The actual level of traffic flow will be at Q_1, where marginal private costs and benefits are equal (point *e*). The socially efficient level of traffic flow, however, will be at the lower level of Q_2, where marginal social costs and benefits are equal (point *d*). In other words, the existing system of allocating road space is likely to lead to an excessive level of road usage.

Identifying a socially optimum level of road space (long run)

In the long run, the supply of road space is not fixed. The authorities must therefore assess what new road schemes (if any) to adopt. This will involve the use of some form of *cost–benefit analysis*.

> ### Definition
>
> **Cost–benefit analysis** The identification, measurement and weighing-up of the costs and benefits of a project in order to decide whether or not it should go ahead.

The socially efficient level of construction will be where the marginal social benefit from construction is equal to the marginal social cost. This means that schemes should be adopted as long as their marginal social benefit exceeds their marginal social cost. But how are these costs and benefits assessed in practice? Case study H.15 in MyEconLab examines the procedure used in the UK.

We now turn to look at different solutions to traffic congestion. These can be grouped into three broad types.

Solution 1: direct provision (supply-side solutions)

The road solution

One obvious solution to traffic congestion is to build more roads. At first sight this may seem an optimum strategy, provided the costs and benefits of road-building schemes are carefully assessed and only those schemes where the benefits exceed the costs are adopted.

However, there are serious problems with this approach.

The objective of equity. The first problem concerns that of *equity*. After all, social efficiency is not the only possible economic objective. For example, when an urban motorway is built, those living beside it will suffer from noise and fumes. Motorway users gain, but the local residents lose. The question is whether this is fair.

The more the government tries to appeal to the car user by building more and better roads, the fewer will be the people who use public transport, and thus the more will public transport decline. Those without cars lose, and these tend to be from the most vulnerable groups – the poor, the elderly, children and the disabled.

Congestion may not be solved. Increasing the amount of road space may encourage more people to use cars. A good example is the London orbital motorway, the M25. In planning the motorway, not only did the government underestimate the general rate of traffic growth, but it also underestimated the direct effect it would have on encouraging people to use the motorway rather than some alternative route, or some alternative means of transport, or even not making the journey at all. It also underestimated the effect it would have on encouraging people to live further from their place of work and to commute along the motorway. The result is that there is now serious congestion on the M25.

Thus new roads may simply generate extra traffic, with little overall effect on congestion.

The environmental impact of new roads. New roads lead to loss of agricultural land, the destruction of many natural habitats, noise, the splitting of communities and disruption to local residents. To the extent that they encourage a growth in traffic, they add to atmospheric pollution and a depletion of oil reserves.

Government or local authority provision of public transport

An alternative supply-side solution is to increase the provision of public transport. If, for example, a local authority ran a local bus service and decided to invest in additional buses, open up new routes, including park-and-ride, and operate a low-fare policy, these services might encourage people to switch from using their cars.

To be effective, this would have to be an attractive alternative. Many people would switch only if the buses were frequent, cheap, comfortable and reliable, and if there were enough routes to take people close to where they wanted to go.

Solution 2: regulation and legislation

An alternative strategy is to restrict car use by various forms of regulation and legislation.

Restricting car access

One approach involves reducing car access to areas that are subject to high levels of congestion. The following measures are widely used: bus and cycle lanes, no entry to side streets, 'high-occupancy vehicle lanes' (confined to cars with one or more passengers) and pedestrian-only areas.

However, there is a serious problem with these measures. They tend not to solve the problem of congestion, but merely to divert it. Bus lanes tend to make the car lanes more congested; no entry to side streets tends to make the main roads more congested; and pedestrian-only areas often make the roads round these areas more congested.

Parking restrictions

An alternative to restricting road access is to restrict parking. If cars are not allowed to park along congested streets, this will improve the traffic flow. Also, if parking is difficult, this will discourage people from using their cars to come into city centres. The problems with this solution include:

- possibly increased congestion as people drive round and round looking for parking spaces;
- illegal parking;
- parking down side streets, causing a nuisance for local residents.

Solution 3: changing market signals

The solution favoured by many economists is to use the price mechanism. As we have seen, one of the causes of traffic congestion is that road users do not pay the full marginal social costs of using the roads. If they could be forced to do so, a social optimum usage of road space could be achieved.

In Figure 22.3 this would involve imposing a charge on motorists of $d - c$. By 'internalising' the congestion and environmental externalities in this way, traffic flow will be reduced to the social optimum of Q_2.

So how can these external costs be charged to the motorist? There are several possible ways.

Extending existing taxes

Three major types of tax are levied on the motorist: fuel tax, taxes on new cars and car licences. Could increasing these taxes lead to the optimum level of road use being achieved?

Increasing the rates of new car tax and car licences may have some effect on reducing the total level of car ownership, but will probably have little effect on car use. The problem is that these taxes do not increase the marginal cost of car use. They are fixed costs. Once you have paid these taxes, there is no extra to pay for each extra journey you make. They do not discourage you from using your car.

Unlike the other two, fuel taxes are a marginal cost of car use. The more you use your car, the more fuel you use and the more fuel tax you pay. They are also mildly related to the level of congestion, since fuel consumption tends to increase as congestion increases. Nevertheless, they are not ideal. The problem is that all motorists would pay an increase in fuel tax, even those travelling on uncongested roads. To have a significant effect on congestion, there would have to be a very large increase in fuel taxes and this would be very unfair on those who are not causing congestion, especially those who have to travel long distances. There is also a political problem. Most motorists regard fuel taxes as too high and would resent paying higher rates.

Pause for thought

Would a tax on car tyres be a good way of restricting car usage?

Road pricing

Charging people for using roads is a direct means of achieving an efficient use of road space. The higher the congestion, the higher should be the charge.

Area charges. One simple and practical means of charging people to use congested streets is the area charge. People would have to pay (normally by the day) for using their car in a city centre. Earlier versions of this scheme involved people having to purchase and display a ticket on their car, rather like a 'pay-and-display' parking system.

More recently, electronic versions have been developed. The London Congestion Charge is an example. Car drivers must pay £10 per day to enter the inner London area (or 'congestion zone') any time between 7.00 and 18.00, Monday to Friday. Payment can be made by various means, including post, Internet, telephone, text message, and at various shops and petrol stations. Payment can be in advance or up to midnight on the day of travel, or up to midnight the next day for an extra £2. Alternatively, owners can register for auto-pay (for an annual fee of £10), being billed in arrears for all charges and receiving a £1 per day discount.

Cars entering the congestion zone have their number plate recorded by camera and a computer check then leads to a fine of £120 being sent to those who have not paid.

The London congestion charging system has reduced traffic in the zone by nearly 20 per cent and has significantly increased the rate of traffic flow. The charge is not a marginal one, however, in the sense that it does not vary with the degree of congestion or the amount of time spent or distance travelled by a motorist within the zone. This is an intrinsic problem of area charges. Nevertheless, their simplicity makes the system easy to understand and relatively cheap to operate.

The London system does not address pollution directly. However, the original scheme did exempt electric (or petrol–electric hybrid) cars, and those fuelled by natural gas or LPG, from paying the charge under an 'alternative fuel discount'. The alternative fuel discount was subsequently replaced by a 'greener vehicle discount' exempting cars that emit 100 g/km of CO_2 or less. This approach recognises that new technologies are likely to result in continual improvements in emissions, even of cars fuelled by petrol. The scheme is to be kept under review, to ensure that both the congestion and environmental benefits are being maintained.

Variable electronic road pricing. The scheme most favoured by many economists and traffic planners is that of variable electronic road pricing. It is the scheme that can most directly relate the price that the motorist is charged to the specific level of marginal social cost. The greater the congestion, the greater the charge imposed on the motorist. Ideally, the charge would be equal to the marginal congestion cost plus any marginal environmental costs additional to those created on non-charged roads.

Various systems have been adopted in various parts of the world, or are under consideration. One involves devices in the road which record the number plates of cars as they pass; alternatively cars must be fitted with sensors. A charge is registered to that car on a central computer. The car owner then receives a bill at periodic intervals, in much the same way as a telephone bill. Several cities around the world are already operating such schemes, including Barcelona, Dallas, Orlando, Lisbon, Oklahoma City and Oslo.

Another system involves having a device installed in the car into which a 'smart card' (like a telephone or photocopying card) is inserted. The cards have to be purchased and contain a certain number of units. Beacons or overhead gantries automatically deduct units from the smart cards at times of congestion. If the card is empty, the number of the car is recorded and the driver fined. Such a system was introduced in 1997 on Stockholm's ring road, and in 1998 in Singapore (see Box 22.2).

With both these types, the rate can easily be varied electronically according to the level of congestion (and pollution too). The rates could be in bands and the current bands displayed by the roadside and/or broadcast on local radio so that motorists knew what they were being charged.

BOX 22.2 ROAD PRICING IN SINGAPORE

Part of an integrated transport policy

It takes only one hour to drive from one end of Singapore to the other. Yet the average Singaporean driver travels an estimated 18 600 km per year, only slightly less than the average US driver, and over 50 per cent more than the average Japanese driver. In 2012 there were estimated to be 594 000 passenger cars in use on Singapore's 3400 kilometres of roads. Yet, despite this, the average car speed on main roads during peak hours is estimated to be as high as 27 km/h. Part of the reason is that it has an integrated transport policy. This includes the following:

- Restricting the number of new car licences, and allowing their price to rise to the corresponding equilibrium. This makes cars in Singapore among the most expensive in the world.
- A 130-kilometre-long mass rail transit (MRT) system with subsidised fares. Trains are comfortable, clean and frequent. Stations are air-conditioned.
- A programme of building new estates near MRT stations.
- Cheap, frequent buses, serving all parts of the island.

But it is in respect to road usage that the Singaporean authorities have been most innovative.

The first innovation came in 1975. The city centre was made a restricted zone. Motorists who wished to enter this zone had to buy a ticket (an 'area licence') at any one of 33 entry points. Police were stationed at these entry points to check that cars had paid and displayed.

Then in 1990 a quota system for new cars was established. The government decides the total number of cars the country should have, and issues just enough licences each month to maintain that total. These licences (or 'Certificates of Entitlement') are for ten years and are offered at auction. Their market price varies from around £10 000 to £30 000.

A problem with the licences is that they are a once-and-for-all payment, which does not vary with the amount people use their car. In other words, their marginal cost (for additional miles driven) is zero. Many people feel that, having paid such a high price for their licence, they ought to use their car as much as possible in order to get value for money!

With traffic congestion steadily worsening, it was recognised that something more had to be done. Either the Area Licensing Scheme had to be widened, or some other form of charging had to be adopted. The decision was taken to introduce electronic road pricing (ERP). This alternative would not only save on police labour costs, but enable charge rates to be varied according to levels of congestion, times of the day, and locality.

What, then, would be the optimum charge? If the objective is to reduce traffic from Q_1 to Q_2 in Figure 22.3 on page 356, then a charge of $d - c$ should be levied.

Since 1998 all vehicles in Singapore have been fitted with an in-vehicle unit (IU). Every journey made requires the driver to insert a smart card into the IU. On specified roads, overhead gantries read the IU and deduct the appropriate charge from the card. If a car does not have sufficient funds on its smart card, the car's details are relayed to a control centre and a fine is imposed. The system has the benefit of operating on three-lane highways and does not require traffic to slow down.

The ERP system operates on Mondays to Fridays from 8 a.m. to 8.00 p.m. in the central area and from 7.30 a.m. to 9.30 a.m. on the expressways and outer ring roads, with charges varying every 5, 20 or 30 minutes within these times. Rates are published in advance but are reviewed every three months. The system is thus very flexible to allow traffic to be kept at the desired level.

The system was expensive to set up, however. Cheaper schemes have been adopted elsewhere, such as Norway and parts of the USA. These operate by funnelling traffic into a single lane in order to register the car, but they have the disadvantage of slowing the traffic down.

One message is clear from the Singapore solution. Road pricing alone is not enough. Unless there are fast, comfortable and affordable public transport alternatives, the demand for cars will be highly price inelastic. People have to get to work!

 Explain how, by varying the charge debited from the smart card according to the time of day or level of congestion, a socially optimal level of road use can be achieved.

The most sophisticated scheme, still under development, involves equipping all vehicles with a receiver. Their position is located by satellites, which then send this information to a dashboard unit that deducts charges according to location, distance travelled, time of day and type of vehicle. The charges can operate through either smart cards or central computerised billing. It is likely that such schemes would initially be confined to lorries.

Despite the enthusiasm for such schemes amongst economists, there are nevertheless various problems associated with them:

- Estimates of the level of external costs are difficult to make.

- Motorists will have to be informed in advance what the charges will be, so that they can plan the timing of their journeys.
- There may be political resistance. Politicians may therefore be reluctant to introduce road pricing for fear of losing popular support.
- If demand is relatively inelastic, the charges might have to be very high to have a significant effect on congestion.
- The costs of installing road-pricing equipment could be very high.
- If road pricing were introduced only in certain areas, shoppers and businesses would tend to move to areas without the charge.
- A new industry in electronic evasion may spring up!

Subsidising alternative means of transport

An alternative to charging for the use of cars is to subsidise the price of alternatives, such as buses and trains. But cheaper fares alone may not be enough. The government may also have to invest directly in or subsidise an *improved* public transport service: more frequent services, more routes, more comfortable buses and trains.

Subsidising public transport need not be seen as an alternative to road pricing: it can be seen as complementary. If road pricing is to persuade people not to travel by car, the alternatives must be attractive. Unless public transport can be made to be seen by the traveller as a close substitute for cars, the elasticity of demand for car use is likely to remain low.

Subsidising public transport can also be justified on grounds of equity. It benefits poorer members of society who cannot afford to travel by car.

It is unlikely that any one policy can provide the complete solution. Certain policies or combinations of policies are better suited to some situations than others. It is important for governments to learn from experiences both within their own country and in others, in order to find the optimum solution to each specific problem.

22.3 PRIVATISATION AND REGULATION

One solution to market failure, advocated by some on the political left, is nationalisation. If industries are not being run in the public interest by the private sector, then bring them into public ownership. This way, so the argument goes, the market failures can be corrected. Problems of monopoly power, externalities, inequality, etc. can be dealt with directly if these industries are run with the public interest, rather than private gain, at heart.

In the late 1940s and early 1950s the Labour government of the time nationalised many of the key transport, communications and power industries, such as the railways, freight transport, airlines, coal, gas, electricity and steel.

From the early 1980s, however, the Conservative governments under Margaret Thatcher and John Major engaged in an extensive programme of 'privatisation', returning most of the **nationalised industries** in the UK to the private sector. Other countries have followed similar programmes of privatisation in what has become a worldwide phenomenon. Privatisation has been seen as a means of revitalising ailing industries and as a golden opportunity to raise revenues to ease budgetary problems.

The arguments for and against privatisation

The following are the major arguments that have been used for and against privatisation.

Arguments for privatisation

Market forces. The first argument is that privatisation will expose these industries to market forces, from which will flow the benefits of greater efficiency, faster growth and greater responsiveness to the wishes of the consumer.

If privatisation involved splitting an industry into competing companies, this greater competition in the goods market would force the companies to keep their costs as low as possible in order to stay in business.

Privatised companies do not have direct access to government finance. To finance investment they must now go to the market: they must issue shares or borrow from banks or other financial institutions. In doing so, they will be competing for funds with other companies, and thus must be seen as capable of using these funds profitably.

Market discipline will also be enforced by shareholders. Shareholders want a good return on their shares and will thus put pressure on the privatised company to perform well. If the company does not make sufficient profits, shareholders will sell their shares. The share price will fall, and the company will be in danger of being taken over. The market for corporate control (see page 170) thus provides incentives for firms to be efficient.

Reduced government interference. In nationalised industries, managers may frequently be required to adjust their targets for political reasons. At one time they may have to keep prices low as part of a government drive against inflation. At another they may have to raise their prices substantially in order to raise extra revenue for the government and help finance tax cuts. Privatisation frees the company from these constraints and allows it to make more rational economic decisions and plan future investments with greater certainty.

Financing tax cuts. The privatisation issue of shares directly earns money for the government and thus reduces the amount it needs to borrow. Effectively, then, the government can use the proceeds of privatisation to finance tax cuts. There is a danger here, however, that in order to raise the maximum revenue the government will want to make the industries as potentially profitable as possible. This may involve selling them as monopolies. But this, of course, would probably be against the interests of the consumer.

Definition

Nationalised industries State-owned industries that produce goods or services that are sold in the market.

Arguments against privatisation

Natural monopolies. The market forces argument for privatisation largely breaks down if a public monopoly is simply replaced by a private monopoly, as in the case of the water companies, each of which has a monopoly in its own area. Critics of privatisation argue that at least a public-sector monopoly is not out to maximise profits and thereby exploit the consumer.

The public interest. Will the questions of externalities and social justice not be ignored after privatisation? Critics of privatisation argue that only the most glaring examples of externalities and injustice can be taken into account, given that the whole ethos of a private company is different from that of a nationalised one: private profit rather than public service is the goal. Externalities, they argue, are extremely widespread and need to be taken into account by the industry itself and not just by an occasionally intervening government. A railway or an underground line, for example, may considerably ease congestion on the roads, thus benefiting road as well as rail users. Other industries may cause substantial external costs. Nuclear power stations may produce nuclear waste that is costly to dispose of safely, and/or provides hazards for future generations. Coal-fired power stations may pollute the atmosphere and cause acid rain.

In assessing these arguments, a lot depends on the toughness of government legislation and the attitudes and powers of regulatory agencies after privatisation.

> ### Pause for thought
>
> *To what extent can the problems with privatisation be seen as arguments in favour of nationalisation?*

Regulation

Identifying the short-run optimum price and output

Privatised industries, if left free to operate in the market, will have monopoly power; they will create externalities; and they will be unlikely to take into account questions of fairness. An answer to these problems is for the government or some independent agency to regulate their behaviour so that they produce at the socially optimum price and output. This has been the approach adopted for the major privatisations in the UK.

Regulation in practice

The behaviour of privatised industries is generally governed by the Competition and Enterprise Acts (see section 21.1) and overseen by a separate regulatory office and the Office of Fair Trading. Currently, the privatised utility regulators are as follows: the Office for Gas and Electricity Markets (Ofgem), the Office of Communications (Ofcom), the Office

of Rail Regulation (ORR) and the Office of Water Services (Ofwat).

As well as supervising the competitive behaviour of the privatised utility, they set terms under which the industries have to operate. For example, the ORR sets the terms under which rail companies have access to track and stations. The terms set by the regulator can be reviewed by negotiation between the regulator and the industry. If agreement cannot be reached, the Competition Commission acts as an appeal court and its decision is binding.

The regulator for each industry also sets limits to the prices that certain parts of the industry can charge. These parts are those where there is little or no competition: for example, the charges made to electricity and gas retailers by National Grid, the owner of the electricity grid and major gas pipelines.

The price-setting formulae are essentially of the '*RPI* minus X' variety. What this means is that the industries can raise their prices by the rate of increase in the retail price index (i.e. by the rate of inflation) *minus* a certain percentage (X) to take account of expected increases in efficiency. Thus if the rate of inflation were 6 per cent, and if the regulator considered that the industry (or firm) could be expected to reduce its costs by 2 per cent ($X = 2\%$), then price rises would be capped at 4 per cent. The *RPI* − *X* system is thus an example of **price-cap regulation**. The idea of this system of regulation is that it forces the industry to pass cost savings on to the consumer.

> ### Pause for thought
>
> *If an industry regulator adopts an RPI − X formula for price regulation, is it desirable that the value of X should be adjusted as soon as cost conditions change?*

Assessing the system of regulation in the UK

The system that has evolved in the UK has various advantages over that employed in the USA and elsewhere, where regulation often focuses on the level of *profits* (see Web Case H.17).

■ It is a discretionary system, with the regulator able to judge individual examples of the behaviour of the industry on their own merits. The regulator has a detailed knowledge of the industry which would not be available to government ministers or other bodies such as the Office of Fair Trading. The regulator could thus be argued to be the best person to decide on whether the industry is acting in the public interest.

> ### Definition
>
> **Price-cap regulation** Where the regulator puts a ceiling on the amount by which a firm can raise its price.

BOX 22.3 THE RIGHT TRACK TO REFORM?

Reorganising the railways in the UK

Few train routes across Europe are profitable and thus they have to be subsidised by governments. Such has been the strain placed upon public finances that European governments in recent years have been looking for ways of reforming their railways. The most radical approach has been adopted in the UK, which involved dividing up the rail system and privatising its various parts.

Privatisation of the rail system in the UK

The UK Conservative government in 1993 stated that the aim of rail privatisation was to 'improve the quality of rail services for the travelling public and for freight customers'. The 1993 Railways Act detailed the privatisation programme. The management of rail infrastructure, such as track, signalling and stations, was to be separated from the responsibility for running trains. There would be 25 passenger train operating companies (TOCs), each having a franchise lasting between seven and fifteen years. These companies would have few assets, being forced to rent track and lease stations from the infrastructure owner (Railtrack), and to lease trains and rolling stock from three new rolling-stock companies. There would be three freight companies, which would also pay Railtrack for the use of track and signalling. In practice, the 25 franchises were operated by just 11 companies (with one, National Express, having nine of the franchises).

Railtrack would be responsible for maintaining and improving the rail infrastructure, but rather than providing this itself, it would be required to purchase the necessary services from private contractors.

To oversee the new rail network, two new posts were created. The first was a rail franchising director, who would be responsible for specifying the length and cost of franchises, as well as for outlining passenger service requirements, including minimum train frequency, stations served and weekend provision. The second post created was that of the rail regulator, who would be responsible both for promoting competition and for protecting consumer interests, which might include specifying maximum permitted fares.

Although the individual train operators generally have a monopoly over a given route, many saw themselves directly competing with coaches and private cars. Several began replacing or refurbishing rolling stock and running additional services.

Developments in the UK since privatisation

Crisis in the early 2000s. Following the Hatfield rail disaster in October 2000, when lives were lost as a result of a faulty rail, the UK rail network was reduced to a virtual state of crisis. Trains were unreliable; fares were rising by more than the rate of inflation; services were being reduced; and passenger complaints were increasing. There seemed to be few, if any, benefits from privatisation. Six of the train operating companies were operating under short-term management contracts, and seven were given government subsidies totalling some £100 million to prevent them going bust.

In fact, part of the industry was 'semi' renationalised, when Railtrack, the privatised track owner, was placed into receivership in 2002. It was replaced by Network Rail, which is a not-for-profit company, wholly dependent upon the UK Treasury for any shortfall in its funds. Any profits are reinvested in the rail infrastructure.

In June 2003 the Strategic Rail Authority (SRA) decided to withdraw the operating licence of the French company Connex South Eastern. Not only was one in every five of its trains running late but, following the receipt of £58 million of public money, the company had failed to turn around its failing financial position. In fact, Connex was asking for a further £200 million in state aid.

Many critics claimed that running the privatised rail network was becoming increasingly difficult, with Connex's failure signalling that yet more public money might be required to keep the network afloat.

Turning the railways around? With the formation of Network Rail, considerable government money has been pumped into the rail system to improve track and signalling. Between 2002 and 2006 over £8 billion of public money was invested. At the same time, the government took more direct control

---

- The system is flexible, since it allows for the licence and price formula to be changed as circumstances change.
- The 'RPI minus X' formula provides an incentive for the privatised firms to be as efficient as possible. If they can lower their costs by more than X, they will, in theory, be able to make larger profits and keep them. If, on the other hand, they do not succeed in reducing costs sufficiently, they will make a loss. There is thus a continuing pressure on them to cut costs. (In the US system, where *profits* rather than *prices* are regulated, there is little incentive to increase efficiency, since any cost reductions must be passed on to the consumer in lower prices, and do not, therefore, result in higher profits.)

There are, however, some inherent problems with the way in which regulation operates in the UK:

- The 'RPI minus X' formula was designed to provide an incentive for the firms to cut costs. But if X is too low, the firm might make excessive profits. Frequently, regulators have underestimated the scope for cost reductions resulting from new technology and reorganisation, and have thus initially set X too low. As a result, instead of X remaining constant for a number of years, as intended, new higher values for X have been set after only one or two years. Alternatively, one-off price cuts have been ordered, as happened when the water companies were required by Ofwat to cut prices by an average of 10 per cent in 2000. In either case, the incentive for the industry

of the railways by winding up the Strategic Rail Authority and passing most of its functions, including the awarding of franchises, to the Department of Transport.

As new franchises came up for renewal, so some contracts were merged, so that by 2007, the 25 franchises had been reduced to 20, with the number of TOCs reduced to nine (four held by National Express, four by the First Group, three by Govia and two each by Stagecoach, Arriva and SercoNS). It was recognised that the benefits of economies of scale and coordinated services within a region exceeded any reduction in competition from having fewer franchises and fewer operators.

What is required, however, is a tight regulatory regime, both in setting minimum standards at the time of granting the franchises and in setting maximum fares on a yearly basis. Given that some of the largest train operators also have a monopoly, or near monopoly, on bus services in the areas, there seems to be less scope for competition than in the past.

Looking forward, the Labour government committed to £15 billion of investment until 2013, including £10 billion investment to increase capacity. With the formation of the Coalition government in 2010, however, these figures were considered to be too high in the context of high levels of government borrowing (see Chapter 30).

Fares have increased since privatisation (by 6 to 7 per cent per year on average) to contribute toward investment costs. The government's aim is to shift the balance of paying for the railway to the customer and the TOCs. Indeed, the government plans to reduce subsidies to the TOCs. In 2011, such subsidies amounted to some £5.2 billion. The government hopes to reduce this by £3.6 billion per year by 2019.

At the same time, it is looking at ways in which to reduce the costs of running the railways. In May 2011, Sir Roy McNulty, in a report jointly commissioned by the Department for Transport and the Office of the Rail Regulator,[1] argued

[1] *Realising the Potential of GB Rail*, Report of the Rail Value for Money Study: Summary Report (Crown Copyright, 2011).

that the rail industry should be looking to reduce its unit costs, i.e. costs per passenger kilometre, by 30 per cent by 2018/19.

With improvements in the infrastructure, investment by the TOCs in new rolling stock and building more slack into timetables, rail punctuality improved and passenger numbers and freight tonnage increased. By 2011, 90.8 per cent of trains were recorded as arriving on time, compared with 79 per cent in 2002/3. Between 1994 and 2010, passenger kilometres increased by some 85 per cent and between 2001 and 2010 by 38 per cent. Freight kilometre tonnage increased by some 48 per cent between 1994 and 2010, despite falling back during the recession of 2008/9.

Has the model been adopted elsewhere?

Other countries, such as Japan and Germany, have rejected the UK model in favour of maintaining a vertically integrated rail network, where rail infrastructure and train services are managed by the same company. It is suggested that a single management would be far more capable of successfully coordinating infrastructure and train service activities than two. Indeed, the 2011 McNulty Report recognises that the fragmentation of the UK rail structure and the lack of an effective supply chain are the principal reasons why there is an 'efficiency gap' in the costs of running the UK rail industry compared with other countries.

Nevertheless, some aspects of the UK model have been adopted under EC Directive 91/440, which allows European train operators access to the rail networks of other companies. This means that several companies (say, from different EU countries) can offer competing services on the same international route.

 Why are subsidies more likely to be needed for commuter and regional services than for medium-to-long-distance passenger services?

to cut costs is reduced. What is the point of being more efficient if the regulator is merely going to insist on a higher value for X and thus take away the extra profits?

■ Regulation is becoming increasingly complex. This makes it difficult for the industries to plan and may lead to a growth of 'short-termism'. One of the claimed advantages of privatisation was to give greater independence to the industries from short-term government interference, and allow them to plan for the longer term. In practice, one type of interference may have been replaced by another.

■ As regulation becomes more detailed and complex and as the regulator becomes more and more involved in the detailed running of the industry, so managers and regulators will become increasingly involved in a game

of strategy: each trying to outwit the other. Information will become distorted and time and energy will be wasted in playing this game of cat and mouse.

■ There may also be the danger of ***regulatory capture***. As regulators become more and more involved in their industry and get to know the senior managers at a personal level, so they are increasingly likely to see the

Definition

Regulatory capture Where the regulator is persuaded to operate in the industry's interests rather than those of the consumer.

managers' point of view and become less and less tough. Commentators do not believe that this has happened yet: the regulators are generally independently minded. But it remains a potential danger.

■ Alternatively, regulators could be captured by government. Instead of being totally independent, there to serve the interests of the consumer, they might bend to pressures from the government to do things which might help the government win the next election.

One way in which the dangers of ineffective or over-intrusive regulation can be avoided is to replace regulation with competition wherever this is possible. Indeed, one of the major concerns of the regulators has been to do just this. (See Case Study H.16 in MyEconLab for ways in which competition has been increased in the electricity industry.)

Increasing competition in the privatised industries

Where natural monopoly exists (see page 167), competition is impossible in a free market. Of course, the industry *could* be broken up by the government, with firms prohibited from owning more than a certain percentage of the industry. But this would lead to higher costs of production. Firms would be operating further back up a downward-sloping long-run average cost curve.

But many parts of the privatised industries are not natural monopolies. Generally it is only the *grid* that is a natural monopoly. In the case of gas and water, it is the pipelines. It would be wasteful to duplicate these. In the case of electricity, it is the power lines: the national grid and the local power lines. In the case of the railways, it is the track.

Other parts of these industries, however, have generally been opened up to competition (with the exception of water). Thus there are now many producers and sellers of electricity and gas. This is possible because they are given access, by law, to the national and local electricity grids and gas pipelines.

To help the opening up of competition, regulators have sometimes restricted the behaviour of the established firms (like BT or British Gas), to prevent them using their dominance in the market as a barrier to entry of new firms. For example, an agreement was reached with British Gas in 1995 to limit its share of the industrial gas market to 40 per cent.

As competition has been introduced into these industries, so price-cap regulation has been progressively abandoned. For example, in 2006 Ofcom abandoned price control of BT and other phone companies over line rentals and phone charges. This was in response to the growth in competition from cable operators, mobile phones and free Internet calls from companies such as Skype via VoiP (voice internet protocol).

Even for the parts of industry where there is a natural monopoly, they could be made contestable monopolies. One way of doing this is by granting operators a licence for a specific period of time. This is known as *franchising*. This has been the approach used for the railways (see Box 22.3). Once a company has been granted a franchise, it has the monopoly of passenger rail services over specific routes. But the awarding of the franchise can be highly competitive, with rival companies putting in competitive bids, in terms of both price (or, in the case of railways, the level of government subsidy required) and the quality of service.

Another approach is to give all companies equal access to the relevant grid. For example, regional electricity companies have to charge the same price for using their local power lines to both rival companies and themselves.

But despite attempts to introduce competition into the privatised industries, they are still dominated by giant companies. Even if they are no longer strictly monopolies, they still have considerable market power and the scope for price leadership or other forms of oligopolistic collusion is great. Thus although regulation through the price formula has been progressively abandoned as elements of competition have been introduced, the regulators have retained their role of preventing cases of collusion and the abuse of monopoly power. The companies, however, do have the right of appeal.

Definition

Franchising Where a firm is granted the licence to operate a given part of an industry for a specified length of time.

SUMMARY

1a Pollution is a negative externality, and due to the lack of property rights over the environment, it will be treated as a free good and hence overused. Environmental policy attempts to ensure that the full costs of production or consumption are paid for by those who produce and consume.

1b The environment is difficult to value, so it is difficult to estimate the costs of environmental pollution. This is a major problem in being able to devise an efficient environmental policy.

1c Environmental policy can be either market based or non-market based, or a mixture of the two. Market-based solutions focus upon the use of taxes and subsidies to correct market signals. Non-market-based solutions involve the use of regulations and controls over polluting activities.

1d The problem with using taxes and subsidies is in identifying the appropriate rates, since these will vary according to the environmental impact.

1e Command-and-control systems, such as making certain practices illegal or putting limits on discharges, are a less sophisticated alternative to taxes or subsidies. However, they may be preferable when the environmental costs of certain actions are unknown and it is wise to play safe.

1f Tradable permits are a mix of command-and-control and market-based systems. Firms are given permits to emit a certain level of pollution and then these can be traded. A firm that can relatively cheaply reduce its pollution below its permitted level can sell this credit to another firm which finds it more costly to do so. The system is an efficient and administratively cheap way of limiting pollution to a designated level. It can, however, lead to pollution being concentrated in certain areas and can reduce the pressure on firms to find cleaner methods of production.

2a The allocation of road space depends on demand and supply. Demand depends on the price to motorists of using their cars, incomes, the cost of alternative means of transport, the price of cars and complementary services (such as parking), and the comfort and convenience of car transport. The price and cross-price elasticities of demand for car usage tend to be low: many people are unwilling to switch to alternative modes of transport. The income elasticity, on the other hand, is high. The demand for cars and car usage grows rapidly as incomes grow.

2b With road space fixed (at least in the short term), allocation depends on the private decisions of motorists. The problem is that motorists create two types of external cost: pollution costs and congestion costs. Thus $MSC > MC$. Because of these externalities, the actual use of road space (where $MB = MC$) is likely to be greater than the optimum (where $MSB = MSC$).

2c There are various types of solution to traffic congestion. These include direct provision by the government or local authorities (of additional road space or better public transport); regulation and legislation (such as restricting car access – by the use of bus and cycle lanes, no entry to side streets and pedestrian-only areas – and various forms of parking restrictions); and changing market signals (by the use of taxes, by road pricing, and by subsidising alternative means of transport).

2d Problems associated with building additional roads include the decline of public transport, attracting additional traffic on to the roads and environmental costs.

2e The main problem with restricting car access is that it tends merely to divert congestion elsewhere. The main problem with parking restrictions is that they may actually increase congestion.

2f Increasing taxes is effective in reducing congestion only if it increases the *marginal* cost of motoring. Even when it does, as in the case of additional fuel tax, the additional cost is only indirectly related to congestion costs, since it applies to all motorists and not just those causing congestion.

2g Road pricing is the preferred solution of many economists. By the use of electronic devices, motorists can be charged whenever they add to congestion. This should encourage less essential road users to travel at off-peak times or to use alternative modes of transport, while those who gain a high utility from car transport can still use their cars, but at a price. Variable tolls and area charges are alternative forms of congestion pricing, but are generally less effective than the use of variable electronic road pricing.

2h If road pricing is to be effective, there must be attractive substitutes available. A comprehensive policy, therefore, should include subsidising efficient public transport. The revenues required for this could be obtained from road pricing.

3a From around 1983 the Conservative government in the UK embarked on a large programme of privatisation. Many other countries followed suit.

3b The economic arguments for privatisation include: greater competition, not only in the goods market but in the market for finance and for corporate control; reduced government interference; and raising revenue to finance tax cuts.

3c The economic arguments against privatisation are largely the market failure arguments that were used to justify nationalisation. In reply, the advocates of privatisation argue that these problems can be overcome through appropriate regulation and increasing the amount of competition.

3d Regulation in the UK has involved setting up regulatory offices for the major privatised utilities. These generally operate informally, using negotiation and bargaining to persuade the industries to behave in the public interest. They also set the terms under which the firms can operate (e.g. access rights to the respective grid).

3e As far as prices are concerned, the industries are required to abide by an '*RPI* minus *X*' formula. This forces them to pass potential cost reductions on to the consumer. At the same time they are allowed to retain any additional profits gained from cost reductions greater than *X*. This provides them with an incentive to achieve even greater increases in efficiency.

3f Many parts of the privatised industries are not natural monopolies. In these parts, competition may be a more effective means of pursuing the public interest. Various attempts have been made to make the privatised industries more competitive, often at the instigation of the regulator. Nevertheless, considerable market power remains in the hands of many privatised firms, and thus the need for regulation will continue.

REVIEW QUESTIONS

1 Why is it so difficult to value the environment? What are the implications of this for government policy on the environment?

2 Is it a good idea to use the revenues from green taxes to subsidise green alternatives (e.g. using petrol taxes for subsidising rail transport)?

3 Compare the relative merits of increased road fuel taxes, electronic road pricing and tolls as means of reducing urban traffic congestion. Why is the price inelasticity of demand for private car transport a problem here, whichever of the three policies is adopted? What could be done to increase the price elasticity of demand?

4 How would you set about measuring the external costs of road transport?

5 Consider the argument that whether an industry is in the public sector or private sector has far less bearing on its performance than the degree of competition it faces.

6 To what extent do the various goals of privatisation conflict?

7 Is it desirable after an industry has been privatised for profitable parts of the industry to cross-subsidise unprofitable parts if they are of public benefit (e.g. profitable railway lines cross-subsidising unprofitable ones)?

8 Should regulators of utilities that have been privatised into several separate companies permit (a) horizontal mergers (within the industry); (b) vertical mergers; (c) mergers with firms in other related industries (e.g. gas and electricity suppliers)?

ADDITIONAL PART H CASE STUDIES IN THE *ECONOMICS FOR BUSINESS* MyEconLab (www.pearsoned.co.uk/sloman)

H.1 **The police as a public service.** The extent to which policing can be classified as a public good.

H.2 **Should health care provision be left to the market?** An examination of the market failures that would occur if health care provision were left to the free market.

H.3 **Corporate social responsibility.** An examination of social responsibility as a goal of firms and its effect on business performance.

H.4 **Public choice theory.** This examines how economists have attempted to extend their analysis of markets to the field of political decision making.

H.5 **Cartels set in concrete, steel and cardboard.** This examines some of the best-known Europe-wide cartels of recent years.

H.6 **Taking your vitamins – at a price.** A case study of a global vitamins cartel.

H.7 **Productivity performance and the UK economy.** A detailed examination of how the UK's productivity compares with that in other countries.

H.8 **Technology and economic change.** How to get the benefits from technological advance.

H.9 **The economics of non-renewable resources.** An examination of how the price of non-renewable resources rises as stocks become depleted, and of how the current price reflects this.

H.10 **A deeper shade of green.** This looks at different perspectives on how we should treat the environment.

H.11 **Perverse subsidies.** An examination of the use of subsidies around the world that are harmful to the environment.

H.12 **Can the market provide adequate protection for the environment?** This explains why markets generally fail to take into account environmental externalities.

H.13 **Environmental auditing.** Are businesses becoming greener? A growing number of firms are subjecting themselves to an 'environmental audit' to judge just how 'green' they are.

H.14 **Restricting car access to Athens.** A case study that examines how the Greeks have attempted to reduce local atmospheric pollution from road traffic.

H.15 **Evaluating new road schemes.** The system used in the UK of assessing the costs and benefits of proposed new roads.

H.16 **Selling power to the people.** Attempts to introduce competition into the UK electricity industry.

H.17 **Regulation US-style.** This examines rate-of-return regulation: an alternative to price-cap regulation.

H.18 **Price-cap regulation in the UK.** How $RPI - X$ regulation has applied to the various privatised industries.

H.19 **Competition on the buses.** An examination of the impact of the deregulation of UK bus services in the mid 1980s.

H.20 **A lift to profits?** The EC imposes a record fine on four companies operating a lift and escalator cartel.

H.21 **Are we all green now?** Changing attitudes to the environment.

H.22 **Selling the environment.** The market-led solution to the Kyoto Protocol.

WEBSITES RELEVANT TO PART H

Numbers and sections refer to websites listed in the Web appendix and hotlinked from this book's website at
www.pearsoned.co.uk/sloman

- For news articles relevant to Part H, see the Economics News Articles link from the book's website.

- For general news on market failures and government intervention, see websites in section A, and particularly A1–5, 18, 19, 24, 31. See also links to newspapers in A38, 39 and 43; and see A42 for links to economics news articles from newspapers worldwide.

- Sites I7 and 11 contain links to Competition and monopoly, Policy and regulation and Transport in the Microeconomics section; they also have an Industry and commerce section. Site I4 has links to Environmental and Environmental Economics in the EconDirectory section. Site I17 has several sections of links in the Issues in Society section.

- Sites I7 and 11 also contain links to sites related to corporate social responsibility: see Industry and Commerce > Fair Trade > Corporate Social Responsibility.

- For information on taxes and subsidies, see E30, 36; G13. For use of green taxes, see H5; G11; E2, 14, 30.

- For information on health and the economics of health care (Case Study H.2 in MyEconLab: see above), see E8; H9. See also links in I8 and 17.

- For sites favouring the free market, see C17; D34. See also C18 for the development of ideas on the market and government intervention.

- For information on training, see E5; G14; H3.

- For the economics of the environment, see links in I4, 7, 11, 17. For policy on the environment and transport, see E2, 7, 11, 14, 29; G10, 11. See also H11.

- UK and EU departments relevant to competition policy can be found at sites E10; G7, 8.

- UK regulatory bodies can be found at sites E4, 11, 15, 16, 18, 19, 21, 22, 25, 29.

- For student resources relevant to this chapter, see sites C1–7, 9, 10, 19.

Business in the international environment

The FT Reports . . .

The Financial Times, 8 May 2009

FT

Big rise in anti-dumping probes

By Frances Williams

The number of new anti-dumping investigations jumped by more than a quarter last year from 2007 as recession-hit industries such as steel felt the squeeze from low-priced competitors, especially China.

Governments opened 208 investigations into unfairly priced imports in 2008, compared with an 11-year low of 163 in 2007, the World Trade Organisation said on Thursday.

The latest figures will reinforce fears that creeping protectionism through anti-dumping actions and other measures could prolong the economic downturn and inhibit recovery. The WTO is already predicting that world trade will slump this year by 9 per cent, the sharpest decline in more than 60 years.

India was by far the biggest instigator of anti-dumping actions in 2008, accounting for a quarter of the total, followed by Brazil and Turkey. Imported steel products were the largest industry target, while more than a third of investigations involved exports from China.

Anti-dumping actions tend to lag behind the economic cycle, suggesting that there could be a further spurt this year as more industries seek protection through legal trade remedies.

Last year's total was well below the peak of 366 investigations recorded in 2001 after the bursting of the dot-com bubble.

However, trade experts point out that imports have fallen faster than exports in many countries. That makes it harder for industries to claim they have been injured by low-priced imports.

Under WTO rules, for anti-dumping duties to be levied, the investigation has to show not only that there has been dumping – goods priced more cheaply abroad than at home – but also that the industry has been hurt by it.

Complaints that anti-dumping actions and other trade remedies have been applied unfairly account for more than half the 147 WTO dispute panel reports adopted since the trade watchdog's creation in 1995.

The state of the steel industry, the biggest source of anti-dumping action over the past 15 years, is seen as a barometer for investigations.

'The big question is going to be what happens to steel,' said one trade expert, noting that actions by the 'big boys' such as the US tended to be copied by others.

Anti-dumping machinery was once almost the exclusive preserve of industrialised countries but developing nations are now the biggest users. Since 1995, India has initiated more cases than any other country and, while the US and the European Union are in second and third place, developing countries such as Argentina, Brazil and Turkey have been catching up . . .

> *Globalization is the target of many critics today. The young see it as a malign force in regard to social agendas. The workers see it as a pernicious force in regard to their economic well-being. But both sets of fears, and resulting opposition to (economic) globalization, especially via trade and multinationals, are mistaken.*
>
> Jagdish Bhagwati, 'Why the critics of globalization are mistaken', *Handelsblatt*, August 2008. Available at www.columbia.edu/~jb38/

With falling barriers to international trade, with improved communications and with an increasingly global financial system, so nations have found that their economies have become ever more intimately linked. Economic events in one part of the world, such as changes in interest rates or a downturn in economic growth, will have a myriad of knock-on effects for the international community at large – from the international investor, to the foreign exchange dealer, to the domestic policy-maker, to the business which exports or imports, or which has subsidiaries abroad.

In Part I we explore the international environment and its impact on business. Chapter 23 considers the issue of globalisation and the rise and spread of multinational enterprises within the world economy. It not only looks at why certain businesses become multinational, but evaluates their impact upon host nations, within both the developed and the developing worlds.

In Chapter 24 we focus on international trade. We consider why trading is advantageous and why, nevertheless, certain countries feel the need to restrict trade and protect domestic industries by raising tariffs or dumping goods on foreign markets at prices below marginal cost (see the *Financial Times* article opposite).

Finally, in Chapter 25, we examine one of the most significant trends in international trade over the past 50 years – namely, the rise of the trade bloc. We outline the advantages and disadvantages of regional trading. We also look briefly at trading blocs in North America and South-East Asia and the Pacific. Then, as an extended case study, we consider the position of the European Union and the effects of the creation of a single European market on both businesses and consumers.

Key terms

Globalisation
Foreign direct investment (FDI)
Multinational corporation
Transnationality index
Comparative advantage
The gains from trade
Terms of trade
Protectionism
Tariffs
Quotas
Infant and senile industries
World Trade Organization (WTO)
Trade bloc
Preferential trading
Free trade areas, customs unions and common markets
Trade creation and diversion
North America Free Trade Association (NAFTA)
Asian-Pacific Economic Cooperation forum (APEC)
European Union (EU)
Single European market

Globalisation and multinational business

Business issues covered in this chapter

- ■ What is meant by globalisation and what is its impact on business?
- ■ What is driving the process of globalisation?
- ■ Does the world benefit from the process of the globalisation of business?
- ■ What forms do multinational corporations take?
- ■ What is the magnitude and pattern of global foreign direct investment?
- ■ For what reasons do companies become multinational ones? Are there any disadvantages for companies of operating internationally?
- ■ How can multinationals use their position to gain the best deal from the host state?
- ■ What is the impact on developing countries of multinational investment?

23.1 GLOBALISATION: SETTING THE SCENE

The nature of global production is changing. In the past, many multinational companies had located much of their manufacturing in developing countries. Now they are increasingly locating service and 'knowledge-based' jobs there too. Such jobs range from telesales to research and development.

Some of these jobs require high levels of skills and training, once seen as the preserve of the rich economies and the source of their competitive advantage in international trade. However, countries such as India and China, as well as many others, produce a massive number of well-trained and well-educated engineers and IT specialists every year. Such workers are predictably cheap to employ compared to their US, European and Japanese counterparts, many of whom have lost their jobs or find their wages being driven down. But it is not all bad news for the developed economies. By outsourcing to developing countries, many companies have seen their costs fall and their profits rise. At the same time, consumers benefit from lower prices.

For developing economies, such as India and China, the benefits of this new wave of globalisation are substantial. Foreign companies invest in high-value-added, knowledge-rich production, most of which is subsequently exported. Economic growth is stimulated and wages rise. Increased consumption then spreads the benefits more widely throughout the economy. There are, however, costs. Many are left behind by the growth and inequalities deepen. There are also often significant environmental externalities as rapid growth leads to increased pollution and environmental degradation.

The exodus of jobs from developed to developing countries is a good example of the process of globalisation. In this chapter we are going to explore what globalisation is, how it is evolving, the impacts it is likely to have on different groups of people throughout the world and the motivations behind the increasing 'multinationalisation' of business.

Defining globalisation

Economically we are bound through trade, investment, production and finance. Politically we are bound through organisations such as the United Nations, the World Trade Organization (WTO), the IMF and the G20. Through such organisations we attempt to establish frameworks and rules to govern almost every aspect of our lives. Culturally we are subject to the same advertising and branding; we migrate; we go on holiday; we share ideas, fashions and music; we compete in global sporting events, such as the Olympics; and increasingly we communicate globally through the Internet.

Globalisation is, then, the process of developing these links. As Phillipe Legrain suggests, globalisation is 'shorthand for how our lives are becoming increasingly intertwined with those of distant people and places around the world – economically, politically and culturally'.[1]

Supporters and critics of globalisation alike tend to agree that globalisation is nothing new. There has always been a degree of economic, political and cultural interdependence. What makes globalisation an issue today is the speed at which interdependence is growing. This is partly the result of unprecedented technological change, particularly in respect to transport and communication, and partly the result of a political drive to remove barriers between countries and embrace foreign influences.

Business, caught within this process of globalisation, will invariably seek to take advantage of what it has to offer, which is essentially a borderless world or one that is increasingly so. A global economy enables a business to locate the different dimensions of its value chain wherever it might get the best deal to lower costs or improve quality or both. Globalisation encourages this process of relocation and the framing of business strategy within a global context.

What is driving globalisation?

Within any global system, certain industries and markets are likely to be more prone to the forces of globalisation than others. This becomes apparent when you attempt to identify the conditions influencing the globalisation process. These globalisation drivers can be categorised in a number of ways. George Yip suggests that the globalisation potential of an industry – that is, its ability to set global strategy and compete in a global marketplace – can be analysed under four headings:

- market drivers;
- cost drivers;
- government drivers;
- competitive drivers.

These are shown in Table 23.1.

Market drivers. Market drivers focus on the extent to which markets throughout the world are becoming similar. The more similar consumers are in respect to income and taste, the more significant globalisation market drivers will become.

Cost drivers. Cost drivers present the business with the potential to reorganise its operations globally and reduce costs as a consequence. Global economies of scale, and transport and distribution issues, will be significant.

Government drivers. Governments often play a key role in driving the process of globalisation, especially when they are positively welcoming to trade and inward investment.

Table 23.1	The drivers of globalisation

Market drivers
Per capita income converging among industrialised nations
Convergence of lifestyles and tastes
Organisations beginning to behave as global customers
Increasing travel creating global consumers
Growth of global and regional channels
Establishment of world brands
Push to develop global advertising

Cost drivers
Continuing push for economies of scale
Accelerating technological innovation
Advances in transportation
Emergence of newly industrialised countries with productive capability and low labour costs
Increasing cost of product development relative to market life

Government drivers
Reduction of tariff barriers
Reduction of non-tariff barriers
Creation of blocs
Decline in role of governments as producers and customers
Privatisation in previously state-dominated economies
Shift to open market economies from closed communist systems in eastern Europe
Increasing participation of China and India in the global economy

Competitive drivers
Continuing increases in the level of world trade
Increased ownership of corporations by foreign acquirers
Rise of new competitors intent upon becoming global competitors
Growth of global networks making countries interdependent in particular industries
More companies becoming globally centred rather than nationally centred
Increased formation of global strategic alliances

Other drivers
Revolution in information and communication
Globalisation of financial markets
Improvements in business travel

Source: G. Yip, *Total Global Strategy* (Prentice Hall, 1995)

---

[1] P. Legrain, *Open World: The Truth about Globalisation* (Abacus, 2003).

Global political agreements, such as those made at the WTO covering world trade and related issues, not only directly affect the operation of markets, but also help establish global rules and protocols.

Competition drivers. As competitiveness builds, whether in the domestic market or overseas, businesses will be forced to consider how to maintain their competitive position. This often involves embracing a global business strategy, which invariably contributes towards globalisation. Global business networks and cross-border strategic alliances are key reflections of this growing competitive global process.

What is clear is that globalisation is driven forward by a wide variety of conditions. Such conditions will vary from industry to industry, reflecting why certain industries are more global than others.

Globalisation: the good and the bad

Even though supporters and critics of globalisation are in agreement that globalisation is nothing new, and that it is primarily driven by technological change and shifting political attitudes, they are far from agreeing about the consequences of globalisation and whether these are beneficial or harmful.

The supporters

Supporters of globalisation argue that it has massive potential to benefit the entire global economy. With freer trade and greater competition, countries and businesses within them are encouraged to think, plan and act globally. Technology spreads faster; countries specialise in particular products and processes, and thereby exploit their core competitive advantages.

Both rich and poor, it is argued, benefit from such a process. Politically, globalisation brings us closer together. Political ties help stabilise relationships and offer the opportunity for countries to discuss their differences. However imperfect the current global political system might be, the alternative of independent nations is seen as potentially far worse. The globalisation of culture is also seen as beneficial, as a world of experience is opened, whether in respect of our holiday destinations, or the food we eat, or the music we listen to or the movies we watch.

Supporters of globalisation recognise that not all countries benefit equally from globalisation: those that have wealth will, as always, possess more opportunity to benefit from the globalisation process, whether from lower prices, global political agreements or cultural experience. However, long term, supporters of globalisation see it as ultimately being for the benefit of all – rich and poor alike.

The critics

Critics of globalisation argue that it contributes to growing inequality and further impoverishes poor nations. As an economic philosophy, globalisation allows multinational corporations (MNCs), based largely in the USA, Europe and Japan, to exploit their dominant position in foreign markets. Without effective competition in these markets, such companies are able to pursue profit with few constraints.

By 'exploiting' low-wage labour, companies are able to compete more effectively on world markets. As competitive pressures intensify and companies seek to cut costs further, this can put downward pressure on such wages.

In political terms, critics of globalisation see the world being dominated by big business. Multinationals put pressure on their home governments to promote their interests in their dealings with other countries, thereby heightening the domination of rich countries over the poor.

Critics are no less damning of the cultural aspects of globalisation. They see the world dominated by multinational brands, Western fashion, music and TV. Rather than globalisation fostering a mix of cultural expression, critics suggest that cultural differences are being replaced by the dominant (Western) culture of the day.

The above views represent the extremes, and to a greater or lesser degree both have elements of truth within them. The impact of globalisation on different groups is not even, and never will be. However, to suggest that big business rules is also an unrealistic exaggeration. Clearly big business is influential, but it is a question of degree. Influence will invariably fluctuate over time, between events, and between and within countries.

In recent years, at least until the global financial crisis of 2008/9, the momentum has been for barriers to come down. This has had profound effects on both multinational business and the peoples of the world.

In the following sections we consider why it is that businesses decide to go multinational, and evaluate what impact they have on their host countries. Before we do this we shall first offer a definition of multinational business and assess the importance of multinational investment within the global economy.

23.2 WHAT IS A MULTINATIONAL CORPORATION?

According to the 2009 World Investment Report there are some 82 000 *multinational corporations* (MNCs)[2] worldwide. Between them they control a total of 810 000 foreign

> **Definition**
>
> **Multinational corporations** Businesses that own and control foreign subsidiaries in more than one country.

---

[2] Also known as transnational corporations (TNCs).

subsidiaries. MNCs account for around two-thirds of international trade, of which around half takes place within the same MNC.

In 2011, the global stock of foreign direct investment (FDI) was around $20.4 trillion. Sales by foreign affiliates accounted for $28.0 trillion in 2011 (40 per cent of world GDP) while their value added, a measure of their output, was estimated at $7.0 trillion (10 per cent of world GDP). Foreign affiliates employed 69 million people in 2011.

Even given their obvious gigantic size and overwhelming importance within the global economy, MNCs defy simple definition. At the most basic level, an MNC is a business that owns and controls foreign subsidiaries in more than one country.

It is this ownership and control of productive assets in other countries which makes the MNC distinct from an enterprise that does business overseas by simply exporting goods or services. Control is important because it distinguishes the MNC as an instrument of FDI rather than portfolio investment.[3] With FDI, managers have complete strategic and operational control over the firm's investment decisions, such as building a new subsidiary overseas or expanding an existing one, or acquiring an existing business operation through either merger or acquisition.

Moreover, there is immense diversity in what constitutes an MNC.

Diversity among MNCs

Size. All of the world's largest firms in the Fortune Global 500 list – Wal-Mart, Shell, Toyota, etc. – are multinationals. Indeed, the turnover of some of them exceeds the national income of many smaller countries (see Table 23.2). And yet there are also thousands of very small, often specialist multinationals, which are a mere fraction of the size of the giants.

The nature of business. MNCs cover the entire spectrum of business activity, from manufacturing to extraction, agricultural production, chemicals, processing, service provision and finance. There is no 'typical' line of activity of a multinational.

Overseas business relative to total business. MNCs differ in respect of how extensive their overseas operations are relative to their total business. Just over one-fifth of Wal-Mart's sales come from overseas subsidiaries, while over four-fifths of BP's sales come from its foreign affiliates. Some smaller MNCs also have a large global presence. The Canadian firm Barrick Gold Corporation, for example, had the highest ranking on the United Nation's transnationality index in 2006 but had sales of less than 2 per cent of those achieved by Wal-Mart.

Table 23.2	Comparison of the ten largest multinational corporations (by gross revenue) and selected countries (by GDP): 2011	
MNC rank	**Country or company (headquarters)**	**GDP ($b) or gross revenue ($b)**
	USA	15 094.0
	UK	2 417.6
1	Wal-Mart Stores	421.8
	South Africa	408.1
2	Royal Dutch/Shell group	378.2
3	Exxon Mobil	354.7
	Thailand	345.6
	Denmark	333.2
4	BP	308.9
	Greece	303.1
	Malaysia	278.7
5	Sinopec Group	273.4
	Finland	266.6
	Singapore	259.8
6	China National Petroleum	240.2
	Portugal	238.9
7	State Grid	226.3
8	Toyota Motor	221.8
	Ireland	217.7
9	Japan Post Holdings	204.0
10	Chevron	196.3
	New Zealand	161.9
	Iceland	14.0
	Albania	12.8

Sources: Companies: Fortune Global 500 (http://money.cnn.com/magazines/fortune/global500/2011/full_list/); Countries: *World Economic Outlook database*, IMF. GDP data are estimates

Production locations. Some MNCs are truly 'global', with production located in a wide variety of countries and regions. Other MNCs, by contrast, only locate in one other region, or in a very narrow range of countries.

There are, however, a number of potentially constraining factors on the location of multinational businesses. For example, businesses concerned with the extraction of raw materials will locate as nature dictates. Businesses that provide services will tend to locate in the rich markets of developed regions of the world economy, where the demand for services is high. Others locate according to the factor intensity of the stage of production. Thus, a labour-intensive stage might be located in a developing country where wage rates are relatively low, while another stage which requires a high level of automation might be located in an industrially advanced country.

---
[3] Portfolio investment involves purchasing shares and other financial assets in overseas organisations but with little or no strategic and operational control over their investment decisions.

Ownership patterns. As businesses expand overseas, they are faced with a number of options. They can decide to go it alone and create wholly owned subsidiaries. Alternatively, they might share ownership, and hence some of the risk, by establishing joint ventures. In such cases the MNC might have a majority or minority stake in the overseas enterprise. Increasingly though, MNCs are looking at a third option: non-equity modes of operation. In this scenario, the MNC has no ownership stake in the partner firm overseas, but exerts control over operations through contractual arrangements such as franchising or strategic alliances. This non-equity mode of operation by MNCs begins to challenge our understanding and, hence, our definition of MNCs.

In certain countries, where MNC investment is regulated, many governments insist on owning or controlling a share in the new enterprise. Whether governments insist on domestic companies (or themselves) having a majority or minority stake varies from country to country. It also depends on the nature of the business and its perceived national importance.

An emerging issue is the increasing significance of state-owned MNCs for cross-border investment. State-owned MNCs are those where the government has a controlling interest in the parent enterprise and its foreign affiliates. The 2011 World Investment Report defines this to be those MNCs where the government has at least 10 per cent of the voting power or is the single largest shareholder. In 2010, it estimated that there were 650 state-owned MNCs with in excess of 8500 foreign affiliates. While in 2010 state-owned MNCS accounted for less than 1 per cent of all MNCs they were responsible for 11 per cent of global FDI flows.

Organisational structure. We discussed (see Chapter 3) the variety of organisational forms that MNCs might adopt – from the model where the headquarters, or parent company, is dominant and the overseas subsidiary subservient, to that where international subsidiaries operate as self-standing organisations, bound together only in so far as they strive towards a set of global objectives.

The above characteristics of MNCs reveal that they represent a wide and very diverse group of enterprises. Beyond sharing the common link of having production activities in more than one country, MNCs differ widely in the nature and forms of their overseas business, and in the relationship between the parent and its subsidiaries.

> ### Pause for thought
>
> *Given the diverse nature of multinational business, how useful is the definition given on page 372 for describing a multinational corporation?*

23.3 TRENDS IN MULTINATIONAL INVESTMENT

Successful multinational businesses are constantly adapting to the economic environment. In recent times they have been shrinking the size of their headquarters, removing layers of bureaucracy, and reorganising their global operations into smaller autonomous profit centres. Gone is the philosophy that big companies will inevitably do better than small ones. Many modern multinationals are organisations that combine the advantages of size (i.e. economies of scale) with the responsiveness and market knowledge of smaller firms.

The key for the modern multinational is flexibility, and to be at one and the same time both global and local.

The size of multinational investment

We can estimate the size of multinational investment by looking at figures for foreign direct investment (FDI). Figure 23.1 shows FDI inflows in $ billions. Global FDI inflows in 2011 reached $1.52 trillion with 51 per cent of flows towards developing and transition economies.

From the chart we also can observe relatively rapid rates of increase in FDI between 1998 and 2000 and again between 2004 and 2007. Both periods saw a surge in cross-border merger and acquisition (M&A) activity. In contrast, when the value of M&A activity contracted sharply following the financial crisis of 2008/9, global FDI inflows fell. Box 23.1 looks in more detail at M&A activity and at greenfield FDI investment, which involves a multinational company setting up a new subsidiary or expanding an existing one.

The significance of inward investment relative to total investment (or 'gross fixed capital formation' – GFCF) is shown in Figure 23.2. Increasing globalisation has meant that the trend in inward investment as a proportion of GFCF has been upwards for both developed and developing nations. However, for the majority of the period since the 1990s the proportion of inward FDI to total investment has been lower in developed than in developing and transition economies.

This feature is echoed in Table 23.3, which shows that the distribution of FDI towards developing and transition economies has grown from, on average, 17.0 per cent in the period 1986 to 1990 to 51.8 per cent in the period 2010 to 2011.

Over the period 2010 to 2011, the four largest host countries in the developing world received 43 per cent of

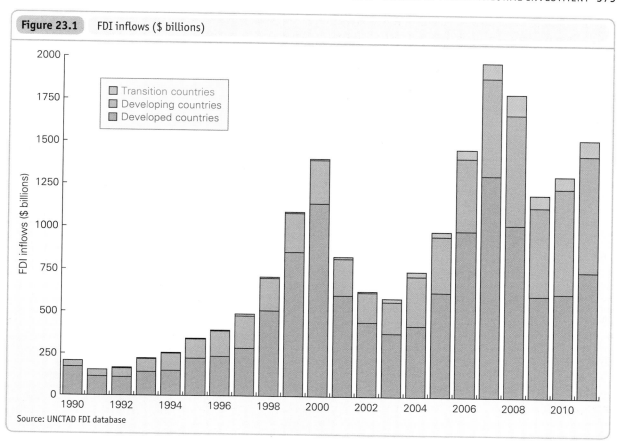

Figure 23.1 FDI inflows ($ billions)

Source: UNCTAD FDI database

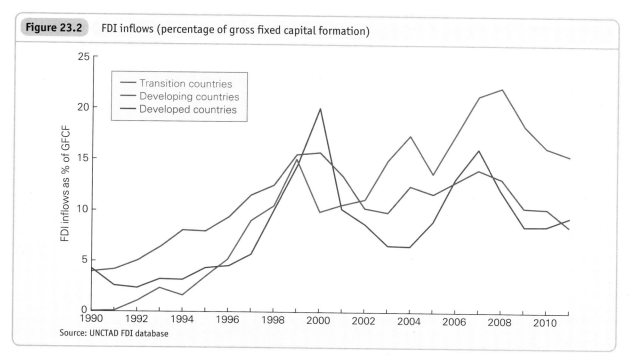

Figure 23.2 FDI inflows (percentage of gross fixed capital formation)

Source: UNCTAD FDI database

all FDI inflows to developing economies, with China (including Hong Kong) accounting for around 30 per cent. FDI is highly concentrated – so much so that Africa as a whole accounts for a mere 5 per cent of global FDI and much of this flows to the resource-rich countries of Nigeria, Angola and South Africa. Transition economies have also seen a growth in their share of global inward FDI to around 6 per cent by 2011.

BOX 23.1 | M&As AND GREENFIELD FDI

Modes of FDI entry

There are two principal forms of Foreign Direct Investment (FDI), known as 'modes of FDI entry'. The first is *greenfield investment*. This involves multinational companies investing in a new subsidiary overseas or expanding an existing one. The second mode of entry is through *cross-border mergers and acquisitions* (M&As).

Table (a) shows the global value of these two modes of FDI entry. Typically, the value of greenfield FDI is higher than investment through M&As. The exception was in 2007 when the value of M&A activity was 0.7 per cent higher than greenfield FDI.

The geography of M&A and greenfield FDI

The geography of the two modes of FDI entry is significantly different. Consider chart (a) which shows the value of

cross-border M&As by the *destination* economy, i.e. the economy of the acquired company.

The host economy for the majority of cross-border M&As is typically a developed economy. Since 1990, 85 per cent of M&A activity by value has typically been in developed economies. Since the financial crisis and subsequent economic downturn, M&A activity has centred less on developed economies. In 2011, 22 per cent of M&A activity by value involved companies in developing and transition economies.

As well as the growing importance of developing and transition economies as a destination for cross-border M&As, especially since the late 2000s, investors from these

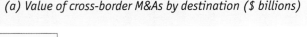

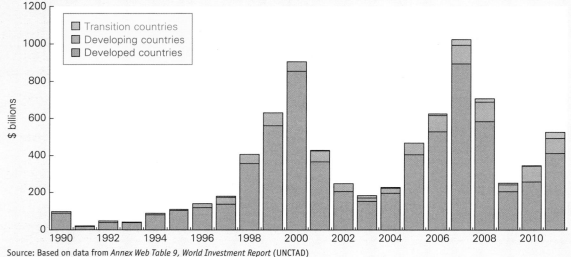

(a) Value of cross-border M&As by destination ($ billions)

Source: Based on data from *Annex Web Table 9, World Investment Report* (UNCTAD)

Table 23.3 Distribution of world FDI inflows, 1982–2011 (percentage of world FDI inflows)

Region	1982–5[a]	1986–90	1991[a]	1992–8	1999–00[b]	2001–3[a]	2004–7	2008–9[a]	2010–11
Developed countries	65.8	83.0	74.0	63.7	79.7	69.2	33.6	53.8	48.2
Europe	25.2	37.8	53.7	37.8	49.9	49.6	22.0	32.5	27.6
Euro area	16.1	21.8	35.4	23.9	32.6	38.4	32.5	20.2	19.8
Germany	1.8	1.9	3.1	1.8	9.6	5.7	1.5	1.2	3.1
Japan	0.7	0.2	0.8	0.5	0.9	1.1	0.3	1.2	−0.1
UK	7.3	12.4	9.6	7.0	8.3	4.3	6.3	5.5	3.7
USA	32.1	35.9	14.8	19.5	24.2	13.4	7.0	14.5	15.0
Developing countries	34.2	17.0	25.9	35.0	19.7	28.7	66.4	39.8	46.0
Africa	3.5	1.9	2.3	2.0	0.9	2.6	33.0	3.8	3.0
Caribbean	0.6	0.3	0.6	1.0	1.6	0.9	5.8	5.3	4.9
South America	5.6	2.5	3.5	6.7	5.2	4.3	3.3	4.9	7.4
Brazil	3.3	0.8	0.7	2.1	2.5	2.4	0.9	2.3	4.0
Asia (excl. Japan)	20.3	10.2	15.7	22.1	10.5	17.0	12.5	23.8	28.5
China (incl. Hong Kong)	3.6	4.4	3.5	12.4	6.6	9.9	8.2	10.9	13.8
India	0.1	0.1	0.0	0.5	0.2	0.8	0.7	2.7	2.0
Least developed countries	0.6	0.4	1.0	0.7	0.4	1.2	16.4	1.3	1.1
Transition economies	0.0	0.0	0.1	1.3	0.6	2.1	18.3	6.4	5.8
Russia				0.6	0.2	0.7	1.4	3.6	3.4

Notes: [a] Years of declining global FDI; [b] Years characterised by exceptionally high cross-border M&A activity
Source: Based on data from UNCTADstat (UNCTAD)

Table (a) Value of cross-border M&As and greenfield FDI projects

	2003	2004	2005	2006	2007	2008	2009	2010	2011
Greenfield FDI ($bn)	801.8	751.6	754.9	989.6	1015.7	1634.4	1051.6	904.6	904.3
M&As ($bn)	182.9	227.2	462.3	625.3	1022.7	706.5	249.7	344.0	525.9
M&As as % of Greenfield	*22.8*	*30.2*	*61.2*	*63.2*	*100.7*	*43.2*	*23.7*	*38.0*	*58.2*

Source: Based on data from *World Investment Report*, Annex Web Tables 9 and 19 (UNCTAD, 2012)

economies are themselves becoming an important *source* of global M&A activity. In both 2009 and 2010, one-third of cross-border M&As involved investors from developing and

(b) Value of greenfield FDI projects by destination, $ billions

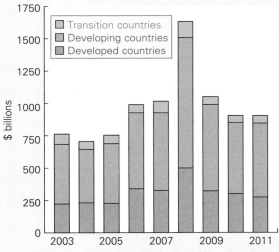

Source: Based on data from *Annex Web Table 1.8, World Investment Report 2012* (UNCTAD)

transition economies. This is roughly double their share of global M&A activity prior to the global financial crisis.

Consider now chart (b) which shows the value of greenfield FDI projects by *destination*. From it, we observe that developing and transition economies have consistently attracted the majority of global greenfield FDI investment. In 2011, these economies received just under 70 per cent of global greenfield FDI investment.

Despite the growth of cross-border M&A activity in developing and transition economies, the value of greenfield FDI remains substantially higher in these economies. In 2011, the value of greenfield FDI investment in developing and transition economies was over five times greater than that from cross-border M&A activity. In contrast, in developed countries the value of investment through greenfield FDI was roughly two-thirds of that through M&A activity.

The share of global greenfield FDI originating *from* developing and transition economies has, in recent years, been consistently around the 30 per cent mark. When viewed alongside the growing funds these countries now contribute to global M&A activity, it is clear that developing and transition economies have become important investors in cross-border investment.

 What factors might explain the significance of developing and transition economies not only as a destination for FDI but also increasingly as a source of FDI?

23.4 WHY DO BUSINESSES GO MULTINATIONAL?

There are many reasons why companies choose to go multinational. These depend on the nature of their business and their corporate strategy.

One motivation for a company becoming multinational is to cut costs. A vertically integrated multinational may be able to locate each part of the production process in the country where the relevant factor prices are lowest.

The other major motivation is to tap into new markets. Once markets within the domestic economy have become saturated, and opportunities for growth diminish, dynamic firms may seek new markets and hence new opportunities by expanding production overseas.

Businesses can look to expand in one of two ways: through either internal or external expansion (see Chapter 15). MNCs are no exception to this rule. They can expand overseas, either by creating a new production facility from scratch (such as Nissan in the north-east of England), or by merging with or taking over existing foreign producers (such as the acquisition of ASDA by Wal-Mart). They can also engage in an international strategic alliance (e.g. the joint venture in 2006 between Finland's Nokia and Japan's Sanyo to produce mobile phones for the North American market).

We noted earlier in the chapter that MNCs are a diverse group of enterprises and their motives for going overseas depend upon individual circumstances. We will examine two theories that have been used to explain the development of the MNC: the product life cycle and the Eclectic Paradigm.

The product life cycle and the multinational company

The product life cycle hypothesis was discussed at length (Chapter 17). However, it is worth reviewing its elements here in order to identify how an MNC, by altering the geographical production of a good, might extend its profitability.

A product's life cycle can be split into four phases: launch, growth, maturity and decline.

The launch phase. This will tend to see the new product produced in the economy where the product is developed. It will be exported to the rest of the world. At this stage of the product's life cycle, the novelty of the product and the monopoly position of the producer enable the business to charge high prices and make high profits.

The growth phase. As the market begins to grow, other producers will seek to copy or imitate the new product. Prices begin to fall. In order to maintain competitiveness, the business will look to reduce costs, and at this stage might consider shifting production overseas to lower-cost production centres.

Maturity. At the early stage of maturity, the business is still looking to sell its product in the markets of the developed economies. Thus it may still be happy to locate some of its plants in such economies. As the original market becomes increasingly saturated, however, the MNC will seek to expand into markets overseas which are at an earlier stage of development. Part of this expansion will be by the MNC simply exporting to these economies, but increasingly it will involve relocating its production there too.

Maturity and decline. By the time the original markets are fully mature and moving into decline, the only way to extend the product's life is to cut costs and sell the product in the markets of developing countries. The location of production may shift once again, this time to even lower-cost countries. By this stage, the country in which the product was developed will almost certainly be a net importer (if there is a market left for the product), but it may well be importing the product from a subsidiary of the same company that produced it within that country in the first place!

Thus the product life cycle model explains how firms might first export and then engage in FDI. It explains how firms transfer production to different locations to reduce costs and enable profits to be made from a product that could have become unprofitable if its production had continued from its original production base.

The theory was developed in the 1960s when MNC activity was less sophisticated than it is today. It can be useful in explaining horizontally and vertically integrated MNCs, but it cannot explain the more modern forms of MNC growth through strategic alliances. We thus turn to the second theory.

The Eclectic Paradigm

John Dunning[4] developed an organising framework, known as the Eclectic Paradigm. This helps to explain the pattern and growth of international production as well as identifying the gains to firms from being multinational. Dunning identifies three categories of gains:

- MNCs can exploit their core competencies in competing with companies in other countries. These are described by Dunning as 'ownership advantages': in other words, advantages deriving from ***ownership-specific assets***.
- They can exploit ***locational advantages*** in host countries, such as the availability of key raw materials or high demand for the good.
- They may also derive ***internalisation advantages***. These occur when the MNC gains from investing overseas rather than exporting to an overseas agent or licensing a foreign firm (i.e. using a market solution). In other words, the MNC gains from keeping control of the product within its organisation.

As firms and nations evolve the distribution of ownership, location and internalisation advantages between firms and nations change so that we observe ever-changing patterns of international production.

Ownership advantages

An MNC may be able to exploit its ownership of assets that reflect its core competencies and which give the business a specific advantage over its foreign rivals in their home markets. Such advantages might include the following:

The ownership of superior technology. Such ownership will not only enhance the productivity levels of the MNC, but probably also contribute to the production of superior-quality products.

Definitions

Ownership-specific assets Assets owned by the firm – such as technology, product differentiation and managerial skills – which reflect its core competencies.

Locational advantages Those features of a host economy that MNCs believe will lower costs, improve quality and/or facilitate greater sales.

Internalisation advantages Where the net benefits of extending the organisational structure of the MNC by setting up an overseas subsidiary are greater than those of arranging a contract with an external part.

---

[4] J. H. Dunning, *The Globalisation of Business* (Routledge, 1993).

Research and development capacity. MNCs are likely to invest heavily in R&D in an attempt to maintain their global competitiveness. The global scale of their operations allows them to spread the costs of this R&D over a large output (i.e. the R&D has a low average fixed cost). MNCs, therefore, are often world leaders in process innovation and product development.

Product differentiation. MNCs often combine innovation with successful product differentiation in international markets. They may invest heavily in advertising and often develop global brand names (e.g. Kellogg's, Ikea, Samsung).

Entrepreneurial and managerial skills. Managers in MNCs are often innovative in the way they do business and organise the value chain. With the arrival of Japanese multinationals in the UK, it became instantly apparent that Japanese managers conducted business in a very different way from their British counterparts. The most fundamental difference concerned working practices. Japanese MNCs quickly established themselves as among the most efficient and productive businesses in the UK (see section 18.7 on the flexible firm).

Pause for thought

Before reading on, can you think of the host country locational advantages that might be attractive to MNCs?

Locational advantages

MNCs will take advantage of the most appropriate locations to make their goods and services. Locational advantages are those features of a host economy that MNCs believe will lower costs, improve quality and/or facilitate greater sales relative to investing in their home country. In addition, by going overseas a firm must be effective at using its ownership-specific advantages over domestic firms, otherwise the locational advantage is muted. MNCs will consider a range of factors when comparing potential locations.

The availability of raw materials. Nations, like individuals, are not equally endowed with factors of production. Some nations are rich in labour, some in capital, some in raw materials. In other words, individual nations might have specific advantages over others. Because such factors of production are largely immobile, especially between nations, businesses respond by becoming multinational: that is, they locate where the necessary factors of production they require can be found. In the case of a business that wishes to extract raw materials, it has little choice but to do this.

The relative cost of inputs. Although it is possible that firms seek out lower-cost land and capital, perhaps because of host government subsidies, one of the main reasons firms want to move overseas is because labour is relatively cheaper. For example, a firm might locate an assembly plant in a developing country (i.e. a country with relatively low labour costs), if that plant uses large amounts of labour relative to the value

added to the product at that stage. Thus foreign countries, with different cost conditions, are able to provide business with a more competitive environment within which to produce its products.

As an example, take the case of Nike, the American sportswear manufacturer. It ruthlessly exploits cost differences between countries. Nike has organised itself globally so that it can respond rapidly to changing cost conditions in its international subsidiaries. Its product development operations are carried out in the USA, but all of its production operations are subcontracted out to over 40 overseas locations, mostly in south and south-east Asia. If wage rates, and hence costs, rise in one host country, then production is simply transferred to a more profitable subsidiary. So long as Nike headquarters has adequate information regarding the cost conditions of its subsidiaries, management decision-making concerning the location of production simply follows the operation of market forces.

The quality of inputs. The location of multinational operations does not simply depend on factor prices: it also depends on factor quality. For example, a country might have a highly skilled or highly industrious workforce, and it is this, rather than simple wage rates, that attracts multinational investment. The issue here is still largely one of costs. Highly skilled workers might cost more to employ per hour, but if their productivity is higher, they might well cost less to employ per unit of output. It is also the case, however, that highly skilled workers might produce a better-quality product, and thus increase the firm's sales.

If a country has both lower-priced factors and high-quality factors, it will be very attractive to multinational investors. In recent years, the UK government has sought to attract multinational investment through having lower labour costs and more flexible employment conditions than its European rivals, while still having a relatively highly trained labour force compared with those in developing countries. As Box 23.2 illustrates, however, such advantages are disappearing rapidly.

Avoiding transport and tariff costs. Locating production in a foreign country can also reduce costs in other ways. For example, a business locating production overseas would be able to reduce transport costs if those overseas plants served local or regional markets, or used local raw materials. One of the biggest cost advantages concerns the avoidance of tariffs (customs duties). If a country imposes tariffs on imports, then, by locating *within* that country (i.e. behind the 'tariff wall'), the MNC gains a competitive advantage over its rivals which are attempting to import their products from outside the country and are thus having to pay the tariff.

Government policy towards FDI. In order to attract FDI, a government might offer an MNC a whole range of financial and cost-reducing incentives, many of which help reduce the fixed (or 'sunk') costs of the investment, thereby reducing the investment's risk. The granting of favourable tax differentials and depreciation allowances, and the provision of premises, are all widely used government strategies to attract foreign business. A fairly recent case in the UK saw a potential investor offered financial incentives valued at £37 000 per employee to locate production in an area of Wales!

The general economic climate in host nations. FDI is more likely to occur if a nation has buoyant economic growth, large market size, high disposable income, an appropriate demographic mix, low inflation, low taxation, few restrictive regulations on business, a good transport network, an excellent education system, a significant research culture, etc. In highly competitive global markets, such factors may make the difference between success and failure.

The financial crisis of the late 2000s, the subsequent economic downturn and fiscal measures to reduce levels of government borrowing (see Chapter 30) affected developed economies, particularly in Europe, especially hard. This only helped to make developing economies even more attractive to foreign investors, including investors based in developing economies.

Internalisation advantages

As well as ownership and locational advantages, FDI can bring internalisation advantages. These are where the benefits of setting up an overseas subsidiary (thereby internalising its production in that country) are greater than the costs of arranging a contract with an external party (e.g. an overseas import agent or a firm in a host country which would make the product under licence).

In the language of sections 3.1 and 15.7 (see pages 238–40), FDI occurs where the *transaction costs* of using the market in an overseas country are too high. Thus, the problems of finding the right partner to contract with, agreeing the terms of the contract, determining the price of the transaction and monitoring the contractual agreement are all compounded in foreign locations where different cultures and legal systems create uncertainties for firms considering expansion overseas. In order to minimise on opportunistic behaviour in such situations (i.e. to reduce moral hazard), the firm will engage in FDI rather than exporting via an overseas import agent or licensing a domestic firm in the host nation.

Of course, many firms that start to venture into overseas markets will engage in exporting, rather than FDI, and use an import agent. However, it is also the case that many of the first multinational subsidiaries are sales and distribution outlets. The first plant set up by Hoover in the UK during the 1930s, for example, was a sales establishment through which it distributed its vacuum cleaners. Hoover found it more profitable to control sales than to use a third party.

Many firms go through a sequence from exporting to overseas investment. Toyota, for example, exported its cars to the UK using local motor vehicle retailers to distribute them prior to establishing a greenfield manufacturing site in Burnaston in Derbyshire in the early 1990s. Honda also set up a manufacturing plant in Swindon, Wiltshire, in 1992 after years of exporting cars to the UK.

The usefulness of the Eclectic Paradigm

The Eclectic Paradigm is thus a useful tool for explaining why MNCs arise. It explains how firms use combinations of ownership, locational and internalisation advantages to engage in various forms of FDI and strategic alliance.

Horizontally integrated multinationals. It can explain the development of **horizontally integrated multinationals**. Firms may initially manufacture in their home nation and export to a foreign location but then decide to switch out of exporting and establish a subsidiary producing the same product overseas.

Thus, FDI may be part of a sequence of expansion into new markets. The sequence may begin with exporting and then involve investment in one or more countries. Firms see that by combining their ownership-specific assets (e.g. technology and managerial skills) with locational advantages in the host nation (e.g. market size and government grants) their revenue streams will be greatest from internalising those assets and establishing an overseas subsidiary instead of exporting to it.

Alternatively, firms that engage in a cross-border horizontal merger or acquisition may do so to take advantage of the potential synergies in ownership-specific assets.

Vertically integrated multinationals. Likewise the eclectic paradigm can also explain **vertically integrated multinationals** with various stages of production taking place in different countries. Following similar reasoning to that presented in section 15.7, consider two firms – one a manufacturer and the other a raw material producer – each with its own set of ownership-specific assets, but located in different countries. Further, these two firms are locked into a contract whereby they trade with each other on a frequent basis and have invested heavily in maintaining the relationship. If there is incomplete information or uncertainty about the other's activities and one firm feels that the other is not fulfilling its side of the bargain, then vertical FDI may take place. Here the driving force in the FDI process is the internalisation advantage achieved by vertical integration because the transaction costs of continuing the market relationship are too high.

Oil companies such as Shell and Exxon (Esso) are good examples of vertically integrated multinationals, undertaking in a global operation the extraction of crude oil, controlling its transportation, refining it and producing by-products, and controlling the retail sale of petrol and other oil products.

Definitions

Horizontally integrated multinational A multinational that produces the same product in many different countries.

Vertically integrated multinational A multinational that undertakes the various stages of production for a given product in different countries.

Conglomerate multinationals. Many of the big MNCs have become **conglomerate multinationals** and the Eclectic Paradigm helps to explain this organisational form. Conglomerates exist because firms have specialised managerial talent (i.e. ownership-specific advantages). Such managers can deal with establishing and running large, complex organisations. Further, there are internalisation advantages from establishing a conglomerate MNC because operating across a number of unrelated sectors and locations using market solutions would be prohibitively costly. Conglomerate expansion overseas allows the firm to spread its risks and gain other economies of scope (see page 137).

Unilever is a good example of a conglomerate multinational. It employs over 171 000 people in 190 countries, producing various food, home care and personal care products. It has around 400 brands including: Walls and Ben & Jerry's ice cream; Slimfast diet foods; Knorr soups; Hellman's mayonnaise; Bovril; Marmite; Lipton, PG Tips tea; Flora margarine; Domestos; Persil, Cif, Omo, Radiant and Surf detergents; Comfort; Timotei and SunSilk shampoos; Vaseline, Dove and Lux soaps; Ponds skin care products; Impulse and Lynx fragrances and deodorants.

Joint ventures. Finally, the Eclectic Paradigm offers insights into the establishment of joint ventures (see page 234). Evidence shows that new-product joint ventures, where risks and development costs are high, occur among the larger MNCs that have complementary ownership-specific assets.[5] Because the costs and risks are great, these investments are likely to take place in markets with high perceived growth. This would help to explain, for example, the decision by Samsung and Sony to produce a sixth-generation LCD TV production plant jointly in South Korea in recent times.

Joint ventures also occur among new and smaller MNCs that have limited ownership-specific assets. These firms look for suitable partners that can complement their resources in countries with high market potential. In addition, all joint ventures require that there are limited contractual disadvantages in signing an agreement to share resources and develop products, indicating that the joint venture relationship is built on trust as well as sound strategic reasoning.

Problems facing multinationals

Although multinational corporations are successful in developing overseas subsidiaries, they also face a number of problems resulting from their geographical expansion:

- *Language barriers.* The problem of working in different languages is a necessary barrier for the MNC to overcome. Clearly this problem varies according to the degree to which a common language is spoken. Further, if an MNC tends to employ expatriates, communication will be more difficult and local staff may feel alienated and thus be less productive.
- *Selling and marketing in foreign markets.* Strategies that work at home might fail overseas, given wide social and cultural differences. Many US multinationals, such as McDonald's and Coca-Cola, are frequently accused of imposing American values in the design and promotion of their products, irrespective of the country and its culture. This can lead to resentment and hostility in the host country, which may ultimately backfire on the MNC.
- *Attitudes of host governments.* Governments will often try to get the best possible deal for their country from multinationals. This could result in governments insisting on part ownership in the subsidiary (either by themselves or by domestic firms), or tight rules and regulations governing the MNC's behaviour, or harsh tax regimes. In response, the MNC can always threaten to locate elsewhere.
- *Communication and coordination between subsidiaries.* Diseconomies of scale may result from an expanding global business. Lines of communication become longer and more complex. These problems are likely to be greater, the greater is the attempted level of control exerted by the parent company: in other words, the more the parent company attempts to conduct business as though the subsidiaries were regional branches. Multinational organisational structures where international subsidiaries operate largely independently of the parent state will tend to minimise such problems.

Definition

Conglomerate multinational A multinational that produces different products in different countries.

---

[5] See S. Agarwal and S. N. Ramaswami, 'Choice of foreign market entry mode: impact of ownership, location and internalization factors', *JIBS*, vol. 23, no. 1 (1992), pp. 1–28. See also A. Madhok, 'Revisiting multinational firms' tolerance for joint ventures: a trust-based approach', *JIBS*, vol. 26, no. 1 (1995), pp. 117–37.

23.5 THE ADVANTAGES OF MNC INVESTMENT FOR THE HOST STATE

As mentioned previously, host governments are always on the lookout to attract foreign direct investment, and are prepared to put up considerable finance and make significant concessions to attract overseas business. So what benefits do MNCs bring to the economy? (See Box 23.2 for examples relating to the UK experience.)

Employment

If MNC investment is in new plant (as opposed to merely taking over an existing company), this will generate employment. Most countries attempt to entice MNCs to depressed regions where investment is low and unemployment is high. Often these will be regions where a major industry has closed (e.g. the coal mining regions of South Wales). The employment that MNCs create is both direct, in the form of people employed in the new production facility, and indirect, through the impact that the MNC has on the local economy. This might be the consequence of establishing a new supply network, or simply the result of the increase in local incomes and expenditure, and hence the stimulus to local business.

It is possible, however, that jobs created in one region of a country by a new MNC venture, with its superior technology and working practices, might cause a business to fold elsewhere, thus leading to increased unemployment in that region.

> **Pause for thought**
>
> *Why might the size of these regional 'knock-on effects' of inward investment be difficult to estimate?*

The balance of payments

A country's balance of payments (see Chapter 27) is likely to improve on a number of counts as a result of inward MNC investment. First, the investment will represent a direct flow of capital into the country. Second, and perhaps more important (especially in the long term), MNC

BOX 23.2 | **LOCATION. LOCATION. LOCATION**

The potential benefits and risks of inward FDI to the UK

Countries that have a large foreign multinational sector, such as the UK, are significantly affected by the actions of foreign companies – their product designs, the technologies they use, their management expertise and their decisions about where to locate and invest.

In 2011, global flows of FDI amounted to $1.52 trillion. Inward FDI to the UK was $53.9 billion. As the chart shows, this was equivalent to 3.5 per cent of world FDI. We also observe considerable variability in the ability of the UK to attract inward investment.

The USA is the largest source of inward investment into the UK. At the end of 2011, American companies held £203.8 billion of investment in the UK, roughly 27 per cent of the UK's inward FDI stock. Meanwhile, it is the service sector that dominates inward investment, accounting for about 71 per cent of the UK's stock of foreign investment.

According to an Ernst & Young's survey:

> The UK's long-standing leadership in European FDI is a direct result of two key factors: its position as the

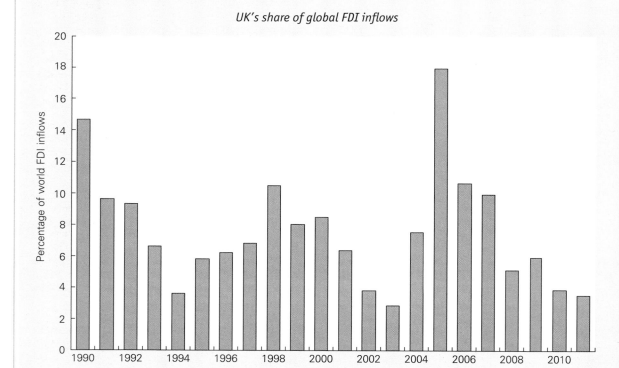

UK's share of global FDI inflows

Source: Based on data from *UNCTADstat* (UNCTAD)

investment is likely to result in both **import substitution** and export promotion. Import substitution will occur as products, previously purchased as imports, are now produced domestically. Export promotion will be enhanced as many multinationals use their new production facilities as export platforms. For example, many Japanese MNCs invest in the UK in order to gain access to the European Union.

The beneficial effect on the balance of payments, however, will be offset to the extent that profits earned from the investment are repatriated to the parent country, and to the extent that the exports of the MNC displace the exports of domestic producers.

Technology transfer

Technology transfer refers to the benefits gained by domestic producers from the technology imported by the MNC. Such benefits can occur in a number of ways. The

> ## Definitions
>
> **Import substitution** The replacement of imports by domestically produced goods or services.
>
> **Technology transfer** Where a host state benefits from the new technology that an MNC brings with its investment.

investment location of choice for US companies, and its strength in several key sectors, including the seemingly-declining financial services industry. The UK performs less well in winning projects from the stronger European economies, and is now lagging behind Germany in winning projects from both China and Japan.

Given these circumstances, the UK must adopt a more strategic approach to FDI that places inward investment within the overall economic context. Both the survey responses and the FDI data make it clear that strong domestic demand, good export links and investment in human and physical capital are key drivers of success in attracting FDI.[1]

Effects on productivity and R&D

As well as offering employment, it is argued that foreign firms have higher rates of productivity than domestic firms, which puts competitive pressure on domestic firms to increase their productivity. Some work by Hubert and Pain in 2000 showed that a 1 per cent rise in the output of foreign firms in a particular industry will raise technical progress by 0.53 per cent in domestic firms in that industry.[2]

It is evident that foreign investment, largely through foreign firms operating in the UK, is crucial for research and development expenditure by businesses in the UK. Annual surveys of business research and development conducted by the Office for National Statistics typically show around one-quarter of all R&D expenditure in the UK is funded from overseas.

Competition for FDI

Because of the huge potential benefits, the competition between nations to attract new investment, whether from indigenous or foreign firms, is intense. Highly mobile MNCs seek out those locational opportunities that allow them to gain a competitive advantage over other global producers.

This exposure to international competition, however, can bring personal and economic hardship when there is multinational divestment. In April 2006, the French motor manufacturer PSA Peugeot-Citroën announced the closure of its car factory in Coventry with the loss of 2300 jobs. Why? The factory was old; cheaper, more productive, factories could be built elsewhere. The Coventry plant cost some €450 per car more than its sister subsidiary at Poissy in France and was almost €1000 per car above the production cost at Peugeot's joint venture factory with Toyota in the Czech Republic.[3]

Nevertheless, despite occasional job losses from MNC disinvestment, the UK has had the highest job creation from FDI of any EU country 'in every year since records began in 1997, with the exception of 2006 when it was briefly overtaken by Poland'.[4]

However, the UK's position in attracting FDI is increasingly under threat. As well as eastern European countries, developing nations such as China and India are increasingly attractive to mobile MNCs and this is only partly due to low relative wage costs. More important in recent times are the additional locational advantages these nations have gained through substantial investments in education and science, thereby raising the quality of their skills base and enhancing their technological capability. As companies become more effective in managing these distant locations and different cultures, higher value-added activities are increasingly likely to be located there.

Thus, globalisation has aided the development of other nations as attractors of internationally mobile capital projects. Further, as FDI flows to developing nations and transition economies continue to rise as a proportion of all inward FDI flows (see Figure 23.1 and Box 23.1), the success of the UK in maintaining its locational attractiveness for inward investment cannot be guaranteed.

 What do you think the UK government might do either to minimise FDI outflows, or to attract a greater volume of FDI inflow?

---

[1] 'Staying ahead of the game: Ernst & Young's 2012 attractiveness survey, UK' (Ernst & Young, 2012).
[2] F. Hubert and N. Pain, 'Inward investment and technical progress in the UK manufacturing sector', OECD Economics Department, Working Paper no. 268 (2000).

[3] 'Anger at Peugeot decision to quit Britain', *Guardian*, 19 April 2006.
[4] Ernst & Young, *op. cit.*

most common is where domestic producers copy the production technology and working practices of the MNC. This is referred to as the 'demonstration effect' and has occurred widely in the UK as British businesses have attempted to emulate many of the practices brought into the country by Japanese multinationals.

In addition to copying best practice, technology might also be transferred through the training of workers. When workers move jobs from the MNC to other firms in the industry, or to other industrial sectors, they take their newly acquired technical knowledge and skills with them.

Taxation

MNCs, like domestic producers, are required to pay tax and therefore contribute to public finances. Given the highly profitable nature of many MNCs, the level of tax revenue raised from this source could be highly significant (but see section 23.6 on ways in which MNCs can avoid tax).

23.6 THE DISADVANTAGES OF MNC INVESTMENT FOR THE HOST STATE

Thus far we have focused on the positive effects resulting from multinational investment. However, multinational investment may not always be beneficial in either the short or the long term.

Uncertainty. MNCs are often 'footloose', meaning that they can simply close down their operations in foreign countries and move (see Box 23.2 for an example relating to the closure of the Peugeot plant in Coventry). This is especially likely with older plants which would need updating if the MNC were to remain, or with plants that can be easily sold without too much loss. The ability to close down its business operations and shift production, while being a distinct economic advantage to the MNC, is a prime concern facing the host nation. If a country has a large foreign multinational sector within the economy, it will become very vulnerable to such footloose activity, and face great uncertainty in the long term. It may thus be forced to offer the multinational 'perks' (e.g. grants, special tax relief or specific facilities) in order to persuade it to remain. These perks are clearly costly to the taxpayer.

Control. The fact that an MNC can shift production locations not only gives it economic flexibility, but enables it to exert various controls over its host. This is particularly so in many developing countries, where MNCs are not only major employers but in many cases the principal wealth creators. Thus attempts by the host state to improve worker safety or impose pollution controls, for example, may be against what the MNC sees as its own best interests. It might thus oppose such measures or even threaten to withdraw from the country if such measures are not modified or dropped. The host nation is in a very weak position.

Transfer pricing. MNCs, like domestic producers, are always attempting to reduce their tax liabilities. One unique way that an MNC can do this is through a process known as *transfer pricing* (see pages 264–5). The practice of transfer pricing is pervasive and governments are losing vast sums in tax revenue every day because of it. The practice enables

the MNC to reduce its profits in countries with high rates of profit tax, and increase them in countries with low rates of profit tax. This can be achieved by simply manipulating its internal pricing structure.

For example, take a vertically integrated MNC where subsidiary A in one country supplies components to subsidiary B in another. The price at which the components are transferred between the two subsidiaries (the 'transfer price') will ultimately determine the costs and hence the levels of profit made in each country. Assume that in the country where subsidiary A is located, the level of corporation tax is half that of the country where subsidiary B is located. If components are transferred from A to B at very high prices, then B's costs will rise and its profitability will fall. Conversely, A's profitability will rise. The MNC clearly benefits as more profit is taxed at the lower rather than the higher rate. Had it been the other way around, with subsidiary B facing the lower rate of tax, then the components would be transferred at a low price. This would increase subsidiary B's profits and reduce A's.

The practice of transfer pricing was mostly starkly revealed in the *Guardian* newspaper in February 2009. Citing a paper that examined the flows of goods priced from US subsidiaries in Africa back to the USA, it stated that 'the public may be horrified to learn that companies have priced flash bulbs at $321.90 each, pillow cases at $909.29 each and a ton of sand at $1993.67, when the average world trade price was 66 cents, 62 cents and $11.20 respectively'.[6]

The environment. Many MNCs are accused of simply investing in countries to gain access to natural resources, which are subsequently extracted or used in a way that is not sensitive to the environment. Host nations, especially developing countries, that are keen for investment are frequently prepared to allow MNCs to do this. They often put more store on the short-run gains from the MNC's

---

[6] 'Shifting profits across borders', *Guardian*, 12 February 2009. Available at www.guardian.co.uk/commentisfree/2009/feb/11/taxavoidance-tax

presence than on the long-run depletion of precious natural resources or damage to the environment. Governments, like many businesses, often have a very short-run focus: they are concerned more with their political survival (whether through the ballot box or through military force) than with the long-term interests of their people.

23.7 MULTINATIONAL CORPORATIONS AND DEVELOPING ECONOMIES

Many of the benefits and costs of MNC investment that we have considered so far are most acutely felt in developing countries. The poorest countries of the world are most in need of investment and yet are most vulnerable to exploitation by multinationals and have the least power to resist it. There tends, therefore, to be a love–hate relationship between the peoples of the developing world and the giant corporations that are seen to be increasingly dominating their lives: from the spread of agribusiness into the countryside through the ownership and control of plantations, to international mining corporations despoiling vast tracts of land; from industrial giants dominating manufacturing, to international banks controlling the flow of finance; from international tour operators and hotels bringing the socially disruptive effects of affluent tourists from North America, Japan, Europe and Australasia, to the products of the rich industrialised countries fashioning consumer tastes and eroding traditional culture.

Although MNCs employ only a small proportion of the total labour force in most developing countries, they have a powerful effect on these countries' economies, often dominating the import and export sectors. They also often exert considerable power and influence over political leaders and their policies and over civil servants, and are frequently accused of 'meddling' in politics.

It is easy to see the harmful social, environmental and economic effects of multinationals on developing countries, and yet governments in these countries are so eager to attract overseas investment that they are frequently prepared to offer considerable perks to MNCs and to turn a blind eye to many of their excesses.

Does MNC investment aid development?

Whether investment by multinationals in developing countries is seen to be a net benefit or a net cost to these countries depends on what are perceived to be their development goals. If maximising the growth in national income is the goal, then MNC investment has probably made a positive contribution. If, however, the objectives of development are seen as more wide-reaching, and include goals such as greater equality, the relief of poverty, a growth in the provision of basic needs (such as food, health care, housing and sanitation) and a general growth in the freedom and sense of well-being of the mass of the population, then the net effect of multinational investment could be argued to be anti-developmental.

Advantages to the host country

In order for countries to achieve economic growth, there must be investment. In general, the higher the rate of investment, the higher will be the rate of economic growth. The need for economic growth tends to be more pressing in developing countries than in advanced countries. One obvious reason is their lower level of income. If they are ever to aspire to the living standards of the rich North, then income per head will have to grow at a considerably faster rate than in rich countries and for many years. Another reason is the higher rates of population growth in developing countries – often some 2 percentage points higher than in the rich countries. This means that for income per head to grow at merely the *same* rate as in rich countries, developing countries will have to achieve growth rates 2 percentage points higher.

Investment requires finance. But developing countries are generally acutely short of funds: FDI can help to make up the shortfall. Specifically, there are key 'gaps' that FDI can help to fill.

The savings gap. A country's rate of economic growth (g) depends crucially on two factors:

- The amount of extra capital that is required to produce an extra unit of output per year: i.e. the marginal capital/output ratio (k). The greater the marginal capital/output ratio, the lower will be the output per year that results from a given amount of investment.
- The proportion of national income that a country saves (s). The higher this proportion, the greater the amount of investment that can be financed.

There is a simple formula that relates the rate of economic growth to these two factors. It is known as the **Harrod–Domar model** (after the two economists, Sir Roy Harrod and Evsey Domar, who independently developed the model). The formula is:

$$g = s/k$$

Thus if a developing country saved 10 per cent of its national income ($s = 10\%$), and if £4 of additional capital

---

Definition

Harrod–Domar model A model that relates a country's rate of economic growth to the proportion of national income saved and the ratio of capital to output.

were required to produce £1 of extra output per annum ($k = 4$), then the rate of economic growth would be 10%/4 = 2.5 per cent.

If that developing country wanted to achieve a rate of economic growth of 5 per cent, then it would require a rate of saving of 20 per cent (5% = 20%/4). There would thus be a shortfall of savings: a *savings gap*. Most, if not all, developing countries perceive themselves as having a savings gap. Not only do they require relatively high rates of economic growth in order to keep ahead of population growth and to break out of poverty, but they tend to have relatively low rates of saving. Poor people cannot afford to save much out of their income.

This is where FDI comes in. It can help to fill the savings gap by directly financing the investment required to achieve the target rate of growth.

The foreign exchange gap. There are many items, especially various raw materials and machinery, that many developing countries do not produce themselves and yet which are vital if they are to develop. Such items have to be imported. But this requires foreign exchange, and most developing countries suffer from a chronic shortage of foreign exchange. Their demand for imports grows rapidly: they have a high income elasticity of demand for imports – for both capital goods and consumer goods. Yet their exports tend to grow relatively slowly. Reasons include: the development of synthetic substitutes for the raw material exports of developing countries (e.g. plastics for rubber and metal) and the relatively low income elasticity of demand for certain primary products (the demand for things such as tea, coffee, sugar cane and rice tends to grow relatively slowly).

FDI can help to alleviate the shortage of foreign exchange: it can help to close the *foreign exchange gap*. Not only will the MNC bring in capital which might otherwise have had to be purchased with scarce foreign exchange, but any resulting exports by the MNC will increase the country's future foreign exchange earnings.

Public finance gap. Governments in developing countries find it difficult to raise enough tax revenues to finance all the projects they would like to. MNC profits provide an additional source of tax revenue.

Skills and technology gaps. MNCs bring management expertise and often provide training programmes for local labour. The capital that flows into the developing countries with MNC investment often embodies the latest technology,

access to which the developing country would otherwise be denied.

Disadvantages to the host country

Whereas there is the potential for MNCs to make a significant contribution to closing the above gaps, in practice they often close them only slightly, or even make them bigger! The following are the main problems:

- They may use their power in the markets of host countries to drive domestic producers out of business, thereby lowering domestic profits and domestic investment.
- They may buy few, if any, of their components from domestic firms, but import them instead: perhaps from one of their subsidiaries.
- The bulk of their profits may simply be repatriated to shareholders in the rich countries, with little, if any, reinvested in the developing country. This, plus the previous point, will tend to make the foreign exchange gap worse.
- Their practice of transfer pricing may give little scope for the host government to raise tax revenue from them. Governments of developing countries are effectively put in competition with each other, each trying to undercut the others' tax rates in order to persuade the MNC to price its intermediate products in such a way as to make its profits in their country.
- Similarly, governments of developing countries compete with each other to offer the most favourable terms to MNCs (e.g. government grants, government contracts, tax concessions and rent-free sites). The more favourable the terms, the less the gain for developing countries as a whole.
- The technology and skills brought in by the multinationals may be fiercely guarded by the MNC. What is more, the dominance of the domestic market by MNCs may lead to the demise of domestic firms and indigenous technology, thereby worsening the skill and technology base of the country.

In addition to these problems, MNCs can alter the whole course of development in ways that many would argue are undesirable. By locating in cities, they tend to attract floods of migrants from the countryside looking for work, but of whom only a small fraction will find employment in these industries. The rest swell the ranks of the urban unemployed, often dwelling in squatter settlements on the outskirts of cities and living in appalling conditions.

More fundamentally, they are accused of distorting the whole pattern of development and of worsening the gap between the rich and poor. Their technology is capital intensive (compared with indigenous technology). The result is too few job opportunities. Those who are employed, however, receive relatively high wages, and are able to buy their products. These are the products consumed in affluent countries – from cars, to luxury foodstuffs, to household appliances – products that the MNCs often advertise

Definitions

Savings gap The shortfall in savings to achieve a given rate of economic growth.

Foreign exchange gap The shortfall in foreign exchange that a country needs to purchase necessary imports such as raw materials and machinery.

heavily, and where they have considerable monopoly/oligopoly power. The resulting 'coca-colanisation', as it has been called, creates wants for the mass of people, but wants that they have no means of satisfying.

> ## Pause for thought
>
> *What problems is a developing country likely to experience if it adopts a policy of restricting, or even preventing, access to its markets by multinational business?*

What can developing countries do?

Can developing countries gain the benefits of FDI while avoiding the effects of growing inequality and inappropriate products and technologies? If a developing country is large

and is seen as an important market for the multinational, if it would be costly for the multinational to relocate, and if the government is well informed about the multinational's costs, then the country's bargaining position will be relatively strong. It may be able to get away with relatively high taxes on the MNC's profits and tight regulation of its behaviour (e.g. its employment practices and its care for the environment). If, however, the country is economically weak and the MNC is footloose, then the deal it can negotiate is unlikely to be very favourable.

The bargaining position of developing countries would be enhanced if they could act jointly in imposing conditions on multinational investment and behaviour. Such agreement is unlikely, however, given the diverse nature of developing countries' governments and economies, and the pro-free market, deregulated world of the early twenty-first century.

BOX 23.3   GROCERS GO GLOBAL

Carrefour has a fresh snake counter alongside the fish department in its Chinese stores. Wal-Mart boasts that in its Chinese stores you can find local delicacies such as whole roasted pigs and live frogs. Are fresh snakes and live frogs what's needed to succeed in China? It would seem so. Global companies thinking local, customising themselves to each market, are increasingly seen as the key to success in Asia and elsewhere around the world.

The expansion of European and American grocer retailers into global markets has been under way for a number of years. Driven by stagnant markets at home with limited growth opportunities, the major players in Europe, such as Carrefour and Casino from France, Tesco in the UK, Ahold from Holland and Metro from Germany, have been looking to expand their overseas operations – but with mixed success.

In recent times, Asia has been the market's growth sector. Tesco entered the Thai market in 1998. Tesco Lotus, the company's regional subsidiary, is now the country's number-one retailer. In 2012 it had over 660 stores, including 88 hypermarkets, employing over 36 000 people. Carrefour and the US-based Wal-Mart have also opened hundreds of new outlets within the region over recent times.

The advantages that international retailers have over their domestic competitors are expertise in systems, distribution, the range of products and merchandising. However, given the distinctive nature of markets within Asia, business must learn to adapt to local conditions. Joint ventures and local knowledge are seen as the key ingredients to success. Even the most closed markets, such as those of Japan, are not immune from the global grocers' onslaught. Wal-Mart acquired a large stake in the ailing 400-store food and clothing chain Seiyu, and Tesco had opened 125 stores by early 2009, employing 3604 people.

Facing up to the big boys

With the rapid expansion of hypermarkets throughout Asia, the retail landscape is undergoing revolutionary change. With a wide range of products all under one roof, from groceries to pharmaceuticals to white goods, and at cut-rate prices, local

neighbourhood stores stand little chance in the competitive battle. 'Mom and pop operations have no economies of scale.' As well as local retailers, local suppliers are also facing a squeeze on profits, as hypermarkets demand lower prices and use their buying power as leverage.

Such has been the dramatic impact these stores have had upon the retail and grocery sector that a number of Asian economies, such as Malaysia and Thailand, have introduced restrictions on the building of new outlets. China, one of the toughest markets to enter, restricted foreign companies to joint venture arrangements until 2004. Now there are no restrictions on how many shops a retailer can operate or where it may open them. However, domestic retailers are still offered tax incentives and other subsidies to compete against their foreign rivals.

Tesco's answer was to go into partnership in 2004 with Taiwanese food supplier Ting Hsing, initially on a 50:50 basis, but in 2006 Tesco raised its stake to 90 per cent. In 2012 Tesco employed more than 26 000 people in 124 stores in mainland China.[1] Initially the stores bore none of the hallmarks of Tesco in the UK. The stores were called Happy Shopper; the colour scheme was orange; and there were few brands that the average British shopper would recognise. The staff up to middle management are all Chinese. Only the most senior executives are British. Since 2006, however, the stores have been rebranded as Tesco and have adopted the familiar red, blue and white colour scheme.

Other international retailers, such as Carrefour and Wal-Mart, have used their own names and brands right from the start. By June 2012, Carrefour, the biggest international retailer in the Chinese market, had opened 208 hypermarkets. These figures are still dwarfed, however, by the domestic leader, Hualian, which operates some 2000 stores.

 What are the ownership, location and internalisation advantages associated with retail FDI in Asia?

---

[1] Data on Tesco's and Carrefour's store numbers are taken from their websites.

SUMMARY

1a The process of globalisation can have profound effects on economies. One current feature of globalisation is the relocating of various service and knowledge-based jobs from developed to developing countries.

1b There are various drivers of globalisation, including market, cost, government and competitive drivers.

1c Supporters of globalisation point to its potential to lead to faster growth and greater efficiency through trade, competition and investment. It also has the potential to draw the world closer together politically.

1d Critics of globalisation argue that it contributes to growing inequality and further impoverishes poor nations. It also erodes national cultures and can have adverse environmental consequences.

2 There is great diversity among multinationals in respect of size, nature of business, size of overseas operations, location, ownership and organisational structure.

3 Foreign direct investment (FDI) tends to fluctuate with the ups and downs of the world economy. Thus in 2001 and 2008/9, years of global economic slowdown, worldwide FDI fell. Over the years, however, FDI has grown substantially, and has accounted for a larger and larger proportion of total investment.

4a Why businesses go multinational depends largely upon the nature of their business and their corporate strategy.

4b One theoretical explanation of MNC development is the product life cycle hypothesis. In this theory, a business will shift production around the world seeking to reduce costs and extend a given product's life. The phases of a product's life will be conducted in different countries. As the product nears maturity and competition grows, reducing costs to maintain competitiveness will force businesses to locate production in low-cost markets, such as developing economies.

4c A more modern approach to explaining international production and MNC development is provided by the

Eclectic Paradigm. According to this approach, firms have certain ownership-specific advantages (core competencies), such as managerial skills, product differentiation and technological advantages, which they can use in the most appropriate locations. They internalise their ownership-specific advantages and engage in FDI because the costs and risks are lower than licensing an overseas firm or using an import agent (i.e. engaging in an external market transaction).

4d Although becoming an MNC is largely advantageous to the business, it can experience problems with language barriers, selling and marketing in foreign markets, attitudes of the host state and the communication and coordination of global business activities.

5 Host states find multinational investment advantageous in respect to employment creation, contributions to the balance of payments, the transfer of technology and the contribution to taxation.

6 Host states find multinational investment disadvantageous in so far as it creates uncertainty; foreign business can control or manipulate the country or regions within it; tax payments can be avoided by transfer pricing; and MNCs might misuse the environment.

7a The benefits of MNCs to developing countries depend upon the developing countries' development goals.

7b MNCs bring with them investment, which is crucial to economic growth. They also provide the host state with foreign exchange, which might be crucial in helping purchase vital imports.

7c MNCs might prove to be disadvantageous to developing economies if they drive domestic producers out of business, source production completely from other countries, repatriate profits, practise transfer pricing to avoid tax, force host states to offer favourable tax deals or subsidies for further expansion, and guard technology to prevent its transfer to domestic producers.

REVIEW QUESTIONS

1 What are the advantages and disadvantages to an economy, like that of the UK, of having a large multinational sector?

2 How might the structure of a multinational differ depending upon whether its objective of being multinational is to reduce costs or to grow?

3 If reducing costs is so important for many multinationals, why is it that many locate production not in low-cost developing economies, but in economies within the developed world?

4 Explain the link between the life cycle of a product and multinational business.

5 Assess the advantages and disadvantages facing a host state when receiving MNC investment.

6 Debate the following: 'Multinational investment can be nothing but good for developing economies seeking to grow and prosper.'

International trade

Business issues covered in this chapter

■ How has international trade grown over the years? Have countries become more or less interdependent?
■ What are the benefits to countries and firms of international trade?
■ Which goods should a country export and which should it import?
■ Why do countries sometimes try to restrict trade and protect their domestic industries?
■ What is the role of the World Trade Organization (WTO) in international trade?

Without international trade we would all be much poorer. There would be some items like pineapples, coffee, cotton clothes, foreign holidays and uranium that we would simply have to go without. Then there would be other items like pineapples and spacecraft that we could produce only very inefficiently.

International trade has the potential to benefit *all* participating countries. This chapter explains why.

Totally free trade, however, may bring problems to countries or to groups of people within those countries. Many people argue strongly for restrictions on trade. Textile workers see their jobs threatened by cheap imported cloth. Car manufacturers worry about falling sales as customers switch to Japanese models or other east Asian ones. This chapter, therefore, also examines the arguments for restricting trade. Are people justified in fearing international competition, or are they merely trying to protect some vested interest at the expense of everyone else?

24.1 TRADING PATTERNS

International trade has been growing as a proportion of countries' national income for many years. This is illustrated in Figure 24.1, which shows the growth in the global volume of exports of goods and in world real GDP. It shows that exports have been growing much more rapidly than GDP.

From 1970 to 2012 the average annual growth in world output was 3.1 per cent, whereas the figure for world exports was 5.1 per cent. The chart also shows the signifi-cant negative impact of the global financial crisis at the end of the 2000s on both world output and, in particular, the volume of exports. The fall in total world output in 2009 was the first since the 1930s.

Despite the impact of the global slowdown at the end of the 2000s, it is likely that trade will continue to increase as a percentage of world GDP. This will increase countries' interdependence and their vulnerability to world trade fluctuations.

Figure 24.1 Annual growth in volume of world exports and GDP

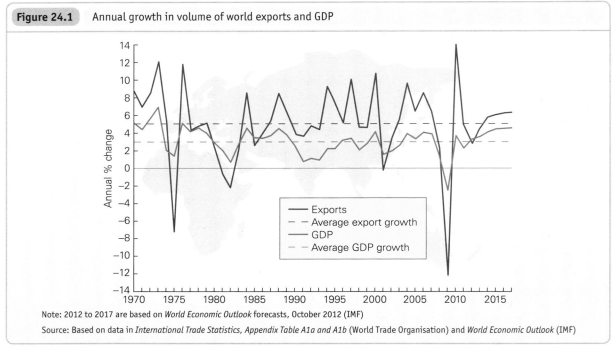

Note: 2012 to 2017 are based on *World Economic Outlook* forecasts, October 2012 (IMF)

Source: Based on data in *International Trade Statistics, Appendix Table A1a and A1b* (World Trade Organisation) and *World Economic Outlook* (IMF)

The geography of international trade

The developed economies dominate world trade. In 2011, they accounted (by value) for 53 per cent of world exports and 58 per cent of world imports (see Figure 24.2). Their share of world trade, however, has declined over time because many of the countries with the most rapid *growth* in exports can be found in the developing world.

Figure 24.2 Share of world merchandise exports, by value (2011)

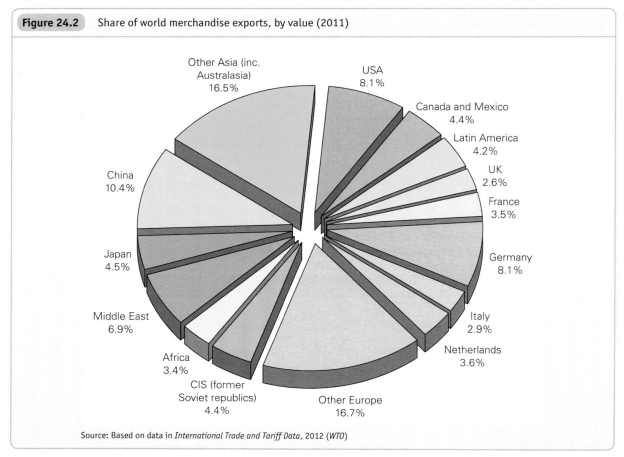

Source: Based on data in *International Trade and Tariff Data*, 2012 (*WTO*)

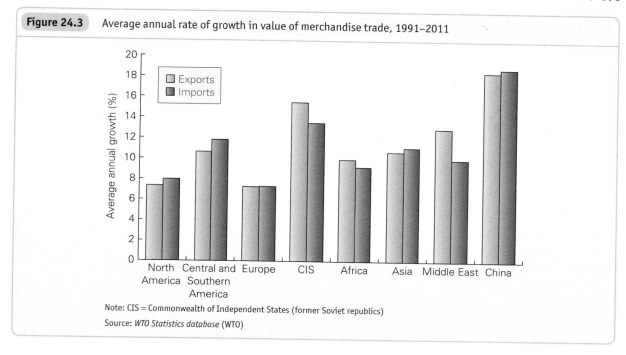

Figure 24.3 Average annual rate of growth in value of merchandise trade, 1991–2011

Note: CIS = Commonwealth of Independent States (former Soviet republics)

Source: *WTO Statistics database* (WTO)

The growth in exports from the group of developing nations collectively known as the BRICS[1] (Brazil, Russia, India, China and South Africa) has been especially rapid. Between them they accounted for just 6.5 per cent of world exports in 1994. By 2011 this had grown to 17.3 per cent.

Figure 24.3 shows the *growth* of exports and imports by region. It is a measure of the openness of economies and further recognition that nations are becoming increasingly interdependent. It illustrates the spectacular growth rate in trade witnessed by China: its exports increased in value by an average of 18 per cent per year from 1991 to 2011.

Despite more rapid growth in trade values in other regions, Europe remains an important geographical centre for trade (see Figure 24.4). In 2011 it accounted for 37.7 per cent of world exports. While Africa, as a whole, has experienced significant growth in exports since the early 1990s, many of the poorest African countries have seen negligible

---

[1] Sometimes the term is used to refer just to the first four countries. When South Africa is excluded, the term is written BRICs rather than BRICS.

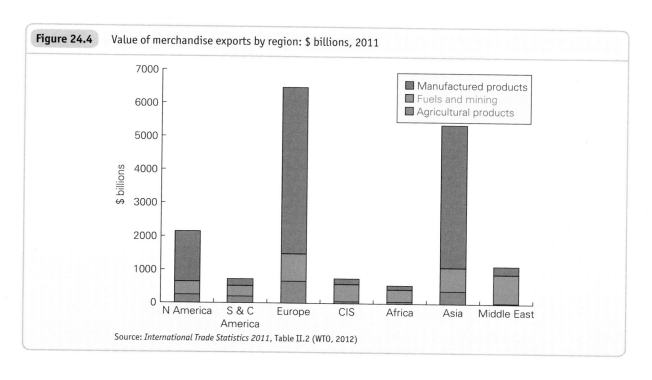

Figure 24.4 Value of merchandise exports by region: $ billions, 2011

Source: *International Trade Statistics 2011*, Table II.2 (WTO, 2012)

growth in exports and imports over the period. In 2011, Africa accounted for only 3.4 per cent of world exports.

Middle Eastern countries experienced virtually no growth in export earnings during much of the 1990s, thanks to the generally falling price of oil. This changed over the periods 1999–2000, 2003–2008 and 2010–11 as world oil prices surged. As a result, the growth in merchandise export values averaged 20 per cent over the period from 1998 to 2011 compared with only 1.4 per cent from 1991 to 1997.

The composition of international trade

Trade in goods

By far the largest category of traded goods is that of manufactured products (see Figure 24.4). In 2011, manufactured products accounted for 67 per cent of all merchandise exports and 55 per cent of *total* exports (which include services). Agricultural products accounted for 9 per cent of merchandise exports and fuels and mining products 20 per cent.

Trade in services

Services in 2011 accounted for 20 per cent of total trade. As with trade in manufactured products, trade in services is concentrated in the hands of the largest industrial nations. The USA is by far the largest exporter with some 13.9 per cent of all service exports, followed by the UK (6.6 per cent) and Germany (6.1 per cent). The largest importer of services is the USA with 10.1 per cent of the total, followed by Germany (7.3 per cent), China (6.1 per cent) and the UK (4.6 per cent).

Trade and the UK

In 2011, the UK sold 2.7 per cent of world exports of goods and consumed 3.7 per cent of world imports of goods.

In 2011, 53.8 per cent of the UK's exports of goods went to EU countries, 14.3 per cent to the USA and 2.8 per cent to China.

UK imports, like UK exports, are strongly tied to Europe. In 2011, 51.9 per cent of the imports of goods came from EU countries, 9.3 per cent from China and 8.9 per cent from the USA.

24.2 THE ADVANTAGES OF TRADE

Specialisation as the basis for trade

Why do countries trade with each other and what do they gain out of it? The reasons for international trade are really only an extension of the reasons for trade *within* a nation. Rather than people trying to be self-sufficient and do everything for themselves, it makes sense to specialise.

Firms specialise in producing certain types of goods. This allows them to gain economies of scale and to exploit their entrepreneurial and management skills and the skills of their labour force. It also allows them to benefit from their particular location and from the ownership of any particular capital equipment or other assets they might possess. With the revenues that firms earn, they buy in the inputs they need from other firms and the labour they require. Firms thus trade with each other.

Countries also specialise. They produce more than they need of certain goods. What is not consumed domestically is exported. The revenues earned from the exports are used to import goods which are not produced in sufficient amounts at home.

But which goods should a country specialise in? What should it export and what should it import? The answer is that it should specialise in those goods in which it has a *comparative advantage*. Let us examine what this means.

The law of comparative advantage

Countries have different endowments of factors of production. They differ in population density, labour skills, climate, raw materials, capital equipment, etc. These differences tend to persist because factors are relatively immobile between countries. Obviously land and climate are totally immobile, but even with labour and capital there tend to be more restrictions (physical, social, cultural or legal) on their international movement than on their movement within countries. Thus the ability to supply goods differs between countries.

What this means is that the relative costs of producing goods will vary from country to country. For example, one country may be able to produce 1 fridge for the same cost as 6 tonnes of wheat or 3 compact disc players, whereas another country may be able to produce 1 fridge for the same cost as only 3 tonnes of wheat but 4 CD players. It is these differences in relative costs that form the basis of trade.

At this stage we need to distinguish between *absolute advantage* and *comparative advantage*.

Absolute advantage

When one country can produce a good with fewer resources than another country, it is said to have an **absolute advantage** in that good. If France can produce

---

Definition

Absolute advantage A country has an absolute advantage over another in the production of a good if it can produce it with less resources than the other country.

Table 24.1	Production possibilities for two countries				
		Kilos of wheat			**Metres of cloth**
Less developed country	Either	2	or		1
Developed country	Either	4	or		8

wine with fewer resources than the UK, and the UK can produce gin with fewer resources than France, then France has an absolute advantage in wine and the UK an absolute advantage in gin. Production of both wine and gin will be maximised by each country specialising and then trading with the other country. Both will gain.

Comparative advantage

The above seems obvious, but trade between two countries can still be beneficial even if one country could produce *all* goods with fewer resources than the other, providing the *relative* efficiency with which goods can be produced differs between the two countries.

Take the case of a developed country that is absolutely more efficient than a less developed country at producing both wheat and cloth. Assume that with a given amount of resources (labour, land and capital) the alternatives shown in Table 24.1 can be produced in each country.

Despite the developed country having an absolute advantage in both wheat and cloth, the less developed country (LDC) has a ***comparative advantage*** in wheat, and the developed country has a *comparative* advantage in cloth. This is because wheat is relatively cheaper in the LDC: only 1 metre of cloth has to be sacrificed to produce 2 kilos of wheat, whereas 8 metres of cloth would have to be sacrificed in the developed country to produce 4 kilos of wheat. In other words, the opportunity cost of wheat is 4 times higher in the developed country (8/4 compared with 1/2).

On the other hand, cloth is relatively cheaper in the developed country. Here the opportunity cost of producing 8 metres of cloth is only 4 kilos of wheat, whereas in the LDC 1 metre of cloth costs 2 kilos of wheat. Thus the opportunity cost of cloth is 4 times higher in the LDC (2/1 compared with 4/8).

To summarise: countries have a comparative advantage in those goods that can be produced at a lower opportunity cost than in other countries.

KI 3
p 20

Pause for thought

Draw up a similar table to Table 24.1, only this time assume that the figures are: LDC 6 wheat or 2 cloth; DC 8 wheat or 20 cloth. What are the opportunity cost ratios now?

If countries are to gain from trade, they should export those goods in which they have a comparative advantage and import those goods in which they have a comparative disadvantage. Given this, we can state a *law of comparative advantage*.

> **KEY IDEA 37** ***The law of comparative advantage.*** Provided opportunity costs of various goods differ in two countries, both of them can gain from mutual trade if they specialise in producing (and exporting) those goods that have relatively low opportunity costs compared with the other country.

But why do they gain if they specialise according to this law? And just what will that gain be? We will consider these questions next.

The gains from trade based on comparative advantage

Before trade, unless markets are very imperfect, the prices of the two goods are likely to reflect their opportunity costs. For example, in Table 24.1, since the less developed country can produce 2 kilos of wheat for 1 metre of cloth, the *price* of 2 kilos of wheat will roughly equal 1 metre of cloth.

Assume, then, that the pre-trade exchange ratios of wheat for cloth are as follows:

LDC   : 2 wheat for 1 cloth
Developed country : 1 wheat for 2 cloth (i.e. 4 for 8)

Both countries will now gain from trade, provided the exchange ratio is somewhere between 2:1 and 1:2. Assume, for the sake of argument, that it is 1:1. In other words, 1 wheat trades internationally for 1 cloth. How will each country gain?

The LDC gains by exporting wheat and importing cloth. At an exchange ratio of 1:1, it now has to give up only 1 kilo of wheat to obtain a metre of cloth, whereas before trade it had to give up 2 kilos of wheat.

Definitions

Comparative advantage A country has a comparative advantage over another in the production of a good if it can produce it at a lower opportunity cost: i.e. if it has to forgo less of other goods in order to produce it.

The law of comparative advantage Trade can benefit all countries if they specialise in the goods in which they have a comparative advantage.

The developed country gains by exporting cloth and importing wheat. Again at an exchange ratio of 1:1, it now has to give up only 1 metre of cloth to obtain a kilo of wheat, whereas before it had to give up 2 metres of cloth.

Thus both countries have gained from trade.

The actual exchange ratios will depend on the relative prices of wheat and cloth after trade takes place. These prices will depend on total demand for and supply of the two goods. It may be that the trade exchange ratio is nearer to the pre-trade exchange ratio of one country than the other. Thus the gains to the two countries need not be equal.

> ### Pause for thought
>
> *Show how each country could gain from trade if the LDC could produce (before trade) 3 wheat for 1 cloth and the developed country could produce (before trade) 2 wheat for 5 cloth, and if the exchange ratio (with trade) was 1 wheat for 2 cloth. Would they both still gain if the exchange ratio was (a) 1 wheat for 1 cloth; (b) 1 wheat for 3 cloth?*

The limits to specialisation and trade

Does the law of comparative advantage suggest that countries will completely specialise in just a few products? In practice, countries are likely to experience *increasing* opportunity costs. The reason for this is that, as a country increasingly specialises in one good, it will have to use resources that are less and less suited to its production and which were more suited to other goods. Thus ever-increasing amounts of the other goods will have to be sacrificed. For example, as a country specialises more and more in grain production, it will have to use land that is less and less suited to growing grain.

These increasing costs as a country becomes more and more specialised will lead to the disappearance of its comparative cost advantage. When this happens, there will be no point in further specialisation. Thus, whereas a country like Germany has a comparative advantage in capital-intensive manufactures, it does not produce only manufactures. It would make no sense not to use its fertile lands to produce food or its forests to produce timber. The opportunity costs of diverting all agricultural labour to industry would be very high.

Other reasons for gains from trade

Decreasing costs. Even if there are no initial comparative cost differences between two countries, it will still benefit both to specialise in industries where economies of scale can be gained, and then to trade. Once the economies of scale begin to appear, comparative cost differences will also appear, and thus the countries will have gained a comparative advantage in these industries.

This reason for trade is particularly relevant for small countries where the domestic market is not large enough to support large-scale industries. Thus exports form a much higher percentage of GDP in small countries such as Singapore than in large countries such as the USA.

Differences in demand. Even with no comparative cost differences and no potential economies of scale, trade can benefit both countries if demand conditions differ.

If people in country A like beef more than lamb, and people in country B like lamb more than beef, then rather than A using resources better suited for lamb to produce beef, and B using resources better suited for producing beef to produce lamb, it will benefit both to produce beef *and* lamb and to export the one they like less in return for the one they like more.

Increased competition. If a country trades, the competition from imports may stimulate greater efficiency at home. This extra competition may prevent domestic monopolies/oligopolies from charging high prices. It may stimulate greater research and development and the more rapid adoption of new technology. It may lead to a greater variety of products being made available to consumers.

Trade as an 'engine of growth'. In a growing world economy, the demand for a country's exports is likely to grow over time, especially when these exports have a high income elasticity of demand. This will provide a stimulus to growth in the exporting country.

Non-economic advantages. There may be political, social and cultural advantages to be gained by fostering trading links between countries.

The terms of trade

What price will our exports fetch abroad? What will we have to pay for imports? The answer to these questions is given by the terms of trade. The **terms of trade** are defined as:

$$\frac{\text{the average price of exports}}{\text{the average price of imports}}$$

expressed as an index, where prices are measured against a base year in which the terms of trade are assumed to be 100. Thus if the average price of exports relative to the

> ### Definition
>
> **Terms of trade** The price index of exports divided by the price index of imports and then expressed as a percentage. This means that the terms of trade will be 100 in the base year.

Figure 24.5 Terms of trade for selected countries (2005 = 100)

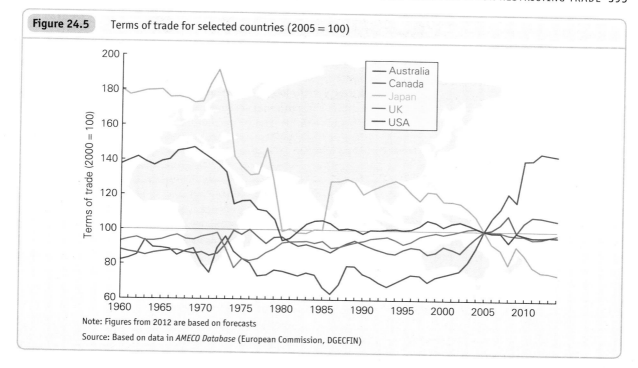

Note: Figures from 2012 are based on forecasts

Source: Based on data in *AMECO Database* (European Commission, DGECFIN)

average price of imports has risen by 20 per cent since the base year, the terms of trade will now be 120. The terms of trade for selected countries are shown in Figure 24.5 (with 2000 as the base year).

If the terms of trade rise (export prices rising relative to import prices), they are said to have 'improved', since fewer exports now have to be sold to purchase any given quantity of imports. Changes in the terms of trade are caused by changes in the demand and supply of imports and exports, and by changes in the exchange rate.

Pause for thought

In Figure 24.5, which countries have experienced an improvement in their terms of trade in recent years?

24.3 ARGUMENTS FOR RESTRICTING TRADE

We have seen how trade can bring benefits to all countries. But when we look around the world, we often see countries erecting barriers to trade. Their politicians know that trade involves costs as well as benefits.

Possible barriers to imports include the following:

- customs duties (or 'tariffs') on imports;
- restrictions on the amount of certain goods that can be imported ('quotas');
- subsidies on domestic products to give them a price advantage over imports;
- administrative regulations designed to exclude imports, such as customs delays or excessive paperwork;
- governments favouring domestic producers when purchasing equipment (e.g. defence equipment).

Alternatively, governments may favour domestic producers by subsidising their exports in a process known as *dumping*. The goods are 'dumped' at artificially low prices in the foreign market.

In looking at the costs and benefits of trade, the choice is not the stark one of whether to have free trade or no trade at all. Although countries may sometimes contemplate having completely free trade, typically countries limit their trade. However, they certainly do not ban it altogether.

Arguments in favour of restricting trade

Arguments having some general validity

The infant industry argument. Some industries in a country may be in their infancy but have a potential comparative advantage. This is particularly likely in developing

KI 37
p 393

Definition

Dumping Where exports are sold at prices below marginal cost – often as a result of government subsidy.

countries. Such industries are too small yet to have gained economies of scale; their workers are inexperienced; there is a lack of back-up facilities – communications networks, specialist research and development, specialist suppliers, etc. – and they may have only limited access to finance for expansion. Without protection, these **infant industries** will not survive competition from abroad.

Protection from foreign competition, however, will allow them to expand and become more efficient. Once they have achieved a comparative advantage, the protection can then be removed to enable them to compete internationally.

To reduce reliance on goods with little dynamic potential. Many developing countries have traditionally exported primaries: foodstuffs and raw materials. The world demand for these, however, is fairly income inelastic, and thus grows relatively slowly. In such cases, free trade is not an engine of growth. Instead, if it encourages countries' economies to become locked into a pattern of primary production, it may prevent them from expanding in sectors like manufacturing which have a higher income elasticity of demand. There may thus be a valid argument for protecting or promoting manufacturing industry.

To prevent 'dumping' and other unfair trade practices. A country may engage in dumping by subsidising its exports. Alternatively, firms may practise price discrimination by selling at a higher price in home markets and a lower price in foreign markets in order to increase their profits. Either way, prices may no longer reflect comparative costs. Thus the world would benefit from tariffs being imposed by importers to counteract the subsidy.

It can also be argued that there is a case for retaliating against countries which impose restrictions on your exports. In the *short* run, both countries are likely to be made worse off by a contraction in trade. But if the retaliation persuades the other country to remove its restrictions, it may have a longer-term benefit. In some cases, the mere threat of retaliation may be enough to get another country to remove its protection.

KI 21
p 161

To prevent the establishment of a foreign-based monopoly. Competition from abroad could drive domestic producers out of business. The foreign company, now having a monopoly of the market, could charge high prices with a resulting misallocation of resources. The problem could be tackled either by restricting imports or by subsidising the domestic producer(s).

All the above arguments suggest that governments should adopt a 'strategic' approach to trade. **Strategic trade theory** argues that protecting certain industries allows a net gain in the *long* run from increased competition in the market (see Box 24.1).

To spread the risks of fluctuating markets. A highly specialised economy – Zambia with copper, Cuba with sugar – will be highly susceptible to world market fluctuations. Greater diversity and greater self-sufficiency, although maybe leading to less efficiency, can reduce these risks.

To reduce the influence of trade on consumer tastes. The assumption of fixed consumer tastes dictating the pattern of production through trade is false. Multinational companies through their advertising and other forms of sales promotion may influence consumer tastes. Many developing countries object to the insidious influence of Western consumerist values expounded by companies such as Coca-Cola and McDonald's. Thus some restriction on trade may be justified in order to reduce this 'producer sovereignty'.

To prevent the importation of harmful goods. A country may want to ban or severely curtail the importation of things such as drugs, pornographic literature and live animals.

To take account of externalities. Free trade will tend to reflect private costs. Both imports and exports, however, can involve externalities. The mining of many minerals for export may adversely affect the health of miners; the production of chemicals for export may involve pollution; the importation of juggernaut lorries may lead to structural damage to houses.

Arguments having some validity for specific groups or countries

The arguments considered so far are of general validity: restricting trade for such reasons could be of net benefit to the world. There are two other arguments, however, that are used by individual governments for restricting trade, where their country will gain, but at the *expense* of other countries, such that there will be a net loss to the world.

The first argument concerns taking advantage of market power in world trade. If a country, or a group of countries, has monopsony power in the purchase of imports (i.e. they are individually or collectively a very large economy, such as the USA or the EU), then they could gain by restricting imports so as to drive down their price. Similarly, if countries have monopoly power in the sale of some export (e.g. OPEC countries with oil), then they could gain by forcing up the price.

The second argument concerns giving protection to declining industries. The human costs of sudden industrial

---

Definitions

Infant industry An industry which has a potential comparative advantage, but which is as yet too underdeveloped to be able to realise this potential.

Strategic trade theory The theory that protecting/supporting certain industries can enable them to compete more effectively with large monopolistic rivals abroad. The effect of the protection is to increase long-run competition and may enable the protected firms to exploit a comparative advantage that they could not have done otherwise.

closures can be very high. In such circumstances, temporary protection may be justified to allow the industry to decline more slowly, thus avoiding excessive structural unemployment. Such policies will be at the expense of the consumer, who will be denied access to cheaper foreign imports.

'Non-economic' arguments for restricting trade. A country may be prepared to forgo the direct economic advantages of free trade in order to achieve objectives that are often described as 'non-economic':

■ It may wish to maintain a degree of self-sufficiency in case trade is cut off in times of war. This may apply particularly to the production of food and armaments.

■ It may decide not to trade with certain countries with which it disagrees politically.

■ It may wish to preserve traditional ways of life. Rural communities or communities built round old traditional industries may be destroyed by foreign competition.

■ It may prefer to retain as diverse a society as possible, rather than one too narrowly based on certain industries.

Pursuing such objectives, however, will involve costs. Preserving a traditional way of life, for example, may mean that consumers are denied access to cheaper goods from abroad. Society must therefore weigh up the benefits against the costs of such policies.

BOX 24.1   STRATEGIC TRADE THEORY

The case of Airbus

Supporters of *strategic trade theory* hold that comparative advantage need not be the result of luck or circumstance, but may in fact be created by government. By diverting resources into selective industries, usually high tech and high skilled, a comparative advantage can be created through intervention.

An example of such intervention was the European aircraft industry, and in particular the creation of the European Airbus Consortium.

The European Airbus Consortium was established in the late 1960s, its four members being Aérospatiale (France), British Aerospace (now BAE Systems) (UK), CASA (Spain) and DASA (Germany). The setting up of this consortium was seen as essential for the future of the European aircraft industry for three reasons:

■ to share high R&D costs;
■ to generate economies of scale;
■ to compete successfully with the market's major players in the USA – Boeing and McDonnell Douglas (which have since merged).

The consortium, although privately owned, was sponsored by government and received state aid, especially in its early years when the company failed to make a profit. Then, in 2000, the French, German and Spanish partners merged to form the European Aeronautic Defence and Space Company (EADS), which had an 80 per cent share of Airbus (BAE Systems having the remaining 20 per cent share). Shortly afterwards, it was announced that enough orders had been secured for the new 550+ seater A380 for production to go ahead. This new jumbo, which had its maiden flight in April 2005, is a serious competitor to the long-established Boeing 747. In 2006, BAE Systems announced that it was planning to sell its 20 per cent stake in Airbus to EADS to concentrate on its core transatlantic defence and aerospace business.

In recent years Airbus has become very successful, capturing a larger share of the world commercial aircraft market. In 2003, for the first time, Airbus delivered more passenger aircraft than Boeing (305 compared with 281 for Boeing), a lead it then maintained until 2012, when Boeing once again delivered more: 601 compared with 588 by Airbus. In the light of Airbus's success, it should come as no surprise to find that the Americans, and Boeing in particular, have brought accusations that Airbus is founded upon unfair trading practices and ought not to receive the level of governmental support that it does (see Box 25.1).

So does the experience of Airbus support the arguments of the strategic trade theorists? Essentially three kinds of benefit were expected to flow from Airbus and its presence in the aircraft market: lower prices, economic spillovers and profits.

■ Without Airbus the civil aircraft market would have been monopolised by two American firms, Boeing and McDonnell Douglas (and possibly one, if the 1997 merger had still gone ahead). Therefore the presence of Airbus would be expected to promote competition and thereby keep prices down. Studies in the 1980s and 1990s tended to support this view, suggesting that consumers have made significant gains from lower prices. One survey estimated that without Airbus commercial aircraft prices would have been 3.5 per cent higher than they currently are, and without both Airbus and McDonnell Douglas they would have been 15 per cent higher.

■ Economic spillovers from the Airbus Consortium, such as skills and technology developments, might be expected to benefit other industries. Findings are inconclusive on this point. It is clear, however, that although aggregate R&D in the whole aircraft industry has risen, so has the level of R&D duplication.

On balance it appears that Airbus has had many positive effects and that the strategic trade theory that has underpinned state aid, in this instance, has been largely vindicated. Boeing has a genuine competitor in Airbus and passengers worldwide have benefited from this competition.

1. *In what other industries could the setting up of a consortium, backed by government aid, be justified as a means of exploiting a potential comparative advantage?*
2. *Is it only in industries that could be characterised as world oligopolies that strategic trade theory is relevant?*

Problems with protection

Tariffs and other forms of protection impose a cost on society. Figure 24.6 illustrates the case of a good that is partly home produced and partly imported. Domestic demand and supply are given by D_{dom} and S_{dom}. It is assumed that firms in the country produce under perfect competition and that therefore the supply curve is the sum of the firms' marginal cost curves.

Let us assume that the country is too small to affect world prices: it is a price taker. The world price is given, at P_w. At P_w, Q_2 is demanded, Q_1 is supplied by domestic suppliers and hence $Q_2 - Q_1$ is imported.

Now a tariff is imposed. This increases the price to consumers by the amount of the tariff. Price rises to $P_w + t$. Domestic production increases to Q_3, consumption falls to Q_4, and hence imports fall to $Q_4 - Q_3$.

What are the costs of this tariff to the country? Consumers are having to pay a higher price, and hence

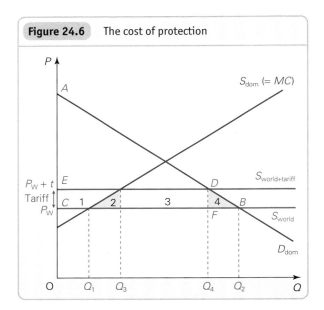

Figure 24.6 The cost of protection

BOX 24.2 **TAKEN TO THE CLEANERS**

Looking after the US steel wire garment hanger industry

The USA is well aware of the dangers of tariffs and other restrictions on trade. In a 2007 report entitled *The Economic Effects of Significant US Import Restraints*, it estimates that:

> US welfare, as defined by public and private consumption, would increase by about $3.7 billion annually if all of the significant restraints quantified in this report were removed unilaterally. Exports would expand by $13.5 billion and imports by $19.6 billion, while about 60,000 workers would move from contracting sectors to expanding sectors as a result of liberalization.[1]

However, the US International Trade Commission (USITC) is constantly embroiled in trade disputes with international partners and does not shirk from retaliatory action if it finds that other nations are engaged in anti-competitive behaviour. Failure to respond firmly would be seen as damaging to the international reputation of a world superpower.

Over the period 1980 to 2006 there were 1569 original cases filed with the USITC, of which 37 per cent were found to require the imposition of trade restrictions, usually a tariff.[2] In 2008, 25 cases were filed against China, including off-road tyres, various chemicals, laminated woven sacks, steel nails and steel pipes.

One of the more interesting cases, though, centres on steel wire garment hangers (SWGH) that are mainly used in the dry cleaning trade. The case against Chinese SWGH manufacturers dates back to 2003 when the USITC recommended an *ad valorem* tariff over three years that began at 25 per cent and

reduced in the third year to 15 per cent. The rationale for this was that imports had risen from 28.8 million units in 1997 to almost half a billion units in 2002.

Tariffs were duly imposed, but the level of imports kept rising to 2.7 billion units in 2007. According to the USITC, Chinese imports had a significant effect on US market share. Import prices fell and so did employment by US hanger manufacturers; from 1345 in 1997 to 564 in 2004 and to 139 in 2007.[3] Some US manufacturers moved their production to Mexico where labour costs were cheaper.

Following a further complaint from one of the US hanger manufacturers, the USITC investigated the market once more and, in March 2008, found that US SWGH manufacturers had been 'materially injured' by Chinese imports, ruling that these had been dumped on US markets at prices that were below 'fair value'. That is, Chinese manufacturers were selling in the USA at prices below what they would charge in China, after allowing for transport and exchange variations. One reason for the lower price was that Chinese manufacturers are given an export tax rebate by the Chinese government, though this fell from 13 per cent to 5 per cent in July 2007.

In March 2008 the USITC imposed tariffs of between 34 per cent and 221 per cent on individual Chinese firms (who were required to pay a bond to US customs when they brought imports into the USA). On publication of the final report in August 2008 it reduced these to between 15 per cent and 187 per cent based on representations made by the Chinese. The end result, though, was a substantial penalty, but not just for the Chinese exporters.

---

[1] USITC, *The Economic Effects of Significant US Import Restraints*, Publication 3906, February 2007. Available at www.usitc.gov/publications/pub3906.pdf

[2] USITC, *Import Injury Investigations. Case Statistics, 1980–2006*. January 2008. Available at www.usitc.gov/trade_remedy/Report-01-08-PUB.pdf

[3] USITC, *Steel Wire Garment Hangers from China*. Publication 3951. October 2007. Available at http://hotdocs.usitc.gov/docs/pubs/701_731/pub3951.pdf

consumer surplus falls from area *ABC* to *ADE* (see pages 83–4 and 314 if you are unsure about consumer surplus). The cost to consumers in lost consumer surplus is thus *EDBC* (i.e. areas 1 + 2 + 3 + 4). *Part* of this cost, however, is redistributed as a *benefit* to other sections in society. *Firms* get a higher price, and thus gain extra profits (area 1): where profit is given by the area between the price and the *MC* curve. The *government* receives extra revenue from the tariff payments (area 3): i.e. $Q_4 - Q_3 \infty$ tariff. These revenues can be used, for example, to reduce taxes.

But *part* of this cost is not recouped elsewhere. It is a net cost to society (areas 2 and 4).

Area 2 represents the extra costs of producing $Q_3 - Q_1$ at home, rather than importing it. If $Q_3 - Q_1$ were still imported, the country would only be paying P_w. By producing it at home, however, the costs are given by the domestic supply curve (= *MC*). The difference between *MC* and P_w (area 2) is thus the efficiency loss on the production side.

Area 4 represents the loss of consumer surplus by the reduction in consumption from Q_2 to Q_4. Consumers have saved area FBQ_2Q_4 of expenditure, but have sacrificed area DBQ_2Q_4 of utility in so doing – a net loss of area 4.

The government should ideally weigh up such costs against any benefits that are gained from protection. (See Box 24.2 for an example relating to tariffs imposed by the USA on Chinese steel wire garment hangers.)

Apart from these direct costs to the consumer, there are several other problems with protection. Some are a direct effect of the protection; others follow from the reactions of other nations.

Protection as 'second-best'. Many of the arguments for protection amount merely to arguments for some type of government intervention in the economy. Protection, however, may not be the best way of dealing with the problem, since protection may have undesirable side-effects. There may be a more direct form of intervention that has no

---

The consequences of tariffs are outlined on pages 398–400. In this case the costs of tariffs were not particularly onerous for dry cleaning customers – it will only add a few cents to a dry cleaning bill and customers do not feel the pain of this sort of rise. The biggest losers were the dry cleaning firms, of which there are some 30 000 in the USA. The *New York Times* quotes one dry cleaner, Mr Jung, thus: 'We do 4000 pieces a week, so obviously we need 4000 hangers. Raise the price a little, OK, but not 60 percent. It's a lot of upset.' In just a few weeks, he said, the price of a box of 500 hangers rose to almost $40 from $17.50.[4]

Assuming that 60 per cent of the rise in the box of hangers was due to the tariff (the rest of the rise may have been due to steel price increases at the time), this would indicate that Mr Jung's annual costs from the tariff increased by $4368 per annum.[5] From what we noted above, this 60 per cent tariff is a little on the low side but an alternative estimate put the additional cost to dry cleaners at around $4000 dollars per year or $120 million for the 30 000 in the industry,[6] so perhaps this is not an unreasonable estimate of the overall cost.

If this is correct, the annual subsidy for maintaining employment in the US wire hanger industry at 2007 levels was around $860 000 per job ($120m/139) or around $213 000 per job at 2004 levels ($120m/564), which is far greater than the industry average wage of just over $30 000 per year in 2007.

For a tariff to have any merit it must have some redistributive qualities. However, any gains from the tariff did not stop the demise of the industry. The falls in both employment and the number of firms, in spite of previous tariffs, indicated that there were other difficulties, such as high energy and labour costs, which were more likely to be domestic in nature. It may have been that the tariff was spent on helping workers who lost their jobs to find new work, but this seems unlikely given the small numbers involved and that the factories were geographically dispersed across the USA. It is more probable that workers found new jobs through existing institutions and networks.

Revenues raised from the tariffs were also not redirected to those bearing the brunt of the costs – in this case the dry cleaner industry. One solution that the dry cleaners came up with to offset the costs of the tariff was to encourage customers to recycle their hangers to save costs. As one customer put it, '[if] somebody brings me in a box full of hangers, that's like putting $10 on the counter before they even do business with me.'[7]

Are there any winners? Well, libertarians and cynics might argue that the biggest winners from the imposition of tariffs are lawyers and civil servants who have to represent the parties involved and investigate the case.

1. *What alternative economic strategy might the US government have adopted to improve the competitiveness of domestic producers?*
2. *How can the USA counter the export rebate given to Chinese SWGH manufacturers by the Chinese government?*

[4] *'Dry cleaners feel an ill wind from China'*, New York Times, 27 April 2008. Available at www.nytimes.com/2008/04/27/nyregion/thecity/ 27hang.html?_r=1

[5] A box of 500 hangers increases by $17.5 × 1.6 = $28. If Mr Jung needs 4000 hangers per week, his extra weekly cost is $10.5 × 8 = $84. This is an extra annual cost of $4368.

[6] *'Costs up, so dry cleaners want their hangers back'*, National Public Radio, 8 May 2008. Available at www.npr.org/templates/story/story.php?storyId=90259986

[7] Ibid.

side-effects. In such a case, protection will be no more than a *second-best* solution.

For example, using tariffs to protect old inefficient industries from foreign competition may help prevent unemployment in those parts of the economy, but the consumer will suffer from higher prices. A better solution would be to subsidise retraining and investment in those areas of the country in *new efficient* industries – industries with a comparative advantage. In this way, unemployment is avoided, but the consumer does not suffer.

Pause for thought

1. Protection to allow the exploitation of monopoly/monopsony power can be seen as a 'first-best' policy for the country concerned. Similarly, the use of tariffs to counteract externalities directly involved in the trade process (e.g. the environmental costs of an oil tanker disaster) could be seen to be a first-best policy. Explain why.
2. Most of the other arguments for tariffs or other forms of protection that we have considered can really be seen as arguments for intervention, with protection being no more than a second-best form of intervention. Go through each of the arguments and consider what would be a 'first-best' form of intervention.

Retaliation. If the USA imposes restrictions on, say, imports from the EU, then the EU may impose restrictions on imports from the USA. Any gain to US firms competing with EU imports is offset by a loss to US exporters. What is more, US consumers suffer, since the benefits from comparative advantage have been lost.

The increased use of tariffs and other restrictions can lead to a trade war, with each country cutting back on imports from other countries. In the end, with retaliation, everyone loses.

Protection may allow firms to remain inefficient. By removing or reducing foreign competition, tariffs etc. may reduce firms' incentive to reduce costs. Thus if protection is being given to an infant industry, the government must ensure that the lack of competition does not prevent it 'growing up'. Protection should not be excessive and should be removed as soon as possible.

Bureaucracy. If a government is to avoid giving excessive protection to firms, it should examine each case carefully. This can lead to large administrative costs.

24.4 THE WORLD TRADING SYSTEM AND THE WTO

After the Wall Street crash of 1929 (when share prices on the US stock exchange plummeted), the world plunged into the Great Depression. Countries found their exports falling dramatically and many suffered severe balance of payments difficulties. The response of many countries was to restrict imports by the use of tariffs and quotas. Of course, this reduced other countries' exports, which encouraged them to resort to even greater protectionism. The net effect of the Depression and the rise in protectionism was a dramatic fall in world trade. The volume of world trade in manufactures fell by more than a third in the three years following the Wall Street crash. Clearly there was a net economic loss to the world from this decline in trade.

After the Second World War there was a general desire to reduce trade restrictions, so that all countries could gain the maximum benefits from trade. There was no desire to return to the beggar-my-neighbour policies of the 1930s.

In 1947, 23 countries got together and signed the General Agreement on Tariffs and Trade (GATT). By February 2013, there were 158 members of its successor organisation, the World Trade Organization (WTO), which was formed in 1995. Russia was the last big country to join (in 2012). Between them, the members of the WTO account for nearly 98 per cent of world trade. The aims of GATT, and now the WTO, have been to liberalise trade. But, whereas GATT focused on the trade in goods, the WTO and its agreements also relate to the trade in services and in inventions and designs, sometimes referred to as intellectual property.

WTO rules

The WTO requires its members to operate according to various rules. These include the following:

■ *Non-discrimination.* Under the 'most favoured nations clause', any trade concession that a country makes to one member must be granted to *all* signatories. The only exception is with free-trade areas and customs unions (such as the EU). Here countries are permitted to abolish tariffs between themselves while still maintaining them with the rest of the world.

- *Reciprocity.* Any nation benefiting from a tariff reduction made by another country must reciprocate by making similar tariff reductions itself.
- *The general prohibition of quotas.*
- *Fair competition.* If unfair barriers are erected against a particular country, the WTO can sanction retaliatory action by that country. The country is not allowed, however, to take such action without permission.
- *Binding tariffs.* Countries cannot raise existing tariffs without negotiating with their trading partners.

Unlike the GATT, the WTO has the power to impose sanctions on countries breaking trade agreements. If there are disputes between member nations, these will be settled by the WTO, and if an offending country continues to impose trade restrictions, permission will be granted for other countries to retaliate.

For example, in March 2002, the Bush administration imposed tariffs on steel imports into the USA in order to protect the ailing US steel industry (see Case Study I.15 in MyEconLab). The EU and other countries referred the case to the WTO, which in December 2003 ruled that they were illegal. This ruling made it legitimate for the EU and other countries to impose retaliatory tariffs on US products. President Bush consequently announced that the steel tariffs would be abolished.

The greater power of the WTO has persuaded many countries to bring their disputes to it. From January 1995 to January 2013 the WTO dealt with 455 disputes (compared with 300 by GATT over the whole of its 48 years).

Pause for thought

Could US action to protect its steel industry from foreign competition be justified in terms of the interests of the USA as a whole (as opposed to the steel industry in particular)?

Trade rounds

Periodically, member countries have met to negotiate reductions in tariffs and other trade restrictions. There have been eight 'rounds' of such negotiations since the signing of GATT in 1947. The last major round to be completed was the Uruguay Round, which began in Uruguay in 1986, continued at meetings around the world and culminated in a deal being signed in April 1994. By that time, the average tariff on manufactured products was 4 per cent and falling. In 1947 the figure was nearly 40 per cent. The Uruguay Round agreement also involved a programme of phasing in substantial reductions in tariffs and other restrictions up to the year 2002 (see Case Study I.6 in MyEconLab).

Despite the reduction in tariffs, many countries have still tried to restrict trade by various other means, such as quotas and administrative barriers. Also, barriers have been particularly high on certain non-manufactures. Agricultural protection in particular has come in for sustained criticism by developing countries. High fixed prices and subsidies given to farmers in the EU, the USA and other advanced countries mean that the industrialised world continues to export food to many developing countries which have a comparative advantage in food production! Farmers in developing countries often find it impossible to compete with subsidised food imports from the rich countries.

The most recent round of trade negotiations began in Doha, Qatar, in 2001 (see Box 24.3). The negotiations have focused on both trade liberalisation and measures to encourage development of poorer countries. In particular, the Doha Development Agenda, as it is called, is concerned with measures to make trade fairer so that its benefits are spread more evenly around the world. This would involve improved access for developing countries to markets in the rich world. The Agenda is also concerned with the environmental impacts of trade and development. The negotiations were originally due to be completed in 2005, but deadlines continued to be missed and eight years later agreement had still not been reached.

BOX 24.3 THE DOHA DEVELOPMENT AGENDA

A new direction for the WTO?

Globalisation, based on the free play of comparative advantage, economies of scale and innovation, has produced a genuinely radical force, in the true sense of the word. It essentially amplifies and reinforces the strengths, but also the weaknesses, of market capitalism: its efficiency, its instability, and its inequality. If we want globalisation not only to be efficiency-boosting but also fair, we need more international rules and stronger multilateral institutions.[1]

In November 1999, the members of the World Trade Organization met in Seattle in the USA. What ensued became known as the 'battle of Seattle' (see Case Study I.3 in MyEconLab). Anti-globalisation protesters fought with police; the world's developing economies fell out with the world's developed economies; and the very future of the WTO was called into question. The WTO was accused of being a free trader's charter, in which the objective of free trade was allowed to ride rough-shod over anything that might stand in its way. Whatever the issue – the environment, the plight of developing countries, the dominance of trade by multinationals – free trade was king.

At Seattle, both the protesters and developing countries argued that things had gone far enough. The WTO must redefine its role, they argued, to respect *all* stakeholders. More radical voices called for the organisation to be scrapped. As Pascal Lamy, then EU Trade Commissioner, made clear in the quote above, rules had to be strengthened, and the WTO had to ensure that the gains from trade were more fair and sustainable.

The rebuilding process of the WTO began in Doha, Qatar in November 2001. The meeting between the then 142 members of the WTO concluded with the decision to launch a new round of WTO trade talks, to be called the 'Doha Development Agenda'. The talks are designed to increase the liberalisation of trade. However, such a goal is to be tempered by a policy of strengthening assistance to developing economies.

The Doha Development Agenda moves the WTO into a new era: one which allows the organisation to play a fuller role in the pursuit of economic growth, employment and poverty reduction, in global governance, and in the promotion of sustainable development, while maintaining its key function of increasing and improving the conditions for world-wide trade and investment.[2]

At Doha it was agreed that the new trade talks would address questions such as:

- *Sustainable development and the environment.* In the past, international trade agreements always seemed to take precedence over international environmental agreements, even though they are legally equivalent. In the new Doha round, this relationship is to be clarified. The hope is to achieve greater coherence between various areas of international policy making.
- *Trade and development.* The Doha Round will attempt to address a number of issues of concern to developing countries as they become more integrated into the world's trading system. For example, it will seek to extend special provisions to developing economies to improve their access to markets in developed countries. It will also attempt to strengthen the current special treatment that developing countries receive, such as the ability to maintain higher rates of tariff protection.

Other areas identified for discussion include: greater liberalisation of agriculture; rules to govern foreign direct investment; the coordination of countries' competition policies; the use and abuse of patents on medicines and the needs of developing countries.

---

[1] *'Global policy without democracy'* (speech by Pascal Lamy, EU Trade Commissioner, given in 2001).

[2] EU summary of Doha Ministerial Conference (http://trade-info.cec.eu.int/europa/2001newround/compas.htm).

SUMMARY

1a World trade has grown, for many years, significantly faster than the growth in world output.

1b World trade is highly concentrated in the developed world and in particular between the top few trading nations.

1c The composition of world trade is largely dominated by manufacturing products, although trade in services has expanded over recent years.

2a Countries can gain from trade if they specialise in producing those goods in which they have a comparative advantage, i.e. those goods that can be produced at relatively low opportunity costs. This is merely an extension of the argument that gains can be made from the specialisation and division of labour.

2b If two countries trade, then, provided that the trade price ratio of exports and imports is between the pre-trade price ratios of these goods in the two countries, both countries can gain.

2c With increasing opportunity costs there will be a limit to specialisation and trade. As a country increasingly specialises, its (marginal) comparative advantage will eventually disappear.

2d Gains from trade also arise from decreasing costs (economies of scale), differences in demand between countries, increased competition from trade and the transmission of growth from one country to another. There may also be non-economic advantages from trade.

2e The terms of trade give the price of exports relative to the price of imports expressed as an index, where the base year is 100.

3a Countries use various methods to restrict trade, including tariffs, quotas, exchange controls, import licensing, export taxes, and legal and administrative barriers. Countries may also promote their own industries by subsidies.

The talks were originally scheduled for completion by January 2005, but this deadline was extended several times as new talks were arranged and failed to reach agreement. A particular sticking point was the unwillingness of rich countries, and the USA and the EU in particular, to liberalise trade in agricultural products, given the pressure from their domestic farmers. The USA was unwilling to make substantial cuts in agricultural subsidies and the EU in agricultural tariffs.

There was also an unwillingness by large developing countries, such as India and Brazil, to reduce protection of their industrial and service sectors. What is more, there were large divergences in opinion between developing countries on how much they should reduce their own agricultural protection.

Breakdown of the talks

The talks seemed finally to have broken down at a meeting in Geneva in July 2008. Despite the willingness of developing countries to reduce industrial tariffs by more than 50 per cent, and by the USA and the EU to make deep cuts in agricultural subsidies and tariffs, the talks foundered over the question of agricultural protection for developing countries. This was item 18 on a 'to-do' list of 20 items; items 1 to 17 had already been agreed. China and India wanted to protect poor farmers by retaining the ability to impose temporary tariffs on food imports in the event of a drop in food prices or a surge in imports. The USA objected. When neither side would budge, the talks collapsed.

But even 'success' would not have addressed some thorny issues, such as achieving equal access to rich countries' markets by all banana-producing countries (see Box 25.1) and protecting cotton producers in developing countries from cheap subsidised cotton grown in the USA. And Africa's interests would not have been properly addressed. In fact, no African country was present in the inner circle of talks at the end.

Many commentators, however, argued that failure was no catastrophe. The gain from total liberalisation of trade would have boosted developing countries' GDP by no more than

1 per cent. And anyway, tariffs were generally falling and were already at an all-time low. But, with the global economic downturn of 2008/9, there were worries that protectionism would begin to rise again. This was a classic prisoner's dilemma (see page 189). Policies that seemed to be in the interests of countries separately would be to the overall detriment of the world. The Nash equilibrium of such a 'game', therefore, is one where countries are generally worse off. As it turned out, the worries were largely unfounded

A final push to agreement?

Whilst there was a pledge at the G20 meeting in London is 2009 to complete the Doha round, a year later no agreement was in sight. Instead, in March 2010, a deadline for a new trade deal was dropped. In November 2010, the governments of the UK, Germany, Indonesia and Turkey created an 'Experts Group' to report on actions to be taken to combat protectionism and to boost global trade. The group's interim report in early 2011 articulated the case for a meaningful deadline and the need for 'one final push' arguing that 'everyone would gain'. On the delay in concluding the DDA, the Experts Group noted:

> Even by the standards of earlier trade rounds, many of which took years to complete, the DDA has been particularly disappointing in the progress of the negotiations taking ten years to reach this point. If the DDA is not completed by the end of this year it will at best lie in the doldrums for a prolonged period.[3]

By the time you read this, a final agreement may have been reached – or perhaps not!

 Outline the advantages and drawbacks of adopting a free trade strategy for developing economies. How might the Doha Development Agenda go some way to reducing these drawbacks?

---

[3] 'The Doha Round; Setting a deadline, defining a fine deal', *High level trade experts group, Interim Report*, January 2011.

3b Reasons for restricting trade that have some validity in a world context include the infant industry argument, the problems of relying on exporting goods whose market is growing slowly or even declining, dumping and other unfair trade practices, the danger of the establishment of a foreign-based monopoly, the need to spread the risks of fluctuating export prices, and the problems that free trade may adversely affect consumer tastes, may allow the importation of harmful goods and may not take account of externalities.

3c Often, however, the arguments for restricting trade are in the context of one country benefiting even though other countries may lose more. Countries may intervene in trade in order to exploit their monopoly/monopsony power or to protect declining industries.

3d Finally, a country may have other objectives in restricting trade, such as remaining self-sufficient in certain strategic products, not trading with certain countries

of which it disapproves, protecting traditional ways of life or simply retaining a non-specialised economy.

3e Arguments for restricting trade, however, are often fallacious. In general, trade brings benefits to countries, and protection to achieve one objective may be at a very high opportunity cost. Even if government intervention to protect certain parts of the economy is desirable, restricting trade is unlikely to be a first-best solution to the problem, since it involves side-effect costs. What is more, restricting trade may encourage retaliation; it may allow inefficient firms to remain inefficient; it may involve considerable bureaucracy.

4 Most countries of the world are members of the WTO and in theory are in favour of moves towards freer trade. The WTO is more powerful than its predecessor, GATT. It has a disputes procedure and can enforce its rulings. In practice, however, countries have been very unwilling to abandon restrictions if they believe that they can gain from them, even though they might be at the expense of other countries.

REVIEW QUESTIONS

1 What is likely to be the impact of rising levels of intra-regional trade for the world economy?

2 Imagine that two countries, Richland and Poorland, can produce just two goods, computers and coal. Assume that for a given amount of land and capital, the output of these two products requires the following constant amounts of labour:

	Richland	Poorland
1 computer	2	4
100 tonnes of coal	4	5

Assume that each country has 20 million workers.

(a) Draw the production possibility curves for the two countries (on two separate diagrams).

(b) If there is no trade, and in each country 12 million workers produce computers and 8 million workers produce coal, how many computers and tonnes of coal will each country produce? What will be the total production of each product?

(c) What is the opportunity cost of a computer in (i) Richland; (ii) Poorland?

(d) What is the opportunity cost of 100 tonnes of coal in (i) Richland: (ii) Poorland?

(e) Which country has a comparative advantage in which product?

(f) Assuming that price equals marginal cost, which of the following would represent possible exchange ratios?
   (i)   1 computer for 40 tonnes of coal;
   (ii) 2 computers for 140 tonnes of coal;
   (iii) 1 computer for 100 tonnes of coal;
   (iv) 1 computer for 60 tonnes of coal;
   (v)   4 computers for 360 tonnes of coal.

(g) Assume that trade now takes place and that 1 computer exchanges for 65 tonnes of coal. Both countries specialise completely in the product in which they have a comparative advantage.

How much does each country produce of its respective product?

(h) The country producing computers sells 6 million domestically. How many does it export to the other country?

(i) How much coal does the other country consume?

3 Why doesn't the USA specialise as much as General Motors or Texaco? Why doesn't the UK specialise as much as Glaxa Smith Kline? Is the answer to these questions similar to the answer to the questions, 'Why doesn't the USA specialise as much as Luxembourg?', and 'Why doesn't ICI or Unilever specialise as much as the local florist?'

4 To what extent are the arguments for countries specialising and then trading with each other the same as those for individuals specialising in doing the jobs to which they are relatively well suited?

5 The following are four items that are traded internationally: wheat; computers; textiles; insurance. In which one of the four is each of the following most likely to have a comparative advantage: India; the UK; Canada; Japan? Give reasons for your answer.

6 Go through each of the arguments for restricting trade (both those of general validity and those having some validity for specific countries) and provide a counter-argument for not restricting trade.

7 If countries are so keen to reduce the barriers to trade, why do many countries frequently attempt to erect barriers?

8 Debate the following: 'All arguments for restricting trade boil down to special pleading for particular interest groups. Ultimately there will be a net social cost from any trade restrictions.'

9 If rich countries stand to gain substantially from freer trade, why have they been so reluctant to reduce the levels of protection of agriculture?

10 Make out a case for restricting trade between the UK and Japan. Are there any arguments here that could not equally apply to a case for restricting trade between Scotland and England or between Liverpool or Manchester?

Trading blocs

Business issues covered in this chapter

- Why do countries form free trade areas and other types of trading alliance, and what forms can they take?
- Do they result in a creation of trade or a mere diversion of trade from outside to inside the area?
- What trading alliances exist around the world and what are their features?
- How has the EU evolved and to what extent is it a true common market?
- How has the single market in the EU benefited companies and member states?

The world economy seems to have been increasingly forming into a series of trade blocs, based upon regional groupings of countries: a European region centred on the European Union, an Asian region on Japan, a North American region on the USA and a Latin American region. Such trade blocs are examples of *preferential trading arrangements*. These arrangements involve trade restrictions with the rest of the world, and lower or zero restrictions between the members.

Although trade blocs clearly encourage trade between their members (intra-regional trade has been growing significantly faster than trade between regions), many countries outside these blocs complain that they benefit the members at the expense of the rest of the world. For many developing economies, in need of access to the most prosperous nations in the world, this represents a significant check on their ability to grow and develop.

In this chapter we shall first consider why groups of countries might wish to establish trade blocs, and what they seek to gain beyond the benefits that result from free and open trade. We will then look at the world's trade blocs as they currently stand, paying particular attention to the European Union, which is by far the most advanced in respect to establishing a high level of regional integration.

Definition

Preferential trading arrangement A trading arrangement whereby trade between the signatories is freer than trade with the rest of the world.

25.1 PREFERENTIAL TRADING

Types of preferential trading arrangement

There are three possible forms that such trading arrangements might take.

Free trade areas

A *free trade area* is where member countries remove tariffs and quotas between themselves, but retain whatever restrictions *each member chooses* with non-member countries. Some provision will have to be made to prevent imports from outside coming into the area via the country with the lowest external tariff.

Customs unions

A *customs union* is like a free trade area, but in addition members must adopt *common* external tariffs and quotas with non-member countries.

Common markets

A *common market* is where member countries operate as a *single* market. Like a customs union there are no tariffs and quotas between member countries and there are common external tariffs and quotas. But a common market goes further than this. A full common market includes the following features: a common system of taxation, and common laws and regulations governing production, employment and trade. It also includes the free movement of labour and capital. It might also include features such as a single currency or fixed exchange rates between members, and the pursuit of a common macroeconomic policy.

The direct effects of a customs union: trade creation and trade diversion

By joining a customs union (or free trade area), a country will find that its trade patterns change. Two such changes can be distinguished: trade creation and trade diversion.

Trade creation

Trade creation is where consumption shifts from a high-cost producer to a low-cost producer. The removal of trade barriers allows greater specialisation according to comparative advantage. Instead of consumers having to pay high prices for domestically produced goods in which the country has a comparative disadvantage, the goods can now be obtained more cheaply from other members of the customs union. In return, the country can export to them goods in which it has a comparative advantage.

Trade diversion

Trade diversion is where consumption shifts from a lower-cost producer outside the customs union to a higher-cost producer within the union.

Assume that the most efficient producer of good y in the world is New Zealand – outside the EU. Assume that before membership of the EU, the UK paid a similar tariff on good y from any country, and thus imported the product from New Zealand rather than from the EU.

After the UK joined the EU, however, the removal of the tariff made the EU product cheaper, since the tariff remained on the New Zealand product. Consumption thus switched to a higher-cost producer. There was thus a net loss in world efficiency. As far as the UK was concerned, consumers still gained, since they were paying a lower price than before. However, there was a loss to domestic producers (from the reduction in protection, and hence reduced prices and profits) and to the government (from reduced tariff revenue). These losses may have been smaller or larger than the gain to consumers: in other words, there may have still been a net gain to the UK, but there could have been a net loss, depending on the circumstances.

> ### Pause for thought
>
> *Is joining a customs union more likely to lead to trade creation or trade diversion in each of the following cases? (a) The union has a very high external tariff. (b) Cost differences are very great between the country and members of the union.*

Definitions

Free trade area A group of countries with no trade barriers between themselves.

Customs union A free trade area with common external tariffs and quotas.

Common market A customs union where the member countries act as a single market with free movement of labour and capital, common taxes and common trade laws.

Trade creation Where a customs union leads to greater specialisation according to comparative advantage and thus a shift in production from higher-cost to lower-cost sources.

Trade diversion Where a customs union diverts consumption from goods produced at a lower cost outside the union to goods produced at a higher cost (but tariff free) within the union.

Longer-term effects of a customs union

Over the longer term, there may be other gains and losses from being a member of a customs union.

Longer-term advantages

- Increased market size may allow a country's firms to exploit *(internal) economies of scale*. This argument is more important for small countries, which therefore have more to gain from an enlargement of their markets.
- *External economies of scale*. Increased trade may lead to improvements in the infrastructure of the members of the customs union (better roads, railways, financial services, etc.). This, in turn, could then bring greater long-term benefits from trade between members, and from external trade too, by making the transport and handling of imports and exports cheaper.
- The bargaining power of the whole customs union with the rest of the world may allow member countries to gain *better terms of trade*. This, of course, will necessarily involve a degree of political cooperation between the members.
- *Increased competition* between member countries may stimulate efficiency, encourage investment and reduce

monopoly power. Of course, a similar advantage could be gained by the simple removal of tariffs with any competing country.

- Integration may encourage a *more rapid spread of technology*.

Longer-term disadvantages

- Resources may flow from the country to more efficient members of the customs union, or to the geographical centre of the union (so as to minimise transport costs). This can be a major problem for a *common market* (where there is free movement of labour and capital). The country could become a depressed 'region' of the community.
- If integration encourages greater cooperation between firms in member countries, it may also encourage *greater oligopolistic collusion*, thus keeping prices higher to the consumer. It may also encourage mergers and takeovers, which would increase monopoly power.
- *Diseconomies of scale*. If the union leads to the development of very large companies, they may become bureaucratic and inefficient.
- *The costs of administering* the customs union may be high. This problem is likely to worsen the more intervention there is in the affairs of individual members.

25.2 PREFERENTIAL TRADING IN PRACTICE

Preferential trading has the greatest potential to benefit countries whose domestic market is too small, taken on its own, to enable them to benefit from economies of scale, and where they face substantial barriers to their exports. Most developing countries fall into this category and as a result many have attempted to form preferential trading arrangements.

Examples in Latin America and the Caribbean include the Latin American Integration Association (LAIA), the Andean Community, the Central American Common Market (CACM) and the Caribbean Community (CARICOM). A Southern Common Market (MerCoSur) was formed in 1991, consisting of Argentina, Brazil, Paraguay and Uruguay. It has a common external tariff and most of its internal trade is free of tariffs.

In 1993, the six ASEAN nations (Brunei, Indonesia, Malaysia, the Philippines, Singapore and Thailand) agreed to work towards an ASEAN Free Trade Area (AFTA). ASEAN (the Association of South-East Asian Nations) now has ten members – the new ones being Vietnam (1995), Laos (1997), Myanmar (1997) and Cambodia (1999) – and is dedicated to increased economic cooperation within the region.

What progress has been made in achieving AFTA? Virtually all tariffs between the six original members were eliminated by 2010 and there are plans to eliminate them for the remaining countries by 2015. ASEAN also plans

to establish a common market, the ASEAN Economic Community (AEC), by 2020.

In Africa the Economic Community of West African States (ECOWAS)[1] has been attempting to create a common market between its 15 members. The West African franc is used in eight of the countries and another six plan to introduce a common currency, the eco, by 2015. The ultimate goal is to combine the two currency areas and adopt a single currency for all member states.

The most significant and advanced trade blocs, however, are to be found not in the developing world but in the developed, notably in Europe and North America.

North America Free Trade Agreement (NAFTA)

NAFTA is a trilateral agreement between the USA, Canada and Mexico and came into force in 1994. The three NAFTA members have agreed to abolish tariffs between themselves in the hope that increased trade and cooperation will follow. Tariffs between the USA and Canada were phased out by 1999 and tariffs between all three countries were eliminated as of 1 January 2008. New non-tariff restrictions will not be permitted either, but many existing ones can remain in force, thus preventing the development of

---
[1] www.ecowas.int.

true free trade between the members. Indeed, some industries, such as textiles and agriculture, will continue to have major non-tariff restrictions.

NAFTA members hope that, with a market similar in size to the EU, they will be able to rival the EU's economic power in world trade. Other countries may join in the future, so NAFTA may eventually develop into a Western Hemisphere free trade association.

NAFTA is principally a free trade area and not a common market. Unlike the EU, it does not seek to harmonise laws and regulations, except in very specific areas such as environmental management and labour standards. Member countries are permitted total legal independence, subject to the one proviso that they must treat firms of other member countries equally with their own firms – the principle of 'fair competition'. Nevertheless, NAFTA has encouraged a growth in trade between its members, most of which is trade creation rather than trade diversion.

Of the three countries in NAFTA, Mexico potentially has the most to gain from the agreement. With easier access to US and Canadian markets, and the added attractiveness it now has to foreign investors, especially US multinationals looking to reduce labour costs, the Mexican economy could reap huge benefits.

NAFTA has made Mexico a thriving export economy that attracts sufficient foreign direct investment to finance its total current account deficit. Many EU and south-east Asian businesses are using the Mexican economy to gain access to the USA, although strong demand within Mexico itself is fast making it a valuable market in its own right.

However, the Mexican economy has faced a number of real threats from the agreement. For example, as trade barriers fall, Mexican companies are being faced with competition from bigger and more efficient US and Canadian rivals.

Disputes do arise between the members. In 2009, for example, the USA reneged on a pilot scheme that would allow some Mexican trucks to travel over the US border.[2] In response, Mexico imposed tariffs of up to 45 per cent on

90 US agricultural and industrial imports, ranging from strawberries and wine to cordless telephones. The list was carefully chosen to avoid pushing up prices of staples in Mexico, while hitting goods that are important exports for a range of American states. Such disputes have to be resolved through the trade dispute mechanism at NAFTA.

The Asia-Pacific Economic Cooperation forum (APEC)

The most significant move towards establishing a more widespread regional economic organisation in east Asia appeared with the creation of the Asia-Pacific Economic Cooperation forum (APEC) in 1989. APEC links 21 economies of the Pacific rim, including Asian, Australasian and North and South American countries (19 countries, plus Hong Kong and Taiwan). These countries account for around 55 per cent of the world's total output and 45 per cent of world trade. At the 1994 meeting of APEC leaders, it was resolved to create a free trade area across the Pacific by 2010 for the developed industrial countries, and by 2020 for the rest.

Unlike the EU and NAFTA, APEC is likely to remain solely a free trade area and not to develop into a customs union, let alone a common market. Within the region there exists a wide disparity in GDP per capita, ranging in 2011 from $65 500 in Australia, $48 400 in the USA and $45 900 in Japan to a mere $1900 in Papua New Guinea and $1370 in Vietnam. Such disparities create a wide range of national interests and goals. Countries are unlikely to share common economic problems or concerns. In addition, political differences and conflicts within the region are widespread, reducing the likelihood that any organisational agreement beyond a simple economic one would succeed. However, the economic benefits from free trade and the resulting closer regional ties could be immense.

By far the most developed trading bloc is the EU. In the remainder of this chapter we will consider the development of the EU and its implications for business.

25.3 THE EUROPEAN UNION

The European Economic Community (EEC) was formed by the signing of the Treaty of Rome in 1957 and came into operation on 1 January 1958.

The original six member countries of the EEC (Belgium, France, Italy, Luxembourg, Netherlands and West Germany) had already made a move towards integration with the formation of the European Coal and Steel Community in 1952. This had removed all restrictions on trade in coal, steel and iron ore between the six countries. The aim had been to gain economies of scale and allow

more effective competition with the USA and other foreign producers.

The EEC extended this principle and aimed eventually to be a full common market with completely free trade between members in all products, and with completely free movement of labour, enterprise and capital.

All internal tariffs between the six members had been abolished and common external tariffs established by 1968. But this still only made the EEC a *customs union*, since a number of restrictions on internal trade remained (legal, administrative, fiscal, etc.). Nevertheless, the aim was eventually to create a full common market.

---

[2] 'Don't keep on trucking', *The Economist*, 19 March 2009.

In 1973 the UK, Denmark and Ireland became members. Greece joined in 1981, Spain and Portugal in 1986, and Sweden, Austria and Finland in 1995. Then in May 2004, a further ten countries joined: Cyprus, the Czech Republic, Estonia, Hungary, Latvia, Lithuania, Malta, Poland, Slovakia and Slovenia. With Bulgaria and Romania joining in 2007, the European Union (EU), as it is now called, currently has 27 members.

From customs union to common market

The EU is clearly a customs union. It has common external tariffs and no internal tariffs. But is it also a common market? For years there have been certain common economic policies.

The Common Agricultural Policy (CAP). The EU has traditionally set common high prices for farm products. This has involved charging variable import duties to bring foreign food imports up to EU prices and intervention to buy up surpluses of food produced within the EU at these above-equilibrium prices. Although the main method of support has shifted to providing subsidies (or 'income support') unrelated to current output, this still represents a common economic policy of agricultural support.

Regional policy. EU regional policy provides grants to firms and local authorities in relatively deprived regions of the Union.

Competition policy. EU policy here has applied primarily to companies operating in more than one member state (see section 21.1). For example, Article 101 of the Treaty of Lisbon prohibits agreements between firms operating in more than one EU country (e.g. over pricing or sharing out markets) which adversely affect competition in trade between member states.

Harmonisation of taxation. VAT is the standard form of indirect tax throughout the EU. However, there are substantial differences in VAT rates between member states, as there are with other tax rates.

Social policy. In 1989 the European Commission presented a social charter to the EU heads of state (see Case Study I.13 in MyEconLab). This spelt out a series of worker and social rights that should apply in all member states. These rights were grouped under 12 headings covering areas such as the guarantee of decent levels of income for both the employed and the non-employed, freedom of movement of labour between EU countries, freedom to belong to a trade union and equal treatment of women and men in the labour market. The social charter was only a recommendation and each element had to be approved separately by the European Council of Ministers.

The social chapter of the Maastricht Treaty (1991) attempted to move the Community forward in implementing the details of the social charter in areas such as maximum working hours, minimum working conditions, health and safety protection, the provision of information to and consultation with workers, and equal opportunities.

The UK Conservative government at the time refused to sign this part of the Maastricht Treaty. It maintained that such measures would increase costs of production and would, therefore, make EU goods less competitive in world trade and increase unemployment. Critics of the UK position argued that the refusal to adopt minimum working conditions (and also a minimum wage rate) would make the UK the 'cheap labour sweat-shop' of Europe. One of the first acts of the incoming Labour government in 1997 was to sign up to the social chapter.

Pause for thought

Does the adoption of laws enforcing improved working conditions necessarily lead to higher costs per unit of output?

Despite these various common policies, in other respects the Community of the 1970s and 1980s was far from a true common market: there were all sorts of non-tariff barriers, such as high taxes on wine by non-wine-producing countries, special regulations designed to favour domestic producers, governments giving contracts to domestic producers (e.g. for defence equipment), and so on.

The Single European Act of 1986, however, sought to remove these barriers and to form a genuine common market by the end of 1992. One of the most crucial aspects of the Act was its acceptance of the principle of **mutual recognition**. This is the principle whereby if a firm or individual is permitted to do something under the rules and regulations of *one* EU country, it must thereby also be permitted to do it in all other EU countries. This means that firms and individuals can choose the country's rules that are least constraining. It also means that individual governments can no longer devise special rules and regulations that keep out competitors from other EU countries.

The benefits and costs of the single market

It is difficult to quantify the benefits and costs of the single market, given that many occur over a long period. Also it is difficult to know to what extent the changes taking place are the direct result of the single market. Nevertheless, it is possible to identify the *types* of benefit that have resulted, many of which have been substantial.

Definition

Mutual recognition The EU principle that one country's rules and regulations must apply throughout the Union. If they conflict with those of another country, individuals and firms should be able to choose which to obey.

BOX 25.1   BEYOND BANANAS

EU/US trade disputes

Trade relations between the EU and USA have been strained in recent years. The World Trade Organization (WTO), set up to manage trade and prevent such disputes arising, has been slow in resolving the issues and restoring order.

The problems between the EU and USA started over bananas.

Bananas

The EU/US 'banana war' began in 1993 when the EU adopted a tariff and quota system that favoured banana producers in African, Caribbean and Pacific (ACP) countries, mostly ex-European colonies. Predictably, Latin American banana producers, owned by large American multinationals like Chiquita and Dole, took exception to this move. Latin American producers, with huge economies of scale, were able to produce bananas at considerably lower cost than producers in the ACP countries. But, faced with significant tariffs on entry into the EU market, their bananas became more expensive. Championed by the USA, the Latin American producers won the case at the WTO for removing the agreement.

The EU, however, failed to comply, arguing that the preferential access to EU markets for ACP producers was part of a general development strategy, known as the 'Lomé Convention', to support developing economies. Without preferential access, it was argued, ACP banana producers could simply not compete on world markets. As a European Commission document highlighted, 'The destruction of the Caribbean banana industry would provoke severe economic hardship and political instability in a region already struggling against deprivation.'

As the EU refused to comply with the WTO ruling, the USA imposed $191 million worth of tariffs on EU exports in March 1999. After a series of battles over the issue at the WTO, the EU finally agreed to reform its banana protocol.

A Treaty was eventually signed in December 2009 between the EU, the USA and Latin American and ACP banana producers. This involved a cut in EU tariffs on Latin American bananas from €176 per tonne to €114 per tonne over a seven-year period, with an initial cut to €148 per tonne.

The deal also included compensation of some €200 million by the EU to ACP nations. The deal, however, is dependent on agreement in the Doha round of trade negotiations.

Hormone-treated beef

If the banana dispute could be resolved, many equally contentious issues could be found to take its place. The dispute between the EU and USA over hormone-treated beef has been going on for a staggering 18 years. In 1998, the WTO panel ruled against a ban by the EU on imports of hormone-treated beef from the USA and Canada. The ruling permitted the two countries to impose retaliatory sanctions on EU imports. After a process of arbitration, the values were set at $116.8 million for the USA and CDN$11.1 million for Canada.

Despite this, the EU continued to refuse to import any animal products, live or processed, that had received growth hormones. The ban was made on grounds of public health, and this remains the crux of the dispute. The EU argues that it has not been proven that hormone-treated beef is safe. In reply, the Americans argue that the EU has not provided evidence that it is otherwise.

Following an independent assessment of the risks to consumers of hormone-treated meat, which resulted in the EU banning certain hormones by its farmers, the EU argued that the sanctions should be lifted as it was no longer in breach of the WTO rules. In November 2004, the EU asked the WTO to rule that continued US and Canadian sanctions related to the beef hormone ruling were illegal. In February 2005, a WTO panel was set up to consider the case. The EU, Canada and the USA would all make representations. In addition Australia, Mexico, China and Taiwan were permitted to make 'third-party' representations.

In April 2008, a WTO disputes panel ruled that the EU violated WTO rules in continuing to ban one of the hormones at issue, but also ruled that the USA and Canada were wrong in taking unilateral actions in imposing sanctions against the EU.

In January 2009, the outgoing Bush Administration published an extended list of EU products that would be

---

Trade creation. Costs and prices have fallen as a result of a greater exploitation of comparative advantage. Member countries can now specialise further in those goods and services that they can produce at a comparatively low opportunity cost.

Reduction in the direct costs of barriers. This category includes administrative costs, border delays and technical regulations. Their abolition or harmonisation has led to substantial cost savings.

Economies of scale. With industries based on a Europe-wide scale, many firms and their plants can be large enough to gain the full potential economies of scale. Yet the whole European market is large enough for there still to be adequate competition. Such gains have varied from industry

to industry depending on the minimum efficient scale of a plant or firm (see Box 9.4 on p. 142). Economies of scale have also been gained from mergers and other forms of industrial restructuring.

Greater competition. Increased competition between firms has led to lower costs, lower prices and a wider range of products available to consumers. This has been particularly so in newly liberalised service sectors such as transport, financial services, telecommunications and broadcasting. In the long run, greater competition can stimulate greater innovation, the greater flow of technical information and the rationalisation of production.

Despite these gains, the single market has not received universal welcome within the EU. Its critics argue that, in

subject to sanctions. However, following talks in early 2009, both parties notified the WTO's Dispute Settlement Body of a Memorandum of Understanding. The USA agreed not to impose new sanctions on imports from the EU and would eliminate all sanctions by 2013. The EU agreed to permit additional duty-free imports of US beef not treated with growth-promoting hormones.

Genetically modified (GM) foods

A more recent trade dispute, again in the field of public health, concerns the development of GM food. GM strains of maize and soya have been available in the USA for many years, but the export of such products, whether as seed or food, is banned from the EU. The US position is that EU consumers should be free to choose whether they have GM food or not. This, not surprisingly, is rejected by the EU on the basis that GM foods might contaminate the entire food supply once introduced. In July 2000, the EU decided to continue with its GM food ban indefinitely.

In response to a complaint to the WTO by the USA, Canada and Argentina, a panel was set up in March 2004 to consider the case. In 2006 the WTO concluded that the EU's GM ban was illegal because the risks shown by the scientific evidence did not warrant the ban. Accordingly, WTO rules should apply across EU member states.

In January 2008, the US and the EU informed the Dispute Settlement Board that they had reached an agreement on 'procedures' for the EU implementing the WTO's ruling. However, this has not prevented individual member states such as Austria, France, Germany Greece, Hungary and Luxembourg banning GM maize produced by the US firm Monsanto.

The European Commission initiated proceedings against Austria and Hungary but was overruled by environment ministers, reacting to domestic political pressures. In response, Monsanto has mounted legal challenges in the French and German courts. There is a danger, therefore, that new complaints may be made to the WTO by GM seed-producing countries.

Airbus

Another recent branch of the current EU/US trade dispute concerns Airbus and EU industrial policy (an area which has been a bone of contention for the USA for many years). The issue concerns the new superjumbo, the A380. The Americans are very unhappy with the loans and subsidies, claimed to be $15 billion, that have been provided by EU members to companies within the Airbus Consortium to develop the aircraft. The American complaint is that such subsidies have broken the WTO subsidy code and, as such, are unfair.

In October 2004, the USA requested the establishment of a WTO panel to consider the case. This provoked a counter-request by Airbus, claiming unfair support for Boeing by the USA. In July 2005, two panels were set up to deal with the two sets of allegations.

In March 2010, the WTO ruled on Boeing's case against Airbus. It found Airbus guilty of using some illegal subsidies to win contracts through predatory pricing, but nevertheless dismissed most of Boeing's claims, as many of the subsidies were reimbursable at commercial rates of interest. However, some of the 'launch aid' for research and development was given at below market rates and hence did violate WTO rules.

The report evoked appeal and counter-appeal from both sides, but the WTO's Appellate Body reported in May 2011 upholding the case that 'certain subsidies' provided by the EU and member states were incompatible with WTO rules. In June 2011, the EU accepted the findings.

In March 2011, the WTO ruled on Airbus's case against Boeing. The panel upheld the EU's claim that some payments or tax breaks by US municipalities to Boeing constituted specific subsidies which adversely affected Airbus's ability to compete in 'third country markets', potentially resulting in significant lost sales.

Again the findings were challenged. The WTO Appellate Body reported in March 2012 and, while some of the Panel's initial findings were overturned, it remained of the view that that certain payments did prejudice Airbus sales. In April 2012, the USA accepted the findings.

 Why does the WTO appear to be so ineffective in resolving the disputes between the EU and USA?

---

a Europe of oligopolies, unequal ownership of resources, rapidly changing technologies and industrial practices, and factor immobility, the removal of internal barriers to trade has merely exaggerated the problems of inequality and economic power. More specifically, the following criticisms are made.

Radical economic change is costly. Substantial economic change is necessary to achieve the full economies of scale and efficiency gains from a single European market. These changes necessarily involve redundancies – from bankruptcies, takeovers, rationalisation and the introduction of new technology. The severity of this 'structural' and 'technological' unemployment (see section 26.3) depends on (a) the pace of economic change and (b) the mobility of labour – both occupational and geographical. Clearly, the more integrated markets become across the EU, the less the costs of future economic change.

Adverse regional effects. Firms are likely to locate as near as possible to the 'centre of gravity' of their markets and sources of supply. If, before barriers are removed, a firm's prime market is the UK, it might well locate in the Midlands or the north of England. If, however, with barriers now removed, its market has become Europe as a whole, it may choose to locate in the south of England or in France, Germany or the Benelux countries instead. The creation of a single European market thus tends to attract capital and jobs away from the edges of the Union to its geographical centre.

In an ideal market situation, areas like Cornwall, the south of Italy, Portugal and parts of eastern Europe should attract resources from other parts of the Union. As these are relatively depressed areas, wage rates and land prices are lower. The resulting lower industrial costs should encourage firms to move there. In practice, however, as capital and labour (and especially young and skilled workers) leave the extremities of the Union, so these regions are likely to become more depressed. If, as a result, their infrastructure is neglected, they then become even less attractive to new investment.

The development of monopoly/oligopoly power. The free movement of capital can encourage the development of giant 'Euro-firms' with substantial economic power. Indeed, recent years have seen some very large European mergers (see Box 15.1). This can lead to higher, not lower prices and less choice for the consumer. It all depends on just how effective competition is, and how effective EU competition policy is in preventing monopolistic and collusive practices.

Trade diversion. Just as trade creation has been a potential advantage of completing the internal market, so trade diversion has been a possibility too. This is more likely if *external* barriers remain high (or are even increased) and internal barriers are *completely* abolished.

Pause for thought

Why may the newer members of the EU have the most to gain from the single market, but also the most to lose?

Perhaps the biggest objection raised against the single European market is a political one: the loss of national sovereignty. Governments find it much more difficult to intervene at a microeconomic level in their own economies.

Completing the internal market

Despite the reduction in barriers, the internal market is still not 'complete'. In other words, various barriers to trade between member states still remain.

To monitor progress an 'Internal Market Scoreboard' was established in 1997. This is published every six months and shows progress towards the total abandonment of any forms of internal trade restrictions (see Box 25.2). It shows the percentage of EU Internal Market Directives still to be transposed into national law. In addition to giving each country's 'transposition deficit', the Scoreboard identifies the number of infringements of the internal market that have taken place. The hope is that the 'naming and shaming' of countries will encourage them to make more rapid progress towards totally free trade within the EU.

In 1997, the average transposition deficit of member countries was 35 per cent. By 1999, this had fallen to 3.5 per cent and by 2012, to just 1.2 per cent. Despite this success, national governments continued to introduce *new* technical standards, several of which have had the effect of erecting new barriers to trade. Also, infringements of single market rules by governments have not always been dealt with. The net result is that, although trade is much freer today than in the early 1990s, especially given the transparency of pricing with the euro, there still exist various barriers, especially to the free movement of goods.

The effect of the new member states

Given the very different nature of the economies of many of the new entrants to the EU, and their lower levels of GDP per head, the potential for gain from membership has been substantial. The gains come through trade creation, increased competition, technological transfer and inward investment, both from other EU countries and from outside the EU.

A study in 2004[3] concluded that Poland's GDP would rise by 3.4 per cent and Hungary's by almost 7 per cent. Real wages would rise, with those of unskilled workers rising faster than those of skilled workers, in accordance with these countries' comparative advantage. There would also be benefits for the 15 pre-2004 members from increased trade and investment, but these would be relatively minor in comparison to the gains to the new members.

---

[3] M. Maliszewska, *Benefits of the Single Market Expansion for Current and New Member States* (Centrum Analiz Spoleczno-Ekonomicznych, 2004).

BOX 25.2 | **THE INTERNAL MARKET SCOREBOARD**

Keeping a tally on progress to a true single market

This success or otherwise of implementing EU internal market directives is measured by the Internal Market Scoreboard. The Scoreboard tracks the *transposition deficit* for each country. This is the percentage of directives that have failed to be implemented into national law by their agreed deadline.

The Scoreboard has been published every six months since 1997 and, in addition to tracking the deficit for each country, also shows the average deficit across all EU countries. The chart shows that the average deficit was falling until May 2002, but then rose somewhat. Part of the problem is that new directives are being issued as existing ones are being implemented.

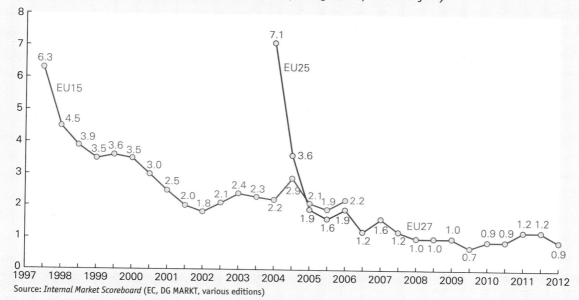

Internal Market Scoreboard (average transposition deficit)

Source: *Internal Market Scoreboard* (EC, DG MARKT, various editions)

After 2004, the transposition deficit tended to fall, even with the accession of ten new members in 2004 and two more in 2007. An average deficit target of 1 per cent was set in 2007 and this was reached by 2008. The average deficit fell further in 2009 to 0.7 per cent. But then it rose to 0.9 per cent in 2010 and to 1.2 in 2011. As of November 2011, only 11 of the 27 Member States were meeting the 1 per cent transposition deficit target.

Behind the rise in the average deficit in 2010 and 2011 was a reduction in the speed with which directives were being enacted. The 24th edition of the Scoreboard, referring to transposition as of November 2011, noted that:

In May 2011, Member States took an extra 5.5 months on average to transpose EU directives after the transposition deadline has passed. Today, member states take almost an extra 8 months.

The transposition deficit fell again in 2012 despite, as of May 2012, Member States taking an extra 9 months to transpose EU directives after the deadline. The increase in the average transposition time was the result of an increase in the number of long-overdue directives.

As well as the transposition deficit, the Scoreboard also measures the *compliance deficit*: the percentage of

transposed directives where infringement proceedings for non-conformity have been initiated by the Commission. The target for the compliance deficit is 0.5 per cent. In November 2011 the compliance deficit was 0.8 per cent. By May 2012 it had fallen to 0.7 per cent. The 25th edition of the Scoreboard reiterates a point made consistently in previous editions when it argues:

Timely transposition of EU legislation represents only the first step towards the proper functioning of the Internal Market. Member States also need to transpose EU Directives correctly into national law *to ensure that citizens and businesses can benefit from the Internal Market's full potential.*

1. *What value are scoreboards for member states and the European Commission?*
2. *Why do you think that it is so important that legislation, such as that governing the Internal Market, is in place in all member states at the same time?*

Note: Internal Market Scoreboards can be accessed at http://ec.europa.eu/internal_market/score/index_en.htm

SUMMARY

1a Countries may make a partial movement towards free trade by the adoption of a preferential trading system. This involves free trade between the members, but restrictions on trade with the rest of the world. Such a system can be either a simple free trade area, or a customs union (where there are common restrictions with the rest of the world), or a common market (where in addition there is free movement of capital and labour, and common taxes and trade laws).

1b A preferential trading area can lead to trade creation where production shifts to low-cost producers within the area, or to trade diversion where trade shifts away from lower-cost producers outside the area to higher-cost producers within the area.

1c Preferential trading may bring dynamic advantages of increased external economies of scale, improved terms of trade from increased bargaining power with the rest of the world, increased efficiency from greater competition between member countries, and a more rapid spread of technology. On the other hand, it can lead to increased regional problems for members, greater oligopolistic collusion and various diseconomies of scale. There may also be large costs of administering the system.

2 There have been several attempts around the world to form preferential trading systems. The two most powerful are the European Union and the North America Free Trade Association (NAFTA).

3a The European Union is a customs union in that it has common external tariffs and no internal ones. But virtually from the outset it has also had elements of a common market, particularly in the areas of agricultural policy, regional policy and competition policy, and to some extent in the areas of tax harmonisation, transport policy and social policy.

3b The Single European Act of 1986 sought to sweep away any remaining restrictions and to establish a genuine free market within the EU: to establish a full common market. Benefits from completing the internal market have included trade creation, cost savings from no longer having to administer barriers, economies of scale for firms now able to operate on a Europe-wide scale, and greater competition leading to reduced costs and prices, greater flows of technical information and more innovation.

3c The actual costs and benefits of EU membership to the various countries vary with their particular economic circumstances – for example, the extent to which they gain from trade creation, or lose from adverse regional effects – and with their contributions to and receipts from the EU budget.

3d These costs and benefits in the future will depend on just how completely the barriers to trade are abolished, on the extent of monetary union and on the effects of the enlargement of the Union.

REVIEW QUESTIONS

1 What factors will determine whether a country's joining a customs union will lead to trade creation or trade diversion?

2 Assume that a group of countries forms a customs union. Is trade diversion in the union more likely or less likely in the following cases?

(a) Producers in the union gain monopoly power in world trade.

(b) Modern developments in technology and communications reduce the differences in production costs associated with different locations.

(c) The development of an internal market within the union produces substantial economies of scale in many industries.

3 Are NAFTA and APEC likely to develop along the same lines as the EU? Explain your answer.

4 Why is it difficult to estimate the magnitude of the benefits of completing the internal market of the EU?

5 Look through the costs and benefits that we identified from the single European market. Do the same costs and benefits arise from a substantially enlarged EU?

6 To what extent do non-EU countries gain or lose from the existence of the EU?

7 If there have been clear benefits from the single market programme, why do individual member governments still try to erect barriers, such as new technical standards?

ADDITIONAL PART I CASE STUDIES IN THE *ECONOMICS FOR BUSINESS* MyEconLab (www.pearsoned.co.uk/sloman)

I.1 **Investing in Wales.** The factors influencing the investment in Wales by the Korean multinational, Lucky Goldstar (LG).

I.2 **The Maharaja Mac.** An examination of activities of McDonald's in India.

I.3 **Ethical business.** An examination of the likelihood of success of companies which trade fairly with developing countries.

I.4 **Fallacious arguments for restricting trade.** Some of the more common mistaken arguments for protection.

I.5 **Free trade and the environment.** Do whales, the rainforests and the atmosphere gain from free trade?

I.6 **The Uruguay round.** An examination of the negotiations that led to substantial cuts in trade barriers.

I.7 **The Battle of Seattle.** This looks at the protests against the WTO at Seattle in November 1999 and considers the arguments for and against the free trade policies of the WTO.

I.8 **The World Trade Organization.** This looks at the various opportunities and threats posed by this major international organisation.

I.9 **High oil prices.** What is their effect on the world economy?

I.10 **Crisis in south-east Asia.** Causes of the severe recession in many south-east Asian countries in 1997/8.

I.11 **A miracle gone wrong.** Lessons from east Asia.

I.12 **Assessing NAFTA.** Who are the winners and losers from NAFTA?

I.13 **The social dimension of the EU.** The principles of the Social Charter.

I.14 **The Internal Market Scoreboard.** Keeping a tally on progress to a true single market.

I.15 **Steel barriers.** Looking after the US steel industry.

I.16 **The transnationality Index.** An index designed to capture how globally orientated countries and businesses are.

WEBSITES RELEVANT TO PART I

Numbers and sections refer to websites listed in the Web appendix and hotlinked from this book's website at **www.pearsoned.co.uk/sloman**

■ For news articles relevant to Part I, see the *Economics News Articles* link from the book's website.

■ For general news on business in the international environment, see websites in section A, and particularly A1–5, 7–9, 24, 25, 31. See also links to newspapers worldwide in A38, 39 and 43, and the news search feature in Google at A41. See also links to economics news in A42.

■ For articles on various aspects of trade and developing countries, see A27, 28; I9.

■ For international data on imports and exports, see site H16 > *Resources* > *Trade statistics*. See also *World Economic Outlook* in H4 and trade data in B23. See also the trade topic in I14.

■ For details of individual countries' structure of imports and exports, see B32.

■ For UK data, see B1, *1. National Statistics* > the fourth link > *Compendia and Reference* > *Annual Abstract* > *External trade and investment.* See also B3 and 34. For EU data, see G1 > *The Statistical Annex* > *Foreign trade and current balance.*

■ For discussion papers on trade, see H4 and 7.

■ For trade disputes, see H16.

■ For various pressure groups critical of the effects of free trade and globalisation, see H12–14.

■ For information on various preferential trading arrangements, see H20–22.

■ For EU sites, see G1, 3, 7–14, 16–18.

■ For information on trade and developing countries, see H4, 7, 9, 10, 16, 17. See also links to development sites in I9.

■ Sites I7 and 11 contain links to various topics in *International Economics* (*International trade, International agreements, Economic cooperation* and *EU Economics*) and to *Trade and trade policy* in *Economic Development*. Site I4 has links to *International economics, Development economics* and *Economic development*. Site I17 has links to *International economics, Trade policy* and *Development economics*.

■ For student resources relevant to this chapter, see sites C1–7, 9, 10, 19.

The macroeconomic environment

The FT Reports . . .

The Financial Times, 13 June 2009

FT

City confident of recovery amid tide of positive figures

By Chris Giles

'Don't be fooled by one month's data' is one of the first lessons taught on any good economics course. Figures bob up and down like a boat at sea, and distinguishing the tide from a freak wave can be perilous.

The accumulation of unexpectedly favourable economic data in the past month, however, can no longer be ignored. Rather than the odd green shoot, the economic landscape now resembles a fragile carpet of green . . .

In a snap FT poll of 20 City economists this week, a majority thought the recession was over for now. When official figures showing that industrial production and manufacturing stabilised in March and began to grow in April were released on Wednesday, the National Institute of Economic and Social Research estimated the economy grew by 0.1 per cent in May and 0.2 per cent in April after contracting 0.5 per cent in March . . .

In official circles there is much pleasure at the recent economic data, including the apparent end of steep house price declines. But there is also an acute fear of appearing to rejoice prematurely. 'We are getting ourselves ready for the "false dawn" stories,' said one senior Treasury official.

His fear is shared by economists outside government. While the economy is probably growing already, the concern is that the green shoots will have shallow roots . . .

The durability of the recovery will become clearer after the summer but is currently very difficult to predict, because powerful forces are encouraging both economic growth and continued weakness.

Despite sterling's recent recovery, its fall since late 2007 has improved Britain's competitiveness and reduced the attractiveness of imports and outsourcing; exceptionally loose monetary policy is boosting the spending power of borrowers and reducing the attractiveness of saving; confidence has recovered from rock-bottom levels as the chances of a depression have receded; government spending is enjoying a last hurrah before the next decade's inevitable retrenchment; and lower oil and utility prices compared with last year are boosting household incomes.

But these forces are counterbalanced by concerns that the recession, and the banks' woes in particular, will lead to a dearth of lending, restraining business activity and investment. Paul Fisher, the Bank of England's head of markets, said yesterday that were this to happen 'even for a few years, then unemployment will stay higher for longer and living standards generally will be lower than they would have been'.

> *Banks are dangerous institutions. They borrow short and lend long. They create liabilities which promise to be liquid and hold few liquid assets themselves. That though is hugely valuable for the rest of the economy. Household savings can be channelled to finance illiquid investment projects while providing access to liquidity for those savers who may need it.*

Mervyn King, Governor of the Bank of England, '*Finance: a return from risk*', speech to the Worshipful Company of International Bankers, at the Mansion House, 17 March 2009 (www.bankofengland.co.uk) see http://www.bankofengland.co.uk/mfsd/iadb/notesiadb/Revisions.htm for the Revisions Policy.

The success of an individual business depends not only on its own particular market and its own particular decisions. It also depends on the whole *macroeconomic* environment in which it operates, as can be seen in the *Financial Times* article opposite.

If the economy is booming, then individual businesses are likely to be more profitable than if the economy is in recession. If the exchange rate rises (or falls), this will have an impact on the competitiveness of businesses trading overseas, and on the costs and profitability of business in general. Similarly, business profitability will be affected by interest rates, the general level of prices and wages and the level of unemployment.

It is thus important for managers to understand the forces that affect the performance of the economy. In the remaining chapters of the book, we will examine these macroeconomic forces and their effects on the business sector.

In Chapter 26 we identify the main macroeconomic objectives that governments pursue and examine how these objectives are related. In particular, we look at the objectives of economic growth, low unemployment and low inflation.

Chapter 27 looks at macroeconomic issues arising from a country's economic relationships with the rest of the world. In particular, it looks at the balance of payments and the role of exchange rates in influencing economic performance.

Chapter 28 looks at the significance of the financial system for both individual businesses and the economy. In particular, it looks at the behaviour of financial institutions and the role of money. You will be able to judge whether 'Banks are dangerous institutions', as Mervyn King states.

Finally, in Chapter 29 we examine various theories about how the economy operates and the implications for business. We look at the relationship between inflation and unemployment and examine the possible causes of the business cycle. We also see the important role played by the expectations of both business and consumers.

Key terms

- Actual and potential economic growth
- Output gap
- Aggregate demand
- Aggregate supply
- Business cycle
- Unemployment
- Inflation
- Circular flow of income
- Injections and withdrawals
- The balance of payments
- The exchange rate
- Fixed and floating exchange rates
- Functions of money
- Assets and liabilities (of banks)
- Central bank
- Money market
- Money supply
- Credit creation
- Deposits multiplier
- Money multiplier
- Demand for money
- Keynesian
- New classical
- Aggregate expenditure
- Marginal propensity to consume
- The multiplier
- The accelerator
- The quantity theory of money
- Expectations
- The Phillips curve
- Real business cycles

The macroeconomic environment of business

Business issues covered in this chapter

- What determines the level of activity in the economy and hence the overall business climate?
- If a stimulus is given to the economy, what will be the effect on business output?
- Why do economies experience periods of boom followed by periods of recession? What determines the length and magnitude of these 'phases' of the business cycle?
- What are the causes of unemployment and how does unemployment relate to the level of business activity?
- What are the causes of inflation and how does inflation relate to the level of business activity?
- What is meant by 'GDP' and how is it measured?

Government macroeconomic policy aims primarily to achieve two goals:

- to ensure that the key macroeconomic variables (such as economic growth and inflation) are at acceptable levels;
- to create a *stable* economic environment in which the economy can flourish: i.e. to minimise fluctuations in economic activity.

In this chapter we shall identify what the main macroeconomic variables are and how they are related. We shall also have a preliminary look at how the government can influence these variables in order to create a more favourable environment for business. Government macroeconomic policy will be discussed in more detail in Part K.

26.1 MACROECONOMIC OBJECTIVES

There are several macroeconomic variables that governments seek to control, but these can be grouped under four main headings.

Economic growth. Governments try to achieve high *rates of economic growth* over the long term: in other words, growth that is sustained over the years and is not just a temporary phenomenon. Governments also try to achieve *stable* growth, avoiding both recessions and excessive

short-term growth that cannot be sustained. In practice, however, this can often prove difficult to achieve, as recent history has shown.

Definition

Rate of economic growth The percentage increase in output over a 12-month period.

KEY IDEA 38

Economies suffer from inherent instability. As a result, economic growth and other macroeconomic indicators tend to fluctuate.

Unemployment. Reducing unemployment is another major macroeconomic aim of governments not only for the sake of the unemployed themselves, but also because it represents a waste of human resources and because unemployment benefits are a drain on government revenues.

Inflation. By **inflation** we mean a general rise in prices throughout the economy. The rate of inflation is the percentage increase in prices over a 12-month period. Government policy here is to keep inflation both low and stable. One of the most important reasons for this is that it will aid the process of economic decision making. For example, businesses will be able to set prices and wage rates, and make investment decisions, with far more confidence. We have become used to low inflation rates and in some countries, like Japan, periods of deflation, where prices in general fall. Even though inflation rates rose in many countries in 2008 and then again in 2010–11, figures remained much lower than in the past; in 1975, UK inflation reached over 23 per cent.

In most developed countries, governments have a particular target for the rate of inflation. In the UK the target is 2 per cent. The Bank of England then adjusts interest rates to try to keep inflation on target (we see how this works in section 30.3).

The balance of payments. Governments aim to provide an environment in which exports can grow without an excessive growth in imports. They also aim to make the economy attractive to inward investment. In other words, they seek to create a climate in which the country's earnings of foreign currency at least match, or preferably exceed, the country's expenditure of foreign currency: they seek to achieve a favourable **balance of payments**.

In order to achieve these various goals, the government may seek to control several 'intermediate' variables. These include interest rates, the supply of money, taxes, government expenditure and exchange rates.

For example, the achievement of a favourable balance of payments depends, in part, on whether changes in **exchange rates** allow the country's goods and services to remain price competitive on international markets. A lower exchange rate (i.e. fewer dollars, yen, euros, etc. to the pound) will make UK goods cheaper to overseas buyers, and thus help to boost UK exports. The government may thus seek to manipulate exchange rates to make them 'more favourable'.

In later chapters we will be looking at the various types of macroeconomic policy that governments can adopt. First we will look at the four macroeconomic objectives and identify their main determinants. In this chapter we will examine economic growth, unemployment and inflation. In Chapter 27 we will focus on the balance of payments and its relation to the exchange rate.

26.2 ECONOMIC GROWTH

The distinction between actual and potential growth

Before examining the causes of economic growth, it is essential to distinguish between *actual* and *potential* economic growth.

KI 38
p 419

Actual growth is the percentage annual increase in national output or 'GDP' (gross domestic product): in other words, the rate of growth in actual output produced. When statistics on GDP growth rates are published, it is actual growth they are referring to. (We examine the measurement of GDP in the appendix to this chapter.)

Potential growth is the speed at which the economy *could* grow. It is the percentage annual increase in the economy's *capacity* to produce: the rate of growth in **potential output**.

KEY IDEA 39

Living standards are limited by a country's ability to produce. Potential national output depends on the country's resources, technology and productivity.

Definitions

Rate of inflation The percentage increase in prices over a 12-month period.

Balance of payments account A record of the country's transactions with the rest of the world. It shows the country's payments to or deposits in other countries (debits) and its receipts or deposits from other countries (credits). It also shows the balance between these debits and credits under various headings.

Exchange rate The rate at which one national currency exchanges for another. The rate is expressed as the amount of one currency that is necessary to purchase one unit of another currency (e.g. £1 = €1.20).

Actual growth The percentage annual increase in national output actually produced.

Potential growth The percentage annual increase in the capacity of the economy to produce.

Potential output The output that could be produced in the economy if all firms were operating at their normal level of capacity utilisation.

Potential output (i.e. potential GDP) is the level of output when the economy is operating at 'normal capacity utilisation'. This allows for firms having a planned degree of spare capacity to meet unexpected demand or for hold-ups in supply. It also allows for some unemployment as people move from job to job. Potential output is thus somewhat below full-capacity output, which is the absolute maximum that could be produced with firms working flat-out.

The difference between actual and potential output is known as the ***output gap***. Thus if actual output exceeds potential output, the output gap is positive: the economy is operating above normal capacity utilisation. If actual output is below potential output, the output gap is negative: the economy is operating below normal capacity utilisation. Box 26.1 looks at the output gap for the UK and four other economies since the mid 1980s.

If the actual growth rate is less than the potential growth rate, there will be an increase in spare capacity and an increase in unemployment: the output gap will become more negative (or less positive). To close a negative output gap, the actual growth rate would temporarily have to exceed the potential growth rate. In the long run, however, the actual growth rate will be limited to the potential growth rate.

Definitions

Output gap Actual output minus potential output.
Business cycle or **trade cycle** The periodic fluctuations of national output round its long-term trend.

There are thus two major issues concerned with economic growth: the short-run issue of ensuring that actual growth is such as to keep actual output as close as possible to potential output; and the long-run issue of what determines the rate of potential economic growth.

Actual economic growth and the business cycle

Although growth in potential output varies to some extent over the years – depending on the rate of advance of technology, the level of investment and the discovery of new raw materials – it nevertheless tends to be much steadier than the growth in actual output.

Actual growth tends to fluctuate. In some years there is a high rate of economic growth: the country experiences a boom. In other years, economic growth is low or even negative: the country experiences a recession.[1] This cycle of booms and recessions is known as the ***business cycle*** or ***trade cycle***.

There are four 'phases' of the business cycle. They are illustrated in Figure 26.1.

1. *The upturn*. In this phase, a stagnant economy begins to recover and growth in actual output resumes.
2. *The rapid expansion*. During this phase, there is rapid economic growth: the economy is booming. A fuller use is made of resources and the gap between actual and full-capacity output narrows.
3. *The peaking out*. During this phase, growth slows down or even ceases.

---

[1] In official statistics, a recession is defined as when an economy experiences falling national output (negative growth) for two or more quarters.

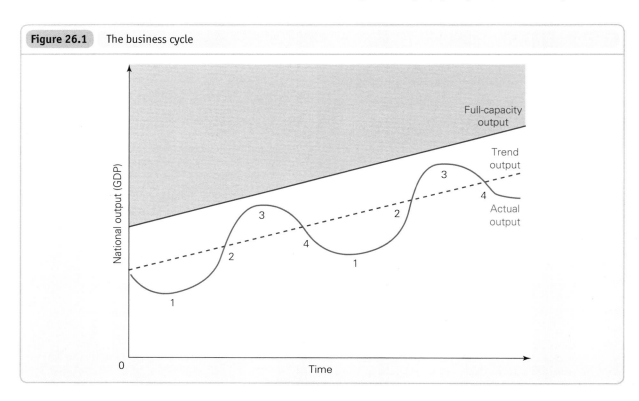

Figure 26.1 The business cycle

4. *The slowdown, recession or slump.* During this phase, there is little or no growth or even a decline in output. Increasing slack develops in the economy.

Long-term output trend. A line can be drawn showing the trend of national output over time (i.e. ignoring the cyclical fluctuations around the trend). This is shown as the dashed line in Figure 26.1. If, over time, firms on average operate with a 'normal' degree of capacity utilisation, the trend output line will be the same as the potential output line. If the average level of capacity that is unutilised stays constant from one cycle to another, the trend line will have the same slope as the full-capacity output line. In other words, the trend (or potential) rate of growth will be the same as the rate of growth of capacity.

If, however, the level of unutilised capacity changes from one cycle to another, then the trend line will have a different slope from the full-capacity output line. For example, if unemployment and unused industrial capacity *rise* from one peak to another, or from one trough to another, then the trend line will move further away from the full-capacity output line (i.e. it will be less steep).

Pause for thought

If the average percentage (as opposed to the average level) of full-capacity output that was unutilised remained constant, would the trend line have the same slope as the potential output line?

The business cycle in practice

The business cycle illustrated in Figure 26.1 is a 'stylised' cycle. It is nice and smooth and regular. Drawing it this way allows us to make a clear distinction between each of the four phases. In practice, however, business cycles are highly irregular. They are irregular in two ways.

The magnitude of the phases. Sometimes in phase 2 there is a very high rate of economic growth, considerably higher than the economy's longer-term average. On other occasions in phase 2 growth is much gentler. Sometimes in phase 4 there is a recession, with an actual decline in output as occurred in 2008/9. On other occasions, phase 4 is merely a 'pause', with growth simply being low.

The length of the phases. Some booms are short lived, lasting only a few months or so. Others are much longer, lasting perhaps three or four years. Likewise some recessions are short, while others are long. Sometimes a recession can be closely followed by another recession with the economic upturn only short-lived. Economists refer to this as a double-dip recession. Such a situation occurred when the recession of 2008/9 was followed by another recession in 2011/12.

Nevertheless, despite the irregularity of the fluctuations, cycles are still clearly discernible, especially if we plot *growth* on the vertical axis rather than the *level* of output. This is done in Figure 26.2, which shows the business cycles of four economies.

Figure 26.2   Growth rates in selected industrialised economies

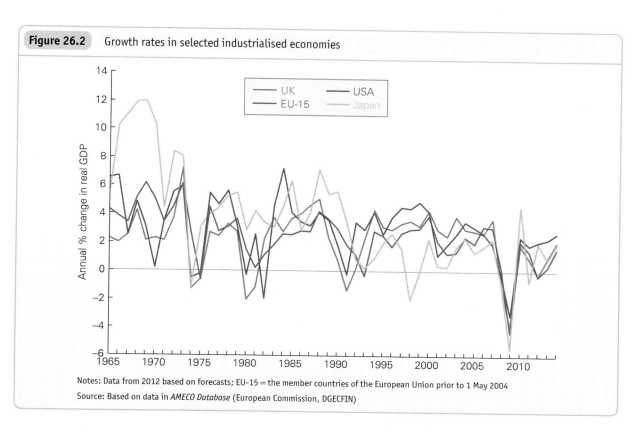

Notes: Data from 2012 based on forecasts; EU-15 = the member countries of the European Union prior to 1 May 2004

Source: Based on data in *AMECO Database* (European Commission, DGECFIN)

BOX 26.1 OUTPUT GAPS

An alternative measure of excess or deficient demand

If the economy grows, how fast and for how long can it grow before it runs into inflationary problems? On the other hand, what minimum rate must be achieved to avoid rising unemployment?

To answer these questions, economists have developed the concept of 'output gaps'.[1] The output gap is the difference between actual output and potential output.

If actual output is below potential output (the gap is negative), there will be a higher than normal level of unemployment as firms are operating below their normal level of capacity utilisation. There will, however, be a downward pressure on inflation, resulting from a lower than normal level of demand for labour and other resources. If actual output is above potential output (the gap is positive), there will be excess demand and a rise in inflation.

Generally, the gap will be negative in a recession and positive in a boom. In other words, output gaps follow the course of the business cycle.

But, how do we measure output gaps? There are two principal statistical techniques.

De-trending techniques. This approach is a purely mechanical exercise which involves smoothing the actual GDP figures. In doing this, it attempts to fit a trend growth path along the lines of the dashed line in Figure 26.1. The main disadvantage of this approach is that it is not grounded in economic theory and therefore does not take into consideration those factors that economists consider to be important in determining output levels over time.

Production function approach. Many forecasting bodies use an approach which borrows ideas from economic theory. Specifically, it uses the idea of a production function which relates output to a set of inputs. Estimates of potential output are generated by using statistics on the size of a country's capital stock, the potential available labour input and, finally, the productivity or effectiveness of these inputs in producing output.

In addition to these statistical approaches, use could be made of *business surveys*. In other words, we ask businesses directly. However, survey-based evidence can provide only a broad guide to rates of capacity utilisation and whether there is deficient or excess demand.

International evidence

The diagram shows output gaps for five economies since the mid 1980s estimated using a production function approach. What is apparent from the chart is that all the economies have experienced significant output gaps, both positive and negative. This helps to illustrate that economies are inherently volatile. However, while output gaps vary from year to year, over the longer term the average output gap tends towards zero.

The diagram shows how the characteristics of countries' business cycles can differ, particularly in terms of depth and duration. But, we also see evidence of an *international business cycle* (see page 546), where national cycles appear to share characteristics. This is true of the late 2000s and into the 2010s. Increasing global interconnectedness from financial and trading links meant that the financial crisis of the late 2000s spread like a contagion.

 How might the behaviour of firms differ during periods of negative and positive output gaps?

[1] See C. Giorno et al., 'Potential output, output gaps and structural budget balances', *OECD Economic Studies*, no. 24, 1995, p. 1.

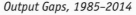
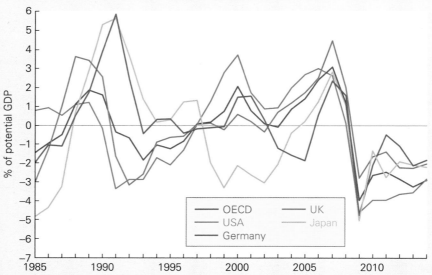

Output Gaps, 1985–2014

Notes: OECD = Organisation for Economic Cooperation and Development and represents the aggregate across 34 national economies; figures for Germany up to 1991 based on West Germany only; Figures from 2012 are forecasts

Source: Based on data from *Economic Outlook December 2012* (OECD)

KI 38
p 419

Causes of fluctuations in actual growth

Economists typically focus on variations in the growth of 'aggregate demand' in explaining variations in the rate of actual growth in the *short run*.

Aggregate demand (*AD*) is the total spending on goods and services made within the country. This spending consists of four elements: consumer spending (*C*), investment expenditure by firms (*I*), government spending (*G*) and the expenditure by foreign residents on the country's goods and services (i.e. their purchases of its exports) (*X*). From these four must be subtracted any expenditure that goes on imports (*M*), since this is expenditure that 'leaks' abroad and is not spent on domestic goods and services. Thus:

$$AD = C + I + G + X - M$$

A rapid rise in aggregate demand will create shortages. This will tend to stimulate firms to increase output, thereby reducing slack in the economy. Likewise, a reduction in aggregate demand will leave firms with increased stocks of unsold goods. They will therefore tend to reduce output.

Aggregate demand and actual output therefore tend to fluctuate together in the short run. A boom is associated with a rapid rise in aggregate demand: the faster the rise in aggregate demand, the higher the short-run growth rate. A recession, by contrast, is associated with a reduction in aggregate demand.

While much of the analysis of business cycles focuses on fluctuations in aggregate demand, shifts in 'aggregate supply' can also lead to fluctuations in the rate of economic growth. *Aggregate supply* (*AS*) is the total amount of goods and services supplied by firms within the country. Sudden sharp changes to input prices could affect firms' output decisions. For instance, increases in input costs, such as those in employing labour, could result in firms reducing production levels.

When viewing economic growth over the longer term, aggregate supply takes on increasing importance. This is because a rapid rise in aggregate demand is not enough to ensure a continuing high level of growth over a *number* of years. Without an expansion of potential output too, rises in actual output must eventually come to an end as spare capacity is used up.

In the long run, therefore, there are two determinants of actual growth:

- the growth in aggregate demand, which determines whether potential output will be realised;
- the growth in potential output.

Potential economic growth

We now focus on the *supply* question. Here we are concerned with the capacity of the economy to produce. There are two main determinants of potential output: (a) the amount of resources available and (b) their productivity.

Increases in the quantity of resources

Capital. The nation's output depends on its stock of capital (*K*). An increase in this stock (through investment) will increase output. If we ignore the problem of machines wearing out or becoming obsolete and needing replacing, then the stock of capital will increase by the amount of investment. The rise in output that results will depend on the productivity of capital.

As we saw in section 23.7 (page 385), the rate of growth depends on the marginal capital/output ratio (*k*). This is the amount of extra capital (ΔK) divided by the amount of extra annual output that it produces (ΔY). The lower the value of *k*, the higher is the productivity of capital (i.e. the less extra capital you need to produce extra output). The rate of growth in potential output also depends on the proportion of national income that is invested (*i*), which, assuming that all saving is invested, will equal the proportion of national income that is saved (*s*). The formula for growth becomes:

$$g = i/k \text{ (or } g = s/k\text{)}$$

Thus if 20 per cent of national income went in new investment (*i* = 20%), and if each £1 of new investment yielded 25p of extra income per year (*k* = 4), then the growth rate would be 5 per cent. A simple example will demonstrate this. If national income is £100 billion, then £20 billion will be invested (*i* = 20%). This will lead to extra annual output of £5 billion (*k* = 4). Thus national income grows to £105 billion: a growth of 5 per cent.

But what determines the rate of investment? There are a number of determinants. These include the confidence of business people about the future demand for their products, the ability of firms to finance investment projects, the profitability of business, the tax regime, the rate of growth in the economy and the rate of interest.

Over the long term, if investment is to increase, then *saving* must increase in order to finance that investment. Put another way, people must be prepared to forgo a certain amount of consumption in order to allow resources to be diverted into producing more capital goods: factories, machines, etc.

Note that if investment is to increase, there may also need to be a steady increase in *aggregate demand*. In other words, if firms are to be encouraged to increase their capacity

KI 19
p 130

Definitions

Aggregate demand Total spending on goods and services made in the economy. It consists of four elements: consumer spending (*C*), investment (*I*), government spending (*G*) and the expenditure on exports (*X*), less any expenditure on foreign goods and services (*M*): *AD* = *C* + *I* + *G* + *X* − *M*.

Aggregate supply The total amount of goods and services produced in the economy.

by installing new machines or building new factories, they may need first to see the *demand* for their products growing. Here a growth in *potential* output is the result of a growth in aggregate demand and hence *actual* output.

Labour. If there is an increase in the working population, there will be an increase in potential output. This increase in working population may result from a larger 'participation rate': a larger proportion of the total population in work or seeking work. For example, if a greater proportion of women with children decide to join the labour market, the working population will rise.

Alternatively, a rise in the working population may be the result of an increase in total population. There is a problem here. If a rise in total population does not result in a greater *proportion* of the population working, output *per head of the population* may not rise at all. In practice, many developed countries are faced with a growing proportion of their population above retirement age, and thus a potential *fall* in output per head of the population.

Land and raw materials. The scope for generating growth here is usually very limited. Land is virtually fixed in quantity. Land reclamation schemes and the opening up of marginal land can add only tiny amounts to GDP. Even if new raw materials are discovered (e.g. oil), this will only result in *short-term* growth: i.e. while the rate of extraction is building up. Once the rate of extraction is at a maximum, economic growth will cease. Output will simply remain at the new higher level, until eventually the raw materials begin to run out. Output will then fall back again.

The problem of diminishing returns. If a single factor of production increases in supply while others remain fixed, diminishing returns will set in. For example, if the quantity of capital increases with no increase in other factors of production, then diminishing returns to capital will set in. The rate of return on capital will fall. Unless *all* factors of production increase, therefore, the rate of growth is likely to slow down.

Then there is the problem of the environment. If a rise in labour and capital leads to a more *intensive* use of land and natural resources, the resulting growth in output may be environmentally unsustainable. The solution to the problem of diminishing returns is for there to be an increase in the *productivity* of resources.

Increases in the productivity of resources

Technological improvements can increase the marginal productivity of capital. Much of the investment in new machines is not just in extra machines, but in superior machines producing a higher rate of return. Consider the microchip revolution of recent years. Modern computers can do the work of many people and have replaced many machines which were cumbersome and expensive to build. Improved methods of transport have reduced the costs of moving goods and materials. Improved communications (such as the Internet) have reduced the costs of transmitting information. The high-tech world of today would seem a wonderland to a person of 100 years ago.

As a result of technical progress, the productivity of capital has tended to increase over time. Similarly, as a result of new skills, improved education and training, and better health, the productivity of labour has also tended to increase over time.

But technical progress on its own is not enough. There must also be the institutions and attitudes that encourage *innovation*. In other words, the inventions must be exploited.

> **Pause for thought**
>
> *Will the rate of actual growth have any effect on the rate of potential growth?*

Policies to achieve growth

How can governments increase a country's growth rate? Policies differ in two ways.

First, they may focus on the demand side or the supply side of the economy. In other words, they may attempt to create sufficient *aggregate demand* to ensure that firms wish to invest and that potential output is realised. Or alternatively, they may seek to increase *aggregate supply* by concentrating on measures to increase potential output: measures to encourage research and development, innovation and training. (Chapter 30 looks at demand-side policies, while Chapter 31 looks at supply-side ones.)

Second, they may be market-orientated or interventionist policies. Many economists and politicians, especially those on the political right, believe that the best environment for encouraging economic growth is one where private enterprise is allowed to flourish: where entrepreneurs are able to reap substantial rewards from investment in new techniques and new products. Such economists therefore advocate policies designed to free up the market. Others, however, argue that a free market will be subject to considerable cyclical fluctuations and market distortions. Such economists, therefore, tend to advocate intervention by the government to reduce these fluctuations and compensate for market failures.

26.3 UNEMPLOYMENT

The meaning of unemployment

Unemployment can be expressed either as a number (e.g. 3 million) or as a percentage (e.g. 10 per cent). But just who should be included in the statistics? Should it be everyone without a job? The answer is clearly no, since we would not want to include children and pensioners. We would probably also want to exclude those who were not looking for work, such as parents choosing to stay at home to look after children.

The most usual definition that economists use for the **number unemployed** is: *those of working age who are without work, but who are available for work at current wage rates*. If the figure is to be expressed as a percentage, then it is a percentage of the total **labour force**. The labour force is defined as: *those in employment plus those unemployed*. Thus if 30 million people were employed and 3 million people were unemployed, the **unemployment rate** would be:

$$\frac{3}{30+3} \times 100 = 9.1\%$$

Official measures of unemployment

Two common measures of unemployment are used in official statistics. The first is **claimant unemployment**. This is simply a measure of all those in receipt of unemployment-related benefits. In the UK, claimants receive the 'job-seeker's allowance'.

The second measure is the **standardised unemployment rate**. Since 1998, this has been the main measure used by the UK government. It is the measure used by the International Labour Organisation (ILO) and the Organisation for Economic Cooperation and Development (OECD), two international organisations that publish unemployment statistics for many countries.

In this measure, the unemployed are defined as people of working age who are without work, available to start work within two weeks and *actively seeking employment* or waiting to take up an appointment. The figures are compiled from the results of national labour force surveys. In the UK the labour force survey is conducted quarterly.

But is the standardised unemployment rate likely to be higher or lower than the claimant unemployment rate?

The standardised rate is likely to be higher to the extent that it includes people seeking work who are nevertheless not entitled to claim benefits, but lower to the extent that it excludes those who are claiming benefits and yet who are not actively seeking work. Clearly, the tougher the benefit regulations, the lower the claimant rate will be relative to the standardised rate. In the three months to November 2012 standardised unemployment in the UK (for those aged 16 and over) was estimated at 2.49 million (7.7 per cent) while the claimant count in November 2012 was 1.54 million (4.7 per cent).

The costs of unemployment

The most obvious cost of unemployment is to the *unemployed themselves*. There is the direct financial cost of the loss in their earnings, measured as the difference between their previous wage and their unemployment benefit. Then there are the personal costs of being unemployed. The longer people are unemployed, the more dispirited they may become. Their self-esteem is likely to fall, and they are more likely to succumb to stress-related illness.

Then there are the costs to the *family and friends* of the unemployed. Personal relations can become strained, and there may be an increase in domestic violence and the number of families splitting up.

Then there are the *broader costs to the economy*. Unemployment benefits are a cost borne by taxpayers. There may also have to be extra public spending on benefit offices, social services, health care and the police. What is more, unemployment represents a loss of output. Apart from the lack of income to the unemployed themselves, this under-utilisation of resources leads to lower incomes for other people too:

- Firms lose the profits that could have been made, had there been full employment.
- The government loses tax revenues, since the unemployed pay no income tax and national insurance, and, given that the unemployed spend less, they pay less VAT and excise duties.
- Other workers lose any additional wages they could have earned from higher national output.

Definitions

Number unemployed (economist's definition) Those of working age who are without work, but who are available for work at current wage rates.

Labour force The number employed plus the number unemployed.

Unemployment rate The number unemployed expressed as a percentage of the labour force.

Claimant unemployment Those in receipt of unemployment-related benefits.

Standardised unemployment rate The measure of the unemployment rate used by the ILO and OECD. The unemployed are defined as people of working age who are without work, available for work and actively seeking employment.

The costs of unemployment are to some extent offset by benefits. If workers voluntarily quit their job to look for a better one, then they must reckon that the benefits of a better job more than compensate for their temporary loss of income. From the nation's point of view, a workforce that is prepared to quit jobs and spend a short time unemployed will be a more adaptable, more mobile workforce – one that is responsive to changing economic circumstances. Such a workforce will lead to greater allocative efficiency in the short run and more rapid economic growth over the longer run.

Long-term involuntary unemployment is quite another matter. The costs clearly outweigh any benefits, both for the individuals concerned and for the economy as a whole. A demotivated, deskilled pool of long-term unemployed is a serious economic and social problem.

Unemployment and the labour market

We now turn to the causes of unemployment. These causes fall into two broad categories: *equilibrium* unemployment and *disequilibrium* unemployment. To make clear the distinction between the two, it is necessary to look at how the labour market works.

Figure 26.3 shows the aggregate demand for labour and the aggregate supply of labour: that is, the total demand and supply of labour in the whole economy. The *real* average wage rate is plotted on the vertical axis. This is the average wage rate expressed in terms of its purchasing power: in other words, after taking inflation into account.

The *aggregate supply of labour curve* (AS_L) shows the number of workers *willing to accept jobs* at each wage rate. This curve is relatively inelastic, since the size of the workforce at any one time cannot change significantly. Nevertheless, it is not totally inelastic because (a) a higher wage rate will encourage some people to enter the labour market (e.g. parents raising children) and (b) the unemployed will be more willing to accept job offers rather than continuing to search for a better-paid job.

The *aggregate demand for labour curve* (AD_L) slopes downward. The higher the wage rate, the more will firms

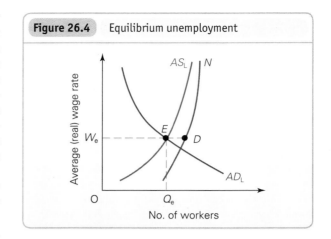

Figure 26.4 Equilibrium unemployment

attempt to economise on labour and to substitute other factors of production for labour.

The labour market is in equilibrium at a wage of W_e in Figure 26.3, where the demand for labour equals the supply. If the wage were above W_e, the labour market would be in a state of disequilibrium. At a wage rate of W_1, there is an excess supply of labour of $A – B$. This is called **disequilibrium unemployment**.

For disequilibrium unemployment to occur, two conditions must hold:

- The aggregate supply of labour must exceed the aggregate demand.
- There must be a 'stickiness' in wages. In other words, the wage rate must not immediately fall to W_e.

Even when the labour market *is* in equilibrium, however, not everyone looking for work will be employed. Some people will hold out, hoping to find a better job. The curve N in Figure 26.4 shows the total number in the labour force. The horizontal difference between it and the aggregate supply of labour curve (AS_L) represents the excess of people looking for work over those actually willing to accept jobs. Q_e represents the equilibrium level of employment and

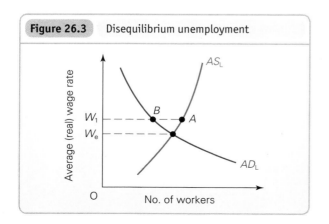

Figure 26.3 Disequilibrium unemployment

Definitions

Aggregate supply of labour curve A curve showing the total number of people willing and able to work at different average real wage rates.

Aggregate demand for labour curve A curve showing the total demand for labour in the economy at different average real wage rates.

Disequilibrium unemployment Unemployment resulting from real wages in the economy being above the equilibrium level.

Equilibrium ('natural') unemployment The difference between those who would like employment at the current wage rate and those willing and able to take a job.

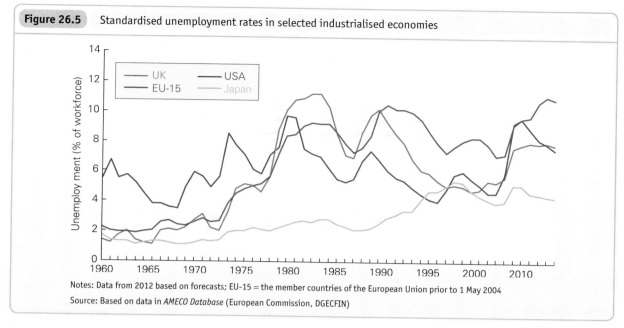

Figure 26.5 Standardised unemployment rates in selected industrialised economies

Notes: Data from 2012 based on forecasts; EU-15 = the member countries of the European Union prior to 1 May 2004

Source: Based on data in *AMECO Database* (European Commission, DGECFIN)

the distance $D – E$ represents the **equilibrium level of unemployment**. This is sometimes known as the *natural level of unemployment*.

Types of disequilibrium unemployment

There are three possible causes of disequilibrium unemployment.

Real-wage unemployment

This is where trade unions use their monopoly power to drive wages above the market-clearing level. In Figure 26.3, the wage rate is driven up above W_e. Excessive real wage rates were blamed by the Thatcher and Major governments for the high unemployment of the 1980s and early 1990s. The possibility of higher real-wage unemployment was also one of the reasons for their rejection of a national minimum wage.

Even though unions have the power to drive up wages in some industries, their power to do so has waned in recent years. Labour markets have become more flexible (see section 18.7). What is more, the process of globalisation has meant that many firms face intense competition from rivals in China, India and many other countries. This makes it impossible for them to concede large pay increases. In many cases, they can simply use labour in other countries if domestic labour is too expensive. For example, many firms employ call-centre workers in India, where wages are much lower.

As far as the national minimum wage is concerned, evidence from the UK suggests that the rate has not been high enough to have significant adverse effects on employment (see Box 18.2 on page 283).

Demand-deficient or cyclical unemployment

Demand-deficient or **cyclical unemployment** is associated with recessions, such as that of 2008/9. As the economy

moves into recession, consumer demand falls. Firms find that they are unable to sell their current level of output. For a time they may be prepared to build up stocks of unsold goods, but sooner or later they will start to cut back on production and cut back on the amount of labour they employ. In Figure 26.3 the AD_L curve shifts to the left. The deeper the recession becomes and the longer it lasts, the higher will demand-deficient unemployment become.

Later, as the economy recovers and begins to grow again, so demand-deficient unemployment will start to fall. Because demand-deficient unemployment fluctuates with the business cycle, it is sometimes referred to as 'cyclical unemployment'. Figure 26.5 shows the fluctuations in unemployment in various industrial countries. If you compare this figure with Figure 26.2, you can see how unemployment tends to rise in recessions and fall in booms.

Growth in the labour supply

If labour supply rises with no corresponding increase in the demand for labour, the equilibrium real wage rate will fall. If the real wage rate is 'sticky' downwards, unemployment will occur. This tends not to be such a serious cause of unemployment as demand deficiency, since the supply of labour changes relatively slowly. Nevertheless, there is a problem of providing jobs for school leavers each year with the sudden influx of new workers on to the labour market.

Definition

Demand-deficient or **cyclical unemployment**
Disequilibrium unemployment caused by a fall in aggregate demand with no corresponding fall in the real wage rate.

KI 38
p 419

BOX 26.2	THE DURATION OF UNEMPLOYMENT

Taking a dip in the unemployment pool

A few of the unemployed may never have had a job and maybe never will. For most, however, unemployment lasts only a certain period. For some it may be just a few days while they are between jobs. For others it may be a few months. For others – the long-term unemployed – it could be several years. Long-term unemployment negatively affects a country's potential output, particularly by reducing a country's stock of human capital. Therefore, the length of time people spend unemployed is an important labour market issue.

Long-term unemployment is normally defined as those who have been unemployed for over 12 months. Chart (a) shows the composition of standardised unemployment in the UK by duration since the early 1990s. It shows how long-term unemployment fell from the mid 1990s until the economic downturn in the late 2000s. As a result, the percentage of unemployed people classified as long-term unemployed, which had hit 45 per cent

in 1994, fell to 20 per cent by 2005, before rising to 36 per cent in 2012.

But, what determines the average duration of unemployment? There are three important factors here.

The number unemployed (the size of the stock of unemployment)

Unemployment is a 'stock' concept: It measures a *quantity* of people unemployed at a particular *point in time*. The higher the stock of unemployment, the longer will tend to be the duration of unemployment. There will be more people competing for vacant jobs.

The rate of inflow and outflow from the stock of unemployment

The people making up the unemployment total are constantly changing. Each week some people are made redundant or

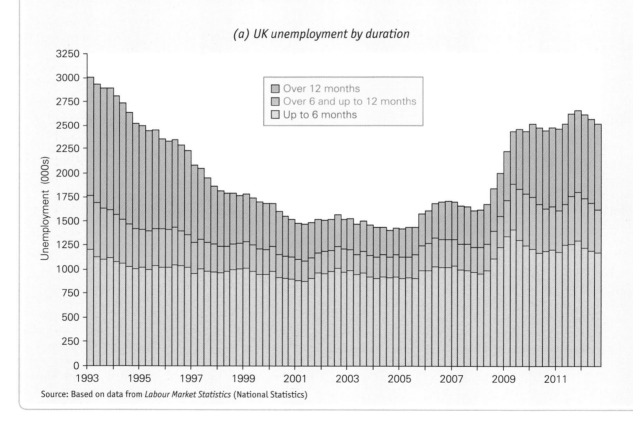

(a) UK unemployment by duration

Legend:
- Over 12 months
- Over 6 and up to 12 months
- Up to 6 months

Source: Based on data from *Labour Market Statistics* (National Statistics)

There is also a potential problem over the longer term if social trends lead more women with children to seek employment. In practice, however, with the rapid growth of part-time employment and the lower average wage rate paid to women, this has not been a major cause of excess labour supply.

Equilibrium unemployment

If you look at Figure 26.5, you can see how unemployment was higher in the 1980s and 1990s than in the 1970s. Part of the reason for this was the growth in equilibrium unemployment. In the 2000s, unemployment fell in many

quit their jobs. They represent an inflow to the stock of unemployment. Other people find jobs and thus represent an outflow from the stock of unemployment. Unemployment is often referred to as 'the pool of unemployment'.

If the inflow of people into unemployment pool exceeds the outflow, the pool of unemployed people will rise. The duration of unemployment will depend on the *rate* of inflow and outflow. The rate is expressed as the number of people per period of time. Chart (b) shows the total inflows and outflows in the UK since 1989.

In each of the years, the outflows (and inflows) exceed the total number unemployed. The bigger the flows are relative to the total number unemployed, the less will be the average duration of unemployment. This is because people move into and out of the unemployment pool more quickly, and hence their average stay will be shorter.

The phase of the business cycle

The duration of unemployment will also depend on the phase of the business cycle. At the onset of a recession, unemployment will rise, but as yet the average length of unemployment is likely to have been relatively short. Once a recession has lasted for a period of time, however, people will on average have been out of work longer; and this long-term unemployment is likely to persist even when the economy is pulling out of recession.

1. *If the number unemployed exceeded the total annual outflow, what could we conclude about the average duration of unemployment?*
2. *Make a list of the various inflows to and outflows from employment from and to (a) unemployment; (b) outside the workforce?*

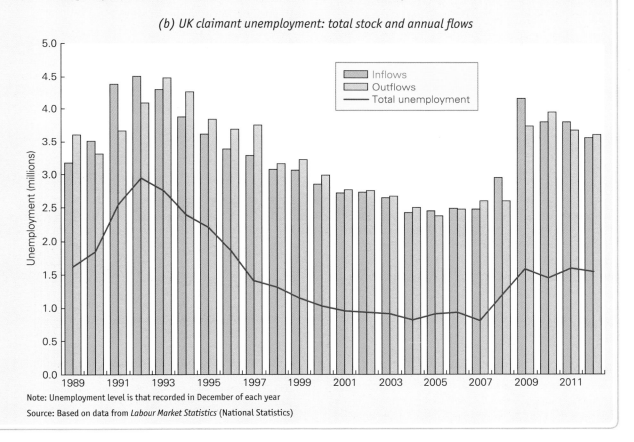

(b) UK claimant unemployment: total stock and annual flows

Note: Unemployment level is that recorded in December of each year

Source: Based on data from *Labour Market Statistics* (National Statistics)

countries – at least until the financial crisis of 2007/8. Again, part of the reason for this was a change in equilibrium unemployment, but this time a fall.

Although there may be overall *macro*economic equilibrium, with the *aggregate* demand for labour equal to the *aggregate* supply, and thus no disequilibrium unemployment, at a *micro*economic level supply and demand may not match. In other words, there may be vacancies in some parts of the economy, but an excess of labour (unemployment) in others. This is equilibrium unemployment. There are various types of equilibrium unemployment.

Frictional (search) unemployment

Frictional unemployment occurs when people leave their jobs, either voluntarily or because they are sacked or made redundant, and are then unemployed for a period of time while they are looking for a new job. They may not get the first job they apply for, despite a vacancy existing. The employer may continue searching, hoping to find a better-qualified person. Likewise, unemployed people may choose not to take the first job they are offered. Instead they may continue searching, hoping that a better one will turn up.

The problem is that information is imperfect. Employers are not fully informed about what labour is available; workers are not fully informed about what jobs are available and what they entail. Both employers and workers, therefore, have to search: employers search for the right labour and workers search for the right jobs.

Structural unemployment

Structural unemployment is where the structure of the economy changes. Employment in some industries may expand while in others it contracts. There are two main reasons for this.

A change in the pattern of demand. Some industries experience declining demand. This may be due to a change in consumer tastes. Certain goods may go out of fashion. Or it may be due to competition from other industries. For example, consumer demand may shift away from coal and to other fuels. This will lead to structural unemployment in mining areas.

A change in the methods of production (technological unemployment). New techniques of production often allow the same level of output to be produced with fewer workers. This is known as 'labour-saving technical progress'. Unless output expands sufficiently to absorb the surplus labour, people will be made redundant. This creates **technological unemployment**. An example is the job losses in the banking industry caused by the increase in the number of cash machines and by the development of telephone and Internet banking.

Structural unemployment often occurs in particular regions of the country. When it does, it is referred to as **regional unemployment**. This is most likely to occur when particular industries are concentrated in particular areas. For example, the decline in the South Wales coal mining industry led to high unemployment in the Welsh valleys.

Seasonal unemployment

Seasonal unemployment occurs when the demand for certain types of labour fluctuates with the seasons of the year. This problem is particularly severe in holiday areas such as Cornwall, where unemployment can reach very high levels in the winter months.

26.4 INFLATION

Inflation refers to rising price levels; deflation refers to falling price levels. The annual rate of inflation measures the annual percentage *increase* in prices. If the rate of inflation is negative, then prices are falling and we are measuring the rate of deflation.

Typically inflation relates to *consumer* prices. The government publishes a 'consumer prices index' (CPI) each month, and the rate of inflation is the percentage increase in that index over the previous 12 months.

A broader measure of inflation relates to the rate at which the prices of all domestically produced goods and services are changing. The price index used in this case is known as the **GDP deflator**. Figure 26.6 shows the annual rates of change in the GDP deflator for the USA, Japan, the UK and the EU-15. As you can see, inflation was particularly severe in the mid-1970s, but rates have been relatively low in more recent years and indeed Japan has experienced deflation.

You will also find rates of inflation reported for a variety of goods and services. For example, inflation rates are published for wages (wage inflation), commodity prices, food prices, house prices, import prices, prices after taking taxes into account and so on.

Definitions

Frictional (search) unemployment Unemployment that occurs as a result of imperfect information in the labour market. It often takes time for workers to find jobs (even though there are vacancies) and in the meantime they are unemployed.

Structural unemployment Unemployment that arises from changes in the pattern of demand or supply in the economy. People made redundant in one part of the economy cannot immediately take up jobs in other parts (even though there are vacancies).

Technological unemployment Structural unemployment that occurs as a result of the introduction of labour-saving technology.

Regional unemployment Structural unemployment occurring in specific regions of the country.

Seasonal unemployment Unemployment associated with industries or regions where the demand for labour is lower at certain times of the year.

GDP deflator The price index of all final domestically produced goods and services: i.e. all items that contribute towards GDP.

Figure 26.6 Inflation rates in selected industrialised economies

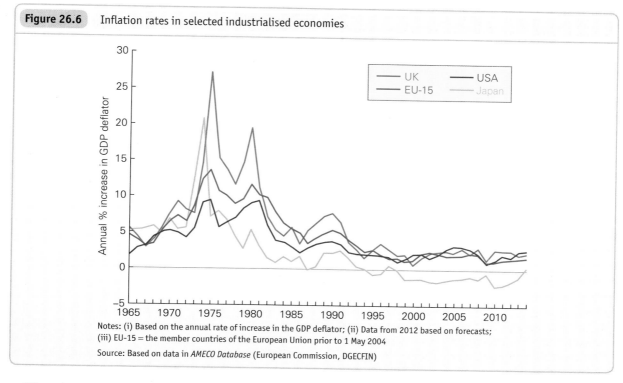

Notes: (i) Based on the annual rate of increase in the GDP deflator; (ii) Data from 2012 based on forecasts;
(iii) EU-15 = the member countries of the European Union prior to 1 May 2004

Source: Based on data in *AMECO Database* (European Commission, DGECFIN)

When there is inflation, we have to be careful in assessing how much national output, consumption, wages, etc. are increasing. Take the case of GDP. GDP in year 2 may seem higher than in year 1, but this may be partly (or even wholly) the result of higher prices. Thus GDP in money terms may have risen by 5 per cent, but if inflation is 3 per cent, *real growth in GDP* will be only 2 per cent. In other words, the volume of output will be only 2 per cent higher.

The distinction between nominal and real figures.
Nominal figures are those using current prices, interest rates, etc. Real figures are figures corrected for inflation.

Before we proceed, a word of caution: be careful not to confuse a rise or fall in *inflation* with a rise or fall in *prices*. A rise in inflation means a *faster* increase in prices. A fall in inflation means a *slower* increase in prices (but still an increase as long as inflation is positive).

The costs of inflation

A lack of growth is obviously a problem if people want higher living standards. Unemployment is obviously a problem, both for the unemployed themselves and also for society, which suffers a loss in output and has to support the unemployed. But why is inflation a problem? If firms are faced with rising costs, does it really matter if they can simply pass them on in higher prices? Similarly for workers, if their wages keep up with prices, there will not be a cut in their living standards.

If people could correctly anticipate the rate of inflation and fully adjust prices and incomes to take account of it, then the costs of inflation would indeed be relatively small. For us as consumers, they would simply be the relatively minor inconvenience of having to adjust our notions of what a 'fair' price is for each item when we go shopping. For firms, they would again be the relatively minor costs of having to change price labels, or prices in catalogues or on menus, or to adjust slot machines. These are known as *menu costs*.

In reality, people frequently make mistakes when predicting the rate of inflation and are not able to adapt fully to it. This leads to the following problems, which are likely to be more serious the higher the rate of inflation becomes and the more the rate fluctuates.

Redistribution. Inflation redistributes income away from those on fixed incomes and those in a weak bargaining position, to those who can use their economic power to gain large pay, rent or profit increases. It redistributes wealth to those with assets (e.g. property) that rise in value

Definitions

Real growth values Values of the rate of growth of GDP or any other variable after taking inflation into account. The real value of the growth in a variable equals its growth in money (or 'nominal') value minus the rate of inflation.

Menu costs of inflation The costs associated with having to adjust price lists or labels.

particularly rapidly during periods of inflation, and away from those with savings that pay rates of interest below the rate of inflation and hence whose value is eroded by inflation. Pensioners may be particularly badly hit by rapid inflation.

Uncertainty and lack of investment. Inflation tends to cause uncertainty in the business community, especially when the rate of inflation fluctuates. (Generally, the higher the rate of inflation, the more it fluctuates.) If it is difficult for firms to predict their costs and revenues, they may be discouraged from investing. This will reduce the rate of economic growth. On the other hand, as will be explained below, policies to reduce the rate of inflation may themselves reduce the rate of economic growth, especially in the short run. This may then provide the government with a policy dilemma.

Balance of payments. Inflation is likely to worsen the balance of payments. If a country suffers from relatively high inflation rates, its exports will become less competitive in world markets. At the same time, imports will become relatively cheaper than home-produced goods. Thus exports will fall and imports will rise. As a result the balance of payments will deteriorate and/or the exchange rate will fall, or interest rates will have to rise. Each of these effects can cause problems. This is examined in more detail in the next chapter.

Resources. Extra resources are likely to be used to cope with the effects of inflation. Accountants and other financial experts may have to be employed by companies to help them cope with the uncertainties caused by inflation.

The costs of inflation may be relatively mild if the inflation rate is kept to single figures. They can be very serious, however, if inflation gets out of hand. If inflation develops into 'hyperinflation', with prices rising perhaps by several hundred or even thousand per cent per year, the whole basis of the market economy will be undermined. Firms constantly raise prices in an attempt to cover their rocketing costs. Workers demand huge pay increases in an attempt to stay ahead of the rocketing cost of living. Thus prices and wages chase each other in an ever-rising inflationary spiral. People will no longer want to save money. Instead they will spend it as quickly as possible before its value falls any further. People may even resort to barter in an attempt to avoid using money altogether.

Hyperinflation has occurred in various countries. Extreme examples include Germany in the early 1920s, Serbia and Montenegro in 1993–5 and Zimbabwe in 2006–8. In each case, inflation peaked at several million percent.

Pause for thought

Do you personally gain or lose from inflation? Why?

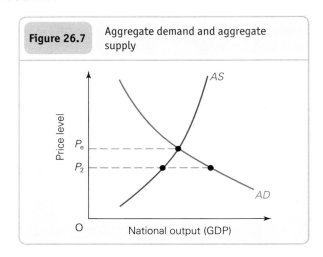

Figure 26.7 Aggregate demand and aggregate supply

Aggregate demand and supply and the level of prices

The level of prices in the economy is determined by the interaction of aggregate demand and aggregate supply. The analysis is similar to that of demand and supply in individual markets, but there are some crucial differences. Figure 26.7 shows aggregate demand and supply curves. Let us examine each in turn.

Aggregate demand curve

The aggregate demand curve shows how much national output (real GDP) will be demanded at each level of prices (GDP deflator). But why does the *AD* curve slope downwards: why do people demand fewer products as prices rise? There are three main reasons:

- If prices rise, people will be encouraged to buy fewer of the country's products and more imports instead (which are now relatively cheaper); also the country will sell fewer exports. Thus aggregate demand will be lower.
- As prices rise, people will need more money to pay for their purchases. With a given supply of money in the economy, this will have the effect of driving up interest rates (we will explore this in Chapter 28). The effect of higher interest rates will be to discourage borrowing and encourage saving. Both will have the effect of reducing spending and hence reducing aggregate demand.
- If prices rise, the value of people's savings will be eroded. They may thus save more (and spend less) to compensate.

The above three effects are *substitution effects* of the rise in prices (see page 49). They involve a switch to *alternatives* – either imports or saving.

There may also be an *income effect*. This will occur provided consumers' incomes do not rise as fast as prices, causing a fall in consumers' *real* incomes. Consumers cut down on consumption as they cannot afford to buy so much. Firms, on the other hand, with falling real wage costs, are likely to find their profit per unit rising. However, they are unlikely to spend much more on investment, if at all, as consumer expenditure is falling. The net effect is a fall in aggregate demand.

Aggregate supply curve

The aggregate supply curve slopes upwards – at least in the short run. In other words, the higher the level of prices, the more will be produced. The reason is simple: provided that factor prices (and, in particular, wage rates) do not rise as rapidly as product prices, firms' profitability at each level of output will be higher than before. This will encourage them to produce more.

Equilibrium

The equilibrium price level will be where aggregate demand equals aggregate supply. To demonstrate this, consider what would happen if aggregate demand exceeded aggregate supply: for example, at P_2 in Figure 26.7. The resulting shortages throughout the economy would drive up prices. This would cause a movement up along both the *AD* and *AS* curves until *AD = AS* (at P_e).

Shifts in the AD or AS curves

If there is a change in the price level there will be a movement *along* the *AD* and *AS* curves. If any other determinant of *AD* or *AS* changes, the respective curve will shift. The analysis here is very similar to shifts and movements along demand and supply curves in individual markets (see pages 51 and 53).

The aggregate demand curve will shift if there is a change in any of its components: consumption, investment, government expenditure or exports minus imports. Thus if the government decides to spend more, or if consumers spend more as a result of lower taxes, or if business confidence increases so that firms decide to invest more, the *AD* curve will shift to the right.

Similarly, the aggregate supply curve will shift to the right if there is a rise in labour productivity or in the stock of capital: in other words, if there is a rise in potential output.

Pause for thought

Give some examples of events that could shift (a) the AD curve to the left; (b) the AS curve to the left.

Causes of inflation

Demand-pull inflation

Demand-pull inflation is caused by continuing rises in aggregate demand. In Figure 26.7, the *AD* curve shifts to the right, and continues doing so. Firms will respond to the rise in aggregate demand partly by raising prices and partly by increasing output (there is a move up along the *AS* curve). Just how much they raise prices depends on how much their costs rise as a result of increasing output. This in turn depends upon how close actual output is to potential output. The less slack there is in the economy, the more will firms respond to a rise in demand by raising their prices (the steeper will be the *AS* curve).

Demand-pull inflation is typically associated with a booming economy. Many economists therefore argue that it is the counterpart of demand-deficient unemployment. When the economy is in recession, demand-deficient unemployment will be high, but demand-pull inflation will be low. When, on the other hand, the economy is near the peak of the business cycle, demand-pull inflation will be high, but demand-deficient unemployment will be low.

Cost-push inflation

Cost-push inflation is associated with continuing rises in costs and hence continuing leftward (upward) shifts in the *AS* curve. Such shifts occur when costs of production rise *independently* of aggregate demand. If firms face a rise in costs, they will respond partly by raising prices and passing the costs on to the consumer, and partly by cutting back on production (there is a movement back along the *AD* curve).

Just how much firms raise prices and cut back on production depends on the shape of the aggregate demand curve. The less elastic the *AD* curve, the less sales will fall as a result of any price rise, and hence the more will firms be able to pass on the rise in their costs to consumers as higher prices.

Note that the effect on output and employment is the opposite of demand-pull inflation. With demand-pull inflation, output and hence employment tend to rise. With cost-push inflation, however, output and employment tend to fall.

It is important to distinguish between *single* shifts in the aggregate supply curve (known as 'supply shocks') and *continuing* shifts. If there is a single leftward shift in aggregate supply, there will be a single rise in the price level. For example, if the government raises the excise duty on petrol and diesel, there will be a single rise in road fuel prices and hence in industry's fuel costs. This will cause *temporary* inflation while the price rise is passed on through the economy. Once this has occurred, prices will stabilise at the new level and the rate of inflation will fall back to zero again. If cost-push inflation is to continue over a number of years, therefore, the aggregate supply curve must *continually* shift to the left. If cost-push inflation is to *rise*, these shifts must get more rapid.

Definitions

Demand-pull inflation Inflation caused by persistent rises in aggregate demand.

Cost-push inflation Inflation caused by persistent rises in costs of production (independently of demand).

BOX 26.3 INFLATION OR DEFLATION

Where's the danger?

During the first half of the 2000s it appeared that inflation was no longer a serious worry in many developed economies. Instead, 'deflation' (i.e. falling prices) had become a source of concern. The Japanese economy has been in deflation for a decade or so and central banks, including the US Federal Reserve and the European Central Bank, were sounding warnings that deflation was a real and present danger to us all. A quote from *The Sunday Times* of 11 May 2003 captures the concerns of the time:

> Consumers have had a good run in America. Twenty years ago a Burger King Whopper cost $1.40. Today the same burger costs 99c. Ten years ago Delta Airlines charged $388 for a flight from New York to San Francisco; this weekend flights are available for $302. Five years ago the average new car cost $25 000; now it is $24 500.

> The same is true for clothes, computers, holidays and television sets. As wages have risen, prices seem to have fallen across the board. But can you have too much of a good thing?

> Last week, America's central bankers warned that falling prices could harm the US economy. The Federal Reserve even went as far as to raise the spectre of deflation – an economic malaise that has paralysed the Japanese economy for a decade and was last seen in America during the Great Depression of the 1930s.

> Consumers normally welcome falling prices, but in a deflating economy such falls can create a damaging downward spiral. Profits fall as companies are unable to offset costs by raising prices. Companies then cut staff to save money. Job losses lead to falling sales.

> Declining sales also make it harder for companies and people to meet their debts, leading to further declines in sales and a rise in bankruptcies. Falling prices also lead

people to defer purchases in the belief that prices will come down further.[1]

One of the main causes of declining prices was the process of globalisation. Imports from low-cost countries, such as China and India, drove prices down. What is more, outsourcing call-centre, back-office and IT work to developing countries put downward pressure on wages. This downward effect on prices and wages in the USA and other developed economies was dubbed the 'China price' effect.

A return of inflation?

The USA and other OECD economies staged a rapid recovery after 2003. Between 2004 and 2006, US economic growth averaged 3.8 per cent and the OECD countries' averaged 3.1 per cent. These rates, however, were dwarfed by China and India, which experienced growth rates of 10.1 per cent and 8.4 per cent respectively over the same period.

The rapid growth in aggregate demand in many OECD countries put upward pressure on prices and wages but, unlike previously, the 'China price' effect was beginning to *reinforce* this upward pressure. By 2007/8, the growth in China, India and other rapidly developing countries was causing significant inflation in commodity prices, i.e. in the prices of raw material and primary agricultural products. This emergence of rapid commodity price inflation can be clearly seen in the chart.

However, with the onset of recession in mid-2008, inflation started to fall and the 'China effect' seemed to have gone away. Once more there seemed to be a spectre of deflation. By 2009, many people were asking themselves why they

---

[1] From 'Deflation turns into biggest economic risk', *The Times*, 11 May 2003. © NI Syndication Limited. Reproduced with permission.

Rises in costs may originate from a number of different sources, such as trade unions pushing up wages, firms with monopoly power raising prices in order to increase their profits, or increases in international commodity prices. With the process of globalisation and increased international competition, cost-push pressures have tended to decrease in recent years. The major exception is the price of various commodities and especially oil. For example, the near tripling of oil prices from $51 per barrel in January 2007 to $147 per barrel in July 2008 and again from $41 a barrel in January 2009 to $126 a barrel in April 2011 put upward pressure on costs and prices around the world.

Demand-pull and cost-push inflation can occur together, since wage and price rises can be caused both by increases in aggregate demand and by independent causes pushing up costs. Even when an inflationary process *starts* as either demand-pull or cost-push, it is often difficult to separate the two. An initial cost-push inflation may encourage the government to expand aggregate demand to offset rises in unemployment. Alternatively, an initial demand-pull inflation may strengthen the power of certain groups, who then use this power to drive up costs. Either way, the result is likely to be continuing rightward shifts in the *AD* curve and leftward shifts in the *AS* curve. Prices will carry on rising.

should buy now when, by delaying, they might be able to get an item more cheaply later on. The effect of this would be a leftward shift in the *AD* curve, which forces prices down even further.

But the worry about deflation was short-lived. As the world economy pulled out of recession and China resumed double-digit growth, so commodity and other prices began rising more rapidly. In the UK, the annual rate of CPI inflation

peaked at 5.2 per cent in the 12 months to September 2011, significantly above the Bank of England's central inflation target of 2 per cent.

1. *What long-term economic benefits might deflation generate for business and the economy in general?*
2. *Would an inflationary China price effect be an example of demand-pull or cost-push inflation?*

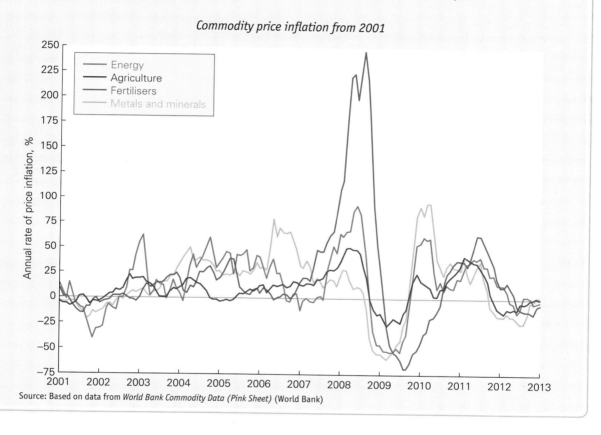

Commodity price inflation from 2001

Source: Based on data from *World Bank Commodity Data (Pink Sheet)* (World Bank)

Expectations and inflation

KI 13
p 71

Workers and firms take account of the *expected* rate of inflation when making decisions.

Imagine that a union and an employer are negotiating a wage increase. Let us assume that both sides expect a rate of inflation of 5 per cent. The union will be happy to receive a wage rise somewhat above 5 per cent. That way the members would be getting a *real* rise in incomes. The employers will be happy to pay a wage rise somewhat below 5 per cent. After all, they can put their price up by 5 per cent, knowing that their rivals will do approximately the same. The actual wage rise that the two sides agree on will thus be somewhere around 5 per cent.

Now let us assume that the expected rate of inflation is 10 per cent. Both sides will now negotiate around this benchmark, with the outcome being somewhere round about 10 per cent.

Thus the higher the expected rate of inflation, the higher will be the level of pay settlements and price rises, and hence the higher will be the resulting actual rate of inflation.

In recent years the importance of expectations in explaining the actual rate of inflation has been increasingly recognised by economists. (We examine this in Chapter 29.)

26.5 THE BUSINESS CYCLE AND MACROECONOMIC OBJECTIVES

In the short term (up to about two years), the four objectives of faster growth in output, lower unemployment, lower inflation and achieving a favourable balance of payments are all related. They all depend on aggregate demand and vary with the course of the business cycle. This is illustrated in Figure 26.8.

In the expansionary phase of the business cycle (phase 2), aggregate demand grows rapidly. There will be relatively rapid growth in output, with a positive output gap emerging, and (demand-deficient) unemployment will fall. Thus two of the problems are getting better. On the other hand, the other two problems will be getting worse. The growing shortages lead to higher (demand-pull) inflation and a deteriorating balance of payments as the extra demand 'sucks in' more imports and as higher prices make domestic goods less competitive internationally.

At the peak of the cycle (phase 3), unemployment is probably at its lowest and output at its highest (for the time being). But growth has already ceased or at least slowed down. Inflation and balance of payments problems are probably acute.

As the economy moves into phase 4 (let us assume that this is an actual recession with falling output), the reverse will happen to that of phase 2. Falling aggregate demand will make growth negative and demand-deficient unemployment higher, but inflation is likely to slow down and the balance of payments will improve. These two improvements may take some time to occur, however.

Governments are thus faced with a dilemma. If they reflate the economy, they will make two of the objectives better (growth and unemployment), but the other two worse (inflation and balance of payments). If they deflate the economy, it is the other way round: inflation and the balance of payments will improve, but unemployment will rise and growth, or even output, will fall.

Societies face trade-offs between economic objectives. For example, the goal of faster growth may conflict with that of greater equality; the goal of lower unemployment may conflict with that of lower inflation (at least in the short run). This is an example of opportunity cost: the cost of achieving more of one objective may be achieving less of another. The existence of trade-offs means that policy-makers must make choices.

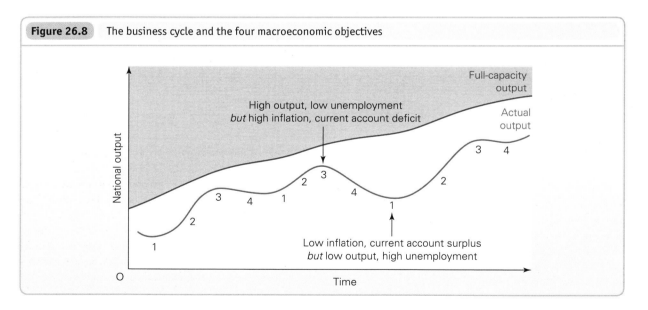

Figure 26.8 The business cycle and the four macroeconomic objectives

26.6 THE CIRCULAR FLOW OF INCOME

Another way of understanding the relationship between the four objectives is to use a simple model of the economy. This is the circular flow of income, which is shown in Figure 26.9. In the diagram, the economy is divided into two major groups: *firms* and *households*. Each group has two roles. Firms are producers of goods and services; they are also the employers of labour and other factors of production. Households (which is the word we use for individuals) are the consumers of goods and services; they are also the suppliers of labour and various other factors of production. In the diagram there is an inner flow and various outer flows of income between these two groups.

Figure 26.9 The circular flow of income

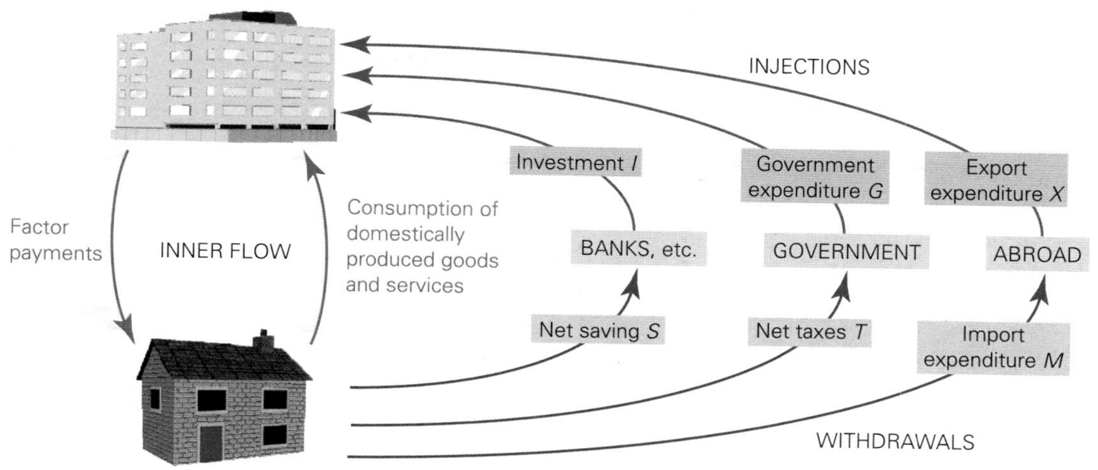

Before we look at the various parts of the diagram, a word of warning. Do not confuse *money* and *income*. Money is a stock concept. At any given time, there is a certain quantity of money in the economy (e.g. £500 billion). But that does not tell us the level of national *income*. Income is a flow concept (as is expenditure). It is measured as so much *per period of time*.

The relationship between money and income depends on how rapidly the money *circulates*: its 'velocity of circulation'. (We will examine this concept in detail later on.) If there is £500 billion of money in the economy and each £1 on average is paid out as income three times each year, then annual national income will be £1.5 trillion.

The inner flow, withdrawals and injections

The inner flow

Firms pay money to households in the form of wages and salaries, dividends on shares, interest and rent. These payments are in return for the services of the factors of production – labour, capital and land – that are supplied by households. Thus on the left-hand side of the diagram money flows directly from firms to households as 'factor payments'.

Households, in turn, pay money to domestic firms when they **consume domestically produced goods and services** (C_d). This is shown on the right-hand side of the inner flow. There is thus a circular flow of payments from firms to households to firms and so on.

If households spend *all* their incomes on buying domestic goods and services, and if firms pay out *all* this income they receive as factor payments to domestic households, and if the velocity of circulation does not change, the flow will continue at the same level indefinitely. The

money just goes round and round at the same speed and incomes remain unchanged.

In the real world, of course, it is not as simple as this. Not all income gets passed on round the inner flow; some is *withdrawn*. At the same time, incomes are injected into the flow from outside. Let us examine these withdrawals and injections.

> **Pause for thought**
>
> *Would this argument still hold if prices rose?*

Withdrawals

Only part of the incomes received by households will be spent on the goods and services of domestic firms. The remainder will be withdrawn from the inner flow. Likewise, only part of the incomes generated by firms will be paid to domestic households. The remainder of this will also be withdrawn. There are three forms of **withdrawals (W)** (or 'leakages' as they are sometimes called).

> ### Definitions
>
> **The consumption of domestically produced goods and services (C_d)** The direct flow of money payments from households to firms.
>
> **Withdrawals (W) (or leakages)** Incomes of households or firms that are not passed on round the inner flow. Withdrawals equal net saving (S) plus net taxes (T) plus import expenditure (M): $W = S + T + M$.

Net saving (S). Saving is income that households choose not to spend but to put aside for the future. Savings are normally deposited in financial institutions such as banks and building societies. This is shown in the bottom right of the diagram. Money flows from households to 'banks, etc'. What we are seeking to measure here, however, is the net flow from households to the banking sector. We therefore have to subtract from saving any borrowing or drawing on past savings by households in order to get the *net* saving flow. Of course, if household borrowing exceeded saving, the net flow would be in the other direction: it would be negative.

Net taxes (T). When people pay taxes (to either central or local government), this represents a withdrawal of money from the inner flow in much the same way as saving: only in this case people have no choice. Some taxes, such as income tax and employees' national insurance contributions, are paid out of household incomes. Others, such as VAT and excise duties, are paid out of consumer expenditure. Others, such as corporation tax, are paid out of firms' incomes before being received by households as dividends on shares. (For simplicity, however, we show taxes being withdrawn at just one point. It does not affect the argument.)

When, however, people receive *benefits* from the government, such as working tax credit, child benefit and pensions, the money flows the other way. Benefits are thus equivalent to a 'negative tax'. These benefits are known as **transfer payments**. They transfer money from one group of people (taxpayers) to others (the recipients).

In the model, 'net taxes' (T) represent the *net* flow to the government from households and firms. It consists of total taxes minus benefits.

Import expenditure (M). Not all consumption is of totally home-produced goods. Households spend some of their incomes on imported goods and services, or on goods and services using imported components. Although the money that consumers spend on such goods initially flows to domestic retailers, it will eventually find its way abroad, either when the retailers or wholesalers themselves import them, or when domestic manufacturers purchase imported inputs to make their products. This expenditure on imports constitutes the third withdrawal from the inner flow. This money flows abroad.

Total withdrawals are simply the sum of net saving, net taxes and the expenditure on imports:

$$W = S + T + M$$

Injections

Only part of the demand for firms' output arises from consumers' expenditure. The remainder comes from other sources outside the inner flow. These additional components of aggregate demand are known as **injections (J)**. There are three types of injection.

Investment (I). This consists of investment in plant and equipment. It also includes the building up of stocks of inputs, semi-finished or finished goods. When firms invest, they obtain the money from various financial institutions, either from past savings or from loans, or through a new issues of shares.

Government expenditure (G). When the government spends money on goods and services produced by firms, this counts as an injection. Examples of such government expenditure are spending on roads, hospitals and schools. (Note that government expenditure in this model does not include state benefits. These transfer payments, as we saw above, are the equivalent of negative taxes and have the effect of reducing the T component of withdrawals.)

Export expenditure (X). Money flows into the circular flow from abroad when residents abroad buy our exports of goods and services.

Total injections are thus the sum of investment, government expenditure and exports:

$$J = I + G + X$$

Aggregate demand, which is the total spending on output, is thus $C_d + J$.

The relationship between withdrawals and injections

There are indirect links between saving and investment via financial institutions, between taxation and government expenditure via the government (central and local), and between imports and exports via foreign countries. These links, however, do not guarantee that $S = I$ or $G = T$ or $M = X$.

Take investment and saving. The point here is that the decisions to save and invest are made by different people, and thus they plan to save and invest different amounts. Likewise the demand for imports may not equal the demand for exports. As far as the government is concerned, it may choose not to make $T = G$. It may choose not to spend all its tax revenues: to run a 'budget surplus' ($T > G$); or it may choose to spend more than it receives in taxes: to run a 'budget deficit' ($G > T$), by borrowing or printing money to make up the difference.

Thus planned injections (J) may not equal planned withdrawals (W).

Definitions

Transfer payments Moneys transferred from one person or group to another (e.g. from the government to individuals) without production taking place.

Injections (J) Expenditure on the production of domestic firms coming from outside the inner flow of the circular flow of income. Injections equal investment (I) plus government expenditure (G) plus expenditure on exports (X).

The circular flow of income and the four macroeconomic objectives

If planned injections are not equal to planned withdrawals, what will be the consequences? If injections exceed withdrawals, the level of expenditure will rise. The extra aggregate demand will generate extra incomes. In other words, *actual* national income will rise. If this rise in actual income exceeds any rise there may have been in potential income, there will be the following effects upon the four macroeconomic objectives:

- There will be economic growth. The greater the initial excess of injections over withdrawals, the bigger will be the rise in national income.
- Unemployment will fall as firms take on more workers in order to meet the extra demand for output.
- Inflation will tend to rise. The more the gap is closed between actual and potential income, the more difficult will firms find it to meet extra demand, and the more likely they will be to raise prices.
- The exports and imports part of the balance of payments will tend to deteriorate. The higher demand sucks more imports into the country, and higher domestic inflation makes exports less competitive and imports relatively cheaper compared with home-produced goods. Thus imports will tend to rise and exports will tend to fall.

Changes in injections and withdrawals thus have a crucial effect on the whole macroeconomic environment in which businesses operate. We will examine some of these effects in more detail in the following chapters.

Pause for thought

What will be the effect on each of the four objectives if planned injections are less than planned withdrawals?

SUMMARY

1   The four main macroeconomic goals that are generally of most concern to governments are economic growth, reducing unemployment, reducing inflation, and avoiding balance of payments and exchange rate problems.

2a Actual growth must be distinguished from potential growth. The actual growth rate is the percentage annual increase in the output that is actually produced, whereas potential growth is the percentage annual increase in the capacity of the economy to produce (whether or not it is actually produced).

2b Actual growth will fluctuate with the course of the business cycle. The cycle can be broken down into four phases: the upturn, the rapid expansion, the peaking-out, and the slowdown or recession. In practice the length and magnitude of these phases will vary: the cycle is thus irregular.

2c Actual growth is determined by potential growth and by the level of aggregate demand. If actual output is below potential output, actual growth can temporarily exceed potential growth, if aggregate demand is rising sufficiently. In the long term, however, actual output can only grow as fast as potential output will permit.

2d Potential growth is determined by the rate of increase in the *quantity* of resources: capital, labour, land and raw materials; and by the *productivity* of resources. The productivity of capital can be increased by technological improvements and the more efficient use of the capital stock; the productivity of labour can be increased by better education, training, motivation and organisation.

3a The two most common measures of unemployment are claimant unemployment (those claiming unemployment-related benefits) and ILO/OECD standardised unemployment (those available for work and actively seeking work or waiting to take up an appointment).

3b The costs of unemployment include the financial and other personal costs to the unemployed person, the costs to relatives and friends, and the costs to society at large in terms of lost tax revenues, lost profits and lost wages to other workers, and in terms of social disruption.

3c Unemployment can be divided into disequilibrium and equilibrium unemployment.

3d Disequilibrium unemployment occurs when the average real wage rate is above the level that will equate the aggregate demand and supply of labour. It can be caused by unions or government pushing up wages (real-wage unemployment), by a fall in aggregate demand but a downward 'stickiness' in real wages (demand-deficient unemployment), or by an increase in the supply of labour.

3e Equilibrium unemployment occurs when there are people unable or unwilling to fill job vacancies. This may be due to poor information in the labour market and hence a time lag before people find suitable jobs (frictional unemployment), to a changing pattern of demand or supply in the economy and hence a mismatching of labour with jobs (structural unemployment – specific types being technological and regional unemployment), or to seasonal fluctuations in the demand for labour.

4a Inflation redistributes incomes from the economically weak to the economically powerful; it causes uncertainty in the business community and as a result reduces investment; it tends to lead to balance of payments problems and/or a fall in the exchange rate; it leads to resources being used to offset its effects. The costs of inflation can be very great indeed in the case of hyperinflation.

4b Equilibrium in the economy occurs when aggregate demand equals aggregate supply. Inflation can occur if there is a rightward shift in the aggregate demand curve or an upward (leftward) shift in the aggregate supply curve.

4c Demand-pull inflation occurs as a result of increases in aggregate demand. This can be due to monetary or non-monetary causes.

4d Cost-push inflation occurs when there are increases in the costs of production independent of rises in aggregate demand. Cost-push inflation can be of a number of different varieties: wage-push, profit-push or import-price-push.

▶

4e Cost-push and demand-pull inflation can interact to form spiralling inflation.

4f Expectations play a crucial role in determining the level of inflation. The higher people expect inflation to be, the higher it will be.

5 In the short run, the four macroeconomic objectives are related to aggregate demand and the business cycle. In the expansion phase, growth is high and unemployment is falling, but inflation is rising and the current account of the balance of payments is moving into deficit. In the recession, the reverse is the case.

6a The circular flow of income model depicts the flows of money round the economy. The inner flow shows the direct flows between firms and households. Money flows from firms to households in the form of factor payments, and back again as consumer expenditure on domestically produced goods and services.

6b Not all income gets passed on directly round the inner flow. Some is withdrawn in the form of saving, some is paid in taxes, and some goes abroad as expenditure on imports.

6c Likewise not all expenditure on domestic firms is by domestic consumers. Some is injected from outside the inner flow in the form of investment expenditure, government expenditure and expenditure on the country's exports.

6d Planned injections and withdrawals are unlikely to be the same. If injections exceed withdrawals, national income will rise, unemployment will tend to fall, inflation will tend to rise and the current account of the balance of payments will tend to deteriorate. The reverse will happen if withdrawals exceed injections.

REVIEW QUESTIONS

1 The following table shows index numbers for real GDP (national output) for various countries (2007 = 100).

Using the formula $g = (Y_t - Y_{t-1})/Y_{t-1} \times 100$ (where g is the rate of growth, Y is the index number of output, t is any given years and $t - 1$ is the previous year):

	2007	2008	2009	2010	2011	2012	2013
Australia	100.0	101.1	102.3	104.8	107.2	110.4	113.6
France	100.0	99.9	97.2	98.6	100.3	100.8	102.1
Germany	100.0	101.1	95.9	99.4	102.4	103.1	104.8
Greece	100.0	99.8	96.6	93.2	86.8	82.7	82.6
Ireland	100.0	97.0	90.2	89.9	90.5	91.0	92.7
Japan	100.0	99.0	93.5	97.6	96.9	98.7	100.4
UK	100.0	98.9	94.6	96.6	97.2	97.7	99.4
USA	100.0	99.6	96.1	99.0	100.7	102.7	104.9

Source: Based on data from AMECO (European Commission, DGECFIN)

(a) (i) Work out the growth rate (g) for each country for each year from 2008 to 2013.
   (ii) Plot the figures on a graph.
   (iii) Describe the patterns that emerge.
(b) (i) For each country work out the percentage increase in real GDP between 2007 and 2013.
   (ii) Prepare a column chart showing the percentage increase in output over this period with the countries ranked from largest to smallest by the size of increase.
   (iii) Comment on your findings.

2 Will the rate of actual growth have any effect on the rate of potential growth?

3 Figure 26.1 shows a decline in actual output in recessions. Redraw the diagram, only this time show a mere slowing down of growth in phase 4.

4 At what point of the business cycle is the country now? What do you predict will happen to growth over the next two years? On what basis do you make your prediction?

5 For what possible reasons may one country experience a persistently faster rate of economic growth than another?

6 Would it be desirable to have zero unemployment?

7 What major structural changes have taken place in the UK economy in the past 10 years that have contributed to structural unemployment?

8 What would be the benefits and costs of increasing the rate of unemployment benefit?

9 Do any groups of people gain from inflation?

10 If everyone's incomes rose in line with inflation, would it matter if inflation were 100 per cent or even 1000 per cent per annum?

11 Imagine that you had to determine whether a particular period of inflation was demand pull, or cost push, or a combination of the two. What information would you require in order to conduct your analysis?

12 In terms of the UK circular flow of income, are the following net injections, net withdrawals or neither? If there is uncertainty, explain your assumptions.

(a) Firms are forced to take a cut in profits in order to give a pay rise.
(b) Firms spend money on research.
(c) The government increases personal tax allowances.
(d) The general public invests more money in building societies.
(e) UK investors earn higher dividends on overseas investments.
(f) The government purchases US military aircraft.
(g) People draw on their savings to finance holidays abroad.
(h) People draw on their savings to finance holidays in the UK.
(i) The government runs a budget deficit (spends more than it receives in tax revenues) and finances it by borrowing from the general public.

APPENDIX: MEASURING NATIONAL INCOME AND OUTPUT

Three routes: one destination

KI 27
p 292

To assess how fast the economy has grown, we must have a means of *measuring* the value of the nation's output. The measure we use is called *gross domestic product* (GDP).

GDP can be calculated in three different ways, which should all result in the same figure. These three methods are illustrated in the simplified circular flow of income shown in Figure 26.10.

The product method

This first method of measuring GDP is to add up the value of all the goods and services produced in the country, industry by industry. In other words, we focus on firms and add up all their production. This method is known as the *product method*.

In the national accounts these figures are grouped together into broad categories such as manufacturing, construction and distribution. The figures for the UK economy for 2010 are shown in the top part of Figure 26.11.

When we add up the output of various firms, we must be careful to avoid *double counting*. For example, if a manufacturer sells a television to a retailer for £200 and the retailer sells it to the consumer for £300, how much has this television contributed to GDP? The answer is *not* £500. We do not add the £200 received by the manufacturer to the £300 received by the retailer: that would be double counting. Instead we either just count the final value (£300) or the value added at each stage (£200 by the manufacturer + £100 by the retailer).

The sum of all the values added by all the various industries in the economy is known as *gross value added (GVA) at basic prices*.

How do we get from GVA to GDP? The answer has to do with taxes and subsidies on products and is shown in the bottom part of Figure 26.11. Taxes paid on goods and services (such as VAT and duties on petrol and alcohol) and any subsidies on products are *excluded* from gross value added (GVA), since they are not part of the value added in production. Nevertheless, the way GDP is measured throughout the EU is at *market prices*: i.e. at the prices actually paid at each stage of production. Thus **GDP at market prices** (sometimes referred to simply as GDP) is GVA *plus* taxes on products *minus* subsidies on products.

The income method

The second approach is to focus on the incomes generated from the production of goods and services. A moment's reflection will show that this must be the same as the sum of all values added at each stage of production. Value added is simply the difference between a firm's revenue from sales and the costs of its purchases from other firms. This difference is made up of wages and salaries, rent, interest and profit. In other words, it consists of the incomes earned by those involved in the production process.

Since GVA is the sum of all values added, it must also be the sum of all incomes generated: the sum of all wages and salaries, rent, interest and profit.

The second part of Figure 26.11 shows how these incomes are grouped together in the official statistics. As you can see, the total is the same as that in the top part Figure 26.11, even though the components are quite different.

Note that we do not include *transfer payments* such as social security benefits and pensions. Since these are not payments for the production of goods and services, they are excluded from GVA. Conversely, part of people's gross income is paid in income taxes. Since it is this *gross* (pre-tax) income that arises from the production of goods and services, we count wages, profits, interest and rent *before* the deduction of income taxes.

| Figure 26.10 | The circular flow of income and expenditure |

(1) Production

(2) Incomes

(3) Expenditure

Definitions

Gross value added (GVA) at basic prices The sum of all the values added by all industries in the economy over a year. The figures exclude taxes on products (such as VAT) and include subsidies on products.

Gross domestic product (GDP) (at market prices) The value of output produced within a country over a 12-month period in terms of the prices actually paid. GDP = GVA + taxes on products − subsidies on products.

Figure 26.11 UK GDP: 2010

UK GVA (product-based measure): 2010

	Percentage of GVA
Agriculture, forestry and fishing £7 569 m	0.6
Mining, energy and water supply £60 950 m	4.7
Manufacturing £130 611 m	10.0
Construction £90 685 m	7.0
Wholesale and retail trade; repairs £140 171 m	10.8
Hotels and restaurants £36 936 m	2.8
Transport and communication £146 510 m	11.3
Banking, finance, insurance, etc. £115 161 m	8.9
Letting of property £119 691 m	9.2
Public administration and defence £68 756 m	5.3
Education, health and social work £193 082 m	14.8
Other services £190 996 m	14.7
Total GVA £1 301 118 m	100.0

UK GVA by category of income: 2010

	Percentage of GVA
Compensation of employees (wages and salaries) £799 974 m	61.5
Operating surplus (gross profit, rent and interest of firms government and other institutions) £395 380 m	30.4
Mixed incomes £81 047 m	6.2
Tax less subsidies on production (other than those on products) plus statistical discrepancy £24 717 m	1.9
Total GVA £1 301 118 m	100.0

UK GDP (product-based measure): 2010

GVA (gross value added at basic prices)	£1 301 118 m
plus Taxes on products	£163 898 m
less Subsidies on products	£6 564 m
GDP (at market prices)	£1 458 452 m

Source: *Annual Abstract of Statistics*, Q4 2011 (National Statistics, 2012)

As with the product approach, if we are working out GVA, we measure incomes before the payment of taxes on products or the receipt of subsidies on products, since it is these pre-tax-and-subsidy incomes that arise from the value added by production. When working out GDP, however, we add in these taxes and subtract these subsidies to arrive at a *market price* valuation.

Pause for thought

If a retailer buys a product from a wholesaler for £80 and sells it to a consumer for £100, then the £20 of value that has been added will go partly in wages, partly in rent and partly in profits. Thus £20 of income has been generated at the retail stage. But the good actually contributes a total of £100 to GDP. Where, then, is the remaining £80 worth of income recorded?

The expenditure method

The final approach to calculating GDP is to add up all expenditure on final output (which will be at market prices). This will include the following:

- Consumer expenditure (C). This includes all expenditure on goods and services by households and by non-profit institutions serving households (NPISH) (e.g. clubs and societies).

- Government expenditure (G). This includes central and local government expenditure on final goods and services. Note that it includes non-marketed services (such as health and education), but excludes transfer payments, such as pensions and social security payments.

- Investment expenditure (I). This includes investment in capital, such as buildings and machinery. It also includes the value of any increase (+) or decrease (−) in inventories, whether of raw materials, semi-finished goods or finished goods.

- Exports of goods and services (X).

- Imports of goods and services (M). These have to be *subtracted* from the total in order to leave just the expenditure on *domestic* product. In other words, we subtract the part of consumer expenditure, government expenditure and investment that goes on imports. We also subtract the imported component (e.g. raw materials) from exports.

$$GDP \text{ (at market prices)} = C + G + I + X - M$$

Table 26.1 shows the calculation of UK GDP by the expenditure approach.

From GDP to national income

Gross national income

Some of the incomes earned in the country will go abroad. These include wages, interest, profit and rent earned in this country by foreign residents and remitted abroad, and taxes on production paid to foreign governments and institutions (e.g. the EU). On the other hand, some of the incomes earned by domestic residents will come from abroad. Again, these can be in the form of wages, interest, profit or rent, or in the form of subsidies received from governments or institutions abroad. Gross domestic product, however, is concerned with those incomes generated within the country, irrespective of ownership. If, then, we are to take 'net income from abroad' into account (i.e. these inflows minus outflows), we need a new measure. This is *gross national income (GNY)*.[2] It is defined as follows:

GNY at market prices = GDP at market prices
+ net income from abroad

Thus GDP focuses on the value of domestic production, whereas GNY focuses on the value of incomes earned by domestic residents.

Net national income

The measures we have used so far ignore the fact that each year some of the country's capital equipment will wear out or become obsolete: in other words, they ignore capital *depreciation*. If we subtract an allowance for depreciation (or 'capital consumption') we get *net national income (NNY)*:

NNY at market prices = GNY at market prices
− depreciation

Table 26.2 shows GDP, GNY and NNY figures for the UK.

Table 26.2	UK GDP, GNY and NNY at market prices: 2010	
		£ million
Gross domestic product (GDP)		1 458 452
Plus net income from abroad		20 885
Gross national income (GNY)		1 479 337
Less capital consumption (depreciation)		−164 006
Net national income (NNY)		1 315 331

Source: *United Kingdom National Accounts: The Blue Book – 2011 Edition* (National Statistics, 2011)

Table 26.1	UK GDP at market prices by category of expenditure: 2010	
	£ million	% of GDP
Consumption expenditure of households and NPISH (C)	937 906	64.3
Gross capital formation (I)	224 579	15.4
Government final consumption (G)	338 067	23.2
Exports of goods and services (X)	436 796	29.9
Imports of goods and services (M)	−476 480	−32.7
Statistical discrepancy	−2 415	−0.2
GDP at market prices	1 458 452	100.0

Source: *United Kingdom National Accounts: The Blue Book – 2011 Edition* (National Statistics, 2011)

Definitions

Gross national income (GNY) GDP plus net income from abroad.

Depreciation The decline in value of capital equipment due to age or wear and tear.

Net national income (NNY) GNY minus depreciation.

---

[2] In the official statistics, this is referred to as *GNI*. We use Y to stand for income, however, to avoid confusion with investment.

Households' disposable income

Finally, we come to a term called **households' disposable income**. It measures the income people have available for spending (or saving): i.e. after any deductions for income tax, national insurance, etc. have been made. It is the best measure to use if want to see how changes in household income affect consumption.

How do we get from GNY at market prices to households' disposable income? We start with the incomes that firms receive[3] from production (plus income from abroad) and then deduct that part of their income that is *not* distributed to households. This means that we must deduct taxes that firms pay – taxes on goods and services (such as VAT), taxes on profits (such as corporation tax) and any other taxes – and add in any subsidies they receive. We must then subtract allowances for depreciation and any undistributed profits. This gives us the gross income that households receive from firms in the form of wages, salaries, rent, interest and distributed profits.

To get from this what is available for households to spend we must subtract the money households pay in income taxes and national insurance contributions, but add all benefits to households such as pensions and child benefit.

Households' = GNY at market prices – taxes paid by
disposable   firms + subsidies received by firms
income   – depreciation – undistributed profits
                   – personal taxes + benefits

Definition

Households' disposable income The income available for households to spend: i.e. personal incomes after deducting taxes on incomes and adding benefits.

---

[3] We also include income from any public-sector production of goods or services (e.g. health and education) and production by non-profit institutions serving households.

SUMMARY TO APPENDIX

1 National income is usually expressed in terms of gross domestic product. This is simply the value of domestic production over the course of the year. It can be measured by the product, expenditure or income methods.

2 The product method measures the values added in all parts of the economy.

3 The income method measures all the incomes generated from domestic production: wages and salaries, rent and profit.

4 The expenditure method adds up all the categories of expenditure: consumer expenditure, government expenditure, investment and exports. We then have to deduct the element of each that goes on imports in order to arrive at expenditure on *domestic* products. Thus $GDP = C + G + I + X - M$.

5 GDP at *market prices* measures what consumers pay for output (including taxes and subsidies on what they buy). Gross value added (GVA) measures what factors of production actually receive. GVA, therefore, is GDP at market prices minus taxes on products plus subsidies on products.

6 Gross *national* income (GNY) takes account of incomes earned from abroad (+) and incomes earned by people abroad from this country (–). Thus GNY = GDP plus net income from abroad.

7 Net national income (NNY) takes account of the depreciation of capital. Thus NNY = GNY – depreciation.

8 Households' disposable income is a measure of household income after the deduction of income taxes and the addition of benefits.

REVIEW QUESTIONS TO APPENDIX

1 Should we include the sale of used items in the GDP statistics? For example, if you sell your car to a garage for £2000 and it then sells it to someone else for £2500, has this added £2500 to GDP, or nothing at all, or merely the value that the garage adds to the car, i.e. £500?

2 What items are excluded from national income statistics which would be important to take account of if we were to get a true indication of a country's standard of living?

COUNTRY	CURRENCY	WE SELL	WE BUY
Australia	Dollar	1.4036	1.7463
China	Yuan	9.214	12.096
East Carib.	Dollar	3.7042	5.1517
Hungary	Forint	272.78	360.87
Japan	Yen	116.40	144.64
Maldives	Rufiyaa	23.148	29.100

The balance of payments and exchange rates

Business issues covered in this chapter

- What is meant by 'the balance of payments' and how do trade and financial movements affect it?
- How are exchange rates determined?
- What are the implications for business of changes in the exchange rate?
- What is the relationship between the balance of payments and exchange rates?
- How do governments and/or central banks seek to influence the exchange rate and what are the implications for other macroeconomic policies and for business?

In Part I we examined the role of international trade for a country and for business, and saw how trade has grown rapidly since 1945. The world economy has become progressively more interlinked, with multinational corporations dominating a large proportion of international business. In this chapter we return to look at international trade and the financial flows associated with it. In particular, we shall examine the relationship between the domestic economy and the international trading environment. This will involve considering both the balance of payments and the exchange rate.

We will first explain what is meant by the balance of payments. In doing so, we will see just how the various monetary transactions between the domestic economy and the rest of the world are recorded.

Then we will examine how rates of exchange are determined, and how they are related to the balance of payments. Then we will see what causes exchange rate fluctuations, and what will happen if the government intervenes in the foreign exchange market to prevent these fluctuations. Finally, we will consider how exchange rates have been managed in practice.

27.1 THE BALANCE OF PAYMENTS ACCOUNT

KI 27
p 292

A country's balance of payments account records all the flows of money between residents of that country and the rest of the world. *Receipts* of money from abroad are regarded as *credits* and are entered in the accounts with a positive sign. *Outflows* of money from the country are regarded as *debits* and are entered with a negative sign.

There are three main parts of the balance of payments account: the *current account*, the *capital account* and the *financial account*. Each part is then subdivided. We shall look at each part in turn, and take the UK as an example. Table 27.1 gives a summary of the UK balance of payments for 2011.

Table 27.1	UK balance of payments: 2011		
	2011		**Average 1987–2011 as % of GDP**
	£m	**% of GDP**	
CURRENT ACCOUNT			
Balance on trade in goods	−100 014	−6.6	−3.6
Balance on trade in services	76 305	5.0	1.9
Balance of trade	**−23 709**	**−1.6**	**−1.7**
Income balance	16 849	1.1	0.5
Net current transfers	−22 142	−1.5	−0.8
Current account balance	**−29 002**	**−1.9**	**−2.0**
CAPITAL ACCOUNT			
Capital account balance	**3 444**	**0.2**	**0.1**
FINANCIAL ACCOUNT			
Net direct investment	−32 470	−2.1	−1.5
Portfolio investment balance	−48 173	−3.2	1.9
Other investment balance	94 600	6.2	1.7
Balance of financial derivatives	6 988	0.5	−0.1
Reserve assets	−4 948	−0.3	−0.1
Financial account balance	**15 997**	**1.1**	**1.9**
Net errors and omissions	**9 561**	**0.6**	**0.1**
Balance	*0*	*0*	*0*

Source: Based on *Balance of Payments, Q2 2012* and *Quarterly National Accounts, Q2 2012* (Office for National Statistics). Contains public sector information licensed under the Open Government Licence (OGL) v.1.0. http://www.nationalarchives.gov.uk/doc/open-government-licence.

The current account

The **current account** records payments for imports and exports of goods and services, plus incomes flowing into and out of the country, plus net transfers of money into and out of the country. It is normally divided into four subdivisions.

The trade in goods account. This records imports and exports of physical goods (previously known as 'visibles'). Exports result in an inflow of money and are therefore a credit item. Imports result in an outflow of money and are therefore a debit item. The balance of these is called the **balance on trade in goods** or **balance of visible trade** or **merchandise balance**. A *surplus* is when exports exceed imports. A *deficit* is when imports exceed exports.

The trade in services account. This records imports and exports of services (such as transport, tourism and insurance). Thus the purchase of a foreign holiday would be a debit since it represents an outflow of money, whereas the purchase by an overseas resident of a UK insurance policy would be a credit to the UK services account. The balance of these is called the **services balance**.

The balance of both the goods and services accounts together is known as the **balance on trade in goods and services** or simply the **balance of trade**.

Income flows. These consist of wages, interest and profits flowing into and out of the country. For example, dividends earned by a foreign resident from shares in a UK company would be an outflow of money (a debit item).

Definitions

Current account of the balance of payments The record of a country's imports and exports of goods and services, plus incomes and transfers of money to and from abroad.

Balance on trade in goods or **balance of visible trade** or **merchandise balance** Exports of goods minus imports of goods.

Services balance Exports of services minus imports of services.

Balance of trade in goods and services or **balance of trade** Exports of goods and services minus imports of goods and services.

Figure 27.1 Current account balance as a percentage of GDP in selected countries

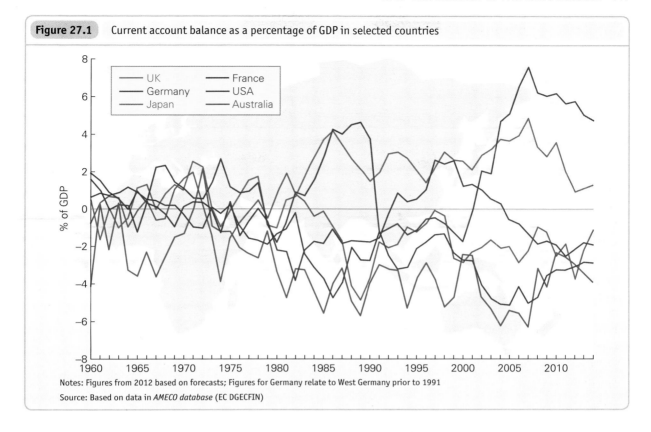

Notes: Figures from 2012 based on forecasts; Figures for Germany relate to West Germany prior to 1991

Source: Based on data in *AMECO database* (EC DGECFIN)

Current transfers of money. These include government contributions to and receipts from the EU and international organisations, and international transfers of money by private individuals and firms. Transfers out of the country are debits. Transfers into the country (e.g. money sent from Greece to a Greek student studying in the UK) would be a credit item.

The **current account balance** is the overall balance of all the above four subdivisions. A *current account surplus* is where credits exceed debits. A *current account deficit* is where debits exceed credits.

Figure 27.1 shows the current account balance expressed as a percentage of GDP for a sample of countries. Since 1984, the UK has consistently experienced a current account deficit.

Definitions

Balance of payments on current account The balance on trade in goods and services plus net incomes and current transfers.

Capital account of the balance of payments The record of transfers of capital to and from abroad.

Financial account of the balance of payments The record of the flows of money into and out of the country for the purpose of investment or as deposits in banks and other financial institutions.

The capital account

The **capital account** relates to the acquisition and disposal of non-financial assets. This comprises two elements.

First, *capital transfers* are the flows of funds, into the country (credits) and out of the country (debits), associated with the transfer of ownership of fixed assets (e.g. land). These transfers include money that migrants bring into the country and official debt forgiveness by governments.

Second, the *acquisition or disposal of non-produced, non-financial assets* covers intangibles such as the sales and purchases of patents, copyrights and trademarks. As Table 27.1 shows, the balance on the capital account is small in comparison to that on the current and financial accounts.

The financial account[1]

The **financial account** of the balance of payments records cross-border changes in the holding of shares, property, bank deposits and loans, government securities, etc. In other words, unlike the current account which is concerned

---

[1] Prior to October 1998, this account was called the 'capital account'. The account that is *now* called the capital account used to be included in the transfers section of the current account. This potentially confusing change of names was adopted in order to bring the UK accounts in line with the system used by the International Monetary Fund (IMF), the EU and most individual countries.

with money incomes, the financial account is concerned with the purchase and sale of assets. Table 27.1 shows that since the late 1980s current account deficits in the UK have been offset by surpluses on the financial account.

Direct investment. This involves a significant and lasting interest in a business in another country. If a foreign company invests money from abroad in one of its branches or associated companies in the UK, this represents an inflow of money when the investment is made and is thus a credit item. (Any subsequent profit from this investment that flows abroad will be recorded as an investment income outflow on the current account.) Investment abroad by UK companies represents an outflow of money when the investment is made. It is thus a debit item. Note that what we are talking about here is the acquisition or sale of assets: e.g. a factory or farm, or the takeover of a whole firm, not the imports or exports of equipment.

Portfolio investment. This relates to transactions in debt and equity securities (shares) which do not result in the investor having any significant influence on the operations of a particular business. If a UK resident buys shares in an overseas company, this is an outflow of funds and is hence a debit item.

Portfolio investment is likely to be affected by sentiment and by relative interest rates. For instance, there was an increase in the demand for UK bonds (debt securities) in the middle part of the 2000s reflecting relatively higher interest rates in the UK compared to other economies, such as the USA and the eurozone.

Other investment and financial flows. While direct and portfolio investments are concerned primarily with long-term investment, these consist primarily of various types of short-term monetary flows between the UK and the rest of the world. Deposits by overseas residents in banks in the UK and loans to the UK from abroad are credit items, since they represent an inflow of money. Deposits by UK residents in overseas banks and loans by UK banks to overseas residents are debit items. They represent an outflow of money.

Short-term monetary flows are common between international financial centres to take advantage of differences in countries' interest rates and changes in exchange rates. Again, sentiment is also important. The financial crisis of the late 2000s contributed to a large disinvestment by non-residents of financial assets in UK financial institutions.

Flows to and from the reserves. The UK, like all other countries, holds reserves of gold and foreign currencies. From time to time the Bank of England (acting as the government's agent) will sell some of these reserves to purchase sterling on the foreign exchange market. It does this normally as a means of supporting the rate of exchange (as we shall see below). Drawing on reserves represents a *credit* item in the balance of payments accounts: money drawn from the reserves represents an *inflow* to the balance of payments (albeit an outflow from the reserves account). The reserves can thus be used to support a deficit elsewhere in the balance of payments.

Conversely, if there is a surplus elsewhere in the balance of payments, the Bank of England can use it to build up the reserves. Building up the reserves counts as a debit item in the balance of payments, since it represents an outflow from it (to the reserves).

When all the components of the balance of payments account are taken together, the balance of payments should exactly balance: credits should equal debits. As we shall see below, if they were not equal, the rate of exchange would have to adjust until they were, or the government would have to intervene to make them equal.

When the statistics are compiled, however, a number of errors are likely to occur. As a result there will not be a balance. To 'correct' for this, a **net errors and omissions item** is included in the accounts. This ensures that there will be an exact balance. The main reason for the errors is that the statistics are obtained from a number of sources, and there are often delays before items are recorded and sometimes omissions too.

> ### Pause for thought
>
> *With reference to Table 27.1, compare the 2011 balance of payments figures (as percentages of GDP) with the averages for the period from 1987. In what senses were the 2011 figures more or less favourable than the averages since 1987?*

> ### Pause for thought
>
> *Where would interest payments on short-term foreign deposits in UK banks be entered on the balance of payments account?*

> ### Definition
>
> **Net errors and omissions** A statistical adjustment to ensure that the two sides of the balance of payments account balance. It is necessary because of errors in compiling the statistics.

27.2 THE EXCHANGE RATE

An exchange rate is the rate at which one currency trades for another on the foreign exchange market.

If you want to go abroad, you will need to exchange your pounds into euros, dollars, Swiss francs or whatever. To do this you may go to a bank. The bank will quote you that day's exchange rates: for example, €1.25 to the pound, or $1.50 to the pound. It is similar for firms. If an importer wants to buy, say, some machinery from Japan, it will require yen to pay the Japanese supplier. It will thus ask the foreign exchange section of a bank to quote it a rate of exchange of the pound into yen. Similarly, if you want to buy some foreign stocks and shares, or if companies based in the UK want to invest abroad, sterling will have to be exchanged into the appropriate foreign currency.

Likewise, if Americans want to come on holiday to the UK or to buy UK assets, or American firms want to import UK goods or to invest in the UK, they will require sterling. They will be quoted an exchange rate for the pound in the USA: say, £1 = $1.55. This means that they will have to pay $1.55 to obtain £1 worth of UK goods or assets.

Exchange rates are quoted between each of the major currencies of the world. These exchange rates are constantly changing. Minute by minute, dealers in the foreign exchange dealing rooms of the banks are adjusting the rates of exchange. They charge commission when they exchange currencies. It is therefore important for them to ensure that they are not left with a large amount of any currency unsold. What they need to do is to balance the supply and demand of each currency: to balance the amount they purchase to the amount they sell. To do this they will need to adjust the price of each currency, namely the exchange rate, in line with changes in supply and demand.

Not only are there day-to-day fluctuations in exchange rates, but also there are long-term changes in them. Figure 27.2 shows the average quarterly exchange rates between the pound and various currencies since 1985.

One of the problems in assessing what is happening to a particular currency is that its rate of exchange may rise against some currencies (weak currencies) and fall against others (strong currencies). In order to gain an overall picture of its fluctuations, therefore, it is best to look at a weighted average exchange rate against all other currencies. This is known as the *exchange rate index* or the *effective exchange rate*.

Definition

Exchange rate index or **effective exchange rate** A weighted average exchange rate expressed as an index, where the value of the index is 100 in a given base year. The weights of the different currencies in the index add up to 1.

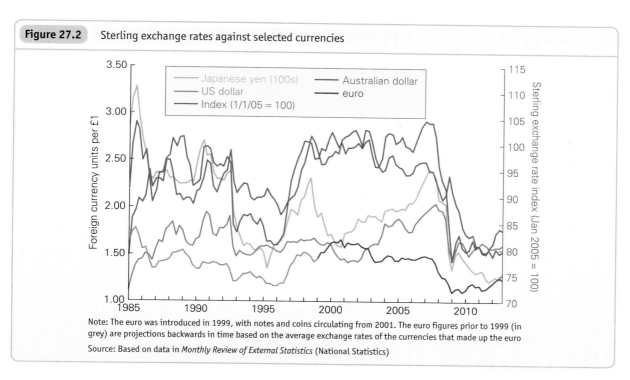

Figure 27.2 Sterling exchange rates against selected currencies

Note: The euro was introduced in 1999, with notes and coins circulating from 2001. The euro figures prior to 1999 (in grey) are projections backwards in time based on the average exchange rates of the currencies that made up the euro

Source: Based on data in *Monthly Review of External Statistics* (National Statistics)

The weight given to each currency in the index depends on the proportion of trade done with that country. Figure 27.2 also shows the sterling exchange rate index based on January 2005 = 100.

The determination of the rate of exchange in a free market

In a free foreign exchange market, the rate of exchange is determined by demand and supply. Thus the sterling exchange rate is determined by the demand and supply of pounds. This is illustrated in Figure 27.3.

For simplicity, assume that there are just two countries: the UK and the USA. When UK importers wish to buy goods from the USA, or when UK residents wish to invest in the USA, they will *supply* pounds on the foreign exchange market in order to obtain dollars. In other words, they will go to banks or other foreign exchange dealers to buy dollars in exchange for pounds. The higher the exchange rate, the more dollars they will obtain for their pounds. This will effectively make American goods cheaper to buy, and investment more profitable. Thus the *higher* the exchange rate, the *more* pounds will be supplied. The supply curve of pounds therefore typically slopes upwards.

When US residents wish to purchase UK goods or to invest in the UK, they will require pounds. They *demand* pounds by selling dollars on the foreign exchange market. In other words, they will go to banks or other foreign exchange dealers to buy pounds in exchange for dollars. The lower the dollar price of the pound (the exchange rate), the cheaper it will be for them to obtain UK goods and assets, and hence the more pounds they are likely to demand. The demand curve for pounds, therefore, typically slopes downwards.

The equilibrium exchange rate will be where the demand for pounds equals the supply. In Figure 27.3 this will be at an exchange rate of £1 = $1.60. But what is the mechanism that equates demand and supply?

If the current exchange rate were above the equilibrium, the supply of pounds being offered to the banks would exceed the demand. For example, in Figure 27.3 if the exchange rate were $1.80, there would be an excess supply of pounds of a – b. Banks would not have enough dollars to exchange for all these pounds. But the banks make money by *exchanging* currency, not by holding on to it. They would thus lower the exchange rate in order to encourage a greater demand for pounds and reduce the excessive supply. They would continue lowering the rate until demand equalled supply.

Similarly, if the rate were below the equilibrium, say at $1.40, there would be a shortage of pounds of c – d. The banks would find themselves with too few pounds to meet all the demand. At the same time, they would have an excess supply of dollars. The banks would thus raise the exchange rate until demand equalled supply.

In practice, the process of reaching equilibrium is extremely rapid. The foreign exchange dealers in the banks are continually adjusting the rate as new customers make new demands for currencies. What is more, the banks have to watch closely what each other is doing. They are constantly in competition with each other and thus have to keep their rates in line. The dealers receive minute-by-minute updates on their computer screens of the rates being offered round the world.

Shifts in the currency demand and supply curves

Any shift in the demand or supply curves will cause the exchange rate to change. This is illustrated in Figure 27.4,

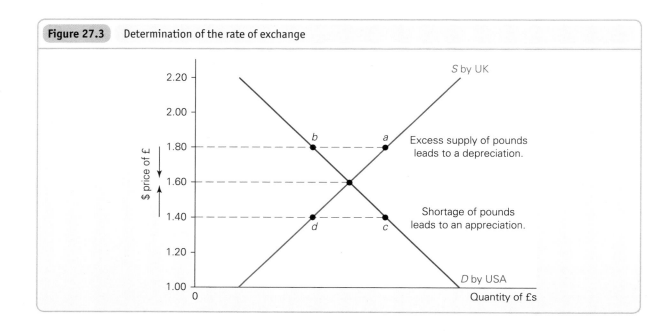

Figure 27.3 Determination of the rate of exchange

BOX 27.1 DEALING IN FOREIGN EXCHANGE

A daily juggling act

Imagine that a large car importer in the UK wants to import 5000 cars from Japan costing ¥15 billion. What does it do?

It will probably contact a number of banks' foreign exchange dealing rooms in London and ask them for exchange rate quotes. It thus puts all the banks in competition with each other. Each bank will want to get the business and thereby obtain the commission on the deal. To do this it must offer a higher rate than the other banks, since the higher the ¥/£ exchange rate, the more yen the firm will get for its money. (For an importer a rate of, say, ¥150 to £1 is better than a rate of, say, ¥120.)

Now it is highly unlikely that any of the banks will have a spare ¥15 billion. But a bank cannot say to the importer 'Sorry, you will have to wait before we can agree to sell them to you.' Instead the bank will offer a deal and then, if the firm agrees, the bank will have to set about obtaining the ¥15 billion. To do this it must offer Japanese who are *supplying* yen to obtain pounds at a sufficiently *low* ¥/£ exchange rate.

(The lower the ¥/£ exchange rate, the fewer yen the Japanese will have to pay to obtain pounds.)

The banks' dealers thus find themselves in the delicate position of wanting to offer a *high* enough exchange rate to the car importer in order to gain its business, but a *low* enough exchange rate in order to obtain the required amount of yen. The dealers are thus constantly having to adjust the rates of exchange in order to balance the demand and supply of each currency.

In general, the more of any foreign currency that dealers are asked to supply (by being offered sterling), the lower will be the exchange rate they will offer. In other words, a higher supply of sterling pushes down the foreign currency price of sterling.

 Assume that an American firm wants to import Scotch whisky from the UK. Describe how foreign exchange dealers will respond.

which this time shows the euro/sterling exchange rate. If the demand and supply curves shift from D_1 and S_1 to D_2 and S_2 respectively, the exchange rate will fall from €1.20 to €1.10. A fall in the exchange rate is called a *depreciation*. A rise in the exchange rate is called an *appreciation*.

But why should the demand and supply curves shift? The following are the major possible causes of a depreciation:

- *A fall in domestic interest rates.* UK rates would now be less competitive for savers and other depositors. More UK residents would be likely to deposit their money

abroad (the supply of sterling would rise), and fewer people abroad would deposit their money in the UK (the demand for sterling would fall).

Definitions

Depreciation A fall in the free-market exchange rate of the domestic currency with foreign currencies.

Appreciation A rise in the free-market exchange rate of the domestic currency with foreign currencies.

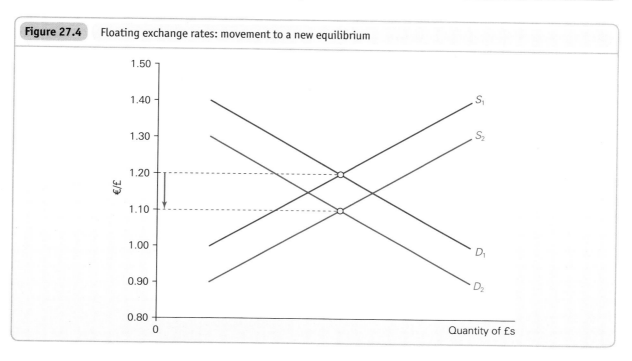

Figure 27.4 Floating exchange rates: movement to a new equilibrium

- *Higher inflation in the domestic economy than abroad.* UK exports will become less competitive. The demand for sterling will fall. At the same time, imports will become relatively cheaper for UK consumers. The supply of sterling will rise.
- *A rise in domestic incomes relative to incomes abroad.* If UK incomes rise, the demand for imports, and hence the supply of sterling, will rise. If incomes in other countries fall, the demand for UK exports, and hence the demand for sterling will fall.
- *Relative investment prospects improving abroad.* If investment prospects become brighter abroad than in the UK, perhaps because of better incentives abroad, or because of worries about an impending recession in the UK,

again the demand for sterling will fall and the supply of sterling will rise.

- *Speculation that the exchange rate will fall.* If businesses involved in importing and exporting, and also banks and other foreign exchange dealers, think that the exchange rate is about to fall, they will sell pounds now before the rate does fall. The supply of sterling will thus rise.

> **Pause for thought**
>
> *Go through each of the above reasons for shifts in the demand for and supply of sterling and consider what would cause an appreciation of the pound.*

27.3 EXCHANGE RATES AND THE BALANCE OF PAYMENTS

Exchange rates and the balance of payments: no government or central bank intervention

In a free foreign exchange market, the balance of payments will *automatically* balance. But why?

The credit side of the balance of payments constitutes the demand for sterling. For example, when people abroad buy UK exports or assets they will demand sterling in order to pay for them. The debit side constitutes the supply of sterling. For example, when UK residents buy foreign goods or assets, the importers of them will require foreign currency to pay for them. They will thus supply pounds. A *floating exchange rate* will ensure that the demand for pounds is equal to the supply. It will thus also ensure that the credits on the balance of payments are equal to the debits: that the balance of payments balances.

This does not mean that each part of the balance of payments account will separately balance, but simply that any current account deficit must be matched by a capital plus financial account surplus and vice versa.

For example, suppose initially that each part of the balance of payments did separately balance. Then let us assume that interest rates rise. This will encourage larger short-term financial inflows as people abroad are attracted

> **Definition**
>
> **Floating exchange rate** When the government does not intervene in the foreign exchange markets, but simply allows the exchange rate to be freely determined by demand and supply.

BOX 27.2 THE IMPORTANCE OF INTERNATIONAL FINANCIAL MOVEMENTS

How a current account deficit can coincide with an appreciating exchange rate

Since the early 1970s, most of the major economies of the world have operated with floating exchange rates. The opportunities that this gives for speculative gain have led to a huge increase in short-term international financial movements. Vast amounts of money transfer from country to country in search of higher interest rates or a currency that is likely to appreciate. This can have a bizarre effect on exchange rates.

If a country pursues an expansionary fiscal policy (i.e. cutting taxes and/or raising government expenditure), the current account will tend to go into deficit as extra imports are 'sucked in'. What effect will this have on exchange rates? You might think that the answer is obvious: the higher demand for imports will create an extra supply of domestic currency on the foreign exchange market and hence drive down the exchange rate.

In fact the opposite is likely. The higher interest rates resulting from the higher domestic demand can lead to a massive inflow of short-term finance. The financial account can thus move sharply into surplus. This is likely to outweigh the current account deficit and cause an *appreciation* of the exchange rate.

Exchange rate movements, especially in the short term, are largely brought about by changes on the financial rather than the current account.

 Why do high international financial mobility and an absence of exchange controls severely limit a country's ability to choose its interest rate?

to deposit money in the UK: the demand for sterling would shift to the right (e.g. from D_2 to D_1 in Figure 27.4). It will also cause smaller short-term financial outflows as UK residents keep more of their money in the country: the supply of sterling shifts to the left (e.g. from S_2 to S_1 in Figure 27.4). The financial account will go into surplus. The exchange rate will appreciate.

As the exchange rate rises, this will cause imports to be cheaper and exports to be more expensive. The current account will move into deficit. There is a movement up along the new demand and supply curves until a new equilibrium is reached. At this point, any financial account surplus is matched by an equal current (plus capital) account deficit.

Exchange rates and the balance of payments: with government or central bank intervention

The government or central bank (the Bank of England in the UK) may be unwilling to let the country's currency float freely. Frequent shifts in the demand and supply curves would cause frequent changes in the exchange rate. This, in turn, might cause uncertainty for businesses, which might curtail their trade and investment.

The central bank may thus intervene in the foreign exchange market. But what can it do? The answer to this will depend on its objectives. It may simply want to reduce the day-to-day fluctuations in the exchange rate, or it may want to prevent longer-term, more fundamental shifts in the rate.

Reducing short-term fluctuations

Assume that the UK government believes that an exchange rate of €1.20 to the pound is approximately the long-term equilibrium rate. Short-term leftward shifts in the demand for sterling and rightward shifts in the supply, however, are causing the exchange rate to fall below this level (see Figure 27.4). What can the government do to keep the rate at €1.20?

Using reserves. The Bank of England can sell gold and foreign currencies from the reserves to buy pounds. This will shift the demand for sterling back to the right.

Borrowing from abroad. The government can negotiate a foreign currency loan from other countries or from an international agency such as the International Monetary Fund. It can then use these moneys to buy pounds on the foreign exchange market, thus again shifting the demand for sterling back to the right.

Raising interest rates. If the Bank of England raises interest rates, it will encourage people to deposit money in the UK and encourage UK residents to keep their money in the country. The demand for sterling will increase and the supply of sterling will decrease.

Maintaining a fixed rate of exchange over the longer term

Governments may choose to maintain a fixed rate over a number of months or even years. The following are possible methods it can use to achieve this (we are assuming that there are downward pressures on the exchange rate: e.g. as a result of higher aggregate demand and higher inflation).

Contractionary policies. This is where the government deliberately curtails aggregate demand by either *fiscal policy* or *monetary policy* or both.

Contractionary fiscal policy will involve raising taxes and/or reducing government expenditure. Contractionary monetary policy involves raising interest rates. Note that in this case we are not just talking about the temporary raising of interest rates to prevent a short-term outflow of money from the country, but the use of higher interest rates to reduce borrowing and hence dampen aggregate demand.

A reduction in aggregate demand will work in two ways:

■ It reduces the level of consumer spending. This will directly cut imports since there will be reduced spending on Japanese Blu-ray players, German cars, Spanish holidays and so on. The supply of sterling coming on to the foreign exchange market thus decreases.
■ It reduces the rate of inflation. If inflation falls below that of other countries, this will make UK goods more competitive abroad, thus increasing the demand for sterling. It will also cut back on imports as UK consumers switch to the now more competitive home-produced goods. The supply of sterling falls.

Supply-side policies. This is where the government attempts to increase the long-term competitiveness of UK goods by encouraging reductions in the costs of production and/or improvements in the quality of UK goods. For example, the government may attempt to improve the quantity and quality of training and research and development.

Controls on imports and or foreign exchange dealing. This is where the government restricts the outflow of money, either by restricting people's access to foreign exchange, or by the use of tariffs (customs duties) and quotas. For instance, the Icelandic government put in place controls on foreign currency exchanges in the aftermath of the collapse of its largest banks in 2008 in order to bolster the krona and to build up foreign reserves.

Pause for thought

What problems might arise if the government were to adopt this third method of maintaining a fixed exchange rate?

27.4 FIXED VERSUS FLOATING EXCHANGE RATES

Are exchange rates best left free to fluctuate and be determined purely by market forces, or should the government or central bank intervene to fix exchange rates, either rigidly or within bands?

Advantages of fixed exchange rates

Surveys reveal that most business people prefer relatively rigid exchange rates: if not totally fixed, then pegged for periods of time, or at least where fluctuations are kept to a minimum. The following arguments are used to justify this preference.

Certainty. With fixed exchange rates, international trade and investment become much less risky, since profits are not affected by movements in the exchange rate.

Assume a firm correctly forecasts that its product will sell in the USA for $1.50. It costs 80p to produce. If the rate of exchange is fixed at £1 = $1.50, each unit will earn £1 and hence make a 20p profit. If, however, the rate of exchange were not fixed, exchange fluctuations could wipe out this profit. If, say, the rate appreciated to £1 = $2, and if units continued to sell for $1.50, they would now earn only 75p each, and hence make a 5p loss.

Little or no speculation. Provided the rate is *absolutely* fixed – and people believe that it will remain so – there is no point in speculating. For example, between 1999 and 2001, when the old currencies of the eurozone countries were still used, but were totally fixed to the euro, there was no speculation that the German mark, say, would change in value against the French franc or the Dutch guilder.

Prevents governments pursuing 'irresponsible' macroeconomic policies. If a government deliberately and excessively expands aggregate demand – perhaps in an attempt to gain short-term popularity with the electorate – the resulting balance of payments deficit will force it to constrain demand again (unless it resorts to import controls).

Governments cannot allow their economies to have a persistently higher inflation rate than competitor countries without running into balance of payments crises, and hence a depletion of reserves. Fixed rates thus force governments (in the absence of trade restrictions) to keep the rate of inflation roughly to world levels.

Disadvantages of fixed exchange rates

Exchange rate policy may conflict with the interests of domestic business and the economy as a whole. A balance of payments deficit can occur even if there is no excess demand. For example, there can be a fall in the demand for the country's exports as a result of an external shock or because of increased foreign competition. If protectionism is to be avoided, and if supply-side policies work only over the long run, the government (or central bank) will be forced to raise interest rates. This is likely to have two adverse effects on the domestic economy:

- Higher interest rates may discourage business investment. This in turn will lower firms' profits in the long term and reduce the country's long-term rate of economic growth. The country's capacity to produce will be restricted and businesses are likely to fall behind in the competitive race with their international rivals to develop new products and improve existing ones.
- Higher interest rates will have a dampening effect on the economy by making borrowing more expensive and thereby cutting back on both consumer demand and investment. This can result in a recession with rising unemployment.

The problem is that, with fixed exchange rates, domestic policy is entirely constrained by the balance of payments. Any attempt to cure unemployment by cutting interest rates will simply lead to a balance of payments deficit and thus force governments to raise interest rates again.

Competitive contractionary policies leading to world depression. If deficit countries pursued contractionary policies, but surplus countries pursued expansionary policies, there would be no overall world contraction or expansion. Countries may be quite happy, however, to run a balance of payments surplus and build up reserves. Countries may thus competitively deflate – all trying to achieve a balance of payments surplus. But this is beggar-my-neighbour policy. Not all countries can have a surplus. Overall the world must be in balance. The result of these policies is to lead to general world recession and a restriction in growth.

Problems of international liquidity. If trade is to expand, there must be an expansion in the supply of currencies acceptable for world trade (dollars, euros, pounds, gold, etc.): there must be adequate ***international liquidity***. Countries' reserves of these currencies must grow if they are to be sufficient to maintain a fixed rate at times of balance of payments disequilibrium. Conversely, there must not be excessive international liquidity. Otherwise the extra demand that would result would lead to world inflation. It is important under fixed exchange rates, therefore, to avoid too much or too little international liquidity. The

---

Definition

International liquidity The supply of currencies in the world acceptable for financing international trade and investment.

problem is whether there is adequate control of international liquidity. The supply of dollars, for example, depends largely on US policy, which may be dominated by its internal economic situation rather than by a concern for the well-being of the international community.

 Inability to adjust to shocks. With sticky prices and wage rates, there is no swift mechanism for dealing with sudden balance of payments crises – like that caused by a sudden increase in oil prices. In the short run, countries will need huge reserves or loan facilities to support their currencies. There may be insufficient international liquidity to permit this. In the longer run, countries may be forced into a depression, by having to deflate. The alternative may be to resort to protectionism, or to abandon the fixed rate and ***devalue***.

 Speculation. If speculators believe that a fixed rate simply cannot be maintained, speculation is likely to be massive. If, for example, there is a large balance of payments deficit, speculative selling will worsen the deficit, and may itself force a devaluation.

Advantages of a free-floating exchange rate

The advantages and disadvantages of free-floating rates are to a large extent the opposite of fixed rates.

 Automatic correction. The government simply lets the exchange rate move freely to the equilibrium. In this way, balance of payments disequilibria are automatically and instantaneously corrected without the need for specific government policies.

No problem of international liquidity and reserves. Since there is no central bank intervention in the foreign exchange market, there is no need to hold reserves. A currency is automatically convertible at the current market exchange rate.

Insulation from external economic events. A country is not tied to a possibly unacceptably high world inflation rate, as it could be under a fixed exchange rate. It is also to some extent protected against world economic fluctuations and shocks.

Governments are free to choose their domestic policy. Under a floating rate the government can choose whatever level of domestic demand it considers appropriate, and simply leave exchange rate movements to take care of any balance of payments effect. Similarly, the central bank can choose whatever rate of interest is necessary to meet domestic objectives, such as achieving a target rate of inflation. The exchange rate will simply adjust to the new rate of interest – a rise in interest rates causing an appreciation, a fall causing a depreciation. This freedom for the government and central bank is a major advantage, especially when the effectiveness of contractionary policies under fixed exchange rates is reduced by downward wage and price rigidity, and when competitive contractionary policies between countries may end up causing a world recession.

Disadvantages of a free-floating exchange rate

Despite these advantages there are still some potentially serious problems with free-floating exchange rates.

Unstable exchange rates. The less elastic are the demand and supply curves for the currency in Figure 27.4, the greater the change in exchange rate that will be necessary to restore equilibrium following a shift in either demand or supply. In the long run, in a competitive world with domestic substitutes for imports and foreign substitutes for exports, demand and supply curves are relatively elastic. Nevertheless, in the short run, given that many firms have contracts with specific overseas suppliers or distributors, the demands for imports and exports are less elastic.

Speculation. In an uncertain world, where there are few restrictions on currency speculation, where the fortunes and policies of governments can change rapidly, and where large amounts of short-term deposits are internationally 'footloose', speculation can be highly destabilising in the short run. If people think that the exchange rate will fall, then they will sell the currency, and this will cause the exchange rate to fall even further, perhaps overshooting the eventual equilibrium. At times of international currency turmoil (see Box 27.3), such speculation can be enormous. Worldwide, over a trillion dollars on average pass daily across the foreign exchanges: greatly in excess of countries' foreign exchange reserves!

> ### Pause for thought
>
> *If speculators on average gain from their speculation, who loses?*

Uncertainty for traders and investors. The uncertainty caused by currency fluctuations can discourage international trade and investment. To some extent this problem can be overcome by using the ***forward exchange market***. Here traders agree with a bank *today* the rate of exchange for some point in the *future* (say, six months' time). This allows traders to plan future purchases of imports or sales of exports at a known rate of exchange. Of course, banks charge for this service, since they are taking on the risks themselves of adverse exchange rate fluctuations.

> ### Definitions
>
> **Devaluation** Where the government refixes the exchange rate at a lower level.
>
> **Forward exchange market** Where contracts are made today for the price at which a currency will be exchanged at some specified future date.

BOX 27.3   THE EURO/DOLLAR SEESAW

Ups and downs in the currency market

For periods of time, world currency markets can be quite peaceful, with only modest changes in exchange rates. But with the ability to move vast sums of money very rapidly from one part of the world to another and from one currency to another, speculators can suddenly turn this relatively peaceful world into one of extreme turmoil.

In this box we examine the huge swings of the euro against the dollar since the euro's launch in 1999. In Case Study J.12 in MyEconLab we examine other examples of currency turmoil.

First the down . . .

On 1 January 1999, the euro was launched and exchanged for $1.16. By October 2000 the euro had fallen to $0.85. What was the cause of this 27 per cent depreciation? The main cause was the growing fear that inflationary pressures were increasing in the USA and that, therefore, the Federal Reserve Bank would have to raise interest rates. At the same time, the eurozone economy was growing only slowly and inflation was well below the 2 per cent ceiling set

by the ECB. There was thus pressure on the ECB to cut interest rates.

The speculators were not wrong. As the diagram shows, US interest rates rose, and ECB interest rates initially fell, and when eventually they did rise (in October 1999), the gap between US and ECB interest rates soon widened again.

In addition to the differences in interest rates, a lack of confidence in the recovery of the eurozone economy and a continuing confidence in the US economy encouraged investment to flow to the USA. This inflow of finance (and lack of inflow to the eurozone) further pushed up the dollar relative to the euro.

The low value of the euro against the dollar meant a high value of the other currencies, including the pound, relative to the euro. This made it very difficult for companies outside the eurozone to export to eurozone countries and also for those competing with imports from the eurozone (which had been made cheaper by the fall in the euro).

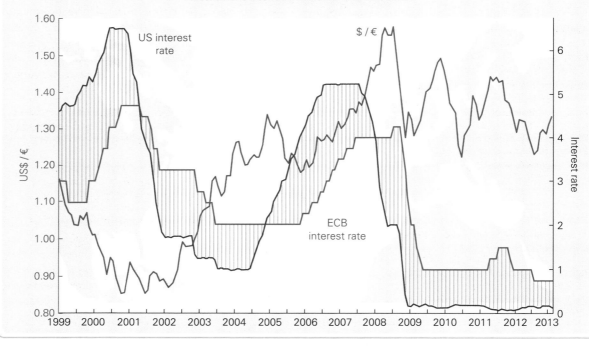

Fluctuations between the euro and the dollar

But dealing in the futures market only takes care of short-run uncertainty. Banks will not be prepared to take on the risks of offering forward contracts for several years hence. Thus firms simply have to live with the uncertainty over exchange rates in future years. This may discourage long-term investment. For example, the possibility of exchange rate appreciation may well discourage firms from investing abroad, since a higher exchange rate will mean

that foreign exchange earnings will be worth less in the domestic currency.

As Figure 27.2 showed (see page 449), there have been large changes in exchange rates. Such changes not only make it difficult for exporters. Importers too will be hesitant about making long-term deals. For example, a UK manufacturing firm signing a contract to buy US components in March 2008, when $2.00 worth of components could be

In October 2000, with the euro trading at around 85¢, the ECB plus the US Federal Reserve Bank, the Bank of England and the Japanese central bank all intervened on the foreign exchange market to buy euros. This arrested the fall, and helped to restore confidence in the currency. People were more willing to hold euros, knowing that central banks would support it.

. . . then the up

The position changed completely in 2001. With the US economy slowing rapidly and fears of an impending recession, the Federal Reserve Bank reduced interest rates 11 times during the year: from 6.5 per cent at the beginning of the year to 1.75 per cent at the end (see the chart). Although the ECB also cut interest rates, the cuts were relatively modest: from 4.75 at the beginning of the year to 3.25 at the end. With eurozone interest rates now considerably above US rates, the euro began to rise.

In addition, a massive deficit on the US current account, and a budget deficit nearing 4 per cent of GDP, made foreign investors reluctant to invest in the US economy. In fact, investors were pulling out of the USA. One estimate suggests that European investors alone sold $70 billion of US assets during 2002. The result of all this was a massive depreciation of the dollar and appreciation of the euro, so that by December 2004 the euro had risen to $1.36: a 60 per cent appreciation since July 2001!

In 2004–5, the US economy began to experience strong economic growth once more (an annual average of 3.4 per cent) and consequently the Fed raised interest rates several times, from 1 per cent in early 2004 to 5.25 by June 2006. With growth in the eurozone averaging just 1.8 per cent in 2004–5, the ECB kept interest rates constant at 2 per cent until early 2006. The result was that the euro depreciated against the dollar in 2005. But then the rise of the euro began again as the US growth slowed and eurozone growth rose and people anticipated a narrowing of the gap between US and eurozone interest rates.

In 2007 and 2008, worries about the credit crunch in the USA led the Fed to make substantial cuts in interest rates to stave off recession. In August 2007 the US federal funds rate was 5.25 per cent. It was then reduced on several occasions to stand at between 0 and 0.25 per cent per cent by December 2008. The ECB, in contrast, kept the eurozone rate constant at 4 per cent for the first part of this period and even raised it to 4.25 temporarily in the face of rapidly

rising commodity prices (see Box 26.3). As a result, short-term finance flooded into the eurozone and the euro appreciated again, from $1.37 in mid-2007 to $1.58 in mid-2008.

Eventually, in September 2008, with the eurozone on the edge of recession and predictions that eurozone rates would fall, the euro at last began to fall. It continued to do so as the ECB cut rates. However, with monetary policy in the eurozone remaining tighter than in the USA, the euro began to rise again, only falling once more at the end of 2009 and into 2010 as US growth accelerated and speculators anticipated a tightening of US monetary policy.

. . . then seesawing on the back of fiscal concerns

The early 2010s was characterised by concerns over levels of government borrowing and the growing stocks of national debt. These concerns contributed to the volatility of the euro. In particular, its value was to be affected by swings in investor confidence over countries' financial health and the adequacy of the mechanisms in place to deal with them (see Box 12.2).

Consequently, the euro would tend to weaken on fears of debt default as investors became increasingly reluctant to hold the currency. For instance, in early 2010, fear of a Greek default and growing worries about contagion to other highly indebted eurozone countries, such as Portugal, Ireland, Italy and Spain, led to speculation against the euro. In January 2010, the euro stood at $1.44; by early June, it had fallen to $1.19. This represented a 17 per cent depreciation. But, then the euro strengthened as discussions began over the design of funding mechanisms for eurozone countries in financial distress. By the end of October the euro was trading at $1.39.

The path of the euro shows that interest-rate volatility and the relative level of interest rates in the USA and the eurozone have been a major contributory factor to exchange-rate volatility between the euro and the dollar. However, more recently concerns over the fiscal health of national eurozone governments have played a particularly important role in explaining fluctuations in the euro.

 Find out what has happened to the euro/dollar exchange rate over the past 12 months. (You can find the data from the Bank of England's Statistical Interactive Database at www.bankofengland.co.uk/statistics/index.htm). Explain why the exchange rate has moved the way it has.

purchased for £1, would find it a struggle to make a profit some four years later when less than $1.60 worth of US components could be purchased for £1!

Lack of discipline on the domestic economy. Governments may pursue irresponsibly inflationary policies (e.g. for short-term political gain). This will have adverse effects over the longer term as the government will at some point have to deflate

the economy again, with a resulting fall in output and rise in unemployment.

Exchange rates in practice

Most countries today have a relatively free exchange rate. Nevertheless, the problems of instability that this can bring are well recognised, and thus many countries seek to regulate or manage their exchange rate.

There have been many attempts to regulate exchange rates since 1945. By far the most successful was the Bretton Woods system, which was adopted worldwide from the end of the Second World War until 1971. This was a form of **adjustable peg** exchange rate, where countries pegged (i.e. fixed) their exchange rate to the US dollar, but could repeg it at a lower or higher level ('devalue' or 'revalue' their exchange rate) if there was a persistent and substantial balance of payments deficit or surplus.

With growing world inflation and instability from the mid-1960s, it became more and more difficult to maintain fixed exchange rates, and the growing likelihood of devaluations and revaluations fuelled speculation. The system was abandoned in the early 1970s. What followed was a period of exchange rate management known as **managed flexibility**. Under this system, exchange rates were not pegged but allowed to float. However, central banks intervened from time to time to prevent excessive exchange rate fluctuations. This system largely continues to this day.

However, on a regional basis, especially within Europe, there were attempts to create greater exchange rate stability. The European system, which began in 1979, involved establishing exchange rate bands: upper and lower limits within which exchange rates were allowed to fluctuate. The name given to the EU system was the **exchange rate mechanism (ERM)**. The hope was that this would eventually lead to a single European currency. With a single currency there can be no exchange rate fluctuations between the member states, any more than there can be fluctuations between the Californian and New York dollar, or between the English, Scottish and Welsh pound.

The single currency, the euro, finally came into being in January 1999 (although notes and coins were not introduced until January 2002). (We examine the euro and its effects on the economies of the member states, and those outside too, in section 32.3.)

Definitions

Adjustable peg A system whereby exchange rates are fixed for a period of time, but may be devalued (or revalued) if a deficit (or surplus) becomes substantial.

Managed flexibility (dirty floating) A system of flexible exchange rates, but where the government intervenes to prevent excessive fluctuations or even to achieve an unofficial target exchange rate.

ERM (exchange rate mechanism) A semi-fixed system whereby participating EU countries allowed fluctuations against each other's currencies only within agreed bands. Collectively they floated freely against all other currencies.

SUMMARY

1a The balance of payments account records all payments to and receipts from foreign countries. The current account records payments for imports and exports, plus incomes and transfers of money to and from abroad. The capital account records all transfers of capital to and from abroad. The financial account records inflows and outflows of money for investment and as deposits in banks and other financial institutions. It also includes dealings in the country's foreign exchange reserves.

1b The whole account must balance, but surpluses or deficits can be recorded on any specific part of the account. Thus the current account could be in deficit but it would have to be matched by an equal and opposite capital plus financial account surplus.

2a The rate of exchange is the rate at which one currency exchanges for another. Rates of exchange are determined by demand and supply in the foreign exchange market. Demand for the domestic currency consists of all the credit items in the balance of payments account. Supply consists of all the debit items.

2b The exchange rate will depreciate (fall) if the demand for the domestic currency falls or the supply increases. These shifts can be caused by a fall in domestic interest rates, higher inflation in the domestic economy than abroad, a rise in domestic incomes relative to incomes abroad, relative investment prospects improving abroad, or the belief among speculators that the exchange rate will fall. The opposite in each case would cause an appreciation (rise).

3a The government can attempt to prevent the rate of exchange from falling by central bank purchases of the domestic currency in the foreign exchange market, either by selling foreign currency reserves or by using foreign loans. Alternatively, the central bank can raise interest rates. The reverse actions can be taken if the government wants to prevent the rate from rising.

3b In the longer term it can prevent the rate from falling by pursuing contractionary policies, protectionist policies, or supply-side policies to increase the competitiveness of the country's exports.

4a Fixed exchange rates bring the advantage of certainty for the business community, which encourages trade and foreign investment. They also help to prevent governments from pursuing irresponsible macroeconomic policies.

4b Fixed exchange rates bring the disadvantages of conflicting policy goals, the tendency to lead to competitive contractionary policies, the problems of ensuring adequate international liquidity to enable intervention, and the restrictions that fixed rates place upon countries when attempting to respond to system shocks.

4c The advantages of free-floating exchange rates are that they automatically correct balance of payments disequilibria; they eliminate the need for reserves; and they give governments a greater independence to pursue their chosen domestic policy.

4d On the other hand, a completely free exchange rate can be highly unstable, especially when the elasticities of demand for imports and exports are low; also speculation may be destabilising. This may discourage firms from trading and investing abroad. What is more, a flexible exchange rate, by removing the balance of payments constraint on domestic policy, may encourage

governments to pursue irresponsible domestic policies for short-term political gain.

4e There have been various attempts to manage exchange rates, without them being totally fixed. One example was the Bretton Woods system: a system of pegged exchange rates, but where devaluations or revaluations were allowed from time to time. Another was the ERM, which was the forerunner to the euro. Member countries' currencies were allowed to fluctuate against each other within a band.

REVIEW QUESTIONS

1 The table below shows the items in the UK's 2007 balance of payments.

(a) Fill in the missing totals for (i) the balance of trade, (ii) the current account balance, (iii) the portfolio investment balance; and (iv) for net errors and omissions.

(b) UK's GDP in 2007 was estimated at £1 405 796 million. Calculate each item on the balance of payments as a percentage of GDP.

(c) Compare the value of each item in £ millions and as percentages of GDP with those for 2011 in Table 27.1.

	£ millions
Current account:	
Balance on trade in goods	−90 605
Balance on trade in services	47 956
Balance of trade	
Income balance	21 369
Net current transfers	−13 546
Current account balance	
Capital account:	
Capital account balance	2 566
Financial account:	
Net direct investment	−62 665
Portfolio investment balance	
Other investment balance	−10 573
Balance of financial derivatives	−26 990
Reserve assets	−1 191
Financial account net flows	24 982
Net errors and omissions	

2 Assume that there is a free-floating exchange rate. Will the following cause the exchange rate to appreciate or depreciate? In each case you should consider whether there is a shift in the demand or supply curves of sterling (or both) and which way the curve(s) shift(s).

(a) More Blu-ray players are imported from Japan.
Demand curve *shifts left/shifts right/does not shift*
Supply curve *shifts left/shifts right/does not shift*
Exchange rate *appreciates/depreciates*

(b) Non-UK residents increase their purchases of UK government securities.
Demand curve *shifts left/shifts right/does not shift*
Supply curve *shifts left/shifts right/does not shift*
Exchange rate *appreciates/depreciates*

(c) UK interest rates fall relative to those abroad.
Demand curve *shifts left/shifts right/does not shift*
Supply curve *shifts left/shifts right/does not shift*
Exchange rate *appreciates/depreciates*

(d) The UK experiences a higher rate of inflation than other countries.
Demand curve *shifts left/shifts right/does not shift*
Supply curve *shifts left/shifts right/does not shift*
Exchange rate *appreciates/depreciates*

(e) The result of a further enlargement of the EU is for investment in the UK by the rest of the EU to increase by a greater amount than UK investment in other EU countries.
Demand curve *shifts left/shifts right/does not shift*
Supply curve *shifts left/shifts right/does not shift*
Exchange rate *appreciates/depreciates*

(f) Speculators believe that the rate of exchange will fall.
Demand curve *shifts left/shifts right/does not shift*
Supply curve *shifts left/shifts right/does not shift*
Exchange rate *appreciates/depreciates*

3 Explain how the current account of the balance of payments is likely to vary with the course of the business cycle.

4 Is it a 'bad thing' to have a deficit on the direct investment part of the financial account?

5 Why may credits on a country's short-term financial account create problems for its economy in the future?

6 What is the relationship between the balance of payments and the rate of exchange?

7 Consider the argument that in the modern world of large-scale short-term international financial movements, the ability of individual countries to affect their exchange rate is very limited.

8 To what extent can dealing in forward exchange markets remove the problems of a free-floating exchange rate?

9 What adverse effects on the domestic economy may follow from (a) a depreciation of the exchange rate and (b) an appreciation of the exchange rate?

10 What will be the effects on the domestic economy under free-floating exchange rates if there is a rapid expansion in world economic activity? What will determine the size of these effects?

28 Chapter

Banking, money and interest rates

Business issues covered in this chapter

- What are the functions of money?
- Why do banks play such a crucial role in the functioning of economies?
- What determines the amount of money in the economy? What causes it to grow and what is the role of banks in this process?
- What is the relationship between money and interest rates?
- How will a change in the money supply and/or interest rates affect the level of business activity?

In this chapter we are going to look at the important role that the banking system plays in the economy. The financial crisis that developed during the late 2000s vividly demonstrated the significance of the financial system to modern-day economies. It is generally recognised that changes in the amount of money can have a powerful effect on all the major macroeconomic indicators, including business activity, employment and economic growth. But, the financial crisis did more than this: it demonstrated the systemic importance of financial institutions.

As a result of the financial crisis, governments, central banks and regulators worldwide are grappling with many very important questions. For instance, are some financial institutions simply too big to fail? How can we ensure that banks operate with sufficient loss-absorbing capacity? Can we better align the incentives of banks with those of the wider community? These and other questions about financial institutions are considered here.

The chapter begins by defining what is meant by money and examining its functions. Then we look at the operation of the financial sector and its role in determining the supply of money.

We then turn to look at the demand for money. Here we are not asking how much money people would like. What we are asking is: how much of people's assets do they want to hold in the form of money?

Next, we put supply and demand together to show how interest rates are determined, or how money supply must be manipulated to achieve a chosen rate of interest. Finally, we see how changes in money supply and/or interest rates affect aggregate demand and the level of business activity.

28.1 THE MEANING AND FUNCTIONS OF MONEY

KI 27
p 292

Before going any further we must define precisely what we mean by 'money' – not as easy a task as it sounds. Money is more than just notes and coins. In fact the main component of a country's money supply is not cash, but deposits in banks and other financial institutions. The bulk of the deposits appear merely as bookkeeping entries in the banks' accounts.

People can access and use this money in their accounts through debit cards, cheques, standing orders, direct debits, etc. without the need for cash. Only a very small proportion of these deposits, therefore, need to be kept by the banks in their safes or tills in the form of cash.

What items should be included in the definition of money? To answer this we need to identify the *functions* of money.

The functions of money

The main purpose of money is for buying and selling goods, services and assets: i.e. as a ***medium of exchange***. It also has two other important functions. Let us examine each in turn.

A medium of exchange

In a subsistence economy where individuals make their own clothes, grow their own food, provide their own entertainments, etc., people do not need money. If people want to exchange any goods, they will do so by barter. In other words, they will do swaps with other people.

The complexities of a modern developed economy, however, make barter totally impractical for most purposes. What is necessary is a medium of exchange which is generally acceptable as a means of payment for goods and services, and as a means of payment for labour and other factor services. 'Money' is any such medium.

To be a suitable physical means of exchange, money must be light enough to carry around, come in a number of denominations, large and small, and not be easy to forge. Alternatively, money must be in a form that enables it to be transferred *indirectly* through some acceptable mechanism. For example, money in the form of bookkeeping entries in bank accounts can be transferred from one account to another by the use of such mechanisms as debit cards, cheques, standing orders and direct debits.

A means of evaluation

Money allows the value of goods, services and assets to be compared. The value of goods is expressed in terms of prices, and prices are expressed in money terms. Money also allows dissimilar things, such as a person's wealth or a company's assets, to be added up. Similarly, a country's GDP is expressed in money terms. Money thus serves as a 'unit of account'.

A means of storing wealth

Individuals and businesses need a means whereby the fruits of today's labour can be used to purchase goods and services in the future. People need to be able to store their wealth: they want a means of saving. Money is one such medium in which to hold wealth. It can be saved.

What should count as money?

What items, then, should be included in the definition of money? Unfortunately, there is no sharp borderline between money and non-money.

Cash (notes and coin) obviously counts as money. It readily meets all the functions of money. Goods (fridges, cars and cabbages) do not count as money. But what about various financial assets such as savings accounts, bonds and shares? Do they count as money? The answer is: it depends on how narrowly money is defined.

> ### Pause for thought
>
> *Why are debit and credit cards not counted as money?*

Countries thus use several different measures of money supply. All include cash, but they vary according to what additional items are included. To understand their significance and the ways in which money supply can be controlled, it is first necessary to look at the various types of account in which money can be held and at the various financial institutions involved.

> ### Definition
>
> **Medium of exchange** Something that is acceptable in exchange for goods and services.

28.2 THE FINANCIAL SYSTEM

In order to understand the role of the financial sector in determining the supply of money, it is important to distinguish different types of financial institution. Each type has a distinct part to play in determining the size of the money supply.

The key role of banks in the monetary system

By far the largest element of money supply is bank deposits. It is not surprising then that banks play an absolutely crucial role in the monetary system. Banking can be divided into two main types: *retail banking* and *wholesale banking* (see Chapter 19). Most banks today conduct both types of business and are thus known as 'universal banks'.

Retail banking is the business conducted by the familiar high street banks, such as Barclays, Lloyds TSB, HSBC, Santander, Royal Bank of Scotland and NatWest (part of the RBS group). They operate bank accounts for individuals and businesses, attracting deposits and granting loans at published rates of interest.

The other major type of banking is **wholesale banking**. This involves receiving large deposits from and making large loans to companies or other banks and financial institutions; these are known as *wholesale deposits and loans*. (See section 19.4 for a more detailed account of their activities.)

In the past, there were many independent wholesale banks, known as *investment banks*. These included famous names such as Morgan Stanley, Rothschild, S G Hambros and Goldman Sachs. With the worldwide financial crisis of 2008, however, most of the independent investment banks merged with universal banks, which conduct both retail and wholesale activities.

The rise of large universal banks has caused concern, however. In the UK, the Independent Commission on Banking (ICB), set up in 2010 by the Coalition government to investigate the structure of the banking system, proposed *functional separation*: the ring-fencing of retail and wholesale banking. The argument here is that the supply of vital retail banking activities needed isolating from the potential contagion from risky wholesale banking activities.

The Coalition government accepted the ICB recommendations and agreed to prepare legislation for functional separation.

Building societies are UK institutions that historically have specialised in granting loans (mortgages) for house purchase. But, like banks, they too are deposit-taking financial institutions and so compete for the deposits of the general public. In recent years, many building societies have converted to banks.

Banks and building societies are both examples of what are called **monetary financial institutions (MFIs)**. This term is used to describe all deposit-taking institutions, which also includes central banks (e.g. the Bank of England).

Balance sheets

Banks and building societies provide a range of **financial instruments**. These are financial claims, either by customers on the bank (e.g. deposits) or by the bank on its customers (e.g. loans). They are best understood by analysing the balance sheets of financial institutions, which itemise their liabilities and assets.

A financial institution's **liabilities** are those financial instruments involving a financial claim on the financial institution itself. As we shall see, these are largely *deposits* by customers, such as current and savings accounts. Its **assets** are financial instruments involving a financial claim on a third party: these are *loans*, such as personal and business loans and mortgages.

The total liabilities and assets for UK banks and building societies are set out in the balance sheet in Table 28.1. The aggregate size of the balance sheet in 2012 was equivalent to around $5^{1}/_{2}$ times the UK's annual GDP. This is perhaps the simplest indicator of the significance of banks in modern economies, like the UK.

Liabilities

As we have seen, customers' deposits in banks (and other MFIs) are liabilities to these institutions. This means simply that the customers have the claim on these deposits and thus the institutions are legally liable to meet the claims.

There are four major types of deposit: sight deposits, time deposits, certificates of deposit and 'repos'.

Definitions

Retail banking Branch, telephone, postal and Internet banking for individuals and businesses at published rates of interest and charges. Retail banking involves the operation of extensive branch networks.

Wholesale banking Where banks deal in large-scale deposits and loans, mainly with companies and other banks and financial institutions. Interest rates and charges may be negotiable.

Monetary financial institutions (MFIs) Deposit-taking financial institutions including banks, building societies and central banks.

Financial instruments Financial products resulting in a financial claim by one party over another.

Liabilities All legal claims for payment that outsiders have on an institution.

Assets Possessions, or claims held on others.

BOX 28.1   FINANCIAL INTERMEDIATION

What is it that banks do?

Banks and other financial institutions are known as *financial intermediaries*. They all have the common function of providing a link between those who wish to lend and those who wish to borrow. In other words, they act as the mechanism whereby the supply of funds is matched to the demand for funds. In this process, they provide four important services.

Expert advice

Financial intermediaries can advise their customers on financial matters: on the best way of investing their funds and on alternative ways of obtaining finance. This should help to encourage the flow of savings and the efficient use of them.

Expertise in channelling funds

Financial intermediaries have the specialist knowledge to be able to channel funds to those areas that yield the highest return. This too encourages the flow of savings as it gives savers the confidence that their savings will earn a good rate of interest. Financial intermediaries also help to ensure that projects that are potentially profitable will be able to obtain finance. They help to increase allocative efficiency.

Maturity transformation

Many people and firms want to borrow money for long periods of time, and yet many depositors want to be able to withdraw their deposits on demand or at short notice. If people had to rely on borrowing directly from other people, there would be a problem here: the lenders would not be prepared to lend for a long enough period. If you had £100 000 of savings, would you be prepared to lend it to a friend to buy a house if the friend was going to take 25 years to pay it back? Even if there was no risk whatsoever of your friend defaulting, most people would be totally unwilling to tie up their savings for so long.

This is where a bank or building society comes in. It borrows money from a vast number of small savers, who are able to withdraw their money on demand or at short notice. It then lends the money to house purchasers for a long period of time by granting mortgages (typically these are paid back over 20 to 30 years). This process whereby financial intermediaries lend for longer periods of time than they borrow is known as *maturity transformation*. They are able to do this because with a large number of depositors it is highly unlikely that they would all want to withdraw their deposits at the same time. On any one day, although some people will be withdrawing money, others will be making new deposits.

Risk transformation

You may be unwilling to lend money directly to another person in case they do not pay up. You are unwilling to take the risk. Financial intermediaries, however, by lending to large numbers of people, are willing to risk the odd case of default. They can absorb the loss because of the interest they earn on all the other loans. This spreading of risks is known as *risk transformation*. What is more, financial intermediaries may have the expertise to be able to assess just how risky a loan is.

Transmitting payments

In addition to channelling funds from depositors to borrowers, certain financial institutions have another important function. This is to provide a means of transmitting payments. Thus by the use of debit cards, credit cards, standing orders, cheques, etc., money can be transferred from one person or institution to another without having to rely on cash.

 Which of the above are examples of economies of scale?

Sight deposits. **Sight deposits** are any deposits that can be withdrawn on demand by the depositor without penalty. In the past, sight accounts did not pay interest. Today, however, there are some sight accounts that do.

The most familiar form of sight deposits are current accounts at banks. Depositors are normally issued with cheque books and/or debit cards (e.g. Visa debit or Mastercard's Maestro) which enable them to spend the money directly without first having to go to the bank and draw the money out in cash. In the case of debit cards, the person's account is electronically debited when the purchase is made and the card is 'swiped' across the machine. This process is known as EFTPOS (electronic funds transfer at point of sale).

An important feature of current accounts is that banks often allow customers to be overdrawn. That is, they can draw on their account and make payments to other people in excess of the amount of money they have deposited.

Time deposits. **Time deposits** require notice of withdrawal. However, they normally pay a higher rate of interest than sight accounts. With some types of account, a depositor can withdraw a certain amount of money on demand, but will have to pay a penalty of so many days' interest. They are not cheque-book or debit-card accounts. The most familiar forms of time deposits are the deposit and savings accounts in banks and the various savings accounts in building societies. No overdraft facilities exist with time deposits.

Definitions

Sight deposits Deposits that can be withdrawn on demand without penalty.

Time deposits Deposits that require notice of withdrawal or where a penalty is charged for withdrawals on demand.

Table 28.1 Balance sheet of UK banks (end of March 2012)

Sterling liabilities	£bn	%	Sterling assets	£bn	%
Sight deposits		33.8	Notes and coins	9.0	0.2
UK banks, etc.	197.7		Balances with UK central bank		6.0
UK public sector	10.5		Cash ratio deposits	2.4	
UK private sector	897.3		Reserve balances	218.4	
Non-residents	126.9		Loans		15.6
Time deposits		40.2	UK banks, etc.	437.5	
UK banks, etc.	245.7		UK banks' CDs, etc.	10.9	
UK public sector	13.4		Non-residents	124.2	
UK private sector	956.2		Bills	26.8	0.7
Non-residents	253.6		Reverse repos	217.3	5.9
Repos	230.1	6.3	Investments	522.7	14.2
CDs and other short-term papers	174.3	4.8	Advances	2014.8	54.8
Capital and other internal funds	514.3	14.1	Other assets	95.5	2.6
Other liabilities	29.9	0.8			
Total sterling liabilities	**3649.9**	**100.0**	**Total sterling assets**	**3679.5**	**100.0**
Foreign currency liabilities	4623.0		Total foreign currency assets	4593.3	
Total liabilities	8272.9		Total assets	8272.8	

Note: Data are not seasonally adjusted
Source: Based on data in *Bankstats (Monetary and Financial Statistics)*, (Bank of England), May 2012

A substantial proportion of time deposits are from the *banking sector*: i.e. other banks and other financial institutions. Inter-bank lending, including that involving foreign banks, has grown over the years with the deregulation of financial markets. But, inter-bank lending virtually dried up in 2008/9. Banks became increasingly fearful that if they lent money to other banks, the other banks might default on payment.

Sale and repurchase agreements ('repos'). If banks have a temporary shortage of funds, they can sell some of their financial assets to other banks or to the central bank – the Bank of England in the UK and the European Central Bank in the eurozone (see below), and later repurchase them on some agreed date, typically a fortnight later. These **sale and repurchase agreements (repos)** are in effect a form of loan, the bank borrowing for a period of time using some of its financial assets as the security for the loan. One of the major assets to use in this way are government bonds, normally called 'gilt-edged securities' or simply 'gilts' (see below). Sale and repurchase agreements involving gilts are known as *gilt repos*. Gilt repos play a vital role in the operation of monetary policy (see section 30.1).

Certificates of deposit. **Certificates of deposit** (CDs) are certificates issued by banks to customers (usually firms) for large deposits of a fixed term (e.g. £100 000 for 18 months). They can be sold by one customer to another, and thus provide a means whereby the holders can get money quickly if they need it without the *banks* that have issued

the CD having to supply the money. (This makes them relatively 'liquid' to the depositor but 'illiquid' to the bank: we examine this below.) The use of CDs has grown rapidly in recent years. Their use by firms has meant that, at a wholesale level, sight accounts have become *less* popular.

Capital and other funds. This consists largely of the share capital in banks. Since shareholders cannot take their money out of banks, it provides a source of funding to meet sudden increases in withdrawals from depositors and to cover bad debts. As we shall see below, it is vital that banks have sufficient capital. Indeed, since the financial crisis of 2008, banks have strengthened their capital base to guard against future problems. At the end of 2008, 'capital and other funds' were less than 10 per cent of sterling liabilities. As you can see from Table 28.1, by March 2012, this had risen to around 14 per cent.

Definitions

Sale and repurchase agreements (repos) An agreement between two financial institutions whereby one in effect borrows from another by selling it assets, agreeing to buy them back (repurchase them) at a fixed price and on a fixed date.

Certificates of deposit Certificates issued by banks for fixed-term interest-bearing deposits. They can be resold by the owner to another party.

Assets

Banks' financial assets are its claims on others. There are three main categories of assets.

Cash and reserve balances in the central bank (Bank of England in the UK, ECB in the eurozone). Banks need to hold a certain amount of their assets as cash. This is largely used to meet the day-to-day demands of customers.

They also keep 'reserve balances' in the central bank. In the UK these earn interest at the Bank of England's repo rate (or 'Bank Rate' as it is called), if kept within an agreed target range. These are like the banks' own current accounts and are used for clearing purposes (i.e. for settling the day-to-day payments between banks). They can be withdrawn in cash on demand. With inter-bank lending being seen as too risky during the crisis of 2008, many banks resorted to depositing surplus cash in the Bank of England, even though the Bank Rate was lower than the inter-bank rate (known as 'LIBOR', which stands for the London Inter-Bank Offered Rate).

In the UK, banks and building societies are also required to deposit a small fraction of their assets as 'cash ratio deposits' with the Bank of England. These cannot be drawn on demand and earn no interest.

Short-term loans. These are in the form of market loans, bills of exchange or reverse repos. The market for these various types of loan is known as the **money market**.

■ *Market loans* are made primarily to other banks or financial institutions. They consist of (a) money lent 'at call' (i.e. reclaimable on demand or at 24 hours' notice), (b) money lent 'at short notice' (i.e. money lent for a few days) and (c) CDs (i.e. certificates of deposit made in other banks or building societies).

■ *Bills of exchange* are loans either to companies (commercial bills) or to the government (Treasury bills). As explained in section 19.4, these are, in effect, an IOU, with the company issuing them (in the case of commercial bills) or the Bank of England (in the case of Treasury bills) promising to pay the holder a specified sum on a particular date (typically three months later). Since bills do not pay interest, they are sold below their face value (at a 'discount') but redeemed on maturity at face value. This enables the purchaser, in this case the bank, to earn a return. The market for new or existing bills is therefore known as the **discount market**.

■ *Reverse repos.* When a sale and repurchase agreement is made, the financial institution *purchasing* the assets (e.g. gilts) is, in effect, giving a short-term loan. The other party agrees to buy back the assets (i.e. pay back the loan) on a set date. The assets temporarily held by the bank making the loan are known as 'reverse repos'.

Longer-term loans. These consist primarily of loans to customers, both personal customers and businesses. These loans, also known as *advances*, are of four main types: fixed-term (repayable in instalments over a set number of

years, typically six months to five years), overdrafts (often for an unspecified term), outstanding balances on credit-card accounts and mortgages (typically for 25 years).

Banks also make *investments*. These are partly in government bonds ('gilts'), which are effectively loans to the government. The government sells bonds, which then pay a fixed sum each year in interest. Once issued, bonds can then be bought and sold on the Stock Exchange. Banks are normally only prepared to buy bonds that have less than five years to maturity. Banks also invest in other financial institutions, including subsidiary financial institutions.

Taxing the balance sheets

In January 2011, the UK Coalition government introduced the bank levy: a tax on the liabilities of banks and building societies operating in the UK. The design of the levy built on proposals presented by the International Monetary Fund in June 2010. There were two key principles. First, the revenues raised should be able to meet the full fiscal costs of any future support for financial institutions. Second, it should provide banks with incentives to reduce risk-taking behaviour and so reduce the likelihood of future financial crises.

The UK bank levy has two rates: a full rate on taxable liabilities with a maturity of less than 1 year and a half rate on taxable liabilities with a maturity of more than 1 year. The intention is to discourage excessive short-term borrowing by the banks in their use of wholesale funding. The tax levy rates are also designed to raise at least £2.5 billion each year. The March 2012 Budget announced that from January 2013, the full rate would rise from 0.088 to 0.105 per cent and the half rate from 0.044 to 0.0525 to offset reductions in the rate of corporation tax (see Chapter 31, page 534).

Not all liabilities are subject to the levy. First, it is not imposed on the first £20 billion of liabilities. This is to encourage small banks (note that the largest UK banks, such as HSBC, Barclays and RBS, each have liabilities of over £2 trillion). Second, various liabilities are excluded.

Definitions

Money market The market for short-term loans and deposits.

Market loans Loans made to other financial institutions.

Bill of exchange A certificate promising to repay a stated amount on a certain date, typically three months from the issue of the bill. Bills pay no interest as such, but are sold at a discount and redeemed at face value, thereby earning a rate of discount for the purchaser.

Discount market An example of a money market in which new or existing bills are bought and sold.

Reverse repos When gilts or other assets are *purchased* under a sale and repurchase agreement. They become an asset of the purchaser.

BOX 28.2 **GROWTH OF BANKS' BALANCE SHEETS**

The rise of wholesale funding

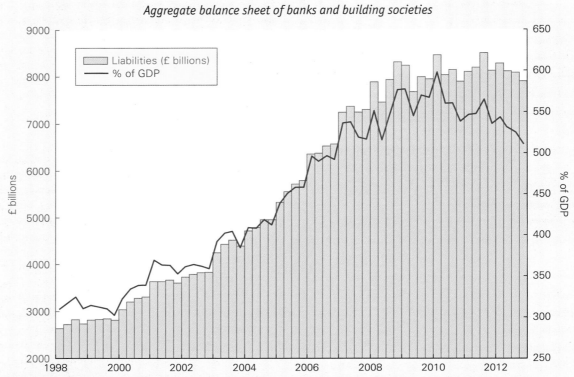

Aggregate balance sheet of banks and building societies

Sources: (i) Data showing liabilities of banks and building societies based on series LPMALOA and RPMTBJF (up to the end of 2009) and RPMB3UQ (from 2010) from *Statistical Interactive Database* (Bank of England) (www.bankofengland.co.uk). See http://www.bankofengland.co.uk/mfsd/iadb/notesiadb/Revisions.htm for the Revisions Policy. Data published 30 January 2013. Data are not seasonally adjusted. (ii) GDP data from *Quarterly National Accounts* (Office for National Statistics). Contains public sector information licensed under the Open Government Licence (OGL) v.1.0. http://www.nationalarchives.gov.uk/doc/open-government-licence. GDP figures are the sum of the latest four quarters

The traditional funding model for banks relied heavily on deposits as the source of funds for loans. However, new ways for financial institutions to access funds to generate new loans have evolved. These reflect the deregulation of financial markets and the rapid pace of financial innovation.

Increasingly financial institutions have made greater use of wholesale funds. These are funds obtained mainly from other financial institutions. This has coincided too with the emergence of a process known as securitisation. This involves the conversion of non-marketable banks' assets, such as residential mortgages, which have regular income streams (e.g. from payments of interest and capital) into tradable financial instruments. In other words, banks' housing and other loans are bundled together to create new securities. The funds raised from their sale can provide the capital to secure further loans. Therefore, securitisation is another means of obtaining funds from other financial institutions. Securitisation is discussed further in Box 28.3.

The rise in wholesale funding provided banks with vast sums of funds for lending. One consequence of this is illustrated in the chart: the expansion of the aggregate balance sheet. The balance sheet grew from £2$\frac{1}{2}$ trillion (3 times GDP) in 1998 to over £8 trillion (5$\frac{1}{2}$ times GDP) in 2012.

Increased wholesale funding and securitisation have meant that many banks have not only witnessed growth in their balance sheets but also a change in their composition.

First, the profile of banks' assets has become less liquid as they have extended more long-term credit to households and firms. This has often been accompanied by an increase in the risk-profile of banks' assets.

Second, securitisation has helped to fuel a general increase in the use of fixed-interest bonds as opposed to ordinary shares (equities) for raising capital. The ratio of bonds to equity capital is known as gearing (or leverage) (see page 298). The increase in leverage meant that, prior to the financial crisis, banks had been operating with lower and lower levels of loss-absorbing capital, such as ordinary shares. If banks run at a loss, dividends on shares can be suspended; the payment of interest on fixed interest bonds cannot. Thus banks were exposed to a greater degree of risk. One of the main global policy responses to the financial crisis has been to require banks to hold more equity capital relative to their assets.

Why do you think banks became reluctant to deposit moneys with other banks during the financial crisis of the late 2000s?

These are: (a) gilt repos; (b) retail deposits insured by public schemes such as the UK's Financial Services Compensation Scheme, which guarantees customers' deposits of up to £85,000; (c) a large part of a bank's capital known as Tier 1 capital (see below) – the argument here is that it is important for banks to maintain sufficient funds to meet the demands of its depositors.

Banks are also able to offset against their taxable liabilities holdings of highly liquid assets, such as Treasury bills and cash reserves at the Bank of England. It is hoped that these exclusions and deductions will encourage banks to engage in less risky lending.

Liquidity, profitability and capital adequacy

As we have seen, banks keep a range of liabilities and assets. The balance of items in this range is influenced by three important considerations: profitability, liquidity and capital adequacy.

Profitability

Profits are made by lending money out at a higher rate of interest than that paid to depositors. The average interest rate received by banks on their assets is greater than that paid by them on their liabilities.

Liquidity

The *liquidity* of an asset is the ease with which it can be converted into cash without loss. Cash itself, by definition, is perfectly liquid.

Some assets, such as money lent at call to other financial institutions, are highly liquid. Although not actually cash, these assets can be converted into cash on demand with no financial penalty. Other short-term inter-bank lending is also very liquid. The only issue here is one of confidence that the money will actually be repaid. This was a worry in the financial crisis of 2008/9, when many banks stopped lending to each other on the inter-bank market for fear that the borrowing bank might become insolvent.

Other assets, however, are much less liquid. Personal loans to the general public or mortgages for house purchase can only be redeemed by the bank as each instalment is paid. Other advances for fixed periods are only repaid at the end of that period.

Banks must always be able to meet the demands of their customers for withdrawals of money. To do this, they must hold sufficient cash or other assets that can be readily turned into cash. In other words, banks must maintain sufficient liquidity.

Capital adequacy

Banks must have sufficient capital (i.e. funds) to allow them to meet all demands from depositors and to cover losses if borrowers default on payment. In the 2007/8 global banking crisis, it became clear that many banks had too little capital and required rescuing by governments. Regulators around the world have thus sought to ensure that banks now have adequate capital.

Capital adequacy refers to a bank's capital relative to its assets, where the assets are weighted according to the degree of risk. The more risky the assets, the greater the amount of capital that will be required.

A measure of capital adequacy is given by the *capital adequacy ratio (CAR)*. This is given by the following formula:

$$CAR = \frac{\text{Common Equity Tier 1 capital} + \text{Additional Tier 1 capital} + \text{Tier 2 capital}}{\text{Risk-weighted assets}}$$

Common Equity Tier 1 (CET1) capital includes bank reserves and ordinary share capital ('equities'), where dividends to shareholders vary with the amount of profit the bank makes. Such capital thus places no burden on banks in times of losses as no dividend need be paid. What is more, unlike depositors, shareholders cannot ask for their money back.

Additional Tier 1 (AT1) capital consists largely of preference shares. These pay a fixed dividend (like company bonds), but although preference shareholders have a prior claim over ordinary shareholders on company profits, dividends need not be paid in times of loss.

Tier 2 capital is subordinated debt with a maturity greater than 5 years. Subordinated debt holders only have a claim on a company after the claims of all other bondholders have been met.

Risk-weighted assets are the total value of assets, where each type of asset is multiplied by a risk factor. Under the internationally agreed Basel II accord, cash and government bonds have a risk factor of zero and are thus not included. Inter-bank lending between the major banks has a risk factor of 0.2 and is thus included at only 20 per cent of its value; residential mortgages have a risk factor of 0.35; personal loans, credit-card debt and overdrafts have a risk factor of 1; loans to companies carry a risk factor of 0.2, 0.5, 1 or 1.5, depending on the credit rating of the company. Thus the greater the average risk factor of a bank's assets, the greater will be the value of its risk weighted assets, and the lower will be its CAR.

The greater the CAR, the greater the capital adequacy of a bank.

Basel III. International capital adequacy requirements were strengthened by the *Basel Committee on Banking Supervision*

Definitions

Liquidity The ease with which an asset can be converted into cash without loss.

Capital adequacy ratio The ratio of a bank's capital (reserves and shares) to its risk-weighted assets.

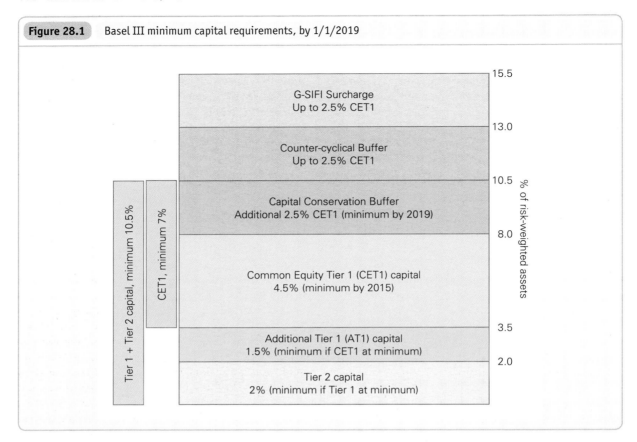

Figure 28.1 Basel III minimum capital requirements, by 1/1/2019

in 2010/11. The new 'Basel III' capital requirements, as they are called, will be phased in by 2019. They are summarised in Figure 28.1.

From 2013, banks will continue to need a CAR of at least 8 per cent (i.e. 0.08). But, by 2015 they will also be required to operate with a ratio of CET1 to risk-weighted assets of at least 4.5 per cent. The phased introduction of a *capital conservation buffer* from 2016 will raise the CET1 ratio to no less than 7 per cent by 2019. This will take the overall CAR to at least 10.5 per cent.

On top of this, national regulators will be required to assess the financial resilience across all financial institutions under its jurisdiction, particularly in light of economic conditions. This is ***macro-prudential regulation***. If necessary, it will then apply a *counter-cyclical buffer* to all banks so increasing the CET1 ratio by up to a further 2.5 per cent. The idea is to build up a capital buffer in boom times to allow it to be drawn on in times of recession or financial difficulty.

Large global financial institutions, known as global systemically important financial institutions (G-SIFIs), will be required to operate with a CET1 ratio of up to 2.5 per cent higher than other banks. The reason for this extra capital requirement is that the failure of such an institution could trigger a global financial crisis. This would potentially take the overall CAR for very large financial institutions in 2019 to 15.5 per cent (see Figure 28.1).

In the UK, capital requirements may be even higher for *retail* banks. The UK's Independent Commission on Banking has proposed that retail banks, which will be legally, economically and operationally independent of the investment parts of banks, should operate with an overall CAR of between 17 and 20 per cent and with a CET1 ratio of at least 10 per cent.

Finally, under Basel III, banks would be required to hold Tier 1 capital of at least 3 per cent of total lending; or, put another way, banks' lending must be no more than $33^{1/3}$ times their Tier 1 capital.

All these details demonstrate the determination of banking regulators to ensure that banks have sufficient capital and that there will be no repeat of the excessive lending and risk taking that led to the banking crisis of 2007/8.

The balance between profitability and liquidity

Profitability is the major aim of banks and most other financial institutions. However, the aims of profitability and liquidity tend to conflict. In general, the more liquid an asset, the less profitable it is, and vice versa. Personal and business loans to customers are profitable to banks,

469 THE FINANCIAL SYSTEM

but highly illiquid. Cash is totally liquid, but earns no profit. Thus financial institutions like to hold a range of assets with varying degrees of liquidity and profitability.

For reasons of *profitability*, the banks will want to 'borrow short' (at low rates of interest, such as people's deposits in current accounts) and 'lend long' (at higher rates of interest, such as on personal loans or mortgages). The difference in the average maturity of loans and deposits is known as the ***maturity gap***. In general terms, the larger the maturity gap between loans and deposits, the greater the profitability. For reasons of *liquidity*, however, banks will want a relatively small gap: if there is a sudden withdrawal of deposits, banks will need to be able to call in enough loans.

The ratio of an institution's liquid assets to total assets is known as its ***liquidity ratio***. For example, if a bank had £100 million of assets, of which £10 million were liquid and £90 million were illiquid, the bank would have a 10 per cent liquidity ratio. If a financial institution's liquidity ratio is too high, it will make too little profit. If the ratio is too low, there is a risk that customers' demands may not be able to be met: this would cause a crisis of confidence and possible closure. Institutions thus have to make a judgement as to what liquidity ratio is best – one that is neither too high nor too low.

Balances in the central bank, short-term loans (i.e. those listed above) and government bonds with less than 12 months to maturity would normally be regarded as liquid assets.

Over the years, banks had reduced their liquidity ratios (i.e. the ratio of liquid assets to total assets). This was not a problem as long as banks could always finance lending to customers by borrowing on the inter-bank market. In 2008, however, banks became increasingly worried about bad debt. They thus felt the need to increase their liquidity ratios and hence cut back on lending and chose to keep a higher proportion of deposits in liquid form. In the UK, for example, banks substantially increased their level of reserves in the Bank of England.

Pause for thought

Why are government bonds that still have 11 months to run regarded as liquid, whereas overdrafts granted for a few weeks are not?

Secondary marketing and securitisation

Another way of reconciling the two conflicting aims of liquidity and profitability is through the ***secondary marketing*** of assets. This is where holders of assets sell them to someone else before the maturity date. This allows banks to close the maturity gap for *liquidity* purposes, but maintain the gap for *profitability* purposes.

Certificates of deposit (CDs) are a good example of secondary marketing. CDs are issued for fixed-period deposits in a bank (e.g. one year) at an agreed interest rate. The bank does not have to repay the deposit until the year is up. CDs are thus illiquid liabilities for the bank, and they allow it to increase the proportion of illiquid assets without having a dangerously high maturity gap. But the holder of the CD in the meantime can sell it to someone else (through a broker). It is thus liquid to the holder. Because CDs are liquid to the holder, they can be issued at a relatively *low* rate of interest and thus allow the bank to increase its profitability.

Another example of secondary marketing is when a financial institution sells some of its assets to another financial institution. The advantage to the first institution is that it gains liquidity. The advantage to the second one is that it gains profitable assets. The most common method for the sale of assets has been through a process known as ***securitisation***.

Securitisation occurs when a financial institution pools some of its assets, such as residential mortgages, and sells them to an intermediary known as a ***special purpose vehicle (SPV)***. SPVs are legal entities created by the financial institution. In turn, the SPV funds its purchase of the assets by issuing bonds to investors (noteholders). These bonds are known as ***collateralised debt obligations (CDOs)***. The sellers (e.g. banks) get cash now rather than having to wait and can use it to fund loans to customers. The buyers make a profit if the income yielded by the CDOs is as expected. Such bonds can be very risky, however, as the future cash flows may be *less* than anticipated.

The securitisation chain is illustrated in Figure 28.2. The financial institution looking to sell its assets is referred to as the 'originator' or the 'originator-lender'. Working from left to right, we see the originator-lender sells its assets to another financial institution, the SPV, which then bundles assets together into CDOs and sells them to investors (e.g. banks or pension funds) as bonds. Now working from right

Definitions

Maturity gap The difference in the average maturity of loans and deposits.

Liquidity ratio The proportion of a bank's total assets held in liquid form.

Secondary marketing Where assets are sold before maturity to another institution or individual.

Securitisation Where future cash flows (e.g. from interest rate or mortgage payments) are turned into marketable securities, such as bonds.

Special purpose vehicle (SPV) Legal entities created by financial institutions for conducting specific financial functions, such as bundling assets together into fixed-interest bonds and selling them.

Collateralised debt obligations (CDOs) These are a type of security consisting of a bundle of fixed-income assets, such as corporate bonds, mortgage debt and credit-card debt.

Figure 28.2   Securitisation chain

---

to left, we see that by purchasing the bonds issued by the SPV, the investors provide the funds for the SPV's purchase of the lender's assets. The SPV is then able to use the proceeds from the bond sales (CDO proceeds) to provide the originator-lender with liquidity.

The effect of secondary marketing is to reduce the liquidity ratio that banks feel they need to keep. It has the effect of increasing their maturity gap.

KI 14 p 74

Dangers of secondary marketing. There are dangers to the banking system, however, from secondary marketing. To the extent that banks individually feel that they can operate with a lower liquidity ratio, so this will lead to a lower national liquidity ratio. This may lead to an excessive expansion of credit (illiquid assets) in times of economic boom.

Also, there is an increased danger of banking collapse. If one bank fails, this will have a knock-on effect on those banks which have purchased its assets. In the specific case of securitisation, the strength of the chain is potentially weakened if individual financial institutions move into riskier market segments, such as **sub-prime** residential

---

BOX 28.3   **RESIDENTIAL MORTGAGES AND SECURITISATION**

Was this the cause of the credit crunch?

The conflict between profitability and liquidity may have sown the seeds for the credit crunch that affected economies across the globe in the second half of the 2000s.

To understand this, consider the size of the 'advances' item in the banking sector's balance sheet – around 55 per cent of the value of sterling assets (see Table 28.1). The vast majority of these are to households. Advances secured against property have, in recent times, accounted for around 80 per cent by value of all household advances. *Residential mortgages* involve institutions lending long.

Securitisation of mortgages

One way in which individual institutions can achieve the necessary liquidity to expand the size of their mortgage lending (illiquid assets) is through *securitisation*. Securitisation grew especially rapidly in the UK and USA. In the UK this was particularly true amongst banks; building societies have historically made greater use of retail deposits to fund advances.

Figures from the Bank of England show that the value of lending to individuals which was securitised increased from just over £0.8 billion in 1998 to £103.6 billion in 2008 (see chart). Most of this securitised debt has been secured debt, i.e. residential mortgages.

KI 7 p 35

Securitisation is a form of financial engineering. It provides banks (originator-lenders) with liquidity and enables them to engage in further lending opportunities. It provides the special purpose vehicles with the opportunity to issue profitable securities.

The increase in securitisation up to 2008 highlights the strong demand amongst investors for these securities. The attraction of these fixed-income products for the noteholders was the potential for higher returns than on (what were) similarly-rated products. However, investors have no recourse should people with mortgages fall into arrears or, worse still, default on their mortgages.

Risks and the sub-prime market

The securitisation of assets is not without risks for all those in the securitisation chain and consequently for the financial system as a whole.

The pooling of advances in itself *reduces* the cash-flow risk facing investors. However, there is a **moral hazard** problem here (see page 89). The pooling of the risks may encourage originator-lenders to lower their credit criteria by offering higher income multiples (advances relative to annual household incomes) or higher loan-to-value ratios (advances relative to the price of housing).

KI 17 p 89

Towards the end of 2006 the USA witnessed an increase in the number of defaults by households on residential mortgages. This was a particular problem in the sub-prime market – higher-risk households with poor credit ratings. Similarly, the number falling behind with their payments rose. This was on the back of rising interest rates.

These problems in the US sub-prime market were the catalyst for the liquidity problem that beset financial systems in 2007 and 2008. Where these assets were securitised, investors, largely other financial institutions, suffered from the contagion arising from arrears and defaults.

Securitisation also internationalised the contagion. Investors are global so that advances, such as a US family's residential mortgage, can cross national borders. This resulted in institutions writing off debts, a deterioration of their balance sheets, the collapse in the demand for securitised assets and the drying up of liquidity.

mortgage markets. Should the income streams of the originator's assets dry up – for instance, if individuals default on their loans – then the impact is felt by the whole of the chain. In other words, institutions and investors are exposed to the risks of the originator's lending strategy.

The issue of securitisation and its impact on the liquidity of the financial system during the 2000s is considered in Box 28.3.

Definitions

Sub-prime debt Debt where there is a high risk of default by the borrower (e.g. mortgage holders who are on low incomes facing higher interest rates and falling house prices).

Moral hazard The temptation to take more risks when you know that someone else will cover the risks if you get into difficulties. In the case of banks taking risks, the 'someone else' may be another bank, the central bank or the government.

The central bank

The Bank of England is the UK's central bank. The European Central Bank (ECB) is the central bank for the countries using the euro. The Federal Reserve Bank of America (the Fed) is the USA's central bank. All countries have a central bank and they fulfil two vital roles in the economy.

The first is to oversee the whole monetary system and ensure that banks and other financial institutions operate as stably and as efficiently as possible.

The second is to act as the government's agent, both as its banker and in carrying out monetary policy. The Bank of England traditionally worked in very close liaison with the Treasury and there used to be regular meetings between the Governor of the Bank of England and the Chancellor of the Exchequer. Although the Bank may have disagreed with Treasury policy, it always carried it out. With the election of the Labour government in 1997, however, the Bank of England was given independence to decide the course of monetary policy. In particular, this

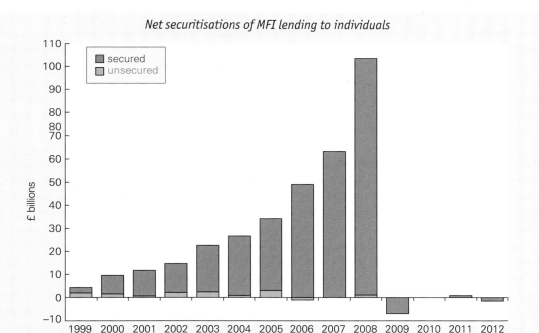

Net securitisations of MFI lending to individuals

Note: Negative totals indicate acquisition of secured and unsecured debt portfolios

Source: Based on data from Bank of England Statistical Interactive Database (series LPQB3XE and LPQB3HK), data published 30 Jan 2013 (www.bankofengland.co.uk). See http://www.bankofengland.co.uk/mfsd/iadb/notesiadb/Revisions.htm for the Revisions Policy.

The chart shows the collapse of the market for securitised assets. 2009 saw banks acquiring debt portfolios. This occurred because banks had to buy back from SPVs unsold debt portfolios. 2010 and 2011 saw only a very modest recovery in securitised markets with each year seeing just £1 billion of lending to individuals securitised. Does securitisation necessarily involve a moral hazard problem?

meant that the Bank of England and not the government would now decide interest rates.

Another example of an independent central bank is the European Central Bank (ECB). The ECB operates monetary policy for the countries using the euro and it alone, not the member governments, determines common interest rates for these countries. Similarly, the Fed is independent of both President and Congress, and its chairman is generally regarded as having great power in determining the country's economic policy. Although the degree of independence of central banks from government varies considerably around the world, there has nevertheless been a general trend to make central banks more independent.

If the UK were ever to adopt the euro, there would be a much reduced role for the Bank of England. At present, however, within its two broad roles, it has a number of different functions. Although we shall consider the case of the Bank of England, the same principles apply to other central banks.

It issues notes

The Bank of England is the sole issuer of banknotes in England and Wales (in Scotland and Northern Ireland retail banks issue banknotes). The amount of banknotes issued by the Bank of England depends largely on the demand for notes from the general public. If people draw more cash from their bank accounts, the banks will have to draw more cash from their balances in the Bank of England.

It acts as a bank

To the government. It keeps the two major government accounts: 'The Exchequer' and the 'National Loans Fund'. Taxation and government spending pass through the Exchequer. Government borrowing and lending pass

---

| BOX 28.4 | RESPONSES TO THE CREDIT CRUNCH |

Cleansing the banking system

We consider here a package of measures introduced in the UK during the financial crisis to provide stability for the financial system and to support ailing financial institutions. These and other measures were mirrored in various aspects around the world.

Supplying liquidity

The Bank of England provides liquidity to banks via 'open-market operations'. This involves the use of repos. The Bank of England offers funds for a fixed term against eligible collateral of a financial institution, such as government bonds (gilt repos).

In normal circumstances these repo operations are designed to help meet a key monetary policy objective: the level of interest rates. Consequently, repo operations are ordinarily very short term, such as overnight 'fine-tuning' repo operations. But, in the period from summer 2007 circumstances ceased to be 'normal' as a massive liquidity shortage in the financial system developed.

During the autumn of 2007, in response to the liquidity shortage, the Bank of England began undertaking *Extended collateral three-month repo operations* (eLTRs). In simple terms, the eligible collateral for lending to banks was widened and included, for instance, mortgage-backed securities (see Box 28.3). As the crisis continued, the size of the funds released through eLTRs continued to grow. It is estimated that in January 2009 the stock of eLTRs outstanding reached £180 billion.

This, however, was still not enough and on 21 April 2008 the Bank of England introduced a *Special Liquidity Scheme* (SLS). This enabled banks to swap or upgrade their holdings of illiquid securities, including mortgage-backed securities, for UK Treasury bills. These bills could then be exchanged for cash in the money markets. Banks could renew the swaps annually for up to three years. The scheme was funded by the government through issues of Treasury bills. Lending under

SLS totalled £185 billion by the time it officially ended on 30 January 2012.

In October 2008 the Bank introduced a further lending facility knows as the *Discount Window Facility* (DWF). It has now become a permanent feature of the Bank's monetary framework. The DWF enables asset swaps: banks and building societies can borrow gilts (government bonds) for 30 or 364 days against a wide range of collateral for a fee. Again, banks can then obtain liquidity by lending gilts in the money market.

Injecting equity

As we saw in Box 28.2, by the mid-2000s, many banks had inadequate capital ratios, holding more illiquid assets but with less loss-absorbing capital. Consequently, they had become less financially resilient. In response, the UK government made available up to £50 billion of extra capital. The new capital was to be in the form of new shares owned by the government – a form of partial nationalisation. The government ended up owning large stakes in some financial institutions, which, as a result, were to be classified as 'public monetary financial institutions'.

Northern Rock. The Northern Rock had made heavy use of the money markets, including large-scale securitisation (see pages 469–70) of its existing mortgage book as a means of funding new mortgages. As the money markets began to seize up in 2007, it suffered acute liquidity shortages in trying to roll-over its short-term borrowing.

In the autumn of 2007 it entered into loan agreements totalling £27 billion with the Bank of England, which were guaranteed by the government. After failing to find a private-sector buyer, Northern Rock was taken into full government ownership on 22 February 2008. In August 2008, to comply with European Law, the Bank of England loans were replaced with a loan from the government. The Northern Rock was split into two separate companies in January 2010: a bank, Northern Rock plc, and a non-deposit taking financial

through the National Loans Fund. The government tends to keep its deposits in the Bank of England to a minimum. If the deposits begin to build up (from taxation), the government will probably spend them on paying back government debt. If, on the other hand, the government runs short of money, it will simply borrow more.

To the banks. Banks' deposits in the Bank of England consist of reserve balances and non-interest bearing cash ratio deposits (see Table 28.1). The reserve balances are largely used for clearing purposes between the banks and to provide them with a source of liquidity. However, in times of uncertainty, banks may choose to hold greater reserve balances.

To overseas central banks. The Bank of England holds deposits of sterling (and similarly the European Central Bank holds

deposits of euros) made by overseas authorities as part of their official reserves and/or for purposes of intervening in the foreign exchange market in order to influence the exchange rate of their currency.

It provides liquidity, as necessary, to banks

It attempts to ensure that there is always an adequate supply of liquidity to meet the legitimate demands of depositors in banks. As we shall see below, it does this through the discount and repo markets. The financial crisis placed incredible pressure on the aggregate liquidity of the financial system. This meant that the usual mechanisms for supplying liquidity had to be adapted and the end result was that the Bank of England, along with other central banks around the world, supplied massive amounts of extra liquidity (see Box 28.4).

institution, Northern Rock (Asset Management) plc. In November 2011, the government announced that Northern Rock plc was being sold to Virgin Money for £747 million.

Bradford and Bingley. Like the Northern Rock, the Bradford and Bingley had made significant use of wholesale funding. By 27 September 2008, the Financial Services Authority deemed that it no longer met the conditions to operate as a deposit-taker. It was too risky. The Bank was nationalised two days later. But, its retail deposit business and its branch network were transferred to the Abbey National, now part of the Santander group. The transfer of the deposits involved a payment to Abbey of £19 billion, thereby providing all depositors with insurance cover for their deposits. The cost of this was ultimately met by a government loan. In March 2010 it was decided that Northern Rock (Asset Management) and Bradford and Bingley would be integrated into a single holding company to be known as UK Asset Resolution and owned by the government.

Royal Bank of Scotland. Towards the end of 2008, the UK government undertook an initial capital injection of £20 billion (£15 billion of ordinary shares and £5 billion of preference shares). At the start of 2009, the government exchanged its holdings of preference shares for ordinary shares and, in so doing, took its share ownership of RBS to 70 per cent. By the end of 2009, the government agreed to a further capital injection of £25.5 billion through non-voting ordinary shares.

Lloyds Banking Group. The Lloyds Banking Group arose out of the merger of HBOS (Halifax Bank of Scotland) and Lloyds TSB, which was announced on 19 January 2009. Just prior to the formal announcement of the merger, the government injected £11.5 billion of capital into HBOS (£8.5 billion of ordinary shares and £3 billion of preference shares) and £5.5 billion into Lloyds TSB (£4.5 billion of ordinary shares and £1 billion of preference shares). After the merger, the £4 billion of preference shares were converted into ordinary shares by a rights issue to existing shareholders. The UK

government acquired £1.7 billion of them. At the end of 2009, Lloyds Banking Group announced plans to raise £21 billion. Of this, £13.5 billion came from another rights issue, with the government purchasing another £5.9 billion of ordinary shares, taking its shareholding to 43 per cent.

Guaranteeing loans on the inter-bank market

In October 2008 the Government introduced the *Credit Guarantee Scheme*. £250 billion was made available for loan guarantees for new inter-bank lending. In other words, if bank A lends to bank B and bank B then defaults, the government would pay bank A. The guarantees were provided by HM Treasury for a fee payable each quarter and were designed to assist with the refinancing of maturing wholesale funding. The guarantees could be rolled over, but the scheme closed to new guarantees as of 28 February 2010. The final guarantee matured in October 2012 and the scheme closed on 1 November.

In January 2009 the government announced details of its *Asset Protection Scheme*. Under the scheme financial institutions, in return for a fee, could insure themselves against future losses incurred on assets, including collateralised debt obligations (CDOs). In November 2009 the Government announced the terms on which the Royal Bank of Scotland would participate in the scheme. The RBS insured assets valued at £282 billion at end of 2008, paying an annual fee for the first 3 years of £0.7 billion and £0.5 billion, thereafter. The agreement saw RBS shoulder the first £60 billion of any losses, with any loses beyond this borne 90 per cent by government and 10 per cent by RBS.

1. *Why may supplying extra liquidity to banks not necessarily be successful in averting a slow-down in borrowing and spending?*
2. *Why is there a potential 'moral hazard' in supporting failing banks? How could the terms of a bailout help to reduce this moral hazard?*

KI 17
p 89

It oversees the activities of banks and other financial institutions

The Bank of England requires all recognised banks to maintain adequate liquidity: this is called **prudential control**.

In May 1997, the Bank of England ceased to be responsible for the detailed supervision of banks' activities. This responsibility passed to the Financial Services Authority (FSA). But, the financial crisis of the late 2000s raised concerns about whether the FSA, the Bank of England and HM Treasury were sufficiently watchful of banks' liquidity and the risks of liquidity shortage. Some commentators argued that a much tighter form of prudential control should have been imposed.

The Coalition government, formed in 2010, quickly outlined plans for a new regulatory framework to be operative within two years. The Bank of England became central to the new framework. First, the Bank's *Financial Policy Committee (FPC)* was made responsible for **macro-prudential regulation**: i.e. regulation which takes a broader view of the financial system. It considers, for instance, the resilience of the financial system to possible shocks and its capacity to create macroeconomic instability through excessive credit creation. Second, the prudential regulation of individual firms was transferred from the FSA to the *Prudential Regulation Authority (PRA)*, a subsidiary of the Bank of England. Third, the *Financial Conduct Authority (FCA)* took responsibility for consumer protection and the regulation of markets for financial services.

It operates the country's monetary and exchange rate policy

Monetary policy. The Bank of England's Monetary Policy Committee (MPC) sets interest rates (the rate on gilt repos) at its monthly meetings. This nine-member committee consists of four experts appointed by the Chancellor of the Exchequer and four senior members of the Bank of England, plus the Governor in the chair.

The Bank of England conducts **open-market operations** to keep interest rates in line with the level decided by the MPC. By purchasing securities (gilts and/or Treasury bills), for example through reverse repos (repos to the banks), the Bank of England provides liquidity, thereby putting downward pressure on interest rates. If it is looking to raise interest rates, the Bank of England will sell securities to banks so reducing banks' reserves in the Bank. In the process of influencing interest rates through open-market operations the Bank of England affects the size of the money supply. (This is explained in Chapter 30.)

Exchange rate policy. The Bank of England manages the country's gold and foreign currency reserves. This is done through the **exchange equalisation account**. By buying and selling foreign currencies on the foreign exchange market, the Bank of England can affect the exchange rate (see Chapter 27).

The role of the money market

It is through the money market that the central banks exercise control of the economy. The market deals in short-term lending and borrowing.

We take the case of the London money market, which is normally divided into the 'discount and repo' markets and the 'parallel' or 'complementary' markets.

The discount and repo markets

The discount market is the market for commercial or government bills. The discount market is also known as the traditional market because it was the market in which many central banks traditionally used to supply central bank money to financial institutions. For instance, if the Bank of England wanted to increase liquidity in the banking system it could purchase from the banks Treasury bills which had yet to reach maturity. This process is known as **rediscounting**. The Bank of England would pay a price below the face value, thus effectively charging interest to the banks. The price could be set so that the 'rediscount rate' reflected the interest rate set by the MPC (see section 30.2).

The emergence of the repo market is a more recent development dating back in the UK to the 1990s. Repos have become an important potential source of wholesale funding for financial institutions (see Box 28.2). By entering into a repo agreement the Bank of England buys gilts from the banks (thereby supplying them with money) on the condition that the banks buy the gilts back at a fixed price and on a fixed date. The repurchase price will be above the sale price. The difference is the equivalent of the interest that the banks are being charged for having what amounts to a loan from the Bank of England. The repurchase price (and hence the 'repo rate') is set by the Bank of England to reflect the rate chosen by the MPC.

The financial crisis caused the Bank to modify its repo operations to manage liquidity for both purposes of monetary policy and increasingly to ensure financial stability. These changes included a widening of the securities

> ### Definitions
>
> **Prudential control** The insistence by the Bank of England that banks maintain adequate liquidity.
>
> **Macro-prudential regulation** Regulation of the financial system as a whole to ensure that it is resilient to shocks.
>
> **Open market operations** The sale (or purchase) of government securities in the open market which aim to reduce (or increase) the money supply and thereby affect interest rates.
>
> **Exchange equalisation account** The gold and foreign exchange reserves account in the Bank of England.
>
> **Rediscounting bills of exchange** Buying bills before they reach maturity.

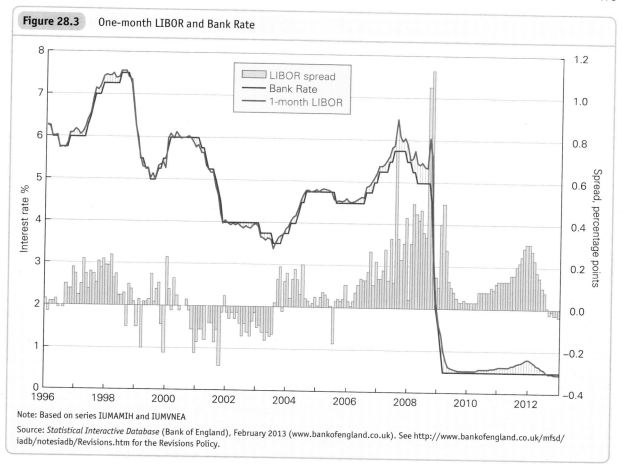

Figure 28.3 One-month LIBOR and Bank Rate

Note: Based on series IUMAMIH and IUMVNEA

Source: *Statistical Interactive Database* (Bank of England), February 2013 (www.bankofengland.co.uk). See http://www.bankofengland.co.uk/mfsd/iadb/notesiadb/Revisions.htm for the Revisions Policy.

eligible as collateral for loans, a suspension of short-term repo operations and an increased focus on longer-term repo operations (see Box 28.4).

So central banks, like the Bank of England, are prepared to provide central bank money through the creation of reserves. Central banks are thus the ultimate guarantor of sufficient liquidity in the monetary system and is known as *lender of last resort*.

As a means of supplying liquidity to troubled banks in various eurozone countries, the ECB in late 2011 and into 2012 issued a large amount of 3-year repo loans (just over €1 trillion). These long-term repo operations, or LTROs, were seen as vital for staving off a liquidity crisis and potential collapse of certain banks struggling with bad debts.

The parallel money markets

One of the most important parallel markets is the *inter-bank market*. This market involves wholesale loans from one bank to another from one day to up to several months.

Definition

Lender of last resort The role of the Bank of England as the guarantor of sufficient liquidity in the monetary system.

Inter-bank lending has traditionally been a major source of liquidity. Bank with surplus liquidity lend to other banks, which then use this as the basis for loans to individuals and companies. Inter-bank interest rates tend to be higher than those in the discount and repo markets and sensitive to the aggregate level of liquidity in the financial system.

As Figure 28.3 shows, during the financial crisis of 2008 inter-bank lending rates rose significantly above the Bank Rate. At the same time lending virtually ceased as banks became worried that the bank they were lending to might default. In response, the government set aside up to £250 billion in loan guarantees under the *Credit Guarantee Scheme* (see Box 28.4). The intention was to guarantee loans on the inter-bank market, removing the risk of default and so encouraging banks to start lending to each other again.

Other parallel money markets include the following:

- The market for certificates of deposit (CDs).
- The inter-companies deposit market (short-term loans from one company to another arranged through the market).
- The foreign currencies market (dealings in foreign currencies deposited short term in London).
- The building society market (wholesale borrowing by the building societies).

- The commercial paper market borrowing in sterling by companies, banks and other financial institutions by the issue of short-term (less than one year) 'promissory notes'. These, like bills of exchange, are sold at a discount and redeemed at their face value, but in the interim can be traded on the market at any time.

The parallel markets have grown in size and importance in recent years. The main reasons for this are (a) the opening-up of markets to international dealing, given the abolition of exchange controls in 1979, (b) the deregulation of banking and money-market dealing and (c) the volatility of interest rates and exchange rates, and thus the desire of banks to keep funds in a form that can be readily switched from one form of deposit to another, or from one currency to another. The main areas of growth have been in inter-bank deposits, certificates of deposit and the foreign currency markets.

28.3 THE SUPPLY OF MONEY

If money supply is to be monitored and possibly controlled, it is obviously necessary to measure it. But what should be included in the measure? Here we need to distinguish between the *monetary base* and *broad money*.

The **monetary base** (or 'high-powered money' or 'narrow money') consists of cash (notes and coin) in circulation outside the central bank.[1] In 1970, the stock of notes and coins in circulation in the UK was around £4 billion, equivalent to 8 per cent of annual GDP. By 2013 this had grown to over £66 billion, but equivalent to only just over 4 per cent of annual GDP.

But the monetary base gives us a very poor indication of the effective money supply, since it excludes the most important source of liquidity for spending: namely, bank deposits. The problem is which deposits to include. We need to answer three questions:

- Should we include just sight deposits, or time deposits as well?
- Should we include just retail deposits, or wholesale deposits as well?
- Should we include just bank deposits, or building society (savings institution) deposits as well?

In the past there has been a whole range of measures, each including different combinations of these accounts. However, financial deregulation, the abolition of foreign exchange controls and the development of computer technology have led to huge changes in the financial sector throughout the world. This has led to a blurring of the distinctions between different types of account. It has also made it very easy to switch deposits from one type of account to another. For these reasons, the most usual measure that countries use for money supply is **broad money**, which in most cases includes both time and sight deposits, retail and wholesale deposits, and bank and building society deposits.

In the UK this measure of broad money is known as M4. In most other European countries and the USA it is known as M3. There are, however, minor differences between countries in what is included.

In 1970, the stock of M4 in the UK was around £26 billion, equivalent to 50 per cent of annual GDP. By 2013 this had grown to £2.1 trillion, equivalent to about 140 per cent of annual GDP. As we have seen, bank deposits of one form or another constitute by far the largest component of (broad) money supply. To understand how money supply expands and contracts, and how it can be controlled, it is thus necessary to understand what determines the size of bank deposits. Banks can themselves expand the amount of bank deposits, and hence the money supply, by a process known as 'credit creation'.

The creation of credit

To illustrate this process in its simplest form, assume that banks have just one type of liability – deposits – and two types of asset – balances with the central bank (to achieve liquidity) and advances to customers (to earn profit).

Banks want to achieve profitability while maintaining sufficient liquidity. Assume that they believe that sufficient liquidity will be achieved if 10 per cent of their assets are held as balances with the central bank. The remaining 90 per cent will then be in advances to customers. In other words, the banks operate a 10 per cent liquidity ratio.

Assume initially that the combined balance sheet of the banks is as shown in Table 28.2. Total deposits are £100 billion, of which £10 billion (10 per cent) are kept in balances with the central bank. The remaining £90 billion (90 per cent) are lent to customers.

---

[1] Before 2006, there used to be a measure of narrow money called M0. This included cash in circulation outside the Bank of England and banks' non-interest-bearing 'operational balances' in the Bank of England, with these balances accounting for a tiny proportion of the whole. Since 2006, the Bank of England has allowed banks to hold interest-bearing reserve accounts, which are much larger than the former operational balances. The Bank of England thus decided to discontinue M0 as a measure and focus on cash in circulation as its measure of the monetary base.

Definitions

Monetary base Notes and coin outside the central bank.

Broad money Cash in circulation plus retail and wholesale bank and building society deposits.

Table 28.2	Banks' original balance sheet		
Liabilities	**£bn**	**Assets**	**£bn**
Deposits	100	Balances with the central bank	10
	___	Advances	90
Total	100	Total	100

Table 28.3	The initial effect of an additional deposit of £10 billion		
Liabilities	**£bn**	**Assets**	**£bn**
Deposits (old)	100	Balances with the central bank (old)	10
Deposits (new)	10	Balances with the central bank (new)	10
		Advances	90
Total	110	Total	110

Now assume that the government spends more money – £10 billion, say, on roads or education. It pays for this with cheques drawn on its account with the central bank. The people receiving the cheques deposit them in their banks. Banks return these cheques to the central bank and their balances correspondingly increase by £10 billion. The combined banks' balance sheet now is shown in Table 28.3.

But this is not the end of the story. Banks now have surplus liquidity. With their balances in the central bank having increased to £20 billion, they now have a liquidity ratio of 20/110, or 18.2 per cent. If they are to return to a 10 per cent liquidity ratio, they need only retain £11 billion as balances at the central bank (£11 billion/£110 billion = 10 per cent). The remaining £9 billion they can lend to customers.

Assume now that customers spend this £9 billion in shops and the shopkeepers deposit the cheques in their bank accounts. When the cheques are cleared, the balances in the central bank of the customers' banks will duly be debited by £9 billion, but the balances in the central bank of the shopkeepers' banks will be credited by £9 billion: leaving *overall balances in the central bank unaltered*. There is still a surplus of £9 billion over what is required to maintain the 10 per cent liquidity ratio. The new deposits of £9 in the shopkeepers' banks, backed by balances in the central bank, can thus be used as the basis for *further* loans. Ten per cent (i.e. £0.9 billion) must be kept back in the central bank, but the remaining 90 per cent (i.e. £8.1 billion) can be lent out again.

When the money is spent and the cheques are cleared, this £8.1 billion will still remain as surplus balances in the central bank and can therefore be used as the basis for yet more loans. Again, 10 per cent must be retained and the remaining 90 per cent can be lent out. This process goes on and on until eventually the position is as shown in Table 28.4.

The initial increase in balances with the central bank of £10 billion has allowed banks to create new advances (and hence deposits) of £90 billion, making a total increase in money supply of £100 billion.

This effect is known as the **bank (or bank deposits) multiplier**. In this simple example with a liquidity ratio of $^1/_{10}$ (i.e. 10 per cent), the bank deposits multiplier is 10. An initial increase in deposits of £10 billion allowed total deposits to rise by £100 billion. In this simple world, therefore, the deposits multiplier is the inverse of the liquidity ratio (L).

bank deposits multiplier = $1/L$

Table 28.4	The full effect of an additional deposit of £10 billion		
Liabilities	**£bn**	**Assets**	**£bn**
Deposits (old)	100	Balances with the central bank (old)	10
Deposits (new: initial) (new: subsequent)	10 90	Balances with the central bank (new)	10
		Advances (old)	90
	___	Advances (new)	90
Total	200	Total	200

Pause for thought

If banks choose to operate with a 5 per cent liquidity ratio and receive an extra £100 million of cash deposits: (a) What is the size of the deposits multiplier? (b) How much will total deposits have expanded after the multiplier has worked through? (c) How much will total credit have expanded?

The creation of credit: the real world

In practice, the creation of credit is not as simple as this. There are three major complications.

Banks' liquidity ratio may vary

Banks may choose a different liquidity ratio. At certain times, banks may decide that it is prudent to hold a bigger proportion of liquid assets. If Christmas or the summer holidays are approaching and people are likely to make bigger cash withdrawals, banks may decide to hold more liquid assets.

Definition

Bank (or bank deposits) multiplier The number of times greater the expansion of bank deposits is than the additional liquidity in banks that caused it: $1/L$ (the inverse of the liquidity ratio).

On the other hand, there may be an upsurge in consumer demand for credit. Banks may be very keen to grant additional loans and thus make more profits, even though they have acquired no additional assets. They may simply go ahead and expand credit, and accept a lower liquidity ratio.

Customers may not want to take up the credit on offer. Banks may wish to make additional loans, but customers may not want to borrow. There may be insufficient demand. But will the banks not then lower their interest rates, thus encouraging people to borrow? Possibly, but if they lower the rate they charge to borrowers, they must also lower the rate they pay to depositors. But then depositors may switch to other institutions such as building societies.

Banks may not operate a simple liquidity ratio

The fact that banks hold a number of fairly liquid assets, such as money at call, bills of exchange and certificates of deposit, makes it difficult to identify a simple liquidity ratio. If the banks use extra cash to buy such liquid assets, can they then use these assets as the basis for creating credit? It is largely up to banks' judgements on their overall liquidity position. In practice, therefore, the size of the bank deposits multiplier will vary and is thus difficult to predict in advance.

Some of the extra cash may be withdrawn from the banks

If extra cash comes into the banking system, and as a result extra deposits are created, part of them may be held by the public as cash *outside* the banks. In other words, some of the extra cash leaks out of the banking system. This will result in an overall ***money multiplier*** effect that is smaller than the full bank deposits multiplier.

The broad money multiplier in the UK

In the UK, the broad money multiplier is usually given by ΔM4/Δcash in circulation with the public *and* banks' interest-bearing deposits (reserve accounts) at the Bank of England.

Another indicator of the broad money multiplier is simply the ratio of the *level* of M4 relative to the cash in circulation with the public and banks' reserve accounts at the central bank. This is shown in Figure 28.4. From it, we can see how the broad money multiplier grew rapidly during the 1980s and into the beginning of the 1990s. From the early 1990s to the mid-2000s, the level of M4 relative to the monetary base fluctuated in a narrow range.

From May 2006 the Bank of England began remunerating banks' reserve accounts at the official Bank Rate. This encouraged banks to increase their reserve accounts at the Bank of England and led to a sharp fall in the broad money multiplier. But, it declined further from 2009. The significant decreases in 2009 and again in 2011/12 coincided with the Bank of England's programme of asset purchases

Definition

Money multiplier The number of times greater the expansion of money supply is than the expansion of the monetary base that caused it: ΔM4/Δmonetary base.

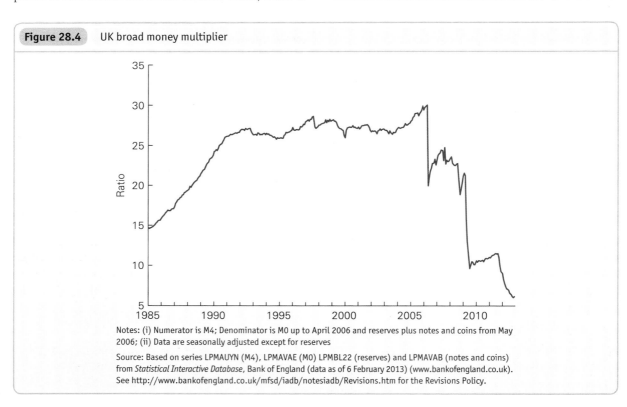

Figure 28.4 UK broad money multiplier

Notes: (i) Numerator is M4; Denominator is M0 up to April 2006 and reserves plus notes and coins from May 2006; (ii) Data are seasonally adjusted except for reserves

Source: Based on series LPMAUYN (M4), LPMAVAE (M0) LPMBL22 (reserves) and LPMAVAB (notes and coins) from *Statistical Interactive Database*, Bank of England (data as of 6 February 2013) (www.bankofengland.co.uk). See http://www.bankofengland.co.uk/mfsd/iadb/notesiadb/Revisions.htm for the Revisions Policy.

(quantitative easing) which led to an increase in banks' reserves at the Bank of England. The point is that the increase in the monetary base did not lead to the same percentage increase in broad money, as banks were more cautious about lending and chose to keep higher reserves.

In the next section we look at factors which help explain movements in the money multiplier and changes in the money supply.

What causes money supply to rise?

There are four sets of circumstances in which the money supply can rise.

Banks choose to hold a lower liquidity ratio

If banks collectively choose to hold a lower liquidity ratio, they will have surplus liquidity. The banks have tended to choose a lower liquidity ratio over time because of the increasing use of direct debits and debit-card and credit-card transactions.

Surplus liquidity can be used to expand advances, which will lead to a multiplied rise in broad money supply (e.g. M4).

An important trend in recent years has been the growth in *inter-bank lending*. Table 28.1 (see p. 464) showed that short-term loans to other banks (including overseas banks) is the largest elements in banks' liquid assets. These assets may be used by a bank as the basis for expanding loans and thereby starting a chain of credit creation. But although these assets are liquid to an *individual bank*, they do not add to the liquidity of the banking system *as a whole*. By using them for credit creation, the banking system is operating with a lower *overall* liquidity ratio.

This was a major element in the banking crisis of 2008. By operating with a collectively low liquidity ratio, banks were vulnerable to people defaulting on debt, such as mortgages. The problem was compounded by the holding of sub-prime debt in the form of securitised assets. Realising the vulnerability of other banks, banks became increasingly unwilling to lend to each other. The resulting decline in inter-bank lending reduced the amount of credit created.

Pause for thought

What effects do debit cards and cash machines (ATMs) have on (a) banks' prudent liquidity ratios; (b) the size of the bank deposits multiplier?

The non-bank private sector chooses to hold less cash

Households and firms, known collectively as the ***non-bank private sector***, may choose to hold less cash. Again, the reason may be a greater use of cards, direct debits, etc. This means that a greater proportion of the cash base will be held as deposits in banks rather in people's wallets, purses or safes outside banks. The extra cash deposits allow banks to create more credit.

The above two reasons for an expansion of broad money supply (M4) are because more credit is being created for a given monetary base. As Figure 28.4 showed, the money multiplier rose substantially in the late 1980s and early 1990s and then gradually up to 2006. The other two reasons for an expansion of money supply are reasons why the monetary base itself might expand.

An inflow of funds from abroad

Sometimes the Bank of England will choose to build up the foreign currency reserves. To do this it will buy foreign currencies on the foreign exchange market using sterling. When the recipients of this extra sterling deposit it in UK banks, or spend it on UK exports and the exporters deposit in UK banks, credit will be created on the basis of it, leading to a *multiplied* increase in money supply.

A public-sector deficit

A public-sector deficit is the difference between public-sector expenditure and public-sector receipts. To meet this deficit, the government has to borrow money by selling interest-bearing securities (Treasury bills and gilts). In general, the bigger the public sector's deficit, the greater will be the growth in the money supply. Just how the money supply will be affected, however, depends on who buys the securities.

Consider first the case where government securities are purchased by the 'non-bank private sector' (the name given to the general public and non-bank firms). The money supply will remain unchanged. When people or firms buy the bonds or bills, they will draw money from their banks. When the government spends the money, it will be redeposited in banks. There is no increase in money supply. It is just a case of existing money changing hands.

This is not the case, however, when the securities are purchased by the banking sector, including the central bank. Consider the purchase of Treasury bills by commercial banks: there will be a multiplied expansion of the money supply. The reason is that, although banks' balances at the central bank will go down when the banks purchase the bills, they will go up again when the government spends the money. In addition, the banks will now have additional liquid assets (bills), which can be used as the basis for credit creation.

The government could attempt to minimise the boost to money supply by financing the deficit through the sale of gilts, since, even if these were partly purchased by the banks, they could not be used as the basis for credit creation.

Definition

Non-bank private sector Household and non-bank firms. The category thus excludes the government and banks.

KI 27
p 292

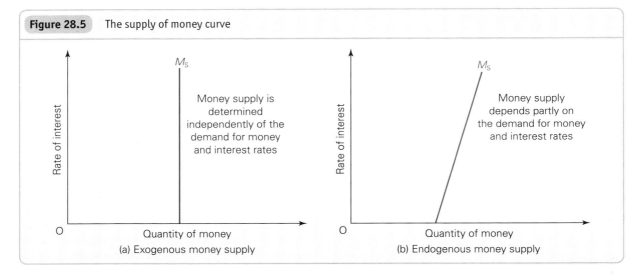

Figure 28.5 The supply of money curve

(a) Exogenous money supply — Money supply is determined independently of the demand for money and interest rates

(b) Endogenous money supply — Money supply depends partly on the demand for money and interest rates

The relationship between money supply and the rate of interest

Simple monetary theory often assumes that the supply of money is totally independent of interest rates: that money supply is *exogenous*. This is illustrated in Figure 28.5(a). The supply of money is assumed to be determined by the government or central bank ('the authorities'): what the

authorities choose it to be, or what they allow it to be by their choice of the level and method of financing the PSNCR.

In practice, money supply is *endogenous*, with higher interest rates leading to increases in the supply of money. This is illustrated in Figure 28.5(b). The argument is that the supply of money is responding to the demand for money. If people start borrowing more money, the resulting shortage of money in the banks will drive up interest rates. But if banks have surplus liquidity or are prepared to operate with a lower liquidity ratio, they will create extra credit in response to the increased demand and higher interest rates: money supply has expanded. If banks find themselves short of liquidity, they can always borrow from the central bank through repos.

28.4 THE DEMAND FOR MONEY

The demand for money refers to the desire to *hold* money: to keep your wealth in the form of money, rather than spending it on goods and services or using it to purchase financial assets such as bonds or shares. It is usual to distinguish three reasons why people want to hold their assets in the form of money.

The transactions motive. Since money is a medium of exchange, it is required for conducting transactions. But since people only receive money at intervals (e.g. weekly or

monthly) and not continuously, they require to hold balances of money in cash or in current accounts.

The precautionary motive. Unforeseen circumstances can arise, such as a car breakdown. Thus individuals often hold some additional money as a precaution. Firms too keep precautionary balances. This may be because of uncertainties about the timing of their receipts and payments. If a large customer is late in making a payment, a firm may be unable to pay its suppliers unless it has spare liquidity. But,

Definitions

Exogenous money supply Money supply that does not depend on the demand for money but is set by the authorities (i.e. the central bank or the government).

Endogenous money supply Money supply that is determined (at least in part) by the demand for money.

firms may also hold precautionary balances because of uncertainty surrounding the economic environment in which they operate.

The assets or speculative motive. Money is not just a medium of exchange, it is also a means of storing wealth (see page 461). Keeping some or all of your wealth as money in a bank account has the advantage of carrying no risk. It earns a relatively small, but safe rate of return. Some assets, such as company shares or bonds, may earn you more on average, but there is a chance that their price will fall. In other words, they are risky.

What determines the size of the demand for money?

What would cause the demand for money to rise? We now turn to examine the various determinants of the size of the demand for money (M_D). In particular we will look at the role of the rate of interest. First, however, let us identify the other determinants of the demand for money.

Money national income. The more money people earn, the greater will be their expenditure and hence the greater the transactions demand for money. A rise in money ('nominal') incomes in a country can be caused either by a rise in real GDP (i.e. real output) or by a rise in prices, or by some combination of the two.

The frequency with which people are paid. The less frequently people are paid, the greater the level of money balances that will be required to tide them over until the next payment.

Financial innovations. The increased use of credit cards, debit cards and cash machines, plus the advent of interest-paying current accounts, have resulted in changes in the demand for money. The use of credit cards reduces both the transactions and precautionary demands. Paying once a month for goods requires less money on average than paying separately for each item purchased. Moreover, the possession of a credit card reduces or even eliminates the need to hold precautionary balances for many people. On the other hand, the increased availability of cash machines, the convenience of debit cards and the ability to earn interest on current accounts have all encouraged people to hold more money in bank accounts. The net effect has been an increase in the demand for money.

Speculation about future returns on assets. The assets motive for holding money depends on people's expectations. If they believe that share prices are about to fall on the stock market, they will sell shares and hold larger balances of money in the meantime. The assets demand, therefore, can be quite high when the price of securities is considered certain to fall. Some clever (or lucky) individuals anticipated the 2007–8 stock market decline. They sold shares and 'went liquid'.

Generally, the more risky such alternatives to money become, the more will people want to hold their assets as money balances in a bank or building society.

People also speculate about changes in the exchange rate. If businesses believe that the exchange rate is about to appreciate (rise), they will hold greater balances of domestic currency in the meantime, hoping to buy foreign currencies with them when the rate has risen (since they will then get more foreign currency for their money).

The rate of interest. In terms of the operation of money markets, this is the most important determinant. It is related to the opportunity cost of holding money. The opportunity cost is the interest forgone by not holding higher interest-bearing assets, such as shares, bills or bonds. With most bank accounts today paying interest, this opportunity cost is less than in the past and thus the demand for money for assets purposes has increased.

But what is the relationship between money demand and the rate of interest? Generally, if rates of interest rise, they will rise more on shares, bills and bonds than on bank accounts. The demand for money will thus fall. The demand for money is thus *inversely* related to the rate of interest.

The demand-for-money curve

The demand-for-money curve with respect to interest rates is shown in Figure 28.6. It is downward sloping, showing that lower interest rates will encourage people to hold additional money balances (mainly for speculative purposes).

> ### Pause for thought
>
> *Which way is the demand-for-money curve likely to shift in each of the following cases? (a) Prices rise, but real incomes stay the same. (b) Interest rates abroad rise relative to domestic interest rates. (c) People anticipate that share prices are likely to fall in the near future.*

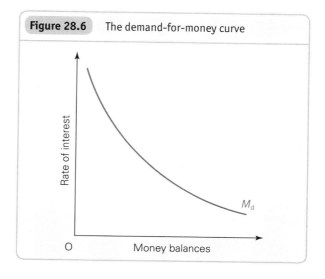

Figure 28.6 The demand-for-money curve

A change in interest rates is shown by a movement along the demand-for-money curve. A change in any other determinant of the demand for money (such as national income or expectations about exchange rate movements) will cause the whole curve to shift: a rightward shift represents an increase in demand; a leftward shift represents a decrease.

28.5 EQUILIBRIUM

Equilibrium in the money market

KI 11
p 55

Equilibrium in the money market occurs when the demand for money (M_d) is equal to the supply of money (M_s). This equilibrium is achieved through changes in the rate of interest.

In Figure 28.7, assume that the demand and supply of money are given by M_s and M_d. The equilibrium rate of interest is r_e and the equilibrium quantity of money is M_e. But why?

If the rate of interest were above r_e, people would have money balances surplus to their needs. They would use these to buy shares, bonds and other assets. This would drive up the price of these assets. But the price of assets is inversely related to interest rates. The higher the price of an asset (such as a government bond), the less will any given interest payment be as a percentage of its price (e.g. £10 as a percentage of £100 is 10 per cent, but as a percentage of £200 is only 5 per cent). Thus a higher price of assets will correspond to lower interest rates.

As the rate of interest fell, so there would be a contraction of the money supply (a movement down along the M_s curve) and an increase in the demand for money balances, especially speculative balances (a movement down along the M_d curve). The interest rate would go on falling until it reached r_e. Equilibrium would then be achieved.

Similarly, if the rate of interest were below r_e, people would have insufficient money balances. They would sell securities, thus lowering their prices and raising the rate of interest until it reached r_e.

KI 10
p 48

A shift in either the M_s or the M_d curve will lead to a new equilibrium quantity of money and rate of interest at the new intersection of the curves. For example, a rise in the supply of money will cause the rate of interest to fall, whereas a rise in the demand for money will cause the rate of interest to rise.

In practice, there is no one single interest rate. Rather equilibrium in the money markets will be where demand and supply of the various financial instruments separately balance. Nonetheless, we would generally expect different interest rates to tend to move together.

Equilibrium in the foreign exchange market

KI 10
p 48

Changes in the money supply will not only affect interest rates, they will also have an effect on exchange rates. Assume, for example, that the money supply increases. This has three direct effects:

- *Part* of the excess balances will be used to purchase foreign assets. This will therefore lead to an increase in the supply of domestic currency coming on to the foreign exchange markets.
- The excess supply of money in the domestic money market will push down the rate of interest. This will reduce the return on domestic assets below that on foreign assets. This, like the first effect, will lead to an increased demand for foreign assets and thus an increased supply of domestic currency on the foreign exchange market.
- Speculators will anticipate that the higher supply of domestic currency will cause the exchange rate to depreciate. They will therefore sell domestic currency and buy foreign currencies.

KI 13
p 71

The effect of all three is to cause the exchange rate to depreciate.

The full effect of changes in the money supply

KI 10
p 48

The effect of changes in the money supply on interest rates and exchange rates will in turn affect the level of activity in the economy. Assume that there is a rise in UK money supply. The sequence of events is as follows and is illustrated in Figure 28.8:

- A rise in money supply will lead to a fall in the rate of interest: this is necessary to restore equilibrium in the money market.

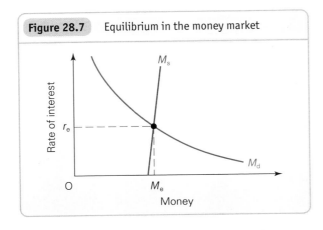

Figure 28.7 Equilibrium in the money market

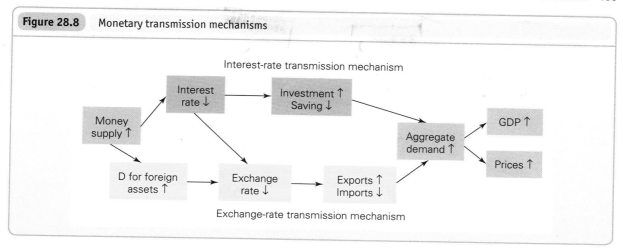

Figure 28.8 Monetary transmission mechanisms

- The fall in the rate of interest will make borrowing cheaper. This will lead to a rise in investment and other forms of borrowing. There may also be a fall in saving as saving now gives a poorer return. (See the top part of Figure 28.8.)

- The fall in the domestic rate of interest and the resulting outflow of money from the country, plus the increased demand for foreign assets resulting from the increased money supply, will cause the exchange rate to depreciate. The fall in the exchange rate will make UK exports cheaper and hence more will be sold. People in the UK will get less foreign currency for a pound. This will make imports more expensive and hence less will be purchased. (See the bottom part of Figure 28.8.)

- The rise in investment and exports will mean increased injections into the circular flow of income (see section 26.6), and the fall in imports will mean reduced withdrawals from it. The effect will be a rise in aggregate demand and a resulting rise in national income and output, and possibly a rise in prices too.

> ### Pause for thought
>
> *What determines the amount that real output rises as a result of a rise in the money supply?*

Just how much will aggregate demand, national income and prices change as a result of changes in the money supply? We will examine this in the next chapter. Then in Chapter 30 we will examine how the government can attempt to *control* the level of aggregate demand: both by changing interest rates and the money supply ('monetary policy') and by changing taxation and/or government expenditure ('fiscal policy').

SUMMARY

1   Money's main function is as a medium of exchange. In addition it is a means of storing wealth, a means of evaluation and a means of establishing the value of future claims and payments.

2a Central to the financial system are the retail and wholesale arms of banks. Between them they provide the following important functions: giving expert advice, channelling capital to areas of highest return, maturity transformation, risk transformation and the transmission of payments. Some of these banks had to be rescued by the government in 2008 – they were too important to the health of the economy to allow them to fail.

2b Banks' liabilities include both sight and time deposits. They also include certificates of deposit and repos. Their assets include: notes and coin, balances with the central bank, market loans, bills of exchange (Treasury bills and commercial bills), reverse repos, advances to customers (the biggest item – including overdrafts, personal loans, credit card debt and mortgages) and investments

(government bonds and inter-bank investments). In the years up to 2008 they had increasingly included securitised assets.

2c Banks aim to make profits, but they must also have a sufficient capital base and maintain sufficient liquidity. Liquid assets, however, tend to be relatively unprofitable and profitable assets tend to be relatively illiquid. Banks therefore need to keep a balance of profitability and liquidity in their range of assets.

2d The Bank of England is the UK's central bank. It issues notes; it acts as banker to the government, to banks and to various overseas central banks; it ensures sufficient liquidity for the financial sector; it operates the country's monetary and exchange rate policy.

2e The money market is the market in short-term deposits and loans. It consists of the discount and repo markets and the parallel money markets.

2f Through repos the Bank of England provides liquidity to the banks at the rate of interest chosen by the Monetary

▶

Policy Committee (Bank Rate). It is always prepared to lend in this way in order to ensure adequate liquidity in the economy. The financial crisis saw the Bank of England supply vast amounts of liquidity to ensure the stability of the financial system. It also adapted its operations in the money market.

2g The parallel money markets consist of various markets in short-term finance between various financial institutions.

3a Money supply can be defined in a number of different ways, depending on what items are included. A useful distinction is between narrow money and broad money. Narrow money includes just cash, and possibly banks' balances at the central bank. Broad money also includes deposits in banks and possibly various other short-term deposits in the money market. In the UK, M4 is the preferred measure of broad money. In the eurozone it is M3.

3b Bank deposits are a major proportion of broad money supply. The expansion of bank deposits is the major element in the expansion of the money supply.

3c Bank deposits expand through a process of credit creation. If banks' liquid assets increase, they can be used as a base for increasing loans. When the loans are redeposited in banks, they form the base for yet more loans, and thus takes place a process of multiple credit expansion. The ratio of the increase of deposits to an expansion of banks' liquidity base is called the 'bank multiplier'. It is the inverse of the liquidity ratio.

3d In practice it is difficult to predict the precise amount by which money supply will expand if there is an increase in cash. The reasons are that banks may choose to hold a different liquidity ratio; customers may not take up all the credit on offer; there may be no simple liquidity ratio given

the range of near money assets; and some of the extra cash may leak away into extra cash holdings by the public.

3e (Broad) money supply will rise if (a) banks choose to hold a lower liquidity ratio and thus create more credit for an existing amount of liquidity; (b) the non-bank private sector chooses to hold less cash; (c) the government runs a deficit and some of it is financed by borrowing from the banking sector; (d) there is an inflow of funds from abroad.

3f Simple monetary theory assumes that the supply of money is independent of interest rates. In practice, a rise in interest rates will often lead to an increase in money supply. But conversely, if the government raises interest rates, the supply of money may fall in response to a lower demand for money.

4a The three motives for holding money are the transactions, precautionary and assets (or speculative) motives.

4b The demand for money will be higher, (a) the higher the level of money national income (i.e. the higher the level of real national income and the higher the price level), (b) the less frequently people are paid, (c) the greater the advantages of holding money in bank accounts, such as access to cash machines and the use of debit cards, (d) the more risky alternative assets become and the more likely they are to fall in value, and the more likely the exchange rate is to rise, and (e) the lower the opportunity cost of holding money in terms of interest forgone on alternative assets.

4c The demand for money curve with respect to interest rates is downward sloping.

5 Equilibrium in the money market is where the supply of money is equal to the demand. Equilibrium is achieved through changes in the interest rate and the exchange rate.

REVIEW QUESTIONS

1 Imagine that the banking system receives additional deposits of £100 million and that all the individual banks wish to retain their current liquidity ratio of 20 per cent.

(a) How much will banks choose to lend out initially?
(b) What will happen to banks' liabilities when the money that is lent out is spent and the recipients of it deposit it in their bank accounts?
(c) How much of these latest deposits will be lent out by the banks?
(d) By how much will total deposits (liabilities) eventually have risen, assuming that none of the additional liquidity is held outside the banking sector?
(e) How much of these are matched by (i) liquid assets; (ii) illiquid assets?
(f) What is the size of the bank multiplier?
(g) If one half of any additional liquidity is held outside the banking sector, by how much less will deposits have risen compared with (d) above?

2 What is meant by the terms *narrow money* and *broad money*? Does broad money fulfil all the functions of money?

3 Why do banks hold a range of assets of varying degrees of liquidity and profitability?

4 What is meant by the securitisation of assets? How might this be (a) beneficial and (b) harmful to banks and the economy?

5 What were the causes of the credit crunch and the banking crisis of the late 2000s?

6 Define the term 'liquidity ratio'. How will changes in the liquidity ratio affect the process of credit creation? Why might a bank's liquidity ratio vary over time?

7 What is measured by the CET1 ratio? What measures would a bank need to take in order to increase its CET1 ratio?

8 Analyse the possible effects on banks' balance sheets of the following:

(a) the Basel III regulatory requirements;
(b) the UK bank levy.

9 Why might the relationship between the demand for money and the rate of interest be an unstable one?

10 What effects will the following have on the equilibrium rate of interest? (You should consider which way the demand and/or supply curves of money shift.)

(a) Banks find that they have a higher liquidity ratio than they need.
(b) A rise in incomes.
(c) A growing belief that interest rates will rise from their current level.

Business activity, employment and inflation

> ## Business issues covered in this chapter
>
> - If there is an increase in investment, how will this affect the economy?
> - Why does an increase in aggregate demand of £x lead to a rise in GDP of more than £x?
> - To what extent does a rise in the money supply lead to a rise in the economy's output (real GDP) rather than merely a rise in prices?
> - What is the relationship between unemployment and inflation? Is the relationship a stable one?
> - How do business and consumer expectations affect the relationship between inflation and unemployment? How are such expectations formed?
> - How does a policy of targeting the rate of inflation affect the relationship between inflation and unemployment?
> - What determines the course of a business cycle and its turning points? Is the business cycle caused by changes in aggregate demand, changes in aggregate supply or both?

In this chapter we examine what determines the level of business activity and why it fluctuates. We also look at the effects of business activity on employment and inflation.

We start, in section 29.1, by looking at the determinants of GDP and, in particular, the role of aggregate demand. After all, the higher the level of aggregate demand, the more will business produce in response to that demand.

In the first section we ignore the role of money and interest rates. In section 29.2, however, we show that changes in money and interest rates can have important, but possibly uncertain, effects on aggregate demand and business activity.

In sections 29.3 and 29.4, we turn to the problems of unemployment and inflation and the relationship between the two. An important influence on both of them is what people *expect* to happen. Generally, if people are optimistic and believe that the economy will grow and unemployment will fall, this will happen. Similarly, if people expect inflation to stay low, it will do. In other words, people's expectations tend to be self-fulfilling. Getting people to expect low rates of inflation is something that can lead central banks to adopt inflation rate targets (the subject of section 29.4).

Finally, in section 29.5, we examine why GDP and business activity fluctuate. In other words, we examine possible causes of the business cycle.

29.1 THE DETERMINATION OF BUSINESS ACTIVITY

How much will business as a whole produce? How many people will be employed? The analysis of output and employment, at least in the short run (one or two years), can be explained most simply in terms of the circular flow of income diagram that we examined on page 437. Figure 29.1 shows a simplified version of the circular flow with injections entering at just one point, and likewise withdrawals leaving at just one point (this simplification does not affect the argument).

If injections (*J*) do not equal withdrawals (*W*), a state of disequilibrium exists. What will bring them back into equilibrium is a change in national income (GDP) and employment.

Start with a state of equilibrium, where injections equal withdrawals. If there is now a rise in injections – say, firms decide to invest more – aggregate demand (i.e. the consumption of domestic products (C_d) plus injections (*J*)) will be higher. Firms will respond to this increased demand by using more labour and other resources and thus paying out more incomes (*Y*) to households. Household consumption will rise and so firms will sell more.

Firms will respond by producing more, and thus using more labour and other resources. Household incomes will rise again. Consumption and hence production will rise again, and so on. There will thus be a multiplied rise in incomes and employment. This is known as the ***multiplier effect***.

> **KEY IDEA 42**
> *The principle of cumulative causation.* An initial event can cause an ultimate effect which is much larger.

The process, however, does not go on for ever. Each time household incomes rise, households save more, pay more taxes and buy more imports. In other words, withdrawals rise. When withdrawals have risen to match the increase in injections, equilibrium will be restored and national income (GDP) and employment will stop rising. The process can be summarised as follows:

$$J > W \rightarrow Y\uparrow \rightarrow W\uparrow \text{ until } J = W$$

Similarly, an initial fall in injections (or rise in withdrawals) will lead to a multiplied fall in GDP and employment:

$$J < W \rightarrow Y\downarrow \rightarrow W\downarrow, \text{ until } J = W$$

Thus equilibrium in the circular flow of income can be at *any* level of GDP and employment.

Identifying the equilibrium level of GDP

KI 11 p 55

Equilibrium can be shown on a 'Keynesian 45° line diagram'. This is named after the great economist, John Maynard Keynes (1883–1946). Keynes argued that GDP is determined by aggregate demand. A rise in aggregate demand will cause GDP to rise; a fall in aggregate demand will cause GDP to fall.

Equilibrium GDP can be at any level of capacity. If aggregate demand is buoyant, equilibrium GDP can be where businesses are operating at full capacity with full employment. If aggregate demand is low, however, equilibrium GDP can be at well below full capacity with high unemployment (i.e. a recession). Keynes argued that it is important, therefore, for governments to manage the level of aggregate demand to avoid recessions.

The 45° line diagram plots various elements of the circular flow of income, such as consumption, withdrawals, injections and aggregate demand, against GDP (national income).

In Figure 29.2 two continuous lines are shown. The 45° line out from the origin plots $C_d + W$ against GDP. It is a 45° line because, by definition, GDP = $C_d + W$. To understand this, consider what can happen to the income earned from GDP: either it must be spent on domestically produced goods (C_d) or it must be withdrawn from the circular flow – there is nothing else that can happen to it. Thus if GDP were £100 billion, then $C_d + W$ must also be £100 billion. If you draw a line such that whatever value is plotted on the horizontal axis (GDP) is also plotted on the vertical axis ($C_d + W$), the line will be at 45° (assuming that the axes are drawn to the same scale).

The other continuous line plots aggregate demand. In this diagram it is known as the *aggregate expenditure line* (*E*). It consists of $C_d + J$: in other words, the total spending on domestic firms.

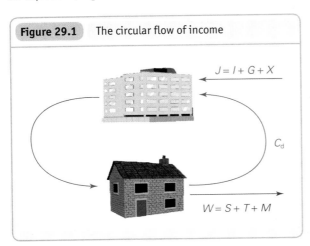

Figure 29.1 The circular flow of income

$J = I + G + X$

C_d

$W = S + T + M$

> **Definition**
>
> **Multiplier effect** An initial increase in aggregate demand of £*xm* leads to an eventual rise in national income that is greater than £*xm*.

Figure 29.2 Equilibrium GDP

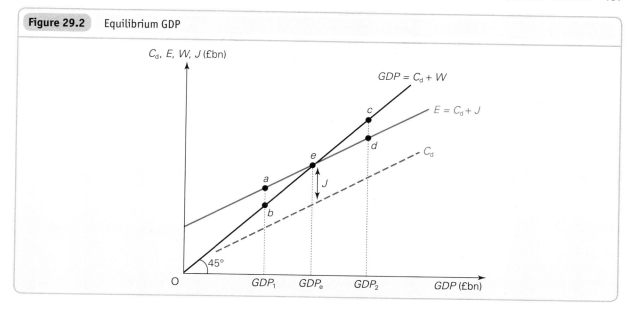

To show how this line is constructed, consider the dashed line. This shows C_d. It is flatter than the 45° line. The reason is that for any given rise in GDP and hence people's incomes, only *part* will be spent on domestic products, while the remainder will be withdrawn: i.e. C_d rises less quickly than GDP. The E line consists of $C_d + J$. But we have assumed that J is constant with respect to changes in GDP. Thus the E line is simply the C_d line shifted upward by the amount of J.

If aggregate expenditure exceeded GDP, at say GDP_1, there would be excess demand in the economy (of $a - b$). In other words, people would be buying more than was currently being produced. Firms would thus find their stocks dwindling and would therefore increase their level of production. In doing so, they would employ more factors of production. GDP would thus rise. As it did so, C_d and hence E would rise. There would be a movement up along the E line. But because not all the extra incomes earned from the rise in GDP would be consumed (i.e. some would be withdrawn), expenditure would rise less quickly than income: the E line is flatter than the GDP line. As income rises towards GDP_e, the gap between the GDP and E lines gets smaller. Once point e is reached, GDP = E. There is then no further tendency for GDP to rise.

If GDP exceeded aggregate expenditure, at say GDP_2, there would be insufficient demand for the goods and services currently being produced ($c - d$). Firms would find their stocks of unsold goods building up. They would thus respond by producing less and employing less factors of production. GDP would thus fall and go on falling until GDP_e was reached.

The multiplier

KI 42
p 486 When aggregate expenditure rises, this will cause GDP to rise. But by how much? The answer is that there will be a *multiplied* rise in GDP: i.e. it will rise by more than the rise in aggregate expenditure. The size of the **multiplier** is given by the letter k, where:

$$k = \Delta GDP/\Delta E$$

Thus, if aggregate expenditure rose by £10 million (ΔE) and as a result GDP rose by £30 million (ΔGDP), the multiplier would be 3. Figure 29.3 is drawn on the assumption that the multiplier is 3.

Assume in Figure 29.3 that aggregate expenditure rises by £20 billion, from E_1 to E_2. This could be caused by a rise in injections, or by a fall in withdrawals (and hence a rise in consumption of domestically produced goods) or by some combination of the two. Equilibrium GDP rises by £60 billion, from £100 billion to £160 billion (where the E_2 line crosses the GDP line).

What determines the size of the multiplier? The answer is that it depends on the 'marginal propensity to consume domestically produced goods' (mpc_d). The mpc_d is the proportion of any rise in GDP that gets spent on domestically produced goods (in other words the proportion that is not withdrawn as saving, taxes or spending on imports).

$$mpc_d = \Delta C_d/\Delta GDP$$

In Figure 29.3, $mpc_d = \Delta C_d/\Delta GDP = £40bn/£60bn = 2/3$ (i.e. the slope of the C_d line). The higher the mpc_d the greater the proportion of income generated from GDP that

Definition

The multiplier The number of times a rise in GDP (ΔGDP) is bigger than the initial rise in aggregate expenditure (ΔE) that caused it. Using the letter k to stand for the multiplier, the multiplier is defined as $k = \Delta GDP/\Delta E$.

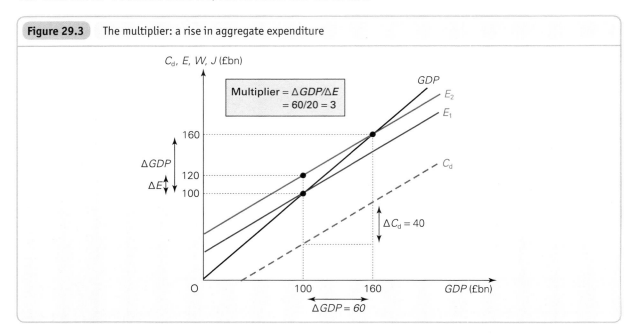

Figure 29.3 The multiplier: a rise in aggregate expenditure

recirculates around the circular flow of income and thus generates extra output.

The **multiplier formula** is given by:

$$k = \frac{1}{1 - mpc_d}$$

In our example, with $mpc_d = {}^2\!/_3$

$$k = \frac{1}{1 - {}^2\!/_3} = \frac{1}{{}^1\!/_3} = 3$$

If the mpc_d were ${}^3\!/_4$, the multiplier would be 4. Thus the higher the mpc_d, the higher the multiplier.

29.2 THE RELATIONSHIP BETWEEN MONEY AND GDP

In this section we examine how changes in the money supply affect GDP. One of the simplest ways of understanding this relationship is in terms of the 'equation of exchange'.

The equation of exchange

The **equation of exchange** shows the relationship between the money value of spending and the money value of output (nominal GDP). This identity may be expressed as follows:

$$MV = PY$$

M is the supply of money in the economy (e.g. M4). V is its **velocity of circulation**. This is the number of times per year that money is spent on buying goods and services that have been produced in the economy that year (real GDP). P is the level of prices of domestically produced goods and services, expressed as an index, where the index is 1 in a chosen base year (e.g. 2000). Thus if prices

today are double those in the base year, P is 2. Y is *real* national income (real GDP): in other words, the quantity of national output produced in that year measured in base-year prices.

PY is thus *nominal* GDP: i.e. GDP measured at current prices. For example, if GDP at base-year prices (Y) is £1 trillion and the price index is 2, then GDP at current prices (PY) is £2 trillion.

> ### Pause for thought
>
> *If the money supply is cut by 10 per cent, what must happen to the velocity of circulation if there is no change in GDP at current prices?*

MV is the total spending on the goods and services that make up GDP – in other words, (nominal) aggregate demand. For example, if money supply is £500 billion, and money, as it passes from one person to another, is spent on average three times a year on national output, then total spending (*MV*) is £1.5 trillion a year. But this too *must* equal GDP at current prices. The reason is that what is spent on output (by consumers, by firms on investment, by the government or by people abroad on exports) must equal the value of goods produced (*PY*).

The equation of exchange (or 'quantity equation') is true by definition. *MV* is *necessarily* equal to *PY* because of the way the terms are defined. Thus a rise in *MV* *must* be accompanied by a rise in *PY*. What a change in *M* does to *P*, however, is a matter of debate. The controversy centres on the impact of changes in the money supply on aggregate demand and then on the impact of changes in aggregate demand on output.

Money supply and aggregate demand

The short run

Chapter 28 identified two ways in which changes in the money supply could affect aggregate demand: the interest-rate and exchange-rate transmission mechanisms. Taken together, the impact of an increase in the money supply can be summarised as follows:

1. A rise in money supply will lead to a fall in the rate of interest.
2. The fall in the rate of interest will lead to a rise in investment and other forms of borrowing. It will also lead to a fall in the exchange rate and hence a rise in exports and a fall in imports.
3. The rise in investment, and the rise in exports and fall in imports, will mean a rise in aggregate demand.

However, there is considerable debate over how these transmission mechanisms function.

How interest-rate sensitive is money demand? The demand for money as a means of storing wealth (the assets motive) can be large and highly responsive to changes in interest rates on alternative assets. Indeed, large sums of money move around the money market as firms and financial institutions respond to and anticipate changes in interest rates. Thus, with an increase in money supply, only a relatively small fall in interest rates on bonds and other assets may be necessary to persuade people to hold all the extra money in bank accounts, thereby greatly slowing down

the average speed at which money circulates. The fall in *V* may virtually offset the rise in *M*.

In other words, the more sensitive is the demand for money to changes in the rate of interest, the less impact changes in money supply have on aggregate demand.

How stable is the money demand function? Another criticism is that the demand for money is unstable. People hold speculative balances of money when they anticipate that the prices of other assets, such as shares, bonds and bills, will fall (and hence the rate of return or interest on these assets will rise).

There are many factors that could affect such expectations, such as changes in foreign interest rates, changes in exchange rates, statements of government intentions on economic policy, good or bad industrial news, or newly published figures on inflation or money supply. With an unstable demand for money, it is difficult to predict the effect of a change in money supply on interest rates and so aggregate demand.

It is largely for this reason that most central banks usually prefer to control interest rates directly, rather than indirectly by controlling the money supply. (We examine the conduct of monetary policy in section 30.2.)

How interest-rate sensitive is spending? The problem here is that investment may be insensitive to changes in interest rates. Businesses are more likely to be influenced in their decision to invest by predictions of the future buoyancy of markets. Interest rates do have *some* effect on businesses' investment decisions, but the effect is unpredictable, depending on the confidence of investors.

Where interest rates are likely to have a stronger effect on spending is via mortgages. If interest rates go up, and mortgage rates follow suit, people will suddenly be faced with higher monthly repayments (debt servicing costs) and will therefore have to cut down their expenditure on goods and services.

How interest-rate sensitive is the exchange rate? Also the amount that the exchange rate will depreciate is uncertain, since exchange rate movements (as we saw in Chapter 27) depend crucially on expectations about trade prospects and about future world interest rate movements. Thus the effects on imports and exports are also uncertain.

To summarise: the effects on total spending of a change in the money supply *might* be quite strong, but they could be weak. In other words, the effects are highly unpredictable. Therefore, the control of the money supply can be an unreliable means of controlling aggregate demand – at least in the short run.

And yet (as we shall see in Chapter 30), at the end of the 2000s and into the early 2010s central banks around the world, including the Bank of England, embarked on a process of increasing the money supply. As national economies shrank and growth remained elusive, the hope was that financial institutions would ease the very tight credit conditions that had resulted from the global financial crisis and so help to boost aggregate demand. Its impact was to depend crucially on the behaviour of the private sector as, in many countries, governments were simultaneously tightening the purse strings in order to reduce often very large public-sector deficits. The private-sector response was to depend, in part, on the willingness of banks to provide additional credit and the willingness of households and businesses to accept this credit and to increase their spending.

The long run

In the long run, there is a stronger link between money supply and aggregate demand. In fact, 'monetarists' claim that in the long run V is determined *totally independently* of the money supply (M). Thus an increase in M will leave V unaffected and hence will directly increase expenditure (MV). But why do they claim this?

If money supply increases over the longer term, people will have more money than they require to hold. They will spend this surplus. Much of this spending will go on goods and services, thereby directly increasing aggregate demand.

The theoretical underpinning for this is given by the *theory of portfolio balance*. People have a number of ways of holding their wealth. They can hold it as money, or as financial assets such as bills, bonds and shares, or as physical assets such as houses, cars and televisions. In other words, people hold a whole portfolio of assets of varying degrees of liquidity – from cash to central heating.

If money supply expands, people will find themselves holding more money than they require: their portfolios are 'unnecessarily liquid'. Some of this money will be used to purchase financial assets and some, possibly after a period of time, to purchase *goods and services*. As more assets are purchased, this will drive up their price. This will effectively reduce their 'yield'. For bonds and other *financial* assets, this means a reduction in their rate of interest. For goods and services, it means an increase in their price relative to their usefulness.

The process will stop when a balance has been restored in people's portfolios. In the meantime, there will have been extra consumption and hence an increase in aggregate demand.

How will a change in aggregate demand affect output and prices?

So if changes in the money supply were to affect aggregate demand – though our discussion above shows that this cannot be taken as given – how would this then affect the economy's output? What effect would it have on prices?

Many economists argue that aggregate supply (GDP) is relatively responsive in the short run to increases in aggregate demand, provided there is slack in the economy. Similarly, reductions in aggregate demand are likely to lead to reductions in GDP. Many also argue, however, that aggregate supply is inelastic in the *long run*; that potential GDP is determined largely or wholly independently of aggregate demand. In the long run, therefore, any rise in MV will be mainly or totally reflected in a rise in prices (P).

In the long run, according to this view, the stock of money therefore determines the price level, and the rate of increase in money supply determines the rate of inflation. It is thus important to ensure that money supply is kept under control if inflation is to be avoided.

(We examine monetary policy in section 30.2.)

29.3 UNEMPLOYMENT AND INFLATION

We turn now to examine the relationship between aggregate demand and both inflation and unemployment. (You might find it useful first to revise sections 26.3 to 26.5.)

Unemployment and inflation in the simple Keynesian model

'Full-employment' GDP

In the simple 'Keynesian' theory that we outlined in section 29.1, it is assumed that there is a maximum normal level of GDP that can be obtained at any one time. If equilibrium GDP is at this level, there will be no deficiency of aggregate demand and hence no disequilibrium unemployment. This level of GDP is referred to as the *full-employment level of GDP* (GDP_F). (In practice, there would still be some unemployment at this level because of the existence of equilibrium unemployment – structural, frictional and seasonal.)

The deflationary gap

If the equilibrium level of GDP (GDP_e) is below the full-employment level (GDP_F), there will be excess capacity in the economy and hence demand-deficient unemployment. This situation is illustrated in Figure 29.4(a). If GDP is to be raised from GDP_e to GDP_F, aggregate expenditure (E) will have to be raised, either by increasing injections or by reducing withdrawals, so as to close the gap $a - b$. This gap is known as the *recessionary or deflationary gap*.

> ### Definitions
>
> **Full-employment level of GDP** The level of GDP at which there is no deficiency of demand.
>
> **Recessionary or deflationary gap** The shortfall of aggregate expenditure below GDP at the full-employment level of GDP.

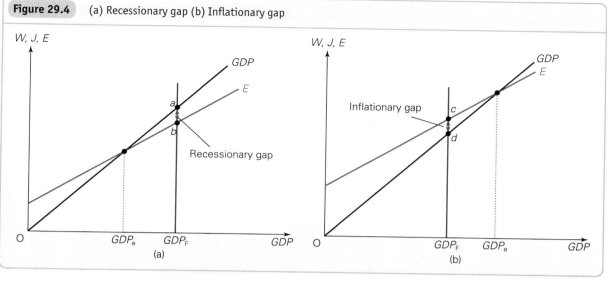

Figure 29.4 (a) Recessionary gap (b) Inflationary gap

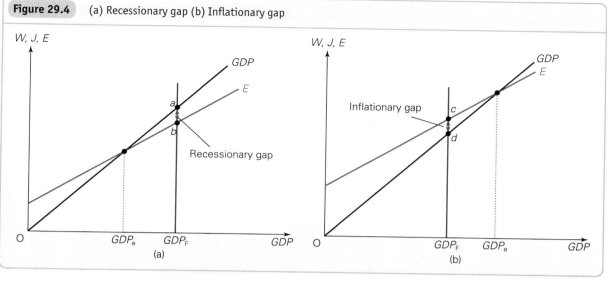

Note that the size of the recessionary gap is *less* than the amount by which GDP_e falls short of GDP_F. This is another illustration of the multiplier. If aggregate expenditure is raised by $a - b$, GDP will rise by $GDP_F - GDP_e$. The multiplier is thus given by:

$$\frac{GDP_F - GDP_e}{a - b}$$

The inflationary gap

If, at the full-employment level of GDP, aggregate expenditure *exceeds* GDP, there will be a problem of excess demand. GDP_e will be above GDP_F. The problem is that GDP_F represents an effective limit to output, other than in the very short term. GDP can only expand beyond this point by firms operating at above normal capacity levels – by employing people overtime or taking other temporary measures to boost output. The result will be demand-pull inflation.

This situation involves an ***inflationary gap***. This is the amount by which aggregate expenditure exceeds national income at the full-employment level of national income. It is illustrated by the gap $c - d$ in Figure 29.4(b). To eliminate this inflation, the inflationary gap must be closed, either by raising withdrawals or by lowering injections.

Many economists thus advocate an active policy of 'demand management': raising aggregate demand (for example, by raising government expenditure or lowering taxes) to close a deflationary gap, and reducing aggregate demand to close an inflationary gap. We explore these 'demand-side' policies in the next chapter).

Unemployment and inflation at the same time

The simple analysis of recessionary and inflationary gaps implies that the aggregate supply curve looks like AS_1 in Figure 29.5. (See pages 432–3 to remind yourself about aggregate demand and supply analysis.) Up to GDP_F, output and employment can rise with no rise in prices at all. The deflationary gap is being closed. At GDP_F no further rises in output are possible. Any further rise in aggregate demand is entirely reflected in higher prices. An inflationary gap opens. In other words, this implies that either inflation *or* unemployment can occur, but not both simultaneously.

> ### Pause for thought
>
> *Assume that full-employment GDP is £500 billion and that current GDP is £450 billion. Assume also that the mpcd is ⁴/₅. (a) Is there an inflationary or deflationary gap? (b) What is the size of this gap?*

> ### Definition
>
> **Inflationary gap** The excess of aggregate expenditure over GDP at the full-employment level of GDP.

Figure 29.5 Unemployment and inflation

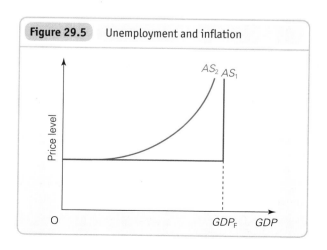

Two important qualifications need to be made to this analysis to explain the occurrence of both unemployment *and* inflation at the same time.

First, there are *other* types of inflation and unemployment not caused by an excess or deficiency of aggregate demand:

for example, cost-push and expectations-generated inflation; frictional and structural unemployment. Box 29.1 looks at the actual relationship between the rate of inflation and the amount of excess or deficient demand, as measured by output gaps, in the UK since the early 1970s.

BOX 29.1 | **MIND THE GAP**

Do output gaps explain inflation?

Chapter 26 introduced the concept of output gaps. An output gap measures the difference between an economy's actual level of output and its potential output (the output level when the economy is operating at 'normal capacity utilisation'). A positive output gap shows that the level of actual output is *greater* than the potential level, while a negative output gap shows that the level of output is *below* the potential level.

The magnitude of the output gap, which is usually expressed as a percentage of potential output, enables us to assess the extent of any demand-deficiency (negative output gap) or the extent of excess demand (positive output gap).

In Chapter 26 we also introduced the aggregate supply curve: the relationship between the economy's general price level and the total output by firms. The slope of the short-run aggregate supply is thought to be affected by the amount of slack in the economy. As the economy approaches or exceeds its potential output, the aggregate supply curve is likely to get steeper as firms' marginal costs rise faster. Consequently, increases in demand at output levels close to or in excess of an economy's potential output will exert more upward pressure on prices than if the economy has a more significant amount of slack. This suggests that the rate of price inflation is positively related to the size of the output gap.

The chart plots the output gap (as a percentage of potential output) and the annual rate of economy-wide inflation (rate of increase of the GDP deflator) for the UK since the early 1970s.

It would appear that for the period from the early 1970s to the end of the 1980s there was a *positive* correlation between output gaps and inflation rates, albeit that turning points in the rates of inflation lag those in the size of output gaps – in other words, it took time for price pressure to fully work through the economy. This reflects, in part, the fact that some prices, such as wage rates, are adjusted relatively infrequently.

Since the 1990s, however, the relationship between output gaps and inflation rates is less clear. Indeed, for much of the rest of the period, there is a general reduction in inflation rates regardless of the size of output gaps. This demonstrates that there are several potential influences on rates of inflation.

One explanation is a *reduction in cost-push pressures* – at least until the mid to late 2000s (see Box 26.3). First, labour markets became more competitive and flexible. Second, firms faced greater competition from the EU, China and many other countries in an increasingly globalised market.

Another explanation is *inflation rate expectations*. If policy-makers are perceived as making credible (i.e. trusted) low inflation rate announcements by those that enter into discussions on prices, such as unions and firms when negotiating wage rates, then inflation rates will be lower. A good example of this is the adoption of clear inflation targets by central banks, such as the Bank of England and the ECB.

 What factors may have resulted in the lower inflation rates experienced by the UK and France from the 1990s?

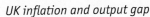

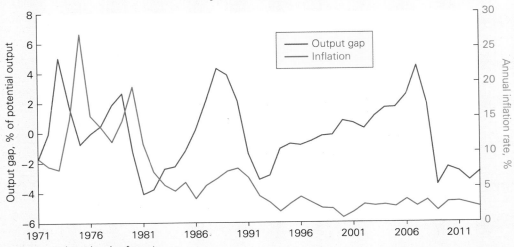

UK inflation and output gap

Notes: 2012 and 2013 based on forecasts

Source: Output gap data from *Economic Outlook* (OECD); Inflation series based on data from *AMECO database*, European Commission, DGECFIN

Thus, even if a government could manipulate GDP so as to get GDP_e and GDP_F to coincide, this would not eliminate all inflation and unemployment – only demand-pull inflation and demand-deficient unemployment. For this reason governments may choose to use a whole package of policies, each tailored to the specific type of problem.

Second, not all firms operate with the same degree of slack. A rise in aggregate demand can lead to *both* a reduction in unemployment *and* a rise in prices: some firms responding to the rise in demand by taking up slack and hence increasing output; other firms, having little or no slack, responding by raising prices; others doing both. Similarly, labour markets have different degrees of slack and therefore the rise in demand will lead to various mixes of higher wages and lower unemployment.

Thus the *AS* curve will look like AS_2 in Figure 29.5.

The Phillips curve

The relationship between inflation and unemployment was examined by A. W. Phillips in 1958. He showed the statistical relationship between wage inflation and unemployment in the UK from 1861 to 1957. With wage inflation on the vertical axis and the unemployment rate on the horizontal axis, a scatter of points was obtained. Each point represented the observation for a particular year. The curve that best fitted the scatter has become known as the **Phillips curve**. It is illustrated in Figure 29.6 and shows an inverse relationship between inflation and unemployment.

Given that wage increases over the period were approximately 2 per cent above price increases (made possible by increases in labour productivity), a similar-shaped, but lower curve could be plotted showing the relationship between *price* inflation and unemployment.

The curve has often used to illustrate the short-run effects of changes in (real) aggregate demand. When aggregate demand rose (relative to potential output), inflation rose and unemployment fell: there was an upward movement along the curve. When aggregate demand fell, there was a downward movement along the curve.

The Phillips curve was bowed in to the origin. The usual explanation for this is that as aggregate demand expanded, at first there would be plenty of surplus labour, which could be employed to meet the extra demand without the need to raise wage rates very much. But as labour became increasingly scarce, firms would find that they had to offer increasingly higher wage rates to obtain

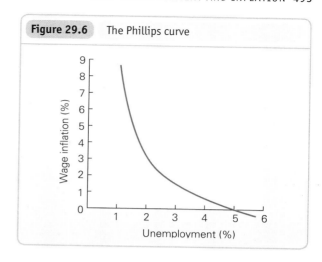

Figure 29.6 The Phillips curve

the labour they required, and the position of trade unions would be increasingly strengthened.

The *position* of the Phillips curve depended on *non-demand* factors causing inflation and unemployment: frictional and structural unemployment; and cost-push, and expectations-generated inflation. If any of these non-demand factors changed so as to raise inflation or unemployment, the curve would shift outward to the right.

The Phillips curve seemed to present governments with a simple policy choice. They could trade off inflation against unemployment. Lower unemployment could be bought at the cost of higher inflation, and *vice versa*. Unfortunately, the experience since the late 1960s has suggested that no such simple relationship exists beyond the short run.

From about 1967 the Phillips curve relationship seemed to break down. The UK, along with many other countries in the Western world, began to experience growing unemployment *and* higher rates of inflation as well.

Figure 29.7 shows price inflation and unemployment in the UK from 1960 to 2012. From 1960 to 1967 a curve similar to the Phillips curve can be fitted through the data. From 1967 to the early 1990s, however, no simple picture emerges. Certainly the original Phillips curve could no longer fit the data; but whether the curve shifted to the right and then back again somewhat (the broken lines), or whether the relationship broke down completely, or whether there was some quite different relationship between inflation and unemployment, is not clear by simply looking at the data.

Since 1997 the Bank of England has been targeting consumer price inflation (see section 29.4). For much of this period, the 'curve' would seem to have become a virtually horizontal straight line at the targeted rate! However, from the late 2000s, against a backdrop of marked economic volatility, the range of inflation rates increased despite inflation rate targeting. Nonetheless, many economists continue to argue that expectations concerning future inflation rates are an important influence on the inflation–unemployment relationship.

Definition

Phillips curve A curve showing the relationship between (price) inflation and unemployment. The original Phillips curve plotted *wage* inflation against unemployment for the years 1861–1957.

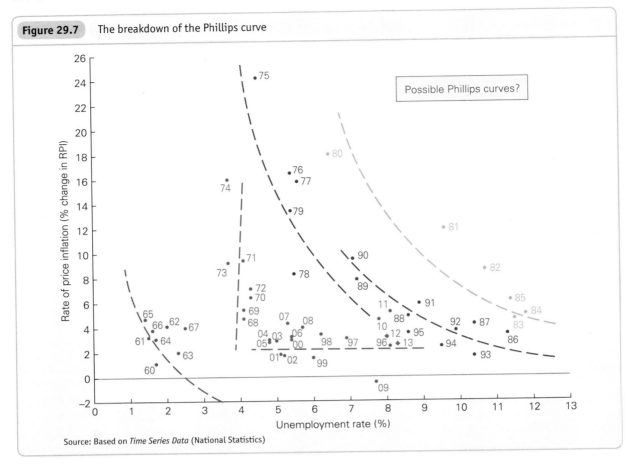

Figure 29.7 The breakdown of the Phillips curve

Source: Based on *Time Series Data* (National Statistics)

One way of incorporating expectations into this relationship is through an 'expectations-augmented' Phillips curve.

The effect of expectations

In its simplest form, the ***expectations-augmented Phillips curve*** is given by the following:

$$\pi = f(1/U) + \pi^e$$

What this states is that inflation (π) depends on two things:

- The inverse of unemployment ($1/U$). This is simply the normal Phillips curve relationship. The higher the rate of (demand-deficient) unemployment, the lower the rate of inflation.
- The expected rate of inflation (π^e). The higher the rate of inflation that people expect, the higher will be the

level of wage demands and the more willing will firms be to raise prices. Thus the higher will be the actual rate of inflation and thus the vertically higher will be the whole Phillips curve.

Let us assume for simplicity that the rate of inflation people expect this year (π_t^e) (where t represents the current time period: i.e. this year) is the same rate that inflation actually was last year (π_{t-1}).

$$\pi_t^e = \pi_{t-1}$$

Thus if unemployment is such as to push up prices by 4 per cent ($f(1/U) = 4\%$) and if last year's inflation was 6 per cent, then inflation this year will be 4 per cent + 6 per cent = 10 per cent.

The accelerationist theory of inflation

Let us trace the course of inflation and expectations over a number of years in an imaginary economy. To keep the analysis simple, assume there is no growth in the economy.

Year 1. Assume that at the outset, in year 1, there is no inflation at all; that none is expected; that $AD = AS$; and that equilibrium unemployment is 8 per cent. The economy will be at point a in Figure 29.8 and Table 29.1.

Definition

Expectations-augmented Phillips curve A (short-run) Phillips curve whose position depends on the expected rate of inflation.

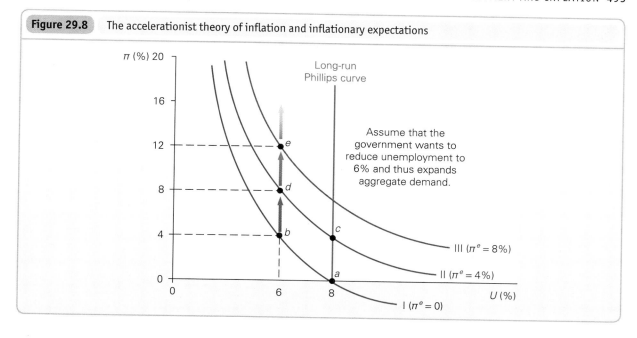

Figure 29.8 The accelerationist theory of inflation and inflationary expectations

Table 29.1 The accelerationist theory of inflation and inflationary expectations

Year	Point on graph	π	=	$f(1/U)$	+	π^e
1	a	0	=	0	+	0
2	b	4	=	4	+	0
3	c	4	=	0	+	4
4	d	8	=	4	+	4
5	e	12	=	4	+	8

Year 2. Now assume that the government expands aggregate demand in order to reduce unemployment. Unemployment falls to 6 per cent. The economy moves to point *b* along curve I. Inflation has risen to 4 per cent, but people, basing their expectations of inflation on year 1, still expect zero inflation. There is therefore no shift as yet in the Phillips curve. Curve I corresponds to an expected rate of inflation of zero.

Year 3. People now revise their expectations of inflation to the level of year 2. The Phillips curve shifts up by 4 percentage points to position II. If nominal aggregate demand (i.e. demand purely in money terms, irrespective of the level of prices) continues to rise at the same rate, the whole of the increase will now be absorbed in higher prices. *Real* aggregate demand will fall back to its previous level and the economy will move to point *c*. Unemployment will return to 8 per cent. There is no *demand-pull* inflation now ($f(1/U) = 0$), but inflation is still 4 per cent due to expectations ($\pi^e = 4\%$).

Year 4. Assume now that the government expands *real* aggregate demand again so as to reduce unemployment once

more to 6 per cent. This time it must expand nominal aggregate demand *more* than it did in year 2, because this time, as well as reducing unemployment, it also has to validate the 4 per cent expected inflation. The economy moves to point *d* along curve II. Inflation is now 8 per cent.

Year 5 onwards. Expected inflation is now 8 per cent (the rate of actual inflation in year 4). The Phillips curve shifts up to position III. If at the same time the government tries to keep unemployment at 6 per cent, it must expand nominal aggregate demand 4 per cent faster in order to validate the 8 per cent expected inflation. The economy moves to point *e* along curve III. Inflation is now 12 per cent.

To keep unemployment at 6 per cent, the government must continue to increase nominal aggregate demand by 4 per cent more than the previous year. As the expected inflation rate goes on rising, the Phillips curve will go on shifting up each year.

Thus in order to keep unemployment below the initial equilibrium rate, inflation must go on *accelerating* each year. For this reason, this theory of the Phillips curve is sometimes known as the ***accelerationist theory***.

The more the government reduces unemployment, the greater the rise in inflation that year, and the more the rise in expectations the following year and each subsequent year; and hence the more rapidly will price rises accelerate. Thus the true longer-term trade-off is between unemployment and the rate of increase in inflation.

Definition

Accelerationist theory The theory that unemployment can only be reduced below the natural rate at the cost of accelerating inflation.

Pause for thought

What determines how rapidly the short-run Phillips curves in Figure 29.8 shift upwards?

The long-run Phillips curve and the natural rate of unemployment

As long as there are demand-pull pressures ($f(1/U) > 0$), inflation will accelerate as the expected rate of inflation (π^e) rises. In the long run, therefore, the Phillips curve will be vertical at the rate of unemployment where *real* aggregate demand equals *real* aggregate supply. This is the *equilibrium* rate of unemployment. It is also known as the **natural rate** or the **non-accelerating-inflation rate of unemployment (NAIRU)**. In Figure 29.8 the equilibrium rate of unemployment is 8 per cent.

The implication for government policy is that expanding aggregate demand can reduce unemployment below the equilibrium rate only in the *short* run. In the long run, the effect will be purely inflationary. On the other hand, a policy of restraining aggregate demand, for example by restraining the growth in the money supply, will *not* in the long run lead to higher unemployment: it will simply lead to lower inflation at the equilibrium rate of unemployment. The implication is that governments should make it a priority to control money supply, perhaps through targeting the size of the public-sector deficit, and thereby nominal aggregate demand and inflation.

Rational expectations

One group, known as 'new classical' economists, go further than the monetarist theory described above. They argue that even the short-run Phillips curve is vertical: that there is *no* trade-off between unemployment and inflation, even in the short run. They base their arguments on two key assumptions:

■ Prices and wage rates are flexible and thus markets clear very rapidly. This means that there will be no disequilibrium unemployment, even in the short run. All unemployment will be equilibrium unemployment – or 'voluntary unemployment' as new classical economists prefer to call it.

■ Expectations are 'rational', but are based on imperfect information.

In the accelerationist theory, expectations are based on *past* information and thus take time to catch up with changes in aggregate demand. Thus for a short time a rise in nominal aggregate demand will raise output and reduce unemployment below the equilibrium rate, while prices and wages are still relatively low.

The new classical analysis is based on **rational expectations**. Rational expectations are not based on past rates of inflation. Instead they are based on the current state of the economy and the current policies being pursued by the government. Workers and firms look at the information available to them – at the various forecasts that are published, at various economic indicators and the assessments of them by various commentators, at government pronouncements, and so on. From this information they predict the rate of inflation as well as they can. It is in this sense that the expectations are 'rational': people use their reason to assess the future on the basis of current information.

But forecasters frequently get it wrong, and so do economic commentators! And the government does not always do what it says it will. Thus workers and firms will be basing expectations on *imperfect information*. The crucial point about the rational expectations theory, however, is that these errors in prediction are *random*. People's predictions of inflation are just as likely to be too high as too low.

If the government raises aggregate demand in an attempt to reduce unemployment, people will anticipate that this will lead to higher prices and wages, and that there will be *no* effect on output and employment. If their expectations of higher inflation are correct, this will thus *fully* absorb the increase in nominal aggregate demand such that there will have been no increase in *real* aggregate demand at all. Firms will not produce any more output or employ any more people: after all, why should they? If they anticipate that people will spend 10 per cent more money but that prices will rise by 10 per cent, their *volume* of sales will remain the same.

Output and employment will only rise, therefore, if people make an error in their predictions (i.e. if they underpredict the rate of inflation and interpret an increase in money spent as an increase in *real* demand). But they are as likely to *over*predict the rate of inflation, in which case output and employment will fall! Thus there is no systematic trade-off between inflation and unemployment, even in the short run.

Definitions

Natural rate of unemployment or **non-accelerating-inflation rate of unemployment (NAIRU)** The rate of unemployment consistent with a constant rate of inflation: the rate of unemployment at which the vertical long-run Phillips curve cuts the horizontal axis.

Rational expectations Expectations based on the *current* situation. These expectations are based on the information people have to hand. While this information may be imperfect and therefore people will make errors, these errors will be random.

Pause for thought

For what reasons would a new classical economist support the policy of the Bank of England publishing its inflation forecasts and the minutes of the deliberations of the Monetary Policy Committee?

Expectations of output and employment

Many economists, especially those who would describe themselves as 'Keynesian', criticise the approach of focusing exclusively on price expectations. Expectations, they argue, influence *output* and *employment* decisions, not just pricing decisions.

If there is a gradual but sustained expansion of aggregate demand, firms, seeing the economy expanding and seeing their orders growing, will start to invest more and make longer-term plans for expanding their labour force. Business and consumers will generally *expect* a higher level of output,

and this optimism will cause businesses to produce more. In other words, expectations will affect output and employment as well as prices. Similarly, if businesses anticipate a recession, they are likely to cut back on production and investment.

Graphically, the increased output and employment from the recovery in investment will shift the Phillips curve to the left, offsetting (partially, wholly or more than wholly) the upward shift from higher inflationary expectations.

The lesson here for governments is that a sustained, but moderate, increase in aggregate demand can lead to a sustained growth in aggregate supply. What should be avoided is an excessive and unsustainable expansion of aggregate demand. In turn, this raises questions about the role that governments should play in managing aggregate demand in order to affect levels of business activity. This has become especially relevant since the financial crisis and subsequent economic downturn of the late 2000s. (Chapter 30 looks at government policy in more detail.)

29.4 INFLATION TARGETING AND UNEMPLOYMENT

The Phillips curve appeared to have shifted to the right in the 1970s and 1980s and then back to the left in the 1990s. It also seems to have changed its shape. Far from being vertical in the long run, it appears now to have become horizontal. Figure 29.9 traces out the path of inflation and unemployment from 1967 to 2013.

What explains the shape of this path? Part of the explanation lies in long-term changes in unemployment. Part lies in the policy of inflation targeting, pursued in the UK since 1992.

Changes in equilibrium unemployment

Why was there a substantial rise in unemployment from the early 1970s to the mid-1980s? Why, as a result, was there an apparent rightward shift in the Phillips curve? Why was there then a substantial fall in unemployment from the mid-1990s? To answer this, we need to look at the labour market and the determinants of the equilibrium level of unemployment (i.e. the natural rate of unemployment or NAIRU).

Structural unemployment. The 1970s and 1980s were a period of rapid industrial change. The changes included the following:

■ Dramatic changes in technology. The microchip revolution, for example, has led to many traditional jobs becoming obsolete.
■ Competition from abroad. The introduction of new products from abroad, often of superior quality to domestic goods, or produced at lower costs, has led to the decline of many older industries: e.g. the textile industry.

■ Shifts in demand away from the products of older labour-intensive industries to new capital-intensive products.

The free market seemed unable to cope with these changes without a large rise in structural/technological unemployment. Labour was not sufficiently mobile – either geographically or occupationally – to move to industries where there were labour shortages or into jobs where there were skill shortages. A particular problem here was the lack of investment in education and training, with the result that the labour force was not sufficiently flexible to respond to changes in demand for labour.

From the mid-1980s, however, there were increasing signs that the labour market was becoming more flexible (see section 18.7). People seemed more willing to accept that they would have to move from job to job throughout their career. At the same time, policies were introduced to improve training (see section 31.3).

Another explanation for first the rise of equilibrium unemployment and later the fall is the phenomenon of 'hysteresis'.

Hysteresis. If a recession causes a rise in unemployment which is not then fully reversed when the economy recovers, then there is a problem of **hysteresis**. This term, used in physics,

KI 35
p 316

Definition

Hysteresis The persistence of an effect even when the initial cause has ceased to operate. In economics it refers to the persistence of unemployment even when the demand deficiency that caused it no longer exists.

Figure 29.9   Phillips loops in the UK

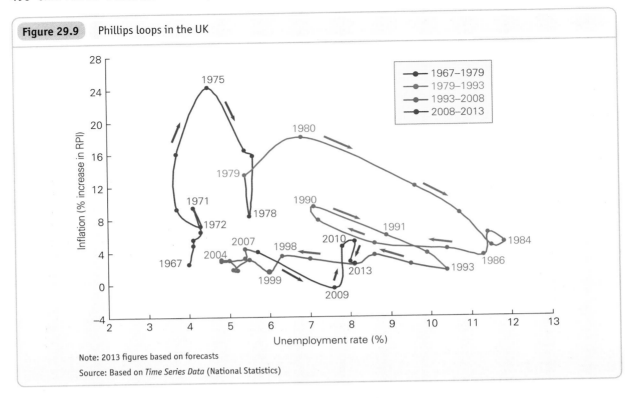

Note: 2013 figures based on forecasts

Source: Based on *Time Series Data* (National Statistics)

refers to the lagging or persistence of an effect, even when the initial cause has been removed. In our context it refers to the persistence of unemployment even when the initial demand deficiency no longer exists.

The recessions of the early 1980s and early 1990s created a growing number of long-term unemployed who were both deskilled and demotivated. What is more, many firms, in an attempt to cut costs, cut down on training programmes. In these circumstances, a rise in aggregate demand would not simply enable the long-term unemployed to be employed again.

The recessions also caused a lack of investment and a reduction in firms' capacity. When demand recovered, many firms were unable to increase output and instead raised prices. Unemployment thus only fell modestly and inflation rose. The NAIRU had increased: the Phillips curve had shifted to the right.

After 1992, however, the economy achieved sustained expansion, with no recession. Equilibrium unemployment began to fall. In other words, the hysteresis was not permanent. As firms increased their investment, the capital stock expanded; firms engaged in more training; the number of long-term unemployed fell.

There is a danger that the problem of hysteresis may recur in the present time. The higher unemployment in the early 2010s, especially in those European countries where measures to reduce public-sector deficits have resulted in a prolonging of recession, may persist once economic growth has resumed.

Inflation targeting

As we have seen, a major determinant of the actual rate of inflation is the rate of inflation that people expect. Since 1992, a policy of inflation targeting has been adopted, and in 1997 the Bank of England was given independence in setting interest rates to achieve the target rate of inflation.

The target was initially set in October 1992 as a range from 1 to 4 per cent for RPIX inflation.[1] With the election of the Labour government in 1997, a single point target of 2.5 per cent was adopted. This was changed to a 2 per cent target for CPI inflation in December 2003. CPI inflation is typically about 0.5 to 0.8 percentage points below RPI inflation.

The public's inflation rate expectations appear to have been affected by inflation rate targeting. Figure 29.10 shows forecast and actual RPI inflation from 1998 to 2014. The forecasts are the average of at least 20 independent forecasts and thus can be taken as an indicator of expectations. As you can see, until the credit crunch of 2008, inflation forecasts were pretty accurate and reflected belief that the Bank of England would be successful in meeting its inflation target.

---

[1] RPIX is the retail prices index, excluding mortgage interest payments. CPI is the consumer prices index. Differences in how CPI is compiled means that CPI inflation is typically about 0.5 percentage points below RPIX inflation. Thus the current target of 2 per cent CPI inflation is approximately equivalent to 2.5 per cent RPIX inflation – the target that was used prior to December 2003.

Figure 29.10   Actual and forecast RPI inflation

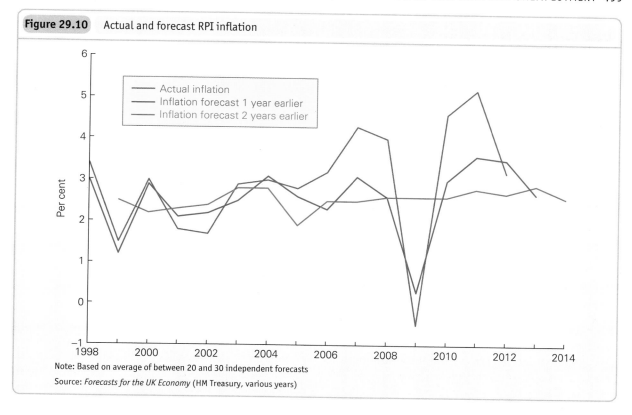

Note: Based on average of between 20 and 30 independent forecasts

Source: *Forecasts for the UK Economy* (HM Treasury, various years)

The credit crunch and the onset of recession began to affect the accuracy of 24-month forecasts. Subsequently, the 12-month forecasts became less accurate too as inflation rose as a result of rapid rises in food, oil and other commodity prices (see Box 26.3). If this were to continue for any length of time then confidence in the central bank's ability to maintain inflation at the target rate may be shaken. Both inflation and unemployment may rise.

Even if the central bank does succeed in achieving the target rate of inflation, in the short term unemployment will fluctuate with the business cycle. Thus there may be movements left or right from one year to the next depending on the level of economic activity. Such fluctuations in unemployment are consistent with stable inflation, provided that the fluctuations are mild and are not enough to alter people's expectations of inflation. Thus there was a very slight rise in unemployment, from 5.1 to 5.2 per cent, from 2001 to 2002 as economic growth slowed slightly and a fall again to 4.8 per cent in 2004 as growth picked up somewhat.

Over the medium term (3 to 6 years), there may be a leftward movement if the economy starts in recession and then the output gap is gradually closed through a process of steady economic growth (growth that avoids 'boom and bust'). Demand-deficient unemployment will be gradually eliminated. Thus between 1992 (the trough of the recession) and 2002, the output gap was closed from −3.1 to +0.2 (see the chart in Box 29.1). Provided the process is gradual, inflation can stay on target.

Over the longer term, movements left (or right) will depend on what happens to equilibrium unemployment. A reduction in equilibrium unemployment will result in a leftward movement. Evidence suggests that since the mid-1980s, there has been a significant reduction in equilibrium unemployment from around 11 per cent to around 5 per cent. The precise amount, however, is not certain as it is subject to measurement errors.

What if inflation targeting were abandoned?

If inflation targeting were abandoned and aggregate demand expanded rapidly, perhaps through tax cuts or a cut in interest rates, the short-run Phillips curve could re-emerge. A rapid expansion of aggregate demand would both reduce unemployment below the equilibrium rate and raise inflation. There would be a positive output gap.

This position could not be sustained, however, as inflationary expectations would rise and the short-run Phillips curve would begin shifting upwards (as in Figure 29.8 on page 495). A long-run vertical Phillips curve would once more become apparent at the natural (equilibrium) rate of unemployment.

29.5 BUSINESS CYCLES

Business cycles and aggregate demand

Many economists, particularly Keynesian, blame fluctuations in output and employment largely on fluctuations in aggregate demand. Theirs is therefore a 'demand-side' explanation of the business cycle. In the upturn (phase 1), aggregate demand starts to rise (see Figure 26.1 on page 420). It rises rapidly in the expansionary phase (phase 2). It then slows down and may start to fall in the peaking-out phase (phase 3). It then falls or remains relatively stagnant in the recession (phase 4).

Consumption cycles

Spending by the household sector is the largest component by value of aggregate demand. In the UK, household spending has averaged around 60 per cent of GDP over the past 50 years. Consequently, even relatively small changes in consumer behaviour can have a significant impact on the overall demand for firms' goods and services and so on the level of business activity. Figure 29.11 shows the similarity in annual rates of economic growth and in household spending for the UK.

While household consumption is affected by a series of factors, here we consider two that help to explain the contribution of consumption to the business cycle.

The first is *expectations*. If consumers believe that their incomes are likely to rise and that their jobs are secure, they are likely to spend more. Thus when the economy booms, consumer confidence is likely to rise, thereby further stimulating the economy. If, however, the economy is in recession and consumers are worried about their future income or that they may lose their job, they will probably cut back on spending. This is then likely to deepen the recession.

The second factor is the *availability of credit*. In a boom, with bank deposits increasing and banks relatively confident about the future, banks may be willing to lend more, thereby further stimulating consumer spending. In a recession, however, banks may fear people's ability to repay loans and may thus cut back on lending, thereby further dampening consumer demand.

Instability of investment: the accelerator

Investment is typically the most volatile component of aggregate demand (see Box 29.2 on page 503). Therefore, investment is an important factor contributing to the ups and downs of the business cycle.

In a recession, investment in new plant and equipment can all but disappear. After all, what is the point of investing in additional capacity if you cannot even sell what you are currently producing? When an economy begins to recover from a recession, however, and confidence returns, investment can rise very rapidly. In percentage terms the rise in investment may be *several times that of the rise in income*. When the growth of the economy slows down, however, investment can fall dramatically.

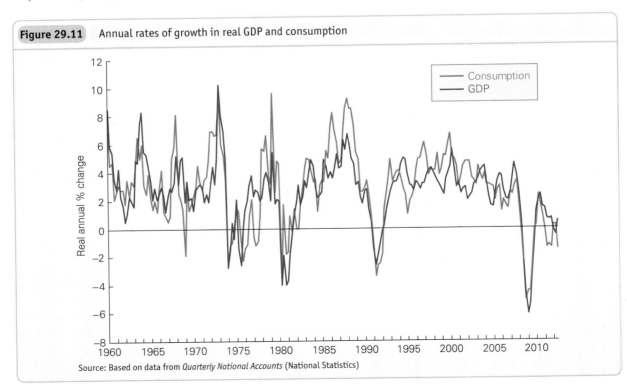

Figure 29.11 Annual rates of growth in real GDP and consumption

Source: Based on data from *Quarterly National Accounts* (National Statistics)

The point is that investment depends not so much on the *level* of GDP and consumer demand, as on their *rate of change*. The reason is that investment (except for replacement investment) is to provide *additional* capacity, and thus depends on how much demand has risen, not on its level. But growth rates change by much more than the level of output. For example, if economic growth is 1 per cent in 2014 and 2 per cent in 2015, then in 2015 output has gone up by 2 per cent, but growth has gone up by 100 per cent! (i.e. it has doubled). Thus percentage changes in investment tend to be much more dramatic than percentage changes in GDP. This is known as the **accelerator theory**.

> ### Pause for thought
>
> *Under what circumstances would you expect a rise in GDP to cause a large accelerator effect?*

These fluctuations in investment, being injections into the circular flow of income, then have a multiplied effect on GDP, thereby magnifying the upswings and downswings of the business cycle.

Fluctuations in stocks

Firms hold stocks of finished goods. These stocks tend to fluctuate with the course of the business cycle, and these fluctuations in stocks themselves contribute to fluctuations in output.

Imagine an economy that is recovering from a recession. At first, firms may be cautious about increasing production. Doing so may involve taking on more labour or making additional investment. Firms may not want to make these commitments if the recovery could soon peter out. They may therefore run down their stocks rather than increase output. Initially, the recovery from recession will be slow.

If the recovery continues, however, firms will start to gain more confidence and will increase their production. Also they will find that their stocks have got rather low and will need building up. This gives a further boost to production, and for a time the growth in output will exceed the growth in demand. This extra growth in output will then, via the multiplier, lead to a further increase in demand.

Once stocks have been built up again, the growth in output will slow down to match the growth in demand. This slowing down in output will, via the accelerator and multiplier, contribute to the ending of the expansionary phase of the business cycle.

> ### Definition
>
> **Accelerator theory** The *level* of investment depends on the *rate of change* of national income, and the result tends to be subject to substantial fluctuations.

As the economy slows down, firms may for a time be prepared to carry on producing and build up stocks. The increase in stocks thus cushions the effect of falling demand on output and employment.

If the recession continues, firms will be unwilling to go on building up stocks. But as firms attempt to reduce their stocks back to the desired level, production will fall *below* the level of sales, despite the fact that sales themselves are lower. This could therefore lead to a dramatic fall in output and, via the multiplier, to an even bigger fall in sales.

Eventually, once stocks have been run down to the minimum, production will have to rise again to match the level of sales. This will contribute to a recovery and the whole cycle will start again.

Aggregate demand and the course of the business cycle

Why do booms and recessions last for several months or even years, and why do they eventually come to an end? Let us examine each in turn.

Why do booms and recessions persist for a period of time?

Time lags. It takes time for changes in injections and withdrawals to be fully reflected in changes in GDP, output and employment. The multiplier process takes time. Moreover, consumers, firms and government may not all respond immediately to new situations. Their responses are spread out over a period of time.

'Bandwagon' effects. Once the economy starts expanding, expectations become buoyant. People think ahead and adjust their expenditure behaviour: they consume and invest more *now*. Likewise in a recession, a mood of pessimism may set in. The effect is cumulative.

The multiplier and accelerator interact: they feed on each other. A rise in GDP causes a rise in investment (the accelerator). This, being an injection into the circular flow, causes a multiplied rise in income. This then causes a further accelerator effect, a further multiplier effect, and so on.

Why do booms and recessions come to an end? What determines the turning points?

Ceilings and floors. Actual output can go on growing more rapidly than potential output only as long as there is slack in the economy. As full employment is approached and as more and more firms reach full capacity, so a ceiling to output is reached.

At the other extreme, there is a basic minimum level of consumption that people tend to maintain. During a recession, people may not buy much in the way of luxury and durable goods, but they will continue to buy food and other basic goods. There is thus a floor to consumption.

The industries supplying these basic goods will need to maintain their level of replacement investment. Also there will always be some minimum investment demand as firms, in order to survive competition, need to install the latest equipment. There is thus a floor to investment too.

Echo effects. Durable consumer goods and capital equipment may last several years, but eventually they will need replacing. The replacement of goods and capital purchased in a previous boom may help to bring a recession to an end.

The accelerator. For investment to continue rising, consumer demand must rise at a *faster and faster* rate. If this does not happen, investment will fall back and the boom will break.

Random shocks. National or international political, social or natural events can affect the mood and attitudes of firms, governments and consumers, and thus affect aggregate demand.

Changes in government policy. In a boom, a government may become most worried by inflation and balance of trade deficits and thus pursue contractionary policies. In a recession, it may become most worried by unemployment and lack of growth and thus pursue expansionary policies. These government policies, if successful, will bring about a turning point in the cycle.

> ### Pause for thought
>
> *Why is it difficult to predict precisely when a recession will come to an end and the economy will start growing rapidly?*

KI 36
p 316
Some economists argue that governments should attempt to reduce cyclical fluctuations by the use of active demand-management policies. These could be either fiscal or monetary policies, or both (see Chapter 30). A more stable economy will provide a better climate for long-term investment, which will lead to faster growth in both potential and actual output.

Aggregate supply and 'real business cycles'

While the mainstream view of business cycles stresses the importance of fluctuations in aggregate demand, it recognises that shifts in the aggregate supply curve in Figure 26.7 (p. 432) can also cause fluctuations in output. Sudden sharp changes to input prices, such as in the price of oil, could be one such cause.

But some economists go further and argue that shifts in aggregate supply are the *primary* source of economic volatility. Their theory is known as **real business cycle theory**. In a recession, according to the theory, aggregate supply curves will shift to the left (output falls), while in a boom aggregate supply curves shift to the right (output rises).

But what causes aggregate supply to change in the first place, and why, once there has been an initial change,

will the aggregate supply curve *go on* changing, causing a recession or boom to continue?

The initial change in aggregate supply could come from a structural change, such as a shift in demand from older manufacturing industries to new service industries. Because of the immobility of labour, not all those laid off in the older industries will find work in the new industries. Structural unemployment (part of equilibrium unemployment) rises and output falls. *Aggregate* demand may be the same, but because of a change in its pattern, aggregate supply falls and the Phillips curve shifts to the right.

Alternatively, the initial shift in aggregate supply could come from a change in technology. For example, a technological breakthrough in telecommunications could increase aggregate supply. Or it could come from an oil price increase, reducing aggregate supply.

The persistence of supply-side effects

But why, when a change in aggregate supply occurs, does the effect persist? Why is there not a single rise or fall? There are two main reasons. The first is that several changes may take months to complete. For example, a decline in demand for certain older industries, perhaps caused by growing competition from abroad, does not take place overnight. Likewise, a technological breakthrough does not affect all industries simultaneously.

The second reason is that these changes will affect the profitability of investment. If investment rises, this will increase firms' capacity and aggregate supply will increase. If investment falls (as a result, say, of the election of a government less sympathetic to industry), aggregate supply will fall. In other words, investment is causing changes in output not through its effect on aggregate *demand* (through the multiplier), but rather through its effect on aggregate *supply*.

Turning points

So far we have seen how the theory of real business cycles explains persistent rises or falls in aggregate supply. But how does it explain *turning points*? Why do recessions and booms come to an end? The most likely explanation is that, once a shock has worked its way through, aggregate supply will stop shifting. If there is then any shock in the other direction, aggregate supply will start moving back again. For example, after a period of recession, gluts in various commodities could lead to falls in commodity prices, thereby reducing industries' costs. Since these 'reverse shocks' are likely to occur at irregular intervals, they can help to explain why real-world business cycles are themselves irregular.

> ### Definition
>
> **Real business cycle theory** The new classical theory which explains cyclical fluctuations in terms of shifts in aggregate supply, rather than aggregate demand.

| **BOX 29.2** | **HAS THERE BEEN AN ACCELERATOR EFFECT OVER THE PAST 50 YEARS?** |

Since 1960, the sum of public and private investment expenditure has averaged around 15 per cent of gross domestic product in the UK. But the level of this investment expenditure – also known as gross capital formation – is highly volatile.

We can see from the chart that it is subject to far more violent swings than national income. If we look at the period from 1960 to 2012, the maximum annual rate of increase in output (real GDP) was 10 per cent while the maximum rate of decline was around 7 per cent. By contrast, the maximum annual rate of increase in constant-price investment was 40 per cent and the maximum rate of decline was 33 per cent. In other words, the range (or spread) of annual rates of change in investment is considerably larger than that for national income.

These figures are consistent with the accelerator theory, which argues that the *level* of investment depends on the *rate of change* of national income. A relatively small percentage change in national income can give a much bigger percentage change in investment.

The ups and downs in GDP and investment do not completely match because there are other factors that help to determine investment other than simply changes in national income. For starters, capital expenditure by the public sector is determined in a political arena and can also be sensitive to the state of the nation's public finances (see Chapter 30). As far as private-sector investment expenditure is concerned, it will be influenced by a variety of factors including: the availability of finance, interest rates, exchange rates, sentiment and business expectations of future demand.

1. *Can you identify any time lags in the graph? Why might there be time lags?*
2. *In what particular industries might we expect investment expenditure to be particularly volatile?*

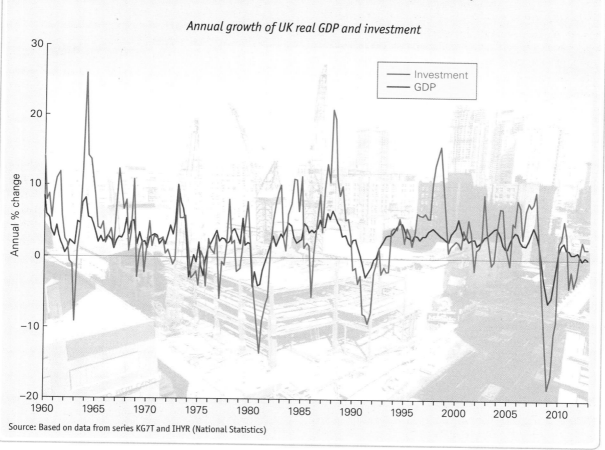

Annual growth of UK real GDP and investment

Source: Based on data from series KG7T and IHYR (National Statistics)

SUMMARY

1a In the simple circular flow of income model, equilibrium national income (GDP) is where withdrawals equal injections: where $W = J$.

1b Equilibrium can be shown on a Keynesian 45° line diagram. Equilibrium is where GDP (shown by the 45° line) is equal to aggregate expenditure (E).

1c If there is an initial increase in aggregate expenditure (ΔE), which could result from an increase in injections or a reduction in withdrawals, there will be a multiplied rise in GDP. The multiplier is defined as $\Delta GDP/\Delta E$.

1d The size of the multiplier depends on the marginal propensity to consume domestically produced goods (mpc_d). The larger the mpc_d, the more will be spent each time incomes are generated round the circular flow, and thus the more will go round again as *additional* demand for domestic product. The multiplier formula is $1/1 - mpc_d$.

2a The quantity equation $MV = PY$ can be used to analyse the possible relationship between money and prices.

2b In the short run, V tends to vary inversely, but unpredictably, with M. Thus the effect of a change in money supply on nominal GDP (PY) is uncertain.

2c The reason is that the interest-rate transmission mechanism between changes in money and changes in GDP is unreliable and possibly weak. The reasons are (a) an unstable and possibly elastic demand for money and (b) an unstable and possibly inelastic investment demand.

2d The exchange-rate transmission mechanism is stronger but still very unpredictable.

2e In the long run, the transmission mechanisms are stronger and relatively stable. If people have an increase in money in their portfolios, they will attempt to restore portfolio balance by purchasing assets, including goods. Thus an increase in money supply is transmitted directly into an increase in aggregate demand. The interest rate and exchange rate mechanisms are also argued to be strong. The demand for money is seen to be more stable in the long run. This leads to a long-run stability in V (unless it changes as a result of other factors, such as institutional arrangements for the handling of money).

2f The short-run effect of a change in money supply on *real* GDP (Y) depends on the degree of slack in the economy. In the long run, Y is determined largely independently of the money supply. A faster growth in the money supply over a long period is likely to result merely in higher inflation.

3a If equilibrium GDP (GDP_e) is below the full-employment level of GDP (GDP_F), there will be a recessionary gap. This gap is equal to $GDP - E$ at GDP_F. This gap can be closed by expansionary fiscal or monetary policy, which will then cause a multiplied rise in GDP (up to a level of GDP_F) and will eliminate demand-deficient unemployment.

3b If equilibrium GDP exceeds the full-employment level of income, the excess demand gives an inflationary gap, which is equal to $E - GDP$ at GDP_F. This gap can be closed by contractionary policies.

3c This simple analysis tends to imply that the AS curve is horizontal up to GDP_F and then vertical. If allowance is made for other types of inflation and unemployment,

however, the AS curve will be upward sloping but getting steeper as full employment is approached and as bottlenecks increasingly occur.

3d The Phillips curve showed the apparent trade-off between inflation and unemployment for more than 100 years prior to 1958. However, after the mid-1960s, the relationship appeared to break down as both inflation and unemployment rose.

3e An explanation for this is given by the adaptive expectations hypothesis. In its simplest form the hypothesis states that the expected rate of inflation this year is what it actually was last year: $\pi_t^e - \pi_{t-1}$.

3f If there is excess demand in the economy, producing upward pressure on wages and prices, initially unemployment will fall. The reason is that workers and firms will believe that wage and price increases represent *real* wage and price increases. Thus workers are prepared to take jobs more readily and firms choose to produce more. But as people's expectations adapt upwards to these higher wages and prices, so ever increasing rises in nominal aggregate demand will be necessary to maintain unemployment below the equilibrium rate. Price and wage rises will accelerate: i.e. inflation will rise.

3g According to this analysis, the Phillips curve is thus vertical at the natural rate of unemployment.

3h The new classical theory assumes flexible prices and wages in the short run as well as in the long run. It also assumes that people base their expectations of inflation on a rational assessment of the *current* situation. People may predict wrongly, but they are equally likely to underpredict or to overpredict. On average over the years they will predict correctly.

3i The rational expectations theory implies that not only the long-run but also the short-run Phillips curve will be vertical. If people correctly predict the rate of inflation, they will correctly predict that any increase in *nominal* aggregate demand will simply be reflected in higher prices. Total output and employment will remain the same: at the equilibrium level.

3k Expectations can also impact upon output and employment. If business is confident that demand will be healthy and that order books will be healthy, then firms are likely to gear up production and take on extra labour.

4a The Phillips curve shifted to the right in the 1970s and 1980s. Reasons include a growth in equilibrium unemployment caused by rapid technological changes and a persistence of unemployment beyond the recessions of the early 1980s and early 1990s (hysteresis).

4b More recently, equilibrium unemployment has fallen as labour markets have become more flexible and as the lagged effects of the recessions of the early 1980s and early 1990s have faded.

4c Inflation targeting, until recently, has successfully kept inflation very close to the target level. Expected inflation is close to the target too.

4d Evidence shows that the effect of inflation targeting on expectations has tended to make the time-path of the Phillips curve horizontal at the target rate of inflation – at least until the recession of 2009. This does not mean, however, that a vertical long-run Phillips curve would not soon become apparent if inflation targeting were abandoned.

5a Many economists, particularly those in the Keynesian tradition, explain cyclical fluctuations in the economy by examining the causes of fluctuations in the level of *demand*.

5b The instability of private-sector spending is a significant cause of the business cycle. The most volatile component of aggregate demand is investment. The accelerator theory explains the instability in investment. It relates the level of investment to *changes* in GDP and consumer demand. An initial increase in consumer demand can result in a very large percentage increase in investment; but as soon as the rise in consumer demand begins

to level off, investment will fall; and even a slight fall in consumer demand can reduce investment to virtually zero.

5c Investment in stocks is also unstable and tends to amplify the business cycle.

5d Booms and recessions can persist because of time lags, 'bandwagon' effects and the *interaction* of the multiplier and accelerator. Turning points are explained by ceilings and floors to output, echo effects, the accelerator, swings in government policy and random shocks.

5e Real business cycle theory focuses on aggregate supply shocks, which then persist for a period of time. Eventually their effect will peter out, and supply shocks in the other direction can lead to turning points in the cycle.

REVIEW QUESTIONS

1 Assume that the multiplier has a value of 3. Now assume that the government decides to increase aggregate demand in an attempt to reduce unemployment. It raises government expenditure by £100 million with no increase in taxes. Firms, anticipating a rise in their sales, increase investment by £200 million, of which £50 million consists of purchases of foreign machinery. How much will GDP rise? (Assume *ceteris paribus*.)

2 What factors could explain why some countries have a higher multiplier than others?

3 What are the implications of the relationship between the money supply (M) and the V and Y terms in the quantity equation $MV = PY$ for the effectiveness of controlling the amount of money in the economy as a means of controlling inflation?

4 In the adaptive expectations model of the Phillips curve, if the government tries to maintain unemployment below the equilibrium rate, what will determine the speed at which inflation accelerates?

5 For what reasons might the equilibrium rate of unemployment increase?

6 How can adaptive expectations of inflation result in clockwise Phillips loops? Why would these loops not be completely regular?

7 What implications would a vertical short-run aggregate supply curve have for the effectiveness of demand management policy?

8 Explain the persistence of high levels of unemployment after the 1980s recession. What policies would you advocate to reduce unemployment?

9 How can the interaction of the multiplier and accelerator explain cyclical fluctuations in GDP?

10 What is meant by 'real business cycle' theory? How can such theory account for (a) the persistence of periods of rapid or slow growth; (b) turning points in the cycle?

ADDITIONAL PART J CASE STUDIES IN THE *ECONOMICS FOR BUSINESS* MyEconLab (www.pearsoned.co.uk/sloman)

J.1 **Theories of economic growth.** An overview of classical and more modern theories of growth.

J.2 **The costs of economic growth.** Why economic growth may not be an unmixed blessing.

J.3 **Technology and unemployment.** Does technological progress destroy jobs?

J.4 **The GDP deflator.** An examination of how GDP figures are corrected to take inflation into account.

J.5 **Comparing national income statistics.** The importance of taking the purchasing power of local currencies into account.

J.6 **The UK's balance of payments deficit.** An examination of the UK's persistent trade and current account deficits.

J.7 **Making sense of the financial balances on the balance of payments.** An examination of the three main components of the financial account.

J.8 **A high exchange rate.** This case looks at whether a high exchange rate is necessarily bad news for exporters.

J.9 **The Gold Standard.** A historical example of fixed exchange rates.

J.10 **The importance of international financial movements.** How a current account deficit can coincide with an appreciating exchange rate.

J.11 **Argentina in crisis.** An examination of the collapse of the Argentine economy in 2001/2.

J.12 **Currency turmoil in the 1990s.** Two examples of speculative attacks on currencies: first on the

▶

Mexican peso in 1995; then on the Thai baht in 1997.

J.13 **The attributes of money.** What makes something, such as metal, paper or electronic records, suitable as money?

J.14 **Secondary marketing.** This looks at one of the ways of increasing liquidity without sacrificing profitability. It involves selling an asset to someone else before the asset matures.

J.15 **Consolidated MFI balance sheet.** A look at the consolidated balance sheet of UK monetary financial institutions (banks, building societies and the Bank of England).

J.16 **John Maynard Keynes (1883–1946).** Profile of the great economist.

J.17 **The rational expectations revolution.** A profile of two of the most famous economists of the new classical rational expectations school.

J.18 **The phases of the business cycle.** A demand-side analysis of the factors contributing to each of the four phases.

J.19 **How does consumption behave?** The case looks at evidence on the relationship between consumption and disposable income from the 1950s to the current day.

J.20 **The household sector balance sheet** This looks at the wealth of the UK household sector detailing the sector's net financial wealth and physical assets before considering ways in which the balance sheet may impact on spending.

J.21 **UK monetary aggregates.** This case shows how UK money supply is measured using both UK measures and eurozone measures.

J.22 **Credit and the business cycle.** This case traces cycles in the growth of credit and relates them to the business cycle. It also looks at some of the implications of the growth in credit.

WEBSITES RELEVANT TO PART J

Numbers and sections refer to websites listed in the Web appendix and hotlinked from this book's website at
www.pearsoned.co.uk/sloman

■ For news articles relevant to Part J, see the *Economics News Articles* link from the book's website.

■ For general news on macroeconomic issues, both national and international, see websites in section A, and particularly A1–5, 7–9. For general news on money, banking and interest rates, see again A1–5, 7–9 and also 20–22, 25, 26, 31, 35, 36. For all of Part J, see also links to macroeconomic and financial news in A42. See also links to newspapers worldwide in A38, 39 and 43, and the news search feature in Google at A41.

■ For macroeconomic data, see links in B1 or 2; also see B4 and 12. For UK data, see B3 and 34. For EU data, see G1 > *The Statistical Annex*. For US data, see *Current economic indicators* in B5 and the *Data* section of B17. For international data, see B15, 21, 24, 31, 33. For links to data sets, see B28; I14.

■ For national income statistics for the UK (Appendix), see B1, *1. National Statistics* > the fourth link > *Economy* > *United Kingdom Economic Accounts* and *United Kingdom National Accounts – The Blue Book*.

■ For the Human Development Index (Box 7.2), see site H17.

■ For data on UK unemployment, see B1, *1. National Statistics* > the fourth link > *Labour Market* > *Labour Market Trends*. For International data on unemployment, see G1; H3 and 5.

■ For international data on balance of payments and exchange rates, see *World Economic Outlook* in H4 and *OECD Economic Outlook* in B21 (also in section 6 of B1). See also the trade topic in I14.

■ For details of individual countries' balance of payments, see B32.

■ For UK data on balance of payments, see B1, *1. National Statistics* > the fourth link > *Economy* > *United Kingdom Balance of Payments – the Pink Book*. See also B3, 34; F2. For EU data, see G1 > *The Statistical Annex* > *Foreign trade and current balance*.

■ For exchange rates, see A3; B34; F2, 6, 8.

■ For discussion papers on balance of payments and exchange rates, see H4 and 7.

■ Sites I7 and 11 contain links to *Balance of payments and exchange rates* in *International economics*.

■ For monetary and financial data (including data for money supply and interest rates), see section F and particularly F2. Note that you can link to central banks worldwide from site F17. See also the links in B1 or 2.

■ For links to sites on money and monetary policy, see the *Financial Economics* sections in I4, 7, 11, 17.

■ For information on the development of ideas, see C12, 18; also see links under *Methodology and History of Economic Thought* in C14; links to economists in I4 and 17. See also sites I7 and 11 > *Economic Systems and Theories* > *History of Economic Thought*.

■ For student resources relevant to this chapter, see sites C1–7, 9, 10, 12, 13, 19.

Macroeconomic policy

The FT Reports . . .

The Financial Times, 29 October 2012

FT

Heseltine attempts revamp of regions

By Brian Groom and Jim Pickard

Lord Heseltine will on Wednesday attempt to inject fresh energy into Britain's tortuous, 80-year quest to unlock the economic potential of regions outside London and the southeast. It is bound to cause controversy.

In a government-commissioned report, the 79-year-old Conservative former deputy prime minister is expected to recommend a significant strengthening of England's 39 local enterprise partnerships, the public–private bodies that replaced Labour's regional development agencies (RDAs).

He is also likely to argue for a bigger role for business leaders and chambers of commerce in setting policy and deciding how money is spent.

Few doubt Lord Heseltine's credentials. As environment secretary under Margaret Thatcher in the 1980s, he was a bold champion of regional development in the aftermath of the Brixton and Toxteth riots.

He established high-spending urban development corporations in London Docklands and Merseyside, and created enterprise zones offering tax breaks for companies that brought jobs to deprived regions.

In his quest to reverse decades of creeping centralism, Lord Heseltine has been unafraid to challenge views in his own party. He described the coalition's decision to scrap the RDAs as a 'mistake', though he is likely to stop short of urging their restoration.

But in attempting to galvanise the coalition's pledge to 'rebalance' the economy by unlocking private sector growth in poorer regions, both he and the government face a stiff task. . . .

Incentives reached their height in the 1970s but the effectiveness of that type of intervention became widely questioned. Many grant-aided plants closed in the early 1980s recession.

The Thatcher era was controversial in different ways. Thirty-eight enterprise zones were set up in the 1980s and 1990s to boost growth by offering tax breaks. They helped to transform London's Docklands, but elsewhere the zones were criticised for creating only a short-term boost and moving jobs from one area to another.

Labour created RDAs in each of England's nine regions after it came to power in 1997 – the biggest expansion of regionalism since the second world war. But its hopes of moving towards regional government foundered when voters in the northeast rejected an assembly by four to one in a 2004 referendum.

RDAs failed to halt the widening gap between London and other regions, but they had substantial business support in parts of the north. The coalition is also trying to stimulate growth through its £2.4bn regional growth fund, to which companies in poorer areas could bid for grants.

> *When the world economy was plunged into deep crisis in the 1930s, the response, both nationally and internationally, was too little and too late. This failure to act turned a serious downturn into a prolonged depression. We will not repeat those mistakes again.*

Alistair Darling. Chancellor of the Exchequer, Budget speech, 21 April 2009

The role of government in managing macroeconomic affairs has always been a contentious one. Economists keenly debate the extent to which governments should intervene in economies. Such debates concern not only national economies, but groups of economies (e.g. the 27 member states of the European Union) and also regional economies (as the *Financial Times* article points out). Economists debate both the potential role of governments in reducing the inherent volatility of economies or in fostering more rapid long-term economic growth.

In this final part of the book, we consider the alternative policies open to government in its attempt to manage or influence the macroeconomy. Chapter 30 focuses on fiscal and monetary policy, which are used by government to regulate aggregate demand. We shall consider how such policies are supposed to work and how effective they are in practice.

Up to the financial crisis of the late 2000s, policy-makers had taken a more passive approach towards policy, often advocating policy rules. The financial crisis saw fiscal rules relaxed, suspended or even abandoned. Many central banks continue to rely on policy rules; for example, the Bank of England sets interest rates so as to achieve a target rate of inflation of 2 per cent. Nonetheless, even here there is renewed interest in the merit of such rules.

Chapter 31, by contrast, focuses on aggregate supply and considers the role of government in attempting to improve economic performance by supply-side reforms: i.e. reforms designed to increase productivity and efficiency and achieve a growth in potential output. Both free-market and interventionist supply-side strategies will be considered.

Finally Chapter 32 takes an international perspective. We shall see how, in a world of interdependent economies, national governments try to harmonise their policies so as to achieve international growth and stability. Unfortunately, there is frequently a conflict between the broader interests of the international community and the narrow interests of individual countries, and in these circumstances, national interests normally dictate policy.

Key terms

Fiscal policy
Fiscal stance
Fine tuning
Automatic fiscal stabilisers and discretionary fiscal policy
Pure fiscal policy
Crowding out
Monetary policy
Open-market operations
Demand management
Inflation targeting
Market-orientated and interventionist supply-side policies
Regional and urban policy
Industrial policy
International business cycle
Policy coordination
International convergence
Economic and monetary union in Europe (EMU)
Single European currency
Currency union

Demand-side policy

Business issues covered in this chapter

- What sorts of government macroeconomic policy are likely to impact on business and in what way?
- What will be the impact on the economy and business of various fiscal policy measures?
- What determines the effectiveness of fiscal policy in smoothing out fluctuations in the economy?
- What fiscal rules are adopted by governments and is following them a good idea?
- How does monetary policy work in the UK and the eurozone, and what are the roles of the Bank of England and the European Central Bank?
- How does targeting inflation influence interest rates and hence business activity?
- Are there better rules for determining interest rates than sticking to a simple inflation target?

There are two major types of demand-side policy: fiscal and monetary. In each case, we shall first describe how the policy operates and then examine its effectiveness. We shall also consider the more general question of whether the government and central bank ought to intervene actively to manage the level of aggregate demand, or whether they ought merely to set targets or rules for various indicators – such as money supply, inflation or government budget deficits – and then stick to them.

30.1 FISCAL POLICY

Fiscal policy involves the government manipulating the level of government expenditure and/or rates of tax so as to affect the level of aggregate demand. An *expansionary* fiscal policy will involve raising government expenditure (an injection into the circular flow of income) or reducing taxes (a withdrawal from the circular flow). A *deflationary*

Definition

Fiscal policy Policy to affect aggregate demand by altering government expenditure and/or taxation.

(i.e. a contractionary) fiscal policy will involve cutting government expenditure and/or raising taxes.

But why might a government use fiscal policy?

First, it can try to remove any severe deflationary or inflationary gaps. For instance, an expansionary fiscal policy could be used to try to prevent an economy experiencing a severe or prolonged recession. This was the approach taken around the world from 2008 when substantial tax cuts and increases in government expenditure were undertaken. Likewise, deflationary fiscal policy could be used to prevent rampant inflation, such as that experienced in the 1970s.

Table 30.1	General government deficits/surpluses and debt as percentage of GDP			
	General government deficits (−) or surpluses (+)		General government debt	
	Average 1995–2007	**Average** 2008–2013	**Average** 1995–2007	**Average** 2008–2013
Belgium	−1.2	−4.0	106.5	96.3
France	−3.0	−6.2	60.6	82.6
Germany	−2.9	−1.8	62.2	77.9
Greece	−5.7	−9.9	100.9	157.8
Ireland	1.2	−13.3	43.3	91.8
Italy	−3.6	−3.3	110.2	116.6
Japan	−6.1	−6.6	137.7	199.6
Netherlands	−1.4	−3.4	57.6	62.9
Portugal	−3.8	−5.5	56.5	95.4
Spain	−1.4	−7.2	54.2	62.7
Sweden	0.0	0.5	57.7	37.4
UK ·	−1.9	−8.3	43.8	77.2
USA	−1.9	−8.7	62.2	94.4
EU-15	−2.3	−4.6	65.3	81.1

Note: 2012 and 2013 figures are forecasts

Source: Based on data from *AMECO* database, Tables 16.3 and 18.1 (European Commission, DG ECFIN)

Second, it can try to smooth out the fluctuations in the economy associated with the business cycle by *fine-tuning*. Stabilisation policies involve the government adjusting the level of aggregate demand so as to prevent the economy's actual output level deviating too far from its potential output level – to keep output gaps to a minimum.

Fiscal policy can also be used to try to influence aggregate *supply*. For example, government can increase its expenditure on infrastructure, or give tax incentives to encourage businesses to invest or to engage in research and development. In so doing, the hope is that government can positively affect an economy's potential output.

Deficits and surpluses

Central government deficits and surpluses

Since an expansionary fiscal policy involves raising government expenditure and/or lowering taxes, this has the effect of either increasing the **budget deficit** or reducing the **budget surplus**. A budget deficit in any one year is where central government's expenditure exceeds its revenue from taxation. A budget surplus is where tax revenues exceed central government expenditure.

For most of the past 50 years, governments around the world have run budget deficits. In recent years, however, many countries, the UK included, made substantial efforts to reduce their budget deficits, and some achieved budget surpluses for periods of time. The position changed dramatically in 2008–9, however, as governments around the world increased their expenditure and cut taxes in an attempt to stave off recession. Budget deficits soared.

General government

'General government' includes central and local government. Table 30.1 shows general government deficits/surpluses and debt for selected countries. They are expressed as a proportion of GDP. Deficits refer to the debt that a government incurs in one year when its spending exceeds its receipts. If the government runs persistent deficits over many years, these debts will accumulate.

As you can see, in the period from 1995 to 2007, all countries, with the exception of Ireland and Sweden, averaged a deficit. Nevertheless, for most countries, these deficits and debts were smaller than in the early 1990s. However, in the period from 2008 to 2013, the average deficit increased for most countries. And, the bigger the deficit, the faster debt increased.

The whole public sector

To get a more complete view of public finances, we would need to look at the spending and receipts of the entire public sector: namely, central government, local government and public corporations.

Total public expenditure. First, we need to distinguish between **current** and **capital expenditures**. Current expenditures include items such as wages and salaries of public-sector staff, administration and the payments of welfare benefits. Capital expenditure (gross capital formation) gives rise to a stream of benefits *over time*. Examples include expenditure on roads, hospitals and schools.

Second, we must distinguish between **final expenditure** on goods and services, and **transfers**. This distinction recognises that the public sector directly adds to the economy's aggregate demand through its spending on goods and services, including the wages of public sector workers, but also that it redistributes incomes between individuals and firms. Transfers include subsidies and benefit payments, such as payments to the unemployed.

Between 1990 and 2011, the UK's public expenditure was typically split 93 to 7 per cent between current and capital expenditure, and 62 to 38 per cent between final expenditure and transfers.

Public-sector deficits. If the public sector spends more than it earns, it will have to finance the deficit through borrowing: known as **public-sector net borrowing (PSNB)**. The difference between the expenditures of the public sector and its receipts from taxation, the revenues of public corporations and the scale of assets. If expenditures exceed receipts (a deficit), then the government has to borrow to make up the difference.

The precise amount of money the public sector requires to borrow in any one year is known as the **public-sector net cash requirement (PSNCR)**. It differs slightly from the PSNB because of time lags in the flows of public-sector incomes and expenditure.

If the public sector runs a surplus (a negative PSNB), it will be able to repay some of the public-sector debts that have accumulated from previous years. Figure 30.1 shows public-sector net borrowing and the public-sector net cash requirement since the 1960s. It shows that public-sector deficits are the norm.

The use of fiscal policy

Automatic fiscal stabilisers

To some extent, government expenditure and taxation will have the effect of *automatically* stabilising the economy. For example, as national income rises, the amount of tax people pay automatically rises. This rise in withdrawals from the circular flow of income will help to damp down the rise in national income. This effect will be bigger if taxes are *progressive* (i.e. rise by a bigger percentage than national income). Some government transfers will have a

similar effect. For example, the total paid in unemployment benefits will fall, if rises in national income cause a fall in unemployment. This again will have the effect of dampening the rise in national income.

Discretionary fiscal policy

Automatic stabilisers cannot *prevent* fluctuations; they merely reduce their magnitude. If there is a fundamental disequilibrium in the economy or substantial fluctuations in national income, these automatic stabilisers will not be enough. The government may thus choose to *alter* the level of government expenditure or the rates of taxation. This is known as **discretionary fiscal policy**. Case Study K.4 in MyEconLab looks at discretionary fiscal policy in the UK and USA since the financial crisis of the late 2000s. Case Study K.5 in MyEconLab examines the use of discretionary fiscal policy in Japan during the 1990s and the 2000s.

If government expenditure on goods and services (roads, health care, education, etc.) is raised, this will create a full multiplied rise in national income. The reason is that all the money gets spent and thus all of it goes to boosting aggregate demand.

Cutting taxes (or increasing benefits), however, will have a smaller effect on national income than raising government expenditure on goods and services by the same amount. The reason is that cutting taxes increases people's *disposable* incomes, of which only part will be spent. Part will be withdrawn into extra saving, imports and other taxes. In other words, not all the tax cuts will be passed on round the circular flow of income as extra expenditure. Thus if one-fifth of a cut in taxes is withdrawn and only four-fifths is spent, the tax multiplier will be only four-fifths as big as the government expenditure multiplier.

KI 36 p 316

KI 42 p 486

Definitions

Current expenditure Recurrent spending on goods and factor payments.

Capital expenditure Investment expenditure; expenditure on assets.

Final expenditure Expenditure on goods and services. This is included in GDP and is part of aggregate demand.

Transfers Transfers of money from taxpayers to recipients of benefits and subsidies. They are not an injection into the circular flow but are the equivalent of a negative tax (i.e. a negative withdrawal).

Public-sector net borrowing The difference between the expenditures of the public sector and its receipts from taxation and the revenues from public corporations.

Public-sector net cash requirement (PSNCR) The (annual) deficit of the public sector, and thus the amount that the public sector must borrow.

Discretionary fiscal policy Deliberate changes in tax rates or the level of government expenditure in order to influence the level of aggregate demand.

| Figure 30.1 | UK public-sector deficit measures (percent of GDP) |

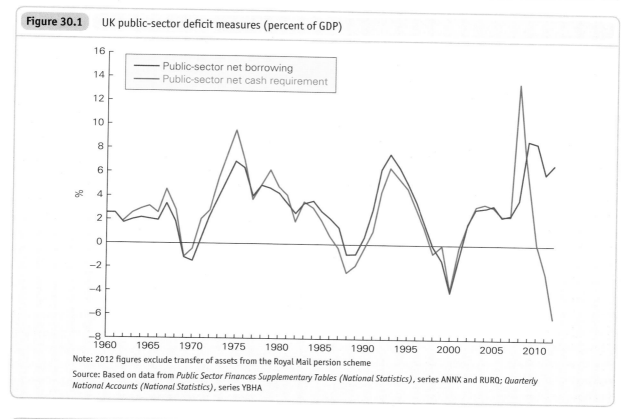

Note: 2012 figures exclude transfer of assets from the Royal Mail persion scheme

Source: Based on data from *Public Sector Finances Supplementary Tables (National Statistics)*, series ANNX and RURQ; *Quarterly National Accounts (National Statistics)*, series YBHA

Pause for thought

Why will the multiplier effect of government transfer payments, such as child benefit, pensions and social security benefits, be less than the full multiplier effect from government expenditure on goods and services?

The effectiveness of fiscal policy

How successful will fiscal policy be? Will it be able to 'fine tune' demand? Will it be able to achieve the level of GDP that the government would like it to achieve?

There are various problems with using fiscal policy to manage the economy. These can be grouped under two broad headings: problems of magnitude and problems of timing.

Problems of magnitude

Before changing government expenditure or taxation, the government will need to calculate the effect of any such change on national income, employment and inflation. Predicting these effects, however, is often very unreliable for a number of reasons.

Predicting the effect of changes in government expenditure

A rise in government expenditure of £x may lead to a rise in total injections (relative to withdrawals) that is smaller than £x. This will occur if the rise in government expendi-

ture *replaces* a certain amount of private expenditure. For example, a rise in expenditure on state education may dissuade some parents from sending their children to private schools. Similarly, an improvement in the National Health Service may lead to fewer people paying for private treatment.

Crowding out. Another reason for the total rise in injections being smaller than the rise in government expenditure is a phenomenon known as **crowding out**. If the government relies on **pure fiscal policy** – that is, if it does not finance an increase in the budget deficit by increasing the money supply – it will have to borrow the money from the non-bank private sector. It will thus be competing with the private sector for finance and will have to offer higher interest rates. This will force the private sector also to offer higher interest rates, which may discourage firms from investing and individuals from buying on credit. Thus government borrowing *crowds out* private borrowing. In the extreme case, the fall in consumption and investment may completely offset the rise in government expenditure, with the result that aggregate demand does not rise at all.

Definitions

Crowding out Where increased public expenditure diverts money or resources away from the private sector.

Pure fiscal policy Fiscal policy which does not involve any change in money supply.

BOX 30.1 THE EVOLVING FISCAL FRAMEWORKS IN THE UK AND EUROZONE

Constraining the discretion over fiscal policy

If the government persistently runs a budget deficit, the national debt will rise. If it rises faster than GDP, it will account for a growing proportion of GDP. There is then likely to be an increasing problem of 'servicing' this debt: i.e. paying the interest on it. The government could find itself having to borrow more and more to meet the interest payments, and so the national debt could rise faster still. As the government borrows more and more, so it has to pay higher interest rates to attract finance. Even if it is successful in this, borrowing and hence investment by the private sector could be crowded out.

The possibility of financial crowding out contributed to many governments embarking on a strategy of fiscal consolidation during the early 2010s. But the recognition of this problem and the need for a fiscal framework had been shaping fiscal policy across Europe for some time. However, the financial crisis called into question how rigid any framework should be and hence how much discretion over fiscal policy national governments should have.

Preparing for the euro

In signing the Maastricht Treaty in 1992, the EU countries agreed that to be eligible to join the single currency (i.e. the euro), they should have sustainable deficits and debts. This was interpreted as follows: the general government deficit should be no more than 3 per cent of GDP and general government debt should be no more than 60 per cent of GDP, or should at least be falling towards that level at a satisfactory pace.

But in the mid-1990s, several of the countries that were subsequently to join the euro had deficits and debts substantially above these levels (see Chart (a)). Getting them down proved a painful business. Government expenditure had to be cut and taxes increased. These fiscal measures, unfortunately, proved to be powerful! Unemployment rose and growth remained low.

The EU Stability and Growth Pact (SGP)

In June 1997, at the European Council meeting in Amsterdam, the EU countries agreed that governments adopting the euro should seek to balance their budgets (or even aim for a surplus) averaged over the course of the business cycle, and that deficits should not exceed 3 per cent of GDP in any one year. A country's deficit was permitted to exceed 3 per cent only if its GDP had declined by at least 2 per cent (or 0.75 per cent with special permission from the Council of Ministers). Otherwise, countries with deficits exceeding 3 per cent were required to make deposits of money with the European Central Bank. These would then become fines if excessive budget deficits were not eliminated within two years.

There were two main aims of targeting a zero budget deficit over the business cycle. The first was to allow automatic stabilisers to work without 'bumping into' the 3 per cent deficit ceiling in years when economies were slowing. The second was to allow a reduction in government debts as a proportion of GDP (assuming that GDP grew on average at around 2–3 per cent per year).

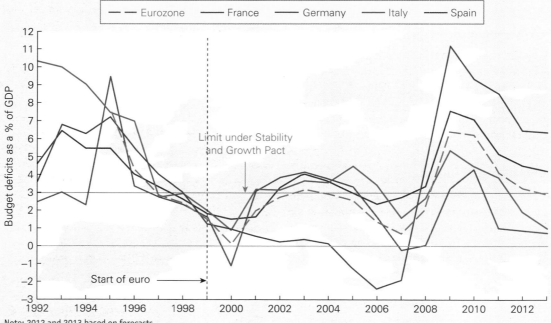

(a) General government deficits in the eurozone

Note: 2012 and 2013 based on forecasts

Source: Based on data in *European Economy* (European Commission)

From 2002, with slowing growth, Germany, France and Italy breached the 3 per cent ceiling. By 2007, however, after two years of relatively strong growth, deficits had been reduced well below the ceiling.

But then the credit crunch hit. As the EU economies slowed, so deficits rose. To combat the recession, in November 2008 the European Commission announced a €200 billion fiscal stimulus plan, mainly in the form of increased public expenditure. €170 billion of the money would come from member governments and €30 billion from the EU, amounting to a total of 1.2 per cent of EU GDP. The money would be for a range of projects, such as job training, help to small businesses, developing green energy technologies and energy efficiency. Most member governments quickly followed by announcing how their specific plans would accord with the overall plan.

The combination of the recession and the fiscal measures pushed most eurozone countries' budget deficits well above the 3 per cent ceiling (see Chart (a)). The recession in EU countries deepened markedly in 2009, with GDP declining by 4.3 per cent in the eurozone as a whole, and by 5.1 per cent in Germany and Italy, 3.7 in Spain and 2.7 per cent in France. Consequently, the deficits were not seen to breach SGP rules.

The Fiscal Compact

As the European economy began to recover in 2010, there was tremendous pressure on member countries to begin reining in their deficits. The average eurozone deficit had risen to 6.2 per cent of GDP, and some countries' deficit was much higher. Indeed, with the Greek, Spanish and Irish deficits being 9.3, 10.8 and 31.3 per cent respectively, reining in the deficits would prove to be especially painful for these and several other eurozone countries.

The SGP was now seen as needing reform. The result was an intense period of negotiation culminating in early 2012 with a new inter-governmental treaty to limit spending and borrowing. The treaty, known as the Fiscal Compact, requires that from January 2013 national governments not only abide by the excessive deficit procedure of the SGP but also keep structural deficits – that part of the deficit which would occur even if the economy were operating at its potential output – at no higher than 0.5 per cent of GDP.

In the cases of countries with a debt-to-GDP ratio significantly below 60 per cent, the structural deficit is permitted to reach 1 per cent of GDP. Finally, where the debt-to-GDP ratio exceeds 60 per cent, countries should, on average, reduce it by one-twentieth per year.

Where a national government is found by the European Court of Justice not to comply with the Fiscal Compact, it has the power to fine that country up to 0.1 per cent of GDP payable to the European Stability Mechanism (ESM). The ESM is a fund from which loans are provided to support a eurozone government in severe financing difficulty, or alternatively is used to purchase that country's bonds in the primary market.

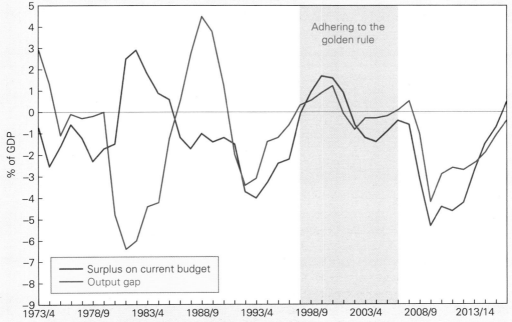

(b) Cyclically-adjusted current budget surplus and the output gap

Note: 2012/13 onwards based on forecasts; output gap is measured as a percentage of *potential* GDP

Source: *Public Sector Finances Databank* (HM Treasury)

The UK Labour government's golden rule

On being elected in 1997, the Labour government in the UK adopted a similar approach to that of the SGP. It introduced two fiscal rules.

First, under its 'golden rule', the government pledged that over the economic cycle, it would borrow only to invest (e.g. in roads, hospitals and schools) and not to fund current spending (e.g. on wages, administration and benefits). Investment was exempted from the zero borrowing rule because it contributes towards the growth of GDP.

Second, under its 'sustainable investment rule', the government also set itself the target of maintaining a public-sector net debt of no more than 40 per cent of GDP averaged over the economic cycle.

As with the Stability and Growth Pact, the argument for the golden rule was that by using an averaging rule over the cycle, automatic stabilisers would be allowed to work. Deficits of receipts over current spending could occur when the economy was in recession or when growth was sluggish (as in 2001–3), helping to stimulate the economy.

Figure (b) shows how the cyclically adjusted current budget was in balance across the economic cycle from 1997/8 to 2006/7. In other words, *after* removing the estimated effects of the economic cycle on the public finances, such as increased welfare payments and lower tax receipts when output is below its potential, the public sector's current expenditures were matched by its receipts.

However, in the Pre-Budget Report of November 2008, the government suspended its golden rule and the sustainable investment rule. It argued that its 'immediate priority' was to support the economy by using discretionary fiscal policy. These measures included a 13-month cut in VAT from 17.5 per cent to 15 per cent and bringing brought forward from 2010/11 £3 billion of capital spending, including spending on motorways, new social housing and schools.

The fiscal approach of the Coalition government

The fiscal priority of the incoming Coalition government in 2010 was to get the public-sector borrowing down, which by 2010 had reached 10.4 per cent of GDP, one of the highest percentages in the developed world. The government set itself a 'fiscal mandate': to achieve a cyclically adjusted current balance by 2015/16. This was, therefore, very similar to the golden rule. The fiscal mandate was supplemented by a target for the ratio of public-sector debt to GDP to be falling by 2015/16.

To achieve its fiscal mandate meant sharp government expenditure cuts and tax rises. The government announced a total consolidation of £128 billion per year by 2015/16. Around 77 per cent (£99 billion per year) would come from spending cuts and the remaining 23 per cent (£29 billion per year) from tax increases.

On its own, the much tighter fiscal policy would substantially dampen aggregate demand. The question was whether the recovery in exports, investment and consumer demand would be sufficient to offset this. That, in turn, depended on confidence – of consumers, business and international financiers – and on monetary policy (see section 30.2).

 What effects will an increase in government investment expenditure have on public-sector debt (a) in the short run; (b) in the long run?

Predicting the effect of changes in taxes

 A cut in taxes, by increasing people's real disposable income, increases not only the amount they spend, but also the amount they save. The problem is that it is not easy to predict the relative size of these two increases. In part it will depend on whether people feel that the cut in tax is only temporary, in which case they may simply save the extra disposable income, or permanent, in which case they may adjust their consumption upwards.

Predicting the resulting multiplied effect on national income

Even if the government *could* predict the net initial effect on injections and withdrawals, the extent to which national income will change is still hard to predict for the following reasons:

 ■ The size of the *multiplier* may be difficult to predict, since it is difficult to predict how much of any rise in income will be withdrawn. For example, the amount of a rise in income that households save or consume will depend on their expectations about future price and income changes. The amount of a rise in income spent on imports will depend on the exchange rate, which may fluctuate considerably.

 ■ Induced investment through the *accelerator* (see page 501) is also extremely difficult to predict. It may be that a relatively small fiscal stimulus will be all that is necessary to restore business confidence, and that induced investment will rise substantially. In such a case, fiscal policy can be seen as a 'pump primer'. It is used to *start* the process of recovery, and then the *continuation* of the recovery is left to the market. But for pump priming to work, businesspeople must *believe* that it will work. Business confidence can change very rapidly and in ways that could not have been foreseen a few months earlier.

Random shocks

Forecasts cannot take into account the unpredictable, such as the attack on the World Trade Center in New York in September 2001. Even events that, with hindsight, should have been predicted, such as the banking crisis of 2007–9, often are not. Unfortunately, unpredictable or unpredicted events do occur and may seriously undermine the government's fiscal policy.

Pause for thought

Gives some other examples of 'random shocks' that could undermine the government's fiscal policy.

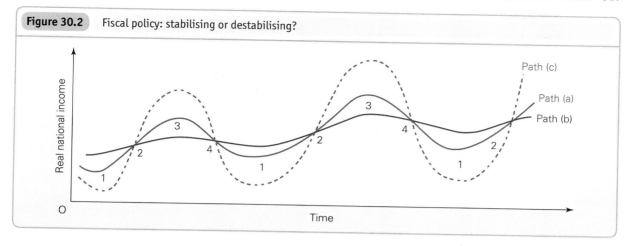

Figure 30.2 Fiscal policy: stabilising or destabilising?

Problems of timing

KI 35
p 316

Fiscal policy can involve considerable time lags. It may take time to recognise the nature of the problem before the government is willing to take action; tax or government expenditure changes take time to plan and implement – changes will have to wait until the next Budget to be announced and may come into effect some time later; the effects of such changes take time to work their way through the economy via the multiplier and accelerator.

If these time lags are long enough, fiscal policy could even be *de*stabilising. Expansionary policies taken to cure a recession may not come into effect until the economy has *already* recovered and is experiencing a boom. Under these circumstances, expansionary policies are quite inappropriate: they simply worsen the problems of overheating. Similarly, deflationary policies taken to prevent excessive expansion may not take effect until the economy has already peaked and is plunging into recession. The deflationary policies only deepen the recession.

This problem is illustrated in Figure 30.2. Path (a) shows the course of the business cycle without government intervention. Ideally, with no time lags, the economy should be dampened in stage 2 and stimulated in stage 4. This would make the resulting course of the business cycle more like path (b), or even, if the policy were perfectly stabilising, a line that purely reflected the growth in potential output.

With the presence of time lags, however, deflationary policies taken in stage 2 may not come into effect until stage 4, and reflationary policies taken in stage 4 may not come into effect until stage 2. In this case the resulting course of the business cycle will be more like path (c). Quite obviously, in these circumstances 'stabilising' fiscal policy actually makes the economy *less* stable.

If the fluctuations in aggregate demand can be forecast, and if the lengths of the time lags are known, then all is not lost. At least the fiscal measures can be taken early and their delayed effects can be taken into account.

Fiscal rules

Given the problems of pursuing active fiscal policy, many governments today take a much more passive approach. Instead of changing the policy as the economy changes, a rule is set for the level of public finances. This rule is then applied year after year, with taxes and government expenditure being planned to meet that rule. For example, a target could be set for the public-sector deficit, with government expenditure and taxes being adjusted to keep borrowing at or within its target level. Box 30.1 looks at recent attempts to apply fiscal targets in the UK and in the eurozone. (Fiscal (and monetary) rules are examined in more detail in section 30.3.)

30.2 MONETARY POLICY

Each month the Bank of England's Monetary Policy Committee meets to set interest rates. The event gets considerable media coverage. Pundits, for two or three days before the meeting, try to predict what the MPC will do and economists give their 'considered' opinions about what the MPC *ought* to do.

The fact is that changes in interest rates have gained a central significance in macroeconomic policy. And it is not just in the UK. Whether it is the European Central Bank set-

ting interest rates for the eurozone countries, or the Federal Reserve Bank setting US interest rates, or any other central bank around the world choosing what the level of interest rates should be, monetary policy is seen as having a major influence on a whole range of macroeconomic indicators.

But is monetary policy simply the setting of interest rates? In reality, it involves the central bank intervening in the money market to ensure that the interest rate that has been announced is also the *equilibrium* interest rate.

The policy setting

In framing its monetary policy, the government must decide on what the goals of the policy are. Is the aim simply to control inflation, or does the government wish also to affect output and employment, or does it want to control the exchange rate?

The government must also decide where monetary policy fits into the total package of macroeconomic policies. Is it seen as the major or even sole macroeconomic policy instrument, or is it merely one of several?

A decision also has to be made about who is to carry out the policy. There are three possible approaches here.

In the first, the government both sets the policy and decides the measures necessary to achieve it. Here the government would set the interest rate, with the central bank simply influencing money markets to achieve this rate. This first approach was used in the UK before 1997.

The second approach is for the government to set the policy *targets*, but for the central bank to be given independence in deciding interest rates. This is the approach adopted in the UK today. The government has set a target rate of inflation of 2 per cent, but then the MPC is free to choose the rate of interest.

The third approach is for the central bank to be given independence not only in carrying out policy, but in setting the policy targets itself. The ECB, within the statutory objective of maintaining price stability over the medium term, has decided on the target of keeping inflation below, but close to, 2 per cent over the medium term.

Finally, there is the question of whether the government or central bank should take a long-term or short-term perspective. Should it adopt a target for inflation or money supply growth and stick to it come what may? Or should it adjust its policy as circumstances change and attempt to 'fine tune' the economy?

We will be looking primarily at *short-term* monetary policy: that is, policy used to keep to a set target for inflation or money supply growth, or policy used to smooth out fluctuations in the business cycle. It is important first, however, to take a longer-term perspective. Governments generally want to prevent an excessive growth in the money supply over the longer term. If money supply does grow rapidly, then inflation is likely to be high. Likewise they want to ensure that money supply grows enough and that there is not a shortage of credit, such as that during the credit crunch. If money supply grows too rapidly, then inflation is likely to be high; if money supply grows too slowly, or even falls, then recession is likely to result.

Control of the money supply over the medium and long term

In section 28.3 we identified two major sources of monetary growth: (a) banks choosing to hold a lower liquidity ratio; (b) public-sector borrowing financed by borrowing from the banking sector. If the government wishes to restrict monetary growth over the longer term, it could attempt to control either or both of these.

Liquidity of banks

The central bank could impose a statutory **minimum reserve ratio** on the banks, *above* the level that banks would otherwise choose to hold. Such ratios come in various forms. The simplest is where the banks are required to hold a given minimum percentage of deposits in the form of cash or deposits with the central bank.

The effect of a minimum reserve ratio is to prevent banks choosing to reduce their cash or liquidity ratio and creating more credit. This was a popular approach of governments in many countries in the past. Some countries imposed very high ratios indeed in their attempt to slow down the growth in the money supply.

A major problem with imposing restrictions of this kind is that banks may find ways of getting round them. After all, banks would like to lend and customers would like to borrow. It is very difficult to regulate and police every single part of countries' complex financial systems.

Nevertheless, attitudes changed substantially after the excessive lending of the mid-2000s. The expansion of credit had been based on 'liquidity' achieved through secondary marketing between financial institutions and the growth of securitised assets containing sub-prime debt (see Box 28.3). After the credit crunch and the need for central banks or governments to rescue ailing banks, such as Northern Rock and later the Royal Bank of Scotland in the UK and many other banks around the world, there were calls for greater regulation of banks to ensure that they had sufficient capital and operated with sufficient liquidity, and that they were not exposed to excessive risk of default. As we saw in Box 28.4 on page 472, a number of measures were taken.

Public-sector deficits

Section 28.3 showed how government borrowing tends to lead to an increase in money supply. To prevent this, public-sector deficits must be financed by selling *bonds* (as opposed to bills, which could well be taken up by the banking sector, thereby increasing money supply). However, to sell extra bonds the government will have to offer higher interest rates. This will have a knock-on effect on private-sector interest rates. The government borrowing will thus crowd out private-sector borrowing and investment. This is known as **financial crowding out**.

Definitions

Minimum reserve ratio A minimum ratio of cash (or other specified liquid assets) to deposits (either total or selected) that the central bank requires banks to hold.

Financial crowding out Where an increase in government borrowing diverts money away from the private sector.

If governments wish to reduce monetary growth and yet avoid financial crowding out, they must therefore reduce the size of public-sector deficits.

It is partly for this reason that many governments have constrained fiscal policy choices by applying fiscal rules or agreements, such as the Stability and Growth Pact and then the Fiscal Compact in the eurozone, or Labour's 'golden rule' and then the Coalition's 'fiscal mandate' in the UK (see Box 30.1).

Short-term monetary measures

Inflation may be off target. Alternatively, the government (or central bank) may wish to alter its monetary policy. What can it do? There are various techniques that could be used. These can be grouped into three categories: (a) altering the money supply; (b) altering interest rates; (c) rationing credit. These are illustrated in Figure 30.3, which shows the demand for and supply of money. The equilibrium quantity of money is initially Q_1 and the equilibrium interest rate is r_1.

Assume that the central bank wants to tighten monetary policy in order to reduce inflation. It could (a) seek to shift the supply of money curve to the left: e.g. from M_s to M'_s (resulting in the equilibrium rate of interest rising from r_1 to r_2), (b) raise the interest rate directly from r_1 to r_2, and then manipulate the money supply to reduce it to Q_2, or (c) keep interest rates at r_1, but reduce money supply to Q_2 by rationing the amount of credit granted by banks and other institutions.

Credit rationing was widely used in the past, especially during the 1960s. The aim was to keep interest rates low, so as not to discourage investment, but to restrict credit to more risky business customers and/or to consumers. In the UK, the Bank of England could order banks to abide by such a policy, although in practice it always relied on persuasion. The government also, from time to time, imposed restrictions on hire-purchase credit, by specifying minimum deposits or maximum repayment periods.

Such policies were progressively abandoned around the world from the early 1980s. They were seen as stifling competition and preventing efficient banks from expanding. Hire-purchase controls may badly hit certain industries (e.g. cars and other consumer durables), whose products are bought largely on hire-purchase credit. What is more, with the deregulation and globalisation of financial markets up to 2007, it had become very difficult to ration credit. If one financial institution was controlled, borrowers could simply go elsewhere.

With the excessive lending in sub-prime markets that had triggered the credit crunch of 2007–9, there were calls around the world for tighter controls over bank lending. But this was different from credit rationing as we have defined it. Tighter controls would be used to prevent reckless behaviour by banks, rather than to achieve a particular level of money at a lower rate of interest.

We thus focus on controlling the money supply and controlling interest rates.

Techniques to control the money supply

There are four possible techniques that a central bank could use to control money supply. They have one major feature in common: they involve manipulating the liquid assets of the banking system. The aim is to influence the total money supply by affecting the amount of credit that banks can create.

Open-market operations. **Open-market operations** are the most widely used of the four techniques around the world. They alter the monetary base. This then affects the amount of credit banks can create and hence the level of broad money (M4 in the UK; M3 in the eurozone).

Open-market operations involve the sale or purchase by the central bank of government securities (bonds or bills) in the open market. These sales (or purchases) are *not* in response to changes in the public-sector deficit and are thus best understood in the context of an unchanged deficit.

If the central bank wishes to *reduce* the money supply, it sells more securities. When people buy these securities, they pay for them with cheques drawn on banks. Thus banks' balances with the central bank are reduced. If this brings bank reserves below their prudent ratio (or statutory ratio, if one is in force), banks will reduce advances. There will be a multiple contraction of credit and hence of (broad) money supply. (Details of how open-market operations work in the UK are given in Box 30.2.)

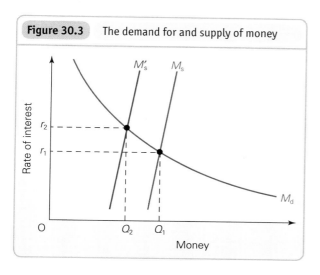

Figure 30.3   The demand for and supply of money

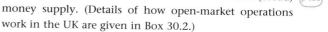

Definition

Open-market operations The sale (or purchase) by the authorities of government securities in the open market in order to reduce (or increase) money supply.

BOX 30.2   THE DAILY OPERATION OF MONETARY POLICY

What goes on at Threadneedle Street?

The Bank of England (the 'Bank') does not normally attempt to control money supply directly. Instead it seeks to control interest rates by conducting open-market operations (OMOs) through short-term and longer-term repos and through the outright purchase of high-quality bonds, These operations, as we shall see, determine short-term interest rates, which then have a knock-on effect on longer-term rates, as returns on different forms of assets must remain competitive with each other.

Let us assume that the Monetary Policy Committee (MPC) of the Bank of England forecasts that inflation will fall below target as a result of a low level of aggregate demand. At its monthly meeting, therefore, it decides to reduce interest rates. What does the Bank do?

The first thing is that it will announce a cut in Bank Rate. It then has to back up the announcement by using OMOs to ensure that its announced interest rate is the equilibrium rate.

Short-term open-market operations

Central to the process is banks' reserves with the Bank of England. Since March 2006, commercial banks set their own reserve targets for the period between the Bank's interest rate decisions (the 'maintenance period'). If on average across the period their reserve balance fell within a narrow range of ±1% of the target, the reserves would be remunerated at the policy rate (Bank Rate).

The Bank of England conducts short-term OMOs every week (on a Thursday) at Bank Rate. In other words, if banks start running short of reserves, as they may well do if lower interest rates encourage customers to spend more from their accounts, they can borrow at Bank Rate through short-term repos (with a one-week maturity).

The size of the weekly OMO is adjusted to help banks maintain reserves at their agreed target levels and reflect variations in the amount of cash withdrawn or deposited in banks. Fluctuations in banknotes in circulation, and hence in banks' reserves, are accepted *within* the week as the reserve target is a weekly *average*.

Although there is usually a shortage of liquidity in the banking system, in some weeks there may be a surplus. To prevent this driving market interest rates down too far, the Bank will look to drain banks' reserves. It can do this in three ways. First, it could sell some of its bond portfolio on a repo basis. Second, it could invite banks to bid for Bank of England one-week sterling bills. Third, it could sell outright some if its bond portfolio.

At the end of the monthly period between MPC interest rate decisions, the Bank of England conducts a 'fine-tuning' OMO. This is conducted on a Wednesday – the day before the MPC

decision on interest rates. The idea is to ensure that banks meet their reserve targets as closely as possible. This OMO could expand or contract liquidity as appropriate.

Longer-term open-market operations

Normally once per month – on a Tuesday at 10 a.m. mid-month – the Bank of England conducts longer-term OMOs. This involves repos at 3-, 6-, 9- and 12-month maturities. In other words, the Bank of England lends money to banks to provide longer-term liquidity.

The rate of interest is market determined. Banks bid for the money and the funds are offered to the successful bidders. The bigger the demand for these funds by banks and the lower the supply by the Bank of England, the higher will be the interest rate that banks must pay. By adjusting the supply, therefore, the Bank of England can influence longer-term interest rates.

Since 2006, the Bank of England has also been willing to make outright purchases of gilts and high-quality foreign-currency government bonds. This has been used as a means of offsetting the drying up of liquidity in the credit crunch of 2007–9. Such purchases are normally made monthly on a Monday.

Financial crisis and open market operations

The financial crisis meant that normal OMOs were no longer sufficient to maintain liquidity for purposes of monetary policy. There was a severe liquidity crisis – one which posed grave risks for financial stability. In response, from January 2009 the Bank of England deliberately injected narrow money in a process known as 'quantitative easing' (see Box 30.4). This involved the Bank of England purchasing assets, largely gilts, from banks. Between January 2009 and February 2012 the Bank of England injected £325 billion by such means. Quantitative easing thus massively extended the scope of OMOs.

As a result of the increase in aggregate reserves, short-term OMOs were temporarily suspended. Long-term repo operations continued but these were modified to allow financial institutions to sell a wider range of securities. Furthermore, as we saw in Box 28.4, the Bank of England introduced the Discount Window Facility (DWF) to its monetary framework. This new permanent feature enables banks to borrow government bonds against a wide range of collateral for up to three years. Banks can then lend these gilts in exchange for liquidity.

 Assume that the Bank of England wants to raise interest rates. Trace through the process by which it achieves this.

Pause for thought

Explain how open-market operations could be used to increase the money supply.

Central bank lending to the banks. The central bank in most countries is prepared to provide extra money to banks (through gilt repos, rediscounting bills or straight loans). In some countries, it is the policy of the central bank to keep its interest rate to banks *below* market rates, thereby encouraging banks to borrow (or sell back securities) whenever such facilities are available. By cutting back the amount it is willing to provide, the central bank can reduce banks' liquid assets and hence the amount of credit they can create.

In other countries, such as the UK and the eurozone countries, it is not so much the amount of money made available that is controlled, but rather the rate of interest (or discount). The higher this rate is relative to other market rates, the less will banks be willing to borrow, and the lower, therefore, will be the monetary base. Raising this rate, therefore, has the effect of reducing the money supply.

In response to the credit crunch of 2007–9, central banks in several countries extended their willingness to lend to banks. As we saw in Box 28.4 on page 472, under its 'Special Liquidity Scheme', the Bank of England was willing to swap, on a temporary basis, banks' mortgage and other debt (an illiquid asset) for special 12-month Treasury bills (a liquid asset). The Bank was effectively lending Treasury bills against the security of mortgage and other debt. Normally banks could securitise and sell these mortgage assets on the money markets as a means of raising finance. With the credit crunch, however, such markets dried up as lenders became more cautious.

Funding. Rather than focusing on controlling the monetary base (as in the case of the above two techniques), an alternative is for the authorities (the Debt Management Office in the UK) to alter the overall liquidity position of the banks. An example of this approach is a change in the balance of **funding** government debt. To reduce money supply the authorities issue more bonds and fewer bills. Banks' balances with the central bank will be little affected, but to the extent that banks hold fewer bills, there will be a reduction in their liquidity. Funding is thus the conversion of one type of government debt (liquid) into another (illiquid).

Variable minimum reserve ratios. In some countries (such as the USA), banks are required to hold a certain proportion of their assets in liquid form. The assets which count as liquid are known as 'reserve assets'. These include assets such as balances in the central bank, bills of exchange, certificates of deposit and money market loans. The ratio of such assets to total liabilities is known as the **minimum reserve ratio**. If the central bank raises this ratio (in other words, requires the banks to hold a higher proportion of liquid assets), then banks will have to reduce the amount of credit they grant. The money supply will fall.

Difficulties in controlling money supply

Targets for the growth in broad money were an important part of UK monetary policy from 1976 to 1985. Money targets were then abandoned and have not been used since. The European Central Bank targets the growth of M3 (see Box 30.3), but this is a subsidiary policy to that of setting interest rates in order to keep inflation under control. If, however, a central bank did choose to target money supply as its main monetary policy, how would the policy work?

Assume that money supply is above target and that the central bank wishes to reduce it. It would probably use open-market operations: i.e. it would sell more bonds or bills. The purchasers of the bonds or bills would draw liquidity from the banks. Banks would then supposedly be forced to cut down on the credit they create. But is it as simple as this?

The problem is that banks will normally be unwilling to cut down on loans if people want to borrow – after all, borrowing by customers earns profits for the banks. Banks can always 'top up' their liquidity by borrowing from the central bank and then carry on lending. True, they will have to pay the interest rate charged by the central bank, but they can pass on any rise in the rate to their customers.

The point is that as long as people *want* to borrow, banks and other financial institutions will normally try to find ways of meeting the demand. In other words, in the short run at least, the supply of money is to a large extent demand determined. It is for this reason that central banks prefer to control the *demand* for money by controlling interest rates.

As we shall see in Box 30.4, there are similar difficulties in *expanding* broad money supply by a desired amount. Following the credit crunch, various central banks around the world engaged in a process of quantitative easing. The process results in an increase in the monetary base (narrow money); banks' liquidity increases. But just how much this results in an increase in broad money depends on the willingness of banks to lend and customers to borrow. In the recessionary climate after 2008, confidence was low. Much of the extra liquidity remained in banks and the money multiplier fell (see Figure 28.4 on page 472). In 2009–10, the growth of M4 in the UK fell, despite quantitative easing, and actually became negative in October 2010 and remained negative throughout 2011 and 2012.

Techniques to control interest rates

The approach to monetary control today in most countries is to focus directly on interest rates. Normally an interest rate change will be announced, and then open-market operations will be conducted by the central bank to ensure that the money supply is adjusted so as to make the announced interest rate the *equilibrium* one. Thus, in Figure 30.3 (on

---

Definitions

Funding Where the authorities alter the balance of bills and bonds for any given level of government borrowing.

Minimum reserve ratio A minimum ratio of cash (or other specified liquid assets) to deposits (either total or selected) that the central bank requires banks to hold.

BOX 30.3   MONETARY POLICY IN THE EUROZONE

The role of the ECB

The European Central Bank (ECB) is based in Frankfurt and is charged with operating the monetary policy of those EU countries that have adopted the euro. Although the ECB has the overall responsibility for the eurozone's monetary policy, the central banks of the individual countries, such as the Bank of France and Germany's Bundesbank, were not abolished. They are responsible for distributing euros and for carrying out the ECB's policy with respect to institutions in their own countries. The whole system of the ECB and the national central banks is known as the European System of Central Banks (ESCB).

In operating the monetary policy of a 'euro economy' roughly the size of the USA, and in being independent from national governments, the ECB's power is enormous and is equivalent to that of the Fed. So what is the structure of this giant on the European stage, and how does it operate?

The structure of the ECB

The ECB has two major decision-making bodies: the Governing Council and the Executive Board.[1]

The Governing Council consists of the members of the Executive Board and the governors of the central banks of each of the eurozone countries. The Council's role is to set the main targets of monetary policy and to take an oversight of the success (or otherwise) of that policy.

The Executive Board consists of a president, a vice-president and four other members. Each serves for an eight-year, non-renewable term. The Executive Board is responsible for implementing the decisions of the Governing Council and for preparing policies for the Council's consideration.

[1] See www.ecb.int/ecb/orga/decisions/govc/html/index.en.html

Each member of the Executive Board has a responsibility for some particular aspect of monetary policy.

The targets of monetary policy

The overall responsibility of the ECB is to achieve price stability in the eurozone. The target is a rate of inflation below, but close to, 2 per cent over the medium term. It is a weighted average rate for all the members of the eurozone, not a rate that has to be met by every member individually.

The ECB also sets a reference value for the annual growth of M3, the broad measure of the money supply. This was set at $4\frac{1}{2}$ per cent at the launch of the euro in 1999 and was still the same value in 2012. The reference value is not a rigid target, but is used as a guide to whether monetary policy is consistent with long-run price stability. In setting the reference value, three things are taken into account: the target for inflation, assumptions about the rate of growth of GDP (assumed to have a trend growth rate of 2 to $2\frac{1}{2}$ per cent per year) and the velocity of circulation of M3 (assumed to be declining at a rate of between $\frac{1}{2}$ and 1 per cent per year). The reference value is reviewed in December each year.

On the basis of its inflation target and M3 reference value, the ECB then sets the rates of interest. In June 2012, the rates were as follows: 1 per cent for the main 'refinancing operations' of the ESCB (i.e. the minimum rate of interest at which liquidity is offered once per week to 'monetary financial institutions' (MFIs) by the ESCB); a 'marginal lending' rate of 1.75 per cent (for providing overnight support to the MFIs); and a 'deposit rate' of 0.25 per cent (the rate paid to MFIs for depositing overnight surplus liquidity with the ESCB).

Interest rates are set by the Governing Council by simple majority. In the event of a tie, the president has the casting vote.

---

page 519), the central bank might announce a rise in interest rates from r_1 to r_2 and then conduct open-market operations to ensure that the money supply is reduced from Q_1 to Q_2.

Let us assume that the central bank decides to raise interest rates. What does it do? In general, it will seek to keep banks short of liquidity. This will happen automatically on any day when tax payments by banks' customers exceed the money they receive from government expenditure. This excess is effectively withdrawn from banks and ends up in the government's account at the central bank. Even when this does not occur, the issuing of government debt will effectively keep the banking system short of liquidity, at least in the short run.

This 'shortage' can then be used as a way of forcing through interest rate changes. Banks will obtain the necessary liquidity from the central bank through repos (see page 464) or by selling it back bills. The central bank can *choose the rate of interest to charge* (i.e. the repo rate or the

bill price). This will then have a knock-on effect on other interest rates throughout the banking system. (See Box 30.2 for more details on just how the Bank of England manipulates interest rates on a day-to-day basis.)

The effectiveness of changes in interest rates

Even though central bank adjustment of the repo rate is the current preferred method of monetary control in most countries, it is not without its difficulties. The problems centre on the nature of the demand for loans. If this demand is (a) unresponsive to interest rate changes or (b) unstable because it is significantly affected by other determinants (such as anticipated income or foreign interest rates), then it will be very difficult to control by controlling the rate of interest.

Problem of an inelastic demand for loans. If the demand for loans is inelastic (i.e. a relatively steep M_d curve in Figure 30.3 on page 519), any attempt to reduce demand

The operation of monetary policy

The ECB sets a minimum reserve ratio for eurozone banks of 2 per cent. This applies to loans funded by deposits with a maturity of up to 2 years. The ratio is designed primarily to prevent excessive lending.

The main instrument for keeping the ECB's desired interest rate as the equilibrium rate is open-market operations in government bonds and other recognised assets, mainly in the form of repos. These repo operations are conducted by the national central banks, which must ensure that the repo rate does not rise above the marginal overnight lending rate or below the deposit rate.

The ECB uses four types of open-market operation:

Main refinancing operations. These are short-term repos with a maturity of one week. They take place weekly and are used to maintain liquidity consistent with the chosen ECB interest rate.

Longer-term refinancing operations (LTROs). These take place monthly and normally have a maturity of three months but, as we shall see below, three-year LTROs were introduced in 2011. They are to provide additional longer-term liquidity to banks as required at rates determined by the market, not the ECB.

Fine-tuning operations. These can be short-term sales or purchases of short-term assets. They are designed to combat unexpected changes in liquidity and hence to keep money-market rates at the ECB's chosen rate.

Structural operations. These are used as necessary to adjust the amount of liquidity in the eurozone. They can involve either the purchase or sale of various assets.

ECB independence

The ECB is one of the most independent central banks in the world. It has very little formal accountability to elected politicians. Although its president can be called before the European Parliament, the Parliament has virtually no powers to influence the ECB's actions. Also, its deliberations are secret. Unlike meetings of the Bank of England's Monetary Policy Committee, the minutes of the Council meetings are not published.

Financial crisis

The financial crisis put incredible strains on commercial banks in eurozone and, hence, on the ECB's monetary framework. Consequently, monetary operations were gradually modified.

A Securities Market Programme (SMP) began in May 2010 designed to supply liquidity to the ailing banking system. It allowed for ECB purchases of central government debt in the secondary market (i.e. not directly from governments) as well as purchases both in primary and secondary markets of private-sector debt instruments. By June 2012, €214 billion of purchases had been made, largely of government bonds issued by countries experiencing financing difficulties, including Portugal, Ireland, Greece and Spain.

The reserve ratio was reduced in January 2012 from 2 per cent to 1 per cent, so helping to alleviate some of the constraints on the volume of bank lending by banks. This move was preceded in December 2011 by three-year refinancing operations (LTROs) worth €529.5 billion and involving some 800 banks. By the end of February 2012, a further €489.2 billion of three-year loans to 523 banks took place, taking the ECB's repo operations to over €1 trillion. The hope was that the funds would help financially distressed banks pay off maturing debt and again increase their lending.

 What are the arguments for and against publishing the minutes of the meetings of the ECB's Governing Council and Executive Board?

---

will involve large rises in interest rates. The problem will be compounded if the demand curve shifts to the right, due, say, to a consumer spending boom. High interest rates lead to the following problems:

- They may discourage business investment and thereby reduce long-term growth.
- They add to the costs of production, to the costs of house purchase and generally to the cost of living. They are thus cost inflationary.
- They are politically unpopular, since the general public do not like paying higher interest rates on overdrafts, credit cards and mortgages.
- The necessary bond issue to restrain liquidity will commit the government to paying high rates on these bonds for the next 20 years or so.
- High interest rates encourage inflows of money from abroad. This drives up the exchange rate. A higher exchange rate makes domestically produced goods expensive relative to goods made abroad. This can be very damaging for export industries and industries competing with imports. Many firms in the UK suffered badly between 1997 and 2007 from a high exchange rate, caused partly by higher interest rates in the UK than in the eurozone and the USA.

Evidence suggests that the demand for loans may indeed be quite inelastic. Especially in the short run, many firms and individuals simply cannot reduce their borrowing commitments. What is more, although high interest rates may discourage many firms from taking out long-term fixed-interest loans, some firms may merely switch to shorter-term variable-interest loans.

Problem of an unstable demand. Accurate monetary control requires the central bank to be able to predict the demand curve for money (in Figure 30.3). Only then can they set the appropriate level of interest rates. Unfortunately, the demand curve may shift unpredictably, making control very

BOX 30.4   QUANTITATIVE EASING

Rethinking monetary policy in hard times

As the economies of the world slid into recession in 2008, central banks became more and more worried that the traditional instrument of monetary policy – controlling interest rates – was insufficient to ward off a slump in demand.

Running out of options?

Interest rates had been cut at an unprecedented rate and central banks were reaching the end of the road for cuts. The Fed was the first to be in this position. By December 2008 the target federal funds rate (the overnight rate at which the Fed lends to banks) had been cut to a range between 0 and 0.25 per cent in December. But you cannot cut nominal rates below zero – otherwise you would be paying people to borrow money, which would be like giving people free money.

The problem was that there was an acute lack of willingness of banks to lend, and firms and consumers to borrow, as people saw the oncoming recession.

Increasing the money supply

So what were central banks to do? The answer was to increase money supply directly, in a process known as *quantitative easing*. This involves an aggressive version of open-market operations, where the central bank buys up a range of assets, such as securitised mortgage debt and long-term government bonds. The effect is to pump large amounts of additional cash into the economy in the hope of stimulating demand and, through the process of credit creation, to boost broad money too.

In the USA, in December 2008, at the same time as the federal funds rate was cut to a range of 0 to 0.25 per cent, the Fed embarked on large-scale quantitative easing. It began buying hundreds of billions of dollars' worth of mortgage-backed securities on the open market and planned also to buy large quantities of long-term government debt. The result was that considerable quantities of new money were injected into the system.

In the UK, in January 2009, the Bank of England was given powers by the Treasury to buy up to £50 billion of high-quality private-sector assets, such as corporate bonds, commercial paper and various viable securitised assets. These purchases were funded by the issuance of Treasury Bills. The aim was directly to increase money supply. But this was only the start.

In March 2009, as the recession deepened, the Chancellor agreed to increase the scale and range of assets to be purchased. This effectively marked the beginning of the second and substantive phase of quantitative easing. These purchases, mainly government bonds (gilts), were financed by the creation of new electronic money. As this was deposited by the sellers of assets in their bank accounts, so banks' reserves with the Bank of England increased, allowing for credit creation. By November 2009 the MPC had sanctioned asset purchases of £200 billion.

The MPC was subsequently to vote for further asset purchases. By May 2012 they had reached £325 billion.

The transmission mechanism of asset purchases

Quantitative easing involves directly increasing the amount of narrow money. It can also, indirectly, increase broad money. There are two main ways this can happen.

The first is through the effects on asset prices and yields. When non-bank financial companies, including insurance companies and pension funds, sell assets to the central bank, they can use the money to purchase other assets. In doing so this will drive up their prices. This, in turn, reduces the yields on these assets (at a higher price there is less dividend or interest per pound spent on them), which should help to reduce interest rates generally and make the cost of borrowing cheaper for households and firms, thereby boosting aggregate demand.

The second mechanism is through bank lending. Commercial banks will find their reserve balances increase at the central bank as the sellers of assets to the central bank deposit the money in their bank accounts. This will increase the liquidity ratio of banks, which, other things being equal, should encourage them to grant more credit.

Of course, a key question is just how much credit creation will take place. As we saw in Figure 28.4 (see page 478), the broad money multiplier fell markedly in 2009 and again in 2011/12 indicating that the increase in the monetary base was proportionately greater than that in broad money. In other words, it is all very well increasing the monetary base, but a central bank cannot force banks to lend or people to borrow. That requires confidence. Indeed from July 2010 to March 2012, a lack of confidence caused M4 to fall by 6.5 per cent – a real fall of 12.5 per cent.

This is not to say that quantitative easing failed in the UK: the decline in broad money could have been greater still. Nonetheless, it does illustrate the potential danger of this approach if, in the short run, little credit creation takes place. In the equation $MV = PY$, the rise in (narrow) money supply (M) may be largely, or more than, offset by a fall in the velocity of circulation (V) (see page 488).

On the other hand, there is also the danger that if this policy is conducted for too long, the growth in broad money supply could ultimately prove to be excessive, resulting in inflation rising above the target level. It is therefore important for central banks to foresee this and turn the monetary 'tap' off in time.

 Would it be appropriate to define the policy of quantitative easing as 'monetarist'?

Definition

Quantitative easing A deliberate attempt by the central bank to increase the money supply by buying large quantities of securities through open-market operations. These securities could be securitised mortgage and other private-sector debt or government bonds.

difficult. The major reason is *speculation*. For example, if people think interest rates will rise and bond prices fall, in the meantime they will demand to hold their assets in liquid form. The demand for money will rise. Alternatively, if people think exchange rates will rise, they will demand the domestic currency while it is still relatively cheap. The demand for money will rise.

It is very difficult for the central bank to predict what people's expectations will be. Speculation depends so much on world political events, rumour and 'random shocks'.

If the demand curve shifts very much, and if it is inelastic, then monetary control will be very difficult. Furthermore, the central bank will have to make frequent and sizeable adjustments to interest rates. These fluctuations can be very damaging to business confidence and may discourage long-term investment.

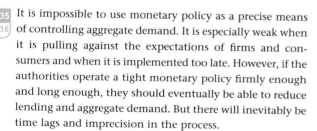

Pause for thought

Assume that the central bank announces a rise in interest rates and backs this up with open-market operations. What determines the size of the resulting fall in aggregate demand?

The net result of an inelastic and unstable demand for money is that substantial interest rate changes may be necessary to bring about the required change in aggregate demand. For example, central banks had to cut interest rates to virtually zero in their attempt to tackle the global recession of the late 2000s. Indeed, as we see in Box 30.4, central banks took to other methods as the room for further interest rate cuts simply disappeared.

Using monetary policy

It is impossible to use monetary policy as a precise means of controlling aggregate demand. It is especially weak when it is pulling against the expectations of firms and consumers and when it is implemented too late. However, if the authorities operate a tight monetary policy firmly enough and long enough, they should eventually be able to reduce lending and aggregate demand. But there will inevitably be time lags and imprecision in the process.

An expansionary monetary policy is even less reliable. If the economy is in recession, no matter how low interest rates are driven, or however much the monetary base is expanded, people cannot be forced to borrow if they do not wish to. Firms will not borrow to invest if they predict a continuing recession.

A particular difficulty in using interest rate reductions to expand the economy arises if the repo rate is nearly zero but this is still not enough to stimulate the economy. The problem is that (nominal) interest rates cannot be negative, for clearly nobody would be willing to lend in these circumstances. Japan was in such a situation in the early 2000s. It was caught in what is known as the **liquidity trap**. The UK and many eurozone countries were in this position in the early 2010s. Despite record low interest rates and high levels of liquidity, borrowing and lending remained low given worries about fiscal austerity and its dampening effects on economic growth.

Despite these problems, changing interest rates can often be quite effective in the medium term. After all, they can be changed very rapidly. There are not the time lags of implementation that there are with fiscal policy. Indeed, since the early 1990s, most governments or central banks in OECD countries have used interest rate changes as the major means of keeping aggregate demand and inflation under control.

In the UK, the eurozone and many other countries, a target is set for the rate of inflation. As we have seen, in the UK the target is 2 per cent; in the eurozone it is 'close to' 2 per cent. If forecasts suggest that inflation is going to be above the target rate, the government or central bank raises interest rates. The advantage of this is that it sends a very clear message to people that inflation *will* be kept under control. People will therefore be more likely to adjust their expectations accordingly and keep their borrowing in check.

Definition

Liquidity trap When interest rates are at their floor and thus any further increases in money supply will not be spent but merely be held in idle balances as people wait for the economy to recover and/or interest rates to rise.

30.3 ATTITUDES TOWARDS DEMAND MANAGEMENT

Debates over the control of demand have shifted ground somewhat in recent years. There is now less debate over the relative effectiveness of fiscal and monetary policy in influencing aggregate demand. There is general agreement that a *combination* of fiscal and monetary policies will have a more powerful effect than either used separately.

The debate today is much more concerned with the extent to which governments ought to pursue an active

demand management policy or adhere to a set of policy rules.

Those in the Keynesian tradition prefer discretionary policy – changing policy as circumstances change. Those in the monetarist tradition prefer to set firm rules (e.g. targets for inflation, public deficits or growth in the money supply) and then stick to them. The financial crisis of the late 2000s helped to fuel the debate about the *type* and *flexibility* of policy rules and the extent to which governments should have discretion over policy.

The case for rules and policy frameworks

Why should governments commit to rules or design policy frameworks which may involve their giving up control of economic instruments? Well, there are two important arguments against discretionary policy.

Political behaviour. The first concerns the motivation of government. Politicians may attempt to manipulate the economy for their own political purposes – such as the desire to be re-elected. The government, if not constrained by rules, may overstimulate the economy some time before an election so that growth is strong at election time. After the election, the government strongly dampens the economy to deal with the higher inflation and rising public-sector debt, and to create enough slack for another boost in time for the next election.

 When politicians behave in this way, they may lose *credibility* for sound economic management. This can lead to higher inflationary expectations, uncertainty and lower long-term investment.

Time lags with discretionary policy. Both fiscal and monetary policies can involve long and variable time lags, which can make the policy at best ineffective and at worst destabilising. Taking the measures before the problem arises, and thus lessening the problem of lags, is no answer since forecasting tends to be unreliable.

In contrast, by setting and sticking to rules, and then not interfering further, the government can provide a sound monetary framework in which there is maximum freedom for individual initiative and enterprise, and in which firms are not cushioned from market forces and are therefore encouraged to be efficient. By the government setting a target for a steady reduction in the growth of money supply, or a target for the rate of inflation, and then resolutely sticking to it, people's expectations of inflation will be reduced, thereby making the target easier to achieve.

This sound and stable monetary environment, with no likelihood of sudden contractionary or expansionary fiscal or monetary policy, will encourage firms to take a longer-term perspective and to plan ahead. This could then lead to increased capital investment and raise long-term growth rates.

The optimum situation is for all the major countries to adhere to mutually consistent rules, so that their economies do not get out of line. This will create more stable exchange rates and provide the climate for world growth.

Advocates of this point of view in the 1970s and 1980s were the monetarists, but in recent years support for the setting of targets has become widespread. As we have seen, in both the UK and the eurozone countries, targets are set for both inflation and public-sector deficits.

The case for discretion

 Many economists, especially those in the Keynesian tradition, reject the argument that rules provide the environment for high and stable growth. Demand, they argue, is subject to many and sometimes violent shocks: e.g. changes in expectations, domestic political events (such as an impending election), world economic factors (such as the world economic recession of 2008–9) or world political events (such as a war). The resulting shifts in injections or withdrawals cause the economy to deviate from a stable full-employment growth path.

 Any change in injections or withdrawals will lead to a cumulative effect on national income via the multiplier and accelerator and via changing expectations. These effects take time and interact with each other, and so a process of expansion or contraction can last many months before a turning point is eventually reached.

Since shocks to demand occur at irregular intervals and are of different magnitudes, the economy is likely to experience cycles of irregular duration and of varying intensity.

 Given that the economy is inherently unstable and is buffeted around by various shocks, Keynesians argue that the government needs actively to intervene to stabilise the economy. Otherwise, the uncertainty caused by unpredictable fluctuations will be very damaging to investment and hence to long-term economic growth (quite apart from the short-term effects of recessions on output and employment).

Difficulties with choice of target under a rules-based policy

Assume that the government or central bank sets an inflation target. Should it then stick to that rate, come what may? Might not an extended period of relatively low inflation warrant a lower inflation target? The government must at least have the discretion to *change* the rules, even if only occasionally.

Then there is the question of whether success in achieving the target will bring success in achieving other macroeconomic objectives, such as low unemployment and stable economic growth? The problem is that something called **Goodhart's Law** is likely to apply. The law, named after Charles Goodhart, formerly of the Bank of England, states that attempts to control an *indicator* of a problem may, as a result, make it cease to be a good indicator of the problem.

> ### Definition
>
> **Goodhart's Law** Controlling a symptom of a problem, or only part of the problem, will not cure the problem: it will simply mean that the part that is being controlled now becomes a poor indicator of the problem.

KEY IDEA 43

Goodhart's law. Controlling a symptom (i.e. an indicator) of a problem will not cure the problem. Instead, the indicator will merely cease to be a good indicator of the problem.

Targeting inflation may make it become a poor indicator of the state of the economy. If people believe that the central bank will be successful in achieving its inflation target, then those expectations will feed into their inflationary expectations, and not surprisingly the target will be met. But that target rate of inflation may now be consistent with both a buoyant and a depressed economy. As we saw for the UK in Figure 29.7, it is possible that the Phillips curve may become *horizontal*.

In extreme cases, as occurred in 2008, the economy may slow down rapidly and yet cost-push factors cause inflation to rise. Targeting inflation in these circumstances will demand *higher* interest rates, which will help to deepen the recession. Thus achieving the inflation target may not tackle the much more serious problem of creating stable economic growth and an environment which will therefore encourage long-term investment.

Use of a Taylor rule. For this reason, many economists have advocated the use of a **Taylor rule**,[1] rather than a simple inflation target. A Taylor rule takes *two* objectives into account – (1) inflation and (2) either the rate of economic growth or unemployment – and seeks to get the optimum degree of stability of the two. The degree of importance attached to each of the two objectives can be decided by the government or central bank. The central bank adjusts interest rates when either the rate of inflation diverges from its target or the rate of economic growth (or unemployment) diverges from its sustainable (or equilibrium) level.

Take the case where inflation is above its target level. The central bank following a Taylor rule will raise the rate of interest. It knows, however, that this will reduce economic growth. This, therefore, limits the amount that the central bank is prepared to raise the rate of interest. The more weight it attaches to stabilising inflation, the more it will raise the rate of interest. The more weight it attaches to maintaining stable economic growth, the less it will raise the rate of interest.

KI 41
p 436

Thus the central bank has to trade off inflation stability against real income stability.

Constrained discretion in the UK

Many countries have, in recent times, been operating economic policy within a framework of rules. This is known as *constrained discretion*.

On being elected in 1997 the UK Labour government set about reforming the frameworks within which fiscal and monetary policies operated.

Fiscal policy. The Labour government set targets for government expenditure, not for just one year, but for a three-year period. It also adopted two operational rules: the golden rule and the sustainable investment rule. These were examined in Box 30.1.

Monetary policy. As far as monetary policy is concerned, this involved granting operational independence to the Bank of England.

Operational independence for the Bank of England means that it sets interest rates in order to meet a government-set inflation rate target. Since December 2003, the target has been that CPI inflation should be 2 per cent in 24 months' time.

To help it achieve this target two years in the future, the Bank of England publishes a quarterly *Inflation Report*, which contains projections for inflation for the next three years. These projections assume that interest rates follow market expectations. They form the basis for the Monetary Policy Committee's monthly deliberations. If the projected inflation in 24 months' time is off target, the MPC will change interest rates accordingly.

Two key projections from the *Inflation Report* are shown in Figure 30.4. They are known as 'fan charts'. The first plots the forecast range of inflation. The second plots the forecast range of real GDP growth. In each case, the darkest central band represents a 10 per cent likelihood, as does each of the eight subsequent pairs of lighter areas out from the central band. Thus inflation and GDP growth are considered to have a 90 per cent probability of being within their respective fan. The bands get wider as the time horizon is extended, indicating increasing uncertainty about the outcome. Also, the less reliable are considered to be the forecasts by the MPC, the wider will be the fan. The dashed line indicates the two-year target point. Thus in quarter 1 of 2013, the 2 per cent inflation target was for quarter 1 of 2015.

Although projections are made for GDP growth, these are to help inform the forecast for inflation. GDP growth is not itself an explicit target.

Definitions

Taylor rule A rule adopted by a central bank for setting the rate of interest. It will raise the interest rate if (a) inflation is above target or (b) economic growth is above the sustainable level (or unemployment is below the equilibrium rate). The rule states how much interest rates will be changed in each case.

Constrained discretion A set of principles or rules within which economic policy operates. These can be informal or enshrined in law.

---

[1] Named after John Taylor, from Stanford University, who proposed that for every 1 per cent that GDP rises above sustainable GDP, real interest rates should be raised by 0.5 percentage points, and that for every 1 per cent that inflation rises above its target level, real interest rates should be raised by 0.5 percentage points (i.e. nominal rates should be raised by 1.5 percentage points).

Figure 30.4 Fan chart of CPI inflation and GDP growth projections (made in 2013 Q1, based on market interest rate expectations and £375 billion of asset purchases)

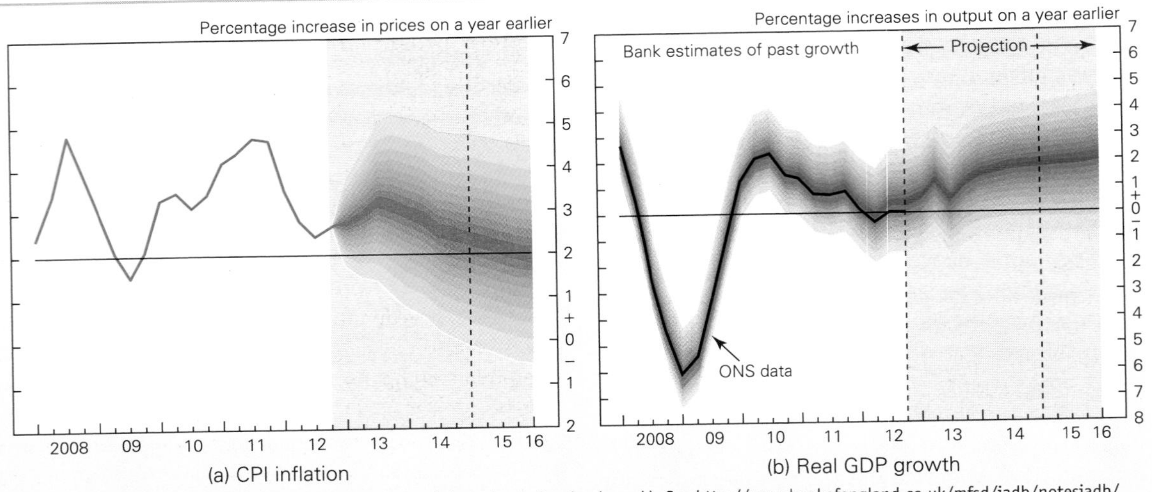

(a) CPI inflation

(b) Real GDP growth

Source: *Inflation Report* (Bank of England, February 2013) (www.bankofengland.co.uk). See http://www.bankofengland.co.uk/mfsd/iadb/notesiadb/Revisions.htm for the Revisions Policy.

Pause for thought

If people believe that the central bank will be successful in keeping inflation on target, does it matter whether a simple inflation rule or a Taylor rule is used? Explain.

Another aim of central bank independence is to enhance transparency in policy making. In the UK, transparency is enhanced by the publication of the minutes of the monthly meetings of the MPC, at which interest rates are set. One of the main purposes of transparency is to convince people of the seriousness with which the Bank of England will adhere to its targets. This, it is hoped, will keep people's *expectations* of inflation low: the lower expected inflation is, the lower will be the actual rate of inflation.

In both fiscal and monetary policy, therefore, rules appeared to have replaced discretion. There was, however, a new form of fine tuning: the frequent adjustment of interest rates, not to smooth out the business cycle, but to make sure that the inflation rule is adhered to. Nevertheless, with automatic fiscal stabilisers still operating, and with interest rate changes to stabilise inflation also having the effect of stabilising aggregate demand, cyclical fluctuations had become less pronounced. Between 1997 and 2007, the average annual economic growth rate was 3.3 per cent, with the rate varying between 2.1 per cent (2005) and 4.5 per cent (2000).

Growing problems in 2008

The global crisis, which started in 2007 with the credit crunch and then developed into the worldwide recession

of 2008–9, highlighted differences between countries in their monetary and fiscal frameworks. It also raised the question of whether rules should be abandoned – at least in exceptional circumstances.

Monetary policy responses. In 2007–8, many countries were faced with a possible return of stagflation (low or no growth accompanied by rapidly rising prices). World food and other commodity prices were rising rapidly. This supply-side shock meant that inflation rates rose. For example, in the UK by September 2008, the annual CPI inflation rate had reached 5.2 per cent while general food prices were rising at an annual rate in excess of 10 per cent. At the same time, the credit crunch that started in the USA spread like a contagion around the world.

To meet their inflationary target, central banks were under pressure to raise interest rates. But, to avert a recession they were under pressure to cut them.

Eventually, with confidence in the banking system plummeting and inter-bank markets virtually frozen, the Bank of England (along with several other central banks) began cutting interest rates. At least now the rate of inflation was forecast to be below 2 per cent in 24 months' time. The Bank of England reduced the Bank Rate from 4.25 per cent in September 2008 to just 0.5 per cent by March 2009, where it stayed through the rest of 2009 and on into 2012. In addition (as we saw in Box 28.4), massive amounts of liquidity and capital were pumped into the banking system to stimulate lending and hence aggregate demand.

But despite general agreement that both inflation and GDP were falling, the extent and speed of the interest rates cuts varied across countries. In part, this reflects differences in the frameworks within which central banks operate. This is explored in Case Study K.10 in MyEconLab.

Fiscal policy responses. The extent of the downturn put governments under pressure to give their economies a fiscal stimulus. In the UK, with the current budget already in deficit (see Box 30.1), the government was in danger of breaching its golden rule and thus would seem to have limited scope for increased expenditure or tax cuts to stimulate aggregate demand.

But the problem was seen to be too serious to stick to rules for rules sake and the golden and sustainable investments rules were abandoned – at least temporarily. The hope was that the rules would be reintroduced once the economy had recovered. As Box 30.1 illustrates, fiscal policy was relaxed with a package of tax cuts and increases in government expenditure, though increases in taxes further down the line were pre-announced.

Fiscal consolidation

The fiscal priority of the Coalition government, formed following the general election in May 2010, was to reduce borrowing and, later in the parliamentary session, to make a start in bringing down the stock of public-sector debt relative to GDP. Public-sector net borrowing in 2010 was in excess of 10 per cent of GDP. Meanwhile the stock of public-sector debt, excluding the liabilities of those banking groups temporarily within the public sector, had reached 59 per cent of GDP.

The government's policy was therefore one of fiscal consolidation with a 'fiscal mandate' to achieve a cyclically adjusted current balance by 2015/16, supplemented by a target for public-sector debt as a percentage of GDP to be falling by 2015/16. The relatively short time span within which these objectives were to be met meant significant expenditure cuts and tax rises. The government announced a total 'consolidation' of £128 billion per year by 2015/16 with, as explained in Box 30.1, the bulk of the consolidation coming from spending cuts.

The debate surrounding the fiscal consolidation had echoes from the past. The prevailing view of the Treasury in the 1920s and early 1930s had been that governments should look to balance their books. In effect, by not doing so it was felt that governments would be competing with the private sector for scarce financial resources and thereby forcing up interest rates and the cost of borrowing. Furthermore, it was argued that governments compete with the private sector for other resources too, notably labour and raw materials. The Coalition government hoped that, by pursuing a rapid fiscal deficit reduction strategy focused on expenditure cuts, it could foster a private-sector-led recovery.

The Labour opposition, taking a more Keynesian line, argued that cutting the deficit too rapidly might not enable rises in consumer expenditure, exports and investment to offset the cuts in government expenditure and that aggregate demand could fall. Indeed, the cuts in government expenditure and rises in tax would curtail the growth in consumer expenditure and hence private-sector investment. There was a severe danger, argued the opposition, that the cuts would significantly weaken growth and, in turn, cause a fall in confidence that would further weaken aggregate demand. The lack of economic growth would actually exacerbate the level of government borrowing.

KI 42
p 486

SUMMARY

1a Fiscal policy affects the size of government budget deficits or surpluses.

1b Automatic fiscal stabilisers are tax revenues that rise and benefits that fall as national income rises. They have the effect of reducing the size of the multiplier and thus reducing cyclical upswings and downswings.

1c Discretionary fiscal policy is where the government deliberately changes taxes or government expenditure in order to alter the level of aggregate demand. Changes in government expenditure on goods and services will have a full multiplier effect. Changes in taxes and benefits will have a smaller multiplier effect as some of the tax/benefit changes will merely affect other withdrawals and thus have a smaller net effect on consumption of domestic product.

1d There are problems in predicting the magnitude of the effects of discretionary fiscal policy. Expansionary fiscal policy can act as a pump primer and stimulate increased private expenditure, or it can crowd out private expenditure. The extent to which it acts as a pump primer depends crucially on business confidence – something that is very difficult to predict beyond a few weeks or months. The extent of crowding out depends on monetary conditions and monetary policy.

1e There are various time lags involved with fiscal policy, which make it difficult to use fiscal policy to 'fine tune' the economy.

1f In recent years, many governments around the world preferred a more passive approach towards fiscal policy. Targets were set for one or more measures of the public-sector finances, and then taxes and government expenditure were adjusted so as to keep to the target.

1g Nevertheless, in extreme circumstances, as occurred in 2008/9, governments were prepared to abandon rules and give a fiscal stimulus to their economies.

2a Control of the growth of the money supply over the longer term will normally involve governments attempting to restrict the size of the budget deficit. This will be difficult to do, however, in a period of recession.

2b In the short term, the authorities can use monetary policy to restrict the growth in aggregate demand in one of two major ways: (a) reducing money supply directly, (b) reducing the demand for money by raising interest rates.

▶

2c The money supply can be reduced directly by using open-market operations. This involves the authorities selling more government securities and thereby reducing banks' reserves when their customers pay for them from their bank accounts. Alternatively, the authorities can reduce the amount it is prepared to lend to banks (other than as a last-resort measure).

2d The money supply is difficult to control precisely, however, and even if it is successfully controlled, there then arises the problem of severe fluctuations in interest rates if the demand for money fluctuates and is relatively inelastic.

2e The current method of control involves the Bank of England's Monetary Policy Committee announcing the interest rate and then the Bank of England bringing this rate about by its operations in the repo and discount markets. It keeps banks short of liquidity, and then supplies them with liquidity largely through gilt repos, at the chosen interest rate (gilt repo rate). This then has a knock-on effect on interest rates throughout the economy.

2f With an inelastic demand for loans, there may have to be substantial changes in interest rates in order to bring the required change in aggregate demand. What is more, controlling aggregate demand through interest rates is made even more difficult by fluctuations in the demand for money. These fluctuations are made more severe by speculation against changes in interest rates, exchange rates, the rate of inflation, etc.

2g Nevertheless, controlling interest rates is a way of responding rapidly to changing forecasts, and can be an important signal to markets that inflation will be kept under control, especially when, as in the UK and the eurozone, there is a firm target for the rate of inflation.

3a The case against discretionary policy is that it involves unpredictable time lags that can make the policy

destabilising. Also, the government may *ignore* the long-run adverse consequences of policies designed for short-run political gain.

3b The case in favour of rules is that they help to reduce inflationary expectations and thus create a stable environment for investment and growth.

3c The case against sticking to money supply or inflation rules is that they may cause severe fluctuations in interest rates and thus create a less stable economic environment for business planning.

3d Although perfect fine tuning may not be possible, Keynesians argue that the government must have the discretion to change its policy as circumstances demand.

3e The UK Labour government, elected in 1997, enshrined in law monetary and fiscal frameworks that involved constraining some of its discretion over economic policy. This included making the Bank of England independent. This now targets a 2 per cent rate of inflation, and adjusts interest rates in order to meet that target. To meet its Code for Fiscal Stability, the UK government set a golden rule to balance its current (as opposed to capital) budget over the course of the business cycle. There seemed to be little scope for discretionary demand-management policy.

3f This became a serious problem in 2008 with rising inflation and falling growth. In November 2008, however, the government abandoned its golden rule and gave a fiscal boost to the economy to combat the slide into recession.

3g The Coalition government, which took power in 2010, embarked on a strategy of fiscal consolidation, focusing on expenditure cuts. Its fiscal mandate was to achieve a balanced cyclically adjusted current budget by 2015/16. This was supplemented by a target for public-sector debt as a share of GDP to be falling by the same date.

REVIEW QUESTIONS

1 'The existence of a budget deficit or a budget surplus tells us very little about the stance of fiscal policy.' Explain and discuss.

2 Adam Smith remarked in *The Wealth of Nations* concerning the balancing of budgets, 'What is prudence in the conduct of every private family can scarce be folly in that of a great kingdom.' What problems might there be if the government decided to follow a balanced budget approach to its spending?

3 What factors determine the effectiveness of discretionary fiscal policy?

4 Why is it difficult to use fiscal policy to 'fine tune' the economy?

5 When the Bank of England announces that it is putting up interest rates, how will it achieve this, given that interest rates are determined by demand and supply?

6 How does the Bank of England attempt to achieve the target rate of inflation of 2 per cent? What determines its likelihood of success in meeting the target?

7 Imagine you were called in by the government to advise on whether it should adopt a policy of targeting the money supply. What advice would you give and how would you justify the advice?

8 Imagine you were called in by the government to advise on whether it should attempt to prevent cyclical fluctuations by the use of fiscal policy. What advice would you give and how would you justify the advice?

9 What do you understand by the term 'constrained discretion'? Illustrate your answer with reference to the UK and the eurozone.

10 Is there a compromise between purely discretionary policy and adhering to strict targets?

11 Under what circumstances would adherence to an inflation target lead to (a) more stable interest rates, (b) less stable interest rates than pursuing discretionary demand management policy?

31 Chapter

Supply-side policy

Business issues covered in this chapter

- How can supply-side policy influence business and the economy?
- What types of supply-side policy can be pursued and what is their effectiveness?
- What will be the impact on business of a policy of tax cuts?
- How can the government encourage increased competition?
- What is the best way of tackling regional problems and encouraging business investment in relatively deprived areas?
- What is meant by 'industrial policy' and what forms can it take?

31.1 SUPPLY-SIDE PROBLEMS

In considering economic policy up to this point we have focused our attention on the demand side of the economy, where unemployment and slow growth are the result of a lack of aggregate demand, and where inflation and a balance of trade deficit are the result of excessive aggregate demand. Many of the causes of these problems, however, lie on the *supply side* and, as such, require an alternative policy approach.

KI 36 **p 316** If successful, ***supply-side policies*** will shift the aggregate supply curve to the right, thus increasing output for any given level of prices (or reducing the price level for any given level of output).

Definition

Supply-side policies Government policies that attempt to influence aggregate supply directly, rather than through aggregate demand.

Effective supply-side initiatives increase an economy's *potential output*: the economy's output when firms are operating at normal levels of capacity utilisation. But, more than this, economists and policy-makers are concerned with how supply-side policies might raise the rate at which the level of potential output grows over time. Therefore, supply-side policies can be evaluated on their ability to affect an economy's long-run economic *growth*.

The quantity and productivity of factors of production

The aggregate supply curve is fundamentally related to an economy's factors of production (i.e. its resources, such as labour and capital). Therefore, policies which influence the *quantities* of factors employed and their *productivity* constitute supply-side policies. The quantity and productivity of factors of production are key supply-side variables.

The labour market

Consider first the labour market. Can policies be designed, for instance, which over time will raise the productivity or effectiveness of the labour force? Can policies be put in place which will make workers more responsive to job opportunities? And how long will it take for such policies to be effective?

> ### Pause for thought
>
> *How can increasing the effectiveness of labour improve both the productivity of labour and the productivity of capital?*

Supply-side policies can also be used to reduce unemployment. In section 26.3 we introduced the concept of equilibrium unemployment: the difference between those who would like to work at the current wage rate and those willing and able to take a job. We saw how this is caused by various rigidities or imperfections in the market. There is a mismatching of aggregate supply and demand, and vacancies are not filled despite the existence of unemployment. Perhaps workers have the wrong qualifications, or are poorly motivated, or are living a long way away from the job, or are simply unaware of the jobs that are vacant. Generally, the problem is that labour is not sufficiently mobile, either occupationally or geographically, to respond to changes in the job market. Labour supply for particular jobs is too inelastic.

Supply-side policies might look to increasing labour market flexibility, to providing better job information or to supporting retraining. Alternatively, they may aim to make employers more adaptable and willing to operate within existing labour constraints.

Investment

For decades, the UK has had a lower level of investment relative to national income than other industrialised countries. This is illustrated in Table 31.1. In particular, investment by the private sector has been weak by international standards: a trend that seems to have persisted over four decades.

> ### Pause for thought
>
> *How can the UK's low level of investment relative to national income be explained?*

To some extent the UK's poor investment performance has been offset by the fact that wage rates have been lower than in competing countries. This has at least made the UK relatively attractive to inward investment, especially by US, Japanese, Korean and more recently by Chinese and Indian companies seeking to set up production plants within the EU.

The poor performance of UK manufacturing firms has resulted in a growing import penetration of the UK market. Imports of manufactured products have grown more rapidly than UK manufactured exports, and since 1983 the UK has been a net importer of manufactured products.

Of course, it might not be just the *quantity* of investment that matters, but also the *type* and *quality* of that investment. Increasingly, the debate concerning the drivers of economic growth has focused on what influences the rate of technological progress. For instance, can countries achieve higher rates of growth by investing in 'cutting-edge' technologies or by raising the shares of national income devoted to education, training, and research and development? Some economists argue that under certain conditions

Table 31.1	Gross fixed capital formation as a percentage of GDP: 1970–2013					
	1970–91		**1992–2013**		**1970–2013**	
	General government	**Private**	**General government**	**Private**	**General government**	**Private**
Japan	5.9	28.9	4.6	20.4	5.2	24.4
Spain	3.0	20.5	3.6	21.0	3.3	20.8
Belgium	3.9	19.7	1.8	19.6	2.9	19.6
Italy	3.0	20.8	2.2	17.9	2.6	19.3
France	3.7	20.0	3.3	16.3	3.5	18.1
Germany	3.3	18.3	1.9	17.9	2.6	18.1
Netherlands	3.7	18.7	3.2	17.1	3.5	17.9
Denmark	3.0	18.8	2.2	17.0	2.6	17.9
Ireland	4.0	18.2	3.2	15.9	3.6	17.1
USA	2.5	16.6	2.4	15.3	2.4	15.9
UK	3.1	16.2	1.8	14.6	2.4	15.4

Source: AMECO database, European Commission, DGECFIN, Tables 3.2 and 6.1

new innovations and new ideas will result in further new innovations and ideas. A key question is what policies can best achieve the conditions for the most effective propagation of innovation and technological progress.

Some economists believe that the UK's low-investment economy highlights the need for more government intervention, especially in the fields of education and training, research and development, and the provision of infrastructure. This has been the approach in many countries, including France, Germany and Japan.

Inflation and supply-side policies

Supply-side policies can impact on prices too. For instance, if inflation is caused by cost-push pressures, supply-side policy can help to reduce these cost pressures in at least two ways:

■ by encouraging more *competition* in the supply of labour and/or goods and services – perhaps through reducing the power of unions and/or firms (e.g. by anti-monopoly legislation);

| BOX 31.1 | GETTING INTENSIVE WITH PHYSICAL CAPITAL |

Economic growth and capital accumulation

In this box we look at the growth of the physical capital stock in a sample of countries and then compare this with their growth in GDP per worker.

Capital recorded in a country's national account consists of non-financial *fixed assets*. It does not include goods and services transformed or used up in the course of production known as *intermediate goods and services*. A country's stock of capital can be valued at its replacement cost, regardless of its age: this is its *gross* value. It can also be valued at its written-down value, known as its *net* value. The net value takes into account the *consumption of capital* which occurs through wear and tear (depreciation) or when capital becomes naturally obsolescent.

In models of economic growth an important measure of capital is the stock of capital per person employed (per worker). This is also known as *capital intensity*. In the chart

we plot the ratio of capital per worker in 2013 to that in 1960 (y-axis) against the ratio of output per worker (x-axis) in 2013 to that in 1960 for a sample of developed countries. For instance, the UK's capital intensity was 2.3 times higher in 2013 while its output per worker was 2.7 times higher.

We would expect that the higher the level of capital per worker, the greater will be the level of output (real GDP) per worker. This appears to be borne out by the evidence in the chart. However, a word of caution: while there is a statistical association between capital accumulation and economic growth, it is the role of economic theory to help us understand this relationship and to consider the other variables affecting long-term growth.

 Does the type of capital being accumulated impact affect the rate of long-run economic growth?

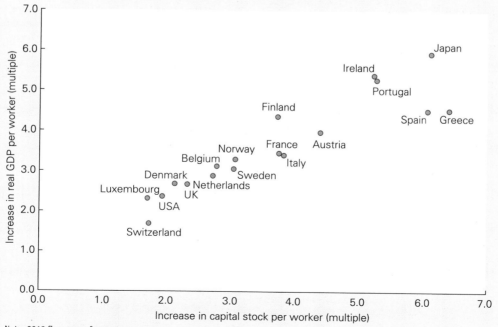

Capital and output per worker in 2013 relative to 1960

Note: 2013 figures are forecasts

Source: Based on data from *AMECO database*, European Commission

KI 9
p 47

■ by encouraging increases in *productivity* through the retraining of labour, or by investment grants to firms, or by tax incentives, etc.

Types of supply-side policy

Supply-side policies can take various forms. Section 31.2 examines *market-orientated* supply-side policies. These policies focus on ways of 'freeing up' the market, such as encouraging private enterprise, risk taking and competition; policies that provide incentives and reward initiative, hard work and productivity.

Then, in section 31.3, we look at *interventionist* supply-side policies. These focus on means of counteracting the deficiencies of the free market.

Regional imbalances. It is all too easy to view supply-side policies and initiatives solely in terms of *national* objectives. But, there are often marked differences in incomes, unemployment rates and other measures of economic and social well-being *within* a country. Therefore, both national governments and international bodies, such as the EU, may adopt supply-side projects and initiatives that help to tackle regional inequalities. We look at regional policy in the final section of this chapter.

> **Pause for thought**
>
> *Why might it take time for the benefits of supply-side policies to become evident?*

31.2 MARKET-ORIENTATED SUPPLY-SIDE POLICIES

Radical market-orientated supply-side policies were first adopted in the early 1980s by the Thatcher government in the UK and the Reagan administration in the USA, but were subsequently copied by other right and centre-right governments around the world. The essence of these supply-side policies is to encourage and reward individual enterprise and initiative, and to reduce the role of government; to put more reliance on market forces and competition, and less on government intervention and regulation.

> **Pause for thought**
>
> *Why might a recovering economy (and hence a fall in government expenditure on social security benefits) make the government feel even more concerned to make discretionary cuts in government expenditure?*

Reducing government expenditure

The desire of many governments to cut government expenditure is not just to reduce the size of the public-sector deficit and hence reduce the growth of money supply; it is also an essential ingredient of their supply-side strategy.

The public sector is portrayed by some as more bureaucratic and less efficient than the private sector. What is more, it is claimed that a growing proportion of public money has been spent on administration and other 'non-productive' activities, rather than on the direct provision of goods and services.

Two things are needed, it is argued: (a) a more efficient use of resources within the public sector and (b) a reduction in the size of the public sector. This would allow private investment to increase with no overall rise in aggregate demand. Thus the supply-side benefits of higher investment could be achieved without the demand-side costs of higher inflation.

In practice, governments have found it very difficult to cut their expenditure relative to GDP. However, many countries were faced with trying to do this after the financial crisis and global economic slowdown of the late 2000s (see Figure 31.1). Governments have found that this means making difficult choices, particularly concerning the levels of services and the provision of infrastructure.

Tax cuts

The imposition of taxation can distort a variety of choices that individuals make. Changes to the rates of taxation can lead individuals to substitute one activity for another. Three commonly referred to examples in the context of aggregate supply are:

KI 9
p 47

■ taxation of labour income and its impact on labour supply (including hours worked and choice of occupation);
■ taxation of interest income earned on financial products (savings) and its impact on the funds available for investment;
■ taxation of firms' profits and its impact on capital expenditure by firms.

Over time, the UK has witnessed a decline in the marginal rates of taxation associated with each of these cases. For example, in 1979, the standard rate of income tax in the UK was 33 per cent and the top rate was 83 per cent. By 2013 the basic rate was only 20 per cent and the top rate was only 45 per cent having been only 40 per cent prior to 2010. In 1983 the main rate of corporation tax in the UK stood at 52 per cent. By 2014 this was 22 per cent.

Substitution effects of tax cuts. The argument for reducing tax rates on incomes and profits is that it contributes to higher levels of economic output. Specifically, it encourages

KI 9
p 47

| **Figure 31.1** | General government expenditure (% of GDP) |

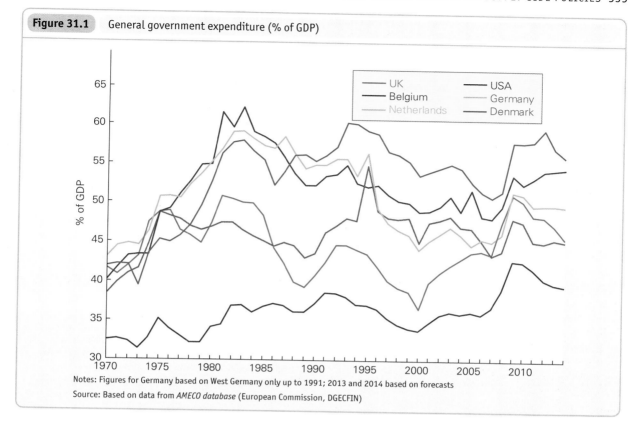

Notes: Figures for Germany based on West Germany only up to 1991; 2013 and 2014 based on forecasts

Source: Based on data from *AMECO database* (European Commission, DGECFIN)

an increased supply of labour hours, more moneys invested with financial institutions and more capital expenditure by firms than would otherwise be the case. The reason is that tax cuts increase the return on such activities. In other words, there is a *substitution effect* inducing more of these beneficial activities. In the case of labour, people are encouraged to substitute work for leisure as their after-tax wage rate is now higher.

Income effects of tax cuts. However, in each case there is a counteracting incentive. This is the *income effect*. Tax cuts increase the returns to working, saving and undertaking capital expenditure. This means that less of each activity needs to be undertaken to generate the same income flow as before. Take the case of labour: if a tax cut increases your hourly take-home pay, you may feel that you can afford to work fewer hours.

Because economic theory offers no firm conclusions as to the benefit of tax cuts, economists and policy-makers often look to empirical evidence for guidance. In the case of whether or not tax cuts encourage people to work longer hours, the evidence suggests that the substitution and income effects just about cancel each other out. Anyway, for many people there is no such choice in the short run. There is no chance of doing overtime or working a shorter week. In the long run, there may be some flexibility in that people can change jobs.

Pause for thought

If tax receipts as a proportion of national income have generally risen since 1979, does this mean that there can have been no positive incentive effects of the various tax measures taken by governments since then?

Reducing the power of labour

The argument here is that if labour costs to employers are reduced, their profits will probably rise. This could encourage and enable more investment and hence economic growth. If the monopoly power of labour is reduced, then cost-push inflation will also be reduced.

The Thatcher government in the 1980s took a number of measures to curtail the power of unions. These included introducing the right of employees not to join unions, preventing workers taking action other than against their direct employers, and enforcing secret ballots on strike proposals (see pages 279–80). It set a lead in resisting strikes in the public sector.

As labour markets have become more flexible, with increased part-time working and short-term contracts, and as the process of globalisation has exposed more companies to international competition, so this has further eroded the power of labour in many sectors of the economy (see section 18.7).

Reducing welfare

New classical economists claim that a major cause of unemployment is the small difference between the welfare benefits of the unemployed and the take-home pay of the employed. This causes voluntary unemployment (i.e. frictional unemployment). People are caught in a 'poverty trap': if they take a job, they lose their benefits.

A dramatic solution to this problem would be to cut unemployment benefits. A major problem with this approach, however, is that, with changing requirements for labour skills, many of the redundant workers from the older industries are simply not qualified for new jobs that are created. What is more, the longer people are unemployed, the more demoralised they become. Employers would probably be prepared to pay only very low wages to such workers. To persuade these unemployed people to take low-paid jobs, the welfare benefits would have to be slashed. A 'market' solution to the problem, therefore, may be a very cruel solution. A fairer solution would be an interventionist policy: a policy of retraining labour.

Another alternative is to make the payment of unemployment benefits conditional on the recipient making a concerted effort to find a job. In the Jobseeker's Allowance introduced in the UK in 1996, claimants must be available for and actively seeking work and must complete a Jobseeker's Agreement, which sets out the types of work the person is willing to do and the plan to find work. Payment can be refused if the claimant refuses to accept jobs offered.

BOX 31.2 LABOUR PRODUCTIVITY

How effective is a British worker?

A country's potential output depends on the productivity of its factors of production, including labour. There are two common ways of measuring labour productivity. The first is output per worker. This is the most straightforward measure to calculate. All that is required is a measure of total output and employment.

A second measure is output per hour worked. This has the advantage that it is not influenced by the *number* of hours worked. So for an economy like the UK, with a very high percentage of part-time workers on the one hand, and long average hours worked by full-time employees on the other, such a measure would be more accurate in gauging worker efficiency.

Both measures focus solely on the productivity of labour. If we want to account directly for the productivity of capital

we need to consider the growth in *total* factor productivity (*TFP*). This measure analyses output relative to the amount of all factors used. Changes in total factor productivity over time provide a good indicator of technical progress.

Chart (a) shows comparative labour productivity levels of various countries and the G7 group of leading industrialised countries using GDP per hour worked. It plots labour productivity *relative* to the UK. As you can see, GDP per hour worked is lower in the UK than the other countries with the exception of Japan. For example, in 2011, compared with the UK, output per hour worked was 27 per higher in the USA, 22 per cent higher in Germany and 18 per cent higher in France. A major explanation of lower productivity in the UK is the fact that for decades it has invested a smaller proportion of its national income than most other industrialised nations.

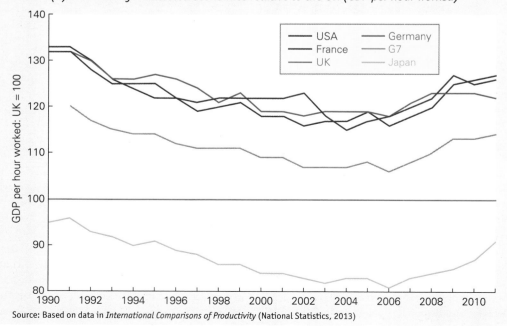

(a) Productivity in selected economies relative to the UK (GDP per hour worked)

Source: Based on data in *International Comparisons of Productivity* (National Statistics, 2013)

Policies to encourage competition

If the government can encourage more competition, this should have the effect of increasing national output and reducing inflation. Five major types of policy were pursued under this heading.

Privatisation. If privatisation simply involves the transfer of a natural monopoly to private hands (e.g. the water companies), the scope for increased competition is limited. However, where there is genuine scope for increased competition (e.g. in the supply of gas and electricity), privatisation can lead to increased efficiency, more consumer choice and lower prices.

Alternatively, privatisation can involve the introduction of private services into the public sector (e.g. private contractors providing cleaning services in hospitals, or refuse collection for local authorities). Private contractors may compete against each other for the franchise. This may well lower the cost of provision of these services, but the quality of provision may suffer unless closely monitored. The effects on unemployment are uncertain. Private contractors may offer lower wages and thus may use more labour. But if they are trying to supply the service at minimum cost, they are likely to employ less labour.

Deregulation. This involves the removal of monopoly rights: again, largely in the public sector. The deregulation of the bus industry in the 1980s, opening it up to private operators, is a good example of this initiative.

Introducing market relationships into the public sector. This is where the government tries to get different departments or

---

Nevertheless, until 2006 the gap had been narrowing. This was because UK productivity, although lower than in many other countries, was growing faster. Part of the reason for this was the inflow of investment from abroad. Since 2006, the productivity gap has widened again. This is the result partly of comparatively low levels of domestic investment (see Table 31.1 on page 532) and partly of lower levels of inward investment. Inward direct investment to the UK in 2011 was only 24 per cent of that in 2007. In France, Germany, Italy and the USA, the figures were 43, 50, 66 and 105 per cent respectively.

Chart (b) compares labour productivity across both measures. Workers in the USA and the UK work longer hours than those in France and Germany. Thus whereas output *per hour worked* in the USA is only about 5 per cent higher than in Germany and 1 per cent higher than in France, output *per person employed* in the USA is about 33 per cent higher than in Germany and 24 per cent higher than in France. The evidence points to UK labour productivity being lower than that in the USA, France and across the G7 group of countries on both measures but higher than that in Japan.

 What could explain the differences in productivity between the countries in chart (b)? What do you think governments can do to help businesses raise productivity levels?

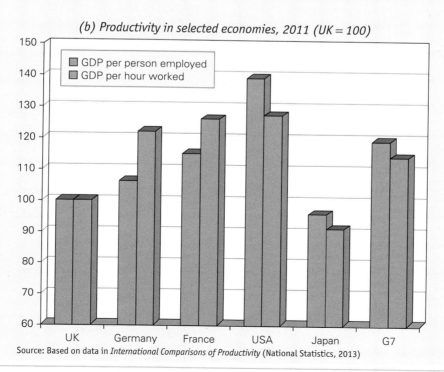

(b) Productivity in selected economies, 2011 (UK = 100)

Source: Based on data in *International Comparisons of Productivity* (National Statistics, 2013)

elements within a particular part of the public sector to 'trade' with each other, so as to encourage competition and efficiency. The best-known examples are within health and education.

One example is in the National Health Service. In 2003, the UK government introduced a system of 'foundation trusts'. Hospitals can apply for foundation trust status. If successful, they are given much greater financial autonomy in terms of purchasing, employment and investment decisions. By May 2012, there were 144 foundation trusts. Critics argue that funds have been diverted to foundation hospitals away from the less well-performing hospitals where greater funding could help that performance. In the 2012 Health and Social Care Act the government plans for all NHS hospitals to become NHS foundation trusts or part of an existing NHS foundation trust by April 2014.

The Private Finance Initiative (PFI). This is where a private company, after a competitive tender, is contracted by a government department or local authority to finance and build a project, such as a new road or a prison. The government then pays the company to maintain and/or run it, or simply rents the assets from the company. The public sector thus becomes a purchaser of services rather than a direct provider itself.

The aim of these 'public–private partnerships' (PPPs) is to introduce competition (through the tendering process) and private-sector expertise into the provision of public services (see Case Study K.14 in MyEconLab). By doing so, the objective is to achieve gains in efficiency which outweigh any extra burden to the taxpayer from private-sector profits.

Critics, however, claim that PPPs result in a poorer quality of provision with weak cost control too, resulting in a higher burden for the taxpayer in the long term. Given mounting criticisms of PPPs and general concerns over levels of government borrowing, the Coalition government in November 2011 set up a review of the PFI. The intention was to develop a new model for delivering public investment and services which, while taking advantage of private-sector expertise, did so at a lower cost than the PFI.

Free trade and capital movements. The opening up of international trade and investment is central to a market-orientated supply-side policy. One of the first measures of the Thatcher government (in October 1979) was to remove all controls on the purchase and sale of foreign currencies, thereby permitting the free inflow and outflow of capital, both long term and short term. Most other industrialised countries also removed or relaxed exchange controls during the 1980s and early 1990s.

The Single European Act of 1987, which came into force in 1993, was another example of international liberalisation. As we saw in section 25.3, it created a 'single market' in the EU: a market without barriers to the movement of goods, services, capital and labour.

31.3 INTERVENTIONIST SUPPLY-SIDE POLICIES

The basis of the case for government intervention is that the free market is likely to provide too little research and development, training and investment.

There are potentially large external benefits from research and development. Firms investing in developing and improving products, and especially firms engaged in more general scientific research, may produce results that provide benefits to many other firms. Thus the *social* rate of return on investment may be much higher than the *private* rate of return. Investment that is privately unprofitable for a firm may therefore still be economically desirable for the nation.

Similarly, investment in training may continue yielding benefits to society that are lost to the firms providing the training when the workers leave.

Investment often involves risks. Firms may be unwilling to take those risks, since the costs of possible failure may be too high. When looked at nationally, however, the benefits of investment might well have substantially outweighed the costs, and thus it would have been socially desirable for firms to have taken the risk. Successes would have outweighed failures.

Even when firms do wish to make such investments, they may find difficulties in raising finance. Banks may be unwilling to lend. Alternatively, if firms rely on raising finance by the issue of new shares, this makes them very dependent on the stock market performance of their shares. This depends largely on current profitability and expected profitability in the near future, not on *long-term* profitability. Similarly, the fear of takeovers may make managers over-concerned to keep shareholders happy, further encouraging 'short-termism'.

Types of interventionist supply-side policy

Nationalisation. This is the most extreme form of intervention, and one that most countries had tended to reject, given a worldwide trend for privatisation. Nevertheless, many countries have stopped short of privatising certain key transport and power industries, such as the railways and electricity generation.

Nationalisation may also be a suitable solution for rescuing vital industries suffering extreme market turbulence. This was the case with the banks in the late 2000s (and beyond) as the financial crisis unfolded. With the credit crunch and the over-exposure to risky investments in securitised sub-prime debt, inadequate levels of capital, declining confidence and plummeting share prices, several banks were taken into full or partial public ownership.

Direct provision. Improvements in infrastructure, such as a better motorway system, can be of direct benefit to industry. Alternatively, the government could provide factories or equipment to specific firms.

Funding research and development. Around about one-third of UK R&D is financed by the government, but around half of this has been concentrated in the fields of defence, aerospace and the nuclear power industry. As a result, there has been little government sponsorship of research in the majority of industry. Since the mid-1970s, however, there have been several government initiatives in the field of information technology. Even so, the amount of government support in this field has been very small compared with Japan, France and the USA. What is more, the amount of support declined between the mid-1980s and the late 1990s.

The UK provides financial support for R&D expenditure through corporation tax relief. In other words, firms can reduce the profits liable for tax by engaging in R&D. As of April 2012, the rate of relief for small and medium-sized enterprises (SMEs) was 225 per cent: taxable profits are reduced by £225 for every £100 of R&D expenditure. For larger companies the rate of relief was 130 per cent.

In 2009, the UK government announced proposals for a Patent Box. The idea is firms will be provided with financial support to innovate where this results in their acquiring patents. Patents provide protection for intellectual property rights. From April 2013, firms are liable to corporation tax on the profits attributable to qualifying patents at a reduced rate of 10 per cent.

Training and education. The government may set up training schemes, or encourage educational institutions to make their courses more vocationally relevant, or introduce new vocational qualifications (such as GNVQs, NVQs and foundation degrees in the UK). Alternatively, the government can provide grants or tax relief to firms which themselves provide training schemes. The UK invests little in training programmes compared with most of its industrial competitors. Alternative approaches to training in the UK, Germany, France and the USA are examined in Case Study K.14 in MyEconLab.

Assistance to small firms. UK governments in recent years have recognised the importance of small firms to the economy and have introduced various forms of advisory services, grants and tax concessions. For example, in 2013

BOX 31.3   A NEW APPROACH TO INDUSTRIAL POLICY

Industrial policy attempts to increase investment and halt or slow the shrinking of the industrial sector. As with many other areas of economic policy, industrial policy throughout most of the world has undergone a radical reorientation in recent years. The government's role has shifted from one of direct intervention in the form of subsidies and protecting industry from competition, to one of focusing upon the external business environment and the conditions that influence its competitiveness.

The reasons for such a change are both philosophical and structural:

■ The rise of the political right in the 1980s led to a shift away from interventionist and towards market-based supply-side policy.
■ Growing government debt, and a desire to curb public expenditure, acted as a key incentive to reduce the state's role in industrial affairs. This was argued to be one of the driving forces behind the European privatisation process in the 1980s and 1990s.
■ During the 1980s, industry became progressively more global in its outlook. As such, its investment decisions were increasingly being determined by external environmental factors, especially the technology, productivity and labour costs of its international competitors.

The new approach to industrial policy, being widely adopted by many advanced countries, is to focus on improving those factors which shape a nation's competitiveness. This involves shifting away from particular sectors to targeting what are referred to as 'framework conditions for industry'. Policies include the following:

■ The promotion of investment in physical and human capital. Human capital in particular, and the existence of a sound skills base, are seen as crucial for attracting global business and ensuring long-run economic growth.
■ A reduction in non-wage employment costs, such as employers' social security and pension contributions. Many governments see these costs as too high and as a severe limitation on competitiveness and employment creation.
■ The promotion of innovation and the encouragement of greater levels of R&D.
■ Support for small and medium-sized enterprises. SMEs have received particular attention due to their crucial role in enhancing innovation, creating employment and contributing to skills development, especially in high-tech areas (see Chapter 16).
■ The improvement of infrastructure. This includes both physical transport, such as roads and railways, and information highways.
■ The protection of intellectual property by more effective use of patents and copyright. By reinforcing the law in these areas, it is hoped to encourage firms to develop new products and commit themselves to research.

These policies, if they are to be truly effective, are likely to require coordination and integration, since they represent a radical departure from traditional industrial policy.

1. In what senses could these new policies be described as (a) non-interventionist; (b) interventionist?
2. Does globalisation, and in particular the global perspective of multinational corporations, make industrial policy in the form of selective subsidies and tax relief more or less likely?

KI 9
p47

small firms paid a 20 per cent rate of corporation tax compared with 23 per cent for larger companies. In addition, small firms are subject to fewer planning and other bureaucratic controls than large companies. Support to small firms in the UK is examined in Case Study K.16 in MyEconLab.

Advice and persuasion. The government may engage in discussions with private firms in order to find ways to improve efficiency and innovation. It may bring firms together to exchange information, so as to coordinate their decisions and create a climate of greater certainty. It may bring firms

and unions together to try to create greater industrial harmony.

Information. The government may provide various information services to firms: technical assistance, the results of public research, information on markets, etc.

In addition to adopting supply-side measures that focus on the economy as a whole, governments might decide to target specific regions of the economy, or specific industries for policy initiatives. Such initiatives are often more interventionist in nature, as the next section shows.

31.4 REGIONAL POLICY

Within most countries, unemployment is not evenly distributed. Take the case of the UK. Northern Ireland and parts of the north and west of England, parts of Wales and parts of Scotland have unemployment rates substantially higher than in the south-east of England.

Similarly, countries experience regional disparities in average incomes, rates of growth and levels of prices, as well as in health, crime, housing, etc. In the UK, these disparities grew wider in the mid-1980s as the recession hit the north, with its traditional heavy industries, much harder than the south. In the recession of the early 1990s, however, it was the service sector that was hardest hit, a sector more concentrated in the south. Regional disparities therefore narrowed somewhat. Disparities are not only experienced at regional level. They are often more acutely felt in specific *areas*, especially inner cities and urban localities subject to industrial decline.

Within the European Union differences exist not only within individual countries, but between them. For example, in the EU some countries are much less prosperous than others. Thus, especially with the opening up of the EU in 1993 to the free movement of factors of production, capital and labour may flow to the more prosperous regions of the Union, such as Germany, France and the Benelux countries, and away from the less prosperous regions, such as Portugal, Greece and southern Italy. With enlargement of the EU in 2004 and 2007 to include twelve new members, mainly from central and eastern Europe, regional disparities within the EU have widened further.

Causes of regional imbalance and the role of regional policy

If the market functioned perfectly, there would be no regional problem. If wages were lower and unemployment were higher in the north, people would simply move to the south. This would reduce unemployment in the north and help to fill vacancies in the south. It would drive up wage rates in the north and reduce wage rates in the south.

The process would continue until regional disparities were eliminated.

The capital market would function similarly. New investment would be located in the areas offering the highest rate of return. If land and labour were cheaper in the north, capital would be attracted there. This too would help to eliminate regional disparities.

A similar argument applies between countries. Take the case of the EU. Labour should move from the poorer countries, such as those of eastern Europe, to the richer ones and capital should flow in the opposite direction until disparities are eliminated.

In practice, the market does not always behave as just described. There are three major problems.

Labour and capital immobility. Labour may be geographically immobile. The regional pattern of industrial location may change more rapidly than the labour market can adjust to it. Thus jobs may be lost in the depressed areas more rapidly than people can migrate.

Similarly, the existing capital stock is highly immobile. Buildings and most machinery cannot be moved to where the unemployed are! *New* capital is much more mobile. But there may be insufficient new investment, especially during a recession, to halt regional decline, even if some investors are attracted into the depressed areas by low wages and cheap land.

Regional multiplier effects. The continuing shift in demand may in part be due to *regional multiplier effects*. In the prosperous regions, the new industries and the new workers attracted there create additional demand. This

Definition

Regional multiplier effects When a change in injections into or withdrawals from a particular region causes a multiplied change in income in that region. The regional multiplier is given by $1/(1 - mpc_r)$, where mpc_r is the marginal propensity to consume products from the region.

creates additional output and jobs and hence more migration. There is a multiplied rise in income. In the depressed regions, the decline in demand and loss of jobs causes a multiplied downward effect. Loss of jobs in manufacturing leads to less money spent in the local community; transport and other service industries lose custom. The whole region becomes more depressed.

KI 33
p 311

Externalities. Labour migration imposes external costs on non-migrants. In the prosperous regions, the new arrivals compete for services with those already there. Services become overstretched; house prices rise; council house waiting lists lengthen; roads become more congested, etc. In the depressed regions, services decline, or alternatively local taxes must rise for those who remain if local services are to be protected. Dereliction, depression and unemployment cause emotional stress for those who remain.

Approaches to regional policy

Market-orientated solutions

Supporters of market-based solutions argue that firms are the best judges of where they should locate. Government intervention would impede efficient decision taking by firms. It is better, they argue, to remove impediments to the market achieving regional and local balance. For example, they favour either or both of the following.

Locally negotiated wage agreements. A problem with nationally negotiated wage rates is that that wages are not driven down in the less prosperous areas and up in the more prosperous ones. This discourages firms from locating in the less prosperous areas. At the same time, firms find it difficult to recruit labour in the more prosperous ones, where wages are not high enough to compensate for the higher cost of living there.

Reducing unemployment benefits. A general reduction in unemployment benefits and other welfare payments would encourage the unemployed in the areas of high unemployment to migrate to the more prosperous areas, or enable firms to offer lower wages in the areas of high unemployment.

KI 9
p 47

The problem with these policies is that they attempt initially to widen the economic divide between workers in the different areas in order to encourage capital and labour to move. Such policies would hardly be welcomed by workers in the poorer areas!

> ### Pause for thought
>
> 1. *Think of some other 'pro-market' solutions to the regional problem.*
> 2. *Do people in the more prosperous areas benefit from pro-market solutions?*

BOX 31.4 **EU REGIONAL POLICY**

The 2007–13 spending programme

An interesting case study of the use of regional policy is the European Union. The EU allocated around 35 per cent of its total budget to regional policy over the period 2007–13, spending some €347 billion.

The EU implements a regional policy because of the existence of economic and social disparities. The EU estimated, prior to the programme starting, that about 154 million inhabitants (one in three EU citizens) had a GDP per head below the 'convergence level' of 75 per cent of the EU-27 average. These disparities had grown with the accession of ten new members in 2004 and two more in 2007.

The 2007–13 programme focused primarily on the poorest member states and regions of the EU: i.e. those below the convergence level of GDP per head. The amount available under the convergence objective was €282.8 billion.

Outside of the convergence regions, significant funds were allocated according to the regional competitiveness and employment objective. This focused on promoting innovation, human capital and job creation. The amount given to this objective was €55 billion.

In order to allocate its resources and meet its objectives, the EU operates a series of interrelated funds, collectively known as the Structural and Cohesion Funds.

The European Regional Development Fund (ERDF). This fund is managed by the Directorate-General for Regional Policy. It allocates grants for projects designed to aid development

in poorer regions of the EU. It focuses upon investment in companies to create and maintain employment, investment in infrastructure and funds to support local development and to foster cooperation between regions.

The European Social Fund (ESF). The ESF is managed by the Directorate-General for Employment and Social Affairs. It allocates funds to help workers and businesses adapt to industrial change, to encourage the social integration of disadvantaged people, to help the unemployed into work, and to strengthen the stock of human capital: i.e. the skills and knowledge base of the workforce.

Cohesion Fund. This is aimed at member states whose national income per head is less than 90 per cent of the EU average. Its aim is to support the development of infrastructure projects, particularly trans-European transport networks, and enhance measures that help protect and improve the quality of the environment.

The next spending programme runs from 2014 to 2020. It is designed to meet the EU's *Europe 2020 strategy*. This includes objectives to reduce youth unemployment, encourage research and development, increase numbers in tertiary education, reduce poverty and to meet climate/energy targets.

 To what extent is the EU's regional policy consistent with those theories of long-term growth theory stressing the importance of innovation and technological progress?

Interventionist solutions

KI 36
p 316

Interventionist policies involve encouraging firms to move. Such policies include the following.

KI 9
p 47

Subsidies and tax concessions in the depressed regions. Businesses could be given general subsidies, such as grants to move, or reduced rates of corporation tax. Alternatively, grants or subsidies could be specifically targeted at increasing employment (e.g. reduced employer's national insurance contributions) or at encouraging investment (e.g. investment grants or other measures to reduce the costs of capital).

The provision of facilities in depressed regions. The government or local authorities could provide facilities such as land and buildings at concessionary, or even zero, rents to incoming firms; or spend money on improving the infrastructure of the area (roads and communications, technical colleges, etc.).

The siting of government offices in the depressed regions. The government could move some of its own departments out of the capital and locate them in areas of high unemployment. The siting of the vehicle licensing centre in Swansea is an example.

It is important to distinguish policies that merely seek to *modify* the market by altering market signals, from policies that *replace* the market. *Regulation* replaces the market, and unless very carefully devised and monitored may lead to ill-thought-out decisions being made. *Subsidies* and *taxes* merely modify the market, leaving it to individual firms to make their final location decisions.

KI 43
p 527

Pause for thought

If you were the government, how would you set about deciding the rate of subsidy to pay a firm thinking of moving to a less prosperous area?

SUMMARY

1a Supply-side policies, if successful, will shift the aggregate supply curve to the right. Supply-side policies look to influence the quantity and productivity of factors of production.

1b The UK has had a lower rate of investment than most other industrialised countries. This has contributed to a historically low rate of economic growth and a growing trade deficit in manufactures.

2a Market-orientated supply-side policies aim to increase the rate of growth of aggregate supply and reduce the rate of unemployment by encouraging private enterprise and the freer play of market forces.

2b Reducing government expenditure as a proportion of GDP is a major element of such policies.

2c Tax cuts can be used to encourage people to work more and more efficiently, and to encourage investment. The effects of tax cuts will depend on how people respond to incentives. The substitution effect will result in greater output; the income effect in lower output.

2d Reducing the power of trade unions and a reduction in welfare benefits, especially those related to unemployment, may force workers to accept jobs at lower wages, thereby decreasing equilibrium unemployment.

2e Various policies can be introduced to increase competition. These include privatisation, deregulation, introducing market relationships into the public sector, the Private Finance Initiative, and freer international trade and capital movements.

3 Interventionist supply-side policy can take the form of grants for investment and research and development, advice and persuasion, the direct provision of infrastructure and the provision, funding or encouragement of various training schemes.

4a Regional and local disparities arise from a changing pattern of industrial production. With many of the older industries concentrated in certain parts of the country and especially in the inner cities, and with an acceleration in the rate of industrial change, so the gap between rich and poor areas has widened.

4b Regional disparities can in theory be corrected by the market, with capital being attracted to areas of low wages and workers being attracted to areas of high wages. In practice, regional disparities persist because of capital and labour immobility and regional multiplier effects.

REVIEW QUESTIONS

1 Define demand-side and supply-side policies. Are there any ways in which such policies are incompatible?

2 Outline the main supply-side policies that have been introduced in the UK since 1979. Does the evidence suggest that they have achieved what they set out to do?

3 What types of tax cuts are likely to create the greatest (a) incentives, (b) disincentives to effort?

4 Compare the relative merits of pro-market and interventionist solutions to regional imbalances.

5 Is the decline of older industries necessarily undesirable?

6 In what ways can interventionist supply-side policy work with the market, rather than against it? What are the arguments for and against such policy?

32 Chapter

International economic policy

Business issues covered in this chapter

- How does the level of business activity in one country impact on that in other countries?
- How do the major economies of the world seek to coordinate their policies and what difficulties arise in the process?
- How did the euro evolve and how effective was the system of exchange rates in Europe that preceded the birth of the euro?
- What are the advantages and disadvantages of the euro for members of the eurozone and for businesses both inside and outside the eurozone?
- How can greater currency stability be achieved, thereby creating a more certain global environment for business?

32.1 GLOBAL INTERDEPENDENCE

KI 42 p 486 We live in an interdependent world. Countries are affected by the economic health of other countries and by their governments' policies. Problems in one part of the world can spread like a contagion to other parts, with perhaps no country immune. This was clearly illustrated by the credit crunch of 2007–8. A crisis that started in the sub-prime market in the USA soon snowballed into a worldwide recession.

There are two major ways in which this process of 'globalisation' affects individual economies. The first is through trade. The second is through financial markets.

Interdependence through trade

So long as nations trade with one another, the domestic economic actions of one nation will have implications for those that trade with it. For example, if the US administration feels that the US economy is growing too fast, it might adopt various contractionary fiscal and monetary measures,

such as higher tax rates or interest rates. US consumers will not only consume fewer domestically produced goods, but also reduce their consumption of imported products. But US imports are other countries' exports. A fall in these other countries' exports will lead to a multiplier effect in these countries. Output and employment will fall.

Changes in aggregate demand in one country thus send ripples throughout the global economy. The process whereby changes in imports into (or exports from) one country affect national income in other countries is known as the *international trade multiplier*. **KI 42** p 486

Definition

International trade multiplier The effect on national income in country B of a change in exports (or imports) of country A.

The more open an economy, the more vulnerable it will be to changes in the level of economic activity in the rest of the world. This problem will be particularly acute if a nation is heavily dependent on trade with one other nation (e.g. Canada on the USA) or one other region (e.g. Switzerland on the EU).

In Chapter 24, we saw that while, since 1970, global GDP has grown by 3.6 per cent per year, export volumes have grown by 5.9 per cent per year. Despite the impact of the global slowdown at the end of the 2000s, it is likely that trade will continue to increase as a percentage of world GDP. This will increase countries' interdependence and their vulnerability to world trade fluctuations.

> **Pause for thought**
>
> *Assume that the US economy expands. What will determine the size of the multiplier effect on other countries?*

BOX 32.1 DOCTOR, THE WORLD HAS CAUGHT A COLD!

Global answers to global problems?

We don't have to look far to see how much economic and financial interdependence affects our daily lives. As you walk down the street to the supermarket, many of the passing cars originate overseas or perhaps were built here by foreign-owned companies. You look up and the plane flying overhead is taking passengers to some far-flung corner of the world for business and pleasure. As you enter the supermarket you see an array of goods from all over the world. Clearly, interdependence through trade connects economies.

The late 2000s have helped also to demonstrate just how interdependent financial systems and financial institutions have become. Financial products had been given a passport to travel, and travel they do!

Increasing economic and financial interdependence means that problems in one part of the world rapidly spread to other parts. Just look at what happened when the US sub-prime mortgage market collapsed. America's illness turned into the world's flu!

But who should dish out the medicine? How potent can the medicine of national governments be in isolation? What role is there for coordinated monetary and fiscal policies and does it require stronger international institutions to deal with world problems?

Iceland's cold

The decline in output in Iceland in 2009, at nearly 7 per cent, was especially stark. The country had been badly hit by the global financial crisis.

An aggressive strategy of credit expansion had seen the liabilities of the three largest Icelandic banks rise from 100 per cent of GDP in 2004 to 923 per cent in 2007. Some of the funds from this expansion came from the inter-bank market but also from deposits overseas in subsidiaries of these banks in the Nordic countries and the UK. When the credit crunch hit, they found it increasingly difficult to roll over loans on the inter-bank market. What is more, the sheer scale of the banks' expansion made it virtually impossible for the Central Bank to guarantee repayments of the loans.

The result was that four of its largest banks were nationalised and run by Iceland's Financial Supervisory Authority.

In November 2008 the International Monetary Fund's executive board approved a US$2.1 billion loan to Iceland to support an economic recovery programme. An initial payment of US$827 million was made with subsequent payments to be spread over time, subject to IMF quarterly reviews of the recovery programme.

A Greek Tragedy?

Greece has been struggling with the burden of a huge budget deficit for some years and following the credit crunch of 2008, its general government deficit soared. In 2008 it was 9.8 per cent of GDP; by 2009, it was 15.6 per cent – the highest in the EU at the time and over five times higher than EU rules allow. The annual cost to Greece of servicing the debt was running at about 12 per cent of GDP. In early 2010 the government estimated that it would need to borrow €53 billion to cover budget shortfalls. Greece, like many other countries, also experienced rising unemployment. By 2010 the unemployment rate was 12.5 per cent, up from 7.7 per cent in 2008.

Austerity measures, as part of an IMF and EU rescue package, aimed to reduce this deficit to less than 3 per cent of GDP by 2014. This would be achieved through a variety of spending cuts and tax rises and is the price that Greece has had to pay to receive a £95 billion bailout. However, the costs of the austerity measures in terms of falling disposable income and rising unemployment have been very high and there have been widespread strikes by public-sector workers.

Subsequent events demonstrated that the debt crisis was not just confined to Greece. For instance, in November 2010 Ireland agreed a rescue package of up to €100 billion with the IMF and EU member states. The general government deficit in Ireland in 2010 was estimated at 31.2 per cent of GDP, up from 14.0 per cent in 2009. The aim was to reduce to this to 3 per cent of GDP by 2015.

IMF to the rescue

We have seen how the IMF has been a major player in helping to finance rescue packages for countries like Iceland, Ireland and Greece. But what is the IMF? And what does it do?

The IMF is a 'specialised agency' of the United Nations and is financed by its 188 member countries (as of 2012). The role of the IMF is to ensure macroeconomic stability – as in the cases above – and to foster global growth.

It also works with developing nations to alleviate poverty and to achieve economic stability. To do this it provides countries with loans.

The IMF has not been without controversy, however. Conditions attached to loans have often been very harsh, especially for some of the most indebted developing countries.

Financial interdependence

International trade has grown rapidly, but international financial flows have grown much more rapidly. Each day, some $4 trillion of assets are traded across the foreign exchanges. Many of the transactions are short-term financial flows, moving to where interest rates are most favourable or to currencies where the exchange rate is likely to appreciate. This again makes countries interdependent.

Pause for thought

Are exports likely to continue growing faster than GDP indefinitely? What will determine the outcome?

Financial interdependency impacts not only on financial institutions around the world, but also on national economies. It also illustrates how global responses can be

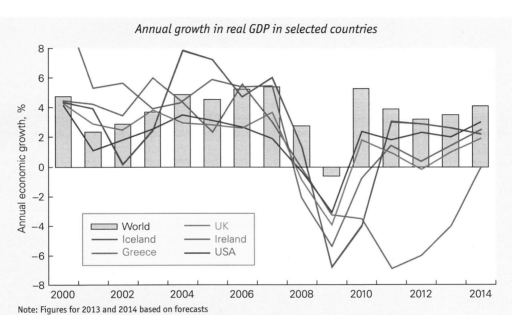

Annual growth in real GDP in selected countries

Annual economic growth, %

Legend: World, Iceland, Greece, UK, Ireland, USA

Note: Figures for 2013 and 2014 based on forecasts

Source: Based on data in *World Economic Outlook*, October 2012 and January 2013 (International Monetary Fund)

The global economic and financial crisis provided the IMF with a challenge: which countries to support with a limited budget? Between 2007 and spring 2012, the IMF provided some $300 billion of loans to member countries. During this period an increasing amount of assistance was being given to developed economies, especially within the EU.

Following crisis talks with finance ministers in Europe in May 2010, the IMF agreed to set aside €250 billion to support eurozone countries in financial difficulty. This would be in addition to €440 billion supplied by eurozone countries under the 'European Financial Stability Facility' and €60 billion from EU funds under the 'European Financial Stabilisation Mechanism'.

In October 2010 the EU agreed to establish a more permanent funding mechanism for eurozone countries in financial difficulties, known as the European Stability Mechanism (see Box 30.1). The Mechanism became operational in 2013. The IMF is a crucial stakeholder in the funding mechanism, both in committing funds but also in assessing, alongside the European Commission and the European Central Banks, the financial position of any country requesting help. This assessment includes possible 'macroeconomic adjustment programmes' for countries in receipt of funds.

Strengthening the IMF

World leaders meeting as part of the G20 in London in April 2009 announced the need to strengthen global financial institutions. They agreed that the resources available to the IMF should be trebled to US$750 billion. They also agreed that the IMF would work with a new Financial Stability Board (FSB), made up, amongst others, of the G20 countries and the European Commission, so as to help in identifying potential economic and financial risks. Essentially, the G20 countries were looking for a better 'early warning system' to meet some of the challenges of an increasingly interdependent world.

However, the ongoing financial problems facing governments, particularly in the eurozone, led the international community in April 2012 to pledge a further increase of $430 billion in resources for the IMF. The intention was to create a credible 'firewall' to contain future financial crisis.

Do you see any problems arising from a strengthening of global economic and financial institutions?

needed. As a result of the credit crunch, world leaders were seriously worried that the whole world would plunge into deep recession. A coordinated policy response from governments and central banks began in earnest in October 2008 when governments in Britain, Europe, North America and other parts of the world injected some $2 trillion of extra capital into banks.

Global policy response

As a consequence of both trade and financial interdependence, the world economy, like the economy of any individual country, tends to experience periodic fluctuations in economic activity – an *international* business cycle. The implication of this is that countries will tend to share common problems and concerns at the same time.

This can aid the process of international cooperation between countries. Countries frequently meet in various groupings – from the narrow group of the world's seven richest countries (the G7) to broader groups such as the G20, which, in addition to the G7 and other rich countries, also includes larger developing countries, such as China, India and Brazil.

Global interdependence also raises important questions about the role of international organisations like the World Trade Organization (see Chapter 24) and the International Monetary Fund (IMF).

The IMF's remit is to promote global growth and stability, to help countries through economic difficulty and to help developing economies achieve macroeconomic stability and reduce poverty. In response to the global economic and financial crisis of the late 2000s, the IMF's budget was substantially increased and it became more actively involved with what were previously defined as 'strong performing economies' (see Box 32.1).

32.2 INTERNATIONAL HARMONISATION OF ECONOMIC POLICIES

What is of crucial importance is to avoid major exchange rate movements between currencies. But imbalances between the major economies of the world, such as the USA, Japan and the eurozone countries, can cause huge swings in exchange rates. Such movements, which are often amplified by speculation, can play havoc with the profits of importers and exporters.

The four main underlying causes of exchange rate movements are divergences in *interest rates, growth rates, inflation rates* and *current account balance of payments*. Table 32.1 shows the variation in the levels of these indicators across a sample of countries. Although the divergences between the countries have narrowed somewhat since the early 1990s, they are still considerable.

Pause for thought

Referring to Table 32.1, in what respects was there greater convergence between the countries in the period 2007–11 than in the period 2002–6?

In trying to generate world economic growth without major currency fluctuations it is important that there is a **harmonisation** of economic policies between nations. In other words, it is important that all the major countries are pursuing consistent policies aiming at common international goals.

But how can policy harmonisation be achieved? As long as there are significant domestic differences between the major economies, there is likely to be conflict, not harmony. For example, if one country, say the USA, is worried about the size of its budget deficit, it may be unwilling to respond to world demands for a stimulus to aggregate demand to pull the world economy out of recession. What is more, speculators, seeing differences between countries, are likely to exaggerate them by their actions, causing large changes in exchange rates. The G8 countries have therefore sought to achieve greater **convergence** of their economies. But whilst convergence may be a goal of policy, in practice it has proved elusive.

Because of a lack of convergence, there are serious difficulties in achieving international policy harmonisation:

- Countries' budget deficits and national debt differ substantially as a proportion of their national income. This puts very different pressures on the interest rates necessary to service these debts.
- Harmonising rates of monetary growth or inflation targets would involve letting interest rates fluctuate with the demand for money. Without convergence in the demand for money, interest rate fluctuations could be severe.
- Harmonising interest rates would involve abandoning money, inflation and exchange rate targets (unless interest rate 'harmonisation' meant adjusting interest rates so as to maintain money or inflation targets or a fixed exchange rate).

Definitions

International harmonisation of economic policies Where countries attempt to coordinate their macroeconomic policies so as to achieve common goals.

Convergence of economies When countries achieve similar levels of growth, inflation, budget deficits as a percentage of GDP, balance of payments, etc.

Table 32.1 International macroeconomic indicators

		Australia	China	France	Germany	Japan	UK	USA
Nominal exchange rate index (average annual % change)	1992–96	2.0	−8.1	2.0	2.0	8.2	−3.0	4.2
	1997–2001	−3.7	4.3	−2.0	−1.7	2.3	3.8	4.7
	2002–06	4.4	−1.8	1.7	1.9	−1.7	0.3	−3.1
	2007–11	4.2	2.2	0.4	0.3	6.2	−4.6	−2.3
Short-term (3-month) average nominal interest rate (%)	1992–96	6.4	9.4	7.1	6.0	1.6	6.8	4.6
	1997–2001	5.3	4.6	3.7	3.7	0.4	6.1	5.3
	2002–06	5.4	2.4	2.6	2.6	0.1	4.3	2.6
	2007–11	5.3	3.4	2.5	2.5	0.6	2.8	1.9
Economic growth (average annual % change in real GDP)	1992–96	3.9	12.4	1.2	1.2	1.3	2.5	3.3
	1997–2001	3.8	8.3	2.9	2.0	0.5	3.7	3.8
	2002–06	3.4	10.6	1.7	1.0	1.7	2.8	2.7
	2007–11	2.6	10.5	0.5	1.2	−0.3	0.1	0.6
Consumer price inflation (average annual % change in CPI)	1992–96	2.4	14.1	2.0	3.1	0.7	2.8	2.9
	1997–2001	2.3	0.3	1.1	1.4	0.1	1.3	2.5
	2002–06	2.9	1.5	1.9	1.4	−0.2	1.7	2.6
	2007–11	2.9	3.7	1.6	1.7	−0.2	3.2	2.2
Current account balance (% of GDP)	1992–96	−4.0	0.3	0.7	−1.1	2.4	−1.4	−1.4
	1997–2001	−3.7	2.3	2.3	−0.8	2.5	−1.5	−3.1
	2002–06	−5.2	4.7	0.3	4.0	3.4	−2.3	−5.2
	2007–11	−4.5	7.4	−1.6	6.3	3.4	−2.2	−3.8

Note: Chinese and Japanese short-term interest rates for 1992–2001 are their central bank policy rates

Sources: OECD *Stat Extracts* and IMF *Principal Economic* Indicators

- Countries have different internal structural relationships. A lack of convergence here means that countries with higher endemic *cost* inflation would require higher interest rates and higher unemployment if international inflation rates were to be harmonised, or higher inflation if interest rates were to be harmonised.
- Countries have different rates of productivity increase, product development, investment and market penetration. A lack of convergence here means that the growth in exports (relative to imports) will differ for any given level of inflation or growth.

- Countries may be very unwilling to change their domestic policies to fall into line with other countries. They may prefer the other countries to fall into line with them!

If any one of the four – interest rates, growth rates, inflation rates or current account balance of payments – could be harmonised across countries, it is likely that the other three would then not be harmonised.

Total convergence and thus total harmonisation may not be possible. Nevertheless, most governments favour some movement in that direction; some is better than none.

32.3 EUROPEAN ECONOMIC AND MONETARY UNION

European economic and monetary union (EMU) involves the complete economic and financial integration of the EU countries. It is not just a common market, but a market with a single currency, a single central bank and a single monetary policy.

The ERM

The forerunner to EMU was the exchange rate mechanism (ERM). This came into existence in March 1979 and the majority of the EU countries were members. The UK, however, chose not to join. Spain joined in 1989, the UK joined in 1990 and Portugal in April 1992. Then in September 1992, the UK and Italy indefinitely suspended their membership of the ERM, but Italy rejoined in November 1996 as part of its bid to join the single European currency. Austria joined in 1995, Finland in 1996 and Greece in 1998. By the time the ERM was replaced by the single currency in 1999, only Sweden and the UK were outside the ERM.

Features of the ERM

Under the system, each currency was given a central exchange rate with each of the other ERM currencies in a grid. However, fluctuations were allowed from the central rate within specified bands. For most countries these bands were set at $\pm 2^{1}/_{4}$ per cent. The central rates could be adjusted from time to time by agreement, thus making the ERM an *adjustable peg* system. All the currencies floated jointly with currencies outside the ERM.

If a currency approached the upper or lower limit against *any* other ERM currency, intervention would take place to maintain the currencies within the band. This would take the form of central banks in the ERM selling the strong currency and buying the weak one. It could also involve the weak currency countries raising interest rates and the strong currency countries lowering them.

The ERM in practice

In a system of pegged exchange rates, countries should harmonise their policies to avoid excessive currency mis-alignments and hence the need for large devaluations or revaluations. There should be a convergence of their economies: they should be at a similar point on the business cycle and have similar inflation rates and interest rates.

The ERM in the 1980s. In the early 1980s, however, French and Italian inflation rates were persistently higher than German rates. This meant that there had to be several realignments (devaluations and revaluations). After 1983 realignments became less frequent, and then from 1987 to 1992 they ceased altogether. This was due to a growing convergence of members' internal policies.

By the time the UK joined the ERM in 1990, it was generally seen by its existing members as being a great success. It had created a zone of currency stability in a world of highly unstable exchange rates, and had provided the necessary environment for the establishment of a truly common market by the end of 1992.

Crisis in the ERM. Shortly after the UK joined the ERM, strains began to show. The reunification of Germany involved considerable reconstruction in the eastern part of the country. Financing this reconstruction was causing a growing budget deficit. The Bundesbank (the German central bank) thus felt obliged to maintain high interest rates in order to keep inflation in check. At the same time, the UK was experiencing a massive current account deficit (partly the result of entering the ERM at what many

commentators argued was too high an exchange rate). It was thus obliged to raise interest rates in order to protect the pound, despite the fact that the economy was sliding rapidly into recession. The French franc and Italian lira were also perceived to be overvalued, and there were the first signs of worries as to whether their exchange rates within the ERM could be retained.

At the same time, the US economy was moving into recession and, as a result, US interest rates were cut. This led to a large outflow of capital from the USA. With high German interest rates, much of this capital flowed to Germany. This pushed up the value of the German mark and with it the other ERM currencies. In September 1992, things reached crisis point. First the lira was devalued. Then two days later, on 'Black Wednesday' (16 September), the UK and Italy were forced to suspend their membership of the ERM: the pound and the lira were floated. At the same time, the Spanish peseta was devalued by 5 per cent.

Turmoil returned in the summer of 1993. The French economy was moving into recession and there were calls for cuts in French interest rates. But this was only possible if Germany was prepared to cut its rates too, and it was not. Speculators began to sell francs and it became obvious that the existing franc/mark parity could not be maintained. In an attempt to rescue the ERM, the EU finance ministers agreed to adopt very wide ± 15 per cent bands. The result was that the franc and the Danish krone depreciated against the mark.

> ### Pause for thought
>
> *Under what circumstances may a currency bloc like the ERM (a) help to prevent speculation; (b) aggravate the problem of speculation?*

A return of calm. The old ERM appeared to be at an end. The new ± 15 per cent bands hardly seemed like a 'pegged' system at all. However, the ERM did not die. Within months, the members were again managing to keep fluctuations within a very narrow range (for most of the time, within $\pm 2^{1}/_{4}$ per cent!). The scene was being set for the abandonment of separate currencies and the adoption of a single currency: the euro.

The Maastricht Treaty and the road to the single currency

Details of the path towards EMU were finalised in the Maastricht Treaty, which was signed in February 1992. The timetable for EMU involved adoption of a single currency by 1999 at the latest.

One of the first moves was to establish a European Monetary Institute (EMI) as a forerunner of the European Central Bank. Its role was to coordinate monetary policy and encourage greater cooperation between EU central

> ### Definition
>
> **Adjustable peg** A system whereby exchange rates are fixed for a period of time, but may be devalued (or revalued) if a deficit (or surplus) becomes substantial.

KI 13
p 71

banks. It also monitored the operation of the ERM and prepared the ground for the establishment of a European central bank in time for the launch of the single currency.

Before they could join the single currency, member states were obliged to achieve convergence of their economies. Each country had to meet five convergence criteria:

- Inflation: should be no more than $1^{1}/_{2}$ per cent above the average inflation rate of the three countries in the EU with the lowest inflation.
- Interest rates: the rate on long-term government bonds should be no more than 2 per cent above the average of the three countries with the lowest inflation.
- Budget deficit: should be no more than 3 per cent of GDP.
- General government debt: should be no more than 60 per cent of GDP.
- Exchange rates: the currency should have been within the normal ERM bands for at least two years with no realignments or excessive intervention.

Before the launch of the single currency, the Council of Ministers had to decide which countries had met the convergence criteria and would thus be eligible to form a *currency union* by fixing their currencies permanently to the euro. Their national currencies would effectively disappear.

At the same time, a European System of Central Banks (ESCB) would be created, consisting of a European Central Bank (ECB) and the central banks of the member states. The ECB would be independent, both from governments and from EU political institutions. It would operate the monetary policy on behalf of the countries which had adopted the single currency.

Birth of the euro

In March 1998, the European Commission ruled that 11 of the 15 member states were eligible to proceed to EMU in January 1999. The UK and Denmark were to exercise their opt-out, negotiated at Maastricht, and Sweden and Greece failed to meet one or more of the convergence criteria. (Greece joined the euro in 2001.)

All 11 countries unambiguously met the interest rate and inflation criteria, but doubts were expressed by many 'Eurosceptics' as to whether they all genuinely met the other three criteria.

The euro came into being on 1 January 1999, but euro banknotes and coins were not introduced until 1 January 2002. In the meantime, national currencies continued to exist alongside the euro, but at irrevocably fixed rates. The

Definition

Currency union A group of countries (or regions) using a common currency.

old notes and coins were withdrawn a few weeks after the introduction of euro notes and coins.

In May 2004, ten new members joined the EU and in January 2007 another two. Under the Maastricht Treaty, they should all make preparations for joining the euro by meeting the convergence criteria. Estonia, Lithuania and Slovenia were the first to join ERM2 in June 2004, with Latvia, Cyprus, Malta and Slovakia following in 2005. They adopted the wide band of ±15 per cent against the euro. Slovenia adopted the euro in 2007, Malta and Cyprus in 2008, Slovakia in 2009 and Estonia in 2011, making a total of 17 countries using the euro.

How desirable is EMU?

Advantages of the single currency

Elimination of the costs of converting currencies. With separate currencies in each of the EU countries, costs were incurred each time one currency was exchanged into another. The elimination of these costs, however, was probably the least important benefit from the single currency. The European Commission estimated that the effect was to increase the GDP of the countries concerned by an average of only 0.4 per cent. The gains to countries like the UK, which have well-developed financial markets, would be even smaller.

Increased competition and efficiency. Despite the advent of the single market, large price differences remained between member states. Not only has the single currency eliminated the need to convert one currency into another (a barrier to competition), but it has brought more transparency in pricing, and has put greater downward pressure on prices in high-cost firms and countries.

Elimination of exchange rate uncertainty (between the members). Removal of exchange rate uncertainty has helped to encourage trade between the eurozone countries. Perhaps more importantly, it has encouraged investment by firms that trade between these countries, given the greater certainty in calculating costs and revenues from such trade.

In times of economic uncertainty, exchange rate volatility between currencies can be high, as the experience of sterling showed during the credit crunch of 2008. The associated uncertainty for the UK in its trade with eurozone countries would have been eliminated had it adopted the euro. Without the euro, countries throughout Europe could have suffered considerably during the banking turmoil from wildly diverging exchange rates and interest rates.

Increased inward investment. Investment from the rest of the world is attracted to a eurozone of over 300 million inhabitants, where there is no fear of internal currency movements. By contrast, the UK, by not joining, has found that inward investment has been diverted away to countries within the eurozone. From 1990 to 1998, the UK's share of inward investment to EU countries (including from other EU countries) was 21.0 per cent. From 1999 to 2003, it was 12.5 per cent, and it fell throughout this period, from 26.2 per cent in 1998 to 6.3 per cent in 2003. From 2003 to 2005, its share rose to 35 per cent as the UK economy grew more strongly than other major economies in the EU. But this was relatively short-lived and since then it has fallen again, with the volatility of sterling acting as a deterrent to investment. In 2010, the UK's share of inward investment to EU countries stood at 15 per cent.

Lower inflation and interest rates. A single monetary policy forces convergence in inflation rates (just as inflation rates are very similar between the different regions within a country). With the ECB being independent from short-term political manipulation, this has resulted in a lower average inflation rate in the eurozone countries. This, in turn, has helped to convince markets that the euro will be strong relative to other currencies. The result is lower long-term rates of interest. This, in turn, further encourages investment in the eurozone countries, both by member states and by the rest of the world.

Opposition to EMU

European monetary union has, however, attracted considerable criticism. 'Eurosceptics' see within it a surrender of national political and economic sovereignty. Others, including those more sympathetic to monetary union in principle, raise concerns about the design of the monetary and financial systems within which monetary union operates – a design that, in principle, can be amended (see Boxes 30.1 and 30.3).

We begin with those arguments against EMU in principle.

The lack of national currencies. This can be a serious problem if an economy is at all out of harmony with the rest of the Union. For example, if countries such as Greece and Spain have lower productivity growth or higher endemic rates of inflation (due, say, to greater cost-push pressures), then how are they to make their goods competitive with the rest of the Union? With separate currencies these countries could allow their currencies to depreciate. With a single currency, however, they could become depressed 'regions' of Europe, with rising unemployment and all the other regional problems of depressed regions *within* a country.

keeping separate currencies and allowing periodic depreciations, with all the uncertainty that they bring.

What is more, the high-inflation countries tend to be the poorer ones with lower wage levels (albeit faster wage *increases*). With the high mobility of labour and capital that will accompany the development of the single market, resources are likely to be attracted to such countries. This could help to narrow the gap between the richer and poorer member states.

The critics of EMU argue that labour is relatively immobile, given cultural and language barriers. Thus an unemployed worker in Cork or Kalamata could not easily move to a job in Turin or Helsinki. What the critics are arguing here is that the EU is not an *optimal currency area* (see Box 32.2).

Loss of separate monetary policies. The second problem identified is that the same central bank rate of interest must apply to all eurozone countries: the 'one size fits all' criticism. The trouble is that while some countries might require a lower rate of interest in order to ward off recession (such as Portugal, Ireland and Greece in 2010–11), others might require a higher one to prevent inflation. The greater the divergence between economies within the eurozone, the greater this problem becomes. It was hoped, however, that, with common fiscal rules and free trade, these divergences would diminish over time.

Asymmetric shocks. A third and related problem for members of a single currency occurs in adjusting to a shock when that shock affects members to different degrees. These are known as *asymmetric shocks*. For example, the banking crisis affected the UK more severely than other countries, given that London is a global financial centre. This problem is more serious, the less the factor mobility between member countries and the less the price flexibility within member countries.

Even when shocks are uniformly felt in the member states, however, there is still the problem that policies adopted centrally will have different impacts on each country. This is because the transmission mechanisms of economic policy (i.e. the way in which policy changes impact of economic variables like growth and inflation) vary across countries.

Pause for thought

Is greater factor mobility likely to increase or decrease the problem of cumulative causation associated with regional multipliers? (See p. 540.)

Definitions

Optimal currency area The optimal size of a currency area is one that maximises the benefits from having a single currency relative to the costs. If the area were to be increased or decreased in size, the costs would rise relative to the benefits.

Asymmetric shocks Shocks (such as an oil price increase or a recession in another part of the world) that have different-sized effects on different industries, regions or countries.

Proponents of EMU argue that it is better to tackle the problem of high inflation or low productivity in such countries by the discipline of competition from other eurozone countries, than merely to feed that inflation by

BOX 32.2 **OPTIMAL CURRENCY AREAS**

When it pays to pay in the same currency

Imagine that each town and village used a different currency. Think how inconvenient it would be having to keep exchanging one currency into another, and how difficult it would be working out the relative value of items in different parts of the country.

Clearly there are benefits of using a common currency, not only within a country but across different countries. The benefits include greater transparency in pricing, more open competition, greater certainty for investors and the avoidance of having to pay commission when you change one currency into another. There are also the benefits from having a single monetary policy if that is delivered in a more consistent and effective way than by individual countries.

So why not have a single currency for the whole world? The problem is that the bigger a single currency area gets, the more likely the conditions are to diverge in the different parts of the area. Some parts may have high unemployment and require expansionary policies. Others may have low unemployment and suffer from inflationary pressures. They may require *contractionary* policies.

What is more, different members of the currency area may experience quite different shocks to their economies, whether from outside the union (e.g. a fall in the price of one of their major exports) of from inside (e.g. a prolonged strike). These 'asymmetric shocks' would imply that different parts of the currency area should adopt different policies. But with a common monetary policy and hence common interest rates, and with no possibility of devaluation/revaluation of the currency of individual members, the scope for separate economic policies is reduced.

The costs of asymmetric shocks (and hence the costs of a single currency area) will be greater, the less the mobility of labour and capital, the less the flexibility of prices and wage rates, and the fewer the alternative policies there are that can be turned to (such as fiscal and regional policies).

So is the eurozone an optimal currency area? Certainly strong doubts have been raised by many economists.

- Labour is relatively immobile.
- There are structural differences between the member states.
- The transmission effects of interest rate changes are different between the member countries, given that countries have different proportions of consumer debt relative to GDP and different proportions of debt at variable interest rates.
- Exports to countries outside the eurozone account for different proportions of the members' GDP and thus their economies are affected differently by a change in the rate of exchange of the euro against other currencies.
- Wage rates are relatively inflexible.
- Under the Stability and Growth Pact and the Fiscal Compact (see Box 30.1), the scope for using discretionary fiscal policy is curtailed, except in times of severe economic difficulty (as in 2009).

This does not necessarily mean, however, that the costs of having a single European currency outweigh the benefits. Also, the problems outlined above should decline over time as the single market develops. Finally, the problem of asymmetric shocks can be exaggerated. European economies are highly diversified; there are often more differences *within* economies than between them. Thus shocks are more likely to affect different industries or localities, rather than whole countries. Changing the exchange rate, if that were still possible, would hardly be an appropriate policy in these circumstances.

 Why is a single currency area likely to move towards becoming an optimal currency area over time?

There are others who are critical of the design of EMU, but who argue, that with appropriate changes, the problems could be significantly reduced.

Monetary policy. In the case of monetary policy, it is argued that the ECB was not as proactive in tackling the recession that followed the aftermath of the financial crisis. Large-scale programmes of quantitative easing were adopted by the US Federal Reserve and the Bank of England (see Box 30.4). The ECB, by contrast, was seen as more cautious. Nonetheless (as we saw in Box 30.3), the ECB did begin to modify its monetary operations. Between December 2011 and March 2012, over €1 trillion of long-term (3-year) repo loans were given to banks. The hope was that this would encourage them to buy government bonds, especially of those countries in greatest financial distress.

Critics point to the underlying weakness of a single currency operating alongside separate *national* government debt issues. The greater the divergence of the eurozone countries, in terms of growth, inflation, deficits, debt and the proportions of debt securities maturing in the short term, the greater this problem becomes.

Fiscal policy. Under the Stability and Growth Pact (SGP), countries were supposed to keep public-sector deficits below 3 per cent of GDP and their stocks of debt below 60 per cent of GDP (see Box 30.1). However, the Pact was not rigidly enforced. Furthermore, because the rules allowed for discretion in times of recession, deficits and debt rose sharply in the late 2000s (see Table 30.1 on page 511).

Subsequently, efforts have been made to change the framework within which national governments make their fiscal choices. The result is the Fiscal Compact, signed in March 2012. This reaffirmed the SGP rules, but added other requirements. For example, eurozone countries would now be required to keep structural deficits at or below 0.5 per cent of GDP and tougher penalties would be imposed on countries breaking the rules.

There are those who argue that for eurozone members to benefit fully from monetary union tighter fiscal rules alone are insufficient. Instead, they advocate greater fiscal harmonisation. In other words, the problem, they say, is one of incomplete integration.

The problem for economists is that the issue of monetary union is a very emotive one. 'Europhiles' often see monetary union as a vital element in their vision of a united Europe. Many Eurosceptics, however, see EMU as a surrender of sovereignty and a threat to nationhood. In such an environment, a calm assessment of the arguments and evidence is very difficult.

32.4 ALTERNATIVE POLICIES FOR ACHIEVING CURRENCY STABILITY

One important lesson of recent years is that concerted speculation has become virtually unstoppable. This was made clear by the expulsion of the UK and Italy from the ERM in 1992, the dramatic fall of the Mexican peso and rise of the yen in 1995, the collapse of various south-east Asian currencies and the Russian rouble in 1997–8, and the collapse of the Argentine peso in 2002. In comparison with the vast amounts of short-term finance flowing across the foreign exchanges each day, the reserves of central banks seem trivial.

If there is a consensus in the markets that a currency will depreciate, there is little that central banks can do. For example, if there were a 50 per cent chance of a 10 per cent depreciation in the next week, then selling that currency now would yield an 'expected' return of just over 5 per cent for the week (i.e. 50 per cent of 10 per cent): equivalent to 1200 per cent at an annual rate!

For this reason, many commentators have argued that there are only two types of exchange rate system that can work over the long term. The first is a completely free-floating exchange rate, with no attempt by the central bank to support the exchange rate. With no intervention, there is no problem of a shortage of reserves!

The second is to share a common currency with other countries: to join a common-currency area, such as the eurozone, and let the common currency float freely. The country would give up independence in its monetary policy, but at least there would be no problem of exchange rate instability within the currency area. A similar alternative is to adopt a major currency of another country, such as the US dollar or the euro. Many smaller states have done this. For example, Kosovo has adopted the euro and Ecuador has adopted the US dollar.

An attempt by a country to peg its exchange rate is likely to have one of two unfortunate consequences. Either it will end in failure as the country succumbs to a speculative attack, or the country's monetary policy will have to be totally dedicated to maintaining the exchange rate.

So is there any way of 'beating the speculators' and pursuing a policy of greater exchange rate rigidity without establishing a single currency? Or must countries be forced to accept freely floating exchange rates, with all the uncertainty for traders that such a regime brings?

We shall examine two possible solutions. The first is to reduce international financial mobility, by putting various types of restriction on foreign exchange transactions. The second is to move to a new type of exchange rate regime which offers the benefits of a degree of rigidity without being susceptible to massive speculative attacks.

Controlling exchange transactions

Until the early 1990s, many countries retained restrictions of various kinds on financial flows. Such restrictions made it more expensive for speculators to gamble on possible exchange rate movements. It is not the case, as some commentators argue, that it is impossible to reimpose controls. Indeed Malaysia did just that in 1998 when the ringgit was under speculative attack. Many countries in the developing world still retain controls, and the last ERM countries to give them up only did so in 1991. It is true that the complexity of modern financial markets provides the speculator with more opportunity to evade controls, but they will still have the effect of dampening speculation.

In September 1998, the IMF said that controls on inward movements of capital could be a useful tool, especially for countries which were more vulnerable to speculative attack. In its 1998 annual report it argued that the Asian crisis of 1997–8 was the result not only of a weak banking system, but also of open capital accounts, allowing massive withdrawals of funds.

> ### Pause for thought
>
> *Before you read on, see if you can identify (a) the ways exchange transactions might be controlled; (b) the difficulties in using such policy.*

The aim of capital controls is not to prevent capital flows. After all, capital flows are an important source of financing investment. Also, if capital moves from countries with a lower marginal productivity of capital to countries where it is higher, this will lead to an efficient allocation of world savings. The aim of capital controls must therefore be to prevent speculative flows which are based on rumour or herd instinct rather than on economic fundamentals.

Types of control

In what ways can movements of short-term capital be controlled? There are various alternatives, each one with strengths and drawbacks.

Quantitative controls. Here the authorities would restrict the amount of foreign exchange dealing that could take place. Perhaps financial institutions would be allowed to exchange only a certain percentage of their assets. Developed countries and most developing countries have rejected this approach, however, since it is seen to be far too anti-market.

The exception is the use of special emergency measures to restrict capital movements in times of a currency crisis. According to Article 57 of the Treaty of Amsterdam, the EU Council of Ministers may 'adopt measures on the movement of capital to or from third countries'. Article 59 allows 'safeguard measures' to be taken if 'in exceptional circumstances, movements of capital to or from third countries cause . . . serious difficulties for the operation of economic and monetary union'. Article 60 allows member states to take 'unilateral measures against a third country with regard to capital movements and payments'.

A Tobin tax. This is named after James Tobin, who in 1972 advocated the imposition of a small tax of 0.1 to 0.5 per cent on all foreign exchange transactions, or on just capital account transactions.[1] This would discourage destabilising speculation (by making it more expensive) and would thus impose some 'friction' in foreign exchange markets, making them less volatile.

In November 2001 the French National Assembly became the first national legislature to incorporate into law a Tobin tax of up to 0.1 per cent. This was followed by Belgium in 2002.

Calls for the use of Tobin taxes have become more frequent in recent years (see Box 32.3), particularly following the financial crisis of the late 2000s. Some have advocated the use of Tobin taxes to curb destabilising financial transactions. Such taxes would not be confined to foreign exchange transactions but would apply to a whole range of financial securities. The calls for such a move have been particularly strong in parts of Europe, with some arguing that part of the money raised should be used in stabilising the continent's financial system.

Non-interest-bearing deposits. Here a certain percentage of inflows of finance would have to be deposited with the central bank in a non-interest-bearing account for a set period of time. Chile in the late 1990s used such a system. It required that 30 per cent of all inflows be deposited with Chile's central bank for a year. This clearly amounted to a considerable tax (i.e. in terms of interest sacrificed) and

had the effect of discouraging short-term speculative flows. The problem was that it meant that interest rates in Chile had to be higher in order to attract finance.

One objection to all these measures is that they are likely only to dampen speculation, not eliminate it. If speculators believe that currencies are badly out of equilibrium and will be forced to realign, then no taxes on capital movements or artificial controls will be sufficient to stem the flood.

There are two replies to this objection. The first is that if currencies are badly out of line then exchange rates *should* be adjusted. The second is that *dampening* speculation is probably the ideal. Speculation *can* play the valuable role of bringing exchange rates to their long-term equilibrium more quickly. Controls are unlikely to prevent this aspect of speculation: adjustments to economic fundamentals. If they help to lessen the wilder forms of destabilising speculation, so much the better.

Exchange rate target zones

One type of exchange rate regime that has been much discussed in recent years is that proposed by John Williamson, of Washington's Institute for International Economics.[2] Williamson advocates a form of 'crawling peg' within broad bands. This system would involve a pegged central rate, where fluctuations around that rate would be allowed within bands (i.e. like the ERM). Unlike the ERM, however, the central value could be adjusted frequently, but only by small amounts: hence the term 'crawling'. The system would have four major features:

■ Wide bands. For example, currencies could be allowed to fluctuate by 10 per cent of their central parity.
■ Central parity set in *real* terms, at the 'fundamental equilibrium exchange rate' (FEER): i.e. a rate that is consistent with long-run balance of payments equilibrium.
■ Frequent realignments. In order to stay at the FEER, the central parity would be adjusted frequently (e.g. monthly) to take account of the country's rate of inflation. If its rate of inflation were 2 per cent per annum above the trade-weighted average of other countries, then the central parity would be devalued by 2 per cent per annum. Realignments would also reflect other changes in fundamentals, such as changes in the levels of protection, or major political events, such as German reunification.
■ 'Soft buffers'. Governments would not be forced to intervene at the 10 per cent mark or at some specified fraction of it. In fact, from time to time the rate might be allowed to move outside the bands. The point is that the closer the rate approached the band limits, the greater would be the scale of intervention.

[1] J. Tobin, 'A proposal for international monetary reform', *Eastern Economic Journal*, 4, no. 3–4, 1978, pp. 153–9.

[2] See, for example, J. Williamson and M. Miller, 'Targets and indicators: a blueprint for the coordination of economic policy', *Policy Analyses in International Economics*, no. 22 (IIE, 1987).

BOX 32.3 THE TOBIN TAX

Adding a bit of friction

In the mid-1980s, the daily turnover in the world's foreign exchange markets was approximately $150 billion. By 2008, it had risen to a truly massive $4 trillion. But only some 5 per cent of this is used for trade in goods and services.

With the massive growth in speculative flows, it is hardly surprising that this can cause great currency instability and financial crises at times of economic uncertainty. Global financial markets have often been decisive in both triggering and intensifying economic crises. The ERM crisis in 1992, the Mexican peso crisis in 1994, the south-east Asian crisis in 1997, the Russian rouble meltdown in 1998, the crisis in Argentina in 2001–2002 and the currency instability of 2008/9 in the wake of the credit crunch are the most significant in a long list.

The main issue is one of volatility of exchange rates. If currency markets responded to shifts in economic fundamentals, then currency volatility would not be so bad. However, it is increasingly the case that vast quantities of money flow around the global economy purely speculatively, with the herd instinct often driving speculative waves. Invariably, given the volume of speculative flows, exchange rates overshoot their natural equilibrium, intensifying the distortions created. Such currency movements are a huge destabilising force, not just for individual economies but for the global economy as a whole.

So is there anything countries can do to reduce destabilising speculation? One suggestion is the introduction of a Tobin tax.

The Tobin tax

Writing in 1972, James Tobin proposed a system for reducing exchange rate volatility without fundamentally impeding the operation of the market. This involved the imposition of an international tax of some 0.1 to 0.5 per cent payable on all spot or cash exchange rate transactions. He argued that this would make currency trading more costly and would therefore reduce the volume of destabilising short-term financial flows, which would invariably lead to greater exchange rate stability.

Tobin's original proposal suggested that the tax rate would need to be very low so as not to affect 'normal business'. Even if it was very low, speculators working on small margins would be dissuaded from regular movements of money, given that the tax would need to be paid per transaction. If a tax rate of 0.2 per cent was set, speculators who moved a sum of money once a day would face a yearly tax bill of approximately 50 per cent. An investor working on a weekly movement of money would pay tax of 10 per cent per annum, and a monthly movement of currency would represent a tax of 2.4 per cent for the year. Given that 40 per cent of currency transactions have only a two-day time horizon, and 80 per cent a time horizon of fewer than seven days, such a tax would clearly operate to dampen speculative currency movements.

In addition to moderating volatility and speculation, the Tobin tax might yield other benefits. It would, in the face of globalisation, restore to the nation state an element of control over monetary policy. In the face of declining governance over international forces, this might be seen as a positive advantage of the Tobin proposals.

The tax could also generate significant revenue. Estimates range from $150 to 300 billion annually. Many of the world's leading pressure groups, such as War on Want and Stamp out Poverty, have argued that the revenue from such an international tax could be used to tackle international problems, such as world poverty and environmental degradation. The World Bank estimates that some $225 billion is needed to eliminate the world's worst forms of poverty. The revenue from a Tobin tax would, in a relatively short period of time, easily exceed this amount. Even with a worldwide rate as low as 0.005 per cent (the rate recommended by Stamp out Poverty), the tax could still raise some $50 billion per year.

Problems with the Tobin tax

How far would a tax on currency transactions restrict speculative movements of money? The issue here concerns the rate of return investors might get from moving their

---

This system has two main advantages. First, the exchange rate would stay at roughly the equilibrium level, and therefore the likelihood of large-scale devaluation or revaluation, and with it the opportunities for large-scale speculative gains, would be small. The reason why the narrow-banded ERM broke down in 1992 and 1993 was that the central parities were *not* equilibrium rates.

Second, the wider bands would leave countries freer to follow an independent monetary policy: one that could therefore respond to domestic needs.

The main problem with the system is that it may not allow an independent monetary policy. If the rate of exchange has to be maintained within the zone, then monetary policy may sometimes have to be used for that purpose rather than controlling inflation.

Nevertheless, crawling bands have been used relatively successfully by various countries, such as Chile and Israel over quite long periods of time. What is more, in 1999, Germany's finance minister at the time, Oskar Lafontaine, argued that they might be appropriate for the euro relative to the dollar and yen. A world with three major currencies, each changing gently against the other two in an orderly way, has a lot to commend it.

Pause for thought

Would the Williamson system allow countries to follow a totally independent monetary policy?

money. If a currency was to devalue by as little as 3 to 4 per cent, a Tobin tax of 0.2 per cent would do little to deter a speculative transaction based upon such a potential return. Given devaluations of 50 per cent in Thailand and Indonesia following the 1997 crash and an 82 per cent appreciation of the euro against the dollar from 2002 to 2008, along with severe short-term fluctuations, a 3 to 4 per cent movement in the currency appears rather modest. Raising the rate of the Tobin tax would be no solution, as it would begin to impinge upon 'normal business'.

One response to such a situation has been proposed by a German economist, Paul Bernd Spahn. He suggests that a two-tier system is used. On a day-to-day basis, a minimal tax rate, as originally envisaged by Tobin, is charged against each transaction conducted. However, during periods when exchange rates are highly unstable, a tax surcharge is levied. This would be at a far higher rate, and would only be triggered once a currency moved beyond some predetermined band of exchange rate variation.

A further problem identified with the Tobin tax concerns the costs of its administration. However, given interlinked computer systems and the progressive centralisation of foreign exchange markets, in terms of marketplaces, traders and currencies, effective administration is becoming easier. Most foreign exchange markets are well monitored already and extending such monitoring to include overseeing tax collection would not be overly problematic.

Another problem is tax avoidance. For example, the Tobin tax is a tax payable on spot exchange rate transactions. This could encourage people to deal more in futures. Foreign exchange futures are a type of 'derivative' that allows people to trade currencies in the future at a price agreed today. These would be far more difficult to monitor, since no currency is exchanged *today*, and hence more difficult to tax. One solution would be to apply a tax on a notional value of a derivative contract. However, derivatives are an important way through which businesses hedge against future risk. Taxing them might seriously erode their use to a business and damage the derivatives market as a whole, making business more risky.

Even with avoidance, however, supporters of the Tobin tax argue that it is still likely to be successful. The main problem is one of political will.

Although some countries, such as France, Canada, Belgium, Brazil and Venezuela, have supported the introduction of a Tobin tax, most of the major economies are opposed to it. With reservations being expressed by the IMF, any concerted international action to control global financial movements will be difficult to put on the agenda, let alone put in place and administer.

Financial transactions tax

In 2009, Adair Turner, chairman of the Financial Services Authority, the UK's financial sector regulator, proposed the possible use of Tobin taxes to curb destabilising financial transactions. This was met with criticism from many bankers that the tax would be unworkable at a global level and if applied solely to the UK would divert financial business away from London.

To date, international opinion on the imposition of a Tobin tax remains divided. But, there is some momentum behind the sort of Financial Transactions Tax (FTT) identified by Adair Turner. While American opinion on an FTT is generally less favourable, South Africa, and some EU member countries, including France and Germany, have been pushing for some form of FTT. The IMF too has come out in favour of taxes on the global financial sector designed to reduce speculation. This has led some commentators to suggest that it is only a matter of time before an FTT is introduced in Europe and possibly elsewhere.

 George Soros, multi-millionaire currency speculator, has referred to global capital markets as being like a wrecking ball rather than a pendulum, suggesting that such markets are becoming so volatile that they are damaging to all concerned, including speculators. What might lead Soros to such an observation?

SUMMARY

1a The more open the world economy, the more effect changes in economic conditions in one part of the world economy will have on world economic performance.

1b Changes in aggregate demand in one country will affect the amount of imports purchased and thus the amount of exports sold by other countries and hence their GDP. There is thus an international trade multiplier effect.

1c Changes in interest rates in one country will affect financial flows to and from other countries, and hence their exchange rates, interest rates and GDP.

2a Currency fluctuations can be lessened if countries harmonise their economic policies. Ideally this will involve achieving common growth rates, inflation rates, balance of payments (as a percentage of GDP) and interest rates. The attempt to harmonise one of these goals, however, may bring conflicts with one of the other goals.

2b Leaders of the G8 and G20 countries meet regularly to discuss ways of harmonising their policies. Usually, however, domestic issues are more important to the leaders than international ones, and frequently they pursue policies that are not in the interests of the other countries.

3a One means of achieving greater currency stability is for a group of countries to peg their internal exchange rates and yet float jointly with the rest of the world. The exchange rate mechanism of the EU (ERM) was an example. Members' currencies were allowed to fluctuate

►

against other member currencies within a band. The band was $\pm 2^1/_4$ per cent for the majority of the ERM countries until 1993.

3b The need for realignments seemed to have diminished in the late 1980s as greater convergence was achieved between the members' economies. Growing strains in the system, however, in the early 1990s, led to a crisis in September 1992. The UK and Italy left the ERM. There was a further crisis in July 1993 and the bands were widened to ± 15 per cent.

3c Thereafter, as convergence of the economies of ERM members increased, fluctuations decreased and remained largely within $\pm 2^1/_4$ per cent.

3d The ERM was seen as an important first stage on the road to complete economic and monetary union (EMU) in the EU.

3f The Maastricht Treaty set out a timetable for achieving EMU. This would culminate with the creation of a currency union: a single European currency with a common monetary policy operated by an independent European Central Bank.

3g The euro was born on 1 January 1999. Twelve countries adopted it, having at least nominally met the Maastricht convergence criteria. Euro notes and coins were introduced on 1 January 2002, with the notes and coins of the old currencies withdrawn a few weeks later.

3h The advantages claimed for EMU are that it eliminates the costs of converting currencies and the uncertainties associated with possible changes in former inter-EU exchange rates. This encourages more investment, both inward and by domestic firms. What is more, a common central bank, independent from domestic governments, will provide the stable monetary environment necessary for a convergence of the EU economies and the encouragement of investment and inter-Union trade.

3i Critics claim, however, that it might make adjustment to domestic economic problems more difficult. The loss of independence in policy making is seen by such people to be a major issue, not only because of the loss of political sovereignty, but also because domestic economic concerns may be at variance with those of the Union as a whole. A single monetary policy is claimed to be inappropriate for dealing with asymmetric shocks. What is more, countries and regions at the periphery of the Union may become depressed unless there is an effective regional policy.

4a Many economists argue that, with the huge flows of short-term finance across the foreign exchanges, governments are forced to adopt one of two extreme forms of exchange rate regime: free floating or being a member of a currency union.

4b If financial flows could be constrained, however, exchange rates could be stabilised somewhat.

4c Forms of control include: quantitative controls, a tax on exchange transactions (a Tobin tax) and non-interest-bearing deposits of a certain percentage of capital inflows with the central bank. Such controls can dampen speculation, but may discourage capital flowing to where it has a higher marginal productivity.

4d An alternative means of stabilising exchange rates is to have exchange rate target zones. Here exchange rates are allowed to fluctuate within broad bands around a central parity which is adjusted to the fundamental equilibrium rate in a gradual fashion.

4e The advantage of this system is that, by keeping the exchange rate at roughly its equilibrium level, destabilising speculation is avoided, and yet there is some freedom for governments to pursue an independent monetary policy. Monetary policy, however, may still from time to time have to be used to keep the exchange rate within the bands.

REVIEW QUESTIONS

1 What are the implications for a country attempting to manage its domestic economy if it is subject to an international business cycle? How might it attempt to overcome such problems?

2 What are the economic (as opposed to political) difficulties in achieving an international harmonisation of economic policies so as to avoid damaging currency fluctuations?

3 To what extent can international negotiations over economic policy be seen as a game of strategy? Are there any parallels between the behaviour of countries and the behaviour of oligopolies?

4 What are the causes of exchange rate volatility? Have these problems become greater or lesser in the last ten years? Explain why.

5 Why did the ERM with narrow bands collapse in 1993? Could this have been avoided?

6 Did the exchange rate difficulties experienced by countries under the ERM strengthen or weaken the arguments for progressing to a single European currency?

7 By what means would a depressed country in an economic union with a single currency be able to recover? Would the market provide a satisfactory solution or would (union) government intervention be necessary? If so, what form would the intervention take?

8 Is the eurozone likely to be an optimal currency area now? Is it more or less likely to be so over time? Explain your answer.

9 Assume that just some of the members of a common market like the EU adopt full economic and monetary union, including a common currency. What are the advantages and disadvantages to those members joining the full EMU and to those not joining?

10 Assess the difficulties in attempting to control exchange transactions. Might such a policy restrict the level of trade?

11 Would the Williamson system allow countries to follow a totally independent monetary policy?

12 If the euro were in a crawling peg system against the dollar, what implications would this have for the ECB in sticking to its inflation target of no more than 2 per cent?

ADDITIONAL PART K CASE STUDIES IN THE *ECONOMICS FOR BUSINESS* MyEconLab (www.pearsoned.co.uk/sloman)

K.1 **The national debt.** This explores the question of whether it matters if a country has a high national debt.

K.2 **Trends in public expenditure.** This case examines attempts to control public expenditure in the UK and relates them to the crowding-out debate.

K.3 **The crowding-out effect.** The circumstances in which an increase in public expenditure can replace private expenditure.

K.4 **The financial crisis and British and American fiscal policy.** An examination of the use of active fiscal and monetary policy during and after the financial crisis of the late 2000s.

K.5 **Discretionary fiscal policy in Japan.** How the Japanese government used fiscal policy on various occasions throughout the 1990s and early 2000s in an attempt to bring the economy out of recession.

K.6 **Central banking and monetary policy in the USA.** This case examines how the Fed conducts monetary policy.

K.7 **Goodhart's Law.** An examination of Key Idea 43.

K.8 **Should central banks be independent of government?** An examination of the arguments for and against independent central banks.

K.9 **Monetary targeting: its use around the world.** An expanded version of Box 30.4.

K.10 **Interest rate responses and the financial crisis of 2007/8.** A comparison of the policy responses of the Fed, the ECB and the Bank of England to the credit crunch.

K.11 **Using interest rates to control both aggregate demand and the exchange rate.** A problem of one instrument and two targets.

K.12 **The USA: is it a 'new economy'?** An examination of whether US productivity increases are likely to be sustained.

K.13 **Welfare to work.** An examination of the policy of the UK Labour government whereby welfare payments are designed to encourage people into employment.

K.14 **Assessing PFI.** Has this been the perfect solution to funding investment for the public sector without raising taxes?

K.15 **Alternative approaches to training and education.** This compares the approaches to training and education – a crucial element in supply-side policy – in the UK, France, Germany and the USA.

K.16 **Assistance to small firms in the UK.** An examination of current government measures to assist small firms.

K.17 **Attempts at harmonisation.** A look at the meetings of the G7 economies where they attempt to come to agreement on means of achieving stable and sustained worldwide economic growth.

K.18 **The UK Labour government's convergence criteria for euro membership.** An examination of the five tests set by the UK government that would have to be passed before the question of euro membership would be put to the electorate in a referendum.

K.19 **Balance of trade and the public finances.** An examination of countries' budget and balance of trade balances.

WEBSITES RELEVANT TO PART K

Numbers and sections refer to websites listed in the Web appendix and hotlinked from this book's website at **www.pearsoned.co.uk/sloman**

■ For news articles relevant to Part K, see the *Economics News Articles* link from the book's website.

■ For general news on macroeconomic policy, see websites in section A, and particularly A1–5. See also links to newspapers worldwide in A38, 39 and 43, and the news search feature in Google at A41. See also links to economics news in A42.

■ For information on UK fiscal policy and government borrowing, see sites E30, 36; F2. See also sites A1–8 at Budget time. For fiscal policy in the eurozone, see *Public Finances in EMU* in H1.

■ For a model of the economy (based on the Treasury model), see *The Virtual Economy* (site D1). In addition to the model, where you can devise your own Budget, there are worksheets and outlines of theories and the work of famous economists.

■ Sites I7 and 11 contain links to fiscal policy: go to *Macroeconomics > Macroeconomic Policy > Taxes and Taxation*.

■ For monetary policy in the UK, see F1 and E30. For monetary policy in the eurozone, see F6 and 5. For monetary policy in the USA, see F8. For monetary policy in other countries, see the respective central bank site in section F.

■ For links to sites on money and monetary policy, see the *Financial Economics* sections in I4, 7, 11, 17.

■ For demand-side policy in the UK, see the latest Budget Report (e.g. section on maintaining macroeconomic stability) at site E30.

■ For inflation targeting in the UK and eurozone, see sites F1 and 6.

■ For the current approach to UK supply-side policy, see the latest Budget Report (e.g. sections on productivity and training) at site E30. See also sites E5 and 9.

■ For information on training in the UK and Europe, see sites D7; E5; G5, 14.

■ For support for a market-orientated approach to supply-side policy, see C17 and E34.

■ For European Union policies, see sites G1, 3, 6, 16, 17, 18.

■ For information on international harmonisation, see sites H4 and 5.

■ For student resources relevant to this chapter, see sites C1–7, 9, 10, 12, 13, 19. See also '2nd floor – economic policy' in site D1. See also the *Labour market reforms* simulation in D3.

Web appendix

All the following websites can be accessed from the home page of this book's own website (www.pearsoned.co.uk/sloman). When you enter the site, click on **Hotlinks** button. You will find all the following sites listed. Click on the one you want and the 'hotlink' will take you straight to it.

The sections and numbers below refer to the ones used in the web references at the end of each Part of the text. Thus if the reference were to A21, this would refer to the Moneyextra site.

A General news sources

As the title of this section implies, websites here can be used for finding material on current news issues or tapping into news archives. Most archives are offered free of charge. However, some do require you to register. As well as key UK and American sources, you will also notice some slightly different places from where you can get your news, such as the St Petersburg Times and Kyodo News (from Japan). Check out site numbers 38. *MyRefdesk*, 43. *Guardian World News Guide* and 44. *Online Newspapers* for links to newspapers across the world. Try searching for an article on a particular topic by using site number 41. *Google News Search.*

1. BBC news
2. The Economist
3. The Financial Times
4. The Guardian
5. The Independent
6. ITN
7. The Observer
8. The Telegraph
9. Aljazeera
10. The New York Times
11. Fortune
12. Time Magazine
13. The Washington Post
14. Moscow Times (English)
15. St Petersburg Times (English)
16. Straits Times
17. New Straits Times
18. The Scotsman
19. The Herald
20. Euromoney
21. Moneyextra
22. Market News International
23. Bloomberg Businessweek
24. International Business Times
25. CNN Money
26. Wall Street Journal
27. Asia News Network
28. allAfrica.com
29. Greek News Sources (English)
30. Kyodo News: Japan (English)
31. Euronews
32. The Australian
33. Sydney Morning Herald
34. Japan Times
35. Reuters
36. Bloomberg
37. David Smith's Economics UK.com
38. Refdesk (links to a whole range of news sources)
39. Newspapers and Magazines on the World Wide Web
40. Yahoo News Search
41. Google News Search
42. ABYZ News Links
43. Guardian World News Guide
44. Onlinenewspapers

B Sources of economic and business data

Using websites to find up-to-date data is of immense value to the economist. The data sources below offer you a range of specialist and non-specialist data information. Universities have free access to MIMAS (site 12) and UK Data Service (site 35), which are huge databases of statistics. Site 34 in this set, the Treasury Pocket Data Bank, is a very useful source of key UK and world statistics, and is updated monthly. It downloads as an Excel file. The Economics Network's *Economic data freely available online* (site 1) gives links to various sections in 39 UK and international sites.

1. Economics Network gateway to economic data
2. Biz/ed Gateway to economic and company data
3. National Statistics
4. Data Archive (Essex)
5. Bank of England Statistical Database
6. Economic Resources (About)
7. Nationwide House Prices Site
8. House Web (data on housing market)

9. Economist global house price data
10. Halifax House Price Index
11. House price indices from ONS
12. Manchester Information and Associated Services (MIMAS)
13. Economist economic and financial indicators
14. FT market data
15. Economagic
16. Groningen Growth and Development Centre
17. AEAweb: Resources for economists on the Internet (RFE): data
18. Joseph Rowntree Foundation
19. Intute: Economics resources (archive site)
20. Energy Information Administration
21. OECD Statistics (StatExtracts)
22. CIA world statistics site (World Factbook)
23. UN Millennium Country Profiles
24. World Bank statistics
25. Federal Reserve Bank of St Louis, US Economic Datasets (FRED)
26. Ministry of Economy Trade and Industry (Japan)
27. Financial data from Yahoo
28. DataMarket
29. Index Mundi
30. Oanda Currency Converter
31. World Economic Outlook Database (IMF)
32. Telegraph shares and markets
33. OFFSTATS links to data sets
34. Treasury Pocket Data Bank (source of UK and world economic data)
35. UK Data Service (incorporating ESDS)
36. BBC News, market data
37. NationMaster
38. Statistical Annex of the European Economy
39. Business and Consumer Surveys (all EU countries)
40. Gapminder
41. WebEc Economics Data
42. WTO International Trade Statistics database
43. UNCTAD trade, investment and development statistics (UNCTADstat)
44. London Metal Exchange
45. Bank for International Settlements, global nominal and real effective exchange rate indices
46. EconStats from EconomyWatch
47. AMECO database

C Sites for students and teachers of economics

The following websites offer useful ideas and resources to those who are studying or teaching economics. It is worth browsing through some just to see what is on offer. Try out the first four sites, for starters. The *Internet for Economists* (site 8) is a very helpful tutorial for economics students on making best use of the Internet for studying the subject.

1. The Economics Network
2. Biz/ed
3. Ecedweb
4. Studying Economics
5. Economics and Business Education Association
6. Tutor2U
7. Council for Economic Education
8. Internet for Economics (tutorial on using the Web)
9. Econoclass: Resources for economics teachers
10. Teaching resources for economists (RFE)
11. METAL – Mathematics for Economics: enhancing Teaching And Learning
12. Federal Reserve Bank of San Francisco: Economics Education
13. Excel in Economics Teaching
14. WebEc resources
15. Dr. T's EconLinks: Teaching Resources
16. Online Opinion (Economics)
17. The Idea Channel
18. History of Economic Thought
19. Resources For Economists on the Internet (RFE)
20. Classroom Expernomics
21. Bank of England education resources
22. Why Study Economics?
23. Economic Classroom Experiments
24. Veconlab: Charles Holt's classroom experiments
25. Embedding Threshold Concepts
26. MIT Open Courseware in Economics

D Economic models and simulations

Economic modelling is an important aspect of economic analysis. There are a number of sites that offer access to a model for you to use, e.g. Virtual economy (where you can play being Chancellor of the Exchequer). Using such models can be a useful way of finding out how economic theory works within an environment that claims to reflect reality.

1. Virtual economy
2. Virtual factory
3. Virtual Learning Arcade
4. About.com Economics
5. Classic Economic Models
6. Economics Network Handbook, chapter on simulations, games and role-play
7. Classroom Experiments, Internet Experiments, and Internet Simulations
8. Simulations
9. Experimental economics: Wikipedia
10. Software available on the Economics Network site
11. RFE Software
12. Virtual Worlds
13. Veconlab: Charles Holt's classroom experiments
14. EconPort
15. Denise Hazlett's Classroom Experiments in Macroeconomics
16. Games Economists Play
17. Finance and Economics Experimental Laboratory at Exeter (FEELE)

18. Classroom Expernomics
19. The Economics Network's Guide to Classroom Experiments and Games
20. Economic Classroom Experiments (Wikiversity)

E UK Government and UK Organisations' sites

If you want to see what a government department is up to, then look no further than the list below. Government departments' websites are an excellent source of information and data. They are particularly good at offering information on current legislation and policy initiatives.

1. Gateway site (GOV.UK)
2. Department for Communities and Local Government
3. Prime Minister's Office
4. Competition Commission
5. Department for Education
6. Department for International Development
7. Department for Transport
8. Department of Health
9. Department for Work and Pensions
10. Department for Business, Innovation and Skills
11. Environment Agency
12. Department of Energy and Climate Change
13. Low Pay Commission
14. Department for Environment, Food and Rural Affairs (DEFRA)
15. Office of Communications (Ofcom)
16. Office of Gas and Electricity Markets (Ofgem)
17. Official Documents OnLine
18. Office of Fair Trading (OFT)
19. Office of Rail Regulation (ORR)
20. The Takeover Panel
21. Sustainable Development Commission
22. OFWAT
23. National Statistics (NS)
24. National Statistics Datasets and Reference Tables
25. HM Revenue and Customs
26. UK Intellectual Property Office
27. Parliament website
28. Scottish Government
29. Scottish Environment Protection Agency
30. HM Treasury
31. Equality and Human Rights Commission
32. Trades Union Congress (TUC)
33. Confederation of British Industry
34. Adam Smith Institute
35. Chatham House
36. Institute for Fiscal Studies
37. Advertising Standards Authority
38. Businesses and Self-employed
39. Campaign for Better Transport
40. New Economics Foundation

F Sources of monetary and financial data

As the title suggests, here is a list of useful websites for finding information on financial matters. You will see that the list comprises mainly central banks, both within Europe and further afield.

1. Rank of England
2. Bank of England Monetary and Financial Statistics
3. Banque de France (in English)
4. Bundesbank (German central bank) (in English)
5. Central Bank of Ireland
6. European Central Bank
7. Eurostat
8. US Federal Reserve Bank
9. Netherlands Central Bank (in English)
10. Bank of Japan (in English)
11. Reserve Bank of Australia
12. Bank Negara Malaysia (in English)
13. Monetary Authority of Singapore
14. Bank of Canada
15. National Bank of Denmark (in English)
16. Reserve Bank of India
17. Links to central banks from the Bank for International Settlements
18. The London Stock Exchange

G European Union and related sources

For information on European issues, the following is a wide range of useful sites. The sites maintained by the European Union are an excellent source of information and are provided free of charge.

1. Economic and Financial Affairs (EC DG)
2. European Central Bank
3. EU official Website
4. Eurostat
5. Employment, Social Affairs and Inclusion (EC DG)
6. Booklets on the EU
7. Enterprise and Industry (EC DG)
8. Competition (EC DG)
9. Agriculture and Rural Development (EC DC)
10. Energy and Transport (EC DG)
11. Environment (EC DG)
12. Regional Policy (EC DG)
13. Taxation and Customs Union (EC DG)
14. Education and Culture (EC DG)
15. European Patent Office
16. European Commission
17. European Parliament
18. European Council
19. Mobility and Transport (EC DG)
20. Trade (EC DG)
21. Internal Market and Services (EC DG)

H International organisations

This section casts its net beyond Europe and lists the Web addresses of the main international organisations in the global economy. You will notice that some sites are run by charities, such as Oxfam, while others represent organisations set up to manage international affairs, such as the International Monetary Fund and the United Nations.

1. Food and Agriculture Organisation
2. United National Conference on Trade and Development (UNCTAD)
3. International Labour Organization (ILO)
4. International Monetary Fund (IMF)
5. Organisation for Economic Cooperation and Development (OECD)
6. OPEC
7. World Bank
8. World Health Organization
9. United Nations
10. United Nations Industrial Development Organisation
11. Friends of the Earth
12. Institute of International Finance
13. Oxfam
14. Christian Aid (reports on development issues)
15. European Bank for Reconstruction and Development (EBRD)
16. World Trade Organization (WTO)
17. United Nations Development Programme
18. UNICEF
19. EURODAD – European Network on Debt and Development
20. NAFTA
21. South American free trade areas
22. ASEAN
23. APEC

I Economics search and link sites

If you are having difficulty finding what you want from the list of sites above, the following sites offer links to other sites and are a very useful resource when you are looking for something a little bit more specialist. Once again, it is worth having a look at what these sites have to offer in order to judge their usefulness.

1. Gateway for UK official sites
2. Alta Plana
3. Data Archive Search
4. Inomics (search engine for economics information)
5. RePEc bibliographic database
6. Estima: Links to economics resources sites
7. Intute: Social Sciences (Economics) (archive site)
8. WebEc
9. One World (link to economic development sites)
10. Economic development sites (list) from OneWorld.net
11. DMOZ Open Directory: Economics
12. Web links for economists from the Economics Network
13. Yahoo's links to economic data
14. OFFSTATS links to data sets
15. Excite Economics links
16. Internet Resources for Economists
17. National Association of Business Economics links
18. Resources for Economists on the Internet
19. UK university economics departments
20. Economics education links
21. Development Gateway Foundation
22. Find the Best

J Internet search engines

The following search engines have been found to be useful.

1. Google
2. Bing
3. Whoosh UK
4. Excite
5. Infoseek
6. Search.com
7. MSN
8. Economics Search Engine from RFE
9. Yahoo
10. Ask
11. Kartoo
12. Blinkx (for videos and audio podcasts)

Key ideas

1. **The behaviour and performance of firms is affected by the business environment.** The business environment includes economic, political/legal, social/cultural and technological factors (page 7).

2. **Scarcity** is the excess of human wants over what can actually be produced. Because of scarcity, various choices have to be made between alternatives (page 16).

3. The **opportunity cost** of something is what you give up to get it/do it. In other words, it is cost measured in terms of the best alternative forgone (page 20).

4. **Rational decision making involves weighing up the marginal benefit and marginal cost of any activity.** If the marginal benefit exceeds the marginal cost, it is rational to do the activity (or to do more of it). If the marginal cost exceeds the marginal benefit, it is rational not to do it (or to do less of it) (page 22).

5. **Transactions costs.** The costs incurred when firms buy inputs or services from other firms as opposed to producing them themselves. They include the costs of searching for the best firm to do business with, the costs of drawing up, monitoring and enforcing contracts and the costs of transporting and handling products between the firms. These costs should be weighed against the benefits of outsourcing through the market (page 33).

6. **The nature of institutions and organisations is likely to influence behaviour.** There are various forces influencing people's decisions in complex organisations. Assumptions that an organisation will follow one simple objective (e.g. short-run profit maximisation) is thus too simplistic in many cases (page 34).

7. **The principal–agent problem.** Where people (principals), as a result of a lack of knowledge, cannot ensure that their best interests are served by their agents. Agents may take advantage of this situation to the disadvantage of the principals (page 35).

8. **Good decision making requires good information.** Where information is poor, or poorly used, decisions and their outcomes may be poor. This may be the result of bounded rationality (page 38).

9. **People respond to incentives.** It is important, therefore, that incentives are appropriate and have the desired effect (page 47).

10. **Changes in demand or supply cause markets to adjust.** Whenever such changes occur, the resulting 'disequilibrium' will bring an automatic change in prices, thereby restoring equilibrium (i.e. a balance of demand and supply) (page 48).

11. **Equilibrium is the point where conflicting interests are balanced.** Only at this point is the amount that demanders are willing to purchase the same as the amount that suppliers are willing to supply. It is a point which will be automatically reached in a free market through the operation of the price mechanism (page 55).

12. **Elasticity.** The responsiveness of one variable (e.g. demand) to a change in another (e.g. price). This concept is fundamental to understanding how markets work. The more elastic variables are, the more responsive is the market to changing circumstances (page 63).

13. **People's actions are influenced by their expectations.** People respond not just to what is happening now (such as a change in price), but to what they anticipate will happen in the future (page 71).

14. **People's actions are influenced by their attitudes towards risk.** Many decisions are taken under conditions of risk or uncertainty. Generally, the lower the probability of (or the more uncertain) the desired outcome of an action, the less likely will people be to undertake the action (page 74).

15. **The principle of diminishing marginal utility.** The more of a product a person consumes over a given period of time, the less will be the additional utility gained from one more unit (page 83).

16. **Adverse selection.** Where information is imperfect, high-risk groups will be attracted to profitable market opportunities to the disadvantage of the average buyer (or seller). In the context of insurance, it refers to those who are most likely to take out insurance posing the greatest risks to the insurer (page 89).

17. **Moral hazard.** Following a deal, there is an increased likelihood that one party will engage in problematic (immoral and hazardous) behaviour to the detriment of another. In the context of insurance, it refers to people taking more risks when they have insurance (page 89).

18. **The 'bygones' principle** states that sunk (fixed) costs should be ignored when deciding whether to produce or sell more or less of a product. Only variable costs should be taken into account (page 129).

19. **Output depends on the amount of resources and how they are used.** Different amounts and combinations of inputs will lead to different amounts of output. If output is to be produced efficiently, then inputs should be combined in the optimum proportions (page 130).

20. **The law of diminishing marginal returns.** When increasing amounts of a variable factor are used with a given amount of a fixed factor, there will come a point when each extra unit of the variable factor will produce less extra output than the previous unit (page 130).

21. **Market power benefits the powerful at the expense of others.** When firms have market power over prices, they can use this to raise prices and profits above the perfectly competitive level. Other things being equal, the firm will gain at the expense of the consumer. Similarly, if consumers or workers have market power, they can use this to their own benefit (page 161).

22. **Economic efficiency** is achieved when each good is produced at the minimum cost and where consumers get maximum benefit from their income (page 165).

23. **People often think and behave strategically.** How you think others will respond to your actions is likely to influence your own behaviour. Firms, for example, when considering a price or product change will often take into account the likely reactions of their rivals (page 181).

24. **Nash equilibrium.** The position resulting from everyone making their optimal decision based on their assumptions about their rivals' decisions. Without collusion, there is no incentive for any firm to move from this position (page 189).

25. **Core competencies.** The key skills of a business that underpin its competitive advantage. A core competence is valuable, rare, costly to imitate and non-substitutable. Firms will normally gain from exploiting their core competencies (page 208).

26. **Flexible firm.** A firm that has the flexibility to respond to changing market conditions by changing the composition of its workforce and its working practices (page 286).

27. **Stocks and flows.** A stock is a quantity of something at a given point in time. A flow is an increase or decrease in something over a specified period of time. This is an important distinction and a common cause of confusion (page 292).

28. **The principle of discounting.** People generally prefer to have benefits today than in the future. Thus future benefits have to be reduced (discounted) to give them a present value (page 295).

29. **Efficient capital markets.** Capital markets are efficient when the prices of shares accurately reflect information about companies' current and expected future performance (page 304).

30. **Allocative efficiency in any activity is achieved where any reallocation would lead to a decline in net benefit.** It is achieved where marginal benefit equals marginal cost. Private efficiency is achieved where marginal private benefit equals marginal private cost ($MB = MC$). Social efficiency is achieved where marginal social benefit equals marginal social cost ($MSB = MSC$) (page 311).

31. **Markets generally fail to achieve social efficiency.** There are various types of market failure. Market failures provide one of the major justifications for government intervention in the economy (page 311).

32. **Equity** is where income is distributed in a way that is considered to be fair or just. Note that an equitable distribution is not the same as a totally equal distribution and that different people have different views on what is equitable (page 311).

33. **Externalities are spillover costs or benefits.** Where these exist, even an otherwise perfect market will fail to achieve social efficiency (page 311).

34. **The free-rider problem.** People are often unwilling to pay for things if they can make use of things other people have bought. This problem can lead to people not purchasing things which would be to the benefit of them and other members of society to have (page 313).

35. **The problem of time lags.** Many economic actions can take a long time to take effect. This can cause problems of instability and an inability of the economy to achieve social efficiency (page 316).

36. **Government intervention may be able to rectify various failings of the market.** Government intervention in the market can be used to achieve various economic objectives which may not be best achieved by the market. Governments, however, are not perfect, and their actions may bring adverse as well as beneficial consequences (page 316).

37. **The law of comparative advantage.** Provided opportunity costs of various goods differ in two countries, both of them can gain from mutual trade if they specialise in producing (and exporting) those goods that have relatively low opportunity costs compared with the other country (page 393).

38. **Economies suffer from inherent instability.** As a result, economic growth and other macroeconomic indicators tend to fluctuate (page 419).

39. **Living standards are limited by a country's ability to produce.** Potential national output depends on the country's resources, technology and productivity (page 419).

40. **The distinction between nominal and real figures.** Nominal figures are those using current prices, interest rates, etc. Real figures are figures corrected for inflation (page 431).

41. **Societies face trade-offs between economic objectives.** For example, the goal of faster growth may

conflict with that of greater equality; the goal of lower unemployment may conflict with that of lower inflation (at least in the short run). This is an example of opportunity cost: the cost of achieving more of one objective may be achieving less of another. The existence of trade-offs means that policy-makers must make choices (page 436).

42. **The principle of cumulative causation.** An initial event can cause an ultimate effect which is much larger (page 486).

43. **Goodhart's Law.** Controlling a symptom (i.e. an indicator) of a problem will not cure the problem. Instead, the indicator will merely cease to be a good indicator of the problem (page 527).

Glossary

Absolute advantage A country has an absolute advantage over another in the production of a good if it can produce it with less resources than the other country.

Accelerationist theory The theory that unemployment can only be reduced below the natural rate at the cost of accelerating inflation.

Accelerator theory The *level* of investment depends on the *rate of change* of national income, and the result tends to be subject to substantial fluctuations.

Actual growth The percentage annual increase in national output actually produced.

Ad valorem tariffs Tariffs levied as a percentage of the price of the import.

Adjustable peg A system whereby exchange rates are fixed for a period of time, but may be devalued (or revalued) if a deficit (or surplus) becomes substantial.

Adverse selection Where information is imperfect, high risk groups will be attracted to profitable market opportunities to the disadvantage of the average buyer (or seller).

Advertising/sales ratio A ratio that reflects the intensity of advertising within a market.

Aggregate demand (*AD*) Total spending on goods and services made in the economy. It consists of four elements, consumer spending (*C*), investment (*I*), government spending (*G*) and the expenditure on exports (*X*), less any expenditure on foreign goods and services (*M*): $AD = C + I + G + X - M$.

Aggregate demand for labour curve A curve showing the total demand for labour in the economy at different average real wage rates.

Aggregate supply The total amount of output in the economy.

Aggregate supply of labour curve A curve showing the total number of people willing and able to work at different average real wage rates.

Ambient-based standards Pollution control that requires firms to meet minimum standards for the environment (e.g. air or water quality).

Appreciation A rise in the free-market exchange rate of the domestic currency with foreign currencies.

Assets Possessions, or claims held on others.

Assisted areas Areas of high unemployment qualifying for government regional selective assistance (RSA and SFI) and grants from the European Regional Development Fund (ERDF).

Asymmetric information A situation in which one party in an economic relationship knows more than another.

Asymmetric shocks Shocks (such as an oil price increase or a recession in another part of the world) that have different-sized effects on different industries, regions or countries.

Average (total) cost (*AC*) Total cost (fixed plus variable) per unit of output: $AC = TC/Q = AFC + AVC$.

Average cost pricing Where a firm sets its price by adding a certain percentage for (average) profit on top of average cost.

Average fixed cost (*AFC*) Total fixed cost per unit of output: $AFC = TFC/Q$.

Average physical product (*APP*) Total output (*TPP*) per unit of the variable factor in question: $APP = TPP/Qv$.

Average revenue Total revenue per unit of output. When all output is sold at the same price, average revenue will be the same as price: $AR = TR/Q = P$.

Average variable cost (*AVC*) Total variable cost per unit of output: $AVC = TVC/Q$.

Balance of payments account A record of the country's transactions with the rest of the world. It shows the country's payments to or deposits in other countries (debits) and its receipts or deposits from other countries (credits). It also shows the balance between these debits and credits under various headings.

Balance of payments on current account The balance on trade in goods and services plus net incomes and current transfers.

Balance of trade Exports of goods and services minus imports of goods and services. If exports exceed imports, there is a 'balance of trade surplus' (a positive figure). If imports exceed exports, there is a 'balance of trade deficit' (a negative figure).

Balance on trade in goods and services or balance of trade Exports of goods and services minus imports of goods and services.

Balance on trade in goods or balance of visible trade or merchandise balance Exports of goods minus imports of goods.

Bank (or bank deposits) multiplier The number of times greater the expansion of bank deposits is than the additional liquidity in banks that caused it $1/L$ (the inverse of the liquidity ratio).

Barometric firm price leadership Where the price leader is the one whose prices are believed to reflect market conditions in the most satisfactory way.

Barometric forecasting A technique used to predict future economic trends based upon analysing patterns of time-series data.

Barter economy An economy where people exchange goods and services directly with one another without any payment of money. Workers would be paid with bundles of goods.

Base year (for index numbers) The year whose index number is set at 100.

Behavioural theories of the firm Theories that attempt to predict the actions of firms by studying the behaviour of various groups of people within the firm and their interactions under conditions of potentially conflicting interests.

Bill of exchange A certificate promising to repay a stated amount on a certain date, typically three months from the issue of the bill. Bills pay no interest as such, but are sold at a discount and redeemed at face value, thereby earning a rate of discount for the purchaser.

Bounded rationality Individuals are limited in their ability to absorb and process information. People think in ways conditioned by their experiences (family, education, peer groups, etc.).

Broad money Cash in circulation plus retail and wholesale bank and building society deposits.

Budget deficit The excess of central government's spending over its tax receipts.

Budget surplus The excess of central government's tax receipts over its spending.

Business cycle or trade cycle The periodic fluctuations of national output round its long-term trend.

By-product A good or service that is produced as a consequence of producing another good or service.

Capital All inputs into production that have themselves been produced (e.g. factories, machines and tools).

Capital account of the balance of payments The record of transfers of capital to and from abroad.

Capital adequacy ratio The ratio of a bank's capital (reserves and shares) to its risk-weighted assets.

Cartel A formal collusive agreement.

Certificates of deposit Certificates issued by banks for fixed-term interest-bearing deposits. They can be resold by the owner to another party.

Change in demand The term used for a shift in the demand curve. It occurs when a determinant of demand *other* than price changes.

Change in supply The term used for a shift in the supply curve. It occurs when a determinant other than price changes.

Change in the quantity demanded The term used for a movement along the demand curve to a new point. It occurs when there is a change in price.

Change in the quantity supplied The term used for a movement along the supply curve to a new point. It occurs when there is a change in price.

Characteristics (or attributes) theory The theory that demonstrates how consumer choice between different varieties of a product depends on the characteristics of these varieties, along with prices of the different varieties, the consumer's budget and the consumer's tastes.

Claimant unemployment Those in receipt of unemployment-related benefits.

Closed shop Where a firm agrees to employ only members of a recognised union.

Collusive oligopoly When oligopolists agree (formally or informally) to limit competition between themselves. They may set output quotas, fix prices, limit product promotion or development, or agree not to 'poach' each other's markets.

Collusive tendering Where two or more firms secretly agree on the prices they will tender for a contract. These prices will be above those which would be put in under a genuinely competitive tendering process.

Command-and-control (CAC) systems The use of laws or regulations backed up by inspections and penalties (such as fines) for non-compliance.

Commercial bill A certificate issued by a firm promising to repay a stated amount on a certain date, typically three months from the issue of the bill. Bills pay no interest as such, but are sold at a discount and redeemed at their face value, thereby earning a rate of discount for the purchaser.

Common market A customs union where the member countries act as a single market with free movement of labour and capital, common taxes and common trade laws.

Comparative advantage A country has a comparative advantage over another in the production of a good if it can produce it at a lower opportunity cost, i.e. if it has to forgo less of other goods in order to produce it.

Competition for corporate control The competition for the control of companies through takeovers.

Complementary goods A pair of goods consumed together. As the price of one goes up, the demand for both goods will fall.

Compounding The process of adding interest each year to an initial capital sum.

Conglomerate merger Where two firms in different industries merge.

Conglomerate multinational A multinational that produces different products in different countries.

Consortium Where two or more firms work together on a specific project and create a separate company to run the project.

Consumer durable A consumer good that lasts a period of time, during which the consumer can continue gaining utility from it.

Consumer prices index (CPI) An index of the prices of goods bought by a typical household.

Consumer surplus The excess of what a person would have been prepared to pay for a good (i.e. the utility measured in money terms) over what that person actually pays. Total consumer surplus equals total utility minus total expenditure.

Consumption The act of using goods and services to satisfy wants. This will normally involve purchasing the goods and services.

Consumption of domestically produced goods and services (Cd) The direct flow of money payments from households to firms.

Convergence of economies When countries achieve similar levels of growth, inflation, budget deficits as a percentage of GDP, balance of payments, etc.

Core competence The key skills of a business that underpin its competitive advantage.

Corporate Social responsibility Where a firm takes into account the interests and concerns of a community rather than just its shareholders.

Cost–benefit analysis The identification, measurement and weighing-up of the costs and benefits of a project in order to decide whether or not it should go ahead.

Cost-push inflation Inflation caused by persistent rises in costs of production (independently of demand).

Countervailing power When the power of a monopolistic/oligopolistic seller is offset by powerful buyers who can prevent the price from being pushed up.

Cournot model A model of duopoly where each firm makes its price and output decisions on the assumption that its rival will produce a particular quantity.

Credible threat (or promise) One that is believable to rivals because it is in the threatener's interests to carry it out.

Cross-price elasticity of demand The responsiveness of demand for one good to a change in the price of another; the proportionate change in demand for one good divided by the proportionate change in price of the other.

Cross-section data Information showing how a variable (e.g. the consumption of eggs) differs between different groups or different individuals at a given time.

Crowding out Where increased public expenditure diverts money or resources away from the private sector.

Currency union A group of countries (or regions) using a common currency.

Current account of the balance of payments The record of a country's imports and exports of goods and services, plus incomes and transfers of money to and from abroad.

Customs union A free trade area with common external tariffs and quotas.

Deadweight welfare loss The loss of consumer plus producer surplus in imperfect markets (when compared with perfect competition).

Debt/equity ratio The ratio of debt finance to equity finance.

Decision tree (or game tree) A diagram showing the sequence of possible decisions by competitor firms and the outcome of each combination of decisions.

Deflation (definition 1) A period of falling prices: negative inflation.

Deflation (definition 2) A period of falling real aggregate demand. Note that 'deflation' is more commonly used nowadays to mean negative inflation.

Deflationary or recessionary gap The shortfall of aggregate expenditure below GDP at the full-employment level of GDP.

Deindustrialisation The decline in the contribution to production of the manufacturing sector of the economy.

Demand curve A graph showing the relationship between the price of a good and the quantity of the good demanded over a given time period. Price is measured on the vertical axis; quantity demanded is measured on the horizontal axis. A demand curve can be for an individual consumer or a group of consumers, or more usually for the whole market.

Demand function An equation showing the relationship between the demand for a product and its principal determinants.

Demand schedule for an individual A table showing the different quantities of a good that a person is willing and able to buy at various prices over a given period of time.

Demand: change in demand The term used for a shift in the demand curve. It occurs when a determinant of demand *other* than price changes.

Demand: change in the quantity demanded The term used for a movement along the demand curve to a new point. It occurs when there is a change in price.

Demand-deficient or cyclical unemployment Disequilibrium unemployment caused by a fall in aggregate demand with no corresponding fall in the real wage rate.

Demand-pull inflation Inflation caused by persistent rises in aggregate demand.

Demand-side policy Government policy designed to alter the level of aggregate demand, and thereby the level of output, employment and prices.

Dependent variable That variable whose outcome is determined by other variables within an equation.

Depreciation (capital) The decline in value of capital equipment due to age or to wear and tear.

Depreciation (currency) A fall in the free-market exchange rate of the domestic currency with foreign currencies.

Derived demand The demand for a factor of production depends on the demand for the good which uses it.

Destabilising speculation This is where the actions of speculators tend to make price movements larger.

Devaluation Where the government refixes the exchange rate at a lower level.

Diminishing marginal rate of substitution of characteristics The more a consumer gets of characteristic A and the less of characteristic B, the less and less of B the consumer will be willing to give up to get an extra unit of A.

Diminishing marginal utility of income Where each additional pound earned yields less additional utility.

Discount market An example of a money market in which new or existing bills are bought and sold.

Discounting The process of reducing the value of future flows to give them a present valuation.

Discretionary fiscal policy Deliberate changes in tax rates or the level of government expenditure in order to influence the level of aggregate demand.

Diseconomies of scale Where costs per unit of output increase as the scale of production increases.

Disequilibrium unemployment Unemployment resulting from real wages in the economy being above the equilibrium level.

Diversification A business growth strategy in which a business expands into new markets outside of its current interests.

Dominant firm price leadership When firms (the followers) choose the same price as that set by a dominant firm in the industry (the leader).

Dominant strategy game Where the *same* policy is suggested by different strategies.

Downsizing Where a business reorganises and reduces its size, especially in respect to levels of employment, in order to cut costs.

Dumping Where exports are sold at prices below marginal cost – often as a result of government subsidy.

Duopoly An oligopoly where there are just two firms in the market.

Econometrics The branch of economics which applies statistical techniques to economic data.

Economies of scale When increasing the scale of production leads to a lower cost per unit of output.

Economies of scope When increasing the range of products produced by a firm reduces the cost of producing each one.

Efficiency frontier A line showing the maximum attainable combinations of two characteristics for a given budget. These characteristics can be obtained by consuming one or a mixture of two brands or varieties of a product.

Efficiency wage hypothesis A hypothesis that states that a worker's productivity is linked to the wage he or she receives.

Efficiency wage rate The profit-maximising wage rate for the firm after taking into account the effects of wage rates on worker motivation, turnover and recruitment.

Efficient (capital) market hypothesis The hypothesis that new information about a company's current or future performance will be quickly and accurately reflected in its share price.

Elastic If demand is (price) elastic, then any change in price will cause the quantity demanded to change proportionately more. (Ignoring the negative sign) it will have a value greater than 1.

Endogenous money supply Money supply that is determined (at least in part) by the demand for money.

Enterprise culture One in which individuals are encouraged to become wealth creators through their own initiative and effort.

Envelope curve A long-run average cost curve drawn as the tangency points of a series of short-run average cost curves.

Environmental policy Initiatives by government to ensure a specified minimum level of environmental quality.

Environmental scanning Where a business surveys social and political trends in order to take account of changes in its decision-making process.

Equation of exchange $MV = PQ$. The total level of spending on GDP (MV) equals the total value of goods and services produced (PQ) that go to make up GDP.

Equilibrium A position of balance. A position from which there is no inherent tendency to move away.

Equilibrium ('natural') unemployment The difference between those who would like employment at the current wage rate and those willing and able to take a job.

Equilibrium price The price where the quantity demanded equals the quantity supplied; the price where there is no shortage or surplus.

Equity The fair distribution of a society's resources.

ERM (the exchange rate mechanism) A semi-fixed system whereby participating EU countries allowed fluctuations against each other's currencies only within agreed bands. Collectively they floated freely against all other currencies.

Ethical consumerism Where consumers' decisions about what to buy are influenced by ethical concerns such as the producer's human rights record and care for the environment.

Excess burden (of a tax on a good) The amount by which the loss in consumer plus producer surplus exceeds the government surplus.

Excess capacity (under monopolistic competition) In the long run, firms under monopolistic competition will produce at an output below that which minimises average cost per unit.

Exchange equalisation account The gold and foreign exchange reserves account in the Bank of England.

Exchange rate The rate at which one national currency exchanges for another. The rate is expressed as the amount of one currency that is necessary to purchase one unit of another currency (e.g. £1 = €1.40).

Exchange rate index A weighted average exchange rate expressed as an index, where the value of the index is 100 in a given base year. The weights of the different currencies in the index add up to 1.

Exogenous money supply Money supply that does not depend on the demand for money but is set by the authorities (i.e. the central bank or the government).

Expectations-augmented Phillips curve A (short-run) Phillips curve whose position depends on the expected rate of inflation.

Explicit costs The payments to outside suppliers of inputs.

External benefits Benefits from production (or consumption) experienced by people *other* than the producer (or consumer).

External costs Costs of production (or consumption) borne by people *other* than the producer (or consumer).

External diseconomies of scale Where a firm's costs per unit of output increase as the size of the whole industry increases.

External economies of scale Where a firm's costs per unit of output decrease as the size of the whole *industry* grows.

External expansion Where business growth is achieved by merger, takeover, joint venture or an agreement.

Externalities Costs or benefits of production or consumption experienced by society but not by the producers or consumers themselves. Sometimes referred to as 'spillover' or 'third-party' costs or benefits.

Factors of production (or resources) The inputs into the production of goods and services labour, land and raw materials, and capital.

Financial account of the balance of payments The record of the flows of money into and out of the country for the purpose of investment or as deposits in banks and other financial institutions.

Financial crowding out Where an increase in government borrowing diverts money away from the private sector.

Financial flexibility Where employers can vary their wage costs by changing the composition of their workforce or the terms on which workers are employed.

Financial instruments Financial products resulting in a financial claim by one party over another.

Financial intermediaries The general name for financial institutions (banks, building societies, etc.) which act as a means of channelling funds from depositors to borrowers.

Fine tuning The use of demand management policy (fiscal or monetary) to smooth out cyclical fluctuations in the economy.

Firm An economic organisation that co-ordinates the process of production and distribution.

First-degree price discrimination Where a firm charges each consumer for each unit the maximum price which that consumer is willing to pay for that unit.

First-mover advantage When a firm gains from being the first one to take action.

Fiscal policy Policy to affect aggregate demand by altering government expenditure and/or taxation.

Fiscal stance How deflationary or reflationary the Budget is.

Fixed costs Total costs that do not vary with the amount of output produced.

Fixed factor An input that cannot be increased in supply within a given time period.

Flat organisation One in which technology enables senior managers to communicate directly with those lower in the organisational structure. Middle managers are bypassed.

Flexible firm A firm that has the flexibility to respond to changing market conditions by changing the composition of its workforce.

Floating exchange rate When the government does not intervene in the foreign exchange markets, but simply allows the exchange rate to be freely determined by demand and supply.

Flow An increase or decrease in quantity over a specified period.

Foreign exchange gap The shortfall in foreign exchange that a country needs to purchase necessary imports such as raw materials and machinery.

Forward exchange market Where contracts are made today for the price at which a currency will be exchanged at some specified future date.

Franchise A formal contractual agreement whereby a company uses another company to produce or sell some or all of its product.

Franchising Where a firm is granted the licence to operate a given part of an industry for a specified length of time.

Free market One in which there is an absence of government intervention. Individual producers and consumers are free to make their own economic decisions.

Free trade area A group of countries with no trade barriers between themselves.

Free-rider problem When it is not possible to exclude other people from consuming a good that someone has bought.

Frictional (search) unemployment Unemployment that occurs as a result of imperfect information in the labour market. It often takes time for workers to find jobs (even though there are vacancies) and in the meantime they are unemployed.

Full-employment level of GDP The level of GDP at which there is no deficiency of demand.

Full-range pricing A pricing strategy in which a business, seeking to improve its profit performance, assesses the pricing of its goods as a whole rather than individually.

Functional flexibility Where employers can switch workers from job to job as requirements change.

Functional relationships The mathematical relationships showing how one variable is affected by one or more others.

Funding Where the authorities alter the balance of bills and bonds for any given level of government borrowing.

Future price A price agreed today at which an item (e.g. commodities) will be exchanged at some set date in the future.

Futures or forward market A market in which contracts are made to buy or sell at some future date at a price agreed today.

Game theory (or the theory of games) The study of alternative strategies that oligopolists may choose to adopt, depending on their assumptions about their rivals' behaviour.

GDP deflator The price index of all final domestically produced goods and services: i.e. all items that contribute towards GDP.

Gearing ratio The ratio of debt finance to total finance.

General government debt The accumulated central and local government deficits (less surpluses) over the years, i.e. the total amount owed by central and local government, both to domestic and overseas creditors.

Global sourcing Where a company uses production sites in different parts of the world to provide particular components for a final product.

Goodhart's Law Controlling a symptom of a problem, or only part of the problem, will not cure the problem it will simply mean that the part that is being controlled now becomes a poor indicator of the problem.

Goods in joint supply These are two goods where the production of more of one leads to the production of more of the other.

Government surplus (from a tax on a good) The total tax revenue earned by the government from sales of a good.

Grandfathering Where each firm's emission permit is based on its *current* levels of emission (e.g. permitted levels for all firms could be 80 per cent of their current levels).

Gross domestic product (GDP) The value of output produced within the country over a 12-month period.

Gross domestic product (GDP) (at market prices) The value of output produced within a country over a 12-month period in terms of the prices actually paid. GDP = GVA + taxes on products − subsidies on products.

Gross national income (GNY) GDP plus net income from abroad.

Gross value added (GVA) at basic prices The sum of all the values added by all industries in the economy over a year. The figures exclude taxes on products (such as VAT) and include subsidies on products.

Growth maximisation An alternative theory which assumes that managers seek to maximise the growth in sales revenue (or the capital value of the firm) over time.

Growth vector matrix A means by which a business might assess its product/market strategy.

Harrod–Domar model A model that relates a country's rate of economic growth to the proportion of national income saved and the ratio of capital to output.

Historic costs The original amount the firm paid for factors it now owns.

Holding company A business organisation in which the present company holds interests in a number of other companies or subsidiaries.

Horizontal merger Where two firms in the same industry at the same stage of the production process merge.

Horizontal product differentiation Where a firm's product differs from its rivals' products, although the products are seen to be of a similar quality.

Horizontal strategic alliances A formal or informal arrangement between firms to jointly provide a particular activity at a similar stage of the same technical process.

Horizontally integrated multinational A multinational that produces the same product in many different countries.

Households' disposable income The income available for households to spend, i.e. personal incomes after deducting taxes on incomes and adding benefits.

Hysteresis The persistence of an effect even when the initial cause has ceased to operate. In economics it refers to the persistence of unemployment even when the demand deficiency that caused it no longer exists.

Imperfect competition The collective name for monopolistic competition and oligopoly.

Implicit costs Costs which do not involve a direct payment of money to a third party, but which nevertheless involve a sacrifice of some alternative.

Import substitution The replacement of imports by domestically produced goods or services.

Income effect The effect of a change in price on quantity demanded arising from the consumer becoming better or worse off as a result of the price change.

Income effect of a rise in wages Workers get a higher income for a given number of hours worked and may thus feel they need to work fewer hours as wages rise.

Income elasticity of demand The responsiveness of demand to a change in consumer incomes; the proportionate change in demand divided by the proportionate change in income.

Independence (of firms in a market) When the decisions of one firm in a market will not have any significant effect on the demand curves of its rivals.

Independent risks Where two risky events are unconnected. The occurrence of one will not affect the likelihood of the occurrence of the other.

Independent variables Those variables that determine the dependent variable, but are themselves determined independently of the equation they are in.

Index number The value of a variable expressed as 100 plus or minus its percentage deviation from a base year.

Indifference curve A line showing all those combinations of two characteristics of a good between which a consumer is indifferent, i.e. those combinations that give a particular level of utility.

Indifference map A diagram showing a whole set of indifference curves. The further away a particular curve is from the origin, the higher the level of utility it represents.

Indivisibilities The impossibility of dividing a factor of production into smaller units.

Industrial concentration The degree to which an industry is dominated by large business enterprises.

Industrial policies Policies to encourage industrial investment and greater industrial efficiency.

Industrial sector A grouping of industries producing similar products or services.

Industry A group of firms producing a particular product or service.

Industry's infrastructure The network of supply agents, communications, skills, training facilities, distribution channels, specialised financial services, etc. that support a particular industry.

Inelastic If demand is (price) inelastic, then any change will cause the quantity demanded to change by a proportionately smaller amount. (Ignoring the negative sign) it will have a value less than 1.

Infant industry An industry which has a potential comparative advantage, but which is as yet too underdeveloped to be able to realise this potential.

Inferior goods Goods whose demand falls as people's incomes rise.

Inflationary gap The excess of aggregate expenditure over GDP at the full-employment level of GDP.

Injections (J) Expenditure on the production of domestic firms coming from outside the inner flow of the circular flow of income. Injections equal investment (I) plus government expenditure (G) plus expenditure on exports (X).

Integrated international enterprise One in which an international company pursues a single business strategy. It co-ordinates the business activities of its subsidiaries across different countries.

Interdependence (under oligopoly) Each firm will be affected by its rivals' decisions. Likewise its decisions will affect its rivals. Firms recognise the importance of this interdependence and it affects their decisions. It is one of the two key features of oligopoly.

Internal expansion Where a business adds to its productive capacity by adding to existing or by building new plant.

Internal funds Funds used for business expansion that come from ploughed-back profit.

Internal rate of return (IRR) The rate of return of an investment: the discount rate that makes the net present value of an investment equal to zero.

Internalisation advantages Where the benefits of extending the organisational structure of the MNC by setting up an overseas subsidiary are greater than the costs of arranging a contract with an external party.

International harmonisation of economic policies Where countries attempt to coordinate their macroeconomic policies so as to achieve common goals.

International liquidity The supply of currencies in the world acceptable for financing international trade and investment.

International trade multiplier The impact of changing levels of international demand on levels of production and output.

Inter-temporal pricing This occurs where different groups have different price elasticities of demand for a product at different points in time.

Investment The purchase by the firm of equipment or materials that will add to its stock of capital.

Joint-stock company A company where ownership is distributed between a large number of shareholders.

Just-in-time methods Where a firm purchases supplies and produces both components and finished products as they are required. This minimises stock holding and its associated costs.

Kinked demand theory The theory that oligopolists face a demand curve that is kinked at the current price demand being significantly more elastic above the current price than below. The effect of this is to create a situation of price stability.

Labour All forms of human input, both physical and mental, into current production.

Labour force The number employed plus the number unemployed.

Land (and raw materials) Inputs into production that are provided by nature (e.g. unimproved land and mineral deposits in the ground).

Law of comparative advantage Trade can benefit all countries if they specialise in the goods in which they have a comparative advantage.

Law of demand The quantity of a good demanded per period of time will fall as the price rises and rise as the price falls, other things being equal (*ceteris paribus*).

Law of diminishing (marginal) returns When one or more factors are held fixed, there will come a point beyond which the extra output from additional units of the variable factor will diminish.

Law of large numbers The larger the number of events of a particular type, the more predictable will be their average outcome.

Leading indicators Indicators that help predict future trends in the economy.

Lender of last resort The role of the Bank of England as the guarantor of sufficient liquidity in the monetary system.

Leverage The extent to which a company relies upon debt finance as opposed to equity finance.

Liabilities All legal claims for payment that outsiders have on an institution.

Licensing Where the owner of a patented product allows another firm to produce it for a fee.

Limit pricing Where a business keeps prices low, restricting its profits, so as to deter new rivals entering the market.

Liquidity The ease with which an asset can be converted into cash without loss.

Liquidity ratio The proportion of a bank's total assets held in liquid form.

Liquidity trap When interest rates are at their floor and thus any further increases in money supply will not be spent but merely be held in idle balances as people wait for the economy to recover and/or interest rates to rise.

Locational advantages Those features of a host economy that MNCs believe will lower costs, improve quality and/or facilitate greater sales.

Lock-outs Union members are temporarily laid off until they are prepared to agree to the firm's conditions.

Logistics The process of managing the supply of inputs to a firm and the outputs from a firm to its customers.

Long run The period of time long enough for *all* factors to be varied.

Long run under perfect competition The period of time which is long enough for new firms to enter the industry.

Long-run average cost (LRAC) curve A curve that shows how average cost varies with output on the assumption that *all* factors are variable. (It is assumed that the least-cost method of production will be chosen for each output.)

Long-run profit maximisation An alternative theory which assumes that managers aim to shift cost and revenue curves so as to maximise profits over some longer time period.

Long-run shut-down point This is where the *AR* curve is tangential to the *LRAC* curve. The firm can just make normal profits. Any fall in revenue below this level will cause a profit-maximising firm to shut down once all costs have become variable.

Loss leader A product whose price is cut by the business in order to attract custom.

Macro-prudential regulation Regulation which focuses on the financial system as a whole and which monitors its impact on the wider economy and ensures that it is resilient to shocks.

Macroeconomics The branch of economics that studies economic aggregates (grand totals), for example the overall level of prices, output and employment in the economy.

Managed flexibility (dirty floating) A system of flexible exchange rates, but where the government intervenes to prevent excessive fluctuations or even to achieve an unofficial target exchange rate.

Managerial utility maximisation An alternative theory which assumes that managers are motivated by self-interest. They will adopt whatever policies are perceived to maximise their own utility.

Marginal benefits The additional benefits of doing a little bit more (or *1 unit* more if a unit can be measured) of an activity.

Marginal consumer surplus The excess of utility from the consumption of one more unit of a good (*MU*) over the price paid: $MCS = MU - P$.

Marginal cost (MC) The cost of producing one more unit of output: $MC = \Delta TC/\Delta Q$.

Marginal cost of capital The cost of one additional unit of capital.

Marginal costs The additional cost of doing a little bit more (or *1 unit* more if a unit can be measured) of an activity.

Marginal disutility of work The extra sacrifice/hardship to a worker of working an extra unit of time in any given time period (e.g. an extra hour per day).

Marginal efficiency of capital (MEC) or **internal rate of return (IRR)** The rate of return of an investment the discount rate that makes the net present value of an investment equal to zero.

Marginal physical product (MPP) The extra output gained by the employment of one more unit of the variable factor: $MPP = \Delta TPP/\Delta Qv$.

Marginal productivity theory The theory that the demand for a factor depends on its marginal revenue product.

Marginal revenue The extra revenue gained by selling one or more unit per time period: $MR = \Delta TR/\Delta Q$.

Marginal revenue product of capital The additional revenue earned from employing one additional unit of capital.

Marginal revenue product of labour The extra revenue a firm earns from employing one more unit of labour.

Marginal utility The extra satisfaction gained from consuming one extra unit of a good within a given time period.

Market The interaction between buyers and sellers.

Market clearing A market clears when supply matches demand, leaving no shortage or surplus.

Market demand schedule A table showing the different total quantities of a good that consumers are willing and able to buy at various prices over a given period of time.

Market experiments Information gathered about consumers under artificial or simulated conditions. A method used widely in assessing the effects of advertising on consumers.

Market loans Loans made to other financial institutions.

Market niche A part of a market (or new market) that has not been filled by an existing brand or business.

Market segment A part of a market for a product where the demand is for a particular variety of that product.

Market surveys Information gathered about consumers, usually via a questionnaire, that attempts to enhance the business's understanding of consumer behaviour.

Marketing mix The mix of product, price, place (distribution) and promotion that will determine a business's marketing strategy.

Mark-up pricing A pricing strategy adopted by business in which a profit mark-up is added to average costs.

Maturity transformation The transformation of deposits into loans of a longer maturity.

Maximax The strategy of choosing the policy which has the best possible outcome.

Maximin The strategy of choosing the policy whose worst possible outcome is the least bad.

Medium of exchange Something that is acceptable in exchange for goods and services.

Menu costs of inflation The costs associated with having to adjust price lists or labels.

Merger The outcome of a mutual agreement made by two firms to combine their business activities.

Merit goods Goods which the government feels that people will underconsume and which therefore ought to be subsidised or provided free.

M-form business organisation One in which the business is organised into separate departments, such that responsibility for the day-to-day management enterprise is separated from the formulation of the business's strategic plan.

Microeconomics The branch of economics that studies individual units (e.g. households, firms and industries). It studies the interrelationships between these units in determining the pattern of production and distribution of goods and services.

Minimum efficient scale (MES) The size of the individual factory or of the whole firm, beyond which no significant additional economies of scale can be gained. For an individual factory the MES is known as the *minimum efficient plant size* (MEPS).

Minimum reserve ratio A minimum ratio of cash (or other specified liquid assets) to deposits (either total or selected) that the central bank requires banks to hold.

Mobility of labour The ease with which labour can either shift between jobs (occupational mobility) or move to other parts of the country in search of work (geographical mobility).

Monetary base Notes and coin in circulation (i.e. outside the central bank).

Monetary financial institutions (MFIs) Deposit-taking financial institutions including banks, building societies and central banks.

Money market The market for short-term loans and deposits.

Money multiplier The number of times greater the expansion of money supply is than the expansion of the monetary base that caused it: $\Delta M4/\Delta$Monetary base.

Monopolistic competition A market structure where, like perfect competition, there are many firms and freedom of entry into the industry, but where each firm produces a differentiated product and thus has some control over its price.

Monopoly A market structure where there is only one firm in the industry.

Monopsony A market with a single buyer or employer.

Moral hazard Following a deal, there is an increased likelihood that one party will engage in problematic (immoral and hazardous) behaviour to the detriment of another.

Multinational corporations Businesses that either own or control foreign subsidiaries in more than one country.

Multiplier The number of times a rise in GDP (ΔGDP) is bigger than the initial rise in aggregate expenditure (ΔE) that caused it. Using the letter k to stand for the multiplier, the multiplier is defined as: $k = \Delta GDP/\Delta E$.

Multiplier effect An initial increase in aggregate demand of £xm leads to an eventual rise in national income that is greater than £xm.

Multiplier formula The formula for the multiplier is: $k = 1/(1 - mpc_d)$.

Mutual recognition The EU principle that one country's rules and regulations must apply throughout the Union. If they conflict with those of another country, individuals and firms should be able to choose which to obey.

Nash equilibrium The position resulting from everyone making their optimal decision based on their assumptions about their rivals' decisions. Without collusion, there is no incentive for any firm to move from this position.

Nationalised industries State-owned industries that produce goods or services that are sold in the market.

Natural monopoly A situation where long-run average costs would be lower if an industry were under monopoly than if it were shared between two or more competitors.

Natural rate of unemployment or non-accelerating-inflation rate of unemployment (NAIRU) The rate of unemployment consistent with a constant rate of inflation; the rate of unemployment at which the vertical long-run Phillips curve cuts the horizontal axis.

Net errors and omissions A statistical adjustment to ensure that the two sides of the balance of payments account balance. It is necessary because of errors in compiling the statistics.

Net national income (NNY) GNY minus depreciation.

Net present value (NPV) of an investment The discounted benefits of an investment minus the cost of the investment.

Network The establishment of formal and informal multi-firm alliances across sectors.

Non-bank private sector Household and non-bank firms. The category thus excludes the government and banks.

Non-collusive oligopoly When oligopolists have no agreement between themselves – formal, informal or tacit.

Non-excludability Where it is not possible to provide a good or service to one person without it thereby being available for others to enjoy.

Non-price competition Competition in terms of product promotion (advertising, packaging, etc.) or product development.

Non-rivalry Where the consumption of a good or service by one person will not prevent others from enjoying it.

Normal goods Goods whose demand rises as people's incomes rise.

Normal profit The opportunity cost of being in business. It consists of the interest that could be earned on a riskless asset, plus a return for risk taking in this particular industry. It is counted as a cost of production.

Numerical flexibility Where employers can change the size of their workforce as their labour requirements change.

Observations of market behaviour Information gathered about consumers from the day-to-day activities of the business within the market.

Oligopoly A market structure where there are few enough firms to enable barriers to be erected against the entry of new firms.

Oligopsony A market with just a few buyers or employers.

Open-market operations The sale (or purchase) by the authorities of government securities in the open market in order to reduce (or increase) money supply and thereby affect interest rates.

Opportunity cost The cost of any activity measured in terms of the best alternative forgone.

Optimal currency area The optimal size of a currency area is one that maximises the benefits from having a single currency relative to the costs. If the area were to be increased or decreased in size, the costs would rise relative to the benefits.

Organisational slack When managers allow spare capacity to exist, thereby enabling them to respond more easily to changed circumstances.

Output gap Actual output minus potential output.

Outsourcing or **subcontracting** Where a firm employs another firm to produce part of its output or some of its input(s).

Overheads Costs arising from the general running of an organisation, and only indirectly related to the level of output.

Ownership-specific assets Assets owned by the firm, such as technology, product differentiation and managerial skills, which reflect its core competencies.

Peak-load pricing The practice of charging higher prices at times when demand is highest because the constraints on capacity lead to higher marginal cost.

Perfect competition A market structure in which there are many firms; where there is freedom of entry to the industry; where all firms produce an identical product; and where all firms are price takers.

Perfectly contestable market A market where there is free and costless entry and exit.

PEST analysis Where the political, economic, social and technological factors shaping a business environment are assessed by a business so as to devise future business strategy.

Phillips curve A curve showing the relationship between (price) inflation and unemployment. The original Phillips curve plotted *wage* inflation against unemployment for the years 1861–1957.

Picketing Where people on strike gather at the entrance to the firm and attempt to dissuade workers or delivery vehicles from entering.

Plant economies of scale Economies of scale that arise because of the large size of the factory.

Potential growth The percentage annual increase in the output that would be produced if all firms were operating at their normal level of capacity utilisation.

Potential output The output that could be produced in the economy if all firms were operating at their normal level of capacity utilisation.

Predatory pricing Where a firm sets its average price below average cost in order to drive competitors out of business.

Preferential trading arrangement A trading arrangement whereby trade between the signatories is freer than trade with the rest of the world.

Present value approach to appraising investment This involves estimating the value *now* of a flow of future benefits (or costs).

Price benchmark This is a price which is typically used. Firms, when raising prices, will usually raise them from one benchmark to another.

Price discrimination Where a firm sells the same product at different prices.

Price elasticity of demand The responsiveness of quantity demanded to a change in price: the proportionate change in quantity demanded divided by the proportionate change in price.

Price elasticity of supply The responsiveness of quantity supplied to a change in price: the proportionate change in quantity supplied divided by the proportionate change in price.

Price maker (Price chooser) A firm that has the ability to influence the price charged for its good or service.

Price mechanism The system in a market economy whereby changes in price in response to changes in demand and supply have the effect of making demand equal to supply.

Price taker A firm that is too small to be able to influence the market price.

Price to book ratio or **Valuation ratio** The ratio of stock market value to book value. The stock market value is an assessment of the firm's past and anticipated future performance. The book value is a calculation of the current value of the firm's assets.

Price-cap regulation Where the regulator puts a ceiling on the amount by which a firm can raise its price.

Primary labour market The market for permanent full-time core workers.

Primary market in capital Where shares are sold by the issuer of the shares (i.e. the firm) and where, therefore, finance is channelled directly from the purchasers (i.e. the shareholders) to the firm.

Primary production The production and extraction of natural resources, plus agriculture.

Principal–agent problem One where people (principals), as a result of lack of knowledge, cannot ensure that their best interests are served by their agents.

Principle of diminishing marginal utility As more units of a good are consumed, additional units will provide less additional satisfaction than previous units.

Prisoners' dilemma Where two or more firms (or people), by attempting independently to choose the best strategy, based upon what other(s) are likely to do, end up in a worse position than if they had cooperated from the start.

Producer surplus The excess of a firm's total revenue over its total (variable) cost.

Product differentiation Where a firm's product is in some way distinct from its rivals' products.

Production The transformation of inputs into outputs by firms in order to earn profit (or meet some other objective).

Production function The mathematical relationship between the output of a good and the inputs used to produce it. It shows how output will be affected by changes in the quantity of one or more of the inputs.

Productivity deal Where, in return for a wage increase, a union agrees to changes in working practices that will increase output per worker.

Profit satisficing Where decision makers in a firm aim for a target level of profit rather than the absolute maximum level.

Profit-maximising rule Profit is maximised where marginal revenue equals marginal cost.

Public good A good or service which has the features of non-rivalry and non-excludability and as a result would not be provided by the free market.

Public-sector net borrowing The difference between the expenditures of the public sector and its receipts from taxation, the revenues of public corporations and the sale of assets. If expenditures exceed receipts (a deficit), then the government has to borrow to make up the difference.

Public-sector net cash requirement (PSNCR) The (annual) deficit of the public sector (central government, local government and public corporations), and thus the amount that the public sector must borrow.

Pure fiscal policy Fiscal policy which does not involve any change in money supply.

Quantity demanded The amount of a good that a consumer is willing and able to buy at a given price over a given period of time.

Quantity supplied The amount of a good that a firm is willing and able to sell at a given price over a given period of time.

Quantity theory of money The price level (P) is directly related to the quantity of money in the economy (M).

Quota (set by a cartel) The output that a given member of a cartel is allowed to produce (production quota) or sell (sales quota).

Random walk Where fluctuations in the value of a share away from its 'correct' value are random, i.e. have no systematic pattern. When charted over time, these share price movements would appear like a 'random walk' – like the path of someone staggering along drunk!

Rate of discount The rate that is used to reduce future values to present values.

Rate of economic growth The percentage increase in output over a 12-month period.

Rate of inflation The percentage increase in the level of prices over a 12-month period.

Rate of return approach The benefits from investment are calculated as a percentage of the costs of investment.

This rate is then compared to the rate at which money has to be borrowed in order to see whether the investment should be undertaken.

Rational choices Choices that involve weighing up the benefit of any activity against its opportunity cost.

Rational consumer behaviour The attempt to maximise total consumer surplus.

Rational expectations Expectations based on the *current* situation. These expectations are based on the information people have to hand. While this information may be imperfect and therefore people will make errors, these errors will be random.

Rationalisation The reorganising of production (often after a merger) so as to cut out waste and duplication and generally to reduce costs.

Real business cycle theory The new classical theory which explains cyclical fluctuations in terms of shifts in aggregate supply, rather than aggregate demand.

Real growth values Values of the rate of growth of GDP or any other variable after taking inflation into account. The real value of the growth in a variable equals its growth in money (or 'nominal') value minus the rate of inflation.

Recession A period where national output falls for a few months or more. The official definition is where output declines for two or more quarters.

Recessionary or deflationary gap The shortfall of aggregate expenditure below GDP at the full-employment level of GDP.

Rediscounting bills of exchange Buying bills before they reach maturity.

Regional Development Agencies (RDAs) Nine agencies, based in English regions, which initiate and administer regional policy within their area.

Regional multiplier effects When a change in injections into or withdrawals from a particular region causes a multiplied change in income in that region. The regional multiplier is given by $1/(1 - mpc_r)$, where mpc_r is the marginal propensity to consume products from the region.

Regional unemployment Structural unemployment occurring in specific regions of the country.

Regression analysis A statistical technique which shows how one variable is related to one or more other variables.

Regulatory capture Where the regulator is persuaded to operate in the industry's interests rather than those of the consumer.

Replacement costs What the firm would have to pay to replace factors it currently owns.

Repo Short for 'sale and repurchase agreement'. An agreement between two financial institutions whereby one in effect borrows from another by selling it assets, agreeing to buy them back (repurchase them) at a fixed price and on a fixed date.

Resale price maintenance Where the manufacturer of a product (legally) insists that the product should be sold at a specified retail price.

Reserve capacity A range of output over which business costs will tend to remain relatively constant.

Reverse repos When gilts or other assets are *purchased* under a sale and repurchase agreement. They become an asset of the purchaser.

Risk This is when an outcome may or may not occur, but where its probability of occurring is known.

Risk premium As a business's gearing rises, investors require a higher average dividend from their investment.

Risk transformation The process whereby banks can spread the risks of lending by having a large number of borrowers.

Sale and repurchase agreements (repos) An agreement between two financial institutions whereby one in effect borrows from another by selling it assets, agreeing to buy them back (repurchase them) at a fixed price and on a fixed date.

Sales revenue maximisation An alternative theory of the firm which assumes that managers aim to maximise the firm's short-run total revenue.

Saving gap The shortfall in savings to achieve a given rate of economic growth.

Scarcity The excess of human wants over what can actually be produced to fulfil these wants.

Seasonal unemployment Unemployment associated with industries or regions where the demand for labour is lower at certain times of the year.

Secondary action Industrial action taken against a firm not directly involved in the dispute.

Secondary labour market The market for peripheral workers, usually employed on a temporary or part-time basis, or a less secure 'permanent' basis.

Secondary market in capital Where shareholders sell shares to others. This is thus a market in 'second-hand' shares.

Secondary production The production from manufacturing and construction sectors of the economy.

Second-degree price discrimination Where a firm charges a consumer so much for the first so many units purchased, a different price for the next so many units purchased, and so on.

Self-fulfilling speculation The actions of speculators tend to cause the very effect that they had anticipated.

Semi-strong efficiency (of share markets) Where share prices adjust quickly, fully and accurately to publicly available information.

Sensitivity analysis Assesses how sensitive an outcome is to different variables within an equation.

Services balance Exports of services minus imports of services.

Short run The period of time over which at least one factor is fixed.

Short run under perfect competition The period during which there is too little time for new firms to enter the industry.

Short-run shut-down point This is where the *AR* curve is tangential to the *AVC* curve. The firm can only just cover its variable costs. Any fall in revenue below this level will cause a profit-maximising firm to shut down immediately.

Short-termism Where firms and investors take decisions based on the likely short-term performance of a company, rather than on its long-term prospects. Firms may thus sacrifice long-term profits and growth for the sake of quick return.

Sight deposits Deposits that can be withdrawn on demand without penalty.

Social benefit Private benefit plus externalities in consumption.

Social cost Private cost plus externalities in production.

Social efficiency Production and consumption at the point where *MSB* = *MSC*.

Social responsibility Where a firm takes into account the interests and concerns of a community rather than just its shareholders.

Social-impact standards Pollution control that focuses on the effects on people (e.g. on health or happiness).

Specialisation and division of labour Where production is broken down into a number of simpler, more specialised tasks, thus allowing workers to acquire a high degree of efficiency.

Speculation This is where people make buying or selling decisions based on their anticipations of future prices.

Spot price The current market price.

Spreading risks (for an insurance company) The more policies an insurance company issues and the more independent the risks of claims from these policies are, the more predictable will be the number of claims.

Stabilising speculation This is where the actions of speculators tend to reduce price fluctuations.

Stakeholders (in a company) People who are affected by a company's activities and/or performance (customers, employees, owners, creditors, people living in the neighbourhood, etc.). They may or may not be in a position to make decisions, or influence decision making, in the firm.

Standard Industrial Classification (SIC) The name given to the formal classification of firms into industries used by the government in order to collect data on business and industry trends.

Standardised unemployment rate The measure of the unemployment rate used by the ILO and OECD. The unemployed are defined as people of working age who are without work, available for work and actively seeking employment.

Stock The quantity of something held.

Strategic alliance Where two or more firms work together, formally or informally, to achieve a mutually desirable goal.

Strategic management The management of the strategic long-term activities of the business, which includes strategic analysis, strategic choice and strategic implementation.

Strategic trade theory The theory that protecting/supporting certain industries can enable them to compete more effectively with large monopolistic rivals abroad.

The effect of the protection is to increase long-run competition and may enable the protected firms to exploit a comparative advantage that they could not have done otherwise.

Strong efficiency (of share markets) Where share prices adjust quickly, fully and accurately to all available information, both public and that available only to insiders.

Structural unemployment Unemployment that arises from changes in the pattern of demand or supply in the economy. People made redundant in one part of the economy cannot immediately take up jobs in other parts (even though there are vacancies).

Subcontracting The business practice where various forms of labour (frequently specialist) are hired for a given period of time. Such workers are not directly employed by the hiring business, but either employed by a third party or self-employed.

Substitute goods A pair of goods which are considered by consumers to be alternatives to each other. As the price of one goes up, the demand for the other rises.

Substitutes in supply These are two goods where an increased production of one means diverting resources.

Substitution effect The effect of a change in price on quantity demanded arising from the consumer switching to or from alternative (substitute) products.

Substitution effect of a rise in wages Workers will tend to substitute income for leisure as leisure now has a higher opportunity cost. This effect leads to *more* hours being worked as wages rise.

Sunk costs Costs that cannot be recouped (e.g. by transferring assets to other uses).

Supernormal profit (also known as **pure profit, economic profit, abnormal profit** or simply **profit**) The excess of total profit above normal profit.

Supply curve A graph showing the relationship between the price of a good and the quantity of the good supplied over a given period of time.

Supply schedule A table showing the different quantities of a good that producers are willing and able to supply at various prices over a given time period. A supply schedule can be for an individual producer or group of producers, or for all producers (the market supply schedule).

Supply: change in supply The term used for a shift in the supply curve. It occurs when a determinant other than price changes.

Supply: change in the quantity supplied The term used for a movement along the supply curve to a new point. It occurs when there is a change in price.

Supply-side policy Government policy that attempts to alter the level of aggregate supply directly.

Tacit collusion A situation where firms have an unspoken agreement to engage in a joint strategy. For example, oligopolists take care not to engage in price cutting, excessive advertising or other forms of competition. There may be unwritten 'rules' of collusive behaviour such as price leadership.

Takeover Where one business acquires another. A takeover may not necessarily involve mutual agreement between the two parties. In such cases, the takeover might be viewed as 'hostile'.

Takeover bid Where one firm attempts to purchase another by offering to buy the shares of that company from its shareholders.

Takeover constraint The effect that the fear of being taken over has on a firm's willingness to undertake projects that reduce distributed profits.

Tapered vertical integration Where a firm is partially integrated with an earlier stage of production; where it produces *some* of an input itself and buys some from another firm.

Taylor rule A rule adopted by a central bank for setting the rate of interest. It will raise the interest rate if (a) inflation is above target or (b) economic growth is above the sustainable level (or unemployment is below the equilibrium rate). The rule states how much interest rates will be changed in each case.

Technical or productive efficiency The least-cost combination of factors for a given output.

Technological unemployment Structural unemployment that occurs as a result of the introduction of labour-saving technology.

Technology policy Involves government initiatives to affect the process and rate of technological change.

Technology transfer Where a host state benefits from the new technology that an MNC brings with its investment.

Technology-based standards Pollution control that requires firms' emissions to reflect the levels that could be achieved from using the best available pollution control technology.

Terms of trade The price index of exports divided by the price index of imports and then expressed as a percentage. This means that the terms of trade will be 100 in the base year.

Tertiary production The production from the service sector of the economy.

Third-degree price discrimination Where a firm divides consumers into different groups and charges a different price to consumers in different groups, but the same price to all the consumers within a group.

Tie-in-sales Where a firm is only prepared to sell a first product on the condition that its customers buy a second product from it.

Time deposits Deposits that require notice of withdrawal or where a penalty is charged for withdrawals on demand.

Time-series data Information depicting how a variable (e.g. the price of eggs) changes over time.

Tit-for-tat Where a firm will cut prices, or make some other aggressive move, *only* if the rival does so first. If the rival knows this, it will be less likely to make an initial aggressive move.

Total (sales) revenue (*TR*) The amount a firm earns from its sales of a product at a particular price: $TR = P \times Q$.

Note that we are referring to *gross* revenue; that is, revenue before the deduction of taxes or any other costs.

Total consumer surplus The excess of a person's total utility from the consumption of a good (*TU*) over the amount that person spends on it (*TE*): $TCS = TU - TE$.

Total cost (*TC*) The sum of total fixed costs (*TFC*) and total variable costs (*TVC*): $TC = TFC + TVC$.

Total physical product The total output of a product per period of time that is obtained from a given amount of inputs.

Total revenue A firm's total earnings from a specified level of sales within a specified period: $TR = P \times Q$.

Total utility The total satisfaction a consumer gets from the consumption of all the units of a good consumed within a given time period.

Tradable permits Each firm is given a permit to produce a given level of pollution. If less than the permitted amount is produced, the firm is given a credit. This can then be sold to another firm, allowing it to exceed its original limit.

Trade creation Where a customs union leads to greater specialisation according to comparative advantage and thus a shift in production from higher-cost to lower-cost sources.

Trade diversion Where a customs union diverts consumption from goods produced at a lower cost outside the union to goods produced at a higher cost (but tariff free) within the union.

Transactions costs The costs incurred when firms buy inputs or services from other firms as opposed to producing them themselves. They include the costs of searching for the best firm to do business with, the costs of drawing up, monitoring and enforcing contracts and the costs of transporting and handling products between the firms.

Transfer payments Moneys transferred from one person or group to another (e.g. from the government to individuals) without production taking place.

Transfer pricing The pricing system used within a business organisation to transfer intermediate products between the business's various divisions.

Transnational association A form of business organisation in which the subsidiaries of a company in different countries are contractually bound to the parent company to provide output to or receive inputs from other subsidiaries.

Two-part tariff A pricing system that requires customers to pay an access and a usage price for a product.

U-form business organisation One in which the central organisation of the firm (the chief executive or a managerial team) is responsible both for the firm's day-to-day administration and for formulating its business strategy.

Uncertainty This is when an outcome may or may not occur and where its probability of occurring is not known.

Unemployment The number of people who are actively looking for work but are currently without a job. (Note that there is much debate as to who should officially be counted as unemployed.)

Unemployment rate The number unemployed expressed as a percentage of the labour force.

Unit elasticity When the price elasticity of demand is unity, this is where quantity demanded changes by the same proportion as the price. Price elasticity is equal to -1.

Valuation ratio or **Price to book ratio** The ratio of stock market value to book value. The stock market value is an assessment of the firm's past and anticipated future performance. The book value is a calculation of the current value of the firm's assets.

Value chain The stages or activities that help to create product value.

Variable costs Total costs that do vary with the amount of output produced.

Variable factor An input that *can* be increased in supply within a given time period.

Velocity of circulation The number of times annually that money on average is spent on goods and services that make up GDP.

Vertical integration A business growth strategy that involves expanding within an existing market, but at a different stage of production. Vertical integration can be 'forward', such as moving into distribution or retail, or 'backward', such as expanding into extracting raw materials or producing components.

Vertical merger Where two firms in the same industry at different stages in the production process merge.

Vertical product differentiation Where a firm's product differs from its rivals' products in respect to quality.

Vertical restraints Conditions imposed by one firm on another which is either its supplier or its customer.

Vertical strategic alliance A formal or informal arrangement between firms operating at different stages of an activity to jointly provide a product or service.

Vertically integrated multinational A multinational that undertakes the various stages of production for a given product in different countries.

Wage taker The wage rate is determined by market forces.

Weak efficiency (of share markets) Where share dealing prevents cyclical movements in shares.

Weighted average The average of several items where each item is ascribed a weight according to its importance. The weights must add up to 1.

Wholesale deposits and loans Large-scale deposits and loans made by and to firms at negotiated interest rates.

Withdrawals (*W*) (or leakages) Incomes of households or firms that are not passed on round the inner flow. Withdrawals equal net saving (*S*) plus net taxes (*T*) plus import expenditure (*M*): $W = S + T + M$.

Working to rule Workers do no more than they are supposed to, as set out in their job descriptions.

Yield on a share The dividend received per share expressed as a percentage of the current market price of the share.

Index